SWIMMING

MEN

Event	Time	Name and Country	Date
Freestyle			
100 metres	49.99	James Montgomery (U.S.A.)	25 July 1976
200 metres	1:50.29	Bruce Furniss (U.S.A.)	19 July 1976
400 metres	3:51.93	Brian Stuart Goodell (U.S.A.)	22 July 1976
1,500 metres	15:02.40	Brian Stuart Goodell (U.S.A.)	20 July 1976
4 × 200 m Relay	7:23.22	United States of America	21 July 1976
Breaststroke			
100 metres	1:03.11	John Hencken (U.S.A.)	20 July 1976
200 metres	2:15.11	David Andrew Wilkie (G.B. & N.I.)	24 July 1976
Butterfly			
100 metres	54.27	Mark Spitz (U.S.A.)	31 Aug. 1972
200 metres	1:59.23	Michael Bruner (U.S.A.)	18 July 1976
Backstroke			
100 metres	55.49	John Naber (U.S.A.)	19 July 1976
200 metres	1:59.19	John Naber (U.S.A.)	24 July 1976
Medley			
400 metres	4:23.68	Rod Strachan (U.S.A.)	25 July 1976
4 × 100 m Relay	3:42.22	United States of America	22 July 1976

WOMEN

Event	Time	Name and Country	Date
Freestyle			
100 metres	55.65	Kornelia Ender (East Germany)	19 July 1976
200 metres	1:59.26	Kornelia Ender (East Germany)	22 July 1976
400 metres	4:09.89	Petra Thumer (East Germany)	20 July 1976
800 metres	8:37.14	Petra Thumer (East Germany)	25 July 1976
4 × 100 m Relay	3:44.82	United States of America	25 July 1976
Breaststroke			
100 metres	1:10.86	Hannelore Anke (East Germany)	22 July 1976
200 metres	2:33.35	Marina Koshevaia (U.S.S.R.)	21 July 1976
Butterfly			
100 metres	1:00.13	Kornelia Ender (East Germany)	22 July 1976
200 metres	2:11.41	Andrea Pollack (East Germany)	19 July 1976
Backstroke			
100 metres	1:01.83	Ulrike Richter (East Germany)	21 July 1976
200 metres	2:13.43	Ulrike Richter (East Germany)	25 July 1976
Medley			
400 metres	4:42.77	Ulrike Tauber (East Germany)	24 July 1976
4 × 100 m Relay	4:07.95	East Germany	18 July 1976

America's Brian Goodell set Olympic and world records in winning both the 400 m and 1,500 m freestyle events at Montreal. (*George Herringshaw, Provincial Sports Photography*)

WEIGHTLIFTING

Event	Total weight Kilos	Total weight lb.	Name and Country	Date
Flyweight	242.5	534½	Alexander Voronin (U.S.S.R.)	18 July 1976
Bantamweight	262.5	578½	Norair Nurikyan (Bulgaria)	19 July 1976
Featherweight	285.0	628¼	Nikolai Kolesnikov (U.S.S.R.).	20 July 1976
Lightweight	305	672¼	Piotr Korol U.S.S.R.)	21 July 1976
Middleweight	335.0	738½	Yordan Mitkov (Bulgaria)	22 July 1976
Light Heavyweight	365.0	804½	Valeri Shary (U.S.S.R.)	24 July 1976
Middle Heavyweight	382.5	843¼	David Rigert (U.S.S.R.)	25 July 1976
Heavyweight	385	848¾	Yuri Zaitsev (U.S.S.R.)	26 July 1976
Super Heavyweight	440.0	970	Vasili Alexeev (U.S.S.R.)	27 July 1976

ARCHERY

Event	Points	Name and Country	Date
Men's Double F.I.T.A.	2,571 points	Darrell Pace (U.S.A.)	30 July 1976
Women's Double F.I.T.A.	2,499 points	Luann Ryon (U.S.A.)	30 July 1976

1976 Olympic Flyweight weightlifting champion, Alexander Voronin (USSR) current world record holder. (*Associated Press*)

SPEED SKATING

MEN

Event	Time	Name and Country	Date
500 metres	39.17	Evgeniy Kulikov (U.S.S.R.)	10 Feb. 1976
1,000 metres	1:19.32	Peter Mueller (U.S.A.)	12 Feb. 1976
1,500 metres	1:59.38	Jan Egil Storholt (Norway)	13 Feb. 1976
5,000 metres	7:22.4	Fred Anton Maier (Norway)	15 Feb. 1968
10,000 metres	14:50.59	Piet Kliene (Netherlands)	14 Feb. 1976

WOMEN

Event	Time	Name and Country	Date
500 metres	42.76	Sheila Young (U.S.A.)	6 Feb. 1976
1,000 metres	1:28.43	Tatyana Averina (U.S.S.R.)	7 Feb. 1976
1,500 metres	2:16.58	Galina Stepanskaya (U.S.S.R.)	5 Feb. 1976
3,000 metres	4:45.19	Tatyana Averina (U.S.S.R.)	8 Feb. 1976

D0946612

GUINNESS MUSEUMS

A number of permanent exhibit halls have been established in various parts of the world. They seek to bring world records from the realm of imagination to stark reality.

Those already established are

Empire State Building, New York City, U.S.A.
Myrtle Beach, South Carolina, U.S.A.
Lake of the Ozarks, Missouri, U.S.A.
Gatlinburg, Tennessee, U.S.A.
Niagara Falls, Ontario, Canada

Plans for new museums are being advanced for

Lake George, New York State, U.S.A.
Boston, Massachusetts, U.S.A.
San Francisco, California, U.S.A.
Kyoto, Japan
London, England

ACKNOWLEDGEMENTS

J. W. Arblaster, A.I.M.; Richard Ayling; Howard Bass; Pat Besford; James Bond; British Airways; British Museum (Natural History); British Rail; British Travel; British Waterworks Association; L. J. Boughey; Henry G. Button; Kenneth H. Chandler; Central Electricity Generating Board; Central Office of Information; Dr. A. J. C. Charig; Sq. Ldr. D. H. Clarke, D.F.C., A.F.C.; Clerk of Dail Eireann; The late Peter T. Cunningham (Chairman 1975–1978); Albert Dormer; Clive Everton; Fédération Aéronautique Internationale; Fédération Internationale de l'Automobile; Fédération Internationale des Hopitaux; Frank L. Forster, Esq.; M. H. Ford; Darryl Francis; Dr. Francis C. Fraser; Colin W. Graham; Norman Graveson; General Post Office; A. Herbert, (New Zealand); Dr. Arthur H. Hughes (Chairman Guinness Superlatives Ltd., 1954–1966); Derek Hurst; Imperial War Museum; Institute of Strategic Studies; Sir Peter Johnson; Erich Kamper; Michael Kelly; Kline Iron and Steel Company; Mr. Michael D. Lampen; John Lees; The Library of Congress, Washington D.C.; *Lloyd's Register of Shipping;* London Transport Board; The late T. L. Marks, O.B.E., T.D. (Chairman 1966–71); K. G. McWhirter, M.A., M.SC.; Dr. G. T. Meaden, editor *Journal of Meteorology*; Meteorological Office; Metropolitan Police; Alan Mitchell, B.A., B.Ag. (For); David Mondey; Music Research Bureau; National Aeronautics and Space Administration; National Geographic Society; National Maritime Museum; National Physical Laboratory; David Norrie; Doug Nye; Mrs. Susann Palmer; Christopher Plumridge; E. T. Pugh, Editor *Manned Spacecraft*; A. J. R. Purssell (Chairman 1971–75); *The Racing Pigeon*, London; John Randall; Jean Reville; Tim Rice; Irving Rosenwater; Jack Rollin; Royal Astronomical Society; Royal Botanic Gardens; Royal Geographic Society; Royal National Life-boat Institution; Alan Russell; SAS City Profiles; Wm. L. Schultz; Graham Snowdon; John H. Stephens; John W. R. Taylor; Dave Terry; Lance Tingay; U.N. Statistical Office; Juhani Virola; J. N. P. Watson; Baruch H. Wood; Gerry L. Wood F.Z.S.; World Meteorological Organization; Francis Albert Young; Zoological Society of London, and various sports associations and governing bodies.

Amanda Clark (Editor's Secretary); Moira F. Stowe (Editor's Assistant); Colin C. Smith (Correspondence Editor); Beverley Waites (Sports Editor's Assistant); Mary Crowder, Lucie Phillippo, Peter J. Matthews and Bernadette Bidwell; the late A. Ross McWhirter (Co-editor 1954–1975).

Also to Barbara Anderson, Anne Belsham, Sally V. Bennett, Christine Bethlehem, Rosemary Bevan, D. Richard Bowen, Signa. Wendy Cirillo, Pamela Croome, Trudy Doyle, Mlle. Béatrice Frei, G. Howard Garrard D.S.C. Jacqueline Gould, Susan Gullen, Tessa Hegley, E. C. Henniker, David N. Hewlett, Angela Hoaen, David F. Hoy, (Managing Director), Eileen Jackson, Hilary Leavey, Diana Lloyd, Jane Mayo, G. M. Nutbrown, W. E. Nutbrown, Margaret Orr-Deas, Peter B. Page, (1954–57), John Rivers, Suzi M. Ross-Browne, Judith Sleath, Anne Symonds, Andrew Thomas, (Associate Editor 1964–68), Gillian Turner, Martin Turner, Winnie Ulrich, Peter Whatley, Stephen James Clarke, (1948–1976) (Management Accountant).

Cover photographs—top left: Largest Lemon 3 lb 9 oz *1,628 kg* (see p 53) (*T. C. Buckeridge*); top right: Cheetah (*Jonathan Kenworthy: Tryon Gallery*); bottom left: The Blue Flame (see p 135) (*Pat Gibbon*); bottom right: Vasili Alexeev (*Gerry Cranham*); centre: Jean Chapman (see pp 23 & 24).

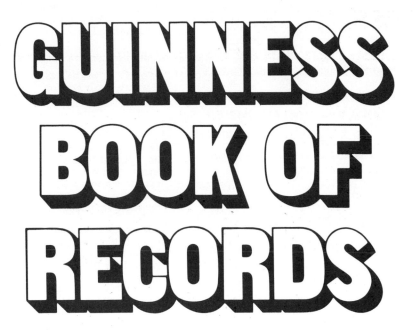

GUINNESS
BOOK OF
RECORDS

EDITION 26

Editor and Compiler
NORRIS McWHIRTER
Sports Editor
STAN GREENBERG

GUINNESS SUPERLATIVES LIMITED
2 CECIL COURT, LONDON ROAD, ENFIELD, MIDDLESEX

OVERSEAS AGENTS

CANADA David Drew Associates, 9 Birchcroft Road, Islington, Ontario, M9A 2L3, Canada
CARIBBEAN Wm. Collins Sons & Co. Ltd., P.O. Box 881, Kingston, Jamaica and P.O. Box 582, Port of Spain, Trinidad.
EUROPE D. Richard Bowen, Post Box 30037, 5–200 61, Malmö 30, Sweden
FAR EAST Nicholas Fulcher 10 Pokfield Road, Lower Ground Floor, Pok Fulham, Hong Kong
REPUBLIC OF IRELAND J. A. McGarry, 5 Second Avenue, Douglas, Isle of Man
KENYA J. L. Morison Son & Jones (Kenya) Ltd., P.O. Box 30198, Nairobi, Kenya
LATIN AMERICA Eti Feeny, c/o Wm. Collins Sons & Co. Ltd., 14 St. James's Place, London, S.W.1.
MIDDLE EAST Nigel M. Ealand, Ealand Enterprises, Platanidia, Volos, Greece

OVERSEAS SOLE DISTRIBUTORS

AUSTRALIA Wm. Collins Pty. Ltd. in Brisbane; Sydney; Melbourne; Adelaide and Perth
CHANNEL ISLANDS L.S.T., 9 Patriotic Street, St. Helier, Jersey
INDIA UBS Publishers Distributors Ltd., 5 Ansari Road, New Delhi, 110002, India
MALTA Agius & Agius Ltd., 42a South Street, Valetta, Malta
NEW ZEALAND Whitcoulls Ltd., Private Bag, Christchurch, New Zealand
OMAN Family Bookshop & Co., P.O. Box 3376 Ruwi, Oman
PAKISTAN Mirza Book Agency, P.O. Box 729, Lahore 3, Pakistan
SOUTH AFRICA Wm. Collins (Africa) (Pty) Ltd., Johannesburg, Cape Town and Durban
SOUTH EAST ASIA Times Distributors, 390 Kim Seng Road, Singapore 9
UNITED ARAB EMIRATES Alnasr Novelty Stores, P.O. Box 1949, Riqa, Dubai, U.A.E.

Standard Book Number ISBN: 0 900424 96 6
Standard Book Number ISBN: 0 900424 97 4 (Australian Edition)

Copyright © 1979 Guinness Superlatives Ltd

World Copyright Reserved
Twenty Sixth Edition

No part of this book may be reproduced or transmitted in any form or by any means electronic, chemical or mechanical, including photocopying, any information storage or retrieval system without a licence or other permission in writing from the copyright owners. Reviewers are welcome to quote brief passages should they wish.

This book is sold subject to the Standard Conditions of Sale of Net Books and may not be resold in the United Kingdom below the net price fixed by the publishers and ascertainable from their 1979 Catalogue.

"Guinness" is a registered trade mark of Guinness Superlatives Ltd.

Note
Back numbers are not available from the publishers but may be obtainable through the second hand book trade. Orders for current editions published overseas will willingly be passed on to the publishers concerned.

OVERSEAS AND FOREIGN LANGUAGE EDITIONS

Language		Title	Latest Publication	Publisher
American	(Casebound)	Guinness Book of World Records	1979	Sterling Publishing Co. Inc., New York City, N.Y., U.S.A.
American	(Paperback)	Guinness Book of World Records	1979	Bantam Books Inc., New York City, N.Y., U.S.A.
Arabic		Contracted for publication	1979	Near East Business Development Company, Beirut, Lebanon.
Chinese	(Paperback)	Contracted for publication	1979	Sing Tao Newspapers Ltd., Hong Kong
Czech	(Casebound)	Guinnessova Kniha Rekordů	1975	Olympia, Prague, Czechoslovakia
Danish	(Casebound)	Guiness Rekordbog	1979	Forlaget Komma A/S, Copenhagen, Denmark
Dutch	(Casebound)	Het Groot Guinness Record Boek	1979	Uitgeverij Luitingh BV., Laren, Netherlands
Finnish	(Casebound)	Guinness Suuri Ennätys Kirja	1976	Sanoma Osakeyhtio, Helsinki, Finland
French	(Casebound)	Guinness Le Livre des Records	1979	Éditions Denoël, Paris, France
German	(Casebound)	Contracted for publication	—	Verlag Ullstein GmbH , Berlin, West Germany
Greek	(Paperback)	τα ηαραξεγα κοιί τά ρεκόρ του κοσψου	1979	Imex Rigas Athanasios Ltd., Thessaloniki, Greece
Hebrew		Guinness Sēfēr Ha'siim	1979	Carta, The Israel Map & Publishing Company, Jerusalem, Israel
Icelandic	(Casebound)	Heimsmetabok Guinness	1977	Bokautgafan Örn og Örlygur h.f., Reykjavik, Iceland
Indonesian	(Paperback)	Guinness Rekaman Rekor Dunia	1979	P. T. Gramedia, Jakarta, Indonesia
Japanese	(Casebound)	Guinness Korega Sekai Ichi	1978	Kodan Sha Limited, Tokyo, Japan
Norwegian	(Casebound)	Guinness Rekordboken Først og Størst Sist og Minst.	1978	Chr. Schibsteds Forlag, Oslo, Norway
Portuguese		Contracted for publication	—	Augusto Sa Da Costa., Lda., Lisbon, Portugal
Serbo-Croat	(Casebound)	Guinnessova Knjiga Rekorda	1977	Prosvjeta, Zagreb, Yugoslavia
Slovenian	(Casebound)	Guinnessova Knjiga Rekordov	1978	Mladinska Knjiga, Ljubljana, Yugoslavia
Spanish (S. American)	(Paperback)	Enciclopedia Guinness de Records Mundiales	1978	Editors Press Service Inc., New York City, N.Y., U.S.A.
Spanish (European)	(Casebound)	El Libro Guinness de los Records	1978	Editorial Minon, Valladolid, Spain
Swedish	(Casebound)	Guinness Rekordbok Först och Störst	1979	Bokforlaget Forum AB., Stockholm, Sweden
Turkish		Guinness Rekorlar Kitabi	1979	Milliyet Yayinlari, Istanbul, Turkey

Future editions in Russian and Italian (re-issue) are under negotiation.

Made and produced in Great Britain by
REDWOOD BURN LIMITED Trowbridge & Esher

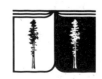

FOREWORD by the Rt. Hon. the Earl of Iveagh

Now that our *Guinness Book of Records* has reached its 26th edition it has long since moved from the status of an annual to that of a perennial.

When we first brought out this book, twenty-four years ago, we did so in the hope of providing a means for peaceful settling of arguments about record performances in this record-breaking world in which we live. We realise, of course, that much joy lies in the argument, but how exasperating it can be if there is no final means of finding the answer.

About a quarter of the many thousands of records listed have to be changed from one edition to the next. In this edition we are again obliged to revise our own entry that records that the global sales of this book, now being published in 23 languages, have surpassed the 36,000,000 mark.

Whether the discussion concerns the highest that any man has jumped over his own height, the greatest weight lifted by a woman, the nationality of the first woman to climb Everest, or—an old bone of contention—the longest time for anyone to become a Saint, I can but quote the words used in introducing the first edition, "How much heat these innocent questions can raise: Guinness, in producing this book, hopes that it may assist in resolving many such disputes, and may, we hope, turn heat into light".

Iveagh

Joint Chairman
Arthur Guinness, Son & Co., Ltd.   October 1979

NOTES ON THE ACCEPTABILITY OF RECORDS

We are *likely* to publish only those records which improve upon previous records or which are newly significant in having become the subject of widespread and preferably international competitiveness.

It should be stressed that unique occurrences and interesting peculiarities are not in themselves necessarily records. Records in our sense essentially have to be both measurable and comparable. Records which are *qualified* in some way, for example, by age, day of the week, county, etc cannot be accommodated in a reference work so general as *The Guinness Book of Records*.

Claimants should send independent corroboration in the form of local or national newspaper cuttings, radio or TV coverage reports and signed authentication by independent adult witnesses or representatives of organisations of standing in their community. Signed log books should show there has been unremitting surveillance in the case of endurance events. Action photographs (preferably colour transparencies) should also be supplied. Five minutes rest intervals (optional but aggregable) are *permitted* after each completed hour in marathon events except for those very few "non-stop" categories in which minimal intervals may be taken only for purposes other than for resting.

If an activity is one controlled by a recognised world or national governing body that body should be consulted and involved in ratifying it.

The publishers do *not* normally supply personnel to invigilate record attempts but reserve the right to do so.

PREFACE

This 26th Edition has been not only completely revised but re-illustrated throughout.

Due to the significant fluctuations in comparative foreign exchange rates, currency conversions have been converted at the rate ruling at the time of the event or record. To indicate this the word "*then*" has been inserted before the relevant conversion.

There has been in recent years a marked increase in efforts to establish records for sheer endurance in many activities. In the very nature of record breaking the duration of such 'marathons' will tend to be pushed to greater and greater extremes and it should be stressed that marathon attempts are not without possible dangers. Organizers of marathon events would be well counselled to seek medical advice before and surveillance during marathons which involve extended periods with little or no sleep. (See above for notes on rest periods).

If there are discrepancies between entries in one edition and another, it may be generally assumed that the *later* entry is the product of the more up to date research. Readers should consult the Stop Press section and the index, where an asterisk indicates that there is an additional entry in the Stop Press.

Finally the editorial office, which is concerned with maintaining and improving the quality of each succeeding edition, is unable to perform also the function of a free general information bureau for quiz competitions and the like, by telephone or by correspondence.

Norris McWhirter

Editor and compiler

October 1979
Guinness Superlatives Limited, 2 Cecil Court, London Road, Enfield, Middlesex

Artwork by Don Roberts

Design and Layout by David Roberts *(no kin)*

Additional Artwork by John Cooper, Eddie Botchway, and Pat Gibbon

Colour Film supplied by NEWSELE Litho Ltd. (Director Janice Tennant)

CONTENTS

THE HUMAN BEING

1. DIMENSIONS

TALLEST GIANTS

The height of human giants is a subject on which accurate information is frequently obscured by exaggeration and commercial dishonesty. The only admissible evidence on the true height of giants is that collected in the last 100 years under impartial medical supervision. Some medical papers have themselves, however, published fanciful, as opposed to measured heights as recently as 1962.

The assertion that Goliath of Gath (*c.* 1060 B.C.) stood 6 cubits and a span (9 ft 6½ in *290 cm*) suggests a confusion of units or some over-zealous exaggeration by the Hebrew chroniclers. The Jewish historian Flavius Josephus (born A.D. 37 or 38, died *post* A.D. 93) and some of the manuscripts of the Septuagint (the earliest Greek translation of the Old Testament) attribute to Goliath the quite credible height of 4 Greek cubits and a span (6 ft 10 in *208 cm*).

Extreme mediaeval data, taken from bone measurements, invariably refer to specimens of extinct whale, giant cave bear, mastodon, woolly rhinoceros or other prehistoric non-human remains.

Circus giants and others who are exhibited are normally under contract not to be measured and are, almost traditionally, billed by their promoters at heights up to 18 in *45 cm* in excess of their true heights. There are many notable examples of this, and 23 instances were listed in the *Guinness Book of Records* (14th edition). The acromegalic giant Eddie Carmel (b. Tel Aviv, Israel, 1938), formerly "The Tallest Man on Earth" of Ringling Bros. and Barnum & Bailey's Circus (1961–68) was allegedly 9 ft 0⅝ in *275 cm* tall (weighing 38 st. 3 lb. *242 kg*), but photographic evidence suggests that his true height was about 7 ft 6⅝ in *229,6 cm*. He died in New York City on 14 Aug. 1972 when his standing height due to severe kyphoscoliosis, was *c.* 7 ft *212 cm*.

An extreme case of exaggeration concerned Siah Khān ibn Kashmir Khān (b. 1913) of Bushehr (Bushire), Iran. Prof. D. H. Fuchs showed photographs of him at a meeting of the Society of Physicians in Vienna, Austria, in January 1935, claiming that he was 320 cm *10 ft 6 in* tall. Later, when Siah Khān entered the Imperial Hospital in Teheran for an operation, it was revealed that his actual height was a full metre less at 220 cm *7 ft 2.6 in*.

World

Modern opinion is that the tallest recorded man of whom there is irrefutable evidence was the pre-acromegalic giant Robert Pershing Wadlow, born at 6.30 a.m. on 22 Feb. 1918 in Alton, Illinois, U.S.A.

Weighing 8½lb. *3,85 kg* at birth, his abnormal growth started at the age of 2 following a double hernia operation. His height progressed as follows:

Age in Years	Height		Weight in lb.	kg	Age in Years	Height		Weight in lb.	kg
5	5′4″	163 cm	105	48	15	7′8″	234 cm	355	161
8	6′0″	183 cm	169	77	16	7′10½″	240 cm	374	170
9	6′2½″	189 cm	180	82	17	8′0½″	245 cm	315[1]	143
10	6′5″	196 cm	210	95	18	8′3½″	253 cm	—	
11	6′7″	200 cm	—		19	8′5½″	258 cm	480	218
12	6′10½″	210 cm	—		20	8′6¾″	261 cm	—	
13	7′1¾″	218 cm	255	116	21	8′8¼″	265 cm	491	223
14	7′5″	226 cm	301	137	22.4[2]	8′11″	272 cm	439	199

[1] *Following severe influenza and infection of the foot.*
[2] *Wadlow was still growing during his terminal illness.*

Dr. C. M. Charles, Associate Professor of Anatomy at Washington University's School of Medicine in St. Louis, Missouri and Dr Cyril MacBryde measured Robert Wadlow at 272 cm *8 ft 11.1 in* in St. Louis on 27 June 1940. Wadlow died 18 days later, at 1.30 a.m. on 15 July 1940, in Manistee, Michigan, as a result of cellulitis (inflammation of cellular tissue) of the right ankle aggravated by a poorly fitted brace, which had been fitted only a week earlier.

He was buried in Oakwood Cemetery, Alton, Illinois in a coffin measuring 10 ft 9 in *328 cm* in length, 32 in *81 cm* wide and 30 in *76 cm* deep. His greatest recorded weight was 35 st. 1 lb. *222,71 kg*, on his 21st birthday. He weighed 31 st. 5 lb. *199 kg* at the time of his death. His shoes were size 37AA (18½ in *47 cm* long) and his hands measured 12¾ in *32,5 cm* from the wrist to the tip of the middle finger (c.f. the depth of this page at 11¼ in *28,6 cm*).

His arm span was 9 ft 5¾ in *2,88 m* and his peak daily consumption attained 8,000 calories. At the age of 9 he was able to carry his father, the Mayor of Alton, who stood 5 ft 11 in *1,82 m* and weighed 170 lb. *72 kg*, up the stairs of the family home.

The only other men for whom heights of 8 ft *244 cm* or more have been reliably reported are the eight listed below. In six cases, gigantism was followed by acromegaly, a disorder which causes an enlargement of the nose, lips, tongue, lower jaw, hands and feet, due to renewed activity by an already swollen pituitary gland, which is located at the base of the brain.

John F. Carroll (1932–69) of Buffalo, New York State, U.S.A. ([1]) 8 ft 7¾ in *263,5 cm.*

John William Rogan (1871–1905), a Negro of Gallatin, Tennessee, U.S.A. ([2]) 8 ft 6 in *259,1 cm.*

Don Koehler (b. 1925–*fl.* 1979) of Denton, Montana, U.S.A. ([3]) 8 ft 2 in *248,9 cm,* now lives in Chicago.

Bernard Coyne (1897–1921) of Anthon, Iowa U.S.A. ([4]) 8 ft 2 in *248,9 cm*

Vainö Myllyrinne (1909–63) of Helsinki, Finland ([5]) 8 ft 1.2 in *247 cm.*

Patrick Cotter O'Brien (1760–1806) of Kinsale, County Cork, Ireland ([6]) 8 ft 1 in *246 cm.*

"Constantine" (1872–1902) of Reutlingen, West Germany ([7]) 8 ft 0.8 in *245,8 cm.*

Sulaimān 'Alī Nashnush (1943–*fl.* 1979) of Tripoli, Libya ([8]) 8 ft 0.4 in *245 cm.*

([1]) *Severe kypho-scoliosis (two dimensional spinal curvature). The figure represents his height with assumed normal spinal curvature, calculated from a standing height of 8 ft 0 in 244 cm, measured on 14 Oct. 1959. His standing height was 7 ft 8¼ in 234 cm shortly before his death.*
([2]) *Measured in a sitting position. Unable to stand owing to ankylosis (stiffening of the joints through the formation of adhesions) of the knees and hips.*
([3]) *Same spinal curvature. Present standing height c. 7 ft 10 in 238,4 cm. He has a twin sister who is 5 ft 9 in 175 cm tall. His father was 6 ft 2 in 1,87 m and his mother 5 ft 10 in 1,77 m.*
([4]) *Eunuchoidal giant (Daddy-long legs syndrome). Rejected by Army in 1918 when 7 ft 9 in 236 cm.*
([5]) *Stood 7 ft 3½ in 222 cm at the age of 21 years. Experienced a second phase of growth in his late thirties and may have stood 8 ft 3 in 251 cm at one time.*
([6]) *Revised height based on skeletal remeasurement in 1975.*
([7]) *Eunuchoidal. Height estimated, as both legs were amputated after they turned gangrenous. He claimed a height of 8 ft 6 in 259 cm.*
([8]) *Operation in Rome to correct abnormal growth was successful in 1960.*

A table of the tallest giants of all-time in the 31 countries with men taller than 7 ft 4 in *223,5 cm* was listed in the 15th edition of the *Guinness Book of Records* (1968) at page 9.

An uncomfirmed height of 8 ft 6 in *259 cm* has been claimed for Gabriel Estevão Monjane (b. 1944) of Monjacaze, Mozambique. Photographic evidence suggests he may have reached 8 ft *245 cm.* Eunuchoidal giants sometimes grow well into their fourth decade.

England
The tallest Englishman ever recorded was William Bradley (1787–1820), born in Market Weighton, Humberside. He stood 7 ft 9 in *236 cm.* John Middleton (1578–1623), the famous Childe of Hale, from near Liverpool, was credited with a height of 9 ft 3 in *282 cm* but a life-size impression of his right hand (length 11½ in *29,2 cm* c.f. Wadlow's 12¾ in *32,4 cm*) painted on a panel in Brasenose College, Oxford indicates his true stature was nearer 7 ft 8 in *233,3 cm.* James Toller (1795–1819) of St. Neots, Cambridgeshire was alleged to be 8 ft 6 in *259 cm* but was actually 7 ft 6 in *229 cm.* Albert Brough (1871–1919), a publican of Nottingham, reached a height of 7 ft 7½ in *232 cm.* Frederick Kempster (1889–1918) of Bayswater, London, was reported to have measured 8 ft 4½ in *255 cm* at the time of his death, but photographic evidence suggests that his height was 7 ft 8½ in *235 cm.* He measured 234 cm *7 ft 8.1 in* in 1913. Henry Daglish, who stood 7 ft 7 in *231 cm.* died in Upper Stratton, Wiltshire, on 16 March 1951, aged 25. The much-publicized Edward (Ted) Evans (1924–58) of Englefield Green, Surrey, was reputed to be 9 ft 3 in *282 cm* but actually stood 7 ft 8½ in *235 cm.* The tallest fully mobile man now living in Great Britain is Christopher Paul Greener (b. New Brighton, Merseyside, 21 Nov. 1943) of Hayes, Kent, who measures 7 ft 5¼ in *226,6 cm.* Terence Keenan (b. 1942) of Rock Ferry, Merseyside measures 7 ft 6 in *229 cm,* but is unable to stand erect owing to a leg condition. His abnormal growth began at the age of 17 when he was only 5 ft 4 in *163 cm* tall.

Scotland
The tallest Scotsman, and the tallest recorded "true" (non-pathological) giant, was Angus Macaskill (1825–63), born on the island of Berneray, in the Sound of Harris, in the Western Isles. He stood 7 ft 9 in *236 cm* and died in St. Anns', on Cape Breton Island, Nova Scotia, Canada. Lambert Quételet (1796–1874), a Belgian anthropometrist, considered that a Scotsman named MacQuail, known as "the Scotch Giant", stood 8 ft 3 in *251 cm.* He served in the famous regiment of giants of Frederick William I (1688–1740), King of Prussia. His skeleton, now in the Staatliche Museum zu Berlin, East Germany, measures 220 cm *7 ft 2.6 in.* Sam McDonald (1762–1802) of Lairg in Sutherland, was reputed to be 8 ft *244 cm* tall but actually stood 6 ft 10 in *208 cm.* The tallest Scotsman now living is George Gracie (b. 1938) of Forth, Strathclyde. He stands 7 ft 3 in *221 cm* and weighs 28 st. *178 kg.* His brother Hugh (b. 1941) is 7 ft 0½ in *215 cm.*

Wales
The tallest Welshman on record was William Evans (1599–1634) of Monmouthshire, who was porter to King James I. He stood 7 ft 6 in *228,2 cm.*

Ireland
The tallest Irishman was Patrick Cotter O'Brien (1760–1806), born in Kinsale, County Cork. He died at Hotwells, Bristol. (See Table opposite) The tallest Irishman now living is believed to be Jim Cully (b. 1926) of Tipperary, a former boxer and wrestler. He stands 7 ft 2 in *218 cm.*

TALLEST GIANTESSES
World *All-time*
Giantesses are rarer than giants but their heights are still spectacular. The tallest woman in medical history was the acromegalic giantess Jane ('Ginny') Bunford, born on 26 July 1895 at Bartley Green, Northfield, West Midlands. Her abnormal growth started at the age of 11 following a head injury, and on her 13th birthday she measured 6 ft 6 in *198 cm.* Shortly before her death on 1 April 1922 she stood 7 ft 7 in *231 cm* tall, but she had severe kypho-scoliosis and would have measured about 7 ft 11 in *241 cm* with assumed normal spinal curvature. Her skeleton, now preserved in the Anatomical Museum in the Medical School at Birmingham University, has a mounted height of 7 ft 4 in *223,5 cm.* Anna Hanen Swan (1846–88) of Nova Scotia, Canada, was billed at 8 ft 1 in *246 cm* but actually measured 7 ft 5½ in *227 cm.* In London on 17 June 1871 she married Martin van Buren Bates (1845–1919) of Whitesburg, Letcher County, Kentucky, U.S.A., who stood 7 ft 2½ in *220 cm* making them the tallest married couple on record. The eunuchoidal giantess Ella Ewing (b. Mar. 1872) of Gorin, Missouri, U.S.A., was billed at 8 ft 2 in *249 cm* and reputedly measured 6 ft 9 in *206 cm* at the age of 10 (*cf.* 6 ft 5 in *196 cm* for Robert Wadlow at this age). She measured 7 ft 4½ in *225 cm* at the age of 23 and may have attained 7 ft 6 in *229 cm* before her death in January 1913.

Living
The tallest living woman is Sandy Allen (b. 18 June 1955, Chicago). She now lives in Shelbyville, Indiana, U.S.A. On 14 July 1977 she underwent a pituitary gland operation, which inhibited further growth at 7 ft 7¼ in *231,7 cm.* A 6½ lb. *2,910 kg* baby, her acromegalic growth began soon after birth. She now weighs 31½ st. *200 kg* and takes a size 16EEE American shoe (= 14½ [U.K.] or 50PP [Continental]).

SHORTEST DWARFS
The strictures which apply to giants apply equally to dwarfs, except that exaggeration gives way to understatement. In the same way as 9 ft *274 cm* may be regarded as the limit towards which the tallest giants tend, so 23 in *58 cm* must be regarded as the limit towards which the shortest mature dwarfs tend (*cf.* the average length of new-born babies is 18–20 in *46–50 cm*). In the case of child dwarfs their *ages* are often enhanced by their agents or managers.

There are many forms of human dwarfism. Ateleiotic dwarfs, known as midgets, have essentially normal proportions but suffer from growth hormone deficiency. Such dwarfs tended to be even shorter at a time when human stature was generally shorter due to lower nutritional standards.

World *All-time*

The shortest mature human of whom there is independent evidence was Pauline Musters ('Princess Pauline'), a Dutch midget. She was born at Ossendrecht, on 26 Feb. 1876 and measured 30 cm *12 in* at birth. At the age of 9 she was 55 cm *21.65 in* tall and weighed only 1,5 kg *3 lb. 5 oz.* She died, at the age of 19, of pneumonia, with meningitis, her heart weakened from alcoholic excesses, on 1 March 1895 in New York City, N.Y., U.S.A. Although she was billed at 48 cm *19 in*, she had earlier been medically measured to be 59 cm *23.2 in* tall. A *post mortem* examination showed her to be exactly 61 cm *24 in* (there was some elongation after death). Her mature weight varied from 3,4 kg to 4 kg *7½ lb. to 9 lb.* and her "vital statistics" were 47–48–43 cm *18½–19–17 in*, which suggests she was overweight.

The Italian girl Caroline Crachami, born in Palermo, Sicily, in 1815, was only 20.2 in *51,3 cm* tall when she died in London in 1824, aged 9. At birth she measured 7 in *18 cm* long and weighed 1 lb. *450 g.* Her skeleton, measuring 19.8 in *50,3 cm*, is now part of the Hunterian collection in the Museum of the Royal College of Surgeons, London.

Male *All-time*

The shortest recorded adult male dwarf was Calvin Phillips, born on 14 Jan. 1791 in Bridgewater, Massachusetts, U.S.A. He weighed 2 lb. *907 g* at birth and stopped growing at the age of 5. When he was 19 he measured 26½ in *67 cm* tall and weighed 12 lb. *5,4 kg* with his clothes on. He died two years later, in April 1812, from progeria, a rare disorder characterised by dwarfism and premature senility.

The most famous midget in history was Charles Sherwood Stratton, *alias* "General Tom Thumb", born on 4 Jan. 1838. When he got into the clutches of the circus proprietor Mr. Barnum his birth date was changed to 4 Jan. 1832 so that when billed at 30½ in *77 cm* at the age of 18 he was in fact 12. He died in his birthplace of Bridgeport, Connecticut, U.S.A. of apoplexy on 15 July 1883 aged 45 (not 51) and was 3 ft 4 in *102 cm*.

Another celebrated midget was Józef ('Count') Boruwalaski (b. November 1739) of Poland. He measured only 8 in *20 cm* long at birth, growing to 14 in *36 cm* at the age of one year. He stood 17 in *43 cm* at 6 years, 21 in *53 cm* at 10, 25 in *64 cm* at 15, 35 in *89 cm* at 25 and 39 in *99 cm* at 30. He died near Durham, England, on 5 Sept. 1837, aged 97.

William E. Jackson, *alias* "Major Mite", born on 2 Oct. 1864 in Dunedin, New Zealand, measured 9 in *23 cm* long and weighed 12 oz. *340 g* at birth. In November 1880 he stood 21 in *53 cm* and weighed 9 lb. *4 kg.* He died in New York City, N.Y., U.S.A., on 9 Dec. 1900, when he measured 27 in *70 cm.*

Living

The world's shortest living mature human reported is Nruturam (b. 28 May 1929) a rachitic dwarf in Naydwar, India, who measures 28 in *71 cm*. The circus acrobatic dancer Süleyman Eris (b. 24 Jan. 1955 in Turkey) was medically measured on 3 Mar. 1977 to be 76,5 cm *30.1 in* and weighed 11,4 kg *25 lb. 2 oz.* He and his brother (83,5 cm *32.8 in*) and sister (96,5 cm *38 in*) are primordial dwarfs.

United Kingdom

The shortest mature human ever recorded in Britain was Miss Joyce Carpenter (b. 21 Dec. 1929), a rachitic dwarf of Charford, Hereford and Worcester, who stood 29 in *74 cm* tall and weighed 30 lb. *13,60 kg.* She died on 7 Aug. 1973 aged 43. Hopkins Hopkins (1737–54) of Llantrisant, Mid Glamorgan was 31 in *79 cm.* Hopkins, who died from progeria (see below) weighed 19 lb. *8,62 kg* at the age of 7 and 13 lb. *6 kg* at the time of his death. There are an estimated 2,000 people of severely restricted growth i.e. under 4 ft 8 in *142 cm* living in Britain today.

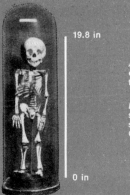

19.8 in

0 in

Above: A Victorian poster advertising the exhibiting of the most famous midget of all time—Tom Thumb.

Left: Measuring only 20.2 in *51,3 cm* when she died aged 9, Caroline Crachami's skeleton is now preserved by the Royal College of Surgeons in London.

The shortest adult in Britain is Norman Goodwin (b. 16 May 1937) of Broom Hayes, South Yorkshire, who is 3 ft 3 in *99 cm* tall. He stopped growing at 14.

Oldest

There are only two centenarian dwarfs on record. The first was Miss Anne Clowes of Matlock, Derbyshire, who died on 5 August 1784 aged 103 years. She was 3 ft 9 in *114 cm* tall and weighed 48 lb. *21,7 kg*. On 6 April 1979 Hungarian–born Miss Susanna Bokoyni ('Princess Susanna') of Newton, New Jersey, U.S.A. celebrated her 100th birthday. She is 3 ft 2 in *96 cm* tall and weighs 40 lb. *18,14 kg*.

Most variable stature

Adam Rainer, born in Graz, Austria, in 1899, measured 118 cm *3 ft 10.45 in* at the age of 21. But then he suddenly started growing upwards at a rapid rate, and by 1931 he had reached 218 cm *7 ft 1¾ in*. He became so weak as a result that he was bed-ridden for the rest of his life. He died on 4 March 1950 aged 51.

TRIBES
Tallest

The tallest major tribe in the world is the Tutsi (also Watussi), Nilotic herdsmen of Rwanda and Burundi, Central Africa whose young adult males average 180 cm *5 ft 10¾ in*. The Tehuelches of Patagonia, long regarded as of gigantic stature (*i.e.* 7 to 8 ft *213* to *244 cm*), have in fact an average height (males) of 5 ft 10 in *178 cm*. A tribe with an average height of more than 6 ft *183 cm* reported from the inland region of Passis Manua of New Britain in December 1956 may be wholly discounted. The Montenegrins of Yugoslavia, with a male average of 5 ft 10 in *178 cm* (in the town of Trebinje the average height is 6 ft *183 cm*), compares with the men of Sutherland, at 5 ft 9½ in *176,5 cm*. In 1912 the average height of the men living in Balmaclellan, Kircudbrightshire was reported to be 5 ft 10.4 in *179 cm*.

Shortest

The smallest pygmies are the Mbuti, with an average height of 4 ft 6 in *137 cm* for men and 4 ft 5 in *135 cm* for women, with some groups averaging only 4 ft 4 in *132 cm* for men and 4 ft 1 in *124 cm* for women. They live in the forests near the river Ituri in the Congo (Kinshasa), Africa.

WEIGHT
Heaviest Men *World*

The greatest weight ever attributed to a human has been 84 st. 11 lb. (1,187 lb.) *538 kg* in the case of Francis John Lang (b. 1934) *alias* Michael Walker of Clinton, Iowa, U.S.A. He could not be admitted for treatment for inflammation of the gall bladder to the Veteran's Administration Hospital, Houston, Texas U.S.A. because of the impossibility of getting him through the doors. He was treated in a caravan in the car park and discharged on 5 Jan. 1972 unweighed but estimated to be between 900 and 1,000 lb. *408–453 kg*. The more precise weight above was claimed for him, while suffering from drug-induced bulimia, in the summer of 1971 when he was working with the Christian Farms of Killeen, Texas. There is, however, no independent corroboration for this precise upper weight quoted, although photographic evidence suggests the weight was possibly reliable.

The highest undisputed weight for a human remains 76 st. 5 lb. (1,069 lb.) *485 kg* for Robert Earl Hughes (b. Monticello, Missouri, U.S.A., 4 June 1926) buried in a coffin the size of a piano crate in Benville Cemetery, Illinois, U.S.A. on 10 July 1958.

Great Britain

The heaviest recorded man in Great Britain was William Campbell, who was born in Glasgow in 1856 and died on 16 June 1878, when a publican at High Bridge, Newcastle upon Tyne, Tyne and Wear. He was 6 ft 3 in *191 cm* tall and weighed 53 st. 8 lb. *340 kg* with an 85-in *216 cm* waist and a 96-in *244 cm* chest. His coffin weighed 1,500 lb. *680 kg*. He was "a man of considerable intelligence and humour". The only other British man with a recorded weight of more than 50 st. *317,5 kg* was the celebrated Daniel Lambert (1770–1809) of Leicester. He stood 5 ft 11 in *180 cm* tall, weighed 52 st. 11 lb. *335 kg* shortly before his death and had a girth of more than 92 in *234 cm*.

The highest weight attained by any man living in Britain today was that of Eric Keeling (born 1933) of Islington, Greater London who scaled 47 st. *299 kg* in mid-1971. An 11 lb. *5 kg* baby he weighed 18 st. *114,5 kg* at the age of 13. By November 1973 he had reduced by dieting (600 calories per day) to 33 st. *210 kg*. He is 6 ft 5 in *195,5 cm* tall.

George McAree (b. 24 Dec. 1923) of Newham, Greater London, is the heaviest man in Britain. In August 1978 he scaled 40 st. 4 lb. *256 kg*. He is 5 ft 10½ in *179 cm* tall and has vital statistics of 83-75-86 in *211-190-218 cm*.

Ireland

The heaviest Irishman is reputed to have been Roger Byrne, who was buried in Rosenallis, County Laoighis (Leix), on 14 March 1804. He died in his 54th year and his coffin and its contents weighed 52 st. *330 kg*. Another Irish heavyweight was Lovelace Love (1731–66), born in Brook Hill, County Mayo. He weighed "upward of 40 st. *254 kg*" at the time of his death.

The only other men for whom weights of more than 55 stone (770 lb.) *350 kg* have been reliably reported are the nine listed below:

	Stone	lb.	kg
Mills Darden (1798–1857) U.S.A. (7 ft 6 in *2,29 m*)	72	12	463
John Hanson Craig (1856–94) U.S.A. (6 ft 5 in *1,95 m*)[1]	64	11	411
Arthur Knorr (1914–60) U.S.A. (6 ft 1 in *1,85 m*)[2]	64	4	408
John Minnoch (b. 1941) USA (5 ft 10 in *1,78 m*)[3]	64	4	408
Toubi (b. 1946) Cameroon	61	3½	389
T. A. Valenzuela (1895–1937) Mexico (5 ft 11 in *1,80 m*)	60	10	386
David Maguire (1904–*fl.* 1935) U.S.A. (5 ft 10 in *1,78 m*)	57	12	367
William J. Cobb (b. 1926) U.S.A. (6 ft 0 in *1,83 m*)[4]	57	4	363
Unnamed Patient (b. 1936) Richmond, Virginia, U.S.A. Aug. 1973	57	2¼	363

[1] Won $1,000 in a "Bonny Baby" contest in New York City in 1858.
[2] Gained 300 lb. *136 kg* in the last 6 months of his life.
[3] Weight unconfirmed by Seatte Hospital, March 1978.
[4] Reduced to 16 st. 8 lb. *105 kg* by July 1965.

Heaviest Women *World*

The heaviest woman ever recorded was the late Mrs. Percy Pearl Washington, 46 who died in a hospital in Milwaukee, on 9 Oct. 1972. The hospital scales registered only up to 800 lb. (57 st. 2 lb.) *362,8 kg* but she was believed to weigh about 880 lb. (62 st. 12 lb.) *399,1 kg*. The previous feminine weight record had been set 84 years earlier at 850 lb. (60 st. 10 lb.) *386 kg* although a wholly unsubstantiated report exists of a woman Mrs. Ida Maitland (1898–1932) of Springfield, Mississippi, U.S.A., who reputedly weighed 65 st. 1 lb. (911 lb.) *413,2 kg*.

A more reliable and better documented case was that of Mrs. Flora Mae Jackson (*née* King), a 5 ft 9 in *175 cm* negress born in 1930 at Shuqualak, Mississippi, U.S.A. She weighed 10 lb. *4,5 kg* at birth, 19 st. 1 lb. (267 lb.) *121 kg* at the age of 11, 44 st. 5 lb. (621 lb.) *282 kg* at 25 and 60 st. (840 lb.) *381 kg* shortly before her death in Meridian, Mississippi, on 9 Dec. 1965. She was known in show business as "Baby Flo".

Great Britain and Ireland

The heaviest woman ever recorded in Great Britain was Mrs. Muriel Hopkins (b. 1931) of Tipton, West Midlands who weighed 43 st. 11 lb. *278 kg* (height 5 ft 11 in *1,8 m*) in

Billy and Benny McCrary, the world's heaviest twins currently weighing in at 53 st 1 lb. *337 kg* and 51 st. 11 lb. *328 kg* respectively. *(Dale Scherfling)*

1978. Shortly before her death on 22 Apr. 1979 she reportedly scaled 52 st. *330 kg*, but this was only an estimate and her actual weight was believed to have been about 47½ st. *301 kg*. Her coffin measured 6 ft 3 in *1,90 m* in length, 4ft 6 in *1,37 m* wide and 3 ft *91 cm* deep. The heaviest weight of a woman living in Britain today was that of Miss Jean Renwick (b. 1939) of Brixton, London, who weighed 40 st. 2 lb. *254 kg* (height 5 ft 3½ in *161 cm*) in January 1972. Since dieting her lowest weight has been 22 st. 2 lb. *141 kg*.

Heaviest twins
The heaviest twins in the world are Billy Leon and Benny Loyd McCrary *alias* McGuire (b. 7 Dec. 1946) of Hendersonville, North Carolina, U.S.A., who in November 1978 were weighed at 743 lb. *337 kg* (Billy) and 723 lb. *328 kg* (Benny) and had 84 in *2,13 m* waists. As professional tag wrestling performers they were *billed* at weights up to 770 lb. *349 kg*. After one 6 week strict slimming course in a hospital, they emerged weighing 5 lb. *2,26 kg* more.

Lightest World
The lightest adult human on record was Lucia Zarate (b. San Carlos, Mexico 2 Jan. 1863, d. October 1889), an emaciated Mexican ateleiotic dwarf of 26½ in *67 cm*, who weighed 2,125 kg *4.7 lb.* at the age of 17. She "fattened up" to 13 lb. *5 kg 90* by her 20th birthday. At birth she weighed 2½ lb. *1,1 kg*. The lightest adult ever recorded in the United Kingdom was Hopkins Hopkins (Shortest dwarfs, see p. 11).

The thinnest recorded adults of normal height are those suffering from Simmonds' Disease (Hypophyseal cachexia). Losses up to 65 per cent of the original body-weight have been recorded in females, with a "low" of 3 st. 3 lb. *20 kg* in the case of Emma Shaller (b. St. Louis, Missouri 8 July 1868, d. 4 Oct. 1890), who stood 5 ft 2 in *1,57 m*. Edward C. Hagner (1892–1962), *alias* Eddie Masher (U.S.A.) is alleged to have weighed only 3 st. 6 lb. *22 kg* at a height of 5 ft 7 in *170 cm*. He was also known as "the Skeleton Dude". In August 1825

the biceps measurement of Claude-Ambroise Seurat (b. 10 April 1797, d. 6 April 1826) of Troyes, France was 4 in *10 cm* and the distance between his back and his chest was less than 3 in *8 cm*. According to one report he stood 5 ft 7½ in *171 cm* and weighed 5 st. 8 lb. *35 kg*, but in another account was described as 5 ft 4 in *163 cm* and only 2 st. 8 lb. *16 kg*. It was recorded that the American exhibitionist Rosa Lee Plemons (b. 1873) weighed 27 lb. *12 kg* at the age of 18. In cases of anorexia nervosa, weights of under 5 st. *32 kg* have also been reported.

Lightest Great Britain
Robert Thorn (b. 1842) of March, Cambridgeshire weighed 49 lb. *22 kg* at the age of 32. He was 4 ft 6 in *137 cm* tall and had a 27 in *68 cm* chest (expanded) and 4½ in *11 cm* biceps.

Slimming
The greatest recorded slimming feat was that of William J. Cobb (b. 1926), *alias* "Happy Humphrey", a professional wrestler of Macon, Georgia, U.S.A. It was reported in July 1965 that he had reduced from 57 st. 4 lb. *364 kg* to 16 st. 8 lb. *105 kg*, a loss of 40 st. 10 lb. *259 kg* in 3 years. His waist measurement declined from 101 in to 44 in *257 cm* to *112 cm*. In October 1973 it was reported that "Happy" was back to his normal weight of 46½ st. or 650 lb. *295 kg*.

The U.S. circus fat lady Mrs. Celesta Geyer (b. 1901), *alias* Dolly Dimples, reduced from 553 lb. *251 kg* to 152 lb. *69 kg* in 1950–51, a loss of 401 lb. *182 kg* in 14 months. Her vital statistics diminished *pari passu* from 79-84-84 in *200-213-213 cm* to a *svelte* 34-28-36 in *86-71-91 cm*. Her book "How I lost 400 lbs." was not a best-seller because of the difficulty of would-be readers identifying themselves with the dressmaking problems of losing more than 28 st. *178 kg* when 4 ft 11 in *150 cm* tall. In December 1967 she was reportedly down to 7 st. 12 lb. *50 kg*. The speed record for slimming was established by Paul M. Kimelman, 21, of Pittsburgh, Pennsylvania, U.S.A., who from 25 Dec. 1966 to August

1967 went on a crash diet of 300 to 600 calories per day to reduce from 487 lb. (34 st. 11 lb.) *215,9 kg* to 130 lb. (9 st. 4 lb.) *59 kg*—a total loss of 357 lb. (25 st. 7 lb.) *156,9 kg*. He has now stabilised at 175 lb. (12 st. 7 lb.) *79 kg*. On 4–8 February 1951 Mrs. Gertrude Levandowski (b. 1893) of Burnips, Michigan, U.S.A. successfully underwent a series of operations to reduce her weight from 44 st. *280 kg* to 22 st. *140 kg*.

Claude Halls (b. 1937) of Sible Hedingham, Essex reduced from 33 st. 6¾ lb. *212,6 kg* to 12 st. 10 lb. *80,7 kg*—a loss of 20 st. 10¾ lb. *131,8 kg*—in the 14 months January 1974 to March 1975. In the first 7 days with Weight Watchers he lost 5 st. 7 lb. *35 kg*.

The feminine Weight Watchers champion in Britain was Mrs. Dolly Wager (b. 1933) of Charlton, London, who, between Sept. 1971 and 22 May 1973 reduced from 31 st. 7 lb. *197 kg* to 11 st. 7 lb. *69,8 kg* so losing 20 st. 7 lb. *130 kg*.

Weight gaining
A probable record for gaining weight was set by Arthur Knorr (b. 17 May 1914), who died on 7 July 1960, aged 46, in Reseda, California, U.S.A. He gained 21 st. 6 lb. *136 kg* in the last 6 months of his life and weighed 64 st. 4 lb. *408 kg* when he died. Miss Doris James of San Francisco, California, U.S.A. is alleged to have gained 23 st. 3 lb. *147 kg* in the 12 months before her death in August 1965, aged 38, at a weight of 48 st. 3 lb. *306 kg*. She was only 5 ft 2 in *157 cm* tall.

Greatest Differential
The greatest weight differential recorded for a married couple is 65 st. 12 lb. *419 kg* in the case of Mills Darden (72 st. 12 lb. *463 kg*—see p. 12) and his wife Mary (7 st. *44,5 kg*). Despite her diminutiveness, however, Mrs. Darden bore her husband 3 (perhaps 5) children before her death in 1837.

---

2. ORIGINS

EARLIEST MAN
SCALE OF TIME
If the age of the Earth-Moon system (latest estimate at least 4,700 million years) is likened to a single year, Handy Man appeared on the scene at about 8.35 p.m. on 31 December, Britain's earliest known inhabitants arrived at about 11.32 p.m., the Christian era began about 13 sec before midnight and the life span of a 114-year-old person (pp. 15 & 16) would be about three-quarters of a second. Present calculations indicate that the Sun's increased heat, as it becomes a "red giant", will make life insupportable on Earth in about 10,000 million years. Meanwhile there may well be colder epicycles. The period of 1,000 million years is sometimes referred to as an aeon.

Man (*Homo sapiens*) is a species in the sub-family Homininae of the family Hominidae of the super-family Hominoidea of the sub-order Simiae (or Anthropoidea) of the order Primates of the infra-class Eutheria of the sub-class Theria of the class Mammalia of the sub-phylum Vertebrata (Craniata) of the phylum Chordata of the sub-kingdom Metazoa of the animal kingdom.

Earliest *Primate*
The earliest known primates appeared in the Palaeocene period of about 80,000,000 years ago. The sub-order of higher primates, called Simiae (or Anthropoidea) evolved from the catarrhine or old-world sect more than 40,000,000 years later in the Lower Oligocene period. During the Middle and Upper Oligocene the super-family Hominoidea emerged. This contains three accepted families, *viz* Hominidae (bipedal, ground-dwelling man or near man), Pongidae (brachiating forest apes) and Oreopithecidae. The earliest known hominoid (man-like) fossil found is the *Oligopithecus savagei* found in El Faiyum, Egypt and dated to *c* 33 million years ago.

Earliest *Hominid* (*Near Man*)
The characteristics of the Hominidae, such as a large brain, very fully distinguish them from any of the other Hominoidea. Evidence published in August 1969 indicated that *Ramapithecus*, discovered by G. Edward Lewis at Siwalik Hills, northern India in 1932 can be dated from 8–13 million years ago.

Earliest *Genus* Homo (*True Man*)
The greatest age attributed to fossils of the genus *Homo* is for the remains of 8 adults and 3 children discovered in the

summer of 1975 at Laetolil, Tanzania by Dr. Mary Leakey and dated by the University of California, Berkeley to between 3,350,000 and 3,750,000 B.C. An arm bone fragment from Kanapoi has been tentatively regarded as from *Homo* and has been dated *c* 4 million years ago.

The most complete of the earliest skeletons of *Homo* is that of "Lucy" (40% complete) found by Dr Donald C. Johanson and named *Australopithecus afarensis* found in the Afar region of Ethiopia in Nov. 1974 dating 3–4 million years B.P.

Earliest *Homo sapiens*
The earliest recorded remains of the species *Homo sapiens*, variously dated from 300,000 to 450,000 years ago in the Middle Pleistocene, were discovered on 24 Aug. 1965 by Dr. László Vértes in a limestone quarry at Vértasszöllös, about 30 miles west of Budapest, Hungary. The remains, designated *Homo sapiens palaeo-hungaricus*, comprised an almost complete occipital bone, part of a skull with an estimated cranial capacity of nearly 1 400 cm³ *85 in³*.

Earliest man in the Americas date from at least 50,000 B.C. and "more probably 100,000 B.C." according to the late Dr. Leakey after the examination of some hearth stones found in the Mojave Desert, California and announced in October 1970. The earliest human relic is a skull found in the area of Los Angeles, California dated in December 1970 to be from 22,000 B.C.

Great Britain
The earliest evidence for the presence of humans in Great Britain dates from the time of the Cromerian interglacial (400,000–500,000 B.C.) Five Worked flint artifacts of this period were found in deposits of this interglacial in a quarry near Westbury-sub-Mendip, Somerset, and described in 1975 by Michael J. Bishop. The oldest human remains ever found in Britain are pieces of a brain case from a specimen of *Homo sapiens fossilis*, believed to be a woman, recovered in June 1935 and March 1936 by Dr. Alvan T. Marston from the Boyn Hill terrace in the Barnfield Pit, near Swanscombe, northern Kent. This find is attributed to Acheulian man, type *III* or *IV*, dating from the Hoxnian interglacial period.

---

3. LONGEVITY

No single subject is more obscured by vanity, deceit, falsehood and deliberate fraud than the extremes of human longevity. Extreme claims are generally made on behalf of the very aged rather than *by* them.

Many hundreds of claims throughout history have been made for persons living well into their second century and some, insulting to the intelligence, for people living even into their third. Centenarians surviving beyond their 110th year are in fact of the extremest rarity and the present absolute proven limit of human longevity does not yet admit of anyone living to celebrate any birthday after their 114th.

It is highly significant that in Sweden, where alone proper and thorough official investigations follow the death of every allegedly very aged citizen, none has been found to have surpassed 108 years. The most reliably pedigreed large group of people in the world, the British peerage, has, after ten centuries, produced only two centenarian peers, but only one reached his 101st birthday. However, this is possibly not unconnected with the extreme draughtiness of many of their residences and the amount of lead in their game.

Scientific research into extreme old age reveals that the correlation between the claimed density of centenarians in a country and its regional illiteracy is 0.83 ± 0.03. In late life, very old people often tend to advance their ages at the rate of about 17 years per decade. This was nicely corroborated by a cross analysis of the 1901 and 1911 censuses of England and Wales. Early claims must necessarily be without the elementary corroboration of birth dates. England was among the earliest of all countries to introduce compulsory local registers (Sept. 1538) and official birth registration (1 July 1837)

AUTHENTICATED NATIONAL LONGEVITY RECORDS

	Years	Days		Born		Died	
Japan	114	—	Shigechiyo Izumi	29 June	1865	fl.29 June	1979
United States[1]	113	214	Delina Filkins (née Ecker)	4 May	1815	4 Dec.	1928
Canada[2]	113	124	Pierre Joubert	15 July	1701	16 Nov.	1814
United Kingdom[3]	112	39	Alice Stevenson	10 July	1861	18 Aug.	1973
Morocco	>112		El Hadj Mohammed el Mokri (Grand Vizier)		1844	16 Sept.	1957
Ireland	111	327	The Hon. Katherine Plunket	22 Nov.	1820	14 Oct.	1932
France	111	c 210	Virginie Duhem	Aug.	1866	1 May	1978
South Africa[4]	111	151	Johanna Booyson	17 Jan.	1857	16 June	1968
Czechoslovakia	111	+	Marie Bernatkova	22 Oct.	1857	fl.Oct.	1968
Channel Islands	110	321	Margaret Ann Neve (née Harvey)	18 May	1792	4 April	1903
Northern Ireland	110	234	Elizabeth Watkins (Mrs.)	10 Mar.	1863	31 Oct.	1973
Yugoslavia	110	150+	Demitrius Philipovitch	9 Mar.	1818	fl.Aug.	1928
Netherlands	110	113	Geert Adriaans Boomgaard	23 Sept.	1788	3 Feb.	1899
Australia[5]	110	39	Ada Sharp (Mrs.)	6 April	1861	15 May	1971
U.S.S.R.[6]	110	+	Khasako Dzugayev	7 Aug.	1860	fl.Aug.	1970
Tasmania (State of)	109	179	Mary Ann Crow (Mrs.)	2 Feb.	1836	31 July	1945
Italy	109	179	Rosalia Spoto	25 Aug.	1847	20 Feb.	1957
Scotland	109	14	Rachel MacArthur (Mrs.)	26 Nov.	1827	10 Dec.	1936
Norway	109	+	Marie Olsen (Mrs.)	1 May	1850	fl.May	1959
Belgium	108	327	Mathilda Vertommen-Hellemans	12 Aug.	1868	4 July	1977
Germany[7]	108	128	Luise Schwarz	27 Sept.	1849	2 Feb.	1958
Portugal[8]	108	+	Maria Luisa Jorge	7 June	1859	fl.July	1967
Finland	107	221	Amalia Wallenius (Mrs.)	6 Aug.	1867	24 Mar.	1975
Sweden	107	94	Anna Johansson	21 Nov.	1865	23 Feb.	1973
Austria	106	231	Anna Migschitz	3 Feb.	1850	1 Nov.	1956
Spain[9]	106	14	Jose Palido	15 Mar.	1866	29 Mar.	1972
Malaysia	106	+	Hassan Bin Yusoff	14 Aug.	1865	fl.Jan.	1972
Isle of Man	105	221	John Kneen	12 Nov.	1852	9 June	1958

[1] The U.S. Veteran Administration was in March 1974 paying pensions to 272 women attested to be widows of veterans of the Civil War (1860–65), the last soldier having died 15 years earlier in 1959. The oldest of these is Angela Felicia Virginia Davalos (Mrs. Harry Harrison Moran), who filed a claim dated 1928 with a baptismal certificate showing 17 May 1856 in Morelia, Mexico as her date and place of birth.

[2] Mrs. Ellen Carroll died in North River, Newfoundland, Canada on 8 December 1943, reputedly aged 115 years 49 days.

[3] London-born Miss Isabella Shepheard was allegedly 115 years old when she died at St. Asaph, Clwyd, North Wales, on 20 Nov. 1948, but her actual age was believed to have been 109 years 90 days. Charles Alfred Nunez Arnold died in Liverpool on 15 Sept. 1941 reputedly aged 112 years 66 days based on a baptismal claim (London, 10 Nov. 1829·; Mrs. Elizabeth Cornish (née Veale) who was buried at Stratton, Cornwall on 10 Mar. 1691/2 was reputedly baptized on 16 Oct. 1578, 112/3 years 4 months earlier.

[4] Mrs. Susan Johanna Deporter of Port Elizabeth, South Africa, was reputedly

114 years old when she died on 4 August 1954. Mrs. Sarah Lawrence, Cape Town, South Africa was reputedly 112 on 3 June 1968.

[5] Reginald Beck of Sydney, New South Wales, Australia was allegedly 111 years old when he died on 13 April 1928.

[6] There are allegedly 21,700 centenarians in U.S.S.R. (c.f. 7,000 in U.S.A.). Of these 21,000 are ascribed to the Georgian S.S.R. i.e. one in every 232. In July 1962 it was reported that 128, mostly male, were in the one village of Medini.

[7] Friedrich Sadowski of Heidelberg reputedly celebrated his 111th birthday on 31 October 1936. Franz Joseph Eder d. Spitzburg 3 May 1911 allegedly aged 116.

[8] Senhora Jesuina da Conceicao of Lisbon was reputedly 113 years when she died on 10 June 1965.

[9] Juana Ortega Villarin, Madrid, Spain, was allegedly 112 in February 1962. Ana Maria Parraga of Murcia was reportedly 107 in Nov. 1969.

which was made fully compulsory only in 1874. Even in the United States, 45 per cent of births occurring between 1890 and 1920 were unregistered.

Several celebrated super-centenarians are believed to have been double lives (father and son, relations with the same names or successive bearers of a title). The most famous example is Christian Jakobsen Drackenberg allegedly born in Stavanger, Norway on 18 Nov. 1626 and died in Aarhus, Denmark aged seemingly 145 years 326 days on 9 Oct. 1772. A number of instances have been commercially sponsored, while a fourth category of recent claims are those made for political ends, such as the 100 citizens of the Russian Soviet Federative Socialist Republic (population about 132,000,000 at mid-1967) claimed in March 1960 to be between 120 and 156. From data on documented centenarians, actuaries have shown that only one 115-year life can be expected in 2,100 million lives (cf. world population was estimated to be 4,205 million at mid-1978).

The height of credulity was reached on 5 May 1933, when a newsagency solemnly filed a story from China with a Peking date-line that Li Chung-yun, the "oldest man on Earth", born in 1680, had just died aged 256 years (sic). Recently the most extreme case of longevity claimed in the U.S.S.R. has been 168 years for Shirali "Baba" Mislimov of Barzavu, Azerbaijan, who died on 2 Sept. 1973 and was reputedly born on 26 Mar. 1805. No interview of this man has ever been permitted to any Western journalist or scientist. He was said to have celebrated the 100th birthday of his third wife Hartun, in 1966, and that of one of his grandchildren in August 1973. It was reported in 1954 that in the Abkhasian Republic of Georgia U.S.S.R., where aged citizens are invested with an almost saint-like status, 2.58 per cent of the population was aged over 90—25 times the proportion in the U.S.A.

Dr. Zhores A. Medvedev, the expelled Soviet gerontologist, in Washington D.C., on 30 Apr. 1974 referring to U.S.S.R.

claims stated "The whole phenomenon looks like a falsification" adding "He (Stalin) liked the idea that (other) Georgians lived to be a 100 or more". "Local officials tried hard to find more and more cases for Stalin". He points out (a) the average life span in the regions claiming the highest incidence of centenarians is lower than the U.S.S.R. average and (b) the number of centenarians claimed in the Caucasus has declined rapidly from 8,000 in 1950 to 4,500 in 1970. Dr. I. M. Spector, of the Institute of Traumatology, Kazan, U.S.S.R. quoted the maximum life-span of man in Apr. 1974 as "110–115 years", though Dr. Medvedev, in Dec. 1977, put the proven limit in the U.S.S.R as low as 108 years.

After 4 years the Andean valley of Vilcabamba in Ecuador ceased, from February 1978, to be the source of highly publicized and uncritical reports about very aged humans. These, it was said, lived up to 25 years beyond the so far acceptable limit of about 115 years. The discovery by Mazess and Forman was published in March 1978 that inhabitants had pointed to baptismal entries of their fathers, and even their grandfathers as their own, reduced the age of the valley's oldest man from 140 to 96. The lucrative income from tourism is expected to decline pari passu.

Charlie Smith of Bartow, Florida, U.S.A. obtained a Social Security card in 1955 when claiming to be born on 4 July 1842 in Liberia. The U.S. Department of Health, Education and Welfare state that they are "unable to disclose the type of evidence used" to determine Mr. Smith's age because such disclosure "would infringe on the confidentiality of the individual's record". He celebrated what he reckoned to be his 136th birthday on 4 July 1978. However a reference to the county records at Arcadia, Florida (Book 2, page 392) reveals a marriage contracted aged 35 on 8 Jan. 1910 and hence an exaggeration of some 33 years.

George Fruits, a War of Independence veteran, reputedly born in Baltimore, Maryland on 2 Feb. 1762 died on 6 Aug.

1876 at Alamo, Indiana at a putative age of 114 years. New research by A. Ross Eckler in 1978 indicates however that he was 17 years younger than his gravestone age. The 1900 U.S. Federal Census for Crawfish Springs Militia District of Walker County, Georgia, records a Mark Thrash aged 77. If the Mark Thrash (reputedly born in Georgia in Dec. 1822) who died near Chattanooga, Tennessee on 17 Dec. 1943 was he, then he would have survived for 121 years.

Oldest authentic centenarian *World*
The greatest authenticated age to which a human has ever lived is a 114th birthday in the case of Shigechiyo Izumi of Tokunoshima, Kagoshima Prefecture. He was born on 29 June 1865 and recorded as a 6 year old in Japan's first census of 1871. He watches television and says the best way to a long life is "not to worry".

In the face of the above data the claim published in the April 1961 issue of the Soviet Union's *Vestnik Statistiki* ('Statistical Herald') that there were 224 male and 368 female Soviet citizens aged in excess of 120 recorded at the census of 15 Jan. 1959, indicates a reliance on hearsay rather than evidence. Official Soviet insistence on the unrivalled longevity of the country's citizenry is curious in view of the fact that the 592 persons in their unique "over 120" category must have spent at least the first 78 years of their prolonged lives under Tsarism. It has recently been suggested that the extreme ages claimed by some men in Georgia, U.S.S.R., are the result of attempts to avoid military service when they were younger, by assuming the identities of older men.

Oldest authentic centenarian *Great Britain*
The United Kingdom has an estimated population of 2,900 (2,360 women and 540 men) centenarians. The number of centenarians reported in Britain was only 140 in 1951, but 520 in 1961 and 2,430 in the 1971 census. Miss Alice Stevenson (1861–1973) (see table p. 15) is the only U.K. citizen with birth and death certificates more than 112 years apart. In April 1706 a John Bailes was buried at All Saints Church, Northampton, having apparently been baptized on 20 Aug. 1592. If the same person, he would have been 113 years 8 months. The oldest centenarian known in Britain who was alive entering 1979, was Mrs Lilias Browning Williams (*née* Hooper) born in Camelford on 30 Nov. 1868, of Launceston, Cornwall, who died on 13 Feb. 1979 aged 110 years 75 days. However, Mrs. Florence Pannell (*née* Neate) of Holland Park, London (born Westminster, 26 Dec. 1868) reached 110 years 175 days on 19 June 1979.

Oldest Triplets
The longest lived triplets on record were Faith, Hope and Charity Caughlin born at Marlboro, Massachusetts, U.S.A. on 27 Mar. 1868. The first to die was Mrs. (Ellen) Hope Daniels aged 93 on 2 Mar. 1962.

Oldest Twins *World*
The chances of identical twins both reaching 100 are said to be one in 700 million. The oldest recorded twins were Eli and John Phipps (b. 14 Feb. 1803, Affinghton, Virginia). Eli died at Hennessey, Oklahoma, U.S.A. on 23 Feb. 1911 aged 108 years 9 days on which day John was still living in Shenandoah, Iowa.

Great Britain
The oldest twins on record in Great Britain have been the Bean twins Robert, of Birkenhead, Merseyside and Mary (now Mrs. Simpson) of Etton, Cambridgeshire who celebrated their 100th birthday on 19 Oct. 1973. Robert died before the end of 1973.

Last 18th Century Link
The last known Briton with 18th century paternity was Miss Alice J. Grigg of Belvedere, Kent (d. 28 Apr. 1970) whose father William was born on 26 Oct. 1799.

Most reigns
The greatest number of reigns during which any English subject could have lived is ten. A person born on the day (11 April) that Henry VI was deposed in 1471 had to live to only the comparatively modest age of 87 years 7 months and 6 days

to see the accession of Elizabeth I on 17 Nov. 1558. Such a person could have been Thomas Carn of London, reputedly born in 1471 and died 28 Jan. 1578 in his 107th year.

---

4. REPRODUCTIVITY

MOTHERHOOD
Most children *World*
The greatest officially recorded number of children produced by a mother is 69 by the first of the two wives of Feodor Vassilyev (b. 1707– *fl.*1782), a peasant from Shuya, 150 miles *241 km* east of Moscow, who, in 27 confinements, gave birth to 16 pairs of twins, 7 sets of triplets and 4 sets of quadruplets. The case was reported by the Monastry of Nikolskiy on 27 Feb. 1782 to Moscow. At least 67 survived infancy. Empress Ekaterina II (The Great) (1762–1796) was reputed to have evinced interest. The children of whom almost all survived to their majority were born in the period *c.*1725–1765.

Currently the highest reported figure is a 32nd child born to Raimundo Carnauba, and his wife Madalena of Ceilandia, Brazil. She was married at 13 and has had 24 sons and 8 daughters. The mother in May 1972 said "They have given us a lot of work and worry but they are worth it", and the father "I don't know why people make such a fuss", The above figures are tentative since no two published interviews with this family seem to produce entirely consistent data.

Great Britain
The British record is seemingly held by Elizabeth, wife of John Mott married in 1676 of Monks Kirby, Warwickshire who produced 42 live-born children. She died in 1720, 44 years later. According to an inscription on a gravestone in Conway Church cemetery, Gwynedd, North Wales, Nicholas Hookes (d. 27 March 1637) was the 41st child of his mother Alice Hookes, but further details are lacking. It has not been possible to corroborate or refute this report. The highest recent reported figure is 24 children born to Mrs. Emily Jane Lucas (b. 1881) of Tonbridge, Kent who died in July 1967.

Great Britain's champion mothers of today are believed to be Mrs. Margaret McNaught (b. 1923), of Balsall Heath, Birmingham (12 boys and 10 girls, all single births) and Mrs. Mabel Constable (b. 1920), of Long Itchington, Warwickshire who also has had 22 children including a set of triplets and two sets of twins.

Oldest mother *World*
Medical literature contains extreme but unauthenticated cases of septuagenarian mothers, such as Mrs. Ellen Ellis, aged 72, of Four Crosses, Clwyd, who allegedly produced a still-born 13th child on 15 May 1776 in her 46th year of marriage. Many cases are cover-ups for illegitimate grandchildren. The oldest recorded mother of whom there is certain evidence is Mrs. Ruth Alice Kistler (*née* Taylor), formerly Mrs. Shepard, of Portland, Oregon, U.S.A. She was born at Wakefield, Massachusetts, on 11 June 1899 and gave birth to a daughter, Suzan, at Glendale, near Los Angeles, California, on 18 Oct. 1956, when her age was 57 years 129 days. The incidence of quinquagenarian births varies widely with the highest purported rate being in Albania (with nearly 5,500 per million) compared with 2 per million in England & Wales.

Great Britain
The oldest British mother reliably recorded is Mrs. Winifred Wilson (*née* Stanley) of Eccles, Greater Manchester. She was born in Wolverhampton on 11 Nov. 1881 or 1882 and had her tenth child, a daughter Shirley, on Nov. 14 1936, when aged 54 or 55 years and 3 days. She died aged 91 or 92 in January 1974. At Southampton on 10 Feb. 1916, Mrs. Elizabeth Pearce gave birth to a son when aged 54 years 40 days.

Ireland
The oldest Irish mother recorded was Mrs. Mary Higgins of

Cork, County Cork (b. 7 Jan. 1876) who gave birth to a daughter, Patricia, on 17 March 1931 when aged 55 years 69 days.

Descendants

In polygamous countries, the number of a person's descendants can become incalculable. The last Sharifian Emperor of Morocco, Moulay Ismail (1672–1727), known as "The Bloodthirsty", was reputed to have fathered a total of 548 sons and 340 daughters.

Capt. Wilson Kettle (b. 1860) of Grand Bay, Port aux Basques, Newfoundland, Canada, died on 25 Jan. 1963, aged 102, leaving 11 children by two wives, 65 grandchildren, 201 great-grandchildren and 305 great-great-grandchildren, a total of 582 living descendants. Mrs. Johanna Booyson (see page 15), of Belfast, Transvaal, was estimated to have 600 living descendants in South Africa in January 1968.

Mrs. Sarah Crawshaw (d. 25 Dec. 1844) left 397 descendants according to her gravestone in Stones Church, Ripponden, Halifax, West Yorkshire.

Multiple great-grandparents

Theoretically a great-great-great-great-grandparent is a possibility, though in practice countries in which young mothers are common, generally have a low expectation of life. At least eleven cases of great-great-great-grandparents have been reported in the last 20 years. Of these cases the youngest person to learn that their great-granddaughter had become a grandmother was Mrs. Ann V. Weirick (1888–1978) of Paxtonville, Pennsylvania, U.S.A., who received news of her great-great-great-grandson Matthew Stork (b. 9 Sept. 1976) when aged only 88. She died on 6 Jan. 1978.

Most Ascendants

In 1916 Arline Neugart aged 10 months, was photographed in Jackson, Minnesota, U.S.A. with a complete set of parents, grandparents and great-grandparents—14 ascendants. This is believed to be the first such case recorded.

MULTIPLE BIRTHS
Lightest Twins

The lightest recorded birthweight for a pair of surviving twins has been 2 lb. 3 oz. *992 g* in the case of Mary 16 oz. *453 g* and Margaret 19 oz. *538 g* born to Mrs. Florence Stimson, Queens Road, Old Fletton, Peterborough, England, delivered by Dr. Macaulay on 16 Aug. 1931. Margaret is now Mrs. M. J. Hurst.

"Siamese" Twins

Conjoined twins derived the name "Siamese" from the celebrated Chang and Eng Bunker (known in Thailand as Chan and In) born at Maklong, on 11 May 1811. They were joined by a cartilaginous band at the chest and married in April 1843 the Misses Sarah and Adelaide Yates and fathered ten and twelve children respectively. They died within three hours of each other on 17 Jan. 1874, aged 62. The only known British example to reach maturity were the "Scottish brothers", who were born near Glasgow in 1490. They were brought to the Court of King James IV of Scotland the following year, and lived under the king's patronage for the rest of his reign. They died in 1518 aged 28 years. The earliest successful separation of Siamese twins was performed on Prisma and Napit Atkinson (b. May 1953 in Thailand) by Dr. Dragstedt at the University of Chicago on 29 March 1955.

The rarest form of conjoined twins is Dicephales tetrabrachius dipus (two heads, four arms and two legs) of which only two examples are known today. They are the pair Masha and Dasha born in the U.S.S.R. on 4 Jan. 1950 and an unnamed pair separated in a 10 hour operation in Washington, D.C., U.S.A. on 23 June 1977.

Fastest Triplet Birth

The fastest recorded natural birth of triplets has been 2 minutes in the case of Mrs. James E. Duck of Memphis, Tennessee (Bradley, Christopher and Carmon) on 21 March 1977.

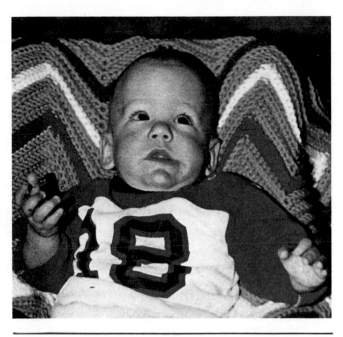

Carmon Scott Duck the sole surviving triplet of the fastest recorded triplet birth.

Quindecaplets

It was announced by Dr. Gennaro Montanino of Rome that he had removed the foetuses of 10 girls and 5 boys from the womb of a 35-year-old housewife on 22 July 1971. A fertility drug was responsible for this unique and unsurpassed instance of quindecaplets.

Longest pregnancy

Claims up to 413 days have been widely reported but accurate data are bedevilled by the increasing use of oral contraceptive pills which is a cause of amenorrhoea. Some women on becoming pregnant erroneously add some preceding periodless months to their pregnancy. In the pre-pill era English law has accepted pregnancies with extremes of 174 days (*Clark* v. *Clark*, 1939) and 349 days (*Hadlum* v. *Hadlum*, 1949).

Most Proximate Births and Shortest Pregnancies

Mrs. Wendra Orr of East Kilbride, Strathclyde gave birth to a son Calum-Stewart on 3 Mar. 1967, and twin daughters Susan Wendra and Sanda Carol on 16 Oct. 1967, 227 days later.

BABIES
Heaviest *World*

The heaviest normal new-born child reported in modern times was a boy weighing 11 kg *24 lb. 4 oz.*, born on 3 June 1961 to Mrs. Saadat Cor of Cegham, Southern Turkey. It was revealed in January 1978 however that, although relayed by a major news agency, no reliance can be placed on this report. Mrs. Anna Bates *née* Swan (see Giantesses) produced a baby weighing 23¾ lb. *10,77 kg* reported in the *New York Medical Record* of 22 Mar. 1879. A deformed baby weighing 29¼ lb. *13,28 kg* was born in May 1939 in a hospital at Effingham, Illinois, U.S.A., but only lived for 2 hours.

Heaviest *United Kingdom*

The greatest recorded live birth weight in the United Kingdom is 21 lb. *9,53 kg* for a child born on Christmas Day, 1852. It was reported in a letter to the *British Medical Journal* (1 Feb. 1879) from a doctor in Torpoint, Cornwall. The only other reported birth weight in excess of 20 lb. *9,07 kg* is 20 lb. 2 oz. *9,13 kg* for a boy born to a 33-year-old schoolmistress in Crewe, Cheshire, on 12 Nov. 1884 with a 14½ in *36,8 cm* chest. A baby of 33 lb. *14,97 kg* was reportedly born to a Mrs. Lambert of Wandsworth Road, London *c.* 1930 but its measurements indicate a weight of about 17 lb. *7,7 kg*.

Most Bouncing Baby

The most bouncing baby on record was probably James

Weir (1819–1821) who, according to his headstone in Cambushnethan, Old Parish Cemetery, Wishaw, Strathclyde, Scotland was 8 st. or 112 lb. *50,8 kg* at 13 months, 3 ft 4 in *1,01 m* in height and 39 in *99 cm* in girth.

Therese Parentean, who died in Rouyn, Quebec, Canada on 11 May 1936 aged 9 years, weighed 24 st. 4 lb. *154 kg*.

Lightest

The lowest birth weight for a surviving infant, of which there is definite evidence, is 10 oz. *283 g* in the case of Marion Chapman, born on 5 June 1938 in South Shields, Tyne and Wear. She was 12¼ in *31 cm* long. By her first birthday her weight had increased to 13 lb. 14 oz. *6 kg 290*. She was born unattended and was nursed by Dr. D. A. Shearer, who fed her hourly through a fountain pen filler. Her weight on her 21st birthday was 7 st. 8 lb. *48 kg 080*. The smallest viable baby reported from the United States has been Jacqueline Benson born at Palatine, Illinois, on 20 Feb. 1936, weighing 12 oz. *340 g*.

A weight of 8 oz. *227 g* was reported on 20 Mar. 1938 for a baby born prematurely to Mrs. John Womack, after she had been knocked down by a lorry in East St. Louis, Illinois, U.S.A. The baby was taken alive to St. Mary's Hospital, but further information is lacking. On 23 Feb. 1952 it was reported that a 6 oz. *170 g* baby only 6½ in *17 cm* long lived for 12 hours in a hospital in Indianapolis, Indiana, U.S.A. A twin was still-born.

Coincident Birthdates

The only verified example of a family producing five single children with coincident birthdays is that of Catherine (1952); Carol (1953); Charles (1956); Claudia (1961) and Cecilia (1966), born to Ralph and Carolyn Cummins of Clintwood, Virginia, U.S.A., all on 20 February. The random odds against five single siblings sharing a birthdate are one in 17,797,577,730—almost 4 times the world's population.

Most Southerly Birth

Emilio Marcos Palma born 7 Jan. 1978 at the Sargento Cabral Base, Antarctica is the only infant who can claim to be the first born on any continent.

A unique photograph, enough to give any mere twin an inferiority complex—a picnic exclusive to triplets and quadruplets held in St. Paul, Minnesota, U.S.A. on 30 July 1973. It was convened and photographed by the "Supertwinologist" Lani Pettit of Sioux City, Iowa.

Test Tube Baby *Earliest*

Louise Brown (5 lb. 12 oz. *2,600 kg*) was delivered by Caesarian section from Lesley Brown, 31, in Oldham General Hospital, Lancashire, at 11.47 p.m. on 25 July 1978. She was externally conceived on 10 Nov. 1977.

MULTIPLE BIRTHS

	World	United Kingdom
Highest number reported at single birth	10 (decaplets) (2 male, 8 female) Bacacay, Brazil 22 Apr. 1946 (also report from Spain, 1924 and China 12 May 1936)	
Highest number medically recorded	9 (nonuplets) (5 male, 4 female) to Mrs. Geraldine Broderick at Royal Hospital, Sydney, Australia on 13 June 1971. 2 males stillborn. Richard (12 oz. *340 g*) survived 6 days 9 (all also died) to patient at University of Pennsylvania, Philadelphia 29 May 1972 9 (all died) reported from Bagerhat, Bangladesh c 11 May 1977 to 30 year old mother	6 (sextuplets) (2 male, 4 female) to Mrs. Sheila Ann Thorns (*née* Manning) at New Birmingham Maternity Hospital on 2 Oct. 1968. Three survive 6 (1 male, 5 female) to Mrs. Rosemary Letts (*née* Egerton) at University College Hospital, Greater London on 15 Dec. 1969. One boy and 4 girls survive
Highest number surviving	6 out of 6 (3 males, 3 females) to Mrs. Susan Jane Rosenkowitz (*née* Scoones) (b. Colombo, Sri Lanka, 28 Oct. 1947) at Mowbray, Cape Town, South Africa on 11 Jan. 1974 In order of birth they were: David, Nicolette, Jason, Emma, Grant and Elizabeth. They totalled 24 lb. 1 oz. *10,915 kg*.	5 out of 6 (as above) and also 5 out of 5 (5 females) to Mrs. Irene Mary Hanson (*née* Brown) at Queen Charlotte's Hospital London on 13 Nov. 1969. and 5 out of 5 (1 male, 4 females) to Mrs. James Bostock of Armadale, Lothian, Scotland (no use of fertility drugs) on 14 Apr. 1972
	Heaviest	**Most Sets**
Quintuplets *World*	25 lb. *11,350 kg* Mrs. Lui Saulien, Chekiang, China 7 June 1953 25 lb. *11,350 kg* Mrs. Kamalammal Pondicherry, India, 30 Dec. 1956	No recorded case of more than a single set
Quadruplets *World*	21 lb. 9 oz. *9,760 kg* Mrs. David Bergquist, of Mountain Iron at University of Minnesota Hospital, Minneapolis U.S.A., 7 Sept.1975 (4 girls)	4 Mde. Feodor Vassilyev, Shuya, Russia (d. *ante* 1770)
Triplets *World* *U.K.*	26 lb. 6 oz. *11,960 kg* (unconfirmed) Iranian case (2 male, 1 female) 18 Mar. 1968 24 lb. 0 oz. *10,886 kg* Mrs. Mary McDermott, of Bearpark, Co Durham, 18 Nov. 1914	15 Maddalena Granata (1839–*fl.* 1886)
Twins *World*	35 lb. 8 oz. *16,100 kg* (liveborn) Warren's case (2 males) reported in *The Lancet* from Derbyshire, England on 6 Dec. 1884 27 lb. 12 oz. *12,590 kg* (surviving) Mrs. J. P. Haskin, Fort Smith, Arkansas, U.S.A. 20 Feb. 1924	16 Mde. Vassilyev (see above). *Note also* Mrs. Barbara Zulu of Barbeton, South Africa bore 3 sets of girls and 3 mixed sets in 7 years (1967–73) 15 Mrs. Mary Jonas of Chester (d. 4 Dec. 1899)—all sets were boy and girl

5. PHYSIOLOGY AND ANATOMY

Hydrogen (63%) and oxygen (25.5%) constitute the commonest of the 24 elements in the human body. In 1972 four more trace elements were added—fluorine, silicon, tin and vanadium. The "essentiality" of nickel has not yet been finally pronounced upon.

BONES
Longest
Excluding a variable number of sesamoids, there are 206 bones in the human body. The thigh bone or *femur* is the longest. It constitutes usually 27½ per cent of a person's stature, and may be expected to be 19¾ in *50 cm* long in a 6-ft *183 cm*-tall man. The longest recorded bone was the femur of the German giant Constantine, who died in Mons, Belgium, on 30 Mar. 1902, aged 30 (see p. 8). It measured 76 cm *29,9 in.* The femur of Robert Wadlow, the tallest man ever recorded, measured an estimated 29½ in *75 cm.*

Smallest
The *stapes* or stirrup bone, one of the three auditory ossicles in the middle ear, is the smallest human bone, measuring from 2,6 to 3,4 mm *0.10 to 0.17 in.* in length and weighing from 2,0 to 4,3 mg *0.03 to 0.065 gr.*

MUSCLES
Largest
Muscles normally account for 40 per cent of the body weight and the bulkiest of the 639 muscles in the human body is the *gluteus maximus* or buttock muscle, which extends the thigh.

Smallest
The smallest muscle is the *stapedius*, which controls the *stapes* (see above), an auditory ossicle in the middle ear, and which is less than 1/20th of an inch *0,127 cm* long.

Smallest waists
Queen Catherine de Medici (1519–89) decreed a waist measurement of 13 in *33 cm* for ladies of the French Court. This was at a time when females were more diminutive. The smallest recorded waist among women of normal stature in the 20th century is a reputed 13 in *33 cm* in the case of the French actress Mlle. Polaire (1881–1939) and Mrs. Ethel Granger (b. 12 April 1905) of Peterborough who reduced from a natural 22 in *56 cm* over the period 1929–1939.

Largest chest measurements
The largest chest measurements are among endomorphs (those with a tendency towards globularity). In the extreme case of Hughes (see p. 12) this was reportedly 124 in *315 cm*, but in the light of his known height and weight a figure of 104 in *264 cm* would be more supportable. George McAree (see Britain's heaviest man) has a chest measurement of 83 in *211 cm*. Among muscular subjects (mesomorphs) of normal height *expanded* chest measurements above 56 in *142 cm* are extremely rare. Louis Cyr (1865–1912), the famous French-Canadian strongman, had a chest measurement of 59 in *150 cm* at his best weight of 300 lb. *136 kg.* Arnold Schwarzennegger (b. 1948) of Graz, Austria, former Mr. Universe and "the most perfectly developed man in the history of the world", has a chest measurement of 58 in *147 cm* at a bodyweight of 252 lb. *115 kg.* He also boasts a 22 in *56 cm* upper arm.

Longest necks
The maximum measured extension of the neck by the successive fitting of copper coils, as practised by the Padaung or Karen people of Burma, is 15¾ in *40 cm.*

BRAIN AND BRAIN POWER
Largest
The brain has 10×10^{10} nerve cells or neurons interconnected by dendrites or filaments and 10×10^{11} glia. Some of the brain's chemical reactions require only one millionth of a second. After the age of 18 the brain loses some 10^3 cells per day. The brain of an average adult male (*i.e.* 30–59 years) weighs 1 410 g *3 lb. 1.73 oz.* falling to 1 030 g *2 lb. 4.31 oz.*

Former Mr. Universe, Arnold Schwarzennegger, (Austria), whose physique earned him the description "the most perfectly developed man in the history of the world".

The heaviest brain ever recorded has been that of a 50 year old white male weighing 4 lb. 8.29 oz. *2 049 g* reported by Dr. Thomas F. Hegert, Chief Medical Examiner for District 9, State of Florida on 23 Oct. 1975. The brain of Oliver Cromwell (1599–1658) reputedly weighed 2 222 g *4 lb. 14.8 oz.*, but the size of his head in portraits does not support this extreme figure. The brain of Lord Byron, who died in Greece in 1824 aged 36, reportedly weighed 6 Neopolitan pounds (1 924 g or *4 lb. 3.86 oz.*,) but this also included a certain amount of blood. In January 1891 the *Edinburgh Medical Journal* reported the case of a 75-year-old man in the Royal Edinburgh Asylum whose brain weighed 1 829 g *4 lb. 0.5 oz.*

Smallest
The non-atrophied brain of the writer Anatole France (1844–1924) weighed only 1017 g *35.8 oz.* without the membrane. Brains in extreme cases of microcephaly may weigh as little as 300 g *10,6 oz.* (*cf.* 20 oz. *567 g* for the adult male gorilla, and 16–20 oz. *454–567 g* for other anthropoid apes).

Highest I.Q.
On the Terman index for Intelligence Quotients, 150 represents "genius" level. The indices are sometimes held to be

immeasurable above a level of 200 but a figure of 210 has been attributed to Kim Ung-Yong of Seoul, South Korea (b. 7 March 1963). He composed poetry and spoke four languages (Korean, English, German and Japanese), and performed integral calculus at the age of 4 years 8 months on television in Tokyo on "The World Surprise Show" on 2 Nov. 1967. Both his parents, Dr. and Mrs. Kim Soo Sun, are University professors and were both born at 11 a.m. on 23 May 1934. The International Society for Philosophical Enquiry has 140 members of whom 22% have an I.Q. above 160 and none below 148. Only 100 persons in a million have I.Q's above 160.

The highest mean I.Q. published for a national population is 106.6 (United Kingdom 100) for the Japanese.

Human Computer
The fastest extraction of a 13th root from a 100 digit number is in 3 min 51 sec by Willem Klein (b. 1914, Netherlands) in Stockholm, Sweden on 8 Nov. 1978.

Human memory
Mehmed Ali Halici of Ankara, Turkey on 14 Oct. 1967 recited 6,666 verses of the Koran from memory in six hours. The recitation was followed by six Koran scholars. Rare instances of eidetic memory—the ability to re-project and hence "visually" recall material—are known to science.

The greatest number of places of π
The greatest number of places to which Pi (ratio of circles' circumference to diameter) has been memorised and recited is 15,151 by Hideaki Tomoyori (Japan) on 4 June 1979 and in Britain 7,500 by Creighton Carvello later in June. Note: It is only the *approximation* of π at 22/7 which recurs after its sixth decimal place and can, of course, be recited *ad nauseam*. The true value is a string of random numbers fiendishly difficult to memorize.

HANDS AND HAIR
Touch sensitivity
The extreme sensitivity of the fingers is such that a vibration with a movement of 0.02 of a micron can be detected. On 12 Jan. 1963 the Soviet newspaper *Izvestiya* reported the case of a totally blindfolded girl, Rosa Kulgeshova, who was able to identify colours by touch alone. Later reports in 1970 completely refuted this claim.

Most fingers
In 1938 the extreme case of a baby girl with 14 fingers and 12 toes was reported from St. George's Hospital, Hyde Park, Greater London.

Longest finger nails
The longest finger nail ever reported is one of 25½ in *64,7 cm* grown by Romesh Sharma of Delhi after 13 years, measured on 15 Feb. 1979. On 23 Feb. 1979 Shridhar Chillal, 41, of Poona, India achieved a measured aggregate of 92½ in *235 cm* for the 5 nails on his left hand (thumb 23.2 in *59 cm*) uncut since 1952.

Longest hair
Swami Pandarasannadhi, the head of the Tirudaduturai monastery, Tanjore district, Madras, India was reported in 1949 to have hair 26 ft *7,93 m* in length. From photographs it appears that he was affected with the disease Plica caudiformis. The hair of Jane Bunford (see p. 10) which she wore in two plaits, reached down to her ankles, indicating a length in excess of 8 ft *2,43 m*.

Longest beard
The longest beard preserved was that of Hans N. Langseth (b. 1846 in Norway) which measured 17½ ft *5,33 m* at the time of his death in 1927 after 15 years residence in the United States. The beard was presented to the Smithsonian Institution, Washington, D.C. in 1967. Richard Latter (b. Pembury, Kent, 1831) of Tunbridge Wells, Kent, who died in 1914 aged 83, reputedly had a beard 16 ft *4,87 m* long but contemporary independent corroboration is lacking and photographic evidence indicates this figure was exaggerated. The beard of the bearded lady Janice Deveree (b. Bracken Co., Kentucky, U.S.A., 1842) was measured at 14 in *36 cm* in 1884.

Longest moustache
The longest moustache on record was that of Masuriya Din (b. 1908), a Brahmin of the Partabgarh district in Uttar Pradesh, India. It grew to an extended span of 8 ft 6 in *2,59 m* between 1949 and 1962. Karna Ram Bheel (b. 1928) was granted permission by a New Dehli prison governor in Feb. 1979 to keep his 7 ft 10 in *238 cm* moustache grown since 1949 during his life sentence. The longest moustache in Great Britain is that of Mr. John Roy (b. 14 Jan. 1910), licensee of the "Cock Inn" at Beazely End, near Braintree, Essex. It attained a peak span of 68½ in *174 cm* between 1939 and when measured on the BBC-TV *Nationwide* programme on 2 Apr. 1976.

DENTITION
Earliest
The first deciduous or milk teeth normally appear in infants at five to eight months, these being the mandibular and maxillary first incisors. There are many records of children born with teeth, the most distinguished example being Prince Louis Dieudonné, later Louis XIV of France, who was born with two teeth on 5 Sept. 1638. Molars usually appear at 24 months, but in Pindborg's case published in Denmark in 1970 a 6 week premature baby was documented with 8 natal teeth of which 4 were in the molar region.

Most
Cases of the growth in late life of a third set of teeth have been recorded several times. A reference to an extreme case in France of a fourth dentition, known as Lison's case was published in 1896. A triple row of teeth was noted in 1680 by Albertus Hellwigius.

Most dedicated dentist
Brother Giovanni Battista Orsenigo of the Ospedale Fatebenefratelli, Rome, Italy, a religious dentist, conserved all the teeth he extracted in three enormous cases during the time he exercised his profession from 1868 to 1904. In 1903 the number was counted and found to be 2,000,744 teeth.

OPTICS
Smallest visible object
The resolving power of the human eye is 0.0003 of a radian or an arc of one minute (1/60th of a degree), which corresponds to 100 microns at 10 in. A micron is a thousandth of a millimetre, hence 100 microns is 0.003937, or less than four thousandths, of an inch. The human eye can, however, detect a bright light source shining through an aperture only 3 to 4 microns across. In Oct. 1972 the University of Stuttgart, West Germany reported that their student Frl. Veronica Seider (b. 1953) possessed a visual acuity 20 times better than average. She could identify people at a distance of more than a mile *1,6 km*.

Colour sensitivity
The unaided human eye, under the best possible viewing conditions, comparing large areas of colour, in good illumination, using both eyes, can distinguish 10,000,000 different colour surfaces. The most accurate photo-electric spectrophotometers possess a precision probably only 40 per cent as good as this. About 7.5% of men and 0.1% of women are colour blind. The most extreme form, monochromatic vision, is very rare. The highest recorded rate of red-green colour blindness is in Czechoslovakia and the lowest rate among Fijians and Brazilian Indians.

VOICE
Highest and lowest
The highest and lowest recorded notes attained by the human voice before this century were a staccato E in *alt altissimo* (e^{iv}) by the American Ellen Beach Yaw (1869–1947) in Carnegie Hall, New York City on 19 Jan. 1896, and an A_1 (55 cycles per sec) by Kasper Foster (1617–73). Madeleine Marie Robin (1918–60) the French operatic coloratura could produce and sustain the B above high C in the Lucia mad scene in *Lucia di Lammermoor*. Since 1950 singers have achieved high and low notes far beyond the hitherto accepted extremes. However, notes at the bass and treble extremities of the register tend to lack harmonics and are of little musical value. Frl. Marita Gunther, trained by Alfred Wolfsohn,

has covered the range of the piano from the lowest note, A_{11}, to c^v. Of this range of $7\frac{1}{4}$ octaves, six octaves are considered to be of musical value. Mr. Roy Hart, also trained by Wolfsohn, has reached notes below the range of the piano. Barry Girard of Canton, Ohio in May 1975 reached the e (4,340 Hz) above the piano's top note. The highest note put into song is G^{IV} twice occurring in *Popoli oli Tessacaglia* by Mozart. The lowest note put into song is a D_{11} by the singer Tom King, of King's Langley, Hertfordshire. Stephan Zucker sang A in *alt altissimo* for 3.8 secs in the tenor role of Salvini in the world première of Bellini's *Adelson e Salvini* in New York City, U.S.A. on 12 Sept. 1972.

Greatest range
The normal intelligible outdoor range of the male human voice in still air is 200 yd *180 m*. The *silbo*, the whistled language of the Spanish-speaking Canary Island of La Gomera, is intelligible across the valleys, under ideal conditions, at five miles *8 km*. There is a recorded case, under freak acoustic conditions, of the human voice being detectable at a distance of $10\frac{1}{2}$ miles *17 km* across still water at night. It was said that Mills Darden (see page 12) could be heard 6 miles *9 km* away when he shouted at the top of his voice.

At the "World" Shouting Competition at Scarborough, North Yorkshire on 17 Feb. 1973 the title was won by Skipper Kenny Leader with 111 decibels at $2\frac{1}{2}$ metres *8 ft 1¼ in.* A feminine record of 110 dBA was set by Mrs. Grace Hall at Pathfinder Village, Exeter, Devon on 19 Nov. 1976.

Lowest detectable sound
The intensity of noise or sound is measured in terms of pressure. The pressure of the quietest sound that can be detected by a person of normal hearing at the most sensitive frequency of c. 2,750 Hz is 2×10^{-5} pascal. One tenth of the logarithm to this standard provides a unit termed a decibel. Prolonged noise above 150 decibels will cause immediate permanent deafness while 200 decibels could be fatal. A noise of 30 decibels is negligible.

Highest detectable pitch
The upper limit of hearing by the human ear has long been regarded as 20,000 Hz (cycles per sec), although children with asthma can often detect a sound of 30,000 cycles per sec. It was announced in February 1964 that experiments in the U.S.S.R. had conclusively proved that oscillations as high as 200,000 cycles per sec can be heard if the oscillator is pressed against the skull.

Fastest talker
Few people are able to speak *articulately* at a sustained speed above 300 words per min. The fastest broadcaster has been regarded as Gerry Wilmot (b. Victoria B.C., Canada 6 Oct. 1914) the ice hockey commentator in the post World War II period. Raymond Glendenning (1907–1974), the B.B.C. horseracing commentator, once spoke 176 words in 30 sec. while commentating on a greyhound race. In public life the highest speed recorded is a 327 words per min burst in a speech made in December 1961 by John Fitzgerald Kennedy (1917–1963), then President of the United States. Tapes of attempts to recite Hamlet's 262 word Soliloquy in under 24 secs (655 w.p.m.) have proved unintelligible. Patricia Keeling-Andrich delivered 403 words from W. S. Gilbert's "The Nightmare" in a test in 60 secs. at Chabot College, Hayward, California on 16 Mar. 1978.

BLOOD
Blood groups
The preponderance of one blood group varies greatly from one locality to another. On a world basis Group O is the most common (46 per cent), but in some areas, for example Norway, Group A predominates.

The full description of the commonest sub-group in Britain is O MsNs, P+, Rr, Lu(a−), K−, Le(a−b+), Fy(a+b+), Jk(a+b+), which occurs in one in every 270 people.

The rarest blood group on the ABO system, one of 14 systems, is AB, which occurs in less than three per cent of persons in the British Isles. The rarest type in the world is a type of Bombay blood (sub-type A-h) found so far only in a Czechoslovak nurse in 1961 and in a brother (Rh positive) and sister (Rh negative) named Jalbert in Massachusetts, U.S.A. reported in February 1968. The American male has started a blood bank for himself.

Richest Natural Resources
Joe Thomas of Detroit, Michigan, U.S.A. was reported in August 1970 to have the highest known count of Anti-Lewis B, the rare blood antibody. A U.S. biological supply firm pays him $1,500 per quart *1,13 l.* The Internal Revenue regard this income as a taxable liquid asset.

Champion blood donor
Ed 'Spike' Howard (1877–1946), the professional strongman of Philadelphia, U.S.A. donated a lifetime total of 1,056 U.S. pints or *499,66 litres.* The present day normal limit on donations is 5 pints per annum. A 50-year-old haemophiliac Warren C. Jyrich required 2,400 donor units *1 080 litres* of blood when undergoing open heart surgery at the Michael Reese Hospital, Chicago, U.S.A. in December 1970.

Largest vein
The largest vein in the human body is a cardiac vein, known as the *vena cava*, which returns most of the blood from the body below the level of the heart.

Most alcoholic subject
It is recorded that a hard drinker named Vanhorn (1750–1811), born in London, averaged more than four bottles of ruby port per day for the 23 years from 1788 to his death aged 61 in 1811. The total of his "empties" was put at 35,688.

The youngest recorded death from alcoholic poisoning was that of a 4 year old boy, Joseph Sweet, in Wolverhampton, England in 1827 reported in the Stafford Assizes case *R. v. Martin.*

The United Kingdom's legal limit for motorists is 80 mg of alcohol per 100 ml of blood. The hitherto recorded highest figure in medical literature of 656 mg per 100 ml was submerged when the late Samuel Riley (b. 1922) of Sefton Park, Merseyside, was found by a disbelieving pathologist to have a level of 1220 mg on 28 Mar. 1979. He had expired in his flat and had been an inspector at the plant of a well-known motor manufacturer.

BODY TEMPERATURE
Highest body temperature
In Kalow's case (*Lancet*, 31 Oct. 1970) a woman following halothane anaesthesia ran a temperature of 112° F *44,4° C.* She recovered after a procainamide infusion. Marathon runners in hot weather attain 105.8° F *41° C.*

A temperature of 115° F *46,1° C* was recorded in the case of Christopher Legge in the Hospital for Tropical Diseases, London, on 9 Feb. 1934. A subsequent examination of the thermometer disclosed a flaw in the bulb, but it is regarded as certain that the patient sustained a temperature of more than 110° F *43,3° C.*

Lowest body temperature
There are two recorded cases of patients surviving body temperatures as low as 60.8° F *16,0° C* Dorothy Mae Stevens, (1929–74) was found in an alley in Chicago, Illinois on 1 Feb. 1951 and Vickie Mary Davis aged 2 years 1 month in an unheated house in Marshalltown, Iowa on 21 Jan. 1956 both with this temperature.

ILLNESS AND DISEASE
Commonest disease
The commonest non-contagious disease in the world is dental caries or tooth decay. In Great Britain 13 per cent of people have lost all their teeth before they are 21 years old. During their lifetime few completely escape its effects. Infestation with pinworm (*Enterobius vermicularis*) approaches 100 per cent in some areas of the world.

The commonest contagious disease in the world is coryza (acute nasopharyngitis) or the common cold. Only 2,580,000 working days were reportedly lost as a result of this illness in Great Britain between mid 1976 and mid 1977, since absences of less than three days are not reported. The greatest reported loss of working time in Britain is from bronchitis, which accounted for 28,062,000, or 8.7 per cent, of the total of 321,450,000 working days lost in the same period.

The most resistant recorded case to being infected at the Medical Research Council Common Cold Unit, Salisbury, Wiltshire is J. Brophy, who has had one mild reaction in 24 visits.

Rarest disease
Medical literature periodically records hitherto undescribed diseases. A disease as yet undescribed but predicted by a Norwegian doctor is podocytoma of the kidney—a tumour of the epithelial cells lining the glomerulus of the kidney.

Kuru, or laughing sickness, afflicts only the Fore tribe of eastern New Guinea and is 100 per cent fatal. It is transmitted by the cannibalistic practice of eating human brains. The rarest fatal diseases in England and Wales have been those from which the last deaths (all males) were all recorded more than 40 years ago—yellow fever (1930), cholera nostras (1928) and bubonic plague (1926).

Most and least infectious disease
The most infectious of all diseases is the pneumonic form of plague, which also has a mortality rate of about 99.99 per cent. Leprosy transmitted by *Mycobacterium leprae* is the least infectious and most bacilliferous of communicable diseases.

Highest mortality
Rabies in humans has been regarded as uniformly fatal when associated with the hydrophobia symptom. A 25-year-old woman Candida de Sousa Barbosa of Rio de Janeiro, Brazil, was believed to be the first ever survivor of the disease in November 1968, though some sources give priority to Matthew Winkler, 6, on 10 Oct. 1970 bitten by a rabid bat.

Leading Cause of Death
The leading cause of death in industrialized countries is arteriosclerosis (thickening of the arterial wall) which underlies much coronary and cerebrovascular disease.

Most notorious carrier
The most notorious of all typhoid carriers has been Mary Mallon, known as Typhoid Mary, of New York City, N.Y., U.S.A. She was the source of the 1903 outbreak, with 1,300 cases. Because of her refusal to leave employment, often under assumed names, involving the handling of food, she was placed under permanent detention from 1915 until her death in 1938.

Parkinson's disease
The most protracted case of Parkinson's disease (named after Dr. James Parkinson's essay of 1817) for which the earliest treatments were not published until 1946, is 56 years in the case of Frederick G. Humphries of Croydon, Greater London whose symptoms became detectable in 1923.

MEDICAL EXTREMES
Heart stoppage
The longest recorded heart stoppage is a minimum of 3 hours 32 minutes in the case of Miss Jean Jawbone, 20, who was revived by a team of 26, using peritoneal dialysis, in Winnipeg Medical Centre, Manitoba, Canada on 19 Jan. 1977. In February 1974 Vegard Slettmoen, 5, fell through the ice on the river Nitselv, Norway. He was found 40 minutes later *2,5 m* 8 ft down but was revived in Akerhaus Central Hospital without brain-damage.

The longest recorded interval in a *post mortem* birth was one of at least 80 minutes in Magnolia, Mississippi, U.S.A. Dr. Robert E. Drake found Fanella Anderson, aged 25, dead in her home at 11.40 p.m. on 15 Oct. 1966 and he delivered her of a son weighing 6 lb. 4 oz. *2 kg 830* by Caesarean operation in the Beacham Memorial Hospital on 16 Oct. 1966.

Pulse Rates
A normal adult pulse rate is 70–72 beats per minute at rest for males and 78–82 for females. Rates increase to 200 or more during violent exercise and drop to as low as 12 in the extreme case of Dorothy Mae Stevens (see Lowest temperature above).

Longest coma
The longest recorded coma was that undergone by Elaine Esposito (b. 3 Dec. 1934) of Tarpon Springs, Florida, U.S.A. She never stirred since an appendicectomy on 6 Aug. 1941, when she was six, in Chicago, Illinois, U.S.A. and she died on 25 Nov. 1978 aged 43 years 357 days having been in a coma for 37 years 111 days.

Longest Dream
Dreaming sleep is characterized by rapid eye movements known as REM. The longest recorded period of REM is one of 2 hours 23 minutes on 15 Feb. 1967 at the department of Psychology, University of Illinois, Chicago on Bill Carskadon, who had had his previous sleep interrupted.

Largest stone
The largest stone or vesical calculus reported in medical literature was one of 13 lb. 14 oz. *6 294 g* removed from an 80-year-old woman by Dr. Humphrey Arthure at Charing Cross Hospital, London, on 29 Dec. 1952.

Vegard Slettmoen (Norway) defied death when he fell through ice into a river. He was revived successfully after being found 40 minutes later 8 ft *2,5 m* down in the water. (*Aftenposten*)

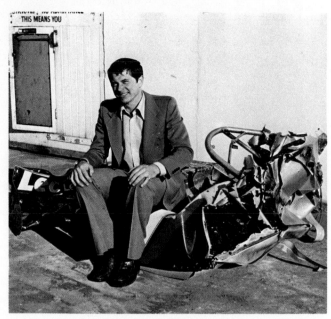

David Purley, seated on the wreck of his car in which he survived a crash at a speed of 108 m.p.h. *173,8 km/h* and experienced a g force of 179.8 (see p. 24).

Jean Chapman, the human fire extinguisher who "ate" 1,921 torches of flame successively in 120 minutes (see p. 24).

Longest in iron lung

The longest recorded survival by an "iron lung" patient is 31 years 9 months by Howard Lee Hale (1912–76) of Crockett, Virginia, U.S.A., from Aug. 1944 to his death on 10 May 1976. The longest survival in an "iron lung" in Britain is since 5 Oct. 1949 by Mr. Dennis Atkin in Lodge Moor Hospital, Sheffield, South Yorkshire. Paul Bates of Horsham, West Sussex was harnessed to a mechanical positive pressure respirator on 13 Aug. 1954. He has received an estimated 183,676,868 respirations into his lungs *via* his trachea up to 1 May 1979.

Fastest reflexes

The results of experiments published in 1966 have shown that the fastest messages transmitted by the human nervous system travel as fast as 180 mph *288 km h*. With advancing age impulses are carried 15 per cent more slowly.

Hiccoughing

The longest recorded attack of hiccoughs was that afflicting Charles Osborne (b. 1894) of Anthon, Iowa, U.S.A., from 1922 to date. He contracted it when slaughtering a hog. His first wife left him and he is unable to keep in his false teeth. The infirmary at Newcastle upon Tyne is recorded to have admitted a young man from Long Witton, Northumberland on 25 March 1769 suffering from hiccoughs which were reportedly audible at a range of more than a mile.

Sneezing

The most chronic sneezing fit ever recorded was that of June Clark, aged 17, of Miami, Florida, U.S.A. She started sneezing on 4 Jan. 1966, while recovering from a kidney ailment in the James M. Jackson Memorial Hospital, Miami. The sneezing was stopped by electric "aversion" treatment administered by Dr. Malcolm Rushmer on 8 June 1966, after 155 days. The highest speed at which expelled particles have been measured to travel is 103.6 m.p.h. *167 km/h*.

Snoring *Loudest*

Research at the Ear, Nose and Throat Department of St. Mary's Hospital, London, published in November 1968, shows that a rasping snore can attain a loudness of 69 decibels (*cf.* 70–90 for a pneumatic drill).

Yawning

In Lee's case, reported in 1888, a fifteen-year-old female patient yawned continuously for a period of five weeks.

Sleeplessness

Researches indicate that on the Circadian cycle for the majority peak efficiency is attained between 8 p.m. and 9 p.m. and the low point comes at 4 a.m. The longest recorded period for which a person has voluntarily gone without sleep is 449 hr (14 days 13 hours) by Mrs. Maureen Weston of Peterborough, Cambridgeshire in a rocking chair marathon on 14 Apr.–2 May 1977. Though she tended to hallucinate toward the end of this surely ill-advised test, she surprisingly suffered no lasting ill-effects.

Motionlessness

The longest that anyone has voluntarily remained motionless is 6 hr 31 min by William Fuqua at Dillards Department Store, Fort Worth, Texas, U.S.A. on 22 July 1978. The longest recorded case of involuntarily being made to stand to attention was when Staff Sgt. Samuel B. Moody U.S.A.F. was so punished in Narumi prison camp, Nagoya, Japan for 53 hours in spring of 1945. He survived to write *Reprieve from Hell*.

Swallowing

The worst reported case of compulsive swallowing was an insane female Mrs. H. aged 42, who complained of a "slight abdominal pain". She proved to have 2,533 objects, including 947 bent pins, in her stomach. These were removed by Drs. Chalk and Foucar in June 1927 at the Ontario Hospital, Canada. The heaviest object extracted from a human stomach has been a 5 lb. 3 oz. *2,530 kg* ball of hair in Swain's case from a 20 year female in the South Devon and East Cornwall Hospital, England on 30 Mar. 1895.

Sword

The longest length of sword able to be "swallowed" by a

practised exponent, after a heavy meal, is 27 in *69 cm*. Perhaps the greatest exponent is Alex Linton, born on 25 Oct. 1904 in Boyle, County Roscommon, Ireland. King Daredevil (real name Larsson) swallowed nine 23 in *58,4 cm* blades below the Xiphisternum.

Fasting

Most humans experience considerable discomfort after an abstinence from food for even 12 hr but this often passes off after 24–48 hr. Records claimed without unremitting medical surveillance are of little value. The longest period for which anyone has gone without solid food is 382 days by Angus Barbieri (b. 1940) of Tayport, Fife, who lived on tea, coffee, water, soda water and vitamins in Maryfield Hospital, Dundee, Angus, from June 1965 to July 1966. His weight declined from 33 st. 10 lb. *214,1 kg* to 12 st. 10 lb. *80 kg 740*. Sister Therese Neumann survived 35 years on the "bread" of the Holy Eucharist wafer at Mass each morning at Konnersreuth, Germany.

Hunger strike

The longest recorded hunger strike was one of 94 days by John and Peter Crowley, Thomas Donovan, Michael Burke, Michael O'Reilly, Christopher Upton, John Power, Joseph Kenny and Seán Hennessy in Cork Prison, Ireland, from 11 Aug. to 12 Nov. 1920. These nine survivors from 12 prisoners owed their lives to expert medical attention and an appeal by Arthur Griffith. The longest recorded hunger strike in a British gaol is 385 days from 28 June 1972 to 18 July 1973 by Denis Galer Goodwin in Wakefield Prison, West Yorkshire protesting his innocence of a rape charge. He was fed by tube orally.

The longest recorded case of survival without food *and* water is at least 321 hrs (13 days 9 hrs) by stowaways Privates Randy Boutaain and Dennis E. Feathers (U.S. Army) in Container No. 303454 aboard S.S. *Sea-Land Economy* from Rotterdam, Netherlands to Houston, Texas, U.S.A. on 7–22 Dec. 1977.

Most voracious fire eaters

Jack Sholomir (G.B.) blew a flame from his mouth to a distance of 23 ft *7 m* at the Eardisley & District Royal British Legion Stampede, at Kinnersley, Hereford and Worcester on 6 June 1977. Mrs. Jean Chapman, at the Six Bells, Stoke Poges, Buckinghamshire, England on 29 Oct. 1977 extinguished successively 1,921 torches of flame in her mouth in 120 minutes. Fire eating is potentially a most dangerous activity.

Human salamanders

The highest dry-air temperature endured by naked men in the U.S. Air Force experiments in 1960 was 400° F *204,4° C* and for heavily clothed men 500° F *260° C*. Steaks require only 325° F *162,8° C*. Temperatures of 140° C *284° F* have been found quite bearable in *Sauna* baths.

The highest temperature recorded by pyrometer for the coals in any fire walk was 1,494° F *812° C* for a walk by "Komar" (Vernon E. Craig) of Wooster, Ohio at the International Festival of Yoga and Esoteric Sciences, Maidenhead, England on 14 Aug. 1976.

Underwater

The world record for voluntarily staying underwater is 13 min 42.5 sec by Robert Foster, aged 32, an electronics technician of Richmond, California, who stayed under 10 ft *3,05 m* of water in the swimming pool of the Bermuda Palms Motel at San Rafael, California, U.S.A., on 15 March 1959. He hyperventilated with oxygen for 30 min before his descent.

g forces

The acceleration g, due to gravity, is 32 ft 1.05 in per sec per sec *978,02 cm/sec²* at sea-level at the Equator. A *sustained* acceleration of 25 g was withstood in a dry capsule during astronautic research by Dr. Carter Collins of California, U.S.A. The highest g value endured on a water-braked rocket sled is 82.6 g for 0.04 of a sec by Eli L. Beedin Jr. at Holloman Air Force Base, New Mexico, U.S.A., on 16

An average of 79 prescribed pills per day are swallowed by Mr. C. Kilner following an operation in 1967.

May 1958. He was put in hospital for 3 days. A man who fell off a 185 ft *56,39 m* cliff (before 1963) has survived a *momentary* g of 209 in decelerating from 68 mp.h. *109 km/h* to stationary in 0.015 of a sec.

The racing driver David Purley G.M. survived a deceleration from 108 mph *173 km/h* to zero in 26 in *66 cm* in a crash at Silverstone on 13 July 1977 which involved a force of 179.8 g.

The land divers of Penecost Island, New Hebrides dive from Platforms 70 ft *21,3 m* high with liana vines attached to their ankles. The jerk can transmit a momentary g force in excess of 100.

Electric Shock *Highest voltage*

Excluding lightning bolts, the highest reported voltage electric shock survived was one of 230,000 volts by Brian Latasa, 17 on the tower of an ultra-high voltage power line in Griffith Park, Los Angeles on 9 Nov. 1967. Highly insulated individuals have touched 1,200,000 volt cables in bare-hand live cable work without harm.

Isolation

The longest recorded period for which any volunteer has been able to withstand total deprivation of all sensory stimulation (sight, hearing and touch) is 92 hr, recorded in 1962 at Lancaster Moor Hospital, Lancashire.

The farthest that any human has been isolated from all other humans has been the lone pilots of lunar command modules when antipodal to their Apollo missions, two lunar explorers 2,200 miles *3 540 km* distant.

Pill-taking

The highest recorded total of pills swallowed by a patient is 331,211 between 9 June 1967 to 1 Jan. 1979 by C. H. A. Kilner (b. 1926) of Malawi, following a successful pancreatectomy.

Most Injections

The diabetic Mrs. Evelyn Ruth Winder of Invercargill, New Zealand made an estimated 52,730 insulin injections of herself over 48 years to May 1979.

Most tattoos

Vivian "Sailor Joe" Simmons, a Canadian tattoo artist, had 4,831 tattoos on his body. He died in Toronto on 22 Dec. 1965 aged 77. Britain's most tattooed man is George Bone (b. 10

Nov. 1946) of Ealing, Greater London whose last few gaps have been blocked in by the Aldershot tattoo artist Bill Skuse. Britain's most decorated woman is Mrs. Rusty Skuse *née* Field (b. 1944) of Aldershot, Hampshire, who after 12 years under the needle of Mr. Skuse, came within 15 per cent of totality. He stated he always had designs on her.

OPERATIONS
Longest
The most protracted operations are those involving brain surgery. Such an operation lasting 31 hours was performed on Victor Zazueta, 19, of El Centro at San Diego Hospital, California by Drs. John F. Alksne and Randall Smith on 17–18 Jan. 1972.

Most major
On 20 August 1975 Mr. Charles Hill (b. 1914) of Sydney, New South Wales, Australia underwent his 87th major operation. Most of the surgery has been abdominal.

Oldest subject
The greatest recorded age at which a person has been subjected to an operation is 111 years 105 days in the case of James Henry Brett, Jr. (b. 25 July 1849, d. 10 Feb. 1961) of Houston, Texas, U.S.A. He underwent a hip operation on 7 Nov. 1960. The oldest age established in Britain was the case of Miss Mary Wright (b. 28 Feb. 1862) who died during a thigh operation at Boston, Lincolnshire on 22 April 1971 aged 109 years 53 days.

Earliest Heart Transplant
The first human heart transplant operation was performed on Louis Washkansky, aged 55, at the Groote Schuur Hospital Cape Town, South Africa, between 1.00 a.m. and 6 a.m., on 3 Dec. 1967, by a team of 30 headed by Prof. Christiaan Neethling Barnard (b. Beaufort West, South Africa, 8 Oct. 1922). The donor was Miss Denise Ann Darvall, aged 25. Washkansky died on 21 Dec. 1967. The longest surviving heart transplantee has been Emmanuel Vitria, 57 of Marseilles, France who received a heart transplant on 28 Nov. 1968 and entered the tenth of his new life in 1977. Britain's longest-surviving heart transplant patient has been Mr. Charles Hendrick who died in Guy's Hospital of a lung infection on 31 Aug. 1969, 107 days after his operation.

Eighty-five per cent of Mrs Rusty Skuse has been tattooed by her husband in twelve years.

Earliest Kidney Transplant
R. H. Lawler (b. 1895) (U.S.A.) performed the first homo transplantation of the kidney in the human in 1950. The longest survival, as between identical twins, has been 20 years.

Earliest appendicectomy
The earliest recorded successful appendix operation was performed in 1736 by Claudius Amyand (1680–1740). He was Serjeant Surgeon to King George II (reigned 1727–60).

Earliest anaesthesia
The earliest recorded operation under general anaesthesia was for the removal of a cyst from the neck of James Venable by Dr. Crawford Williamson Long (1815–78), using diethyl ether $(C_2H_5)_2O$, in Jefferson, Georgia, U.S.A., on 30 March 1842. The earliest amputation under an anaesthetic in Great Britain was by Dr. William Scott and Dr. James McLauchlan at the Dumfries and Galloway Infirmary, Scotland on 19 Dec. 1846.

Most Durable Cancer Patient
The most extreme recorded case of survival from diagnosed cancer is that of Mrs. Winona Mildred Melick, (*née* Douglass) (b. 22 Oct. 1876) of Long Beach, California. She had four cancer operations in 1918, 1933, 1966 and 1968 but celebrated her 102nd birthday in 1978.

Laryngectomy
On 24 July 1924 John I. Poole of Plymouth, Devon after diagnosis of carcinoma then aged 33 underwent total laryngectomy in Edinburgh. In July 1978 he entered his 55th year as a "neck-breather".

Fastest amputation
The shortest time recorded for a leg amputation in the pre-anaesthetic era was 13 to 15 seconds by Napoleon's chief surgeon Dominique Larrey. There could have been no ligation.

Surgical instruments
The largest surgical instruments are robot retractors used in abdominal surgery introduced by Abbey Surgical Instruments of Chingford, Essex in 1968 and weighing 11 lb. *5 kg*. Some bronchoscopic forceps measure 60 cm *23½ in* in length. The smallest are Elliot's eye trephine, which has a blade 0.078 in *0.20 cm* in diameter and "straight" stapes picks with a needle type tip or blade of 0,3 mm *0.013 in* long.

PSYCHIC FORCES
Extra-sensory perception
The highest consistent performer in tests to detect powers of extra-sensory perception is Pavel Stepánek (Czechoslovakia) known in parapsychological circles as "P.S.". His performance on nominating hidden white or green cards from May 1967 to March 1968 departed from a chance probability yielding a Chi^2 value corresponding to $P < 10^{-50}$ or odds of more than 100 octillion to one against the achievement being one of chance. One of the two appointed referees recommended that the results should not be published. The highest published scores in any E.S.P. test were those of a 26-year-old female tested by Prof. Bernard F. Reiss of Hunter College, New York in 1936. In 74 runs of 25 guesses each she scored one with 25 all correct, two with 24 and an average of 18.24 instead of the random 5.00. Such a result would depart from chance probability by a factor $>10^{700}$. This produced the comment from some that there might be a defect in the theory of probability.

Most durable ghosts
Ghosts are not immortal and, according to the *Gazetteer of British Ghosts*, seem to deteriorate after 400 years. The most outstanding exception to their normal "half-life" would be the ghosts of Roman soldiers thrice reported still marching through the cellars of the Treasurer's House, York Minster after nearly 19 centuries. The book's author, Peter Underwood, states that Britain has more reported ghosts per square mile than any other country with Borley Rectory near Long Melford, Suffolk the site of unrivalled activity between 1863 and its destruction by fire in 1939.

ANIMAL: Most valuable

THE ANIMAL AND PLANT KINGDOMS

2

ANIMAL KINGDOM
GENERAL RECORDS

Note—Guinness Superlatives Ltd. has published a specialist volume entitled *The Guinness Book of Animal Facts and Feats* (2nd Edition) (price £6.50). This work treats the dimensions and performances of the Classes of the Animal Kingdom in greater detail, giving also the sources and authorities for much of the material in this chapter.

Largest and heaviest

The largest and heaviest animal in the world is the Blue or Sulphur-bottom whale (*Balaenoptera musculus*), also called Sibbald's rorqual. The largest specimen ever recorded was a female landed at the Cia Argentina de Pesca, South Georgia some time in the period 1904–1920 which measured 107 Norwegian fot *33,58 m 110 ft 2½ in* in length. Another female measuring 96¾ ft *29,48 m* brought into the shore station at Prince Olaf, South Georgia in *c.* 1931 was calculated to have weighed 163.7 tons *166 tonnes*, exclusive of blood and other body fluids, judging by the number of cookers that were filled by the animal's blubber, meat and bones and internal organs. The total weight of this whale was believed to have been 174 tons *177 tonnes*.

On the principle that the weight should vary as the cube of linear dimensions, a 100 ft *30,48 m* Blue whale in good condition should weigh about 160 tons *163 tonnes*, but in the case of pregnant females the weight could be as much as 190–200 tons *193–203 tonnes*—equivalent to 35 adult bull African elephants.

Tallest

The tallest living animal is the Giraffe (*Giraffa camelopardalis*), which is now found only in the dry savannah and semi-desert areas of Africa south of the Sahara. The tallest ever recorded was a Masai bull (*G. camelopardalis tippelskirchi*) named "George", received at Chester Zoo, England on 8 Jan. 1959 from Kenya. His head *almost* touched the roof of the 20 ft *6,09 m* high Giraffe House when he was 9 years old. George died on 22 July 1969. Less credible heights of up to 23 ft *7 m* (between pegs) have been claimed for bulls shot in the field.

Longest

The longest animal ever recorded is the ribbon worm *Lineus longissimus* also known as the "Boot-lace worm", which is found in the shallow coastal waters of the North Sea. In 1864 a specimen measuring more than 180 ft *54 m* was washed ashore at St. Andrews, Fifeshire, Scotland after a storm.

Rarest

The best claimants to the title of the world's rarest land animal are those species which are known only from a single (type) specimen. One of these is the tenrec *Dasogale fontoynonti*, which is known only from a specimen collected in eastern Madagascar (Malagasy Republic) and now preserved in the Museum d'Histoire Naturelle, Paris.

Commonest

It has been estimated that man shares the earth with about 3,000,000,000,000,000,000,000,000,000,000,000 (3,000 quintillion or 3×10^{33}) other living things. The number of nematode sea-worms has been estimated at 4×10^{25}.

Fastest

The fastest reliably measured speed (air) of any animal is 106.25 m.p.h. *171 km/h* for the Spine-tailed swift (*Chaetura caudacuta*) reported from the U.S.S.R. in 1942. In 1934 ground speeds ranging from 171.8 to 219.5 m.p.h. *276,5–353,3 km/h* were recorded by stop-watch for spine-tailed swifts over a 2-mile *3 km* course in the Cachar Hills of north-eastern India, but scientific tests have since revealed that this species of bird cannot be seen at a distance of 1 mile *1,6 km*, even with a standard binocular. This bird is the fastest moving living creature and has a blood temperature of 112.5° F *44,7° C*. Speeds even higher than a "free fall" maximum of 185 m.p.h. *297 km/h* have been ascribed to the Peregrine falcon (*Falco peregrinus*) in a stoop, but in recent experiments in which miniature air speedometers were fitted, the maximum recorded diving speed was 82 m.p.h. *132 km/h*.

Longest lived

Few non-bacterial creatures live longer than humans. It would appear that tortoises are the longest lived such animals. The greatest authentic age recorded for a tortoise is 152-plus years for a male Marion's tortoise (*Testudo sumeirii*) brought from the Seychelles to Mauritius in 1766 by the Chevalier de Fresne, who presented it to the Port Louis army garrison. This specimen (it went blind in 1908) was accidentally killed in 1918. When the famous Royal Tongan tortoise "Tu'malilia" (believed to be a specimen of *Testudo radiata*) died on 19 May 1966 it was reputed to be over 200 years old, having been presented to the then King of Tonga by Captain James Cook (1728–79) on 22 Oct. 1773, but this record may well have been compiled from two (or more) overlapping residents.

The bacteria *Thermoactinomyces vulgaris* has been found alive in cores of mud taken from the bottom of Windermere, Cumbria, England which have been dated to 1,500 yrs before the present.

Heaviest brain

The Sperm whale (*Physeter catodon*) has the heaviest brain of any living animal. The brain of a 49 ft *14,93 m* bull processed in the Japanese factory ship *Nissin Maru No. 1* in the Antarctic on 11 Dec. 1949 weighed 9,2 kg *20.24 lb.* compared with 6,9 kg *15.38 lb.* for a 90 ft *27 m* Blue whale. The heaviest brain recorded for an elephant was an exceptional 16.5 lb. *7,5 kg* in the case of a 1.94 ton *1957 kg* Asiatic cow. The brain of the adult bull African elephant is normally 9¼–12 lb. *4,2–5,4 kg.*

Largest eye

The giant squid (*Architeuthis sp.*) has the largest eye of any living animal. The ocular diameter may exceed 38 cm *15 in* (cf. 30 cm *11,81 in* for a 33⅓ long-playing record).

Largest egg

The largest egg of any living animal is that of the Whale shark (*Rhiniodon typus*). One egg case measuring 12 in by 5.5 in by 3.5 in *30 × 14 × 9 cm* was picked up by the shrimp trawler "Doris" on 29 June 1953 at a depth of 31 fathoms (186 ft *56,6 m*) in the Gulf of Mexico 130 miles *209 km* south of Port Isabel, Texas, U.S.A. The egg contained a perfect embryo of a Whale shark 13.78 in *35 cm* long.

Longest gestation

The viviparous Alpine black salamander (*Salamandra atra*) has a gestation period of up to 38 months at altitudes above 1 400 m *4,600 ft* in the Swiss Alps, but this drops to 24–26 months at lower altitudes.

Fastest and slowest growth

The fastest growth in the Animal Kingdom is that of the Blue whale calf (see p. 26). A barely visible ovum weighing a fraction of a milligramme (0.000035 of an oz.) grows to a weight of *c.* 26 tons *26 tonnes* in 22¾ months, made up of 10¾ months gestation and the first 12 months of life. This is equivalent to an increase of 30,000 million-fold. The slowest growth in the Animal Kingdom is that of the deep-sea clam *Tindaria callistiformis* of the North Atlantic, which takes an estimated 100 years to reach a length of 8 mm *0.31 in.*

Greatest size difference between sexes

The largest female deep-sea angler fish of the species *Ceratias holboelki* on record weighed half a million times as much as the smallest known parasitic male. It has been suggested that this fish would make an appropriate emblem for the Women's Lib. Movement.

Highest G Force

The highest force encountered in nature is the 400 g *averaged* by the Click beetle *Athous haemorrhoidalis* (a common British species) when "jack-knifing" into the air to escape predators. One example measuring 12 mm *0,47 in* in length and weighing 40 mg *0.00014 oz* which jumped to a height of 30 cm *11¾ in* was calculated to have "endured" a peak brain deceleration of 2300 g at the end of the movement.

Blood temperatures

The highest mammalian blood temperature is that of the Domestic goat (*Capra hircus*) with an average of 103.8° F *39,9° C*, and a normal range of from 101.7° to 105.3° F *38,7° to 40,7° C*. The lowest mammalian blood temperature is that of the Spiny anteater (*Tachyglossus aculeatus*), a monotreme found in Australia and New Guinea, with a normal range of 72° to 87° F *22,2° to 24,4° C*. The blood temperature of the Golden hamster (*Mesocricetus auratus*) sometimes falls as low as 38.3° F *3,5° C* during hibernation, and an extreme figure of 29.6° F *−1,3° C* has been reported for a myotis bat (family Vespertilionidae) during a deep sleep.

Most valuable furs

The highest-priced animal pelts are those of the Sea otter (*Enhydra lutris*), also known as the Kamchatka beaver, which fetched up to $2,700 (then £675) before their 55-year-long protection started in 1912. The protection ended in 1967, and at the first legal auction of sea otter pelts at Seattle, Washington, U.S.A. on 31 January 1968 Neiman-Marcus, the famous Dallas department store, paid $9,200 (then £3,832) for four pelts from Alaska. In May 1970 a Kojah (a mink–sable cross) coat costing $125,000 £52,083 was sold by Neiman-Marcus to Welsh actor Richard Burton for his wife, Elizabeth Taylor.

Heaviest ambergris

The heaviest piece of ambergris (a fatty deposit in the intestine of the Sperm whale) on record was a 1,003 lb. *455 kg* lump recovered from a Sperm whale (*Physeter catodon*) taken in Australian waters on 3 Dec. 1912 by a Norwegian whaling fleet. It was later sold in London for £23,000.

Most valuable

The most valuable animals in cash terms are thoroughbred racehorses. It was announced in Nov. 1978 that *Affirmed* (see Chap. XII Horseracing) would be syndicated for $14.4 million (£7.2 million). The most valuable zoo exhibit is the Giant Panda (*Ailuropoda melanoleuca*) for which $250,000 (£104,160) was offered by the San Diego Zoological Gardens for a fertile pair in 1971. The most valuable marine exhibit is the Killer Whale (*Orcinus orca*). In September 1975 the 6,500 lb. *2 948 kg* female "Newtka" was flown from Dallas, Texas, U.S.A. to Niagara Falls insured for £71,400.

---

1. MAMMALS

Largest and heaviest *World*

For details of the Blue whale (*Balaenoptera musculus*) see page 26. Further information: the tongue and heart of a 27,6 m *90 ft 8 in* long female Blue whale taken by the Slava whaling fleet in the Antarctic on 17 March 1947 weighed 4.22 tons *4,29 tonnes* and 1,540 lb. *698,5 kg* respectively.

Largest and heaviest *British waters*

The largest Blue whale ever recorded in British waters was probably an 88 ft *26,8 m* specimen killed near the Bunaveneader station in Harris in the Western Isles, Scotland in 1904. In Sept. 1750 a Blue whale allegedly measuring 101 ft *30,75 m* in length ran aground in the River Humber estuary. Another specimen stranded on the west coast of Lewis, Western Isles, Scotland in *c.* 1870 was credited with a length of 105 ft *32 m* but the carcase was cut up by the local people before the length could be verified. In both cases the length was probably exaggerated or taken along the curve of the body instead of in a straight line from the tip of the snout to the notch in the flukes. Four Blue whales have been stranded on British coasts since 1913, at least two of them after being harpooned by whalers. The last occurrence (*c.* 60 ft *18 cm*) was at Wick, Highland, Scotland on 15 Oct. 1923.

Blue whales inhabit the colder seas and migrate to warmer waters in the winter for breeding. Observations made in the Antarctic in 1947–48 showed that a Blue whale can maintain a speed of 20 knots (23 m.p.h. *37 km/h*) for ten minutes when frightened. It has been calculated that a 90 ft *27 m* Blue whale travelling at 20 knots *37 km/h* would develop 520 h.p. *527 c.v.* Newborn calves measure 6,5 to 8,6 m *21 ft 3½ in* to *28 ft 6 in* in length and weigh up to 3,000 kg *2.95 tons.*

It has been estimated that there were between 17,500 and 19,000 Blue whales living throughout the oceans in 1977. The species has been protected *de jure* since, 1967, although non-member countries of the International Whaling Commission, *e.g.* Chile and Peru, are not bound by this agreement.

Deepest dive

The greatest *recorded* depth to which a whale has dived is 620 fathoms (3,720 ft *1 134 m*) by a 47 ft *14,32 m* bull Sperm whale (*Physeter catodon*) found with its jaw entangled with a submarine cable running between Santa Elena, Ecuador and Chorillos, Peru, on 14 Oct. 1955. At this depth the whale withstood a pressure of 1,680 lb/in² *118 kg.f/cm²* of body surface. On 25 Aug. 1969 another bull sperm whale was killed 100 miles *160 km* south of Durban after it had surfaced from a dive lasting 1 hr 52 min, and inside its stomach were found two small sharks which had been swallowed about an hour earlier. These were later identified as *Scymnodon sp.*, a species found only on the sea floor. At this point from land the depth of water is in excess of 1,646 fathoms (10,476 ft *3 193 m*) for a radius of 30–40 miles *48–64 km*, which now suggests that the sperm whale sometimes may descend to a depth of over 10,000 ft *3 000 m* when seeking food.

Largest on land *World*
The largest living land animal is the African bush elephant (*Loxodonta africana africana*). The average adult bull stands 10 ft 6 in *3,20 m* at the shoulder and weighs 5.6 tons *5,7 tonnes*. The largest specimen ever recorded, and the largest land animal of modern times, was a bull shot 25 miles *40 km* north-northeast of Mucusso, southern Angola on 7 Nov. 1974. Lying on its side this elephant measured 13 ft 8 in *4,16 m* in a projected line from the highest point of the shoulder to the base of the forefoot, indicating that its standing height must have been about 13 ft *3,96 m*. Other measurements included an over-all length of 35 ft *10,67 m* (tip of extended trunk to tip of extended tail) and a forefoot circumference of 5 ft 11 in *1,80 m*. The weight was computed to be 26,328 lb. (11.75 tons, *11,96 tonnes*), (see also Shooting, Chapter 12).

Largest on land *Britain*
The largest wild mammal in the British Isles is the Red deer (*Cervus elephus*). A full-grown stag stands 3 ft 8 in *1,11 m* at the shoulder and weighs 230–250 lb. *104–113 kg*. The heaviest ever recorded was probably a stag killed at Glenfiddich, Banff, Scotland in 1831, which weighed 525 lb. *238 kg*. The heaviest park Red deer on record was a stag weighing 476 lb. *215 kg* (height at shoulder 4 ft 6 in *1,37 m*) killed at Woburn, Bedfordshire in 1836. The wild pony (*Equus caballus*) may weigh up to 700 lb. *320 kg* but now lives under semi-feral conditions.

Tallest
The tallest mammal is the Giraffe (*Giraffa camelopardalis*). For details see p. 26.

Smallest *Land*
The smallest recorded land mammal is the rare Kitti's hog-nosed bat (*Craseonycteris thonglongyai*) or Bumblebee bat, which is restricted to two caves near the forestry station at Ban Sai Yoke on the Kwae Noi River, Kanchanaburi, Thailand. Mature specimens (both sexes) have a wing span of *c* 160 mm *6.29 in* and weigh 1.75–2 g *0.062–0.071 oz*. The smallest mammal found in the British Isles is the European pygmy shrew (*Sorex minutus*). Mature specimens have a head and body length of 43–64 mm *1.69–2.5 in*, a tail length of 31–46 mm *1.22–1.81 in* and weigh between 2,4 and 6,1 g *0.084* and *0.213 oz*.

Smallest *Marine*
The smallest totally marine mammal is probably Heaviside's dolphin (*Cephalorhynchus heavisidei*) of the South Atlantic. Adult specimens have an average length of 4 ft *1,22 m* and weigh up to 90 lb. *41 kg*. The Sea otter (*Enhydra lutris*) is even smaller (55–81.4 lb. *25–38,5 kg*), but this species sometimes comes ashore during storms.

Rarest
The rarest placental mammal in the world is the tenrec *Dasogale fontoynonti* (see p. 26). Among sub-species, the Javan tiger (*Panthera tigris sondaica*) was reduced to 4 or 5 specimens by 1977, all of them in the Meru Betiri reserve in eastern Java. The Arabian oryx (*Oryx leucoryx*) has not been reported in the wild since 3 were killed and 4 captured in South Oman in 1972.

The total British population of the now fully-protected Common otter (*Lutra lutra*) is now less than 300, compared to 14,000 before the Second World War. No otters have been killed in England since 1975, but three were killed in Wales in 1976.

Fastest *World*
The fastest of all land animals over a short distance (*i.e.* up to 600 yds *549 m*) is the Cheetah or Hunting Leopard (*Acinonyx jubatus*) of the open plains of East Africa, Iran, Turkmenia and Afghanistan, with a probable maximum speed of 60–63 m.p.h. *96–101 km/h* over suitably level ground. Speeds of 71,

84 and even 90 m.p.h. *114, 135 and 145 km/h* have been claimed for this animal, but these figures must be considered exaggerated. Tests in London in 1937 showed that on an oval greyhound track over 345 yds *316 m* a female cheetah's average speed over three runs was 43.4 m.p.h. *69,8 km/h* (cf. 43.26 m.p.h. *69,6 km/h* for the fastest racehorse), but this specimen was not running flat out. The fastest land animal over a sustained distance (*i.e.* 1,000 yds *914 m* or more) is the Pronghorn antelope (*Antilocapra americana*) of the western United States. Specimens have been observed to travel at 35 m.p.h. for 4 miles *56 km/h for 6 km*, at 42 m.p.h. for 1 mile *67 km/h for 1,6 km* and 55 m.p.h. for half a mile *88,5 km/h for 0,8 km*. On 14 Aug. 1936 at Spanish Lake, in Lake County, Oregon a hard-pressed buck was timed by a car speedometer at 61 m.p.h. *98 km/h* over 200 yds *183 m*.

Fastest *Britain*
The fastest British land mammal over a sustained distance is the Roe deer (*Capreolus capreolus*), which can cruise at 25–30 m.p.h. *40–48 km/h* for more than 20 miles *32 km*, with occasional bursts of up to 40 m.p.h. *64 km/h*. On 19 Oct. 1970 a frightened runaway Red deer (*Cervus elaphus*) registered a speed of 42 m.p.h. *67,5 km/h* on a police radar trap as it charged through a street in Stalybridge, Greater Manchester.

Slowest
The slowest moving land mammal is the Ai or Three-toed sloth (*Bradypus tridactylus*) of tropical America. The average ground speed is 6 to 8 ft *1,83–2,44 m* a minute (0.068–0.098 m.p.h. *0,109–0,158 km/h*), but in the trees it can "accelerate" to 15 ft *4,57 m* a minute (0.170 m.p.h. *0,272 km/h*) (cf. these figures with the 0.03 m.p.h. *0,05 km/h* of the common garden snail and the 0.17 m.p.h. *0,27 km/h* of the giant tortoise.

Longest lived
No other mammal can match the extreme proven 114 years attained by Man (*Homo sapiens*) (see pp. 15 & 16). It is probable that the closest approach is among Blue and Fin whales (*Balaenoptera musculus* and *B. physalus*). Studies of the annual growth layers or laminations found in the wax-like plug deposited in the outer ear indicate a maximum life-span of 90–100 years.

The longest-living land mammal, excluding Man, is the Asiatic elephant (*Elephas maximus*). The greatest age that has been verified with certainty is 70 years in the case of a bull timber elephant "Kyaw Thee" (Tusker 1342), who died in the Taunggyi Forest division, southern Shan States, Burma in 1965. The famous circus cow elephant "Modoc" was reportedly 78 years old when she died in Santa Clara, California, U.S.A. on 17 July 1975, but this claim has not yet been fully authenticated.

Highest living
The highest living wild mammal in the world is probably the Yak (*Bos grunniens*), of Tibet and the Szechwanese Alps, China, which occasionally climbs to an altitude of 20,000 ft *6,100 m* when foraging. The Bharal (*Pseudois nayaur*) and the Pika or Mouse hare (*Ochotona thibetana*) may also reach this height in the Himalayas. In 1890 the tracks of an elephant were found at 15,000 ft *4 750 m* on Kilimanjaro, Tanzania.

Largest herds
The largest herds on record were those of the Springbok (*Antidorcas marsupialis*) during migration across the plains of the western parts of southern Africa in the 19th century. In 1849 John (later Sir John) Fraser observed a *trekbokken* that took three days to pass through the settlement of Beaufort West, Cape Province. Another herd seen moving near Nels Poortje, Cape Province in 1888 was estimated to contain 100,000,000 head, although 10,000,000 is probably a more realistic figure. A herd estimated to be 15 miles *24 km* wide and more than 100 miles *160 km* long was reported from Karree Kloof, Orange River, South Africa in July 1896.

The largest concentration of wild mammals found living anywhere in the world today is that of the Guano Bat (*Tadarida brasiliensis*) in Bracan Cave, San Antonio, Texas,

U.S.A., where twenty million animals assemble after migration from Mexico.

Longest and shortest gestation periods
The longest of all mammalian gestation periods is that of the Asiatic elephant (*Elephas maximus*), with an average of 609 days or just over 20 months and a maximum of 760 days—more than two and a half times that of a human. The gestation period of the American opossum (*Didelphis marsupialis*), also called the Virginian opossum, is normally 12 to 13 days but may be as short as eight days.

The gestation periods of the rare Water opossum or Yapok (*Chironectes minimus*) of Central and northern South America (average 12–13 days) and the Eastern native cat (*Dasyurus viverrinus*) of Australia (average 12 days) may also be as short as 8 days.

Largest litter
The greatest recorded number of young born to a *wild* mammal at a single birth is 32 (not all of which survived) in the case of the Common tenrec (*Centetes ecaudatus*) found in Madagascar and the Comoro Islands. The average litter size is 12–16. In March 1961 a litter of 32 was also reported for a House mouse (*Mus musculus*) at the Roswell Park Memorial Institute in Buffalo, N.Y., U.S.A. (average litter size 13–21) (see also Chapter 9 Agriculture, prolificacy records—pigs).

Youngest breeder
The Streaked tenrec (*Hemicentetes semispinosus*) of Madagas-

car is weaned after only 5 days, and females are capable of breeding 3–4 weeks after birth.

CARNIVORES
Largest Land *World*
The largest living terrestrial carnivore is the Kodiak bear (*Ursus arctos middendorffi*), which is found on Kodiak Island and the adjacent Afognak and Shuyak islands in the Gulf of Alaska, U.S.A. The average adult male has a nose to tail length of 8 ft *2,4 m* (tail about 4 in *10 cm*), stands 52 in *132 cm* at the shoulder and weighs between 1,050 and 1,175 lb. *476–533 kg*. In 1894 a weight of 1,656 lb. *751 kg* was recorded for a male shot at English Bay, Kodiak Island, whose *stretched* skin measured 13 ft 6 in *4,11 m* from the tip of the nose to the root of the tail. This weight was exceeded by a "cage-fat" male in the Cheyenne Mountain Zoological Park, Colorado Springs, Colorado, U.S.A. which scaled 1,670 lb. *757 kg* at the time of its death on 22 Sept. 1955.

Weights in excess of 1,600 lb. *725 kg* have also been reported for the Polar bear (*Ursus maritimus*), but the average adult male weighs 850–900 lb. *386–408 kg* and measures 7¾ ft *2,4 m* nose to tail. In 1960 a polar bear allegedly weighing 2,210 lb. *1 002 kg* before skinning was shot at the polar entrance to Kotzebue Sound, north-west Alaska. In April 1962 the 11 ft 1½ in *3,39 m* tall over-mounted specimen was put on display at the Seattle World Fair, Washington, U.S.A.

Largest Land *Britain*
The largest land carnivore found in Britain is the Badger

Simba, the 826 lb. *375 kg* lion with his owner Adrian Nyoka who stands 5 ft 8 in *1,72 m* (see p. 30). (*Gerald L. Wood*)

(*Meles meles*). The average adult boar (sows are slightly smaller) measures 3 ft *90 cm* in length—including a 4 in *10 cm* tail—and weighs 27 lb. *12,3 kg* in the early spring and 32 lb. *14,5 kg* at the end of the summer when it is in "grease". In Dec. 1952 a boar weighing exactly 60 lb. *27,2 kg* was killed near Rotherham, South Yorkshire.

Largest Marine

The largest toothed mammal ever recorded is the Sperm whale (*Physeter catodon*), also called the cachalot. The average adult bull measures 47 ft *14,30 m* in length and weighs about 33 tons *33,5 tonnes*. The largest accurately measured specimen on record was a 67 ft 11 in *20,7 m* bull captured off the Kurile Islands, north-west Pacific, by a U.S.S.R. whaling fleet in the summer of 1950. Twelve cachalots have been stranded on British coasts since 1913. The largest, a bull measuring 61 ft 5 in *19 m* was washed ashore at Birchington, Kent on 18 Oct. 1914. Another bull estimated at 65 ft *19,8 m* but badly decomposed was stranded at Ferryloughan, Co. Galway, Ireland on 2 Jan. 1952.

Smallest

The smallest living member of the Order Carnivora is the Least weasel (*Mustela rixosa*), also called the Dwarf weasel, which is circumpolar in distribution. Four races are recognised, the smallest of which is *M.r.pygmaea* of Siberia. Mature specimens have an overall length of 177–207 mm *6.96–8,14 in* and weigh between 35 and 70 g *1¼ to 2½ oz*.

Largest feline

The largest member of that cat family (Felidae) is the long-furred Siberian tiger (*Panthera tigris altaica*), also called the Amur or Manchurian tiger. Adult males average 10 ft 4 in *3,15 m* in length (nose to tip of extended tail), stand 39–42 in *99–107 cm* at the shoulder and weigh about 585 lb. *265 kg*. In 1950 a male weighing 384 kg *846.5 lb*. was shot in the Sikhote Alin Mts., Maritime Territory, U.S.S.R. In Nov. 1967 David H. Hasinger of Philadelphia, U.S.A. shot an outsized Indian tiger (*Panthera tigris tigris*) in northern Uttar Pradesh which measured 10 ft 7 in *3,22 m* between pegs (11 ft 1 in *3,37 m* over the curves) and weighed 857 lb. *388,7 kg* (cf. 9 ft 3 in *2,82 m* and 420 lb. *190 kg* for average adult male). It is now on display in the U.S. Museum of Natural History, Smithsonian Institution, Washington, DC.

The average adult African lion (*Pantheria leo*) measures 9 ft *2,7 m* overall, stands 36–38 in *91–97 cm* at the shoulder and weighs 400–410 lb. *181–185 kg*. The heaviest wild specimen on record was one weighing 690 lb. *313 kg* shot by Mr. Lennox Anderson just outside Hectorspruit in the eastern Transvaal, South Africa in 1936. In July 1970 a weight of 826 lb. *375 kg* was reported for a black-maned lion named "Simba" (b. Dublin Zoo, 1959) at Colchester Zoo, Essex. He died on 16 Jan. 1973 at Knaresborough Zoo, North Yorkshire, where his stuffed body is currently on display.

Smallest feline

The smallest member of the cat family is the Rusty-spotted cat (*Felis rubiginosa*) of southern India and Ceylon. The average adult male has an overall length of 25–28 in *64–71 cm* (tail 9–10 in *23–25 cm*) and weighs about 3 lb. *1,350 kg*.

PINNIPEDS (Seals, Sea-lions and Walruses)

Largest *World*

The largest of the 32 known species of pinniped is the Southern elephant seal (*Mirounga leonina*), which inhabits the sub-Antarctic islands. Adult bulls average 16½ ft *5 m* in length (tip of inflated snout to the extremities of the outstretched tail flippers), 12 ft *3,7 m* in maximum bodily girth and weigh about 5,000 lb. (2.18 tons *2 268 kg*). The largest accurately measured specimen on record was a bull killed in Possession Bay, South Georgia on 28 Feb. 1913 which measured 21 ft 4 in *6,50 m* after flensing (original length about 22½ ft *6,85 m*) and probably weighed at least 4 tons/*tonnes*. There are old records of bulls measuring 25–30 ft *7,62–9,14 m* and even 35 ft *10,66 m* but these figures must be considered exaggerated.

Largest British

The largest pinniped among British fauna is the Grey seal (*Halichoerus grypus*), also called the Atlantic seal. In 1772 an extremely bulky bull measuring 9 ft *2,74 m* in length, 7 ft 6 in *2,28 m* in maximum bodily girth and weighing 658 lb. *298 kg* was killed in the Farne Islands.

Smallest

The smallest pinnipeds are the Baikal seal (*Pusa sibirica*) of Lake Baikal, U.S.S.R. and the Ringed seal (*Pusa hispida*) of the Arctic. Adult specimens measure up to 5 ft 6 in *1,67 m* and weigh up to 280 lb. *127 kg*.

Rarest

The Caribbean or West Indian monk seal (*Monachus tropicalis*) has not been recorded since 1962 when a single specimen was sighted on the beach of Isla Mujeres off the Yucatan Peninsula, Mexico, and the species is now believed to be on the verge of extinction.

Fastest and deepest

The highest swimming speed recorded for a pinniped is 25 m.p.h. *40 km/h* for a Californian sea lion (*Zalophus californianus*). The deepest dive recorded for a pinniped is 600 m *1,968 ft* for a bull Weddell seal (*Leptonychotes weddelli*) in McMurdo Sound, Antarctica in March 1966. At this depth the seal withstood a pressure of 875 lb./in² *6 033 k Pa* of body area. The exceptionally large eyes of the Southern elephant seal (*Mirounga leonina*), point to a deep-diving ability, and unconfirmed measurements down to 2,000 ft *609 m* have been claimed.

Longest lived

A female Grey seal (*Halichoerus grypus*) shot at Shunni Wick in the Shetland Islands on 23 April 1969 was believed to be "at least 46 years old" based on a count of dental annuli.

BATS

Largest *World*

The only flying mammals are bats (order Chiroptera), of which there are about 1,000 living species. That with the greatest wing span is the Kalong (*Pteropus vampyrus*), a fruit bat found in Malaysia and Indonesia. It has a wing span of up to 170 cm *5 ft 7 in* and weighs up to 900 g *31.7 oz*.

Largest *Britain*

The largest bat found in Britain is the very rare Large mouse-eared bat (*Myotis myotis*). Mature specimens have a wing span of 355–450 mm *13.97–17.71 in* and weigh up to 45 g *1.58 oz*.

Smallest *World*

For details of Kitti's hog-nosed bat see p. 28.

Smallest *Britain*

The smallest native British bat is the Pipistrelle (*Pipistrellus pipistrellus*). Mature specimens have a wing span of 190–250 mm *7.48–9.84 in* and weigh between 3 and 8 g *0.10–0.28 oz*.

Rarest *Britain*

The rarest native British bat is Bechstein's bat (*Myotis bechsteini*), with Dorset and Hampshire as the main centres of population. There have been about thirty records to date. In January 1965 fifteen specimens of the Grey long-eared bat (*Plecotus austriacus*) were discovered in the roof of the Nature Conservancy's Research Station at Furzebrook, Dorset. Up to then this species, which is found all over Europe, had only been recorded once in Britain (Hampshire, 1875).

Fastest

Because of the great practical difficulties few data on bat speeds have been published. The greatest speed attributed to a bat is 32 m.p.h. *51 km/h* in the case of a Free-tailed or Guano bat (*Tadarida mexicana*). This speed is closely matched by the Noctule bat (*Nyctalus noctula*) and the Long-winged bat (*Miniopterus schreibersi*), both of which have been timed at 31 m.p.h. *50 km/h*.

Longest lived

The greatest age reliably reported for a bat is "at least 24 years" for a female Little brown bat (*Myotis lucifugus*) found on 30 April 1960 in a cave on Mount Aeolis, East Dorset, Vermont, U.S.A. It had been banded at a summer colony in

A comparison of the life-spans of contrasting animals from six classes.
ARACHNIDS (Tarantula Spider) see p. 44; AMPHIBIANS (Japanese Giant Salamander) see p. 41; MAMMALS (Asiatic or Indian Elephant) see p. 28; BIRDS (Andean Condor) see p. 37; FISH (European Eel) see p. 43; REPTILES (Marion's Tortoise) see p. 26.

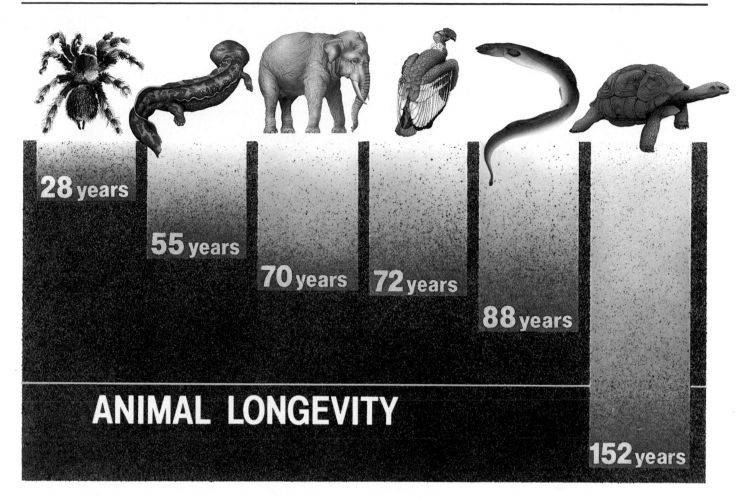

28 years

55 years

70 years

72 years

88 years

ANIMAL LONGEVITY

152 years

Mashpee, Massachusetts on 22 June 1937. There is an unconfirmed French report of a 26–27 year old Greater horseshoe bat (*Rhinolophus ferrumequinum*).

Highest detectable pitch

Because of their ultrasonic echolocation bats have most acute hearing of any terrestrial animal. Vampire bats (*Desmodontidae*) and fruit bats (*Pteropodidae*) can hear frequencies as high as 150 k Hz (*cf.* 20 k Hz for the adult human limit but 153 k Hz for the Bottle-nosed dolphin (*Tursiopis truncatus*)).

PRIMATES
Largest

The largest living primate is the Eastern lowland gorilla (*Gorilla gorilla grauei*) which inhabits the lowlands of the eastern part of Zaïre (formerly Democratic Republic of the Congo) and south-western Uganda. The average adult bull stands 5 ft 9 in *1,75 m* tall (including crest) and measures 58 to 60 in *147–152 cm* round the chest and weighs about 360 lb. *163 kg*. The greatest height (top of crest to heel) recorded for a gorilla is 6 ft 2 in *1,88 m* for a bull of the Mountain race (*Gorilla g. beringei*) shot in the eastern Congo in *c.* 1921.

The heaviest gorilla ever kept in captivity was an Eastern lowland bull named "Mbongo", who died in San Diego Zoological Gardens, California, U.S.A. on 15 March 1942. During an attempt to weigh him shortly before his death the platform scales "fluctuated from 645 pounds to nearly 670 (*293–304 kg*)". This specimen measured 5 ft 7½ in *1,71 m* in height and 69 in *175 cm* around the chest. The heaviest gorilla living in captivity today has been the Western lowland (*Gorilla g. gorilla*) bull "Samson" (b. 1949) of Milwaukee County Zoological Park, Wisconsin, U.S.A. He has weighed as much as 658 lb. *299 kg* but is now down to 485 lb. *220 kg*.

Smallest

The smallest known primate is the rare Feather-tailed tree shrew (*Ptiolcercus lowii*) of Malaysia, Adult specimens have a total length of 230–330 mm *9–13 in* (head and body 100–140 mm *3.93 5.51 in.*, tail 130 190 mm *5.1–7.5 in*) and weigh 35–50 g *1.23–1.76 oz*. The mouse lemur (*Microcebus murinus*) of Madagascar is approximately the same length (274–300 mm *10.8–11.8 in*) but heavier, adults weighing 45–80 grammes, *1.58–2.82 oz*.

Rarest

The rarest primate is the Hairy-eared mouse lemur (*Cheirogaleus trichotis*) of Madagascar which, until fairly recently, was known only from the type specimen and two skins. In 1966, however, a live example was found on the east coast near Mananara.

Longest lived

The greatest irrefutable age reported for a non-human primate is 57 years in the case of a male Orang-utan (*Pongo pygmaeus*) named "Guas", who died in Philadelphia Zoological Garden, Pennsylvania, U.S.A. on 9 Feb. 1977. He was received on 1 May 1931 after having been kept for some time in Cuba. The world's oldest living primate is the Western lowland bull gorilla "Massa" of Philadelphia Zoological Garden, Pennsylvania, U.S.A., who was still alive in March 1979 aged 48 years 3 months. He was received as a five-year-old on 30 Dec. 1935.

Strength

In 1924 "Boma", a 165 lb. *74,80 kg* male chimpanzee at Bronx Zoo, New York, N.Y., U.S.A. recorded a right-handed pull (feet braced) of 847 lb. *384 kg* on a dynamometer (*cf.* 210 lb. *95 kg* for a man of the same weight). On another occasion an adult female chimpanzee named "Suzette" (estimated weight 135 lb. *61 kg*) at the same zoo registered a right-handed pull of 1,260 lb. *572 kg* while in a rage. A record from the U.S.A. of a 100 lb. *45 kg* chimpanzee achieving a two-handed dead lift of 600 lb. *272 kg* with ease suggests that a male gorilla could with training raise 1,800 lb. *816 kg*!

MONKEYS

Largest
The only species of monkey reliably credited with a weight of more than 100 lb. *45 kg* is the Mandrill (*Mandrillus sphinx*) of equatorial West Africa. The greatest reliable weight recorded is 119 lb. *54 kg* but an unconfirmed weight of 130 lb. *59 kg* has been reported.

Smallest
The smallest known monkey is the Pygmy marmoset (*Cebuella pygmaea*) of Ecuador, northern Peru and western Brazil. Mature specimens have a maximum total length of 304 mm *12 in* half of which is tail, and weigh from 49 to 80 g *1.7 to 2.81 oz*. which means it rivals the mouse lemur for the title of the smallest living primate (see p. 31).

RODENTS

Largest
The world's largest rodent is the Capybara (*Hydrochoerus hydrochaeris*), also called the Carpincho or Water Hog, which is found in tropical South America. Mature specimens have a head and body length of 3¼ to 4½ ft *0,99–1,4 m* and weigh up to 174 lb *79 kg*. Britain's largest rodent is now the Coypu (*Myocastor coypus*), also known as the Nutria, which was introduced from Argentina by East Anglian fur-breeders in 1927. In 1937 four escaped from a nutria-farm near Ipswich, Suffolk and by 1978 there were an estimated 8,000 coypu living in Britain, all of them in East Anglia. Adult males measure 30–36 in *76–91 cm* in length (including short tail) and weigh up to 28 lb. *13 kg* in the wild state (40 lb. *18 kg* in captivity).

Smallest
The smallest rodent is probably the Old World harvest mouse (*Micromys minutus*), of which the British form measures up to 135 mm *5.3 in* in total length and weighs between 4,2 and 10,2 g *0.15 to 0.36 of an oz*. In June 1965 it was announced that an even smaller rodent had been discovered in the Asian part of the U.S.S.R. (probably a more diminutive form of *M. minutus*), but further information is lacking.

Rarest
The rarest rodent in the world is believed to be the James Island rice rat (*Oryzomys swarthi*), also called Swarth's rice rat. Four specimens were collected on this island in the Galapagos group in 1906, and it was not heard of again until January 1966 when a recent skull was found.

Longest lived
The greatest reliable age reported for a rodent is 22 years 10 months for a female Bushtailed porcupine (*Atherurus africanus*), which died in Philadelphia Zoological Garden, Pennsylvania, U.S.A. on 6 May 1933. It was received as a young adult on 5 July 1910.

Fastest Breeder
The female Meadow vole (*Microtus agrestis*) found in Britain, can reproduce from the age of 25 days and have up to 17 litters of 6 to 8 young in a year.

INSECTIVORES

Largest
The largest insectivore is the Moon rat (*Echinosorex gymnurus*), also known as Raffles' gymnure, which is found in Burma, Thailand, Malaysia, Sumatra and Borneo. Mature specimens have a head and body length of 265–445 mm *10.43–17.52 in*, a tail measuring 200–210 mm *7.87–8.26 in* and weigh up to 1 400 g *3.08 lb*. Although Anteaters (family Myrmecophagidae) feed on termites and other soft-bodied insects they are not insectivores, but belong to the order Edentata, which means "without teeth".

Smallest
The smallest insectivore is Savi's white-toothed pygmy shrew (*Suncus etruscus*), also called the Etruscan shrew, which is found along the coast of the northern Mediterranean and southwards to Cape Province, South Africa. Mature specimens have a head and body length of 36–52 mm *1.32–2.04 in*, a tail length of 24–29 mm *0.94–1.14 in* and weigh between 1,5 and 2,5 g *0.052 and 0.09 oz*.

Longest lived
The greatest reliable age recorded for an insectivore is 10½ years for a Hedgehog tenrec (*Setifer setosus*), which died in London Zoo in 1971. There is an unconfirmed record of a Hedgehog (*Erinaceus europaeus*) living for 14 years.

ANTELOPES

Largest
The largest of all antelopes is the rare Derby eland (*Taurotragus derbianus*), also called the Giant eland, of West and north-central Africa, which may surpass 2,000 lb. *907 kg*. The Common eland (*T. oryx*) of East and South Africa has the same shoulder height of up to 5 ft 10 in *1,78 m* but is not quite so massive, although there is one record of a 5 ft 5 in *1,65 m* bull shot in Nyasaland (now Malawi) in *c.* 1937 which weighed 2,078 lb. *943 kg*.

Smallest
The smallest known antelope is the Royal antelope (*Neotragus pygmaeus*) of West Africa. Mature specimens measure 10–12 in *25–31 cm* at the shoulder and weigh only 7–8 lb. *3–3,6 kg* which is the size of a large Brown hare (*Lepus europaeus*). The slender Swayne's dik-dik (*Madoqua swaynei*) of Somalia, East Africa weighs only 5–6 lb. *2–2,7 kg* when adult, but this species stands about 13 in *33 cm* at the shoulder.

Rarest
The rarest antelope is probably Jentink's duiker (*Cephalophus jentinki*), also known as the Black-headed duiker, which is found only in a restricted area of tropical West Africa. There are only four in captivity, Alpha, Beta and their two offspring, in the Gladys Porter Zoo, Brownsville, Texas, U.S.A.

DEER

Largest
The largest deer is the Alaskan moose (*Alces alces gigas*). A bull standing 7 ft 8 in *2,3 m* at the withers and weighing an estimated 1,800 lb. *816 kg* was shot on the Yukon River in the Yukon Territory, Canada in Sept. 1897. Unconfirmed measurements up to 8½ ft *2,59 m* at the withers and estimated weights up to 2,600 lb. *1 180 kg* have been claimed. The record antler span is 78½ in *199 cm*.

Smallest
The smallest true deer (family Cervidae) is the Pudu (*Pudu mephistophiles*) of Ecuador the male of which stands 13–15 in *33–38 cm* at the shoulder and weighs 18–20 lb. *8–9 kg*. The smallest known ruminant is the Lesser Malayan chevrotain or Mouse deer (*Tragulus javanicus*) of south-eastern Asia. Adult specimens measure 8–10 in *20–25 cm* at the shoulder and weigh 6–7 lb. *2,7–3,2 kg*.

Rarest
The rarest deer in the world is Fea's muntjac (*Muntiacus feae*), which is known only from two specimens collected on the borders of Tenasserim, Lower Burma and Thailand.

Oldest
The greatest reliable age recorded for a deer is 26 years 6 months 2 days for a Red deer (*Cervus elephus*) which died in the National Zoological Park, Washington, D.C., U.S.A. on 24 March 1941.

MARSUPIALS

Largest
The largest of all marsupials is the Red kangaroo (*Macropus rufus*) of southern and eastern Australia. Adult males or "boomers" stand 6–7 ft *1,83–2,13 m* tall, weigh 150–175 lb. *68–79 kg* and measure up to 8 ft 11 in *2,71 m* in a straight line from the nose to the tip of the extended tail.

Smallest

The smallest known marsupial is the rare Kimberley planigale or flat-skulled marsupial mouse (*Planigale subtilissima*), which is found only in the Kimberley district of Western Australia. Adult males have a head and body length of 44,5 mm *1.75 in*, a tail length of 51 mm *2 in* and weigh about 4 g *0.141 oz*. Females are smaller than males.

Rarest

The rarest marsupial is probably the Thylacine (*Thylacinus cynocephalus*), also known as the "Tasmanian tiger", the largest of the carnivorous marsupials, which reportedly became extinct some time in the mid-1930's (the last captive specimen died in Hobart Zoo, Tasmania in 1934). In 1961, however, a young male was accidentally killed by fishermen at Sandy Cape, western Tasmania, and in July 1977 a positive sighting was made of another specimen near Derby on the north-western side of the island.

Longest Lived

The greatest reliable age recorded for a marsupial is 19 years 7 months for a South Australian wallaroo (*Macropus robustus erubescens*), which died in New York Zoological Park (Bronx Zoo) in 1968.

Highest and longest jumps

The greatest measured height cleared by a hunted kangaroo is 10 ft 6 in *3,20 m* over a pile of timber. During the course of a chase in January 1951 a female Red kangaroo (*Macropus rufus*) made a series of bounds which included one of 42 ft *12,80 m*. There is also an unconfirmed report of a Great grey kangaroo (*M. canguru*) jumping nearly 13,5 m *44 ft 8½ in* on the flat.

TUSKS
Longest

The longest recorded elephant tusks (excluding prehistoric examples) are a pair from the eastern Congo (Zaire) preserved in the National Collection of Heads and Horns kept by the New York Zoological Society in Bronx Park, New York City, N.Y., U.S.A. The right tusk measures 11 ft 5½ in *3,49 m* along the outside curve and the left 11 ft *3,35 m*. Their combined weight is 293 lb. *133 kg*. A single tusk of 11 ft 6 in *3,50 m* has been reported, but further details are lacking.

Heaviest

The greatest weight ever recorded for an elephant tusk is 117 kg. *258 lb*. for a specimen collected in Benin (formerly Dahomey), West Africa and exhibited at the Paris Exposition in 1900.

HORNS
Longest

The longest recorded animal horn was one measuring 81¼ in *206 cm* on the outside curve, with a circumference of 18¼ in *46 cm*, found on a specimen of domestic Ankole cattle (*Bos taurus*) near Lake Ngami, Botswana (formerly Bechuanaland). The largest head (horns measured from tip to tip across the forehead) is one of 13 ft 11 in *4,24 m* for a specimen of wild buffalo (*Bubalus bubalus*) shot in India in 1955. The maximum recorded for a Texas Longhorn steer is 9 ft 9 in *2,97 m* from tip to tip.

Longest *Rhinoceros*

The longest recorded anterior horn for a rhinoceros is one of 62¼ in *158 cm* found on a female southern race White rhinoceros (*Ceratotheriam simum simum*) shot in South Africa in *c*. 1848. The interior horn measured 22¼ in *57 cm*. There is also an unconfirmed record of an anterior horn measuring 81 in *206 cm*.

HORSES AND PONIES

The worlds' horse population is estimated to be 75,000,000.

Largest

The heaviest horse ever recorded was a 19.2-hand (6 ft 6 in *1,98 m*) pure-bred Belgian stallion named "Brooklyn Supreme" (foaled 12 April 1928) owned by Ralph Fogleman of Callender, Iowa, U.S.A. which weighed 3,200 lb. 1.42 tons *1,44 tonnes* shortly before his death on 6 Sept. 1948 aged 20.

Measuring a combined length of 22 ft 5½ in *6,84 m*, this pair of elephant tusks are the longest ever recorded

In April 1973 the Belgian mare "Wilma du Bos" (foaled 15 July 1966), owned by Mrs. Virgie Arden of Reno, Nevada, U.S.A. was reported to weigh slightly in excess of 3,200 lb. *1 451 kg* when in foal and being shipped from Antwerp. The normal weight of this 18.2 hand *1,88 m* mare is about 2,400 lb. *1 088 kg*. The British weight record is held by the 17.2 hand (5 ft 10 in *1,78 m*) Shire stallion "Honest Tom 5123" (foaled in 1884), owned by James Forshaw of Littleport, Cambridgeshire, which scaled 2,912 lb. *1 325 kg* in 1891. This poundage may have been exceeded by another huge Shire stallion named "Great Britain 978", bred by Henry Bultitaft of Ely, Cambridgeshire in 1876, but no weight details are available. In 1888 this horse was sold to Phineas T. Barnum, the American showman, for exhibition purposes.

Tallest

The tallest horse documented was the Percheron-Shire cross "Firpon" (foaled 1959), owned by Julio Falabella which stood 21.1 hands (7 ft 1 in *2,16 m*) and weighed 2,976 lb. *1 350 kg*. He died on the Recco de Roca Ranch near Buenos Aires, Argentina on 14 Mar. 1972. A height of 21.1 hands was also claimed for the Clydesdale gelding "Big Jim" (foaled 1950) bred by Lyall M. Anderson of West Broomley, Montrose, Scotland. He died in St. Louis, Missouri in 1957. A claim for 21.2 hands (7 ft 2 in *2,18 m*) was made in 1908 for a horse named "Morocco" weighing 2,835 lb. *1 286 kg* in Allentown, Pennsylvania, U.S.A. The tallest living horse bred in Britain today is the Shire stallion "Ladbrook Invader" (foaled 17 Apr. 1968), owned by Mr. Arthur Lewis of Tamworth, Staffordshire. He stands 19.1½ hands (6 ft 5½ in *1,97 m*) and weighs about 22 cwt. (2,464 lb. *1 120 kg*). He was shipped to the U.S.A. in 1976. "Wandle Henry Cooper" (foaled 1965) owned by Young & Co Brewery Ltd, Wandsworth, Greater London, stands 18.2½ hands (6 ft 2½ in *1,89 m*) and weighs *c*. 20 cwt *1 018 kg*.

Smallest

The smallest breed of horse (sic) is the Falabella of Argentina which was developed over a period of 45 years by crossing and recrossing a small group of undersized English Thoroughbreds with Shetland ponies. Adult specimens stand 15–30 in *38–74 cm* at the shoulder and weigh 40–80 lb. *18–36 kg*. Foals of 3 hands (12 in *30,4 cm*) have been twice recorded by Norman J. Mitchell of Glenorie, N.S.W., Australia in the cases of "Tung Dynasty" (8 Feb. 1978) and "Quicksilver" (1975).

Oldest

The greatest reliable age recorded for a horse is 62 years in the case of "Old Billy" (foaled 1760), believed to be a cross between a Cleveland and Eastern blood, who was bred by Mr. Edward Robinson of Wild Grave Farm in Woolston, Lancashire. In 1762 or 1763 he was sold to the Mersey and Irwell Navigation Company and remained with them in a working capacity (i.e. marshalling and towing barges) until 1819 when he was retired to a farm at Latchford, near Warrington, where he died on 27 Nov. 1822. The skull of this horse is preserved in the Manchester Museum, and his stuffed head is now on display in the Bedford Museum. The greatest reliable age recorded for a pony is 54 years for a stallion owned by a farmer in Central France which was still alive in 1919. The greatest age recorded for a thoroughbred racehorse is 42 years in the case of the bay gelding "Tango Duke" (foaled 1935), owned by Mrs. Carmen J. Koper of Barongarook, Victoria, Australia. The horse died on 25 Jan. 1978.

Strongest *draught*

The greatest load ever hauled by a pair of draught-horses was 48 short tons *43,5 tonnes* (= 50 pine logs or 36,055 board-feet of timber) on a special sledge litter *pulled across snow* for a distance of 275 yds *251 m* at the Nester Estate, Ewen, Ontanagon County, Michigan, U.S.A. on 26 Feb. 1893. The two horses, both Clydesdales, had a combined weight of 3,500 lb. *1 587 kg*. On 4 Sept. 1924 a pair of Shire geldings owned by Liverpool Corporation registered a much more impressive *maximum* pull equivalent to a starting load of 50 tons *51 tonnes* on a dynamometer at the British Empire Exhibition at Wembley, London.

The three year old Great Dane "Shamgret Danzas" the world's tallest living dog. (*Kentish Mercury South East.*)

DOGS—(*U.K. dog population 5,500,000 (1979 estimate) compared with 41,000,000 for the U.S.A.*).

Largest

The heaviest breed of domestic dog (*Canis familiaris*) is the St. Bernard. The heaviest recorded example was "Schwarzwald Hof Duke", owned by Dr. A. M. Bruner of Oconomowoc, Wisconsin, U.S.A. He was whelped on 8 Oct. 1964 and weighed 21 st. 1 lb. *133,8 kg* on 2 May 1969, dying three months later aged 4 years 10 months. The largest St. Bernard ever weighed in Britain was "Burton Black Magician", also called "Shane" (1969–1976), owned by Mrs. Sheila Bangs of Animal Mayday of Mitcham, Surrey. In Oct. 1973 he scaled a peak 19 st. 0 lb. 4¾ oz. *120,79 kg*.

Tallest

The tallest breeds of dog are the Great Dane and the Irish wolfhound, both of which can exceed 39 in *99 cm* at the shoulder. In the case of the Great Dane the extreme recorded example is "Shamgret Danzas" (whelped in 1975), owned by Mrs. G. Comley of Milton Keynes, Bucks. He stands 40½ in *102,9 cm* and weighs 16 stone *101,6 kg*. The Irish Wolfhound "Broadbridge Michael" (whelped in 1920), owned by Mrs. Mary Beynon of Sutton-at-Hone, Kent, stood 39½ in *100,3 cm* at the age of two years.

Smallest

The world's smallest breeds of dog are the Yorkshire terrier, the short-haired Chihuahua and the Toy poodle, *miniature* versions of which have been known to weigh less than 16 oz. *453 g* when adult. In April 1971 a weight of 10 oz. *283 g* was reliably reported for a fully-grown Yorkshire terrier called "Sylvia" (shoulder height 3½ in 89 *mm*) owned by Mrs. Connie Hutchins of Walthamstow, Greater London.

Oldest

Authentic records of dogs living over 20 years are extremely rare, but even 34 years has been accepted by one authority. The greatest reliable age recorded for a dog is 29 years 5 months for a Queensland "heeler" named "Bluey", owned by Mr. Les Hall of Rochester, Victoria, Australia. The dog was obtained as a puppy in 1910 and worked among cattle and sheep for nearly 20 years. He was put to sleep on 14 Nov. 1939. The British record is 27 years 10 months for a Welsh sheepdog cross called "Toots", who was whelped in January 1948 and died on 4 Nov. 1975 in the care of her life-time owner Barry Tuckey at Glebe Farm, Stockton, Warwickshire.

Strength and Endurance

The greatest load ever shifted by a dog was 6,400½ lb. *2 905 kg* of railroad steel pulled by a 176 lb. *80 kg* St. Bernard named "Ryettes Brandy Bear" at Bothell, Washington, U.S.A. on 21 July 1978. The four-year-old dog, owned by Douglas Alexander of Monroe, Washington, pulled the weight on a four-wheeled carrier across a cement surface for a distance of 15 ft *4,57 m* in less than 90 seconds. The record time for the annual 1,049 mile *1 680 km* dog sled race from Anchorage to Nome, Alaska is 14 days 14 hrs 43 min by "Emitt Peters" in the 1975 race.

Rarest

The rarest breed of dog in the world is the Tahl-Tan bear dog of Canada. In May 1978 there were reportedly only 3 pure bred examples still living, all of them in Atlin, British Columbia. The rarest breed recognised by the Kennel Club (i.e. with British registration) is the Portuguese water dog (Cao de Agua). In March 1978 the world population was 237, including 213 in the U.S.A. and only 17 in Portugal.

Guide Dog

The longest period of *active service* reported for a guide dog is 13 years 2 months in the case of a Labrador-retriever bitch named "Polly" (whelped 10 Oct. 1956), owned by Miss Rose Resnick of San Rafael, California, U.S.A. The dog was put to sleep on 15 Dec. 1971.

Largest litter

The largest recorded litter of puppies is one of 23 thrown on 19 June 1944 by "Lena", a foxhound bitch owned by Commander W. N. Ely of Ambler, Pennsylvania, U.S.A. On 6–7th Feb. 1975 "Careless Ann", a St. Bernard bitch, owned by Robert and Alice Rodden of Lebanon, Missouri, U.S.A. also produced a litter of 23, 14 of which survived. The British record is held by "Settrina Baroness Medina", a Red Setter bitch owned by Mgr. M. J. Buckley, Director of the Wood Hall Centre, Wetherby, West Yorkshire, who gave birth to 22 puppies, 15 of which survived, on 10 Jan. 1974. All 17 puppies born in Feb. 1977 to "Trudi", an Irish setter owned by Mr. Alan Jenkins of Wolverhampton, survived.

Most prolific
The greatest sire of all time was the champion greyhound "Low Pressure", nicknamed "Timmy", whelped in September 1957 and owned by Mrs. Bruna Amhurst of Regent's Park, London. From December 1961 until his death on 27 Nov. 1969 he fathered 2,414 registered puppies, with at least 600 others unregistered.

Most valuable
In June 1972 Mrs. Judith Thurlow of Great Ashfield, Suffolk turned down an offer of £14,000 for her racing greyhound "Super Rory" (b. Oct. 1970). Show dogs have also fetched extremely high prices, and in July 1976 Mrs. Eiselle Banks of Rayleigh, Essex turned down an American offer of £10,000 for her international champion Lowchen "Cluneen Adam Adamant" (b. 13 Aug. 1969).

"Top dog"
The greatest altitude attained by a mammal is 1,050 miles 1 690 km by the Samoyed husky bitch fired as a passenger in Sputnik II on 3 Nov. 1957. The dog was variously named "Kudryavka" (feminine form of "Curly"). "Limonchik" (dimunitive of lemon), "Malyshka", "Zhuchka" or by the Russian breed name for husky, "Laika".

Highest and longest jump
The canine "high jump" record is held by an Alsatian named "Crumstone Danko" owned by the De Beers mining company, who scaled an 11 ft 3 in 3,43 m high wall without a springboard in Pretoria, South Africa in May 1942. He was also credited with 16½ ft 5,03 m off a springboard. The British record is 10 ft 6 in 3,20 m by the Lancashire Police dog "Lancon Sultan VI", handled by P.C. John Evans at Hutton, near Preston, Lancashire on 8 Aug. 1973. The longest recorded canine long jump was one of 30 ft 9,14 m by a greyhound named "Bang" made in jumping a gate in coursing a hare at Brecon Lodge, Gloucestershire in 1849.

Ratting
The greatest ratter of all time was Mr. James Searle's bull terrier bitch "Jenny Lind", who killed 500 rats in 1 hr 30 min at "The Beehive", Old Crosshall Street, Liverpool on 12 July 1853. Another bull terrier named "Jacko", owned by Mr. Jemmy Shaw, was credited with killing 1,000 rats in 1 hr 40 min, but the feat was performed over a period of ten weeks in batches of 100 at a time. The last 100 were accounted for in 5 min 28 sec in London on 1 May 1862.

Tracking
The greatest tracking feat on record was performed by a Dobermann Pinscher named "Sauer", trained by Detective-Sergeant Herbert Kruger. In 1925 he tracked a stock-thief 100 miles 160 km across the Great Karroo, South Africa by scent alone. In 1923 a collie dog named "Bobbie", lost by his owners while they were on holiday in Wolcott, Indiana, U.S.A., turned up at the family home in Silverton, Oregon six months later, after covering a distance of some 2,000 miles 3 200 km. The dog, later identified by householders who had looked after him along the route, had apparently travelled back through the states of Illinois, Iowa, Nebraska and Colorado, before crossing the Rocky Mountains in the depths of winter and then continuing through Wyoming and Idaho.

Top Show Dog
The record number of "Best in Show" awards won by any dog in all breed shows is 127 compiled by the Pekinese International Champion Chik T'Sun of Caversham, owned by Mr. & Mrs. Charles C. Venable of Marietta, Georgia, in North America from January 1957 to February 1960.

Top Trainer
The most successful dog trainer in the world—and the fastest—is Mrs. Barbara Woodhouse of Rickmansworth, Hertfordshire, who has trained 16,867 dogs to a high standard during the period 1951 to 19 Mar. 1979. Her record for a single day is 80 dogs (Denver, Colorado, U.S.A., June 1973).

Police Dogs
The world's top police dog is "Trep" of Dade County Crime Force, Florida U.S.A. with $63 million (then £36 million) worth of narcotics sniffed out. Demonstrating at a school with 10 hidden packets, Trep once found 11. "Sergeant Blitz", a drug-sniffing police dog in Savannah, Georgia, U.S.A. was the subject of a $10,000 (£5,250) "contract" in January 1977.

Greatest Dog Funeral
The greatest dog funeral on record was for the mongrel dog "Lazaras" belonging to the eccentric Emperor Norton I of the United States, Protector of Mexico, held in San Francisco, California in 1862 which was attended by an estimated 10,000 people.

CATS
Heaviest
The heaviest domestic cat (Felis catus) on record is a 9 year old long-haired part-persian named "Tiger", who scales a constant 42–43 lbs. 19,05–19,50 kg (neck 12½ in 31,75 cm, waist 33 in 83,8 cm, length 37 in 94 cm). He is owned by Mrs. Phyllis Dacey of Billericay, Essex. In Dec. 1978 an unconfirmed weight of 44 lb. 19,9 kg (neck 15½ in 39,3 cm, waist 28 in 71,1 cm, length 41 in 104,1 cm) was reported for a 6 year-old male cat named "Tiddles" living in Cardiff, South Wales.

Oldest
Cats are generally longer-lived than dogs. Information on this subject is often obscured by two or more cats bearing the same nickname in succession. The oldest cat ever recorded was probably the tabby "Puss", owned by Mrs. T. Holway of Clayhidon, Devon who celebrated his 36th birthday on 28 Nov. 1939 and died the next day. A more recent and better-documented case was that of the female tabby "Ma", owned by Mrs. Alice St. George Moore of Drewsteignton, Devon. She was put to sleep on 5 Nov. 1957 aged 34.

Rarest breed
The rarest of the 72 recognised breeds of cat in Britain is the Red self Persian or Long-haired red self.

Largest kindle
The largest litter ever recorded was one of 19 kittens (4 stillborn) delivered by Caesarean section to "Tarawood Antigone", a four-year-old brown Burmese, on 7 Aug. 1970. Her owner, Mrs. Valerie Gane of Church Westcote, Kingham, Oxfordshire, said the result was a mis-mating with a half-Siamese. Of the 15 survivors, 14 were males and one female.

The largest live litter (all of which survived) was one of 14 kittens born in Dec. 1974 to a Persian cat named "Bluebell", owned by Mrs. Elenore Dawson of Wellington, Cape Province, South Africa.

Most prolific
A cat named "Dusty", aged 17, living in Bonham, Texas, U.S.A., gave birth to her 420th kitten on 12 June 1952. A 21-year-old cat "Tippy" living in Kingston-upon-Hull, Humberside gave birth to her 343rd kitten in June 1933.

Richest and most valuable
Dr. William Grier of San Diego, California, U.S.A. died in June 1963 leaving his entire estate of $415,000 (then £148,000) to his two 15-year-old cats "Hellcat" and "Brownie". When the cats died in 1965 the money went to the George Washington University in Washington, D.C. In 1967 Miss Elspeth Sellar of Grafham, Surrey turned down an offer of 2,000 guineas (£2,100) from an American breeder for her champion copper-eyed white Persian tom "Coylum Marcus" (b. 28 Mar. 1965) who died on 14 April 1978.

Mousing Champion

The greatest mouser on record was a tabby named "Mickey", owned by Shepherd & Sons Ltd. of Burscough, Lancashire who killed more than 22,000 mice during 23 years with the firm. He died in November 1968.

Cat population

The largest cat population is that of the U.S.A. with 23,000,000. Of Britain's cat population of 4,900,000 an estimated 100,000 are "employed" by the Civil Service.

RABBITS
Largest

The largest breed of domestic rabbit (*Oryctolagus cuniculus*) is the British giant. Adult specimens average 18–20 lb. *8,16–9,07 kg* but weights up to 30 lb. *13,6 kg* have been reliably reported for bucks. The heaviest recorded wild rabbit is one of 6 lb. 12 oz. *3,06 kg* shot by Mr. Monty Forest in the Swinford Estate, Burford, Oxfordshire in February 1976.

Smallest

The smallest breeds of domestic rabbit are the Netherlands dwarf and the Polish, both of which average 2½ lb. *1,13 kg* at maturity.

Most prolific

The most prolific domestic breeds are the New Zealand white and the Californian. Does produce 5 to 6 litters a year, each containing 8–12 young (*cf.* five litters and three to seven young for the wild rabbit).

HARES
Largest

In November 1956 a Brown hare (*Lepus europaeus*) weighing 15 lb. 1 oz. *6,83 kg* was shot near Welford, Northamptonshire.

LARGEST PET LITTERS

Animal	Number	Breed	Owner
Cat	15	Burmese/Siamese	Mrs. Valerie Gane, Church Westcote, Kingham, Oxfordshire.
Dog	23	Foxhound	Cdr. W. N. Ely, Ambler, Pennsylvania, U.S.A.
	23	St. Bernard	R. and A. Rodden, Lebanon, Missouri, U.S.A.
Rabbit	24	New Zealand White	Joseph Filek, Sydney, Cape Breton, Nova Scotia, Canada.
Guinea Pig	12	—	Laboratory Specimen
Hamster	18	Golden Hamster	Laboratory Specimen
Mouse	32	House Mouse	Laboratory Specimen (U.S.A.)
Gerbil	10	—	Julie Lock, Bridgwater, Somerset.

CAGED PET LONGEVITY TABLE
The greatest recorded ages for commonly kept pets are as follows:

	Years	Months	
Rabbit (*Oryctolagus cuniculus*)	18*		European rabbit *fl.* Aug. 1977.
Guinea Pig (*Cavia porcellus*)	14	10½	"Snowball" (M. A. Wall) Bingham, Notts., Died 14 Feb. 1979
Gerbil (*Gerbillus gerbillus*)	7	9½	"Squirt" (Tom Clouser) Brookfield, Wisconsin, U.S.A. Died 22 Sept. 1977.
House Mouse (*Mus musculus*)	5	11	"Hercules" (R. Hair), Purley, Surrey. Jan. 1971–26 Dec. 1976.
Rat (*Rattus sp.*)	5	8	Philadelphia, Pennsylvania, U.S.A. *c.* 1924.

* 18 years also reported for a doe still living in 1947.

Note: A report of 10 years 2 months for a hamster has been published but details are lacking.

2. BIRDS (*Aves*)

Largest *Ratite*

The largest living bird is the North African ostrich (*Struthio camelus camelus*), which is found in reduced numbers south of the Atlas Mountains from Upper Senegal and Niger across to the Sudan and central Ethiopia. Male examples of this flightless or ratite sub-species have been recorded up to 9 ft 2,74 m in height and 345 lb. *156,5 kg* in weight.

Largest *Carinate*

The heaviest flying bird or carinate is the Kori bustard or Paauw (*Otis kori*) of East and South Africa. Weights up to 40 lb. *18 kg* have been reliably reported for cock birds shot in South Africa. The Mute swan (*Cygnus olor*), which is resident in Britain, can also reach 40 lb. *18 kg* on occasion, and there is a record from Poland of a cob weighing 22,5 kg *49.5 lb.* which was probably too heavy to fly. The heaviest bird of prey is the Andean condor (*Vultur gryphus*), adult males averaging 20–25 lb. *9,09–11,30 kg*. An unconfirmed weight of 31 lb. *14,1 kg* has been claimed for a California condor (*Gymnogyps californianus*) (average weight 20 lb. *9 kg*) now preserved in the California Academy of Sciences, Los Angeles.

Largest wing span

The Wandering albatross (*Diomedea exulans*) of the southern oceans has the largest wing span of any living bird, adult males averaging 10 ft 4 in 3,15 m with wings tightly stretched. The largest recorded specimen was a male measuring 11 ft 10 in 3,60 m caught by banders in Western Australia in *c.* 1957, but some unmeasured birds may reach or possibly just exceed 13 ft 3,96 m. The only other bird reliably credited with a wingspan in excess of 11 ft 3,35 m is the vulture-like Marabou or Adjutant stork (*Leptoptilus crumeniferus*) of Africa. In the 1930's an extreme measurement of 13 ft 4 in 4,06 m was reported for a specimen shot in Central Africa, but this species rarely exceeds 9 ft 2,43 m.

Smallest *World*

The smallest bird in the world is Helena's hummingbird (*Mellisuga helenae*) of Cuba and the Isle of Pines. An average adult male measures 58 mm 2.28 in in total length—bill 15 mm 0.59 in, head and body 15 mm 0.59 in and tail 28 mm 1.10 in—and weighs about 2 g 0.07 oz., which means it is lighter than a Sphinx moth (0.08 oz. 2,2 g). The smallest bird of prey is the 1¼ oz. 35 g Bornean falconet (*Microhierax latifrons*) which is sparrow-sized.

The smallest sea bird is the Least storm petrel (*Halocyptena microsoma*), which breeds only on San Benito Island, Lower California, U.S.A. Adult specimens average 140 mm 5½ in in total length.

Smallest *Great Britain*

The smallest regularly-breeding British bird is the Goldcrest (*Regulus regulus*), also known as the Golden crested wren or Kinglet. Adult specimens measure 90 mm 3.5 in in total length and weigh between 3,8 and 4,5 g 0.108 and 0.127 oz.

Most abundant *Wild*

The most abundant species of wild bird is the Red-billed quelea (*Quelea quelea*) of the drier parts of Africa south of the Sahara with a population estimated at 10,000,000,000 of which a tenth are destroyed each year by pest control units.

Most abundant *Domestic*

The most abundant species of domesticated bird is the Chicken, the domesticated form of the wild Red jungle fowl (*Gallus gallus*) of south-east Asia. In 1974 there were believed to be about 4,000,000,000 in the world, or about one chicken for every member of the human race. The fowl stock in Britain was estimated at 130,000,000 in 1972, producing 270,000,000 chicks annually. The most abundant sea bird is Wilson's petrel (*Oceanites oceanicus*). No population estimates have been published, but the number runs into hundreds—possibly thousands—of millions. The top-breeding British sea-bird is the Guillemot (*Uria aalge*) with an estimated 577,000 breeding pairs in 1973.

Most abundant *Great Britain*
The commonest wild breeding land bird in Great Britain was, according to a survey published in 1977, the wren (*Troglodytes troglodytes*) when 10,000,000 pairs survived a mild winter. It was estimated in 1967 that 250,000 pigeon fanciers owned an average of 40 racing pigeons per loft, making a population of *c.* 10,000,000 in Great Britain. At the start of the shooting season there may in some years be 2 million reared pheasants (*Phasianus colchicus*) in addition to *c.* 8 million wild birds.

Rarest *World*
Because of the practical difficulties involved in assessing bird populations in the wild, it is virtually impossible to establish the identity of the world's rarest living bird. One of the strongest contenders, however, must be the Kauai O-o (*Moho braccatus*) of Kauai, Hawaiian Islands, of which only a single pair survived in 1976. In Jan. 1978 a New Zealand ornithological expedition exploring Chatham Island, positively identified and photographed three Magenta petrels (*Pterodroma magentae*). The only previous *claimed* sighting had been in 1868 about 500 miles *800 km* east of Chatham Island. In Dec. 1977 the White-winged guan (*Penelope albinennis*), thought to have become extinct about 100 years ago, was rediscovered in considerable numbers in north-western Peru. The world's rarest raptor (bird of prey) is the Mauritius kestrel (*Falco punctatus*). In Dec. 1978 the total wild population was 18, with another 5 being raised in captivity.

Rarest *Great Britain*
According to the British Ornithologists Union there are 28 species of birds which have been recorded only once in the British Isles—18 of them since the end of the Second World War in 1945. That which has not recurred for the longest period is the Black-capped petrel (*Pterodroma hasitata*), also known as the "Diablotin". A specimen was caught alive on a heath at Southacre, near Swaffham, Norfolk in March or April 1850. In Feb. 1978 a solitary example of the rare Franklin gull (*Larus pipixcan*) of North America was sighted near Great Yarmouth, Norfolk and 10 months later a Greater sand plover (*Charadrius leschenaultii*) from Central Southern Asia was recorded at Pagham Harbour Nature Reserve near Chichester, Sussex. The most tenuously established British bird is the Snowy owl (*Nyctea scandiaca*), with one pair breeding recurringly on Fetlar, Shetland Islands. Another pair introduced into the Highland Wildlife Park, near Aviemore, Scotland reared two chicks in 1975.

Fastest flying
The fastest flying bird is the Spine-tailed swift (*Chaetura caudacuta*). For details see page 26.

The bird which presents the hunter with the greatest difficulty is the Red-breasted merganser (*Mergus serrator*). On 29 May 1960 a specimen flushed from the Kukpuk River, Cape Thompson, northern Alaska, U.S.A. by a light aircraft recorded an air speed of 80 m.p.h. *128 km/h* in level flight for nearly 13 secs before turning aside.

Fastest and slowest wing beat
The fastest recorded wing beat of any bird is that of the hummingbird (*Heliactin cornuta*) of tropical South America with a rate of ninety beats a second. This rate is probably exceeded by the Bee hummingbirds (*Mellisuga helenae*) and (*Acestrura bombus*) but no figures have yet been published. Large vultures (family Vulturidae) and albatrosses (Diomedeidae) can soar for hours without beating their wings, but sometimes exhibit a flapping rate as low as one beat per sec.

Longest lived
The greatest irrefutable age reported for any bird is 72+ years in the case of a male Andean condor (*Vultur gryphus* named "Kuzya", which died in Moskovskii Zoologicheskii Park, Moscow, U.S.S.R. in 1964. This bird had been received as an adult in 1892. The British record is 68+ years in the case of a female European eagle-owl (*Bubo bubo*) which was still alive in 1899. Other records which are regarded as *probably* reliable include 73 years (1818–91) for a Greater sulphur-crested cockatoo (*Cacatua galerita*); 72 years (1797–

Fledglings being fed by the Goldcrest—the smallest regularly-breeding bird in Great Britain (see p. 36). (*James F. Young*).

1869) for an African grey parrot (*Psittacus erithacus*); 70 years (1770–1840) for a Mute swan (*Cygnus olor*) and 69 years for a Raven (*Corvus corax*). In 1972 a Southern Ostrich (*Struthio camelus australis*) aged 62 years and 3 months was killed in the Ostrich Abattoir at Oudtshoorn, Cape Province, South Africa.

"Jimmy", a red and green Amazon parrot owned by Mrs. Bella Ludford of Liverpool, England was allegedly hatched in captivity on 3 Dec. 1870 and lived 104 years in his original brass cage dying on 5 Jan. 1975.

Eggs *Largest*
The largest egg produced by any living bird is that of the Ostrich (*Struthio camelus*). The average example measures 6 to 8 in *15–20 cm* in length, 4 to 6 in *10–15 cm* in diameter and weighs 3.63 to 3.88 lb. *1,65–1,78 kg* (equal to the volume of two dozen hen's eggs). It requires about 40 min for boiling. The shell though $\frac{1}{16}$ in *1,5 mm* thick can support the weight of a 20 st. *127 kg* man. The largest egg laid by any bird on the British list is that of the Mute swan (*Cygnus olor*), which measures from 4.3 to 4.9 in *109–124 mm* in length and between 2.8 and 3.1 in *71–78,5 mm* in diameter. The weight is 12–13 oz. *340–368 g.*

Eggs *Smallest*
The smallest egg laid by any bird is that of Helena's hummingbird *Mellisuga helenae*, the world's smallest bird (see page 34). A specimen collected at Boyate, Santiago de Cuba on 8 May 1906 and later presented to the U.S. National Museum, Washington, D.C., U.S.A. measures 11,4 mm *0.45 in* in length, 8 mm *0.32 in* in diameter and weighs 0,5 g *0.176 oz.* The smallest egg laid by a bird on the British list is that of the Goldcrest (*Regulus regulus*), which measures 12,2–14,5 mm *0.48–0.57 in* in length and between 9,4 and 9,9 mm *0.37 and 0.39 in* in diameter. Eggs emitted from the oviduct before maturity, known as "sports", are not reckoned to be of significance in discussion of relative sizes.

Incubation *Longest and shortest*
The longest normal incubation period is that of the Wander-

ing albatross (*Diomedea exulans*), with a normal range of 75 days to 82 days. There is a case of an egg of the Mallee fowl (*Leipoa ocellata*) of Australia taking 90 days to hatch against its normal incubation of 62 days. The shortest incubation period is the 10 days of the Great spotted woodpecker (*Dendrocopus major*) and the Black-billed cuckoo (*Coccyzus erythropthalmus*). The idlest of cock birds include hummingbirds (family Trochilidae), Eider duck (*Somateria mollissima*) and Golden pheasant (*Chrysolophus pictus*) among whom the hen bird does 100 per cent of the incubation, whereas the female Common kiwi (*Apteryx australis*) leaves this entirely to the male for 75 to 80 days.

Longest flights

The greatest distance covered by a ringed bird during migration is 12,000 miles *19 300 km* by an Arctic tern (*Sterna paradisaea*), which was banded as a nestling on 5 July 1955 in the Kandalaksha Sanctuary on the White Sea coast and was captured alive by a fisherman 8 miles *13 km* south of Fremantle, Western Australia on 16 May 1956.

Highest flying

The celebrated example of a skein of 17 Egyptian geese (*Alopochen aegyptiacus*) photographed by an astronomer at Dehra Dun, northern India on 17 Sept. 1919 as they crossed the sun at an estimated height of between 11 and 12 miles (58,080–63,360 ft *17 700–19 310 m*), has been discredited by experts.

The highest acceptable altitude recorded for a bird is 8 200 m *26,900 ft* for a small number of Alpine choughs (*Pyrrhocorax graculus*) which followed the British Everest expedition of 1924 to Camp V. On 23 May 1960 a Steppe eagle (*Aquila nipalensis*) and two other raptors were found dead at nearly 26,000 ft *7 924 m* on the South Col. On three separate occasions in 1959 a radar station in Norfolk picked up flocks of small passerine night migrants flying in from Scandinavia at heights up to 21,000 ft *6 400 m*. They were probably Warblers (*Sylviidae*), Chats (*Turdidae*) and Flycatchers (*Muscicapidae*).

Most airborne

The most aerial of all birds is the Sooty tern (*Sterna fuscata*) which, after leaving the nesting grounds, remains continuously aloft for three or four years before returning to the breeding grounds. The most aerial land bird is the Common swift (*Apus apus*) which remains "airborne" for at least 9 months of the year.

Fastest swimmer

The fastest swimming bird is the Gentoo penguin (*Pygoscelis papua*). In January 1913 a small group were timed at 10 m/sec *22.3 m.p.h.* under water near the Bay of Isles, South Georgia. This is a respectable flying speed for some birds. The deepest diving bird is the Emperor penguin (*Aptenodytes forsteri*) of the Antarctic which can reach a depth of 265 m *870 ft* and remain submerged for up to 18 minutes.

Most acute vision

Birds of prey (Falconiformes) have the keenest eyesight in the avian world, and their visual acuity is at least 8–10 times stronger than that of human vision. The Golden eagle (*Aquila chrysaetos*) can detect an 18 in *46 cm* long hare at a range of 2,150 yds *1 966 m* (possibly even 2 miles *3,2 km*) in good light and against a contrasting background, and a Peregrine falcon (*Falco peregrinus*) a pigeon at a range of over 3500 ft *1066 m*.

Feathers *Longest*

The longest feathers grown by any bird are those of the cock Long-tailed fowl or Onagadori (a strain of *Gallus gallus*) which have been bred in south-western Japan since the mid 17th century. In 1973 a tail covert measuring 10,60 m *34 ft 9½ in* was reported by Masashi Kubota of Kochi, Shikoku. The tail feathers of the flying Reeve's pheasant (*Syrmaticus reevesi*) of north and west China can exceed 8 ft *2,43 m*.

Feathers *Most*

In a series of "feather counts" on various species of bird a Whistling swan (*Cygnus columbianus*) was found to have 25,216 feathers. The ruby-throated hummingbird (*Archilochus colubris*) has only 940, although hummingbirds have more feathers per area of body surface than any other living bird.

Earliest and latest cuckoo

It is unlikely that the Cuckoo (*Cuculus canorus*) has ever been *heard and seen* in Britain earlier than 2 March, on which date one was observed under acceptable conditions by Mr. William A. Haynes of Trinder Road, Wantage, Oxfordshire in 1972. The two latest dates are 16 Dec. 1912 at Anstey's Cove, Torquay, Devon and 26 Dec. 1897 or 1898 in Cheshire.

Champion Bird Spotter

The world's leading bird-spotter is G. Stuart Keith (G.B.), who works in the American Museum of Natural History, New York. In 32 years to Mar. 1979 his score is 5,450 species of the 8,650 known species of birds.

Nests, *Largest*

The largest bird's nest on record is one 9½ ft *2,9 m* wide and 20 ft *6 m* deep built by Bald eagles (*Haliaeetus leucocephalus*) near St. Petersburg, Florida, U.S.A. reported in 1963 and estimated to weigh more than 2 tons/*tonnes*. The incubation mounds built by Scrubfowl (family Megapodidae) have however been measured up to 50 ft *15,25 m* in diameter and 20 ft *6 m* in height.

DOMESTICATED BIRDS

Chicken *Heaviest*

The heaviest breed of chicken is one called the White Sully developed by Mr. Grant Sullens of West Point, California, U.S.A. over a period of seven years. One monstrous rooster named "Weirdo" reportedly weighed 22 lb. *10 kg* in January 1973, and was so ferocious that he had already killed two cats and crippled a dog which came too close. The heaviest British breed is the Dorking, with roosters weighing up to 14 lb. *6,36 kg*.

Chicken Flying *for distance*

The record distance flown by a chicken is 297 ft 2 in *90,57 m* by Kung Flewk at the International Chicken Flying Association Meet at Rio Grande, Ohio, U.S.A. on 21 May 1977.

Turkey *Heaviest*

The greatest *live* weight recorded for a Turkey (*Meleagris gallopavo*) is 75 lb. *34,02 kg* reported in Dec. 1973 for a "holiday" bird reared by Signe Olsen of Salt Lake City, Utah, U.S.A. The British record for a dressed bird is 72 lb. *32,65 kg* for an 18 month old stag reared by British United Turkeys Ltd of Chester, Cheshire. It won the annual "heaviest turkey" competition held in London on 8 Dec. 1978. Turkeys were introduced into Britain *via* Spain from Mexico in 1549.

Most Expensive

The highest price reached at auction (auctioneers "The Goodies") for a turkey was the £1,300 paid by Thornhill Poultry Packers of Great Longstone, Derbyshire for the 72 lb. *32,65 kg* stag (see above) at The Glazier's Hall, London on 8 Dec. 1978.

Longest lived

The longest lived domesticated bird (excluding the Ostrich) is the domestic goose (*Anser anser domesticus*) which normally lives about 25 years. On 16 Dec. 1976 a gander named "George" owned by Mrs. Florence Hull of Thornton, Lancashire, died aged 49 years 8 months. He was hatched out in April 1927. The longest lived small cagebird is the Canary (*Serinus canaria*). The oldest example on record was a 34 year old cock bird named "Joey" owned by Mrs. K. Ross of Hull. The bird was purchased in Calabar, Nigeria in 1941 and died on 8 April 1975. The oldest Budgerigar (*Melopsittacus undulatus*) on record was a hen bird named "Charlie" owned by Miss J. Dinsey of Stonebridge, London, which lived for 29 years 2 months. She died on 20 June 1977.

Most talkative

The world's most talkative bird is a male African grey parrot

(*Psittacus erythacus*) named "Prudle", owned by Mrs. Lyn Logue of Golders Green, London, which won the "Best talking parrot-like bird" title at the National Cage and Aviary Bird Show held in London each December for 12 consecutive years (1965–1976). Prudle, who has a vocabulary of nearly 1,000 words, was taken from a nest in a tree about to be felled at Jinja, Uganda in 1958. He retired undefeated in 1977.

3. REPTILES (*Reptilia*)

(Crocodiles, snakes, turtles, tortoises and lizards.)

Largest and heaviest

The largest reptile in the world is the Estuarine or Salt-water crocodile (*Crocodylus porosus*) of south-east Asia, northern Australia, New Guinea, the Philippines and the Solomon Islands. Adult bulls average 12–14 ft *3,7–4,3 m* in length and scale about 1,100 lb. *499 kg.* In 1823 a notorious man-eater 27 ft *8,23 m* in length and weighing an estimated 2 tons/*tonnes* was shot at Jala Jala on Luzon Island in the Philippines after terrorising the neighbourhood for many years. Its skull, the largest on record if we exclude fossil remains, is now preserved in the Museum of Comparative Zoology at Harvard University, Cambridge, Massachusetts, U.S.A. Another outsized example with a reputed length of 33 ft *10,05 m* and a maximum bodily girth of 13 ft 8 in *4,16 m* was shot in the Bay of Bengal in 1840, but the dimensions of its skull (preserved in the British Museum of Natural History, London) suggest that it must have come from a crocodile measuring about 24 ft *7,31 m.* The holder of the "official" record is a 20 ft 2 in *6,14 m* bull harpooned by Mr. Keith Adams in the McArthur River near Borroloola, Northern Territory Australia on 26 June 1960. In July 1957 an unconfirmed length of 28 ft 4 in *8,63 m* was reported for an Estuarine crocodile shot by Mrs. Kris Pawlowski on MacArthur Bank in the Norman River, north-western Queensland.

Smallest

The smallest known species of reptile is believed to be *Sphaerodactylus parthenopion*, a tiny gecko found only on the island of Virgin Gorda, one of the British Virgin Islands, in the West Indies. It is known only from 15 specimens, including some gravid females found between 10 and 16 Aug. 1964. The three largest females measured 18 mm *0.71 in* from snout to vent, with a tail of approximately the same length. It is possible that another gecko, *Sphaerodactylus elasmorhynchus*, may be even smaller. The only known specimen was an apparently mature female with a snout-vent length of 17 mm *0.67 in* and a tail the same measurement found on 15 March 1966 among the roots of a tree in the western part of the Massif de la Hotte in Haiti. A species of dwarf chameleon, *Evoluticauda tuberculata* found in Madagascar, and known only from a single specimen, has a snout-vent length of 18 mm *0.71 in* and a tail length of 14 mm *0.55 in.* Chameleons, however, are more bulky than geckos, and it is not yet known if this specimen was fully grown.

The smallest reptile found in Britain is the Viviparous or Common lizard (*Lacerta vivipara*). Adult specimens have an overall length of 108–178 mm *4.25–7 in.*

Fastest

The highest speed measured for any reptile on land is 18 m.p.h. *29 km/h* for a Six-lined racerunner (*Cnemidophorus sexlineatus*) pursued by a car near McCormick, South Carolina, U.S.A. in 1941. The highest speed claimed for any reptile in water is 22 m.p.h. *35 km/h* by a frightened Pacific leatherback turtle (see below).

Lizards *Largest*

The largest of all lizards is the Komodo monitor or Ora (*Varanus komodoensis*), a dragonlike reptile found on the Indonesian islands of Komodo, Rintja, Padar and Flores. Adult males average 8 ft *2,43 m* in length and weigh 175–200 lb. *79–91 kg.* Lengths up to 23 ft *7 m (sic)* have been quoted for this species, but the largest specimen to be accurately measured was a male presented to an American zoologist in 1928 by the Sultan of Bima which taped 3,05 m *10 ft 0.8 in.*

In 1937 this animal was put on display in St. Louis Zoological Gardens, Missouri, U.S.A. for a short period. It then measured 10 ft 2 in *3,10 m* in length and weighed 365 lb. *166 kg.* The longest lizard in the world is the slender Salvadori dragon (*Varanus salvadori*) of New Guinea which has been reliably measured up to 15 ft 7 in *4,75 m* long.

Lizards *Oldest*

The greatest age recorded for a lizard is more than 54 years for a male Slow worm (*Anguis fragilis*) kept in the Zoological Museum in Copenhagen, Denmark from 1892 until 1946.

Chelonians *Largest*

The largest of all chelonians is the Pacific leatherback turtle (*Dermochelys coriacea schlegelii*). The average adult measures 6–7 ft *1,83–2,13 m* in overall length (length of carapace 4–5 ft *122–152 cm*) and weighs between 660 and 800 lb. *299–363 kg.* The greatest weight reliably recorded is 1,908 lb. *865 kg* for a specimen captured off Monterey, California, U.S.A. on 29 Aug. 1961 measuring 8 ft 4 in *2,54 m* overall. The largest chelonian found in British waters is the Atlantic leatherback turtle (*Dermochelys coriacea coriacea*). One weighing 997 lb. *425 kg* and measuring more than 7 ft *2,13 m* in length was caught by a French fishing trawler in the English Channel on 8 May 1958.

The largest living tortoise is *Geochelone* (*Testudo*) *gigantea* of the Indian Ocean islands of Aldabra, Mauritius, Réunion and Seychelles (introduced 1874). Adult males sometimes exceed 350 lb. *158 kg* in weight and a specimen weighing 900 lb. *408 kg.* was allegedly collected in Aldabra in 1847. The largest desert tortoise is the protected *Gopherus agassizi* of the south-western United States which normally scales about 10–12 lb. *4,53–5,44 kg* when adult. In Jan. 1976 a weight of 23 lb. 14 oz. *10,8 kg* (shell length 15 in *38 cm*) was recorded for a huge male collected in the Mojave Desert, California.

Chelonians *Longest lived*

Tortoises are the longest lived of all vertebrates. (See Animal Kingdom Records above.) Other reliable records over 100 years include a Common box tortoise (*Testudo carolina*) of 138 years and a European pond-tortoise (*Emys orbicularis*) of 120+ years. The greatest proven age of a continuously observed tortoise is 116+ years for a Mediterranean spur-thighed tortoise (*Testudo graeca*) which died in Paignton Zoo, Devon in 1957.

Chelonians *Slowest moving*

In a recent "speed" test carried out in the Seychelles a male giant tortoise (*Geochelone gigantea*) could only cover 5 yds *4,57 m* in 43.5 sec (0.23 m p h *0,37 km/h*) despite the enticement of a female tortoise. The National Tortoise Championship record is 18 ft *5,48 m* up a 1 : 12 gradient in 43.7 sec by "Charlie" at Tickhill, South Yorkshire on 2 July 1977.

SNAKES

Longest *World*

The longest of all snakes (average adult length) is the Reticulated python (*Python reticulatus*) of south-east Asia, Indonesia and the Philippines which regularly exceeds 20 ft *6 m.* In 1912 a specimen measuring exactly 10 m *32 ft 9½ in* was shot near a mining camp on the north coast of Celebes in the Malay Archipelago. Lengths of 37½ ft *11,43 m*, 42 ft *12,8 m* and even 45 ft *13,7 m* have been claimed for the Anaconda (*Eunectes murinus*) of tropical South America, but these extreme measurements were probably based on stretched skins. The greatest authenticated length recorded for an anaconda is 27 ft 9 in *8,48 m* for a female killed in Brazil in c. 1960.

Longest *In Captivity*

The longest snake living in captivity anywhere in the world today is probably a female Reticulated python (*Python reticulatus*) named "Cassius" owned by Mr. Adrian Nyoka of Knaresborough Zoo, North Yorkshire which measures c. 27 ft *8,23 m* and scales 240 lb. *109 kg.* It was collected in Malaysia in 1972.

Longest *British*

The longest snake found in Britain is the Grass snake (*Natrix*

natrix), which is found throughout southern England, parts of Wales and in Dumfries and Galloway, Scotland. Adult males average 660 mm *26 in* in length and adult females 760 mm *29.92 in.* The longest accurately measured specimen was probably a female killed in South Wales in 1887 which measured 1 775 mm *5 ft 10 in.*

Shortest

The shortest known snake is the Thread snake *Leptotyphlops bilineata,* which is found on the islands of Martinique, Barbados and St. Lucia in the West Indies. It has a maximum recorded length of 11,9 cm *4.7 in.* The shortest venomous snake is the Striped dwarf garter snake (*Elaps dorsalis*) of South Africa, adults average 6 in *152 mm* in length.

Heaviest

The heaviest snake is the Anaconda (*Eunectes murinus*) which is nearly twice as heavy as a Reticulated python (*Python reticulatus*) of the same length. The specimen shot in Brazil in *c.* 1960 (see page 39) was not weighed, but as it had a maximum bodily girth of 44 in *111 cm* it must have scaled nearly 500 lb. *227 kg.* The heaviest venomous snake is the Eastern diamond-back rattlesnake (*Crotalus adamanteus*) of the south-eastern United States. One specimen measuring 7 ft 9 in *2,36 m* in length weighed 34 lb. *15 kg.* Less reliable lengths up to 8 ft 9 in *2,66 m* and weights up to 40 lb. *18 kg* have been reported. In Feb. 1973 a posthumous weight of 28 lb. *12,75 kg* was reported for a 14 ft 5 in *4,39 m* long King cobra (*Ophiophagus hannah*) at New York Zoological Park (Bronx Zoo).

Venomous *Longest and Shortest*

The longest venomous snake in the world is the King cobra (*Ophiophagus hannah*), also called the Hamadryad, of southeast Asia and the Philippines. A specimen collected near Port Dickson in the state of Negri Sembilan, Malaya in April 1937 grew to 18 ft 9 in *5,71 m* in London Zoo. It was destroyed at the outbreak of war in 1939.

Oldest

The greatest irrefutable age recorded for a snake is 40 years

A mock fight with Susie, a 22 ft *6,7 m* python, the longest species of snake in the world (see p. 39). (*Camera Press Ltd*).

3 months and 14 days

3 months and 14 days for a male Common boa (*Boa constrictor constrictor*) named "Popeye" at Philadelphia Zoological Garden, Pennsylvania, U.S.A., who was euthanazed on 15 April 1977 because of medical problems associated with advanced age. He was purchased from a London dealer in December 1936.

Fastest moving

The fastest moving land snake is probably the slender Black mamba (*Dendroaspis polylepis*). On 23 April 1906 an angry Black mamba was timed at a speed of 7 m.p.h. *11 km/h* over a measured distance of 47 yds *43 m* near Mbuyuni on the Serengeti Plains, Tanzania. Stories that Black mambas can overtake galloping horses (maximum speed 43.26 m.p.h. *69,62 km/h*) are wild exaggerations, though a speed of 15 m.p.h. *24 km/h* may be possible for short bursts over level ground. The British grass snake (*Natrix natrix*) has a maximum speed of 4.2 m.p.h. *6,8 km/h.*

Most venomous

The world's most venomous snake is the sea snake (*Hydrophis belcheri*) which has a venom one hundred times as toxic as that of the Australian taipan (*Oxyuranus scutellatus*). The snake abounds round Ashmore Reef in the Timor Sea, off the coast of North West Australia. The most venomous land snake is the Small scaled or Fierce Snake (*Parademansia microlepidotus*) of south-western Queensland and north-eastern South Australia which has a venom nine times as toxic as that of the Tiger snake (*Notechis scutatus*) of South Australia and Tasmania (one specimen yielded 110 mg *0,00385 oz.* after milking, a quantity sufficient to kill at least 125,000 mice. Until 1976 this 2 m *6 ft 6¾ in* long snake was regarded as a western form of the taipan, but its venom differs significantly from the latter. It is estimated that between 30,000 and 40,000 people (excluding Chinese and Russians) die from snakebite each year, 75 per cent of them in densely populated India. Burma has the highest mortality rate with 15.4 deaths per 100,000 population per annum.

Most venomous *Britain*

The only venomous snake in Britain is the Adder (*Vipera berus*). Since 1890 ten people have died after being bitten by this snake, including six children. The most recently recorded death was on 1 July 1975 when a 5 year old was bitten at Callandar, Central, Scotland and died 44 hours later. The longest recorded specimen was a female measuring 43½ in *110,5 cm* which was killed by Graham Perkins of Paradise Farm, Pontrilas, Hereford and Worcester in August 1977.

Longest fangs

The longest fangs of any snake are those of the Gaboon viper (*Bitis gabonica*) of tropical Africa. In a 6 ft *1,83 m* long specimen they measured 50 mm *1.96 in.* On 12 Feb. 1963 a Gaboon viper bit itself to death in the Philadelphia Zoological Gardens, Philadelphia, Pennsylvania, U.S.A. Keepers found the dead snake with its fangs deeply embedded in its own back.

4. AMPHIBIANS (*Amphibia*)

Largest *World*

The largest species of amphibian is the Chinese giant salamander (*Megalobatrachus davidianus*), which lives in the cold mountain streams and marshy areas of north-eastern, central and southern China. The average adult measures 1 m *39 in* in total length and weighs 11–13 kg *24.2 to 28.6 lb.* One huge individual collected in Kweichow (Guizhou) Province in southern China in the early 1920s measured 5 ft *1,52 m* in total length and weighed nearly 100 lb. *45 kg.* The Japanese giant salamander (*Megalobatrachus japonicus*) is slightly smaller, but one captive specimen weighed 40 kg *88 lb.* when alive and 45 kg *100 lb.* after death, the body having absorbed water from the aquarium.

Largest *Britain*

The heaviest British amphibian is the Common toad (*Bufo bufo*) of which a female has been weighed at 114 g *4 oz.*

The longest is the Warty or Great crested newt (*Triturus cristatus*). One female specimen collected at Hampton, Greater London measured 162 mm *6.37 in* in total length.

Smallest *World*

The smallest species of amphibian is believed to be the arrow-poison frog (*Sminthillus limbatus*), found only in Cuba. Adult specimens have a snout-vent length of 8,5–12,4 mm *0.44–0.48 in.*

Smallest *Britain*

The smallest amphibian found in Britain is the Palmate newt (*Triturus helveticus*). Adult specimens measure 7,5–9,2 cm *2.95–3.62 in* in total length and weigh up to 2,39 g *0.083 oz.* The Natterjack or Running toad (*Bufo calamita*) has a maximum snout-vent length of only 8 cm *3.14 in.* but it is a bulkier animal.

Longest lived

The greatest authentic age recorded for an amphibian is about 55 years for a male Japanese giant salamander (*Megalobatrachus japonicus*) which died in the aquarium at Amsterdam Zoological Gardens on 3 June 1881. It was brought to Holland in 1829, at which time it was estimated to be three years old.

Highest and lowest

The greatest altitude at which an amphibian has been found is 8 000 m *26,246 ft* for a Common toad (*Bufo vulgaris*) collected in the Himalayas. This species has also been found at a depth of 340 m *1,115 ft* in a coal mine.

Most poisonous

The most active known poison is the batrachotoxin derived from the skin secretions of the Kokoi (*Phyllobates latinasus*), an arrow-poison frog found in north-western Colombia, South America. Only about 1/100,000th of a gramme *0.0000004 oz.* is sufficient to kill a man.

Newt *Largest World*

The largest newt in the world is the Pleurodele or Ribbed newt (*Pleurodeles waltl*), which is found in Morocco and on the Iberian Peninsula. Specimens measuring up to 40 cm *15.74 in* in total length and weighing over 1 lb. *450 g* have been reliably reported.

Newt *Smallest World*

The smallest newt in the world is believed to be the Striped newt (*Notophthalmus perstriatus*) of the south-eastern United States. Adult specimens average 51 mm *2.01 in* in total length.

Frog *Largest World*

The largest known frog is the rare Goliath frog (*Rana goliath*) of Cameroun and Equatorial Guinea. A female weighing 3 306 g *7 lb. 4.5 oz.* was caught in the rapids of the River Mbia, Equatorial Guinea on 23 Aug. 1960. It had a snout-vent length of 34 cm *13.38 in* and measured 81,5 cm *32.08 in* overall with legs extended. In December 1960 another giant frog known locally as "agak" or "carn-pnag" and said to measure 12–15 in *30–38 cm* snout to vent and weigh over 6 lb. *2,7 kg* was reportedly discovered in central New Guinea, but further information is lacking. In 1969 a new species of giant frog was discovered in Sumatra.

Frog *Largest Britain*

The largest frog found in Britain is the *introduced* Marsh frog (*Rana r. ridibunda*). Adult males have been measured up to 96 mm *3.77 in* snout to vent, and adult females up to 133 mm *5.25 in*, the weight ranging from 60 to 95 g *1.7 oz.* to *3 oz.*

Longest jump

The record for three consecutive leaps is 10,3 m *33 ft 5½ in* by a female South African sharp-nosed frog (*Rana oxyrhyncha*) named "Santjie" at a frog Derby held at Lurula Natal Spa, Paulpietersburg, Natal on 21 May 1977. At the annual Calaveras County Jumping Frog Jubilee at Angels Camp, California, U.S.A. in 1975 "Ex Lax" made a *single* leap of 17 ft 6¾ in *5,35 m* for its owner Bill Moniz.

Bufo taitanus beiranus, the smallest toad in the world which was first discovered in Mozambique c. 1906. (*J. P. Coates Palgrave*)

Tree frog *Largest*

The largest species of tree frog is *Hyla vasta*, found only on the island of Hispaniola (Haiti and the Dominican Republic) in the West Indies. The average snout-vent length is about 9 cm *3.54 in* but a female collected from the San Juan River, Dominican Republic, in March 1928 measured 14,3 cm *5.63 in.*

Tree frog *Smallest*

The smallest tree frog in the world is the Least tree frog (*Hyla ocularis*), found in the south-eastern United States. It has a maximum snout-vent length of 15,8 mm *0.62 in.*

Toad *Largest World*

The most massive toad in the world is probably the Marine toad (*Bufo marinus*) of tropical South America. An enormous female collected on 24 Nov. 1965 at Miraflores Vaupes, Colombia and later exhibited in the Reptile House at Bronx Zoo, New York City, U.S.A. had a snout vent length of 23,8 cm *9.37 in* and weighed 1 302 g *2 lb. 11¼ oz.* at the time of its death in 1967.

Toad *Largest Britain*

The largest toad and heaviest amphibian found in Britain is the Common toad (*Bufo bufo*). Females of up to 102 mm *3.94 in* in length and 114 g *3.2 oz.* have been recorded.

Toad *Smallest World*

The smallest toad in the world is the sub-species *Bufo taitanus beiranus*, first discovered in *c.* 1906 near Beira, Mozambique, East Africa. Adult specimens have a maximum recorded snout-vent length of 24 mm *0.94 in.*

Salamander *Smallest*

The smallest species of salamander is the Pygmy salamander (*Desmognathus wrighti*), which is found only in Tennessee, North Carolina and Virginia, U.S.A. Adult specimens measure from 37 to 50,8 mm *1.45 to 2.0 in* in total length.

5. FISHES (*Pisces, Bradyodonti, Selachii, Marsipoli*)

Largest Marine *World*

The largest fish in the world is the rare plankton-feeding Whale shark (*Rhiniodon typus*), which is found in the warmer areas of the Atlantic, Pacific and Indian Oceans. It is not, however, the largest marine animal, since it is smaller than the larger species of whales (mammals). In 1919 a Whale shark measuring 10 *wa* (= 60 ft 9 in, *18,5 m*) in length and weighing an estimated 42.4 tons *43 tonnes* was trapped in a bamboo stake-trap at Koh Chik, in the Gulf of Siam. The largest carnivorous fish (excluding plankton eaters) is the comparatively rare Great white shark (*Carcharodon charcharias*), also called the "Maneater", which ranges from the tropics to temperate zone waters. In June 1930 a specimen measuring 37 ft *11,27 m* in length was reportedly trapped in a herring weir at White Head Island, New Brunswick, Canada but may have been a wrongly identified Basking shark (see below). In May 1948 a great white shark measuring 21 ft *6,40 m* in length was captured after a fierce battle by fishermen off Havana, Cuba. It weighed 7,302 lb. *3 312 kg*. The longest of the bony or "true" fishes (Pisces) is the Russian sturgeon (*Acipenser huso*), also called the Beluga, which is found in the temperate areas of the Adriatic, Black and Caspian Seas but enters large rivers like the Volga and the Danube for spawning. Lengths up to 8 m *26 ft 3 in* have been reliably reported, and a gravid female taken in the estuary of the Volga in 1827 weighed 1 474,2 kg *1.44 tons*. The heaviest bony fish in the world is the Ocean sunfish (*Mola mola*), which is found in all tropical, sub-tropical and temperate waters. On 18 Sept. 1908 a huge specimen was accidentally struck by the S.S. *Fiona* off Bird Island about 40 miles *65 km* from Sydney, New South Wales, Australia and towed to Port Jackson. It measured 14 ft *4,26 m* between the anal and dorsal fins and weighed 2.24 tons *2,28 tonnes*.

Britain

The largest fish ever recorded in the waters of the British Isles was a 36 ft 6 in *11,12 m* Basking shark (*Cetorhinus maximus*) washed ashore at Brighton, East Sussex in 1806. It weighed an estimated 8 tons/*tonnes*. The largest bony fish found in British waters is the Ocean sunfish (*Mola mola*). A specimen weighing 800 lb. *363 kg* stranded near Montrose, Scotland on 14 Dec. 1960 and was sent to the Marine Research Institute in Aberdeen.

Largest Freshwater *World*

The largest fish which spends its whole life in fresh or brackish water is the rare Pa beuk or Pla buk (*Pangasianodon gigas*), a giant catfish, which is found in the deep waters of the Mekong River of Laos and Thailand. Adult males average 8 ft *2,43 m* in length and weigh about 360 lb. *163 kg*. This size was exceeded by the European catfish or Wels (*Silurus glanis*) in earlier times (in the 19th century lengths up to 15 ft *4,57 m* and weights up to 720 lb. *336,3 kg* were reported for Russian specimens), but today anything over 6 ft *1,83 m* and 200 lb. *91 kg* is considered large. The Arapaima (*Arapaima glanis*), also called the Pirarucu, found in the Amazon and other South American rivers and often claimed to be the largest freshwater fish, averages 6½ ft *2 m* and 150 lb. *68 kg*. The largest "authentically recorded" measured 8 ft 1½ in *2,48 m* in length and weighed 325 lb. *147 kg*. It was caught in the Rio Negro, Brazil in 1836. In September 1978, a Nile perch (*Lates niloticus*) weighing 416 lb. *188,6 kg* was netted in the eastern part of Lake Victoria, Kenya.

Largest Freshwater *Britain*

The largest fish ever caught in a British river was a Common sturgeon (*Acipenser sturio*) weighing 507½ lb. *230 kg* measuring 9 ft *2,74 m* which was accidentally netted in the Severn at Lydney, Gloucestershire on 1 June 1937. Larger specimens have been taken at sea—notably one weighing 700 lb. *317 kg* and 10 ft 5 in *3,18 m* long netted by the trawler *Ben Urie* off Orkney and landed at Aberdeen on 18 Oct. 1956.

Smallest *Marine*

The smallest recorded marine fishes are the Marshall Islands goby (*Eviota zonura*) measuring 12 to 16 mm *0.47 to 0.63 in* and *Schindleria praematurus* from Samoa, measuring 12 to 19 mm *0.47 to 0.74 in*, both in the Pacific Ocean. Mature specimens of the latter fish, which was not described until 1940, have been known to weigh only 2 mg, equivalent to 17,750 to the oz—the lightest of all vertebrates and the smallest catch possible for any fisherman. The smallest British marine fish is the goby (*Lebutus orca*), which grows to a length of 39 mm *1.53 in*. It has been recorded off south-west Cornwall and in the Irish Sea. The smallest known shark is the Long-faced dwarf shark (*Squaliolus laticaudus*) of the western Pacific. Adult specimens measure about 110 mm *4.33 in* in length.

Smallest *Freshwater*

The shortest known fish, and the shortest of all vertebrates, is the Dwarf pygmy goby (*Pandaka pygmaea*), a colourless and nearly transparent fish found in the streams and lakes of Luzon in the Philippines. Adult males measure only 7,5 to 9,9 mm *0.28 to 0.38 in* in length and weigh 4 to 5 mg *0.00014 to 0.00017 oz*.

Fastest

The Sailfish (*Istiophorus platypterus*) is generally considered to be the fastest species of fish, although the practical difficulties of measurement make data extremely difficult to secure. A figure of 68.1 m.p.h. *109,7 km/h* (100 yds *91 m* in 3 sec) has been cited for one off Florida, U.S.A. The swordfish (*Xiphias gladius*) has also been credited with very high speeds, but the evidence is based mainly on bills that have been found deeply embedded in ships' timbers. A speed of 50 knots (57.6 m.p.h. *92,7 km/h*) has been calculated from a penetration of 22 in *56 cm* by a bill into a piece of timber, but 30 to 35 knots (35 to 40 m.p.h. *56–64 km/h* is the most conceded by some experts. Speeds in excess of 35 knots (40 m.p.h. *64 km/h*) have also been attributed to the Marlin (*Tetrapturus sp.*), the Wahoo (*Acanthocybium solandri*), the Great blue shark (*Prionace glauca*) and the Bonefish (*Albula vulpes*), and the Bluefin tuna (*Tunnus thynnus*) has been scientifically clocked at 43.4 m.p.h. *69,8 km/h* in a 20 sec dash. The Four-winged flying fish (*Cypselurus heterururs*) may also exceed 40 m.p.h. *64 km/h* during its rapid rush to the surface before take-off (the average speed in the air is about 35 m.p.h. *56 km/h*). Record flights of 90 sec, 36 ft *11 m* in altitude and 1 110 m *3,640 ft* length have been recorded in the tropical Altantic.

Longest lived

Aquaria are of too recent origin to be able to establish with certainty which species of fish can be regarded as being the longest lived. Early indications are, however, that it is the Lake sturgeon (*Acipenser fulvescens*) of North America. In one study of the growth rings (annuli) of 966 specimens caught in the Lake Winnebago region, Wisconsin, U.S.A. between 1951 and 1954 the oldest sturgeon was found to be a male (length 2.01 m *6 ft 7 in*) which gave a reading of 82 years and was still growing. In July 1974 a growth ring count of 228 years (*sic*) was reported for a female Koi fish, a form of fancy carp, named "Hanako" living in a pond in Higashi Shirakawa, Gifu Prefecture, Japan, but the greatest authoritatively accepted age for this species is "more than 50 years".

In 1948 the death was reported of an 88-year-old female European eel (*Anguilla anguilla*) named "Putte" in the aquarium at Halsingborn Museum, southern Sweden. She was allegedly born in the Sargasso Sea, North Atlantic in 1860, and was caught in a river as a three-year-old elver.

Oldest goldfish

While goldfish (*Carassius auratus*) have been reported to live for over 40 years in China, the British record is held by a specimen named "Goldie" owned by Mr. H. S. Taylor of Sleaford, Lincolnshire, which died on 27 Feb. 1978, aged 36 years.

Shortest lived

The shortest-lived fishes are probably certain species of the sub-order Cyprinodontei (killifish) found in Africa and South America which normally live about eight months in the wild state.

Deepest

The greatest depth from which a fish has been recovered is 8 300 m *27,230 ft* in the Puerto Rico Trench (27,488 ft *8 366 m*) in the Atlantic by Dr. Gilbert L. Voss of the U.S. research vessel *John Elliott* who took a 6½ in *16,5 cm* long *Bassogigas profundissimus* in April 1970. It was only the fifth such brotulid ever caught. Dr. Jacques Piccard and Lieutenant Don Walsh, U.S. Navy, reported they saw a sole-like fish about 1 ft *33 cm* long (tentatively identified as *Chascanopsetta lugubris*) from the bathyscaphe *Trieste* at a depth of 35,802 ft *10 912 m* in the Challenger Deep (Marianas Trench) in the western Pacific on 24 Jan. 1960. This sighting, however, has been questioned by some authorities, who still regard the brotulids of the genus *Bassogigas* as the deepest-living vertebrates.

Most and least eggs

The Ocean sunfish (*Mola mola*) produces up to 300,000,000 eggs, each of them measuring about 0.05 in *1,3 mm* in diameter. The egg yield of the tooth carp *Jordanella floridae* of Florida, U.S.A. is only *c.* 20 over a period of several days.

Most venomous

The most venomous fish in the world are the Stonefish (family Synanceidae) of the tropical waters of the Indo-Pacific. Direct contact with the spines of their fins, which contain a strong neurotoxic poison, often proves fatal.

Most electric

The most powerful electric fish is the Electric eel (*Electrophorus electricus*), which is found in the rivers of Brazil, Colombia, Venezuela and Peru. An average sized specimen can discharge 400 volts at 1 ampere, but measurements up to 650 volts have been recorded.

River Thames

The first salmon caught in the Thames since June 1833 was taken at West Thurrock Power Station, Essex in November 1974 and weighed 8 lb. 4½ oz. *3,757 kg.*

6. STARFISHES (*Asteroidea*)

Largest

The largest of the 1,600 known species of starfish in terms of total arm span is the very fragile brisingid *Midgardia xandaros*. A specimen collected by the Texas A & M University research vessel *Alaminos* in the southern part of the Gulf of Mexico in the late summer of 1968, measured 1 380 mm *54.33 in* tip to tip, but the diameter of its disc was only 26 mm *1.02 in.* Its dry weight was 70 g *2.46 oz.* The heaviest species of starfish is the five-armed *Thromidia catalai* of the Western Pacific. One specimen collected off Ilot Amedee, New Caledonia on

below: The Rhinoceros starfish (*Thromidia catalai*) the heaviest species in the world which can weigh up to 6 kg *13.2 lb.*

above: Contact with the well-camouflaged stonefish, the most venomous of all fish, can prove lethal.

14 Sept. 1969 and later deposited in Noumea Aquarium weighed an estimated 6 kg *13.2 lb.* (total arm span 630 mm *24.8 in*). The largest starfish found in British waters is the Spiny starfish (*Marthasterias glacialis*), which has been measured up to 665 mm *26.18 in* arm tip to arm tip.

Smallest
The smallest known starfish is *Marginaster capreenis*, found deep in the Mediterranean, which is not known to exceed 20 mm *0.78 in* in diameter. The smallest starfish found in British waters is the Cushion starfish (*Asterina gibbosa*) which measures up to c. 60 mm *2.36 in* in diameter but is usually c. 25 mm *1 in* across.

Deepest
The greatest depth from which a starfish has been recovered is 7 584 m *24,881 ft* for a specimen of *Porcellanaster ivanovi* collected by the U.S.S.R. research ship *Vityaz* in the Marianas Trench, in the West Pacific c. 1962.

7. ARACHNIDS (*Arachnida*)

SPIDERS (order Araneae)
Largest *World*
The world's largest known spider is the bird-eating spider *Theraphosa blondi* of northern South America. A male specimen with a leg span of 10 in *25 cm* when fully extended and a body length of 3½ in *8,9 cm* was collected at Montagne la Gabrielle, French Guiana in April 1925. It weighed nearly 2 oz. *56 g*. The heaviest spider ever recorded was a female "tarantula" of the long haired species *Lasiodora klugi* collected at Manaos, Brazil in 1945. It measured 9½ in *241 mm* across the legs and weighed almost 3 oz. *85 g*.

Largest *Britain*
Of the 617 known British species of spider covering an estimated population of over 500,000,000,000,000, the Cardinal spider (*Tegenaria parietina*) has the greatest leg span. In 1974 one spanning 5.3 in *13,4 cm* was trapped in a house in Wokingham, Berkshire but later escaped. This spider is found only in southern England. The well-known "Daddy Longlegs" spider (*Pholcus phalangioides*) rarely exceeds 3 in *75 mm* in leg span, but one outsized specimen collected in England measured 6 in *15,2 cm* across. The heaviest spider found in Britain is the orb weaver (*Araneus quadratus*) (formerly called *Araneus reaumuri*). A female, not of extreme size, collected in October 1943 weighed 1,174 g *0.041 oz.* and measured 15 mm *0.58 in* in body length.

Smallest *World*
The smallest known spider is *Patu marplesi* (family Symphytognathidae) of Western Samoa. The type specimen (male) found in moss at c. 2,000 ft *610 m* altitude near Malolelei, Upolu in January 1956 measure 0,43 mm *0.016 in* overall— or half the size of this full stop . The smallest spider found in Britain is the money spider *Glyphesis cottonae*, which is confined to a swamp near Beaulieu Road Station, New Forest, Hampshire and Thursley Common, Surrey. Adult specimens of both sexes have a body length of 1 mm *0.039 in*.

Rarest
The most elusive of all spiders are the primitive atypical tarantulas of the genus *Liphistius*, which are found in Southeast Asia. The most elusive spider in Britain is the handsome crimson and black Lace web eresus spider (*Eresus niger*), found in Hampshire, Dorset and Cornwall, which is known only from eight specimens (seven males and one female). In the early 1950's one was reportedly seen at Sandown on the Isle of Wight, but it escaped.

Fastest
The highest speed recorded for a spider on a level surface is 1.73 ft/sec *53 cm/sec* (1.17 m.p.h. *1,88 km/h*) in the case of a specimen of *Tegenaria atrica*. This is 33 times her body length per sec compared with the human record of 5½ times.

Longest lived
The longest lived of all spiders are the primitive *Mygalo-*

morphae (tarantulas and allied species). One mature female tarantula collected at Mazatland, Mexico in 1935 and estimated to be 12 years old at the time, was kept in a laboratory for 16 years, making a total of 28 years. The longest-lived British spider is probably the purse web spider (*Atypus affinis*). One specimen was kept in a greenhouse for nine years.

Largest webs
The largest webs are the aerial ones spun by the tropical orb weavers of the genus *Nephila*, which have been measured up to 18 ft 9¾ in *573 cm* in circumference. The smallest webs are spun by spiders like *Glyphesis cottonae*, etc. which are about the size of a postage stamp.

Most venomous
The most venomous spider in the world is probably *Latrodectus mactans* of the Americas, which is better known as the "Black widow" in the United States. Females of this species, measuring up to 6,35 mm *2.5 in* overall have a bite capable of killing a human being, but deaths are rare. The Funnel web spider (*Atrax robustus*) of Australia, the Jockey spider (*Latrodectus hasseltii*) of Australia and New Zealand, the Button spider (*Latrodectus indistinctus*) of South Africa, the Podadora (*Glyptocranium gasteracanthoides*) of Argentina and the Brown recluse spider (*Loxosceles reclusa*) of the central and southern United States have also been credited with fatalities.

Smallest and largest tick
The smallest known tick is a male *Ixodes soricis* from a British Columbian shrew, and the largest an engorged female, *Amblyomma varium* from a Venezuelan sloth.

8. CRUSTACEANS (*Crustacea*)

(Crabs, lobsters, shrimps, prawns, crayfish, barnacles, water fleas, fish lice, woodlice, sandhoppers, krill, etc.)

Largest *World*
The largest of all crustaceans (although not the heaviest) is the giant spider crab (*Macrocheira kaempferi*), also called the stilt crab, which is found in deep waters off the south-eastern coast of Japan. Mature specimens usually have a 12–14 in *30–35 cm* wide body and a claw-span of 8–9 ft *2,43–2,74 m* but unconfirmed measurements up to 19 ft *5,79 m* have been reported. A specimen with a claw span of 12 ft 1½ in *3,69 m* weighed 41 lb. *18,6 kg*.

The largest species of lobster, and the heaviest of all crustaceans, is the American or North Atlantic lobster (*Homarus americanus*). On 11 Feb. 1977 a specimen weighing 44 lb. 6 oz. *20,14 kg* and measuring 3 ft 6 in *1,06 m* from the end of the tail-fan to the tip of the largest claw was caught off Nova Scotia, Canada and later sold to a New York restaurant owner.

Largest *Britain*
The largest crustacean found in British waters is the Common or European lobster (*Homarus vulgarus*), which averages 2–3 lb. *900–1 360 g*. In June 1931 an outsized specimen weighing 20½ lb. *5,80 kg* and measuring 4 ft 1½ in *1,26 m* in total length, was caught in a caisson during the construction of No. 3 jetty at Fowey, Cornwall. Its crushing claw weighed 2 lb. 10 oz. *1,188 g* after the meat had been removed. The largest crab found in British waters is the Edible or Great crab (*Cancer pagurus*). In 1895 a crab measuring 11 in *279 mm* across the shell and weighing 14 lb. *6,35 kg* was caught off the coast of Cornwall.

Smallest
The smallest known crustaceans are water fleas of the genus *Alonella*, which may measure less than 0,25 mm *0.0098 in* in length. They are found in British waters. The smallest known lobster is the Cape lobster (*Homarus capensis*) of South Africa which measures 10–12 cm *3.9–4.7 in* in total length. The smallest crabs in the world are the aptly named pea crabs

(family Pinnotheridae). Some species have a shell diameter of only 0.25 in *6,3 mm,* including *Pinnotheres pisum* which is found in British waters.

Longest lived

The longest lived of all crustaceans is the American lobster (*Homarus americanus*). Very large specimens may be as much as 50 years old.

Vertical Distribution

The greatest depth from which a crustacean has been recovered is 9 790 m *32,119 ft* for an amphipod (order Amphipoda) collected by the Galathea Deep Sea Expedition in the Philippine Trench in 1951. The marine crab *Ethusina abyssicola* has been taken at a depth of 14,000 ft *4 265 m.* Amphiopods have also been collected in the Ecuadorean Andes at a height of 13,300 ft *4 053 m.*

9. INSECTS (*Insecta*)

Heaviest *World*

The heaviest insects in the world are the Goliath beetles (family *Scarabaeidae*) of equatorial Africa. The largest member of the group is *Goliathus goliathus,* and in one series of fully-grown males the weight ranged from 70 to 100 g *2.5–3.5 oz.*

Heaviest *Britain*

The heaviest beetle found in Britain is the Stag beetle (*Lucanus cervus*) which is widely distributed over southern England. The largest specimen on record was a male collected at Sheerness, Kent, in 1871 and now preserved in the British Museum (Natural History), London, which measures 87.4 mm *3.04 in* in length (body plus mandibles) and probably weighed over 6 000 mg *0.21 oz.* when alive.

Longest

The longest insect in the world is the tropical stick-insect *Pharnacia serratipes,* females of which have been measured up to 330 mm *12.99 in* in body length. The longest known beetle (excluding antenae) is the Hercules beetle (*Dynastes hercules*) of Central and South America, which has been measured up to 180 mm *7.08 in* but only half of this length is accounted for by the "prong" from the thorax. The longhorn beetle *Batocera wallacei* of New Guinea has been measured up to 267 mm *10.5 in,* but 190 mm *7.5 in* of this was antenna.

Smallest *World*

The smallest insects recorded so far are the "Hairy-winged" beetles of the family Ptiliidae (= Trichopterygidae) and the "battledore-wing fairy flics" (parasitic wasps) of the family Myrmaridae. They measure only 0,2 mm *0.008 in* in length, and the fairy flies have a wing span of only 1 mm *0.04 in.* This makes them smaller than some of the protozoa (single-celled animals). The male bloodsucking banded louse *Enderleinellus zonatus,* ungorged, and the parasitic wasp (*Caraphractus cinctus*) may each weigh as little as 0,005 mg, or *5,670,000 to an oz.* The eggs of the latter each weigh 0,0002 mg, *or 141,750,000 to an oz.*

Commonest

The most numerous of all insects are the Springtails (Order Collembola), which have a very wide geographical range. It has been calculated that the top 9 in *288 mm* of soil in one acre of grassland contain 230,000,000 springtails or more than 5,000 per square foot *465/m².*

Fastest flying

Experiments have proved that the widely publicised claim by an American entomologist in 1926 that the Deer bot-fly (*Cephenemyia pratti*) could attain a speed of 818 m.p.h. *1 316 km/h* (sic) was wildly exaggerated. If true it would have generated a supersonic 'pop'! Acceptable modern experiments have now established that the highest maintainable air-speed of any insect, including the Deer bot-fly, is 24 m.p.h. *39 km/h,* rising to a maximum of 36 m.p.h. *58 km/h* for short bursts. A relay of bees (maximum speed 11 m.p.h. *18 km/h*)

would use only a gallon of nectar in cruising 4,000,000 miles *6,5 million km* at an average speed of 7 m.p.h. *11 km/h.*

Longest lived

The longest-lived insects are queen termites (*Isoptera*), which have been known to lay eggs for up to 50 years.

Loudest

The loudest of all insects is the male cicada (family Cicadidae). At 7,400 pulses/min its tymbal organs produce a noise (officially described by the United States Department of Agriculture as "Tsh-ee-EEEE-e-ou") detectable more than a quarter of a mile *400 m* distant. The only British species is the very rare Mountain cicada (*Cicadetta montana*), which is confined to the New Forest area in Hampshire.

Southernmost

The farthest south at which any insect has been found is 77° S (900 miles *1 450 km* from the South Pole) in the case of a springtail (order Collembola).

Largest locust swarm

The greatest swarm of Desert locusts (*Schistocera gregaria*) ever recorded was one covering an estimated 2,000 miles² *5 180 km²* observed crossing the Red Sea in 1889. Such a swarm must have contained about 250,000,000,000 insects weighing about 500,000 tons *508 000 tonnes.*

Fastest wing beat

The fastest wing beat of any insect under natural conditions is 62,760 a min by a tiny midge of the genus *Forcipomyia.* In experiments with truncated wings at a temperature of 37° C *98.6° F* the rate increased to 133,080 beats/min. The muscular contraction-expansion cycle in 0.00045 or 1/2,218th of a sec, further represents the fastest muscle movement ever measured.

Slowest wing beat

The slowest wing beat of any insect is 300 a min by the swallowtail butterfly (*Papilio machaon*). Most butterflies beat their wings at a rate of 460 to 636 a min.

Hive record

The greatest reported amount of wild honey ever extracted from a single hive is 404 lb. *183,2 kg* recorded by Ormond R. Aebi of Santa Cruz, California on 29 Aug. 1974.

Bush-cricket *Largest*

The bush-cricket with the largest wing span is the New Guinean grasshopper *Siliquofera grandis* with female examples measuring more than 10 in *254 mm. Pseudophyllanax imperialis,* found on the island of New Caledonia in the south-western Pacific has antennae measuring up to 8 in *203 mm.* The largest bush-cricket found in Britain is *Tettigonia viridissima,* which normally has a body length of 1¼ in *31,8 mm.* In August 1953 a female measuring 77 mm *3.03 in* in body length (including ovipositor) was caught in a sand pit at Grays, Essex and later presented to London Zoological Gardens. The largest of the 14 true grasshoppers found in Britain is *Mecostethus grossus,* females of which measure up to 39 mm *1.53 in* in body length.

Dragonflies *Largest*

The largest dragonfly in the world is *Megaloprepes caeruleata* of Central and South America, which has been measured up to 191 mm *7.52 in* across the wings and 120 mm *4.72 in* in body length. The largest dragonfly found in Britain is *Anax imperator,* which has a wing span measurement of up to 106 mm *4.17 in.* The smallest British dragonfly is *Lestes dryas,* which has a wing span of 20–25 mm *0.78–0.98 in.*

Flea *Largest*

The largest known flea is *Hystrichopsylla schefferi schefferi,* which was described from a single specimen taken from the nest of a Mountain beaver (*Aplodontia rufa*) at Puyallup, Washington, U.S.A. in 1913. Females measure up to 8 mm *0,31 in* in length which is the diameter of a pencil. The largest flea (61 species) found in Britain is the Mole and Vole flea (*H. talpae*), females of which have been measured up to 6 mm *0.23 in.*

Flea *Longest jump*

The champion jumper among fleas is the common flea (*Pulex irritans*). In one American experiment carried out in 1910 a specimen allowed to leap at will performed a long jump of 13 in *330 mm* and a high jump of 7¾ in *197 mm*. In jumping 130 times its own height a flea subjects itself to a force of 200 g. Siphonapterologists recognise 1,830 varieties.

BUTTERFLIES AND MOTHS (order Lepidoptera)
Largest *World*

The largest known butterfly is the Queen Alexandra birdwing (*Ornithoptera alexandrae*) of New Guinea. Females may have a wing span exceeding 280 mm *11.02 in* and weigh over 5 g *0.176 oz*. The largest moth in the world (although not the heaviest) is the Hercules moth (*Cosdinoscera hercules*) of tropical Australia and New Guinea. A wing area of up to 40.8 in² *263,2 cm²* and a wing span of 280 mm *11 in* have been recorded. In 1948 an unconfirmed measurement of 360 mm *14.17 in* was reported for a female captured near the post office at the coastal town of Innisfail, Queensland, Australia. The rare Owlet moth (*Thysania agrippina*) of Brazil has been measured up to 300 mm *11.81 in* in wing span, and the Philippine atlas moth (*Attacus crameri caesar*) up to 280 mm *11.02 in*, but both these species are lighter than *C. hercules*.

Largest *Britain*

The largest (but not the heaviest) of the 21,000 species of insect found in Britain is the very rare Death's head hawk-moth (*Acherontia atropos*). One female found dead in a garden at Tiverton, Devon, in 1931 had a wing span of 5.75 in *145 mm* and weighed nearly 3g *0.10 oz*. The largest butterfly found in Britain is the Monarch butterfly (*Danaus plexippus*), also called the Milkweed or Black-veined brown butterfly, a rare vagrant which breeds in the southern United States and Central America. It has a wing span of up to 5 in *127 mm* and weighs about 1 g *0.04 oz*. The largest *native* butterfly is the Swallowtail (*Papilo machaon*), females of which have a wing span of 70–100 mm *2.75–3.93 in*. This species is now confined to a small area of the Norfolk Broads.

Smallest *World and Britain*

The smallest of the 140,000 known species of Lepidoptera are the moth *Johanssonia acetosae* (*Stainton*) found in Britain, and *Stigmella ridiculosa* from the Canary Islands, which have a wing span of *c.* 2 mm *0.08 in* with a similar body length. The world's smallest known butterfly is the Dwarf blue (*Brephidium barberae*) of South Africa. It has a wing span of 14 mm *0.55 in*. The smallest butterfly found in Britain is the Small blue (*Cupido minimus*), which has a wing span of 19–25 mm *0.75–1.0 in*.

Rarest

The rarest British butterfly is the Large blue (*Maculinea arion*), which is now confined to a few localities in north Devon. In 1978 less than ten specimens were sighted and it is now believed to be on the verge of extinction. The rarest moth found in Britain is the Tree-lichen beauty (*Briophila algae*), which was last recorded in Greater Manchester in July 1858.

Most acute sense of smell

The most acute sense of smell exhibited in nature is that of the male Emperor moth (*Eudia pavonia*) which, according to German experiments in 1961, can detect the sex attractant of the virgin female at the almost unbelievable range of 11 km *6.8 miles* upwind. This scent has been identified as one of the higher alcohols ($C_{16}H_{29}OH$), of which the female carries less than 0,0001 mg.

10. CENTIPEDES (*Chilopoda*)

Longest

The longest known species of centipede is a large variant of the widely distributed *Scolopendra morsitans*, found on the Andaman Islands, Bay of Bengal. Specimens have been measured up to 13 in *330 mm* in length and 1½ in *38 mm* in breadth. The longest centipede found in Britain is *Haplophilus subterraneus*, which measures up to 70 mm *2.75 in* in length and 1,4 mm *0.05 in* across the body, but on 1 Nov. 1973 Mr. Ian Howgate claims to have seen a thin amber-coloured specimen in St. Albans, Herts, measuring at least 4½ in *114 mm*.

Shortest

The shortest recorded centipede is an unidentified species which measures only 5 mm *0.19 in* The shortest centipede found in Britain is *Lithobius dubosequi*, which measures up to 9,5 mm *0.374 in* in length and 1,1 mm *0.043 in* across the body.

Most legs

The centipede with the greatest number of legs is *Himantarum gabrielis* of southern Europe which has 171–177 pairs when adult.

Fastest

The fastest centipede is probably *Scutigera coleoptrata* of southern Europe which can travel at a rate of 50 cm *19.68 in* a sec or 1.1 m.p.h. *1,8 km/h*.

11. MILLIPEDES (*Diplopoda*)

Longest

The longest known species of millipede are *Graphidostreptus gigas* of Africa and *Scaphistostreptus seychellarum* of the Seychelles in the Indian Ocean, both of which have been measured up to 280 mm *11.02 in* in length and 20 mm *0.78 in* in diameter. The longest millipede found in Britain is *Cylindroiulus londinensis* which measures up to 50 mm *1.96 in*.

Shortest

The shortest millipede in the world is the British species *Polyxenus lagurus*, which measures 2,1–4,0 mm *0.082–0.15 in* in length.

Most legs

The greatest number of legs reported for a millipede is 355 pairs (710 legs) for an unidentified South African species.

12. SEGMENTED WORMS (*Annelida or Annulata*)

Longest

The longest known species of giant earthworm is *Microchaetus rappi* (=*M. microchaetus*) of South Africa. An average-sized specimen measures 136 cm *4 ft 6 in* in length (65 cm *25½ in* when contracted), but much larger examples have been reliably reported. In *c.* 1937 a giant earthworm measuring 22 ft *6,70 m* in length when naturally extended and 20 mm *0.78 in* diameter was collected in the Transvaal, and in November 1967 another specimen measuring 11 ft *3,35 m* in length and 21 ft *6,40 m* when naturally extended was found reaching over the national road (width 6 m *19 ft 8½ in*) near Debe Nek, eastern Cape Province. The longest segmented worm found in Britain is the King rag worm (*Nereis virens*). On 19 Oct. 1975 a specimen of 38 in *965 mm* was collected by Mr. James Sawyer in Hauxley Bay, Northumberland.

Shortest

The shortest known segmented worm is *Chaetogaster annandalei*, which measures less than 0,5 mm *0.019 in* in length.

13. MOLLUSCS (*Mollusca*)

(Squids, octopuses, shellfish, snails, etc.)

Largest squid

The heaviest of all invertebrate animals is the Atlantic giant squid (*Architeuthis sp.*). The largest specimen ever recorded was one measuring 55 ft *16,75 m* in total length (head and

The only surviving example of the rarest shell, *Tibia serrata* (Perry), measuring 5.1 in *130 mm* in length, recovered in August 1977 in Iran. (*La Conchiglia*)

body 20 ft *6,09 m* tentacles 35 ft *10,66 m*) captured on 2 Nov. 1878 after it had run aground in Thimble Tickle Bay, Newfoundland, Canada. It weighed an estimated 2 tons/ *tonnes*. In October 1887 a giant squid (*Architeuthis longimanus*) measuring 57 ft *17,37 m* in total length was washed up in Lyall Bay, New Zealand, but 49 ft *14,93 m* of this was tentacle. The largest squid ever recorded in British waters was one found at the head of Whalefirth Voe, Shetland on 2 Oct. 1959 which measured 24 ft *7,31 m* in total length.

Largest octopus
In Nov. 1896 the remains of an unknown marine animal weighing an estimated 6–7 tons/*tonnes* were found on a beach near St. Augustine, Florida, U.S.A. Tissue samples were later sent to the U.S. National Museum in Washington, D.C., and in 1970 they were *positively* identified as belonging to a giant form of octopus. It is estimated that this creature had a tentacular span of 200 ft *60,9 m*. The largest octopus found in British waters is the Common octopus (*Octopus vulgaris*), which has been measured up to 7 ft *2,13 m* in radial spread and may weigh more than 10 lb. *4,5 kg*.

Most ancient mollusc
The longest existing living creature is *Neopilina galatheae*, a deep-sea worm-snail which had been believed extinct for about 320,000,000 years. In 1952, however, specimens were found at a depth of 11,400 ft *3 470 m* off Costa Rica by the Danish research vessel *Galathea*. Fossils found in New York State, U.S.A., Newfoundland, Canada, and Sweden show that this mollusc was also living about 500,000,000 years ago.

Longest lived mollusc
The longest lived mollusc is probably the deep-sea clam *Tindaria callistiformis*, which lives an estimated 100 years. The Giant clam (*Tridacna derasa*) lives about 30 years.

SHELLS
Largest
The largest of all existing bivalve shells is the marine Giant clam (*Tridacna gigas*), which is found on the Indo-Pacific coral reefs. A specimen measuring 43 in *109,2 cm* by 29 in *73,6 cm* and weighing 579½ lb. *262,9 kg* (over a quarter of a ton) was collected from the Great Barrier Reef in 1917, and is now preserved in the American Museum of Natural History, New York City, N.Y., U.S.A. Another lighter specimen was measured to be 137 cm *53.9 in* overall. The largest bivalve shell found in British waters is the Fan mussel (*Pinna fragilis*). One specimen found at Tor Bay, Devon measured 37 cm *14.56 in* in length and 20 cm *7.87 in* in breadth at the hind end.

Smallest
The smallest bivalve shell found in British waters is the coin-shell *Neolepton sykesi*, which has an average length of 1,2 mm *0.047 in*. This species is only known from a few examples collected off Guernsey, Channel Islands and West Ireland. The smallest British shell is the univalve *Ammonicera rota*, which measures 0,5 mm *0.02 in* in diameter.

Rarest
A second example of the lost species *Tibia serrata* (Perry) first found in 1811 was reported in August 1977 from Bandar Abbas, Iran by Sg. Franco Perantoni (Italy) It is grey-cream and golden-yellow and 130 mm *5.1 in* in length.

GASTROPODS
Largest
The largest known gastropod is the Trumpet or Baler conch (*Syrinx aruanus*) of Australia. One outsized specimen collected at Bunbury, Western Australia in 1974 and now owned by Morton Hahn of Randolph, New Jersey, U.S.A. weighed 35 lb. *15,9 kg* when live. Its shell measures 28.1 in *71,3 cm* in length and has a maximum girth of 38 in *96,5 cm*.

The largest known land gastropod is the African giant snail (*Achatina sp.*). An outsized specimen "Gee Geronimo" owned by Christopher Hudson of Hove, E. Sussex, measured 15½ in *39,3 cm* from snout to tail (shell) length 10¾ in *27,3 cm*) in Dec. 1978 and weighed exactly 2 lb. *900 g*. The snail was collected in Sierra Leone in June 1976 where shell lengths up to 14 in *35,5 cm* have been reliably reported.

The largest land snail found in Britain is the Roman or Edible snail (*Helix pomatia*), which measures up to 4 in *10 cm* in overall length and weighs up to 3 oz. *85 g*. The smallest British land snail is *Punctum pygmaeum*, which has a shell measuring 0.023–0.035 of an inch *0,6–0,9 mm* by 0.047–0.059 of an inch *1,2–1,5 mm*.

Speed
The fastest-moving species of land snail is probably the common garden snail (*Helix aspersa*). According to tests carried out in the United States of America absolute top speed for *Helix aspersa* is 0.0313 m.p.h. *0,05 km/h* (or 55 yds *50,3 m* per hr.) while some species are at full stretch at 0.00036 m.p.h. *0,0005 km/h* (or 23 in *58 cm* per hr). The snail-racing equivalent of a 4 minute mile is 24 inches in 3 minutes or the 7,920 minute or 5½ day mile.

14. RIBBON WORMS (*Nemertina or Rhynchopods*)

Longest
The longest of the 550 recorded species of ribbon worms, also called nemertines (or nemerteans), is the "Boot-lace worm" (*Lineus longissimus*), which is found in the shallow waters of the North Sea. A specimen washed ashore at St. Andrews, Fife, Scotland in 1864 after a severe storm measured more than 180 ft *55 m* in length, making it easily the longest recorded worm of any variety.

15. JELLYFISHES (*Scyphozoa or Scyphomedusia*)

Largest and smallest
The largest jellyfish is *Cyanea arctica* with tentacles up to 120 ft *36,5 m*. The largest coelenterate found in British waters is the rare "Lion's mane" jellyfish (*Cyanea capillata*), which is also known as the Common sea blubber. One specimen measured at St. Andrew's Marine Laboratory, Fife, Scotland had a bell diameter of 91 cm *35.8 in* and tentacles stretching over 13,7 m *45 ft*. Some true jellyfishes have a bell diameter of less than 20 mm *0.78 in*.

Most venomous
The most venomous coelenterates are the box jellies of the genera *Chiropsalmus* and *Chironex* of the Indo-Pacific region, which carry a neuro-toxic venom similar in strength to that found in the Asiatic cobra. These jellyfish have caused the deaths of at least 60 people off the coast of Queensland, Australia in the past 25 years. Victims die within 1–3 min. A most effective defence is women's panty hose, outsize versions of which are now worn by Queensland life-savers at surf carnivals.

16. SPONGES (*Parazoa, Porifera or Spongida*)

Largest
The largest known sponge is the barrel-shaped Loggerhead sponge (*Spheciospongia vesparium*) of the West Indies and the waters off Florida, U.S.A. Single individuals measure up to 3 ft 6 in *105 cm* in height and 3 ft *91 cm* in diameter. Neptune's cup or goblet (*Poterion patera*) of Indonesia grows to 4 ft *120 cm* in height, but it is a less bulky animal. In 1909 a Wool sponge (*Hippospongia canaliculatta*) measuring 6 ft *183 cm* in circumference was collected off the Bahama Islands. When first taken from the water it weighed between 80 and 90 lb. *36 and 41 kg* but after it had been dried and relieved of all excrescences it scaled 12 lb. *5,44 kg* (this sponge is now preserved in the U.S. National Museum, Washington, D.C., U.S.A.).

Smallest
The smallest known sponge is the widely distributed *Leucosolenia blanca*, which measures 3 mm *0.11 in* in height when fully grown.

Deepest
Sponges have been recovered from depths of up to 18,500 ft *5 637 m*.

17. EXTINCT ANIMALS

Longest *World*
The first dinosaur to be scientifically described was *Megalosaurus* ("large lizard"), a 20 ft *6,09 m* long bipedal theropod, in 1824. A lower jaw and other bones of this animal had been found before 1818 in a slate quarry at Stonesfield, near Woodstock, Oxfordshire, It stalked across what is now southern England about 130,000,000 years ago. The word "dinosaur" ("fearfully great lizard") was not used for such reptiles until 1841. The longest recorded dinosaur was *Diplodocus* ("double-beam"), an attenuated sauropod which ranged over western North America about 150,000,000 years ago. A composite skeleton of three individuals excavated near Split Mountain, Utah between 1909 and 1922 and mounted in the Carnegie Museum of the Natural Sciences in Pittsburgh, Pennsylvania, measures 87½ ft *26,67 m* in total length (neck 22 ft *6,70 m* body 15 ft *4,57 m*, tail 50 ft 6 in *15,40 m*—nearly the length of three London double-decker buses—and 11 ft 9 in *3,6 m* at the pelvis (the highest point on the body). This animal weighed a computed 10,56 tonnes *10.4 tons* in life.

Longest *Britain*
In 1975 an amateur fossil-hunter working on the cliff-face near Brighstone, Isle of Wight, uncovered an unusual 228 mm *9 in* long bone which was later identified as the haemal arch (a bone running beneath the vertebrae of the tail) of a Diplodocus-type sauropod.

Heaviest
The heaviest prehistoric animal, described scientifically so far, was *Brachiosaurus brancai* ("arm lizard") which lived from 135–165 million years ago. Its remains have been found in East Africa (Rhodesia and Tanzania), U.S.A. (Colorado, Oklahoma and Utah) and Europe. A complete skeleton excavated near Tendaguru Hill, southern Tanganyika (Tanzania) in 1909 and now mounted in the Museum für Naturkunde, East Berlin, Germany, measures 74 ft 6 in *22,68 m* in total length and 21 ft *6,40 m* at the shoulder. This reptile weighed a computed 78,26 tonnes *77 tons* in life, but isolated bones have since been discovered in East Africa which indicate that some specimens may have weighed as much as 125 tons *127 tonnes*.

In the summer of 1972 the remains of another enormous sauropod, new to science, were discovered in a flood-plain bonejam in Colorado, U.S.A. by an expedition from Brigham Young University, Provo, Utah. Excavations are still continuing, but a study of the incomplete series of cervical vertebrae indicate that this dinosaur must have had a neck length of approximately 39 ft *11,88 m* (cf. 22 ft *6,70 m* for Diplodocus). If the rest of "Supersaurus" (as it has been nicknamed) is built on Brachiosaurus-type lines, this presupposes an over-all length of *c.* 130 ft *39,6 m* a shoulder height of 37 ft *11,27 m* and a raised head measurement of 75 ft *22,8 m*, and a weight of at least 250 tons *255 tonnes*, making it the largest animal that has ever existed.

Largest land predator
The largest of the carnosaurs (family *Megalosauridae*) was probably *Tyrannosaurus rex* ('tyrant lizard') which stalked over what are now the states of Montana and Wyoming in the U.S.A. about 75,000,000 years ago. No complete skeleton of this dinosaur has ever been discovered, but composite remains indicate that it had a bipedal height of up to 18 ft 6 in *5,63 m*, measured 35 ft *10,65 m* in overall length (in a recent reinterpretation of Tyrannosaurus, 12 ft *3,65 m* was chopped off the tail length to produce a more symmetrical animal), and weighed 6¾ ton/*tonnes*. In 1934 the skeleton of a huge Allosaurus with a body much more massive in proportion to its height than Tyrannosaurus was excavated near Kenton, Oklahoma, U.S.A. This carnosaur had a bipedal height of 16 ft *4,87 m* and measured 42 ft *12,8 m* in overall length.

Most brainless
Stegosaurus ("plated reptile"), which measured up to 30 ft *9 m* in total length and weighed 1¾ ton/*tonnes*, had a walnut-sized brain weighing only 2½ oz. *70 g*, which represented 0.004 of one per cent of its body weight (*cf.* 0.074 of one per cent for an elephant and 1.88 per cent for a human). It roamed widely across the Northern Hemisphere about 150,000,000 years ago.

Largest dinosaur eggs
The largest known dinosaur eggs are those of *Hypselosaurus priscus*, a 30 ft *9,14 m* long sauropod which lived about 80,000,000 years ago. Some specimens found in the valley of the Durance near Aix-en-Provence southern France in

EARLIEST OF THEIR TYPES

Type	Scientific name and year of discovery	Location	Estimated years before present
Ape	*Aegyptopithecus zeuxis* (1966)	El Faiyûm, Egypt	28,000,000
Primate	tarsier-like	Indonesia	70,000,000
	lemur	Madagascar	70,000,000
Social insect	*Sphecomyrma freyi* (1967)	New Jersey, U.S.A.	100,000,000
Bird	*Archaeopteryx lithographica* (1861)	Bavaria, W. Germany	150,000,000
Mammal	*Megazostrodon* (1966)	Thaba-ea-Litau, Lesotho	190,000,000
Reptiles	*Hylonomus, Archerpeton, Protoclepsybrops Romericus*	all in Nova Scotia	290,000,000
Amphibian	*Ichthyostega* (first quadruped)	Greenland	350,000,000
Spider	*Palaeostenzia crassipes*	Tayside, Scotland	370,000,000
Insect	*Rhyniella procursor*	Tayside, Scotland	370,000,000
Mollusc	*Neopilina galatheae* (1952)	off Costa Rica	510,000,000
Vertebrates (Fish scales)	*Anatolepis*	Crook County, Wyoming, U.S.A.	510,000,000
Crustacean	*Karagassiema* (12 legged)	Sayan Mts., U.S.S.R.	c. 650,000,000
Metazoans	Bore hole tracks	Zambia	1,050,000,000

right: A 6 ft 2 in *1,88 m* man standing alongside the carapace (shell) of *Stupendemys geographicus*, the worlds largest known prehistoric chelonian. (*Roger C. Wood, Harvard University*)

October 1961 would have had, uncrushed, a length of 12 in *300 mm* and a diameter of 10 in *255 mm*.

Largest flying creature

The largest flying creature was a winged reptile (not yet named) of the order Pterosauria which glided over what is now the state of Texas, U.S.A. about 70,000,000 years ago. Partial remains (four wings, a neck, hind legs and mandibles) of three specimens discovered in Big Bend National Park, West Texas recently indicate that this pterosaur must have had a wing span of at least 11 m *36.08 ft* and that the maximum expanse may have been as great as 21 m *68.89 ft* (*cf.* 27 ft *8,23 m* for *Pteranodon ingens*.)

Largest marine reptile

The largest marine reptile ever recorded was *Kronosaurus queenslandicus*, a short-necked pliosaur which swam in the seas around what is now Australia about 100,000,000 years ago. It measured up to 55 ft *16,76 m* in length and had an 11½ ft *3,60 m* long skull. *Stretosaurus macromerus*, another short-necked pliosaur, was also of comparable size. A mandible found in Cumnor, Oxfordshire must have belonged to a reptile measuring at least 50 ft *15,23 m* in length.

Largest crocodile

The largest known crocodile was *Deinosuchus riograndensis*, which lived in the lakes and swamps of what is now the state of Texas, U.S.A. about 75,000,000 years ago. Fragmentary remains discovered in Big Bend National Park, West Texas, indicate it must have measured at least 50 ft *15,24 m* in total length. The less bulky gavial *Rhamphosuchus*, which lived in what is now northern India about 7,000,000 years ago, also reached a length of 50 ft *15,24 m*.

Largest chelonians

The largest prehistoric chelonian was the possibly marine pelomedusid turtle *Stupendemys geographicus*, which lived about 80,000,000 years ago. Fossil remains discovered by a Harvard University paleontological expedition in Northern Venezuela in 1972 indicate that this turtle had a carapace (shell) measuring 7½–8 ft *2,28–2,44 m* in mid-line length and probably measured at least 12 ft *3,65 m* in overall length.

THE 250 TON SUPERSAURUS

An artist's impression of the mightiest animal ever to roam the Earth. The 250 ton ''Supersaurus'', the remains of which were discovered in Colorado, U.S.A., in 1972, was taller than a 7 storey building (see p. 48). (Note: Human drawn to scale.)

Largest tortoise

The largest prehistoric tortoise was probably *Geochelone* (= *Colossochelys*) *atlas*, which lived in what is now northern India, Burma, Java, the Celebes and Timor between 1,000,000 and 2,500,000 years ago. In 1923 the fossil remains of a specimen with a carapace 5 ft 5 in *165 cm* long (7 ft 4 in *2,23 m* over the curve) and 2 ft 11 in *89 cm* high were discovered near Chandigarh in the Siwalik Hills. This animal had a total length of 8 ft *2,44 m* and is computed to have weighed 2,100 lb. *852 kg* when it was alive. Recently the fossil remains of other giant tortoises of comparable size have been found in Florida and Texas, U.S.A.

Longest snake

The longest prehistoric snake was the python-like *Gigantophis garstini*, which inhabited what is now Egypt about 50,000,000 years ago. Parts of a spinal column and a small piece of jaw discovered at El Faiyum indicate a length of *c*. 33 ft *10,05 m*, which is comparable with the longest constrictors living today.

Largest amphibian

The largest amphibian ever recorded was the gharial-like *Prionosuchus plummeri* which lived 230,000,000 years ago. In 1972 the fragmented remains of a specimen measuring an estimated 11 m *36 ft* in life, were discovered in North Brazil.

Largest fish

No prehistoric fish larger than living species has yet been discovered. The claim that the Great shark (*Carcharodon megalodon*), which abounded in Miocene seas some 15 million years ago, measured 80 ft *24 m* in length, based on ratios from fossil teeth has now been shown to be in error. The modern estimate is that this shark did not exceed 43 ft *13,1m*.

Largest insect

The largest prehistoric insect was the dragonfly *Meganeura monyi*, which lived about 280,000,000 years ago. Fossil remains (i.e. impressions of wings) discovered at Commentry, central France, indicate that it had a wing expanse of up to 70 cm *27.5 in*.

Britain's largest dragonfly was *Typus sp.* (family *Meganeuridae*), which is only known from a wing impression found on a lump of coal in Bolsover colliery, Derbyshire in July 1978. It had an estimated wing span of 50–60 cm *19.68–23.62 in* and lived about 300,000,000 years ago, making it the oldest flying creature so far recorded.

Most southerly

The most southerly creature yet found is a freshwater salamander-like amphibian *Labyrinthodont*, represented by a 2½ in *63,5 mm* piece of jawbone found near Beardmore Glacier Antarctica, 325 miles *532 km* from the South Pole, dating from the early Jurassic of 200,000,000 years ago. This discovery was made in December 1967.

Largest bird

The largest prehistoric bird was *Dromornis stirtoni*, a huge emu-like creature which lived in central Australia about 10–11 million years ago. Fossil leg bones found near Alice Springs in 1974 indicate that the bird must have stood 9–10 ft *2,74–3,04 m* in height and weighed at least 1,100 lb. *500 kg*. The flightless moa *Dinornis giganteus* of North Island, New Zealand was even taller, attaining a height of over 13 ft *3,96 m* but it only weighed about 500 lb. *227 kg*.

The largest prehistoric bird actually to fly was probably the condor-like *Teratornis incredibilis* which lived in what is now North America about 100,000,000 years ago. Fossil remains discovered in Smith Creek Cave, Nevada in 1952 indicate it had a wing span of 5 m *16 ft 4¾ in* and weighed nearly 50 lb. *22,5 kg*. A wing span measurement of 5 m *16 ft 4¾ in* has also been reported for another flying bird named *Ornithodesmus latidens*, which flew over what is now Hampshire and the Isle of Wight about 90,000,000 years ago. Another gigantic flying bird named *Osteodontornis orri*, which lived in what is now the state of California, U.S.A. about 20,000,000 years ago, had a wing span of 16 ft *4,87 m* and was probably even heavier. It was related to the pelicans and storks.

The albatross-like *Gigantornis eaglesomei*, which flew over what is now Nigeria between 34,000,000 and 58,000,000 years ago, has been credited with a wing span of 20 ft *6,09 m* on the evidence of a single fossilised breastbone.

Largest mammal

The largest known prehistoric marine mammal was *Basilosaurus* (= *Zeuglodon*) of 50,000,000 years ago. A specimen from Alabama measured 70 ft *21,33 m* and weighed an estimated 27 tonnes. The largest prehistoric land mammal ever recorded, was *Baluchitherium* (= *Indricotherium*, *Paraceratherium*, *Aceratherium*, *Thaumastotherium*, *Aralotherium* and *Benaratherium*), a long necked hornless rhinoceros which lived in Europe and central western Asia between 20,000,000 and 40,000,000 years ago. It stood up to 17 ft 9 in *5,41 m* to the top of the shoulder hump, (27 ft *8,23 m* to the crown of the raised head), measured 35–37 ft *10,66–11,27 m* in length and probably weighed nearly 20 tons/*tonnes*. The bones of this gigantic browser were first discovered in 1907–1908 in the Bugti Hills in east Baluchistan, Pakistan.

Largest mammoth

The largest extinct elephant was the Steppe mammoth *Paraelephas* (= *Mammuthus*) *trogontherii*, which roamed over what is now central Europe a million years ago. A fragmentary skeleton found in Mosbach, West Germany indicates a shoulder height of 4,5 m *14 ft 9 in*.

Tusks *Longest*

The longest tusks of any prehistoric animal were those of the straight-tusked elephant *Hesperoloxodon antiquus germanicus*, which lived in what is now northern Germany about 2,000,000 years ago. The average length in adult bulls was 5 m *16 ft 4¾ in*. A single tusk of a woolly mammoth (*Mammonteus primigenius*) preserved in the Franzens Museum at Brno, Czechoslovakia measures 5,02 m *16 ft 5½ in* along the outside curve. In *c*. August 1933, a single tusk of an Imperial mammoth (*Archidiskodon imperator*) measuring 16+ ft *4,87+ m* (anterior end missing) was unearthed near Post, Gorza County, Texas, U.S.A. In 1934 this tusk was presented to the American Museum of Natural History in New York City, N.Y., U.S.A.

Tusks *Heaviest*

The heaviest fossil tusk on record is one weighing 330 lb. *149,7 kg* with a maximum circumference of 35 in *89 cm* now preserved in the Museo Civico di Storia Naturale, Milan, Italy. The specimen (in two pieces) measures 11 ft 9 in *3,58 m* in length. The heaviest recorded mammoth tusks are a pair in the University of Nebraska Museum, Lincoln, Nebraska, U.S.A. which have a combined weight of 498 lb. *226 kg* and measure 13 ft 9 in *4,21 m* and 13 ft 7 in *4,14 m* respectively. They were found near Campbell, Nebraska in April 1915.

Antlers *Greatest Span*

The prehistoric Giant deer (*Megaceros giganteus*), which lived in northern Europe and northern Asia as recently as 50,000 B.C., had the longest horns of any known animal. One specimen recovered from an Irish bog had greatly palmated antlers measuring 14 ft *4,3 m* across.

PLANT KINGDOM (*Plantae*)

PLANTS
Rarest

Plants thought to be extinct are rediscovered each year and there are thus many plants of which specimens are known in but a single locality. The small pink blossoms of *Presidio manzanita* survive in a single specimen reported in June 1978 at an undisclosed site in California. The only known location of the adder's-tongue spearwort (*Ranunculus ophioglossifolius*) in the British Isles is the Badgeworth Nature Reserve, Gloucestershire. *Pennantia baylisiana*, a tree found in 1945 on Three Kings Island, off New Zealand, only exists as a female and cannot fruit.

Northernmost
The yellow poppy (*Papaver radicatum*) and the Arctic willow (*Salix arctica*) survive, the latter in an extremely stunted form, on the northernmost land (83° N).

Southernmost
The most southerly plant life recorded is seven species of lichen found in 1933–34 by the second expedition of Rear-Admiral Richard E. Byrd, U.S. Navy, in latitude 86° 03′ S. in the Queen Maud Mountains, Antarctica. The southernmost recorded flowering plant is the carnation (*Colobanthus crassifolius*), which was found in latitude 67° 15′ S. on Jenny Island, Margaret Bay, Graham Land (Palmer Peninsula), Antarctica.

Highest
The greatest certain altitude at which any flowering plant has been found is 20,130 ft *6 135 m* in the Himalaya for *Stellaria decumbens*. A claim for 23,000 ft *7 000 m* in the Himalaya for *Christolea crassifolia* remains inconclusive. A non-flowering plant of *Androsace microphylla* was recorded by A. Zimmermann at 6 350 m *20,833 ft* on the 1952 Swiss Everest expedition.

Roots
The greatest reported depth to which roots have penetrated is a calculated 400 ft *120 m* in the case of a wild fig tree at Echo Caves, near Ohrigstad, East Transvaal, South Africa.

A single winter rye plant (*Secale cereale*) has been shown to produce 387 miles *622,8 km* of roots in 1.83 cubic feet *0,051 m³* of earth.

Worst weeds
The most intransigent weed is the mat-forming water weed *Salvinia auriculata*, found in Africa. It was detected on the filling of Kariba Lake in May 1959 and within 11 months had choked an area of 77 miles² *199 km²* rising by 1963 to 387 miles² *1 002 km²*. The world's worst land weeds are regarded as purple nut sedge, Bermuda grass, barnyard grass, junglerice, goose grass, Johnson grass, Guinea grass, cogon grass and lantana. The most damaging and widespread cereal weeds in Britain are the wild oats *Avena fatua* and *A. ludoviciana*. Their seeds can withstand temperatures of 240° F *115,6° C* for 15 minutes and remain viable.

Most spreading plant
The greatest area covered by a single clonal growth is that of the wild box huckleberry (*Gaylussacia brachyera*), a mat-forming evergreen shrub first reported in 1796. A colony covering 8 acres *3,2 hectares* was discovered in 1845 near New Bloomfield, Pennsylvania. Another colony, covering about 100 acres, was "discovered" on 18 July 1920 near the Juniata River, Pennsylvania. It has been estimated that this colony began 13,000 years ago.

Largest Philodendron
A Philodendron, 300 ft *91,5 m* in length, now grows in La Carreta Restaurant in San Jacinto, California, U.S.A.

Largest aspidistra
The aspidistra (*Aspidistra elatior*) was introduced to Britain as a parlour palm from Japan and China in 1822. The biggest aspidistra in the world is one 51¾ in *131 cm* tall and grown by Cliff W. Evans at Kiora, Moruya, N.S.W., Australia and measured in December 1977.

Earliest flower
The oldest fossil of a flowering plant with palm-like imprints was found in Colorado, U.S.A., in 1953 and dated about 65,000,000 years old.

Largest cactus
The largest of all cacti is the saguaro (*Cereus giganteus* or *Carnegiea gigantea*), found in Arizona, south eastern California, U.S.A. and Sonora, Mexico. The green fluted column is surmounted by candelabra-like branches rising to a height of 52 ft 5¾ in *16,00 m* in the case of a specimen measured on the boundary of the Saguaro National Monument, Arizona. They have waxy white blooms which are followed by edible crimson fruit. An armless cactus 78 ft *23,77 m* in height was measured in April 1978 by Hube Yates in Cave Creek, Arizona.

Tallest hedge *World*
The world's tallest hedge is the Meikleour beech hedge in Perthshire, Scotland. It was planted in 1746 and has now attained a trimmed height of 85 ft *26 m*. It is 600 yds *550 m* long. Some of its trees now exceed 100 ft *30,48 m*.

Tallest hedge *Yew*
The tallest yew hedge in the world is in Earl Bathurst's Park, Cirencester, Gloucestershire. It was planted in 1720, runs for 170 yds *155 m* reaches 36 ft *11 m*, is 15 ft *4,57 m* thick at its base and takes 20 man-days to trim.

Tallest hedge *Box*
The tallest box hedge is 35 ft *10,7 m* in height at Birr Castle, Offaly, Ireland dating from the 18th century.

Mosses
The smallest of mosses is the pygmy moss (*Ephemerum*) and the longest is the brook moss (*Fontinalis*), which forms streamers up to 3 ft *91 cm* long in flowing water.

Longest seaweed
Claims made that seaweed off Tierra del Fuego, South America, grows to 600 ft *182,5 m* and even to 1,000 ft *305 m* in length have gained currency. More recent and more reliable records indicate that the longest species of seaweed is the Pacific giant kelp (*Macrocystis pyrifera*), which does not exceed 196 ft *60 m* in length. It can grow 45 cm *17¾ in* in a day. The longest of the 700 species of British seaweed is the brown seaweed *Chorda filum* which grows up to a length of 20 ft *6,10 m*. The Japanese seaweed *Sasgassum muticum* introduced c. 1970 can grow to 30 ft *9,15 m*.

Largest vines
The largest recorded grape vine was one planted in 1842 at Carpinteria, California, U.S.A. By 1900 it was yielding more than 9 tons/*tonnes* of grapes in some years, and averaging 7 tons/*tonnes* per year. It died in 1920. Britain's largest vine (1898–1964) was at Kippen, Stirling with a girth, measured in 1956, of 5 ft *1,52 m*. England's largest vine is the Great Vine, planted in 1768 at Hampton Court, Greater London. Its girth is 85 in *215,9 cm* with branches up to 114 ft *34,7 m* long and an average yield of 703 lb. *318,8 kg*.

Most Northerly and Southerly
A vineyard at Sabile, Latvia, U.S.S.R. is just north of Lat. 57° N. The most northerly vineyard in Britain is that at Renishaw Hall, Derbyshire with 2,600 vines. It lies in Lat. 53° 18′ N. The Coonawarra vineyard, South Australia (Lat. 37° 20′ S.) is the world's most southerly.

TREES AND WOOD
Most massive tree
The most massive living thing on Earth is the biggest known California big tree (*Sequoiadendron giganteum*) named the "General Sherman", standing 272 ft 4 in *83 m* tall, in the Sequoia National Park, California, U.S.A. It has a true girth of 79.1 ft *24,11 m* (at 5 ft *1,52 m* above the ground). The "General Sherman" has been estimated to contain the equivalent of 600,120 board feet of timber, sufficient to make 5,000,000,000 matches. The foliage is blue-green, and the red-brown tan bark may be up to 24 in *61 cm* thick in parts. In 1968 the official published figure for its estimated weight was "2,145 tons" (1,915 long tons *2 030 tonnes*). The largest known petrified tree is one of this species with a 295 ft *89,9 m* trunk near Coaldale, Nevada, U.S.A.

The seed of a "big tree" weighs only 1/6,000th of an oz. *4,7 mg*. Its growth at maturity may therefore represent an increase in weight of over 250,000 million fold.

Tallest *World*
The world's tallest known species of tree is the coast redwood (*Sequoia sempervirens*), now found growing indigenously only near the coast of California from just across the Oregon border south to Monterey. The tallest measured example is

TALLEST TREES IN UNITED KINGDOM AND IRELAND—By species

		ft	m			ft	m
Alder (Italian)	Westonbirt, Gloucester	92	28	Lime	Duncombe Park, North Yorks.	150	45
Alder (Common)	Sandling Park, Kent	85	25	Metasequoia	Savill Garden, Berks.	72	22
Ash	Cockington Ct., Devon	121	37	Monkey Puzzle	Bicton House, Devon	90	27,5
Beech	Whitfield Ho., Hereford & Worc.	135	41	Oak (Common)	Petworth House, West Sussex	121	37
Beech (Copper)	Longleat, Wiltshire	112	34	Oak (Sessile)	Whitfield Ho., Hereford & Worcs.	140	42
Birch (Silver)	Woburn Sands, Bedfordshire	97	29	Oak (Red)	Cowdray Park, West Sussex	115	35
Cedar (Blue Atlas)	Brockhampton Pk, Hereford & Worc.	125	38	Pear	Borde Hill, West Sussex	64	19
Cedar (of Lebanon)	Petworth House, West Sussex	132	40	Pine (Corsican)	Stanage Park, Powys	144	43
Chestnut (Horse)	Petworth House, West Sussex	125	38	Plane	Bryanston, Dorset	145	44
Chestnut (Sweet)	Godinton Park, Kent	118	35	Poplar (Black Italian)	Fairlawne, Kent	150	46
Cypress (Lawson)	Endsleigh, Devon	133	40	Poplar (Lombardy)	Marble Hill, Twickenham, G. London	118	35
Cypress (Leyland)	Bicton, Devon	111	34	Redwood (Coast)	Undisclosed site, north Devon	138	42
Cypress (Monterey)	Tregothnan, Cornwall	120	36	Silver Fir	Benmore, Strathclyde	158	48
Douglas Fir	Powis Castle, Powys	181	55	Spruce (Sitka)	Murthly, Tayside	174	53
Elm (Wych)	Rossie Priory, nr. Dundee	128	39	Sycamore	Drumlanrig Castle, Dumfries & Gal.	112	34
Eucalyptus (Blue Gum)	Glengariff, Co. Cork	140	42	Tulip-tree	Taplow House, Buckinghamshire	120	36
Grand Fir	Strone, Cairndow, Strathclyde	188	57	Walnut	Alnwick Castle, Northumberland	80	24
Ginkgo	Linton Park (Maidstone), Kent	93	28	Walnut, (Black)	Garendon Hall, Leicestershire	98	30
Hemlock (Western)	Benmore, Strathclyde	152	46	Wellingtonia	Endsleigh, Devon	165	50
Holly	Staverton Thicks, Suffolk	74	22	Willow (weeping)	Trinity College, Cambridge	76	23
Hornbeam	Wrest Park, Bedfordshire	105	32	Wingnut (Caucasian)	Abbotsbury, Dorset	115	35
Larch (European)	Hascombe, Surrey	146	44,5	Yew	Wardour Old Castle, Wilts.	82	25
Larch (Japanese)	Blair Castle, Tayside	121	36				

the Howard Libbey Tree in Redwood Creek Grove, Humboldt County, California discovered by Dr. Paul A. Zahl in 1963 to be 367.8 ft *112,10 m* with an apparently dead top and re-estimated at 366.2 ft *111,60 m* in 1970. It has a girth of 44 ft *13,41 m*. The nearby tree announced to a Senate Committee by Dr. Rudolf W. Becking on 18 June 1966 to be 385 ft *117,34 m*, proved on remeasurement to be no more than 311.3 ft *94,88 m* tall. The tallest non-sequoia is a Douglas fir at Quinault Lake Park trail, Washington, U.S.A. of *c*. 310 ft *94,5 m*.

The tallest broadleaf tree in the world is a *Euculyptus regnans* measured in Western Australia at 338 ft *103 m*.

Tallest *All-time*
The identity of the tallest tree of all-time has never been satisfactorily resolved. Although there have been claims as high as 525 ft *160 m* (subsequently reduced in May 1889 on re-measurement to 220 ft *67 m*), the now accepted view is that maximum height recorded by a qualified surveyor was the 375 ft *114,3 m* Cornthwaite Tree (*Eucalyptus regnans*, formerly *E. amygdalina*) in Thorpdale, Gippsland, Victoria in 1880. Claims for a Douglas fir (*Pseudotsuga taxifolia*) of 417 ft *127,10 m* with a 77 ft *23,47 m* circumference felled by George Carey in 1895 in British Columbia have been obscured, though not necessarily invalidated by a falsified photograph. The tallest specimen now known is *c*. 310 ft *94,5 m* (see above). A coast redwood of 367 ft 8 in *112,06 m* felled in 1873 near Guerneville, California, U.S.A., was thus almost precisely the same height as the Howard Libbey Tree as originally measured.

Tallest *Great Britain*
The tallest tree in Great Britain is a Grand fir (*Abies grandis*) at Strone, Cairndow, Strathclyde, now 188 ft *57 m* tall. The tallest in England is a Douglas fir (*Pseudotsuga taxifolia*) measured at 172 ft *52,42 m* in 1974 at Dunster, Somerset. The tallest measured in Northern Ireland is a Giant Sequoia (*Sequoiadendron giganteum*, measured in 1976 to be 158 ft *48 m* tall at Caledon Castle, County Tyrone.

Tallest *Ireland*
The tallest tree in Ireland is a Sitka spruce (*Picea sitchensis*) 166 ft *50,59 m* tall at Curraghmore, Waterford, measured in March 1974.

Tallest Christmas Tree
The world's tallest cut Christmas tree was a 221 ft *67,36 m* tall Douglas fir (*Pseudotsuga taxifolia*) erected at Northgate Shopping Center, Seattle, Washington in December, 1950. The tallest Christmas tree erected in Britain was the 85 ft 3¼ in *25,98 m* long spruce from Norway erected for the Canterbury Cathedral appeal on the South Bank, London on 20 Nov. 1975.

Greatest girth *World*
The Santa Maria del Tule Tree, in the state of Oaxaca, in Mexico is a Montezuma cypress (*Taxodium mucronatum*) with a girth of 112–113 ft *34,1–34,4 m* (1949) at a height of 5 ft *1,52 m* above the ground. A figure of 167 ft *51 m* in circumference was reported for the pollarded European chestnut (*Castanea sativa*) known as the "Tree of the 100 Horse" (Castagno di Cento Cavalli) on Mount Etna, Sicily, Italy in 1972.

Measuring 221 ft *67,36 m*, the worlds tallest cut Christmas tree, a Douglas fir was erected in Dec. 1950 in Seattle, U.S.A. (*The Seattle Times*)

from left to right: R. Butcher with his record 11 lb. 8 oz. *5,216 kg.* cucumber and his 225 lb. *102,05 kg* pumpkin. (*Garden News*). The 3 lb. 9 oz. *1,628 kg* lemon grown by T. Buckeridge in 1978, with the grower's daughter, Thomasine. (*T. C. Buckeridge*). Record breaking rhubarb weighing 5 lb. 11 ozs. *2,579 kg* grown by A. C. Setterfield. (*Garden News*)

RECORD DIMENSIONS AND WEIGHTS FOR FRUIT, VEGETABLES AND FLOWERS GROWN IN THE UNITED KINGDOM

Most data subsequent to 1958 comes from the annual *Garden News* Giant Vegetable and Fruit Contest and the Super Sunflower Contest.

Apple	3 lb. 1 oz.	*1,357 kg*	V. Loveridge	Ross-on-Wye, Hereford and Worcester	1965
Artichoke	8 lb.	*3,625 kg*	A. R. Lawson	Tollerton, North Yorkshire	1964
Beetroot	24 lb.	*10,875 kg*	R. G. Arthur	Longlevens, Gloucestershire	1971
Broad Bean	23⅜ in	*59,3 cm*	T. Currie	Jedburgh, Borders	1963
Broccoli	28 lb. 14¾ oz.	*13,100 kg*	J. T. Cooke	Funtington, West Sussex	1964
Brussels Sprout[1]	16 lb. 1 oz.	*7,285 kg*	E. E. Jenkins	Shipston-on-Stour, Warwickshire	1974
Cabbage[2]	114 lb. 3 oz.	*51,8 kg*	P. G. Barton	Cleckheaton, W. Yorkshire	1977
Carrot[3]	7 lb. 5 oz.	*3,300 kg*	R. Clarkson	Freckleton, Lancashire	1970
Cauliflower	52 lb. 11½ oz.	*23,900 kg*	J. T. Cooke	Funtington, West Sussex	1966
Celery	35 lb.	*15,875 kg*	C. Bowcock	Willaston, Merseyside	1973
Cucumber[4]	11 lb. 8 oz. (indoor)	*5,216 kg*	R. Butcher	Stockbridge, Hants.	1978
	8 lb. 4 oz. (outdoor)	*3,740 kg*	C. Bowcock	Willaston, Merseyside	1973
Dahlia[5]	9 ft tall	*2,74 m*	J. Crennan	Abbey Wood, London S.E.	1975
Dwarf Bean	17½ in	*43,4 cm*	C. Bowcock	Willaston, Merseyside	1973
Gladiolus*	7 ft 10½ in	*2,40 m*	W. Wilson	Dunfermline, Fife	1977
Gooseberry	2.06 oz.	*58,5 g*	A. Dingle	Macclesfield, Cheshire	1978
Gourd	196 lb.	*88,900 kg*	J. Leathes	Herringfleet Hall, Suffolk	1846
Grapefruit*	3 lb. 8 oz.	*1,585 kg*	A. J. Frost	Willington, Bedfordshire	1977
Hollyhock	19 ft 7 in	*5,96 m*	G. Palmer	West Clandon, Surrey	1978
Kale	12 ft tall	*3,65 m*	B. T. Newton	Mullion, Cornwall	1950
Leek	9 lb. 5½ oz.	*4,235 kg*	C. Bowcock	Willaston, Merseyside	1973
Leek, Pot	100.38 in^3	*1,644* cm^3	R. S. Bell	Ashington, Northumberland	1977
Lemon[6]	3 lb. 9 oz.	*1,628 kg*	T. Buckeridge	Isfield, E. Sussex	1978
Lettuce	25 lb.	*11,335 kg*	C. Bowcock	Willaston, Merseyside	1974
Lupin*	6 ft 0½ in	*1,84 m*	J. Lawlor	New Maldon, Surrey	1971
Mangold	54½ lb.	*24,720 kg*	P. F. Scott	Sutton, Humberside	1971
Marrow[7]	64 lb.	*29,025 kg*	W. Allingham	Wareham, Dorset	1977
Mushroom[8]	54 in circum.	*1,37 m*	—	Hasketon, Suffolk	1957
Onion	6 lb. 3 oz.	*2,830 kg*	T. Fenton	Preston, Lancashire	1977
Parsnip[9]	10 lb.	*4,525 kg*	C. Bowcock	Willaston, Merseyside	1973
Pea Pod	10⅛ in	*25,7 cm*	T. Currie	Jedburgh, Borders	1964
Pear	2 lb. 10½ oz.	*1,200 kg*	Mrs. K. Loines	Hythe, Hampshire	1973
Petunia	8 ft	*2,43 m*	G. A. Warner	Dunfermline, Fife	1978
Potato[10]	7 lb. 1 oz.	*3,200 kg*	J. H. East	Spalding, Lincolnshire	1963
Pumpkin[11]	225 lb. 0 oz.	*102,05 kg*	R. Butcher	Stockbridge, Hants.	1978
Radish[12]	17 lb.	*7,711 kg*	K. Ayliffe	Brecon, Powys	1976
Red Cabbage	42 lb.	*19,05 kg*	R. Straw	Stavely, Derbyshire	1925
Rhubarb	5 lb 11 oz.	*2,579 kg*	A. C. Setterfield	Englefield, Berkshire	1978
Runner Bean	39 in long	*99 cm*	Mrs. E. Huxley	Churton, Cheshire	1976
Savoy	38 lb. 8 oz.	*17,450 kg*	W. H. Neil	Retford, Nottinghamshire	1966
Shallot*	2 lb. 12 oz.	*1,245 kg*	M. Silverstoff	Falmouth, Cornwall	1977
Strawberry	7¼ oz.	*205 kg*	E. Oxley	Walton-on-the-Naze, Essex	1972
Sugar Beet[13]	28 lb.	*12,7 kg*	W. Featherby	Everingham, Humberside	1977
Sunflower	23 ft 6½ in tall	*7,17 m*	F. Kelland	Exeter, Devon	1976
Swede[14]	42 lb. 6 oz.	*19,220 kg*	J. K. Wallace	Sorbie, Wigtownshire	1979
Tomato[15]	4 lb. 4 oz.	*1,925 kg*	C. Roberts	Eastbourne, East Sussex	1974
Tomato Plant[16]	20 ft tall	*6,09 m 15,400 kg*	—	Southport, Merseyside	1957
Tomato Truss	20 lb. 4 oz.	*9,175 kg*	C. Bowcock	Willaston, Merseyside	1973
Turnip[17]	35 lb. 4 oz.	*15,975 kg*	C. W. Butler	Nafferton, Humberside	1972

[1] *A Brussels Sprout plant measuring 11 ft 8 in 3,55 m was grown by Ralph G. Sadler of Watchbury Farm, Barford, Warwickshire on 6 July 1978.*

[2] *The Swalwell, County Durham Red Cabbage of 1865 grown by William Collingwood (d. 8 Oct. 1867) reputedly weighed 123 lb.* 55,7 kg *and was 259 in 6,57 m in circumference*

[3] *One of 7 lb. 7 oz.* 3,35 kg *(15 in 38 m long) reported grown by Police Sgt. Alfred Garwood of Blidworth, Nottinghamshire in November 1970. A specimen of 11 lb.* 4,79 kg *was grown by Bob McEwan of Beeac, Victoria, Australia in Sept. 1967.*

[4] *A 13 lb.* 5,89 kg *example was grown by George J. Kucera of Mexia, Texas, U.S.A. in July 1978. A Vietnamese variety 6 ft* 1,83 m *long was reported by L. Szabo of Debrecen, Hungary in Sept. 1976.*

[5] *A 9 ft 10 ¾ in* 3,01 m *dahlia was grown by H. W. Deem of Victoria, Australia in 1977.*

[6] *A 6 lb. 4 oz.* 2,83 kg *lemon with a 28¾ in* 73 cm *girth was reported by Mrs. D. Knutzen of Whittier, California U.S.A. in Jan. 1977.*

[7] *A 96 lb.* 43,525 kg *marrow has been reported from Suffolk. A 63½ lb.* 28,000 kg *specimen grown by J. C. Lewis of Blackwood, Gwent, won a contest in 1937.*

[8] *Same size reported by J. Coombes at Mark, Somerset on 28 July 1965. In Sept. 1968 one weighing 18 lb. 10 oz.* 8,425 kg *was reported from Whidbey I. Washington, U.S.A. A mushroom with an estimated circumference of 75 in* 190 cm *was reported by the Lualaba river, Zaire in 1920.*

[9] *One 60 in* 152 cm *long was reported by M. Zaninovich of Waneroo W. Australia.*

[10] *One weighing 18 lb. 4 oz.* 8,275 kg *reported dug up by Thomas Siddal in his garden in Chester on 17 Feb. 1795. A yield of 515 lb.* 233,5 kg *from a 2¼ lb. parent seed by Bowcock planted in April 1977. Six tubers weighing 54 lb. 8 oz.* 24,72 kg *by Alan Nunn of Rhodes, Greater Manchester were reported on 18 Sept. 1949.*

[11] *A squash of 513 lb.* 232,69 kg *was grown by Harold Fulp, Jr., at Ninevah, Indiana, U.S.A. in 1977.*

[12] *A radish of 25 lb.* 11,34 kg *was grown by Glen Tucker of Stanbury, South Australia in Aug. 1974 and by Herbert Breslow of Ruskin, Florida, U.S.A. in 1977.*

[13] *One weighing 45½ lb.* 20,63 kg *was grown by Robert Meyer of Brawley, California in 1974.*

[14] *One weighing 39 lb. 8 oz.* 17,9 kg *claimed by E. R. Reay of Gaitsgill Hall, Dalston, Cumbria, 1940 (unratified).*

[15] *Grace's Gardens reported a 6 lb. 8 oz.* 2,94 kg *tomato grown by Clarence Daily of Monona, Wisconsin in 1977.*

[16] *A 21 ft 3½ in* 6,48 m *plant was grown at Wyckoff, N.J., U.S.A. in July 1976 by David Vibert.*

[17] *A 73 lb.* 33,1 kg *turnip was reported in December 1768.*

* *Not in official contest.*

The heaviest orange is one weighing 3 lb. 11 oz. 1,77 kg *grown by Bill Calendine of Tucson, Arizona, U.S.A., in 1977*

WEDNESDAY, 9 SEPTEMBER, 1925.

A GARDEN PRODIGY.

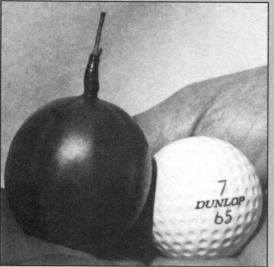

above: In 1925 Mr. R. Straw grew this massive 42 lb. *19,05 kg* red cabbage the largest ever recorded (see p. 53). (*Sheffield Mail*)

left: This gigantic gooseberry 2.06 oz. *58,5 g.* seen at the Marton Gooseberry Show on 5 Aug. 1978 broke all records (see p. 53). (*George Riley*)

Greatest girth *Britain*

The tree of greatest girth in Britain is a Sweet Chestnut (*Castanea sativa*) at Canford, Dorset, with a bole 43 ft 9 in *13,33 m* in circumference. The largest-girthed living British oak is one at Bowthorpe Farm near Bourne, south Lincolnshire, measured in Sept. 1973 to be 39 ft 1 in *11,91 m*. The largest "maiden" (i.e. not pollarded) oak is the Majesty Oak at Fredville Park, near Nonington, Kent, with a girth of (1973) 38 ft 1 in *11,60 m*.

Oldest tree *World*

The oldest recorded tree was a bristlecone pine (*Pinus longaeva*) designated WPN–114, which grew at 10,750 ft *3 275 m* above sea-level on the north-east face of the Wheeler Ridge on the Sierra Nevada, California, U.S.A. During studies in 1963 and 1964 it was found to be about 4,900 years old but was cut down with a chain saw. The oldest known *living* tree is the bristlecone pine named *Methuselah* at 10,000 ft *3 050 m* in the California side of the White Mountains confirmed as 4,600 years old. In March 1974 it was reported that this tree had produced 48 live seedlings. Dendrochronologists estimate the *potential* life-span of a bristlecone pine at nearly 5,500 years, but that of a "Big Tree" at perhaps 6,000 years. A report in March 1976 stated that some enormous specimens of Japanese cedar (*Cryptomeria japonica*) had been dated by carbon-14 to 5,200 B.C.

Oldest tree *Great Britain*

Of all British trees that with the longest life is the yew (*Taxus baccata*), for which a maximum age well in excess of 1,000 years is usually conceded. The oldest known is the Fortingall Yew near Aberfeldy, Tayside, part of which still grows. In 1777 this tree was over 50 ft *15,24 m* in girth and it cannot be much less than 1,500 years old today.

Earliest species

The earliest species of tree still surviving is the maiden-hair tree (*Ginkgo biloba*) of Chekiang, China, which first appeared about 160,000,000 years ago, during the Jurassic era. It was "re-discovered" by Kaempfer (Netherlands) in 1690 and reached England *c.* 1754. It has been grown in Japan since *c.* 1100 where it was known as *ginkyō* ("silver apricot") and is now known as *icho.*

Fastest growing

Discounting bamboo, which is not botanically classified as a tree, but as a woody grass, the fastest rate of growth recorded is 35 ft 3 in *10,74 m* in 13 months by an *Albizzia falcata* planted on 17 June 1974 in Sabah, Malaysia. The youngest recorded age for a tree to reach 100 ft *30,48 m* is 7 years for *Eucalyptus regnans* in Rhodesia.

Slowest growing

The speed of growth of trees depends largely upon conditions, although some species, such as box and yew, are always slow-growing. The extreme is represented by a specimen of Sitka spruce which required 98 years to grow to 11 in *28 cm* tall with a diameter of less than 1 in *2,5 cm* on the Arctic tree-line. The growing of miniature trees or *bonsai* is an oriental cult mentioned as early as *c.* 1320.

Most Leaves

Little work has been done on the laborious task of establishing which species has most leaves. A large oak has perhaps 250,000 but a Cypress may have some 45 to 50 million leaf scales.

Remotest

The tree remotest from any other tree is believed to be one at an oasis in the Ténéré Desert, Niger Republic. In Feb. 1960 it survived being rammed by a lorry driven by a Frenchman. There were no other trees within 50 km *31 miles*. The tree was transplanted and it is now in the Museum at Niamey, Niger.

Most expensive

The highest price ever paid for a tree is $51,000 (then £18,214) for a single Starkspur Golden Delicious apple tree from near Yakima, Washington, U.S.A., bought by a nursery in Missouri in 1959.

Largest forest *World*

The largest afforested areas in the world are the vast coniferous forests of the northern U.S.S.R., lying mainly between latitude 55° N, and the Arctic Circle. The total wooded area amount to 2,700,000,000 acres *1 100 million ha* (25 per cent of the world's forests), of which 38 per cent is Siberian larch. The U.S.S.R. is 34 per cent afforested.

Largest forest *Great Britain*

The largest forest in England is Kielder Forest (72,336 acres *29 273 ha*), in Northumberland. The largest forest in Wales is the Coed Morgannwg (Forest of Glamorgan) (42,555 acres *17 221 ha*). Scotland's most extensive forest is the Glen Trool Forest (51,376 acres *20 791 ha*) in Kirkcudbrightshire. The United Kingdom is 7 per cent afforested.

Wood *Heaviest*

The heaviest of all woods is black ironwood (*Olea laurifolia*), also called South African ironwood, with a specific gravity of up to 1.49, and weighing up to 93 lb./ft³ *1 490 kg/m³*. The heaviest British wood is boxwood (*Buxus sempervirens*) with an extreme of 64 lb./ft³ *1 025 kg/m³*.

Wood *Lightest*

The lightest wood is *Aeschynomene hispida*, found in Cuba, which has a specific gravity of 0.044 and a weight of only 2¾ lb./ft³ *44 kg/m³*. The wood of the balsa tree (*Ochroma pyramidale*) is of very variable density—between 2½ and 24 lb./ft³ *40 and 384 kg/m³*. The density of cork is 15 lb./ft³ *240 kg/m³*.

Bamboo *Tallest*

The tallest recorded bamboo was a Thorny bamboo culm (*Bambusa arundinacea*) felled at Pattazhi, Travancore, Southern India, in November 1904 measuring 121½ ft *37,03 m*.

Bamboo *Fastest growing*

Some species of the 45 genera of bamboo have attained growth rates of up to 36 in *91 cm* per day (0.00002 m.p.h. *0,00003 km/h*), on their way to reaching a height of 100 ft *30 m* in less than three months.

BLOOMS AND FLOWERS

Largest bloom *World*

The mottled orange-brown and white parasitic stinking corpse lily (*Rafflesia arnoldii*) has the largest of all blooms. These attach themselves to the cissus vines of the jungle in south-east Asia and measure up to 3 ft *91 cm* across and ¾ of an in *1,9 cm* thick, and attain a weight of 15 lb. *7 kg*.

The largest known inflorescence is that of *Puya raimondii*, a rare Bolivian plant with an erect panicle (diameter 8 ft *2,4 m*) which emerges to a height of 35 ft *10,7 m*. Each of these bears up to 8,000 white blooms (see also Slowest-flowering plant, p. 56). The flower-spike of an agave was in 1974 measured to be 52 ft *15,8 m* long in Berkeley, California.

The world's largest blossoming plant is the giant Chinese wisteria at Sierra Madre, California, U.S.A. It was planted in 1892 and now has branches 500 ft *152 m* long. It covers nearly an acre, weighs 225 tons *228 tonnes* and has an estimated 1,500,000 blossoms during its blossoming period of five weeks, when up to 30,000 people pay admission to visit it. In November 1974 a Passion plant, fed by a hormone by Dennis and Patti Carlson, was reported to have grown to a length of 600 ft *182 m* at Blaine, Minnesota, U.S.A.

Largest bloom *Great Britain*

The largest bloom of any indigenous British flowering plant is that of the wild white water lily (*Nymphaea alba*), which measures 6 in *15 cm* across. Other species bear much larger inflorescences.

Smallest flowering plant

Many hitherto unsuspected minute flowers have been discovered since 1972 by Mr. and Mrs. Robert I. Gilbreath of California. The smallest 1/72nd of an inch *0,35 mm* in

Weighing over 1¼ tons/tonnes and measuring 39 ft *11,88 m* in diameter this wreath was built by Joe Marrazzo and James Piscopo in Pennsylvania, U.S.A., in Dec. 1977. (*Sircely*)

diameter is the *Pilea microphylla* of Western India. The smallest plant regularly flowering in Britain is the chaffweed (*Cetunculus minimus*), a single seed of which weighs 0.00003 of a gramme.

Rarest Flower

The Burpee Co $20,000 prize offered in 1924 for the first all white marigold was won in 1945 by Alice Vonk of Sully, Iowa, USA.

Fastest Growth

The case of a *Liliacea hesperogucca whipplei* growing 12 ft *3,65 m* in 14 days was reported from Treco Abbey, Isles of Scilly in July 1978.

Slowest flowering plant

The slowest flowering of all plants is the rare *Puyu raimondii*, the largest of all herbs, discovered in Bolivia in 1870. The panicle emerges after about 150 years of the plant's life. It then dies. (See also above under Largest blooms.) Some agaves, erroneously called Century plants, first flower after 40 years.

Largest wreath

The largest wreath ever constructed was the wreath built by Joe Marrazzo and James Piscopo in Morrisville, Pennsylvania, U.S.A. in Dec. 1977. It weighed 2,687 lb. *1 219 kg* and measured 39 ft *11,88 m* in diameter.

Longest daisy chain

The longest daisy chain is one of 4082 ft *1 244 m* at Coediog, Llanelidan, Clwyd, Wales made in 7 hours on 11 June 1978.

Orchid *Largest*

The largest of all orchids is *Grammatophyllum speciosum*, native to Malaysia. Specimens have been recorded up to 25 ft *7,62 m* in height. The largest orchid flower is that of *Phragmipedium caudatum*, found in tropical areas of America, Its petals are up to 18 in *46 cm* long, giving it a maximum outstretched diameter of 3 ft *91 cm*. The flower is, however, much less bulky than that of the stinking corpse lily.

Orchid *Tallest*

The tallest free standing orchid is the *Grammatophyllum speciosum* (see above). *Galeola foliata* may attain 49 ft *15 m* on decaying rainforest trees in Queensland, Australia.

Orchid *Smallest*

The smallest orchid is *Bulbophyllum minutissimum*, found in Australia. Claims have also been made for *Notylia norae* found in Venezuela. The smallest orchid flowers are borne by *Stelis graminea* being less than 1 mm *0.04 in* long.

Orchid *Highest priced*

The highest price ever paid for an orchid is 1,150 guineas (£1,207.50), paid by Baron Schröder to Sanders of St. Albans for an *Odontoglossum crispum* (variety *pittianum*) at an auction by Protheroe & Morris of Bow Lane, London, on 22 March 1906. A Cymbidium orchid called Rosanna Pinkie was sold in the United States for $4,500 (then £1,600) in 1952.

Largest rhododendron

The largest species of rhododendron is the scarlet *Rhododendron arboreum*, examples of which reach a height of 60 ft *18,25 m* at Mangalbaré, Nepal. The cross-section of the trunk of a *Rhododendron giganteum*, reputedly 90 ft *27,43 m* high from Yunnan, China is preserved at Inverewe Garden, Highland. The largest in the United Kingdom is one 25 ft *7,60 m* tall and 272 ft *82,90 m* in circumference at Government House, Hillsborough, Co. Down. A specimen 35 ft *10,65 m* high and 3 ft 3 in in circumference has been measured at Tregothan, Truro, Cornwall.

Largest rose tree

A "Lady Banks" rose tree at Tombstone, Arizona, U.S.A., has a trunk 40 in *101 cm* thick, stands 9 ft *2,74 m* high and covers an area of 5,380 ft² *499 m²* supported by 68 posts and several thousand feet of piping. This enables 150 people to be seated under the arbour. The cutting came from Scotland in 1884.

FRUIT

Most and least nutritive

An analysis of the 38 commonly eaten raw (as opposed to dried) fruits shows that the one with the highest calorific value is avocado (*Persea americana*), with 741 calories per edible lb. or *163 cals* per *100 gr*. That with the lowest value is cucumber with 73 calories per lb. *16 cals per 100 gr*. Avocados probably originated in Central and South America and contain also vitamins A, C, and E and 2.2 per cent protein.

Melon

A watermelon weighing 197 lb. *89,3 kg* was reported by

Grace's Garden in 1975. The grower was Ed Weeks of Tarboro, North Carolina.

Pineapple *Largest*
A pineapple weighing 17 lb *7,71 kg* was picked by H. Retief in Malindi, Kenya in December 1978.

FERNS
Largest
The largest of all the more than 6,000 species of fern is the tree fern (*Alsophila excelsa*) of Norfolk Island, in the South Pacific, which attains a height of up to 60 ft *18,28 m*.

Smallest
The world's smallest ferns are *Hecistopteris pumila*, found in Central America, and *Azolla caroliniana*, which is native to the United States.

GRASSES
Commonest and Fastest Growing
The world's commonest grass is *Cynodon ductylon* or Bermuda grass. The "Callie" hybrid, selected in 1966, grows as much as 6 in *15,2 cm* a day and stolons reach 18 ft *5,5 m* in length. The tallest of the 160 grasses found in Great Britain is the common reed (*Phragmites communis*), which reaches a height of 9 ft 9 in *2,97 m*.

Shortest
The shortest grass native to Great Britain is the very rare sand bent (*Mibora minima*) from Anglesey, Gwynedd which has a maximum growing height of under 6 in *15 cm*.

LEAVES
Largest *World*
The largest leaves of any plant belong to the raffia palm (*Raphia raffia*) of the Mascarene Islands, in the Indian Ocean and the Amazonian bamboo palm (*R. toedigera*) of South America, whose leaf blades may measure up to 65 ft *19,81 m* in length with petioles up to 13 ft *3,96 m*.

The largest undivided leaf is that of *Alocasia macrorrhiza*, found in Sabah, East Malaysia. One found in 1966 was 9 ft 11 in *3,02 m* long and 6 ft 3½ in *1,92 m* wide, with a unilateral area of 34.2 ft² *3,17 m²*.

Largest *Great Britain*
The largest leaves to be found in outdoor plants in Great Britain are those of *Gunnera manicata* from Brazil with leaves 6 to 10 ft *1,82–3,04 m* across on prickly stems 5 to 8 ft *1,52–2,43 m* long.

Fourteen-leafed clover
A fourteen-leafed white clover (*Trifolium repens*) was found by Randy Farland near Sioux Falls, South Dakota, U.S.A. on 16 June 1975.

SEEDS
Largest
The largest seed in the world is that of the double coconut or Coco de Mer (*Lodoicea seychellarum*), the single-seeded fruit of which may weigh 40 lb. *18 kg*. This grows only in the Seychelles, in the Indian Ocean.

Smallest
The smallest seeds are those of *Epiphytic* orchids, at 35,000,000 to the oz. (*cf.* grass pollens at up to 6,000,000,000 grains/oz.). A single plant of the American ragweed can generate 8,000,000,000 pollen grains in five hours.

Most viable
The most protracted claim for the viability of seeds are those of the Arctic lupin (*Lupinus arcticus*) found in frozen silt at Miller Creek in the Yukon, Canada in July 1954. They were germinated in 1966 and were dated by the radio carbon method of associated material to at least 8,000 B.C. and more probably to 13,000 B.C.

Most Conquering Conker
The highest recorded battle honours for an untreated conker (fruit of the Common horse-chestnut or *Aesculus hippo-*

castanum) is a "five thousander plus", which won the BBC Conker Conquest in 1954. A professor of botany has however opined that this heroic specimen might well have been a "ringer", probably an ivory or tagua nut (*Phytelephas macrocarpa*).

KINGDOM PROTISTA

PROTISTA
Protista were first discovered in 1676 by Anton van Leeuwenhoek of Delft (1632–1723), a Dutch microscopist. Among Protista are characteristics common to both plants and animals. The more plant-like are termed Protophyta (protophytes), including unicellular algae, and the more animal-like are placed in the phylum Protozoa (protozoans), including amoeba and flagellates.

Largest
The largest protozoans which are known to have existed were the now extinct Nummulites, which each had a diameter of 0.95 in *24,1 mm*. The largest existing protozoan is *Pelomyxa palustris*, which may attain a length of up to 0.6 of an in *15,2 mm*.

Smallest
The smallest of all protophytes is *Micromonas pusilla*, with a diameter of less than 2 microns or micrometres (2×10^{-6}m) or *0.00008 of an in*.

Fastest moving
The protozoan *Monas stigmatica* has been measured to move a distance equivalent to 40 times its own length in a second. No human can cover even seven times his own length in a second.

Fastest reproduction
The protozoan *Glaucoma*, which reproduces by binary fission, divides as frequently as every three hours. Thus in the course of a day it could become a "six greats grandparent" and the progenitor of 510 descendants.

KINGDOM FUNGI

Largest
The largest recorded specimen of the giant puff ball (*Lycoperdon giganlea*) was one 62 in *157 cm* in diameter and 18 in *45,5 cm* high found at Mellor, Derbyshire in 1971. A flatter specimen 64 in *162,5 cm* in diameter was recorded in New York State, U.S.A. in 1877. A 72 lb *32,6 kg* example of the edible mushroom (*Polyporus frondosus*) was reported by Joseph Opple near Solon, Ohio in Sept. 1976.

The largest officially recorded tree fungus was a specimen of *Oxyporus* (*Fomes*) *nobilissimus*, measuring 56 in *142 cm* by 37 in *94 cm* and weighing at least 300 lb. *136 kg* found by J. Hisey in Washington State, U.S.A., in 1946. The largest recorded in the United Kingdom is an ash fungus (*Fomes fraxineus*) measuring 50 in by 15 in *127 cm* by *38 cm* wide, found by the forester A. D. C. LeSueur on a tree at Waddesdon, Buckinghamshire, in 1954.

Most poisonous toadstool
The yellowish-olive death cap (*Amanita phalloides*) is regarded as the world's most poisonous fungus. It is found in England. From six to fifteen hours after tasting, the effects are vomiting, delirium, collapse and death. Among its victims was Cardinal Giulio de' Medici, Pope Clement VII (b. 1478) on 25 Sept. 1534.

The Registrar General's Report states that between 1920 and 1950 there were 39 fatalities from fungus poisoning in the United Kingdom. As the poisonous types are mostly *Amanita* varieties, it is reasonable to assume that the deaths were predominantly due to *Amanita phalloides*. The most recent fatality was probably in 1960.

KINGDOM FUNGI/PROCARYOTA

Aeroflora
Fungi were once classified in the subkingdom Protophyta of the Kingdom Protista. The highest total fungal spore count was 161,037 per m³ near Cardiff on 21 July 1971. A plant tree pollen count of 2,160 per m³ was recorded near London on 9 May 1971. The lowest counts of airborne allergens are nil. The highest recorded grass pollen count in Britain was one of 2,824 per m³ recorded at Aberystwyth on 29 June 1961.

KINGDOM PROCARYOTA

Earliest Life Form
Spherical Microfossils, unicellular and physically similar to blue-green algae, *Aphanocapsa*, were reported by Dr. Elso S. Barghoorn of Harvard University and Dr. Andrew H. Knoll in October 1977 in chert dateable to 3,400 million years ago, 12 miles *19,3 km* south-west of Barberton, South Africa. Their average diameter is 2.5 microns. There is some evidence that life-forms were first existent even 500 million years earlier.

The earliest life-form reported from Britain is *Kakabekia barghoorniana*, a microorganism similar in form to an orange slice, found near Harlech, Gwynedd, Wales in 1964 and dated to 2,000 million years ago.

BACTERIA
Anton van Leeuwenhoek (1632–1723) was the first to observe bacteria in 1675. The largest of the bacteria is the sulphur bacterium *Beggiatoa mirabilis*, which is from 16 to 45 microns in width and which may form filaments several millimetres long.

Smallest Free-Living Entity
The smallest of all free-living organisms are pleuro-pneumonia-like organisms (P.P.L.O.) of the *Mycoplasma*. One of these, *Mycoplasma laidlawii*, first discovered in sewage in 1936, has a diameter during its early existence of only 100 millimicrons, or 0.000004 of an in. Examples of the strain known as H.39 have a maximum diameter of 300 millimicrons and weigh an estimated 1.0×10^{-16} of a gramme. Thus a 174 ton *177 tonnes* Blue whale would weigh 1.77×10^{23} or 177,000 trillion times as much.

Highest
In April 1967 the U.S. National Aeronautics and Space Administration reported that bacteria had been recently discovered at an altitude of 135,000 ft (25.56 miles) *41 100 m*.

Longest lived
The oldest deposits from which living bacteria are claimed to have been extracted are salt layers near Irkutsk, U.S.S.R., dating from about 600,000,000 years ago. The discovery was not accepted internationally. The U.S. Dry Valley Drilling Project in Antarctica claimed resuscitated rod-shaped bacteria from caves up to a million years old.

Toughest
The bacterium *Micrococcus radiodurans* can withstand atomic radiation of 6.5 million röntgens or 10,000 times that fatal to the average man.

VIRUSES
Largest
Viruses were discovered by Dmitriy Ivanovsky (1864–1920) in 1892. The largest true viruses are the brick-shaped pox viruses (*e.g.* smallpox, vaccina, orf etc.) measuring *c.* 250 × 300 nm (1 nanometer $= 1 \times 10^{-9}$m).

Smallest
Of more than 1,000 identified viruses, the smallest is the sheep scrapie virus with a diameter of 14 nanometers or 14 millionths of a millimetre. Some 40 times smaller still is the nanovariant WSI RNA with a length of 91 nucleotides published by Dr. Walter Schaffner of the University of Zürich in 1977.

PARKS, ZOOS, OCEANARIA and AQUARIA

PARKS, ZOOS, OCEANARIA AND AQUARIA

PARKS
Largest *World*
The world's largest park is the Wood Buffalo National Park in Alberta, Canada (established 1922), which has an area of 11,172,000 acres (17,560 miles² *45 480 km²*).

Largest *Britain*
The largest National Park in Great Britain is the Lake District National Park which has an area of 866 miles² *2 240 km²*. The largest private park in the United Kingdom is Woburn Park (3,000 acres *1 200 ha*), near Woburn Abbey, the seat of the Dukes of Bedford. The largest common in the United Kingdom is Llansantffraed Cwmdauddwr (28,819 acres *11 662 ha*) in Powys, Wales.

ZOOS
Largest game reserve
It has been estimated that throughout the world there are some 500 zoos with an estimated annual attendance of 330,000,000. The largest zoological reserve in the world has been the Etosha Reserve, Namibia established in 1907 with an area which grew to 38,427 miles² *99 525 km²*.

Oldest
The earliest known collection of animals was that set up by Shulgi, a 3rd dynasty ruler of Ur in 2094-2047 B.C. at Puzurish in south-east Iraq. The oldest known zoo is that at Schönbrunn, Vienna, Austria, built in 1752 by the Holy Roman Emperor Franz I for his wife Maria Theresa. The oldest privately owned zoo in the world is that of the Zoological Society of London, founded in 1826. Its collection, housed partly in Regent's Park, London (36 acres *14,5 ha*) and partly at Whipsnade Park, Bedfordshire (541 acres *219 ha*), (opened 23 May 1931) is the most comprehensive in the United Kingdom. The stocktaking on 1 Jan. 1979 accounted for a total of 11,035 specimens. These comprised 2,102 mammals, 2,118 birds, 657 reptiles and amphibians, an estimated total of 2,920 fish and an estimated total of 3,238 invertebrates. Locusts, ants and bees are excluded from these figures. The record annual attendances are 3,031,571 in 1950 for Regent's Park and 756,758 in 1961 for Whipsnade.

OCEANARIA
Earliest and Largest
The world's first oceanarium is Marineland of Florida, opened in 1938 at a site 18 miles *29 km* south of St. Augustine, Florida, U.S.A. Up to 5,800,000 gal *26,3 million litres* of sea-water are pumped daily through two major tanks, one rectangular (100 ft *30,48 m* long by 40 ft *12,19 m* wide by 18 ft *5,48 m* deep) containing 375,000 gal *1,7 million litres* and one circular (233 ft *71 m* in circumference and 12 ft *3,65 m* deep) containing 330,000 gal *1,5 million litres*. The tanks are seascaped, including coral reefs and even a shipwreck. The salt water tank at Hanna-Barbera's Marineland, located on the Palos Verdes Peninsula, U.S.A. is 251½ ft *76,65 m* in circumference and 22 ft *6,7 m* deep, with a capacity of 530,000 gal *2,4 million litres*. The total capacity of this whole oceanarium is 2,080,000 gal *9,4 million litres*. Their killer whale *Orky* at 14,000 lb *6 350 kg* is the largest in captivity.

AQUARIA
Largest aquarium
The world's largest aquarium, as opposed to fish farm, is the John G. Shedd Aquarium at 12th Street and Lake Shore Drive, Chicago, Illinois, U.S.A. completed in November 1929 at a cost of $3,250,000 (then £668,725). The total capacity of its display tanks is 375,000 gal *1,7 million litres* with reservoir tanks holding 1,665,000 gal *7,5 million litres*. Exhibited are 5,500 specimens from 350 species. Most of these specimens are collected by the Aquarium collecting boat based in Miami, Florida, and are shipped by air to Chicago. The record attendances are 78,658 in a day on 21 May 1931, and 4,689,730 visitors in the single year of 1931.

THE NATURAL WORLD

3

THE EARTH

The Earth is not a true sphere, but flattened at the poles and hence an ellipsoid. The polar diameter of the Earth (7,899.809 miles *12 713,510 km*) is 26.576 miles *42,770 km* less than the equatorial diameter (7,926.385 miles *12 756,280 km*). The Earth also has a slight ellipticity of the equator since its long axis (about longitude 37° W) is 174 yds *159 m* greater than the short axis. The greatest departures from the reference ellipsoid are a protuberance of 244 ft *74 m* in the area of Papua/New Guinea and a depression of 354 ft *108 m* south of Sri Lanka, in the Indian Ocean.

The greatest circumference of the Earth, at the equator, is 24,901.47 miles *40 075,03 km*, compared with 24,859.75 miles *40 007,89 km* at the meridian. The area of the surface is estimated to be 196,937,600 miles^2 *510 066 100 km^2*. The period of axial rotation, *i.e.* the true sidereal day, is 23 hrs 56 min 4.0996 sec, mean time.

The mass of the Earth is 5,880,000,000,000,000,000,000 tons *5 974 × 10^{18} tonnes* and its density is 5.515 times that of water. The volume is an estimated 259,875,620,000 miles^3 *1 083 208 840 000 km^3*. The Earth picks up cosmic dust but estimates vary widely with 30,000 tons/*tonnes* a year being the upper limit. Modern theory is that the Earth has an outer shell or lithosphere about 25 miles *40 km* thick, then an outer and inner rock layer or mantle extending 1,800 miles *2 900 km* deep, beneath which there is an iron-nickel core at an estimated temperature of 3 700° C *6,700° F*, and at a pressure of 22,000 tons/*tonnes* per in^2 or 3,400 kb. If the iron-nickel core theory is correct, iron must be by far the most abundant element in the Earth.

1. WEATHER

Guinness Superlatives Ltd. published in 1977 a more specialist volume entitled the *Guinness Book of Weather Facts and Feats* by Ingrid Holford (Price £6.50).

The meteorological records given below necessarily relate largely to the last 130 to 150 years, since data before that time are both sparse and unreliable. Reliable registering thermometers were introduced as recently as *c*. 1820. The longest continuous observations have been maintained at the Radcliffe Observatory, Oxford since 1815.

Palaeo-entomological evidence is that there was a southern European climate in England *c*. 90,000 B.C., while in *c*. 6,000 B.C. the mean summer temperature reached 67° F 19,4° C, or 6 deg F 3,3 *deg C* higher than the present. The earliest authentic British weather records relate to the period 26 Aug.—17 Sept. 55 B.C. The earliest reliably known hot summer was in A.D. 664 during our driest ever century and the earliest known severe winter was that of A.D. 763–4. In 1683–84 there was frost in London from November to April. Frosts were recorded during August in the period 1668–89.

Progressive extremes
The world's extremes of temperature have been noted progressively thus:

PROGRESSIVE LIST OF WORLD'S EXTREME HIGH TEMPERATURES

127.4° F	53,0° C	Ouargla, Algeria	27 Aug. 1884
130° F	54,4° C	Amos, California, U.S.A.	17 Aug. 1885
130° F	54,4° C	Mammoth Tank, California, U.S.A.	17 Aug. 1885
134° F	56,7° C	Death Valley, California, U.S.A.	10 July 1913
136.4° F	58,0° C	Al'Aziziyah (el-Azizia), Libya*	13 Sept. 1922

* Obtained by the U.S. National Geographical Society but not officially recognized by the Libyan Ministry of Communications.

A reading of 140° F 60° C at Delta, Mexico, in August 1953 is not now accepted because of over-exposure to roof radiation. The official Mexican record of 136.4° F 58,0° C at San Luis, Sonora on 11 Aug. 1933 is not internationally accepted.

A freak heat flash reported from Coimbra, Portugal, in September 1933 said to have caused the temperature to rise to 70° C 158° F for 120 seconds is apocryphal.

PROGRESSIVE LIST OF WORLD'S EXTREME LOW TEMPERATURES

−73° F	−58,3° C	Floeberg Bay, Ellesmere I., Canada	1852
−90.4° F	−68° C	Verkhoyansk, Siberia, U.S.S.R.	3 Jan. 1885
−90.4° F	−68° C	Verkhoyansk, Siberia U.S.S.R.	5 & 7 Feb. 1892
−90.4° F	−68° C	Oymyakon, Siberia, U.S.S.R.	6 Feb. 1933
−100.4° F	−73,5° C	South Pole, Antarctica	11 May 1957
−102.1° F	−74,5° C	South Pole, Antarctica	17 Sept. 1957
−109.1° F	−78,34° C	Sovietskaya, Antarctica	2 May 1958
−113.3° F	−80,7° C	Vostok, Antarctica	15 June 1958
−114.1° F	−81,2° C	Sovietskaya, Antarctica	19 June 1958
−117.4° F	−83,0° C	Sovietskaya, Antarctica	25 June 1958
−122.4° F	−85,7° C	Vostok, Antarctica	7–8 Aug. 1958
−124.1° F	−86,7° C	Sovietskaya, Antarctica	9 Aug. 1958
−125.3° F	−87,4° C	Vostok, Antarctica	25 Aug. 1958
−126.9° F	−88,3° C	Vostok, Antarctica	24 Aug. 1960

Most equable temperature
The location with the most equable recorded temperature over a short period is Garapan, on Saipan, in the Mariana Islands, Pacific Ocean. During the nine years from 1927 to 1935, inclusive, the lowest temperature recorded was 19,6° C 67.3° F on 30 Jan. 1934 and the highest was 31,4° C 88.5° F

WEATHER RECORDS

1. **HIGHEST SHADE TEMPERATURE:** *World* 136.4° F *58° C* Al'Aziziyah, Libya, 13.9.1922. *UK & Ireland* 98° F <37° C Raunds Northants; Epsom, Surrey and Canterbury, Kent 9.8.1911(a)

2. **LOWEST SCREEN TEMPERATURE:** *World* —126.9° F —*88,3° C* Vostok, Antarctica, 24.8.1960(b). *UK & Ireland* —17° F —*27,2° C*, Braemar, Grampian, Scotland, 11.2.1895(c)

3. **GREATEST RAINFALL** (24 hours): *World* 73.62 in *1 870 mm*, Cilaos, La Reunion, Indian Ocean, 15–16.3.1952(d) *UK & Ireland* 11.00 in *279 mm*, Martinstown, Dorset, 18–19.7.1955

4. **GREATEST RAINFALL** (Calendar Month): *World* 366.14 in *9 299 mm*, Cherrapunji, Meghalaya, India, July 1861 *UK & Ireland* 56.54 in *1 436 mm*, Llyn Llydau, Snowdon, Gwynedd, October 1909

   GREATEST RAINFALL (12 months): *World* 1,041.78 in *26 461 mm*, Cherrapunji, Meghalaya, 1.8.1860–31.7.1861 *UK & Ireland* 257.0 in *6 527 mm*, Sprinkling Tarn, Cumbria, in 1954(e)

5. **GREATEST SNOWFALL** (f) (12 months): *World* 1,224.5 in *31 102 mm*, Paradise, Mt. Rainier, Washington, U.S.A. 19.2.1971 to 18.2.1972 *UK & Ireland* 60 in *1 524 mm*, Upper Teesdale and Denbighshire Hills, Clwyd, Wales, 1947

6. **MAXIMUM SUNSHINE:**(g) *World* 97%+ (over 4,300 hours), eastern Sahara, annual average *UK & Ireland* 78.3% (382 hours) Pendennis Castle, Falmouth, Cornwall, June 1925

7. **MINIMUM SUNSHINE:** *World* Nil at North Pole—for winter stretches of 186 days *UK & Ireland* Nil in a month at Westminster, London, in December, 1890(h)

8. **BAROMETRIC PRESSURE** (Highest): *World* 1,083.8 mb. (*32.00 in*), Agata Siberia, U.S.S.R. (alt. 862 ft *262 m*), 31.12.1968. *UK & Ireland* 1,054.7 mb. (*31.15 in*), Aberdeen, 31.1.1902

9. **BAROMETRIC PRESSURE** (Lowest):(j) *World* 876 mb. (*25.87 in*), 240 miles *390 km* west of Guam, Pacific Ocean, 19.11.1975 *UK & Ireland* 925.5 mb. (*27.33 in*), Ochtertyre, near Crieff, Tayside, 26.1.1884

10. **HIGHEST SURFACE WIND-SPEED:**(k) *World* 231 m.p.h *371 kmlh*, Mt. Washington (6,288 ft *1 916 m*), New Hampshire, U.S.A., 12.4.1934 *UK & Ireland* 144 m.p.h. *231 kmlh* (125 knots), Coire Cas ski lift (3,525 ft *1 074 m*), Cairn Gorm, Highland, 6.3.1967(l)

11. **THUNDER-DAYS** (Year):(m) *World* 322 days, Bogor (formerly Buitenzorg), Java, Indonesia (average, 1916–19) *UK & Ireland* 38 days, Stonyhurst, Lancashire, 1912 and Huddersfield, West Yorkshire, 1967

12. **HOTTEST PLACE** (Annual mean):(n) *World* Dallol, Ethiopia, 94° F *34,4° C* (1960–66) *UK & Ireland* Penzance, Cornwall, and Isles of Scilly, both 52.7° F *11,5° C*, average 1931–60

13. **COLDEST PLACE** (Annual mean): *World* Polus Nedostupnosti, Pole of Cold (78° S., 96° E.), Antarctica, —72° F —*57,8° C UK & Ireland* Dalwhinnie, Highland 43° F *6,1° C* (alt. 1,151 ft *351 m*)

14. **WETTEST PLACE** (Annual mean): *World* Mt. Wai-'ale-'ale (5,148 ft *1 569 m*), Kauai, Hawaii, 451 in *11 455 mm* (average 1920–72). In 1948 621 in *15 773 mm UK & Ireland* Styhead Tarn (1,600 ft *487 m*), Cumbria, 172.9 in *4 391 mm*

14. **MOST RAINY DAYS** (Year): *World* Mt. Wai-'ale-'ale up to 350 per annum *UK & Ireland* Ballynahinch, Galway, 309 days in 1923

15. **DRIEST PLACE** (Annual mean): *World* Nil—In the Desierto de Atacama, near Calama, Chile *UK & Ireland* Great Wakering, Essex, 19.2 in *487 mm* (1916–50)(o)

15. **LONGEST DROUGHT:** *World* c. 400 years to 1971, Desierto de Atacama, Chile *UK & Ireland* 73 days, Mile End, Greater London, 4.3 to 15.5 1893(p)

16. **HEAVIEST HAILSTONES:**(q) *World* 1.67 lb. *750 g* (7½ in *19 cm* diameter, 17½ in *44,45 cm* circumference), Coffeyville, Kansas, U.S.A, 3.9.1970 *UK and Ireland* 5 oz. *141 g*, Horsham, West Sussex, 5.9.1958

17. **LONGEST SEA LEVEL FOGS** (Visibility less than 1,000 yds *914,4 m*): *World* Fogs persist for weeks on the Grand Banks, Newfoundland, Canada, and the average is more than 120 days per year(r) *UK & Ireland* London duration record was 26.11 to 1.12.1948 and 5.12 to 9.12.1952 (both 4 days 18 hours)

18. **WINDIEST PLACE:** *World* The Commonwealth Bay, George V Coast, Antarctica, where gales reach 200 m.p.h. *320 kmlh UK & Ireland* Tiree, Strathclyde (89 ft *27 m*); annual average 17.4 m.p.h. *28 kmlh*. Data awaited for Fair Isle

EQUATOR

Footnotes to table

(a) *The 101.5° F 38,6 ° C reported from Tonbridge, Kent was a non-standard exposure and is estimated to be equivalent of 97–98° F 36–36,7° C*

(b) *Vostok is 11,220 ft 3 419 m above sea-level. The coldest permanently inhabited place is the Siberian village of Oymyakon (63° 16′ N., 143° 15′ E.), in the U.S.S.R. where the temperature reached –96° F –71,1° C in 1964.*

(c) *The –23° F –30,5° C at Blackadder, Borders, on 4 Dec. 1879, and the –20° F –28,9° C at Grantown-on-Spey on 24 Feb. 1955, were not standard exposures. The –11° F –23,9° C reported from Buxton, Derbyshire on 11 Feb. 1895 was not standard. The lowest official temperature in England is –6° F –21,1° C at Bodiam, West Sussex on 20 Jan. 1940, at Ambleside, Cumbria on 21 Jan. 1940 and at Houghall, Durham on 5 Jan. 1941 and 4 March 1947.*

(d) *This is equal to 7,435 tons 7 554 tonnes of rain per acre. Elevation 1 200 m 3,937 ft.*

(e) *The record for Ireland is 145.4 in 3 921 mm near Derriana Lough, County Kerry in 1948.*

(f) *The record for a single snow storm is 189 in 4 800 mm at Mt. Shasta, Ski Bowl, California, and for 24 hr, 76 in 1 930 mm at Silver Lake, Colorado, U.S.A. on 14–15 April 1921. The greatest depth of snow on the ground was 25 ft 5 in 7,74 m at Paradise on 17 Apr. 1972. London's earliest recorded snow was on 25 Sept. 1885, and the latest on 27 May 1821. Less reliable reports suggest snow on 12 Sept. 1658 (Old Style) and on 12 June 1791.*

(g) *St. Petersburg, Florida, U.S.A., recorded 768 consecutive sunny days from 9 Feb. 1967 to 17 March 1969.*

(h) *The south-eastern end of the village of Lochranza, Isle of Arran, Strathclyde is in shadow of mountains from 18 Nov. to 8 Feb. each winter.*

(j) *The U.S.S. Repose, a hospital ship, recorded 25.55 inches 856 mb. in the eye of a typhoon in 25° 35′ N 128° 20′ E off Okinawa on 16 Sept. 1945.*

(k) *The highest speed yet measured in a tornado is 280 m.p.h. 450 km/h at Wichita Falls, Texas, U.S.A., on 2 April 1958.*

(l) *The figure of 177.2 m.p.h. 285.2 km/h at R.A.F. Saxa Vord, Unst, in the Shetlands, Scotland, on 16 Feb. 1962, was not recorded with standard equipment There were gales of great severity on 15 Jan. 1362 and 26 Nov. 1703.*

(m) *Between Lat. 35° N. and 35° S. there are some 3,200 thunderstorms each 12 night-time hrs, some of which can be heard at a range of 18 miles 29 km.*

(n) *In Death Valley, California, U.S.A., maximum temperatures of over 120° F 48,9° C were recorded on 43 consecutive days—6 July to 17 Aug. 1917. At Marble Bar, Western Australia (maximum 121° F 49,4° C) 160 consecutive days with maximum temperatures of over 100° F 37,8° C were recorded—31 Oct. 1923 to 7 April 1924 at Wyndham, Western Australia, the temperature reached 90° F 32,2° C or more on 333 days in 1946.*

(o) *The lowest rainfall recorded in a single year was 9.29 in 23,6 cm at one station in Margate, Kent in 1921.*

(p) *The longest drought in Scotland was one of 38 days at Port William, Dumfries & Galloway on 3 Apr. to 10 May 1938.*

(q) *Much heavier hailstones are sometimes reported. These are usually not single but coalesced stones. An ice block of 1 to 2 kg 35–70 oz. was reputed at Withington, Manchester on 2 Apr. 1973.*

(r) *Lower visibilities occur at higher altitudes. Ben Nevis is reputedly in cloud 300 days per year.*

on 9 Sept. 1931, giving an extreme range of 11,8 deg C *21.2 deg F*. Between 1911 and 1966 the Brazilian off-shore island of Fernando de Noronha had a minimum temperature of 18,6° C *65.5° F* on 17 Nov. 1913 and a maximum of 32,0° C *89.6° F* on 2 March 1965, an extreme range of 13,4 deg C *24.1 deg F*.

Greatest temperature ranges

The great recorded temperature ranges in the world are around the Siberian "cold pole" in the eastern U.S.S.R. Verkhoyansk (67° 33′ N., 133° 23′ E.) has ranged 192 deg F *106,7 deg C* from –94° F *–70° C* (unofficial) to 98° F *36,7° C*.

The greatest temperature variation recorded in a day is 100 deg F *55,5 deg C* (a fall from 44° F *6,7° C* to –56° F *–48,8° C*) at Browning, Montana, U.S.A., on 23–24 Jan. 1916. The most freakish rise was 49 deg F *27,2 deg C* in 2 min at Spearfish, South Dakota, from –4° F *–20° C* at 7.30 a.m. to 45° F *7,2° C* at 7.32 a.m. on 22 Jan. 1943. The British record is 29 deg C *52.2 deg F* (–7° C *19.4° F* to 22° C *71.6° F*) at Tummel Bridge, Tayside on 9 May 1978.

Longest freeze

The longest recorded unremitting freeze (maximum temperature 32° F *0° C* and below) in the British Isles was one of 34 days at Moor House, Cumbria, from 23 Dec. 1962 to 25 Jan. 1963. This was almost certainly exceeded at the neighbouring Great Dun Fell, where the screen temperature never rose above freezing during the whole of January 1963. Less rigorous early data includes a frost from 5 Dec. 1607 to 14 Feb. 1608 and a 91 day frost on Dartmoor, Devon in 1854–55. No temperature lower than 34° F *1° C* has ever been recorded on Bishop Rock, Isles of Scilly.

Upper atmosphere

The lowest temperature ever recorded in the atmosphere is –143° C *–225.4° F* at an altitude of about 50 to 60 miles

80,5–96,5 km, during noctilucent cloud research above Kronogård, Sweden, from 27 July to 7 Aug. 1963. A jet stream moving at 408 m.p.h. *656 km/h* at 154,200 ft *47 000 m* (29.2 miles *46 km*) was recorded by Skua rocket above South Uist, Outer Hebrides, Scotland on 13 Dec. 1967.

Deepest permafrost

The greatest recorded depth of permafrost is 1,5 km *4,920 ft* reported in April 1968 in the basin of the River Lena, Siberia, U.S.S.R.

Most recent White Christmas and Frost Fair

London has experienced seven "White" Christmas Days since 1900. These have been 1906, 1917 (slight), 1923 (slight), 1927, 1938, 1956 (slight) and 1970. These were more frequent in the 19th century and even more so before the change of the calendar, which, by removing 3–13 Sept. brought forward all dates subsequent to 2 Sept. 1752 by 11 days. The last of the nine recorded Frost Fairs held on the Thames since 1564/65 was in Dec. 1813 to 26 Jan. 1814.

Most intense rainfall

Difficulties attend rainfall readings for very short periods but the figure of 1.50 in *38,1 mm* in 1 min at Barst, Guadaloupe on 26 Nov. 1970, is regarded as the most intense recorded in modern times. The cloudburst of "near 2 ft *609 mm* in less than a quarter of half an hour" at Oxford on the afternoon of 31 May (Old Style) 1682 is regarded as unacademically recorded. The most intense rainfall in Britain recorded to modern standards has been 2.0 in *51 mm* in 12 min at Wisbech, Cambridgeshire on 28 June 1970.

Falsest St. Swithin's Days

The legend that the weather on St. Swithin's Day, celebrated on 15 July (Old and New Style) since A.D. 912, determines the rainfall for the next 40 days is one which has long persisted. There was a brilliant 13½ hrs sunshine in London on 15 July 1924, but 30 of the next 40 days were wet. On 15 July 1913 there was a 15 hour downpour, yet it rained on only 9 of the subsequent 40 days in London.

Best and worst British summers

According to Prof. Gordon Manley's survey over the period 1728 to 1978 the best (i.e. driest and hottest) British summer was that of 1976 and the worst (i.e. wettest and coldest) that of 1879. Temperatures of >32° C (89.8° F) were recorded on 15 consecutive days (25 June–7 July 1976) within Great Britain including 7 such consecutive days in Cheltenham (1–7 July), where 35,9° C *96.6° F* was reached on 3 July.

Humidity and discomfort

Human comfort or discomfort depends not merely on temperature but on the combination of temperature, humidity, radiation and wind-speed. The United States Weather Bureau uses a Temperature-Humidity Index, which equals two-fifths of the sum of the dry and wet bulb thermometer readings plus 15. A THI of 98.2 has been twice recorded in Death Valley, California—on 27 July 1966 (119° F and 31 %) and on 12 Aug. 1970 (117° F and 37 %). A person driving at 45 mph *72 km/h* in a car without a windscreen in a temperature of –45° F *–42,7° C* would, by the chill factor, experience the equivalent of –125° F *–87,2° C*, i.e. within 2 deg F *1,1 deg C* of the world record.

Largest Mirage

The largest mirage on record was that sighted in the Arctic at 83° N 103° W by Donald B. MacMillan in 1913. This type of mirage known as the Fata Morgana appeared as the same "Hills, valleys, snow-capped peaks extending through at least 120 degrees of the horizon" that Peary had named Crocker Land 6 years earlier. On 17 July 1939 a mirage of Snaefells Jokull (4,715 ft *1 437 m*) on Iceland was seen from the sea when 335–350 miles *539–563 km* distant.

Lightning

The visible length of lightning strokes varies greatly. In mountainous regions, when clouds are very low, the flash may be less than 300 ft *91 m* long. In flat country with very high clouds, a cloud-to-earth flash sometimes measures 4 miles *6 km* though in extreme cases such flashes have been measured at 20 miles *32 km*. The intensely bright central core of the lightning channel is extremely narrow. Some authorities suggest that its diameter is as little as half an inch *1,27 cm*. This core is surrounded by a "corona envelope" (glow discharge) which may measure 10 to 20 ft *3–6 m* in diameter.

The speed of a lightning discharge varies from 100 to 1,000 miles/sec *160 to 1 600 km/sec* for the downward leader track, and reaches up to 87,000 miles/sec *140 000 km/sec* (nearly half the speed of light) for the powerful return stroke. In Britain there is an average of 6 strikes/mile² per annum or 3,7 per km² and an average of 4,200 per annum over Greater London alone. Every few million strokes there is a giant discharge, in which the cloud-to-earth and the return lightning strokes flash from the top of the thunder clouds. In these "positive giants" energy of up to 3,000 million joules (3×10^{16} ergs) is sometimes recorded. The temperature reaches about 30,000° C, which is more than five times greater than that of the surface of the Sun. A theory that lightning was triggered by cosmic rays was published in 1977.

Highest waterspout
The highest waterspout of which there is a reliable record was one observed on 16 May 1898 off Eden, New South Wales, Australia. A theodolite reading from the shore gave its height as 5,014 ft *1 528 m*. It was about 10 ft *3 m* in diameter. A waterspout moved around Torbay, Devon on 17 Sept. 1969 which was according to press estimates 1,000 ft *300 m* in height.

Cloud extremes
The highest standard cloud form is cirrus, averaging 27,000 ft *8 250 m* and above, but the rare nacreous or mother-of-pearl formation sometimes reaches nearly 80,000 ft *24 000 m* (see also Noctilucent clouds, Chapter 4). The lowest is stratus, below 3,500 ft *1 066 m*. The cloud form with the greatest vertical range is cumulo-nimbus, which has been observed to reach a height of nearly 68,000 ft *20 000 m* in the tropics.

Tornadoes
Britain's strongest tornado was at Southsea, Portsmouth on 14 Dec. 1810 (Force 8 on the Meaden-TORRO scale). On 19 Oct. 1870 fifteen were reported in one day. The Newmarket tornado (Force 6) of 3 Jan. 1878 caused property damage estimated at up to £1,000,000.

---

2. NATURAL PHENOMENA

EARTHQUAKES
(Note: Seismologists record all dates with the year first, based not on local time but on Greenwich Mean Time)

Greatest *World*
It is estimated that each year there are some 500,000 detectable seismic or micro-seismic disturbances of which 100,000 can be felt and 1,000 cause damage.

Using the new Seismic moment magnitudes (defined in 1977), the world's strongest assessable earthquake has been the cataclysmic Lebu Shock, south of Concepción, Chile on 1960 May 22 assessed at 9.5.

Worst death roll *World*
The greatest loss of life occurred in the earthquake (*ti chen*) in the Shensi, Shansi and Honan provinces of China, of 1556 Feb. 2, (new style) (Jan 23 o.s.) when an estimated 830,000 people were killed. The highest death roll in modern times has been in the Tangshan 'quake (Mag. 8.2) in Eastern China on 1976 July 27 (local time was 3 a.m. July 28). A first figure published on 4 Jan. 1977 revealed 655,237 killed, later adjusted to 750,000. The greatest material damage was in the 'quake on the Kwanto plain, Japan, of 1923 Sept. 1 (Mag. 8.2, epicentre in Lat. 35° 15′ N., Long. 139° 30′ E.). In Sagami Bay the sea-bottom in one area sank 400 m *1,310 ft*. The official total of persons killed and missing in the *Shinsai* or great 'quake and the resultant fires was 142,807. In Tōkyō and Yokohama 575,000 dwellings were destroyed. The cost of the damage was estimated at £1,000 million (now more than £4,000 million).

Worst death roll *Great Britain and Ireland*
The East Anglian or Colchester earthquake of 1884 April 22 (9.18 a.m.) (epicentres Lat. 51° 48′ N., Long. 0° 53′ E., and Lat. 51° 51′ N., Long 0° 55′ E.) caused damage estimated at £10,000 to 1,200 buildings, and according to *The Great English Earthquake* by Peter Haining, the death of at least 3 and possibly 5 people. Langenhoe Church was wrecked. Windows and doors were rattled over an area of 53,000 miles² *137 250 km²* and the shock was felt in Exeter and Ostend, Belgium. The most marked since 1884 and the worst since instruments have been in use (*i.e.* since 1927) occurred in the Midlands at 3.43 p.m. on 1957 Feb. 11, showing a strength of between five and six on the Davison scale. The strongest Scottish tremor occurred at Inverness at 10.45 p.m. on 1816 Aug. 13, and was felt over an area of 50,000 miles² *130 000 km²*. The strongest Welsh tremor occurred in Swansea at 9.45 a.m. on 1906 June 27 (epicentre Lat. 51° 38′ N., Long. 4° W.). It was felt over an area of 37,800 miles² *97 900 km²*. No earthquake with its epicentre in Ireland has ever been instrumentally measured, though the effects of remoter shocks have been felt. However, there was a shock in 1734 August which damaged 100 dwellings and five churches.

VOLCANOES
The total number of known active volcanoes in the world is 455 with an estimated 80 more that are submarine. The greatest active concentration is in Indonesia, where 77 of its 167 volcanoes have erupted within historic times. The name volcano derives from the now dormant Vulcano Island (from the God of fire Vulcanus) in the Aeolian group in the Mediterranean.

Greatest eruption
The total volume of matter discharged in the eruption of Tambora, a volcano on the island of Sumbawa, in Indonesia, 5–7 Apr. 1815, has been estimated at 36.4 miles³ *151,7 km³* The energy of this eruption was 8.4 × 10^{26} ergs. The volcano lost about 4,100 ft *1 250 m* in height and a crater seven miles *11 km* in diameter was formed. This compares with a probable 15 miles³ *62,5 km³* ejected by Santoríni and 4.3 miles³ *18 km³* ejected by Krakatoa (see below). The internal pressure causing the Tambora eruption has been estimated at 46,500,000 lb./in² or more than 20,750 tons/in² *3 270 000 kg/cm²*.

Longest Lava Flow
The longest lava flow in historic times, known as *pahoehoe* (twisted cord-like solidifications), is that from the eruption of Laki in south-east Iceland which flowed 65–70 km *40.5–43.5 miles*. The largest known pre-historic flow is the Roza basalt flow in North America c. 15 million years ago, which had an unsurpassed length (480 km *300 miles*), area (40 000 km² *15,400 miles²*) and volume (1 250 km³ *300 miles³*).

Greatest explosion
The greatest explosion (possibly since Santoríni in the Aegean Sea c. 1470 B.C.) occurred at c. 10 a.m. (local time), or 3.00 a.m. G.M.T., on 27 Aug. 1883, with an eruption of Krakatoa, an island (then 18 miles² *47 km²*) in the Sunda Strait, between Sumatra and Java, in Indonesia. A total of 163 villages were wiped out, and 36,380 people killed by the wave it caused. Rocks were thrown 34 miles *55 km* high and dust fell 3,313 miles *5 330 km* away 10 days later. The explosion was recorded four hours later on the island of Rodrigues, 2,968 miles *4 776 km* away, as "the roar of heavy guns" and was heard over 1/13th part of the surface of the globe. This explosion has been estimated to have had about 26 times the power of the greatest H-bomb test detonation but was still only a fifth part of the Santoríni cataclysm.

Highest *Extinct*
The highest extinct volcano in the world is Cerro Aconcagua (stone centinel) (22,834 ft *6 960 m*) on the Argentine side of the Andes. It was first climbed on 14 Jan. 1897 by Mathias Zurbriggen and was the highest summit climbed anywhere until 12 June 1907.

The Nakwakto Rapids in Slingsby Channel, B.C., Canada are the strongest currents in the world. The flow rate can reach 16 knots *29,6 km/h* (see p. 64). (*Institute of Ocean Sciences*)

Highest *Dormant*

The highest dormant volcano is Volcán Llullaillaco (22,057 ft *6 723 m*), on the frontier between Chile and Argentina.

Highest *Active*

The highest volcano regarded as active is Volcán Antofalla (6 450 m *21,162 ft*), in Argentina, though a more definite claim is made for Volcán Guayatiri or Guallatiri (19,882 ft *6 060 m*), in Chile, which erupted in 1959.

Northernmost and southernmost

The northernmost volcano is Beeren Berg (7,470 ft *2 276 m*) on the island of Jan Mayen (71° 05′ N.) in the Greenland Sea. It erupted on 20 Sept. 1970 and the island's 39 inhabitants (all male) had to be evacuated. It was possibly discovered by Henry Hudson in 1607 or 1608, but definitely visited by Jan Jacobsz May (Netherlands) in 1614. It was annexed by Norway on 8 May 1929. The Ostenso seamount (5,825 ft *1 775 m*) 346 miles *556 km* from the North Pole in Lat. 85° 10′ N., Long 133° W was volcanic. The most southerly known active volcano is Mount Erebus (12,450 ft *3 795 m*) on Ross Island (77° 35′ S.), in Antarctica. It was discovered on 28 Jan. 1841 by the expedition of Captain (later Rear-Admiral Sir) James Clark Ross, R.N. (1800–1862), and first climbed at 10 a.m. on 10 March 1908 by a British party of five, led by Professor (later Lieut.-Col. Sir) Tannatt William Edgeworth David (1858–1934).

Largest crater

The world's largest *caldera* or volcano crater is that of Mount Aso (5,223 ft *1 590 m*) in Kyūshū, Japan, which measures 17 miles *27 km* north to south, 10 miles *16 km* east to west and 71 miles *114 km* in circumference.

GEYSERS

Tallest World

The Waimangu (Maori, *black water*) geyser, in New Zealand, erupted to a height in excess of 1,500 ft *457 m* in 1904, but has not been active since it erupted violently at 6.20 a.m. on 1 Apr. 1917 and killed 4 people. Currently the world's tallest active geyser is the U.S. National Parks' Service Steamboat Geyser, which from 1962–1969 erupted with intervals ranging from 5 days to 10 months to a height of 250–380 ft *76–115 m*. The greatest measured water discharge is 825,000 gals *37 850 hl* by the Giant Geyser, also in

Yellowstone National Park, Wyoming. The *Geysir* ("gusher") near Mount Hekla in south-central Iceland, from which all others have been named, spurts, on occasions, to 180 ft *55 m*, while the adjacent Strokkur, reactivated by drilling in 1963, spurts at 10 to 15 min intervals.

3. STRUCTURE AND DIMENSIONS

OCEANS

Largest

The area of the Earth covered by sea is estimated to be 139,670,000 miles² *361 740 000 km²* or 70.92 per cent of the total surface. The mean depth of the hydrosphere was once estimated to be 12,450 ft *3 795 m*, but recent surveys suggest a lower estimate, of 11,660 ft *3 554 m*. The total weight of the water is estimated to be 1.3×10^{18} tons, or 0.022 per cent of the Earth's total weight. The volume of the oceans is estimated to be 308,400,000 miles³ *1 285 600 000 km³* compared with only 8,400,000 miles³ *35 000 000 km³* of fresh water.

The largest ocean in the world is the Pacific. Excluding adjacent seas, it represents 45.8 per cent of the world's oceans and is about 63,800,000 miles² *165 250 000 km²* in area. The shortest navigable trans-Pacific distance from Guayaquil, Ecuador to Bangkok, Thailand is 10,905 miles *17 550 km*.

Deepest *World*

The deepest part of the ocean was first discovered in 1951 by H.M. Survey Ship *Challenger* in the Marianas Trench in the Pacific Ocean. The depth was measured by sounding and by echo-sounder and published as 5,960 fathoms (35,760 ft *10 900 m*). Subsequent visits to the Challenger Deep have resulted in claims by echo-sounder only, culminating in one of 6,033 fathoms (36,198 ft *11 033 m*) or 6.85 miles by the U.S.S.R.'s research ship *Vityaz* in March 1959. On 23 Jan. 1960 the U.S. Navy bathyscaphe *Trieste* descended to 35,820 ft *10 917 m*. A metal object, say a pound ball of steel, dropped into water above this trench would take nearly 63 min to fall to the sea-bed 6.85 miles *11,03 km* below. The average depth of the Pacific Ocean is 14,000 ft *4 267 m*.

Deepest *British waters*

The deepest point in the territorial waters of the United Kingdom is an area 6 cables (*1 100 m*) off the island of Raasay, Highland, in the Inner Sound at Lat. 57° 30' 33" N., Long. 5° 57' 27" W. A depth of 1,038 ft (173 fathoms, *316 m*) was found in Dec. 1959 by H.M.S. *Yarnton* (Lt.-Cdr. A. C. F. David, R. N.).

Largest sea

The largest of the world's seas is the South China Sea, with an area of 1,148,500 miles² *2 974 600 km²*. The Malayan Sea comprising the waters between the Indian Ocean and the South Pacific, south of the Chinese mainland covering 3,144,000 miles² *8 142 900 km²* is not now an entity accepted by the International Hydrographic Bureau.

Largest gulf

The largest gulf in the world is the Gulf of Mexico, with an area of 580,000 miles² *1 500 000 km²* and a shoreline of 3,100 miles *4 990 km* from Cape Sable, Florida, U.S.A., to Cabo Catoche, Mexico.

Largest bay

The largest bay in the world is Hudson Bay, northern Canada, with a shoreline of 7,623 miles *12 268 km* and with an area of 317,500 miles² *822 300 km²*. Great Britain's largest bay is Cardigan Bay which has a 140 mile *225 km* long shoreline and measures 72 miles *116 km* across from the Lleyn Peninsula, Gwynedd to St. David's Head, Dyfed in Wales.

Longest fjords and sea lochs *World*

The world's longest fjord is the Nordvest Fjord arm of the Scoresby Sund in eastern Greenland, which extends inland 195 miles *313 km* from the sea. The longest of Norwegian fjords is the Sogne Fjord, which extends 183 km *113.7 miles* inland from Sygnefest to the head of the Lusterfjord arm at Skjolden. It averages barely 4,75 km *3 miles* in width and has a deepest point of 1 245 m *4,085 ft*. If measured from Huglo along the Bømlafjord to the head of the Sørfjord arm at Odda, Hardangerfjorden can also be said to extend 183 km *113.7 miles*. The longest Danish fjord is Limfjorden (100 miles *160 km* long).

Longest fjords and sea lochs *Great Britain*

Scotland's longest sea loch is Loch Fyne, which extends 42 miles *67,5 km* inland into Strathclyde (formerly Argyllshire).

Highest seamount

The highest known submarine mountain, or seamount is one discovered in 1953 near the Tonga Trench, between Samoa and New Zealand. It rises 28,500 ft *8 690 m* from the sea bed, with its summit 1,200 ft *365 m* below the surface.

Remotest spot from land

The world's most distant point from land is a spot in the South Pacific, approximately 48° 30' S., 125° 30' W., which is about 1,660 miles *2 670 km* from the nearest points of land, namely Pitcairn Island, Ducie Island and Cape Dart, Antarctica. Centred on this spot, therefore, is a circle of water with an area of about 8,657,000 miles² *22 421 500 km²* —about 7,000 miles² *18 000 km²* larger than the U.S.S.R., the world's largest country (see Chapter 10).

Most southerly

The most southerly part of the oceans is 85° 34' S., 154° W., at the snout of the Robert Scott Glacier, 305 miles *490 km* from the South Pole.

Longest voyage

The longest possible great circle sea voyage is one of 19,860 miles *31 960 km* from a point 150 miles *240 km* west of Karachi, Pakistan to a point 200 miles *320 km* north of Uka' Kamchatka *via* the Mozambique Channel, Drake Passage and Bering Sea.

Sea temperature

The temperature of the water at the surface of the sea varies from −2° C *28.5° F* in the White Sea to 35,6° C *96° F* in the shallow areas of the Persian Gulf in summer. A freak geo-thermal temperature of 56° C *132.8° F* was recorded in February 1965 by the survey ship *Atlantis II* near the bottom of Discovery Deep (7,200 ft *2 195 m*) in the Red Sea. Ice-focused solar rays have been known to heat lake water to nearly 80° F *26,8° C*. The normal Red Sea temperature is 22° C *71.6° F*.

STRAITS

Longest

The longest straits in the world are the Tatarskiy Proliv or Tartar Straits between Sakhalin Island and the U.S.S.R. mainland running from the Sea of Japan to Sakhalinsky Zaliv. This distance is 800 km *497 miles*—thus marginally longer than the Malacca Straits.

Broadest

The broadest named straits in the world are the Davis Straits between Greenland and Baffin Island with a minimum width of 210 miles *338 km*. The Drake Passage between the Diego Ramirez Islands, Chile and the South Shetland Islands is 710 miles *1 140 km* across.

Narrowest

The narrowest navigable straits are those between the Aegean island of Euboea and the mainland of Greece. The gap is only 45 yds *40 m* wide at Khalkis. The Seil Sound, Strathclyde, Scotland, narrows to a point only 20 ft *6 m* wide where a bridge joins the island of Seil to the mainland and is thus said to span the Atlantic.

WAVES

Highest

The highest officially recorded sea wave was measured by Lt. Frederic Margraff U.S.N. from the U.S.S. *Ramapo* proceeding from Manila, Philippines, to San Diego, California, U.S.A., on the night of 6–7 Feb. 1933, during a 68-knot (78.3 m.p.h. *126 km/h*) hurricane. The wave was computed to be 112 ft *34 m* from trough to crest. The highest instrumentally measured wave was one 86 ft *26,2 m* high, recorded by the British ship *Weather Reporter*, in the North Atlantic on 30 Dec. 1972 in Lat. 59° N., Long. 19° W. It has been calculated on the statistics of the Stationary Random Theory that one wave in more than 300,000 may exceed the average by a factor of 4.

On 9 July 1958 a landslip caused a wave to wash 1,740 ft *530 m* high along the fjord-like Lituya Bay, Alaska, U.S.A.

Highest seismic wave

The highest estimated height of a *tsunami* (often wrongly called a tidal wave) was one of 85 m *278 ft*, which appeared off Ishigaki Island, Ryukyu Chain on 24 Apr. 1971. It tossed a 750 ton block of coral more than 2,5 km *1.3 miles*. *Tsunami* (a Japanese word which is singular and plural) have been observed to travel at 490 m.p.h. *790 km/h*. Between 479 B.C. and 1977 there were at least 500 instances of *tsunami* of which 270 were destructive.

CURRENTS

Greatest

The greatest current in the oceans of the world is the Antarctic Circumpolar Current or West Wind Drift Current which was measured in 1969 in the Drake Passage between South America and Antarctica to be flowing at a rate of 9,500 million ft³ *270 000 000 m³* per sec—nearly treble that of the Gulf Stream. Its width ranges from 185 to 1,240 miles *300 to 2 000 km* and has a surface flow rate of ¾ of a knot *1,4 km/h.*

Strongest

The world's strongest currents are the Nakwakto Rapids, Slingsby Channel, British Columbia, Canada (Lat. 51° 05' N., Long. 127° 30' W.) where the flow rate may reach 16.0 knots *29,6 km/h*. The fastest current in British territorial waters is 10.7 knots *19,8 km/h* in the Pentland Firth between the Orkney Islands and Caithness, formerly Scotland's northernmost mainland county.

GREATEST TIDES

Extreme tides are due to lunar and solar gravitational forces affected by their perigee, perihelion and conjunctions. Barometric and wind effects can superimpose an added "surge" element. Coastal and sea-floor configurations can accentuate these forces.

World
The greatest tides in the world occur in the Bay of Fundy, which divides the peninsula of Nova Scotia, Canada, from the United States' north-easternmost state of Maine and the Canadian province of New Brunswick. Burncoat Head in the Minas Basin, Nova Scotia, has the greatest mean spring range with 47.5 ft *14,50 m* and an extreme range of 53.5 ft *16,30 m.*

Great Britain
The place with the greatest mean spring range in Great Britain is Beachley, on the Severn, with a range of 40.7 ft *12,40 m,* compared with the British Isles' average of 15 ft *4,57 m.* Prior to 1933 tides as high as 28.9 ft *8,80 m* above and 22.3 ft *6,80 m* below datum (total range 51.2 ft *15,60 m)* were recorded at Avonmouth though an extreme range of 52.2 ft *15,90 m* for Beachley was officially accepted. In 1883 a freak tide of greater range was reported from Chepstow, Gwent.

Ireland
The greatest mean spring tidal range in Ireland is 17.3 ft *5,27 m* at Mellon, Limerick, on the River Shannon.

ICEBERGS
Largest
The largest iceberg on record was an Antarctic tabular 'berg of over 12,000 miles² *31 000 km²* (208 miles *335 km* long and 60 miles *97 km* wide and thus larger than Belgium) sighted 150 miles *240 km* west of Scott Island, in the South Pacific Ocean, by the U.S.S. *Glacier* on 12 Nov. 1956. The 200 ft *61 m* thick Arctic ice island T.1 (140 miles² *360 km²*) (discovered in 1946) was plotted for 17 years. The tallest iceberg measured was one of 550 ft *167 m* reported off western Greenland by the U.S. icebreaker *East Wind* in 1958.

Most southerly Arctic
The most southerly Arctic iceberg was sighted in the Atlantic by a U.S.N. weather patrol in Lat. 28° 44′ N., Long. 48° 42′ W. in April 1935. The southernmost iceberg reported in British home waters was one sighted 60 miles *96 km* from Smith's Knoll, on the Dogger Bank, in the North Sea.

Most northerly Antarctic
The most northerly Antarctic iceberg was a remnant sighted in the Atlantic by the ship *Dochra* in Latitude 26° 30′ S., Longitude 25° 40′ W., on 30 April 1894.

LAND
There is satisfactory evidence that at one time the Earth's land surface comprised a single primeval continent of 80 million miles² 2×10^8 km², now termed Pangaea, and that this split about 190,000,000 years ago, during the Jurassic period, into two super-continents, termed Laurasia (Eurasia, Greenland and Northern America) and Gondwanaland (Africa, Arabia, India, South America, Oceania and Antarctica) and named after Gondwana, India, which itself split 120 million years ago. The South Pole was apparently in the area of the Sahara as recently as the Ordovician period of *c.* 450 million years ago.

ROCKS
The age of the Earth is generally considered to be within the range of 4600 ± 100 million years, by analogy with directly measured ages of meteorites and of the moon. However, no rocks of this great age have yet been found on the Earth since geological processes have presumably destroyed the earliest record.

Oldest *World*
The greatest reported age for any scientifically dated rock is 3,800 ± 100 million years for granite gneiss rock found near Granite Falls in the Minnesota river valley, U.S.A. as measured by the lead-isotope and rubidium-uranium methods by the U.S. Geological Survey and announced on 26 Jan. 1975. These metamorphic samples compare with the Amitsoq gneiss from Godthaab, Greenland unreservedly accepted to be between 3700 and 3750 million years.

Oldest *Great Britain*
The original volcanic products from which were formed the gneiss and granulite rocks of the Scourian complex in the north west Highlands and the Western Isles may be possibly older than 3,000 million years. They were crystallized 2,800 million years ago.

Largest
The largest exposed rocky outcrop is the 1,237 ft *377 m* high Mount Augustus (3,627 ft *1 105 m* above sea-level), discovered on 3 June 1858, 200 miles *320 km* east of Carnarvon, Western Australia. It is an upfaulted monoclinal gritty conglomerate 5 miles *8 km* long and 2 miles *3 km* across and thus twice the size of the celebrated monolithic arkose Ayer's Rock (1,100 ft *335 m*), 250 miles *400 km* south-west of Alice Springs, in Northern Territory, Australia.

CONTINENTS
Largest
Only 29.08 per cent, or an estimated 57,270,000 miles² *148 328 000 km²* of the Earth's surface is land, with a mean height of 2,480 ft *756 m* above sea-level. The Eurasian land mass is the largest, with an area (including islands) of 21,053,000 miles² *54 527 000 km².*

Smallest
The smallest is the Australian mainland, with an area of about 2,940,000 miles² *7 614 500 km²,* which, together with Tasmania, New Zealand, New Guinea and the Pacific Islands, is described sometimes as Oceania. The total area of Oceania is about 3,450,000 miles² *8 935 000 km²* including West Irian (formerly West New Guinea), which is politically in Asia.

Land remotest from the sea *World*
There is an as yet unpinpointed spot in the Dzoosotoyn Elisen (desert), northern Sinkiang, China, that is more than 1,500 miles *2 400 km* from the open sea in any direction. The nearest large town to this point is Wulumuchi (Urumchi) to its south.

Land remotest from the sea *Great Britain*
The point furthest from the sea in Great Britain is a point near Meriden, West Midlands, England, which is 72½ miles *117 km* equidistant from the Severn Bridge, the Dee and Mersey estuaries and the Welland estuary in the Wash. The equivalent point in Scotland is in the Forest of Atholl, north west Tayside 40½ miles *65 km* equidistant from the head of Loch Leven, Inverness Firth and the Firth of Tay.

Peninsula
The world's largest peninsula is Arabia, with an area of about 1,250,000 miles² *3 250 000 km².*

ISLANDS
Largest *World*
Discounting Australia, which is usually regarded as a continental land mass, the largest island in the world is Greenland (part of the Kingdom of Denmark), with an area of about 840,000 miles² *2 175 000 km².* There is evidence that Greenland is in fact several islands overlayed by an ice cap without which it would have an area of 650,000 miles² *1 680 000 km².*

Largest *Great Britain*
The mainland of Great Britain (Scotland, England and

The Angel waterfall in Venezuela, the highest in the world, having a total drop of 3212 ft *979 m* (see p. 69). (*BBC*)

Wales) is the eighth largest in the world, with an area of 84,186 miles² *218 041 km².* It stretches 603½ miles *971 km* from Dunnet Head in the north to Lizard Point in the south and 287½ miles *463 km* across from Porthaflod, Dyfed to Lowestoft, Suffolk. The island of Ireland (32,594 miles² *84 418 km²*) is the 20th largest in the world.

Freshwater

The largest island surrounded by fresh water is the Ilha de Marajó (13,500 miles² *35 000 km²*), in the mouth of the River Amazon, Brazil. The world's largest inland island (*i.e.* land surrounded by rivers) is Ilha do Bananal, Brazil. The largest island in a lake is Manitoulin Island (1,068 miles² *2 766 km²*) in the Canadian (Ontario) section of Lake Huron. The largest lake island in Great Britain is Inchmurrin in Loch Lomond, Strathclyde/Central, Scotland with an area of 284 acres *115 ha.*

Remotest *World Uninhabited*

The remotest island in the world is Bouvet Øya (formerly Liverpool Island), discovered in the South Atlantic by J. B. C. Bouvet de Lozier on 1 Jan. 1739, and first landed on by Capt. George Norris on 16 Dec. 1825. Its position is 54° 26′ S., 3° 24′ E. This uninhabited Norwegian dependency is about 1,050 miles *1 700 km* from the nearest land—the uninhabited Queen Maud Land coast of eastern Antarctica.

Remotest *World Inhabited*

The remotest inhabited island in the world is Tristan da Cunha, discovered in the South Atlantic by Tristao da Cunha, a Portuguese admiral, in March 1506. It has an area of 38 miles² *98 km²* (habitable area 12 miles² *31 km²*) and was annexed by the United Kingdom on 14 Aug. 1816. After evacuation in 1961 (due to volcanic activity), 198 islanders returned in Nov. 1963. The nearest inhabited land is the island of St. Helena, 1,320 miles *2 120 km* to the north-east. The nearest continent, Africa is 1,700 miles *2 735 km* away.

Remotest *Great Britain*

The remotest of the British islets is Rockall 191 miles *307 km* west of St. Kilda, Western Isles. This 70 ft *21 m* high rock measuring 83 ft *25 m* across was not formally annexed until 18 Sept. 1955. The remotest British island which has ever been inhabited is North Rona which is 44 miles *70,8 km* from the next nearest land at Cape Wrath and the Butt of Lewis. It was evacuated *c.* 1844. Muckle Flugga, off Unst, in the Shetlands, is the northernmost inhabited with a population of 3 (1971) and is in a latitude north of southern Greenland. Just to the north of it is the rock of Out Stack.

above: A dry roomy tunnel, typical of the 190.3 miles of trunk passages, in the Flint Mammoth system, the longest cave system in the world. (see p. 67). (Dr. A. C. Waltham)

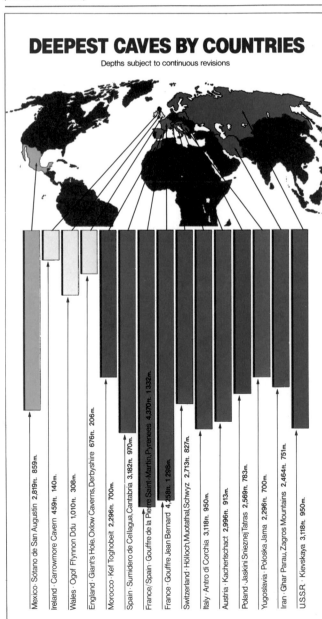

DEEPEST CAVES BY COUNTRIES

Depths subject to continuous revisions

Mexico · Sótano de San Augustin 2,819ft. 859m.

Ireland · Carrowmore Cavern 459ft. 140m.

Wales · Ogof Ffynnon Ddu 1,010ft. 308m.

England · Giant's Hole, Oxlow Caverns, Derbyshire 676ft. 206m.

Morocco · Kef Toghobeit 2,296ft. 700m.

Spain · Sumidero de Cellagua, Cantabria 3,182ft. 970m.

France/Spain · Gouffre de la Pierre Saint-Martin, Pyrenees 4,370ft. 1,332m.

France · Gouffre Jean Bernard 4,258ft. 1,298m.

Switzerland · Hölloch, Muotathal, Schwyz 2,713ft. 827m.

Italy · Antro di Corchia 3,118ft. 950m.

Austria · Kacherlschacht 2,996ft. 913m.

Poland · Jaskini Sniezznej Tatras 2,569ft. 783m.

Yugoslavia · Poloska Jama 2,296ft. 700m.

Iran · Ghar Parau, Zagros Mountains 2,464ft. 751m.

U.S.S.R. · Kievskaya 3,118ft. 950m.

Highest Rock Pinnacle

The world's highest rock pinnacle is Ball's Pyramid near Lord Howe Island, Pacific which is 1,843 ft *561 m* high, but has a base axis of only 200 m *218 yds*. It was first scaled in 1965.

Northernmost land

The most northerly land is Kaffeklubben Øyen (Coffee Club Island) off the north-east of Greenland, 440 miles *708 km* from the North Pole, discovered by Dr. Lange Koch in 1921 but determined only in June 1969 to be in Latitude 83° 40′ 6″.

Southernmost land

The South Pole, unlike the North Pole, is on land. The Amundsen-Scott South Polar station was built there at an altitude of 9,370 ft *2 855 m* in 1957. It is drifting bodily with the ice cap 27–30 ft *8–9 m* per annum in the direction 43° W and was replaced by a new structure in 1975.

Greatest archipelago

The world's greatest archipelago is the 3,500 mile *5 600 km* long crescent of more than 13,000 islands which forms Indonesia.

Largest atoll

The largest atoll in the world is Kwajalein in the Marshall Islands, in the central Pacific Ocean. Its slender 176 mile *283 km* long coral reef encloses a lagoon of 1,100 miles² *2 850 km²*. The atoll with the largest land area is Christmas Atoll, in the Line Islands, in the central Pacific Ocean. It has an area of 184 miles² *477 km²*. Its two principal settlements, London and Paris, are 4 miles *6 km* apart.

Longest reef

The longest reef is the Great Barrier Reef off Queensland, north-eastern Australia, which is 1,260 statute miles *2 027 km* in length. Between 1959 and 1971 a large section between Cooktown and Townsville was destroyed by the proliferation of the Crown of Thorns starfish (*Acanthaster planci*).

DEPRESSIONS

Deepest *World*

The deepest depression so far discovered is beneath the Hollick-Kenyon Plateau in Marie Byrd Land, Antarctica, where, at a point 5,900 ft *1 800 m* above sea-level, the ice depth is 14,000 ft *4 267 m*, hence indicating a bed rock depression 8,100 ft *2 468 m* below sea-level. The greatest submarine depression is a large area of the floor of the north west Pacific which has an average depth of 15,000 ft *4 570 m*. The deepest exposed depression on land is the shore surrounding the Dead Sea, 1,291 ft *593 m* below sea-level. The deepest point on the bed of this lake is 2,600 ft *792 m* below the Mediterranean. The deepest part of the bed of Lake Baykal in Siberia, U.S.S.R., is 4,872 ft *1 484 m* below sea-level.

Deepest *Great Britain*

The lowest lying area in Great Britain is in the Holme Fen area of the Great Ouse, in Cambridgeshire, at 9 ft *2,75 m* below sea-level. The deepest depression in England is the bed of part of Windermere, 94 ft *28,65 m* below sea-level, and in Scotland the bed of Loch Morar, Highland 987 ft *300,8 m* below sea-level.

Largest

The largest exposed depression in the world is the Caspian Sea basin in the Azerbaydzhani, Russian, Kazakh and Turkmen Republics of the U.S.S.R. and northern Iran (Persia). It is more than 200,000 miles² *518 000 km²* of which 143,550 miles² *371 800 km²* is lake area. The preponderant land area of the depression is the Prikaspiyskaya Nizmennost', lying around the northern third of the lake and stretching inland for a distance of up to 280 miles *450 km*.

CAVES

Longest

The most extensive cave system in the world is that under the Mammoth Cave National Park, Kentucky, U.S.A. first discovered in 1799. On 9 Sept. 1972 an exploration group led by Dr. John P. Wilcox completed a connection, pioneered by Mrs. Patricia Crowther on 30 Aug., between the Flint Ridge Cave system and the Mammoth Cave system so making a combined system with a total mapped passageway length of 190.3 miles *306,25 km*. The longest cave system in Great Britain is the Easegill system which reached 27.3 miles *44 km* with the connection of Easegill Caverns, Cumbria with Pippikin Pot, Lancashire on 16 Dec. 1978.

Largest Cavern

The Big Room of Carlsbad Caverns, New Mexico covers 14 acres *5,6 ha* with a ceiling height ranging from 80 to 255 ft *24–77 m*. The longest axis is 1,800 ft *550 m*.

Longest stalactite

The longest known stalactite in the world is a wall-supported column extending 195 ft *59 m* from roof to floor in the Cueva de Nerja, near Málaga, Spain. The rather low tensile strength of calcite (calcium carbonate) precludes very long free-hanging stalactites, but one of 38 ft *11,60 m* exists in the Poll an Ionain cave in County Clare, Ireland.

Tallest stalagmite

The tallest known stalagmite in the world is La Grande Stalagmite in the Aven Armand cave, Lozère, France, which has attained a height of 98 ft *29 m* from the cave floor. It was found in September 1897. The tallest cave column is the 106 ft *32,3 m* tall Bicenntial Column in Ogle Cave in Carlsbad Cavern National Park, New Mexico U.S.A.

MOUNTAINS

A *Guinness Book of Mountaineering Facts and Feats* by Edward Pyatt will be published early in 1980.

Highest *World*

An eastern Himalayan peak of 29,028 ft *8 848 m* above sea-level on the Tibet-Nepal border (in an area first designated Chu-mu-lang-ma on a map of 1717) was discovered to be the world's highest mountain in 1852 by the Survey Department of the Government of India, from theodolite readings taken in 1849 and 1850. In 1860 its height was computed to be 29,002 ft *8 840 m*. On 25 July 1973 the Chinese announced a height of 8 848,1 m or *29,029 ft 3 in*. In practice the altitude can only be justified as 29,028 ft ± 25 feet or a mean *8 848 m*. The 5½ mile *8,85 km* high peak was named Mount Everest after Sir George Everest, C.B. (1790–1866), formerly Surveyor-General of India. After a total loss of 11 lives since the first reconnaissance in 1921, Everest was finally conquered at 11.30 a.m. on 29 May 1953. (For details of ascents, see under Mountaineering in Chapter 12.) The mountain whose summit is farthest from the Earth's centre is the Andean peak of Chimborazo (20,561 ft *6 267 m*), 98 miles *158 km* south of the equator in Ecuador, South America. Its summit is 7,057 ft *2 150 m* further from the Earth's centre than the summit of Mt. Everest. The highest mountain on the equator is Volcán Cayambe (19,285 ft *5 878 m*), Ecuador, in Long. 77° 58′ W.

Highest *Insular*

The highest insular mountain in the world is the unsurveyed Ngga Pulu formerly Mount Sukarno, formerly Carstensz Pyramide in Irian Jaya, Indonesia, once Netherlands New Guinea, according to cross-checked altimeter estimates, it is 16,500 ft *5 030 m* high.

Highest *U.K. and Ireland*

A list of the highest points in the 72 geographical divisions of the United Kingdom and the 26 counties of the Republic of Ireland was given on page 63 of the 23rd (1977) Edition.

The highest mountain in the United Kingdom is Ben Nevis (4,406 ft *1 343 m* excluding the 12 ft *3,65 m* cairn), 4¼ miles *6,85 km* south-east of Fort William, Highland, Scotland. It was climbed before 1720 but though acclaimed the highest in 1790 was not confirmed to be higher than Ben Macdhui (4,300 ft *1 310 m*) until 1847. In 1834 Ben Macdhui and Ben Nevis (Gaelic, Beinn Nibheis) (first reference, 1778) were respectively quoted as 4,570 ft *1 393 m* and 4,370 ft *1 332 m*. The highest mountain in England is Scafell Pike (3,210 ft *978 m*) in Cumbria; in Wales is Snowdon (3,560 ft *1 085 m*) (Yr Wyddfa) in Gwynedd; and in the island of Ireland is Carrauntual (3,414 ft *1 041 m*) in County Kerry.

There is some evidence that, before being ground down by the ice-cap, mountains in the Loch Bà area of the Isle of Mull, Strathclyde were 15,000 ft *4 575 m* above sea-level.

Highest *Peaks over 3,000 ft*

There are 577 peaks and tops over 3,000 ft *915 m* in the whole British Isles and 165 peaks and 136 tops in Scotland higher than England's highest point, Scafell Pike. The highest mountain off the mainland is Sgùrr Alasdair (3,309 ft *1 008 m*) on Skye named after Alexander (in Gaelic Alasdair) Nicolson, who made the first ascent in 1873.

Highest unclimbed

The highest unclimbed mountain is now only the 31st highest—Zemu Gap Peak (22,526 ft *7 780 m*) in the Sikkim Himalaya.

Largest

The world's tallest mountain measured from its submarine base (3,280 fathoms *6 000 m*) in the Hawaiian Trough to peak is Mauna Kea (Mountain White) on the island of Hawaii, with a combined height of 33,476 ft *10 203 m* of which 13,796 ft *4 205 m* are above sea-level. Another mountain whose dimensions, but not height, exceed those of Mount Everest is the volcanic Hawaiian peak of Mauna Loa (Mountain Long) at 13,680 ft *4 170 m*. The axes of its elliptical base, 16,322 ft *4 975 m* below sea-level, have been estimated at 74 miles *119 km* and 53 miles *85 km*. It should be noted that Cerro Aconcagua (22,834 ft *6 960 m*) is more than 38,800 ft *11 826 m* above the 16,000 ft *4 875 m* deep Pacific abyssal plain or 42,834 ft *13 055 m* above the Peru-Chile Trench which is 180 miles *290 km* distant in the South Pacific.

Greatest ranges

The world's greatest land mountain range is the Himalaya-Karakoram, which contains 96 of the world's 109 peaks of over 24,000 ft *7 315 m*. The greatest of all mountain ranges is, however, the submarine Indian/East Pacific Oceans Cordillera extending 19,200 miles *30 720 km* from the Gulf of Aden to the Gulf of California by way of the seabed between Australia and Antarctica with an average height of 8,000 ft *2 430 m* above the base ocean depth.

Longest Lines of Sight

In Alaska Mt. McKinley (20,320 ft *6 193 m*) has been sighted from Mt. Sanford (16,237 ft *4 949 m*) from a distance of 230 miles *370 km*. McKinley, so named in 1896, was Denali (Great One) in Athabascan.

Greatest plateau

The most extensive high plateau in the world is the Tibetan Plateau in Central Asia. The average altitude is 16,000 ft *4 875 m* and the area is 77,000 miles² *200 000 km²*.

Sheerest Wall

The 3,200 ft *975 m* wide northwest face of Half Dome, Yosemite, California, U.S.A. is 2,200 ft *670 m* high but nowhere departs more than 7 degrees from the vertical. It was first climbed (Class VI) in 5 days in July 1957 by Royal Robbins, Jerry Gallwas and Mike Sherrick.

Highest halites

Along the northern shores of the Gulf of Mexico for 725 miles *1 160 km* there exist 330 subterranean "mountains" of salt, some of which rise more than 60,000 ft *18 300 m* from bed rock and appear as the low salt domes first discovered in 1862.

Lowest Hill

The official map of Seria, Brunei shows a hillock named Bukit Thompson on the Padang Golf Course at 15 ft *4,5 m*.

RIVERS
Longest *World*

The two longest rivers in the world are the Amazon (*Amazonas*), flowing into the South Atlantic, and the Nile (*Bahr-el-Nil*) flowing into the Mediterranean. Which is the longer is more a matter of definition than simple measurement.

The true source of the Amazon was discovered in 1953 to be a stream named Huarco, rising near the summit of Cerro Huagra (17,188 ft *5 238 m*) in Peru. This stream progressively becomes the Toro then the Santiago then the Apurimac, which in turn is known as the Ene and then the Tambo before its confluence with the Amazon prime tributary the Ucayali. The length of the Amazon from this source to the South Atlantic *via* the Canal do Norte was measured in 1969 to be 4,007 miles *6 448 km* (usually quoted to the rounded off figure of 4,000 miles *6 437 km*).

If, however, a vessel navigating down the river turns to the south of Ilha de Marajó through the straits of Breves and Boiuci into the Pará, the total length of the water-course becomes 4,195 miles 6 750 km. *The Pará is* not *however a tributary of the Amazon, being hydrologically part of the basin of the Tocantins.*

The length of the Nile watercourse, as surveyed by M. Devroey (Belgium) before the loss of a few miles of meanders due to the formation of Lake Nasser, behind the Aswan High Dam, was 4,145 miles *6 670 km*. This course is the hydrologically acceptable one from the source in Burundi of the Luvironza branch of the Kagera feeder of the Victoria Nyanza *via* the White Nile (*Bahr-el-Jebel*) to the delta.

Longest *Ireland*

The longest river in Ireland is the Shannon, which is longer than any river in Great Britain. It rises 258 ft *78,6 m* above sea-level, in County Cavan, and flows through a series of loughs to Limerick. It is 240 miles *386 km* long, including the 56 mile *90 km* long estuary to Loop Head. The basin area is 6,060 miles² *15 695 km²*.

Longest *Great Britain*

The longest river in Great Britain is the Severn, which empties into the Bristol Channel and is 220 miles *354 km* long. Its basin extends over 4,409 miles² *11 419 km²*. It rises in north-western Powys and flows through Salop, Hereford and Worcester, Gloucestershire and Avon and has a record 17 tributaries. The longest river *wholly* in England is the Thames, which is 215 miles, *346 km* long to the Nore. Its remotest source is at Seven Springs, Gloucestershire, whence the River Churn joins the other head waters. The source of the Thames proper is Trewsbury Mead, Coates, Cirencester, Gloucestershire. The basin measures, 3,841 miles² *9 948 km²*. The Yorkshire Ouse's 11 tributaries aggregate 629 miles *1012 km*. The longest river wholly in Wales is the Towy, with a length of 64 miles *102 km*. It rises in Dyfed and flows out into Carmarthen Bay. The longest river in Scotland is the Tay, with Dundee, Tayside, on the shore of the estuary. It is 117 miles *188 km* long from the source of its remotest head-stream, the River Tummel, Tayside and has the greatest volume of any river in Great Britain, with a flow of up to 49,000 cusecs *1 387 m³* per sec. Of Scottish rivers the Tweed and the Clyde have most tributaries with 11 each.

Shortest river

The world's shortest named river is the D River, Lincoln City, Oregon, U.S.A., which connects Devil's Lake to the Pacific Ocean and is 440 ft *134 m* long at low tide.

Largest basin and longest tributary

The largest river basin in the world is that drained by the Amazon (4,007 miles *6 448 km*). It covers about 2,720,000 miles² *7 045 000 km²*. It has about 15,000 tributaries and subtributaries, of which four are more than 1,000 miles *1 609 km* long. These include the Madeira, the longest of all tributaries, with a length of 2,100 miles *3 380 km*, which is surpassed by only 14 rivers in the whole world.

Longest sub-tributary

The longest sub-tributary is the Pilcomayo (1,000 miles *1 609 km* long) in South America. It is a tributary of the Paraguay (1,500 miles *2 415 km* long), which is itself a tributary of the Paraná (2,500 miles *4 025 km*).

Longest estuary

The world's longest estuary is that of the often frozen Ob', in the northern U.S.S.R., at 550 miles *885 km*. It is up to 50 miles *80 km* wide.

Largest delta

The world's largest delta is that created by the Ganga (Ganges) and Brahmaputra in Bangla Desh (formerly East Pakistan) and West Bengal, India. It covers an area of 30,000 miles² *75 000 km²*.

Greatest flow

The greatest flow of any river in the world is that of the Amazon, which discharges an average of 4,200,000 cusecs *120 000 m³/sec* into the Atlantic Ocean, rising to more than 7,000,000 cusecs *200 000 m³/sec* in full flood. The lowest 900 miles *1 450 km* of the Amazon average 300 ft *90 m* in depth.

Submarine river

In 1952 a submarine river 250 miles *400 km* wide, known as the Cromwell current, was discovered flowing eastward 300 ft *90 m* below the surface of the Pacific for 3,500 miles *5 625 km* along the equator. Its volume is 1,000 times that of the Mississippi.

Subterranean river

In August 1958 a crypto-river was tracked by radio isotopes flowing under the Nile with 6 times its mean annual flow or 500,000 million m³ *20 million million ft³*.

Largest swamp

The world's largest tract of swamp is in the basin of the Pripet or Pripyat River—a tributary of the Dnieper in the U.S.S.R. These swamps cover an estimated area of 18,125 miles² *46 950 km²*.

RIVER BORES
World

The bore on the Ch'ient'ang'kian (Hang-chou-fe) in eastern China is the most remarkable in the world. At Spring tides the wave attains a height of up to 25 ft *7,5 m* and a speed of 13 knots *24 km/h*. It is heard advancing at a range of 14 miles *22 km*. The bore on the Hooghly branch of the Ganges travels for 70 miles *110 km* at more than 15 knots *27 km/h*. The annual downstream flood wave on the Mekong sometimes reaches a height of 46 ft *14 m*. The greatest volume of any tidal bore is that of the Canal do Norte (10 miles *16 km* wide) in the mouth of the Amazon.

Great Britain

The most notable river bore in the United Kingdom is that on the Severn, which attained a measured height of 9¼ ft *2,8 m* on 15 Oct. 1966 downstream of Stone-bench, and a speed of 13 m.p.h. *20 km/h*. It travels as far up as Severn Stoke in Hereford and Worcester.

Fastest rapids

The fastest rapids which have ever been navigated are the Lava Falls on the River Colorado, U.S.A. At times of flood these attain a speed of 30 m.p.h. *48 km/h* (26 knots) with waves boiling up to 12 ft *3,65 m*.

WATERFALLS
Highest

The highest waterfall (as opposed to vaporized 'Bridal Veil') in the world is the Salto Angel in Venezuela, on a branch of the River Carrao, an upper tributary of the Caroni with a total drop of 3,212 ft *979 m*—the longest single drop is 2,648 ft *807 m*. It was re-discovered by a United States pilot named James (Jimmy) Angel (died 8 Dec. 1956), who crashed nearby on 9 Oct. 1937. The falls, known by the Indians as Cherun-Meru, were first reported by Ernesto Sanchez La Cruz in 1910.

Highest *United Kingdom*

The tallest waterfall in the United Kingdom is Eas a'Chùal Aluinn, from Glas Bheinn (2,541 ft *774 m*), Highland, Scotland, with a drop of 658 ft *200 m*. England's highest fall above ground is Caldron (or Cauldron) Snout, on the Tees, with a fall of 200 ft *60 m* in 450 ft *135 m* of cataracts, but no sheer leap. It is on the border of Durham and Cumbria. The cascade in the Gaping Gill Cave descends 365 ft *111 m*.

The highest Welsh waterfall is the Pistyll Rhaiadr (240 ft *73 m*), on the River Rhaiadr, on the Clwyd-Powys border.

Highest *Ireland*

The highest falls in Ireland are the Powerscourt Falls (350 ft *106 m*), on the River Dargle, County Wicklow.

Greatest

On the basis of the average annual flow, the greatest waterfall in the world is the Guairá (374 ft *114 m* high), known also as the Salto dos Sete Quedas, on the Alto Paraná River between Brazil and Paraguay, Although attaining an average height of only 110 ft *33,5 m*, its estimated annual averages flow over the lip (5,300 yds *4 850 m* wide) is 470,000 cusecs *13 300 m³/sec*. The amount of water this represents can be imagined by supposing that it was pouring into the dome of St. Paul's Cathedral—it would fill it completely in three-fifths of a sec. It has a peak flow of 1,750,000 cusecs *50 000 m³/sec*. The seven cataracts of the Boyoma (formerly Stanley) Falls in the Congo (Kinshasa) have an average annual flow of 600,000 cusecs *17 000 m³/sec*.

It has been calculated that, when some 5,500,000 years ago the Mediterranean basins began to be filled from the Atlantic through the Straits of Gibraltar, a waterfall 26 times greater than the Guairá and perhaps 800 m *2,625 ft* high was formed.

Widest

The widest waterfalls in the world are the Khône Falls (50 to 70 ft *15–21m* high) in Laos, with a width of 6.7 miles *10,8 km* and a flood flow of 1,500,000 cusecs *42 500 m³/sec*.

LAKES AND INLAND SEAS
Largest *World*

The largest inland sea or lake in the world is the Kaspiskoye More (Caspian Sea) in the southern U.S.S.R. and Iran (Persia). It is 760 miles *1 225 km* long and its total area is 143,550 miles² *371 800 km²*. Of the total area some 55,280 miles² *143 200 km²* (38.6%) is in Iran, where it is named the Darya-ye-Khazar. Its maximum depth is 980 m *3,215 ft* and its surface is 92 ft *28 m* below sea-level. Its estimated volume is 21,500 miles³ *89 600 km³* of saline water. Since 1930 it has diminished 15,000 miles² *39 000 km²* in area with a fall of 62 ft *18,90 m* while the shore line has retreated more than 10 miles *16 km* in some places. The U.S.S.R. Government plan to reverse the flow of the upper Pechora River from flowing north to the Barents Sea by blasting a 70 mile *112 km* long canal with nuclear explosives into the south-flowing Kolva river so that *via* the Kama and Volga rivers the Caspian will be replenished.

Freshwater Lake *World*

The freshwater lake with the greatest surface area is Lake Superior, one of the Great Lakes of North America. The total area is 31,800 miles² *82 350 km²*, of which 20,700 miles² *53 600 km²* are in Minnesota, Wisconsin and Michigan, U.S.A. and 11,100 miles² *27 750 km²* in Ontario, Canada. It is 600 ft *182 m* above sea-level. The freshwater lake with the greatest volume is Baykal (see also pages 67, 70) with an estimated volume of 5,520 miles³ *23 000 km³*.

Freshwater lake *United Kingdom*

The largest lake in the United Kingdom is Lough Neagh (48 ft *14,60 m* above sea-level) in Northern Ireland. It is 18 miles *28,9 km* long and 11 miles *17,7 km* wide and has an area of 147.39 miles² *381,73 km²*. Its extreme depth is 102 ft *31 m*.

Freshwater lake *Great Britain*

The largest lake in Great Britain, and the largest inland loch in Scotland is Loch Lomond (23 ft *7,0 m* above sea-level), which is 22.64 miles *36,44 km* long and has a surface area of 27.45 miles² *70,04 km²*. It is situated in the Strathclyde and Central regions and its greatest depth is 623 ft *190 m*. The lake with the greatest volume is however Loch Ness with 263,162,000,000 ft³ *7 451 920 000 m³*. The longest lake is Loch Ness which measures 24.23 miles *38,99 km*. The three arms of the Y-shaped Loch Awe aggregate however, 25.47 miles *40,99 km*. The largest lake in England is Windermere, in the county of Cumbria. It is 10½ miles *17 km* long and has a surface area of 5.69 miles² *14,74 km²*. Its greatest depth is 219 ft *66,75 m* in the northern half. The largest *natural* lake in Wales is Llyn Tegid, with an area of 1.69 miles² *4,38 km²*, although it should be noted that the largest lake in Wales is that formed by the reservoir at Lake Vyrnwy, where the total surface area is 1,120 acres *453,25 ha*.

Freshwater lake *Republic of Ireland*
The largest lough in the Republic of Ireland is Lough Corrib in the counties of Mayo and Galway. It measures 27 miles *43,5 km* in length and is 7 miles *11,25 km* across at its widest point with a total surface area of 41,616 acres (65.0 miles² *168 km²*).

Largest Lagoon
The largest lagoon in the world is Lagoa dos Patos in southernmost Brazil. It is 158 miles *254 km* long and extends over 4,110 miles² *10 645 km²*.

Deepest *World*
The deepest lake in the world is Ozero (Lake) Baykal in central Siberia, U.S.S.R. It is 385 miles *620 km* long and between 20 and 46 miles *32–74 km* wide. In 1957 the lake's Olkhon Crevice was measured to be 1 940 m *6,365 ft* deep and hence 1 485 m *4,872 ft* below sea-level (see also p. 69).

Deepest *Great Britain*
The deepest lake in Great Britain is the 10.30 mile *16,57 km* long Loch Morar, in Highland. Its surface is 30 ft *9 m* above sea-level and its extreme depth 1,017 ft *310 m*. England's deepest lake is Wast Water (258 ft *78 m*), in Cumbria. The lake with the greatest mean depth is Loch Ness with *c*. 450 ft *137 m*.

Highest *World*
The highest steam-navigated lake in the world is Lago Titicaca (maximum depth 1,214 ft *370 m*), with an area of about 3,200 miles² *8 285 km²* (1,850 miles² *4 790 km²* in Peru, 1,350 miles² *3 495 km²* in Bolivia), in South America. It is 130 miles *209 km* long and is situated at 12,506 ft *3 811 m* above sea-level. There is an unnamed glacial lake near Everest at 19,300 ft *5 880 m*. Tibet's largest lake Nam Tso of 722 miles² *1 956 km²* is at 15,060 ft *4 578 m*.

Highest *United Kingdom*
The highest lake in the United Kingdom is the 1.9 acre *0,76 ha* Lochan Buidhe at 3,600 ft *1 097 m* above sea-level in the Cairngorm Mountains, Scotland. England's highest is Broad Crag Tarn (2,746 ft *837 m* above sea-level) on Scafell Pike, Cumbria and the highest named freshwater in Wales is The Frogs Pool, a tarn near the summit of Carnedd Llywelyn, Gwynedd at *c*. 2,725 ft *830 m*.

Lake in a lake
The largest lake in a lake is Manitou Lake (41.09 miles² *106,42 km²*) on the world's largest lake island Manitoulin Island (1,068 miles² *2 766 km²*) in the Canadian part of Lake Huron. It contains itself a number of islands.

Underground Lake
Reputedly the world's largest underground lake is the Lost Sea 300 ft *91 m* subterranean in the Craighead Caverns, Sweetwater, Tennessee, U.S.A. measuring 4½ acres *1,8 ha* and discovered in 1905.

Desert *Largest*
Nearly an eighth of the world's land surface is arid with a rainfall of less than 25 cm (*9.8 in*) per annum. The Sahara Desert in N. Africa is the largest in the world. At its greatest length it is 3,200 miles *5 150 km* from east to west. From north to south it is between 800 and 1,400 miles *1 275 and 2 250 km*. The area covered by the desert is about 3,250,000 miles² *8 400 000 km²*. The land level varies from 436 ft *132 m* below sea-level in the Qattâra Depression, Egypt to the mountain Emi Koussi (11,204 ft *3 415 m*) in Chad. The diurnal temperature range in the western Sahara may be more than 80° F or *45° C*.

Sand dunes
The world's highest measured sand dunes are those in the

Saharan sand sea of Isaouane-n-Tifernine of east central Algeria in Lat. 26° 42′ N., Long 6° 43′ E. They have a wave-length of near 3 miles *5 km* and attain a height of 1,410 ft *430 m*.

Gorge *Largest*
The largest land gorge in the world is the Grand Canyon on the Colorado River in north-central Arizona, U.S.A. It extends from Marble Gorge to the Grand Wash Cliffs, over a distance of 217 miles *349 km*. It varies in width from 4 to 13 miles *6 to 20 km* and is up to 7,000 ft *2 133 m* deep. The submarine Labrador Basin canyon is *c*. 2,150 miles *3 440 km* long.

Gorge *Deepest*
The deepest canyon in low relief territory is Hell's Canyon, dividing Oregon and Idaho, U.S.A. It plunges 7,900 ft *2 400 m* from the Devil Mountain down to the Snake River. A stretch of the Kali River in central Nepal flows 18,000 ft *5 485 m* below its flanking summits of the Dhaulagiri and Annapurna groups. The deepest submarine canyon yet discovered is one 25 miles *40 km* south of Esperance, Western Australia, which is 6,000 ft *1 800 m* deep and 20 miles *32 km* wide.

Sea Cliffs *Highest*
The highest sea cliffs yet pinpointed anywhere in the world are those on the north coast of east Molokaʻi, Hawaii near Umilehi Point, which descend 3,300 ft *1 005 m* to the sea at an average gradient of >55°. The highest cliffs in North West Europe are those on the north coast of Achill Island, in County Mayo, Ireland, which are 2,192 ft *668 m* sheer above the sea at Croaghan. The highest cliffs in the United Kingdom are the 1,300 ft *396 m* Conachair cliffs on St. Kilda, Western Isles (1,379 ft *425 m*). The highest sheer sea cliffs on the mainland of Great Britain are at Clo Mor, 3 miles *4,8 km* south-east of Cape Wrath, Highland, Scotland which drop 921 ft *280,7 m*. England's highest cliffs are Holdstone Hill which descends 1,131 ft *344 m* in a ½ mile *800 m* and Great Hangman Hill, near Coombe Martin, also in North Devon, which descends from 1,029 ft *313 m* to the sea in less than ¼ mile *400 m*, the last 700 ft *213 m* of which is sheer.

Natural Arch *Longest*
The longest natural arch in the world is the Landscape Arch in the Arches National Park, 25 miles *40 km* north of Moab, Utah, U.S.A. This natural sandstone arch spans 291 ft *88 m* and is set about 100 ft *30 m* above the canyon floor. In one place erosion has narrowed its section to 6 ft *1,82 m*. Larger, however, is the Rainbow Bridge, Utah discovered on 14 Aug. 1909 with a span of 278 ft *84,7 m* but more than 22 ft *6,7 m* wide.

Natural Bridge *Highest*
The highest natural arch is the sandstone arch 25 miles *40 km* WNW of K'ashih, Sinkiang, China, estimated in 1947 to be nearly 1,000 ft *312 m* tall with a span of about 150 ft *45 m*.

Longest glaciers
It is estimated that 6,020,000 miles² *15 600 000 km²*, or about 10.4 per cent of the Earth's land surface, is permanently glaciated. The world's longest known glacier is the Lambert Glacier, discovered by an Australian aircraft crew in Australian Antarctic Territory in 1956–57. It is up to 40 miles *64 km* wide and, with its upper section, known as the Mellor Glacier, it measures at least 250 miles *402 km* in length. With the Fisher Glacier limb, the Lambert forms a continuous ice passage about 320 miles *514 km* long. The longest Himalayan glacier is the Siachen (47 miles *75,6 km*) in the Karakoram range, though the Hispar and Biafo combine to form an ice passage 76 miles *122 km* long. The fastest moving major glacier is the Quarayaq in Greenland which flows 20–24 m *65–80 ft* per day.

Greatest avalanches
The greatest avalanches, though rarely observed, occur in the Himalaya but no estimates of their volume had been published. It was estimated that 3,500,000 m³ *120 000 000 ft³* of snow fell in an avalanche in the Italian Alps in 1885. (See also Disasters, end of Chapter 10.)

ECLIPSES: Least frequent

THE UNIVERSE AND SPACE

The Guinness Book of Astronomy Facts and Feats by Patrick Moore was published in May 1979 price £6.95.

LIGHT-YEAR—that distance travelled by light (speed 186,282.397 miles/sec *299 792,458 km s⁻¹* or 670,616,629.4 m.p.h. *1 079 258 848,8 km h⁻¹ in vacuo*) in one tropical year (365.24219878 mean solar days at January 0,12 hours Ephemeris time in A.D. 1900) and is 5,878,499,814,000 miles *9 460 528 405 000 km.* The unit was first used in March 1888.

MAGNITUDE—a measure of stellar brightness such that the light of a star of any magnitude bears a ratio of 2.511886 to that of a star of the next magnitude. Thus a fifth magnitude star is 2.511886 times as bright, while one of the first magnitude is exactly 100 (or 2.511886⁵) times as bright, as a sixth magnitude star. In the case of such exceptionally bright bodies as Sirius, Venus, the Moon (magnitude −12.71) or the Sun (magnitude −26.78), the magnitude is expressed as a minus quantity.

PROPER MOTION—that component of a star's motion in space which, at right angles to the line of sight, constitutes an apparent change of position of the star in the celestial sphere.

The universe is the entirety of space, matter and anti-matter. An appreciation of its magnitude is best grasped by working outward from the Earth, through the Solar System and our own Milky Way Galaxy, to the remotest extra-galactic nebulae and quasars.

METEOROIDS
Meteor shower

Meteoroids are of cometary or asteroidal origin. A meteor is the light phenomenon caused by the entry of a meteoroid into the Earth's atmosphere. The greatest meteor "shower" on record occurred on the night of 16–17 Nov. 1966, when the Leonid meteors (which recur every 33¼ years) were visible between western North America and eastern U.S.S.R. It was calculated that meteors passed over Arizona, U.S.A., at a rate of 2,300 per min for a period of 20 min from 5 a.m. on 17 Nov. 1966.

METEORITES
Oldest

It was reported in August 1978 that Dust grains in the Murchison meteorite which fell in Australia in Sept. 1969 pre-date the formation of the Solar System.

Largest *World*

When a meteoroid penetrates to the Earth's surface, the remnant is described as a meteorite. This occurs about 150 times per year over the whole land surface of the Earth. Although the chances of being struck are deemed negligible, the most anxious time of day for meteorophobes is 3 p.m. The largest known meteorite is one found in 1920 at Hoba West, near Grootfontein in south-west Africa. This is a block 9 ft *2,75 m* long by 8 ft *2,43 m* broad, estimated to be 132,000 lb. (59 tons/*tonnes*). The largest meteorite exhibited by any museum is the "Tent" meteorite, weighing 68,085 lb. (30.4 tons *30 882 kg*) found in 1897 near Cape York, on the west coast of Greenland, by the expedition of Commander (later Rear-Admiral) Robert Edwin Peary (1856–1920). It was known to the Eskimos as the Abnighito and is now exhibited in the Hayden Planetarium in New York City, N.Y., U.S.A. The largest piece of stony meteorite recovered is a piece of 1770 kg *3,902 lb.* part of a shower which struck Kirin, Kaoshan Province, China on 8 Mar. 1976. The oldest dated meteorites are from the Allende fall in Chihuahua, Mexico on 8 Feb. 1969.

There was a mysterious explosion of 12½ megatons in Latitude 60° 55′ N., Longitude 101° 57′ E., in the basin of the Podkamennaya Tunguska river, 40 miles north of Vanavar, in Siberia, U.S.S.R., at 00 hrs 17 min 11 sec U.T. on 30 June 1908. The cause was variously attributed to a meteorite (1927), a comet (1930), a nuclear explosion (1961) and to anti-matter (1965). This devastated an area of about 1,500 miles² *3 885 km²* and the shock was felt as far as 1 000 km (more than *600 miles*) away. The comet theory is now favoured.

Largest *United Kingdom and Ireland*

The heaviest of the 22 meteorites known to have fallen on the British Isles since 1623 was one weighing at least 102 lb. *46,25 kg* (largest piece 17 lb. 6 oz. *7,88 kg*), which fell at 4.12 p.m. on 24 Dec. 1965 at Barwell, Leicestershire. Scotland's largest recorded meteorite fell in Strathmore, Tayside on 3 Dec. 1917. It weighed 22¼ lb. *10,09 kg* and was the largest of four stones totalling 29 lb. 6 oz. *13,324 kg.* The largest recorded meteorite to fall in Ireland was the Limerick Stone of 65 lb. *29,5 kg* part of a shower weighing more than 106 lb. *48 kg* which fell near Adare County Limerick, on 10 Sept. 1813. The larger of the two recorded meteorites to land in Wales was one weighing 28 oz. *794 g* of which a piece weighing 25½ oz. *723 g* went through the roof of the Prince Llewellyn Hotel in Beddgelert, Gwynedd, shortly before 3.15 a.m. on 21 Sept. 1949.

Largest craters

A crater 150 miles *241 km* and ½ mile *805 m* deep has been postulated in Wilkes Land, Antarctica since 1962. It would be caused by a 13,000 million ton meteorite striking at 44,000 m.p.h. *70 811 km/h.* U.S.S.R. scientists reported in Dec. 1970 an astrobleme with a 60 mile *95 km* diameter and a maximum depth of 1,300 ft *400 m* in the basin of the River Popigai. There is a possible crater-like formation 275 miles *442,5 km* in diameter on the eastern shore of the Hudson Bay, Canada, where the Nastapoka Islands are just off the coast.

The largest proven crater is the Coon Butte or Barringer crater, discovered in 1891 near Canyon Diablo, Winslow, northern Arizona, U.S.A. It is 4,150 ft *1 265 m* in diameter and now about 575 ft *175 m* deep, with a parapet rising 130 to 155 ft *40–48 m* above the surrounding plain. It has been estimated that an iron-nickel mass with a diameter of 200 to 260 ft *61–79 m* and weighing about 2,000,000 tons/*tonnes* gouged this crater in *c.* 25,000 B.C.

Evidence was published in 1963 discounting a meteoric origin for the crypto-volcanic Vredefort Ring (diameter 26 miles *41,8 km*), to the south-west of Johannesburg, South Africa, but this has now been re-asserted. The New Quebec (formerly the Chubb) "Crater", first sighted on 20 June 1943 in northern Ungava, Canada, is 1,325 ft *404 m* deep and measures 6.8 miles *10,9 km* round its rim.

Fireball *Brightest*
The brightest fireball ever photographically recorded was by Dr. Zdeněk Ceplecha over Sumava, Czechoslovakia on 4 Dec. 1974 with a momentary magnitude of −22 or 10,000 times brighter than a full Moon.

Tektites
The largest tektite of which details have been published has been of 3,2 kg *7.04 lb.* found in 1932 at Muong Nong, Saravane Province, Laos and now in the Paris Museum.

AURORAE
Most frequent
Polar lights, known since 1560 as Aurora Borealis or Northern Lights in the northern hemisphere and since 1773 as Aurora Australis in the southern hemisphere, are caused by electrical solar discharges in the upper atmosphere and occur most frequently in high latitudes. Aurorae are visible at some time on *every* clear dark night in the polar areas within 20 degrees of the magnetic poles. The extreme height of aurorae has been measured at 1,000 km *620 miles*, while the lowest may descend to 45 miles *72,5 km*. Reliable figures exist only from 1952 since when the record high and low number of nights of auroral displays in Shetland (geomagnetic Lat. 63°) has been 203 (1957) and 58 (1965). The most recent great display in northwest Europe was that of 4–5 Sept. 1958.

Lowest Latitudes
Extreme cases of displays in very low latitudes are Cuzco, Peru (2 Aug. 1744); Honolulu, Hawaii (1 Sept. 1859) and questionably Singapore (25 Sept. 1909).

Noctilucent Clouds
Regular observations in Western Europe date only from 1964 since when the record high and low number of nights on which these phenomena (at heights of *c.* 52 miles *85 km*) have been observed have been 41 (1974) and 15 (1970).

THE MOON
The Earth's closest neighbour in space and only natural satellite is the Moon, at a mean distance of 238,855 statute miles *384 400 km* centre to centre or 233,812 miles *376 284 km* surface to surface. Its closest approach (perigee) and most extreme distance away (apogee) measured surface to surface are 216,420 and 247,667 miles *348 294 and 398 581 km* respectively or 221,463 and 252,710 miles *356 410/406 697 km* measured centre to centre. It has a diameter of 2,159.3 miles *3 475,0 km* and has a mass of 7.23 × 10¹⁹ tons *7,35 × 10¹⁹ tonnes* with a mean density of 3.34. The average orbital speed is 2,287 m.p.h. *3 680 km/h.*

The first direct hit on the Moon was achieved at 2 min 24 sec after midnight (Moscow time) on 14 Sept. 1959, by the Soviet space probe *Lunik II* near the *Mare Serenitatis*. The first photographic images of the hidden side were collected by the U.S.S.R.'s *Lunik III* from 6.30 a.m. on 7 Oct. 1959, from a range of up to 43,750 miles *70 400 km* and transmitted to the Earth from a distance of 470 000 km *292,000 miles*. The first "soft" landing was made by the U.S.S.R.'s *Luna IX*, in the area of the Ocean of Storms on 3 Feb. 1966.

"Blue Moon"
Owing to sulphur particles in the upper atmosphere from a forest fire covering 250,000 acres *100 000 ha* between Mile 103 and Mile 119 on the Alaska Highway in northern British Columbia, Canada, the Moon took on a bluish colour, as seen from Great Britain, on the night of 26 Sept. 1950. The Moon also appeared green after the Krakatoa eruption of 27 Aug. 1883 (see page 62) and in Stockholm for 3 min on 17 Jan. 1884.

Crater *Largest*
Only 59 per cent of the Moon's surface is directly visible from the Earth because it is in "captured rotation", *i.e.* the period of rotation is equal to the period of orbit. The largest wholly visible crater is the walled plain Bailly, towards the Moon's South Pole, which is 183 miles *295 km* across, with walls rising to 14,000 ft *4 250 m*. The Orientale Basin, partly on the averted side, measures more than 600 miles *965 km* in diameter.

Crater *Deepest*
The deepest crater is the Newton crater, with a floor estimated to be between 23,000 and 29,000 ft *7 000–8 850 m* below its rim and 14,000 ft *2 250 m* below the level of the plain outside. The brightest directly visible spot on the Moon is *Aristarchus*.

Highest mountains
In the absence of a sea level, lunar altitudes are measured relative to a reference sphere of radius 1 738,000 km or *1,079.943 miles*. Thus the greatest elevation attained by any of the 12 U.S. astronauts has been 7 830 m *25,688 ft* on the Descartes Highlands by Capt. John Walter Young U.S.N. and Major Charles M. Duke Jr. on 27 Apr. 1972.

Temperature extremes
When the Sun is overhead the temperature on the lunar equator reaches 243° F *117,2° C* (31 deg F *17,2 deg C* above the boiling point of water). By sunset the temperature is 58° F *14,4° C* but after nightfall it sinks to −261° F *−162,7° C.*

Moon samples
The age attributed to the oldest of the moon material brought back to Earth by the *Apollo* programme crews has been soil dated to 4,720 million years.

THE SUN
Distance extremes
The Earth's 66,620 m.p.h. *107 220 km/h* orbit of 584,017,800 miles *939 885 500 km* around the Sun is elliptical, hence our distance from the Sun varies. The orbital speed varies between 65,520 m.p.h. *105 450 km/h* (minimum) and 67,750 m.p.h. *109 030 km/h.* The average distance of the Sun is 1.000 000 230 astronomical units or 92,955,829 miles *149 597 906 km.*

The closest approach (perihelion) is 91,402,000 miles *147 097 000 km* and the farthest departure (aphelion) is 94,510,000 miles *152 099 000 km.* The Solar System is revolving around the centre of the Milky Way once in each 225,000,000 years, at a speed of 481,000 m.p.h. *774 000 km/h* and has a velocity of 42,500 m.p.h. *68 400 km/h* relative to stars in our immediate region such as Vega, towards which it is moving.

Temperature and dimensions
The Sun has an internal temperature of about 16 000 000 K, a core pressure of 500,000,000 tons/in² and uses up 4,000,000 tons/*tonnes* of hydrogen per sec. thus providing a luminosity of 3 × 10²⁷ candlepower, with an intensity of 1,500,000 candles/in² *1 530 000 candelas*. The Sun has the stellar classification of a "yellow dwarf" and, although its density is only 1.407 times that of water, its mass is 332,946 times as much as that of the Earth. It has a mean diameter of 865,270 miles *1 392 520 km*. The Sun with a mass of 1.958 × 10²⁷ tons *1,989 × 10²⁷ tonnes* represents more than 99 per cent of the total mass of the Solar System.

Sun-spots *Largest*
To be visible to the *protected* naked eye, a Sun-spot must cover about one two-thousandth part of the Sun's disc

left: Friedrich Wilhelm Bessel (1784–1846) the German astronomer who first proved the immense distances of the stars by his parallax measurements in 1838. (*Radio Times Hulton Picture Library*). *centre:* The English astronomer Edmond Halley (1656–1742), who exactly predicted the return of his great comet 16 years after he died. (*Royal Society of London*). *right:* The first great telescopic observer, Galileo Galilei (1564–1642) whose discoveries included the satellites of Jupiter, the phases of Venus and the starry nature of the Milky Way. (*Royal Society of London*)

and thus have an area of about 500,000,000 miles² *1 300 million km².* The largest recorded Sun-spot occurred in the Sun's southern hemisphere on 8 April 1947. Its area was about 7,000 million miles² *18 000 million km²* with an extreme longitude of 187,000 miles *300 000 km* and an extreme latitude of 90,000 miles *145 000 km.* Sun-spots appear darker because they are more than 1 500 deg C cooler than the rest of the Sun's surface temperature of 5 525° C. The largest observed solar prominence was one protruding 365,000 miles *588 000 km,* observed from Skylab in 1973.

Most frequent

In October 1957 a smoothed Sun-spot count showed 263, the highest recorded index since records started in 1755 (*cf.* previous record of 239 in May 1778). In 1943 one Sun-spot lasted for 200 days from June to December.

ECLIPSES
Earliest recorded

The earliest extrapolated eclipses that have been identified are 1361 B.C. (lunar) and Oct. 2136 B.C. (solar). For the Middle East only, lunar eclipses have been extrapolated to 3450 B.C. and solar ones to 4200 B.C. No centre of the path of totality for a solar eclipse crossed London for the 575 years from 20 March 1140 to 3 May 1715. The next will be on 14 June 2151. The most recent occasion when a line of totality of a solar eclipse crossed Great Britain was on 29 June 1927 for 24.5 sec at 6.23 a.m. at West Hartlepool, Cleveland and the next instance will clip the Cornish coast on the morning of Wednesday 11 Aug. 1999. On 30 June 1954 a total eclipse was witnessed in Unst, Shetland Islands but the centre of the path of totality was to the north of territorial waters.

Longest duration

The maximum *possible* duration of an eclipse of the Sun is 7 min 31 sec. The longest actually *measured* was on 20 June 1955 (7 min 8 sec), seen from the Philippines. One of 7 min 29 sec should occur in mid Atlantic on 16 July 2186, which will then be the longest for 1,469 years. The longest possible in the British Isles is 5½ min. That of 15 June 885 lasted nearly 5 min, as will that of 20 July 2381 in the Border area. Durations can be extended by observers being airborne as on 30 June 1973 when an eclipse was "extended" to 72 min aboard *Concorde.* An annular eclipse may last for 12 min 24 sec. The longest totality of any lunar eclipse is 104 min. This has occurred many times.

Most and least frequent

The highest number of eclipses possible in a year is seven, as in 1935, when there were five solar and two lunar eclipses; or four solar and three lunar eclipses, as will occur in 1982. The lowest possible number in a year is two, both of which must be solar, as in 1944 and 1969.

COMETS
Earliest recorded

The earliest records of comets date from the 7th century B.C. The speeds of the estimated 2,000,000 comets vary from 700 m.p.h. *1 125 km/h* in outer space to 1,250,000 m.p.h. *2 000 000 km/h* when near the Sun. The successive appearances of Halley's Comet have been traced back to 467 B.C. It was first depicted in the Nuremburg Chronicle of A.D. 684. The first prediction of its return by Edmund Halley (1656–1742) proved true on Christmas Day 1758, 16 years after his death. Its next perihelion should be at 9.9 (*viz.* at 9.30 p.m. on the 9th) February 1986, 75.81 years after the last, which was on 19 April 1910. A sighting may occur in Dec. 1984.

Closest approach

On 1 July 1770, Lexell's Comet, travelling at a speed of 23.9 miles/sec *38,5 km/sec* (relative to the Sun), came within 745,000 miles *1 200 000 km* of the Earth. However, the Earth is believed to have passed through the tail of Halley's Comet, most recently on 19 May 1910.

Largest

Comets are so tenuous that it has been estimated that even the head of one rarely contains solid matter much more than *c.* 1 km *0.6 miles* in diameter. Tails, as in the case of the brightest of all, the Great Comet of 1843, may trail for 205,000,000 miles *330 million km.* The head of Holmes Comet of 1892 once measured 1,500,000 miles *2 400 000 km* in diameter. Comet Bennett which appeared in January 1970 was found to be enveloped in a hydrogen cloud measuring some 8,000,000 miles *12 750 000 km* in length.

Shortest period

Of all the recorded periodic comets (these are members of the Solar System), the one which most frequently returns is Encke's Comet, first identified in 1786. Its period of 1,206 days (3.3 years) is the shortest established. Not one of its 51 returns (including 1977) has been missed by astronomers. Now increasingly faint, it is expected to "die" by Feb. 1994. The most frequently observed comets are Schwassmann-Wachmann I, Kopff and Oterma which can be observed every year between Mars and Jupiter.

Longest period

At the other extreme is Delavan's Comet of 1914, whose path was not accurately determined. It is not expected to return for perhaps for 24 million years.

PLANETS
Largest

Planets (including the Earth) are bodies within the Solar System and which revolve round the Sun in definite orbits. Jupiter, with an equatorial diameter of 88,780 miles *142 880*

PROGRESSIVE ROCKET ALTITUDE RECORDS

A) 1,446,403,000 mls. 2 327 760 000 km.
Pioneer 10 · Kennedy Space Centre, Cape
Canaveral, Florida, USA · 2 March 1972

B) 242,000,000 mls. 389 450 000 km.
Mars 1 · USSR · 1 November 1962

C) 215,300,000 mls. 346 480 000 km.
Luna 1 · Tyura Tam, USSR · 2 January 1959

D) 70,700 mls. 113 770 km.
Pioneer 1-B Lunar Probe · Cape Canaveral,
Florida, USA · 11 October 1958

E) >2,700 mls. >4 345 km.
Farside No.5 / 4 stage USA · Eniwetok
Atoll · 20 October 1957

F) >800 mls. >1 300 km.
ICBM test flight · Tyura Tam/ Baikonur,
USSR · August 1957

G) 682 mls. 1097 km.
Jupiter C · Cape Canaveral, Florida, USA
20 September 1956

H) 318 mls. 512 km.
GFR B-5-B · ? Tyura Tam, USSR
1950-52

J) 244 mls. 392.6 km.
V–2/ WAC Corporal 2 stage Bumper No.5
White Sands, N.M., USA · 24 February 1949

K) 118 mls. 190 km.
A.4 rocket Germany · Heidelager, Poland
mid 1944

L) c.85 mls. c.136 km.
A.4 rocket Germany · Heidelager, Poland
early 1944

M) 52.46 mls. 84.42 km.
A.4 rocket · Peenemünde, Germany
3 October 1942

N) 8.1 mls. 13 km.
USSR "Stratosphere" rocket · USSR
1935

O) 3.1 mls. 5 km.
GIRD-X liquid fuel · USSR · 25 November
1933

P) 1.24 mls. 2 km.
Reinhold Tiling solid fuel rocket ·
Osnabruck, Germany · April 1931

Q) 0.71 mls. 1.14 km.
A 3–in rocket · near London, England
April 1750

above: A. Distance by 1 July 1978. A distance of 3,600 million miles *5 800 million km* will be reached by 1987 on its way to crossing the orbit of Pluto and leaving the Solar System's effective gravitational field. Pioneer 11 will fly-by Saturn on 1 Sept. 1979 at 108,000 mph *174 000 km/h* and then chase Pioneer 10 in leaving the Solar System for deep space. Mariner 11 (launch 20 Aug. 1977) and Mariner 12 (1 Sept. 1977) comprise the Jupiter-Saturn Mission. On 27 Aug. 1981 it may prove possible to re-target Mariner 11 to approach Uranus (31 Jan. 1986) and even Neptune (Sept. 1989). B. & C. Apogee in solar orbit. P. There is some evidence that Tiling may shortly after have reached 9,500 m *5.90 miles* with a solid fuel rocket at Wangerooge, East Friesian Islands, West Germany.

Planets

km and a polar diameter of 82,980 miles *133 540 km* is the largest of the nine major planets, with a mass 317.83 times, and a volume 1,318 times that of the Earth. It also has the shortest period of rotation resulting in a Jovian day of only 9 hrs 50 min 30.003 sec in the equatorial zone.

Smallest and Coldest
The coldest planet is Pluto, which has an estimated surface temperature of −360° F *−220° C* (100 deg F *53 deg C* above absolute zero). Its mean distance from the Sun is 3,674,488,000 miles *5 913 514 000 km* and its period of revolution is 248.54 years. Its diameter is c. 3000 km *1,880 miles* and has a mass about 1/500th of that of the Earth. Pluto was first recorded by Clyde William Tombaugh (b. 4 Feb. 1906) at Lowell Observatory, Flagstaff, Arizona, U.S.A., on 18 Feb. 1930 from photographs taken on 23 and 29 Jan. and announced on 13 March. Because of its orbital eccentricity Pluto moved closer to the Sun than Neptune between 23 Jan. 1979 and 15 Mar. 1999.

Fastest
Mercury, which orbits the Sun at an average distance of 35,983,100 miles *57 909 200 km* has a period of revolution of 87.9686 days, so giving the highest average speed in orbit of 107,030 m.p.h. *172 248 km/h.*

Hottest
For Venus a surface temperature of c. 480° C *896° F* has been estimated from measurements made from the U.S.S.R. *Venera 7* and *Venera 8* probes in 1970 and 1972.

Nearest
The fellow planet closest to the Earth is Venus, which is, at times, about 25,700,000 miles *41 360 000 km* inside the Earth's orbit, compared with Mars's closest approach of 34,600,000 miles *55 680 000 km* outside the Earth's orbit. Mars, known since 1965 to be cratered, has temperatures ranging from 85° F *29,4° C* to −190° F *−123° C.*

Surface features
By far the highest and most spectacular is Olympus Mons (formerly Nix Olympica) in the Tharsis region with a diameter of 500–600 km *310–370 miles* and a height of 26 ± 3 km *75,450–95,150 ft.* above the surrounding plain.

Brightest and faintest
Viewed from the Earth, by far the brightest of the five planets visible to the naked eye (Uranus at magnitude 5.7 is only marginally visible) is Venus, with a maximum magnitude of −4.4. The faintest is Pluto, with a magnitude of 14.

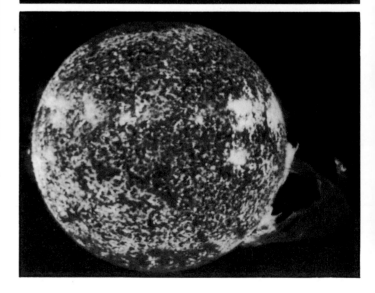

below: The most spectacular solar flare ever recorded, spanning more than 588 000 km *365,000 miles*, and photographed on 19 Dec. 1973, during the third and final manned Skylab mission (see p. 73). *(NASA)*

PROGRESSIVE RECORDS OF THE MOST DISTANT MEASURED HEAVENLY BODIES

The possible existence of galaxies external to our own Milky Way system was mooted in 1789 by Sir William Herschel (1738–1822). These extra-galactic nebulae were first termed "island universes". Sir John Herschel (1792–1871) opined as early as 1835 that some were 48,000 light-years distant. The first direct measurement of any body outside our Solar System was in 1838.

Estimated Distance in Light Years[1]		Object	Method	Astronomer	Observatory	Date
nearly 11 (now 11.08)		61 Cygni	Parallax	F. Bessel	Königsberg, Germany	1838
>20 (now 26)		Vega	Parallax	F. G. W. Struve	Dorpat (now Tartu), Estonia	1840
c. 200		Limit	Parallax			by 1900
750,000 (now 2.2 m)[2]		Galaxy M31	Cepheid variable	E. P. Hubble	Mt. Wilson, Cal., U.S.A.	1923
900,000 (now 2.2 m)[2]		Galaxy M31	Cepheid variable	E. P. Hubble	Mt. Wilson, Cal., U.S.A.	1924

Millions of Light Years*	% of c					
			Red shift[3]			
250	2.5	Ursa Major Galaxy		E. P. Hubble	Mt. Wilson, Cal., U.S.A.	by 1934[4]
>350	3.6			M. L. Humason	Palomar, Cal., U.S.A.	by 1952
	>10			M. L. Humason	Palomar, Cal., U.S.A.	1954
3,000	31	Cluster 1448			Palomar, Cal., U.S.A.	1956
c. 4,500	46	3C 295 in Boötes			Palomar, Cal., U.S.A.	June 1960
5,300	54.5	QSO 3C 147			Palomar, Cal., U.S.A.	April 1964[5]
8,700	80	QSO 3C 9		M. Schmidt	Palomar, Cal., U.S.A.	May 1965
c. 10,000	81			Margaret Burbidge et al.	Palomar, Cal., U.S.A.	Dec. 1965
	82.2	QSO 1116 + 12		M. Schmidt	Palomar, Cal., U.S.A.	Jan. 1966
13,000	82.4	QSO PKS 0237 − 23		J. G. Bolton	Parkes, N.S.W., Australia	March 1967
	83.8	QSO 4C 25.5		E. Olsen	Palomar, Cal., U.S.A.	July 1968
	87.5	QSO 4C 05.34			Kitt Peak, Arizona, U.S.A.	May 1970
15,000	92	QSO OH 471		R. F. Carswell et al.	Steward Observatory, Arizona, U.S.A.	March 1973
15,500	95.5	QSO OQ 172		Margaret Burbidge et al.	Lick Observatory, Cal., U.S.A.	April 1973

Note: c is the notation for the speed of light. (see page 71)
[1] Term first utilised in March 1888.
[2] Re-estimate by W. Baade in Sept. 1952.
[3] Discovered by V. M. Slipher from Flagstaff, Arizona, U.S.A. 1920.
[4] In this year Hubble opined that the observable horizon would be 3,000 m light-years.

[5] Then said that QSO 3C2 and 286 might be more distant—latter claimed by Dr. Shklovsky (USSR) to be receding at 55% of c in Dec. 1963.
* The distances are on a Euclidian model. According to the Schramm model, based on an August 1978 value of the Hubble constant (c. 60 km/sec/megaparsec) the expansion of the Universe began 14,500 ± 1,000 million years ago.

Densest and least dense

Earth is the densest planet with an average figure of 5.515 times that of water, whilst Saturn has an average density only about one eighth of this value or 0.705 times that of water.

Conjunctions

The most dramatic recorded conjunction (coming together) of the other seven principal members of the Solar System (Sun, Moon, Mercury, Venus, Mars, Jupiter and Saturn) occurred on 5 Feb. 1962, when 16° covered all seven during an eclipse in the Pacific area. It is possible that the sevenfold conjunction of September 1186 spanned only 12°. The next notable conjunction will take place on 5 May 2000.

SATELLITES
Most

Of the nine major planets, all but Venus and Mercury have satellites. The planet with the most is Jupiter, with four large and nine small moons. The Earth and Pluto are the only planets with a single satellite. The distance from their parent planets varies from the 5,827 miles *9 378 km* of *Phobos* from the centre of Mars to the 14,730,000 miles *23 705 000 km* of Jupiter's outer satellite Sinope (Jupiter IX). The Solar System has, (excluding Saturn's unproven Xth and XIth, and Jupiter's unproven XIVth, but including Pluto's probable moon *Charon*, announced in July 1978) a total of 33 satellites.

Largest and smallest

The largest satellite is the sixth moon of Saturn, *Titan*, with a diameter of 3,400 miles *5 500 km* and a possible atmospheric thickness of 90 miles *150 km*. The heaviest satellite is the third moon of Jupiter, *Ganymede*, which is 2.02 times heavier than our own Moon, but it is possible that the large satellite of Neptune, *Triton*, is both larger than *Titan* and heavier than *Ganymede*. The smallest satellite is Jupiter XIII with a diameter of only 8 km *5 miles*.

Largest asteroids

In the belt which lies between Mars and Jupiter, there are some 45,000 (only 2,042 numbered to Oct. 1977) minor planets or asteroids which are, for the most part, too small to yield to diameter measurement. The largest and first discovered (by Piazzi at Palermo, Sicily on 1 Jan. 1801) of these is *Ceres*, with a diameter of 623 miles *1 003 km*. The only one visible to the naked eye is *Vesta* (diameter 334 miles *538 km* discovered on 29 Mar. 1807 by Dr. Heinrich Wilhelm Olbers (1758–1840), a German amateur astronomer. The closest measured approach to the Earth by an asteroid was 485,000 miles *780 000 km* in the case of *Hermes* on 30 Oct. 1937. The most distant detected is Object Kowal, found between Saturn and Uranus on 18–19 Oct. 1977, by Charles Kowal from the Hale Observatory, California U.S.A. and tentatively named *Chiron*.

STARS
Largest and most massive

The fainter component of Plaskett's star discovered by J. S. Plaskett from the Dominion Astrophysical Observatory, Victoria, British Columbia, Canada in 1922 is the most massive star known with a mass c. 55 times that of the Sun. Betelgeux (top left star of Orion) has a diameter of > 400 million km *250 million miles* and in 1978 was found to be surrounded by a tenuous "shell" of potassium 1,6 million million km or 11 000 astronomical units. The light from Betelgeux left it in A.D. 1460. The diameter of IRS 5 is believed to be 15 000 million km *9500 million miles*.

Smallest

The least massive stars known are the two components of the binary star *Wolf 424*, a faint star in Virgo. Each of the two stars has only 0.06 solar masses.

Brightest

Sirius A (*Alpha Canis Majoris*), also known as the Dog Star, is apparently the brightest star of the 5,776 stars visible in the heavens, with an apparent magnitude of −1.46. It is in the constellation *Canis Major* and is visible in the winter months of the northern hemisphere, being due south at midnight on the last day of the year. The Sirius system is 8.64 light-years distant and has a luminosity 26 times as much as that of the Sun. It has a diameter of 1,450,000 miles *2,33 million km* and a mass of 4.20×10^{27} tons *$4,26 \times 10^{27}$ tonnes*. The faint white dwarf companion Sirius B has a diameter of only 6,000 miles *10 000 km* but is 350,000 times heavier than the Earth.

Farthest

The Solar System, with its Sun, nine principal planets, 33 satellites, asteroids and comets, was discovered in 1921 to be

The most travelled humans of all time, Col. Vladimir Kovalyonok and Aleksandr Ivanchenkov, who spent 139 days 14 hrs 47 min in space, returning to Earth on 2 Nov. 1978 (see p. 78). (*Novosti*)

about 32,000 light-years from the centre of the lens-shaped Milky Way galaxy (diameter 100,000 light-years) of about 100,000 million stars. The most distant star in our galaxy is therefore about 80,000 light-years distant.

Nearest

Excepting the special case of our own Sun (*q.v.* above) the nearest star is the very faint *Proxima Centauri*, which is 4.28 light-years (25,200,000,000,000 miles *40,5 × 10^{12} km*) away.

The nearest star visible to the naked eye is the southern hemisphere star *Alpha Centauri*, or *Rigel Kentaurus* (4.38 light-years), with a magnitude of −0.29. By A.D. 11,800 the nearest star will be Barnard's Star (see below under Stellar Planets) at a distance of 3.75 light years.

Most and least luminous

If all stars could be viewed at the same distance, the most luminous would be the apparently faint variable *S. Doradûs*, in the Greater Magellanic Cloud (*Nebecula Major*), which can be nearly 1 million times brighter than the Sun, and has an absolute magnitude of −8.9. The variable η Carinae in *c*. 1840 was perhaps 4 million times more luminous than the sun. The faintest star detected visually is a very red star, known as LP 425-140, 23.5 light years distant with about one millionth of the Sun's brightness.

Brightest super-nova
Super-novae, or temporary "stars" which flare and then fade, occur perhaps five times in 1,000 years in our galaxy. The brightest "star" ever seen by historic man is believed to be the super-nova in Apr. 1006 near Lupus β which flared for 2 years and attained a magnitude of −9 to −10. It is now believed to be the radio source G.327.6 + 14.5 nearly 3000 light-years distant.

Constellations
The largest of the 89 constellations is *Hydra* (the Sea Serpent), which covers 1,302.844 deg² or 6.3 per cent of the hemisphere and contains at least 68 stars visible to the naked eye (to 5.5 mag.). The constellation *Centaurus* (Centaur), ranking ninth in area embraces however at least 94 such stars. The smallest constellation is *Crux Australis* (Southern Cross) with an area of 68.477 deg² compared with the 41,252.96 deg² of the whole sky.

Stellar planets
Planetary companions, with a mass of less than 7 per cent of their parent star, have been reported for 61 *Cygni* (1942), *Lalande* 21185 (1960) *Krüger 60*, *Ci 2354*, *BD + 20° 2465* and one of the two components of *70 Ophiuchi*. A planet of 6 times the mass of Jupiter 750 million miles *1 200 million km*, from *Epsilon Eridani* (see below) was reported by Peter van de Kamp in January 1973. In August 1975 van de Kamp reported that Barnard's Star (Munich 15040) possibly had two planets equivalent in mass to Jupiter and Saturn.

Listening operations ("Project Ozma") on *Tau Ceti* and *Epsilon Eridani* were maintained from 4 April 1960 to March 1961, using an 85-ft *25,90 m* radio telescope at Deer Creek Valley, Green Bank, West Virginia, U.S.A. The apparatus was probably insufficiently sensitive for any signal from a distance of 10.7 light-years to be received. Monitoring has been conducted from Gorkiy, U.S.S.R. since 1969.

Longest Name
The longest name for any star is *Shurnarkabtishashutu*, the Arabic for "under the southern horn of the bull".

Black Holes
The first tentative identification of a Black Hole was announced in December 1972 in the binary-star X-ray source Cygnus X-1. This is a small dark companion of some 10 solar masses from which the escape velocity tends to *c* (the velocity of light). The critical size has been estimated to be as low as a diameter of 3.67 miles *5,90 km*. In early 1978 supermassive Black Holes were suggested with a mass of 100 million suns—2×10^{35} tonnes.

THE UNIVERSE
Outside the Milky Way galaxy, which possibly moves around the centre of the local super-cluster of 2,500 neighbouring galaxies at a speed of 1,350,000 m.p.h. *2 172 500 km/h*, there exist 10,000 million other galaxies. These range in size up to the largest known object in the Universe, the radio galaxy 3C-236 in Leo Minor announced from Westerbork Synthesis Radio Telescope, Netherlands in August 1974, which is 18.6 million light-years across. In Oct. 1976 it was suggested that 3C-123 may have a diameter of 120 million light-years.

Farthest visible object
The remotest heavenly body visible with the naked eye is the Great Galaxy in *Andromeda* (Mag. 3.47), known as Messier 31. This is a rotating nebula in spiral form, and its distance from the Earth is about 2,200,000 light-years, or about 13,000,000,000,000,000,000 miles *21×10^{18} km*. It is just possible however that, under ideal seeing conditions, Messier 33, the Spiral in Triangulum (Mag. 5.79), can be glimpsed by the naked eye of keen-sighted people at a distance of 2,300,000 light-years.

Quasars
In November 1962 the existence of quasi-stellar radio sources ("quasars" or QSO's) was established. No satisfactory model has yet been constructed to account for the immensely high luminosity of bodies apparently so distant and of such small diameter. In April 1975 it was announced that 3C-279 had a measured luminosity of 2.75×10^{14} that of the sun.

Pulsars
The earliest observation of a pulsating radio source or "pulsar" CP 1919 by Dr. Jocelyn Bell Burnell was announced from the Mullard Radio Astronomy Observatory, Cambridge-shire, England, on 29 Feb. 1968. The 100th was announced from Jodrell Bank, Cheshire in June 1973. The fastest so far discovered is NP 0532 in the Crab Nebula with a pulse period of 33 milli-sec. The now accepted model is that they are rotating neutron stars with an inner core density of 4.7×10^{15} g/cm³ (*74,400 million tons/in³*).

Remotest object
The interpretation of very large red shifts exhibited by quasars is controversial. The record value of Z = 3.53 for Quasar OQ 172 (see Table p. 75) has been interpreted in Aug. 1978 as between 13,500 and 15,500 million light years. The 3° background radiation discovered in 1965 by Penzias and Wilson appears to be moving at a velocity of 99.9998 % c.

Age of the Universe
In November 1976 a newly published value of Hubble's constant indicated that the age of the Universe lay between 17,500 and 21,300 million years (see also Table p. 75). In Aug. 1978, however, the parameters were re-assessed at between 13,500 and 15,500 million years.

ROCKETRY AND MISSILES
Earliest uses
War rockets, propelled by a charcoal-saltpetre-sulphur gunpowder, were described by Tseng Kung Liang of China in 1042. These early rockets became known in Europe by 1258. The pioneer of military rocketry in Britain was Col. Sir William Congreve, Bt., M.P. (1772–1828), Comptroller of the Royal Laboratory, Woolwich, Greater London and Inspector of Military Machines, whose "six-pound *2,72 kg* rocket" was developed to a range of 2,000 yds *1 825 m* by 1805 and first used by the Royal Navy against Boulogne, France on 8 Oct. 1806.

The first launching of a liquid-fuelled rocket (patented 14 July 1914) was by Dr. Robert Hutchings Goddard (1882–1945) of the United States, at Auburn, Massachusetts, U.S.A., on 16 March 1926, when his rocket reached an altitude of 41 ft *12,5 m* and travelled a distance of 184 ft *56 m*. The U.S.S.R.'s earliest rocket was the semi-liquid fuelled GIRD-IX tested on 17 Aug. 1933.

Longest ranges
On 16 March 1962, Nikita Khrushchyov, then Prime Minister of the U.S.S.R., claimed in Moscow that the U.S.S.R. possessed a "global rocket" with a range of 30 000 km (*about 19,000 miles*) i.e. more than the Earth's semi-circumference and therefore capable of hitting any target from either direction.

Most powerful *World*
It has been suggested that the U.S.S.R. lunar booster which blew up at Tyura Tam in the summer (? July) of 1969 had a thrust of 10 to 14 million lb. *4,5 to 6,35 million kg*. There is some evidence of a launch of a U.S.S.R. "G" class lunar booster, larger than the U.S. *Saturn V* on 11 May 1973.

The most powerful rocket that has been publicized is the *Saturn V*, used for the Project Apollo and Skylab programmes on which development began in January 1962, at the John F. Kennedy Space Center, Merritt Island, Florida, U.S.A. The rocket is 363 ft 8 in *110,85 m* tall, with a payload of 74 783 kg *73.60 tons* in the case of *Skylab I*, and gulps 13.4 tons *13,6 tonnes* of propellant per sec for 2½ min (2,010 tons

2 042 tonnes). Stage I (S-IC) is 138 ft *42,06 m* tall and is powered by five Rocketdyne F-1 engines, using liquid oxygen (LOX) and kerosene, each delivering 1,514,000 lb. *686 680 kg* thrust. Stage II (S-II) is powered by five LOX and liquid hydrogen Rocketdyne J-2 engines with a total thrust of 1,141,453 lb. *517 759 kg* while Stage III (designated S-IVB) is powered by a single 228,290 lb. *103 550 kg* thrust J-2 engine. The whole assembly generates 175,600,000 h.p. and weighs up to 7,600,000 lb. (3,393 tons *3 447 tonnes*) fully loaded in the case of *Apollo 17*. It was first launched on 9 Nov. 1967, from Cape Canaveral (then Kennedy), Florida.

Highest velocity

The first space vehicle to achieve the Third Cosmic velocity sufficient to break out of the Solar System was *Pioneer 10* (see page 74). The Atlas SLV-3C launcher with a modified Centaur D second stage and a Thiokol Te-364-4 third stage left the Earth at an unprecedented 32,114 m.p.h. *51 682 km/h* on 2 March 1972. The highest recorded velocity of any space vehicle has been 240 000 km/h *149,125 m.p.h.* in the case of the U.S.-German solar probe Helios B launched on 15 Jan. 1976. By 10 May 1979 *Pioneer 10* was 2 900 million km distant.

Ion rockets

Speeds of up to 100,000 m.p.h. *160 000 km/h* are envisaged for rockets powered by an ion discharge. An ion thruster has been maintained for 9,715 hours (404 days 19 hrs) at the Lewis Research Center in Cleveland, Ohio, U.S.A. Ion rockets were first used in flight by NASA's SERT I rocket launched on 20 July 1964.

SPACE FLIGHT

The physical laws controlling the flight of artificial satellites were first propounded by Sir Isaac Newton (1642–1727) in his *Philosophiae Naturalis Principia Mathematica* ("Mathematical Principles of Natural Philosophy"), begun in March 1686 and first published in the summer of 1687. The first artificial satellite was successfully put into orbit at an altitude of 142/588 miles *228,5/946 km* and a velocity of more than 17,750 m.p.h. *28 565 km/h* from Tyura Tam, a site located 170 miles *275 km* east of the Aral Sea on the night of 4 Oct. 1957. This spherical satellite *Sputnik* ("Fellow Traveller") 1, officially designated "Satellite 1957 Alpha 2", weighed 83,6 kg *184.3 lb.*, with a diameter of 58 cm *22.8 in*, and its lifetime is believed to have been 92 days, ending on 4 Jan. 1958. It was designed under the direction of Dr. Sergey Pavlovich Korolyov (1907–66). By January 1978 it was estimated that there were 4,470 discreet pieces of hardware in the Earth's orbit. By October 1977 it was estimated that 40 per cent of all launches were from Plesetsk, U.S.S.R.

Earliest successful manned satellite

The first successful manned space flight began at 9.07 a.m. (Moscow time), or 6.08 a.m. G.M.T., on 12 April 1961. Cosmonaut Flight Major (later Colonel) Yuriy Alekseyevich Gagarin (born 9 March 1934) completed a single orbit of the Earth in 89.34 min in the 4.65 ton *4,72 tonnes* space vehicle *Vostok* ('East') I. The take-off was from Tyura Tam in Kazakhstan, and the landing was 108 min later near the village of Smelovka, near Engels, in the Saratov region of the U.S.S.R. The maximum speed was 17,560 m.p.h. *28 260 km/h* and the maximum altitude 327 km *203.2 miles* in a flight of 40 868,6 km *25,394.5 miles*. Major Gagarin, invested a Hero of the Soviet Union and awarded the Order of Lenin and the Gold Star Medal, was killed in a jet plane crash near Moscow on 27 March 1968.

First woman in space

The first and only woman to orbit the Earth was Junior Lieutenant (now Lt.-Col.) Valentina Vladimirovna Tereshkova, now Mme. Nikolayev (b. 6 March 1937), who was launched in *Vostok 6* from Tyura Tam, U.S.S.R., at 9.30 a.m. G.M.T. on 16 June 1963, and landed at 8.16 a.m. on 19 June, after a flight of 2 days 22 hrs 42 min, during which she completed over 48 orbits (1,225,000 miles *1 971 000 km*) and passed momentarily within 3 miles *4,8 km* of *Vostok 5*. She was formerly a textile worker. Her mission was variously reported to be punctuated with pleas to be brought back due to giddiness and of being extended because of her excellent performance.

First in flight fatality

Col. Vladimir Mikhailovich Komarov (b. 16 March 1927) was launched in *Soyuz* ("Union") 1 at 00.35 a.m. G.M.T. on 23 April 1967. The spacecraft was in orbit for about 25½ hrs but he impacted on the final descent due to parachute failure and was thus the first man indisputedly known to have died during space flight.

First "walk" in space

The earliest undoubted instance of an astronaut floating free outside a space vehicle was by Astronaut, the late Edward H. White II (killed 27 Jan. 1967) for 21 min over Hawaii to the U.S. Atlantic coast on 3 June 1965 from Gemini IV. Evidence for the earlier claim of Lt.-Col. Aleksey A. Leonov from *Voshkod 2* on 18 Mar. 1965 is not unreservedly accepted.

Longest manned space flight

The longest time spent in the weightlessness of space has been 139 days 14 hrs 47 mins by Col. Vladimir Kovalyonok (b. 1942) and Aleksandr Sergeyevich Ivanchenkov (b. 1940), who were launched at 11.17 p.m. (Moscow time) on 15 June 1978 from the Baikonur Cosmodrome, to join *Salyut 6* and landed 180 km *112 miles* south east of Dzhezkazgan, Kazakhstan at 2.05 pm on 2 Nov. 1978. During this time they became the most travelled humans of all-time with a mileage of more than 56 million miles *90 million km*. It was reported that on their return to Earth's gravity they had difficulty in re-learning to walk and in picking up cups of tea. Additionally in the mornings they tried to "swim" out of bed.

Astronaut *Oldest and youngest*

The oldest of the 87 people in space has been Donald Kent "Deke" Slayton (b. Sparta, Wisconsin, U.S.A. 1 Mar. 1924) who was aged 51 years 146 days when launched on the Apollo-Soyuz mission on 24 July 1975. The youngest has been Major (later Col.) Gherman Stepanovich Titov (b. 11 Sept. 1935), who was aged 25 years 329 days when launched in *Vostok 2* on 6 Aug. 1961.

Duration record on the Moon

The crew of *Apollo 17* collected a record 253 lb. *114,8 kg* of rock and soil during their 22 hrs 5 min "extra-vehicular activity". They were Capt. Eugene A. Cernan, U.S.N. (b. Chicago, 14 Mar. 1934) and Dr. Harrison H. (Jack) Schmitt (b. Santa Rosa, New Mexico 3 July 1935) who became the 12th man on the moon. The crew were on the lunar surface for 74 hrs 59½ min during this longest of lunar missions which took 12 days 13 hrs 51 min on 7–12 Dec. 1972.

First extra-terrestrial vehicle

The first wheeled vehicle landed on the Moon was *Lunokhod 1* which began its Earth-controlled travels on 17 Nov. 1970. It moved a total of 10,54 km *6.54 miles* on gradients up to 30 deg in the Mare Imbrium and did not become non-functioning until 4 Oct. 1971. The lunar speed and distance record was set by the *Apollo 16* Rover with 11.2 m.p.h. *18 km/h* downhill and 22.4 miles *33,8 km*.

Closest Approach to the Sun

The research spacecraft *Helios B* approached within 27 million miles *43,4 million km* of the Sun, carrying both U.S. and West German instrumentation on 16 Apr. 1976.

Largest Space Object

The heaviest object orbited is the Apollo 15 (spacecraft plus third stage) which, prior to Trans lunar injection in parking orbit weighed 140 512 kg *138.29 tons*. The 442 lb. *200 kg* U.S. R.A.E. (radio astronomy explorer) B or Explorer 49 launched on 10 June 1973 has, however, antennae, 1,500 ft *415 m* from tip to tip.

Most expensive project

The total cost of the U.S. manned space programme up to and including the lunar mission of *Apollo 17* has been estimated to be $25,541,400,000 (£9,823,150,000). The first 15 years of the U.S.S.R. space programme from 1958 to Sept. 1973 has been estimated to have cost $45,000 million.

DRINK: Smallest bottles

WHEN!

THE SCIENTIFIC WORLD

1. ELEMENTS

All known matter in, on and beyond the Earth is made up of chemical elements. The total of naturally-occurring elements so far detected is 94, comprising, at ordinary temperature, two liquids, 11 gases and 81 solids. They so-called "fourth state" of matter is plasma, when negatively charged electrons and positively-charged ions are in flux.

Lightest and heaviest sub-nuclear particles

By January 1979 the existence of 23 "stable particles, 37 meson resonance multiplets and 56 baryon resonance multiplets" was accepted, representing the possible eventual discovery of 221 particles and an equal number of anti-particles. Of SU(3) particles the one with the highest mass is the omega minus, announced on 24 Feb. 1964 from the Brookhaven National Laboratory, near Upton, Long Island, New York State, U.S.A. It has a mass state of 1672.2 ± 0.4 Mev and a lifetime of 1.1×10^{-10} sec. Sub-atomic concepts require that the masses of the graviton, photon, and neutrino should all be zero. Based on the sensitivities of various cosmological theories, upper limits for the masses of these particles are $7,6 \times 10^{-67}$ g for the graviton; $3,0 \times 10^{-53}$ g for the photon and $1,4 \times 10^{-32}$ g for the neutrino (c.f. $9,10953 \times 10^{-28}$ g for the mass of an electron.)

THE 107 ELEMENTS

There are 94 known naturally-occurring elements comprising, at ordinary temperatures, two liquids, 11 gases, 72 metals and 9 other solids. To date the discovery of a further 13 transuranic elements (Elements 95 to 107) has been claimed of which 9 are undisputed.

Category	Name	Symbol	Discovery of Element	Record
Commonest (lithosphere)	Oxygen	O	1771 Scheele (Germany-Sweden)	46.60% by weight
Commonest (atmosphere)	Nitrogen	N	1772 Priestly (G.B.) et al.	78.09% by volume
Commonest (extra-terrestrial)	Hydrogen	H	1776 Cavendish (G.B.)	90% of all matter
Rarest (of the 94)	Astatine	At	1940 Corson (U.S.) et al.	1/100th oz. 0,35 g in Earth's crust
Lightest	Hydrogen	H	1776 Cavendish (G.B.)	0.005612 lb/ft³ 0,00008989 g/cm³
Lightest (Metal)	Lithium	Li	1817 Afrwedson (Sweden)	33.30 lb/ft³ 0,5334 g/cm³
Densest	Osmium	Os	1804 Tennant (G.B.)	1,410 lb/ft³ 22,59 g/cm³
Heaviest (Gas)	Radon	Rn	1900 Dorn (Germany)	0.6299 lb/ft³ 0,01009 g/cm³
Newest*	Unnilseptium	Uns	1976 Oganesyan et al (U.S.S.R.)	highest atomic number (element 107)
Purest	Helium	⁴He	1895 Ramsay (G.B.)	2 parts in 10¹⁵ (1978)
Hardest	Carbon	C	— prehistoric	Diamond allotrope, Knoop value 8,400
Most Expensive	Californium	Cf	1950 Seaborg et al. (U.S.)	Sold in 1968 for $1000 per µg
Most Stable†	Tellurium	Te 130	1782 von Reichenstein (Austro. Hung.)	Half-life of 2.51 × 10²¹ years (1974)
Least Stable	Lithium (isotope 5)	Li 5	1817 Afrwedson (Sweden)	Half-life of 4.4 × 10⁻²² sec.
Most Isotopes	Caesium	Cs	1860 Bunsen & Kirchhoff (Germ)	34
Least Isotopes	Hydrogen	H	1776 Cavendish (G.B.)	3 (confirmed)
Most Ductile	Gold	Au	ante 3000 B.C.	1 oz. drawn to 43 miles 1 g/2,4 km
Highest Ductility in Tension	Lead-tin (1:1.)			
Highest Tensile Strength	Boron	B	1808 Gay-Lussac et al. (France)	3.9 × 10⁶ lb f/in² 26,8 GPa
Lowest Melting/Boiling Point	Helium	⁴He	1895 Ramsay (G.B.)	−272,375°C under pressure 24.985 atm (25320 kPa) and −268.928° C
Highest Melting/Boiling Point	Tungsten	W	1783 J. J. & F. d'Elhuyar (Spain)	3 422° C and 5 730° C
Lowest Expansion (negative)	Plutonium	Pu	1940 Seaborg (U.S.) et al	−5.8 × 10⁻⁵ cm/cm/deg C between 450–480° C (Delta prime allotrope (disc. 1953)
Lowest Expansion (positive)	Carbon (diamond)	C	— Prehistoric	1.0 × 10⁻⁶ cm/cm/deg C (at 20° C)
Highest Expansion (metal)	Caesium	Cs	1860 Bunsen & Kirchhoff (Germ.)	9.7 × 10⁻⁵ cm/cm/deg C (at 20° C)
Highest Expansion (gas)	Nitrogen	N	1916 Beta allotrope	108 × 10⁻³ cm/cm/deg C (c. −210° C)
Most Poisonous	Plutonium	Pu	1940 Seaborg (U.S.) et al.	1 µg or microgramme (1 thirty millionth of an oz.) inhaled or swallowed will cause cancer. With a half-life of 23,640 years, toxicity is retained for a thousand centuries.

* Provisional I.U.P.A.C. name. Evidence alleging the existence of Elements 116, 124 and 126 published on 17 June 1976 subsequently was declared to have been misconceived. Unnilhexium (Unh) or element 106 was identified by Ghiorso et al (USA) on 9 Sept. 1974.

† Double beta decay estimate. Alpha particle record is Lead-204 at 1.4 × 10¹⁷ years (1958) and Beta particle record is Cadmium 113 at 9 × 10¹⁵ years (Greth, Gangadharan and Wolke, 1969).

CHEMICAL COMPOUNDS

It has been estimated that there are 4,040,000 described chemical compounds of which 63,000 are (1978) in common use.

Most Refractory	Tantulum Carbide TaCo-88	Melts at 4 010° ± 75 deg C
Most Refractory (plastics)	Modified polymides	900°F 482°C for short periods
Lowest Expansion	Invar metal (Ni-Fe alloy with C and Mn)	1,3 × 10⁻⁷ cm/cm/deg C at 20° C
Highest Tensile Strength	Sapphire whisker Al_2O_3	6 × 10⁶lb/in² 42,7 GPa
Highest Tensile Strength (plastics)	Polyvinyl alcoholic fibres	1.4 × 10⁵ lbf/in² 1,03 GPa
Most Magnetic	Cobalt-copper-samarium Co_3Cu_2Sm	10,500 oersted coercive force
Least Magnetic alloy	Copper nickel alloy CuNi	963 parts Cu to 37 parts Ni
Most Pungent	Vanillaldehyde	Detectable at 2 × 10⁻⁸ mg/litre
Sweetest	1n-propoxy-2-amino-4-nitro-benzene	5,600 × as sweet as 1% sucrose
Bitterest	Bitrex or Benzyl diethyl ammonium benzoate	200 × as bitter as quinine sulphate
Most Acidic[1]	Perchloric acid ($HClO_4$)	pH value of normal solution tends to 0.
Most Alkaline	Caustic soda (NaOH) and potash (KOH) and tetramethylammonium hydroxide (N(CH₃)₄OH)	pH value of normal solution is 14.
Highest Specific Impulse	Hydrogen with liquid fluorine	447 lb f/sec/lb 4382 N/sec/kg
Most Poisonous	Thiopentone (a barbiturate)	Intracardiac injection will kill in 1 to 2 secs.

[1] *The most powerful acid, assessed on its power as a hydrogen-ion donor, is a solution of antimony pentafluoride in fluorosulphonic acid—$SbF_5 + FSO_3H$.*

Newest particles

After 41 months of experiment the tau lepton (symbol T⁻) was confirmed by Prof. Martin Perl at the Stanford Linear Accelerator Center California, USA in December 1978.

Most and Least stable

The proton was measured to be stable against decay in 1974 for a lifetime in excess of 2×10^{30} years. The least stable or shortest lived nuclear particles discovered are the rho prime meson (definite proof of existence announced on 29 Jan. 1973) and the three baryon resonances N (2650), N (3030), Δ (2850) and Δ (3230), all 1.6×10^{-24} sec.

Substance smelliest

The most evil smelling substance, of the 17,000 smells so far classified, must be a matter of opinion but ethyl mercaptan (C_2H_5SH) and butyl seleno-mercaptan (C_4H_9SeH), are powerful claimants, each with a smell reminiscent of a combination of rotting cabbage, garlic, onions and sewer gas.

Most expensive perfume

The retail prices of the most expensive perfumes tend to be fixed at public relations rather than economic levels. The most expensive ingredient in perfume is pure French middle note jasmine essence at £2,900 per kg or £82.20p per oz.

Most potent poison

The rickettsial disease, Q-fever can be instituted by a *single* organism but is only fatal in 1 in 1,000 cases. About 10 organisms of *Francisella tularenesis* (formerly *Pasteurella tularenesis*) can institute tularaemia variously called alkali disease, Francis disease or deerfly fever, and this is fatal in upwards of 10 cases in 1,000.

Most powerful nerve gas

In the early 1950s substances known as V-agents, notably VX, 300 times more toxic than phosgene ($COCl_2$) used in World War I, were developed at the Chemical Defence Experimental Establishment, Porton Down, Wiltshire. V-agents are lethal at 1 mg per man. Patents were applied for in 1962 and published in February 1974.

Most powerful drugs

The most powerful commonly available drug is d-Lysergic Acid Diethylamide tartrate (LSD-25, $C_{20}H_{25}N_3O$) first produced in 1938 for common cold research and as a hallucinogen by Dr. Albert Hoffmann (Swiss) on 16–19 Apr. 1943. The most potent analgesic drug is Etorphine or M-99, announced in June 1963 by Dr. Kenneth W. Bentley (b. 1925) and D. G. Hardy of Reckitt & Sons Ltd. of Hull, Humberside, with almost 10,000 times the potency of morphine.

Most prescribed drug

The benzodiazepine group tranquillizing drug Valium discovered by Hoffmann-La Roche is the world's most widely used drug.

Most absorbant substance

The U.S. Department of Agriculture Research Service announced on 18 Aug. 1974 that "H-span" or Super Slurper composed of one half starch derivative and one fourth each of acrylamide and acrylic acid can when treated with iron retain water 1,300 times its own weight.

Finest powder

Particulate matter of 25 to 40 Å or $2,564 \times 10^{-6}$ cm was reportedly produced by an electron beam evaporation process at the Atomic Energy Establishment, Harwell in October 1972. The paper was published by Dr. P. RamaKrishnan.

---

2. DRINK

The strength of spirituous liquor is gauged by degrees proof. In the United Kingdom proof spirit is that mixture of ethyl alcohol (C_2H_5OH) and water which at 51° F *10,55° C* weighs in air 12/13ths of an equal measure of distilled water. Such spirit in fact contains 49.28 per cent alcohol by weight, so that pure or absolute alcohol is 75.35° over proof (O.P.). In the U.S.A. proof is double the actual percentage of alcohol by volume at 60°F *15,6°C*. A "hangover" is due to toxic congenerics such as amyl alcohol ($C_5H_{11}OH$).

Most alcoholic

Absolute (or 100%) alcohol is 75.35 degrees over proof (U.K.) or 200% proof spirit (U.S.). During independence (1918–1940) the Estonian Liquor Monopoly marketed 98% potato alcohol (196 proof U.S.). In 31 U.S. states *Everclear* 190 proof 95% alcohol, is marketed by the American Distilling Co. "primarily as a base for home-made cordials". Royal Navy rum introduced in 1692, was 40° O.P. (79.8%) before 1948 but was reduced to 4.5° U.P. (under proof) or 46.3% alcohol by weight, before its abolition on 31 July 1970.

Oldest Wine

The oldest datable wine has been an amphora salvaged and drank by Capt. Jacques Cousteau from the wreck of a Greek trader sunk in the Mediterranean *c* 230 B.C. Wine jars recovered from the Pompeii eruption of A.D. 79 were found labelled VESUVINUM—the oldest known trade mark.

Beer *Strongest world*

The world's strongest and most expensive beer is EKU Kulminator Urtyp Hell from Kulmbach, West Germany which retails for up to 70p per ½ pint *28,4 cl* bottle. It is 13.2% alcohol by volume at 20° C with an original gravity of 1117.6°.

Beer *Strongest Great Britain*

The strongest regularly brewed nationally distributed beer in Britain is Gold Label Barley Wine brewed by Tennant Bros. of Sheffield, a subsidiary of Whitbread & Co. Ltd. It has an alcoholic content of 8.6 per cent by weight, 10.6 per cent by volume and an original gravity of 1098.06°. The strongest regularly brewed draught beer is Fuller's E.S.B. at 1055°.

Beer *Weakest*

The weakest liquid ever marketed as beer was a sweet Ersatz

beer which was brewed in Germany by Sunner, Colne-Kalk, in 1918. It had an original gravity of 1,000.96° and a strength 1/30th that of the weakest beer now obtainable in the United Kingdom.

Most Expensive Wine

The highest price paid for any bottle (meaning a container as opposed to a measure) of wine is $18,000 (then £9,475) for a jeroboam (equivalent to 4 bottles) of 1864 Chateau Lafite claret bought by John A. Grisanti of Grisanti's Restaurant, Memphis, Tennessee at Heublein Inc's 10th Annual Auction at Atlanta, Georgia on 25 May 1978.

Greatest Wine Auction

The largest single sale of wine was conducted by Christie's of King Street, St. James's, London on 10–11 July 1974 at Quaglino's Ballroom, London when 2,325 lots comprising 432,000 bottles realised £962,190. The largest ever wine-tasting was held at Nederburg, South Africa for 1,737 people with 15 openers, 93 pourers and 2,012 bottles on 4 Mar. 1978.

Most expensive liqueurs

The most expensive liqueur in France is *Eau de vie de poire avec poire* at 100 F (now £11 66p) at Fauchon in Paris.

Most expensive spirits

The most expensive bottle of spirits at auction is £780 for a magnum of *Grande Fine Champagne Cognac, 1811* at Christie's Geneva on 13 Nov. 1978. Cognac Coutier (50 years old) retails for 1200 F (now £140) a bottle at Fauchon. In Britain *Hennessy Private Reserve Grande Champagne* retails for £120 (including V.A.T.) for a standard bottle.

Largest bottles

The largest bottle normally used in the wine and spirit trade is the Jeroboam (equal to 4 bottles of champagne or, rarely, of brandy and from 5 to 6½ bottles of claret according whether blown or moulded) and the Double Magnum (equal, since *c.* 1934 to 4 bottles of claret or, more rarely, red Burgundy). A complete set of Champagne bottles would consist of a ¼ bottle, through the ½ bottle, bottle, magnum, Jeroboam, Rehoboam, Methuselah, Salmanazer and Balthazar, to the Nebuchadnezzar, which has a capacity of 16 litres *28.14 pt*, and is equivalent to 20 bottles. In May 1958 a 5 ft *152 cm* tall sherry bottle with a capacity of 20½ Imperial gal *93,19 litres* was blown in Stoke-on-Trent, Staffordshire. This bottle, with the capacity of 131 normal bottles, was named an "Adelaide".

Smallest bottles

The smallest and meanest bottles of liquor sold are the bottles of Scotch whisky marketed by The Cumbrae Supply Co. of Glasgow. They contain 24 minims or $\frac{1}{20}$ of a fl. oz. *1,42 millilitres* and retailed in 1979 for 32p (including the match box in which it is packaged).

Champagne cork flight

The longest distance for a champagne cork to fly from an untreated and unheated bottle 4 ft *1,22 m* from level ground is 102 ft 11 in *31,36 m* by Gary P. Mahan at La Habra Heights, California on 2 Aug. 1975.

Miniature Bottles

The largest reported collection of unduplicated miniature bottles is one of 2125 as at 30 Apr. 1979 owned by B. A. Everest of Tunbridge Wells, Kent.

3. TELESCOPES

Earliest

Although there is evidence that early Arabian scientists understood something of the magnifying power of lenses, their first use to form a telescope has been attributed to Roger Bacon (*c.* 1214–92) in England. The prototype of modern refracting telescopes was that completed by Johannes Lippershey for the Netherlands government on 2 Oct. 1608.

A bottle of wine from the most northerly vineyard in Great Britain, that at Renishaw Hall, Derbyshire, lat. 53° 18' N (see p. 51).

Largest *Reflector World*

The largest telescope in the world is the 6 m *236.2 in* telescope sited on Mount Semirodriki, near Zelenchukskaya in the Caucasus Mountains, U.S.S.R., at an altitude of 6,830 ft *2,080 m*. Work on the mirror, weighing 70 tons/*tonnes* was not completed until the summer of 1974. Regular observations were begun on 7 Feb. 1976 after 16 years work. The weight of the 42 m *138 ft* high assembly is 840 tonnes *827 tons*. Being the most powerful of all telescopes its range, which includes the location of objects down to the 25th magnitude, represents the limits of the observable Universe. Its light-gathering power would enable it to detect the light from a candle at a distance of 15,000 miles *24 000 km*.

Largest *Reflector Great Britain*

The largest reflector in the British Isles is the Isaac Newton 98.2 in *249,4 cm* reflector at the Royal Greenwich Observatory, Herstmonceux Castle, East Sussex. It was built in Newcastle upon Tyne, Tyne and Wear, weighs 92 tons *93,5 tonnes*, cost £641,000 and was inaugurated on 1 Dec. 1967. Plans are now advanced to move it to a new northern hemisphere site—probably in the Canary Islands—and refit a 100 inch *254 cm* reflector.

Largest *Refractor*

The largest refracting (*i.e.* magnification by lenses) telescope in the world is the 62 ft *18,90 m* long 40 in *101,6 cm* telescope completed in 1897 at the Yerkes Observatory, Williams Bay, Wisconsin, and belonging to the University of Chicago, Illinois, U.S.A. In 1900 a 125 cm *49.2 in* refractor *54,85 m 180 ft* in length was built for the Paris Exposition but its optical performance was too poor to justify attempts to use it. The largest in the British Isles is the 28 in *71,1 cm* at the Royal Greenwich Observatory (then in London) completed in 1894.

Radio *Largest steerable dish*
Radio waves of extra-terrestrial origin were first detected by Karl Jansky of Bell Telephone Laboratories, Holmdel, New Jersey, U.S.A. using a 100 ft long shortwave rotatable antenna in 1932. The world's largest trainable dish-type radio telescope is the 100 m *328 ft* diameter, 3,000 ton *3048 tonnes* assembly at the Max Planck Institute for Radio Astronomy of Bonn in the Effelsberger Valley, West Germany; it became operative in May 1971. The cost of the installation begun in November 1967 was 36,920,000 DM £6,150,000.

Radio *Largest Dish*
The world's largest dish radio telescope is the partially-steerable ionospheric assembly built over a natural bowl at Arecibo, Puerto Rico, completed in November 1963 at a cost of about $9,000,000 (£3.75 million). The dish has a diameter of 1,000 ft *304,80 m* and covers 18½ acres *7,28 ha*. Its sensitivity was raised by a factor of 1,000 and its range to the edge of the observable Universe at some 15,000 million light-years by the fitting of new aluminium plates at a cost of $8.8 million. Re-dedication was on 16 Nov. 1974. The RATAN-600 radio telescope being built in the Northern Caucasus, U.S.S.R. will have mirror dishes on a 600 m *1,968.5 ft* perimeter.

Radio *Largest World*
The world's largest radio telescopic installation is the U.S. National Science Foundation VLA (Very Large Array). It is Y-shaped with each arm 13 miles *20,9 km* long with 27 mobile antennae (each of 25 m *82 ft* diameter) on rails. It is 50 miles *80 km* west of Socorro in the Plains of San Augustin, New Mexico and the completion date will be in January 1981 at an estimated cost of $78 million (*now £41 million*).

Radio *Largest Great Britain*
The British Science Research Council 5 km Radio telescope at Lord's Bridge, Cambridgeshire to be operated by the Mullard Radio Astronomy Observatory of Cambridge University will utilize eight mobile 42 ft *12,80 m* rail-borne computer-controlled dish aerials, which will be equivalent to a single steerable dish 5 km *3 miles 188 yds* in diameter. The project cost more than £2,100,000 and was completed in 1973.

Solar
The world's largest solar telescope is the 480 ft *146,30 m* long McMath telescope at Kitt Peak National Observatory near Tucson, Arizona, U.S.A. It has a focal length of 300 ft *91,44 m* and an 80 in *2,03 m* heliostat mirror. It was completed in 1962 and produces an image measuring 33 in *83,8 cm* in diameter.

Observatory *Highest*
The highest altitude observatory in the world is the University of Denver's High Altitude Observatory at an altitude of 14,100 ft *4 297 m*, opened in 1973. The principal instrument is a 24 in *60,48 cm* Ealing Beck reflecting telescope.

Observatory *Oldest*
The oldest astronomical observatory building extant in the world is the Chomsong-dae built in A.D. 632 in Kyongju, South Korea.

Planetaria *World*
The ancestor of the planetarium is the rotatable Gottorp Globe, built by Andreas Busch in Denmark between 1654 and 1664 to the orders of Olearius, court mathematician to Duke Frederick III of Holstein. It is 34.6 ft *10,54 m* in circumference, weighs nearly 3½ tons/*tonnes* and is now preserved in Leningrad, U.S.S.R. The stars were painted on the inside. The earliest optical installation was not until 1923 in the Deutsches Museum, Munich, by Zeiss of Jena, Germany. The world's largest planetarium, is in Moscow, U.S.S.R., and has a diameter of 82½ ft *25,15 m*.

Planetaria *Great Britain*
The United Kingdom's first planetarium was opened at Madame Tussaud's, Marylebone Road, London, on 19 March 1958. Accurate images of 8,900 stars (some below naked eye magnitude) are able to be projected on the 70 ft *21,33 m* high copper dome.

4. GEMS AND OTHER PRECIOUS MATERIALS

The 28¼ ton jade boulder discovered by Karl Ebner in British Columbia, Canada in 1977.

The 170.49 carat Star of Peace, the world's largest flawless diamond owned by Manfredo Horowitz of Geneva, Switzerland.

PRECIOUS STONE RECORDS

Note: The carat was standardised at 205 mg in 1877. The metric carat of 200 mg was introduced in 1914.

Largest

Diamond (pure crystallised carbon)
3,106 metric carats (over $1\frac{1}{4}$ lb.)—*The Cullinan*, found by Capt. M. F. Wells 26 Jan. 1905 in the Premier Mine, Pretoria, South Africa.

Emerald (green beryl) $[Be_3Al_2(SiO_3)_6]$
125 lb. *56 kg 70* crystal (up to $15\frac{3}{4}$ in *40 cm* long and $9\frac{3}{4}$ in *24,75 cm* in diameter) from a Ural, U.S.S.R. mine.

Sapphire (blue corundum) (Al_2O_3)
2,302 carat stone found at Anakie, Queensland, Australia, in *c.* 1935, now a 1,318 carat head of President Abraham Lincoln (1809–65).

Ruby (red corundum) (Al_2O_3)
3,421 carat broken stone reported found in July 1961 (largest piece 750 carats).

Largest Cut Stone

530.2 metric carats. Cleaved from *The Cullinan* in 1908, by Jak Asscher of Amsterdam and polished by Henri Koe known as *The Star of Africa* No. 1 and now in the Royal Sceptre.
In Dec. 1977 top blue-white 5 carat gems were quoted at £35,500 to £71,000.

2,680 carat unguent jar carved by Dionysio Miseroni in the 17th century owned by the Austrian Government. 1,350 carat of *gem* quality, the *Devonshire* stone from Muso, Columbia.

1,444 carat black star stone carved from 2,097 carats in 1953–1955 into a bust of General Dwight David Eisenhower (1890–1969).

1,184 carat natural gem stone of Burmese origin. The largest star ruby is the 138.72 carat Rosser Reeves stone at the Smithsonian Institution.

Other records

Diamond is the *hardest* known naturally-occurring substance, being 90 times as hard as the next hardest mineral, corundum (Al_2O_3). The peak hardness value on the Knoop scale is 8,400 compared with an average diamond of 7,000. The rarest colours for diamond are blue (record—44.4 carat *Hope* diamond) and pink (record—24 carat presented by Dr. John Thoburn Williamson to H.M. The Queen in 1958). The 137.02 ct Premier Rose diamond was bought by Goldberg-Weiss in Dec. 1978 for a reputed $11,500,000. A 353.9 carat uncut stone was found in the Premier Mine in April 1978 and auctioned by De Beers for $5,170,000 in May to a Mouw-Goldberg-Weiss syndicate. The record auction price for a diamond ring is £413,173 (£20,095 or $37,289 per carat) for a 20.56 ct pear shaped flawless 'D' diamond at Sotheby's, Zurich on 22 Nov. 1978.

A necklace of eight major emeralds and one pendant emerald of 75.63 carats with diamonds was sold by Sotheby's in Zurich on 24 Nov. 1971 for £436,550 (*then* $1,090,000).
The Swiss customs at Geneva confirmed on 16 April 1972 the existence of an hexagonal emerald of about 20,000 carats, thus possibly worth more than $100 million.

Note: both the sapphire busts are in the custody of the Kazanjian Foundation of Los Angeles, California, U.S.A.

Since 1955 rubies have been the world's most precious gem attaining a price of up to £4,000 per carat by 1969.
The ability to make corundum prisms for laser technology up to over 12 in *30 cm* in length seems to have little bearing on the market for natural gems.

RECORDS FOR OTHER PRECIOUS MATERIALS

Largest

Pearl (Molluscan consecretion)
14 lb. 1 oz. *6,37 kg* $9\frac{1}{2}$ in *24 cm* long by $5\frac{1}{2}$ in *14 cm* in diameter—*Pearl of Laotze*

Opal $(SiO_2.nH_2O)$
Any stone: 220 troy oz. (yellow-orange).
Gem stone: 17,700 carats (*Olympic Australis*)

Crystal
Any stone: 250 tons/*tonnes* (Beryl)

Ball: $106\frac{3}{4}$ lb. *40,48 kg* $12\frac{3}{4}$ in *32,7 cm* diameter, the *Warner* sphere

Topaz $[(AlSi_2O_4)_4(F,OH)_2]$
"Brazilian Princess" 21,327 carat 221 facets. Light blue.

Amber (Coniferous fossil resin)
33 lb. 10 oz. *15,25 kg.*

Turquoise monolith $(CuAl_6(PO_4)_4(OH)_8 \cdot 4H_2O)$ 218 lb. *98,8 kg.*

Jade $[NaAl(Si_2O_6)]$
Boulder of 63,307 lb. 28.26 tons *28,71 tonnes* discovered by Karl Ebner.

Marble (Metamorphosed $CaCO_3$)
90 tons/*tonnes* (single slab)

Nuggets—Gold (Au)
7,560 oz. $(472\frac{1}{2}$ lb. *214,32 kg*) (reef gold) *Holtermann Nugget*

Silver (Ag)
2,750 lb. troy

Where Found

At Palawan, Philippines, 7 May 1934 in shell of giant clam.

Andamooka, South Australia Jan. 1970.
Coober Pedy, South Australia, Aug. 1956.

Malakialina, Madagascar reported 1964.
Burma, (originally a 1,000 lb. *450 kg* piece).

Brazil.

Reputedly from Burma acquired in 1860.

Riverside County, California, 17 Jan. 1975.

Watson Lake, British Columbia, Canada 1977.

Quarried at Yule, Colorado, U.S.A.

Beyers & Holtermann Star of Hope Gold Mining Co., Hill End, N.S.W., Australia, 19 Oct. 1872.

Sonora, Mexico.

Notes On Present Location, etc.

In a San Francisco bank vault. It is the property since 1936 of Wilburn Dowell Cobb and was valued at $4,080,000 in July 1971.

The Andamooka specimen (34,215 carats) was unearthed by a bulldozer.

Note: Measures 18 m *59 ft* long and 173 m³ *226 yd³* in volume.

U.S. National Museum, in Washington, D.C.

Exhibited by Smithsonian Institution, Nov. 1978. Valued at $1,066,350 or $50 per carat.

Bought by John Charles Bowing (d. 1893) for £300 in Canton, China. Natural History Museum, London, since 1940.

Found by Chester Jastromb and Kenneth Casper. Original weight was probably *c.* 250 lb. *113,4 kg.*

Jadeite can be virtually any colour. The less precious nephrite is $Ca_2(Mg,Fe)_5$ $(OH)_2(Si_4O_{11})_2$.

A piece of over 45 tons/*tonnes* was dressed from this slab for the coping stone of the Tomb of the Unknown Soldier in Arlington National Cemetery, Virginia, U.S.A.

The purest large nugget was the *Welcome Stranger*, found at Moliagul, Victoria, Australia, which yielded 2,248 troy oz. *69,92 kg* of pure gold from $2,280\frac{1}{4}$ oz. *70,92 kg.*

Appropriated by the Spanish Government before 1821.

Other Gems Records:
Largest Stone of Gem Quality:
A 520,000 carat (2 cwt. 5 lb. *103,8 kg*) aquamarine, $Be_3Al_2(SiO_3)_6$ found near Marambaia, Brazil in 1910. Yielded over 200,000 carats of gem quality cut stones.

Rarest:
Taaffeite $(Be_4Mg_4Al_{15}O_{32})$ first discovered in Dublin, Ireland, in November 1945. Only four of these pale mauve stones are known—the largest is of 0.84 of a carat.

Densest Gem Mineral:
Stibiotantalite $[(SbO)_2(Ta,Nb)_2O_6]$ a rare brownish-yellow mineral found in San Diego County, California, has a density of 7.46. The alloy platiniridium has a density of more than 22.0.

5. PHOTOGRAPHY

CAMERAS

Earliest

The earliest photograph was taken in the summer of 1826 by Joseph Nicéphore Niepce (1765–1833), a French physician and scientist. It showed the courtyard of his country house at Gras, near St. Loup-de-Varennes. It probably took eight hours to expose and was taken on a bitumen-coated polished pewter plate measuring 7¾ in by 6½ in *20 × 16,5 cm*. The earliest photograph taken in England was one of a diamond-paned window in Laycock (or Lacock) Abbey, Wiltshire, taken in August 1835 by William Henry Fox Talbot, M.P. (1800–77), the inventor of the negative-positive process. The negative of this was donated to the Science Museum, London in 1937 by his granddaughter Matilda. The world's earliest aerial photograph was taken in 1858 by Gaspard Félix Tournachon (1820–1910), *alias* Nadar, from a balloon near Villacoublay, on the outskirts of Paris, France.

Largest

The largest camera ever built is the 27 ton Rolls Royce camera built for Product Support (Graphics) Ltd., of Derby, England completed in 1959. It measures 8 ft 10 in *2,69 m* high, 8 ft 3 in *2,51 m* wide and 35 ft *10,66 m* in length. The lens is a 63″ f 15 Cooke Apochromatic. Its value after improvements in 1971 was in excess of £100,000.

Smallest

Apart from cameras built for intra-cardiac surgery and espionage, the smallest camera that has been marketed is the circular Japanese "Petal" camera with a diameter of 1.14 in *2,9 cm* and a thickness of 0.65 in *1,65 cm*. It has a focal length of 12 mm *0.47 in*. The B.B.C. T.V. programme *Record Breakers* showed prints from this camera on 3 Dec. 1974.

Fastest

In 1972 Prof. Basor of the U.S.S.R. Academy of Sciences published a paper describing an experimental camera with a time resolution of 5×10^{-13} of a sec or ½ a picosec. The fastest production camera in the world is the Imacon 600 manufactured by John Hadland (P.I.) Ltd of Bovingdon, Hertfordshire which is capable of 600 million pictures per sec. Uses include lasar, ballistic, detonic, plasma and corona research.

Most expensive

The most expensive complete range of camera equipment in the world is that of Nikon of Tokyo, Japan, who marketed in 1979 a range of 19 cameras with 62 lenses and 366 accessories. Fox Talbot of London quoted £62,836.15 plus £7,854.51 V.A.T. for the whole range. A Thomas Sutton wet plate camera, c. 1865, was sold at auction at Sotheby's for £11,500 on 8 Mar. 1974.

6. NUMEROLOGY

In dealing with large numbers, scientists use the notation of 10 raised to various powers to eliminate a profusion of noughts. For example, 19,160,000,000,000 miles would be written 1.916×10^{13} miles. Similarly, a very small number for example 0,0000154324 of a gramme, would be written $1,5432 \times 10^{-5}$ g. Of the prefixes used before numbers the smallest is "atto-" from the Danish atten for 18, indicating a trillionth part (10^{-18}) of the unit, and the highest is "exa" (Greek, hexa, six), symbol E, indicating six groups of 3 zeros 10^{18} or a trillion (U.K.) or a quintillion (U.S.) fold.

Highest Numbers

The highest lexicographically accepted named number in the system of successive powers of ten is the centillion, which is 10 raised to the power 600, or one followed by 600 noughts in the British system or 10^{303} in the U.S. system. The highest named number outside the decimal notation is the Buddhist *asankhyeya*, which is equal to 10^{140} or 100 tertio-virgintillions (British system) or 100 quinto-quadragintillions (U.S. system).

The number 10^{100} (10,000 sexdecillion [U.K.] or 10 duo-trigintillion [U.S.]) is designated a Googol. The term was devised by Dr. Edward Kasner (U.S.) (d. 1955). Ten raised to the power of a Googol is described as a Googolplex. Some conception of the magnitude of such numbers can be gained when it is said that the number of atoms in some models of the observable Universe does not exceed 10^{85}.

The highest number ever used in a mathematical proof is a bounding value published in 1977 and known as Graham's number. It concerns bichromatic hypercubes and is inexpressible without the special "arrow" notation, devised by Knuth in 1976, extended to 64 layers.

Prime numbers

A prime number is any positive integer (excluding 1) having no integral factors other than itself and unity, *e.g.* 2, 3, 5, 7 or 11. The lowest prime number is thus 2. The highest known prime number is 2^{21701} (a number of 6,533 digits) discovered after months of trials by computer by Laura Nickel, 18, and Curt Noll, 18, on 30 Oct. 1978 at California State University, U.S.A.

Perfect numbers

A number is said to be perfect if it is equal to the sum of its divisors other than itself, *e.g.* $1 + 2 + 4 + 7 + 14 = 28$. The lowest perfect number is 6 $(1 + 2 + 3)$. The highest known and the 25th so far discovered, is $(2^{21701} - 1) \times 2^{21700}$. It is a consequence of the highest known prime (see above).

Most Innumerate

The most innumerate people are the Nambiquara of the north west Matto Grosso of Brazil who lack any system of numbers. They do however have a verb which means "they are two alike".

Most accurate and most inaccurate version of "pi"

The greatest number of decimal places to which *pi* (π) has been calculated is 1,000,000 by the French mathematicians Jean Guilloud and Mlle. Martine Bouyer achieved on 24 May 1973 on a CDC 7600 computer but not verified until 3 Sept. 1973. The published value to a million places, in what has been described as the world's most boring 400 page book, was 3.141592653589793 ... (omitting the next 999,975 places) ... 5779458151. In 1897 the General Assembly of Indiana enacted in House Bill No. 246 that *pi* was *de jure* 4.

Earliest measures

The earliest known measure of weight is the *beqa* of the Amratian period of Egyptian civilization c. 3,800 B.C. found at Naqada, United Arab Republic. The weights are cylindrical with rounded ends from 188.7 to 211.2 g *6.65 to 7.45 oz*. The unit of length used by the megalithic tomb-builders in Britain c. 2200 B.C. appears to have been 2.72 ± 0.003 ft *82,90 cm ± 0.09 cm*. This was deduced by Prof. Alexander Thom.

Time Measure *Longest*

The longest measure of time is the *kalpa* in Hindu chronology. It is equivalent to 4,320 million years. In astronomy a cosmic year is the period of rotation of the sun around the centre of the Milky Way galaxy, *i.e.* about 225,000,000 years. In the Late Cretaceous Period of c. 85 million years ago the Earth rotated faster so resulting in 370.3 days per year while in Cambrian times some 600 million years ago there is evidence that the year contained 425 days.

Time Measure *Shortest*

Owing to variations in the length of a day, which is estimated to be increasing irregularly at the average rate of about two milliseconds per century due to the Moon's tidal drag, the second has been redefined. Instead of being 1/86,400th part of a mean solar day, it has, since 1960, been reckoned as

1/31,556,925.9747th part of the solar (or tropical) year at A.D. 1900, January 0. 12 hrs, Ephemeris time. In 1958 the second of Ephemeris time was computed to be equivalent to 9,192,631,770 $\pm$ 20 cycles of the radiation corresponding to the transition of a caesium 133 atom when unperturbed by exterior fields. The greatest diurnal change recorded has been 10 milliseconds on 8 Aug. 1972 due to the most violent solar storm recorded in 370 years of observations. The shortest blip of light is one of 0.2 of a pico-second (0, 2×10^{-12} of a sec.) produced by the Center of Laser Studies, University of Southern California in Aug. 1978. Light travels 0,06 of a millimetre or *0.0023 of an inch.*

Smallest Units
The shortest unit of length is the atto-metre which is 1.0×10^{-16} of a cm. The smallest unit of area is a "shed", used in sub-atomic physics and first mentioned in 1956. It is 1.0×10^{-48} of a cm². A "barn" is equal to 10^{24} "sheds". The interaction of a neutrino with electrons was reported in 1976 to be over the area of 1×10^{-45} of a cm².

Longest Slide Rule
The world's longest slide rule is one 320 ft 11.1 in *97,81 m* in length completed in Mar. 1979 by students of Alvirne High School, Hudson, New Hampshire, U.S.A.

7. PHYSICAL EXTREMES
(*Terrestrial*)

Temperature *Highest*
The highest man-made temperatures yet attained are those produced in the centre of a thermonuclear fusion bomb, which are of the order of 300,000,000 to 400,000,000° C. Of controllable temperatures, the highest effective laboratory figure reported is 50,000,000° C, for 2/100ths of a second by Prof. Lev A. Artsimovich at Tokamuk in the U.S.S.R. in 1969. At very low particle densities even higher figures are obtainable. Prior to 1963 a figure of 3,000 million ° C was reportedly achieved in the U.S.S.R. with Ogra injection-mirror equipment.

Temperature *Lowest*
The lowest temperature reached is 5×10^{-7} degree Kelvin, achieved by Professor A. Abragam (b. 1914) in collaboration with M. Chapellier, M. Goldman, and Vu Hoang Chau at the Centre d'Etudes Nucléaires, Saclay, France, in March 1969. Absolute or thermodynamic temperatures are defined in terms of ratios rather than as differences reckoned from the unattainable absolute zero, which on the Kelvin scale is $-273,15°$ C or $-459.67°$ F. Thus the lowest temperature ever attained is 1 in 5.46×10^8 of the melting point of ice (0° C or 273.15K or 32° F).

The lowest equilibrium temperature ever attained is 0.0003 K by nuclear refrigeration in a *1,4 kg 3 lb.* copper specimen by Prof. Olli V. Lounasmaa (b. 1920) and his team at the Helsinki University of Technology, Otaniemi, Finland, on 17 April 1974.

Solar Power plant
The largest solar furnace in the world is the 5 megawatt Solar Thermal Test Facility at the Sandia Laboratories, Albuquerque, New Mexico, U.S.A. completed in December 1977. Sunlight from 222 heliostats is concentrated on a target 114 ft *34,7 m* up in the power tower.

Highest pressures
The highest sustained laboratory pressures yet reported are of 1.7 mega bars (11,000 tons force/in² *160 GPa*) achieved in the giant hydraulic diamond-faced press at the Carnegie Institution's Geophysical Laboratory, Washington D.C. reported in June 1978. Using dynamic methods and impact speeds of up to 18,000 m.p.h. *29 000 km/h*, momentary pressures of 75,000,000 atmospheres (490,000 tons/in² *7000 GPa*) were reported from the United States in 1958.

Highest vacuum
The highest (or 'hardest') vacuums obtained in scientific research are of the order of 10^{-14} torr at the IBM Thomas J. Watson Research Center, Yorktown Heights, New York, U.S.A. in October 1976 in a cryogenic system with temperatures down to $-269°$ C *$-452°$ F*. This is equivalent to depopulating (baseball sized) molecules from one metre apart to 80 km apart or from 1 yard to 50 miles.

Fastest centrifuge
The highest man-made rotary speed ever achieved and the fastest speed of any earth-bound object is 4,500 m.p.h. *7 250 km/h* by a swirling tapered 6 in *15,2 cm* carbon fibre rod in a vacuum at Birmingham University, England reported on 24 January 1975.

Most Powerful Microscope
The world's most powerful microscope was announced by Dr. Lawrence Bartell and Charles Ritz of the University of Michigan in July 1974 with an image magnification of 260 million fold. It uses an optical laser to decode holograms produced with 40 Kev radiation and has produced photographs of electron clouds of atoms of neon and argon.

Highest measured frequency
It .was announced in July 1977 that K. M. Evenson, D. A. Jennings and F. R. Peterson of the U.S. National Bureau of Standards, Boulder, Colorado, had attained a frequency of $1,97 \times 10^{14}$ Hz (197 terahertz) with a helium-neon laser emission.

Highest note
The highest note yet attained is one of 60000 megahertz (60 GHz) (60,000 million vibrations/sec), generated by a 'laser' beam striking a sapphire crystal at the Massachusetts Institute of Technology in Cambridge, Massachusetts, U.S.A., in September 1964.

Loudest noise
The loudest noise created in a laboratory is 210 decibels or 400,000 acoustic watts reported by NASA from a 48 ft *14,63 m* steel and concrete horn at Huntsville, Alabama, U.S.A. in October 1965. Holes can be bored in solid material by this means.

Quietest place
The "dead room", measuring 35 ft by 28 ft *10,67 × 8,50 m* in the Bell Telephone System laboratory at Murray Hill, New Jersey, U.S.A., is the most anechoic room in the world. eliminating 99,98 per cent of reflected sound.

Finest balance
The most accurate balance in the world is the Sartorius Model 4108 manufactured in Göttingen, West Germany, which can weigh objects of up to 0,5 g to an accuracy of 0,01 µg or 0,00000001 g which is equivalent to little more than one sixtieth of the weight of the ink on this full stop .

Lowest viscosity
The California Institute of Technology, U.S.A. announced on 1 Dec. 1957 that there was no measureable viscosity, *i.e.* perfect flow, in liquid helium II, which exists only at temperatures close to absolute zero ($-273,15°$ C or $-459.67°$ F).

Lowest friction
The lowest coefficient of static and dynamic friction of any solid is 0.02, in the case of polytetrafluoroethylene ($[C_2F_4]_n$), called P.T.F.E.—equivalent to wet ice on wet ice. It was first manufactured in quantity by E. I. du Pont de Nemours & Co. Inc. in 1943, and is marketed from the U.S.A. as Teflon. In the United Kingdom it is marketed by I.C.I. as Fluon.

In the centrifuge at the University of Virginia a 30 lb. *13,60 kg* rotor magnetically supported has been spun at 1,000 revs/sec in a vacuum of 10^{-6} mm of mercury pressure. It loses only one revolution per second per day thus spinning for years.

Most powerful electric current
The most powerful electric current generated is that from the

Zeus capacitor at the Los Alamos Scientific Laboratory, New Mexico, U.S.A. If fired simultaneously the 4,032 capacitors would produce for a few microseconds twice as much current as that generated elsewhere on Earth.

Most powerful particle accelerator

The 1.24 mile *2 km* diameter proton synchrotron at the Fermi National Accelerator Laboratory at Batavia, Illinois, U.S.A. is the highest energy "atom-smasher" in the world. By June 1976 an energy of 500 billion (5×10^{11}) electron volts was attained. Plans to double the energy to nearly 1 Tera electron volts have begun. This will involve constructing 1,000 super-conducting magnets maintained at a temperature of $-452°$ F $-268,8°$ C by means of a 4,000 litre *880 gal* per hour helium liquefying plant.

The £32 million CERN intersecting storage rings (ISR) project near Geneva, Switzerland started on 27 Jan. 1971, using two 28 GeV proton beams, and is designed to yield the equivalent of 1,700 GeV or 1.7 TeV (1.7 million million electron volts) in its centre of mass experiments.

Largest bubble chamber

The largest bubble chamber in the world is the $7 million installation completed in October 1973 at Weston, Illinois (see above). It is 15 ft *4,57 m* in diameter and contains 7,259 gal *33 000 litres* of liquid hydrogen at a temperature of $-247°$ C with a super-conductivity magnet of 30,000 gauss.

Heaviest magnet

The heaviest magnet in the world is one measuring 60 m *196 ft* in diameter, with a weight of 36,000 tons/*tonnes* for the 10 GeV synchrophasotron in the Joint Institute for Nuclear Research at Dubna, near Moscow, U.S.S.R. Intermagnetics General Corporation announced in 1975 plans for a 180 kG vanadium-gallium magnet.

Magnetic fields *Strongest and weakest*

The strongest magnetic field strength achieved has been one of 301 kilogauss *30,1 teslas* at the Francis Bitter National Magnet Laboratory at Massachusetts Institute of Technology, announced in July 1977. The outer magnet is of super-conducting niobium-titanium.

The weakest magnetic field measured is one of 8×10^{-11} gauss in the heavily shielded room at the Francis Bitter National Magnet Laboratory, Cambridge, Massachusetts, U.S.A. It is used for research by Dr. David Cohen into the very weak magnetic field generated in the heart and brain.

Finest cut

Biological specimens embedded in epoxy resin can be sectioned by a glass knife microtome under ideal conditions to a thickness of 1/875,000th of an inch $2,9 \times 10^{-5}$ mm.

Sharpest objects

The University of California Medical Center, San Francisco announced in July 1974 the ultimate in sharpness—glass electrodes more than 200 times slimmer than a diamond phonograph stylus. These can be used for exploring the cells in the eye. The points are 0.05 µm.

Most powerful "laser" beams

The first illumination of another celestial body was achieved on 9 May 1962, when a beam of light was successfully reflected from the Moon by the use of an optical "maser" (microwave amplification by stimulated emission of radiation) or "laser" (light amplification by stimulated emission of radiation) attached to a 48 in *121,9 cm* telescope at Massachusetts Institute of Technology, Cambridge, Massachusetts, U.S.A. The spot was estimated to be 4 miles *6,4 km* in diameter on the Moon. The device was propounded in 1958 by Dr. Charles Hard Townes (born 1915) of the U.S.A. A "maser" light flash is focused into liquid nitrogen-cooled ruby crystal. Its chromium atoms are excited into a high energy state in which they emit a red light which is allowed to escape only in the direction desired. Such a flash for 1/5,000th of a second can bore a hole through a diamond by vaporization at 10,000° C, produced by 2×10^{23} photons.

The "Shiva" laser was reported at the Lawrence Livermore Laboratory, California to be concentrating 2.6×10^{13} watts into a pinhead-sized target for 9.5×10^{-11} of a second in a test on 18 May 1978.

Brightest light

The brightest steady artificial light sources are "laser" beams with an intensity exceeding the Sun's 1,500,000 candles/in² *232 500 candelas/cm²* by a factor well in excess of 1,000. In May 1969 the U.S.S.R. Academy of Sciences announced blast waves travelling through a luminous plasma of inert gases heated to 90,000 K. The flare-up for up to 3 microseconds shone at 50,000 times the brightness of the Sun *viz.* 75,000 million candles/in². Of continuously burning sources, the most powerful is a 200 kW high-pressure xenon arc lamp of 600,000 candle-power, reported from the U.S.S.R. in 1965.

The synchrotron radiation from a 4 by 0.5 in *100 × 2,5 mm* slit in the SPEAR high energy physics plant at the end of the 2 mile *3,2 km* long Stanford Linear Accelerator, California, U.S.A. has been described as the world's most powerful light beam.

The most powerful searchlight ever developed was one produced during the 1939–45 war by the General Electric Company Ltd. at the Hirst Research Centre in Wembley, Greater London. It had a consumption of 600 kW and gave an arc luminance of 300,000 candles/in² and a maximum beam intensity of 2,700,000,000 candles from its parabolic mirror (diameter 10 ft *3,04 m*).

Most durable light

The average bulb lasts for 750 to 1,000 hrs. There is some evidence that a carbon filament bulb burning in the Fire Department, Livermore, south Alameda County, California has been burning since 1901.

Shortest wavelength

On 15 Apr. 1974 I.B.M. researchers E. Spillar and A. Segmüller announced that X-rays with a wavelength of only $4,6 \times 10^{18}$ Hz (390 millionths of an inch) had been harnessed in a device, which may become a "light pipe" to guide X-rays to required locations.

Longest Echo

The longest recorded echo in any building in Great Britain is one of 15 sec. following the closing of the door of the Chapel of the Mausoleum, Hamilton, Strathclyde built in 1840–55.

Largest wind tunnel *World*

The world's largest wind tunnel is a low-speed tunnel with a 40 × 80 ft *12,19 × 24,38 m* test section built in 1944 at the Ames Research Center, Moffett Field, California, U.S.A. The tunnel encloses 800 tons/*tonnes* of air and cost approximately $7,000,000 (*then* £1,735,000). The maximum volume of air that can be moved is 60,000,000 ft³ *1 700 000 m³* per min. On 30 July 1974 NASA announced an intention to increase it in size to 80 × 120 ft *24,38 × 36,57 m* for 345 m.p.h. speeds with a 135,000 h.p. system. The most powerful is the 216,000 h.p. *219 000 c.v.* installation at the Arnold Engineering Test Center at Tullahoma, Tennessee, U.S.A. opened in September 1956. The highest Mach number attained with air is Mach 27 at the works of the Boeing Company in Seattle, Washington State, U.S.A. For periods of micro-seconds, shock Mach numbers of the order of 30 (22,830 m.p.h. *36 735 km/h*) have been attained in impulse tubes at Cornell University, Ithaca, New York State, U.S.A.

Largest wind tunnel *Great Britain*

The most powerful wind tunnel in the United Kingdom is the intermittent compressed air type installation at the B.A.C. plant at Warton, Lancashire which can be run at Mach 4, which is equivalent to 3,044 m.p.h. *4 898 km/h* at sea level.

Smallest Hole

Inco Nickel Co. were reported in Aug. 1977 to have produced a hole with a diameter of a ten millionth of an inch *0,000004 mm* or one thousand times smaller than a human hair.

MUSIC: Bell ringing

6

THE ARTS AND ENTERTAINMENTS

1. PAINTING

Guinness Superlatives has published a more specialist book *Guinness Book of Art Facts and Feats* (£6.95) by John FitzMaurice Mills.

Earliest *Art*
Pieces of ochre with ground facets found at Lake Mungo, N.S.W., Australia reported in 1973 dated *ante* 30,000 B.C. *may* have been used as cave art pigments. If confirmed, these would antedate even the French La Ferrassie, Périgord Aurignacian cave art dated to 25,000 B.C.

Largest World *All time*
Panorama of the Mississippi, completed by John Banvard (1815–91) in 1846, showing the river for 1,200 miles *1 930 km* in a strip probably 5,000 ft *1 525 m* long and 12 ft *3,65 m* wide, was the largest painting in the world, with an area of more than 1.3 acres *0,52 ha*. The painting is believed to have been destroyed when the rolls of canvas, stored in a barn at Cold Spring Harbor, Long Island, New York State, U.S.A., caught fire shortly before Banvard's death on 16 May 1891.

Existing
The largest known painting now in existence is *The Battle of Gettysburg*, completed in 1883, after 2½ yrs of work, by Paul Philippoteaux (France) and 16 assistants. The painting is 410 ft *125 m* long, 70 ft *21,3 m* high and weighs 5.36 tons *5,45 tonnes*. It depicts the climax of the Battle of Gettysburg, in southern Pennsylvania, U.S.A., on 3 July 1863. In 1964 the painting was bought by Joe King of Winston-Salem, North Carolina, U.S.A. after being stored by E. W. McConnell in a Chicago warehouse since 1933.

"Old Master"
The largest "Old Master" is *Il Paradiso*, painted between 1587 and 1590 by Jacopo Robusti, *alias* Tintoretto (1518–94), and his son Domenico (1565–1637) on Wall "E" of the Sala del Maggior Consiglio in the Palazzo Ducale (Doge's Palace) in Venice, Italy. The work is 22 m *72 ft 2 in* long and 7 m *22 ft 11½ in* high and contains more than 100 human figures.

Largest *Great Britain*
The largest painting in Great Britain is the giant oval *Triumph of Peace and Liberty* by Sir James Thornhill (1676–1734), on the ceiling of the Painted Hall in the Royal Naval College, Greenwich. It measures 106 ft *32,3 m* by 51 ft *15,4 m* and took 20 yrs (1707–1727) to complete.

A painting 6,050 ft² *562 m²* in area and weighing more than a ton was painted for the 4th European Youth Games under the direction of David A. Judge and to the design of Norman G. Warner in Colchester, Essex between 29 Oct. 1975 and 24 May 1976 by 365 people.

Smallest
The smallest reported painting in the world is *My Small Country—Holland* executed by Gert Twigt in January 1979 within a circle of diameter 0,15 mm *6/1000th of an inch*.

Most Valuable
The "Mona Lisa" (*La Gioconda*) by Leonardo da Vinci (1452–1519) in the Louvre, Paris, was assessed for insurance purposes at the highest ever figure of $100,000,000 (*then £35.7 million*) for its move for exhibition in Washington, D.C., and New York City, N.Y., U.S.A., from 14 Dec. 1962 to 12 March 1963. However, insurance was not concluded because the cost of the closest security precautions was less than that of the premiums. It was painted in c. 1503–07 and measures 77 × 53 cm *30.5 × 20.9 in*. It is believed to portray Mona (short for Madonna) Lisa Gherardini, the wife of Francesco del Giocondo of Florence, who disliked it and refused to pay for it. Francis I, King of France, bought the painting for his bathroom in 1517 for 4,000 gold florins or 492 oz. *15,30 kg* of gold now worth some £30,000.

HIGHEST PRICE
Auction price *World*
The highest price ever bid in a public auction for any painting is £2,310,000 for *Portrait of Juan de Pareja*, also known as *The Slave of Velázquez*, painted in Rome in 1649 by Diego Rodríguez de Silva Velázquez (1599–1660) and sold on 27 Nov. 1970 at the salerooms of Christie, Manson & Woods, London to the Wildenstein Gallery, New York. The painting had been sold at Christie's at auction in 1801 for 39 guineas (£40.95). It was in the possession of the Earls of Radnor from May 1811 until 1970.

By British Artist
The highest auction price for the work of a British artist is the £340,000 paid at Christie's of London for J. M. W. Turner's *The Bridgewater Sea Piece* from the Trustees of The Ellesmere 1939 Settlement on 18 June 1976.

By A Woman Artist
The highest price ever paid for a painting by a female artist is $150,000 (*then £62,500*), at Parke Bernet, New York on 3

Mar. 1971, for *Summertime* by Mary Cassatt (b. Pensylvania, U.S.A., 1844—d. 1926). She worked mainly from Paris.

Miniature portrait

The highest price ever paid for a portrait miniature is the £65,100 given by an anonymous buyer at a sale held by Christie's, London on 8 June 1971 for a miniature of Frances Howard, Countess of Essex and Somerset by Isaac Oliver (c 1556–1617), painted c. 1605. This miniature, sent for auction by Lord Derby, measured 5⅛ in *13 cm* in diameter.

Modern painting

The highest price paid for a modern painting is $2,000,000 (£1 million) paid by the National Gallery of Australia, Canberra, Australia in 1973 for the 83 × 192½ in *210,8 × 488,9 cm* canvas *Blue Poles* painted in 1953 by Jackson Pollock (1912–1956) of New York.

Living artist *World*

The highest price paid for paintings in the lifetime of the artist is $1,950,000 (*then £812,500*) paid for the two canvases *Two Brothers* (1905) and *Seated Harlequin* (1922) by Pablo Diego José Francisco de Paula Juan Nepomuceno Crispín Crispiano de la Santisima Trinidad Ruiz y Picasso (1881–1973) of Spain. This was paid by the Basle City Government to the Staechelin Foundation to enable the Basle Museum of Arts to retain the painting after an offer of $2,560,000 (*£1,066,666*) had been received from the United States in December 1967.

British and Irish

The highest price for any painting by a living United Kingdom born artist is $160,000 (*then £89,890*) for the painting *Reclining Man with Sculpture* by Francis Bacon (b. Dublin, Ireland, 1909, then part of the United Kingdom) sold on 27 May 1976 at Sotheby Parke Bernet, New York City, U.S.A.

Drawing

The highest price ever attached to any drawing is £804,361 for the cartoon *The Virgin and Child with St. John the Baptist and St. Anne*, measuring 54½ in by 39¼ in *137 by 100 cm*, drawn in Milan, probably in 1499–1500, by Leonardo da Vinci (1452–1519) of Italy, retained by the National Gallery in 1962. Three United States bids of over $4,000,000 (*then £1,428,570*) were reputed to have been made for the cartoon.

MOST PROLIFIC
Painter

Picasso was the most prolific of all painters in a career which lasted 78 years. It has been estimated that Picasso produced about 13,500 paintings or designs, 100,000 prints or engravings, 34,000 book illustrations and 300 sculptures or ceramics. His life-time *oeuvre* has been valued at £500 million.

Portraitist

John A. Wismont Jr. (b. New York City, 20 Sept. 1941),

formerly of Disneyland, Anaheim, California, painted 45,423 water colour paintings in his career (up to 1978) including 9,853 in 1976.

Most Repetitious Painter

Antonio Bin of Paris has painted the *Mona Lisa* on some 300 occasions. These sell for up to £1,000 apiece.

Oldest and youngest R.A.

The oldest ever Royal Academician has been (Thomas) Sidney Cooper C.V.O., who died on 8 Feb. 1902 aged 98 yrs 136 days, having exhibited 266 paintings over the record span of 69 consecutive years (1833–1902). The youngest ever R.A. has been Mary Moser (1744–1819) (later Mrs. Hugh Lloyd), who was elected on the foundation of the Royal Academy in 1768 when aged 24.

Youngest exhibitor

The youngest ever exhibitor at the Royal Academy of Arts Annual Summer Exhibition has been Lewis Melville "Gino" Lyons (b. 30 Apr. 1962). His *Trees and Monkeys* was painted on 4 June 1965, submitted on 17 Mar. 1967 and exhibited to the public on 29 Apr. 1967.

Largest gallery

The world's largest art gallery is the Winter Palace and the neighbouring Hermitage in Leningrad, U.S.S.R. One has to walk 15 miles *24 km* to visit each of the 322 galleries, which house nearly 3,000,000 works of art and objects of archaeological interest. The world's largest modern art museum is the Georges Pompidou National Centre for Art and Culture opened in Paris in 1977 with 17 700 m² *183,000 ft²* of floor space.

Finest brush

The finest standard brush sold is the 000 in Series 7 by Winsor and Newton known as a "triple goose". It is made of 150-200 Kolinsky sable hairs weighing 15 milligrams *.000529 oz*.

MURALS
Earliest

The earliest known murals on man-made walls are those at Çatal Hüyük in southern Anatolia, Turkey, dating from c. 5850 B.C.

Largest

The largest logo and mural painting in the world is the American Revolution Bicentennial symbol, on the curved roof of the Arizona Veterans Memorial Coliseum, Phoenix, Arizona. It occupies 110,000 ft² *10 219 m²* or more than 2½ acres *1,0 ha*. It will be painted over in 1977. After being outlined by aid of a computer, it took 45 man days, under the supervision of its designer John M. Glitsos, to apply the necessary 870 gallons *3 955 l* of patriotic (red, white and blue) paint on 18–26 Aug. 1973.

A ground mural measuring 1,400 ft *426,7 m* long by 100 ft

HIGHEST-PRICE PAINTINGS—Progressive records

Price	Equivalent 1979 Value	Painter, title, sold by and sold to	Date
£6,500	£145,000	Antonio Correggio's *The Magdalen Reading* (in fact spurious) to Elector Friedrich Augustus II of Saxony.	1746
£8,500	£174,000	Raphael's *The Sistine Madonna* to Elector Friedrich Augustus II of Saxony.	1759
£16,000	£196,000	Van Eycks' *Adoration of the Lamb*, 6 outer panels of Ghent altarpiece by Edward Solby to the Government of Prussia.	1821
£24,600*	£445,000	Murillo's *The Immaculate Conception* by estate of Marshall Soult to the Louvre (against Czar Nicholas I) in Paris.	1852
£70,000	£1,960,000	Raphael's *Ansidei Madonna* by the 8th Duke of Marlborough to the National Gallery.	1885
£100,000	£2,840,000	Raphael's *The Colonna Altarpiece* by Seldemeyer to J. Pierpoint Morgan.	1901
£102,880	£2,250,000	Van Dyck's *Elena Grimaldi-Cattaneo* (portrait) by Knoedler to Peter Widener (1834–1915).	1906
£102,880	£1,860,000	Rembrandt's *The Mill* by 6th Marquess of Lansdowne to Peter Widener.	1911
£116,500	£2,110,000	Raphael's smaller *Panshanger Madonna* by Joseph (later Baron) Duveen (1869–1939) to Peter Widener.	1913
£310,400	£5,580,000	Leonardo da Vinci's *Benois Madonna* to Czar Nicholas II in Paris.	1914
£821,429*	£3,620,000	Rembrandt's *Aristotle Contemplating the Bust of Homer* by estate of Mr. and Mrs. Alfred W. Erickson to New York Metropolitan Museum of Art.	1961
£1,785,714	£5,890,000	Leonardo da Vinci's *Ginerva de' Benci* (portrait) by Prince Franz Josef II of Liechtenstein to National Gallery of Art, Washington, D.C., U.S.A.	1967
£2,310,000*	£6,325,000	Velázquez's *Portrait of Juan de Pareja* by the Earl of Radnor to the Wildenstein Gallery, New York.	1970

*Indicates price at auction, otherwise prices were by private treaty.

above: The largest mosaic in the world is on all four walls of the library of this university building in Mexico City. (*Gerry Paknadel*)

right and below right: The world's most expensive sculpture, the $3.9 million *(then £2.4 million)* 4th century bronze statue of a youth, which was bought by J. Paul Getty's £23 million museum (below) in Malibu, California (see p. 90).

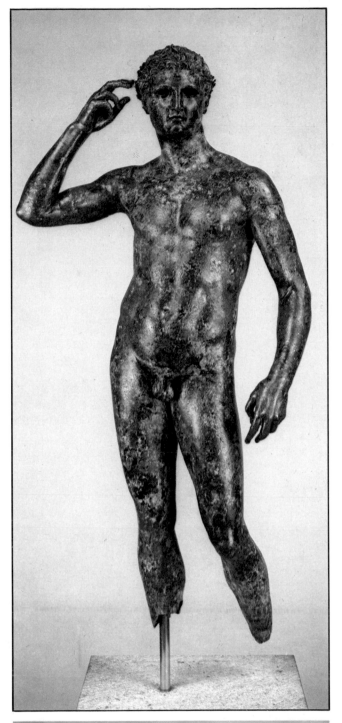

30,4 m named Yellow Brick Road—Leisure Time painted on a disused runway near the Tamiami Stadium, South Dade, Florida U.S.A. was completed on 18 Mar. 1976.

Largest mosaic

The world's largest mosaic is on the walls of the central library of the Universidad Nacional Autónomao de México, Mexico City. There are four walls, the two largest measuring 12,949 ft² *1 203 m²* each representing the pre-Hispanic past. The largest Roman mosaic in Britain is the Woodchester Pavement, Glouccstershire of *c.* A.D. 325, excavated in 1793, now recovered with protective earth until its 8th showing due in 1983. It measures 48 ft 10 in *14,88 m* square comprising 1½ million tesserae.

Largest cartoon

The largest cartoon ever exhibited was one covering five storeys (50 × 150 ft *15 × 45 m*) of a University of Arizona building drawn by Dr. Peter A. Kesling for Mom 'n Dad's Day 1954.

MUSEUMS
Oldest

The oldest museum in the world is the Ashmolean Museum in Oxford built in 1679.

Largest

The largest museum in the world is the American Museum of Natural History on 77th to 81st Streets and Central Park West, New York City, N.Y., U.S.A. Founded in 1874, it comprises 19 interconnected buildings with 23 acres *9 ha* of floor space. The largest museum in the United Kingdom is the British Museum (founded in 1753), which was opened to the public in 1759. The main building in Bloomsbury, London, was built in 1823 and has a total floor area of 17.57 acres *7,11 ha.*

2. SCULPTURE

Earliest *World*

The earliest known examples of sculpture are the so-called Venus figurines from Aurignacian sites, dating to *c.* 25,000–22,000 B.C., *e.g.* the famous Venus of Willendorf from Austria and the Venus of Brassempouy (Landes, France). A piece of ox rib found in 1973 at Pech de l'Aze, Dordogne, France in an early Middle Palaeolithic layer of the Riss glaciation *c.* 105,000 B.C. appears to have several intentional engraved lines on one side.

Great Britain

The earliest British art object is an engraving of a horse's head on a piece of rib-bone from Robin Hood Cave, Creswell Crag, Derbyshire. It dates from the Upper Palaeolithic period (*c.* 15,000 to 10,000 B.C.). The earliest Scottish rock carving from Lagalochan, Strathclyde dates from *c.* 3,000 B.C.

Most expensive *World and Ancient*

The highest price ever paid for a sculpture is $3,900,000 (*then £2,400,000*) paid by private treaty in London in early 1977 by J. Paul Getty's Museum in California for the 4th century B.C. bronze statue of a youth attributed to the school of Lysippus. It was found by fishermen on the seabed off Faro, Italy in 1963. The £23 million Museum, with 38 galleries, opened in Malibu in January 1974, is the world's most heavily endowed with £700 million.

Living sculptor

The highest price paid for the work of a living sculptor is the $260,000 (*then £108,000*) given at Sotheby's Parke-Bernet Galleries, New York on 1 March 1972 by Fischer Fine Arts of London for the 75 in *189 cm* long wooden carving *Reclining Figure* by Henry Moore, O.M., C.H. (b. Castleford, West Yorkshire, 30 July 1898) sold by Cranbrook Academy, Bloomfield Hills, Michigan, U.S.A.

Largest

The world's largest sculptures are the mounted figures of Jefferson Davis (1808–89), Gen. Robert Edward Lee (1807–1870) and Gen. Thomas Jonathan ("Stonewall") Jackson (1824–63), covering 1.33 acres *0,5 ha* on the face of Stone Mountain, near Atlanta, Georgia. They are 90 ft *27,4 m* high. Roy Faulkner was on the mountain face for 8 years 174 days with a thermo-jet torch working with the sculptor Walker Kirtland Hancock and other helpers from 12 Sept. 1963 to 3 Mar. 1972. When completed the world's largest sculpture will be that of the Indian chief Tashunca-Uitco (*c.* 1849–1877), known as Crazy Horse, of the Oglala tribe of the Dakota or Nadowessioux (Sioux) group. The sculpture was begun on 3 June 1948 near Mount Rushmore, South Dakota, U.S.A. A projected 561 ft *170 m* high and 641 ft *195 m* long, it has required blasting 5,800,000 tons *5 890 000 tonnes* of stone and is the life work of one man, Korczak Ziolkowski.

Ground figures

In the Nazca Desert, south of Lima, Peru there are straight lines (one more than 7 miles *11,2 km* long), geometric shapes and of plants and animals drawn on the ground sometime between 100 B.C. and A.D. 700 for an uncertain but probably religious or astronomical purpose by a still unknown civilization. They were first detected from the air in *c.* 1928.

Hill figures

In August 1968 a 330 ft *100 m* tall figure was found on a hill above Tarapacá, Chile.

The largest human hill carving in Britain is the "Long Man" of Wilmington, East Sussex, 226 ft *68 m* in length. The oldest of all White Horses in Britain is the Uffington White Horse in Oxfordshire, dating from the late Iron Age (*c.* 150 B.C.) and measuring 374 ft *114 m* from nose to tail and 120 ft *36 m* from ear to heel.

Most Massive Mobile

The most massive recorded mobile is *Quest* by Jerome Kirk installed at TRW Inc., Redondo Beach, California U.S.A.

in Sept. 1968. It is a 32 ft *9,75 m* long wind-driven pivotal mobile weighing 5.35 tons *5 442 kg*. The term mobile was coined to contrast with "stabile" sculpture by Marcel Duchamp (1887–1968) in 1932.

3. LANGUAGE & LITERATURE

Earliest

Anthropologists have evidence that the truncated pharynx of Neanderthal man precluded his speaking anything akin to a modern language any more than an ape or a modern baby. Cro-Magnon man of 40,000 B.C. had however developed an efficient vocal tract. Clay tablets of the neolithic Danubian culture discovered in Dec. 1966 at Tartaria, Moros River, Romania have been dated to the fifth or fourth millennium B.C. The tablets bear symbols of bows and arrows, gates and combs. Writing tablets bearing an early form of the Elamite language dating from 3,500 B.C. were found in south-eastern Iran in 1970. Tokens or tallies from Tepe Asiab and Ganji-I-Dareh Tepe in Iran have however been dated to 8,500 B.C.

Oldest

The written language with the longest continuous history is Egyptian from the earliest hieroglyphic inscriptions on the palette of Narmer dated to *c.* 3,100 B.C. to Coptic used in Churches at the present day more than 5,000 years later. Hieroglyphs were used until A.D. 394 and thus may be overtaken by Chinese characters as the most durable script in the 21st century.

Oldest words in English

Some as yet unpublished research indicates some words of a pre-Indo-European substrate survive in English—apple (apal), bad (bad), gold (gol) and tin (tin).

Commonest language

Today's world total of languages and dialects still spoken is about 5,000 of which some 845 come from India. The language spoken by more people than any other is Northern Chinese, or Mandarin, by an estimated 68 per cent of the population hence 575 million people in 1975. The so-called national language (*Guóyǔ*) is a standardized form of Northern Chinese (*Běifanghuà*) as spoken in the Peking area. This was

Georges Schmidt, formerly of the United Nations, who has at times in his career been fluent in 31 languages (see p. 91).

alphabetized into *zhùyīn fùhào* of 37 letters in 1918. In 1958 the *pinyin* system, which is a phonetic pronunciation guide, was introduced. The next most commonly spoken language and the most widespread is English, by an estimated 360,000,000 in mid-1975. English is spoken by 10 per cent or more of the population in 34 sovereign countries.

In Great Britain and Ireland there are six indigenous tongues: English, Cornish, Scots Gaelic, Welsh, Irish Gaelic, and Romany (Gipsy). Of these English is, of course, predominant. Mr. Edward (Ned) Maddrell (1877–1974) of Glen Chass, Port St. Mary, Isle of Man, died as the last islander whose professed tongue was Manx. Cornish, now happily saved, came within an ace of extinction but a dictionary was published in 1887, four years before the death of the then last fluent speaker John Davey. In the Channel Islands, apart from Jersey and Guernsey *normand*, there survive words of Sarkese or *Sèrtchais* in which a prayer book was published in 1812, but of which there are very few speakers left.

Rarest Language
There are believed to be 20 or more languages including 6 Indian languages in North America in which no-one can converse because there is only one speaker left. Eyak is still spoken in south east Alaska by two aged sisters if they meet.

Most complex
The following extremes of complexity have been noted: Chippewa, the North American Indian language of Minnesota, U.S.A., has the most verb forms with up to 6,000; Tillamook, the North American Indian language of Oregon, U.S.A., has the most prefixes with 30; Tabassaran, a language in Daghestan, U.S.S.R., uses the most noun cases with 35, while Eskimaux use 63 forms of the present tense and simple nouns have as many as 252 inflections. In Chinese the 40 volume *Chung-wén Tà Tz'u-tiĕn* dictionary lists 49,905 characters. The fourth tone of "i" has 84 meanings, varying as widely as "dress", "hiccough" and "licentious". The written language provides 92 different characters of "i⁴". The most complex written character in Chinese is that representing *xiè* consisting of 64 strokes meaning "talkative". The most complex in current use is *yù* with 32 strokes meaning to urge or implore.

Most and least irregular verbs
Esperanto was first published by Dr. Ludwig Zamenhof (1859–1917) of Warsaw in 1887 without irregular verbs and is now estimated (by text book sales) to have a million speakers. Swahili has a strict 6-class pattern of verbs and no verbs which are irregular to this pattern. According to the more daunting grammars published in West Germany, English has 194 irregular verbs though there are arguably 214.

Rarest and commonest sounds
The rarest speech sound is probably the sound written ř in Czech which occurs in very few languages and is the last sound mastered by Czech children. In the southern Bushman language !xõ there is a click articulated with both lips, which is written ⊙. The *l* sound in the Arabic word *Allah*, in some contexts, is pronounced uniquely in that language. The commonest sound is the vowel *a* (as in the English father); no language is known to be without it.

Literature, smallest
Of written languages, that with the smallest literature is Kamassian. The only surviving fragment from these Samoyed people near Lake Baykal, U.S.S.R., is a 24 line lament translated in *The Elek Book of Oriental Verse*.

Vocabulary
The English language contains about 490,000 words plus another 300,000 technical terms, the most in any language, but it is doubtful if any individual uses more than 60,000. Those in Great Britain who have undergone a full 16 years of education use perhaps 5,000 words in speech and up to 10,000 words in written communications.

Greatest linguist
If the yardstick of ability to speak with fluency and reasonable accuracy is adhered to, it is doubtful whether any human could maintain fluency in more than 20–25 languages concurrently or achieve fluency in more than 40 in a lifetime.

The most multi-lingual living person in the world is Georges Henri Schmidt (b. Strasbourg, France 28 Dec. 1914), the Chief of the U.N. Terminology Section in 1965–71. The 1975 edition of *Who's Who in the United Nations*, listed "only" 19 languages because he was then unable to find time to "revive" his former fluency in 12 others. Britain's greatest linguist is George Campbell (b. 1913), who retired from the B.B.C. Overseas Service where he worked, with 39 languages.

Historically the greatest linguists have been proclaimed as Cardinal Mezzofanti (1774–1849) (fluent in 26 or 27), Professor Rask (1787–1832), Sir John Bowering (1792–1872) and Dr. Harold Williams of New Zealand (1876–1928), who was fluent in 28 languages.

ALPHABET
Earliest
The development of the use of an alphabet in place of pictograms occurred in the Sinaitic world between 1700 and 1500 B.C. This western Semitic language developed the consonantal system based on phonetic and syllabic principles. The oldest letter is "O", unchanged in shape since its adoption in the Phoenician alphabet *c.* 1300 B.C. The newest letters in the English alphabet, are "j" and "v" which are of post Shakespearean use *c.* 1630. There are 65 alphabets now in use.

Longest and shortest
The language with most letters is Cambodian with 72 (including useless ones) and Rotokas in central Bougainville Island has least with 11 (just a, b, e, g, i, k, o, p, ř, t and u). Amharic has 231 formations from 33 basic syllabic forms, each of which has seven modifications, so this Ethiopian language cannot be described as alphabetic.

Most and least consonants and vowels
The language with most consonantal sounds is the Caucasian language Ubyx, with 80 and that with least is Rotokas, with only 6 consonants. The language with the most vowels is Sedang, a central Vietnamese language with 55 distinguishable vowel sounds and those with the least is the Caucasian language Abkhazian with two such. The English record for consecutive vowels is 6 in the musical term *euouae*. The Estonian word jäääärne, meaning the edge of the ice, has the same 4 consecutively. Voiauai, a language in Pará State, Brazil consists solely of 7 vowels. The English word "latchstring" has 6 consecutive consonants.

Largest letter
The largest permanent letters in the world are the giant 600 ft *183 m* letters spelling READYMIX on the ground in the Nullarbor near East Balladonia, Western Australia. This was constructed in Dec. 1971.

WORDS
Longest words *World*
The longest word ever to appear in literature occurs in *The Ecclesiazusae*, a comedy by Aristophanes (448–380 B.C.). In the Greek it is 170 letters long but transliterates into 182 letters in English, thus: lopadotemachoselachogaleokranioleipsanodrimhypotrimmatosilphioparaomelitokatakechymenokichlepikossyphophattoperisteralektryonoptekephalliokigklopeleiolagoiosiraiobaphetraganopterygon. The term describes a fricassee of 17 sweet and sour ingredients including mullet, brains, honey, vinegar, pickles, marrow and ouzo (a Greek drink laced with anisette).

English
The longest word in the Oxford English Dictionary is floccipaucinihilipilification (alternatively spelt in hyphenated form with "n" in seventh place), with 29 letters, meaning "the action of estimating as worthless", first used in 1741, and later by Sir Walter Scott (1771–1832). Webster's Third International Dictionary lists among its 450,000 entries pneumonoultramicroscopicsilicovolcanoconiosis (45 letters) the name of a miners' lung disease.

The nonce word used by Dr. Edward Strother (1675–1737) to describe the spa waters at Bristol was aequeosalinocalcalinoceraceoaluminosocupreovitriolic of 52 letters.

The longest regularly formed English word is praetertranssubstantiationalistically (37 letters), used by Mark McShane in his novel *Untimely Ripped*, published in 1963. The medical term hepaticocholangiocholecystenterostomies (39 letters) refers to the surgical creations of new communications between gallbladders and hepatic ducts and between intestines and gallbladders. The longest words in common use are disproportionableness and incomprehensibilities (21 letters) and interdenominationalism (22 letters).

Longest palindromes

The longest known palindromic word is *saippuakivikauppias* (19 letters), the Finnish word for a dealer in lye (i.e. caustic soda). The longest in the English language is *redivider* (9 letters), while another nine-letter word, *Malayalam*, is a proper noun given to the language of the Malayali people in Kerala, southern India. The nine letter word ROTAVATOR is a registered trade mark belonging to Howard Machinery Ltd. The contrived chemical term *detartrated* has 11 letters. Some baptismal fonts in Greece and Turkey bear the circular 25 letter inscription NIΨON ANOMHMATA MH MONAN OΨIN meaning "wash (my) sins not only (my) face". This appears at St. Mary's Church Nottingham, St. Paul's, Woldingham, Surrey and other churches. The longest palindromic composition devised is one of 11,125 words completed by Jeff Grant of Hastings, New Zealand in Jan. 1979. "No elate man I meet sees a bed". . . and hence predictably ends". . . Debase esteem in a metal eon".

Longest chemical name

The longest chemical term is that describing Bovine NADP-specific Glutamate Dehydrogenase, which contains 500 amino-acids and a resultant name of some 3,600 letters.

Longest anagrams

The longest non-scientific English words which can form anagrams are the 17-letter transpositions "misrepresentation" and "representationism". The longest scientific transposals are cholecystoduodenostomy/duodenocholecystostomy and hydropneumopericardium/pneumohydropericardium each of 22 letters.

Longest abbreviation

The longest known abbreviation is S.K.O.M.K.H.P.K.J.C. D.P.W.B., the initials of the Syarikat Kerjasama Orang-orang Melayu Kerajaan Hilir Perak Kerana Jimat Cermat Dan Pinjaman Wang Berhad. This is the Malay name for the Lower Perak Malay Government Servant's Co-operative Thrift and Loan Society Limited, in Teluk Anson, Perak, West Malaysia (formerly Malaya). The abbreviation for this abbreviation is Skomk. The 55 letter full name of Los Angeles (El Pueblo de Nuestra Señora la Reina de los Angeles de Porciuncula) is abbreviated to L.A. or 3.63% of its length.

Longest Acronym

The longest acronym is NIIOMTPIABOPARMBETZHE-LBETRABSBOMONIMONIMONKONOTDTEKHST-ROMONT with 56 letters (54 in cyrillic) in the *Concise Dictionary of Soviet Terminology* meaning: The laboratory for shuttering, reinforcement, concrete and ferro-concrete operations for composite-monolithic and monolithic constructions of the Department of the Technology of Building—assembly operations the Scientific Research Institute of the Organization for building mechanization and technical aid of the Academy of Building and Architecture of the USSR.

Commonest words and letters

In written English the most frequently used words are in order: the, of, and, to, a, in, that, is, I, it, for *and* as. The most used in conversation is I. The commonest letter is 'e' and the commonest initial letter is 'T'.

Most meanings

The most over-worked word in English is the word *set* which has 58 noun uses, 126 verbal uses and 10 as a participial adjective.

Most Homophones

The most homophonous sounds in English are *air* and *sol* which, according to the researches of Dora Newhouse of Los Angeles, both have 38 homophones. The homonym with most variant spellings is *Air* with Aire, Are, Ayr, E'er, Eir, Ere, Err, Erre, Eyre, Heir, Eire, Eyr *and* Ore.

Most accents

Accents were introduced in French in the reign of Louis XIII (1601–43). The word with most accents is *hétérogénéité*, meaning heterogeneity. An atoll in the Pacific Ocean 320 miles *516 km* E.S.E. of Tahiti is named Héréhérétué.

Shortest holoalphabetic sentence

The contrived headline describing the reaction of despicable

LONGEST WORDS IN VARIOUS LANGUAGES

French	Anticonstitutionnellement (25 letters) —anticonstitutionally.
Croatian	Prijestolonasljednikovica (25 letters) —wife of an heir apparent.
Italian	Precipitevolissimevolmente (26 letters) —as fast as possible.
Portuguese	inconstitucionalissimamente (27 letters) —the highest degree of unconstitutionality.
Icelandic‡	Vaolaheioarvegamannaverkfaerageymsluskur (35 letters) —the door-key hook of the Supreme court barrister's housemaid
Japanese	Ryágū-no-otohime-no-motoyui-no-kirihazushi (36 letters) —a seaweed, literally of small pieces of the paper hair streamers of the underwater princess.
Hungarian	Megszentsegtelenithetetlenseyeskedeseitekert (44 letters) —for your unprofaneable actions.
Russian	ryentgyenoelyektrokardiografichyeskogo (33 Cyrillic letters, transliterating as 38) —of the radioelectrocardiographic.
Dutch‡	Rijksluchtvaartdienstweerschepenpersoneel (41 letters) —Government aviation department weather ship personnel.
Turkish‡	Cekoslovakyalılastıramadıklarımızdanmıymıssınız (47 letters) —"are you not of that group of persons that we were said to be unable to Czechoslovakianise?"
Mohawk*	tkanuhstasrihsranuhwe'tsraaksahsrakaratattsrayeri' (50 letters) —the praising of the evil of the liking of the finding of the house is right.
German†‡	Donaudampfschifffahrtselectricitaetenhauptbetriebswerkbauunterbeamtengesellschaft (81 letters, —The club for subordinate officials of the head office management of the Danube steamboat electrical services (Name of a pre-war club in Vienna).
Swedish‡	Spårvagnsaktiebolagsskensmutsskjutarefackföreningspersonalbeklädnadsmagasinsförrådsförvaltaren (94 letters) —Manager of the depot for the supply of uniforms to the personnel of the track cleaners' union of the tramway company.

* Mohawk forms words of limitless length. Above is an example.
† The longest dictionary word in every day usage is Kraftfahrzeugreparaturwerkstatten (33 letters or 34 if the ä is written as ae) meaning motor vehicle repair shops (or service garages).
‡ Not found in standard dictionaries.

vandals from the valley thwarted by finding a block of quartz with carvings (already) upon it as "Quartz glyph job vex'd cwm finks" represents the ultimate in containing all 26 letters in 26 letters. This was devised by Jeff Grant of Hastings, New Zealand.

Longest sentence

A sentence of 1300 words appears in "Absalom Absalom" by William Faulkner and one of 3,153 words in *History of the Church of God* composed by Sylvester Hassell of Wilson, North Carolina, U.S.A., *c.* 1884 with 86 semi-colons and 390 commas. The longest sentence recorded to have got past the editor of a major newspaper is one of 1,030 words in the *Chicago Tribune* T.V. column by Clarence G. Petersen in the issue of 19 Aug. 1970. The Report of the President of Columbia University 1942–43 contained a sentence of 4,284 words. The first 40,000 words of *The Gates of Paradise* by George Andrzeyevski (Panther) appear to lack any punctuation. Some authors such as James Joyce (1882–1941) appear to eschew punctuation altogether.

PLACE-NAMES
Earliest

The earliest recorded British place-name is Belerion, the Penwith peninsula of Cornwall, referred to as such by Pytheas of Massilia in *c.* 308 B.C. The name Salakee on St. Mary's, Isles of Scilly is however arguably of a pre Indo-European substrate meaning *tin island*. There are reasons to contend that Leicester (Roman, Ligora Castrum) contains an element reflecting its founding by the Western Mediterranean navigators, the Ligurians, as early as *c* 1200 B.C. The earliest distinctive name for what is now Great Britain was Albion by Himilco *c.* 500 B.C. The oldest name among England's 46 counties is Kent, first mentioned in its Roman form of Cantium (from the Celtic *canto*, meaning a rim, *i.e.* a coastal district) from the same circumnavigation by Pytheas. The earliest mention of England is the form *Angelcymn*, which appeared in the Anglo-Saxon Chronicle in A.D. 880.

Longest *World*

The official name for Bangkok, the capital city of Thailand, is Krungtep Mahanakhon. The full name is however: Krungthep Mahanakhon Bovorn Ratanakosin Mahintharayutthaya Mahadilokpop Noparatratchathani Burirom Udomratchanivetmahasathan Amornpiman Avatarnsathit Sakkathattiyavisnukarmprasit (167 letters) which in its most scholarly transliteration emerges with 175 letters. The longest place-name now in use in the world is Taumatawhakatangihangakoauauotamatea(turipukakapikimaungahoronuku)pokaiwhenuakitanatahu, the unofficial 85-letter version of the name of a hill (1,002 ft above sea-level) in the Southern Hawke's Bay district of the North Island, New Zealand. This Maori name means "the hill whereon was played the flute of Tamatea, circumnavigator of lands, for his lady love". The official version has 57 letters (1 to 36 and 65 to 85). Ijouaououene, Morocco has 8 consecutive vowels.

Great Britain

The longest place-name in the United Kingdom is the concocted 58-letter name Llanfairpwllgwyngyllgogerychwyrndrobwllllantysiliogogogoch, which is translated: "St. Mary's Church in a dell of white hazel trees, near the rapid whirlpool, by the red cave of the Church of St. Tysilio". This is the name used for the reopened (April 1973) village railway station in Anglesey, Gwynedd, Wales, but the *official* name consists of only the first 20 letters of what the Welsh would regard as a 51 letter word since "ll" and "ch" may be regarded as one. The longest genuine Welsh place-name listed in the Ordnance Survey Gazetteer is Lower Llanfihangel-y-Creuddyn (26 letters), a village near Aberystwyth, Dyfed, Wales.

England

The longest single word (unhyphenated) place-name in England is Blakehopeburnhaugh, a hamlet between Burness and Rochester in Northumberland, of 18 letters. The hyphenated Sutton-under-Whitestoncliffe, North Yorkshire has 27 letters on the Ordnance Survey but with the insertion of "the" and the dropping of the final "e" 29 letters in the Post Office List. The longest multiple name is North

Leverton with Habblesthorpe (30 letters), Nottinghamshire, while the longest parish name is Saint Mary le More and All Hallows with Saint Leonard and Saint Peter, Wallingford (68 letters) in Oxfordshire formed on 5 April 1971.

Scotland

The longest single word place-names in Scotland are Claddochknockline, on the island of North Uist, Western Isles and the nearby Claddochbaleshare both with 17 letters. Kirkcudbrightshire (18 letters) became merged into Dumfries and Galloway on 16 May 1975. A 12-acre *5 ha* loch 9 miles *14 km* west of Stornoway on Lewes, Western Isles is named Loch Airidh Mhic Fhionnlaidh Dhuibh (31 letters).

Ireland

The longest place-name in Ireland is Muckanagheder-dauhaulia (22 letters), 4 miles *6 km* from Costello in Camus Bay, County Galway. The name means "soft place between two seas".

Shortest

The shortest place names in the world are the French village of Y (population 143), so named since 1241, the Danish village Å on the island Fyn, the Norwegian village of Å (pronounced "Aw"), the Swedish place Å in Vikholandet, U in the Caroline Islands, Pacific Ocean; and the Japanese town of Sosei which is alternatively called Aioi or O. There was once a 6 in West Virginia, U.S.A. The shortest place-names in Great Britain are the two-lettered villages of Ae (population 199 in 1961) Dumfries and Galloway; Oa on the island of Islay, Strathclyde and Bu on Wyre, Orkney Islands. In the Shetland Islands there are skerries called Ve and two stacks called Aa. The island of Iona was originally I. The River E flows into the southern end of Loch Mhór, Inverness-shire, and O Brook flows on Dartmoor, Devon. The shortest place-name in Ireland is Ta (or Lady's Island) Lough, a sea-inlet on the coast of County Wexford. Tievelough, in County Donegal, is also called Ea.

Most Spellings

The Leicestershire village of Shepshed is recorded in 49 spellings since the Scepesvesde of the Doomsday Book in 1086.

PERSONAL NAMES
Earliest

The earliest personal name which has survived is possibly N'armer, the earliest Egyptian Pharaoh, dating from *c.* 3050 B.C. The earliest known name of any resident of Britain is Divitiacus, King of the Suessiones, the Gaulish ruler of the Kent area *c.* 75 B.C. under the name Prydhain. Scotland, unlike England, was never conquered by the Roman occupiers (A.D. 43–410). Calgācus (b. *c.* A.D. 40), who led this last resistance was the earliest native of Scotland whose name has been recorded.

Longest Pedigree

The only non-Royal English pedigree that can with certainty show a clear pre-Conquest descent is that of the Arden family. It is claimed on behalf of the Clan Mackay that their clan can be traced to Loarn, the Irish invader of south west Pictland, now Strathclyde, *c.* A.D. 501.

Longest Single name

The longest Christian or given name on record is Napuamohala-onaona-a-me-ka-wehiwehi-o-na-kuahiwi-a-mena-awawa-ke-hoomaka-ke-hoaala-ke-ea-o-na-aina-naniakea-o-hawaii-i-ka-wanaao (102 letters) in the case of Miss Dawne N. Lee so named in Honolulu, Hawaii, U.S.A. in February 1967. The name means "The abundant, beautiful blossoms of the mountains and valleys begin to fill the air with their fragrance throughout the length and breadth of Hawaii".

Longest Surname *World*

The longest name used by anyone is Adolph Blaine Charles David Earl Frederick Gerald Hubert Irvin John Kenneth Lloyd Martin Nero Oliver Paul Quincy Randolph Sherman Thomas Uncas Victor William Xerxes Yancy Zeus Wolfeschlegelsteinhausenbergerdorff, Senior, who was born at Bergedorf, near Hamburg, Germany, on 29 Feb. 1904. On printed forms he uses only his eighth and second Christian names and the first 35 letters of his surname. The full version of the name of 590 letters appeared in the 12th edition of *The Guinness Book of Records*. He now lives in Philadelphia, Pennsylvania, U.S.A., and has shortened his surname to Mr. Wolfe + 585, Senior.

United Kingdom

The longest surname in the United Kingdom was the six-barrelled one borne by the late Major L.S.D.O.F. (Leone Sextus Denys Oswolf Fraudati filius) Tollemache-Tollemache de Orellana Plantagenet Tollemache Tollemache, who was born in 1884 and died of pneumonia in France on 20 Feb. 1917. Of non-repetitious surnames, the last example of a five-barrelled one was that of the Lady Caroline Jemima Temple-Nugent-Chandos-Brydges-Grenville (1858–1946). The longest single English surname is Featherstonehaugh, correctly pronounced on occasions (but improbably on the correct occasion) Featherstonehaw or Festonhaw or Fessonhay or Freestonhugh or Feerstonhaw or Fanshaw.

Scotland

In Scotland the surname nin (feminine of mac) Achinmacdholicachinskerray (29 letters) was recorded in an 18th century parish register.

Most Christian names

The great great grandson of Carlos III of Spain, Don Alfonso de Borbón y Borbón (1866–1934) had 89 Christian names of which several were lengthened by hyphenation.

Shortest

The single letter surname O, of which 28 examples appear in Belgian telephone directories, besides being the commonest single letter name is the one obviously causing most distress to those concerned with the prevention of cruelty to computers. There are two one-lettered Burmese names E (calm), pronounced aye and U (egg), pronounced Oo. U *before* the name means "uncle". There exist among the 47,000,000 names on the Dept. of Health & Social Security index 5 examples of a one-lettered surname. Their identity has not been disclosed, but they are "A", "B", "J", "N", "O" and "X". Two-letter British surnames include By and On have recently been joined by Oy, Za and others. The Christian name "A" has been used for 5 generations in the Taber family of Essex.

Commonest Family name *World*

The commonest family name in the world is the Chinese name Chang which is borne according to estimates, by between 9.7% and 12.1% of the Chinese population, so indicating even on the lower estimate that there are at least some 75,000,000 Changs—more than the entire population of all but 7 of the 159 other sovereign countries of the world.

English

The commonest surname in the English-speaking world is Smith. The most recent published count showed 659,050 nationally insured Smiths in Great Britain, of whom 10,102 were plain John Smith and another 19,502 were John (plus one or more given names) Smith. Including uninsured persons there were over 800,000 Smiths in England and Wales alone, of whom 81,493 were called A. Smith. There were an estimated 2,382,509 Smiths in the U.S.A. in 1973.

"Macs"

There are, however, estimated to be 1,600,000 persons in Britain with M', Mc or Mac (Gaelic "son of") as part of their surnames. The commonest of these is Macdonald which accounts for about 55,000 of the Scottish population.

Commonest Christian name

From the latest available full year (1976) birth registrations for England and Wales at St. Catherine's House (formerly Somerset House), the most favoured first forename choice of parents bearing the 21 commonest surnames are boys Mark/Marc with the narrowest of leads over Paul followed by Stephen/Steven and girls Sarah/Sara with a very narrow lead over Claire/Clare/Clair. This massive survey of 61,000 names was carried out by C. V. Appleton. From 1196 to at least 1925

William and John were first and second but by 1971 John had sunk to 17th and William failed to make the Top 50.

Most versions

Mr. R. B. McAtee of Arlington, Virginia, U.S.A. has collected 334 versions of the spelling of his family name since 1902. Mzilikazi of Zululand (b. *c.* 1795) had his name chronicled in 325 spellings, according to researches by Dr. R. Kent Rasmussen.

Most contrived name

In the United States the determination to derive commercial or other benefit from being the last listing in the local telephone book has resulted in self-given names, starting with six z's—for example Mr. Vladimir Zzzzzzabakov of the San Francisco book. Last in the book for Madison, Wisconsin is however the 31 year old Hero Zzyzzx (pronounced Ziz-icks) whose name, he claims, is for real. The alpha and omega of Britain's 62 directories are Mrs. Maude E. Aab of Hull, Humberside and Mr. Shamsu Zzaman of Northampton.

TEXTS AND BOOKS

Oldest

The oldest known written text is the pictographic expression of Sumerian speech (see Earliest Language, p. 90). The Samarian papyri, written in Aramaic, found 8½ miles *13,7 km* north of Jericho are dated 375–335 B.C.

Oldest printed

The oldest surviving printed work is a Korean scroll or *sutra* from wooden printing blocks found in the foundations of the Pulguk Sa pagoda, Kyongju, Korea, on 14 Oct. 1966. It has been dated no later than A.D. 704. It was claimed in November 1973 that a 28 page book of Tang dynasty poems at Yonsei University, Korea was printed from metal type *c.* 1160.

Oldest Mechanically printed

It is widely accepted that the earliest mechanically printed full length book was the 42-line Gutenberg Bible, printed at Mainz, Germany, in *c.* 1455 by Johann Henne zum Gensfleisch zur Laden, called "zu Gutenberg" (*c.* 1398 - *c.* 1468). Work on water marks published in 1967 indicates a copy of a surviving printed "Donatus" Latin grammar was made from paper in *c.* 1450. The earliest exactly dated printed work is the Psalter completed on 14 Aug. 1457 by Johann Fust (*c.* 1400–1466) and Peter Schöffer (1425–1502), who had been Gutenberg's chief assistant. The earliest printing by William Caxton (*c.* 1422–1491) though undated would appear to be *The Recuyel of the Historyes of Troye* in late 1473 to spring 1474.

Largest *Book*

The largest book in the world is the *Super Book* measuring 9 ft × 10 ft 2⅛ in *2,74 × 3,07 m* weighing 557 lb. *252,6 kg* consisting of 300 pages published in Denver, Colorado, U.S.A. in 1976.

Publication

The largest publication in the world is the 1,112 volume set of *British Parliamentary Papers* published by the Irish University Press in 1968–1972. A complete set weighs 3¼ tons *3,3 tonnes*, costs £21,000 and would take 6 years to read at 10 hours per day. The production involved the death of 34,000 Indian goats, and the use of £15,000 worth of gold ingots. The total print is 500 sets.

Dictionary

The largest dictionary now published is the 12-volume Royal quarto *The Oxford English Dictionary* of 15,487 pages published between 1884 and 1928 with a first supplement of 963 pages in 1933 with a further 4-volume supplement, edited by R. W. Burchfield, in which the third and fourth volumes covering O–S and T–Z have yet to appear. The work contains 414,825 words, 1,827,306 illustrative quotations and reputedly 227,779,589 letters and figures, 63.8 times more than the Bible.

Smallest Book

The smallest marketed bound printed book with cursive

material is one of 15 pages measuring 2,1 × 2,1 × 0,8 mm $\frac{1}{12}$ × $\frac{1}{12}$ × $\frac{1}{32}$ in, comprising *Three Blind Mice* and produced by Gleniffer Press, of Paisley, Scotland in 1978.

Longest novel
The longest important novel ever published is *Les hommes de bonne volonté* by Louis Henri Jean Farigoule (b. 26 Aug. 1885), *alias* Jules Romains, of France, in 27 volumes in 1932–46. The English version *Men of Good Will* was published in 14 volumes in 1933–46 as a "novel-cycle". The 4,959 page edition published by Peter Davies Ltd has an estimated 2,070,000 words excluding a 100 page index. The novel *Tokuga-Wa Ieyasu* by Sohachi Yamaoka has been serialised in Japanese daily newspapers since 1951. Now completed it will require nearly 40 volumes in book form.

Encyclopaedias *Earliest*
The earliest known encyclopaedia was compiled by Speusippus (*post* 408–c. 338 B.C.) a nephew of Plato, in Athens c. 370 B.C. The earliest encyclopaedia compiled by a Briton was *Liber exerptionum* by the Scottish monk Richard (d. 1173) at St. Victor's Abbey, Paris c. 1140.

Largest
The largest encyclopaedia ever compiled was the *Great Standard Encyclopaedia* of Yung-lo ta tien of 22,937 manuscript chapters (370 still survive), written by 2,000 Chinese scholars in 1403–08.

Most comprehensive
The most comprehensive present day encyclopaedia is the *Encyclopaedia Britannica*, first published in Edinburgh, Scotland, in Dec. 1768–1771. A group of booksellers in the United States acquired reprint rights in 1898 and completed ownership in 1899. In 1943 the *Britannica* was given to the University of Chicago, Illinois, U.S.A. The current 30-volume 15th edition contains 33,141 pages and 43,000,000 words from 4,277 contributors. It is now edited in Chicago and in London.

Longest Index
The Ninth Collective Index of *Chemical Abstracts* completed on 23 Aug. 1978 contains 20.55 million entries in 95,882 pages and 57 volumes, and weighs 251 lb *113,8 kg.*

Maps *Oldest*
The oldest known map of any kind is a clay tablet depicting the river Euphrates flowing through northern Mesopotamia, Iraq, dated c. 3800 B.C. The earliest surviving product of English map-making is the Anglo Saxon *mappa mundi*, known as the Cottonian manuscript from the late 10th century. The earliest printed map in the world dates from Isodore of Sevellés *Etymologiarium* of 1472. The earliest printed map of Britain was Ptolemy's outline printed in Bologna, Italy in 1477.

Most Expensive *Printed Book*
The highest price ever paid for a printed book is $2,400,000 (then £1,265,000) for one of the only 21 complete known copies of the Gutenberg Bible, printed in Mainz, West Germany in c. 1454. It was bought from the Carl and Lily Pforzheimer Foundation by Texas University in a sale arranged by Quaritch of London in New York on 9 June 1978.

Broadsheet
The highest price ever paid for a broadsheet has been $404,000 (then £168,333) for one of the 16 known copies of *The Declaration of Independence*, printed in Philadelphia in 1776 by Samuel T. Freeman & Co., and sold to a Texan in May 1969.

Manuscripts
The highest value ever paid for any manuscript is £280,000 paid at Christie's, London on 17 Nov. 1976 for a single leaf of *The Death of Zahhak* from the 258 page Persian *Shahnameh*, commissioned by Shah Ismai'l in 1522 and sold by Arthur J. Houghton of New York. The splitting of this manuscript has been greatly criticized. It has been estimated that the total value of this manuscript acquired by Mr. Houghton in 1959 may be as high as £32,000,000 (*$60 million*).

An engraving from the world's most expensive atlas, the 16th century Mercator atlas of Europe. (*Sotheby Parke Bernet & Co.*)

Atlas
The highest price paid for an atlas is £340,000 for a 16th century Mercator atlas of Europe, sold at Sotheby's, London, on 13 Mar. 1979.

BIBLE
Oldest
Biblical texts in Hebrew are known to have become stabilized as early as A.D. 70. The oldest leather and papyrus Dead Sea Scrolls date from c. 250 B.C. The oldest known bible is the *Codex Vaticanus* written in Greek *ante* A.D. 350 and preserved in the Vatican Museum, Rome. The earliest Bible printed in English was one edited by Miles Coverdale, Bishop of Exeter (c. 1488–1569), while living in Antwerp, and printed in 1535. William Tyndale's New Testament in English had, however, been printed in Cologne and in Worms, Germany in 1525.

Longest and Shortest books
The longest book in the Authorized version of the Bible is the Book of Psalms, while the longest book including prose is the Book of the Prophet Isaiah, with 66 chapters. The shortest is the Third Epistle of John, with 294 words in 14 verses. The Second Epistle of John has only 13 verses but 298 words.

Longest Psalm, verse sentence and name
Of the 150 Psalms, the longest is the 119th, with 176 verses, and the shortest is the 117th, with two verses. The shortest verse in the Authorized Version (King James) of the Bible is verse 35 of Chapter XI of the Gospel according to St. John, consisting of the two words "Jesus wept". The longest is verse 9 of Chapter VIII of the Book of Esther, which extends to a 90-word description of the Persian empire. The total number of letters in the Bible is 3,566,480. The total number of words depends on the method of counting hyphenated words, but is usually given as between 773,692 and 773,746. The word "and" according to Colin McKay Wilson of the Salvation Army appears 46,227 times. The longest personal name in the Bible is Maher-shalal-hash-baz, the symbolic name of the second son of Isaiah (Isaiah,

Louis Alexander of Haslemere, Surrey, whose school text books sell over 4½ million copies per year. (*Longman Group Ltd.*)

Chapter VIII, verses 1 and 3). The caption of Psalm 22, however, contains a Hebrew title sometimes rendered Al-'Ayyeleth Hash-Shahar (20 letters).

LETTERS
Longest
The longest personal letter based on a word count is one of 1,113,747 words written in 8 months ending May 1976, by Miss Jacqueline Jones of Lindale, Texas, to her sister, Mrs. Jean Stewart, of Springfield, Maine, U.S.A.

To an editor *Longest*
The longest recorded letter to an editor was one of 13,000 words (a third of a modern novel) written to the editor of the *Fishing Gazette* by A.R.I.E.L. and published in 7-point type spread over two issues in 1884.

Most
Britain's, and seemingly the world's, most indefatigable writer of letters to the editors of newspapers is Raymond L. Cantwell, 53, of Oxford, who since 1948 claims 28,549 letters published in print, on the air or in aid of charity.

Shortest
The shortest correspondence on record was that between Victor Marie Hugo (1802–85) and his publisher Hurst and Blackett in 1862. The author was on holiday and anxious to know how his new novel *Les Misérables* was selling. He wrote "?". The reply was "!".

Most Personal Mail
The highest confirmed mail received by any private citizen in a year is 900,000 letters by the baseball star Hank Aaron reported by the US Postal Department in June 1974. About a third were letters of hate engendered by his bettering of Babe Ruth's career record for "home runs". (See Chap. 12.)

Longest Diary
No collated records exist but the diary of T. C. Baskerville of Charlton-cum-Hardy, Manchester maintained since 1939 comprises an estimated 3,390,000 words.

Pen Pals Most Durable
The longest sustained correspondence on record is one of 73 years between Mrs. E. Darlington of Marple, Cheshire and Mrs. Gertrude Walker of Hawthorn, South Australia which started on 5 Jan. 1906.

Birthday Card—Most Parsimonious
Mrs. Amelia Finch (b. 18 Apr. 1912) of Lakehurst, New Jersey, U.S.A. and Mr. Paul E. Warburgh (b. 1 Feb. 1902) of Huntington, New Jersey have been exchanging the same card since 1 Feb. 1927.

Christmas cards
The greatest number of personal Christmas cards sent out is believed to be 62,824 by Mr. Werner Erhard of San Francisco, California in December 1975.

AUTOGRAPHS AND SIGNATURES
Earliest English Regal
The earliest English sovereign whose handwriting is known to have survived is Edward III (1327–1377). The earliest full signature extant is that of Richard II (dated 26 July 1386). The Magna Carta does not bear even the mark of King John (reigned 1199–1216), but carries only his seal. An attested cross of King Cnut (1016–1035) has survived.

Most expensive
The highest price ever paid on the open market for a single autograph letter signed is $51,000 (*then £10,500*), paid in 1927 for a letter written by the Gloucestershire-born Button Gwinnett (1732–77), one of the three men from Georgia to sign the United States' Declaration of Independence in Philadelphia beginning on 4 July 1776. An expense account by Paul Revere, dated 3 Jan 1774 and signed by John Hancock, was auctioned for $70,000 (*then £36,850*) at Sotheby Parke Bernet on 26 Apr. 1978.

The highest price paid for a signed autograph letter of a living person is $6 250 (*then £2430*) for a letter from ex-President Richard M. Nixon to a Brigadier dated 14 Dec. 1971.

AUTHORS
Most prolific
The most prolific writer for whom a word count has been published was Charles Hamilton, *alias* Frank Richards (1875–1961), the Englishman who created Billy Bunter. At his height in 1908 he wrote the whole of the boys' comics *Gem* (founded 1907) and *Magnet* (1908–1940) and most of two others, totalling 80,000 words a week. His lifetime output has been put at 100,000,000 words. He enjoyed the advantages of the use of electric light rather than candlelight and of being unmarried. The champion of the goose quill era was Józef Ignacy Kraszewski (1812–1887) of Poland who produced more than 600 volumes of novels and historical works.

Most Novels
The greatest number of novels published by any author is 904 by Kathleen Lindsay (Mrs. Mary Faulkner) (1903–1973) of Somerset West, Cape Province, South Africa. She wrote under six pen names, two of them masculine. The most prolific living novelist is Lauran Paine of California, who has had some 850 published under 70 pen names. After receiving a probable record 743 rejection slips the British novelist John Creasey M.B.E. (1908–1973), under his own name and 13 *noms de plume* had 564 books totalling more than 40,000,000 words published from 1932 to his death on 9 June 1973. The British authoress with the greatest total of full length titles is Miss Ursula Harvey Bloom (b. Chelmsford, Essex 1892) (Mrs. A. C. G. Robinson, formerly Mrs. Denham-Cookes), who reached 500 by December 1975, starting in 1924 with *The Great Beginning* and including the best sellers *The Ring Tree* (novel) and *The Rose of Norfolk* (non-fiction). Enid Mary Blyton (1898–1968) (Mrs. Darrell Waters) completed 600 titles of children's stories many of them brief with 59 in the single year 1955. She was translated into a record 128 languages.

Most Text Books
Britain's most successful writer of text books is the ex-schoolmaster Ronald Ridout (b. 23 July 1916) who between 1948 and May 1979 had 401 titles published with sales of 68,000,000. His *The First English Workbook* has sold 4,465,000.

The annual aggregate sales of all titles by Louis Alexander of Haslemere, Surrey, reached 4,573,000 in 1977.

Highest paid
In 1958 a Mrs. Deborah Schneider of Minneapolis, Minnesota, U.S.A., wrote 25 words to complete a sentence in a competition for the best blurb for Plymouth cars. She won from about 1,400,000 entrants the prize of $500 (£178) every month for life. On normal life expectations she would have collected $12,000 (£4,285) per word. No known anthology includes Mrs. Schneider's deathless prose.

A modern author of a highly successful 100,000 word filmed novel might expect to earn up to $17.50 per word.

Top selling
It was announced on 13 March 1953 that 672,058,000 copies of the works of Marshal Iosif Vissarionovich Dzhugashvili, *alias* Stalin (1879–1953), had been sold or distributed in 101 languages.

The all-time estimate of book sales by Erle Stanley Gardner (1889–1970) (U.S.) to 1 Jan. 1979 were 310,910,603 copies in 23 languages. The top selling authoress, has been Dame Agatha Christie (*née* Miller) (later Lady Mallowan) (1890–1976) whose 87 crime novels sold an estimated 300,000,000 in 103 languages. *Sleeping Murder* was published posthumously in 1977. Currently the top-selling authoress is Barbara Cartland (Mrs McCorquodale) with global sales exceeding 100,000,000 in 242 novels in 18 languages.

Highest selling title
The authors who have written the highest selling title are Norris Dewar McWhirter (b. 12 Aug. 1925) and his twin brother Alan Ross McWhirter (k. 27 Nov. 1975), editors and compilers of *The Guinness Book of Records* first published from 107 Fleet Street, London in October 1955. Global sales in 19 languages by May 1979 reached over 36,000,000 copies.

Most rejections
The greatest recorded number of publisher's rejections for a manuscript is 109 for the 130,000 word manuscript "World Government Crusade" by Gilbert Young (b. 1906) since 1958. His public meeting in Bath, England in support of his parliamentary candidature as a World Government Candidate, however, drew a crowd of one.

Oldest authoress
The oldest authoress in the world is Mrs. Alice Pollock (*née* Wykeham-Martin, (1868–1971) of Haslemere, Surrey, whose book "Portrait of My Victorian Youth" (Johnson Publications) was published in March 1971 when she was aged 102 years 8 months.

Youngest
The youngest recorded commercially published author is Dorothy Straight (b. 25 May 1958) of Washington D.C., who wrote *How the World Began* in 1962 aged 4 which was published in August 1964 by Pantheon Books, New York.

Longest Literary Gestation
The standard German dictionary *Deutsches Wörterbuch*, begun by the brothers Grimm in 1854, was finished in 1971. *Acta Sanctorum* begun by Jean Bolland in 1643, arranged according to saints' days, reached the month of November in 1925 and an introduction for December was published in 1940.

Poet Laureate *Youngest and oldest*
The youngest Poet Laureate was Laurence Eusden (1688–1730), who received the bays on 24 Dec. 1718 at the age of 30 years and 3 months. The greatest age at which a poet has succeeded is 73 in the case of William Wordsworth (1770–1850) on 6 April 1843. The longest lived Laureate was John Masefield, O.M., who died on 12 May 1967, aged 88 years 345 days. The longest which any poet has worn the laurel is 41 years 322 days, in the case of Alfred (later the 1st Lord) Tennyson (1809–92), who was appointed on 19 Nov. 1850 and died in office on 6 Oct. 1892.

Longest poem
The lengthiest poem ever published has been the Kirghiz folk epics *Manas*, which appeared in printed form in 1958

Nicholas Monsarrat, author of the best-selling novel, *The Cruel Sea* published in 1951 (see p. 98).

but which has never been translated into English. It runs to "more than 500,000 lines". Short translated passages appear in *The Elek Book of Oriental Verse*.

The longest poem ever written in the English language is one on the life of King Alfred by John Fitchett (1766–1838) of Liverpool which ran to 129,807 lines and took 40 years to write. His editor Robert Riscoe added the concluding 2,585 lines

HIGHEST PRINTINGS
World
The world's most widely distributed book is the Bible, portions of which have been translated into 1,659 languages. This compares with 222 languages by Lenin. It has been estimated that between 1815 and 1975 some 2,500,000,000 copies were printed of which 1,500,000,000 were handled by Bible Societies. The total distribution of complete Bibles by the United Bible Societies (covering 150 countries) in the year 1978 was 9,280,222.

It has been reported that 800,000,000 copies of the red-covered booklet *Quotations from the Works of Mao Tse-tung* were sold or distributed between June 1966, when possession became virtually mandatory in China, and Sept. 1971 when their promoter Marshal Lin Piao was killed. The *American Spelling Book* by Noah Webster was distributed in some 75,000,000 copies.

Non fiction
The total disposal through non-commercial channels by Jehovah's Witnesses of the 192 page hard bound book *The Truth That Leads to Eternal Life* published by the Watchtower Bible and Tract Society of Brooklyn, New York, on 8 May 1968, reached 95 million in 112 languages by 1 Jan. 1979.

BEST SELLERS
The world's all-time best *selling* book is the annual reference work *The World Almanac & Book of Facts* first published in 1868 and currently edited by George E. Delury. Its cumulative sale to October 1978 is estimated at 38 million copies increasing by 1,100,000 each year.

Fiction

The novel with the highest sales has been *Valley of the Dolls* (first published March 1966) by Jacqueline Susann (Mrs. Irving Mansfield) (1921–1974) with a world wide total of 21,472,000 to 1 May 1979. In the first 6 months Bantam sold 6.8 million. In the United Kingdom the highest print order has been 3,000,000 by Penguin Books Ltd. for their paperback edition of *Lady Chatterley's Lover*, by D. H. (David Herbert) Lawrence (1885–1930). The total sales to April 1979 were 4,213,500. Alistair Stuart MacLean (b. Scotland April 1922) between 1955 and 1978 wrote 23 books of which the sales of 17 have exceeded a million copies and 12 have been filmed. *The Cruel Sea* by Nicholas Monsarrat (b. 22 Mar. 1910) published in 1951 by Cassells, reached sales of 1,180,000 in its *original* edition by 1976.

Slowest seller

The accolade for the world's slowest selling book (known in U.S. publishing as slooow-sellers) probably belongs to David Wilkins's Translation of the New Testament from Coptic into Latin published by Oxford University Press in 1716 in 500 copies. Selling an average of one each 139 days, it was in print for 191 years.

PUBLISHERS AND PRINTERS
Largest Publisher *World*

The largest publisher in the world is the United States Government Printing Office (founded 1860) in Washington, D.C., U.S.A. The Superintendents of Documents Division dispatches items worth more than $44 million (*£23 million*) every year. The inventory is maintained at 24,500 titles in print.

Great Britain

In terms of new titles per annum Britain's most prolific publisher was Robert Hale Ltd. (founded 1936) with 666 in 1978. The U.K. published a record 38,766 book titles in 1978 of which 9,236 were reprints. The highest figure for reprints was 9,977 in 1970.

Largest Printer *World*

The largest printers in the world are R. R. Donnelley & Sons Co. of Chicago, Illinois, U.S.A. The company, founded in 1864 has plants in 13 main centres, turning out $661,000,000 (*£347 million*) worth of work per year. More than 60,000 tons of inks and 1,000,000 tons of paper and board are consumed every year.

Print order

The initial print order for the 50th Automobile Association Members' Handbook (1978–79) was 4,500,000 copies. The total print since 1908 has been 72,400,000. It is currently printed by web offset by Petty & Sons of Leeds.

LIBRARIES
Largest *World*

The largest library in the world is the United States Library of Congress (founded on 24 Apr. 1800), on Capitol Hill, Washington, D.C. By 1978 it contained 74,387,000 items, including 18,638,633 volumes and pamphlets. The buildings contain 35 acres *14,0 ha* of floor space and contain 350 miles *563 km* of shelving. The James Madison Memorial Extension began in 1971 is due for completion in 1980.

The largest non-statutory library in the world is the New York Public Library (founded 1895) on Fifth Avenue with a floor space of 525,276 ft² *48 800 m²* and 80 miles *128 km* of shelving. Its collection including 83 branch libraries embraces 8,605,610 volumes 10,683,105 manuscripts and 317,183 maps.

Great Britain

The largest library in the United Kingdom is the British Library, dispersed among 17 buildings in London and three at Boston Spa, West Yorkshire, with a total staff of 2000. The British Library Reference Division in Bloomsbury comprises the former library departments of the British Museum. It contains nearly 10 million books, and takes in more than 82,000 *different* journals. Under the Copyright Act a copy of every UK publication must be deposited with the British Library and much is acquired from overseas by purchase or exchange. Stock increases involve 2 miles *3 km* of additional shelving annually. The British Library's Newspaper Library at Colindale, North London, has 496,000 volumes and parcels comprising 35,000 different titles. The British Library Lending Division in West Yorkshire runs the largest library inter-lending operation in the world; it handles annually more than 2 million requests from other libraries (UK and overseas) for items they do not hold in stock. The largest public library in the United Kingdom will be the extended Mitchell Library, North Street, Glasgow with a floor area of 510,000 ft² *47 380 m²* or 11.7 acres *4,7 ha* and an ultimate capacity for 4,000,000 volumes. The oldest public library in Scotland is in Kirkwall, Orkney, founded in 1683.

Overdue books

The most overdue book taken out by a known borrower was one reported on 7 Dec. 1968, checked out in 1823 from the University of Cincinnati Medical Library on Febrile Diseases (London, 1805 by Dr. J. Currie). This was returned by the borrower's great-grandson Richard Dodd. The fine calculated to be $2,264 (*then £1,102 10s*) was waived.

PERIODICALS
Oldest *World*

The oldest continuing periodical in the world is *Philosophical Transactions of the Royal Society*, published in London, which first appeared on 6 Mar. 1665.

Great Britain

The Botanical Magazine has been in continuous publication since 1787, as several "parts" a year forming a series of continuously numbered volumes. Britain's oldest weekly periodical is *Lancet* first published in 1823. The Scottish monthly *Blackwood's Magazine* has not missed an issue since the first in April 1817. The Editor had always been a Blackwood until the appointment of David Fletcher in July 1976. The *Scots Magazine* began publication in 1739 and ran till 1826, and with three breaks has been produced continuously since 1924.

Largest circulation *World*

The largest circulations of any weekly periodical is that of *TV Guide* (U.S.A.) which in 1974 became the first magazine in history to sell a billion (1,000 million) copies in a year. The weekly average for July–Dec. 1978 was 19,495,113. In its 39 basic international editions *The Reader's Digest* (established February 1922) circulates 29,701,000 copies monthly in 15 languages, including a United States edition of more than 17,750,000 copies and a United Kingdom edition (established 1939) of 1,432,795 copies (av. Jan.–Dec. 1978).

Parade, the syndicated Sunday newspaper colour supplement, is distributed with 128 newspapers every Sunday. The current circulation is 21,195,624 (May 1979).

Great Britain

The highest circulation of any periodical in Great Britain is that of the *Radio Times* (instituted on 28 Sept. 1923). The average weekly sale for July–December 1978 was 3,824,675 copies with a readership of 10,663,000. The highest sale of any issue was 9,778,062 copies for the Christmas issue of 1955. *T.V. Times* averaged sales of 3,691,407 in the period July–Dec. 1978 with an estimated readership of 11,078,000 (July–Dec. 1978).

Annual

Old Moore's Almanack has been published annually since 1697, when it first appeared as a broadsheet, by Dr. Francis Moore (1657–1715) of Southwark, London to advertise his "physiks". The annual sale certified by its publishers W. Foulsham & Co. Ltd. of Slough England is 1,096,000 copies and its aggregate sale is estimated to be in excess of 107 million.

NEWSPAPERS
Oldest *World*

The oldest existing newspaper in the world is the Swedish official journal *Post och Inrikes Tidningar*, founded in 1645.

It is published by the Royal Swedish Academy of Letters. The oldest existing commercial newspaper is the *Haarlems Dagblad/Oprechte Haarlemsche Courant*, published in Haarlem, in the Netherlands. The *Courant* was first issued as the *Weeckelycke Courante van Europa* on 8 Jan. 1656 and a copy of issue No. 1 survives.

Great Britain

The oldest continuously produced newspaper in the United Kingdom is *Berrow's Worcester Journal* (originally the *Worcester Post Man*), published in Worcester. It was traditionally founded in 1690 and has appeared weekly since June 1709. The oldest newspaper title is that of the *Stamford Mercury* dating back to at least 1714 and traditionally to 1695. The oldest daily newspaper in the United Kingdom is *Lloyd's List*, the shipping intelligence bulletin of Lloyd's London, established as a weekly in 1726 and as a daily in 1734. The *London Gazette* (originally the *Oxford Gazette*) was first published on 16 Nov. 1665. The oldest Sunday newspaper in the United Kingdom is *The Observer*, first issued on 4 Dec. 1791.

Largest and Smallest

The most massive single issue of a newspaper was the 7½ lb. *3,40 kg New York Times* of Sunday 17 Oct. 1965. It comprised 15 sections with a total of 946 pages, including about 1,200,000 lines of advertising. The largest page size ever used has been 51 in by 35 in *130 cm by 89 cm* for *The Constellation*, printed in 1859 by George Roberts as part of the Fourth of July celebrations in New York City, N.Y., U.S.A. The *Worcestershire Chronicle* was the largest British newspaper. A surviving issue of 16 Feb. 1859 measures 32¼ in by 22½ in *82 cm by 57 cm*. The smallest recorded page size has been 3 × 3¾ in *7,6 × 9,5 cm* of the *Daily Banner* (25 cents per month) of Roseberg, Oregon, U.S.A., issues of which, dated 1 and 2 Feb. 1876, survive. The *Answers to Correspondents* published by Messrs Carr & Co., Paternoster Square, London in 1888 was 3½ × 4½ in *9 × 11 cm*.

Most Expensive

Britain's most expensive paper is *The Observer* at 20p or 4s in the money prior to 15 Feb. 1971.

Most

The United States had 1,756 English language daily newspapers at 1 Oct. 1978. They had a combined net paid circulation of 62,200,000 copies per day at 30 Sept. 1978. The peak year for U.S. newspapers was 1910, when there were 2,202. The leading newspaper readers in the world are the people of Sweden, where 564 newspapers were sold for each 1,000 compared with the U.K. figure of 438.

Longest editorship

The longest editorship of any national newspaper has been more than 59 years by C. P. Scott (1846–1932) of the (then *Manchester*) *Guardian*, who was appointed aged 25 in 1872 and died on 1 Jan. 1932. John Watson was editor of the South Australian newspaper *The Border Watch* from 1863 to Dec. 1925—a span of 62 years. Robert Edwards was 4 times appointed editor of a national paper—*Daily Express* (1961); *Daily Express* (1963); *Sunday People* (1966) and *Sunday Mirror* (1972). Dr. Thomas Riddle D.D. (b. 18 Apr. 1886) was still editor of *The Christian Herald* in May 1979 aged 93 years.

Most durable feature

The longest lasting feature in the British national press from one pen is *Your Stars* by Edward Lyndoe. It has run since 1 Oct. 1933 in *The Sunday People*. "Auntie Rhona" (Miss Rhona Chesters b. 14 Feb. 1900) contributed her Children's Corner in the *Peterborough Standard* from 2 Oct. 1925 until June 1978 when she retired.

Most Syndicated Cartoonist

Ranan R. Lurie (b. 26 May 1932) is the most widely syndicated cartoonist in the world. His work is published in 45 countries.

Longest lived strip

The most durable newspaper comic strip has been the Katzenjammer Kids (Hans and Fritz) created by Rudolph Dirks and first published in the *New York Journal* on 12 Dec.

1897 and perpetuated by his son John. The earliest strip was The Yellow Kid, which first appeared in the New York *Journal* on 18 Oct. 1896. The most widely syndicated is *Blondie* (originated in 1930) appearing in 1,800 newspapers in 55 countries and in 33 languages.

Most Misprints

The record for misprints in *The Times* was set on 22 Aug. 1978 when on page 19 there were 97 in 5½ single column inches. The passage concerned 'Pop' (Pope) Paul VI.

CIRCULATION
Earliest 1,000,000

The first newspaper to achieve a circulation of 1,000,000 was *Le Petit Journal*, published in Paris, France, which reached this figure in 1886, when selling at 5 centimes. The *Daily Mail* first reached a million in May 1900.

Highest *World*

The highest circulation for any newspaper in the world is that for the *Yomiuri Shimbun* (founded 1874) of Japan which attained a figure of 13,029,424 copies in April 1979. This is achieved by totalling the figures for editions published in various centres with a morning figure of 8,190,598 and an evening figure of 4,838,826.

Great Britain

The highest circulation of any single newspaper in Britain is that of the Sunday newspaper *The News of the World*, printed in Bouverie Street, London. Single issues have attained a sale of 9,000,000 copies with an estimated readership of more than 19,000,000. The paper first appeared on 1 Oct. 1843, and surpassed the million mark in 1905. The latest sales figure is 4,905,279 copies per issue (average for 1 July to 31 Dec. 1978), with an estimated readership of 13,090,000.

The highest net sale of any daily newspaper in the United Kingdom is that of *The Sun*, founded in London in 1964. The latest sales figure is 3,989,599 (July–Dec. 1978), with an estimated readership of 12,371,000.

Evening

The highest circulation of any evening newspaper is that of *The Evening News*, established in London in 1881. The latest weekday figure is 537,784 copies per issue (average for March 1979), with an average readership of 1,396,000 (July–Dec. 1978).

Most read

The newspaper which achieves the closest to a saturation circulation is *The Sunday Post*, established in Glasgow in 1914. In 1978 its estimated readership in Scotland of 2,909,000 represented 74 per cent of the entire population aged 15 and over.

CROSSWORDS
First

The earliest crossword was one with 32 clues invented by Arthur Wynne (b. Liverpool, England, d. 1945) and published in the *New York World* on 21 Dec. 1913. The first crossword published in a British newspaper was one furnished by C. W. Shepherd in the *Sunday Express* of 2 Nov. 1924.

Largest

The largest crossword ever published is one with 7,748 clues and 25,000 squares, compiled in 8 years by Henri Blaise (1939–77) (Belgium). It measured 42 × 65 ins (18.95 ft² *1,76 m²*). The largest crosswords regularly published are "Mammoth" crosswords based on grids of 73 × 73 (5,329) squares with up to 828 clues by First Features Ltd of Hastings, East Sussex since 1 May 1970. The longest word included in a crossword has been Arrondissementsschoolopziener—a county school inspector (29 letters).

Fastest and slowest solution

The fastest recorded time for completing *The Times* crossword under test conditions is 3 min 45.0 sec by Roy Dean, 43 of Bromley, Greater London in the B.B.C. "Today" radio studio on 19 Dec. 1970. In May 1966 *The Times* of London received an announcement from a Fijian woman that she had just succeeded in completing their crossword No. 673 in the issue of 4 Apr. 1932. Dr. John Sykes won the Cutty Sark/*Times* championship 4 times (1972–1975). The only woman to reach a final has been Mrs. Morar Ryton.

Most Durable Compilers

Adrian Bell (b. 4 Oct. 1901) of Barsham, Suffolk contributed a record 4,327 crosswords to *The Times* from 2 Jan. 1930 to 1 Mar. 1975. R. J. Baddock of Plymouth (b. 30 Oct. 1894) has been a regular contributor to national newspapers since 13 Aug. 1926. Mrs. Phyllis Harvey, 84, of Brighton from December 1924 to December 1978 completed 54 years of contributions to the *Evening News* Junior Cross Word (now Quick crossword). The most prolific compiler is Roger F. Squires, who compiles 34 published puzzles single-handedly each week. His total output to August 1979 is estimated at nearly 14,000.

ADVERTISING RATES

The highest ever price for a single page has been $142,600 (£*71,300*) for a four-colour back cover in *Parade* (circulation 21 million per week) in May 1979 (see page 98). The current record is $137,600 (£*68,800*) for a four colour page in *Parade* (in May 1979). The advertising revenue from the October 1978 U.S. edition of *Readers Digest* was $10,393,200 (*then £5,196,000*).

The highest expenditure ever incurred on a single advertisement in a periodical is $5,200,000 (£*2,600,000*) by Gulf and Western Industries on 5 Feb. 1979 for insertions in *Time* Magazine (U.S. and selected overseas editions). The British record is some £100,000 for a 20-page colour supplement by Woolworths in *The Radio Times* of 16 Nov. 1972. The colour rate for a single page in *The Radio Times* reached £12,300 on 1 Feb. 1979. The world's highest newspaper advertising rate is 25,704,000 Yen (£*60,480*) for a full page in the morning edition and 20,491,800 Yen (£*48,216*) for the evening edition of the *Asahi Shimbun* of Tokyo (April 1979). The highest rate in Britain is a full page in *The Sunday Express* at £18,000 (April 1979).

4. MUSIC

The Guinness Book of Music Facts and Feats, by Robert and Celia Dearling with Brian Rust (£6.50) contains a more detailed treatment of musical facts and superlatives.

Origins

The world's oldest surviving musical notation dates from *c.* 1800 B.C. A heptonic scale deciphered from a clay tablet by Dr. Duchesne-Guillemin in 1966–67 was found at a site in Nippur, Sumer, now Iraq. An Assyrian love song also *c.* 1800 B.C. to an Ugarit god from a tablet of notation and lyric was reconstructed for an 11 string lyre at the University of California, Berkeley on 6 Mar. 1974. Musical history is, however, able to be traced back to the 3rd millennium B.C., when the yellow bell (*huang chung*) had a recognised standard musical tone in Chinese temple music. Whistles and flutes made from perforated phalange bones have been found at Upper Palaeolithic sites of the Aurignacian period (*c.* 25,000–22,000 B.C.) *e.g.* at Istallóskö, Hungary and in Molodova, U.S.S.R.

INSTRUMENTS

Piano Earliest

The earliest pianoforte in existence is one built in Florence, Italy, in 1720 by Bartolommeo Cristofori (1655–1731) of Padua, and now preserved in the Metropolitan Museum of Art, New York City.

Piano Grandest

The grandest grand piano built was one of 1¼ tons/*tonnes* 11 ft 8 in *3,55 m* in length made by Chas. H. Challen & Son Ltd. of London in 1935. The longest bass string measured 9 ft 11 in *3,02 m* and the tensile stress on the 6½ cwt *330 kg* frame was 30 tons/*tonnes*.

Organ Largest *World*

The largest and loudest musical instrument ever constructed

is the now only partially functional Auditorium Organ in Atlantic City, New Jersey, U.S.A. Completed in 1930, this heroic instrument has two consoles (one with seven manuals and another movable one with five), 1,477 stop controls and 33,112 pipes ranging in tone from $\frac{3}{16}$ of an inch *4,7 mm* to the 64 ft *19 m* tone. It is powered with blower motors of 365 horsepower *370 cv*, cost $500,000 (*then £102,880*) and has the volume of 25 brass bands, with a range of seven octaves. The grand organ at Wanamaker's Store, Philadelphia, installed in 1911, was enlarged until by 1930 it had 6 manuals and 30,067 pipes including a 64 ft *19 m* tone Gravissima. The world's largest church organ is that in Passau Cathedral, Germany. It was completed in 1928 by D. F. Steinmeyer & Co. It was built with 16,000 pipes and five manuals. The world's only five-manual electric organ was installed in the Carnegie Hall, New York City in Sept. 1974.

Great Britain

The largest organ in Great Britain is that completed in Liverpool Anglican Cathedral on 18 Oct. 1926, with two five-manual consoles of which only one is now in use, and 9,704 speaking pipes (originally 10,936) ranging from tones of ¾ in to 32 feet *1,9 cm to 9,75 m*.

Organists *Most Durable*

The longest recorded reign as an organist has been 81 years in the case of Charles Bridgeman (1779–1873) of All Saints Parish Church, Hertford, England, who was appointed in 1792 and who was still playing in 1873. The year in which he reached his crescendo was not recorded.

Loudest Organ stop

The loudest organ stop in the world is the Ophicleide stop of the Grand Great in the Solo Organ in the Atlantic City Auditorium (see above). It is operated by a pressure of 100 in *254 cm* of water (3½ lb./in² *24 kPa*) and has a pure trumpet note of ear-splitting volume, more than six times the volume of the loudest locomotive whistles.

Brass instrument *Largest*

The largest recorded brass instrument is a tuba standing 7½ ft *2,28 m* tall, with 39 ft *11,8 m* of tubing and a bell 3 ft 4 in *1 m* across. This contrabass tuba was constructed for a world tour by the band of John Philip Sousa (1854–1932), the United States composer, in *c.* 1896–98, and is still in use. This instrument is now owned by a circus promoter in South Africa.

Alphorn *Longest*

The longest alphorn is one of 13,4 m *43 ft 11½ in* built from a spruce log by Herr Stocker in Switzerland in 1976. It weighs 32 kg *70½ lb* and was seen on the 1977 B.B.C. T.V. *Christmas Record Breakers* Show.

Stringed instrument *Largest*

The largest movable stringed instrument ever constructed was a pantaleon with 270 strings stretched over 50 ft² *4,6 m²* used by George Noel in 1767. The greatest number of musicians required to operate a single instrument was the six required to play the gigantic orchestrion, known as the Apollonican, built in 1816 and played until 1840.

Guitar *Largest and Most Expensive*

The largest and presumably also the loudest playable guitar in the world is one 9 ft 10 in *3 m* tall weighing 380 lb. *172 kg* built by the Odessey Guitar Co. of Vancouver, B.C., Canada. The most expensive standard sized guitar is the German chittara battente by Jacob Stadler, dated 1624, which was sold for £10,500 at Christies, London on 12 June 1974.

Double bass *Largest*

The largest double bass ever constructed was one 14 ft *4,26 m* tall, built in 1924 in Ironia, New Jersey, U.S.A. by Arthur K. Ferris, allegedly on orders from the Archangel Gabriel. It weighed 11.6 cwt. *590 kg* with a sound box 8 ft *2,43 m* across, and had leathern strings totalling 104 ft *31,7 m*. Its low notes could be felt rather than heard.

'Cello *Most valuable*

The highest ever auction price for a violoncello is £145,000

The largest guitar in the world, measuring 9 ft 10 in *3 m* tall built in Vancouver, BC, Canada (see p. 101). (*Gordon Counsell*)

at Sotheby's, London on 8 Nov. 1978 for a Stradivari made in Cremona, Italy in 1710.

Violin *Most valuable*
The highest ever price paid at auction for a violin is £145,000 the "Huberman" *ex* Kreisler Stradivari dated 1733 at Sotheby's, London on 3 May 1979. Some 700 of the 1,116 violins by Stradivarius (1644–1737) have survived. His inlaid 'Hellier' violin was sold by private treaty in the U.S. in March 1979 for a reputed $400,000 (*£200,000*).

Violinist *Underwater*
The only violinist to surmount the problems of playing the violin underwater has been Mark Gottlieb. Submerged in Evergreen State College swimming bath in Olympia, Washington, U.S.A. in March 1975 he gave a submarine rendition of Handel's Water Music. He is still working on the problem of bow speed and *détaché*.

Most Durable Fiddler
Otto E. Funk, 62, walked 4,165 miles *6 702 km* from New York City to San Francisco, California playing his Hopf violin every step of the way westward. He arrived on 16 June 1929 after 183 days on the road. Rolland S. Tapley retired as a violinist from the Boston Symphony Orchestra after playing for a reputedly unrivalled 58 years from Feb. 1920 to 27 Aug. 1978.

Drum *Largest*
The largest drum in the world is the Disneyland Big Bass Drum with a diameter of 10 ft 6 in *3,2 m* and a weight of 450 lb. *204 kg*. It was built in 1961 by Remo Inc. of North Hollywood, California, U.S.A. and is mounted on wheels and towed by a tractor.

Highest and lowest notes
The extremes of orchestral instruments (excluding the organ) range between a handbell tuned to g^v (6,272 cycles/sec) and the sub-contrabass clarinet, which can reach C_{11} or 16.4 cycles/sec. The highest note on a standard pianoforte is c^v (4,186 cycles/sec), which is also the violinist's limit. In 1873 a sub double bassoon able to reach $B_{111}\sharp$ or 14.6 cycles/sec was constructed but no surviving specimen is known. The extremes for the organ are g^{vi} (the sixth G above middle c)

(12,544 cycles/sec) and C_{111} (8.12 cycles/sec) obtainable from ¾ in *1,9 cm* and 64 ft *19 m* pipes respectively.

Easiest and Most Difficult Instruments
The American Music Conference announced in September 1977 that the easiest instrument is the ukulele, and the most difficult are the French horn and the oboe, which latter has been described as "the ill woodwind that no-one blows good".

ORCHESTRAS
Largest *Orchestra*
The most massive orchestra ever assembled was one of 20,100 at the Ullevaal Stadium, Oslo of Norges Musikkorps Forbund bands from all Norway on 28 June 1964. On 17 June 1872, Johann Strauss the younger (1825–99) conducted an orchestra of 987 pieces supported by a choir of 20,000, at the World Peace Jubilee in Boston, Massachussetts, U.S.A. The number of first violinists was 400.

Marching band
The largest marching band on record was one of 1,976 musicians and 54 drill majors, flag bearers and directors who marched 2 miles *3,2 km* down Pennsylvania Avenue in President Nixon's Inaugural Parade on 20 Jan. 1973.

Most Successful Brass band
Most British Open Championship titles (inst. 1853) have been won by the Black Dyke Mills Band which has won 22 times from 1862 to 1974 including three consecutive wins in 1972–74.

Greatest attendance *Classical Concert*
The greatest attendance at any classical concert has been 400,000 for the Boston Pops Orchestra, conducted by Arthur Fiedler at the Hatch Memorial Shell, Boston, Massachusetts, U.S.A. on 4 July 1977. At the 1978 concert the 83 year old conductor was presented with a testimonial bearing a record 500,000 signatures.

Pop Festival
The greatest claimed attendance at a Pop Festival has been 600,000 for the "Summer Jam" at Watkins Glen, New York, U.S.A., on Sunday 29 July 1973 of whom about 150,000 actually paid. There were 12 "sound towers". The attendance at the third Pop Festival at East Afton Farm, Freshwater, Isle of Wight, England on 30 Aug. 1970 was claimed by its promoters, Fiery Creations, to be 400,000.

Highest gross and audience
The highest recorded paid attendance for a single pop recording group is 76,229 attenders for the concert by the British group Led Zeppelin at the Silver Dome, Pontiac, Michigan, U.S.A. on 30 Apr. 1977. The gross was $792,361 (*£446,094*).

COMPOSERS
Most prolific
The most prolific composer of all time was probably Georg Philipp Telemann (1681–1767) of Germany. He composed 12 complete sets of services (one cantata every Sunday) for a year, 78 services for special occasions, 40 operas, 600 to 700 orchestral suites, 44 Passions, plus concertos and chamber music. The most prolific symphonist was Johann Melchior Molter (c. 1695–1765) of Germany who wrote 165. Joseph Haydn (1732–1809) of Austria wrote 104 numbered symphonies some of which are regularly played today.

Most rapid
Among composers of the classical period the most prolific was Wolfgang Amadeus Mozart (1756–91) of Austria, who wrote *c.* 1,000 operas, operettas, symphonies, violin sonatas, divertimenti, serenades, motets, concertos for piano and many other instruments, string quartets, other chamber music, masses and litanies, of which only 70 were published before he died aged 35. His opera The Clemency of Titus (1791) was written in 18 days and three symphonic masterpieces, *Symphony No. 39 in E flat major, Symphony in G minor* and the *Jupiter Symphony in C*, were reputedly written in the space of 42 days in 1788. His overture Don Giovanni was written in full score at one sitting in Prague in 1787 and finished on the day of its opening performance.

Longest symphony

The longest of all single classical symphonies is the orchestral symphony No. 3 in D minor by Gustav Mahler (1860–1911) of Austria. This work, composed in 1896, requires a contralto, a women's and boys' choir in addition to a full orchestra. A full performance requires 1 hour 34 min, of which the first movement alone takes 45 min. The Symphony No. 2 (the Gothic, or No. 1), composed in 1919–22 by Havergal Brian (1876–1972) was played by over 800 performers (4 Brass Bands) in the Victoria Hall, Hanley, Staffordshire on 21 May 1978 (conductor Trevor Stokes). Brian wrote an even vaster work based on Shelley's "Prometheus Unbound" lasting 4 hrs 11 min but the full score has been missing since 1961.

The symphony *Victory at Sea* written by Richard Rodgers and arranged by Robert Russell Bennett for N.B.C. T.V. in 1952 lasted for 13 hours.

Longest piano composition

The longest continuous non-repetitive piece for piano ever composed has been the Opus Clavicembalisticum by Kaikhosru Shapurji Sorabji (b. 1892). The composer himself gave it its only public performance on 1 Dec. 1930 in Glasgow, Scotland. The work is in 12 movements with a theme and 44 variations and a Passacaglia with 81 and a playing time of $2\frac{3}{4}$ hours.

Longest silence

The most protracted silence in a modern sheet music is one entitled *4 minutes 33 seconds* in a totally silent *opus* by John Cage (U.S.A.). Commenting on this trend among young composers, Igor Fyodorovich Stravinsky (1882–1971) said that he looked forward to their subsequent compositions being "works of major length".

HIGHEST PAID MUSICIANS
Pianist

Wladziu Valentino Liberace (b. West Allis, Wisconsin, U.S.A., 16 May 1917) earns more than $2 million each 26 week season with a peak of $138,000 (*then £49,285*) for a single night's performance at Madison Square Gardens, New York City, U.S.A. in 1954.

The highest paid classical concert pianist was Ignace Jan Paderewski (1860–1941), Prime Minister of Poland (1919–20), who accumulated a fortune estimated at $5,000,000, of which $500,000 (*then £110,000*) was earned in a single season in 1922–23. The *nouveau riche* wife of a U.S. industrialist once required him to play behind a curtain.

Singer *Most Successful*

Of great fortunes earned by singers, the highest on record are those of Enrico Caruso (1873–1921), the Italian tenor, whose estate was about $9,000,000 (*then £1,875,000*) and the Italian-Spanish coloratura soprano Amelita Galli-Curci (1889–1963), who received about $3,000,000 (*£750,000*). In 1850, up to $653 was paid for a single seat at the concerts given in the United States by Johanna ("Jenny") Maria Lind, later Mrs. Otto Goldschmidt (1820–87), the "Swedish Nightingale". She had a range from g to e^{III} of which the middle register is still regarded as unrivalled. The tenor Count John Francis McCormack (1884–1945) of Ireland gave up to 10 concerts to capacity audiences in a single season in New York City.

Worst

While no agreement exists as to the identity of history's greatest singer, there is unanimity on the worst. The excursions of the soprano Florence Foster Jenkins (1868–1944) into lieder and even high coloratura culminated on 25 Oct. 1944 in her sell-out concert at the Carnegie Hall, New York, U.S.A. The diva's (already high) high F was said to have been made higher in 1943 by a crash in a taxi. It is one of the tragedies of musicology that Madame Jenkins' *Clavelitos*, accompanied by Cosme McMoon, was never recorded for posterity. Her latter day rival is Mrs. Hazel Saunders of Clent, Here. & Worcs.

Violinist

The Austrian-born Fritz Kreisler (1875–1962) is reputed to have received more than £1,000,000 in his career.

OPERA
Longest

The longest of commonly performed operas is *Die Meistersinger von Nürnberg* by Wilhelm Richard Wagner (1813–83) of Germany. A normal uncut performance of this opera as performed by the Sadler's Wells company between 24 Aug. and 19 Sept. 1968 entailed 5 hrs 15 min of music. *The Heretics* by Gabriel von Wayditch, a Hungarian-American, is orchestrated for 110 pieces and lasts $8\frac{1}{2}$ hours.

Shortest

The shortest opera written was *The Deliverance of Theseus* by Darius Milhaud (b. Sept. 1892) first performed in 1928 which lasts for 7 min 27 secs.

Aria

The longest single aria, in the sense of an operatic solo, is Brünnhilde's immolation scene in Wagner's *Gotterdammerung*. A well-known recording of this has been precisely timed at 14 minutes 46 seconds.

Opera houses *Largest*

The largest opera house in the world is the Metropolitan Opera House, Lincoln Center, New York City, N.Y., U.S.A., completed in September 1966 at a cost of $45,700,000 (*then £16,320,000*). It has a capacity of 3,800 seats in an auditorium 451 ft *137 m* deep. The stage is 234 ft *71 m* in width and 146 ft *44,5 m* deep. The tallest opera house is one housed in a 42-storey building on Wacker Drive in Chicago, Illinois, U.S.A.

Most tiers

The Teatro della Scala (La Scala) in Milan, Italy, shares with the Bolshoi Theatre in Moscow, U.S.S.R., the distinction of having the greatest number of tiers. Each has six, with the topmost being nicknamed the *Galiorka* by Russians.

Opera Singers *Youngest and Oldest*

The youngest opera singer in the world has been Jeanette Gloria La Bianca, born in Buffalo, New York on 12 May 1934, who sang Rosina in *The Barber of Seville* at the Teatro dell'Opera, Rome on 8 May 1950 aged 15 years 361 days, having appeared as Gilda in *Rigoletto* at Velletri 45 days earlier. Ginetta La Bianca was taught by Lucia Carlino and managed by Angelo Carlino. The tenor Giovanni Martinelli sang Emperor Altoum in *Turandot* in Seattle, Washington, U.S.A. on 4 Feb. 1967 when aged 81.

SONG
Oldest

The oldest known song is the *shaduf* chant, which has been sung since time immemorial by irrigation workers on the man-powered pivoted-rod bucket raisers of the Nile water mills (or *saqiyas*) in Egypt (now the United Arab Republic). The English song *Sumer is icumen in* dates from *c.* 1240.

National anthems

The oldest national anthem is the *Kimigayo* of Japan, in which the words date from the 9th century. The anthem of Greece constitutes the first four verses of the Solomos poem, which has 158 stanzas. The shortest anthems are those of Japan, Jordan and San Marino, each with only four lines. Of the 23 wordless national anthems the oldest is that of Spain dating from 1770.

Longest rendering

"God Save the King" was played non-stop 16 or 17 times by a German military band on the platform of Rathenau Railway Station, Brandenburg, on the morning of 9 Feb. 1909. The reason was that King Edward VII was struggling inside the train with the uniform of a German Field-Marshal before he could emerge.

Top songs of all time

The most frequently sung songs in English are *Happy Birthday to You* (based on the original *Good morning to all*), by Mildred and Patty S. Hill of New York (published in 1935 and in copyright until 2010); *For He's a Jolly Good Fellow* (originally the French *Malbrouk*), known at least as early as 1781, and *Auld Lang Syne* (originally the Strathspey

Music

I fee'd a Lad at Michaelmass), some words of which were written by Robert Burns (1759–96). *Happy Birthday* was sung in space by the Apollo IX astronauts on 8 Mar. 1969.

Top selling sheet music
Sales of three non-copyright pieces are known to have exceeded 20,000,000 namely *The Old Folks at Home* by Stephen Foster, (1855), *Listen to the Mocking Bird* (1855) and *The Blue Danube* (1867). Of copyright material the two top-sellers are *Let Me Call You Sweetheart* (1910, by Whitson and Friedman) and *Till We Meet Again* (1918, by Egan and Whiting) each with some 6,000,000 by 1967. Other huge sellers have been *St. Louis Blues, Stardust* and *Tea for Two*.

Most successful songwriter
In terms of sales of single records, the most successful of all song writers has been Paul McCartney (see also Gramophone, pp. 106 & 107) formerly of the Beatles and now of Wings. Between 1962 and 1 Jan. 1978 he wrote jointly or solo 43 songs which sold a million or more.

Eurovision Contest
In the 24 contests since 1956 France has won 4 (1958–60–62–77) and shared in 1969. Luxembourg also won outright 4 times (1961–65–72–73). The U.K. won in 1967 (Sandie Shaw, *Puppet On A String*) and 1976 (Brotherhood of Man, *Save Your Kisses For Me*) and shared in 1969 (Lulu, *Boom, Bang-a-Bang*).

HYMNS
Earliest
There are more than 950,000 Christian hymns in existence. The earliest exactly datable hymn is the Heyr Rimna Smiour (Hear, the maker of heaven) from 1208 by the Icelandic band and chieftain Kolbeinn Tumason (1173–1208). Hymn 91 in the Methodist School hymnal is attributed to Clement of Alexandria (AD 170–220).

Longest and shortest
The longest hymn is "Hora novissima tempora pessima sunt; vigilemus" by Bernard of Cluny (12th century), which runs to 2,966 lines. In English the longest is "The Sands of Time are sinking" by Mrs. Anne Ross Cousin, *née* Cundell (1824–1906), which is in full 152 lines, though only 32 lines in the Methodist Hymn Book. The shortest hymn is the single verse in Long Metre "Be Present at our Table Lord", anonymous but attributed to "J. Leland".

Most prolific hymnists
Mrs. Frances (Fanny) Jane Van Alstyne *née* Crosby (1820–1915), (U.S.A.) wrote 8,500 hymns although she had been blinded at the age of 6 weeks. She is reputed to have knocked off one hymn in 15 min. Charles Wesley (1707–88) wrote about 6,000 hymns. In the seventh (1950) edition of *Hymns Ancient and Modern* the works of John Mason Neale (1818–66) appear 56 times.

BELLS
Oldest *World*
The oldest bell in the world is reputed to be that found in the Babylonian Palace of Nimrod in 1849 by Mr. (later Sir) Austen Henry Layard (1817–94). It dates from *c.* 1000 B.C.

Great Britain
The oldest *dated* bell in England is one hanging in Lissett church, near Bridlington, Humberside discovered in Oct. 1972 to bear the date MCCLIIII (1254). The oldest inscribed bell is at Caversfield church, Oxfordshire and may be dated *c.* 1210. The uninscribed bell, at the Parish Church of St. Nicholas, Lanark, Strathclyde in daily use was originally founded in 1110 and refounded in 1659, 1740 and 1835.

Heaviest *World*
The heaviest bell in the world is the Tsar Kolokol, cast on 25 Nov. 1735 in Moscow, U.S.S.R. It weighs 193 tons *196 tonnes* measures 5,9 m *19 ft 4¼ in* diameter and 5,87 m *19 ft 3 in* high, and its greatest thickness is 24 in *60 cm*. The bell is cracked, and a fragment, weighing about 11 tons/*tonnes* was broken from it. The bell has stood, unrung, on a platform in the Kremlin, in Moscow, since 1836.

Rolland S. Tapley was an orchestral violinist for 58 years, from Feb. 1920 until his retirement on 27 Aug. 1978 (see p 101).

The heaviest bell in use is the Mingun bell, weighing 55,555 viss or *90,52 tons* with a diameter of 16 ft 8½ in *5,09 m* at the lip, in Mandalay, Burma, which is struck by a teak boom from the outside. It was cast at Mingun late in the reign of King Bodawpaya (1782–1819). The heaviest swinging bell in the world is the Petersglocke in Cologne Cathedral, Germany, cast in 1923 with a diameter of 3,40 m *11 ft 1¾ in* weighing 25,4 tonnes *25.0 tons*.

The heaviest change ringing peal in the world is the ring of 13 bells, cast in 1938–39, weighing 16½ tons *16,7 tonnes*, in Liverpool Anglican Cathedral. The tenor bell, Emmanuel, weighs 82 cwt. 11 lb. *4 170,8 kg.*

Great Britain
The heaviest bell hung in Great Britain is "Great Paul" in St. Paul's Cathedral, London. It was cast in 1881, weighs 16 tons 14 cwt. 2 qrs. 19 lb. *17 tonnes* and has a diameter of 9 ft 6½ in *2,9 m*. "Big Ben", the hour bell in the clock tower of the House of Commons, was cast in 1858 and weighs 13 tons 10 cwt. 3 qrs. 15 lb. *13 761 kg.*

The heaviest bell ever cast in England and the heaviest tuned bell in the world is the bourdon bell of the Laura Spelman Rockefeller Memorial carillon in Riverside Church, New York City, N.Y., U.S.A. It weighs 18 tons 5 cwt. 1 qr. 18 lb. *18,5 tonnes* and is 10 ft 2 in *3 m* in diameter.

Carillon *Largest*
The largest carillon in the world is the Laura Spelman Rockefeller Memorial carillon in Riverside Church, New York City, U.S.A. with 74 bells weighing 102 tons. The Bourdon weighs 40,900 lb. or 18¼ tons.

Heaviest

The heaviest carillon in Great Britain is in St. Nicholas Church, Aberdeen, Scotland. It consists of 48 bells, the total weight of which is 25 tons 8 cwt. 2 qrs. 13 lb. *25 838 kg*. The bourdon bell weighs 4 tons 9 cwt. 3 qrs. 26 lb. *4 571 kg* and the carillon comprises four octaves, less the bottom semi-tone.

Bell Ringing

Eight bells have been rung to their full "extent" (a "Bob Major" of 40,320 changes) only once without relays. This took place in a bell foundry at Loughborough, Leicestershire, beginning at 6.52 a.m. on 27 July 1963 and ending at 12.50 a.m. on 28 July, after 17 hrs 58 min. The peal was composed by Kenneth Lewis of Altrincham, Greater Manchester, and the eight ringers were conducted by Robert B. Smith, aged 25, of Marple, Greater Manchester. Theoretically it would take 37 years 355 days to ring 12 bells (maximus) to their full extent of 479,001,600 changes. The greatest number of peals (minimum of 5,040 changes, all in tower bells) rung in a year is 209 by Mark William Marshall of Ashford, Kent in 1973. The late George E. Fearn rang 2,666 peals from 1928 to May 1974. Matthew Lakin (1801–1899) was a regular bell-ringer at Tetney Church near Grimsby for 84 years.

5. THEATRE

Origins

Theatre in Europe has its origins in Greek drama performed in honour of a god, usually Dionysus. The earliest amphitheatres date from the 5th century B.C. and the largest of all known is one at Megalopolis in central Greece, where the auditorium reached a height of 75 ft *23 m* and had a capacity of 17,000. The first stone built theatre in Rome erected in 55 B.C. could accommodate 40,000 spectators.

Oldest *World*

The oldest indoor theatre in the world is the Teatro Olimpico in Vicenza, Italy. Designed in the Roman style by Andrea di Pietro, *alias* Palladio (1508–80), it was begun three months before his death and finished in 1582 by his pupil Vicenzo Scamozzi (1552–1616). It is preserved today in its original form.

Great Britain

The earliest London theatre was James Burbage's "The Theatre", built in 1576 near Finsbury Fields, London. The oldest theatre still in use in Great Britain is The Royal, Bristol. The foundation stone was laid on 30 Nov. 1764, and the theatre was opened on 30 May 1766 with a "Concert of Music and a Specimen of Rhetorick". The City Varieties Music Hall, Leeds was a singing room in 1762 and so claims to outdate the Theatre Royal. Actors were legally

The smallest theatre in the world, the Mull Little Theatre which regularly performs professional plays.

rogues and vagabonds until the passing of the Vagrancy Act in 1824. The oldest amateur dramatic society is the Amateur Dramatic Club (A.D.C.) in Cambridge founded in the Hoop Hotel, Jesus Lane by F. C. Burnand in May 1855.

Largest *World*

The world's largest building used for theatre is the National People's Congress Building (*Ren min da hui tang*) on the west side of Tian an men Square, Peking, China. It was completed in 1959 and covers an area of 12.9 acres *5,2 ha*. The theatre seats 10,000 and is occasionally used as such as in 1964 for the play "The East is Red". The highest capacity purpose-built theatre is the Perth Entertainment Centre, Western Australia completed at a cost of $A 8.3 million (£4.2 million) in November 1976 with a capacity of 8,003 seats. The stage area is 12,000 ft² *1 148 m²*.

Great Britain

The highest capacity theatre is the Odeon, Hammersmith, Greater London, with 3,485 seats in 1975. The largest theatre stage in Great Britain is the Opera House in Blackpool, Lancashire. It was re-built in July 1939 and has seats for 2,975 people. Behind the 45 ft *14 m* wide proscenium arch the stage is 110 ft *33 m* high, 60 ft *18 m* deep and 100 ft *30 m* wide, and there is dressing room accommodation for 200 artistes.

Britain's largest open air theatre is at Scarborough, North Yorkshire opened in 1932 with a seating capacity of 7,000 plus standing room for 9,000 and a 182 ft *55 m* long stage.

Smallest

The smallest regularly operated professional theatre in Great Britain is the Mull Little Theatre, near Dervaig, Isle of Mull, Scotland with a capacity of 36 seats.

Largest amphitheatre

The largest amphitheatre ever built is the Flavian amphitheatre or Colosseum of Rome, Italy, completed in A.D. 80. Covering 5 acres *2 ha* and with a capacity of 87,000, it has a maximum length of 612 ft *187 m* and maximum width of 515 ft *175 m*.

Longest runs

The longest continuous run of any show in the world is *The Mousetrap* by Dame Agatha Mary Clarissa Christie, D.B.E. (*née* Miller, later Lady Mallowan) (1890–1976). This thriller opened on 25 Nov. 1952, at the Ambassadors Theatre (capacity 453) and moved after 8,862 performances "down the road" to St. Martin's Theatre on 25 Mar. 1974. The Silver Jubilee performance on 25 Nov. 1977 was the 10,390th and the 11,000th was on 9 May 1979.

Revue

The greatest number of performances of any theatrical presentation is 43,310 (to 27 Apr. 1979) in the case of *The Golden Horseshoe Revue*—a show staged at Disneyland Park, Anaheim, California, U.S.A. The show was first put on on 17 July 1955. The three main performers Fulton Burley, Walley Baag and Betty Taylor play as many as five houses a day in a routine lasting 45 minutes. In Britain, the Brighton Corporation's variety show *Tuesday Night at the Dome* reached its 1,460th performance in 33 years on 17 Apr. 1979.

Broadway

The Broadway record is 3,242 performances by *Fiddler on the Roof* which closed, after its first run, on 3 July 1972. It had opened on 22 Sept. 1964. Paul Lipson played 1,811 times as Tevye during which time he had ten "wives" and 58 "daughters". The world gross earnings reached $64,300,000 (£25.7 million) on an original investment of $375,000 (then £133,928). The off-Broadway musical show *The Fantasticks* by Tom Jones and Harvey Schmidt achieved its 7,999th performance as it entered its 20th year at the Sullivan Street Playhouse, Greenwich Village, New York City on 3 May 1979. It has been played in a record 3,788 productions in 55 countries.

Musical shows

The longest-running musical show ever performed in Britain was *The Black and White Minstrel Show* later *Magic* of the Minstrels. The aggregate but discontinuous number of performances was 6,464 with a total attendance of 7,794,552. The show opened at the Victoria Palace, London on 25 May 1962 and closed on 4 Nov. 1972. It re-opened for a season in June 1973 at the New Victoria and finally closed on 8 Dec. 1973.

Jesus Christ Superstar, which opened at Palace Theatre, London on 8 Aug. 1972, passed *Oliver* with its 2,620th performance on 3 Oct. 1978.

Shortest runs *World*
The shortest run on record was that of *The Intimate Revue* at the Duchess Theatre, London, on 11 March 1930. Anything which could go wrong did. With scene changes taking up to 20 min apiece, the management scrapped seven scenes to get the finale on before midnight. The run was described as "half a performance". In a number of Broadway productions the opening and closing nights have coincided.

Broadway
Of the many Broadway shows for which the opening and closing nights coincided, one of the more costly was *Kelly*, a musical costing $700,000 which underwent the double ceremony on 6 Feb. 1965.

Youngest Broadway Producer
Margo Feiden (Margo Eden) (b New York, 2 Dec 1944) produced the musical *Peter Pan*, which opened on 3 Apr. 1961 when she was 16 years 5 months old. She wrote *Out Brief Candle*, which opened on 18 Aug. 1962. She is now a leading art dealer.

One-man shows
The longest run of one-man shows is 849 by Victor Borge (b. Copenhagen, 3 Jan. 1909) in his *Comedy in Music* from 2 Oct. 1953 to 21 Jan. 1956 at the Golden Theatre, Broadway, New York City. The world aggregate record for one-man shows is 1,700 performances of *Brief Lives* by Roy Dotrice (b. Guernsey, 5 May 1923) including 400 straight at the Mayfair Theatre, London ending on 20 July 1974. He was on stage for more than 2½ hours per performance of this 17th century monologue and required 3 hours for make up and 1 hour for removal of make-up so aggregating 40 weeks in the chair.

Most Durable Actor
Richard Hearne O.B.E. (b. Norwich 30 Jan. 1909) played a baby when aged 6 weeks and continuously through childhood in circus, pantomine and musical comedy. In Christmas 1977 he was in Cinderella at the London Palladium.

Most Durable Leading Actress
Dame Anna Neagle, D.B.E., (b. 20 Oct. 1904) played the lead role in *Charlie Girl* at the Adelphi Theatre, London for 2,062 of 2,202 performances between 15 Dec. 1965 and 27 Mar. 1971. She played the role a further 327 times in 327 performances in Australasia.

Most Roles
The greatest recorded number of theatrical, film and television roles is 1,259 from 1951 to May 1979 by Jan Leighton (U.S.).

Longest play
The longest recorded theatrical production has been *The Warp* by Neil Oram directed by Ken Campbell, a 10 part play cycle played at the Institute of Contemporary Art. The Mall, London on 18–20 Jan. 1979. Russell Denton was on stage for all but 5 minutes of the 18 hours 5 mins. The three intermissions totalled 3 hrs 10 mins.

Shakespeare
The first all amateur company to have staged all 37 of Shakespeare's plays was The Southsea Shakespeare Actors, Hampshire, England (founded 1947), when in October 1966 they presented *Cymbeline*. The amateur director throughout was Mr. K. Edmonds Gateloy, M.B.E. Ten members of the Royal Holloway College, Englefield Green, Surrey, completed a dramatic reading of all the 37 plays, 154 sonnets and

Don Ho, who has played over 4,000 cabaret performances in the Reef Towers Hotel in Honolulu.

five narrative poems in 37 hours 22 mins on 15–16 Apr. 1977. The longest is *Hamlet* with 4,042 lines and 29,551 words. Of Shakespeare's 1,277 speaking parts the longest is Hamlet with 11,610 words.

Longest chorus line
The world's longest permanent chorus line was that formed by the Rockettes in the Radio City Music Hall, which opened in December 1932 in New York City, U.S.A. The 36 girls danced precision routines across its 144 ft *43,9 m* wide stage.

Cabaret
The highest night club fee in history has been $100,000 (*then £40,000*) collected by Liza Minnelli (b. 12 Mar. 1946) for the New Year's Eve show at the Colonie Hill Club, Long Island, New York on 1 Jan. 1975. Patrons paid $150 (*£65*) per seat. Don Tai Loy Ho (b. 13 Aug. 1930, Oahu, Hawaii) has played the Polynesian Palace in the Reef Towers Hotel, Honolulu since Sept. 1970. In 4,000 performances to Jan. 1979 he is estimated to have kissed over 250,000 grandmothers.

Ice shows
Holiday on Ice Production Inc., founded by Morris Chalfen in 1945, stages the world's most costly live entertainment with up to seven productions playing simultaneously in several of 75 countries drawing 20,000,000 spectators paying $40 million (*£22.2 million*) in a year. The total skating and other staff exceeds 900. The most prolific producer of Ice Shows is Gerald Palmer with 134 since 1945 including 31 consecutive shows at Empire Pool, Wembley, London with attendances up to 727,000. Hazel Wendy Jolly (b. 1933) has appeared in the Wembley Winter Pantomime for 26 years.

Most Ardent Theatregoers
It has been estimated by the press that H. Howard Hughes (b. 1904) of Fort Worth, Texas, had seen 4,160 shows in the period 1956–1976. Britain's leading "first nighter" Edward Sutro M.C. (1900–78) saw 3,000 first night productions in 1916–56 and possibly more than 5,000 in his 60 years of theatre-going. The highest firmly recorded number of theatre attendances in Britain is 3,325 shows in 26 years from 28 Mar. 1953 to 28 Mar. 1979 by John Iles of Salisbury, Wiltshire. He estimates he has travelled 136,361 miles *221 814 km* and seen 137,829 performers in 8,556 hours (over 50 weeks) inside theatres.

Fashion Shows
The most prolific producer and most durable commentator of fashion shows is Adalene Ross of San Francisco, California with totals over 4,610 in both categories to mid-1979.

Professional Wrestling
The highest paid professional wrestler is reputedly Lars

The Sinclair Microvision, the smallest TV set in the world weighing only 28 oz. *737 g* (see p. 110).

Anderson who has a $2.3 million (£1,150,000) 3 year contract with the Universal Wrestling Alliance in Georgia, U.S.A. Lou Thesz (still active) has won 7 of the world's many "world" titles. "Fabulous" Moolah has won major U.S. women's alliance titles every year since 1956. The heaviest ever wrestler has been William J. Cobb of Macon, Georgia, U.S.A. (b. 1926), who was billed in 1962 as the 802 lb. *363 kg* (57 st. 4 lb.) "Happy" Humphrey. Ed "Strangler" Lewis (1890–1966) *né* Robert H. Friedrich, fought 6,200 bouts in 44 years losing only 33 matches. He won world titles in 1921, 1922, 1928 and 1931–32.

6. GRAMOPHONE

Origins
The gramophone (phonograph) was first *conceived* by Charles Cros (1842–1888) a French poet and scientist, who described his idea in sealed papers deposited in the French Academy of Sciences on 30 Apr. 1877. However the realisation of a practical device was first *achieved* by Thomas Alva Edison (1847–1931) of the U.S.A. The first successful machine was constructed by his mechanic, John Kruesi on 4–6 Dec. 1877, demonstrated on the 7 Dec. and patented on the 19 Feb. 1878. Pre-recorded tapes were first marketed by Recording Associates in New York City, U.S.A. in 1950.

Earliest
The first practical hand cranked, wax coated cylinder phonograph was manufactured in the United States by Chichester Bell and Charles Sumner Tainter in 1886. The forerunner of the modern disc gramophone was patented in 1887 by Emile Berliner (1851–1929), a German immigrant to the U.S.A. Although a toy machine based on his principle was produced in Germany in 1889, the gramophone was not a serious commercial competitor to the cylinder phonograph until 1896.

Most Record Players
The country with the greatest number of record players is the United States, with a total of 75,300,000 by Dec. 1976. A total of more than half a billion dollars (now *£260 million*) is spent annually on 500,000 juke boxes in the United States.

In the United States retail sales of discs and tapes reached $2,740 million in 1976 which included sales of 273 million stereo L.P.'s and 190 million singles and 127.8 million stereo tapes. In Sweden disc and tape sales were a record $17.92 (£9.95) per head in 1976.

Smallest Record
The smallest functional gramophone record is one 1⅜ in *3,5 cm* in diameter of "God Save the King" of which 250 were made by HMV Record Co. in 1924.

Oldest Records
The B.B.C. record library, contains over 750,000 records, including 5,250 with no known matrix. An Edison solid wax cylinder, recorded in Edison's laboratory and dated 26 June 1888 is the oldest record in the library which also contains a collection of early Berliner discs.

Earliest jazz records
The earliest jazz record made was *Indiana* and *The Dark Town Strutters Ball*, recorded for the Columbia label in New York City, N.Y., U.S.A., on or about 30 Jan. 1917, by the Original Dixieland Jazz Band, led by Dominick (Nick) James La Rocca (1889–1961). This was released on 31 May 1917. The first jazz record to be released was the O.D.J.B.'s *Livery Stable Blues* (recorded 24 Feb.), backed by *The Dixie Jass Band One-Step* (recorded 26 Feb.), released by Victor on 7 March 1917.

Most successful solo recording artist
On 9 June 1960 the Hollywood Chamber of Commerce presented Harry Lillis (*alias* Bing) Crosby, Jr. (1904–77) with a platinum disc to commemorate the alleged sale of 200,000,000 records from the 2,600 singles and 125 albums he had recorded. On 15 Sept. 1970 he received a second platinum disc when Decca claimed a sale of 300,650,000 discs. Crosby's first commercial recording was *I've Got the Girl* recorded on 18 Oct. 1926 (master number W142785 [Take 3] issued on the Columbia label) and his first million-seller was *Sweet Leilani* in 1937. No detailed audit of his global life-time sales from his royalty reports has ever been published.

Similarly no independently audited figures have been published for Elvis Aron Presley (1935–77). In view of Presley's 150 major hits on singles and 70 top-selling albums from 1956 continuing after his death, it may be assumed that it was he who succeeded Crosby as the top-selling solo artist.

Most Successful group
The singers with the greatest sales of any group have been the Beatles. This group from Liverpool, Merseyside, comprised George Harrison, M.B.E. (b. 25 Feb. 1943), John Ono (formerly John Winston) Lennon, M.B.E. (b. 9 Oct. 1940), James Paul McCartney, M.B.E. (b. 18 June 1942) and Richard Starkey, M.B.E. *alias* Ringo Starr (b. 7 July 1940). The all-time Beatles sales by the end of 1978 have been estimated at 100 million singles and 100 million albums—a total unmatched by any other recording act.

Golden Discs *Earliest*
The earliest recorded piece eventually to aggregate a total sale of a million copies were performances by Enrico Caruso (b. Naples, Italy, 1873, and d. 2 Aug. 1921) of the aria *Vesti la giubba* (*On with the Motley*) from the opera *I Pagliacci* by Ruggiero Leoncavallo (1858–1919), the earliest version of which was recorded with piano on 12 Nov. 1902. The first single recording to surpass the million mark was Alma Gluck's *Carry me back to old Virginny* on the Red Seal Victor label on the 12-inch *30,48 cm* single faced (later backed) record 74420. The first actual golden disc was one sprayed by R.C.A. Victor for presentation to the U.S. trombonist and band-leader Alton "Glenn" Miller (1904–44) for his *Chattanooga Choo Choo* on 10 Feb. 1942.

Most
The only *audited* measure of million-selling singles and 500,000 selling albums within the United States, is certification by the Recording Industry Association of America introduced 14 Mar. 1958. Out of the 2,390 R.I.A.A. gold

record awards made to 1 Jan. 1979, the most have gone to The Beatles with 42 (plus one with Billy Preston) as a group. McCartney has 16 more awards outside the group and with Wings. The most awards to an individual is 38 to Elvis Presley (1935–77) spanning 1958 to 1 Jan. 1979. Globally however Presley's total of million-selling singles has been authoritatively put at "approaching 80". His twin brother Jesse Garon Presley died at birth.

Most recorded song

Two songs have each been recorded over 1,000 times—*Yesterday* written by Paul McCartney and John Lennon (see above) with 1,186 versions between 1965 and 1 Jan. 1973 and *Tie A Yellow Ribbon Round the old Oak Tree* written by Irwin Levine and L. Russell Brown with more than 1,000 from 1973 to 1 Jan. 1979.

Most recordings

Miss Lata Mangeshker (b. 1928) between 1948 and 1974 has reportedly recorded not less than 25,000 solo, duet and chorus backed songs in 20 Indian languages. She frequently had 5 sessions in a day and has "backed" 1,800 films to 1974.

Biggest sellers *Singles*

The greatest seller of any gramophone record to date is *White Christmas* by Irving Berlin (b. Israel Bailin, at Tyumen, Russia, 11 May 1888) with 25,000,000 for the Crosby single (recorded 29 May 1942) and more than 100,000,000 in other versions. The highest claim for any "pop" record is an unaudited 25,000,000 for *Rock Around the Clock*, copyrighted in 1953 by James E. Myers under the name Jimmy DeKnight and the late Max C. Friedmann and recorded on 12 Apr. 1954 by Bill Haley and the Comets. The top-selling British record of all-time is *I Want to Hold Your Hand* by the Beatles, released in 1963, with world sales of over 13,000,000. The first single to sell over 2,000,000 copies in Great Britain was *Mull of Kintyre*, released in November 1977, by Wings, a group which includes Paul McCartney (see Beatles above), Linda McCartney (b. New York 24 Sept. 1942) and Denny Laine (b. Jersey 29 Oct. 1944). It was written by McCartney and Laine.

Albums

The best selling album of all time is the double album (4 sides) of the soundtrack of the film *Saturday Night Fever* with 25 million copies globally by 1 May 1979. The most popular of the songs were written by the Bee Gees comprising the Manx born Gibb brothers Barry Alan (b. 1 Sept. 1947) and the twins Robin and Maurice (b. 22 Dec. 1949).

The best selling album by a British performer is the double album *Frampton Comes Alive* recorded in the US by Peter Frampton (b. Beckenham, Kent 22 April 1950) with 8 million copies by the end of 1978. The largest selling British album recorded in Britain is *Jesus Christ Superstar* by Andrew Lloyd Webber (b. London, 22 Mar. 1948) and Tim Rice (b. Amersham, Bucks, 10 Nov. 1944) with sales of nearly 6 million double album sets by the end of 1978.

The Charts—*US Singles*

Singles record charts were first published by *Billboard* on 20 July 1940 when the No. 1 was *I'll Never Smile Again* by Tommy Dorsey (b. 19 Nov. 1905, d. 26 Nov. 1956). Three discs have stayed top for a record 13 consecutive weeks—*Frenesi* by Artie Shaw from Dec. 1940; *I've Heard that Song Before* by Harry James from Feb. 1943 and *Goodnight Irene* by Gordon Jenkins and the Weavers from Aug. 1950. *I go crazy* by Paul Davis stayed on the chart for 40 consecutive weeks from Aug. 1977. The Beatles have had most No. 1 records (20) and Elvis Presley has had most hit singles on Billboard's Hot 100—97 from 1956 to May 1979.

US Albums

Billboard first published an chart album on 15 Mar. 1945 when the No. 1 was *King Cole Trio* featuring Nat "King" Cole (b. 17 Mar. 1919, d. 15 Feb. 1965). *South Pacific* was No. 1 for 69 weeks (non-consecutive) from May 1949. *Johnny's Greatest Hits* by Johnny Mathis stayed in the chart for 490 weeks (over 9 years) from April 1958. The Beatles had most No. 1's (15) and Presley most hit albums (75 from 1956 to May 1979).

The Guinness Book of British Hit Singles *by Jo and Tim Rice with Paul Gambaccini and Mike Read (£3.95 paperback; £5.25 hardback) lists every one of the 6,700 plus records by more than 2,000 acts in the British Top 50 from 14 Nov. 1952 to 1 Jan. 1979.*

UK Singles

Singles record charts were first published in Britain on 14 Nov. 1952 by *New Musical Express*. *I Believe* by Frankie Laine (b. 30 Mar. 1913) held No. 1 position for 18 weeks (non-consecutive) from April 1953, with *Rose Marie* by Slim Whitman (b. 20 Jan. 1924) the consecutive record holder with 11 weeks from July 1955. The longest stay has been the 122 weeks of *My Way* by Francis Albert Sinatra (b. 12 Dec. 1917) in 9 separate runs from 2 Apr. 1969 into 1972. The record for an uninterrupted stay is 56 weeks for Englebert Humperdinck's *Release Me* from 26 Jan. 1967. The Beatles and Presley hold the record for most No. 1 hits with 17 each, with Presley having an overall record of 95 hits in the UK singles chart from 1956 to May 1979. The leading British chart maker is Cliff Richard (b. Harry Webb, 14 Oct. 1940) with 68 from 1958 to May 1979.

Fastest selling L.P.s

The fastest selling record of all time is *John Fitzgerald Kennedy—A Memorial Album* (Premium Albums), an L.P. recorded on 22 Nov. 1963, the day of Mr. Kennedy's assassination, which sold 4,000,000 copies at 99 cents (*then 35p*) in six days (7–12 Dec. 1963), thus ironically beating the previous speed record set by the satirical L.P. *The First Family* in 1962–63. The fastest selling British record has been the Beatles' double album *The Beatles* (Apple) with "nearly 2 million" in its first week in November 1968.

Advance sales

The greatest advance sale was 2,100,000 for *Can't Buy Me Love* by the Beatles, released in the United States on 16 Mar. 1964. The Beatles also equalled their British record record of 1,000,000 advance sales, set by *I Want to Hold Your Hand* (Parlophone transferred to Apple Aug. 1968) on 29 Nov. 1963, with this same record on 20 Mar. 1964. The U.K. record for advance sales of an L.P. is 750,000 for the Parlophone album *Beatles for Sale* released on 4 Dec. 1964.

Loudest *Pop Group*

The amplification at *The Who* concert at Charlton Athletic Football Ground, London on 31 May 1976 provided by a Tasco P.A. System had a total power of 76,000 watts from eighty 800 W Crown D.C. 300 A Amplifiers and twenty 600 W Phase Linear 200's. The readings at 50 metres from the front of the sound system were 120 db. *Exposure to such noise levels causes PSH—Permanent Shift of Hearing or partial deafness.*

7. CINEMA

Guinness Superlatives is publishing a more specialist book *Guinness Book of Film Facts and Feats* by Patrick Robinson in the autumn of 1980.

FILMS

Origins

The greatest impetus in the development of cinematography came from the inventiveness of Etienne Jules Marey (1830–1903) of France in the 1870's.

Earliest silent showings

The earliest demonstration of a celluloid cinematograph film on a screen was given at 44 Rue de Rennes, Paris on 22 Mar. 1895 by Auguste Marie Louis Nicolas Lumière (1862–1954) and Louis Jean Lumière (1864–1948). The film was entitled *La Sortie des Ouvriers de l'Usine Lumière* taken probably in August or September 1894 outside the factory gates at Lyons. Louis Aimé Augustin Le Prince, according to evidence in *The Shell Book of Firsts*, achieved dim moving outlines on a whitewashed wall at the Institute for the Deaf, Washington Heights, New York, U.S.A. as early as 1885. The earliest demonstration of film projection in Britain was given by Bert Acres (b. U.S.A. 23 July 1854, d. Walthamstow,

Essex 27 Dec. 1918) at the Royal Photographic Society, 12 Hanover Square, London on 14 Jan. 1896.

Earliest 'Talkie'

The earliest sound-on-film motion picture was achieved by Eugene Augustin Lauste (b. Paris 17 Jan. 1857) who patented his process on 11 Aug. 1906 and produced a workable system using a string galvanometer in 1910 in London. The event is more usually attributed to Dr. Lee de Forest (1873–1961) in New York City, N.Y., U.S.A., on 13 March 1923. The first all-talking picture was *Lights of New York*, shown at The Strand, New York City, on 6 July 1928.

Most expensive film

The most expensive film ever made is the 6 hr 13 min long *War and Peace*, the U.S.S.R. government adaptation of the masterpiece of Tolstoy directed by Sergei Bondarchuk (b. 1921) over the period 1962–67. The total cost has been stated to be more than £40,000,000. More than 165,000 uniforms had to be made. The re-creation of the Battle of Borodino (7 Sept. 1812) involved 120,000 Red Army "extras" at 3 roubles (£1.38) per month.

Most expensive film rights

The highest price ever paid for film rights is $9,500,000 (*then £4,950,000*) announced on 20 Jan. 1978 by Columbia for *Annie*, the Broadway Musical by Charles Strouse starring Andrea McCordle, Dorothy Loudon and Reid Shelton.

Longest film

The longest film ever shown is *The Human Condition*, directed in three parts by Masaki Kobayashi of Japan. It lasts 9 hrs 27 min, excluding breaks. It was exhibited in Tōkyō, Japan in October 1961 at an admission price of 250 yen (24½p). The longest film ever released was **** by Andy Warhol (b. Andrew Warhola, Cleveland, Ohio, 1931) which lasted 24 hrs. It proved not surprisingly, except reportedly to its creator, a commercial failure and was withdrawn and re-released in 90 min form as *The Loves of Ondine*.

Highest box office gross

The film which has had the highest world gross earnings is *Star Wars*, written and produced by Gary Kartz and directed by George Lucas, which from 25 May 1977–1 Jan. 1979 grossed $267 million (*£133.5 million*).

Highest earnings by an actor

The highest rate of pay in cinema history is being contested between Marlon Brando (b. 3 Apr. 1924) for his brief part in *Superman* and Steve McQueen (b. 1930) for his role in *Tai Pan*. Both received in excess of $2,500,000 (*£1,250,000*) but the final amount will depend on box office percentages.

Largest Studios

The largest complex of film studios in the world are those at Universal City, South California. The Back Lot contains 561 buildings and there are 34 sound stages.

Oscars *Most*

Walter (Walt) Elias Disney (1901–1966) won more "Oscars" —the awards of the United States Academy of Motion Picture Arts and Sciences, instituted on 16 May 1929 for 1927–28—than any other person. The physical count comprises 20 statuettes, and nine other plaques and certificates including posthumous awards. The only actress to win three Oscars in a starring rôle has been Miss Katharine Hepburn, formerly Mrs. Ludlow Ogden Smith (b. Hartford, Conn., 9 Nov. 1909) in *Morning Glory* (1932–3), *Guess Who's Coming to Dinner* (1967) and *The Lion in Winter* (1968). She was 11 times nominated. Oscars are named after Mr. Oscar Pierce of Texas, U.S.A. The films with most awards have been *Ben Hur* (1959) with 11, followed by *Gone With the Wind* (1939) with 10 and *West Side Story* (1961) with 10. The film with the highest number of nominations was *All About Eve* (1950) with 14. It won six. The youngest ever winner was Shirley Temple aged 6 in 1934 and the oldest George Burns, 80 for "The Sunshine Boys" in 1976

CINEMAS

Earliest

The earliest structure designed and exclusively used for

exhibiting projected films is believed to be one erected at the Atlanta Show, Georgia U.S.A. in October 1895 to exhibit C. F. Jenkins' phantoscope. The earliest cinema constructed in Great Britain was built without permission at Olympia, London, to house the "Theatregraph" promoted by Robert William Paul (1869–1943). This was completed by 16 April 1896.

Largest *World*

The largest cinema in the world is the Radio City, New York City, with a capacity of 4,400.

Great Britain

Great Britain's largest cinema is the Odeon Theatre, Hammersmith, Greater London, with 3,485 seats. The Playhouse, Glasgow had 4,235 seats.

Drive-In

The world's largest drive-in cinema is that at Newington, New Haven, Connecticut, U.S.A. with a capacity for 4,000 cars.

Most cinema seats

The Falkland Islands and the Cook Islands have more seats used for watching films per total population than any other country in the world, with 250 seats for each 1,000 inhabitants. The Central African Empire has 8 cinemas.

Highest cinema going

The people of Taiwan go to the cinema more often than those of any other country in the world with an average of 66 attendances per person per annum according to the latest data. The Soviet Union claims to have most cinemas in the world, with 163,400 in 1974, but this includes buildings merely equipped with even 16 mm projectors. The U.S.A. has some 16,000 actual cinemas. The number of cinemas in the U.K. reached a peak 4,714 in 1944 declining to 1,566 by April 1979. The average weekly admissions declined from 33,420,000 in 1944 to 2,500,000 in 1978 but picked up on the 1977 figures.

Biggest Screen

The permanently installed cinema screen with the largest area is one of 70 ft *21,33 m* tall by 96 ft *29,26 m* wide installed in the Pictorium Theater, Marriott's Great America Entertainment Center, Santa Clara, California on 16 May 1978. It was made by Harkness Screens Ltd at Boreham Wood, Herts. A temporary screen 297 ft × 33 ft *90,5 × 10 m* was used at the 1937 Paris Exposition.

8. RADIO BROADCASTING

Origins

The earliest description of a radio transmission system was written by Dr. Mahlon Loomis (U.S.A.) (b. Fulton County, N.Y., 21 July 1826) on 21 July 1864 and demonstrated between two kites more than 14 miles *22 km* apart at Bear's Den, Loudoun County, Virginia in October 1866. He received U.S. patent No. 129,971 entitled Improvement in Telegraphing on 20 July 1872. He died in 1886.

Earliest patent

The first patent for a system of communication by means of electro-magnetic waves, numbered No. 12039, was granted on 2 June 1896 to the Italian-Irish Marchese Guglielmo Marconi, G.C.V.O. (Hon.) (1874–1937). A public demonstration of wireless transmission of speech was, however, given in the town square of Murray, Kentucky, U.S.A. in 1892 by Nathan B. Stubblefield. He died destitute on 28 March 1928. The first permanent wireless installation was at The Needles on the Isle of Wight, by Marconi's Wireless Telegraph Co., Ltd., in November 1896.

Earliest broadcast *World*

The world's first advertised broadcast was made on 24 Dec. 1906 by the Canadian born Prof. Reginald Aubrey Fessenden (1868–1932) from the 420 ft *128 m* mast of the National Electric Signalling Company at Brant Rock, Massachusetts,

U.S.A. The transmission included Handel's *Largo*. Fessenden had achieved the broadcast of speech as early as November 1900 but this was highly distorted.

Great Britain

The first experimental broadcasting transmitter in Great Britain was set up at the Marconi Works in Chelmsford, Essex, in December 1919, and broadcast a news service in February 1920. The earliest regular broadcast was made from the Marconi transmitter "2 MT" at Writtle, Essex, on 14 Feb. 1922.

Transatlantic transmissions

The earliest transatlantic wireless signals (the letter S in Morse Code) were received by Marconi, George Stephen Kemp and Percy Paget from a 10 kw station at Poldhu, Cornwall, at Signal Hill, St. John's, Newfoundland, Canada, at 12.30 p.m. on 12 Dec. 1901. Human speech was first heard across the Atlantic in November 1915 when a transmission from the U.S. Navy station at Arlington, Virginia was received by U.S. radio-telephone engineers on the Eiffel Tower.

Earliest Radio-Microphones

The radio-microphone, which was in essence also the first "bug", was devised by Reg. Moores (G.B.) in 1947 and first used on 76 MHz in the ice show *Aladdin* at Brighton Sports Stadium, East Sussex in Sept. 1949.

Longest B.B.C. national broadcast

The longest B.B.C. national broadcast was the reporting of the Coronation of Queen Elizabeth II on 2 June 1953. It began at 10.15 a.m. and finished at 5.30 p.m., after 7 hrs 15 min.

Longest continuous broadcast *World*

The longest continuous broadcast (excluding disc-jockeying) has been one of 336 hrs by Bill Tinsley of WATN Radio, Watertown, New York, U.S.A. on 17–31 Mar. 1979.

Great Britain

The longest local radio transmission has been 45 hrs by B.B.C. Radio Derby's programme broadcast by Paul Baird and Simon Shaw on 30 Mar. to 1 Apr. 1979.

Hospital Radio

Ian Jones completed 60 hours of broadcasting on Hospital Radio Harefield, Uxbridge, Middx. on 2–4 Dec. 1978.

Most durable programmes *B.B.C.*

The longest running B.B.C. radio series is *The Week's Good Cause* beginning on 24 Jan. 1926. The longest running record programme is *Desert Island Discs* which began on 29 Jan. 1942 and on which programme only seven guests have been thrice stranded. The *Desert Island* programme has been presented since its inception by Roy Plomley, O.B.E. who devised the idea. The longest running solo radio feature is *Letter from America* by (Alfred) Alistair Cooke, Hon. K.B.E. (b. Manchester 20 Nov. 1908), first broadcast on 24 March 1946. The longest running radio serial is *The Archers* which was created by Godfrey Baseley and was first broadcast on 7 June 1950. Up to May 1978 the signature tune *Barwick Green* had been played over 29,000 times. The only one of 363 roles which has been played without interruption from the start has been that of Philip Archer by Norman Painting O.B.E. (b. Leamington Spa 23 Apr. 1924).

Earliest Antipodal Reception

Frank Henry Alfred Walker (b. 11 Nov. 1904) on the night of 12 Nov. 1924 received on his home-made 2 valve receiver on 75 metres signals from Marconi's yacht *Electra* (call sign ICCM) in Australian waters at Crown Farm, Cuttimore Lane, Walton-on-Thames, Surrey, England.

Most stations

The country with the greatest number of radio broadcasting stations is the United States, where there were 8,608 authorized broadcast stations in 1978 of which 4,547 were AM (Amplitude modulation) and 4,061 FM (Frequency modulation).

Highest listenership

The peak recorded listenership on B.B.C. Radio was 30,000,000 adults on 6 June 1950 for the boxing fight between Lee Savold (U.S.) and Bruce Woodcock (G.B.).

Highest Response

The highest recorded response from a radio show occurred on 27 Nov. 1974 when on a 5 hour talk show on WCAU, Philadelphia, U.S.A., Howard Sheldon, the astrologist registered a call count of 388,299 calls on the "Bill Corsair Show".

9. TELEVISION

Invention

The invention of television, the instantaneous viewing of distant objects by electrical transmissions, was not an act but a process of successive and inter-dependent discoveries. The first commercial cathode ray tube was introduced in 1897 by Karl Ferdinand Braun (1850–1918), but was not linked to "electric vision" until 1907 by Boris Rosing of Russia in St. Petersburg (now Leningrad). A. A. Campbell Swinton F.R.S. (1863–1930) published the fundament of television transmission on 18 June 1908 in a brief letter to *Nature* entitled "Distant Electric Vision". The earliest public demonstration of television was given on 27 Jan. 1926 by John Logie Baird (1888–1946) of Scotland, using a development of the mechanical scanning system suggested by Paul Nipkov in 1884. He had achieved the transmission of a Maltese Cross over 10 ft *3,05 m* at 8, Queen's Arcade, Hastings, East Sussex in February 1924 and the first facial image (of William Taynton, 15) at Frith Street on 30 Oct. 1925. Taynton had to be bribed with 2s 6d. A patent application for the Iconoscope had been filed on 29 Dec. 1923 by Dr. Vladimir Kosma Zworykin (born in Russia on 30 July 1889, became a U.S. citizen in 1924), though not issued until 20 Dec. 1938. The patent filed by Philo Taylor Farnsworth (US) on 7 Jan. 1927 was however granted on 26 Aug. 1930. Farnsworth succeeded with a low definition image at 202 Green Street, Los Angeles in November 1927. The first experimental transmission in Britain was on 30 Sept. 1929. Public transmissions on 30 lines were made from 22 Aug. 1932 until 11 Sept. 1935.

Earliest service

The world's first high definition (*i.e.* 405 lines) television broadcasting service was opened from Alexandra Palace, Haringey, Greater London, on 2 Nov. 1936, when there were about 100 sets in the United Kingdom. The Chief Engineer was Mr. Douglas Birkinshaw. A television station in Berlin, Germany, made a low definition (180 line) transmission from 22 March 1935. The transmitter burnt out in Aug. 1935.

Transatlantic transmission

The earliest transatlantic transmission by satellite was achieved at 1 a.m. on 11 July 1962, *via* the active satellite *Telstar 1* from Andover, Maine, U.S.A., to Pleumeur Bodou, France. The picture was of Mr. Frederick R. Kappell, chairman of the American Telephone and Telegraph Company, which owned the satellite. The first "live" broadcast was made on 23 July 1962 and the first woman to appear was the *haute couturière*, Ginette Spanier, directrice of Balmain, the next day. On 9 Feb. 1928 the image of J. L. Baird (see above) and of a Mrs. Howe was transmitted from Station 2 KZ at Coulsdon, Surrey, England to Station 2 CVJ, Hartsdale, N.Y., U.S.A.

Longest telecast

The longest pre-scheduled telecast on record was a continuous transmission for 163 hours 18 mins by GTV 9 of Melbourne, Australia covering the Apollo XI moon mission on 19–26 July 1969. The longest continuous TV transmission under a single director was the Avro Television Production *Open Het Dorpe* transmitted in the Netherlands on 26–27 November 1962 for 23 hrs 20 min under the direction of Theo Ordaman.

Video-Tape Recording

Alexander M. Poniatoff first demonstrated video tape recording known as Ampex (his initials plus 'ex' for excellence) in 1956.

Most durable shows *World*

The world's most durable T.V. show is N.B.C.'s *Meet the Press* first transmitted on 6 Nov. 1947 and weekly since 12 Sept. 1948 originated by Lawrence E. Spivak, who appeared weekly as either moderator or panel member until 1975.

Great Britain

The longest running T.V. programme on B.B.C. is *Panorama* which was first transmitted, introduced by Patrick Murphy, on 11 Nov. 1953. *Andy Pandy* was first transmitted on 11 July 1950 but consisted of repeats of a cycle of 26 shows until 1970. The seasonal programme *Come Dancing* was first transmitted on 29 Sept. 1950. "The News" started on 21 Mar. 1938 in sound only. The regular daily T.V. News began on 5 July 1954. The puppet show *Sooty*, devised by Harry Corbett (b. Bradford, 1918) has been transmitted every year since 1952.

Most sets

In 1975 the total estimated number of television transmitters in use or under construction was 19,870 serving 363,770,000 sets (91 for each 1,000 of the world population). In the United States where 99 per cent of the population was reached in 1976, the number of colour sets has grown from 200,000 in 1960 to 56,900,000 by October 1978. The number of licences current in the United Kingdom was 18,440,080 on 31 Mar. 1979 of which 12,101,832 (65.62%) were for colour sets. Black and white sets became rarer than colour sets in 1976.

T.V. Watching

In July 1978 it was estimated that the *average* American child by his or her 18th birthday has watched 710 solid days (17,040 hours) of T.V., seen more than 350,600 commercials and more than 15,000 T.V. murders. There are 571 T.V. sets per 1,000 people in the U.S.A. compared with 348 in Sweden and 315 in Britain.

Most Television Free

Iceland has a T.V. free day on Thursdays to reduce disruption of family life. Otherwise transmissions are normally limited to between 8 and 11 p.m. Upper Volta had by 1974 only one set per 1,000 of the population.

Greatest audience

The greatest estimated number of viewers for a televised event is 1,000 million for the live and recorded transmissions of the XXth and XXIst Olympic Games in Munich, West Germany and Montreal, Canada in 1972 and 1976.

Largest Production

The BBC production of the 37 plays of Shakespeare in 1978–1984 will cost a minimum of £6,800,000. The new series was conceived by its producer Cedric Messina.

Largest Contracts *World*

The largest T.V. contract ever signed was one for $34,000,000 (*then* £14,166,666) in a three-year no-option contract between Dean Martin (b. Dino Paul Crocetti, 7 June 1917) and N.B.C. in 1968.

Currently television's highest-paid performer is Johnny Carson the host of *The Tonight Show*. His current 5 year N.B.C. contract reportedly calls for annual payments of some $2,500,000 (*now* £1,315,000) for a 125 day working year, perhaps double that in percentages on commercial fees. The highest-paid current affairs or news performer is Barbara Walters of A.B.C. *The Evening News* programme, who signed a 5-year $1 million a year contract on or about 21 Apr. 1976.

Mary Tyler Moore (b 29 Dec. 1937) as head of her own production company reputedly earned some $2,250,000 (*now* £1,180,000) in the last series of shows in which she starred which ended in 1977.

Great Britain

The largest contract in British television was one of a reported £9,000,000, inclusive of production expenses, signed by Tom Jones (b. Thomas Jones Woodward, 7 June 1940) of Treforest, Mid Glamorgan, Wales in June 1968 with A.B.C.-T.V. of the United States and A.T.V. in London for 17 one-hour shows per annum from January 1969 to January 1974.

Highest Paid TV Actor

Peter Falk (b. 16 Sept. 1927), the disarmingly persistent detective *Columbo*, was paid from $300,000 to $350,000 for a single episode of his series of six so totalling $1,950,000 (*then* £1,147,000) in 1976.

Largest T.V. prizes *World*

The greatest amount won by an individual in T.V. prizes was $264,000 (*then* £94,286) by Teddy Nadler (b. 1910) of St. Louis, Missouri on quiz programmes in the United States up to September 1958. He reputedly had to pay $155,000 in federal and state taxes and has been unemployed since. On 24 July 1975 WABC-T.V., New York City transmitted the first televised Grand Tier draw of the State Lottery in which the winner took the grand prize of $1,000,000 (*now* £540,500). This was however taxable. Don Chu of El Dorado, Arkansas won $128,000 (*then* £67,000) on a quiz show aired by KTVE-T.V. on 18 June 1977. Barbara Anne Eddy of Vancouver, B.C. won the same amount on this show taped on 1 Feb. 1978 but a Canadian pays no tax.

Most successful appeals

The most successful T.V. appeals in the world are those transmitted in New Zealand. The Telethon appeal on South Pacific T.V., Auckland in 1978 for the Arthritis and Rheumatism Foundation raised $3,002,750 (£1,648,350) from a 2,550,000 audience. The first television appeal response in Britain, from in excess of 1,000,000 viewers, occurred after the Reports Action appeal on 16 Apr. 1978, on behalf of the British Kidney Patient Association, on Granada TV by Joan Bakewell and Bob Greaves. Gifts totalled £400,000 in value.

Biggest sale

The greatest number of episodes of any T.V. programme ever sold has been 1,144 episodes of "Coronation Street" by Granada Television to CBKST Saskatoon, Saskatchewan, Canada, on 31 May 1971. This constituted 20 days 15 hrs 44 min continuous viewing.

Most prolific scriptwriter

The most prolific television writer in the world is the Rt. Hon. Lord Willis known as Ted Willis (b. 13 Jan. 1918), who in the period 1949–79 has created 24 series, including the first seven years and 2,250,000 words of *Dixon of Dock Green* which ran from 1955–1976, 24 stage plays and 21 feature films. He had 20 plays produced. His total output since 1945 can be estimated at 15,500,000 words.

Highest T.V. advertising rates

The highest T.V. advertising rate has been $370,000 per min (*then* £3,083 per sec) for C.B.S. network prime time during the transmission of *Super Bowl* on 14 Jan. 1977. In Great Britain the peak time weekday 60 sec spot rate (6.45–10.15 p.m.) for Thames Television is £9,300 + V.A.T. for a booking within 4 weeks of transmission (May 1979).

Most takes

The highest number of "takes" for a T.V. commercial is 28 in 1973 by Pat Coombs, the commedienne, who has supported Dick Emery on B.B.C. T.V. Her explanation was "Everytime we came to the punch line I just could not remember the name of the product".

Commercials Records

In 1977 James Coburn of Beverly Hills, California was reputed to have been paid $500,000 (£250,000) for uttering two words on a series of Schlitz beer commercials. The words "Schlitz Light" were thus at a quarter of a million dollars per syllable.

Smallest Set

The world's smallest T.V. set is the 28 oz. *737 g* Sinclair Microvision with overall dimensions of 6 × 4 × 1½ in *15,2 × 10,1 × 3,8 mm* and a screen measuring 2 in *5,08 cm* diagonally, manufactured by Sinclair Radionics Ltd. of St. Ives, Cambridgeshire.

THE WORLD'S STRUCTURES

7

EARLIEST STRUCTURES

World

The earliest known human structure is a rough circle of loosely piled lava blocks found in 1960 on the lowest cultural level at the Lower Paleolithic site at Olduvai Gorge in Tanzania. The structure was associated with artifacts and bones and may represent a work-floor, dating to *c.* 1,750,000 B.C. The earliest evidence of *buildings* yet discovered is that of 21 huts with hearths or pebble-lined pits and delimited by stake holes found in October 1965 at the Terra Amata site in Nice, France thought to be belonging to the Acheulian culture of 120,000 years ago. Excavation carried out between 28 June and 5 July 1966 revealed one hut with palisaded walls with axes of 49 ft *15 m* and 20 ft *6 m*. The oldest free standing structures in the world are now believed to be the megalithic temples at Mgarr and Skarba in Malta and Ggantija in Gozo dating from *c.* 3,250 B.C. The remains of a stone tower 20 ft *6,1 m* high built into the walls of Jericho has been excavated and is dated to 5000 B.C.

Great Britain

A rudimentary platform of birch branches, stones and wads of clay thrown down on the edge of a swamp at Star Carr, south of Scarborough, North Yorkshire, may possibly represent the earliest man-made "dwelling" yet found in Britain (Mesolithic, 7607 B.C. ± 210). Remains of the earliest dated stone shelter and cooking pit were discovered in 1967 at Culver Well, Isle of Portland, Dorset (Mesolithic, 5200 B.C. ± 135). On the Isle of Jura, Strathclyde, Scotland a hearth consisting of three linked stone circles has been dated to the Mesolithic period 6013 ± 200 B.C.

Ireland

The earliest known structures in Ireland date from the Mesolithic period *c.* 6850–6500 B.C. A series of pits associated with post-holes have been excavated at a living site at Mount Sandel, Co. Derry.

1. BUILDINGS FOR WORKING

LARGEST BUILDINGS

Commercial *World*

The greatest ground area covered by any building in the world is that by the Ford Parts Redistribution Center, Pennsylvania Avenue, Brownstown Township, Michigan, U.S.A. It encloses a floor area of 3,100,000 ft² or 71.16 acres *28,8 ha*. It was opened on 20 May 1971 and employs 1,400 people. The fire control system comprises 70 miles *112 km* of pipelines with 37,000 sprinklers. The building with the largest cubic capacity in the world is the Boeing Company's main assembly plant at Everett, Washington State, U.S.A. completed in 1968 with a capacity of 200 million ft³ *5,6 million m³*.

Great Britain

The largest building in Britain is the Ford Parts Center at Daventry, Northamptonshire, which measures 1,978 × 780 ft *602 × 237 m* and 1.6 million ft² or 36.7 acres *14,86 ha*. It was opened on 6 Sept. 1972 at a cost of nearly £8 million. It employs 1,600 people and is fitted with 14,000 fluorescent lights.

Scientific

The most capacious scientific building in the world is the Vehicle Assembly Building (VAB) at Complex 39, the selected site for the final assembly and launching of the Apollo moon spacecraft on the Saturn V rocket, at the John F. Kennedy Space Center (KSC) on Merritt Island, Cape Canaveral, Florida, U.S.A. It is a steel-framed building measuring 716 ft *218 m* in length, 518 ft *158 m* in width and 525 ft *160 m* high. The building contains four bays, each with its own door 460 ft *140 m* high. Construction began in April 1963 by the Ursum Consortium. Its floor area is 343,500 ft² (7.87 acres *3,18 ha*) and its capacity is 129,482,000 ft³ *3 666 500 m³*. The building was "topped out" on 14 Apr. 1965 at a cost of $108,700,000 (*then £38.8 million*).

Administrative

The largest ground area covered by any office building is that of the Pentagon, in Arlington County, Virginia, U.S.A. Built to house the U.S. Defense Department's offices it was completed on 15 Jan. 1943 and cost an estimated $83,000,000 (*then £20,595,000*). Each of the outermost sides of the Pentagon is 921 ft *281 m* long and the perimeter of the building is about 1,500 yds *1 370 m*. The five storeys of the building enclose a floor area of 6,500,000 ft² *604 000 m²* (149.2 acres). During the day 29,000 people work in the building. The telephone system of the building has over 44,000 telephones connected by 160,000 miles *257 500 km* of cable and its 220 staff handle 280,000 calls a day. Two restaurants, six cafeterias and ten snack bars and a staff of 675 form the catering department of the building. The corridors measure 17 miles *27 km* in length and there are 7,748 windows to be cleaned.

Office

The largest office buildings in the world are The World

Trade Center in New York City, U.S.A. with a total of 4,370,000 ft² (100.32 acres *40,6 ha*) of rentable space in each of the twin towers of which the taller is 1,350 ft *411,48 m.*

Single Office *Great Britain*
The largest single office in the United Kingdom is that of West Midlands Gas at Solihull, West Midlands, built by Spooners (Hull) Ltd. in 1962. It now measures 753 ft by 160 ft *230 by 49 m* (2.77 acres *1,12 ha*) in one open plan room accommodating 2,170 clerical and managerial workers.

TALLEST BUILDINGS
World
The tallest office building in the world is the Sears Tower, the national headquarters of Sears, Roebuck & Co. in Wacker Drive, Chicago, Illinois with 110 storeys rising to 1,454 ft *443 m* and begun in August 1970. Its gross area is 4,400,000 ft² (101.0 acres *40,8 ha*). It was "topped out" on 4 May 1973. It surpassed the World Trade Center in New York City in height at 2.35 p.m. on 6 Mar. 1973 with the first steel column reaching to the 104th storey. The addition of two T.V. antennae brought the total height to 1,559 ft *475,18 m.* The building's population is 16,700 served by 103 elevators and 18 escalators. It has 16,000 windows.

Asia
Asia's tallest building, where building must be proofed against earthquakes, is the 60 storey "Sunshine 60" in Ikebukuro, Tokyo, Japan completed in 1978 to a height of 240 m *787.4 ft.* (See also Passenger Lifts, fastest).

Great Britain
The tallest office block in Britain is the £72 million National Westminster tower block in Bishopsgate, City of London due for completion in spring 1979. It has 49 storeys and 3 basement levels and is 600 ft 4 in *183 m* tall. The gross floor area is 636,373 ft² *59,121 m²* or 14.6 acres. The view from the top extends over 8 counties.

HABITATIONS
Greatest altitude
The highest inhabited buildings in the world are those in the Indian–Tibet border fort of Bāsisi at *c.* 19,700 ft *5 988 m.* In April 1961, however, a 3-room dwelling was discovered at 21,650 ft *6 600 m* on Cerro Llullaillaco (22,058 ft *6 723 m*), on the Argentine-Chile border, believed to date from the late pre-Columbian period *c.* 1480. An unnamed settlement on the T'e-li-mo trail in southern Tibet is at an apparent altitude of 19,800 ft *6 019 m.*

Northernmost
The most northerly habitation in the world is the Danish Scientific station set up in 1952 in Pearyland, northern Greenland, over 900 miles *1 450 km* north of the Arctic Circle. Eskimo hearths dated to before 1000 B.C. were discovered in Pearyland in 1969. The U.S.S.R. and the United States have maintained research stations on ice floes in the Arctic. The U.S.S.R.'s "North Pole 15", which drifted 1,250 miles *2 000 km,* passed within 1¼ miles *2,8 km* of the North Pole in December 1967.

The most northerly continuously inhabited place is the Canadian Department of National Defence outpost at Alert on Ellesmere Island, Northwest Territories in Lat 82° 30′ N. Long. 62° W set up in 1950.

Southernmost
The most southerly permanent human habitation is the United States' Scott-Amundsen South Polar Station (see page 67) completed in 1957 and replaced in 1975.

EMBASSIES AND CIVIC BUILDINGS
Largest
The largest embassy in the world is the U.S.S.R. embassy on Bei Xiao Jie, Peking, China, in the north-eastern corner of the Northern walled city. The whole 45 acre *18,2 ha* area of the old Orthodox Church mission (established 1728), now known as the *Bei guan,* was handed over to the U.S.S.R. in 1949. The largest in Great Britain is the United States of America Embassy in Grosvenor Square, London. The

Chancery Building, completed in 1960, alone has 600 rooms for a staff of 700 on seven floors with a usable floor area of 255,000 ft² (5.85 acres *2,37 ha*).

Great Britain
The oldest municipal building in Britain is the Exeter Guildhall first referred to in a deed of 1160. The Tudor front was added in 1593.

EXHIBITION CENTRES
Largest *Great Britain*
Britain's largest exhibition centre is the National Exhibition Centre, Birmingham opened in February 1976. Five halls which inter-connect cover 87 180 m² *938,397 ft²* or 21.54 acres with a volume of 1 168 466 m³ or *41.26 million ft³.*

INDUSTRIAL STRUCTURES
Tallest chimneys *World*
The world's tallest chimney is the $5.5 million International Nickel Company's stack 1,245 ft 8 in *379,6 m* tall at Copper Cliff, Sudbury, Ontario, Canada, completed in 1970. It was built by Canadian Kellogg Ltd., in 60 days and the diameter tapers from 116.4 ft *35,4 m* at the base to 51.8 ft *15,8 m* at the top. It weighs 38,390 tons *39 006 tonnes* and became operational in 1971. The world's most massive chimney and Europe's tallest is one of 1,148 ft *350 m* at Puentes, Spain built by M. W. Kellogg Co. It contains 20,600 yd³ *15 750 m³* of concrete and 2.9 million lb. *1 315 tonnes* of steel and has an internal volume of 6.7 million ft³ *189 720 m³.*

Great Britain
The tallest chimney in Great Britain is one of 850 ft *259 m* at Drax Power Station, North Yorkshire, begun in 1966 and topped out on 16 May 1969. It has an untapered diameter of 87 ft 9 in *26 m* and has the greatest capacity of any chimney. The architects were Clifford Tee & Gale of London. The oldest known industrial chimney in Britain is the Stone Edge Chimney, near Chesterfield, Derbyshire built to a height of 55 ft *16,76 m ante* 1771.

Cooling towers
The largest cooling tower in the world is that adjacent to the nuclear power plant at Uentrop, West Germany which is 590 ft *179,8 m* tall. It was completed in 1976. The largest in the United Kingdom are the Ferrybridge "C" power station, West Yorkshire, type measuring 375 ft *114 m* tall and 300 ft *91 m* across the base.

HANGARS
Largest *World*
The world's largest hangar is the Goodyear Airship hangar at Akron, Ohio, U.S.A. which measures 1,175 ft *358 m* long, 325 ft *99 m* wide and 200 ft *61 m* high. It covers 364,000 ft² (8.35 acres *3,38 ha*) and has a capacity of 55,000,000 ft³ *1,6 million m³.* The world's largest single fixed-wing aircraft hangar is the Lockheed-Georgia engineering test center at Marietta, Georgia measuring 630 ft by 480 ft *192 by 146 m* (6.94 acres *2,8 ha*) completed in 1967. The maintenance hangar at Frankfurt/Main Airport, West Germany has a slightly lesser area but a frontage of 902 ft *275 m.* The cable supported roof has a span of 130 m *426.5 ft.* Delta Air Lines' jet base on a 140 acre *56,6 ha* site at Hartsfield International Airport, Atlanta, Georgia, has 36 acres *14,5 ha* under roof.

Great Britain
The largest hangar building in the United Kingdom is the Britannia Assembly Hall at the former Bristol Aeroplane Company's works at Filton, Avon, now part of the British Aircraft Corporation. The overall width of the Hall is 1,054 ft *321 m* and the overall depth of the centre bay is 420 ft *128 m.* It encloses a floor area of 7½ acres *3,0 ha.* The cubic capacity of the Hall is 33,000,000 ft³ *934 000 m³.* The building was begun in April 1946 and completed by September 1949.

GRAIN ELEVATOR
Largest
The world's largest single-unit grain elevator is that operated by the C-G-F-Grain Company at Wichita, Kansas, U.S.A. Consisting of a triple row of storage tanks, 123 on each side of the central loading tower or "head house", the unit is

MAN MADE STRUCTURES

1. Warszawa Radio Mast—the tallest structure in the world 646,38 m *2,120 ft 8 in* (see p 118). 2. The C. N. Tower, Toronto—the tallest self-supporting tower 1,822 ft 1 in *553,3 m* (see p 120). 3. Sears Tower, Chicago—the tallest office building in the world 1,454 ft 443 m (see p 112). 4. The World Trade Centre, New York City—the largest office building in the world 1,350 ft *411,48 m* tall (see pp 111–112). 5. The Empire State Building—the tallest structure in the world (1930–1954) 1,427 ft *449 m* (see p 119). 6. The I.B.A. mast at Belmont, Yorkshire—the U.K's tallest structure at 1,272 ft *387,1 m* (see p 118). 7. The International Nickel Co's smoke stack at Sudbury, Ontario, the tallest in the world 1,245 ft 8 in *379,6 m* (see p. 112). 8. The Drax Power Station smoke stack—the tallest in the U.K., 850 ft *259 m* (see p. 112). 9. The 70 storey Lake Point Towers, Chicago—the tallest block of flats in the world, 645 ft *197 m* (see p 115). 10. The National Westminster Bank, City of London—the tallest office block in Great Britain, 600 ft 4 in *183 m* (see p. 112). 11. The Great Pyramid of Cheops at El Gizeh, Egypt—the tallest pyramid in the world, 480,9 ft *146,5 m* (see p 119). 12. Motherland, the tallest free-standing statue in the world measuring 270 ft *82,3 m* from base to tip of sword (see p 127). 13. The Ferris Wheel at the Midway, Chicago, Illinois—measuring 250 ft *76 m* in diameter (see p 117). 14. The Statue of Liberty on Liberty Island in the Upper Bay of New York Harbor, U.S.A.—standing 151 ft 1 in *46,05 m* from base to torch.

2,717 ft *828 m* long and 100 ft *30 m* wide. Each tank is 120 ft *37 m* high, with an inside diameter of 30 ft *9 m* giving a total storage capacity of 20,000,000 bushels *7,3 million hl* of wheat. The largest collection of elevators in the world are the 23 at City of Thunder Bay, Ontario, Canada, on Lake Superior with a total capacity of 103.9 million bushels *37,4 million hl*.

GARAGES
Largest *World*

The world's largest parking garage is at O'Hare Airport, Chicago with 6 levels and a capacity for 9,250 cars. It is operated by Allright Auto Parks Inc., the world's largest parking company.

Great Britain

Great Britain's highest capacity underground car park is that under the Victoria Centre, Nottingham with a capacity of 1,650 cars opened in June 1972.

Private

The largest private garage ever built was one for 100 cars at the Long Island, New York mansion of William Kissam Vanderbilt (1849–1920).

Parking lot

The largest parking lot in Great Britain is that for 15,000 cars and 200 coaches at the National Exhibition Centre, Birmingham (see page 112).

Filling station

The largest filling station of the 36,000 in the United Kingdom is the Esso service area on the M4 at Leigh Delamere, Wiltshire, opened on 3 Jan. 1972. It has 48 petrol and diesel pumps and extends over 43 acres *17,4 ha*. It cost £650,000, has a staff of 280 and can service two million vehicles a year.

SEWAGE WORKS
Largest *World*

The largest single full treatment sewage works in the world is the West-Southwest Treatment Plant, opened in 1940 on a site of 501 acres *203 ha* in Chicago, Illinois, U.S.A. It serves an area containing 2,940,000 people. It treated an average of 835,000,000 U.S. gal *3.16 million litres* of wastes per day in 1973. The capacity of its sedimentation and aeration tanks is 1 280 000 m^3 *1.6 million yds^3*.

Great Britain

The largest full treatment works in Britain and probably in Europe is the G.L.C. Beckton Works which serves a 2,966,000 population and handles a daily flow of 207 million gal *941 million litres* in a tank capacity of 757,000 ft^3 *21 400 m^3*.

GLASSHOUSE
Largest *Great Britain*

The largest glasshouse in the United Kingdom is one covering 7.34 acres *2,97 ha* owned by Van Heyningen Bros. at Holland Nurseries, Littlehampton, West Sussex.

WOODEN BUILDING
Largest

The world's largest buildings in timber are the two U.S. Navy airship hangers built in 1942–43 at Tillamook, Oregon. Now used by the Louisiana-Pacific Corporation as a saw mill they measure 1,000 ft long; 170 ft high at the crown and 296 ft wide at the base (*304,8 m × 51,81 m × 90,22 m*) and are worth $6 million (£13,150,000).

AIR SUPPORTED BUILDING
Largest

The world's largest air supported roof is the roof of the 80,600 capacity octagonal Pontiac Silverdome Stadium,

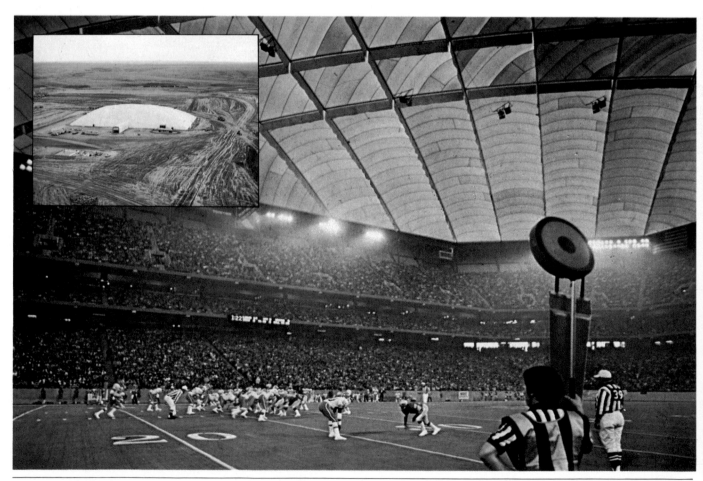

Measuring a total of 10 acres *4 ha*, the roof of the Pontiac Silverdome Stadium, Michigan, is the largest air-supported roof in the world, and inset at Lima, Ohio, U.S.A. is one of the largest standard size air-halls (see p. 115). (*Irvin Industries*)

Michigan, U.S.A. measuring 522 ft *159 m* in width and 722 ft *220 m* in length. The air pressure is 5 lb./in² *34,4 kPa* supporting the 10 acre *4 ha* translucent "Fiberglas" roofing. The structural engineers were Geiger-Berger Associates of New York City. The largest standard size air hall is one 860 ft *262 m* long, 140 ft *42,6 m* wide and 65 ft *19,8 m* high, at Lima, Ohio, U.S.A., made by Irvin Industries of Stamford, Connecticut, U.S.A.

2. BUILDINGS FOR LIVING

WOODEN BUILDINGS
Oldest
The oldest extant wooden buildings in the world are those comprising the Pagoda, Chumanar gate and the Temple of Horyu (Horyu-ji), at Nara, Japan, dating from A.D. 607. The nearby Daibutsuden, built in 1704–11, once measured 285.4 ft long, 167.3 ft wide and 153.3 ft tall *87 × 51 × 46,75 m*. The present dimensions are 187 × 165.6 × 159.7 ft *57 × 50,5 × 48,7 m*.

CASTLES
Earliest *World*
Fortifications existed in all the great early civilizations, including that of ancient Egypt from 3,000 B.C. Fortified castles in the more accepted sense only existed much later. The oldest in the world is that at Gomdan, in the Yemen, which originally had 20 storeys and dates from before A.D. 100.

Great Britain
The oldest stone castle extant in Great Britain is Richmond Castle, Yorkshire, built in *c.* 1075. Iron Age relics from the first century B.C. or A.D. have been found in the lower levels of the Dover Castle site.

Ireland
The oldest Irish castle is Ferrycarrig near Wexford dating from *c.* 1180. The oldest castle in Northern Ireland is Carrickfergus Castle, County Antrim, Northern Ireland, which dates from before 1210.

Largest *United Kingdom and Ireland*
The largest inhabited castle in the world is the Royal residence of Windsor Castle at New Windsor, Berkshire. It is primarily of 12th century construction and is in the form of a waisted parallelogram 1,890 ft by 540 ft *576 by 164 m*. The total area of Dover Castle however covers 34 acres *13,75 ha* with a width of 1,100 ft *335,2 m* and a curtain wall of 1,800 ft *550 m* or if underground works are taken in, 2,300 ft *700 m*. The overall dimensions of Carisbrooke Castle (450 ft by 360 ft *110 by 137 m*), Isle of Wight, if its earthworks are included, are 1,350 ft by 825 ft *411 m by 251 m*. The largest castle in Scotland is Edinburgh Castle with a major axis of 1,320 ft *402 m* and measuring 3,360 ft *1 025 m* along its perimeter wall including the Esplanade. The most capacious of all Irish castles is Carrickfergus (see above) but that with the most extensive fortifications is Trim Castle, County Meath, built in *c.* 1205 with a curtain wall 1,455 ft *443 m* long.

Forts *Largest*
The largest ancient castle in the world is Prague Castle, Czechoslovakia originating in the 9th century. It is a very oblong irregular polygon with an axis of 570 m *1,870 ft* and an average traverse diameter of 128 m *420 ft* with a surface area of 7,28 hectares *18 acres*. Fort George, Ardersier, Highland built in 1748–1769 measures 2,100 ft *640 m* in length and has an average width of 620 ft *189 m*. The total site covers 42½ acres *17,2 ha*.

Thickest walls
The walls of Babylon north of Al Hillah, Iraq, built in 600 B.C., were up to 85 ft *26 m* in thickness. The walls of the Great Tower or Donjon of Flint Castle, built in 1277–80 are 23 ft *7,01 m* thick. The largest Norman keep in Britain is that of Colchester Castle measuring 152½ ft *46 m* by 111½ ft *34 m*.

PALACES
Largest *World*
The largest palace in the world is the Imperial Palace (*Gu*

gong) in the centre of Peking (*Bei jing*, the northern capital), China, which covers a rectangle 1,050 yds by 820 yds *960 by 750 m* an area of 177.9 acres *72 ha*. The outline survives from the construction of the third Ming Emperor, Yung lo of 1402–24, but due to constant re-arrangements most of the intra-mural buildings are 18th century. These consist of 5 halls and 17 palaces of which the last occupied by the last Empress was the Palace of Accumulated Elegance (*Chu xia gong*) until 1924.

Residential
The largest residential palace in the world is the Vatican Palace, in the Vatican City, an enclave in Rome, Italy. Covering an area of 13½ acres *5,5 ha* it has 1,400 rooms, chapels and halls, of which the oldest date from the 15th century.

Great Britain
The largest palace in the United Kingdom in Royal use is Buckingham Palace, London, so named after its site, bought in 1703 by John Sheffield, the 1st Duke of Buckingham and Normandy (1648–1721). Buckingham House was reconstructed in the Palladian style between 1835 and 1836, following the design of John Nash (1752–1835). The 610 ft *186 m* long East Front was built in 1846 and refaced in 1912. The Palace, which stands in 39 acres *15,8 ha* of garden, has 600 rooms including a ballroom 111 ft *34 m* long.

The largest ever Royal palace has been Hampton Court Palace, Greater London, acquired by Henry VIII from Cardinal Wolsey in 1525 and greatly enlarged by the King and later by William III, Anne and George I, whose son George II was its last resident monarch. It covers 4 acres *1,6 ha* of a 669 acre *270,7 ha* site.

Largest moat
The world's largest moats are those which surround the Imperial Palace in Peking (see above). From plans drawn by French sources it appears to measure 54 yds *49 m* wide and have a total length of 3,600 yds *3 290 m*. The city's moats total in all 23½ miles *38 km*.

FLATS
Largest
The largest block of private flats in Britain is Dolphin Square, London, covering a site of 7½ acres *3 ha*. The building occupies the four sides of a square enclosing gardens of about three acres *1,2 ha*. Dolphin Square contains 1,220 separate and self-contained flats, an underground garage for 300 cars with filling and service station, a swimming pool, eight squash courts, a tennis court and an indoor shopping centre. It cost £1,750,000 to build in 1936 but was sold to Westminster City Council for £4,500,000 in January 1963. Its nine storeys house 3,000 people.

The Hyde Park development in Sheffield, South Yorkshire, comprises 1,322 dwellings and an estimated population of 4,675 persons. It was built between 1959 and 1966.

Tallest *World*
The tallest block of flats in the world are Lake Point Towers of 70 storeys, and 645 ft *197 m* in Chicago, Illinois, U.S.A.

Great Britain
The tallest residential block in Great Britain is the Shakespeare Tower in the Barbican in the City of London, which has 116 flats and rises to a height of 419 ft 2½ in *127,77 m* above the street. The first of the three towers was "topped out" in May 1971.

HOTELS
Largest *World*
The hotel with most rooms in the world is the 12 storey Hotel Rossiya in Moscow, U.S.S.R., with 3,200 rooms providing accommodation for 5,350 guests opened in 1967. It would thus require more than 8½ years to spend one night in each room. In addition there is a 21 storey "Presidential" tower in the central courtyard. The hotel employs about 3,000 people, and has 93 lifts. The ballroom is reputed to be the world's largest. Muscovites are not permitted as residents

while foreigners are charged 16 times more than the very low rate charged to U.S.S.R. officials.

The largest commercial hotel building in the world, is The Waldorf Astoria, on Park Avenue, New York City, N.Y., U.S.A. It occupies a complete block of 81,337 ft² (1.87 acres *0,75 ha*) and reaches a maximum height of 625 ft 7 in *191 m*. The Waldorf Astoria has 47 storeys and 1,852 guests' rooms and maintains the largest hotel radio receiving system in the world. The Waldorf can accommodate 10,000 people at one time and has a staff of 1,700. The restaurants have catered for parties up to 6,000 at a time. The coffee-maker's daily output reaches 1,000 U.S. gal *3 785 litres*. The electricity bill is $2,000,000 each year. The hotel has housed 6 Heads of States simultaneously. It was opened on 1 Oct. 1931.

Great Britain
The greatest sleeping capacity of any hotel in Great Britain is 1,859 in the London Penta Hotel, Cromwell Road, London S.W.7 with a staff of 419. It was opened in 1973. The Regent Palace Hotel, Piccadilly Circus, London, opened 20 May 1915, has however 225 more rooms totalling 1,140. The largest hotel is the Grosvenor House Hotel, Park Lane, London, which was opened in 1929. It is of 8 storeys covering 2½ acres *1 ha* and caters for more than 100,000 visitors per year in 470 rooms. The Great Room is the largest hotel room measuring 181 ft by 131 ft *55 by 40 m* with a height of 23 ft *7 m*. Banquets for 1,500 are frequently handled.

Tallest
The tallest hotel in the world, measured from the street level of its main entrance to the top, is the 723 ft *220,3 m* tall 70 storey Peachtree Center Plaza, Atlanta, Georgia, U.S.A. The $50 million, 1,100 room hotel is operated by Western International Hotels and owned by Portman Properties. Their Detroit Plaza measuring from the rear entrance level is however 748 ft *227,9 m* tall. Britain's tallest hotel is the 27 storey 380 ft *132,24 m* tall London Penta Hotel (see above).

Most expensive
The world's costliest hotel accommodation is The Celestial Suite on the ninth floor of the Astroworld Hotel Houston, Texas which is rented for $2,500 (*now £1,250*) a day. This compares with the official New York City Presidential Suite in The Waldorf Astoria at $1,200 (*now £600*) a day.

The most expensive hotel suite in Britain is the Royal Suite on the 8th floor of the Hotel Inter-Continental, London W.1., with 3 bedrooms at £442.28 (incl. V.A.T.).

Spas
The largest spa in the world measured by number of available hotel rooms is Vichy, Allier, France, with 14,000 rooms. Spas are named after the watering place in the Liège province of Belgium where hydropathy was developed from 1626. The highest French spa is Baréges, Hautes-Pyrénées, at 4,068 ft *1 240 m* above sea level.

HOUSING
Largest estate
The largest housing estate in the United Kingdom is the 1,670-acre *675 ha* Becontree Estate, on a site of 3,000 acres *1 214 ha* in Barking and Redbridge, Greater London, built between 1921 and 1929. The total number of homes is 26,822, with an estimated population of nearly 90,000.

New towns
Of the 23 new towns being built in Great Britain that with the largest eventual planned population is Milton Keynes, Buckinghamshire, with 250,000 planned for 1992.

Largest house *World*
The largest private house in the world is the 250-room Biltmore House in Asheville, North Carolina, U.S.A. It is owned by George and William Cecil, grandsons of George Washington Vanderbilt II (1862–1914). The house was built between 1890 and 1895 in an estate of 119,000 acres *48 160 ha*, at a cost of $4,100,000 (now (£1,708,333) and now valued at $55,000,000 with 12,000 acres *4 856 ha*. The most expensive private house ever built is The Hearst Ranch at

San Simeon, California, U.S.A. It was built in 1922–39 for William Randolph Hearst (1863–1951), at a total cost of more than $30,000,000 (*then £6,120,000*). It has more than 100 rooms, a 104 ft *32 m* long heated swimming pool, an 83 ft *25 m* long assembly hall and a garage for 25 limousines. The house required 60 servants to maintain it.

Great Britain
The largest house in Great Britain was Wentworth Woodhouse, near Rotherham, South Yorkshire, formerly the seat of the Earls Fitzwilliam and now a teachers' training college. The main part of the house, built over 300 years ago, has more than 240 rooms with over 1,000 windows, and its principle façade is 600 ft *183 m* long. The Royal residence, Sandringham House, Norfolk, has been reported to have had 365 rooms before the demolition of 73 surplus rooms in 1975. The largest house in Ireland is Castletown in County Kildare, owned by the Hon. Desmond Guinness and is the headquarters of the Irish Georgian Society. Scotland's largest house is Hopetoun House, West Lothian, built between 1696 and 1756 with a west façade 675 ft *206 m* long.

Smallest
The smallest house in Britain is the 19th century fisherman's cottage on Conway Quay, Gwynedd. It has a 72 in *182 cm* frontage, is 122 in *309 cm* high and has two tiny rooms and a staircase.

Most expensive *House*
The highest asking price for a private furnished house has been £3,800,000 by Mr. Ravi Tikkoo, for Kenstead Hall, The Bishop's Avenue, Hampstead, London. The buyer by private treaty on 6 Apr. 1977 was Crown Prince Fahd of Saudi Arabia. The adjacent £500,000 Risinghurst was bought for servants and the total cost of extensions and renovations had passed £8 million by Nov. 1978.

Penthouse
The world's most expensive penthouse is the four storey Galleria International penthouse on 57th Street between Park and Lexington Avenue, Manhattan, New York City with 4 main bedrooms, a 22 ft swimming pool, a library, a sauna and several solariums. It was on the market in March 1976 for £1,750,000.

Stately home most visited
The most visited stately home, for which precise figures are published in the United Kingdom, is Beaulieu, Hampshire, owned by Lord Montagu of Beaulieu with 636,000 (1978/79) visitors. The figures for Woburn Abbey, Bedfordshire, owned by the Duke of Bedford, have not been published since 1963 but the annual attendance including that of the Woburn Wild Animal Kingdom exceeds 1,000,000.

Barracks
The oldest purpose built barracks in the world are believed to be Collins Barracks, formerly the Royal Barracks, Dublin Ireland completed in 1704 and still in use.

---

3. BUILDINGS FOR ENTERTAINMENT

STADIUM
Largest *World*
The world's largest stadium is the Strahov Stadium in Praha (Prague), Czechoslovakia. It was completed in 1934 and can accommodate 240,000 spectators for mass displays of up to 40,000 Sokol gymnasts.

Football
The largest football stadium in the world is the Maracaña Municipal Stadium in Rio de Janeiro, Brazil, where the football ground has a normal capacity of 205,000, of whom 155,000 may be seated. A crowd of 199,854 was accommodated for the World Cup final between Brazil and Uruguay on 16 July 1950. A dry moat, 7 ft *2,13 m* wide and more than 5 ft *1,5 m* deep, protects players from spectators and *vice versa*. Britain's most capacious football stadium is Hampden Park, Glasgow opened on 31 Oct. 1903 and once surveyed to

accommodate 184,000 compared with an attendance of 149,547 on 17 Apr. 1937 and the present licensed limit of 135,000.

Covered

The Azteca Stadium, Mexico City, Mexico, opened in 1968, has a capacity of 107,000 of whom nearly all are under cover. The largest covered stadium in Britain is the Empire Stadium Wembley, Brent, Greater London, opened in April 1923. It was the scene of the 1948 Olympic Games and the final of the 1966 World Cup. In 1962–63 the capacity under cover was increased to 100,000 of whom 45,000 may be seated. The original cost was £1,250,000.

Largest Roof

The transparent acryl glass "tent" roof over the Munich Olympic Stadium, West Germany measures 914,940 ft² *(21.0 acres 8,5 ha)* in area resting on a steel net supported by masts. The roof of longest span in the world is the 680 ft *207,2 m* diameter of the Louisiana Superdome (see below). The major axis of the elliptical Texas Stadium completed in 1971 at Irving, Texas is however 240 m *787 ft 4 in.*

Indoor

The world's largest indoor stadium is the 13 acre *5,26 ha* $173 million *(then £75 million)* 273 ft *83,2 m* tall Superdome in New Orleans, Louisiana completed in May 1975. Its maximum seating capacity for conventions is 97,365 or 76,791 for football. Box suites rent for $35,000 excluding the price of admission. A gondola with six 312 inch *7,92 m* T.V. screens produces instant replay.

Largest ballroom

The largest ballroom in the United Kingdom is Tiffany's, Purley, Croydon, Greater London. The room is over 200 ft *60 m* long and 117 ft *35,7 m* wide, and has a total floor area of 23,320 ft² *2 170 m²*. When laid out for dance championships, the floor of the Earl's Court Exhibition Hall, Kensington, London is 256 ft *78 m* in length

Amusement resort

The world's largest amusement resort is Disney World in 27,443 acres *11 105 ha* of Orange and Osceola counties, 20 miles *32 km* south of west of Orlando in central Florida. It was opened on 1 Oct. 1971. This $400 million investment attracted 10,700,000 visitors in its first year. The most attended resort in the world is Disneyland, Anaheim, California where the total number of visitors reached 175,638,309 by 1 Oct. 1978.

Holiday Camps

The largest holiday camp in Britain is that at Filey, North Yorkshire owned by Butlins Ltd. It extends over 500 acres *200 ha* and can house 10,600 residents.

Largest Pleasure Beach

The largest pleasure beach in the world is Virginia Beach, Virginia, U.S.A. It has 28 miles *45 km* of beach front on the Atlantic and 10 miles *16 km* of estuary frontage. The area embraces 255 miles² *660 km²* and 134 hotels and motels.

Longest pleasure pier

The longest pleasure pier in the world is Southend Pier at Southend-on-Sea in Essex. It is 1.34 miles *2,15 km* in length. It was first opened in August 1889 with final extensions made in 1929. In 1949–50 the pier railway carried 5,750,000 passengers.

Earliest Fair

The earliest major international fair was the Great Exhibition of 1851 in the Crystal Palace, Hyde Park, City of Westminster, Greater London which in 141 days attracted 6,039,195 admissions.

Largest Fair

The largest ever International Fair site was that for the St. Louis, Missouri Louisiana Purchase Exposition which covered 1,271,76 acres *514,66 ha*. It also staged the 1904 Olympic Games and drew an attendance of 19,694,855.

Record Fair attendance

The record attendance for any fair was 64,218,770 for Expo 70 held on an 815 acre *330 ha* site at Osaka, Japan from March to 13 Sept. 1970. It made a profit of 19,439,402,017 yen *(£22.6 million)*.

Big Wheel

The original Ferris Wheel, named after its constructor, George W. Ferris (1859–96), was erected in 1893 at the Midway, Chicago, Illinois, at a cost of $385,000 *(then £79,218)* It was 250 ft *76 m* in diameter, 790 ft *240 m* in circumference, weighed 1,070 tons *1 087 tonnes* and carried 36 cars each seating 60 people, making a total of 2,160 passengers. The structure was removed in 1904 to St. Louis, Missouri, and was eventually sold as scrap for $1,800 *(then £370)*. In 1897 a Ferris Wheel with a diameter of 300 ft *91 m* was erected for the Earl's Court Exhibition, London. It had ten 1st-class and 30 2nd-class cars. The largest wheel now operating is the Riesenrad in the Prater Park, Vienna, Austria with a diameter of 197 ft *60 m*. It was built by the British engineer Walter Basset in 1896 and carried 15 million people in its first 75 years to 13 June 1971.

Fastest switchback

The maximum speeds claimed for switchbacks, scenic railways or roller coasters have in the past been exaggerated for commercial reasons. The highest point on any circuit is of 125 ft *38,1 m* on the Magic Mountain Colossus at Valencia, California whose record 115 ft *35 m* drop produces velocities of 56 m.p.h. *90 km/h*. The dual track racing system extends over 4,631 ft *1 411 m* and was opened in May 1978. The top of the *schuss* on "The Tidal Wave" in Santa Clara, California opened on 8 July 1977 is 140 ft *42,6 m* high. The Fujikyu Highland Amusement Park Giant Coaster track is 1432 m *1,566 yds* long.

Longest Slide

The longest slide in the world is at Bad Tölz, West Germany. This has a length of 1 226 m *0.76 mile* and a vertical drop of 220 m *721 ft*.

Restaurant *Highest*

The highest restaurant in the world is at the Chacaltaya ski resort, Bolivia at 5 340 m *17,519 ft*. The highest in Great Britain is the Ptarmigan Observation Restaurant at 3,650 ft *1 112 m* above sea-level on Cairngorm (4,084 ft *1 244 m*) near Aviemore, Highland, Scotland.

Night Club *Oldest*

The earliest night club *(boite de nuit)* was "Le Bal des Anglais" at 6 Rue des Anglais, Paris, 5e France. It was founded in 1843 but closed *c.* 1960.

Largest

The largest night club in the world is Gilley's Club (formerly Shelly's) built in 1955 and extended in 1971 on Spencer Highway, Houston, Texas, U.S.A. with a seating capacity of more than 3,000 and a total capacity of 5,500. In the more classical sense the largest night club in the world is "The Mikado" in the Akasaka district of Tōkyō, Japan, with a seating capacity of 2,000. It is "manned" by 1,250 hostesses. A binocular is essential to an appreciation of the floor show.

Lowest

The lowest night club is the "Minus 206" in Tiberias, Israel on the shores of the Sea of Galilee. It is 206 m *676 ft* below sea-level. An alternative candidate is "Outer Limits", opposite the Cow Palace, San Francisco, California which was raided for the 151st time on 1 Aug. 1971. It has been called "The Most Busted Joint" and "The Slowest to Get the Message".

PUBLIC HOUSES
Oldest

There are various claimants to the title of the United Kingdom's oldest inn. A foremost claimant is "The Fighting Cocks", St. Albans, Hertfordshire (an 11th century structure on an 8th century site). The timber frame of The Royalist

117

Hotel, Digbeth Street, Stow-on-the-Wold, Gloucestershire has been dated to 1,000 years before the present. It was the inn "The Eagle and the Child" in the 13th century and known to exist in A.D. 947. An origin as early as A.D. 560 has been claimed for "Ye Olde Ferry Boat Inn" at Holywell, Cambridgeshire. There is some evidence that it antedates the local church, built in 980, but the earliest documents are not dated earlier than 1100. There is evidence that the "Bingley Arms", Bardsey, near Leeds, West Yorkshire, restored and extended in 1738 existed as the "Priest's Inn" according to Bardsey Church records dated 905.

The oldest pub in Ireland is "The Brazen Head", Bridge Street, Dublin licensed in 1666 and re-built in 1668. The fact that this former den of iniquity does not sell Draught Guinness is evidence of its antiquity.

Largest *World*

The largest beer-selling establishment in the world is the Mathäser, Bayerstrasse 5, München (Munich), West Germany, where the daily sale reaches 84,470 pts *48 000 litres*. It was established in 1829, was demolished in World War II and re-built by 1955 and now seats 5,500 people. The through-put at the Dube beer halls in the Bantu township of Soweto, Johannesburg, South Africa may, however, be higher on some Saturdays when the average consumption of 6,000 gal (48,000 pts *27 280 litres*) is far exceeded.

Great Britain

The largest public house in Great Britain is "The Swan" at Yardley, West Midlands. It has eight bars with a total drinking area of 13,852 ft² *1 287 m²* with 58 taps and 2 miles *3,2 km* of piping. The sale of beer is equivalent to 31,000 bottles per week. The pub can hold well over 1,000 customers and 320 for banqueting. The permanent staff totals 60 with seven resident. "The Swan" is owned by Allied Breweries and administered by Ansells Limited.

Smallest

The smallest pub in Great Britain is the 17th century "The Nutshell", Bury St. Edmunds, Suffolk with maximum dimensions of 15 ft 10 in by 7 ft 6 in *4,82 × 2,28 m*.

Longest bars *World*

The longest permanent bar with beer pumps is that built in 1938 at the Working Men's Club, Mildura, Victoria, Australia. It has a counter 298 ft *90,8 m* in length, served by 27 pumps. Temporary bars have been erected of greater length. The Falstaff Brewing Corp. put up a temporary bar 336 ft 5 in *102 m* in length on Wharf St., St. Louis, Missouri, U.S.A., on 22 June 1970. The Bar at Erickson's on Burnside Street, Portland, Oregon, in its heyday (1883–1920) possessed a Bar which ran continuously around and across the main saloon measuring 684 feet *208,48 m*. The chief bouncer Edward "Spider" Johnson had a chief assistant named "Jumbo" Reilly who weighed 23 stone and was said to resemble "an ill natured orang-utan". Beer was 5 cents for 16 fluid ounces.

United Kingdom and Ireland

The longest bars in the United Kingdom with beer pumps are the Theatre Bar, The Gaiety Bar and the Princes Bar, at Butlin's Holiday Camp, Filey, North Yorkshire, each measuring 80 ft *24,38 m* in length and each having 40 dispensers (beer & lager). The longest bar in a pub is of 71 ft 11 in *21,92 m* with 29 dispensers in "The Mount Pleasant Inn, Repton, Derbyshire. The Grand Stand Bar at Galway Racecourse, Ireland completed in 1955, measures 210 ft *64 m*.

Longest name

The pub with the longest name is the 39 letter "The Thirteenth Mounted Cheshire Rifleman Inn", at Stalybridge, Greater Manchester, but "The Green Man and Black's Head Royal Hotel" at Ashbourne, Derbyshire has more words.

Longest tenure

There are no collated records on licensees but the "Glan-y-Afon Inn", Milwr near Holywell, North Wales had a 418 year

long (1559–1977) run within a family which ended with the retirement of Mrs. Mary Evans.

Shortest name

Public houses in the United Kingdom with a name of only two letters include the "C.B." Hotel Arkengarthdale, near Richmond, North Yorkshire, The "H.H." at Cheriton, Hampshire, the "Ox" in Lebberston, near Filey, North Yorkshire and the "XL" at Garstang, Lancashire.

Commonest name

The commonest pub name in Britain is "Red Lion" of which there are probably just more than 1,000. John A. Blackwell of Ferndown, Dorset has recorded over 4,600 different pub names.

Highest

The highest public house in the United Kingdom is the "Tan Hill Inn" in North Yorkshire. It is 1,732 ft *528 m* above sea-level, on the moorland road between Reeth, North Yorkshire and Brough, Cumbria. The highest pub open the year round is the "Cat and Fiddle" in Cheshire, near Buxton, Derbyshire at 1,690 ft *515 m*. The White Lady Restaurant, 2,550 ft *777 m* up on Cairngorm (4,084 ft *1 244 m*) near Aviemore, Highland, Scotland is the highest licensed restaurant.

Most Visits

Stanley House of Totterdown, Bristol has visited 3,137 differently named pubs in Britain by way of public transport only to 1 May 1979.

Beer Garden *Largest*

The world's largest beer garden is the Augustiner Biergarten in Munich, West Germany founded in 1901 with space for 5,200 people. It has sold as much as 100 hectolitres *17,600 pints* in a single day.

---

4. TOWERS AND MASTS

TALLEST STRUCTURES

World

The tallest structure in the world is the guyed Warszawa Radio mast at Konstantynow near Gabin and Płock 60 miles *96 km* north-west of the capital of Poland. It is 646,38 m *2,120 ft 8 in* tall or more than four tenths of a mile. The mast was completed on 18 July 1974 and put into operation on 22 July 1974. It was designed by Jan Polak and weighs 550 tons/ *tonnes*. The mast is so high that anyone falling off the top would reach their terminal velocity and hence cease to be accelerating before hitting the ground. Work was begun in July 1970 on this tubular steel construction, with its 15 steel guy ropes. It recaptured for Europe a record held in the U.S.A. since the Chrysler Building surpassed the Eiffel Tower in 1929.

Great Britain

The tallest structure in the United Kingdom is the Independent Broadcasting Authority's mast at Belmont, north of Horncastle, Lincolnshire completed in 1965 to a height of 1,265 ft *385 m* with 7 ft *2,13 m* added by meteorological equipment installed in September 1967. It serves Yorkshire T.V. and weighs 210 tons.

PROGRESSIVE LIST OF HIGHEST STRUCTURES IN GREAT BRITAIN

Feet	Metres		
404	*123*	Salisbury Cathedral Spire	c.1305–
525	*160*	Lincoln Cathedral	1307–1548
489	*149*	St. Paul's Cathedral, London	1315–1561
518.7	*158,1*	Blackpool Tower, Lancashire	1894–
562	*171,29*	New Brighton Tower, Merseyside	1900–1919
820	*250*	G.P.O. Radio Masts, Rugby	1925–
1,000*	*304,8*	I.T.A. Mast, Mendlesham, Suffolk	July 1959
1,265	*385*	I.B.A. Mast, Emley Moor, Yorkshire	1965–
1,265	*385*	I.B.A. Mast, Belmont	1965–
1,272	*387,1*	I.B.A. Mast, Belmont	Sept. 1967

*I.T.A. masts of the same height followed at Lichfield, Staffordshire; Black Hill, Strathclyde; Caldbeck, Cumbria; and Durris, Grampian.

top left: ''The Fighting Cocks'' at St. Albans, Herts, the 11th century inn, one of the claimants to the title of the oldest public house (see p. 117). (*David Roberts*)
below left: The Azteca Stadium in Mexico City, which has the highest covered seating capacity of any stadium in the world (see p. 117). (*Gerry Paknadel*) *right:*
Reaching a height of 723 ft *220,3 m*, the 70 storey Peachtree Center Plaza Hotel in Atlanta, Georgia, U.S.A.—the tallest hotel in the world (see p. 116).

A PROGRESSIVE RECORD OF THE WORLD'S TALLEST STRUCTURES

Height in ft	m	Structure	Location	Material	Building or Completion Dates
204	62	Djoser step pyramid (earliest Pyramid)	Saqqâra, Egypt	Tura limestone casing	c. 2650 B.C
294	89	Pyramid of Meidum	Meidum, Egypt	Tura limestone casing	c. 2600 B.C.
c. 336	102	Snefru Bent pyramid	Dahshûr, Egypt	Tura limestone casing	c. 2600 B.C.
342	104	Snefru North Stone pyramid	Dahshûr, Egypt	Tura limestone casing	c. 2600 B.C.
480.9[1]	146,5	Great Pyramid of Cheops (Khufu)	El Gizeh, Egypt	Tura limestone casing	c. 2580 B.C.
525[2]	160	Lincoln Cathedral, Central Tower	Lincoln, England	lead sheathed wood	c. 1307–1548
489[3]	149	St. Paul's Cathedral spire	City of London, England	lead sheathed wood	1315–1561
465	141	Minster of Notre Dame	Strasbourg, France	Vosges sandstone	1420–1439
502[4]	153	St. Pierre de Beauvais spire	Beauvais, France	lead sheathed wood	–1568
475	144	St. Nicholas Church	Hamburg, Germany	stone and iron	1846–1847
485	147	Rouen Cathedral spire	Rouen, France	cast iron	1823–1876
513	156	Köln Cathedral spires	Cologne, West Germany	stone	–1880
555[5]	169	Washington Memorial	Washington, D.C., U.S.A.	stone	1848–1884
985.9[6]	300,5	Eiffel Tower	Paris, France	iron	1887–1889
1,046	318	Chrysler Building	New York City, U.S.A.	steel and concrete	1929–1930
1,250[7]	381	Empire State Building	New York City, U.S.A.	steel and concrete	1929–1930
1,572	479	KWTV Television Mast	Oklahoma City, U.S.A.	steel	Nov. 1954
1,610[8]	490	KSWS Television Mast	Roswell, New Mexico, U.S.A	steel	Dec. 1956
1,619	493	WGAN Television Mast	Portland, Maine, U.S.A.	steel	Sept. 1959
1,676	510	KFVS Television Mast	Cape Girardeau, Missouri, U.S.A.	steel	June 1960
1,749	533	WTVM & WRBL Television Mast	Columbus, Georgia, U.S.A.	steel	May 1962
1,749	533	WBIR-TV Mast	Knoxville, Tennessee, U.S.A.	steel	Sept. 1963
2,063	628	KTHI-TV Mast	Fargo, North Dakota, U.S.A.	steel	Nov. 1963
2,120.6	646,38	Warszawa Radio Mast	Plock, Poland	galvanised steel	22 July 1974

[1] Original height. With loss of pyramidion (topmost stone) height now 449 ft 6 in 137 m.
[2] Fell in a storm.
[3] Struck by lightning and destroyed 4 June 1561.
[4] Fell April 1573, shortly after completion.
[5] Sinking at a rate of 0.0047 ft per annum or 5 in 12,7 cm since 1884.

[6] Original height. With addition of T.V. antenna in 1957, now 1,052 ft in 320,75 m.
[7] Original height. With addition of T.V. tower on 1 May 1951 now 1,427 ft 449 m. On 11 Oct. 1972 it was revealed that the top 15 storeys might be replaced by 33 to give the old champion 113 storeys and a height of 1,494 ft 455,37 m.
[8] Fell in gale in 1960.

TALLEST TOWERS
World
The tallest self-supporting tower (as opposed to a guyed mast) in the world is the $44 million CN Tower in Metro Centre, Toronto, Canada, which rises to 1,822 ft 1 in *555,33 m*. Excavation began on 12 Feb. 1973 for the 130,000 ton structure of reinforced, post-tensioned concrete topped out on 2 Apr. 1975. The 416-seat restaurant revolves in the Sky Pod at 1,140 ft *347,5 m* from which the visibility extends to hills 74½ miles *120 km* distant. Lightning strikes the top about 200 times (30 storms) per annum.

The tallest tower built before the era of television masts is the Eiffel Tower, in Paris, France, designed by Alexandre Gustav Eiffel (1832–1923) for the Paris exhibition and completed on 31 March 1889. It was 300,51 m *985 ft 11 in* tall, now extended by a T.V. antenna to 320,75 m *1,052 ft 4 in* and weighs 7 340 tonnes *7,224 tons*. The maximum sway in high winds is 12,7 cm *5 in*. The whole iron edifice which has 1,792 steps, took 2 years, 2 months and 2 days to build and cost 7,799,401 francs 31 centimes.

Great Britain
The tallest self-supported tower in Great Britain is the 1,080 ft *329,18 m* tall Independent Broadcasting Authority transmitter at Emley Moor, West Yorkshire, completed in September 1971. The structure, which cost £900,000, has an enclosed room at the 865 ft *263,65 m* level and weighs with its foundations more than 15,000 tons/*tonnes*. The tallest tower of the pre-television era was the New Brighton Tower of 562 ft *171,29 m* built on Merseyside in 1897–1900 and dismantled in 1919–1921.

5. BRIDGES

Oldest *World*
Arch construction was understood by the Sumerians as early as 3200 B.C. and a reference exists to a Nile bridge in 2650 B.C. The oldest surviving dateable bridge in the world is the slab stone single arch bridge over the River Meles in Smyrna (now Izmir), Turkey, which dates from *c.* 850 B.C.

Great Britain
The clapper bridges of Dartmoor and Exmoor (*e.g.* the Tarr Steps over the River Barle, Exmoor, Somerset) are thought to be of prehistoric types although none of the existing examples can be certainly dated. They are made of large slabs of stone placed over boulders. The Romans built stone bridges in England and remains of these have been found at Corbridge (Roman, Corstopitum), Northumberland dating to the 2nd century A.D.; Chester, Northumberland and Willowford, Cumbria. Remains of a very early wooden bridge, have been found at Ardwinkle, Northamptonshire.

LONGEST
Cable suspension *World*
The world's longest bridge span is the main span of the £67 million Humber Estuary Bridge, England at 4,626 ft *1 410 m* due for opening in June 1980. Work began on 27 July 1972. The towers are 162,5 m *533 ft 1⅛ in* tall from datum and are 1⅜ in *36 mm* out of parallel, to allow for the curvature of the Earth. Including the Hessle and the Barton side spans, the bridge stretches 2 220 m or 1.37 miles.

The Mackinac Straits Bridge between Mackinaw City and St. Ignace, Michigan, U.S.A., is the longest suspension bridge in the world measured between anchorages (1.58 miles *2 543 m*) and has an overall length, including viaducts of the bridge proper measured between abutment bearings, of 3.63 miles *5 853,79 m*. It was opened in November 1957 (dedicated 28 June 1958) at a cost of $100 million (*then £35,700,000*) and has a main span of 3,800 ft *1 158 m*.

The double-deck road-rail Akashi-Kaikyo bridge linking Honshū and Shikoku, Japan is planned to be completed in 1988. The main span will be 5,840 ft *1 780 m* in length with an overall suspended length with side spans totalling 11,680 ft *3 560 m*. Work began in Oct. 1978 and the eventual cost is expected to exceed 1 trillion (10^{12}) yen.

Work is expected to start on the Messina Bridge linking Sicily with the Italian mainland in 1980. The towers would be 1,000 ft *304,8 m* high at the span exceeding *1 850 m 6070 ft*. The total cost has been estimated at close to £2,000 million.

Cantilever *World*
The Quebec Bridge (Pont de Québec) over the St. Lawrence River in Canada has the longest cantilever truss span of any in the world—1,800 ft *549 m* between the piers and 3,239 ft *987 m* overall. It carries a railway track and 2 carriageways. Begun in 1899, it was finally opened to traffic on 3 Dec. 1917 at a cost of 87 lives, and $Can.22,500,000 (*then £4,623,000*).

Great Britain
The longest cantilever bridge in Great Britain is the Forth Bridge. Its two main spans are 1,710 ft *521 m* long. It carries a double railway track over the Firth of Forth 156 ft *47,5 m* above the water level. Work commenced in November 1882 and the first test trains crossed on 22 Jan. 1890 after an expenditure of £3 million. It was officially opened on 4 March 1890. Of the 4,500 workers who built it, 57 were killed in various accidents.

Steel arch *World*
The longest steel arch bridge in the world is the New River Gorge bridge, near Fayetteville, West Virginia, U.S.A., completed in 1977 with a span of 1,700 ft *518,2 m*.

Great Britain
The longest steel arch bridge in Great Britain is the Runcorn-Widnes bridge, Cheshire opened on 21 July 1961. It has a span of 1,082 ft *329,8 m*.

Floating bridge
The longest floating bridge in the world is the Second Lake Washington Bridge, Seattle, Washington State, U.S.A. Its total length is 12,596 ft *3 839 m* and its floating section measures 7,518 ft *2 291 m* (1.42 miles *2,29 km*). It was built at a total cost of $15,000,000 (*then £5,357,000*) and completed in August 1963.

Covered bridge
The longest covered bridge in the world is that at Hartland, New Brunswick, Canada measuring 1,282 ft *390,8 m* overall completed in 1899.

Railway bridge
The longest railway bridge in the world is the Huey P. Long Bridge, Metairie, Louisiana, U.S.A. with a railway section 22,996 ft *7 009 m* (4.35 miles *7 km*) long. It was completed on 16 Dec. 1935 with a longest span of 790 ft *241 m*. The Yangtse River Bridge, completed in 1968 in Nanking, China is the world's longest combined highway and railway bridge. The rail deck is 6 772 m *4.20 miles* and the road deck is 4 589 m *2.85 miles*.

Great Britain
The longest railway bridge in Britain is the second Tay Bridge (11,653 ft *3 552 m*), Tayside, Scotland opened on 20 June 1887. Of the 85 spans, 74 (length 10,289 ft *3 136 m*) are over the waterway. The 878 brick arches of the London Bridge to Deptford Creek viaduct built in 1836 extend for 3¾ miles *6,0 km*.

Longest bridging
The world's longest bridging is the Second Lake Pontchartrain Causeway, completed on 23 March 1969, joining Lewisburg and Metairie, Louisiana, U.S.A. It has a length of 126,055 ft *38 422 m* (23.87 miles). It cost $29,900,000 (*then £12.45 million*) and is 228 ft *69 m* longer than the adjoining First Causeway completed in 1956. The longest railway viaduct in the world is the rock-filled Great Salt Lake Railroad Trestle, carrying the Southern Pacific Railroad 11.85 miles *19 km* across the Great Salt Lake, Utah, U.S.A. It was opened as a pile and trestle bridge on 8 Mar. 1904, but converted to rock fill in 1955–60.

The longest stone arch bridging in the world is the 3,810 ft *1 161 m* long Rockville Bridge north of Harrisburg, Pennsylvania, U.S.A., with 48 spans containing 196,000 tons/*tonnes* of stone and completed in 1901.

Widest Bridge

The world's widest long-span bridge is the 1,650 ft *502,9 m* span Sydney Harbour Bridge, Australia (160 ft *48 m* wide). It carries two electric overhead railway tracks, 8 lanes of roadway and a cycle and footway. It was officially opened on 19 Mar. 1932. The Crawford Street Bridge in Providence, Rhode Island, U.S.A., has a width of 1,147 ft *350 m*. The River Roch is bridged for a distance of 1,460 ft *445 m* where the culvert passes through the centre of Rochdale, Greater Manchester and this is sometimes claimed to be a breadth.

HIGHEST
World

The highest bridge in the world is the bridge over the Royal Gorge of the Arkansas River in Colorado, U.S.A. It is 1,053 ft *321 m* above the water level. It is a suspension bridge with a main span of 880 ft *268 m* and was constructed in 6 months, ending on 6 Dec. 1929. The highest railway bridge in the world is the single track span at Fades, outside Clermont-Ferrand, France. It was built in 1901–09 with a span of 472 ft *144 m* and is 435 ft *132,5 m* above the River Sioule.

Great Britain

The highest railway bridge in Great Britain is the Ballochmyle viaduct over the River Ayr, Strathclyde built 169 ft *51,5 m* over the river bed in 1846–48 with the then world's longest masonry arch span of 181 ft *55,16 m*.

AQUEDUCTS
World longest *Ancient*

The greatest of ancient aqueducts was the Aqueduct of Carthage in Tunisia, which ran 87.6 miles *141 km* from the springs of Zaghouan to Djebel Djougar. It was built by the Romans during the reign of Publius Aelius Hadrianus (A.D. 117–138). By 1895, 344 arches still survived. Its original capacity has been calculated at 7,000,000 gal *31,8 million litres* per day. The triple-tiered aqueduct Pont du Gard, built in A.D. 19 near Nîmes, France, is 160 ft *48 m* high. The tallest of the 14 arches of Aguas Livres Aqueduct, built in Lisbon, Portugal, in 1784 is 213 ft 3 in *65 m*.

World longest *Modern*

The world's longest aqueduct, in the modern sense of a water conduit, as opposed to an irrigation canal, is the California State Water Project aqueduct, completed in 1974, to a length of 826 miles *1329 km* of which 385 miles *619 km* is canalized.

Great Britain *longest*

The longest bridged aqueduct in Britain is the Pont Cysylltau in Clwyd on the Frankton to Llantisilio branch of the Shropshire Union Canal. It is 1,007 ft *307 m* long, has 19 arches up to 121 ft *36 m* high above low water on the Dec. It was designed by Thomas Telford (1757–1834) of Scotland, and was opened for use in 1805.

6. CANALS

Earliest *World*

Relics of the oldest canals in the world, dated by archaeologists *c.* 4000 B.C., were discovered near Mandali, Iraq early in 1968.

Earliest *Great Britain*

The earliest canals in Britain were first cut by the Romans. In the Midlands the 11 mile *17 km* long Fossdyke Canal between Lincoln and the River Trent at Torksey was built in about A.D. 65 and was scoured in 1122. Part of it is still in use today. Though the Exeter canal was cut as early as 1564–66, the first wholly artificial major navigation canal in the United Kingdom was the 18½ mile *29,7 km* long canal with 14 locks from Whitecoat Point to Newry, Northern Ireland opened on 28 Mar. 1742. In Great Britain the Sankey Navigation Canal in Lancashire, 8 miles *12,8 km* in length, with 10 locks, was opened in November 1757.

Longest *World*

The longest canalized system in the world is the Volga-Baltic Canal opened in April 1965. It runs 1,850 miles *2 300 km* from Astrakhan up the Volga, *via* Kuybyshev, Gor'kiy and Lake Ladoga, to Leningrad, U.S.S.R. The longest canal of the ancient world has been the Grand Canal of China from Peking to Hangchou. It was begun in 540 B.C. and not completed until 1327 by which time it extended (including canalized river sections) for 1,107 miles *1 781 km*. The estimated work force *c* AD 600 reached 5,000,000 on the Pien section. Having been allowed by 1950 to silt up to the point that it was in no place more than 6 ft *1,8 m* deep, it is now, however, plied by ships of up to 2,000 tons/*tonnes*.

The Beloye More (White Sea) Baltic Canal from Belomorsk to Povenets, in the U.S.S.R., is 141 miles *227 km* long with 19 locks. It was completed with the use of forced labour in 1933 and cannot accommodate ships of more than 16 ft *5 m* in draught.

The world's longest big ship canal is the Suez Canal linking the Red and Mediterranean Seas, opened on 16 Nov. 1869 but inoperative from June 1967 to June 1975. The canal was planned by the French diplomatist Count Ferdinand de Lesseps (1805–94) and work began on 25 April 1859. It is 100.6 miles *161,9 km* in length from Port Said lighthouse to Suez Roads and 197 ft *60 m* wide. The construction work force was 8,213 men and 368 camels. The largest vessel to transit has been S.S. *British Progress* a VLCC (Very Large Crude Carrier) of 228 589 tonnes dwt (length 329,66 m *1081.5 ft*; beam 48,68 m *159.7 ft* at maximum draft 25,60 m *84 ft*). This was Southbound in ballast on 5 July 1976.

Busiest

The busiest big ship canal is the Panama first transited on 15 Aug. 1914. In 1974 there were a record 14,304 ocean-going transits. The largest liner to transit is *Queen Elizabeth 2* (66,851 gross tons) on 25 Mar. 1975 for a toll of $42,077.88. The ships with the greatest beam to transit have been the *Acadia Forest* and the *Atlantic Forest* of 106.9 ft *32,58 m*. The lowest toll was 36 U.S. cents by the swimmer Richard Halliburton in 1928. The fastest transit has been 3 hr 28 min by the destroyer *U.S.S. McDougall DD 358* in April 1941.

Longest *Great Britain*

Inland Waterways in Great Britain, normally defined as non-tidal (except for a few tidal "links" on the Thames, Trent and Yorkshire Ouse) rivers and canals, consist of 2,394 miles *3 852 km* with 110 miles *177 km* being restored. Of this total 2,125 miles *3 420 km* are inter-linked.

The longest possible journey on the system would be one of 415¾ miles *669 km* and 157 locks from Bedford, on the Great Ouse to near Ripon, North Yorkshire.

Largest seaway

The world's longest artificial seaway is the St. Lawrence Seaway (189 miles *304 km* long) along the New York State-Ontario border from Montreal to Lake Ontario, which enables 80 per cent of all ocean-going ships, and bulk carriers with a capacity of 26,000 tons *26 400 tonnes* to sail 2,342 miles *3 769 km* from the North Atlantic, up the St. Lawrence estuary and across the Great Lakes to Duluth, Minnesota, U.S.A., on Lake Superior (602 ft *183 m* above sea level). The project cost $470,000,000 (*then £168 million*) and was opened on 25 Apr. 1959.

Irrigation canal

The longest irrigation canal in the world is the Karakumskiy Kanal, stretching 528 miles *850 km* from Haun-Khan to Ashkhabad, Turkmenistan, U.S.S.R. In September 1971 the "navigable" length reached 280 miles *450 km*. The length of the £370 million project will reach 930 miles *1 300 km*.

LOCKS
Largest *World*

The world's largest single lock is that connecting the Schelde with the Kanaaldok system at Zandvliet, west of Antwerp, Belgium. It is 500 m *1,640 ft* long and 57 m *187 ft* wide and is an entrance to an impounded sheet of water 18 km *11.2 miles* long.

below: Boring work proceeding inside the 33½ mile *53,9 km* long Seikan Tunnel which will become by far the longest vehicular tunnel in the world (see p. 123). (*Nippon Steel Corporation*). *bottom:* Construction of the Oshimizu Tunnel, the world's longest main-line railway tunnel at 22,2 km *13.79 miles*. It was holed through on 25 Jan. 1979 (see p. 123). (*Japan Railway Construction Public Corporation*)

left: The Grand Coulee Dam, on the Columbia River, Washington State, U.S.A., the largest concrete dam in the world. (*Eric Reeves*)

Largest *Great Britain*

The largest lock in the United Kingdom is the West Dock, Bristol which measures 1,200 × 140 ft *366 × 42,7 m* and has a depth of 58 ft *17,7 m*.

Deepest *World*

The world's deepest lock is the John Day dam lock on the Columbia river, Oregon and Washington, U.S.A. completed in 1963. It can raise or lower barges 113 ft *34,4 m* and is served by a 982 ton *998 tonne* gate.

Deepest *Great Britain*

The deepest lock in Britain is the rebuilt Lock 8/9 at Bath on the Kennet and Avon Canal which will lower boats 19½ ft *5,94 m*.

Longest flight

The world's highest lock elevator overcomes a head of 68,58 m *225 ft* at Ronquières on the Charleroi–Brussels Canal, Belgium. The two 236 wheeled caissons each able to carry 1,350 tons take 22 mins to cover the 1,432 m *4,698 ft* long ramp.

The longest flight of locks in the United Kingdom is on the Worcester and Birmingham Canal at Tardebigge, Hereford and Worcester, where in a 2½ mile *4 km* stretch there are the Tardebigge (30) and Stoke (6) flights which together drop the canal 259 ft *78,9 m*.

Largest cut

The Gaillard Cut (known as "the Ditch") on the Panama Canal is 270 ft *82 m* deep between Gold Hill and Contractor's Hill with a bottom width of 500 ft *152 m*. In one day in 1911 as many as 333 dirt trains each carrying 357 tons *363 tonnes* left this site. The total amount of earth excavated for the whole Panama Canal was 8,910,000 tons *9 053 000 tonnes* which total will be raised by the further widening of the Gaillard Cut.

7. DAMS

Earliest

The earliest dam ever built was the Sadd al-Kafara, seven miles *11,3 km* south-east of Helwan, United Arab Republic. It was built in the period 2950 to 2750 B.C. and had a length of 348 ft *106 m* and a height of 37 ft *11 m*.

Most massive

Measured by volume, the largest dam in the world is the 98 ft *29,8 m* high New Cornelia Tailings earthfill dam, Arizona, U.S.A. with a volume of 274,026,000 yd³ *209 506 000 m³* completed in 1973 to a length of 6.74 miles *10,85 km*.

Largest concrete

The world's largest concrete dam, and the largest concrete structure in the world, is the Grand Coulee Dam on the Columbia River, Washington State, U.S.A. Work on the dam was begun in 1933, it began working on 22 Mar. 1941 and was completed in 1942 at a cost of $56 million. It has a crest length of 4,173 ft *1 272 m* and is 550 ft *167 m* high. It contains 10,585,000 yds³ *8 092 000 m³* of concrete and weighs about 19,285,000 tons *19 595 000 tonnes*. The hydro-electric power plant (now being extended) will have a capacity of 9,780,000 kw.

Highest

The highest dam in the world is the Grande Dixence in Switzerland, completed in September 1961 at a cost of 1,600 million Swiss francs (£151,000,000). It is 935 ft *285 m* from base to rim, 2,296 ft *700 m* long and the total volume of concrete in the dam is 7,792,000 yds³ *5 957 000 m³*. The Rogunsky earth-fill dam in the U.S.S.R. is expected to have a final height of 1,066 ft *325 m*. The damning of the Vakhsh river at Nurek, U.S.S.R. with a rock-fill dam is due for completion after 19 years work in late 1979. The final height will be 986 ft *300,5 m*. Many Microseisms have caused the rate of filling to be slowed down.

Longest

The longest river dam in the world is the 62 ft *19 m* high Kiev dam on the river Dnepr, U.S.S.R. which was completed in 1964 to a length of 33.6 miles *54,1 km*. In the early 17th century an impounding dam of moderate height was built in Lake Hungtze, Kiangsu, China, to a reputed length of 100 km *62 miles*.

The longest sea dam in the world is the Afsluitdijk stretching 20.195 miles *32,5 km* across the mouth of the Zuider Zee in two sections of 1.553 miles *2,499 km* (mainland of North Holland to the Isle of Wieringen) and 18.641 miles *30 km* from Wieringen to Friesland. It has a sea-level width of 293 ft *89 m* and a height of 24 ft 7 in *7,5 m*.

Strongest

The world's strongest structure will be the Sayano-Shusens-kaya dam on the River Yenisey, U.S.S.R. which is under construction and designed to bear a load of 18 000 000 tonnes from a fully-filled reservoir.

United Kingdom

The most massive (5,630,000 yds³ *4 304 000 m³*), and longest (2,050 ft *625 m* crest length) high dam in the United Kingdom is the 240 ft *73 m* high Scammonden Dam, West Yorkshire, begun in November 1966 and completed in the summer of 1970. This rock fill dam carries the M62 on its crest and was built by Sir Alfred McAlpine's. The cost of the project together with the 6½ miles *10 km* motorway was £8,400,000. There are longer low dams or barrages of the valley cut-off type notably the Hanningfield Dam, Essex, built from July 1952 to August 1956 to a length of 6,850 ft *2 088 m* and a height of 64.5 ft *19,7 m*. The rock fill Llyn Brianne Dam, Dyfed is Britain's highest dam reaching 298½ ft *91 m* in Nov. 1971 and becoming operational on 20 July 1972.

Largest Reservoir *World*

The most voluminous man-made is Bratsk reservoir (River Angara) U.S.S.R., with a volume of 137,214,000 acre-ft *169,25 km³*. The dam was completed in 1964.

The world's largest artificial lake measured by surface area is Lake Volta, Ghana, formed by the Akosombo dam completed in 1965. By 1969 the lake had filled to an area of 3,275 miles² *8 482 km²* with a shoreline 4,500 miles *7 250 km* in length.

The completion in 1954 of the Owen Falls Dam near Jinja, Uganda, across the northern exit of the White Nile from the Victoria Nyanza marginally raised the level of that *natural* lake by adding 166,000,000 acre-ft *204,75 km³*, and technically turned it into a reservoir with a surface area of 17,169,920 acres *6,9 million ha* (26,828 miles² *69 484 km²*).

Largest Reservoir *Great Britain*

The largest wholly artificial reservoir in Great Britain is the Queen Mary Reservoir, built from August 1914 to June 1925, at Littleton, near Staines, Surrey, with an available storage capacity of 8,130 million gal. *36 960 million litres* and a water area of 707 acres *286 ha*. The length of the perimeter embankment is 20,766 ft *6 329 m* (3.93 miles *6,32 km*). Of the valley cut-off type reservoirs the most capacious is Emping-ham Reservoir (Rutland Water) Leicestershire, with a capacity of 27,300 million gals *124 000 million litres*. It has the largest surface area of any reservoir covering 3,114 acres *1 260 ha*. The deepest reservoir in Europe is Loch Morar, Highland, Scotland, with a maximum depth of 1,017 ft *310 m* (see also page 70).

Largest polder

The largest of the five great polders in the old Zuider Zee, Netherlands, will be the 149,000 acre *60 300 ha* (232.8 miles² *602,9 km²*) Markerwaard. Work on the 66 mile *106 km* long surrounding dyke was begun in 1957. The water area remaining after the erection of the 1927–32 dam (20 miles *32 km* in length) is called IJssel Meer, which will have a final area of 487.5 miles² *1 262,6 km²*

Largest levees

The most massive levees ever built are the Mississippi levees begun in 1717 but vastly augmented by the U.S. Federal Government after the disastrous floods of 1927. These extend for 1,732 miles *2 787 km* along the main river from Cape Girardeau, Missouri, to the Gulf of Mexico and comprise more than 1,000 million yds³ *765 million m³* of earthworks. Levees on the tributaries comprise an additional 2,000 miles *3 200 km*. The Pine Bluff, Arkansas to Venice, Louisiana segment of 650 miles *1 046 km* is continuous.

8. TUNNELS

LONGEST
Water supply *World*

The world's longest tunnel of any kind is the New York City West Delaware water supply tunnel begun in 1937 and completed in 1944. It has a diameter of 13 ft 6 in *4,1 m* and runs for 105 miles *168,9 km* from the Rondout Reservoir into the Hillview Reservoir, in Yonkers, New York City, N.Y., U.S.A.

Water supply *Great Britain*

The longest water supply tunnel in the United Kingdom is the Thames water tunnel from Hampton-on-Thames to Walthamstow, Greater London, completed in 1960 with a circumference of 26 ft 8 in *8,1 m* and a length of 18.8 miles *30,3 km*.

Railway *World*

The world's longest main-line rail tunnel is the 22,2 km (*13 miles 1,397 yds*) long Oshimizu Tunnel on the Tokyo-Niigata Joetsu line in central Honshū under the Tanigawa mountain which was holed through on 25 Jan. 1979. The cost of the whole project will by March 1981 reach £3,150 million. Fatalities in 7 years have been 13.

Railway *Great Britain*

Great Britain's longest main-line railway tunnel is the Severn Tunnel (4 miles 628 yds *6 km*), linking Avon and Gwent completed with 76,400,000 bricks between 1873 and 1886.

Sub-aqueous

The 33.49 mile *53,9 km* long Seikan Rail Tunnel will be 240 m *787 ft* beneath sea level and 100 m *328 ft* below the sea bed of the Tsugaru Strait between Tappi Saki, Honshū, and Fukushima, Hokkaidō, Japan. Once due to be completed by March 1979 at a cost of Yen 200,000 million, major flooding on 6 May 1976 has put back completion beyond 1982. Tests started on the sub-aqueous section (14.5 miles *23,3 km*) in 1963 and construction in June 1972. Currently the world's longest sub-aqueous rail tunnel is the Shin Kanmon Tunnel, completed in May 1974 which runs 11.61 miles *18,7 km* from Honshū to Kyūshū, Japan.

Subway

The world's longest continuous vehicular tunnel is the London Transport Executive underground railway line from Morden to East Finchley, *via* Bank. In use since 1939, it is 17 miles 528 yds *27,8 km* long and the diameter of the tunnel is 12 ft *3,7 m* and the station tunnels 22.2 ft *6,8 m*.

Road *World*

The longest road tunnel is the 8.7 mile *14,0 km* long Arlberg Road Tunnel from St. Anton and Langen in western Austria, opened to traffic on 9 Dec. 1978.

Great Britain

The longest road tunnel in the United Kingdom is the Mersey Tunnel, joining Liverpool and Birkenhead, Merseyside. It is 2.13 miles *3,43 km* long, or 2.87 miles *4,62 km* including branch tunnels. Work was begun in December 1925 and it was opened by H.M. King George V on 18 July 1934. The total cost was £7¾ million. The 36 ft *11 m* wide 4-lane roadway carries nearly 7½ million vehicles a year. The first tube of the second Mersey Tunnel was opened on 24 June 1971.

Largest

The largest diameter road tunnel in the world is that blasted through Yerba Buena Island, San Francisco, California,

U.S.A. It is 76 ft *23 m* wide, 58 ft *17 m* high and 540 ft *165 m* long. More than 35,000,000 vehicles pass through on its two decks every year.

Hydro-Electric or Irrigation *World*

The longest irrigation tunnel in the world is the 51.5 mile *82,9 km* long Orange-Fish Rivers Tunnel, South Africa, begun in 1967 at an estimated cost of £60 million. The boring was completed in April 1973. The lining to a minimum thickness of 9 inches *23 cm* will give a completed diameter of 17 ft 6 in *5,33 m*. The total work force was at times more than 5,000. Some of the access shafts in the eight sections descend more than 1,000 feet *305 m*.

Great Britain

The longest in Great Britain is that at Ben Nevis, Highland, which has a mean diameter of 15 ft 2 in *4,6 m* and a length of 15 miles *24 km*. It was begun in June 1926 and was holed through into Loch Treig on 3 Jan. 1930 for hydroelectric use. The greatest diameter water tunnel is the 23 ft *7,01 m* tunnel at Clunie, Tayside.

Bridge Tunnel

The world's longest bridge-tunnel system is the Chesapeake Bay Bridge-Tunnel, extending 17.65 miles *28,40 km* from Eastern Shore, Virginia Peninsula to Virginia Beach, Virginia, U.S.A. It cost $200,000,000 (*then £71,4 million*) and was completed after 42 months and opened to traffic on 15 Apr. 1964. The longest bridged section is Trestle C (4.56 miles *7,34 km* long) and the longest tunnel is the Thimble Shoal Channel Tunnel (1.09 miles *1,75 km*).

Canal Tunnels *World*

The world's longest canal tunnel is that on the Rove canal between the port of Marseilles, France and the river Rhône, built in 1912–27. It is 4.53 miles *7,29 km* long, 72 ft *22 m* wide and 50 ft *15 m* high, involving 2¼ million yds³ *1,7 million m³* of excavation.

Great Britain

The longest canal tunnel in Great Britain is the Standedge (more properly Stanedge) Tunnel in West Yorkshire on the Huddersfield Narrow Canal built from 1794 to 4 Apr. 1811. It measures 3 miles 418 yds *5,21 km* in length and was closed on 21 Dec. 1944. The longest *continuous* tunnel of the 43 still in use is the 3,056 yd *2 794 m* long Blisworth on the Grand Union. The now closed Huddersfield Narrow Canal is also the highest in the United Kingdom, reaching a height at one point of 638 ft *194 m* above sea-level.

Tunnelling records

The world's records for rapid tunnelling were set in 1967 in the 5 mile *8 km* Oso Irrigation Tunnel, Colorado, U.S.A. when 419 ft *127,7 m* was achieved by the mole on the 57 ft² *5,5 m²* tunnel-face in one day.

9. SPECIALISED STRUCTURES

Advertising sign Highest *World*

The highest advertising sign in the world are the four Bank of Montreal logos atop the 72 storey 935 ft *285 m* tall First Canadian Place, Toronto. Each sign, built by Claude Neon Industries Ltd., measures 20 × 22 ft *6,09 × 6,70 m* and was lifted by helicopter.

Advertising sign Highest *Great Britain*

The highest advertising sign in Great Britain was the revolving name board of the contractors "Peter Lind" on the Post Office Tower, London. The illuminated letters were 12 ft *3,7 m* tall and 563 to 575 ft *171 to 175 m* above the street.

Advertising sign Largest

The greatest advertising sign ever erected was the electric Citroën sign on the Eiffel Tower, Paris. It was switched on on 4 July 1925, and could be seen 24 miles *38 km* away. It was in six colours with 250,000 lamps and 56 miles *90 km* of electric cables. The letter "N" which terminated the name "Citroën" between the second and third levels measured 68 ft

5 in *20,8 m* in height. The whole apparatus was taken down after 11 years in 1936. For the largest ground sign see Chapter 6, page 91—Letters, largest.

The world's largest neon sign was that owned by the Atlantic Coast Line Railroad Company at Port Tampa, Florida, U.S.A. It measured 387 ft 6 in *118 m* long and 76 ft *23 m* high, weighed 175 tons *178 tonnes* and contained about 4,200 ft *1 280 m* of red neon tubing. It was demolished on 19 Feb. 1970. Broadway's largest billboard in New York City is 11,426 ft² *1 062 m²* in area—equivalent to 107 ft *32,6 m* square. Britain's largest illuminated sign is the word PLAY-HOUSE extending 90 ft *27 m* across the frontage of the new theatre in Leeds, West Yorkshire opened in 1970.

The world's largest working sign was that in Times Square, at 44 & 45th Streets, New York City, U.S.A., in 1966. It showed two 42½ ft *13 m* tall "bottles" of Haig Scotch Whisky and an 80 ft *24 m* long "bottle" of Gordon's Gin being "poured" into a frosted glass.

Barn Largest

The largest barn in Britain is one at Manor Farm, Cholsey, near Wallingford, Oxfordshire. It is 303 ft *92 m* in length and 54 ft *16 m* in breadth (16,362 ft² *1 520 m²*). The Ipsden Barn, Oxfordshire, is 385½ ft *117 m* long but 30 ft *9 m* wide (11,565 ft² *1 074 m²*). The longest tithe barn in Britain is one measuring 268 ft *81 m* long at Wyke Farm, near Sherborne, Dorset.

Bonfire Largest

The largest recorded bonfire constructed in Britain was the Coronation bonfire using 600 tons *608 tonnes* of timber and 2,000 gallons *9 100 litres* of petroleum built to a height of 120 ft *36,6 m* in Whitehaven, Cumbria in 1902.

Breakwater Longest *World*

The world's longest breakwater is that which protects the Port of Galveston, Texas, U.S.A. The granite South Breakwater is 6.74 miles *10,85 km* in length.

Breakwater Longest *Great Britain*

The longest breakwater in Great Britain is the North Breakwater at Holyhead, Anglesey, Gwynedd which is 9,860 ft (1.86 miles *3 005 m*) in length and was completed in 1873.

Cemetery Largest

The world's largest cemetery is that in Leningrad, U.S.S.R., which contains over 500,000 of the 1,300,000 victims of the German army's siege of 1941–42. The largest cemetery in the United Kingdom is Brookwood Cemetery, Brookwood, Surrey. It is owned by the London Necropolis Co. and is 500 acres *200 ha* in extent with more than 225,000 interments.

Column Tallest

The tallest columns (as opposed to obelisks) in the world are the 36 fluted pillars 90 ft *27,43 m* tall of Vermont marble in the colonnade of the Education Building, Albany, New York. Their base diameter is 6½ ft *1,98 m*. The tallest load-bearing stone columns in the world are those measuring 69 ft *21 m* in the Hall of Columns of the Temple of Amun at Karnak, opposite Thebes on the Nile, the ancient capital of Upper Egypt. They were built in the 19th dynasty in the reign of Rameses II in *c.* 1270 B.C.

Crematorium Earliest

The oldest crematorium in Britain is one built in 1879 at Woking, Surrey. The first cremation took place there on 20 March 1885, the practice having been found legal after the cremation of Iesu Grist Price on Caerlan fields on 13 Jan. 1884.

Crematorium Largest

The largest crematorium in the world is at the Nikolo-Arkhangelskoye Cemetery, East Moscow, with 7 twin cremators of British design, completed in March 1972. It has several Halls of Farewell for atheists. Britain's largest is the City of London Crematorium, E.12, which extends over 165 acres *66,77 ha* and peaked at 5,290 cremations in 1976.

Britain has the highest percentage (63.6%) in any country where cremation is voluntary.

Dock Gate
The world's largest dock gate is that at Nigg Bay, Cromarty Firth, Highlands, Scotland first operated in March 1974. It measures 408 ft *124 m* long, 50 ft *15,2 m* high with a 4 ft *1,21 m* thick base, is made of reinforced concrete and weighs 16,000 tons *16 257 tonnes* together with its sill, quoins and roundheads. The builders were Brown and Root-Wimpey Highland Fabricators.

Dome Largest *World*
The world's largest dome is the Louisiana Superdome, New Orleans, U.S.A. It has a diameter of 680 ft *207,26 m*. (See page 117 for further details.) The largest dome of ancient architecture is that of the Pantheon, built in Rome in A.D. 112, with a diameter of 142½ ft *43 m*.

Dome Largest *Great Britain*
The largest dome in Britain is that of the Bell Sports Centre, Perth, Scotland, with a diameter of 222 ft *67 m* designed by D. B. Cockburn and constructed in Baltic whitewood by Muirhead & Sons Ltd. of Grangemouth, Central, Scotland.

Door Largest *World*
The largest doors in the world are the four in the Vehicle Assembly Building near Cape Kennedy, Florida, with a height of 460 ft *140 m* (see page 111).

Door Largest *Great Britain*
The largest doors in Great Britain are those to the Britannia Assembly Hall, at Filton airfield, Avon. The doors are 1,035 ft *315 m* in length and 67 ft *20 m* high, divided into three bays each 345 ft *105 m* across. The largest simple hinged door in Britain is that of Ye Old Bull's Head, Beaumaris, Anglesey, Gwynedd, which is 11 ft *3,35 m* wide and 13 ft *3,96 m* high.

Door Oldest
The oldest doors in Britain are those of Hadstock Church, Essex, which date from *c.* 1040 A.D. and exhibit evidence of Danish workmanship.

Dry Dock Largest *World*
The largest dry dock in the world is that at Koyagi, Nagasaki, Japan completed in 1972. It measures 970 m *3,182 ft* long; 100 m *328 ft* in width and has a maximum depth of 14,5 m *47.6 ft*.

The largest shipbuilding dry dock in the U.K. is the Belfast Harbour Commission and Harland and Wolff building dock at Belfast, Northern Ireland. It was excavated by Wimpey's to a length of 1,825 ft *556 m* and a width of 305 ft *93 m* and could accommodate tankers of 1,000,000 tons deadweight. Work was begun on 26 Jan. 1968 and completed on 30 Nov. 1969 and involved the excavation of 400,000 yds³ *306 000 m³*. (See also Largest crane.) The dry dock under construction at Port Rashid, Dubai, Persian Gulf, opened in March 1979 measures 1,722 by 328 ft *525 × 100 m*.

Earthworks Largest *World*
The largest earthworks in the world carried out prior to the mechanical era were the Linear Earth Boundaries of the Benin Empire in the Bendel state of Nigeria. These were first reported in 1900 and partially surveyed in 1967. In April 1973 it was estimated by Mr Patrick Darling that the total length of the earthworks was probably between 4,000 and 8,000 miles *6 400–12 800 km* with the total amount of earth moved estimated at from 500 to 600 million yds³ *380–460 million m³*.

Earthworks Largest *Great Britain*
The greatest prehistoric earthwork in Britain is Wansdyke, originally Woden's Dyke, which ran 86 miles *138 km* from Portishead, Avon to Inkpen Beacon and Ludgershall, south of Hungerford, Berkshire. It is believed to have been built by the pre-Roman Wessex culture. The most extensive single site earthwork is the Dorset Curses near Gussage St. Michael, dating from *c.* 1900 B.C. The workings are 6 miles *9,7 km* in

length, involving an estimated 250,000 yds³ *191 000 m³* of excavations. The largest of the Celtic hill-forts is that known as Mew Dun, or Maiden Castle, 2 miles *3 km* south-west of Dorchester, Dorset. It covers 115 acres *46,5 ha* and was abandoned shortly after A.D. 43.

Fence Largest
The longest fence in the world is the dingo-proof fence enclosing the main sheep areas of Queensland, Australia. The wire fence is 6 ft *1,8 m* high, one foot *30 cm* underground and stretches for 3,437 miles *5 531 km*.

Fountain Tallest *World*
The world's tallest fountain is the Fountain at Fountain Hills, Arizona built at a cost of $1,500,000 for McCulloch Properties Inc. At full pressure of 375 lb./in² *26,3 kg/cm²* and at a rate of 5,828 Imp. gal/min *26 500 litres/min* the 560 ft *170 m* tall column of water weighs more than 8 tons/*tonnes*. The nozzle speed achieved by the three 600 h.p. pumps is 46.7 m.p.h. *75 km/h*.

Fountain Tallest *Great Britain*
The tallest fountain in Great Britain is the Emperor Fountain at Chatsworth, Bakewell, Derbyshire. When first tested on 1 June 1844, it attained the then unprecedented height of 260 ft *79 m*. Since the war it has not been played to more than 250 ft *76 m* and rarely beyond 180 ft *55 m*.

Flagstaff Tallest *World*
The tallest flagstaff ever erected was that outside the Oregon Building at the 1915 Panama-Pacific International Exposition in San Francisco, California, U.S.A. Trimmed from a Douglas fir, it stood 299 ft 7 in *91 m* in height and weighed 45 tons *47 tonnes*. The tallest unsupported flag pole in the world is a 170 ft *51,8 m* tall (plus 10 ft *3,048 m* below ground) metal pole weighing 28,000 lb. *12 700 kg* erected in 1943 at the U.S. Merchant Marine Academy in King's Point, New York, U.S.A. The pole, built by Kearney-National Inc., tapers from 24 in to 5½ in *61 cm to 14 cm* at the jack.

Flagstaff Tallest *Great Britain*
The tallest flagstaff in Great Britain is a 225 ft *68 m* tall Douglas fir staff at Kew, Richmond upon Thames, Greater London. Cut in Canada, it was shipped across the Atlantic and towed up the River Thames on 7 May 1958, to replace the old 214 ft *65 m* tall staff of 1919.

Garbage Dump Biggest
Reclamation Plant No. 1, Fresh Kills, Staten Island, opened in March 1974, is the world's largest sanitary landfill. In its first 4 months 450,000 tons of refuse from New York City was dumped on the site by 700 barges.

Gasholder Largest *World*
The world's largest gasholder is that at Fontaine l'Eveque, Belgium, where disused mines have been adapted to store up to 500 million m³ *17,650 million ft³* of gas at ordinary pressure. Probably the largest conventional gasholder is that at Wien-Simmering, Vienna, Austria, completed in 1968, with a height of 274 ft 8 in *84 m* and a capacity of 10.59 millions ft³ *300 000 m³*.

Gasholder Largest *Great Britain*
The largest gasholder ever constructed in Great Britain is the East Greenwich Gas Works No. 2 Holder built in 1891 with an original capacity for 12,200,000 ft³ *346 000 m³*. As constructed its capacity is 8.9 million ft³ *252 000 m³* with a water tank 303 ft *92 m* in diameter and a full inflated height of 148 ft *45 m*. The No. 1 holder (capacity 8.6 million ft³ *243 500 m³*) has a height of 200 ft *61 m*. The River Tees Northern Gas Board's 1,186 ft *361 m* deep underground storage in use since January 1959 has a capacity of 330,000 ft³ *9 300 m³*.

Globe Largest revolving
The world's largest revolving globe is the 21½ ton/*tonnes* 27 ft 11 in *8,50 m* diameter sphere in the Coleman Map Building, Wellesley, Massachusetts, U.S.A. completed at a cost of $200,000 (*then £71,425*) in 1956.

Henges

There are in Britain some 80 henges built *c.* 2500 B.C. of which the largest was Durrington Walls, Wiltshire with an average diameter of 1,550 ft *472 m*. It has been obliterated by road building.

Jetty Longest

The longest deep water jetty in the world is the Quai Hermann du Pasquier at Le Havre, France, with a length of 5,000 ft *1 524 m*. Part of an enclosed basin, it has a constant depth of water of 32 ft *9,8 m* on both sides.

Kitchen *Largest*

The largest kitchen ever set up has been the Indian Government field kitchen set up in April 1973 at Ahmadnagar, Maharashtra in the famine area which daily provided 1.2 million subsistence meals.

Lighthouse Brightest *World*

The lighthouse with the most powerful light in the world is Créac'h d'Ouessant lighthouse, established in 1638 and last altered in 1939 on l'Ile d'Ouessant, Finistère, Brittany, France. It is 163 ft *50 m* tall and, in times of fog, has a luminous intensity of up to 500 million candelas.

The lights with the greatest visible range are those 1,092 ft *332 m* above the ground on the Empire State Building, New York City, N.Y., U.S.A. Each of the four-arc mercury bulbs has a rate candlepower of 450,000,000, visible 80 miles *130 km* away on the ground and 300 miles *490 km* away from aircraft. They were switched on on 31 Mar. 1956.

Lighthouse Brightest *Great Britain*

The lighthouse in Great Britain with the most powerful light is the shorelight Orfordness, Suffolk. It has an intensity of 7,500,000 candelas. The Irish light with the greatest intensity is Aranmore on Rinrawros Point, County Donegal.

Lighthouse Remotest *Great Britain*

The most remote Trinity House lighthouse is The Smalls, about 16 sea miles (18.4 statute miles *29,6 km*) off the Dyfed coast. The most remote Scottish lighthouse is Sule Skerry, 35 miles *56 km* off shore and 45 miles *72 km* north-west of Dunnet Head, Highland. The most remote Irish light is Blackrock, 9 miles *14 km* off the Mayo coast.

Lighthouse Tallest

The world's tallest lighthouse is the steel tower 348 ft *106 m* tall near Yamashita Park in Yokohama, Japan. It has a power of 600,000 candles and a visibility range of 20 miles *32 km*.

Marquee Largest *World*

The largest tent ever erected was one covering an area of 188,368 ft² (4.32 acres *17 500 m²*) put up by the firm of Deuter from Augsburg, West Germany, for the 1958 "Welcome Expo" in Brussels, Belgium.

Marquee Largest *Great Britain*

The largest marquee in Britain is one made by Piggot Brothers in 1951 and used by the Royal Horticultural Society at their annual show (first held in 1913) in the grounds of the Royal Hospital, Kensington and Chelsea, Greater London. The marquee is 310 ft *94 m* long by 480 ft *146 m* wide and consists of 18¾ miles *30 km* of 36 in *91 cm* wide canvas covering a ground area of 148,800 ft² *13 820 m²*. A tent 407 ft *124 m* long was erected in one lift by twenty men of the Military Corrective Training Centre, Colchester on 25 July 1978.

Maypole

The tallest reported Maypole erected in England was one of Sitka spruce 105 ft 7 in *32,12 m* tall put up in Pelynt, Cornwall on 1 May 1974.

Maze Largest

The worlds largest maze is that at Longleat, nr. Warminster, Wilts., with 1.61 miles *2,59 km* of paths flanked by 16,180 yew trees. It was opened on 6 June 1978.

Monument Prehistoric *Largest*

Britain's largest megalithic prehistoric monuments are the 28½ acre *11,5 ha* earthworks and stone circles of Avebury, Wiltshire, rediscovered in 1646. The earliest calibrated date in the area of this neolithic site is *c.* 4200 B.C. The whole work is 1,200 ft *365 m* in diameter with a 40 ft *12 m* ditch around the perimeter and required an estimated 15 million man-hours of work. The largest trilithons exist at Stonehenge, to the south of Salisbury Plain, Wiltshire, with single sarsen blocks weighing over 45 tons/*tonnes* and requiring over 550 men to drag them up a 9° gradient. The earliest stage of the construction of the ditch has been dated to 2180 ± 105 B.C. Whether Stonehenge was a lunar calendar, a temple or an eclipse-predictor remains debatable.

Monument Tallest

The world's tallest monument is the stainless steel Gateway to the West Arch in St. Louis, Missouri, U.S.A., completed on 28 Oct. 1965 to commemorate the westward expansion after the Louisiana Purchase of 1803. It is a sweeping arch spanning 630 ft *192 m* and rising to the same height of 630 ft *192 m* and costing $29,000,000 (then £10.35 million). It was designed in 1947 by Eero Saarinen (died 1961).

The tallest monumental column in the world is that commemorating the battle of San Jacinto (21 Apr. 1836), on the bank of the San Jacinto river near Houston, Texas, U.S.A. General Sam Houston (1793–1863) and his force of 743 Texan troops killed 630 Mexicans (out of a total force of 1,600) and captured 700 others, for the loss of nine men killed and 30 wounded. Constructed in 1936–39, at a cost of $1,500,000 (then £372,000), the tapering column is 570 ft *173 m* tall, 47 ft *14 m* square at the base, and 30 ft *9 m* square at the observation tower, which is surmounted by a star weighing 196.4 tons *199,6 tonnes*. It is built of concrete, faced with buff limestone, and weighs 31,384 tons *31 888 tonnes*.

Monument, Youngest Ancient

The newest scheduled ancient monuments are a hexagonal pill box and 48 concrete tank traps south of Christchurch, Dorset built in World War II and protected since 1973.

Mound Largest *World*

The gravel mound built as a memorial to the Seleucid King Antiochus I (reigned 69–34 B.C.) on the summit of Nemud Dagi (8,205 ft *2 494 m*) south east of Malatya, Eastern Turkey measures 197 ft *59,8 m* tall and covers 7.5 acres *3 ha*.

Mound Largest *United Kingdom*

The largest artificial mound in Europe is Silbury Hill, 6 miles *9,7 km* west of Marlborough, Wiltshire, which involved the moving of an estimated 670,000 tons *681 000 tonnes* of chalk to make a cone 130 ft *39 m* high with a base of 5½ acres *2 ha*. Prof. Richard Atkinson in charge of the 1968 excavations showed that it is based on an innermost central mound, similar to contemporary round barrows, now dated to 2,745 ± 185 B.C. The largest long barrow in England is that inside the hill-fort at Maiden Castle (see above). It originally had a length of 1,800 ft *548 m* and had several enigmatic features such as a ritual pit with pottery, limpet shells, and animal bones. The longest long barrow containing a megalithic chamber is that at West Kennet (*c.* 2200 B.C.), near Silbury, measuring 385 ft *117 m* in length.

Naturist Resorts

The oldest resort is Der Freilichtpark, Klingberg, West Germany established in 1903. The largest in the world is the Centre Helio-Marin, Montalivet, near Bordeaux, France extending over 1¼ miles *2 km* of coast and 170 ha *420 acres* with 1,200 chalets and 50,000 visitors per annum. However, 100,000 people visit the smaller centre Helio-Marin at Cap d'Agde, southern France, which covers 90 ha *222 acres*. The term 'nudist camp' is deplored by naturists.

Obelisk (Monolithic) Largest

The largest standing obelisk in the world is that in the Piazza of St. John in Lateran, Rome, erected in 1588. It came originally from the Circus Maximus (erected A.D. 357) and before that from Heliopolis, Egypt (erected *c.* 1450 B.C.). It is

110 ft *33 m* in length and weighs 450 tons *457 tonnes*. The largest obelisk in the United Kingdom is Cleopatra's Needle on the Embankment, London, which is 68 ft, 5½ in *20 m* tall and weighs 186.36 tons *189,35 tonnes*. It was towed up the Thames from Egypt on 21 Jan. 1878 and positioned on 13 Sept.

Obelisk (Monolithic) Oldest
The longest an obelisk has remained *in situ* is that at Heliopolis, near Aswan, Egypt, erected by Senusret I *c.* 1750 B.C.

Pier Longest *World*
The world's longest pier is the Damman Pier, Saudi Arabia, on the Persian Gulf. A rock-filled causeway 4.84 miles *7,79 km* long joins the steel trestle pier 1.80 miles *2,90 km* long, which joins the Main Pier (744 ft *226 m* long), giving an overall length of 6.79 miles *10,93 km*. The work was begun in July 1948 and completed on 15 Mar. 1950.

Pier Longest *Great Britain*
The longest pier in Great Britain is the Bee Ness Jetty, completed in 1930, which stretches 8,200 ft *2 500 m* along the west bank of the River Medway, 5 to 6 miles *8 to 9,6 km* below Rochester, at Kingsnorth, Kent.

Pyramid Largest
The largest pyramid, and the largest monument ever constructed, is the Quetzalcóatl at Cholula de Rivadabia, 63 miles *101 km* south-east of Mexico City, Mexico, It is 177 ft *54 m* tall and its base covers an area of nearly 45 acres *18,2 ha*. Its total volume has been estimated at 4,300,000 yds³ *3 300 000 m³* compared with 3,360,000 yds³ *2,5 million m³* for the Pyramid of Cheops (see above). The pyramid-building era here was between the 2nd and 6th centuries A.D.

Pyramid Oldest
The oldest known pyramid is the Djoser step pyramid at Saqqâra, Egypt constructed to a height of 204 ft *62 m* originally with a Tura limestone casing in *c.* 2650 B.C. The oldest New World pyramid is that on the island of La Venta in south-eastern Mexico built by the Olmec people *c.* 800 B.C. It stands 100 ft *30 m* tall with a base diameter of 420 ft *128 m*.

Scaffolding
The greatest scaffolding structure ever erected was one comprising 750,000 ft (152 miles *228,5 km*) of tubing up to 486 ft *148 m* in height used in the reconstruction of Guy's Hospital, London in 1971.

Seven Wonders of the World
The Seven Wonders of the World were first designated by Antipater of Sidon in the 2nd century B.C. They included the Pyramids of Giza, built by three Fourth Dynasty Egyptian Pharaohs, Khwfw (Khufu or Cheops), Kha-f-Ra (Khafre, Khefren or Chepren) and Menkaure (Myccrinus) near El Giza (El Gizeh), south-west of El Qâhira (Cairo) in Egypt. The Great Pyramid ("Horizon of Khufu") was finished *c.* 2580 B.C. Its original height was 480 ft 11 in *146,5 m* (now, since the loss of its topmost stones and the pyramidion, reduced to 449 ft 6 in *137 m*) with a base line of 756 ft *230 m* and thus covering slightly more than 13 acres *5 ha*. It has been estimated that a permanent work force of 4,000 required 30 years to manoeuvre into position the 2,300,000 limestone blocks averaging 2½ tons/*tonnes* each, totalling about 5,750,000 tons *5 840 000 tonnes* and a volume of 90,700,000 ft³ *2 568 000 m³*. A costing exercise published in Dec. 1974, indicated that it would require 405 men 6 years at a cost of $1.13 billion (*then £500 million*).

Of the other six wonders only fragments remain of the Temple of Artemis (Diana) of the Ephesians, built in *c.* 350 B.C. at Ephesus, Turkey (destroyed by the Goths in A.D. 262), and of the Tomb of King Mausolus of Caria, built at Halicarnassus, now Bodrum, Turkey, in *c.* 325 B.C. No trace remains of the Hanging Gardens of Semiramis, at Babylon, Iraq (*c.* 600 B.C.); the 40 ft *12 m* tall marble, gold and ivory statue of Zeus (Jupiter), by Phidias (5th century B.C.) at Olympia, Greece (lost in a fire at Istanbul); the 117 ft *35 m* tall statue by Chares of Lindus of the figure of the god Helios (Apollo)

called the Colossus of Rhodes (sculptured 292–280 B.C., destroyed by an earthquake in 224 B.C.); or the 400 ft *122 m* tall world's earliest lighthouse built by Sostratus of Cnidus *c.* 270 B.C. as a pyramidically shaped tower of white marble (destroyed by earthquake in A.D. 1375) on the island of Pharos (Greek, *pharos* = lighthouse), off the coast of El Iskandariya (Alexandria), Egypt.

Stairs Longest *World*
The world's longest stairs are reputedly at the Aūra power station, Sienndal, western Norway. Built of wood, these are 4,101 ft *1 250 m* in length, rising in 3,875 steps at an angle of 41 degrees inside the pressure shaft. The T'ai Chan temple stairs of 6,600 steps in the Shantung Mountains, China ascend 4,700 feet in 5 miles *1 428 m* in *8 km*.

Stairs Longest *Great Britain*
The longest stairs in Britain are those from the transformer gallery to the surface 1,065 ft *324 m* in the Cruachan Power Station, Argyll, Scotland. They have 1,420 steps and the Work Study Dept. allows 27 mins 41.4 sec for the ascent.

Statue Longest
Near Bamiyan, Afghanistan there are the remains of the recumbent Sakya Buddha, built of plastered rubble, which was "about 1,000 ft *305 m*" long and is believed to date from the 3rd or 4th century A.D.

Statue Tallest
The tallest free-standing statue in the world is that of "Motherland", an enormous pre-stressed concrete female figure on Mamayev Hill, outside Volgograd, U.S.S.R., designed in 1967 by Yevgenyi Vuchetich, to commemorate victory in the Battle of Stalingrad (1942–43). The statue from its base to the tip of the sword clenched in her right hand measures 270 ft *82,30 m*.

The U.S. sculptor Felix de Welton has announced a plan to replicate the Colossus of Rhodes to a height of 308 ft *93,87 m*.

Tomb Largest
The largest tomb in the world is that of Emperor Nintoku (died *c.* A.D. 428) south of Osaka, Japan. It measures 1,594 ft *485 m* long by 1,000 ft *305 m* wide by 150 ft *45 m* high.

Totem Pole Tallest
A totem pole 173 ft *52,73 m* tall was raised on 6 June 1973 at Alert Bay, British Columbia, Canada. It tells the story of the Kwakiutl and took 36 man-weeks to carve.

Vats Largest
The largest vat in the world is named "Strongbow" used by H. P. Bulmer Ltd., the cider makers of Hereford, England. It measures 64½ ft *19,65 m* in height and 75½ ft *23,0 m* in diameter with a capacity of 1,630,000 gallons *74 099 hectolitres*.

Wall Longest *World*
The Great Wall of China, completed during the reign of Chhin Shih Huang-ti (246–210 B.C.), has main line length of 2,150 miles *3 460 km* with a further 1,780 miles *2 860 km* of branches and spurs, with a height of from 15 to 39 ft *4,5 to 12 m* and up to 32 ft *9,8 m* thick. It runs from Shanhaikuan, on the Gulf of Pohai, to Yümên-kuan and Yang-kuan and was kept in repair up to the 16th century.

Wall Longest *Great Britain*
The longest of the Roman Walls built in Britain was the 15–20 ft *4,5–6 m* tall Hadrian's Wall, built in the period A.D. 122–126. It ran across the Tyne-Solway isthmus for 74½ miles *120 km* from Bowness-on-Solway, Cumbria, to Wallsend-on-Tyne, Tyne and Wear, and was abandoned in A.D. 383.

Waterwheel Largest *World*
The largest waterwheel in the world is the Mohammadieh Noria wheel at Hama, Syria with a diameter of 131 ft *40 m* dating from Roman times. The Lady Isabella wheel at Laxey, Isle of Man is the largest in the British Isles and was

The Ayer Hitam No. 2 Dredge at Puchong, Malaysia, which carried out the most productive tin dredging operation ever, in November 1976 (see p. 130). (*Ayer Hitam*)

built for draining a lead mine and completed on 27 Sept. 1854, and dis-used since 1929. It has a circumference of 228 ft *69 m*, a diameter of 72½ ft *22 m* and an axle weighing 9 tons/ *tonnes*. The largest waterwheel in England is claimed to be the pitch-back indoor wheel of 45 ft *13,70 m* diameter which provided power from 1862–1932 for the mill of James Wilson & Son Ltd. of Lothersdale, near Keighley, West Yorkshire.

Window Largest

The largest sheet of glass ever manufactured was one of 50 m² *538.2 ft²*, or 20 m *65 ft 7 in* by 2,5 m *8 ft 2½ in*, exhibited by the Saint Gobian Company in France at the *Journées Internationales de Miroiterie* in March 1958. The largest single windows in the world are those in the Palace of Industry and Technology at Rondpoint de la Défense, Paris, with an extreme width of 218 m *715,2 ft* and a maximum height of 50 m *164 ft*.

Wine cellar

The largest wine cellars in the world are at Paarl, those of the Ko-operative Wijnbouwers Vereeniging, known as K.W.V. near Cape Town, in the centre of the wine-growing district of South Africa. They cover an area of 25 acres *10 ha* and have a capacity of 30 million gal *136 million litres*. Their largest blending vats have a capacity of 45,700 gal *207 750 litres* and are 17 ft *5 m* high, with a diameter of 26 ft *8 m*.

Ziqqurat Largest

The largest surviving ziqqurat (from the verb *zaqaru*, to build high) or stage-tower is the Ziqqurat of Ur (now Muqqayr, Iraq) with a base 200 ft by 150 ft *60 by 45 m* built to at least three storeys of which the first and part of the second now survive to a height of 60 ft *18 m*. It has been variously dated between *c.* 2,050 B.C. and *c.* 2,800 B.C.

10. BORINGS AND MINES

Deepest *World*

Man's deepest penetration into the Earth's crust is under Rig No. 32 gas well at No. 1 Bertha Rogers Field, Washita County, Oklahoma, U.S.A. After 503 days drilling the Loffland Brothers Drilling Co. reached 31,441 ft *9 583 m* (5.95 miles *9,58 km*) on 3 Apr. 1974. The hole temperature at the bottom was 475° F. *246° C*. A conception of the depth of this $6 million (then £2,500,000) hole can be gained by the realization that it was sufficient in depth to lower the CN Tower down it more than 17 times (see page 120).

In May 1976 drilling was begun at Saatly, Azerbaijan, U.S.S.R. in an attempt to reach the Mohorovicic discontinuity. The target here was announced to be 15 km *49,212 ft*.

Deepest *Ocean Drilling*

The deepest recorded drilling into the sea bed by the *Glomar Challenger* of the U.S. Deep Sea Drilling Project is one of 5,709 ft *1 740 m* off N.W. Spain in 1976 and the deepest site is one 20,483 ft *6 243 m* below the surface.

Oil Fields

The largest oil field in the world is the Ghawar field, Saudi Arabia developed by ARAMCO which measures 150 miles by 22 miles *240 km by 35 km*. The Groningen gas field in the Netherlands, exploited since 1965, has reserves of 100×10^{12} ft³. This may be matched by the Dome find of 1972 off Qatar The area of the designated parts of the U.K. Continental shelf as at 1 Apr. 1975 was 223,550 miles² *579 000 km²* with total recoverable reserves of 3,200 million tonnes of oil and 51,000,000 million ft³ *1 443 000 million m³* of gas. Gas was first discovered in the West Sole Field in October 1965 and oil in the Forties Field at 11,000 ft *3 352 m* announced from the drilling barge *Sea Quest* on 7 Oct. 1970, though a small gasfield was detected near Whitby, N. Yorkshire in 1937. The most productive oil field is expected to be Brent (found in July 1971) where the B platform was installed in Aug. 1976. Production in 1979 reached 350,000 barrels a day and should peak to 850,000 bbd in 1983. The whole U.K. production in 1978 was 60,000,000 tonnes or 15,357 million Imperial galls.

The deepest oil exploration is in 4,346 ft *1 324 m* of water 50 miles *80 km* west of Point Noire, Congo by *Discoverer Seven Seas* spudded in on 14 Jan. 1978.

Oil Platforms *Largest*

The deepest fixed leg oil platform in the world sits in 1,025 ft *312 m* of water 100 miles *160 km* southeast of New Orleans, Louisiana, U.S.A. The overall height of the structure in this $275 million enterprise is 1,265 ft *385,5 m*.

The world's most massive oil platform is the Central Ninian production and storage platform built at Loch Kishorn, Highland, Scotland. When towed out to the North Sea site on 5 May 1978 it was the heaviest object ever moved— 600,000 tonnes/tons ballasted weight. She was towed by 8 tugs with a combined strength of 92,000 I.H.P. The height of the concrete structure is 509 ft *155 m* and the overall height 820 ft *250 m*. The tallest fixed leg platform in the North Sea is one 750 ft *228,6 m* in height built by Redpath Dorman Long for Shell-Esso at Methil, Fife and moved to the Brent Field in April 1976.

The deepest water platform is BNOC's Thistle A platform in 530 ft *161,5 m* of water.

Gusher Greatest

The most prolific wildcat recorded is the 1,160 ft *353 m* deep Lucas No. 1, at Spindletop, about 3 miles *4,8 km* south of Beaumont, Texas, U.S.A., on 10 Jan. 1901. The gusher was heard more than a mile *1,6 km* away and yielded 800,000 barrels during the 9 days it was uncapped. The surrounding ground subsequently yielded 142,000,000 barrels.

Oil Spill Greatest

The worst oil spill in history was of 220,000 tons of crude light oil from the Liberian tanker *Amoco Cadiz* (Capt. Pasquale Barardi) which drifted on to the French Brittany coast at Portsall on 16 Mar. 1978. The oil slick stretched more than 100 miles *160 km* from Pointe St. Mathieu to Perros-Guirec.

The worst oil spill in British waters was from the 118,285 dwt *Torrey Canyon* which struck the Pollard Rock off Land's End on 18 Mar. 1967 spilling 30,000 tons of Kuwait "Crude".

Flare Greatest

The greatest gas fire was that which burnt at Gassi Touil in the Algerian Sahara from noon on 13 Nov. 1961 to 9.30 a.m. on 28 Apr. 1962. The pillar of flame rose 450 ft *137 m* and the smoke 600 ft *182 m*. It was eventually extinguished by

An aerial view of the Ten Mile Wash, Arizona, backed up by the world's largest dam—the New Cornelia Tailings Dam (see p. 122). (*Don Green—Kennecott Copper Corporation*).

Paul Neal ("Red") Adair, aged 47, of Austin, Texas, U.S.A., using 550 lb. *245 kg* of dynamite. His fee was understood to be about $1,000,000 (*then £357,000*).

Water Well Deepest *World*
The world's deepest water bore is the Stensvad Water Well 11-W1 of 7,320 ft *2 231 m* drilled by the Great Northern Drilling Co. Inc. in Rosebud County, Montana, U.S.A. in October-November 1961. The Thermal Power Co. geothermal steam well begun in Sonoma County, California in 1955 is now down to 9,029 ft *2 752 m*.

Water Well Deepest *Great Britain*
The deepest well in Great Britain is a water table well 2,842 ft *866 m* deep in the Staffordshire coal measures at Smestow. The deepest artesian well in Britain is that at the White Heather Laundry, Stonebridge Park, Brent, Greater London, bored in 1911 to a depth of 2,225 ft *678 m*. The deepest private well is probably that of Friningham Farm, Thurnham, Kent sunk to 415 ft *126,5 m* and deepened by bore to 818 ft *249,3 m* in 1940.

Water Well *Greatest Flow*
The highest recorded flow rate of any artesian well is 20,000 U.S. gallons (16,650 Imp. galls) per min *757 hectolitres/min* certified in 1973 for a well 20 miles *32 km* north west of Orlando, Florida by the Wekiva river.

MINES
Earliest
The earliest known mining operations were in the Ngwenya Hills of the Hhohho District of north-western Swaziland where haematite (iron ore) was mined for body paint *c.* 41,000 B.C. The earliest known copper mines were reported in February 1977 in the Timna Valley, north of Elat, Israel tentatively dated *ante* 3000 B.C. The earliest known mines in England are the Neolithic flint mines at Church Hill, Findon, West Sussex dated to 3390 B.C. ± 150.

Deepest *World*
The world's deepest mine of any kind is the Western Deep Levels Mine at Carletonville, South Africa. A depth of 12,600 ft *3 840 m* (2.38 miles) was attained by May 1975. At such extreme depths where the rock temperature attains temperatures of 131° F *55° C* refrigerated ventilation is necessary. The other great hazard is rock bursts due to the pressures.

Deepest *Great Britain*
The all-time record depth is 4,132 ft *1 259 m* in the Arley Seam of the Parsonage Colliery, Leigh, Greater Manchester in February 1949. The all-time deepest working in Scotland is at Frances Colliery, Dysart, Fife, (sunk 1877). The Bowhouse seam is under the sea, 3,118 ft *950,36 m* below sea level. The deepest present mine workings are the Bickershaw Colliery, Greater Manchester at 3,690 ft *1 127 m*. The deepest ever shaft in England, is that of the Cleveland Potash Ltd. at Boulby, North Yorkshire at 3,754 ft *1 144 m* completed in February 1973 and the deepest in Scotland is Monktonhall No. 1, Lothian, which is 3,048 ft *929 m* to the sump. The deepest Cornish tin mine was Dolcoath mine, near Camborne. The Williams shaft was completed in 1910 to 550 fathoms (3,300 ft *1 005 m*) from adit or approximately 3,600 ft *1 097 m* from the surface.

Copper Mine
Historically the world's most productive copper mine has been the Bingham Canyon Mine (see opposite) belonging to the Kennecott Copper Corporation with over 9,000,000 short tons *8 million tonnes* in the 65 years 1904–68. Currently the most productive is the Chuquicamata mine of the Anaconda Company 150 miles *240 km* north of Antofagasta, Chile, with more than *300 000 tonnes*.

The world's largest underground copper mine is at El Teniente, 50 miles *80 km* south-east of Santiago, Chile with more than 200 miles *320 km* of underground workings and an annual output of nearly 11,000,000 tons *11 176 000 tonnes* of ore.

Silver, lead and zinc Mine
The world's largest lead, zinc and silver mine is the Kidd Creek Mine of Texasgulf Canada Ltd., located at Timmins, Ontario, Canada. Since 1970 the world's leading lead mine has been the Viburnum Trend, S.E. Missouri, U.S.A. with 489,397 short tons *443 700 tonnes* in 1972, from which is extracted some 10% of the world's output of lead. The world's largest zinc smelter is the Cominco Ltd. plant at Trail, British Columbia, Canada which has an annual capacity of 263,000 tons *267 000 tonnes* of zinc and 800 tons *813 tonnes* of cadmium.

Gold Mine Largest area
The largest goldmining area in the world is the Witwatersrand gold field extending 30 miles *48 km* east and west of Johannesburg, South Africa. Gold was discovered there in 1886 by George Harrison and by 1944 more than 45 per cent of the world's gold was mined there by 320,000 Bantu and 44,000 Europeans. In 1979 50% of the world's supply came from this area whose production reached a peak 1 000 400 kg *984.3 tons* in 1970.

Gold Mine Largest *World*
The largest goldmine in area is the East Rand Proprietary Mines Ltd., whose 8,785 claims cover 12,100 acres *4 900 ha*. The largest, measured by volume extracted, is Randfontein Estates Gold Mine Co. Ltd. with 170 million yds³ *129 million m³*—enough to cover Manhattan Island to a depth of 8 ft *2,4 m*. The main tunnels if placed end to end would stretch a distance of 2,600 miles *4 184 km*.

Gold Mine Largest *Great Britain and Ireland*
The most productive goldmine in Britain was Clogan St. David's, Powys, Wales, in which county gold was discovered in 1836. This mine yielded 120,000 fine oz. in 1854–1914. Alluvial gold deposits are believed to have been worked in the Wicklow Mountains, Ireland, as early as 1800 B.C.

Gold Mine Richest
Historically the richest goldmine has been Crown Mines with nearly 49.4 million ounces *1 400 million g*. The richest in yield in 1977 was West Driefontein with 23,19 grams per tonne milled *0.75 troy oz. per ton*), but Vaal Reefs produced most with 67 tonnes in 1978.

Iron Mine
The world's largest iron-mine is at Lebedinsky, U.S.S.R., in the Kursk Magnetic Anomaly which has altogether an estimated 20,000 million tons *20 320 million tonnes* of rich (45–65 per cent) ore and 10,000,000 million tons $10,16 \times 10^{12}$ *tonnes* of poorer ore in seams up to 2,000 ft *610 m* thick. The world's greatest reserves are, however, those of Brazil, estimated to total 58,000 million tons *58 930 million tonnes* or 35 per cent of the world's total surface stock.

Platinum
The world's largest platinum refinery is the Impala plant at Springs, South Africa. The largest producer is the Rustenburg Group with more than 1,000,000 ounces *28 tonnes* per year.

Uranium Mine
The world's largest uranium mine at Rossing in Namibia (South West Africa) went into full production in 1978.

Tungsten Mine
The largest tungsten mine with published output figures is the Union Carbide mine in Mount Morgan, near Bishop, California opened in 1937 with a capacity of 2,000 tons/*tonnes* per day and a work force of 420.

Spoil dumps
The world's largest artificial spoil dump is the New Cornelia Tailings at Ten Mile Wash, Arizona, U.S.A. with a volume of 274,026,000 yds³ *209,506,000 m³*. The largest colliery tip in Great Britain covers 114 acres *46 ha* (maximum height 130 ft *40 m*) with 18 million tons *18,3 million tonnes* of slag at Cutacre Clough, Lancashire.

Quarry Largest *World*
The world's largest excavation is the Bingham Canyon Copper Mine, 30 miles *48 km* south of Salt Lake City, Utah, U.S.A. From 1906 to mid-1976 the total excavation has been 3,700 million short tons *3 355 million tonnes* over an area of 2.81 miles² *7,21 km²* to a depth of 2,540 ft *774 m*. This is seven times the amount of material moved to build the Panama Canal. Three shifts of 900 men work round the clock with 39 face shovels, 113 dump trucks and 67 locomotives and 17 drilling machines for the 28 tons/*tonnes* of explosive used daily. The record extraction in 24 hours is 504,167 short tons *457 372 tonnes* on 13 Oct. 1974.

The world's deepest open pit of the pre-mechanical pick and shovel era is the Kimberley Open Mine in South Africa, dug over a period of 43 years (1871 to 1914) to a depth of nearly 1,200 ft *365 m* and with a diameter of about 1,500 ft *457 m* and a circumference of nearly a mile, covering an area of 36 acres *14,5 ha*. Three tons/*tonnes* (14,504,566 carats) of diamonds were extracted from the 21,000,000 tons *21 337 000 tonnes* of earth dug out. The inflow of water has now made the depth 845 ft *257 m* to the water surface.

Quarry Largest *England*
The deepest quarry in England is the Old Delabole Slate Quarry, Cornwall, which has been worked since *c.* 1570 and now has a circumference of 1.63 miles *2,6 km* and a depth of 500 ft *152 m*. The largest limestone quarry in Britain is the Imperial Chemical Industries Ltd.'s Tunstead Quarry, near Buxton, Derbyshire. The working face is 1.6 miles *2,57 km* long and up to 180 ft *54,8 m* high. It is producing 6,000,000 long tons of limestone per annum.

Largest stone
The largest mined slab of quarried stone on record is one of 1,800 tons of slate from Spoutcrag Quarry, Langdale Valley, Cumbria, England in May 1969.

Open Cast Mining
The world's largest open cast mine is the Fortuna-Garsdorf lignite mine near Bergheim, West Germany. Since 1955 the cut has been extended to 4 × 3 km *2.5 × 2 miles* and to 250 m *820 ft* deep.

Tin Mining
The most productive dredging for tin ever recorded was 801,26 tonnes *788.3 tons* of concentrate (76.8% Sn) by Ayer Hitam No. 2 Dredge at Puchong, Malaysia in the 30 days of November 1976 at 237 ft *72,2 m* below surface level in a pond lowered 70 ft *21,3 m* by pumping.

THE MECHANICAL WORLD

1. SHIPS

EARLIEST BOATS

Evidence for sea faring between the Greek mainland and Melos to trade obsidian *c.* 7250 B.C. was published in 1971. Oars found in bogs at Magle Mose, Sjaelland, Denmark and Star Carr, North Yorkshire, England, have been dated to the eighth millenium B.C.

The oldest surviving boat is the 142 ft *43,4 m* long 40 ton Nile boat buried near the Great Pyramid of Khufu, Egypt *c.* 2515 B.C. and now re-assembled.

The oldest shipwreck ever found is one of a Cycladic trading vessel located off the islet of Dhókós, near the Greek island of Hydra reported in May 1975 and dated to 2450 B.C. ± 250.

Earliest power

Propulsion by steam engine was first achieved when in 1783 the Marquis Jouffroy d'Abbans ascended a reach of the river Saône near Lyon, France, in the 180 ton *182 tonnes* paddle steamer *Pyroscaphe*.

The tug *Charlotte Dundas* was the first successful power-driven vessel. She was a paddle-wheel steamer built in Scotland in 1801–02 by William Symington (1763–1831), using a double-acting condensing engine constructed by James Watt (1736–1819). The earliest regular steam run was by the paddle-wheeler *Clermont*, built by Robert Fulton (1765–1815), a U.S. engineer, using a Boulton and Watt engine. She maintained a service from New York to Albany (150 miles *240 km* in 32 hrs) from 17 Aug. 1807.

Oldest vessels *World*

The world's oldest active steam ship is the *Skibladner*, which has plied Lake Mjøsa, Norway since 1856. She has had two major refits and was built in Motala, Sweden.

Great Britain

The 48 ton Bristol steam driven dredger *Bertha* of 50 ft *15,42 m* was designed by I. K. Brunel in 1844 and is afloat at Exeter, Devon, England. Mr. G. H. Pattinson's 40 ft *12,20 m* steam launch *Dolly* was raised after 67 years from Ullswater, Cumbria, in 1962 and now on Lake Windermere, also probably dates from the 1840's. The oldest motor vessel afloat in British waters is the *Proven* on the run from the Clyde to the Inner Hebrides. She was built in Norway in 1866. The oldest vessel on *Lloyd's Yacht Register* is the twin screw steam yacht *Esperence* built on the Clyde in 1869 and salvaged from Windermere in 1941.

Earliest turbine

The first turbine ship was the *Turbinia*, built in 1894 at Wallsend-on-Tyne, Tyne and Wear, to the design of the Hon. Sir Charles Algernon Parsons, O.M., K.C.B. (1854–1931). The *Turbinia* was 100 ft *30,48 m* long and of 44½ tons *45,2 tonnes* displacement with machinery consisting of three steam turbines totalling about 2,000 shaft horsepower. At her first public demonstration in 1897 she reached a speed of 34.5 knots (39.7 m.p.h. *63,9 km/h*).

PASSENGER LINERS
Largest active

The world's largest liner is R.M.S. *Queen Elizabeth 2* of 66,851 gross tons and with an overall length of 963 ft *293 m* completed for the Cunard Line Ltd. in 1969. She set a "turn round" record of 8 hrs 3 min at New York on 17 May 1972. In her 1979 World cruise the price of the Queen Mary and the Queen Elizabeth suites was £95,365 (*$181,193*).

Largest ever

The R.M.S. *Queen Elizabeth* (finally 82,998 but formerly 83,673 gross tons), of the Cunard fleet, was the largest passenger vessel ever built and had the largest displacement of any liner in the world, She had an overall length of 1,031 ft *314 m* and was 118 ft 7 in *36 m* in breadth and was powered by steam turbines which developed 168,000 h.p. Her last passenger voyage ended on 15 Nov. 1968. In 1970 she was removed to Hong Kong to serve as a floating marine university and renamed *Seawise University*. On 9 Jan. 1972 she was fired by 3 simultaneous outbreaks. Most of the gutted hull had been cut up and removed by December 1977.

WARSHIPS
Battleships *Largest World*

The largest battleship in the world is now the U.S.S. *New Jersey* with a full load displacement of 59,000 tons *59 900 tonnes* and an overall length of 888 ft *270 m*. She was the last fire support ship on active service in the world and was de-commissioned on 17 Dec. 1969.

Largest all-time

The Japanese battleships *Yamato* (completed on 16 Dec. 1941 and sunk south west of Kyūshū, Japan, by U.S. planes

SUPERLATIVE SHIPS

France II
Largest Sailing Ship, see p. 134.

Curaçao
Earliest Atlantic Crossing, see p. 134.

Le Terrible
Fastest Destroyer, see p. 133.

0   100 ft   200 ft
30,48 m   61 m

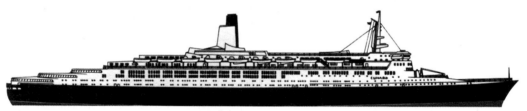

Yamato—Largest Ever Battleship, see p. 131.

Queen Elizabeth II—Largest Present Day Passenger Liner, see p. 131.

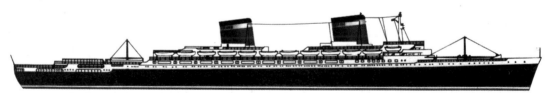

United States—Fastest Atlantic Crossing, see p. 134.

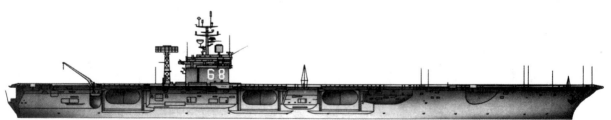

USS Nimitz—Largest Aircraft Carrier, see p. 133.

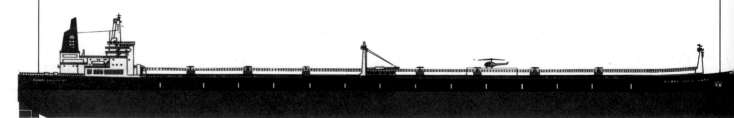

Pierre Guillaumat—Largest Tanker, see p. 133.

on 7 Apr. 1945) and *Musashi* (sunk in the Philippine Sea by 11 bombs and 16 torpedoes on 24 Oct. 1944) were the largest battleships ever commissioned, each with a full load displacement of 72,809 tons *73 977 tonnes*. With an overall length of 863 ft *263 m*, a beam of 127 ft *38,7 m* and a full load draught of 35½ ft *10,8 m* they mounted nine 460 mm *18,1 in* guns and three triple turrets. Each gun weighed 162 tons *164,6 tonnes* and was 75 ft *22,8 m* in length firing a 3,200 lb. *1 451 kg* projectile.

Largest Great Britain

Britain's largest ever and last battleship was H.M.S. *Vanguard* with a full load displacement of 51,420 tons *52 245 tonnes*, overall length 814 ft *248,1 m*, beam 108½ ft *33,07 m*, with a maximum draught of 36 ft *10,9 m*. She mounted eight 15 in *38 cm* and sixteen 5.25 in *13,33 cm* guns. A shaft horsepower of 130,000 gave her a sea speed of 29½ knots (34 m.p.h. *54 km/h*). The *Vanguard* was laid down in John Brown & Co. Ltd.'s yard at Clydebank, Strathclyde, on 20 Oct. 1941, launched on 30 Nov. 1944 and completed on 25 April 1946. She was sold in August 1960 for scrap, having cost a total of £14,000,000.

Guns

The largest guns ever mounted in any of H.M. ships were the 18 in *45 cm* pieces in the light battle cruiser (later aircraft carrier) H.M.S. *Furious* in 1917. In 1918 they were transferred to the monitors H.M.S. *Lord Clive* and *General Wolfe*. The thickest armour ever carried was in H.M.S. *Inflexible* (completed 1881), measuring 24 in *60 cm* backed by teak up to a maximum thickness of 42 in *106,6 cm*.

Fastest destroyer

The highest speed attained by a destroyer was 45.02 knots (51.84 m.p.h. *83,42 km/h*) by the 3,750 ton *3 810 tonnes* French destroyer *Le Terrible* in 1935. She was powered by four Yarrow small tube boilers and two geared turbines giving 100,000 shaft horse-power. She was removed from the active list at the end of 1957.

AIRCRAFT CARRIERS
Largest *World*

The warships with the largest full load displacement in the world are the U.S. Navy aircraft carriers U.S.S. *Nimitz* and *Dwight D. Eisenhower* at 91,400 tons. They are 1,092 ft *332 m* in length overall and have a speed well in excess of 30 knots *56 km/h* from their nuclear-powered 280,000 s.h.p. reactors. They have to be refuelled after about 900,000 miles *1,450 000 km* steaming. Their complement is 6,300 and the total cost of the *Eisenhower*, commissioned on 18 Oct. 1977, exceeded $2 billion (£1,052 million) excluding the 90 plus aircraft carried. U.S.S. *Enterprise* is, however, 1,102 ft *335,8 m* long and thus still the longest warship ever built.

SUBMARINES
Largest

The $1¼ billion (£560 million) nuclear powered submarine U.S.S. *Ohio* was commissioned at Groton, Connecticut in April 1979 with 24 Trident I missiles of 4,600 mile *7 400 km* range and a submerged displacement of 18,700 tons. She is 560 ft *170,6 m* in length. The U.S.S.R. Delta II class submarines with 16 SSN 8 missiles, may be even larger. Four or five were in service by January 1977 when even larger submarines were reported under construction. The largest submarines ever built for the Royal Navy are the four atomic-powered nuclear missile R class boats with a surface displacement of 7,500 tons *7 620 tonnes* and 8,400 tons *8 534 tonnes* submerged, a length of 425 ft *129,5 m* a beam of 33 ft *10 m* and a draught of 30 ft *9,1 m*.

Fastest

The world's fastest submarines are the U.S. Navy's tear-drop hulled nuclear vessels of the Los Angeles class. They have been listed officially as capable of a speed of "30 plus knots" (34 plus m.p.h. *55 plus km/h*) but the true figure is believed to be dramatically higher. The first 4 were commissioned in 1975/76 with a further 19 by 1979–80.

Deepest

The two U.S.N. vessels able to descend 12,000 ft *3 650 m* are the 3 man *Trieste II* (DSV I) of 303 tons recommissioned in November 1973 and the DSV 2 (Deep submergence vessel) U.S.S. *Alvin*. The *Trieste II* was reconstructed from the record-breaking bathyscaphe *Trieste* but without the Krupp built sphere, which enabled it to descend to 35,820 ft *10 917 m*. (see Chapter 11, Greatest ocean descent).

TANKERS
Largest

The world's largest tanker and ship of any kind is the 555 031 tons deadweight (274,838 g.r.t.) *Pierre Guillaumat* completed for Compagnie Nationale de Navigation on 9 Nov. 1977. She is 414,23 m *1,359 ft* long with a beam of 63,05 m *206.6 ft*, has a draught of 28,6 m *93.8 ft* and is powered by 4 turbines delivering 65,000 s.h.p. She can maintain a speed of 16 knots *18.4 m.p.h. Bellamya* (completed for Societe Maritime Shell on 31 Dec. 1976) is 275,276 g.r.t. but 553,662 dwt.

Globtik Tankers U.S. Inc. expect to take delivery of the first of three 600,000 dwt. ton nuclear-powered tankers from Newport News Shipbuilding and Dry Dock Co. at £187 million each in 1985. These 1,303 ft *397,15 m* long tankers will have an annual carrying capacity of 25 million barrels or 5 million tons of crude oil at 22 knots.

CARGO VESSELS
Largest

The largest vessel in the world capable of carrying dry cargo is the Liberian ore/oil carrier *World Gala* of 152,068 g.r.t. *286,981 dwt.* tons with a length of 1,109 ft *338 m* and a beam of 179 ft *54 m* owned by Liberian Trident Transports Inc. completed in 1973. The largest British ore/oil carrier is the Orient Steam Nav. Co's *Lauderdale*, built in Japan in 1972, of 143,959 g.r.t. *264,591 dwt.* and a length of 1,101 ft *335,6 m*.

Largest whale factory

The largest whale factory ship is the U.S.S.R.'s *Sovietskaya Ukraina* (32,034 gross tons), with a summer deadweight of 46,000 tons *46 738 tonnes* completed in October 1959. She is 713.6 ft *217,5 m* in length and 94 ft 3 in *28,7 m* in the beam.

Most powerful tugs

The world's largest and most powerful tugs are the *S. A. Wolraad Waltemade* and her sister ship *John Ross* of 2,822 g.r.t. rated at 19,200 horse-power and with a bollard pull of 150 tons. They have an overall length of 278 ft 10 in *85 m* and a beam of 49 ft 10 in *15,2 m*. They were built to handle the largest tankers and were completed in April 1976 (Leith, Scotland) and in Oct. 1976 (Durban, South Africa).

Largest car ferry

The world's largest car and passenger ferry is the 30.5 knot 24,600 g.r.t. GTS *Finnjet* which entered service across the Baltic between Helsinki and Travemünde, West Germany on 13 May 1977. She can carry 350 cars and 1,532 passengers.

Largest hydrofoil

The world's largest naval hydrofoil is the 212 ft *65 m* long *Plainview* (310 tons *314 tonnes* full load), launched by the Lockheed Shipbuilding and Construction Co. at Seattle, Washington, U.S.A., on 28 June 1965. She has a service speed of 50 knots (57 m.p.h. *92 km/h*). Three 165 ton Supramar PTS 150 Mk III hydrofoils carrying 250 passengers at 40 knots *74 km/h* ply the Malmö–Copenhagen crossing. They were built by Westermoen Hydrofoil Ltd. of Mandal, Norway. A 500 ton wing ground effect vehicle capable of carrying 900 tons has been reported in the U.S.S.R.

Most powerful icebreaker

The world's most powerful icebreaker is the 25,000 ton U.S.S.R. atomic powered *Arktika*, able to smash through ice up to nearly 4 m *13 ft* thick. On 9 Aug. 1977 she sailed from Murmansk and reached the North Pole at 2 a.m. GMT on 17 Aug.

The largest *converted* icebreaker has been the 1,007 ft *306,9 m* long S.S. *Manhattan* (43,000 s.h.p.), which was converted by the Humble Oil Co. into a 150,000 ton *152 407 tonnes* ice-breaker with an armoured prow 69 ft 2 in *21,08 m* long. She made a double voyage through the North-West Passage in arctic Canada from 24 Aug. to 12 Nov. 1969. The North-West Passage was first navigated in 1906.

Yacht Most Expensive

The ultimate in luxury yachts is the 20 knot 212 ft *64,6 m* *Al Riyadh* built at van Lent's yard, Kaag, Netherlands for King Khalid of Saudi Arabia at an estimated cost of £7 million. It has a helicopter pad, satellite communications, a pool, an operating theatre and a crew of 26 for 24 guests.

Largest dredger

The world's most powerful dredger is the 468.4 ft *142,7 m* long *Prins der Nederlanden* of 10,586 g.r.t. She can dredge 20,000 tonnes of sand from a depth of 35 m *115 ft* via two suction tubes in less than an hour.

Wooden ship

The heaviest wooden ship ever built was the *Richelieu*, 333 ft 8 in *101,70 m* long and of 8,534 tons launched in Toulon, France on 3 Dec. 1873. H.M. Battleship *Lord Warden*, completed in 1869, displaced 7,940 tons *8 060 tonnes*. The longest modern wooden ship ever built was the New York built *Rochambeau* (1867–1872) formerly *Dunderberg*. She measured 377 ft 4 in *115 m* overall. It should be noted that the biblical length of Noah's Ark was 300 cubits or, at 18 inches *45,7 cm* to a cubit, 450 ft *137 m* (but see Junks below).

Longest dug-out

The world's longest canoe is the 117 ft *35,7 m* long 20 ton Kauri wood Maori war canoe Nga Toki Matawhaorua built by adzes at Kerikeri Inlet, New Zealand in 1940 for a crew of 70 or more.

SAILING SHIPS
Largest

The largest sailing vessel ever built was the *France II* (5,806 gross tons), launched at Bordeaux in 1911. The *France II* was a steel-hulled, five-masted barque (square-rigged on four masts and fore and aft rigged on the aftermost mast). Her hull measured 418 ft *127,4 m* overall. Although principally designed as a sailing vessel with a stump topgallant rig, she was also fitted with two steam engines. She was wrecked in 1922. The only seven masted sailing schooner ever built was the 375.6 ft *114,4 m* long *Thomas W. Lawson* (5,218 gross tons) built at Quincy, Massachusetts, U.S.A. in 1902 and lost in the English Channel on 15 Dec. 1907.

The largest sailing vessel under the Red Ensign is the three-masted topgallant schooner *Captain Scott* of 144 ft *43,8 m* overall and displacing 380 tons/*tonnes* completed in September 1971 and based in Loch Eil, Highland, Scotland.

The world's only surviving First Rate Ship-of-the-Line is the Royal Navy's 104 gun battleship H.M.S. Victory laid down at Chatham, Kent on 23 July 1759 constructed from the wood of some 2,200 oak trees. She bore the body of Admiral Nelson from Gibraltar to Portsmouth arriving 44 days after serving as his victorious flagship at the Battle of Trafalgar on 21 Oct. 1805. In 1922 she was moved to No. 2 dock, Portsmouth—site of the world's oldest graving dock. The total length of her cordage (both standing and running rigging) is 100,962 ft (19.12 miles *30,77 km.*)

Largest junks

The largest junk on record was the sea-going *Cheng Ho*, flag-ship of Admiral Cheng Ho's 62 treasure ships, of *c.* 1420, with a displacement of 3,100 tons *3 150 tonnes* and a length variously estimated up to 538 ft *164 m* and believed to have had 9 masts.

A river junk 361 ft *110 m* long, with treadmill-operated paddle-wheels, was recorded in A.D. 1161. In *c.* A.D. 280 a floating fortress 600 ft *182,8 m* square, built by Wang Chün on the Yangtze took part in the Chin-Wu river war. Present-day junks do not, even in the case of the Chiangsu traders, exceed 170 ft *51,8 m* in length.

Longest day's run under sail

The longest day's run claimed by any sailing ship was one of 465 nautical miles (535.45 statute miles *861,72 km*) by the clipper *Champion of the Seas* (2,722 registered tons) of the Liverpool Black Ball Line running before a north-westerly gale in the south Indian Ocean under the command of Capt. Alex. Newlands. The elapsed time between the fixes was 23 hrs 17 min giving an average of 19.97 knots *37,00 km/h.*

Largest sails

The largest spars ever carried were those in H.M. Battleship *Temeraire*, completed at Chatham, Kent, on 31 Aug. 1877. The fore and main yards measured 115 ft *35 m* in length. The mainsail contained 5,100 ft *1 555 m* of canvas, weighing 2 tons *2,03 tonnes* and the total sail area was 25,000 ft² *2 322 m²*.

Largest wreck

The largest ship ever wrecked has been the £25 million tanker *Olympic Bravery* (275,000 tons deadweight) which ran aground off Ushant I, N.W. France on 24 Jan. 1976 on her maiden voyage. She broke in two on 12 Mar. 1976.

Largest Collision

The closest approach to an irresistible force striking an immovable object occurred on 19 Dec. 1977, 22 miles *35 km* off the coast of Southern Africa when the tanker *Venoil* (330,954 dwt.) struck her sister ship *Venpet* (330,869 dwt.)

OCEAN CROSSINGS
Atlantic *Earliest*

The earliest crossing of the Atlantic by a power vessel, as opposed to an auxiliary engined sailing ship, was a 22-day voyage begun in April 1827, from Rotterdam, Netherlands, to the West Indies by the *Curaçao*. She was a 127 ft *38,7 m* wooden paddle boat of 438 tons, built in Dundee, Tayside, in 1826 and purchased by the Dutch Government for the West Indian mail service. The earliest Atlantic crossing entirely under steam (with intervals for desalting the boilers) was by H.M.S. *Rhadamanthus* from Plymouth to Barbados in 1832. The earliest crossing of the Atlantic under continuous steam power was by the condenser-fitted packet ship *Sirius* (703 tons *714 tonnes*) from Queenstown (now Cóbh), Ireland, to Sandy Hook, New Jersey, U.S.A., in 18 days 10 hours on 4–22 Apr. 1838.

Atlantic Fastest *World*

The fastest Atlantic crossing was made by the *United States* (then 51,988, now 38,216 gross tons), former flagship of the United States Lines. On her maiden voyage between 3 and 7 July 1952 from New York City N.Y., U.S.A., to Le Havre, France, and Southampton, England, she averaged 35.59 knots, or 40.98 m.p.h. *65,95 km/h* for 3 days 10 hrs 40 min (6.36 p.m. G.M.T. 3 July to 5.16 a.m. 7 July) on a route of 2,949 nautical miles *5 465 km* from the Ambrose Light Vessel to the Bishop Rock Light, Isles of Scilly, Cornwall. During this run, on 6–7 July 1952, she steamed the greatest distance ever covered by any ship in a day's run (24 hrs)—868 nautical miles *1 609 km*, hence averaging 36.17 knots (41.65 m.p.h. *67,02 km/h*). The maximum speed attained from her 240,000 shaft horse-power engines was 38.32 knots (44.12 m.p.h. *71,01 km/h*) on trials on 9–10 June 1952.

Fastest Pacific crossing

The fastest crossing of the Pacific Ocean from Yokohama to Long Beach, California (4,840 nautical miles *8 960 km*) was 6 days 1 hr 27 mins by the container ship *Sea-Land Commerce* (50,315 tons) at an average of 33.27 knots (38.31 m.p.h. *61,65 km/h*).

Southernmost

The farthest south ever reached by a ship was achieved on 15 Feb. 1912 when the *Fram* reached Lat. 78° 41′ S. off the Antarctic coast.

Deepest anchorage

The deepest anchorage ever achieved is one of 24,600 ft *7 498 m* in the mid-Atlantic Romanche Trench by Capt. Jacques-Yves Cousteau's research vessel *Calypso*, with a 5½ mile *8,9 km* long nylon cable, on 29 July 1956.

The GTS *Finnjet*, the largest car and passenger ferry in the world which can attain a speed of 30.5 knots when crossing between Helsinki, Finland and Travemünde, W. Germany (see p. 133).

Greatest Roll

The ultimate in rolling was recorded in heavy seas off Coos Bay, Oregon, U.S.A. on 13 Nov. 1971, when the U.S. Coast Guard motor lifeboat *Intrepid* made a 360 degree roll.

2. ROAD VEHICLES

Guinness Superlatives has now published automotive records in greater detail in the more specialist publication *Car Facts and Feats* (2nd edition price £4.95). The 3rd edition will be published in Spring 1980.

COACHING

Before the widespread use of tarred road surfaces from 1845 coaching was slow and hazardous. The zenith was reached on 13 July 1888 when J. Selby, Esq., drove the "Old Times" coach 108 miles *173 km* from London to Brighton and back with 8 teams and 14 changes in 7 hrs 50 min to average 13.79 m.p.h. *22,19 km/h*. Four-horse carriages could maintain a speed of 21¼ m.p.h. *34 km/h* for nearly an hour. The *Border Union* stage coach, built *c.* 1825, ran 4 in hand from Edinburgh to London (393 miles *632 km*). When it ceased in 1842, due to competition from railways, the allowed schedule was 42 hours 23 min

MOTOR CARS

Most Cars

In 1978 it was estimated that in the United States 138 million drivers drove 147 million vehicles 1,480,000 million miles *2 380 000 million km* or 206.2 miles *331,9 km* per week per driver.

Earliest automobiles *Model*

The earliest automobile of which there is record is a two-foot-long steam-powered model constructed by Ferdinand Verbiest (d. 1687) a Belgian Jesuit priest, and described in his *Astronomia Europaea*. His model of 1668 was possibly inspired either by Giovanni Branca's description of a steam turbine, published in his *La Macchina* in 1629, or by writings on "fire carts" or *Nan Huai-Jen* during the Chu dynasty (*c.* 800 B.C.) in the library of the Emperor Khang-hi of China, to whom he was an astronomer during the period *c.* 1665–80.

Earliest automobiles *Passenger-carrying*

The earliest mechanically-propelled passenger vehicle was the first of two military steam tractors, completed at the Paris Arsenal in 1769 by Nicolas-Joseph Cugnot (1725–1804). This reached 2¼ m.p.h. *3,6 km/h*. Cugnot's second, larger tractor, completed in May 1771, today survives in the *Conservatoire nationale des arts et métiers* in Paris. Britain's first steam carriage carried eight passengers on 24 Dec. 1801 in Camborne, Cornwall and was built by Richard Trevithick (1771–1833).

Earliest automobiles *Internal combustion*

The first true internal-combustion engined vehicle was that built by the Londoner Samuel Brown (Patent 5350, 25 Apr. 1826) whose 4 h.p. *4,05 c.v.* two cylinder atmospheric gas 88 litre engined carriage climbed Shooters Hill, Blackheath, Kent in May 1826. The first successful petrol-driven car, the Motor-wagen, built by Karl-Friedrich Benz (1844–1929) of Karlsruhe, ran at Mannheim, Germany, in late 1885. It was a 5 cwt. *250 kg* 3-wheeler reaching 8–10 m.p.h. *13–16 km/h*. Its single cylinder 4-stroke chain-drive engine (bore 91.4 mm., stroke 160 mm.) delivered 0.85 h.p. *0,86 c.v.* at 200 r.p.m. It was patented on 29 Jan. 1886. Its first 1 kilometre road test was reported in the local newspaper, the *Neue Badische Landeszeitung*, of 4 June 1886, under the heading "Miscellaneous". Two were built in 1885 of which one has been preserved in "running order" at the Deutsches Museum, Munich.

Earliest automobile *British*

In Britain Edward Butler (1863–1940) built a 1,042 c.c. twin-cylinder 2-stroke petrol-engined tricycle at Erith, Kent in 1888 but the earliest successful British built car with an internal combustion engine was the Bremer car built at Walthamstow, Greater London, by the engineer Frederick William Bremer (1872–1941) which first took the road in December 1894 though the body was not completed until the following month. The car has a single cylinder horizontal, water cooled 600 c.c. engine with a two speed chain drive and tiller steering. The maximum speed is about 15 m.p.h. and the car in 1964 completed the London–to–Brighton run. It is now housed in the Vestry House Museum, London E.17. Henry Hewetson drove an imported Benz Velo in the south-eastern suburbs of London in November 1894.

Earliest registrations

The world's first plates were probably introduced by the Parisian police in France in 1893. Registration plates were introduced in Britain in 1903. The original A1 plate was secured by the 2nd Earl Russell (1865–1931) for his 12 h.p. *12,1 c.v.* Napier. This plate, willed in September 1950 to Mr. Trevor T. Laker of Leicester, was sold in August 1959 for £2,500 in aid of charity. It was reported in April 1973 that a "cherished" number plate changed hands for £14,000 in a private deal.

FASTEST CARS
Rocket-engined

The highest speed attained by any wheeled land vehicle is 631.367 m.p.h. *1 016,086 km/h* over the first measured kilometre by *The Blue Flame*, a rocket powered 4-wheeled vehicle driven by Gary Gabelich (b. San Pedro, California 29 Aug. 1940) on the Bonneville Salt Flats, Utah, U.S.A. on 23 Oct. 1970. Momentarily Gabelich exceeded 650 m.p.h. *1 046 km/h*. The car was powered by a liquid natural gas/hydrogen peroxide rocket engine developing a maximum 22,000 lb.s.t. and thus theoretically capable of 900 m.p.h. *1 448 km/h*.

Jet-engined

The highest speed attained by any jet-engined car is 613.995 m.p.h. *988,129 km/h* over a flying 666.386 yds *609,342 m* by the 34 ft 7 in *10,5 m* long 9,000 lb. *4 080 kg Spirit of America —Sonic I*, driven by Norman Craig Breedlove (b. Los Angeles, California, 23 Mar. 1938) on Bonneville Salt Flats, on 15 Nov. 1965. The car was powered by a General Electric J79 GE-3 jet engine, developing 15,000 lb.s.t. *6 080 kg* at sea-level.

Wheel-driven

The highest speed attained by a wheel-driven car is 429.311 m.p.h. *690,909 km/h* over a flying 666.386 yds *609,342 m* by Donald Malcolm Campbell, C.B.E. (1921–67), a British engineer, in the 30 ft *9,10 m* long *Bluebird*, weighing 9,600 lb. *4 354 kg* on the salt flats at Lake Eyre, South Australia, on 17 July 1964. The car was powered by a Bristol-Siddeley Proteus 705 gas-turbine engine developing 4,500 s.h.p. Its *peak* speed was *c.* 445 m.p.h. *716 km/h*. It was rebuilt in 1962, after a crash at about 360 m.p.h. *579 km/h* on 16 Sept. 1960.

Piston-engined

The highest speed attained by a piston-engined car is 418.504

The world's longest car, the 29 ft 6 in *8,99 m* stretched Fleetwood Cadillac. It is owned by Joel D. Nelson of Bakersfield, California.

m.p.h. *673,516 km/h* over a flying 666.386 yds *609,342 m* by Robert Sherman Summers (born Omaha, Nebraska, 4 Apr. 1937) in *Goldenrod* on Bonneville Salt Flats on 12 Nov. 1965. The car, measuring 32 ft *9,75 m* long and weighing 5,500 lb. *2 494 kg* was powered by four fuel-injected Chrysler Hemi engines (total capacity 27,924 c.c.) developing 2,400 b.h.p.

Diesel engined
The prototype 230 h.p. 3 litre Mercedes C 111/3 attained 327,3 km/h *203.3 m.p.h.* in tests on the Nardo Circuit, Southern Italy on 5–15 Oct. 1978.

Racing car
The world's fastest racing car yet produced was the Porsche 917/30 Can-Am Car powered by a 5,374 c.c. flat 12 turbo-charged engine developing 1,100 b.h.p. On the Paul Ricard circuit near Toulon, France, in Aug. 1973 Mark Donohue (U.S.A.) reached 257 m.p.h. *413,6 km/h*. The two models built took 2.2 secs for 0–60 m.p.h. *0–96 km/h*, 4.3 secs for 0–100 m.p.h. *0–160,9 km/h* and 12.6 secs for 0–200 m.p.h. *0–321,8 km/h*. In 1973 the UOP Shadow Can-Am car's 8.1 litre turbocharged Chevrolet V-8 engine developed 1,240 b.h.p.

Road cars
The Ferrari BB Berlinetta Boxer has the highest independently (*Autocar*) road-tested speed for a production car at 163 m.p.h. *262,3 km/h. Motor* has tested a Porsche 3.3 litre Turbo to 160.1 m.p.h. *257,6 km/h*. The Aston Martin Vantage has an *estimated* maximum speed of 170 m.p.h. *273 km/h*. Various detuned track cars have been licensed for road use but are not purchasable production models. The fastest manufacturer's *claim* for a production road car, is 315 km/h *195.7 m.p.h.* for the Lamborghini Countach P400.

The highest road-tested acceleration reported is 0–60 m.p.h. *0–96,5 km/h* in 5.3 secs and 0–100 m.p.h. *0–160,9 km/h* in 12.3 secs by *Motor* (19 May 1979 issue) for a Porsche 3,299 c.c. Turbo at Ehra-Lessien, West Germany. The engine yielded 300 b.h.p. (DIN) at 5,500 r.p.m.

LARGEST CARS
World
Of cars produced for private road use, the largest has been the Bugatti "Royale" type 41, known in Britain as the "Golden Bugatti", of which only six (not seven) were made at Molsheim, France by the Italian Ettore Bugatti, and some survive. First built in 1927, this machine has an 8-cylinder engine of 12.7 litres capacity, and measures over 22 ft *6,7 m* in length. The bonnet is over 7 ft *2 m* long. The special $100,000 stretched 1976 Fleetwood Cadillac, built for Joel D.

Nelson of Bakersfield, California exhibited in April 1979, measures 29 ft 6 in *8,99 m* in length. It carries 2 colour TV sets, an 8 speaker stereo system, refrigerator, bar, videotape recorder and camera, 4 'phones and a safe. The longest present-day limousine is the Stageway Coaches Inc. 10 door "Travelall" 18 seat model measuring 25 ft 4¼ in *7,7 m* overall. (For cars not intended for private use, see Largest engines.)

Largest Engines *All-time and current records*
The world's most powerful piston engine car is "Quad Al." It was designed and built in 1964 by Jim Lytle and was first shown in May 1965 at the Los Angeles Sports Arena. The car featured four Allison V12 aircraft engines with a total of 6 840 in³ *112,087 c.c.* displacement and 12,000 h.p. The car has 4-wheel drive, 8 wheels and tyres, and dual six-disc clutch assemblies. The wheelbase is 160 in *406,4 cm*, and weighs 5,860 lb. *2 658 kg*. It has 96 spark plugs and 96 exhaust pipes.

The largest car ever used was the "White Triplex", sponsored by J. H. White of Philadelphia, Pennsylvania, U.S.A. Completed early in 1928, after two year's work, the car weighed about 4 tons *4,06 tonnes* and was powered by three Liberty V12 aircraft engines with a total capacity of 81,188 c.c., developing 1,500 b.h.p. at 2,000 r.p.m. It was used to break the world speed record but crashed at Daytona, Florida on 13 Mar. 1929.

Currently the most powerful car on the road is the 6 wheeled Jameson-Concorde, powered by a 27,000 cc 1,760 hp Rolls Royce V12 Merlin aero-engine, governed down to a maximum speed of 185 m.p.h. *298 km/h*. It has a range of 300 miles *480 km* with tanks of 60 gal *272 litres* capacity. The vehicle weighs 2.65 tons *2,69 tonnes* overall.

Largest Engines *Production car*
The highest engine capacity of a production car was 13½ litres *824 in³*, in the case of the U.S. Pierce-Arrow 6-66 Race-about of 1912–18, the U.S. Peerless 6-60 of 1912–14 and the Fageol of 1918. The largest currently available is the V8 engine of 500.1 in³ *8,195 c.c.*, developing 235 b.h.p. net, used in the 1972 Cadillac Fleetwood Eldorado.

Petrol consumption
The world record for fuel economy on a closed circuit course (one of 14.076 miles *22,00 km*) was set by Ben Visser (U.S.) in a highly modified 1.5 litre *90.8 in³* 1959 Opel CarAvan station wagon in the annual Shell Research Laboratory contest at Wood River, Illinois, driven by Ben and Carolyn Visser on 2 Oct. 1973 with 451.90 ton miles per U.S. gal. and 376.59 miles *606,0 km* on one U.S. gal. i.e. *3,78 litres*. These figures

are equivalent to 542.70 ton miles and 452.26 miles *727,84 km* on an imperial gallon i.e. *4,54 litres*. The tyre pressure was 200 lb/in² and the maximum speed was 12 m.p.h. *19,3 km/h*.

On 30 July 1977 on the Hockenheim Ring, West Germany a 200 cc diesel engined 3 wheeler covered 674 km on 1 litre of fuel—equivalent to 1,903.8 miles to the gallon.

On 5 July 1978 at Mallory Park, Leicestershire, Michael May, 22 drove a vehicle, designed by Ricardo & Co of Shoreham, West Sussex, for 10 laps. The consumption rate was 1,643 miles per gallon or *581,6 km per litre*.

Champion Mechanic
Leopold Alfonso Villa O.B.E. (1899–1979) acted as racing mechanic or chief engineer for Sir Malcolm Campbell and Donald Campbell at 10 land and 11 water speed world records from 1924 to 1964.

Most Durable Car
The highest recorded mileage for a car is 1,184,880 authenticated miles *1 906 879 km* by August 1978 for a 1957 Mercedes 180 D owned by Robert O'Reilly of Olympia, Washington State, U.S.A.

Taxis
The largest taxi fleet was that of New York City, which amounted to 29,000 cabs in October 1929, compared with the present figure of 12,500 plus an equal number of "gypsies". London's most durable "cabby" was F. Fuller, who drove from 26 Oct. 1908 until he handed in his badge on 16 Sept. 1966—57 years later. On 30 Apr. 1979 there were 12,195 cabs and 16,740 drivers (31 Dec. 1978) in London.

Longest Taxi Ride
The longest cab ride on record is one of 6,753.3 miles *10 868,3 km* by Fred Hamby, hired by Charles Dailie and Herbert Sedinger through 16 of the U.S. states on 9–25 Sept. 1978. They started in Lanette, Alabama.

MOST EXPENSIVE CARS
Special
The most expensive car to build has been the U.S. Presidential 1969 Lincoln Continental Executive delivered to the U.S. Secret Service on 14 Oct. 1968. It has an overall length of 21 ft 6.3 in *6,56 m* with a 13 ft 4 in *4,06 m* wheel-base and with the addition of two tons *2,03 tonnes* of armour plate, weighs 5.35 tons *5,43 tonnes* (12,000 lb. *5 443 kg*). The estimated research, development and manufacture cost was $500,000 (*then £208,000*) but it is rented at $5,000 (*now £2,940*) per annum. Even if all four tyres were shot out it can travel at 50 m.p.h. *80 km/h* on inner rubber-edged steel discs.

Carriage House Motor Cars Ltd. of New York City in March 1978 completed 4 years work on converting a 1973 Rolls Royce including lengthening it by 30 in *76,2 cm*. The price tag was $500,000 (*then £263,157*).

Standard
The most expensive British standard car is the Rolls-Royce 8 cylinder 6,750 c.c. Camargue, quoted in "What Car" (May 1979) at £56,757 (incl. tax). More expensive are custom built models. Jack Barclay Ltd. of Berkeley Square, London W.1 quote £170,000 for an armour-plated Rolls-Royce Phantom VI without tax or number plates.

Used
The greatest price paid for any used car has been $421,040 (*then £210,520*), for a 1936 Mercedes-Benz Roadster from the M. L. Cohn collection, by a telephone bidder in Monaco, at Christie's sale on 25 Feb. 1979 at the Los Angeles Convention Center. The greatest collection of vintage cars is the William F. Harrah Collection of 1,700, estimated to be worth more than $4 million (*£2·3 million*), at Reno, Nevada, U.S.A. Mr. Harrah is still looking for a Chalmer's Detroit 1909 Tourabout, an Owen car of 1910–12 and a Nevada Truck of 1915.

Most inexpensive
The cheapest car of all-time was the 1922 Red Bug Buckboard, built by Briggs and Stratton Co. of Milwaukee, Wisconsin, listed at $150–$125. It had a 62 in *1,57 m* wheel base and weighed 245 lb. *111 kg*. The cheapest model listed in *Autocar's* New Car Prices feature 5 May 1979 was the Fiat 126 at £1,783 (incl. tax). The early models of the King Midget cars were sold in kit form for self-assembly for as little as $100 (*then £24 16s.*) as late as 1948.

Longest production
The longest any car has been in production is 42 years (1910–52), including wartime interruptions, in the case of the "Flat Twin" engined Jowett produced in Britain. The Volkswagen "Beetle" series, originally designed by Ferdinand Porsche, ceased production on 19 Jan. 1978 with 19,200,000 cars produced since May 1938. Britain's all-time champion is the Mini, originally sold for £496 19s 2d (incl. Purchase Tax) in August 1959. Sales reached 4,484,717 by March 1979.

Round the World Driving
The fastest circumnavigation embracing more than an equator's length of driving (26,514.43 road miles *42 670 km*) is one in 102 days 18 hrs 26 min 54.7 secs by Johnnie Parsons in the U.S. Bicentennial Global Record Run from 4 July to 15 Oct. 1976 in a Pontiac G.P. He averaged 47.22 m.p.h. *75,99 km/h*. Paula Murphy *née* Mulhauser finishing on 17 Oct. 1976 drove her Pontiac Sunbird 26,412.30 road miles *42 506 km* in 105 days 2 hrs 29 min 25.0 secs averaging 47.49 m.p.h. *76,42 km/h* also through 28 countries.

Round Britain Driving
The best recorded time for driving the 3664 miles *5 896 km* Round Britain course on an Official Certified Trial under the surveillance of a motoring organisation and with Tachograph readings, is 88 hrs 53 min to average 41.22 m.p.h. *66,33 km/h* in a Chrysler *Alpine* saloon by Alec White, John Bloxham and Toney Cox on 22–26 Apr. 1978. The trial was sponsored by Andrews Industrial Equipment and Wolverhampton Motor Services.

Mountain Driving
Cars have been driven up Ben Nevis, Highland, Scotland (4,406 ft *1 343 m*) on 4 occasions. The record times are 7 hr 23 min (ascent) and 1 hr 55 min (descent) by George F. Simpson in an Austin 7 on 6 Oct. 1928. Henry Alexander accomplished the feat twice in May 1911 (Model T Ford) and on 13 Sept. 1928 (Model A Ford).

Driving in Reverse
Charles Creighton (1908–1970) and James Hargis of Maplewood, Missouri, U.S.A., drove their Ford Model A 1929 roadster in reverse from New York City 3,340 miles *5 375 km* to Los Angeles, California on 26 July–13 Aug. 1930 without once stopping the engine. They arrived back in New York in reverse on 5 Sept. so completing 7,180 miles *11 555 km* in 42 days. Gerald Hoagland drove a 1969 Chevrolet Impala 501 miles *806,2 km* non-stop in 17 hrs 38 mins at Chemung Speed Drome, New York, U.S.A. on 9–10 July 1976.

Oldest driver
Roy M. Rawlins (b. 10 July 1870) of Stockton, California, U.S.A., was warned for driving at 95 m.p.h. *152 km/h* in a 55 m.p.h. *88,5 km/h* zone in June 1974. On 25 Aug. 1974 he was awarded a California State licence valid till 1978 by Mr. John Burrafato but Mr. Rawlings died in 1975 aged 105. Mrs. Maude Tull of Inglewood, California, who took to driving aged 91 after her husband died, was issued a renewal on 5 Feb. 1976 when aged 104. Britain's only recorded centenarian driver was Herbert Warren (1874–1975) of Whatlington, Norfolk, who drove a 1954 Standard 10. The oldest age at which anyone has passed the then Ministry of Transport driving test was on 20 Sept. 1969 at Sutton-in-Derwent, Yorkshire, when Mr. Arthur Daniel (b. 7 Feb. 1884) passed at his second attempt aged 85. The highest year number ever displayed on a Veteran Motorist's badge was "75" by Walter Herbert Weake, who started his accident free career in 1894 and drove daily until his death in 1969, aged 91.

above and below: The exterior and interior of the longest bus in the world which has a capacity for 187 passengers. (*Wayne Corporation*)

below: The world's most powerful fire appliance, the 59 ton, 8-wheeled Oshkosh (see p. 139).

above: Monster No. 2, the world's most powerful wrecker capable of lifting more than 160 tons *163 tonnes*, owned by the Vance Corporation (see p. 139).

Youngest driver

Instances of drivers have been recorded in H.M. Armed Forces much under 17 years. Mrs. P. L. M. Williams (b. 3 Feb. 1926), now of Risca, Gwent, as Private Patterson in the A.T.S. drove a 5 ton truck in 1941 aged 15. Gordon John Graham of Clydebank, Strathclyde passed his advanced driving test aged 17 years 18 days on 20 Nov. 1973.

Driving Tests

The record for persistence in taking the Ministry of Transport's Learners' Test is held by Mrs. Miriam Hargrave, (b. 3 Apr. 1908) of Wakefield. West Yorkshire, who failed her 39th driving test in eight years on 29 Apr. 1970 after "crashing" a set of red lights. She triumphed at her 40th attempt after 212 lessons on 3 Aug. 1970. The examiner was alleged not to have known about her previous 39 tests. In 1978 she was reported to dislike right-hand turns. The world's easiest tests are those in Egypt in which the ability to drive 6 metres *19.64 ft* forward and 6 in reverse has been deemed sufficient. Mrs. Fannie Turner (b. 1903) of Little Rock, Arkansas, U.S.A. passed her *written* test for driver's on her 104th attempt in Oct. 1978.

Buses *Earliest*

The first municipal motor omnibus service in the world was inaugurated on 12 April 1903 between Eastbourne railway station and Meads, East Sussex, England. A steam powered bus named *Royal Patent* ran between Gloucester and Cheltenham for 4 months in 1831.

Longest

The longest buses in the world are the 10.72 ton *10 870 kg* 76 ft *23,16 m* long articulated buses, with 121 passenger seats and room also for 66 "strap-hangers" built by the

Wayne Corporation of Richmond, Indiana, U.S.A. for use in the Middle East.

Longest route

The longest regularly scheduled bus route is the Greyhound "Supercruiser" Miami, Florida, to San Francisco, California, route over 3,240 miles *5 214 km* in 81 hours 50 min (average speed of travel 39.59 m.p.h. *63,71 km/h*). The total Greyhound fleet numbers 5,500 buses.

Caravans *Longest Journey*

The longest continuous motor caravan journey is one of 143,716 miles *231 288 km* by Harry B. Coleman and Peggy Larson in a Volkswagen Camper from 20 Aug. 1976 to 20 Apr. 1978 through 113 countries. Saburo Ouchi (b. 7 Feb. 1942) of Tokyo, Japan drove 270 000 km *167,770 miles* in 91 countries from 2 Dec. 1969 to 10 Feb. 1978. He said Queensland, Australia has the worst roads in the world for his Volkswagen "Kombi".

Largest

The largest caravan built in Britain is one 55 ft *16,76 m* in length completed in 1976 by Nash, Morgan & Co. of Lydney, Gloucestershire for the circus owner Gerry Cottle.

Most massive vehicles

The most massive vehicle ever constructed is the Marion eight-caterpillar crawler used for conveying *Saturn V* rockets to their launching pads at the John F. Kennedy Space Center, Florida (see Chapter 4, Most powerful rocket). It measures 131 ft 4 in *40 m* by 114 ft *34,7 m* and the two built cost $12,300,000 (*then £5,125,000*). The loaded train weight is 8,036 tons *8 165 tonnes*. Its windscreen wipers with 42 in *106 cm* blades are the world's largest.

Most Powerful Wrecker

The world's most powerful wrecker is the Vance Corporation 25 ton *25,4 tonne* 30 ft *9,14 m* long Monster No. 2 stationed at Hammond, Indiana, U.S.A. It can lift in excess of 160 tons *163 tonnes* on its short boom.

Largest Earth Mover

The world's largest earth mover is the Balderson "Double Dude" plow (plough) harnessed to a Caterpillar SXS D9H 820 flywheel horsepower tractor. It can cast 14,185 yd³ *10 845 m³* per hour.

Dumper Truck *Largest*

The world's largest dump truck is the Terex Titan 33–19 manufactured by the Terex Division of General Motors Corporation. It has a loaded weight of 539.9 tons *548,6 tonnes* and a capacity of 312½ tons *317,5 tonnes*. When tipping its height is 56 ft *17,06 m*. The 16 cylinder engine delivers 3,300 h.p. The fuel tank holds 1,300 Imperial gallons *5 904,6 litres*. It went into service in Nov. 1974.

Tractor *Largest*

The world's largest tractor is the $325 000 (*then £162,500*) 58 ton Northern Manufacturing Co 8-wheeled 16V–747. It is 14 ft *4,26 m* tall and 20 ft 7 ins *6,27 m* wide with a 707.7 gallon tank. It was launched in Oct. 1978.

Fire Engine *Most Powerful*

The world's most powerful fire appliance is the 860 h.p. 8 wheel Oshkosh firetruck used for aircraft fires. It can discharge 41,600 gallons of foam through two turrets in just 150 seconds. It weighs 59.0 tons *60 tonnes*.

Load Heaviest *World*

The greatest weight moved on wheels anywhere in the world was 2,142 ton *2 177 tonne* module for the Claymore field North Sea oil platform measuring 200 × 50 × 28 ft *60,9 × 15,2 × 8,5 m* on a 640 wheeled Magnaload platform at Willington Quay, Wallsend in August 1976.

The world's record road load is one of a 741 ton *753 tonne* nuclear reactor vessel 6 miles *9,6 km* from Seneca to Marseilles, Illinois on a 384 wheel Schearele trailer by the Reliance Truck Co. on 12 Feb. 1977.

Great Britain

The heaviest road load moved in the United Kingdom has been a 395 ton *401,4 tonnes* 121 ft 7¾ in *37,08 m* long reheater pressure vessel from the G.E.C. factory in Larne to Belfast docks, Northern Ireland on 17–18 Dec. 1977. The gross weight of the 172 ft 6¾ in *52,6 m* long rig of two pulling and one pushing tractor with the bogies was 625 tons *635,2 tonnes*. The longest load moved on British roads has been a 192 ft *58,5 m* 143 ton Belgian made main wash column to I.C.I. Wilton on 29 July 1976.

Tyres Largest

The world's largest tyres are manufactured in Topeka, Kansas by the Goodyear Co. for giant dumper trucks. They measure 11 ft 6 in *3,50 m* in diameter, weigh 12,500 lb. *5 670 kg* and cost more than $50,000 (*£25,000*). A tyre 17 ft *5,18 m* in diameter is believed to be the limitation of what is practical.

Skid marks Longest

The longest recorded skid marks on a public road have been those 950 ft *290 m* long left by a Jaguar car involved in an accident on the M1 near Luton, Bedfordshire, on 30 June 1960. Evidence given in the High Court case *Hurlock* v. *Inglis and others* indicated a speed "in excess of 100 m.p.h. *160 km/h*" before the application of the brakes. The skid marks made by the jet-powered *Spirit of America*, driven by Craig Breedlove, after the car went out of control at Bonneville Salt Flats, Utah, U.S.A., on 15 Oct. 1964, were nearly 6 miles *9,6 km* long. (see Jet-engined record p. 135)

Amphibious vehicle circumnavigation

The only trans-Atlantic crossing by an amphibious vehicle was achieved by Ben and Elinore Carlin (Australia and U.S.A. respectively) in an amphibious jeep "Half-Safe". He completed the last leg of the Atlantic crossing (the English Channel) on 24 Aug. 1951. He arrived back in Montreal, Canada on 8 May 1958 having completed a circumnavigation of 39,000 miles *62 765 km* over land and 9,600 miles *15 450 km* by sea and river.

Snowmobiles

Fritz Sprandel of Schnecksville, Pennsylvania U.S.A. drove his Scorpion 440 Whip snowmobile from Westport, Washington 5,004.5 miles *8 058,9 km* to Lubec, Maine in 62 days from 4 Dec. 1977 to 4 Feb. 1978.

Petrol Station

The largest gallonage sold claimed through a single pump is 7,813.77 gal *35 521,4 litres* in 24 hours on 25 June 1977 at Mornington Motors Ltd., Dunedin, New Zealand.

Tow Longest

The longest tow on record was one of 4,759 miles *7 658 km* from Halifax, Nova Scotia to Canada's Pacific Coast, when Frank J. Elliott and George A. Scott of Amherst persuaded 168 passing motorists in 89 days to tow their Model T Ford (in fact engineless) to win a $1,000 bet on 15 Oct. 1927.

MOTORCYCLES

Earliest (see also Chapter XII)

The earliest internal combustion-engined motorized bicycle was a wooden-framed machine built at Bad Canstett in Nov. 1885 by Gottlieb Daimler (1834–1900) of Germany and first ridden by Wilhelm Maybach (1846–1929). It had a top speed of 12 m.p.h. *19 km/h* and developed one-half of one horsepower from its single-cylinder 264 c.c. four-stroke engine at 700 r.p.m. The first motorcycles of entirely British production were the 1,046 c.c. Holden flat-four and the 2¾ h.p. Clyde single both produced in 1898. The earliest factory which made motorcycles in quantity was opened in 1894 by Heinrich and Wilhelm Hildebrand and Alois Wolfmüller at Munich, West Germany. In its first two years this factory produced over 1,000 machines, each having a water-cooled 1,488 c.c. twin-cylinder four-stroke engine developing about 2.5 b.h.p. at 600 r.p.m.—the highest capacity motor cycle engine ever put into production.

Fastest road machine

The highest speed returned in an independent road test for a

THE MECHANICAL WORLD

Road Vehicles/Railways

catalogued road machine is 154.2 m.p.h. *248,1 km/h* for a Dunstall Suzuki GS 1000 CS.

Fastest racing machine
There is no satisfactory answer to the identity of the fastest track machine other than to say that the current Kawasaki, Suzuki and Yamaha machines have all been geared to attain speeds marginally in excess of 300 km/h 186.4 m.p.h. under race conditions.

Duration Record
The longest time a solo motorcycle has been kept in non-stop motion is 500 hr by Owen Fitzgerald, Richard Kennett and Don Mitchell who covered 8,432 miles *13 570 km* in Western Australia on 10–31 July 1977.

Most on One Machine
The Huntingdon Park Elks stunt and drill team from California mounted and rode 17 men on a 1200 c.c. Harley Davidson in April 1974. The feat was repeated at Sydney Showground, Australia on 21 May 1976 when Sgt. Henry Brennan drove a Police 750 c.c. Honda 535 metres *585 yd* with 13 other policemen and 3 police women aboard totalling 1,412 kg *1.38 tons*.

Most expensive
The most expensive road motorcycle available in Britain is the twin rotary Wankel engined 2,000 c.c. Van Veen OCR 1000 made in the Netherlands and priced at £6,500.

Circumnavigation
Ernest O'Gaffney 41, departed from New York City on his Kawasaki KZ 1000 "Spirit of America", with pillion passenger Jan Davis on 27 Nov. 1978, and arrived back 79 days later on 15 Feb. 1979, having traversed 25 countries in a 35,000 mile *56 300 km* circumnavigation.

BICYCLES
Earliest
The first design for a machine propelled by cranks and pedals, with connecting rods has been attributed to Leonardo da Vinci (1452–1519) or one of his pupils dated c 1493. The earliest such design actually built was in 1839–40 by Kirkpatrick Macmillan (1810–78) of Dumfries, Scotland. It is now in the Science Museum, Kensington and Chelsea, Greater London.

Longest
The longest tandem "bicycle" ever built is the 1⅛ ton *1 360 kg* Vestergaard multipede built in Koege, Denmark in April 1976. It seats 35 and measures 72 feet *21,94 m* in length and has an additional stabilizing wheel.

Smallest
The world's smallest wheeled rideable bicycle is one with 2⅛ in *5,4 cm* wheels weighing 2 lb. *900 g* built and ridden by Charlie Charles at Circus Circus Hotel, Las Vegas, Nevada U.S.A.

Largest
A classic Ordinary bicycle with wheels of 64 in *162,5 cm* diameter front and 20 in *50,8 cm* back was built c. 1886 by the Pope Manufacturing Co. of Massachusetts, U.S.A. It is now owned by Paul Niquette of Connecticut.

Fastest
The world speed records for human powered vehicles are 49.38 m.p.h. *79,47 km/h* (single rider) by Ralph Therrio in 1977 and 54.43 m.p.h. *87,60 km/h* (multiple riders) by Jan Russell and Butch Stanton aboard "White Lightning" at the Ontario Speedway, California on 7 May 1978 in their supine-supine recumbent stream-lined tricycle.

Unicycle records
The tallest unicycle ever mastered in one 13.97 m *45 ft 10 in* tall ridden (with a safety belt or mechanic) by Carlho Sem Abrahams (b. Paramaribo, Surinam 3 Dec. 1962) in Paramaribo for 7 metres *23 ft* on 26 Nov. 1977. Robert Neil 'Bob' McGuinness (b. 1951) unicycled the 6 400 km *3,976 miles*

across Canada from Halifax to Vancouver in 79 days on 6 June–24 August 1978. Frank R. Williams, 20 of the U.S. Air Force set a record for 100 miles from south of Austin to Waco, Texas in 12 hrs 50 mins on 5 Sept. 1977.

Penny-Farthing record
The record for riding from Land's End to John o'Groats on Ordinary Bicycles, more commonly known in the 1870's as Penny-Farthings, is 10 days 7 hrs 12 min by James Richard Moir, 37 of St. Leonards-on-Sea, East Sussex on 5–15 June 1977.

Lawn Mowers
The widest gang mower in the world is the 5 ton 60 ft *18,28 m* wide 27 unit Big Green Machine used by the sod farmer Jay Edgar Frick of Monroe, Ohio. It mows an acre in 60 sec. On 28 Mar.–1 Apr. 1959 a Ransome *Matador* motor mower was driven for 99 hours non-stop over 375 miles *603 km* Edinburgh to London.

---

3. RAILWAYS

Guinness Superlatives publish railway records in much greater detail in the more specialist publication *Guinness Book of Rail Facts and Feats* (price £6.95, 3rd edition, published Autumn 1979).

TRAINS
Earliest
Railed trucks were used for mining as early as 1550 at Leberthal, Alsace and at the Broseley colliery, Salop in October 1605, but the first self-propelled locomotive ever to run on rails was that built by Richard Trevithick (1771–1833) for the 3 foot gauge plateway at Coalbrookdale, Salop in 1803. The earliest established railway to have a steam powered locomotive was the Middleton Colliery Railway, set up by an Act of 9 June 1758 running between Middleton Colliery and Leeds Bridge, Yorkshire. This line went over to the use of steam locomotives (gauge 4 ft 1 in) built by Matthew Murray (1765–1826), in 1812. The Stockton and Darlington Railway, Cleveland, which ran from Shildon through Darlington to Stockton, opened on 27 Sept. 1825. The 7 ton *7,1 tonne Locomotion* could pull 48 tons *48,7 tonnes* at a speed of 15 m.p.h. *24 km/h*. It was designed and driven by George Stephenson (1781–1848). The first regular steam passenger run was inaugurated over a one mile section (between Bogshole Farm and South Street) on the 6¼ mile *10,05 km* track between Canterbury and Whitstable, Kent, on 3 May 1830 hauled by the engine *Invicta*. The first electric railway was Werner von Siemen's 600 yds *548 m* long Berlin electric track opened for the Berlin Trades' Exhibition on 31 May 1879.

Fastest
The world rail speed record was set up by the U.S. Federal Railroad Administration LIMRV (Linear Induction Motor Research Vehicle) built by the Garrett Corporation on the 6.2 mile *9,97 km* long Pueblo test track, Colorado, U.S.A. when a speed of 254.76 m.p.h. *410 km/h* was attained on 14 Aug. 1974.

A progressive table of railway speed records since 1829 was published in the 23rd edition on page 141.

Steam
The highest speed ever ratified for a steam locomotive was 126 m.p.h. *202 km/h* over 440 yds *402 m* by the L.N.E.R. 4-6-2 No. 4468 *Mallard* (later numbered 60022), which hauled seven coaches weighing 240 tons *243 tonnes* gross, down Stoke Bank, near Essendine, between Grantham, Lincolnshire, and Peterborough, Cambridgeshire on 3 July 1938. Driver Joseph Duddington was at the controls with Fireman Thomas Bray. The engine suffered severe damage. On 12 June 1905 a speed of 127.06 mp.h. *204,48 km/h* was claimed for the "Pennsylvania Special" near Ada, Ohio, U.S.A. but has never been accepted by leading experts.

Regular run World
The fastest point-to-point schedule in the world is that of the

140

Pacific Coast

Atlantic Coast

Westport
(Washington State)

Lubec
(Maine)

UNITED STATES OF AMERICA

Finish 5.13pm
February 4. 1978
Lubec

Start 2am.
December 4. 1977
Westport

LONGEST SNOWMOBILE TRIP

N
200 miles

above: The route taken by Fritz Sprandel on his 5004.5 mile *8 058,9 km* snowmobile trip across the U.S.A. The map also shows the world's longest continuous frontier between the U.S.A. and Canada (see p. 139 and 173). (*Photographs: David Powers*).
below: "White Lightning", the human powered vehicle on which the world non-mechanical speed record was set at Ontario Speedway, California in May 1978. It missed breaking the U.S. National speed limit of 55 m.p.h. by a fraction (see p. 140).

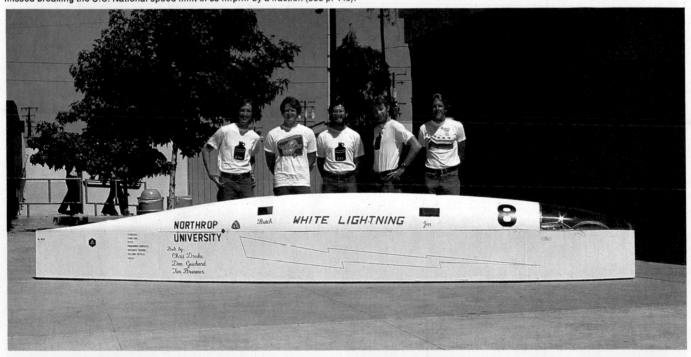

NORTHROP UNIVERSITY   *Butch*   WHITE LIGHTNING   *Jan*   8

King's Cross–Berwick section of British Rail's Eastern Region HST Service introduced on 14 May 1979 at 106.25 m.p.h. *180 km/h.* Speeds of 300 km/h *186.4 m.p.h.* are planned for the SNCF Paris–Lyon electrified line by 1982.

Great Britain
British Rail inaugurated their HST (High Speed Train) daily services between London–Bristol and South Wales on 4 Oct. 1976. On 10 Apr. 1979 one covered the 94 miles *151,2 km* between Paddington, London and Chippenham, Wiltshire in 50 min 31 sec for a start-to-stop average of 111.64 m.p.h. *179,67 km/h.* The peak speed is 125 m.p.h. *201 km/h.* The prototype British Rail gas turbine APT-E (Advanced Passenger Train-Experimental) attained 152 m.p.h. *244,6 km/h,* between Swindon and Reading on the Bristol-London line on 10 Aug. 1975.

Longest Non-Stop

The re-inaugurated Flying Scotsman between London King's Cross and Edinburgh scheduled at 4 hrs 52 mins is to be speeded up to 4 hrs 30 mins. The longest run on British Rail without any advertised stop is the Night Motorail Service from Olympia, Kensington and Chelsea, Greater London to Inverness inaugurated in May 1973. The distance is 565 miles *909 km* and the time taken is 11 hours 15 min.

Most Powerful World

The world's most powerful steam locomotive, measured by tractive effort, was No. 700, a triple articulated or triplex 2-8-8-8-4, the Baldwin Locomotive Co. 6-cylinder engine built in 1916 for the Virginian Railway. It had a tractive force of 166,300 lb. *75 432 kg* working compound and 199,560 lb. *90 518 kg* working simple.

Probably the heaviest train ever hauled by a single engine was one of 15,300 tons *15 545 tonnes* made up of 250 freight cars stretching 1.6 miles *2,5 km* by the *Matt H. Shay* (No. 5014), a 2-8-8-8-2 engine which ran on the Erie Railroad from May 1914 until 1929.

Longest freight train

The longest and heaviest freight train on record was one about 4 miles *6 km* in length consisting of 500 coal cars with three 3,600 h.p. diesels pulling and three more pushing on the Iaeger, West Virginia to Portsmouth, Ohio stretch of 157 miles *252 km* on the Norfolk and Western Railway on 15 Nov. 1967. The total weight was nearly 42,000 tons *42 674 tonnes*.

Greatest load

The heaviest single pieces of freight ever conveyed by rail are limited by the capacity of the rolling stock. The only rail carrier with a capacity of 850 tonnes is a 36 axle 86,3 m *283 ft 1½ in* long "Schnabel" built for a U.S. railway by Krupp, West Germany in 1978.

The heaviest load carried by British Rail was a 122 ft *37,1 m* long boiler drum, weighing 275 tons *279 tonnes* which was carried from Immingham Dock to Killinghome, Humberside in September 1968. They also move their own rails in lengths of 300 feet *91,44 m*.

The heaviest load ever moved on rails is the 10,700 ton Church of the Virgin Mary built in 1548 in the village of

---

The magnetic-lift type linear motor car now being tested in Japan which is designed eventually to attain 500 km/h *310 m.p.h.* (see p. 144). (*Japanese National Railways*)

Most, Czechoslovakia in Oct.-Nov. 1975 because it was in the way of coal deposits. It was moved 800 yds *730 m* at 0.0013 m.p.h. *0,002 km/h* over 4 weeks at a cost of £9 million.

TRACKS

Longest line

The world's longest run is one of 9 438 km *5,864½ miles* on the Trans Siberian line from Moscow to Nakhodka, U.S.S.R. in the Soviet Far East. There are 97 stops in the journey which takes 8 days 4 hrs 25 mins. The Baykal-Amur Magistral (BAM) northern line, begun with forced labour in 1938, is expected to be open in 1983 and will cut 500 km *310 miles* off the route round the southern end of Lake Baykal. A total of 10,000 million ft³ *283,000,000 m³* of earth has to be moved and 3,700 bridges built in this £8,000 million 9 year project.

Longest straight

The longest straight in the world is on the Commonwealth Railways Trans Australian line over the Nullarbor Plain from Mile 496 between Nurina and Loongana, Western Australia, to Mile 793 between Ooldea and Watson, South Australia, 297 miles *478 km* dead straight although not level. The longest straight on British Rail is the 18 miles *29 km* between Barlby and Staddlethorpe Junctions on the Selby, North Yorkshire to Kingston-upon-Hull, Humberside line.

Widest and Narrowest

The widest gauge in standard use is 5 ft 6 in *1,676 m*. This width is used in India, Pakistan, Bangladesh, Sri Lanka, Argentina and Chile. In 1885 there was a lumber railway in Oregon, U.S.A., with a gauge of 8 ft *2,4 m*. The narrowest gauges in use are 1 ft 3 ins *0,381 m* on the Ravenglass & Eskdale Railway, Cumbria (7 miles *11,2 km*) and the Romney, Hythe & Dymchurch line in Kent (14 miles *22,53 km*).

Highest *World*

The highest standard gauge (4 ft 8½ in *1,43 m*) track in the world is on the Peruvian State Railways at La Cima, on the Morocoha Branch at 15,806 ft *4 817 m* above sea-level. The highest point on the main line is 15,688 ft *4 781 m* in the Galera tunnel.

Great Britain

The highest point of the British Rail system is at the pass of Drumochter on the former Perth-Inverness border, where the track reaches an altitude of 1,484 ft *452 m* above sea-level. The highest railway in Britain is the Snowdon Mountain Railway, which rises from Llanberis, Gwynedd to 3,493 ft *1 064 m* above sea-level, just below the summit of Snowdon (Yr Wyddfa). It has a gauge of 2 ft 7½ in *800 mm*.

Lowest

The lowest point on British Rail is in the Severn Tunnel— 144 ft *43,8 m* below sea-level.

Steepest Gradient *World*

The world's steepest standard gauge gradient by adhesion is 1:11 between Chedde and Servoz on the meter gauge SNCF Chamonix line, France.

Great Britain

The steepest sustained adhesion-worked gradient on main line in the United Kingdom is the two-mile Lickey incline of 1:37.7 in Hereford and Worcester. From the tunnel bottom to James Street, Liverpool, on the former Mersey Railway, there is a stretch of 1:27; and between Folkestone Junction and Harbour a mile *1,6 km* of 1:30.

Shallowest Gradient

The shallowest gradient posted on the British Rail system is one indicated as 1 in 14,400 between Pirbright Junction and Farnborough, Hampshire. This could be described alternatively as England's most obtuse summit.

Busiest Rail system

The world's most crowded rail system is the Japanese National Railways, which by 1976 carried 19,487,000 passengers daily. Professional pushers are employed on the

Mr. Roy Catton, during his 37 day continuous model railway marathon in which the train travelled 678 miles (see p. 144). (*Morning Telegraph Sheffield*)

Tōkyō Service to squeeze in passengers before the doors can be closed. Among articles lost in 1970 were 419,929 umbrellas, 172,106 shoes, 250,630 spectacles and hats and also assorted false teeth and artificial eyeballs.

Greatest mileage

The greatest mileage covered with a 7 day all-line roving ticket on British Rail is 10,306½ miles *16 586,7 km* on 18–24 Apr. 1977 by J. Jeffrey of Maidstone, Kent. He carried on another week to reach 19,912½ miles *32 046,0 km*.

Railroad Handcar Pumping

"World" Championships pumped over a 220 yard *201,16 m* shuttle course sponsored by the Jacksonville Jaycees, Illinois, on 12 Sept. 1976 produced best times of 62.177 secs for men (Jerry Johnson and Tom Sheehan) and 81.123 secs for women (Chris Ruyle and Jeanne McCulloch).

STATIONS
Largest *World*

The world's largest railway station is Grand Central Terminal, Park Avenue and 43rd Street, New York City, N.Y., U.S.A., built 1903–13. It covers 48 acres *19 ha* on two levels with 41 tracks on the upper level and 26 on the lower. On average more than 550 trains and 180,000 people per day use it, with a peak of 252,288 on 3 July 1947.

Great Britain

The largest railway station in extent on the British Rail system is the 17-platform Clapham Junction, London covering 27¾ acres *11,22 ha* with a total face of 11,185 ft *3 409 m*. The station with the largest number of platforms is Waterloo, London (24⅜ acres *9,9 ha*), with 21 main line and two Waterloo and City Line platforms, with a total face of 15,352 ft *4 679 m*. Victoria Station (21¾ acres *8,80 ha*) with 17 platforms has, however, a total face length of 18,412 ft *5 611 m*. The oldest station in Britain is Liverpool Road Station, Manchester, first used on 15 Sept. 1830.

Busiest

The busiest railway junction in Great Britain is Clapham Junction, Wandsworth, Greater London on the Southern Region of British Rail, with an average of 2,400 trains passing through each 24 hours (May 1979).

Highest

The highest station in the world is Condor, Bolivia at 15,705 ft *4 786 m* on the metre gauge Rio Mulato to Potosi line. The highest passenger station on British Rail is Corrour, Highland, at an altitude of *1,347* ft *410,5 m* above sea-level.

Waiting rooms

The world's largest waiting rooms are those in Peking Station, Chang'an Boulevard, Peking, China, opened in September 1959, with a capacity of 14,000.

Longest platform

The longest railway platform in the world is the Khargpur platform, West Bengal, India, which measures 2,733 ft *833 m* in length. The State Street Center subway platform staging on "The Loop" in Chicago, Illinois, U.S.A., measures 3,500 ft *1 066 m* in length.

The longest platform in the British Rail system is the 1,981 ft *603,8 m* long platform at Colchester, Essex.

UNDERGROUND RAILWAYS
Most extensive
The earliest (first section opened 10 Jan. 1863) and one of the most extensive underground or rapid transit railway systems of the 67 in the world is that of the London Transport Executive, with 255 miles *410,3 km* of route, of which 77 miles *123 km* is bored tunnel and 21 miles *33,79 km* is "cut and cover". This whole Tube system is operated by a staff of 11,800 serving 279 stations. The 484 trains comprising 4,223 cars carried 569,000,000 passengers in 1978. The greatest depth is 221 ft *67,3 m* near Hampstead on the Northern Line. The longest journey without a change is Epping to West Ruislip—34.1 miles *54,8 km*. The record for touring the then 277 stations was 15 hours precisely by Leslie R. V. Burwood on 3 Sept. 1968.

Busiest
The busiest subway in the world is the New York City Transport Authority (first section opened on 27 Oct. 1904) with a total of 229.76 route miles *369,76 km* and 1,018,833,642 passengers in 1978. The 458 stations are closer set than London's. The record for travelling the whole system was 21 hours 8½ min by Mayer Wiesen and Charles Emerson on 8 Oct. 1973.

MODEL RAILWAYS
The non-stop duration record for a model train (loco plus 6 coaches, is 864 hrs 30 mins from 1 June–7 July 1978, covering 678 miles *1 091 km*, organised by Roy Catton at "Pastimes" Toy Store, Mexborough, S. Yorkshire. The longest train ever operated was one of 501 cars with 9 HO scale engines by The Model Railroad Club of New Jersey at Union, N.J. on 22 July 1978 when it traversed its own length.

TRAMS
Longest tram journey
The longest tramway journey now possible is from Krefeld St Tönis to Witten Annen Nord, West Germany. With luck at the 8 inter-connections the 105,5 km *65.5 mile* trip can be achieved in 5½ hours. By late 1977 there were still some 315 tramway systems surviving of which the longest is that of Leningrad, U.S.S.R. with 2,500 cars on 53 routes.

Oldest
The oldest trams in revenue service in the world are Motor cars 1 and 2 of the Manx Electric Railway dating from 1893.

MONORAIL
Highest Speed
The highest speed ever attained on rails is 3,090 m.p.h. *4 972 km/h* (Mach 4.1) by an unmanned rocket-powered sled on the 6.62 mile *10,65 km* long captive track at the U.S. Air Force Missile Development Center at Holloman, New Mexico, U.S.A., on 19 Feb. 1959. The highest speed reached carrying a chimpanzee is 1,295 m.p.h. *2 084 km/h*.

The highest speed attained by a tracked hovercraft is 411 km/h *255.3 m.p.h.* by the jet-powered *L'Aérotrain 02*, invented by Jean Bertin. An experimental magnetically levitated Japanese National Railway train on a test track near Miyazaki reached 346 km/h *215 m.p.h.* on 10 Nov. 1978 and is expected to touch 500 km/h *310 m.p.h.* in 1979.

4. AIRCRAFT

Guinness Superlatives has published aircraft records in much greater detail in the specialist publication *Guinness Book of Air Facts and Feats* (3rd edition) (price £6.50).

Note—The use of the Mach scale for aircraft speeds was introduced by Prof. Ackeret of Zürich, Switzerland. The Mach number is the ratio of the velocity of a moving body to the local velocity of sound. This ratio was first employed by Dr. Ernst Mach (1838–1916) of Vienna, Austria in 1887. Thus Mach 1.0 equals 760.98 m.p.h. *1 224,67 km/h* at sea-level at 15°C, and is assumed, for convenience, to fall to a constant 659.78 m.p.h. *1 061,81 km/h* in the stratosphere, *i.e.* above 11,000 m *36,089 ft*.

EARLIEST FLIGHTS
World
The first controlled and sustained power-driven flight occurred near the Kill Devil Hill, Kitty Hawk, North Caro-lina, U.S.A., at 10.35 a.m. on 17 December 1903, when Orville Wright (1871–1948) flew the 12 h.p. chain-driven *Flyer I* for a distance of 120 ft *36,5 m* at an airspeed of 30 m.p.h. *48 km/h*, a ground speed of 6.8 m.p.h. *10,9 km/h* and an altitude of 8–12 ft *2,4–3,6 m* for about 12 sec watched by his brother Wilbur (1867–1912), three life savers and two others. Both brothers, from Dayton, Ohio, were bachelors because, as Orville put it, they had not the means to "support a wife as well as an aeroplane". The *Flyer* is now in the National Air and Space Museum at the Smithsonian Institution, Washington D.C.

The first hop by a man-carrying aeroplane entirely under its own power was made when Clément Ader (1841–1925) of France flew in his *Eole* for about 50 m *164 ft* at Armainvilliers, France, on 9 Oct. 1890. Richard William Pearce (1877–1953) flew for at least 50 yards *45 m* along the Main Waitohi Road, South Canterbury, New Zealand in a self-built petrol-engined monoplane on a date, which on best evidence was 31 Mar. 1903. The earliest "rational design" for a flying machine, according to the Royal Aeronautical Society, was that published by Emanuel Swedenborg (1688–1772) in Sweden in 1717.

Great Britain
The first officially recognised flight in the British Isles was made by the U.S. citizen Samuel Franklin Cody (1861–1913) who flew 1,390 ft *423 m* in his own biplane at Farnborough, Hampshire, on 16 Oct. 1908. Horatio Frederick Phillips (1845–1924) almost certainly covered 500 ft *152 m* in his Phillips II *"Venetian blind"* aeroplane at Streatham, in 1907. The first resident British citizen to fly in a powered 'plane was Griffith Brewer (1867–1948), as a passenger of Wilbur Wright, on 8 Oct. 1908 at Auvours, France.

Cross-Channel
The earliest cross-Channel flight by an aeroplane was made on Sunday, 25 July 1909 when Louis Blériot (1872–1936) of France flew his *Blériot XI* monoplane, powered by a 23 h.p. Anzani engine, 26 miles *41,8 km* from Les Baraques, France, to Northfall Meadow near Dover Castle, England, in 36½ minutes, after taking off at 4.41 a.m.

Jet-engined *World*
Proposals for jet propulsion date back to Captain Marconnet (1909) of France, and Henri Coanda (1886–1972) of Romania and to the turbojet proposals of Maxime Guillaume in 1921. The earliest testbed run was that of the British Power Jets Ltd.'s experimental W.U. (Whittle Unit) on 12 Apr. 1937, invented by Flying Officer (now Air Commodore Sir) Frank Whittle (b. Coventry, 1 June 1907), who had applied for a patent on jet propulsion in 1930. The first flight by an aeroplane powered by a turbojet engine was made by the Heinkel He 178, piloted by Flug Kapitan Erich Warsitz, at Marienehe, Germany, on 27 Aug. 1939. It was powered by a Heinkel He S3b engine (834 lb *378 kg* s.t. as installed with long tailpipe) designed by Dr. Hans 'Pabst' von Ohain and first tested in August 1937.

Great Britain
The first British jet flight occurred when Fl. Lt. P. E. G. "Jerry" Sayer, O.B.E., (k. 1942) flew the Gloster-Whittle E.28/39 (wing span 29 ft *8,84 m*, length 25 ft 3 in *7,70 m*) fitted with an 860 lb. *390 kg* s.t. Whittle W-1 engine for 17 min at Cranwell, Lincolnshire, on 15 May 1941. The maximum speed was *c.* 350 m.p.h. *560 km/h*.

Supersonic flight
The first supersonic flight was achieved on 14 Oct. 1947 by Capt. (later Brig.-Gen) Charles ("Chuck") Elwood Yeager, U.S.A.F. retd. (b. 13 Feb. 1923), over Edwards Air Force Base, Muroc, California, U.S.A., in a Bell XS-1 rocket plane ("Glamorous Glennis"), with Mach 1.015 (670 m.p.h. *1 078 km/h*) at an altitude of 42,000 ft *12 800 m*.

The first British aeroplane, and the first turbojet-powered aeroplane in the world, to achieve supersonic speed was a de Havilland D. H. 108 tailless research aircraft which, piloted by John Derry, recorded a Mach number between 1.0 and 1.1 in a dive on 6 Sept. 1948.

Three of the four specially built Douglas World Cruisers. *New Orleans* and *Chicago* (the two nearest the camera) made aviation history's first circumnavigational flight in 1924. (*U.S.A.F.*)

Trans-Atlantic

The first crossing of the North Atlantic by air was made by Lt-Cdr. (later Rear Admiral) Albert Cushion Read (1887–1967) and his crew (Stone, Hinton, Rodd, Rhoads and Breese) in the 84 knot *155 km/h* U.S. Navy/Curtiss flying-boat NC-4 from Trepassey Harbour, Newfoundland, *via* the Azores, to Lisbon, Portugal, on 16 to 27 May 1919. The whole flight of 4,717 miles *7 591 km* originating from Rockaway Air Station, Long Island, N.Y. on 8 May, required 53 hours 58 min, terminating at Plymouth, England, on 31 May.

The Newfoundland-Azores flight of 1,200 miles *1930 km* took 15 hrs 18 min at 81.7 knots *151,4 km/h.*

Non-stop

The first non-stop trans-Atlantic flight was achieved from 4.13 p.m. G.M.T. on 14 June 1919, from Lester's Field, St. John's, Newfoundland, 1,960 miles *3 154 km* to Derrygimla bog near Clifden, County Galway, Ireland, at 8.40 a.m. G.M.T., 15 June, when the pilot Capt. John William Alcock, D.S.C. (1892–1919), and the navigator Lt. Arthur Whitten Brown (1886–1948) flew across in a Vickers *Vimy*, powered by two 360 h.p. Rolls-Royce *Eagle VIII* engines. Both men were created civil K.B.E's on 21 June 1919 when Alcock was aged 26 years 227 days, and won a *Daily Mail* prize of £10,000.

Solo

The 79th man to achieve a trans-Atlantic flight but the first to do so solo was Capt. (later Brig.) Charles Augustus Lindbergh (Hon. A.F.C.) (1902–1974) who took off in his 220 h.p. Ryan monoplane "Spirit of St. Louis" at 12.52 p.m. G.M.T. on 20 May 1927 from Roosevelt Field, Long Island, N.Y., U.S.A. He landed at 10.21 p.m. G.M.T. on 21 May 1927 at Le Bourget airfield, Paris, France. His flight of 3,610 miles *5 810 km* lasted 33 hours 29½ min and he won a prize of $25,000 (*then £5,300*).

Most Flights

John M. Winston, a senior British Airways Flight Engineer, flew 1,277 trans-Atlantic flights from 10 May 1947 to 14 Dec. 1978—a total of 20,100 hours.

Trans-Pacific

The first non-stop Pacific flight was by Major Clyde Pangborn and Hugh Herdon in the Bellanca cabin 'plane *Miss Veedol* from Sabishiro Beach, Japan 4,558 miles *7 335 km* to Wenatchee, Washington, U.S.A. in 41 hrs 13 mins on 3–5 Oct. 1931. (For earliest crossing see 1924 flight below).

Circumnavigational Flights

Strict circumnavigation requires passing through two antipodal points thus with a minimum distance of 24,859.75 miles *40 007,89 km*. The F.A.I. permits flights which exceed the length of the Tropic of Cancer or Capricorn *viz* 22,858.754 miles *36 787,599 km*.

The earliest such flight of 26,345 miles *42 398 km* was by two U.S. Army Douglas D.W.C. amphibians in 57 'hops'. The *Chicago* was piloted by Lt. Lowell H. Smith and Lt. Leslie P. Arnold and the *New Orleans* was piloted by Lt. Erik H. Nelson and Lt. John Harding between 6 Apr. and 28 Sept. 1924 beginning and ending at Seattle, Washington, U.S.A.

The earliest solo claim was by Wiley Hardemann Post (1898–1935) (U.S.) in the Lockheed Vega "Winnie Mae" starting and finishing at Floyd Bennett Field, New York City on 15–22 July 1933 in 10 "hops". The distance of 15,596 miles *25 099 km* with a flying time of 115 hrs 36 min was however at too high a latitude to qualify.

The fastest flight has been the non-stop eastabout flight of 45 hrs 19 min by three flight-refuelled USAF B-52's led by Maj-Gen. Archie J. Old Jr. They covered 24,325 miles *39 147 km* on 16–18 Jan. 1957 finishing at March Air Force Base, Riverside California, having averaged 525 m.p.h. *845 km/h* with four in-flight refuellings by KC-97 aerial tankers.

The first circum-polar flight was solo by Capt. Elgen M. Long, 44, in a Piper Navajo on 5 Nov.–3 Dec. 1971. He covered 38,896 miles *62 597 km* in 215 flying hours. The cabin temperature sank to −40° C *−40° F* over Antarctica.

Circumnavigation *Smallest aircraft*

The smallest aircraft to complete a circumnavigation is the 20 ft 11 in *6,38 m* single-engined 180 h.p. Thorp T-18 built in his garage by its pilot Donald P. Taylor of Sage, California. His 26,190 mile *42 148 km* flight in 37 stages took 176 flying hours ending at Oshkosh, Wisconsin on 30 Sept. 1976.

Largest wing span

The aircraft with the largest wing span ever constructed was the $40 million Hughes H.2 *Hercules* flying-boat, which was raised 70 ft *21,3 m* into the air in a test run of 1,000 yds *914 m*, piloted by Howard Hughes (1905–1976), off Long Beach Harbor, California, U.S.A., on 2 Nov. 1947. The eight-engined 190 ton *193 tonnes* aircraft had a wing span of 320 ft *97,54 m* and a length of 219 ft *66,75 m* and never flew again.

The Tally Birdman TL-1, weighing only 131 kg *288 lb.* at take-off, is the lightest powered aeroplane ever flown.

Heaviest

The third Boeing E-4A advanced airborne command post version of the Boeing 747-200B transport flew for the first time on 6 June 1974 powered by 4 General Electric F103-GE-100 turbofan engines with a total thrust of 210,000 lb. *95 250 kg.* The all-up weight has been put at 379.4 tons *385,6 tonnes* and the cost at $117 million (*then £55½ million*) making it the heaviest and most expensive aircraft of all time.

Lightest

The lightest mechanically powered aeroplane ever flown was the prototype Birdman TL-1, a single-place monoplane designed and built by Emmet M. Tally III (*k.* 1976) of Daytona Beach, Florida and first flown on 25 Jan. 1975. It had a wing span of 34 ft *10,36 m,* a weight of 100 lb. *45 kg* empty, and 288 lb. *131 kg* at normal take-off weight. It was powered by a 15 h.p. Tally Aircraft M.C. 101DT single-cylinder two-stroke engine, driving a pusher propeller and had a maximum speed of 60 m.p.h. *97 km/h* and a range of 200 miles *322 km* on 4 U.S. gallons (15 litres) of fuel. The pilot sat on an open seat.

The lightest and smallest twin-engined aeroplane is the prototype MC 10 Cricri single-seat monoplane designed and built by Michel Colomban of Rueil-Malmaison, France, and first flown on 19 July 1973 by 68-year-old Robert Buisson. It has a wing span of 16 ft 4¾ in *5,00 m,* an empty weight of 139 lb. *63 kg* and take-off weight of 375 lb. *170 kg,* including this pilot. Two 9 h.p. Rowena two-stroke engines give it a maximum speed of 130 m.p.h. *210 km/h* and a range of 248 miles *400 km.* The Cricri is aerobatic.

Smallest

The smallest aeroplane ever flown is the Stits *Skybaby* biplane, designed and built by Ray Stits at Riverside, California, U.S.A., and first flown by Robert H. Starr on 26 May 1952. It was 9 ft 10 in *3 m* long, with a wing span of 7 ft 2 in *2,18 m,* and weighed 452 lb. *205 kg* empty. It was powered by an 85 h.p. Continental C85 engine, giving a top speed of 185 m.p.h. *297 km/h.*

Bombers *Heaviest*

The world's heaviest bomber is the eight-jet swept-wing Boeing B-52H *Stratofortress,* which has a maximum take-off weight of 488,000 lb. (217.86 tons *221,35 tonnes*). It has a wing span of 185 ft *56,38 m* and is 157 ft 6¾ in *48,02 m* in length, with a speed of over 650 m.p.h. *1 046 km/h.* The B-52 can carry twelve SRAM thermonuclear short range attack missiles or twenty four 750 lb. *340 kg* bombs under its wings and eight more SRAMs or eighty four 500 lb. *226 kg* bombs in the fuselage. The ten-engined Convair B-36J, weighing 183 tons *185 tonnes,* had a greater wing span, at 230 ft *70,10 m* but it is no longer in service. It had a top speed of 435 m.p.h. *700 km/h.*

Fastest

The world's fastest operational bombers are the French Dassault *Mirage IV,* which can fly at Mach 2.2 (1,450 m.p.h. *2 333 km/h*) at 36,000 ft *11 000 m;* the American General Dynamics FB-111A, with a maximum speed of Mach 2.5; and the Soviet swing-wing Tupolev Tu-26 known to N.A.T.O.

as "Backfire", which has an estimated over-target speed of Mach 2.0 and a combat radius of up to 3,570 miles *5 745 km.*

Airliner Largest *World*

The highest capacity jet airliner is the Boeing 747 "Jumbo Jet", first flown on 9 Feb. 1969 (see Heaviest aircraft) and has a capacity of from 385 to 500 passengers with a maximum speed of 608 m.p.h. *978 km/h.* Its wing span is 195.7 ft *59,64 m* and its length 231.3 ft *70,5 m.* It entered service on 22 Jan. 1970.

Great Britain

The largest ever British aircraft was the experimental Bristol Type 167 *Brabazon,* which had a maximum take-off weight of 129.4 tons *131,4 tonnes,* a wing span of 230 ft *70,10 m* and a length of 177 ft *53,94 m.* This eight-engined aircraft first flew on 4 Sept. 1949. The *Concorde* (see below) has a maximum take-off weight of 408,000 lb. *185 065 kg* (182.14 tons).

Airliner Fastest

The supersonic BAC/Aerospatiale *Concorde,* first flown on 2 Mar. 1969, with a capacity of 128 passengers, cruises at up to Mach 2.2 (1,450 m.p.h. *2 334 km/h*). It flew at Mach 1.05 on 10 Oct. 1969, exceeded Mach 2 for the first time on 4 Nov. 1970 and became the first supersonic airliner used on passenger services on 21 Jan. 1976 when Air France and British Airways opened services simultaneously between, respectively, Paris-Rio de Janeiro and London–Bahrain. Services between London and New York (record 3 hrs 6 min) and Paris and New York began on 22 Nov. 1977.

The U.S.S.R.'s Tu 144 which first flew on 31 Dec. 1968 began passenger operations between Moscow and Alma Ata (2,190 miles *3 520 km*) on 1 Nov. 1977, offering an average speed of 1,245 m.p.h. *2 004 km/h* (Mach 1.9).

Most Capacious

The capacity of the commercial adaptation of the U.S.A.F. Lockheed C-5A Galaxy known as the Lockheed 500-3 is 51,707 ft³ *1 463 m³* The wing-span is 222.7 ft *67,8 m* and the length 245.9 ft *74,9 m.*

Largest propeller

The largest aircraft propeller ever used was the 22 ft 7½ in *6,9 m* diameter Garuda propeller, fitted to the Linke-Hofmann R II built in Wroclaw, Poland, which flew in 1919. It was driven by four 260 h.p. Mercedes engines and turned at only 545 r.p.m.

Scheduled flights *Longest*

The longest distance scheduled non-stop flight is the weekly Pan-Am Sydney-San Francisco non-stop 13 hr 25 min Flight 816, in a Boeing 747 SP, opened in December 1976, over 7,475 statute miles *12 030 km.* The longest delivery flight by a commercial jet is 8,936 nautical miles or 10,290 statute miles *16 560 km* from Seattle, Washington, U.S.A. to Cape Town, South Africa by the South African Airway's Boeing 747 SP (Special performance) "Matroosberg" with 178 400 kg *175.5 tons* of pre-cooled fuel in 17 hr 22½ min on 23–29 Mar. 1976.

Shortest

The shortest scheduled flight in the world is that by Loganair between the Orkney Islands of Westray and Papa Westray which has been flown with Britten-Norman Islander twin-engined 10-seat transports since September 1967. Though scheduled for 2 min, in favourable wind conditions it has been accomplished in 58 secs by Capt. Andrew D. Alsop.

London–Edinburgh

The F.A.I. ratified flight record between the capitals of Scotland and England is 26 min 25 sec by Sqn. Ldr. R. Peart A.F.C. D.S.M. on 9 Sept. 1977 averaging 750.89 m.p.h. *1 208,45 km/h* for the 330.6 mile *532 km* flight.

HIGHEST SPEED
Official record

The official air speed record is 2,193.167 m.p.h. *3 529,56 km/h* by Capt. Eldon W. Joersz and Maj. George T. Morgan, Jr., in a Lockheed SR-71A near Beale Air Force Base, California, U.S.A. over a 15/25 km course on 28 July 1976.

Air-launched record

The fastest fixed-wing aircraft in the world was the U.S. North American Aviation X-15A-2, which flew for the first time (after modification from X-15A) on 28 June 1964 powered by a liquid oxygen and ammonia rocket propulsion system. Ablative materials on the airframe once enabled a temperature of 3,000° F. to be withstood. The landing speed was 210 knots (242 m.p.h. *389,1 km/h*) momentarily. The highest speed attained was 4,534 m.p.h. *7 297 km/h* (Mach 6.72) when piloted by Major William J. Knight, U.S.A.F. (b. 1930), on 3 Oct. 1967. An earlier version piloted by Joseph A. Walker (1920–66), reached 354,200 ft *107 960 m* (67.08 miles) also over Edwards Air Force Base, California, U.S.A., on 22 Aug. 1963. The programme was suspended after the final flight of 24 Oct. 1968.

Potentially the fastest aircraft ever flown is the Space Shuttle Orbiter built for N.A.S.A. by Rockwell International Corporation and first flown piggyback atop a converted Boeing 747 on 18 Feb. 1977. When flown into space, from 1979, the Orbiter will take off like a rocket, operate in orbit as a spacecraft, at up to 17,600 m.p.h. *28 325 km/h*, and land at speeds as high as 194 knots 223 m.p.h. *359 km/h*.

Fastest jet

The world's fastest jet aircraft is the U.S.A.F. Lockheed SR-71 reconnaissance aircraft (see Official record above) which was first flown on 22 Dec. 1964 and is reportedly capable of attaining an altitude ceiling of close to 100,000 ft *30 480 m*. The SR-71 has a wing span of 55.6 ft *16,94 m* and a length of 107.4 ft *32,73 m* and weighs 170,000 lb. (75.9 tons *77,1 tonnes*) at take-off. Its reported range is 2,982 miles *4 800 km* at Mach 3 at 78,750 ft *24 000 m*. At least 30 are believed to have been built. The fastest combat aircraft in the world is the U.S.S.R. Mikoyan MiG-25 fighter (code name "Foxbat"). The reconnaissance "Foxbat-B" has been tracked by radar at about Mach 3.2 (2,110 m.p.h. *3 395 km/h*). When armed with four large underwing air-to-air missiles known to N.A.T.O. as "Acrid", the fighter "Foxbat-A" is limited to Mach 2.8 (1,845 m.p.h. *2 969 km/h*. The single-seat "Foxbat-A" spans 45 ft 9 in *13,95 m*, is 73 ft 2 in *22,3 m* long and has a maximum take-off weight of 79,800 lb. *36 200 kg*.

Fastest biplane

The fastest recorded biplane was the Italian Fiat C.R.42B, with a 1,010 h.p. Daimler-Benz DB601A engine, which attained 323 m.p.h. *520 km/h* in 1941. Only one was built.

Fastest piston-engined aircraft

The fastest speed at which a piston-engined aeroplane has ever been measured was for a cut-down privately owned Hawker *Sea Fury* which attained 520 m.p.h. *836 km/h* in level flight over Texas, U.S.A., in August 1966 piloted by Mike Carroll (k. 1969) of Los Angeles. The official record for a piston-engined aircraft is 482.463 m.p.h. *776,449 km/h* over Edwards AFB California by Darryl C. Greenamyer (U.S.) in a modified Grumman F8F-2 *Bearcat* on 16 Aug. 1969.

Fastest propeller-driven aircraft

The Soviet Tu-114 turboprop transport is the world's fastest propeller-driven aeroplane. It has achieved average speeds of more than 545 m.p.h. *877 km/h* carrying heavy payloads over measured circuits. It is developed from the Tupolev Tu-95 bomber, known in the West as the "Bear", and has 14,795 h.p. engines. The turboprop-powered Republic XF-84H prototype U.S. Navy fighter which flew on 22 July 1955 had a top *design* speed of 670 m.p.h. *1 078 km/h* but was abandoned.

Fastest Trans-Atlantic flight

The trans-Atlantic flight record is 1 hr. 54 min. 56.4 secs. by Major James V. Sullivan, 37 and Major Noel F. Widdifield, 33 flying a Lockheed SR-71A eastwards on 1 Sept. 1974. The average speed, slowed by refuelling by a KC-135 tanker aircraft, for the New York–London stage of 3,461.53 miles *5 570,80 km* was 1,806.963 m.p.h. *2 908,026 km/h*. The solo record (Gander to Gatwick) is 8 hrs 47 min 32 sec by Capt. John J. A. Smith in a Rockwell 685 on 12 Mar. 1978.

Altitude *Official record*

The official world altitude record by an aircraft taking off from the ground under its own power is 123,524 ft (23.39 miles *37 650 m*) by Aleksandr Fedotov (U.S.S.R.) in a Mikoyan E.266M, (MiG-25) aircraft, powered by two 30,865 lb. *14 000 kg* thrust turbojet engines, on 31 Aug. 1977.

The greatest recorded height by any pilot without a pressure cabin or even a pressure suit has been 49,500 ft *15 085 m* by Sq./Ldr. G. W. H. Reynolds, D.F.C. in a Spitfire Mark VC over Libya in 1942.

Duration

The flight duration record is 64 days, 22 hours, 19 min and 5 sec, set up by Robert Timm and John Cook in a Cessna 172 "Hacienda". They took off from McCarran Airfield, Las Vegas, Nevada, U.S.A., just before 3.53 p.m. local time on 4 Dec. 1958, and landed at the same airfield just before 2.12 p.m. on 7 Feb. 1959. They covered a distance equivalent to six times round the world with continued refuellings, without landing.

The record for duration without refuelling is 84 hrs 32 min, set by Walter E. Lees and Frederic A. Brossy in a Bellanca monoplane with a 225 h.p. Packard Diesel engine, at Jacksonville, Florida, on 25–28 May 1931.

AIRPORTS

Largest *World*

The world's largest airport is the Dallas/Fort Worth Airport, Texas, U.S.A., which extends over 17,500 acres *7 080 ha* in the Grapevine area, midway between Dallas and Fort Worth. It was opened in January 1974 at an initial cost of nearly $800 million. The present 4 runways and 5 terminal buildings are planned to be extended to 9 runways and 13 terminals with 260 gates with an ultimate capacity for 150 million passengers. The total airport reserve area of Mirabel, Montreal's airport, Canada, is 36 000 ha *88,960 acres* of which 7 000 ha *17,300 acres* is operational. The planned area of the Jeddah airport, Saudi Arabia, due to be completed at a cost of £3,800 million by 1982 has been published at 26,250 acres *10 600 ha*.

Great Britain

Seventy-three airline companies from 68 countries operate scheduled services into Heathrow Airport—London (2,819 acres *1 140 ha*), and during 1978 there was a total of 292,055 air transport movements handled by a staff of 56,465 employed by the various companies and the British Airports Authority. The total number of passengers, both incoming and outgoing, was 26,910,068. The most flights yet handled by Heathrow in a day was 986 on 19 July 1974 and the largest number of passengers yet handled in a day was 106,726 on 30 June 1978. Aircraft fly to more than 90 countries.

Busiest

The world's busiest airport is the Chicago International Airport, O'Hare Field, Illinois, U.S.A. with a total of 754,986 movements and 49,151,449 passengers in the year 1978. This represents a take-off or landing every 41.8 seconds round the clock. Heathrow Airport—London handles more *international* traffic than any other.

The busiest landing area ever has been Bien Hoa Air Base, south Vietnam, which handled more than 1,000,000 take-offs and landings in 1970. The world's largest "helipad" was An Khe, south Vietnam.

Highest and lowest

The highest airport in the world is La Sa (Lhasa) Airport, Tibet at 14,315 ft *4 363 m*.

The highest landing ever made by a fixed-wing 'plane is 19,947 ft *6 080 m* on Dhaulagri, Himalaya by a Pilatus Porter, named "Yeti", supplying the 1960 Swiss Expedition. The lowest landing field is El Lisan on the east shore of the Dead Sea, 1,180 ft *360 m* below sea-level, but the lowest international airport is Schiphol, Amsterdam, at 13 ft *3,9 m* below sea-level.

Farthest and Nearest to City Centres

The airport farthest from the city centre it allegedly serves is Mirabel, Quebec, Canada which is 33 miles *53 km* from Montreal. The Gibraltar airport is 800 yards *800 m* from the centre.

Longest Runway *World*

The longest runway in the world is one of 7 miles *11 km* in length (of which 15,000 ft *4 572 m* is concreted) at Edwards Air Force Base on the bed of Rogers Dry Lake at Muroc, California, U.S.A. The whole test centre airfield extends over 65 miles² *168 km²*. In an emergency an auxiliary 12 mile *19 km* strip is available along the bed of the Dry Lake. The world's longest civil airport runway is one of 16,076 ft (3.04 miles *4,89 km*) at Upington, South Africa.

Great Britain

The longest runway available normally to civil aircraft in the United Kingdom is No. 1 at Heathrow Airport—London, measuring 12,800 ft (2.42 miles *3,90 km*).

HELICOPTERS
Fastest

A Bell YUH-1B Model 533 compound research helicopter, boosted by two auxiliary turbojet engines, attained an unofficial speed record of 316.1 m.p.h. *508,7 km/h* over Arlington, Texas, U.S.A., in April 1969. The official world speed record for a pure helicopter is 368,4 km/h *228.9 m.p.h.* set by Gourguen Karapetyan in a MilA-10 on a 15/25 km course near Moscow, U.S.S.R. on 21 Sept. 1978.

Largest

The world's largest helicopter is the Soviet Mil *Mi-12* ("Homer"), also known as the V-12, which set up an international record by lifting a payload of 88,636 lb. (39.5 tons *40,2 tonnes*) to a height of 7,398 ft *2 255 m* on 6 Aug. 1969. It is powered by four 6,500 h.p. turboshaft engines and has a span of 219 ft 10 in *67 m* over its rotor tips with a length of 121 ft 4½ in *37,00 m* and weighs 103.3 tons *105 tonnes*.

Smallest

The Aerospace General Co. one-man rocket assisted minicopter weighs about 160 lb. *72,5 kg* and can cruise 250 miles *400 km* at 85 m.p.h. *137 km/h.*

Highest

The altitude record for helicopters is 40,820 ft *12 442 m* by an Aérospatiale SA315B *Lama*, over France on 21 June 1972. The highest recorded landing has been at 23,000 ft *7 000 m* below the South-East face of Everest in a rescue sortie in May 1971. The World Trade Center helipad is 1,385 ft *422 m* above street level in New York City on the South Tower.

AUTOGYROS
Earliest

The autogyro or gyroplane, a rotorcraft with an unpowered rotor turned by the airflow in flight, preceded the practical helicopter with engine-driven rotor. Juan de la Cierva (Spain), made the first successful autogyro flight with his model C.4 (commercially named an *Autogiro*) at Getafe, Spain, on 9 Jan. 1923. On 6 Dec. 1955, Dr. Igor B. Bensen (U.S.A.) flew his very simple open-seat Gyro-Copter and then made the design available in kit form to amateur constructor/pilots.

Speed Altitude and Distance Records

Wing Cdr. Kenneth H. Wallis (G.B.) holds the straight-line distance record of 543.27 miles *874,32 km* set in his WA-116 F autogyro on 28 Sept. 1975 non-stop from Lydd, Kent to Wick, Highland. Wg. Cdr. Wallis flew his WA-116, with 72 h.p. McCulloch engine, to a record altitude of 15,220 ft *4 639 m* on 11 May 1968, and to a record speed of 111.2 m.p.h. *179 km/h* over a 3 km straight course on 12 May 1969.

FLYING-BOAT
Fastest

The fastest flying-boat ever built has been the Martin XP6M-1 *Seamaster*, the U.S. Navy 4 jet engined minelayer flown in 1955–59 with a top speed of 646 m.p.h. *1 040 km/h.* In Sept.

1946 the Martin JRM-2 *Mars* flying-boat set a payload record of 68,327 lb. *30 992 kg.*

The official flying-boat speed record is 566.69 m.p.h. *912 km/h*, set up by Nikolai Andrievsky and crew of two in a Soviet Beriev M-10, powered by two AL-7 turbojets, over a 15/25 km course on 7 Aug. 1961. The M-10 holds all 12 records listed for jet-powered flying-boats, including an altitude of 49,088 ft *14 962 m* set by Georgiy Buryanov and crew over the Sea of Azov on 9 Sept. 1961.

AIRSHIPS
Earliest

The earliest flight in an airship was by Henri Giffard from Paris in his coal-gas 88,300 ft³ *2 500 m³* 144 ft *43,8 m* long airship on 24 Sept. 1852. The earliest British airship was a 20,000 ft³ *566 m³* 75 ft *22,8 m* long craft built by Stanley Spencer whose maiden flight was from Crystal Palace, Bromley, Greater London on 22 Sept. 1902. The latest airship to be built in Britain is the 181,200 ft³ *5 131 m³* 164 ft *50 m* long Aerospace Development AD-500, assembled at R.A.F. Cardington, Bedfordshire. Its maiden flight was on 3 Feb. 1979.

Largest *Rigid*

The largest rigid airship ever built was the 210.5 ton *213,9 tonne* German *Graf Zeppelin II* (LZ 130), with a length of 245 m *803.8 ft* and a capacity of 7,062,100 ft³ *199 981 m³*. She made her maiden flight on 14 Sept. 1938 and in May and August 1939 made radar spying missions in British air space. She was dismantled in April 1940. Her sister ship *Hindenburg* was 5.6 ft *1,70 m* longer.

British

The largest British airship was the R101 built by the Royal Airship Works, Cardington, Bedfordshire, which first flew on 14 Oct. 1929. She was 777 ft *236, 8 m* in length and had a capacity of 5,508,800 ft³ *155 995 m³*. She crashed near Beauvais, France, killing 48 aboard on 5 Oct. 1930.

Non-Rigid

The largest non-rigid airship ever constructed was the U.S. Navy ZPG 3-W which had a capacity of 1,516,300 ft³ *42 937 m³*, was 403.4 ft *122,9 m* long and 85.1 ft *25,93 m* in diameter, with a crew of 21. She first flew on 21 July 1958, but crashed into the sea in June 1960.

Greatest Passenger Load

The most people ever carried in an airship was 207 in the U.S. Navy *Akron* in 1931. The trans-Atlantic record is 117 by the German *Hindenburg* in 1937. The distance record for airships is 3,967.1 miles *6 384,5 km*, set up by the German *Graf Zeppelin*, captained by Dr. Hugo Eckener, between 29 Oct. and 1 Nov. 1928.

BALLOONING
Earliest

The earliest recorded ascent was by a model hot air balloon invented by Father Bartolomeu de Gusmão (né Lourenço) (b. Santos, Brazil, 1685), which was flown indoors at the Casa da India, Terreiro do Paço, Portugal on 8 Aug. 1709.

Distance record

The record distance travelled by a balloon is 3,107.61 miles *5001,22 km* in 137 hrs 5 min 50 sec by the American Yost HB-72 helium-filled balloon *Double Eagle II* on 12–17 Aug. 1978 from Sprague Farm, Presque Isle, Maine, U.S.A. to Coquerel Farm, Miserey, France. The crew on this first North Atlantic crossing was Ben L. Abruzzo, 48, Maxie L. Anderson, 44 and Larry M. Newman, 31 from Albuquerque, New Mexico, U.S.A.

Highest *Unmanned*

The highest altitude attained by an unmanned balloon was 170,000 ft *51 815 m* by a Winzen balloon of 47.8 million ft³ *1,35 million m³* launched at Chico, California in October 1972.

Manned

The greatest altitude reached in a manned balloon is the

above: The helium-filled balloon *Double Eagle II*, photographed over the French Coast, after completing in 1978 the first ever transatlantic flight by a free balloon. (*Flight International*)

top left & bottom left: Philip Charles Clark who set the world's distance record for hot-air ballooning at 350.7 miles *564,47 km* in just under 11 hours in the Cameron balloon *Sungas* (left) on 25 Jan. 1978 (see p. 150). (*top left: George Gallop; bottom left: Clive Landen*)

unofficial 123,800 ft (23.45 miles *37 735 m*) by Nicholas Piantanida (1933–66) of Bricktown, New Jersey, U.S.A., from Sioux Falls, South Dakota, U.S.A., on 1 Feb. 1966. He landed in a cornfield in Iowa but did not survive. The official record is 113,740 ft *34 668 m* by Cdr. Malcolm D. Ross, U.S.N.R. and the late Lt.-Cdr. Victor E. Prather, U.S.N. in an ascent from the deck of U.S.S. *Antietam* on 4 May 1961, over the Gulf of Mexico.

The record altitude in an open basket is 38,789 ft *11 822 m* by Kingswood Sprott Jr. over Lakeland, Florida, U.S.A. on 27 Sept. 1975.

Largest

The largest balloon built is one with an inflatable volume of 70 million ft³ *2 million m³* by Winzen Research Inc., Minnesota, U.S.A.

Ballooning (*Hot-Air*)

The world's distance record for hot-air ballooning is 350.7 miles *564,47 km* by Philip Charles Clark (G.B.) set on 25 Jan. 1978 in the Cameron balloon *Sungas* from Bristol to Châlons-sur-Marne, France.

The altitude record is 45,837 ft *13 971 m* by Julian R. P. Nott and co-pilot Felix J. C. Pole (both G.B.) over Bhopal, India on 25 Jan. 1974 in *Daffodil II*, the 375,000 ft³ *10 618 m³* Cameron A-375 balloon. The largest hot-air balloon ever built is the U.K. Cameron A-500 500,000 ft³ *14 158 m³* *Gerard A. Heineken* first flown on 18 Aug. 1974. The endurance record is 18 hrs 56 min from Melbury Bubb, Dorset to Angers, France by Donald Allan Cameron (G.B.) and Le Comte Jean Costa de Beauregard (France) in a Cameron A-500 on 21–22 Nov. 1975.

HOVERCRAFT (Skirted Air Cushion Vehicles)
Earliest

The inventor of the ACV (air-cushion vehicle) is Sir Christopher Sydney Cockerell, C.B.E., F.R.S. (b. 4 June 1910), a British engineer who had the idea in 1954, published his Ripplecraft Report 1/55 on 25 Oct. 1955 and patented it on 12 Dec. 1955. The earliest patent relating to an air-cushion craft was applied for in 1877 by John I. Thornycroft (1843–1928) of Chiswick, London. The first flight by a hovercraft was made by the 4 ton/*tonnes* Saunders-Roe SR-N1 at Cowes on 30 May 1959. With a 1,500 lb. *680 kg* thrust Viper turbo-jet engine, this craft reached 68 knots *126 km/h* in June 1961. The first hovercraft public service was run across the Dee Estuary by the 60 knot *111 km/h* 24-passenger Vickers-Armstrong's VA-3 between July and September 1962.

Largest

The world's largest civil hovercraft is the 305 ton British-built SRN 4 Mk III with a capacity of 416 passengers and 60 cars. It is 186 ft *56,69 m* in length, is powered by 4 Bristol Siddeley Marine Proteus engines giving a maximum speed in excess of the permitted operating speed of 65 knots.

Fastest warship

The world's fastest warship is the 78 ft *23,7 m* long 100 ton/*tonnes* U.S. Navy test vehicle SES-100B. She attained 88.88 knots *102.35 m.p.h.* in speed trials in 1976. A contract for a 3,000 ton Large Surface Effect Ship (LSES) was placed by the U.S. Department of Defense with Bell Aerospace in September 1977 for delivery in mid-1981.

Longest flight

The longest hovercraft journey was one of 5,000 miles *8 047 km* through eight West African countries between 15 Oct. 1969 and 3 Jan. 1970 by the British Trans-African Hovercraft Expedition.

Highest

The greatest altitude at which a hovercraft is operating is on Lago Titicaca, Peru, where since 1975 an HM2 Hoverferry is hovering 12,506 ft *3 811 m* above sea level.

Clark O. Palaez from Cebu City, Philippines (left) who flew solo in a Piper Tri-Pacer at the age of 10 yrs. 11 months on 24 Aug. 1968 (see p. 151).

MODEL AIRCRAFT
Altitude, Speed and Duration
The world record for altitude is 26,929 ft *8 208 m* by Maynard L. Hill (U.S.A.) on 6 Sept. 1970 using a radio-controlled model. The free flight speed record is 213.70 m.p.h. *343,92 km/h* by V. Goukoune and V. Myakinin (both U.S.S.R.) with a radio-controlled model at Klementyeva, U.S.S.R., on 21 Sept. 1971. The record duration flight is one of 28 hrs 28 min by B. Laging at Balluvat, Victoria, Australia on 1 Oct. 1978.

Cross Channel
The first cross channel model helicopter flight was achieved by an 11 lb. *5,00 kg* model Bell 212 radio controlled by Dieter Zeigler for 32 miles *52 km* between Ashford, Kent and Ambleteuse, France on 17 July 1974.

Paper Aircraft
The flight duration record for a paper aircraft is 15.0 sec by William Harlan Pryor in the Municipal Auditorium, Nashville, Tennessee, U.S.A. on 26 Mar. 1975. A paper plane was reported and witnessed to have flown 1¼ miles *2,0 km* by "Chick" C. O. Reinhart from a 10th storey office window at 60 Beaver Street, New York City across the East River to Brooklyn in August 1933. It was helped by a thermal from a coffee-roasting plant.

Indoor
An indoor distance of 113 ft 11 in *34,72 m* was recorded by Brad Mickelson in Eby Fieldhouse, Coe College, Cedar Rapids, Iowa, U.S.A. on 2 Apr. 1979.

PERSONAL AVIATION RECORDS
Most Flying Hours
Max Conrad (1903–79) (U.S.A.) between 1928 and mid-1974 totalled 52,929 hr 40 min logged flight—more than 6 years airborne. He completed 150 transatlantic crossings in light aircraft.

Most Take Offs and Landings
Douglas Blair, 34, and Dennis Oliver made 138 take-offs and daylight landings in 14 hrs 54 min on 21 June 1978 from Milwaukee, Wisconsin to Urbana, Ohio, U.S.A. in a single engine Beechcraft Bonanza.

Oldest and Youngest Pilots
The youngest age at which anyone has ever qualified as a military pilot is 15 yrs 5 months in the case of Sgt. Thomas Dobney (b. 6 May 1926) of the R.A.F. He had overstated his age (14 years) on entry. Miss Betty Bennett took off, flew and landed solo at the age of 10 on 4 Jan. 1952 in Cuba. Clark O. Pelaez (b. 4 May 1957) flew a Piper Tri-Pacer solo at Cebu City, Philippines on 24 Apr. 1968 aged 10 years 11 months. The world's oldest pilot is Ed. McCarty (b. 18 Sept. 1885) of Kimberly, Idaho, U.S.A., who in 1977 was flying his rebuilt 30 year old Ercoupe aged 92. Glenn E. Messer of Birmingham, Alabama has been flying "steady" since 13 May 1911. Albert E. Savoy (b. 22 Feb. 1895) was issued with his first PPL aged 82 years 8 months on 8 Nov. 1977.

Human-powered flight
The 70 lb *31,75 kg* Gossamer Condor (96 ft *29,26 m* wingspan) designed by D. Paul MacCready flew the figure-of-8 course between pylons 880 yds *804,6 m* apart powered by the 9¾ stone *61,2 kg* Bryan Allen at Shafter Airport, California on 23 Aug. 1977 to win the £50,000 Kremer prize. The flight lasted 7 mins 27.5 secs.

---

5. POWER PRODUCERS

Oldest Steam Engine
The oldest steam engine in working order is the 1812 Boulton & Watt 26 h.p. 42 in bore beam engine on the Kennet & Avon Canal at Great Bedwyn, Wiltshire. It was restored by the Crofton Society in 1971.

Earliest Atomic Pile
The world's first atomic pile was built in a disused squash court at Stagg Field, University of Chicago, Illinois, U.S.A. It went "critical" at 3.25 p.m. on 2 Dec. 1942.

Power Plant Largest *World*
The world's largest power station is the U.S.S.R.'s hydro-electric station at Krasnoyarsk on the river Yenisey, Siberia, U.S.S.R. with a power of 6,096 MW. Its third generator turned in March 1968 and the twelfth became operative in December 1970. The turbine hall, completed in June 1968, is 1,378 ft *420 m* long. The reservoir backed up by the dam was reported in Nov. 1972 to be 240 miles *386 km* in length.

The largest planned power plant is the Itaipu on the river Paraná on the Brazil–Paraguay border with an ultimate 12,600,000 kW from 18 turbines.

Great Britain
The power station with the greatest installed capacity in Great Britain is Longannet, Fife, Scotland which attained 2,400 MW by December 1972. At Drax, North Yorkshire, 6 × 660 MW sets yielding 3,960 MW are expected to be in commission by 1984. A 3,300 MW oil fired installation on the Isle of Grain, Kent, is due to be commissioned in 1980.

The largest hydro-electric plant in the United Kingdom is the North of Scotland Hydro-electricity Board's Power Station at Loch Sloy, Central. The installed capacity of this station is 130 MW. The Ben Cruachan Pumped Storage Scheme was opened on 15 Oct. 1965 at Loch Awe, Strathclyde, Scotland. It has a capacity of 400 MW and cost £24,000,000. The 1,880 MW underground pumped storage scheme at Dinorwic, Gwynedd will be the largest built in Europe with a head of 1,739 ft *530 m* and a capacity of 13,770 ft³/sec *390 m³/sec*. Completion is due in 1981.

Nuclear Power Station *Largest*
The world's largest atomic power station is the Ontario Hydro's Pickering station which in 1973 attained full output of 2,160 MW.

Nuclear Reactor *Largest*
The largest single nuclear reactor in the world is the 1,098 MW Browns Ferry Unit 1 General Electric boiling water type reactor located on the Wheeler Reservoir, near Decatar, Alabama which became operative in 1973. The Grand Gulf Nuclear Station at Port Gibson, Mississippi will have a capacity of 1,290 MW in 1979.

Tidal Power Station
The world's first major tidal power station is the *Usine marèmotrice de la Rance*, officially opened on 26 Nov. 1966 at the Rance estuary in the Golfe de St. Malo, Brittany, France. It was built in five years at a cost of 420,000,000 francs (£34,685,000), and has a net annual output of 544,000,000 kWh. The 880 yd *804 m* barrage contains 24 turbo alternators. This harnessing of the tides has imperceptibly slowed the Earth's rate of revolution. The $1,000 million (£540 million) Passamaquoddy project for the Bay of Fundy in Maine, U.S.A., and New Brunswick, Canada, is not expected to be operative before 1978.

Boiler Largest
The largest boilers ever designed are those ordered in the United States from The Babcock & Wilcox Company (U.S.A.) with a capacity of 1,330 MW so involving the evaporation of 9,330,000 lb. *4 232 000 kg* of steam per hour. The largest boilers now being installed in the United Kingdom are the three 660 MW units for the Drax Power Station (see p. 151) designed and constructed by Babcock & Wilcox Ltd.

Generator Largest
Generators in the 2,000,000 kW (or 2,000 MW) range are now in the planning stages both in the U.K. and the U.S.A. The largest under construction is one of 1,300 MW by the Brown Boveri Co. of Switzerland for the Tennessee Valley Authority.

Turbines Largest
The largest turbines are those rated at 820,000 h.p. with an

The oldest working mill in England, the post-mill at Outwood, Surrey, built in 1665 (see p. 153).

overload capacity of 1,000,000 h.p., 32 ft *9,7 m* in diameter with a 401 ton *407 tonnes* runner and a 312½ ton *317,5 tonnes* shaft installed at the Grand Coulee "Third Powerplant".

Pump
The world's largest integral reversible pump-turbine is that made by Allis-Chalmers for the $50,000,000 Taum Sauk installation of the Union Electric Co. in St. Louis, Missouri, U.S.A. It has a rating of 240,000 h.p. as a turbine and a capacity of 1,100,000 gallons *5 000 559 litres*/min as a pump. The Tehachapi Pumping Plant, California (1972) pumps 18,300,000 gal/min *83,2 million litres/min* over 1,700 ft *518 m* up.

Gas Works Largest
The flow of natural gas from the North Sea is diminishing the manufacture of gas by the carbonisation of coal and the re-forming process using petroleum derivatives. Britain's largest ever gasworks 300 acres *120 ha* were at Beckton, Newham. Currently the most productive gasworks are at the

oil re-forming plant at Greenwich, Greater London, with an output of 420.5 million ft³ *11 907 298 m³* per day.

Biggest black-out
The greatest power failure in history struck seven north-eastern U.S. States and Ontario, Canada, on 9–10 Nov. 1965. About 30,000,000 people in 80,000 miles² *207 200 km²* were plunged into darkness. Only two were killed. In New York City the power failed at 5.27 p.m. and was not fully restored for 13½ hours. The total consequential losses in the 52 minute New York City power failure of 13 July 1977 including looting was put at $1 billion (*then £580 million*).

Largest Windmill
The biggest windmill in the world is the *53 m* 173 ft 10½ in tall Tvind windmill, Ulfborg, Denmark completed in February 1978. The 3 blades sweep a 54 metre 177 ft 2 in diameter circle. It cost 4 million kroner (£350,000) and has a capacity of 2000 kW. A windmill with 200 foot *6 896 m* blades is reportedly planned at Boone, North Carolina, U.S.A.

Windmill Earliest

The earliest recorded windmills are those used for grinding corn in Iran (Persia) in the 7th century A.D.

The earliest known in England was the post-mill at Bury St. Edmunds, Suffolk, recorded in 1191. The oldest Dutch mill is the towermill at Zeddam, Gelderland built in c. 1450. The oldest working mill in England is the post-mill at Outwood, Surrey, built in 1665, though the Ivinghoe Mill in Pitstone Green Farm, Buckinghamshire, dating from 1627, has been restored.

Windmill *Largest Conventional*

The largest Dutch windmill is the Dijkpolder in Maasland built in 1718. The sails measure 95¾ ft *29 m* from tip to tip. The tallest windmill in the Netherlands is De Walvisch in Schiedam built to a height of 108 ft *33 m* in 1794. The tallest windmill still standing in Britain is the 9 storey Sutton mill, Norfolk built in 1853 which before being struck by lightning in 1941 had sails 73 feet *22,2 m* in diameter with 216 shutters.

---

6. ENGINEERING

Oldest Machinery *World*

The earliest machinery still in use is the *dâlu*—a water raising instrument known to have been in use in the Sumerian civilization which originated c. 3500 B.C. in Lower Iraq even earlier than the *Saqiyas* on the Nile.

Great Britain

The oldest piece of machinery (excluding clocks) operating in the United Kingdom is the snuff mill driven by a water wheel at Messrs. Wilson & Co.'s Sharrow Mill in Sheffield, South Yorkshire. It is known to have been operating in 1797 and more probably since 1730.

Press Largest

The world's two most powerful production machines are forging presses in the U.S.A. The Loewy closed-die forging press, in a plant leased from the U.S. Air Force by the Wyman-Gordon Company at North Grafton, Massachusetts, U.S.A. weighs 9,469 tons *9 620 tonnes* and stands 114 ft 2 in *34,79 m* high, of which 66 ft *20,1 m* is sunk below the operating floor. It has a rated capacity of 44,600 tons *45 315 tonnes*, and went into operation in October 1955. The other similar press is at the plant of the Aluminium Company of America at Cleveland, Ohio. There has been a report of a

press in the U.S.S.R. with a capacity of 75 000 tonnes *73,800 tons* at Novo Kramatorsk. The Bêché and Grohs counterblow forging hammer, manufactured in West Germany are rated at 60,000 tonnes. The most powerful press in Great Britain is the closed-die forging and extruding press installed in 1967 at the Cameron Iron Works, Livingston, Lothian. The press is 92 ft *28 m* tall (27 ft *8,2 m* below gound) and exerts a force of 30,000 tons *30 481 tonnes*.

Lathe Largest

The world's largest lathe is the 72 ft *21,9 m* long 385 ton *391 tonnes* giant lathe built by the Dortmunder Rheinstahl firm of Wagner in 1962. The face plate is 15 ft *4,57 m* in diameter and can exert a torque of 289,000 ft/lb. *39 955 m/kg f* when handling objects weighing up to 200 tons *203 tonnes*.

Excavator Largest

The world's largest excavator is the 13,000 tonne bucket wheel excavator being assembled at the open cast lignite-mine of Hambach, West Germany with a rating of 200 000 m³ *260,000 yd³* per 20 hour working day. It is 210 m *690 ft* in length and 82 m *269 ft* tall. The wheel is 67,88 m *222 ft* in circumference with 5 m³ *6.5 yd³* buckets.

Dragline Largest *World*

The Ural Engineering Works at Ordzhonikidze, U.S.S.R., completed in March 1962, has a dragline known as the ES-25(100) with a boom of 100 m *328 ft* and a bucket with a capacity of 31.5 yds³ *24 m³*. The world's largest walking dragline is the Bucyrus-Erie 4250W with an all-up weight of 12,000 tons *12 192 tonnes* and a bucket capacity of 220 yds³ *168 m³* on a 310 ft *94,4 m* boom. This machine, the world's largest mobile land machine is now operating on the Central Ohio Coal Company's Muskingum site in Ohio, U.S.A.

Great Britain

The largest dragline excavator in Britain is "Big Geordie", the Bucyrus-Erie 1550W 6250 gross h.p., weighing 3,000 tons *3 048 tonnes* with a forward mast 160 ft *48,7 m* high. On open-cast coal workings at Butterwell, Northumberland in September 1975, it proved able to strip 100 tons *101 tonnes* of overburden in 65 secs with its 65 yard³ *49,7 m³* bucket on a 265 ft *80,7 m* boom. It is owned by Derek Crouch (Contractors) Ltd. of Peterborough, Cambridgeshire.

Crane Most Powerful *World*

The world's most powerful crane is the 53,000 tons 584 ft *178 m* long converted tanker *Odin* owned by Heerema Engineering Service of The Hague, Netherlands. On 26 May 1976 she made a test lift on 3000 tonnes *3,048 tons* at a

A 55 ft *16,76 m* long 450,600 lb. *204,4 tonnes* generator shaft, the largest forging on record completed in Oct 1973 (see p. 154). *(Bethlehem Steel Corporation)*

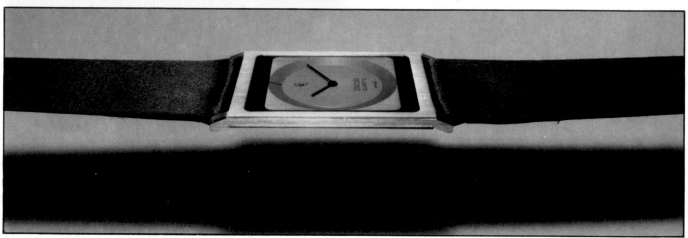

left: The world's largest mobile land machine the Bucyrus-Erie 4250W walking dragline. It weighs 12,000 tons *12,192 tonnes* and has a bucket capacity of 220 yds³ *168 m³* (see p. 153).

below: Delirium I, the thinnest quartz watch in the world, only 1,98 mm *1/16th in* thick, which retails for $4,400 £2,200 (See p. 156). (Concord Watch Corporation)

radius maximum of 105 ft *32 m* in the Calard Canal, Europoort.

Gantry Crane Most Powerful

The 92.3 ft *28,14 m* wide Rahco (R. A. Hanson Disc. Ltd.) gantry crane at the Grand Coulee Dam Third Powerplant was tested to lift a load of 2,232 long tons *2 268 tonnes* in 1975. It lowered a 3,944,000 lb. *1789 tonne* generator rotor with an accuracy of $\frac{1}{32}$ inch *0,8 mm*.

Crane Tallest Mobile

The tallest mobile crane in the world is the 810 tonnes Rosenkranz K10001 with a lifting capacity of 1 000 tonnes *984 tons*, a combined boom and jib height of 202 m *663 ft*. It is carried on 10 trucks each limited to 75 ft 8 in *23,06 m* and an axle weight of 118 tonnes *116 tons*. It can lift 30 tonnes *29.5 tons* to a height of 160 m *525 ft*.

Greatest Lift

The heaviest lifting operation in engineering history was the 41,000 short ton (36,607 long tons *37 194 tonnes*) roof of the Velodrome in Montreal, Canada in 1975. It was raised by jacks some 4 in *10 cm* to strike its centering.

Blast Furnace Largest

The world's largest blast furnace is one with an inner volume 5.070 m³ *179,040 ft³* and a 14,8 m *48 ft 6½ in* diameter hearth at the Oita Works, Kyushu, Japan completed in October 1976 with an annual capacity of 4,380,000 tons *4 451 500 tonnes*.

Forging Largest

The largest forging on record is one of a 450,600 lb. *204,4 tonnes* 55 ft *16,76 m* long generator shaft for Japan, forged by the Bethlehem Steel Corp. Pennsylvania in Oct. 1973.

Pipeline Longest *Oil*

The longest crude oil pipeline in the world is the Interprovincial Pipe Line Company's installation from Edmonton, Alberta, Canada to Buffalo, New York State, U.S.A., a distance of 1,775 miles *2 856 km*. Along the length of the pipe 13 pumping stations maintain a flow of 6,900,000 gal *31 367 145 litres* of oil per day.

The eventual length of the Trans-Siberian Pipeline will be 2,319 miles *3 732 km*, running from Tuimazy through Omsk and Novosibirsk to Irkutsk. The first 30 mile *48 km* section was opened in July 1957.

Submarine Pipelines

The longest submarine pipeline is the Ekofisk-Emden line stretching 260 miles *418 km* under the North Sea and completed in July 1975. The deepest North Sea pipeline is that from the Cormorant Field to Firths Voe, Shetland at 530 ft *162 m*.

Natural Gas

The longest natural gas pipeline in the world is the Trans-Canada Pipeline which by 1974 had 5,654 miles *9 099 km* of pipe up to 42 in *106,6 cm* in diameter.

Pipeline Most Expensive

The world's most expensive pipeline is the Alaska pipeline running 798 miles *1 284 km* Prudhoe Bay to Valdez. By completion of the first phase in 1977 it had cost at least $6,000 million (£3,250 million). The pipe is 48 in *1,21 m* in diameter and will eventually carry up to 2 million barrels of crude oil per day.

Oil Tank Largest

The largest oil tank ever constructed is the Million Barrel Ekofisk Oil Tank completed in Norway in 1973 and implanted in the North Sea measuring 92 × 92 × 102 m high (*301.8 ft square and 335 ft high*) and containing 8 000 tonnes *7,873 tons* of steel and 202 000 tonnes *198,809 tons* of concrete. The capacity of 160 000 m³ *209,272 yds³* is equivalent to 1.42 times the amount of oil which escaped from the *Torrey Canyon*.

Cat Cracker Largest
The world's largest catalyst cracker is the Exxon Co's Bayway Refinery plant at Linden, New Jersey, U.S.A. with a fresh feed rate of 5,040,000 U.S. galls *19 077 000 litres* per day.

Nut Largest
The largest nuts ever made weigh 47 cwt *2,39 tonnes* each and have an outside diameter of 50½ in *128,2 cm* and a 31½ in *80 cm* thread. Known as Moorthrust, they are manufactured by Doncaster Moorside Ltd. of Oldham, Greater Manchester for securing propellers.

Valve Largest
The world's largest valve is the 14 ft *4,26 m* diameter Pratt-Triton XL butterfly valve made in Aurora, Illinois, U.S.A. for water and power systems.

Transformer Largest
The world's largest single phase transformers are rated at 1,500,000 kV of which 8 are in service with the American Electric Power Service Corporation. Of these five stepdown from 765 to 345 kV. Britain's largest transformers are those rated at 1,000,000 kVa 400/275 kV built by Hackbridge & Hewittic Co. Ltd., Walton-on-Thames, Surrey first commissioned for the CEGB in Oct. 1968.

Ropeway or Telepherique Highest *World*
The highest and longest aerial ropeway in the world is the Teleférico Mérida (Mérida téléphérique) in Venezuela, from Mérida City (5,379 ft *1 639,5 m*) to the summit of Pico Espejo (15,629 ft *4 763,7 m*), a rise of 10,250 ft *3 124 m*. The ropeway is in four sections, involving 3 car changes in the 8 mile ascent in one hour. The fourth span is 10,070 ft *3 069 m* in length. The two cars work on the pendulum system—the carrier rope is locked and the cars are hauled by means of three pull ropes powered by a 230 h.p. *233 c.v.* motor. They have a maximum capacity of 45 persons and travel at 32 ft *9,7 m* per sec (21.8 m.p.h. *35,08 km/h*). The longest single span ropeway is the 13,500 ft *4 114 m* long span from the Coachella Valley to Mt. San Jacinto (10,821 ft *3 298 m*), California U.S.A., inaugurated on 12 Sept. 1963.

Great Britain
Britain's longest cabin lift is that at Llandudno, Gwynedd, opened in June 1969. It has 42 cabins with a capacity of 1,000 people per hour and is 5,320 ft *1 621 m* in length.

Passenger Lift Fastest *World*
The fastest domestic passenger lifts in the world are the express lifts to the 60th floor of the 246 m *787.4 ft* tall "Sunshine 60" building, Ikebukuro, Tokyo, Japan completed 5 Apr. 1978. They were built by Mitsubishi Corp. and operate at a speed of 2,000 ft/min *609,6 m/min* or 22.72 m.p.h. *36,56 km/h*. Much higher speeds are achieved in the winding cages of mine shafts. A hoisting shaft 6,800 ft *2 072 m* deep, owned by Western Deep Levels Ltd. in South Africa, winds at speeds of up to 40.9 m.p.h. *65,8 km/h* (3,595 ft *1 095 m* per min). Otitis-media (popping of the ears) presents problems much above even 10 m.p.h. *16 km/h*.

Great Britain
The longest lift in the United Kingdom is one 930 ft long inside the B.B.C. T.V. tower at Bilsdale, West Moor, North Yorkshire, built by J. L. Eve Construction Co. Ltd. It runs at 130 ft *39,6 m/*min. The longest fast lifts are the two 15-passenger cars in the Post Office Tower, Maple Street, London W1 which travel 540 ft *164 m* up at up to 1,000 ft *304 m/*min.

Escalator Longest
The term was registered in the U.S. on 28 May 1900 but the earliest "Inclined Escalator" was installed by Jesse W. Reno on the pier at Coney Island, New York in 1896. The first installation in Britain was at Harrods, Knightsbridge, London in Nov. 1898. The escalators on the Leningrad Underground, U.S.S.R. have a vertical rise of 195 ft *59,4 m*. The longest escalators in Britain are the four in the Tyne Tunnel, Tyne and Wear installed in 1951. They measure 192 ft 8 in *58,7 m* between combs with a vertical lift of 85 ft *25,9 m* and a step speed of up to 1.7 m.p.h. *2,7 km/h*.

The world's longest "moving sidewalks" are those installed in 1970 in the Neue Messe Centre, Dusseldorf, West Germany which measure 225 m *738 ft* between comb plates. The longest in Great Britain is the 375 ft *114,3 m* long Dunlop Starglide at London Airport Terminal 3 installed in March–May 1970.

Printer Fastest
The world's fastest printer is the Radiation Inc. electro-sensitive system at the Lawrence Radiation Laboratory, Livermore, California. High speed recording of up to 30,000 lines each containing 120 alphanumeric characters per minute is attained by controlling electronic pulses through chemically impregnated recording paper which is rapidly moving under closely spaced fixed styli. It can thus print the wordage of the whole Bible (773,692 words) in 65 sec—3,333 times as fast as the world's fastest typist.

Transmission Lines *Longest*
The longest span between pylons of any power line in the world is that across the Sogne Fjord, Norway, between Rabnaberg and Fatlaberg. Erected in 1955 by the Whitecross Co. Ltd. of Warrington, Cheshire, England as part of the high-tension power cable from Refsdal power station at Vik, it has a span of 16,040 ft *4 888 m* and a weight of 12 tons/*tonnes*. In 1967 two further high tensile steel/aluminium lines 16,006 ft *4 878 m* long, and weighing 33 tons *33,5 tonnes*, manufactured by Whitecross and B.I.C.C. were erected here. The longest in Britain are the 5,310 ft *1 618 m* lines built by J. L. Eve Co. across the Severn with main towers each 488 ft *148 m* high.

Highest
The world's highest are those across the Straits of Messina, with towers of 675 ft *205 m* (Sicily side) and 735 ft *224 m* (Calabria) and 11,900 ft *3 627 m* apart. The highest lines in Britain are those made by British Insulated Callender's Cables Ltd. at West Thurrock, Essex, which cross the Thames estuary suspended from 630 ft *192 m* tall towers at a minimum height of 250 ft *76 m*, with a 130 ton *132 tonnes* breaking load. They are 4,500 ft *1 371 m* in length.

Highest voltages
The highest voltages now carried are 1,330,000 volts 1,224 miles *1 970 km* on the D.C. Pacific Inter-tie in the United States. The Ekibastuz D.C. transmission lines in Kazakhstan, U.S.S.R. are planned to be 2400 km *1,490 miles* long with 1,500,000 volt capacity.

Conveyor Belt Longest
The world's longest single flight conveyor belt is one of 9 miles *14 km* installed near Uniontown, Kentucky, U.S.A. by Cable Belt Ltd. of Camberley, Surrey. It has a weekly capacity of 140,000 short tons *142 247 tonnes* of coal on a 42 in *1,06 m* wide 800 ft *243 m/*min belt and forms part of a 12½ miles *20 km* long system. The longest installation in Great Britain is also by Cable Belt Ltd. and of 5½ miles *8,9 km* underground at Longannet Power Station, Fife, Scotland. The world's longest multi-flight conveyor is one of 100 km *62 miles* between the phosphate mine near Bucraa and the port of El Aaiun, Morocco, built by Krupps and completed in 1972. It has 11 flights of between 9 and 11 km *5.6–6.8 miles* and is driven at 4,5 m/sec *10.06 m.p.h.*

Wire Rope Longest
The longest wire rope ever spun in one piece was one measuring 46,653 ft *14 219 m* (8.83 miles) long and 3⅛ in *7,93 cm* in circumference, with a weight of 28½ tons *28,9 tonnes*, manufactured by British Ropes Ltd. of Doncaster, South Yorkshire. The thickest ever made are spliced crane strops 28,2 cm *11¼ in* thick made of 2,392 individual wires in March 1979 by British Ropes at Willington Quay, Tyneside.

Tubing Smallest
The smallest tubing in the world is made by Accles and Pollock, Ltd. of Warley, West Midlands. It is of pure nickel with an outer and inner diameter of 0.0005 in and 0.00013 in and was announced on 9 Sept. 1963. The average human hair measures from 0.002 to 0.003 of an inch *0,05–0,075 mm* diameter. The tubing, which is stainless, can be used for the

artificial insemination of bees and for the medical process of "feeding" nerves, and weighs only 5 oz. *141 gr* per 100 miles *160 km*.

Radar Installation *Largest*
The largest of the three installations in the U.S. Ballistic Missile Early Warning System (B.M.E.W.S.) is that near Thule, in Greenland, 931 miles *1 498 km* from the North Pole, completed in 1960 at a cost of $500,000,000 (*then £178.5 million*). Its sister stations are one at Cape Clear, Alaska, U.S.A., completed in 1961, and a $115,000,000 (*then £41.07 million*) installation at Fylingdales Moor, North Yorkshire, completed in June 1963. The largest scientific radar installation is the 21 acre *84 000 m²* ground array at Jicamarca, Peru.

TIME PIECES
Clock *Oldest*
The earliest mechanical clock, that is one with an escapement, was completed in China in A.D. 725 by I Hsing and Liang Ling-tsan.

The oldest surviving working clock in the world is the faceless clock dating from 1386, or possibly earlier, at Salisbury Cathedral, Wiltshire, which was restored in 1956 having struck the hours for 498 years and ticked more than 500 million times. Earlier dates, ranging back to *c.* 1335, have been attributed to the weight-driven clock in Wells Cathedral, Somerset, but only the iron frame is original. A model of Giovanni de Dondi's heptagonal astronomical clock of 1348–64 was completed in 1962.

Clock Largest *World*
The world's most massive clock is the Astronomical Clock in the Cathedral of St. Pierre, Beauvais, France, constructed between 1865 and 1868. It contains 90,000 parts and measures 40 ft *12,1 m* high, 20 ft *6,09 m* wide and 9 ft *2,7 m* deep. The Su Sung clock, built in China at K'aifeng in 1088–92, had a 20 ton *20,3 tonnes* bronze armillary sphere for 1½ tons, *1,52 tonnes* of water. It was removed to Peking in 1126 and was last known to be working in its 40 ft *12,1 m* high tower in 1136.

Public
The largest four-faced clock in the world is that on the building of the Allen-Bradley Company of Milwaukee, Wisconsin, U.S.A. Each face has a diameter of 40 ft 3½ in *12,28 m* with a minute hand 20 ft *6,09 m* in overall length. The tallest four-faced clock in the world is that of the Williamsburgh Savings Bank in Brooklyn, New York City, N.Y., U.S.A. It is 430 ft *131 m* above street level.

Great Britain
The largest clock in the United Kingdom is that on the Royal Liver Building (built 1908–11) with dials 25 ft *7,62 m* in diameter and the 4 minute hands each 14 ft *4,26 m* long. The mechanism and dials weigh 22 tons and are 220 ft *67 m* above street level.

Longest stoppage "Big Ben"
The longest stoppage of the clock in the House of Commons clock tower, London since the first tick on 31 May 1859 has been 13 days from noon 4 Apr. to noon 17 Apr. 1977. In 1945 a host of starlings slowed the minute hand by 5 minutes.

Clock Most accurate
The most accurate and complicated clockwork in the world is the Olsen clock, installed in the Copenhagen Town Hall, Denmark. The clock, which has more than 14,000 units, took 10 years to make and the mechanism of the clock functions in 570,000 different ways. The celestial pole motion of the clock will take 25,753 years to complete a full circle and is the slowest moving designed mechanism in the world. The clock is accurate to 0.5 of a second in 300 years—50 times more accurate than the previous record.

Clock Most expensive
The highest auction price for any English made clock is £65,000 for a Thomas Tompion bracket clock dating from 1676–1680 at Christie's in London on 7 Feb. 1979.

Watch Oldest
The oldest watch (portable clock-work time-keeper) is one made of iron by Peter Henlein in Nürnberg (Nüremberg), Bavaria, Germany, in *c.* 1504 and now in the Memorial Hall, Philadelphia, Pennsylvania, U.S.A. The earliest wrist watches were those of Jacquet-Droz and Leschot of Geneva, Switzerland, dating from 1790.

Watch Smallest
The smallest watches in the world are produced by Jaeger Le Coultre of Switzerland. Equipped with a 15-jewelled movement they measure just over half-an-inch *1,2 cm* long and three-sixteenths of an inch *0,476 cm* in width. The movement, with its case, weighs under .25 oz *7 g*.

Watch Thinnest
The world's thinnest wrist watch is the Delirium I made by the Concord Watch Corporation of New York, which measures 1,98 mm 1⁄16 *in* thick. It retails with its lizard strap for $4,400 (£2,200) and is manufactured in Bienne, Switzerland.

Watch Most expensive
Excluding watches with jewelled cases, the most expensive standard men's pocket watch is the Swiss *Grande Complication* by Audemars-Piguet which retailed for £38,000 in May 1979. On 1 June 1964, a record £27,500 was paid for the Duke of Wellington's watch made in Paris in 1807 by Abraham Louis Bréguet, (1747–1823) at the salerooms of Sotheby & Co., London, by the dealers Messrs. Ronald Lee for a Portuguese client. The Patek Philippe 18 carat gold minute-repeater, perpetual calendar pocket watch launched by Tiffany's, New York on 28 Sept. 1976 is priced at $48,000 (£28,250).

Time Measurer Most accurate *World*
The most accurate time-keeping devices are the twin atomic hydrogen masers installed in 1964 in the U.S. Naval Research Laboratory, Washington, D.C. They are based on the frequency of the hydrogen atom's transition period of 1,420,450,751,694 cycles/sec. This enables an accuracy to within one sec/1,700,000 years.

COMPUTERS
The modern computer was made possible by the invention of the point-contact transistor by John Bardeen and Walter Brattain announced in July 1948, and the junction transistor by R. L. Wallace, Morgan Sparks and Dr. William Shockley in early 1951.

The computer planned to be the world's biggest by a factor of 40 is the $50 million NASF (Numerical Aerodynamic Simulation Facility) at NASA's Ames Research Center, Palo Alto, California. Rural tenders from CDC at Burroughs call for a capacity of 12.8 gigaflops (12,800 million complex calculations per second).

Most Powerful and Fastest *World*
The world's most powerful and fastest computer is the CRAY-1, designed by Seymour R. Cray of Cray Research, Inc., Minneapolis, Minnesota. The clock period is 12.5 nanoseconds and memory ranges up to 1,048,576 64-bit words, resulting in a capacity of 8,388,608 bytes of main memory. It attains speeds of 200 million floating point operations per second. With 32 CRAY DD-19 disk storage units, it has a storage capacity of 7.7568×10^{10} bits. Floating decimal points may vary between 10^{-2500} to 10^{2500}. The cost of a mid-range system is $6,500,000 (£3,250,000).

Great Britain
The computer with the largest memory built in the United Kingdom is the International Business Machines' IBM System 370 Model 168 MP which is a multiprocessing computer with 16,777,216 bytes of main storage. A 'byte' is a unit of storage comprising 8 'bits' collectively equivalent to one alphabetic letter or two numerals. This machine is produced at Havant, Hampshire. ICL has proposed a computer with 576 separate streams which would be 50 times faster than ILLIAC IV, the $30 million Burroughs computer which comprises 64 separate computing elements in tandem.

THE BUSINESS WORLD

9

1. COMMERCE

The $(US) has in this chapter been converted at a fixed mean rate of $2.00 to the £ Sterling and at the relevant rates at other dates.

The *Guinness Book of the Business World* by Henry Button and Andrew Lampert (£6.50) contains a more detailed treatment of records and facts in the world of commerce and industry.

Oldest Industry

Agriculture is often described as "the oldest industry in the world", whereas in fact there is no evidence that it was practised before *c.* 11,000 B.C. The oldest known industry is flint knapping, involving the production of chopping tools and hand axes, dating from about 1,750,000 years ago. Salt panning is of comparable antiquity.

Oldest Company *World*

The oldest company in the world is the Faversham Oyster Fishery Co., referred to in the Faversham Oyster Fishing Act 1930, as existing "from time immemorial", *i.e.* in English law from before 1189.

Great Britain

The Royal Mint has origins going back to A.D. 287. The Oxford University Press celebrated the 500th anniversary of its origins in 1478 in 1978. The Whitechapel Bell Foundry of Whitechapel Road, London, E.1, has been in business since 1570. The retail business in Britain with the oldest history is the Cambridge bookshop, which, though under various ownership, has traded from the site of 1 Trinity Street since 1581 and since 1907 under its present title Bowes & Bowes. R. Durtnell & Sons, builders, of Brasted, Kent, has been run by the same family since 1591. The first bill of adventure signed by the English East India Co., was dated 21 March 1601.

Greatest Assets *World*

The business with the greatest amount in physical assets is the Bell System, which comprises the American Telephone and Telegraph Company, with headquarters at 195 Broadway, New York City, N.Y., U.S.A., and its subsidiaries. The Bell System's total assets on the consolidated balance sheet at 28 Feb. 1979 were valued at $104,926,359,000 (*then £52,463 million*). The plant involved included 134.3 million telephones. The number of employees is 993,000. A total of 20,109 shareholders attended the Annual Meeting in April 1961, thereby setting a world record.

The first company to have assets in excess of $1 billion was the United States Steel Corporation with $1,400 million (*then £287.73 million*) at the time of its creation by merger in 1900.

Great Britain

The enterprise in the United Kingdom, excluding banks, with the greatest capital employed is the Post Office with £6,881,100,000 in 1977/8. This ranks twelfth in the western world.

The biggest British industrial company is Imperial Chemical Industries Ltd. with assets employed of £3,969 million as at 31 Dec. 1978. Its staff and payroll averaged 151,000 during the year. The company, which has around 350 U.K. and overseas subsidiaries, was formed on 7 Dec. 1926 by the merger of four concerns—British Dyestuffs Corporation Ltd.; Brunner, Mond & Co. Ltd.; Nobel Industries Ltd. and United Alkali Co. Ltd. The first chairman was Sir Alfred Moritz Mond (1868–1930), later the 1st Lord Melchett.

The net assets of The "Shell" Transport and Trading Company, Ltd., at 31 Dec. 1978 were £3,485,000,000, comprising mainly its 40% share in the net assets of the Royal Dutch/Shell Group of Companies which stood at £7,973 million. Group companies employ 158,000. "Shell" Transport was formed in 1897 by Marcus Samuel (1853–1927), later the 1st Viscount Bearsted.

Greatest profit and loss

The greatest net profit ever made by an industrial company in a year is $3,508.0 million (*£1,754.0 million*) by General Motors of Detroit in 1978.

The greatest loss ever recorded by any enterprise in a year was £443,000,000 by the British Steel Corporation in 1977–78. The Bethlehem Steel Corporation loss for the 3rd quarter of 1978 was $477 million (*£238.5 million*).

Greatest sales

The first company to surpass the $1 billion (U.S.) mark in annual sales was the United States Steel Corporation in 1917. Now there are some 250 corporations with sales exceeding £1,000 million including 143 from the United States. The list is headed by General Motors of Detroit with $63,221,100,000 (*£31,610 million*) in 1978.

The top gross profits in the United Kingdom in *The Times 1,000 1978–79* was British Petroleum with £2,393,600,000 million. The biggest loss maker in *The Times 1,000 1978–79* was Texaco with £41,935,000.

above: A petro-chemical plant belonging to the biggest British Industrial Company, ICI. The company has 550 subsidiaries and 151,000 employees (including overseas) (see p. 157).

below: The St. Louis, Missouri plant of Anheuser-Busch Inc, the largest single brewer in the world. Their sales exceed 7,250 million pints per year (see pp. 159–60).

Of nationalized industries the record cost to the taxpayer in a year was £567,600,000 or £1,079 per minute in 1975 by British Rail.

Biggest work force
The greatest payroll of any single civilian organisation in the world is that of the U.S.S.R. National Railway system with a total work force of 2,031,200 in 1976. The biggest employer in the United Kingdom is the Post Office with 408,674 employees (incl. part time workers) on 31 Dec. 1978.

Largest Take-Over
The largest take-over in commercial history has been the bid of £438,000,000 by Grand Metropolitan Hotels Ltd., for the brewers Watney Mann on 17 June 1972. The value of the consideration was £378.2 million.

Largest Merger
The largest merger ever mooted in British business was that of the Hill Samuel Group (£768 million assets) and Slater, Walker Securities (£469 million) in April 1973 with combined assets of £1,237 million. This plan was called off on 19 June 1973.

Biggest Write Off
The largest reduction of assets in the history of private enterprise was the $800 million *£347 million* write off of Tristar aircraft development costs announced on 23 Nov. 1974.

Companies
The number of companies on the register in Great Britain at 31 Dec. 1978 was 692,182 of which 15,825 were public and the balance private companies.

Most directorships
The record for directorships was set in 1961 by Hugh T. Nicholson, formerly senior partner of Harmood Banner & Co., London who as a liquidating chartered accountant became director of all 451 companies of the Jasper group in 1961 and had 7 other directorships.

Advertising Agency
The largest advertising agency in 1978, as listed in *Advertizing Age*, is Dentsu Incorporated of Tokyo with estimated billings of $2,210 million. The MEAL survey ranks J. Walter

Thompson No. 1 in Britain with 1978 Gross Display Advertizing expenditure of £49,700,000.

Biggest advertiser
The world's biggest advertiser is Sears Roebuck and Co., with $528,771,000 (*£264 million*) in 1978 excluding its catalogue.

Aircraft manufacturer
The world's largest aircraft manufacturer is the Boeing Com-

pany of Seattle, Washington, U.S.A. The corporation's sales totalled $5,463,000,000 (£2,731 million) in 1978 and it had 92,200 employees and assets valued at $1,473,600,000 (then 736 million) at 1 Apr. 1979. Cessna Aircraft Company of Wichita, Kansas, U.S.A., produced 7,673 civil aircraft (55 models) in the year 1975, with total sales of $492 million (then £240 million). The company has produced more than 130,000 aircraft since Clyde Cessna's first was built in 1911. Their record year was 1965–66 with 7,922 aircraft completed.

Airline *Largest*
The largest airline in the world is the U.S.S.R. State airline "Aeroflot", so named since 1932. This was instituted on 9 Feb. 1923, with the title of Civil Air Fleet of the Council of Ministers of the U.S.S.R., abbreviated to "Dobrolet". It operates 1,300 aircraft over about 560,000 miles *900 000 km* of routes, employs 400,000 people and carries 100 million passengers to 67 countries. The commercial airline carrying the greatest number of passengers in 1978 was United Airlines of Chicago, Illinois, U.S.A. (formed 1926) with 41,676,260 passengers. The company had 53,831 employees and a fleet of 336 jet planes. In March 1979 British Airways were operating a fleet of 209 aircraft, with 68 on order. Staff employed on airline activities totalled 54,357 and 15.7 million passengers were carried in 1978 on 362,345 miles *583,000 km* of unduplicated routes.

Oldest
The oldest existing national airline is Koninklijke-Luchtvaart-Maatschappij N.V. (KLM) of the Netherlands, which opened its first scheduled service (Amsterdam-London) on 17 May 1920, having been established on 7 Oct. 1919. One of the original constituents of B.O.A.C., Handley-Page Transport Ltd., was founded in May 1919 and merged into Imperial Airways in 1924. Delag (Deutsche Luftschiffahrt A.G.) was founded at Frankfurt am Main on 16 Nov. 1909 and started a scheduled airship service June 1910. Chalk's International Airline has been flying amphibians between Miami, Florida and the Bahamas since July 1919. Albert "Pappy" Chalk flew from 1911 to 1975.

Aluminium producer
The world's largest producer of primary aluminium is the Aluminum Company of America (Alcoa of Pittsburgh, U.S.A.) with its affiliated companies. The company had an output of 1,937,784 short tons *1,757,946 tonnes* in 1978. The Aluminum Company of Canada Ltd. owns the largest aluminium smelter in the western world, at Arvida, Quebec, with a capacity of 465,000 short tons *422 000 tonnes* per annum. Alcoa of Pittsburgh, U.S.A. has the highest sales with $4,051,800,000 (£2,025 million) in 1978.

Art auctioneering
The largest and oldest firm of art auctioneers in the world is the Sotheby Parke Bernet Group of London and New York, founded in 1744. The turnover in 1977–78 was $322,194,000 (£161,097,000 million). The highest total for any house sale auction was theirs from 18–27 May 1977 at the 6th Earl of Rosebery's home at Mentmore, Buckinghamshire which reached £6,389,933 or $10,9 million. H.M. Government had turned down an offer of £2 million.

Bank
The International Bank for Reconstruction and Development (founded 27 Dec. 1945), the United Nations "World Bank" at 1818 H Street N.W., Washington, D.C., U.S.A., has an authorized share capital of $34,000 million (£14,210 million). There were 130 members with a subscribed capital of $25,903,100,000 (£13,633 million) at 31 Dec. 1977. The International Monetary Fund in Washington, D.C., U.S.A. has 138 members with total quotas of SDR 39,011 million ($49,934 million or £24,505 million) at 30 Apr. 1979.

The private commercial bank with the greatest deposits is the Bank of America National Trust and Savings Association, of San Francisco, California, U.S.A., with $75,828,044,000 (£37,914,022,000) at 31 Dec. 1978. Its total assets were $94,902,464,000 (£47,451 million). Barclays Bank (with Barclays Bank International and other subsidiary companies) had some 5,000 branches and offices in 75 countries (3,000 in the United Kingdom) in December 1978. Deposits totalled 20,841 million and assets £23,884 million. The largest bank in the United Kingdom is the National Westminster with total assets of £22,184,000,000 and 3,261 branches as at 31 Dec. 1978. The bank with most branches is The State Bank of India with 7,262 on 1 Jan. 1979 with assets of £6,072,122,395.

Bank building
The world's tallest bank building is the Bank of Montreal's First Bank Tower, Toronto, Canada which has 72 stories and stands 935 ft *284,98 m*. The largest bank vault in the world, measuring 350 × 100 × 8 ft *106,7 × 30,4 × 2,4 m* and weighing 879 tons *893 tonnes* is in the Chase Manhattan Building, New York City, completed in May 1961. Its six doors weigh up to 40 tons *40,6 tonnes* apiece but each can be closed by the pressure of a forefinger.

Banquet Greatest *Outdoors*
The greatest banquet ever staged was that by President Loubet, President of France, in the gardens of the Tuileries, Paris, on 22 Sept. 1900. He invited the mayors of France and their deputies ending up with 22,295 guests. With the Gallic *penchant* for round numbers, the event has always been referred to as "le banquet des 100,000 maires". It was estimated that some 30,000 attended a military feast at Radewitz, Poland on 25 June 1730 thrown by King August II (1709–1733).

Indoors
The greatest number of people served indoors at a single sitting was 18,000 municipal leaders at the Palais de l'Industrie, Paris on 18 Aug. 1889.

Most expensive
The menu for the main 5½ hr banquet at the Imperial Iranian 2500th Anniversary gathering at Persepolis in October 1971 was probably the most expensive ever compiled. It comprised quail eggs stuffed with Iranian caviar, a mousse of crayfish tails in Nantua sauce, stuffed rack of roast lamb, with a main course of roast peacock stuffed with *foie gras*, fig rings and raspberry sweet champagne sherbet, with wines including *Château Lafite-Rothschild* 1945 at £40 per bottle from the cellars of Maxime, Paris.

Barbers
The largest barbering establishment in the world is Norris of Houston, 3303 Audley, Houston, Texas, U.S.A. which employs 60 barbers.

Bicycle factory
The 64-acre *25,9 ha* plant of TI Raleigh Industries Ltd. at Nottingham is the largest cycle factory in the world producing complete bicycles, components and wheeled toys. The company employs 10,000 and has the capacity to make more than 2,000,000 bicycles and 850,000 wheeled toys per year.

Book shop
The book shop with most titles and the longest shelving (30 miles *48 km*) in the world is W. & G. Foyle Ltd., City of Westminster, Greater London. First established in 1904 in a small shop in Islington, the company is now at 119–125 Charing Cross Road. The area on one site is 75,825 ft² *7 044 m²*. The most capacious bookstore in the world measured by square footage is Barnes & Noble Bookstore of Fifth Ave. at 18th Street, New York City, U.S.A. with 154,250 ft² *14 330 m²* and with 12.87 miles *20,71 km* of shelving.

The world's largest second-hand booksellers are Richard Booth (Bookseller) Ltd., of Hay-on-Wye, Powys, Wales with 8.30 miles *13,35 km* of shelving and a running stock of 900,000 to 1,100,000 in 30,091 ft² *2 795 m²* of selling space.

Brewer *Oldest*
The oldest brewery in the world is the Weihenstephan Brewery, Freising, near Munich, West Germany, founded in A.D. 1040.

Largest World
The largest single brewer in the world is Anheuser-Busch,

Inc. in St. Louis, Missouri, U.S.A. In 1978 the company sold 41,600,000 U.S. barrels, equivalent to 8,593 million Imperial pints, the greatest annual volume ever produced by a brewing company. The company's St. Louis plant covers 100 acres *40,5 ha* and after completion of current modernisation projects will have an annual capacity in excess of 12,000,000 U.S. barrels *2,478 million Imperial pints*. The largest brewery on a single site is Adolph Coors Co. of Golden, Colorado, U.S.A. where 12.8 million barrels *3 581 million Imp. pints* were sold in 1978.

Europe

The largest brewery in Europe is the Guinness Brewery at St. James's Gate, Dublin, Ireland, which extends over 57.22 acres *23,16 ha*. The business was founded in 1759.

Great Britain

The largest brewing company in the United Kingdom based on its 8,477 public houses, 885 off-licenses and 76 hotels, is Bass Ltd. The company has net assets of £661,100,000, 61,193 employees (including bar-staff) and controls 13 breweries. Their sales figure for the year ending 30 Sept. 1978 was £1,014,400,000.

Greatest exports

The largest exporter of beer, ale and stout in the world is Arthur Guinness, Son & Co. Ltd., of Dublin, Ireland. Exports of Guinness from the Republic of Ireland in the 52 weeks ending 17 Mar. 1979 were 937,068 bulk barrels (bulk barrel = 36 Imperial gallons), which is equivalent to 1,482,833 half pint glasses *1,404,354 30-centilitre glasses* per day.

Brickworks

The largest brickworks in the world is the London Brick Company plant at Stewartby, Bedfordshire. The works, established in 1898, now cover 221 acres *90 ha* and has a production capacity of 16,000,000 bricks and brick equivalent each week.

Building contractors

The largest construction company in the United Kingdom is George Wimpey Ltd. (founded 1880), of London, who undertake building, civil, mechanical, electrical and chemical engineering work. With gross assets of £502,000,000 and 38,000 employees, worldwide the turnover of work was £853,000,000 in 42 countries in 1978.

Building societies

The biggest building society in the world is the Halifax Building Society of Halifax, West Yorkshire. It was established in 1853 and has total assets exceeding £7,500,000,000. It has over 7,500 employees and over 1,700 offices.

Chemist shop chain

The largest chain of chemist shops in the world is Boots The Chemists, which has 1,157 retail branches. The firm was founded by Jesse Boot (b. Nottingham, 1850), later the 1st Baron Trent, who died in 1931.

Chocolate factory

The world's largest chocolate factory is that built by Hershey Foods Corp. in Hershey, Pennsylvania, U.S.A. in 1903–1905. It now has 2,000,000 ft² *185,800 m²* of floor space.

Computer Company

The world's largest computer firm is International Business Machines (IBM) Corporation of New York which in a 1975 court decision was held to have a 36.7% share in the value of "electronic computers and peripheral equipment, except parts" based on 1971 shipments. In 1978 assets were $20,771,374,000 (*£10,385 million*) and sales were $20,076,089 million (*£10,038 million*).

Department Stores *World*

F. W. Woolworth celebrated its centenary year by announcing a total of 5,788 stores world wide. Frank W. Woolworth opened his first Five and Ten Cent Store in Utica, New York State on 22 Feb. 1879. The 1978/79 earnings were a record $130,300,000 *£65,150,000*.

Great Britain

The largest department store in the United Kingdom is Harrods Ltd. of Knightsbridge, Royal Borough of Kensington and Chelsea, Greater London named after Henry Charles Harrod, who opened a grocery in Knightsbridge Village in 1849. It has a total selling floor space of 16 acres *6,4 ha*, employs 4,000 people and had a total of 15,400,000 transactions in 1978.

Highest sales per unit area

The department store with the fastest-moving stock in the world is the Marks & Spencer premier branch, known as "Marble Arch" at 458 Oxford Street, City of Westminster, Greater London. The figure of £750 worth of goods per square foot of selling space per year is believed to be an understatement. The selling area is 97,400 ft² *9 048 m².* The company has 253 branches in the U.K. and operates on over 6 million ft² *558 000 m²* of selling space and now has stores on the Continent and Canada.

Distillery

The world's largest distilling company is The Seagram Company Ltd., of Canada. Its sales in the year ending 31 July 1978 totalled U.S. $2,272,584,000 (*£1,136 million*) of which $1,886,727,000 (*£943 million*) were from sales by Joseph E. Seagram & Sons, Inc. in the United States. The group employs about 15,000 people, including about 10,800 in the United States.

The largest of all Scotch whisky distilleries is Carsebridge at Alloa, Central Region, Scotland, owned by Scottish Grain Distillers Limited. This distillery is capable of producing more than 20,000,000 proof gallons per annum. The largest establishment for blending and bottling Scotch whisky is owned by John Walker & Sons Limited at Kilmarnock, Strathclyde, where over 3 million bottles are filled each week. "Johnnie Walker" is the world's largest-selling brand of Scotch whisky. The largest malt Scotch whisky distillery is the Tomatin Distillery, Highland, established at 1,028 ft *313 m* above sea level in 1897, with an annual capacity 5.0 million proof gallons. The world's largest-selling brand of gin is Gordon's.

Fisheries

The world's highest recorded catch of fish was 65 700 000 tonnes in 1973. Peru had the largest ever national haul with 12 160 000 tonnes in 1970 comprising mostly anchoveta. The United Kingdom's highest figure was 1 206 000 tonnes in 1948. The world's largest fishmongers are MacFisheries, a subsidiary of Unilever Ltd., with 173 retail outlets as at April 1979.

Largest Net

The largest net yet manufactured is one that can fish 6.8 million m³ *8.8 million yd³* per hour announced from West Germany in March 1974.

Grocery stores

The largest grocery chain in the world is Safeway Stores Incorporated of Oakland, California, U.S.A. with sales in 1978 of $12,550,569,000 (*£6,275 million*) and total current assets valued at $1,183,390,000 (*£591 million*) as at 30 Dec. 1978. The company has 2,436 stores totalling 57,461,000 ft² *5 338 126 m².* The total payroll is 144,243.

Hotelier

The top revenue-earning hotel business is Holiday Inns Inc., with a 1978 revenue of $1,202 million (*£601 million*), from 1,731 inns (284,000 rooms) at 1 March 1979 in 59 countries. The business was founded by Charles Kemmons Wilson with his first inn in Summer Avenue, Memphis, Tennessee in 1952.

Insurance

It was estimated in 1978 that the total premiums paid in the United States had surpassed $100 billion (*£52,600 million*) or $1,400 *£736* per household. The company with the highest volume of insurance in force in the world is the Prudential Insurance Company of America of Newark, New Jersey with $330,364 million (*£165,182 million*) at 31 Dec. 1978, which is nearly twice the U.K. National Debt figure. The admitted assets are $50,054 million (£25,027 million).

Great Britain

The largest life assurance company in the United Kingdom is the Prudential Assurance Co. Ltd. At 1 Jan. 1979 the tangible assets were £5,012,945,000 and the total amount assured was £26,856,000,000.

Life policies Largest

The largest life assurance policy ever written in Britain was one of £10,000,000 $25,000,000 for James Derrick Slater (b. 13 Mar. 1929), Chairman of Slater, Walker Securities, the City of London Investment bankers. The existence of the policy was made known on 3 June 1971.

Highest pay-out

The highest pay-out on a single life has been some $18 million (£3.3 million) to Mrs. Linda Mullendore, wife of an Oklahoma rancher, reported on 14 Nov. 1970. Her murdered husband had paid $300,000 in premiums in 1969.

Marine

The largest ever marine insurance loss was the 125,000 g.r.t. VLCC (Very Large Crude Carrier), *Olympic Bravery*. This vessel which was insured at Lloyds and valued at £25 m, ran aground off Ushant on 24 Jan. 1976. The 83,000 g.r.t. LNG (Liquid Natural Gas) Carrier *Aquarius* built in 1977 by General Dynamics Corporation, Massachusetts, U.S.A. is currently insured for $175 million £103 million. This vessel is owned by Wilmington Trust Company, Delaware, U.S.A., and chartered to the Burmah Oil Co., Ltd.

Land *Owner*

The world's largest landowner is the United States Government, with a holding of 762,192,000 acres (1,190,000 miles² 3 082 000 km²) which is nearly the area of India. The world's largest *private* landowner is reputed to be International Paper Co. with 9 million acres 3,64 million ha. The United Kingdom's greatest ever private landowner was the 3rd Duke of Sutherland, George Granville Sutherland-Leveson-Gower, K.G. (1828–92), who owned 1,358,000 acres 549 560 ha in 1883. Currently the largest landholder in Great Britain is the Forestry Commission (instituted 1919) with 3,089,492 acres 1 250 274 ha. The longest tenure is that by St. Paul's Cathedral of land at Tillingham, Essex, given by King Ethelbert before A.D. 616. Currently the landowner with the largest known acreage is the 9th Duke of Buccleuch (b. 1923) with 336,000 acres 136 035 ha.

Value Highest

Currently the most expensive land in the world is that in the City of London. The freehold price on small prime sites reached £1,950/ft² (£21,230/m²) in mid 1973. The real estate value per square metre of the two topmost French vineyards, Grande and Petite Cognac vineyards in Bordeaux, has not been recently estimated. The China Square Inch Land Ltd. at a charity auction on 2 Dec. 1977 sold 1 cm² 0.155 in² of land at Sha Tau Kok for HK$2,000 (the equivalent of U.S.$17,405,833,737 per acre). The purchasers were Stephen and Tony Nicholson.

Greatest auction

The greatest auction was that at Anchorage, Alaska on 11 Sept. 1969 for 179 tracts 450,858 acres 182 455 ha of the oil-bearing North Slope, Alaska. An all-time record bid of $72,277,133 for a 2,560 acre 1 036 ha lease was made by the Amerada Hess Corporation—Getty Oil consortium. This £30,115,472 bid indicated a price of $28,233 (then £11,763) per acre.

Highest rent

The highest record rentals in the world are for shop premises in Hong Kong at U.S.$20 per ft² per *month* or £120 per ft² p.a. The freehold price for a grave site with excellent *Fung Shui* in Hong Kong may cost H.K.$200,000 for 4 ft × 10 ft or £19,400 per ft².

Lowest rent

The rent for a 3 room apartment in the Fuggerei in Augsburg, West Germany, since it was built by Jacob Fugger in 1519, has been 1 Rhine guilder, now 1.72 DMk or 31½p. Fugger was

the "millionaire" philanthropist who pioneered social welfare.

Mineral water

The world's largest mineral water firm is Source Perrier, near Nimes, France with an annual production of more than 2,100,000,000 bottles, of which 1,000,000,000 now come from Perrier and Contrexeville. The French drink about 50 litres *88 pts* of mineral water per person per year.

Motor Car Manufacturer *Largest World*

The largest manufacturing company in the world is General Motors Corporation of Detroit, Michigan, U.S.A. During its peak year of 1978 world wide sales totalled $63,221,100,000 (£31,610 million). Its assets at 31 Dec. 1978 were valued at $30,598,300,000 (£15,299 million). Its total 1978 payroll was $17,195,500,000 (£8,597 million) to an average of 839,000 employees. Dividends paid in 1978 were $1,725,500,000 (£862,750,000).

Great Britain

The largest British manufacturer was B.L. Ltd. with 771,000 vehicles produced and a sales turnover of £3,073 million of which £1,358 million was overseas sales in 180 markets in 1978. Direct exports of £910 million make B.L. Britain's largest net earner of foreign currency.

Largest plant

The largest single automobile plant in the world is the Volkswagenwerk, Wolfsburg, West Germany, with 55,000 employees and a capacity for over 4,500 vehicles daily. The surface area of the factory buildings is 368 acres *149 ha* and that of the whole plant 4,880 acres *1 975 ha* with 43.5 miles *70 km* of rail sidings.

Salesmanship

The all-time record for automobile salesmanship in units sold individually is 1,425 in 1973 by Joe Girard of Detroit, U.S.A., author of "How to Sell Anything to Anybody" winner of the No. 1 Car Salesman title each year in 1966–77. His lifetime total of one-at-time "belly to belly" selling was 13,001 sales, all retail. He retired on 1 Jan. 1978 to teach others this art.

Oil Company

The world's largest oil company is the Exxon Corporation (formerly Standard Oil Company [New Jersey]), with 130,000 employees and assets valued at $41,530,804,000 (£20,765 million) on 1 Jan. 1979.

Oil refineries *Largest*

The world's largest refinery is the Amerada Hess refinery in St. Croix, Virgin Islands with a capacity of 30.2 million tons *30,7 million tonnes*. The largest oil refinery in the United Kingdom is the Esso Refinery at Fawley, Hampshire. Opened in 1921 and much expanded in 1951, it has a capacity of *19.2 million tonnes* per year. The total investment together with the associated chemical plant, on the 1,300 acre *526 ha* site is £170,000,000.

Paper mills

The world's largest paper mill is that established in 1936 by the Union Camp Corporation at Savannah, Georgia, U.S.A., with an all-time record output in 1974 of 1,002,967 short tons *909 829 tonnes*. The largest paper mill in the United Kingdom is the Bowaters Kemsley Mill near Sittingbourne, Kent with a complex covering an area of 260 acres *105 ha* and a capacity in excess of 300,000 tons/*tonnes* a year.

Pharmaceuticals

The world's leading pharmaceutical company is Hoechst of West Germany with a turnover of £5,802 million (1977). Britain's largest drug *and* food turnover in 1977–78 was by Glaxo with a £488,028,000.

Pop-corn plant

The largest pop-corn plant in the world is The House of Clarks Ltd. (instituted 1933) of Dagenham, Barking, which in 1977/78 produced 65,000,000 packets of pop-corn.

Public relations

The world's largest public relations firm is Hill and Knowlton, Inc. of 633 Third Avenue, New York City, N.Y., U.S.A. and ten other U.S. cities. The firm employs a full-time staff of more than 700 and also maintains offices in 22 overseas cities.

161

The world's pioneer public relations publication is *Public Relations News*, founded by Mrs. Denny Griswold in 1944 and which now circulates in 86 countries.

Publishing

The publishing company generating most net revenue is Time Inc. of New York City with $1,697.6 million (*£848.8 million*) in 1978. Britain's largest publisher is I.P.C. Ltd., a subsidiary of Reed International Ltd., with a publishing turnover of £303 million as at March 1979. The largest book publishing concern in the world is the Book Division of McGraw-Hill Inc. of New York with sales of $305,321,000 (*£152.6 million*) in 1978.

Restaurateurs

The largest restaurant chain in the world is that operated by McDonald's Corporation of Oakbrook, Illinois, U.S.A., founded on 15 Apr. 1955 in Des Plaines, Chicago by Ray A. Kroc B.H. (Bachelor of Hamburgerology). By 1 Jan. 1979 the number of McDonald's restaurants licensed and owned in 25 countries reached 5,185 with an aggregate throughput of 22 billion 100% beef hamburgers under the motto "Q.S.C. & V."—for quality, (fast) service, cleanliness and value. Sales systemwide in 1978 were $4,575 million (*£2,287 million*). The largest hotel, catering and leisure group in the United Kingdom is Trusthouse Forte who employ up to 54,000 full and part-time staff in the U.K., 17,000 overseas, and who had a turnover of £613,800,000 in 1977–78. They had 860 hotels world-wide.

Fish and Chip Restaurant

The world's largest fish and chip shop is Harry Ramsdens, White Cross, Guiseley, West Yorkshire with 180 staff serving 1,510,000 customers per annum, who consumed 311 tons of fish and 450 tons of potatoes.

Retailer

The largest retailing firm in the world is Sears, Roebuck and Co. (founded by Richard Warren Sears in North Redwood railway station, Minnesota in 1886) of Chicago, Illinois, U.S.A. The net sales were $17,946,000,000 (*£8,973 million*) in the year ending 31 Jan. 1979 when the corporation had 866 retail stores and 2,861 catalogue, retail and telephone sales offices and independent catalogue merchants in the U.S.A. and total assets valued at $15,262,112,000 (*£7,631 million*).

Ship-building

In 1978 there were 18,194,120 tons gross of ships, excluding sailing ships, barges and vessels of less than 100 tons, completed throughout the world, excluding the U.S.S.R. and People's Republic of China. Japan completed 6,307,155 tons gross (34.67 per cent of the world total). The United Kingdom ranked third with 1,133,331 tons gross. The world's leading shipbuilding firm in 1977 was the Mitsubishi Heavy Industries Co. of Japan, which launched 81 merchant ships of 1,377,342 gross tons. Physically the largest ship yard in the United Kingdom is Harland and Wolff Ltd. of Queen's Island, Belfast, which covers some 300 acres *120 ha*.

Shipping line

The largest shipping owners and operators in the world are the Royal Dutch/Shell Group of Companies (see page 157), whose fleets of owned/managed and chartered ships at 31 Dec. 1978 comprised 232 oil tankers (totalling 30 million deadweight tons), 11 gas carriers (totalling 732 000 m³ *957,382 yd³* capacity) and 7 dry bulk carriers (600,000 d.wt.).

Shopping Centre

The world's first shopping centre was Roland Park Shopping Center, Baltimore, Maryland built in 1896. The world's largest shopping centre is the Lakewood Center, California with a gross building area of 2,451,438 ft² *227 745 m²* on a 168 acre *67,9 ha* site with parking for 12,500 cars. Britain's largest shopping centre is the £18 million Arndale Centre, Luton, Bedfordshire, opened on 16 Jan. 1972, extending over an area 17 acres *6,8 ha* with parking for 2,200 cars and visited by about 400,000 customers per week. The world's largest wholesale merchandise mart is the Dallas Market center, located on Stemmons Freeway, Dallas, Texas, U.S.A. with more than 7 million ft² *650 300 m²* in 6 buildings. The

complex covers 135 acres *54 ha* with some 3,000 permanent showrooms displaying merchandise of more than 22,000 manufacturers. The center attracts 500,000 buyers each year to its 27 annual markets and trade shows.

Soft drinks

The world's top-selling soft drink is Coca-Cola with over 235,000,000 drinks sold per day by the end of 1978 in more than 135 countries. Coke was launched as a tonic by Dr. John S. Pemberton of Atlanta, Georgia in 1886. The Coca-Cola Company was formed in 1892 and the famous bottle was patented in 1915.

Steel Company *World*

The world's largest producer of steel has been Nippon Steel of Tokyo, Japan which produced 53.24 million tons *54,1 million tonnes* of steel and steel products in 1977/78. The Fukuyama Works of Nippon Kokan has a capacity of more than 16 000 000 tonnes per annum. Its Jan. 1978 work force was 76,034.

Great Britain

Britain's largest steelworks are those at Scunthorpe, Humberside, which have a capacity of 5.64 million tonnes/*tons* and employs 18,000 people on a 3,690 acre *1 493 ha* site.

STOCK EXCHANGES

The oldest Stock Exchange in the world is that at Amsterdam, in the Netherlands, founded in 1602. There were 138 throughout the world as of 22 June 1976.

Most markings

The highest number of markings received in one day on the London Stock Exchange was 32,665 on 14 Oct. 1959 following the 1959 General Election. The record for a year is 4,396,175 "marks" in the year ending 31 Mar. 1960. There were 8,034 securities (*c.f.* 9,749 peak in June 1973) listed at 31 Dec. 1978. Their total nominal value was £110,057 million (gilt-edged £71,689 million) and their market value was £329,385 million (gilt-edged £60,518 million) at peak in September 1978.

The highest figure of *The Financial Times* Industrial Ordinary share index (1 July 1935 = 100) was 558.6 on 4 May 1979. The lowest figure was 49.4 on 26 June 1940. The greatest rise in a day has been 23.7 points to 315.5 on 1 July 1975 in anticipation of anti-inflationary measures, and the greatest fall in a day was 24.0 to 313.8 on 1 Mar. 1974 on the realisation of a fourth post-war Labour Government.

Highest and lowest par values

The highest denomination of any share quoted in the world is a single share in F. Hoffmann–La Roche of Basel worth Sw. Fr. 101 000 (*£21,992*) on 23 Apr. 1976. The record for the London Stock Exchange is £100 for preference shares in Baring Brothers & Co. Ltd., the bankers.

U.S. records

The highest index figure on the Dow Jones average (instituted 8 Oct. 1896) of selected industrial stocks at the close of a day's trading was 1,051.70 on 11 Jan. 1973, when the average of the daily "highs" of the 30 component stocks was 1,067.20. The old record trading volume in a day on the New York Stock Exchange of 16,410,030 shares on 29 Oct. 1929, the "Black Tuesday" of the famous "crash" was unsurpassed until April 1968. The Dow Jones industrial average, which reached 381.71 on 3 Sept. 1929, plunged 30.57 points on 29 Oct. 1929, on its way to the Depression's lowest point of 41.22 on 8 July 1932. The largest decline in a day, 38.33 points, occurred on 28 Oct. 1929. The total lost in security values from 1 Sept. 1929 to 30 June 1932 was $74,000 million (*then £23,000 million*). The greatest paper loss in a year was $209,957 million (*then £87,500 million*) in 1974. The record daily increase of 28.40 on 30 Oct. 1929 was most recently bettered on 1 Nov. 1978 with 35.34 points to 827.79. The record day's trading was 66,370,000 shares on 3 Aug. 1978. The largest transaction on record "share-wise" was on 14 Mar. 1972 for 5,245,000 shares of American Motors at $7.25 each. The largest stock trade in the history of the New York Exchange was a 1,874,300 share block of Cutler-Hammer

The aluminium 31 storey headquarters in Pittsburgh, Pennsylvania of Alcoa, the world's largest producer of aluminium (see p. 159).

stock at $55 in a $103,086,500 (*£54½ million*) transaction on 12 June 1978. The highest price paid for a seat on the N.Y. Stock Exchange was $515,000 (*then £214,580*) in 1969. The lowest 20th century price was $17,000 in 1942.

Largest equity
The greatest aggregate market value of any corporation is $33.5 billion (*£16,420 million*) assuming a closing price of $206⅝ multiplied by the 149,533,813 shares of IBM extant on 31 Dec. 1975.

Greatest Personal Loss
The highest recorded personal paper losses on stock values have been those of Ray A. Kroc, Chairman of McDonald's Corporation with $64,901,718 (*then £27 million*) on 8 July 1974 and Edwin H. Land, President of Polaroid Corporation with $59,397,355 on 28–29 May 1974, when Polaroid stock closed $12.12 down at 43¼ on the day.

Largest new issue
The American Telegraph & Telephone Company offered $1,375 million's worth of shares in a rights offer on 27,500,000 shares of convertible preferred stock on the New York market on 2 June 1971. The largest offering on the London Stock Exchange by a United Kingdom company was the £76 million rights offer of Lloyds Banks Ltd. on 6 Feb. 1976.

Largest investment house
The largest investment company in the U.S.A., and once the world's largest partnership with 124 partners, before becoming a corporation in 1959 is Merrill, Lynch, Pierce, Fenner & Smith Inc. (founded 6 Jan. 1914) of New York City, U.S.A. The assets are $8.6 billion and it has 23,535 employees, 450 offices and 1,770,000 separate accounts. The firm is referred to in the United States stock exchange circles as "We" or "We, the people" or "The Thundering Herd".

Largest store
The world's largest store is R. H. Macy & Co. Inc. at Broadway and 34th Street, New York City, N.Y., U.S.A. It covers 50.5 acres *20,3 ha* and employs 12,000 who handle 400,000 items. The sales of the company and its subsidiaries in 1978 were $1,834,100,000 (*£917 million*). Mr. Rowland Hussey Macy's sales on his first day at his fancy goods store on 6th Avenue, on 27 Oct. 1858, were recorded as $11.06 (*then £2.20*).

Largest supermarket
The largest supermarket in the United Kingdom is Carrefour in Bristol (actually a hypermarket). Currently it has a selling area of 90,000 ft² *18 912 m²* and parking space for 1,700 cars.

Tobacco company
The world's largest tobacco company is the British-American Tobacco Company Ltd. (founded in London in 1902). The Company's subsidiaries and affiliates operate 118 tobacco factories in 53 countries: consolidated turnover in 1977–78 was £5,405 million and total assets were £2,959 million at 30 Sept. 1978. The Group's sales in 1978 topped 550,000 million cigarettes.

The world's largest cigarette plant is the $200 million Philip Morris plant at Richmond, Virginia, U.S.A. opened in October 1974. It has a payroll of 4,000 producing 450 million cigarettes a day.

Toy manufacturer
The world's largest single toy manufacturer is Mattel Inc. of Hawthorne, Los Angeles, U.S.A. founded in 1945. Its total sales for the year ending 3 Feb. 1979 were $496,563,000 (*£248.2 million*) for 6 divisions of which Mattel Toys is the largest.

Toy shop
The world's biggest toy shop is Hamleys of Regent Street Ltd., founded in 1760 in Holborn and removed to Regent Street, London, W.1. in 1901. It has selling space of 30,000 ft² *2 787 m²* on 11 floors with over 300 employees during the Christmas season. It was taken over by Debenhams on 12 May 1976 and has also a Sport and Leisure Centre (occupying 50,000 ft² *4 650 m²*) in Wigmore Street, London, and Model Centres in London and Bristol.

Vintners
The oldest champagne firm is Ruinart Père et Fils founded in 1729. The oldest cognac firm is Augier Frères & Co., established in 1643.

2. MANUFACTURED ARTICLES

Guinness Superlatives Ltd. has published specialist volumes entitled *English Pottery and Porcelain* (price £7.95), *Antique Firearms* (price £7.95) and will be publishing the *Guinness Book of Antiques* by John FitzMaurice Mills in October 1979 (price £7.95).

Antique *Largest*
The largest antique ever sold has been London Bridge in March 1968. The sale was made by Mr. Ivan F. Luckin of the Court of Common Council of the Corporation of London to the McCulloch Oil Corporation of Los Angeles, California, U.S.A. for $2,460,000 (*then £1,029,000*). The 10,000 tons/*tonnes* of facade stonework were re-assembled at a cost of £3 million, at Lake Havasu City, Arizona and "re-dedicated" on 10 Oct. 1971.

Armour
The highest auction price paid for a suit of armour is £25,000 paid in 1924 for the Pembroke suit of armour, made at Greenwich in the 16th century, for the 2nd Earl of Pembroke.

Beds *Largest*
In Bruges, Belgium, Philip, Duke of Burgundy had a bed 12¼ ft wide and 19 ft long *3,81 × 5,79 m* erected for the perfunctory *coucher officiel* ceremony with Princess Isabella of Portugal in 1430. The largest bed in Great Britain is the Great Bed of Ware, dating from *c.* 1580, from the Crown Inn, Ware, Hertfordshire, now preserved in the Victoria and

Measuring 6,800 ft² *631,7 m²*, the world's largest blanket was made in ten months by readers of *Woman's Weekly* in aid of charity (see p. 165). (*"Record Breakers"*)

Albert Museum, London. It is 10 ft 8½ in wide, 11 ft 1 in long and 8 ft 9 in tall *3,26 × 3,37 × 2,66 m*. The largest bed currently marketed in the United Kingdom is a Super Size Diplomat bed, 9 ft wide by 9 ft long, *2,74 m²* from The London Bedding Centre, Sloane Street, S.W.1 which sells for £2,200 (inc. VAT).

Heaviest

The heaviest bed is a water bed 9 ft 7 in × 9 ft 10 in *2,92 × 2,99 m* owned by Milan Vacek of Canyon Country, California since 1977. The thermostatically heated water alone weighs 4,205 lb. *1 907 kg*.

Beer cans

Beer cans date from a test marketing by Krueger Beer of Richmond, Virginia in 1935. The largest collection is claimed by John F. Ahrens of Mount Laurel, New Jersey with 12,000 *different* cans.

Beer mats

The world's largest collection of beer mats is owned by Leo Pisker of Vienna, who had collected 76,000 different mats from 144 countries by Apr. 1979. The largest collection of purely British mats is 19,428 by Charles M. Schofield of Glasgow by 8 Apr. 1978.

Weighing 3½ tons/*tonnes*, this chandelier is the largest ever constructed, having 1,896 electric lights illuminating the Casino Knokke in Belgium (see p. 165). (*Knokke Casino*)

Blanket

The largest blanket ever made measured 68 × 100 ft *20,7 × 30,48 m* weighing 600 lb. *272 kg*. It was knitted in 20,160 6-inch squares in 10 months (Oct. 1977–July 1978) by *Woman's Weekly* readers for Action Research for The Crippled Child. It was shown on B.B.C. T.V. *Record Breakers* in Oct. 1978.

Candle

A candle 80 ft *24,38 m* high and 8½ feet *2,59 m* in diameter was exhibited at the 1897 Stockholm Exhibition by the firm of Lindahls. The overall height was 127 ft *38,70 m*

Carpets and Rugs *Earliest*

The earliest carpet known is a woollen pile-knotted carpet, red on white ground excavated at Pazyryk, U.S.S.R. in 1947, dated to the 5th century B.C. and now preserved in Leningrad.

Largest

Of ancient carpets the largest on record was the gold-enriched silk carpet of Hashim (dated A.D. 743) of the Abbasid caliphate in Baghdad, Iraq. It is reputed to have measured 180 by 300 ft *54,86 × 91,44 m*.

The world's largest carpet now consists of 88,000 ft² (over two acres *or 0,81 ha*) of maroon carpeting in the Coliseum exhibition hall, Columbus Circle, New York City, N.Y., U.S.A. This was first used for the International Automobile Show on 28 Apr. 1956.

Most expensive

The most magnificent carpet ever made was the Spring carpet of Khusraw made for the audience hall of the Sassanian palace at Ctesiphon, Iraq. It was about 7,000 ft² *650 m²* of silk, gold thread and encrusted with emeralds. It was cut up as booty by military looters in A.D. 635 and from the known realisation value of the pieces must have had an original value of some £100,000,000. In 1946 the Metropolitan Museum, New York privately paid $1 million (*then £248,138*) for the 26.5 × 13.6 ft *807 × 414 cm* Anholt Medallion carpet made in Tabriz or Kashan, Persia *c.* 1590. The highest price ever paid at auction for a carpet is £121,000 for a Mamluk carpet 12 ft 5 in × 7 ft 3 in *378 × 220 cm* presumed woven in Cairo *c.* 1500, at Sotheby's Bond Street Salerooms, London on 29 Mar. 1978.

Most finely woven

The most finely woven carpet known is one with more than 2,490 knots per in² *386 per cm²* from a fragment of an Imperial Mughal prayer carpet of the 17th century now in the Altman collections in the Metropolitan Museum of Art, New York City, N.Y., U.S.A.

Ceramics

The auction record for any ceramic object is £420,000 for the 16¼ in *41,2 cm* Ming blue and white bottle dated 1403–24 acquired by Mrs. Helen Glatz, a London dealer, at Sotheby Parke Bernet, London on 2 Apr. 1974. The Greek urn painted by Ueuphromios and thrown by Euxitheos in *c.* 530 B.C. was bought by private treaty by the Metropolitan Museum of Art, New York for $1.3 million (*then £541,666*) in August 1972.

Chair *Largest*

The world's largest chair is the 9 m *9 ft 6¼ in* tall 4,2 m *13 ft 9¼ in* wide chair outside the Edsbyverken furniture factory in Edsbyn, Sweden since 1944.

Most expensive

The highest price ever paid for a single chair is $85,000 (*then £35,000*) for the John Brown Chippendale mahogany corner chair attributed to John Goddard of Newport, Rhode Island, U.S.A. and made in *c.* 1760. This piece was included in the collection of Mr. Lansdell K. Christie dispersed by Sotheby Parke Bernet, New York on 21 Oct. 1972.

Chandelier *Largest*

The world's largest chandelier, was built in Murano, Italy in 1953 for the Casino Knokke, Belgium. It measures 8 m *26 ft 3 in* in circumference and 7 m *23 ft* in height and weighs 3½ tons/tonnes with 1,896 electric lights.

Christmas cracker

The largest cracker ever constructed was one 45 ft *13,71 m* in length and 8 ft *2,43 m* in diameter built for the BBC TV *Record Breakers* Show transmitted on 27 Dec. 1974.

Cigars *Largest*

The largest smokeable cigar in existence is one 2,78 m *9 ft 1½ in* long, 32,4 cm *12¾ in* in circumference and weighing 27,3 kg *60 lb 3 oz*. It was made by J. P. Scmidt Jun., Fredericia, Denmark and exhibited in May 1979.

The largest standard cigar in the world is the 9¾ in *24,1 cm* long "Partagas Visible Immensas". The Partagas factory in Havana, Cuba, manufacturers special gift cigars 50 cm *19.7 in* long, which retail in Europe for £8. Russos' Restaurant, Union Street, San Francisco has the largest known collection of cigar bands with some 5,000 dating from 1860.

Most expensive

The most expensive standard cigar in the world is the Montecristo 'A', which retails in Britain at £5.48.

Most voracious smokers

Scott Case smoked 110 cigarettes simultaneously for 30 secs at the Oddball Olympics in Los Angeles in May 1974. Paul Mears (University of Winnipeg, Manitoba, Canada) won a contest in smoking 35 full-size cigars simultaneously in 1975.

In New York City on 23 Sept. 1973 Simon Argevitch of Oakland, California retained his record for the more esoteric art of smoking 14 cigars while simultaneously whistling.

Cigarettes *Consumption*

The heaviest smokers in the world are the people of the United States, where 665,000 million cigarettes (an average of 3,900 per adult) were consumed at a cost of some $15,000 million (*£7,900 million*) in 1977. The people of China however were estimated to consume 725,000 million in 1977. The peak consumption in the United Kingdom was 3,230 cigarettes per adult in 1973. The peak volume was 243,100,000 lb. *110,2 million kg* in 1961, compared with 218,000,000 lb. *98,9 million kg* in 1978 when 125,200 million cigarettes were sold. The largest single plant is the Philip Morris factory at Richmond, Virginia, U.S.A. opened in October 1974 with 4,500 workers producing 485 million cigarettes per day.

In the United Kingdom 59 per cent of adult men and 42 per cent of adult women smoke.

Tar/Nicotine Content

Of the 121 brands most recently analysed for the Dept. of Health and Social Security the one with highest tar/nicotine content is *Pall Mall King Size* with 36/3.5 *mg* per cigarette. *Silk Cut Ultra Mild, Embassy Ultra Mild* and *John Player King Size Ultra Mild* with < 4/0.3 are at the safer end of the league table.

Most popular

The world's most popular cigarette is "Marlboro", a filter cigarette made by Phillip Morris, which sold 186,598 million units in 1978. The largest selling British cigarette in 1978 was *Benson and Hedges King Size*. The Wills brand "The Three Castles" was introduced in 1878.

Longest and shortest

The longest cigarettes ever marketed were "Head Plays", each 11 in *27,9 cm* long and sold in packets of 5 in the United States in about 1930, to save tax. The shortest were "Lilliput" cigarettes, each 1¼ in *31,7 mm* long, and ⅛ in *3 mm* in diameter, made in Great Britain in 1956.

Largest collection

The world's largest collection of cigarettes is that of Robert E. Kaufman, M.D., of 950 Park Avenue, New York City 28, N.Y., U.S.A. In May 1979 he had 7,225 different cigarettes with 43 kinds of tips made in 167 countries. The oldest brand represented is "Lone Jack", made in the U.S.A. in *c.* 1885. Both the longest and shortest (see above) are represented.

Cigarette cards

The earliest known and most valuable tobacco card is 'Vanity Fair' dated 1876 issued by Wm. S. Kimball & Co., Rochester, New York. The earliest British example appeared c. 1883 in the form of a calendar issued by Allen & Ginter, of Richmond, Virginia, trading from Holborn Viaduct, City of London. The largest known collection is that of Mr. Edward Wharton-Tigar, M.B.E. (b. 1913) of London with a collection of more than 1,000,000 cigarette and trade cards in about 45,000 sets. The highest price paid for a set is £2,000 at Murray's Auction, London on 11 Oct. 1975 for Taddy's "Clowns" by Ian Graham of Leeds.

Cigarette lighter *Most expensive*

The most expensive cigarette pocket lighter in the world is the 18 carat gold and platinum Dunhill lighter, featuring the Union Jack comprising of 73 precious stones (diamonds, rubies and sapphires) and selling for $20,000 (£10,000) at Dunhill's in New York in 1979. The 18 carat lighthouse table lighter, made by Alfred Dunhill Ltd. of St. James's, City of Westminster, Greater London, set on an island of amethyst retails for a record £32,500.

Cigarette packets

The earliest surviving cigarette packet is the Finnish "Petit Canon" packet for 25, made by Tollander & Klärich in 1860, from the Ventegodt Collection. The rarest is the Latvian 700-year anniversary (1201–1901) Riga packet, believed to be unique, from the same collection.

Credit card collection

The largest collection of valid credit cards at 1 May 1979 is one of 932 (all different) by Walter Cavanagh (b. 1943) of Santa Clara, California, U.S.A. The cost of acquisition o "Mr. Plastic Fantastick" was nil, and he keeps them in the world's longest wallet—250 ft 76, m long weighing 28 lb. 12,7 kg worth more than $1 million in credit.

Curtain

The largest curtain ever built has been the bright orange-red 4 ton 4 064 kg 185 ft 56 m high curtain suspended 1,350 ft 411 m across the Rifle Gap, Grand Hogback, Colorado, U.S.A. by the Bulgarian-born sculptor Christo, 36 (né Javacheff) on 10 Aug. 1971. It blew apart in a 50 m.p.h. 80 km/h gust 27 hrs later. The total cost involved in displaying this work of art was $750,000 (then £312,500).

Dolls

The highest price paid at auction for dolls is £16,000 for a pair of William and Mary painted wooden dolls in original clothes 22 in 55,8 cm high at Sotheby's, London on 19 Apr. 1974. After an export licence was refused they were purchased, following a public subscription, by Victoria and Albert Museum, London. A rag doll 23 ft 7 m in height was made at Monterey Adult Education Center, New York in April–June 1977.

Dress *Most expensive*

The dress with the highest price tag ever exhibited by a Paris fashion house was one in the Schiaparelli spring/summer collection on 23 Jan. 1977. "The Birth of Venus" designed by Serge Lepage with 512 diamonds was priced at Fr. 7,500,000 (£880,000).

Emperor Jean-Bédel Bokassa's coronation robe with a 39 foot 11,8 m long train was encrusted with 785,000 pearls and 1,220,000 crystal beads by Guiselin of Paris for £77,125 for use at Bangui, Central African Empire in December 1977.

Fabrics *Earliest and Most expensive*

The oldest surviving fabric discovered from Level VI A at Çatal Hüyük, Turkey has been radio-carbon dated to 5900 B.C.

The most expensive fabric obtainable is an evening-wear fabric 37½ in 95 cm wide, hand embroidered and sequinned on a pure silk ground in a classical flower pattern. It has 194,400 tiny sequins per yard, 46,000 per m² and is designed by Alan Hershman of Duke St., London; it cost £290 per metre in May 1978.

Finest cloth

The most expensive cloth, the brown-grey throat hair of Indian goats, is Shatoosh (or Shatusa), finer, and more expensive than Vicuña. It is sold by Neiman-Marcus of Dallas, Texas, U.S.A., at $1,000 (£526) per yard.

Firework

The most powerful firework obtainable is the Bouquet of Chrysanthemums *hanabi*, marketed by the Marutamaya Ogatsu Fireworks Co. Ltd., of Tōkyō, Japan. It is fired to a height of over 3,000 ft 915 m from a 36 in 914 mm calibre mortar. Their chrysanthemum and peony flower shells produce a spherical flower with "twice-thrice changing colours", 2,000 ft 610 m in diameter. The largest firework produced in Britain is one fired on 8 June 1946 from Brock's 25 in 635 mm, 22 cwt. 1 117 kg mortar. The shell weighs 200 lb. 90,7 kg and is 6½ ft 1,98 m in circumference and was first used in Lisbon in 1886. The world's lowest firework was George Plimpton's 40½ in 102 cm 720 lb. 325 kg Roman candle "Fat Man" intended to break the Japanese record over Long Island, N.Y. in February 1975. It sizzled, hissed and exploded leaving a crater 10 ft 3 m deep.

Flags *Oldest*

The crest in the centre of the Austrian flag has its origins in the 11th century while that of Malta dates from 1090. The origins of the Iranian flag, with its sword-carrying lion and sun, are obscure but "go beyond the 12th century".

Largest

The largest flag in the world, the "Stars and Stripes", was displayed by the Great American Flag Co. of Warren, Vermont on the Verrazano Narrows Bridge, New York, U.S.A. on 28 June 1976. It measured 193 ft 58,82 m by 366½ ft 101,7 m or 1.64 acres 0,66 ha weighing about 1½ tons with 15 ft 4,57 m wide stripes and stars 11 ft 3,35 m in diameter. The largest Union Flag (or Union Jack) was one 240 × 108 ft 73,15 × 32,91 m displayed at the Royal Tournament, Earl's Court, London in July 1976. It weighed more than a ton and was made by Form 4Y at Bradley Rowe School, Exeter, Devon. The largest flag *flown* from a public building in Britain is a Union Flag measuring 40 ft 12,19 m by 20 ft 6,09 m first flown from the Civic Offices, Newcastle-under-Lyme, Staffordshire on 21 Apr. 1977. The study of flags is known as vexillology.

Float

The longest float used in any street carnival is the 200 ft 60 m long dragon *Sun Loon* used in Bendigo, Victoria, Australia. It has 65,000 mirror scales. Six men are needed to carry its head alone. The largest float is the 150 foot 45,7 m long, 22 ft 6,7 m wide 'Agree' Float bearing 51 All-American Homecoming "Queens" used at the Orange Bowl parade, Miami, Florida on 29 Dec. 1977.

Furniture *Most expensive*

The highest price ever paid for a single piece of furniture is £240,000 for a French Louis XVI ormolu mounted ebony *bureau plat* and *cartonnier* 5 ft 4½ in 1,63 m high by 3 ft 1½ in 95 cm wide at Sotheby Parke Bernet, New Bond Street, London on 13 Dec. 1974. At Mentmore, Buckinghamshire on 18 May 1977 a bureau *en pente* of c. 1735 by Bernard van Risen Burgh was bought in at £280,000.

Oldest British

The oldest surviving piece of British furniture is a three-footed tub with metal bands found at Glastonbury, Somerset, and dating from between 300 and 150 B.C.

Largest Piece

The largest item of furniture in the world is the Long Sofa—a wooden bench for old seafarers—measuring 72 m 236 ft in length at Oscarshamn, Sweden.

Glass

The most priceless example of the art of glass-making is usually regarded as the glass Portland Vase which dates from late in the 1st century B.C. or 1st century A.D. It was made in Italy, and was in the possession of the Barberini family in Rome from at least 1642. It was eventually bought by the Duchess of Portland in 1792 but smashed while in the British

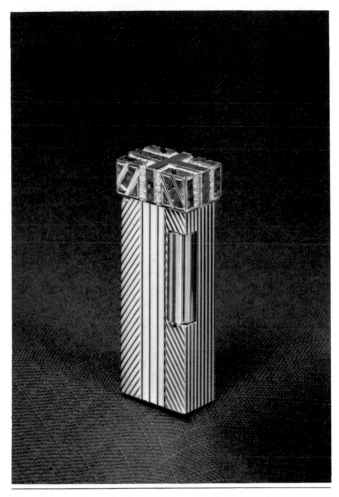

The most expensive pocket lighter in the world, the $20,000 lighter made by Alfred Dunhill Ltd. in 1979 (see p. 166).

A pair of William and Mary wooden dolls which fetched £16,000 at an auction in April 1974—the highest price ever paid (see p. 166). (*Victoria and Albert Museum*)

Museum in 1847. The auction record is £520,000 for a 4th-century Roman glass cage-cup measuring 7 in *17,78 cm* in diameter and 4 in *10,16 cm* in height, sold at Sotheby's, London, on 4 June 1979.

Gold plate

The world's highest auction price for a single piece of gold plate is £40,000 for a 20 oz. 4 dwt. *628,3 g* George II teapot made by James Ker of Edinburgh for the King's Plate Horse race for 100 guineas at Leith, Scotland in 1736. The sale was by Christie's, City of Westminster, Greater London on 13 Dec. 1967 to a dealer from Boston, Massachusetts, U.S.A.

The gold coffin of the 14th century B.C. Pharaoh Tutankhamun discovered by Howard Carter on 16 Feb. 1923 in Luxor, western Thebes, Egypt weighed 2,448 lb. *1 110 kg*. The exhibition at the British Museum attracted 1,656,151 people (of whom 45.7% bought catalogues) from 30 Mar. to 30 Dec. 1972 resulting in a profit of £657,731.22.

Guns

The highest price ever paid for a single gun is £125,000 given by the London dealers F. Partridge for a French flintlock fowling piece made for Louis XIII, King of France in *c.* 1615 and attributed to Pierre le Bourgeoys of Lisieux, France (d. 1627). This piece was included in the collection of the late William Goodwin Renwick of the United States sold by Sotheby's, London on 21 Nov. 1972. (see also Pistols)

Hat *Most expensive*

The highest price ever paid for a hat is 165,570 francs (*then £14,032*) (inc. tax) by Moët et Chandon at an auction by Maîtres Liery, Rheims et Laurin on 23 Apr. 1970 for one last worn by Emperor Napoleon I (1769–1821) on 1 Jan. 1815.

Jade

The highest price ever paid for an item in jade is 1,250,000 Swiss Francs (*then £156,250*) for a necklace set with 31 graduated beads of Imperial green jade. This was sold by Christie's at the Hotel Richmond, Geneva, Switzerland, on 9 May 1973. The highest price paid for jade objects is H.K $1.4 million (*£175,000*) for a pair of 19th-century green jadeite table screens 17¼ in *43,8 cm* in height by Sotheby's in Hong Kong on 2 Nov. 1976.

Jig-saw

The largest jig-saw ever made is one 48 ft 0 $\frac{1}{16}$ in × 24 ft 0⅛ in *14,63 × 7,31 m* built with 9,111 pieces by the 75th Field Artillery Group, U.S. Army at Fort Sill, Oklahoma and exhibited on 3 Nov. 1975. The *Festival of Britain* jig-saw by Efroc Ltd., now in Montserrat though of much lesser area contains an estimated 40,000 pieces.

Matchbox labels

The oldest match label is that of John Walker, Stockton-on-Tees, Cleveland, England in 1827. Collectors of labels are phillumenists, of bookmatch covers philliberumenists and of matchboxes cumyxaphists. Several labels are only uniquely known such as the Byron Match from Roche & Co., Marseilles and the Canadian Allumettes Frontenac from the Eddy Match Co. both in the Frank J. Mrazik Collection in Quebec, Canada.

Medal or Decoration

The highest price paid at auction for an order or decoration is £17,000 at Sotheby's London on 21 Mar. 1979 for the group including the V.C. and the M.M. won by Capt. George Burdon McKean of the 14th Canadian Infantry Bn, Quebec Regt. awarded for gallantry on the Gavrelle sector in France on 27–28 Apr. 1918.

Nylon Sheerest
The lowest denier nylon yarn ever produced is the 6-denier used for stockings exhibited at the Nylon Fair in London in February 1956. The sheerest stockings normally available are 9-denier. An indication of the thinness is that a hair from the average human head is about 50 denier.

Paperweight
The highest price ever paid for a glass paperweight is £33,000 at Sothcby Parke Bernet, London on 4 July 1977 for a Clichy double convolvulus bouquet weight, 2¾ in *7,2 cm* in diameter. The earliest were made in Italy in the 15th century.

Penknife
The penknife with the greatest number of blades is the Year Knife made by the cutlers, Joseph Rodgers & Sons Ltd, of Sheffield, England, whose trade mark was granted in 1682. The knife was built in 1822 with 1,822 blades but had to halt at 1,973 because there was no further space. It was acquired by Britain's largest hand tool manufacturers, Stanley Works (Great Britain) Ltd. of Sheffield, South Yorkshire in 1970.

Pens *Most expensive*
The most expensive writing pens are the 18 carat pair of pens (one fibre-tipped and one ballpoint) capped by diamonds of 3.88 carats sold by Alfred Dunhill (see Cigarette lighter above) for £9,943 the pair (incl. V.A.T.).

Pipe *Most expensive*
A briar root with a silver mounting with Canadian motifs with silver chains and an ivory pushtype stem made by Julius Vesz of Toronto, Canada is priced at U.S. $7,500 *(£3,945)*.

Pistols *Most expensive*
The highest price paid for a pair of pistols at auction is the £78,000 given by the London dealer Howard Ricketts at Sotheby Parke Bernet, London on 17 Dec. 1974 for a pair of English Royal flintlock holster pistols made *c.* 1690–1700 by Pierre Monlong. They were sent for sale by Anne, Duchess of Westminster.

Playing Cards
The rarest pack of playing cards is the 17th century "Lives of the Saints" published by the Bowles family and estimated to be worth £2,000. A 7 of diamonds signed by Edward Gibbon in 1786 as an IOU for £320 has been sold for £500.

Porcelain and Pottery English
The highest price ever paid for a single piece of English porcelain is £32,000 for a Chelsea Boar's Head (of the red anchor period) sold at Sotheby's on 13 Nov. 1973. The pottery record is £15,015 for a Staffordshire 18th century salt-glaze pew group sold at Christie's on 15 Dec. 1975.

Pot Lid
The highest price paid for a pot lid is £2,600 by Richard Cashmore for a 19th century Staffordshire porcelain example at Phillips, London on 18 Oct. 1978.

Ropes largest and longest
The largest rope ever made was a coir fibre launching rope with a circumference of 47 in *119 cm* made in 1858 for the British liner *Great Eastern* by John and Edwin Wright of Birmingham. It consisted of four strands, each of 3,780 yarns. The longest fibre rope ever made without a splice was one of 10,000 fathoms or 11.36 miles *18 288 m* of 6½ in *16,5 cm* circumference manila by Frost Brothers (now British Ropes Ltd.) in London in 1874.

Shoes *Most expensive*
The most expensive standard shoes obtainable are mink-lined golf shoes with 18 carat gold embellishments and ruby-tipped spikes made by Stylo Matchmakers International Ltd., of Northampton, England which retail for £3,575 or $6,800 per pair in the U.S.A.

Largest
Excluding cases of elephantiasis, the largest shoes ever sold are a pair size 42 built for the giant Harley Davidson of Avon Park, Florida, U.S.A. The normal limit is Size 14. The 1887 Jubilee Boot made for the Newark trades procession, Nottinghamshire weighed 81¾ lb. *31,7 kg*, is 4 ft 3½ in *131 cm* long and is Size 141. It is owned by Clarks Shoe Museum, Street, Somerset.

Silver
The highest price ever paid for silver is £612,500 for the Duke of Kingston tureens made in 1735 by Meissonier and sold by Christie's, Geneva on 8 Nov. 1977.

Snuff *Most expensive*
The most expensive snuff obtainable in Britain is "Café Royale" sold by G. Smith and Sons (est. 1869) of 74, Charing Cross Road, City of Westminster, Greater London. It sells at £1.20 per oz.

Box
The highest price ever paid for a snuff box is £89,250 paid by Kenneth Snowman of Wartski's in a sale at Christie's, London on 26 June 1974. This was for the gold and lapis lazuli example uniquely signed by Juste-Oreille Meissonnier (d. 1750) the French master goldsmith and dated Paris 1728. It was made for Marie-Anne de Vaviere-Neubourg, wife o. Charles II of Spain. It measures 83 × 57 mm *3¼ × 2¼ in* It was sent in for sale from the Ortiz-Patino collection.

Spoons Apostle
The highest price ever paid for a set of 12 apostle spoons is £70,000 paid by Mrs. How in a sale at Christie's, London on 26 June 1974. They are Elizabethan silver-gilt spoons, made by Christopher Wace in 1592, known as the "Tichborne Celebrities".

Stuffed bird
The highest price ever paid for a stuffed bird is £9,000. This was given on 4 Mar. 1971 at Messrs Sotheby & Co., London by the Iceland Natural History Museum for a specimen of the Great Auk (*Alca impennis*) in summer plumage, which was

The 1887 Jubilee Boot which measures 4 ft 3½ in *131 cm* long and will fit only a size 141 foot.

taken in Iceland *c.* 1821; this particular specimen stood 22½ in *57 cm* high. The Great Auk was a flightless North Atlantic seabird, which was finally exterminated on Eldey, Iceland in 1844, becoming extinct through hunting. The last British sightings were at Co. Waterford in 1834 and St. Kilda, Western Isles *c.* 1840.

Sword

The highest price paid for a sword is the $145,000 (*then £85,800*) paid for the gold sword of honour presented by the Continental Congress of 1779 to General Marie Jean Joseph Lafayette at Sotheby Parke Bernet, New York City, U.S.A. on 20 Nov. 1976.

Table cloth

The world's largest table cloth is one 219 yds *200 m* long by 2 yds *1,8 m* wide double damask made by John S. Brown & Sons Ltd. of Belfast and shipped to a royal palace in the Middle East. There was also an order for matching napkins for 450 places.

Tapestry *Earliest*

The earliest known examples of tapestry woven linen are three pieces from the tomb of Thutmose IV, the Egyptian Pharaoh and dated to 1483–1411 B.C.

Largest

The largest single piece of tapestry ever woven is "Christ in His Majesty", measuring 72 ft by 39 ft *21,94 × 11,88 m* designed by Graham Vivian Sutherland O.M. (b. 24 Aug. 1903) for an altar hanging in Coventry Cathedral, West Midlands. It cost £10,500, weighs ¾ ton *760 kg* and was delivered from Pinton Frères of Felletin, France, on 1 Mar. 1962.

Longest Embroidery

An uncompleted 8 in *20,3 cm* deep 1,065 ft *324,6 m* embroidery of scenes from C. S. Lewis's Narnia children's stories has been worked by Mrs. Margaret Pollard of Truro, Cornwall to the order of Mr. Michael Maine. The famous Bayeux *Telle du Conquest, dite tapisserie de la reine Mathilde,* a hanging 19½ in *49,5 cm* wide by 231 ft *70,40 m* in length. It depicts events of the period 1064–1066 in 72 scenes and was probably worked in Canterbury, Kent, in *c.* 1086. It was "lost" for 2½ centuries from 1476 until 1724.

Most expensive

The highest price paid for a set of tapestries is £200,000 for four Louis XV pieces at Sotheby & Co., London on 8 Dec. 1967.

Tartan *Earliest*

The earliest evidence of tartan is the so-called Falkirk tartan, found stuffed in a jar of coins in Bells Meadow, Falkirk, Scotland. It is of a dark and light brown pattern and dates from *c.* A.D. 245. The earliest reference to a specific named tartan has been to a Murray tartan in 1618 although Mackay tartan was probably worn earlier.

Time Capsule

The world's largest time capsule is the Tropico Time Tunnel of 10,000 ft³ *283 m³* in a cave in Rosamond, California, sealed by the Kern Antelope Historical Society on 20 Nov. 1966 and intended for opening in A.D. 2866.

Vase *Largest*

The largest vase on record is one 8 ft *2,78 m,* in height weighing 650 lb. *294,8 kg* thrown by Sebastiano Maglio at Haeger Potteries of Dundee, Illinois, U.S.A. (founded 1872) during August 1976.

Wig

The largest wig yet made of human hair is that by Bergmann of 5th Avenue, New York City in 1975. It measures 15 ft *4,57 m* in length.

Wreath *Most expensive*

The most expensive wreath on record was that sent to the funeral of President Kennedy in Washington, D.C. on 25 Nov. 1963 by the civic authority of Paris. It was handled by Interflora Inc. and cost $1,200 (*then £428*). The only rival was a floral tribute sent to the Mayor of Moscow in 1970 by

Sebastiano Maglio of Haeger Potteries of Dundee, Illinois made this 8 ft *2,78 m* vase—the largest such recorded. (*A. P. Moose*)

Umberto Formichello, general manager of Interflora which is never slow to scent an opportunity.

Writing paper

The most expensive writing paper in the world is that sold by Cartier Inc. on Fifth Avenue, New York City at $8,000 (*now £4,570*) per 100 sheets with envelopes. It is of hand made paper from Tervakoski Osakeyhtiö, Finland, with deckle edges and a "personalized" portrait watermark. Second thoughts and mis-spellings tend to be costly.

3. AGRICULTURE

Origins

It has been estimated that only 21 per cent of the world's land surface is cultivable and that only 7.6% is actually under cultivation. Evidence adduced in 1971 from Nok Nok Tha and Spirit Cave, Thailand tends to confirm plant cultivation and animal domestication was part of the Hoabinhian culture *c.* 11,000 B.C. Reindeer may have been domesticated as early as *c.* 18,000 B.C. but definite evidence is still lacking.

The earliest attested evidence for the cultivation of grain comes from Ali Kosh, Iran and Jericho, by *c.* 7000 B.C. Goat was domesticated at Asiab, Iran by *c.* 8050 B.C. and dog at Star Carr, North Yorkshire by *c.* 7700 B.C.: the earliest definite date for sheep is *c.* 7200 B.C. at Argissa-Magula, Thessaly, Greece and for pig and cattle *c.* 7000 B.C. at the same site. The earliest date for horse is *c.* 4350 B.C. from Dereivka, Ukraine, U.S.S.R.

FARMS
Earliest

The earliest dated British farming site is a neolithic one, enclosed within the Iron Age hill-fort at Hembury, Devon, excavated during 1934–5 and now dated to 4210–3990 B.C. Pollen analysis from two sites Oakhanger, Hampshire, and Winfrith Heath, Dorset (Mesolithic *c.* 4300 B.C.) indicates

169

that Mesolithic man may have had herds which were fed on ivy during the winter months.

Largest *World*
The largest farms in the world are collective farms in the U.S.S.R. These have been reduced in number from 235,500 in 1940 to only 36,000 in 1969 and have been increased in size so that units of over 60,000 acres *25 000 ha* are not uncommon. The pioneer farm of Laucidio Coelho near Campo Grande, Mato Grosso, Brazil in *c.* 1901 was 3,358 miles^2 *8 700 km^2* 2.15 million acres with 250,000 head of cattle at the time of his death in 1975.

Great Britain
The largest farms in the British Isles are Scottish hill farms in the Grampians. The largest arable farm is that of Elveden, Suffolk, farmed by the Earl of Iveagh. Here 11,245½ acres *4 550 ha* are farmed on an estate of 22,918 acres *9 274 ha*, the greater part of which was formerly derelict land. The 1978 production included 1,639,298 gal. *7,458,806 litres* of milk, 3,267 tons *3 320 tonnes* of grain and 19,287 tons *19,597 tonnes* of sugar beet. The livestock includes 3,610 cattle, 1,000 ewes and 4,259 pigs.

Cattle station
The world's largest cattle station is Alexandria Station, Northern Territory, Australia, selected in 1873 by Robert Collins, who rode 1,600 miles *2 575 km* to reach it. It has 82 working bores, a staff of 90 and originally extended over 7,207,608 acres *2 916 818 ha*—more than the area of England's four largest counties of North Yorkshire, Cumbria, Devon and Lincoln put together. The present area is 6,500 miles^2 *16 835 km^2* which is stocked with 60,000 shorthorn cattle. Until 1915 the Victoria River Downs Station, Northern Territory, was over three times larger, with an area of 22,400,000 acres (35,000 miles^2 *90 650 km^2*).

Sheep station
The largest sheep station in the world is Commonwealth Hill, in the north-west of South Australia. It grazes between 70,000 and 90,000 sheep, *c.* 700 cattle and 25,000 uninvited kangaroos in an area of 4,080 miles^2 *10 567 km^2* *i.e.* larger than the combined area of Norfolk and Suffolk.

The largest sheep move on record occurred when 27 horsemen moved a mob of 43,000 sheep 40 miles *64 km* from Barcaldine to Beaconsfield Station, Queensland, Australia, in 1886.

Turkey farm
The world's largest turkey farm is that of Bernard Matthews Ltd., centred at Gt. Witchingham, Norfolk, with 1,076 workers tending 5,400,000 turkeys.

Chicken ranch
The world's largest chicken ranch is the 520 acre *210 ha* "Egg City" Moorpark, California established by Jules Goldman in 1961. Some 2 million eggs are laid daily by 3.1 million chickens.

Piggery
The world's largest piggery is the Sljeme pig unit in Yugoslavia which is able to process 300,000 pigs in a year. Even larger units may exist in Romania but details are at present lacking.

Cow shed
The longest cow shed in Britain is that of the Yorkshire Agricultural Society at Harrogate, North Yorkshire. It is 456 ft *139 m* in length with a capacity of 686 cows. The National Agricultural Centre, Kenilworth, Warwickshire, completed in 1967, has, however, capacity for 782 animals.

Foot-and-mouth disease
The worst outbreak of foot-and-mouth disease in Great Britain was that from Salop on 25 Oct. 1967 to 25 June 1968 in which there were 2,364 outbreaks and 429,632 animals slaughtered at a direct and consequential loss of £150,000,000. The outbreak of 1871, when farms were much smaller, affected 42,531 farms. The disease first appeared in Great Britain at Stratford, East London in August 1839.

Sheep Shearing
The highest recorded speed for sheep shearing in a working day was that of G. Phillips who machine-sheared 694 lambs (average 77.1 per hour) in 9 hrs at Tymawr Farm, Libanus, Powys on 25 June 1975. The blade (*i.e.* handshearing) record in a 9 hr working day is 350, set in 1899. In a shearing marathon, four men machine-shore 1,649 sheep in 24 hrs at Brecon, Powys, Wales on 13–14 July 1977.

Great Britain
British records for 9 hrs have been set at 555 by Roger Poyntz-Roberts (300) and John Savery (255) on 9 June 1971 (sheep caught *by* shearers), and 610 by the same pair (sheep caught *for* shearers) in July 1970.

Sheep *Survival*
On 2 Mar. 1978, Peter Boa of Seiberscross, Strath Brora, Sutherland, Scotland dug out 9 sheep buried in snow for 33 days. Two ewes were alive.

Mushroom farm
The largest mushroom farm in the world is the Butler County Mushroom Farm, Inc., founded in 1937 in a disused limestone mine near West Winfield, Pennsylvania, U.S.A. It employs over 1,000 in a maze of underground galleries 110 miles *177 km* long, producing over 45,000,000 lb. *20 411 tonnes* of mushrooms per year.

Largest wheat field
The largest single fenced field sown with wheat was one of 35,000 acres *14 160 ha* sown in 1951 south west of Lethbridge, Alberta, Canada.

Largest vineyard
The world's largest vineyard is that extending over the Mediterranean façade between the Rhône and the Pyrenees in the *départments* Hérault, Gard, Aude, and Pyrenées-Orientales in an area of 840 000 ha *2,075,685 acres* of which 52.3% is *monoculture viticole*.

Largest hop field
The largest hop field in the world is one of 3,945 acres *1 596 ha* at Toppenish, Washington State, U.S.A. It is owned by John I. Haas, Inc., the world's largest hop growers, with hop farms in British Columbia (Canada), California, Idaho, Oregon and Washington, with a total net area of 3,765 acres *1 522 ha*.

Community Garden *Largest*
The largest recorded community garden project is that operated by the City Beautiful Council, and the Benjamin Wegerzyn Garden Center Dayton, Ohio, U.S.A. It comprises 1,173 allotments each of 812¼ ft^2 *74,45 m^2*.

"Beecher Arlinda Ellen", the Holstein who holds the record for the greatest milk yield for one lactation (365 days) at 24.8 tons *25,1 tonnes* (see p. 172).

Agriculture

CROP YIELDS

Wheat
Crop yields for highly tended small areas are of little significance. The British record is 89.8 cwt/acre *11 273 kg/ha* on a field of 20.4 acres *8,25 ha* by A. S. Clark of Langley Mawn, Saffron Walden, Essex in 1977 using Maris Hobbit winter wheat.

Barley
A yield of 82.61 cwt./acre *10 371 kg/ha* of Clermont Spring Barley was achieved in 1972 by John Graham of Kirkland Hall, Wigton, Cumbria from a 13.52 acre *5,47 ha* field.

Corn
A yield of 352.64 U.S. bushels (15½% moisture) from an acre, using De Kalb XL-54, by Roy Lynn, Jr. near Kalamazoo, Michigan on 30 Sept. 1977.

Sugar beet
The highest recorded yield for sugar beet is 62.4 short tons (55.71 long tons) per acre *1 139,8 tonnes/ha* by Andy Christensen and Jon Giannini in the Salinas Valley, California.

Potato picking
The greatest number of U.S. barrels picked in a 9½ hr day is 235 by Walter Sirois (b. 1917) of Caribou, Maine, U.S.A. on 30 Sept. 1950.

Ploughing
The world championship (instituted 1953) has been staged in 17 countries and won by ploughmen of ten nationalities of which the United Kingdom has been most successful with 6 championships. The only man to take the title three times has been Hugh Barr of Northern Ireland in 1954–55–56.

The fastest recorded time for ploughing an acre *0,404 ha* (minimum 32 right-hand turns and depth 9 in *22 cm*) is 13 mins 34 secs by Leslie Painter using a Bamford 5 furrow 12 in *30,5 cm* plough towed by a Massey Ferguson 1155 tractor at West Farm, Appleton, Oxfordshire on 18 Nov. 1977.

The greatest recorded acreage ploughed in 24 hrs is 123.4 acres *49,9 ha* by David Griffiths and Pat Neylan using a Lamborghini R-1056 DT tractor with a 6 furrow plough to a depth of 7 in *17,7 cm* in the Nakuru District, Kenya on 6–7 July 1978. John Frisby of Stoke Golding near Nuneaton, Warwickshire, ploughed for 80 hrs on 3–6 Nov. 1978.

Largest Hay Rick
A rick of some 23,500 straw bales was completed by Birch and Pearman at Billesley, Warwickshire in September 1977.

LIVESTOCK
Note: Some exceptionally high livestock auction sales are believed to result from collusion between buyer and seller to raise the ostensible price levels of the breed concerned. Others are marketing and publicity exercises with little relation to true market prices.

Highest Priced *Bull*
The highest price ever paid for a bull is $2,500,000 (£1,087,000) for the beefalo (a ⅜th buffalo, ⅜ charolais, ¼ Hereford) *Joe's Pride* sold by D. C. Basolo of Burlingame, California to the Beefalo Cattle Co. of Canada of Calgary, Alberta, Canada on 9 Sept. 1974.

The highest price ever paid for a bull in Britain is 60,000 guineas (£63,000), paid on 5 Feb. 1963 at Perth, Scotland, by James R. Dick (1928–74) co-manager of Black Watch Farms, for "Lindertis Evulse", an Aberdeen-Angus owned by Sir Torquil and Lady Munro of Lindertis, Kirriemuir, Tayside, Scotland. This bull failed a fertility test in August 1963 when 20 months old thus becoming the world's most expensive piece of beef.

Cow
The highest price ever paid for a cow is $Can. 235,000 (£131,200) for the Holstein-Friesian "Hanover Hill Barb" by a U.S.-Canadian syndicate at the Sale of Stars, Oakville, Ontario, Canada on 8 Nov. 1976. The British record is

THE BUSINESS WORLD

£14,910 for "Fairthwaite Indiana", a pure-bred Chianina in-calf heifer sold to Mr. Christopher Reeves of Taunton, Somerset by Harrison & Hetherington Ltd. in Carlisle, Cumbria on 21 Sept. 1974.

Sheep
The highest price ever paid for a sheep is $A46,000 (£30,000) for a Merino ram from John Collins & Sons, Mount Bryan, South Australia by Mrs. P. L. Puckridge of White River, Port Lincoln, South Australia at the Royal Adelaide Show on 2 Sept. 1976.

The British auction record is £13,000 paid by A. C. Campbell & Co. of Creetown, Dumfries & Galloway for Graham McClymont's Scottish Blackface ram in Oct. 1976.

The highest price ever paid for wool is $A46 per kg (£11.09 per lb.) for a bale of superfine Merino fleece from the Launceston, Tasmania sales in February 1973 It was sold by Mr. C. Stephen of Mount Morriston estate to Fujii Keori Ltd. of Osaka, Japan.

Pig
The highest price ever paid for a pig is $42,500 (£21,250) for a Duroc boar named "Glacier" owned by Baize Durocs of Stamford, Texas, U.S.A., by Wilbert & Myron Meinhart of Hudson Iowa on 24 Feb. 1979. The U.K. record is 3,300 guineas (£3,465), paid by Malvern Farms for the Swedish Landrace gilt "Bluegate Ally 33rd" owned by Davidson Trust in a draft sale at Reading, Berkshire on 2 Mar. 1955.

Horse
The highest price for a draught horse is $47,500 (*then £9,970*) paid for the 7 year old Belgian stallion *Farceur* by E. G. Good at Cedar Falls, Iowa on 16 Oct. 1917.

Donkey
Perhaps the lowest ever price for livestock was at a sale at Kuruman, Cape Province, South Africa in 1934 where donkeys were sold for less than 2p each.

Heaviest *Cattle*
Of heavyweight cattle the heaviest on record was a Holstein-Durham cross named "Mount Katahdin" exhibited by A. S. Rand of Maine, U.S.A. in 1906–1910 and frequently weighed at an even 5,000 lb. *2 267 kg*. He was 6 ft 2 in at the shoulder with a 13 ft *3,96 m* girth and died in a barn fire c. 1923. The British record is the 4,480 lb. *2 032 kg* of "The Bradwell Ox" owned by William Spurgin of Bradwell, Essex. He was 15 ft *4,57 m* from nose to tail and had a girth of 11 ft *3,35 m* when 6 years old in 1830. The largest breed of heavyweight cattle is the Chianini, brought to Italy from the Middle East in pre Roman times. Mature bulls average 5 ft 8 in *1,73 m* at the forequarters and weigh 2,865 lb. *1 300 kg*. In 1955 a bull named "Donetto" tipped the scales at 3,834 lb. *1 740 kg* at the Arezzo show—a world record for any bull of any breed.

The highest recorded birthweight for a calf is 225 lb. *102 kg* from a British Friesian cow at Rockhouse Farm, Bishopston, Swansea, West Glamorgan, in 1961.

Pigs
The heaviest hog recorded was "Big Bill" of 2,552 lb. *22¾ cwt 11 575 kg* measuring *9 ft 2,75 m* long with a belly on the ground raised in Henderson County, Tennessee, U.S.A. and killed in 1933. He was mounted and displayed by the Wells family in Jackson, Tennessee until 1946. The British record is a hog of 12 cwt. 66 lb. *639,5 kg* bred by Joseph Lawton of Astbury, Cheshire. In 1774 it stood 4 ft 8½ in *1,43 m* in height and was 9 ft 8 in *2,94 m* long. The highest recorded weight for a piglet at weaning (8 weeks) is 81 lb. *36,7 kg* for a boar, one of nine piglets farrowed on 6 July 1962 by the Landrace gilt "Manorport Ballerina 53rd", *alias* "Mary", and sired by a Large White named "Johnny" at Kettle Lane Farm, West Ashton, Trowbridge, Wiltshire.

Sheep
The highest recorded birthweight for a lamb in the world is 38 lb. *17,2 kg* at Clearwater, Miner County near Howard, Kansas, U.S.A. in 1975 but neither this lamb nor the ewe survived.

Broiler Growth
The record for growth for flocks of at least 2,500 at 56 days is 5.902 lb. *2,677 kg* with a conversion rate of 2.085 by Ross Breeders Ltd., Edinburgh reported in April 1979.

Prolificacy *Cattle*
On 25 Apr. 1964 it was reported that a cow named "Lyubik" had given birth to seven calves at Mogilev, U.S.S.R. A case of five live calves at one birth was reported in 1928 by T. G. Yarwood of Manchester. The life-time prolificacy record is 30 in the case of a cross-bred cow owned by G. Page of Warren Farm, Wilmington, East Sussex, which died in November 1957, aged 32. A cross-Hereford calved in 1916 and owned by A. J. Thomas of West Hook Farm, Marloes, Dyfed, Wales, produced her 30th calf in May 1955 and died in May 1956, aged 40.

Pigs
The highest recorded number of piglets in one litter is 34, thrown on 25–26 June 1961 by a sow owned by Aksel Egedee of Denmark. In February 1955 a Wessex sow owned by Mrs. E. C. Goodwin of Paul's Farm, Leigh, near Tonbridge, Kent, had a litter of 34, of which 30 were born dead. A litter of 32 piglets (26 live born) was thrown in February 1971 by a British saddleback owned by Mr. R. Spencer of Toddington, Gloucestershire. A sow, "Bessie" owned by Mr L. Witt of Bath, Avon farrowed litters of 19 (1 stillborn) on 12 Nov. 1975, 19 (3 stillborn) on 5 Apr. 1976 and 21 (3 stillborn) on 16 Sept. 1976 making 59 in a year (52 reared).

Sheep
A case of eight lambs at a birth was reported by D. T. Jones of Priory Farm, Gwent, in June 1956, but none lived. A case of a sheep living to 26 years was recorded in flock book records by H. Poole, Wexford, Ireland. A Greyface ewe at Moss Side Farm, Longtown Cumbria gave birth to live sextuplets in March 1977.

Egg-laying
The highest authenticated rate of egg-laying is by "Princess Te Kawau", a Black Orpington, owned by Mrs. D. M. Waddell, with 361 eggs in 364 days in an official test at Taranaki, New Zealand, ending on 31 Mar. 1930. The U.K. record is 353 eggs in 365 days in a National Laying Test at Milford, Surrey in 1957 by a Rhode Island Red owned by W. Lawson of Welham Grange, Retford, Nottinghamshire.

The heaviest egg reported is one of 16 oz. *454 g*, with double yolk and double shell, laid by a white Leghorn at Vineland, New Jersey, U.S.A., on 25 Feb. 1956. The largest recorded was one of "nearly 12 oz." for a 5 yolked egg 12¼ in *31 cm* around the long axis and 9 in *22,8 cm* around the shorter axis laid by a Black Minorca at Mr. Stafford's Damsteads Farm, Mellor, Lancashire in 1896.

The highest recorded annual average for a flock is 313 eggs in 52 weeks from a flock of 1,000 Warren-Stadler SSL layers (from 21 weeks of age) by Eric Savage, White Lane Farm, Albury, Surrey, England in 1974–75.

Most yolks
The highest claim for the number of yolks in a chicken's egg is 9 reported by Mrs. Diane Hainsworth of Hainsworth Poultry Farms, Mount Morris, New York, U.S.A. in July 1971 and also from a hen in Kirghizia, U.S.S.R. in August 1977.

Goose Egg
The white goose "Speckle" owned by Donny Brandenberg, of Goshen, Ohio, U.S.A., on 3 May 1977 laid a 24 oz. *680 g* egg measuring 13½ × 9½ in *34 × 24 cm* in circumferences.

Milk Yields *Cows*
The world lifetime record yield of milk is 340,578 lb. (152.04 tons *154 479 kg*) at 3.3 per cent butter fat by the U.S. Holstein cow "Or-Win Masterpiece Riva" owned by Willard and Gary Behm at Adrian, Michigan up to 10 Apr. 1975. The greatest yield of any British cow was that given by the British Friesian "Guillyhill Janna 2nd", owned by S. H. West. This cow yielded 330,939 lb. *150 111 kg* up to 1973. The greatest recorded yield for one lactation (365 days) is 55,661 lb. *25 247 kg* by the Holstein "Beecher Arlinda Ellen" owned by Mr. & Mrs. Harold L. Beecher of Rochester, Indiana, U.S.A. in 1975. The British and probably world record for milk yield in a day is 198¼ lb. *89,92 kg* by R. A. Pierson's British Friesian "Garsdon Minnie" in 1948.

Hand milking
Andy Faust at Collinsville, Oklahoma, U.S.A. in 1937 achieved 120 U.S. gallons *99.92 U.K. galls* in 12 hours.

Goats
The highest recorded milk yield for any goat is 7,546 lb. *3 422 kg* in 365 days by "Waiora Frill Q*" bred by Mr. & Mrs. E. L. Collins of Swanson, Auckland, New Zealand in 1972.

Butter fat yield
The world record lifetime yield is 14,651 lb. *6 645 kg* by the Jersey cow *Sunny King Berna* (calved 5 Mar. 1950) in 5,726 days to January 1979 on the J. W. Coppini estate, Ferndale, California. The British record butter fat yield in a lifetime is 12,166 lb. *5 518 kg* by the Ayrshire cow "Craighead Welma" owned by W. Watson Steele from 273,072 lb. at 4.45%. The highest recorded lactation (365 days) yield reported is 2,230 lb. *1 011 kg* by the Holstein "Breezewood Patsy Bar Pontiac" owned by the Gelbke brothers of Vienna, Ohio, U.S.A. announced on 8 Oct. 1976. The United Kingdom record for butter fat in one day is 9.30 lb. *4,218 kg* (79 lb. *35,8 kg* milk at 11.8%) by Queens Letch Farms' Guernsey Cow "Thisbe's Bronwen of Trewollack".

Cheese
The most active cheese-eaters are the people of France, with an annual average in 1978 of 37.7 lb. *17,1 kg* per person. The world's biggest producer is the United States with a factory production of 3,344,300,000 lbs. 1,492,991 tons *1 516 949 tonnes* in 1977. The U.K. cheese consumption in 1978 was 12.09 lb. *5,48 kg* per head.

Oldest
The oldest and most primitive cheeses are the Arabian *kishk*, made of dried curd of goats' milk. There are today 450 named cheeses of 18 major varieties, but many are merely named after different towns and differ only in shape or the method of packing. France has 240 varieties.

Most expensive
The world's most expensive cheese is La Baratte from the Loire Valley, France at 140 francs per kg (£8.60 *per lb.*) Britain's most costly cheese is Dorset Blue at £2.80 per lb. in May 1979.

Largest
The largest cheese ever made was a cheddar of 34,591 lb. *15 190 kg* made in 43 hrs on 20–22 Jan. 1964 by the Wisconsin Cheese Foundation for exhibition at the New York World's Fair, U.S.A. It was transported in a specially designed refrigerated tractor trailer "Cheese Mobile" 45 ft *13,71 m* long.

CHICKEN PLUCKING
Ernest Hausen (1877–1955) of Fort Atkinson, Wisconsin, U.S.A., died undefeated after 33 years as a champion. On 19 Jan. 1939 he was timed at 4.4 secs and reputedly twice did 3.5 secs a few years later.

The record time for plucking 12 chickens clean by a team of 4 women at the annual Chicken Plucking Championship at Marsaryktown, Florida, U.S.A. is 32.9 seconds set on 9 Oct. 1976 by Doreena Cary, Diane Grieb, Kathy Roads and Dorothy McCarthy.

TURKEY PLUCKING
Vincent Pilkington of Cootehill, County Cavan, Ireland killed and plucked 100 turkeys in 7 hrs 32 min on 15 Dec. 1978.

THE HUMAN WORLD

1. POLITICAL AND SOCIAL

Detailed information on all the sovereign and non-sovereign countries of the world will be contained in *The Guinness Book of Answers* (3rd Edition) (To be published Guinness Superlatives March 1980, £5.95).

The land area of the Earth is estimated at 57,270,000 miles[2] *148 328 000 km[2]* (including inland waters), or 29.08 per cent of the world's surface area.

Largest political division
The British Commonwealth of Nations, a free association of 39 independent sovereign states together with their dependencies, covers an area of 13,095,000 miles[2] *33 915 000 km[2]* with a population which in 1978 just surpassed 1000,000,000.

COUNTRIES
Total
The total number of separately administered territories in the world is 221, of which 164 were independent countries (as of 1 Aug. 1979). Of these, 39 sovereign and 42 non-sovereign are insular countries. Only 29 sovereign countries are entirely without a seaboard.

Largest
The country with the greatest area is the Union of Soviet Socialist Republics (the Soviet Union), comprising 15 Union (constituent) Republics with a total area of 22 402 200 km[2] *8,649,500 miles[2]*, or 15.0 per cent of the world's total land area, and a total coastline (including islands) of 106 360 km *66,090 miles*. The country measures 8 980 km *5,580 miles* from east to west and 4 490 km *2,790 miles* from north to south and is 91.8 times the size of the United Kingdom.

The United Kingdom covers 94,221 miles[2] *244 030 km[2]* (including 1,197 miles[2] *3 100 km[2]* of inland water), or 0.16 per cent of the total land area of the world. Great Britain is the world's eighth largest island, with an area of 84,186 miles[2] *218 040 km[2]* and a coastline 4,928 miles *7 930 km* long, of which Scotland accounts for 2,573 miles *4 141 km*, Wales 426 miles *685 km* and England 1,929 miles *3 104 km*.

Smallest
The smallest independent country in the world is the State of the Vatican City or Holy See (Stato della Città del Vaticano), which was made an enclave within the city of Rome, Italy on 11 Feb. 1929. The enclave has an area of 44 hectares *108.7 acres*. The maritime sovereign country with the

shortest coastline is Monaco with 3.49 miles *5,61 km* excluding piers and breakwaters.

The world's smallest republic is Nauru, less than 1 degree south of the equator in the Western Pacific, which became independent on 31 Jan. 1968, has an area of 5,263 acres *2 129 ha* and a population of 8,000 (latest estimate mid-1976). Tuvalu has an area of 6 080 acres *2 460 ha* but a population of 6,000.

The smallest colony in the world is Gibraltar with an area of 2½ miles[2] *5,8 km[2]*. Pitcairn Island, the only inhabited (70 people, 1977) island of a group of 4 (total area 18½ miles[2] *48 km[2]*) has an area of 1½ miles[2] or 960 acres *388 ha*.

The official residence, since 1834, of the Grand Master of the Order of the Knights of Malta totalling 3 acres *1,2 ha* and comprising the Villa del Priorato di Malta on the lowest of Rome's seven hills, the 151 ft *46 m* Aventine, retains certain diplomatic privileges as does 68 Via Condotti. The order has accredited representatives to foreign governments and is hence sometimes cited as the smallest state in the world.

Flattest and Most Elevated
The country with the lowest highest point is the Republic of the Maldives which attains 4 metres *13ft*. The country with the highest lowest point is Lesotho. The egress of the Senqu (Orange) river-bed is 4,530 ft *1 381 m* above sea level.

Most impenetrable boundary
The "Iron Curtain" (858 miles *1 380 km*) dividing the Federal Republican (West) and the Democratic Republican (East) parts of Germany, utilises 2,230,000 land mines and 50,000 miles *80 500 km* of barbed wire, much of it of British manufacture, in addition to many watch-towers containing detection devices. The whole strip of 270 yds *246 m* wide occupies 133 miles[2] *344 km[2]* of East German territory.

Longest and Shortest Frontier
The longest *continuous* frontier in the world is that between Canada and the United States, which (including the Great Lakes boundaries) extends for 3,987 miles *6 416 km* (excluding 1,538 miles *2 547 km* with Alaska). The frontier which is crossed most frequently is that between the United States and Mexico. It extends for 1,933 miles *3 110 km* and there are more than 120,000,000 crossings every year. The Sino-Soviet frontier, broken by the Sino-Mongolian border,

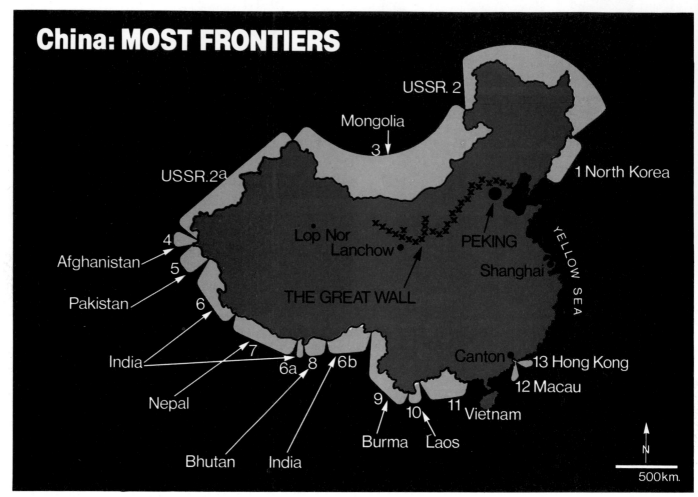

China: MOST FRONTIERS

USSR. 2

Mongolia

3

1 North Korea

USSR.2a

4

Afghanistan

5

Pakistan

6

India

7

6a 8 6b

Nepal

Bhutan   India

Lop Nor

Lanchow

PEKING

Shanghai

THE GREAT WALL

YELLOW SEA

Canton   13 Hong Kong

12 Macau

9   10   11 Vietnam

Burma   Laos

N

500km.

extends for 4,500 miles *7 240 km* with no reported figure of crossings. The "frontier" of the Holy See in Rome measures 2.53 miles *4,07 km*. The land frontier between Gibraltar and Spain at La Linea, closed since 1969, measures 1,672 yds *1,53 km*. Zambia, Rhodesia, Botswana and Namibia (South West Africa) meet at a point.

Most Frontiers

The country with the most land frontiers is China, with 13 —Mongolia, U.S.S.R., North Korea, Hong Kong, Macau, Vietnam, Laos, Burma, India, Bhutan, Nepal, Pakistan and Afghanistan. France, if all her *Départements d'outre-mer* are included, may, on extended territorial waters, have 20 frontiers.

POPULATIONS
World

Estimates of the human population of the world largely hinge on the accuracy of the component figure for the popu-

lation of the People's Republic of China, which has published no census since that of 30 June 1953 (582.6 million). The U.N. estimate for 1978 accounted more closely than hitherto with that of the U.S. Bureau of the Census at 930 million. The daily increase in the world's population has been estimated at 221,900 per day or 154 per minute. It was estimated that 286 were born and 114 died every minute in 1977–78. The world's population has doubled in the last 49 years and is now doubling at a rather faster rate. It is estimated that 75,000,000,000 humans have been born and died in the last 600,000 years.

Most populous country

The largest population of any country is that of China, which in *pinyin* is written Zhogguo. The mid-1977 U.N. estimate was 865,677,000. The rate of natural increase in the People's Republic of China is now estimated between 1.5 and 1.66 per cent and then the 1,000 million mark will be reached during 1980 by U.S. estimates but will not be reached until 1986 by U.N. estimates. The Yugoslav news agency Tanjug reported that on 1 May 1978 the Chinese claimed a population of 900 million.

Least populous

The independent state with the smallest population is the Vatican City or the Holy See (see Smallest country, page 173), with 723 inhabitants at mid 1977 and a nil birth rate.

Most densely populated

The most densely populated territory in the world is the Portuguese province of Macau (or Macao), on the southern coast of China. It has an estimated population of 279,000 (mid-1977) in an area of 6.2 miles^2 *16,05 km^2* giving a density of 44,990 per mile^2 *17 370 per km^2*.

The Principality of Monaco, on the south coast of France, has a population of 25,000 (30 June 1977) in a area of 369,9 acres *149,6 ha* giving a density of 35,800/mile^2 *13 820/km^2*.

WORLD POPULATION—Progressive estimates			
Date	Millions	Date	Millions
10 000 B.C.	c.5	1930	2,070
A.D. 1	c.200	1940	2,295
1000	c.275	1950	2,533*
1250	375	1960	3,049*
1500	420	1970	3,704*
1650	550–600	1975	4,090*
1700	615	1976	4,163*
1750	720	1977	4,314**
1800	900	1978	4,395*
1900	1,625	1980	4,470*
1920	1,862	2000	6,351*†

* *U.S. Bureau of Census data made on medium variants.*

** *The mid 1978 provisional estimate by the U.N. is 4,205 million.*

† *Some demographers maintain that the figure will (or must) stabilize at 10 to 15,000 million but above 8,000 million during the 21st century. The Tsui-Bogue estimate from the University of Chicago for A.D. 2000 is 5,800 million.*

This is being relieved by marine infilling which will increase her area to 447 acres *180 ha*. Singapore has 2,334,000 (mid-1978 estimate) people in an inhabited area of 73 miles² *189 km²*.

Of territories with an area of more than 1,000 km², Hong Kong (405 miles² *1 049 km²*) contains 4,525,000 (estimated mid-1977), giving the territory a density of 11,362/mile² *4 389/km²*. Hong Kong is now the most populous of all colonies. The transcription of the name is from a local pronunciation of the Peking dialect version of Xiang gang (a port for incense). Kowloon, on the mainland, had a density which reached 84 816/km² or *219,559/mile²* in 1961. On the Wah Fu estate there are 55,000 people living on 24 acres giving an unsurpassed spot density of 1,466,600 per mile² *566 280/km²*. In 1959, at the peak of the housing crisis, it was reported that in one house designed for 12 people the number of occupants was 459, including 104 in one room and 4 living on the roof.

Of countries over 1,000 miles² *2 589 km²* the most densely populated is Bangladesh with a population of 84,655,000 (mid 1978, estimate) living in 55,126 miles² *142 775 km²* at a density of 1,535/mile² *592/km²*. The Indonesian island of Java (with an area of 48,763 miles² *126 295 km²*) had a population of 69,037,000 (1971), giving a density of 1,415/mile² *547/km²*.

The United Kingdom (94,221 miles² *244 030 km²*) had an estimated home population of 55,843,000 at 30 June 1978, giving a density of 593.5 people/mile² *229,1/km²*. The population density for England alone (50,869 miles² *131 750 km²*) is 965.3/mile² *372,6/km²*, while that of south-eastern England is more than 1,640/mile² *630/km²*.

Most sparsely populated
Antarctica became permanently occupied by relays of scientists from October 1956. The population varies seasonally and reaches 1,500 at times.

The least populated territory, apart from Antarctica, is Greenland, with a population of 56,000 (estimated mid 1977) in an area of 840,000 miles² *2 175 000 km²* giving a density of one person to every 15.0 miles² *38,8 km²*. Some 84.3% of the island comprises an ice-cap.

Emigration
More people emigrate from Mexico than from any other country. An estimated 800,000 emigrated illegally into the U.S.A. in 1976 alone. A total of 210,300 emigrated from the U.K. in 1976. The largest number of emigrants in any one year was 360,000 in 1852, mainly from Ireland. The number of U.K. citizens leaving from Oct. 1977–Oct 1978 was 133,400.

Immigration
The country which regularly receives the most legal immigrants is the United States, with 462,315 in 1977. It has been estimated that in the period 1820–1977, the U.S.A. has received 42,063,523 *official* immigrants. One in 24 of the U.S. population is however an *illegal* immigrant. The peak year for immigration into the United Kingdom was the 12 months from 1 July 1961 to 30 June 1962, when about 430,000 Commonwealth citizens arrived. The number of non-U.K. immigrants from Oct. 1977–Oct. 1978 was 104,100.

Tourism
The Jubilee Year record of 11.5 million visitors for the United Kingdom was surpassed by the provisional 1978 figure of 11,700,000 who spent an estimated £2,323 million excluding fares to British carriers.

Birth Rate *Highest and Lowest*
The highest 1970–75 figure is 52.2 for the Niger Republic. The rate for the whole world was 30.4 per 1,000 in 1975.

Excluding Vatican City, where the rate is negligible, the lowest recorded rate is 7.5 for Monaco (1977).

The 1977 rate in the United Kingdom was 11.7/1,000 (11.6 in England and Wales, 11.9 in Scotland and 16.6 in Northern Ireland), while the 1977 rate for the Republic of Ireland was 21.4 registered births per 1,000. The highest number of births in England and Wales (since registration in 1837) has been 957,782 in 1920 and the lowest this century 569,000 in 1977. The figure has fallen each year since 1964 (875,972).

Death Rate *Highest and Lowest*
The highest of the latest available recorded death rates is 28.1 deaths per each 1,000 of the population in Bangladesh in 1970–75. The rate for the whole world was 12.3 per 1,000 in 1975.

The lowest of the latest available recorded rates is 1.7 deaths/1,000 in Tonga in 1976.

The 1978 rate in the United Kingdom was 11.7/1,000 (11.9 in England and Wales, 12.5 in Scotland and 11.0 in Northern Ireland). The highest S.M.I. (Standard Mortality Index where the national average is 100) is in Salford, Greater Manchester with a figure of 133. The 1977 rate for the Republic of Ireland was 10.5 registered deaths per 1,000.

Natural Increase
The highest of the latest available recorded rates of natural increase is 40.6 (45.4–4.8) per 1,000 in Syria. The rate for the whole world was 30.4−12.3 = 18.1 per 1,000 in 1975.

The 1977 rate for the United Kingdom was statistically nil (nil in England and Wales, nil in Scotland and 5.9 increase in Northern Ireland). The rate for the first time in the first quarter of 1975 became one of natural decrease. The figure for the Republic of Ireland was 10.9/1,000 in 1977.

The lowest rate of natural increase in any major independent country is in West Germany with a negative figure of −2.0 per 1,000 (9.5 births and 11.5 deaths) for 1977.

Marriage ages
The country with the lowest average ages for marriage is India, with 20.0 years for males and 14.5 years for females. At the other extreme is Ireland, with 31.4 for males and 26.5 for females. In the People's Republic of China the *recommended* age for marriage for men has been 28 and for women 25. In England and Wales the peak age for marriages are 22.8 years (male) and 19.6 years (female).

Divorces
The country with most divorces is the United States with a total of 1,090,000 in 1977—a rate of 50.09% on the current annual total of marriages.

Sex Ratio
There were estimated to be 1,003.5 men in the world for every 1,000 women (1975). The country with the largest recorded shortage of males is the U.S.S.R., with 1,143 females to every 1,000 males (1979 census). The country with the largest recorded woman shortage is Pakistan, with 885 to every 1,000 males in 1972. The figures are, however, probably under-enumerated due to *purdah*. The ratio in the United Kingdom was 1,054.5 females to every 1,000 males at 30 June 1977, and is expected to be 1,014.2/1,000 by A.D. 2000.

Infant Mortality
Based on deaths before one year of age, the lowest of the latest available recorded rates is 8.0 deaths per 1,000 live births in Sweden in 1977. The world rate in 1975 was 98.

The highest recorded infant mortality rate reported has been 195 to 300 for Burma in 1952 and 259 for Zaïre in 1950. Many countries have apparently ceased to make returns. In Ethiopia the infant mortality rate was unofficially estimated to be nearly 550/1,000 live births in 1969.

The United Kingdom figure for 1978 was 13.1/1,000 live births (England and Wales 13.8, Scotland 12.9, Northern Ireland 16.6). The Republic of Ireland figure for 1977 was 15.7.

Life Expectation

There is evidence that life expectation in Britain in the 5th century A.D. was 33 years for males and 27 years for females. In the decade 1890–1900 the expectation of life among the population of India was 23.7 years.

Based on the latest available data, the highest recorded expectation of life at age 12 months is 73.0 years for males and 79.2 years for females in Iceland (1975–76).

The lowest recorded expectation of life at birth is 27 years for both sexes in the Vallée du Niger area of Mali in 1957 (sample survey, 1957–58). The figure for males in Gabon was 25 years in 1960–61 but 45 for females.

The latest available figures for England and Wales (1974) are 69.3 years for males and 75.5 years for females; for Scotland (1968–70) 66.9 years for males and 73.08 years for females; for Northern Ireland (1969–71) 67.9 years for males and 73.7 years for females and for the Republic of Ireland (1970–72) 68.77 years for males and 73.52 years for females. The British figure for 1901–1910 was 48.53 years for males and 52.83 years for females.

Standards of Living

The country with the highest average income per native citizen in 1977 was Abu Dhabi, with some $70,000 £41,200. In 1976 the average income per head in the United Kingdom was £1,813 $3,082.

Housing

For comparison, dwelling units are defined as a structurally separated room or rooms occupied by private households of one or more people and having separate access or a common passageway to the street.

The country with the greatest recorded number of private housing units is India, with 100,251,000 occupied in 1972.

Great Britain comes fourth among reporting countries, with a stock of 20,617,000 dwellings as at 1 Jan. 1979. The record number of permanent houses built has been 413,715 in 1968.

Physicians

The country with the most physicians is the U.S.S.R., with 831,300, or one to every 307 persons. China has more than a million para-medical personnel known as "bare foot doctors". In England and Wales there were 85,000 hospital doctors, general practitioners and dentists working within the National Health Service in 1975.

The country with the lowest recorded proportion is Upper Volta, with 58 physicians (one for every 92,759 people) in 1970.

Dentists

The country with the most dentists is the United States, where 131,000 were registered members of the American Dental Association in 1978.

Psychiatrists

The country with the most psychiatrists is the United States. The registered membership of the American Psychiatric Association was 22,000 in 1978. The membership of the American Psychological Association was 45,000 in 1978.

Hospital Largest *World*

The largest medical centre in the world is the District Medical Center in Chicago, Illinois, U.S.A. It covers 478 acres *193 ha* and includes five hospitals, with a total of 5,600 beds, and eight professional schools with more than 3,000 students.

The largest mental hospital in the world is the Pilgrim State Hospital, West Brentwood, Long Island, N.Y., U.S.A., with 3,816 beds. It formerly contained 14,200 beds.

The busiest maternity hospital in the world is the Mama Yemo Hospital, Kinshasa, Zaire with 41,930 deliveries in 1976. The record "birthquake" occurred on a day in May 1976 with 175 babies born. It has 599 beds.

Great Britain

The largest hospitals of any kind in Great Britain are Winwick Hospital near Warrington, with 1,837 staffed beds, and Rainhill Hospital near Liverpool, which has 1,768 staffed beds for mental patients.

The largest general hospital in Great Britain is the St. James Hospital, Leeds, West Yorkshire, with 1,361 staffed beds.

The largest maternity hospital in Great Britain is the Simpson Memorial Maternity Pavilion, Edinburgh with 219 staffed beds.

The largest children's hospital in Great Britain is Queen Mary's Hospital for Children, at Carshalton, Sutton, Greater London, with 574 staffed beds.

Longest stay in hospital

Miss Martha Nelson was admitted to the Columbus State Institute for the Feeble-Minded in Ohio, U.S.A. in 1875. She died in January 1975 aged 103 years 6 months in the Orient State Institution, Ohio after spending more than 99 years in institutions.

CITIES
Oldest *World*

The oldest known walled town in the world is Arīhā (Jericho). The latest radio-carbon dating on specimens from the lowest levels reached by archaeologists indicate habitation there by perhaps 3,000 people as early as 7800 B.C. The village of Zawi Chemi Shanidar, discovered in 1957 in northern Iraq, has been dated to 8910 B.C. The oldest capital city in the world is Dimashq (Damascus), the capital of Syria. It has been continuously inhabited since *c.* 2500 B.C.

Great Britain

The oldest town in Great Britain is often cited as Colchester, the old British Camulodunum, headquarters of Belgic chiefs in the 1st century B.C. However, the name of the tin trading post Salakee, St. Mary's, Isles of Scilly is derived from pre-Celtic roots and hence *ante* 550 B.C.

Most populous *World*

The most populous city in the world is Tōkyō, Japan with a population in 1977 of 11,649,000. At the census of 1975 the "Keihin Metropolitan Area" (Tōkyō-Yokohama Metropolitan Area) of 1,081 miles² *2 800 km²* however contained 17,037,300 people.

The world's largest city not built by the sea or on a river is Greater Mexico City, (Ciudad de Mexico), Mexico, with a population (1976 estimate) of 11,943,100.

Great Britain

The largest conurbation in Britain is Greater London (established on 1 Apr. 1965), with a population of 6,918,000 (mid-1978). The residential population of the City of London (677.3 acres *274 ha* plus 61.7 acres *24,9 ha* foreshore) is 5,600 compared with 128,000 in 1801. The peak figure for Greater London was 8,615,050 in 1939.

Largest in area

The world's largest town, in area, is Mount Isa, Queensland, Australia. The area administered by the City Council is 15,822 miles² *40 978 km²*. The largest conurbation in the United Kingdom is the county of Greater London with an area of 609.8 miles² *1 579,5 km²*.

Smallest town and hamlet

The smallest place with a town council is Caerwys, Clwyd, Wales with a population of 801. The town has a charter dated 1284.

Highest *World*

The highest capital in the world, before the domination of Tibet by China, was Lhasa, at an elevation of 12,087 ft *3 684 m* above sea-level. La Paz, the administrative and *de facto* capital of Bolivia, stands at an altitude of 11,916 ft *3 631 m* above sea-level. The city was founded in 1548 by

176

The southernmost village in the world, Puerto Williams in Chile, only 680 miles *1 090 km* north of Antarctica.

Currently the highest capital city in the world, La Paz in Bolivia, standing at an altitude of 11,916 ft *3 631 m* above sea level (see p. 176). (*I.C.A.*)

Capt. Alonso de Mendoza on the site of an Indian village named Chuquiapu. It was originally called Ciudad de Nuestra Señora de La Paz (City of Our Lady of Peace), but in 1825 was renamed La Paz de Ayacucho, its present official name. Sucre, the legal capital of Bolivia, stands at 9,301 ft *2 834 m* above sea-level. The new town of Wenchuan, founded in 1955 on the Chinghai-Tibet road, north of the Tangla range is the highest in the world at 5 100 m *16,732 ft* above sea-level. The highest dwellings in the world are those at Bāsisi, India near the Tibet border at *c.* 19,700 ft *5 988 m*.

Great Britain

The highest village in Britain is Flash, in northern Staffordshire, at 1,518 ft *462 m* above sea-level. The highest in Scotland is Wanlockhead, in Dumfries and Galloway at 1,380 ft *420 m* above sea-level.

Lowest

The settlement of Ein Bokek, which has a synagogue, on the shores of the Dead Sea is the lowest in the world at 1,299 ft *395,9 m* below sea-level.

Northernmost

The world's most northerly town with a population of more than 10,000 is the Arctic port of Dikson, U.S.S.R. in 73° 32′ N. The northernmost village is Ny Ålesund (78° 55′ N.), a coalmining settlement on King's Bay, Vest Spitsbergen, in the Norwegian territory of Svalbard, inhabited only during the winter season. The northernmost capital is Reykjavik, the capital of Iceland, in 64° 08′ N. Its population was estimated to be 84,772 in 1 Dec. 1974. The northernmost permanent human occupation is the base at Alert (82° 31′ N.), on Dumb Bell Bay, on the north-east coast of Ellesmere Island, northern Canada.

Southernmost

The world's southernmost village is Puerto Williams (population about 350), on the north coast of Isla Navarino, in Tierra del Fuego, Chile, about 680 miles *1 090 km* north of Antarctica. Wellington, North Island, New Zealand is the southernmost capital city on 41° 17′ S. The world's southernmost administrative centre is Port Stanley (51° 43′ S.), in the Falkland Islands, off South America.

Most remote from the sea

The largest town most remote from the sea is Wulumuch'i (Urumchi) formerly Tihwa, Sinkiang, capital of the Uighur Autonomous Region of China, at a distance of about 1,400 miles *2 250 km* from the nearest coastline. Its population was estimated to be 320,000 in 1974.

WORLD'S MOST POPULOUS CITIES - PROGRESSIVE LIST

Population	Name		Date
c. 150	Chemi Shanidar	Iraq	8910 B.C.
3,000	Jericho (Aríhà)	Samaria	7800 B.C.
50,000	Uruk (Erech) (now Warka)	Iraq	3000 B.C.
250,000	Greater Ur	Iraq	2200 B.C.
350,000	Babylon (now al-Hillah)	Iraq	600 B.C.
500,000	Pataliputra (Paltna) Bihàr	India	400–185 B.C.
600,000	Seleukia (near Baghdad)	Iraq	300 B.C.–165 A.D.
1,100,000	Rome	Italy	133 B.C.
1,500,000	Angkor	Cambodia	900 A.D.
1.0–1.5 million	Hang Chow	China	1279
707,000	Peking (Cambaluc), now Beijing	China	1578
1,117,290	Greater London	United Kingdom	1801
8,615,050	Greater London (peak)	United Kingdom	1939
11,649,000	Tokyo	Japan	1977

Note: The 1975 estimates for the metropolitan areas of Tokyo-Yokohama and for New York are 17,037,300 (census) and 16,848,000. The U.N. projection for A.D. 2000 for Greater Mexico City and Tokyo-Yokohama are 31,616,000 and 26,128,000.

BRITISH AND IRISH LARGEST AND SMALLEST PRIMARY LOCAL GOVERNMENT AREAS
—By size and population

	By Area (in acres/hectares)						By Home Population				
	Largest			Smallest			Most Populous			Least Populous	
England	North Yorkshire	2,055,109	831 661	Isles of Scilly	4,120	1 667	Greater London	6,970,100		Isles of Scilly	2,020
Wales	Dyfed	1,424,668	576 534	South Glamorgan	102,807	41 604	Mid Glamorgan	539,200²		Powys	105,500
Scotland³	Highland⁴	6,214,400	2 514 880	Orkney	217,600	88 059	Strathclyde⁵	2,504,909		Orkney	17,675
Northern Ireland	Tyrone	779,520	315 460	North Down	18,174	7 354	Belfast City	363,000¹		Moyle	13,400
Republic of Ireland	Cork	1,843,408	745 990	Louth	202,806	82 071	Dublin County	799,048		Longford	28,250

¹ Figures based on mid 1976 estimate.
² The most populous town in Wales—the City of Cardiff (pop. 278,900)—is in South Glamorgan.
³ Scotland's 33 Counties were replaced on 16 May 1975 by nine regions and three Island Areas.
⁴ The inclusion by Act of Parliament on 10 February 1972 of Rockall in the District of Harris in Western Isles put the extremities of that Authority at the record distance apart of 302 miles 486 km.
⁵ Includes the most populous town in Scotland—the City of Glasgow (pop. 856,000).

2. ROYALTY AND HEADS OF STATE

The Guinness Book of Kings, Rulers and Statesmen by Clive Carpenter (Guinness Superlatives, £7.95) contains much extra information.

Oldest ruling house

The Emperor of Japan, Hirohito (born 29 Apr. 1901), is the 124th in line from the first Emperor, Jimmu Tenno or Zinmu, whose reign was traditionally from 660 to 581 B.C., but probably from c. 40 to c. 10 B.C.

Her Majesty Queen Elizabeth II (b. 21 Apr. 1926) represents dynasties historically traceable at least back until the 5th century A.D.; notably that of Elesa of whom Alfred The Great was a 13 greats grandson and the Queen is therefore a 49 greats granddaughter. If the historicity of some early Scoto-Irish and Pictish kings were acceptable, the lineage could be named to about 70 generations.

Reigns *Longest*

The longest recorded reign of any monarch is that of Pepi II, a Sixth Dynasty Pharaoh of ancient Egypt. His reign began in c. 2,310 B.C., when he was aged 6, and lasted c. 94 years. Musoma Kanijo, chief of the Nzega district of western Tanganyika (now part of Tanzania), reputedly reigned for more than 98 years from 1864, when aged 8, until his death on 2 Feb. 1963. The 6th Japanese Emperor Koo-an traditionally reigned for 102 years (from 392 to 290 B.C.), but probably his actual reign was from about A.D. 110 to about A.D. 140. The reign of the 11th Emperor Suinin was traditionally from 29 B.C. to A.D. 71 (99 years), but probably from A.D. 259 to 291. The longest reign of any major European monarch was that of King Louis XIV of France, who ascended the throne on 14 May 1643, aged 4 years 231 days, and reigned for 72 years 110 days until his death on 1 Sept. 1715, four days before his 77th birthday. Grand Duke Karl Friederich of Baden (1728–1811) ruled from 12 May 1738 for 73 years 29 days.

BRITISH MONARCHY RECORDS

	Kings	Queens Regnant	Queens Consort
LONGEST REIGN OR TENURE	59 years 96 days¹ George III 1760–1820	63 years 216 days Victoria 1837–1901	57 years 70 days Charlotte 1761–1818 (Consort of George III)
SHORTEST REIGN OR TENURE	77 days² Edward 1483	13 days Jane, July 1553	154 days Yoleta (1285–1286) (2nd consort of Alexander III)
LONGEST LIVED	81 years 239 days³ George III (b. 1738–d. 1820)	81 years 243 days Victoria (b. 1819–d. 1901)	85 years 303 days Mary of Teck (b. 1867–d. 1953) (Consort of George V)
MOST CHILDREN (LEGITIMATE)⁴	18 Edward I 1272-1307	9⁵ Victoria (b. 1819–d. 1901)	15 Eleanor (c. 1244-1290) and Charlotte (b. 1744–d. 1818)
OLDEST TO START REIGN OR CONSORTSHIP	64 years 10 months William IV 1830–1837	37 years 5 months Mary I 1553–1558	56 years 53 days Alexandra (b. 1844–d. 1925) (Consort of Edward VII)
YOUNGEST TO START REIGN OR CONSORTSHIP	269 days Henry VI in 1422	6 or 7 days Mary, Queen of Scots in 1542	6 years 11 months Isabella (second consort of Richard II in 1396)
MOST MARRIED	6 times Henry VIII 1509–1547	3 times Mary, Queen of Scots 1542–1567 (executed 1587)	4 times Catherine Parr (b. c. 1512–d. 1548) (sixth consort of Henry VIII)

Notes (Dates are dates of reigns or tenures unless otherwise indicated).

¹ James Francis Edward, the Old Pretender, known to his supporters as James III, styled his reign from 16 Sept. 1701 until his death 1 Jan. 1766 (i.e. 64 years 109 days).
² There is the probability that in pre-Conquest times Sweyn 'Forkbeard', the Danish King of England, reigned for only 40 days in 1013–1014.
³ Richard Cromwell (b. 4 Oct. 1626), the 2nd Lord Protector from 3 Sept. 1658 until his abdication on 24 May 1659, lived under the alias John Clarke until 12 July 1712 aged 85 years 9 months and was thus the longest lived Head of State.
⁴ Henry I (1068–1135) in addition to one (possibly two) legitimate sons and a daughter had at least 20 bastard children (9 sons, 11 daughters), and possibly 22, by six mistresses.
⁵ Queen Anne (b. 1665–d. 1714) had 17 pregnancies, which produced only 5 live births.

Currently the longest reigning monarch in the world is King Sobhuza II, K.B.E. (b. 4 July 1899), the *Ngwenyama* (Paramount Chief) of Swaziland, under United Kingdom protection since December 1899, and independent since 6 Sept. 1968. At the last published count in 1972 he had 112 wives. Hirohito (see above) has been Emperor in Japan since 25 Dec. 1926.

Roman Occupation

During the 369 year long Roman occupation of England, Wales and parts of Scotland there were 40 sole and 27 co-Emperors of Rome. Of these the longest reigning was Constantinus I (The Great) from 31 Mar. 307 to 22 May 337—30 years 2 months.

Shortest

King Vickramabahu II of the Kalinga Kshatriya dynasty of Ceylon (Sri Lanka) was assassinated a few hours after he was crowned at Polonnaruwa in 1196.

Highest post-nominal numbers

The highest post-nominal number ever used to designate a member of a Royal House was 75 briefly enjoyed by Count Heinrich LXXV Reuss (1800–1801). All male members of this branch of this German family are called Heinrich and are successively numbered from I upwards *each* century.

The highest British regnal number is 8, used by Henry VIII (1509–1547) and by Edward VIII (1936) who died as H.R.H. the Duke of Windsor, K.G., K.T., K.P., G.C.B., G.C.S.I., G.C.M.G., G.C.I.E., G.C.V.O., G.B.E., I.S.O., M.C. on 28 May 1972. Jacobites liked to style Henry Benedict, Cardinal York (born 1725), the grandson of James II, as Henry IX in respect of his "reign" from 1788 to 1807 when he died the last survivor in the male line of the House of Stuart.

Longest lived 'Royals'

The longest life among the Blood Royal of Europe has been that of the late H.R.H. Princess Alicia of Bourbon who was born on 29 June 1876 and died on 20 Jan 1975 aged 98 years 206 days. The greatest age among European Royal Consorts is the 99 years 110 days of H.S.H. Princess Marie Felixovna Romanovsky-Krassinsky, who was born 19 Aug. 1872 and died in Paris 7 Dec. 1971. The longest-lived Queen on record has been the Queen Grandmother of Siam, Queen Sawang (b. 10 Sept. 1862), 27th daughter of King Mongkut (Rama IV), who died on 17 Dec. 1955 aged 93 years 3 months.

H.R.H. Princess Alice Mary, V.A., G.C.V.O., G.B.E. Countess of Athlone (b. 25 Feb. 1883) became the longest lived British "royal" on 15 July 1977 and celebrated her 96th birthday on 25 Feb. 1979.

Youngest King and Queen

Of the world's 25 monarchies that with the youngest King is Bhutan where King Jigme Singye Wangchuk was born 11 Nov. 1955, succeeded on 24 July 1972.

Heaviest Monarch

The world's heaviest monarch is the 6 ft 3 in *1,90 m* tall King Taufa'ahau of Tonga who in Sept. 1976 was weighed on the only adequate scales in the country at the airport recording 33 st. *462 lb. 209,5 kg.*

Most Prolific

The most prolific monogamous "royals" have been Prince Hartmann of Liechtenstein (1613–1686) who had 24 children, of whom 21 were live born, by Countess Elisabeth zu Salm-Reifterscheidt (1623–1688). H.R.H. Duke Roberto I of Parma also had 24 children but by two wives.

Head of State oldest and youngest

The oldest head of state in the world is Marshal Tito of Yugoslavia (b. Josip Broz, 25 May 1892) aged 87. The youngest non-royal head of state is Jean-Claude Duvalier, (b. 3 July 1951) President of Haiti since 21 Apr. 1971.

above: The longest lived British Royal, H.R.H. Princess Alice, Countess of Athlone, last surviving grandchild of Queen Victoria, who was born on 25 Feb. 1883. (*Photograph: Snowdon*)

below: Currently the world's oldest head of state, Marshal Tito of Yugoslavia aged 87.

3. LEGISLATURES

PARLIAMENTS—WORLD
Earliest and Oldest

The earliest known legislative assembly was a bicameral one in Erech, Iraq *c.* 2800 B.C. The oldest legislative body is the *Al ingi* (Althing) of Iceland founded in A.D. 930. This body, which originally comprised 39 local chieftains at Thingvellir, was abolished in 1800, but restored by Denmark to a consultative status in 1843 and a legislative status in 1874. The legislative assembly with the oldest continuous history is the Tynwald Court in the Isle of Man, which is believed to have originated more than 1,000 years ago.

Largest

The largest legislative assembly in the world is the National People's Congress of the People's Republic of China. The fourth Congress, which was convened in January 1975, had 3,500 members.

Smallest quorum

The House of Lords has the smallest quorum, expressed as a percentage of eligible voters, of any legislative body in the world, namely less than one-third of one per cent. To transact business there must be three peers present, including the Lord Chancellor or his deputy. The House of Commons quorum of 40 M.P.'s, including the Speaker or his deputy, is 20 times as exacting.

Highest paid legislators

The most highly paid of all the world's legislators are Members of the U.S. Congress who receive a basic annual salary of $57,500 (now £28,750). Of this, up to $3,000 (£1,500) is exempt from taxation. In addition up to $1,021,167 (£510,583) per annum is allowed for office help, with a salary limit of $49,941 (now £24,970) for any one staff member (limited to 16 in number). Senators are allowed up to $143,000 (£71,500) per annum for an official office expense account from which official travel, telegram, long distance telephone, air mail, postage, stationery, subscriptions to newspapers, and office expenses in home state are paid. They also command very low rates for filming, speech and radio transcriptions and, in the case of women senators, beauty treatment. When abroad they have access to "counterpart funds". A retiring President electing to take also his congressional pension would enjoy a combined pension of $103,500 (£54,475) per annum.

Longest membership

The longest span as a legislator was 83 years by József Madarász (1814–1915). He first attended the Hungarian Parliament in 1832–36 as *oblegatus absentium* (*i.e.* on behalf of an absent deputy). He was a full member in 1848–50 and from 1861 until his death on 31 Jan. 1915.

Best Attendance Record

U.S. Congressman William H. Natcher (Democrat) of Bowling Green, Kentucky on 6 Jan. 1978 completed 25 years (1954–1979) without missing a single vote (3,748 quorum calls and 7,000 votes) to 9 Apr. 1979. State Representative Lucille H. McCollough was elected to the Michigan House of Representatives on 1 Jan. 1955 and had a perfect attendance record into June 1979.

Filibusters

The longest continuous speech in the history of the United States Senate was that of Senator Wayne Morse (1900–74) of Oregon on 24–25 Apr. 1953, when he spoke on the Tidelands Oil Bill for 22 hrs 26 min without resuming his seat. Interrupted only briefly by the swearing-in of a new senator, Senator Strom Thurmond (b. 1902) (South Carolina, Democrat) spoke against the Civil Rights Bill for 24 hrs 19 min on 28–29 Aug. 1957. The United States national record duration for a filibuster is 43 hrs by Texas State senator Bill Meier against nondisclosure of industrial accidents in May 1977.

Treaty *Oldest*

The world's oldest treaty is the Anglo-Portuguese Treaty of Alliance signed in London over 600 years ago on 16 June 1373. The text was confirmed "with my usual flourish" by John de Banketre, Clerk.

PARLIAMENTS—UNITED KINGDOM

Earliest

The earliest known use of the term "parliament" in an official English royal document, in the meaning of a summons to the King's council, dates from 19 Dec. 1241.

The Houses of Parliament of the United Kingdom in the Palace of Westminster, London, had 1,762 members (House of Lords 1,127, House of Commons 635) in June 1975.

Longest

The longest English Parliament was the "Pensioners" Parliament of Charles II, which lasted from 8 May 1661 to 24 Jan. 1679, a period of 17 years 8 months and 16 days. The longest United Kingdom Parliament was that of George V, Edward VIII and George VI, lasting from 26 Nov. 1935 to 15 June 1945, a span of 9 years 6 months and 20 days.

Shortest

The parliament of Edward I, summoned to Westminster for 30 May 1306, lasted only one day. The parliament of Charles II at Oxford from 21–28 March 1681 lasted 7 days. The shortest United Kingdom Parliament was that of George III, lasting from 15 Dec. 1806 to 29 Apr. 1807, a period of only 4 months and 14 days.

Longest sittings

The longest sitting in the House of Commons was one of $41\frac{1}{2}$ hrs from 4 p.m. on 31 Jan. 1881 to 9.30 a.m. on 2 Feb. 1881, on the question of better Protection of Person and Property in Ireland. The longest sitting of the Lords has been 19 hrs 16 min from 2.30 p.m. on 29 Feb. to 9.46 a.m. on 1 Mar. 1968 on the Commonwealth Immigrants Bill (Committee stage).

Longest speech

The longest recorded continuous speech in the House of Commons was that of Henry Peter Brougham (1778–1868) on 7 Feb. 1828, when he spoke for 6 hrs on Law Reform. He ended at 10.40 p.m. and the report of this speech occupied 12 columns of the next day's edition of *The Times*. Brougham, created the 1st Lord Brougham and Vaux on 22 Nov. 1830, also holds the House of Lords record, also with six hours on 7 Oct. 1831, when speaking on the second reading of the Reform Bill. The longest back bench speech under present, much stricter, Standing Orders has been one of 3 hrs 16 min by Sir Bernard Braine (b. 1914) the Conservative member for Essex, South East concerning Canvey Island on 23–24 July 1974.

The longest speech in Stormont, Northern Ireland was one of $9\frac{1}{2}$ hours by Tommy Henderson M.P. on the Appropriations Bill on 26–27 May 1936.

Greatest parliamentary petition

The greatest petition was supposed to be the Great Chartist Petition of 1848 but of the 5,706,000 "signatures" only 1,975,496 were valid. The all time largest was for the abolition of Entertainment Duty with 3,107,080 signatures presented on 5 June 1951.

Most time consuming legislation

The most profligate use of parliamentary time was on the Government of Ireland Bill of 1893–4, which required 82 days in the House of Commons of which 46 days was in Committee. The record for a standing committee is 58 sessions for the Aircraft and Shipbuilding Industries bill which was represented to the House of Commons on 8 June 1976 after the notorious 303–303 tied vote of 27 May 1976.

Divisions

The record number of divisions in the House of Commons is 64 on 23–24 Mar. 1971 including 57 in succession between midnight and noon. The largest division was one of 350–310 on a vote of confidence in 1892.

ELECTIONS—WORLD

Largest

The largest election ever held was that for the Indian *Lok Sabha* (House of the People) on 16–20 Mar. 1977. There were 373,000 polling places for the 320 million voters. The outgoing Prime Minister Mrs Indira Ghandi was better known by her symbol (a cow) than by name.

Closest

The ultimate in close general elections occurred in Zanzibar (now part of Tanzania) on 18 Jan. 1961, when the Afro-Shirazi Party won by a single seat, after the seat of Chake-Chake on Pemba Island had been gained by a single vote.

Most one-sided

North Korea recorded a 100 per cent. turn-out of electors and a 100 per cent vote for the Worker's Party of Korea in the general election of 8 Oct. 1962. The previous record had been set in the Albanian election of 4 June 1962, when all but seven of the electorate of 889,875 went to the polls—a 99.9992 per cent turn-out. Of the 889,868 voters, 889,828 voted for the candidates of the Albanian Party of Labour, *i.e* 99.9955 per cent of the total poll.

Most Bent
In his book *Journey Without Maps* Graham Greene quotes the case of the Liberian presidential election of 1928 in which President Charles D. B. King was returned with a majority over his opponent Mr Thomas J. Faulkner of the People's Party officially announced as 600,000. The total electorate at the time was less than 15,000.

Highest personal majority
The highest ever personal majority by any politician has been 424,545 by Ram Bilas Paswan, 30, the Janata candidate for Hajipur in Bihar, India in March 1977. The electorate was 625,179.

Communist parties
The largest national Communist party outside the Soviet Union (15,000,000 members in 1975) and Communist states has been the Partito Communista Italiano (Italian Communist Party), with a membership of 2,300,000 in 1946. The total was 1,700,000 in 1976. The membership in mainland China was estimated to be 28,000,000 in 1974. The Communist Party of Great Britain, formed on 31 July 1920 in Cannon Street Station Hotel, London, attained its peak membership of 56,000 in December 1942, compared with 28,529 in April 1976.

Longest Term
Members of Taiwan's National Assembly elected in 1947 have been extended in office and include several hundred who celebrated their 32nd year in 1979.

Voting Age Extremes
The eligibility for voting is 15 years of age in the Philippines and 25 years in Andorra.

Smallest vote
Mr. Wideon Pyfrom (Free National Party) standing for the Rolleville constituency, in the Bahamas in the July 1977 elections secured a *nil* vote.

PRIME MINISTERS—WORLD
Oldest
The longest lived Prime Minister of any country is believed to have been Christopher Hornsrud, Prime Minister of Norway from 28 Jan. to 15 Feb. 1928. He was born on 15 Nov. 1859 and died on 13 Dec. 1960, aged 101 years 28 days.

El Hadji Muhammad el Mokri, Grand Vizier of Morocco, died on 16 Sept. 1957, at a reputed age of 116 Muslim (*Hijri*) years, equivalent to 112.5 Gregorian years. The oldest age of appointment has been 81 years in the case of Morarji Ranchhodji Desai (b. 29 Feb. 1896) in March 1977.

Longest term of office
Prof. Dr. António de Oliveirar Salazar, G.C.M.G. (Hon.) (1889–1970) was the President of the Council of Ministers (*i.e.* Prime Minister) of Portugal from 5 July 1932 until 27 Sept. 1968—36 years 84 days. He was superseded 11 days after going into coma. The longest serving democratically elected premier was Tage Erlander of Sweden for 22 years 357 days from 10 Oct. 1946 to 1 Oct. 1969.

ELECTORATES—UNITED KINGDOM
Largest and smallest
The largest electorate of all time was the estimated 217,900 for Hendon, Barnet, Greater London, prior to the redistribution in 1941. The largest electorate for a seat in Great Britain is 104,375 at Bromsgrove and Redditch. In Antrim South, Northern Ireland the figure is 126,444. The smallest electorate of all-time was in Old Sarum (number of houses nil, population nil since *c.* 1540) in Wiltshire, with eight electors who returned two members in 1821, thus being 54,475 times as well represented as the Hendon electorate of 120 years later. There were no contested elections in Old Sarum for the 536 years from 1295 to 1831. The smallest electorate for any seat is Glasgow Central with 19,826 electors, thus making a vote 6.3 times weightier than in Antrim South.

Elections
The record number of candidates in a general election is 2,571 on 3 May 1979. The most in a constituency is 9 in Devon North.

European Parliamentary Election Records
In the first European Parliamentary elections of 7 June 1979 the highest majority in the 81 constituencies was 95,484 for M. Seligman (Con) in Sussex West. The lowest was 302 for W. Hopper (Con) in Greater Manchester West. The largest and smallest electorates were 575,991 in Wight and Hampshire East and 298,802 in Highlands and Islands. The latter had the highest turn out with 39.4%. The lowest turn out was 20.4% in London North East.

MAJORITIES—UNITED KINGDOM
Party
The largest party majorities were those of the Liberals, with 307 seats in 1832 and 356 seats in 1906. In 1931 the Coalition of Conservatives, Liberals and National Labour candidates had a majority of 491. The narrowest party majority was that of the Whigs in 1847, with a single seat.

The largest majority on a division was one of 463 (464 votes to 1), on a motion of "no confidence" in the conduct of World War II, on 29 Jan. 1942. Since the war the largest has been one of 461 (487 votes to 26) on 10 May 1967, during the debate on the government's application for Britain to join the European Economic Community (the "Common Market").

Largest personal *All-time*
The largest individual majority of any Member of Parliament was the 62,253 of Sir A. Cooper Rawson, M.P. (Conservative) at Brighton in 1931. He polled a record 75,205 votes against 12,952 votes for his closest opponent the Labour Candidate, Lewis Coleman Cohen, later Lord Cohen of Brighton (1897–1966), from an electorate of 128,779. The largest majority of any woman M.P. was 38,823 in the same General Election by the Countess of Iveagh (*née* Lady Gwendolen Florence Mary Onslow), C.B.E. (1881–1966), the Conservative member for Southend-on-Sea, Essex, from November 1927 to October 1935.

Current
The largest majority in Parliament is 38,868 held by James H. Molyneaux (Official Unionist Party) in Antrim South where he received 50,782 votes. The highest figure for Great Britain was 31,481 by T. Alec Jones (Lab.) in Rhondda, Wales.

Narrowest personal *All-time*
The closest result occurred in the General Election of 1886 at Ashton-under-Lyne, Greater Manchester when the Conservative and Liberal candidates both received 3,049 votes. The Returning Officer, Mr. James Walker, gave his casting vote for John E. W. Addison (Con.), who was duly returned while Alexander B. Rowley (Gladstone-Liberal) was declared unelected. On 13 Oct. 1892 there was a by-election at Cirencester, Gloucestershire, which resulted in an election petition after which the number of votes cast for the Conservative and Liberal were found to have been equal. A new election was ordered.

Two examples of majorities of one have occurred. At Durham in the 1895 General Election, Matthew Fowler (Lib.) with 1,111 votes defeated the Hon. Arthur R. D. Elliott (Liberal-Unionist) (1,110 votes) after a recount. At Exeter in the General Election of December 1910 a Liberal victory over the Conservatives by 4 votes was reversed on an election petition to a Conservative win by H. E. Duke K.C. (later the 1st Lord Merrivale) (Unionist) with 4,777 votes to R. H. St. Maur's (Lib.) 4,776 votes.

The smallest majority since "universal" franchise was by two votes by Abraham John Flint (1903–71), the National Labour candidate at Ilkeston, Derbyshire, in the 1931 General Election. He received 17,587 votes, compared with 17,585 for G. H. Oliver, D.C.M. (Lab.).

Robert James Atkins, the Tory MP for Preston North who had a majority of only 29 over his Labour opponent, Ronald Henry Atkins.

Current

The finest economy of effort in getting elected by any member of the present Parliament was a majority of 29 by Robert James Atkins (Conservative) over Ronald Henry Atkins (Labour) in Preston North.

Fewest Votes

The record low number of votes in a General Election is 20 by Lt. Cdr. W. G. Boaks D.S.C. R.N. at Devon North on 3 May 1979.

Most recounts

The greatest recorded number of recounts has been 7 in the case of Brighton, Kemptown on 16 Oct. 1964 when Dennis H. Hobden (Labour) won by 7 votes and at Peterborough on 31 Mar–1 Apr. 1966 when Sir Harmar-Nicholls Bt. (Conservative) won by 3 votes. The counts from the point of view of the loser Michael J. Ward (Labour) went $+163$, $+163$, $+2$, -2, -6, $+1$, -2, -3. Lord Harmar-Nicholls, whose final majority was 22, suffered 21 counts in 8 elections as an M.P.

Most rapid change of fortune

On 3 July 1874 Hardinge Stanley Giffard (Con.), later the 1st Earl of Halsbury (1823–1921), received one vote at Launceston, Cornwall having been nominated without his consent. In 1877 he was returned unopposed for the same seat.

Greatest swing

The greatest swing, at least since 1832, was at the Dartford, Kent by-election when on 27 Mar. 1920 Labour turned a Coalition majority of 9,370 to a win by 9,048. This represented a swing of 38.7 per cent.

Highest poll

The highest poll in any constituency since "universal" franchise was 93.42 per cent in Fermanagh and South Tyrone, Northern Ireland, at the General Election of 25 Oct. 1951, when there were 62,799 voters from an electorate of 67,219.

The Anti-Partition candidate, Mr. Cahir Healy (1877–1970), was elected with a majority of 2,635 votes. The highest poll in any constituency in the May 1979 General Election was 86.97 per cent in Fermanagh and South Tyrone. The highest figure in Great Britain was 86.08 per cent in Cornwall North and the lowest in Chelsea with 57.30%.

HOUSE OF LORDS
Oldest Member

The oldest member ever was the Rt. Hon. the 5th Baron Penrhyn, who was born on 21 Nov. 1865 and died on 3 Feb. 1967, aged 101 years 74 days. The oldest now is the Rt. Hon. Walter Egerton George Lucian Keppel, M.C., ninth Earl of Albemarle (b. 28 Feb. 1882). The oldest peer to make a maiden speech was Lord Maenan (1854–1951) aged 94 years 123 days. (see Oldest creation, Chapter 11)

Youngest Member

The youngest present member of the House of Lords has been H.R.H. the Prince Charles Philip Arthur George, K.G., K.T., G.C.B., the Prince of Wales (b. 14 Nov. 1948). All Dukes of Cornwall, of whom Prince Charles is the 24th, are technically eligible to sit, regardless of age—in his case from his succession on 6 Feb. 1952, aged 3. The 20th and 21st holders, later King George IV (b. 1762) and King Edward VII (b. 1841), were technically entitled to sit from birth. The youngest creation of a life peer or peeress under the Peerage Act 1958 has been that of Lady Masham (b. 14 Apr. 1935) who was created Baroness Masham of Ilton at the age of 34 years 262 days.

POLITICAL OFFICE HOLDERS
Premiership *Longest term*

No United Kingdom Prime Minister has yet matched in duration the continuous term of office of Great Britain's first Prime Minister the Rt. Hon. Sir Robert Walpole, K.G., later the 1st Earl of Orford (1676–1745), First Lord of the Treasury and Chancellor of the Exchequer for 20 years 326 days from 3 Apr. 1721 to 12 Feb. 1742. The office was not, however, officially recognised until 1905, since when the longest tenure has been that of Herbert Henry Asquith, later the 1st Earl of Oxford and Asquith (1852–1928), with 8 years 243 days from 8 Apr. 1908 to 7 Dec. 1916. This was 7 days longer than the three terms of Sir Winston Churchill, between 1940 and 1955.

Shortest term

The Rt. Hon. William Pulteney, the Earl of Bath (1684–1764) held office for 3 days from 10–12 Feb. 1746 but was unable to form a ministry. The shortest term of any ministry was that of the 1st Duke of Wellington, K.G., G.C.B., G.C.H. (1769–1852), whose third ministry survived only 22 days from 17 Nov. to 9 Dec. 1834.

Most times

The only Prime Minister to have accepted office five times was the Rt. Hon. Stanley Baldwin, later the 1st Earl Baldwin of Bewdley (1867–1947). His ministries were those of 22 May 1923 to 22 Jan. 1924, 4 Nov. 1924 to 5 June 1929, 7 June 1935 to 21 Jan. 1936, from then until the abdication of 12 Dec. 1936 and from then until 28 May 1937.

Longest lived

The longest lived Prime Minister of the United Kingdom has been the Rt. Hon. Sir Winston Leonard Spencer-Churchill, K.G., O.M., C.H., T.D., (b. 30 Nov. 1874), who surpassed the age of the Rt. Hon. William Ewart Gladstone (1809–98) on 21 Apr. 1963 and died on 24 Jan. 1965, aged 90 years 55 days. Gladstone's last day in office on 3 Mar. 1894 was when he was 84 years 64 days—having been elected on 18 Aug. 1892.

Youngest

The youngest of Great Britain's 50 Prime Ministers has been the Rt. Hon. the Hon. William Pitt (b. 28 May 1759), who accepted the King's invitation to be First Lord of the Treasury on 19 Dec. 1783, aged 24 years 205 days. He had previously declined on 27 Feb. 1783, when aged 23 years 275 days.

Legislatures

Legislatures

Chancellorship *Longest and shortest tenures*
The Rt. Hon. Sir Robert Walpole, K.G., later the 1st Earl of Orford (1676–1745), served 22 years 5 months as Chancellor of the Exchequer, holding office continuously from 12 Oct. 1715 to 12 Feb. 1742, except for the period from 16 Apr. 1717 to 2 Apr. 1721. The briefest tenure of this office was 26 days in the case of the Baron (later the 1st Earl of) Mansfield (1705–93), from 11 Sept. to 6 Oct. 1767. The only man with four terms in this office was the Rt. Hon. William Ewart Gladstone (1809–98) in 1852–55, 1859–66, 1873–74 and 1880–82.

Foreign Secretaryship *Longest tenures*
The longest term of office of any Foreign Secretary has been the 10 years 360 days of Sir Edward Grey K.G., M.P. (later Viscount Grey of Fallodon) from 10 Dec. 1905 to 5 Dec. 1916. The Most Hon. Robert Arthur Talbot Gascoyne-Cecil, Marquis of Salisbury, K.G., G.C.V.O., in two spells in 1887–92 and 1895–1900 aggregated 11 years 87 days in this office.

Colonial Secretaryship *Longest tenures*
The longest term of office has been 19 years 324 days by the Rt. Hon. Henry Bathurst, Earl Bathurst (1762–1834), who was Secretary of State for the Colonial and War Department from 11 June 1812 to 1 May 1827. The longest tenure this century has been the 5 years 78 days of the Rt. Hon. Alan Tindal Lennox-Boyd, Viscount Boyd of Merton, C.H. (b. 18 Nov. 1904) from 28 July 1954 to 13 Oct. 1959.

Speakership *Longest*
Arthur Onslow (1691–1768) was elected Mr. Speaker on 23 Jan. 1728, at the age of 36. He held the position for 33 years 43 days, until 18 Mar. 1761 allowing for the "lost" 11 days (3–13 Sept. 1752).

M.P.s *Youngest*
Edmund Waller (1606–1687) was the Member of Parliament for Amersham, Buckinghamshire, in the Parliament of 1621, in which year he was 15. The official returns, however, do not show him as actually having taken his seat until two years later when, in the Parliament of 1623–24, he sat as Member for Ilchester, Somerset. In 1435 Henry Long (1420–1490) was returned for an Old Sarum seat also at the age of 15. His precise date of birth is unknown. Minors were debarred in law in 1695 and in fact in 1832. Since that time the youngest Member of Parliament has been the Hon. Esmond Cecil Harmsworth (now the 2nd Viscount Rothermere) who was elected for the Isle of Thanet, Kent, on 28 Nov. 1919, when 21 years 183 days. The youngest M P is David Alton (Liberal) M.P. for Liverpool, Edge Hill (born 15 Mar. 1951). He had been elected in a by-election on 29 Mar. 1979.

Oldest
The oldest of all members was Samuel Young (b. 14 Feb. 1822), Nationalist M.P. for East Cavan (1892–1918), who died on 18 Apr. 1918, aged 96 years 63 days. The oldest "Father of the House" in Parliamentary history was the Rt. Hon. Charles Pelham Villiers (b. 3 Jan. 1802), who was the Member for Wolverhampton when he died on 16 Jan. 1898, aged 96 years 13 days. He was a Member of Parliament for 63 years 6 days, having been returned at 16 elections. The oldest member and "Father of the House" is John Parker C.B.E., M.P. (Labour) for Barking, Dagenham (b. 15 July 1906), now the only pre-war M.P. having been elected for Romford, Essex in 1935.

Longest span
The longest span of service of any M.P., is 63 years 10 months (1 Oct. 1900 to 25 Sept. 1964) by the Rt. Hon. Sir Winston Leonard Spencer-Churchill, K.G., O.M., C.H., T.D. (1874–1965), with a break only from November 1922 to October 1924. The longest unbroken span was that of C.P. Villiers (see above). The longest span in the Palace of Westminster (both Houses of Parliament) has been 73 years by the 10th Earl of Wemyss and March G.C.V.O., who, as Sir Francis Wemyss-Charteris-Douglas, served as M.P. for East Gloucestershire (1841–46) and Haddingtonshire (1847–83) and then took his seat in the House of Lords, dying on 30 June 1914, aged 95 years 330 days.

The oldest *ever* MP was Samuel Young, the Nationalist member for East Cavan for 20 years and who died aged 96 years 63 days.

Women M.P.s *Earliest*
The first woman to be elected to the House of Commons was Mme. Constance Georgine Markievicz (*née* Gore Booth). She was elected as member (Sinn Fein) for St. Patrick's Dublin, in December 1918. The first woman to take her seat was the Viscountess Astor, C. H. (1879–1964) (b. Nancy Witcher Langhorne at Danville, Virginia, U.S.A.; formerly Mrs. Robert Gould Shaw), who was elected Unionist member for the Sutton Division of Plymouth, Devon, on 28 Nov. 1919, and took her seat three days later.

Longest Serving
The longest ever serving woman M.P. has been Baroness Irene Mary Bewick Ward C.H., D.B.E., who fought all 12 General elections (1924–1970) and who served as member for Wallsend (1931–45) and for Tynemouth (1950–74). She shared also the 20th century record for introducing 4 Private Members Bills which became Acts with Sir Robert Gower (1880–1953).

Heaviest and Tallest
The heaviest M.P. of all-time is believed to have been Cyril Smith M.B.E., Liberal member for Rochdale since October 1972, whose peak reported weight in early 1976 was 29 st. 12 lb. *189,60 kg.* Sir Louis Gluckstein G.B.E, T.D., Q.C.; who served for East Nottingham (1931–1945), was an unrivalled 6 ft 7½ ins *2,02 m.*

Mayoralties
The longest established mayoralty in Britain is that of the City of London dating from 1192 with the 20 year term of Henry Fitz Ailwyn till 1212. The most elections, since these became annual in 1215, has been 8 by Gregory de Rokesley (1274/5 to 1280/1). Harold E. Johnson has been elected Mayor of Hatton, Washington each year since 1931.

4. MILITARY AND DEFENCE

WAR
Guinness Superlatives Ltd. has published specialist volumes entitled *The Guinness History of Land Warfare* (£4.95) by Kenneth Macksey, *History of Sea Warfare* (£4.95) by Gervis Frere-Cook and Macksey, and *History of Air Warfare* (£6.50) by David Brown, Christopher Shores and Macksey.

Longest
The longest of history's countless wars was the "Hundred Years War" between England and France, which lasted from 1338 to 1453 (115 years), although it may be said that the Holy War, comprising the nine Crusades from the First (1096–1104) to the Ninth (1270–91), extended over 195 years.

Shortest
The shortest war on record was that between the United Kingdom and Zanzibar (now part of Tanzania) from 9.02 to 9.40 a.m. on 27 Aug. 1896. The U.K. battle fleet under Rear-Admiral (later Admiral Sir) Harry Holdsworth Rawson (1843–1910) delivered an ultimatum to the self-appointed Sultan Sa'īd Khalid to evacuate his palace and surrender. This was not forthcoming until after 38 minutes of bombardment. Admiral Rawson received the Brilliant Star of Zanzibar (first class) from the new Sultan Hamud ibn Muhammad. It was proposed at one time that elements of the local populace should be compelled to defray the cost of the ammunition used.

Bloodiest
By far the most costly war in terms of human life was World War II (1939–45), in which the total number of fatalities, including battle deaths and civilians of all countries, is estimated to have been 54,800,000 assuming 25 million U.S.S.R. fatalities and 7,800,000 Chinese civilians killed. The country which suffered most was Poland with 6,028,000 or 22.2 per cent of her population of 27,007,000 killed. The total death roll from World War I was only 17.7 per cent of that of World War II, *viz* 9,700,000.

In the case of the United Kingdom, however, the heaviest armed forces fatalities occurred in World War I (1914–18), with 765,399 killed out of 5,500,000 engaged (13.9 per cent), compared with 265,000 out of 5,896,000 engaged (4.49 per cent) in World War II.

In the Paraguayan war of 1864–70 against Brazil, Argentina and Uruguay, their population was reduced from 1,400,000 to 220,000 of whom only 30,000 were adult males.

Bloodiest civil
The bloodiest civil war in history was the T'ai-p'ing ("Great Peace") rebellion, in which peasant sympathizers of the Southern Ming dynasty fought the Manchu Government troops in China from 1851 to 1864. The rebellion was led by the deranged Hung Hsiu-ch'üan (executed) who imagined himself to be a younger brother of Jesus Christ. His force was named *T'ai-p'ing T'ien Kuo* (Heavenly Kingdom of Great Peace). According to the best estimates, the loss of life was between 20,000,000 and 30,000,000, including more than 100,000 killed by Government forces in the sack of Nanking on 19–21 July 1864.

Most costly
The material cost of World War II far transcended that of the rest of history's wars put together and has been estimated at $1.5 million million. The total cost to the Soviet Union was estimated semi-officially in May 1959 at 2,500,000,000,000 roubles (£100,000 million) while a figure of $530,000 million has been estimated for the U.S.A. In the case of the United Kingdom the cost of £34,423 million was over five times as great as that of World War I (£6,700 million) and 158.6 times that of the Boer War of 1899–1902 (£217 million).

Last battle on British soil
The last pitched land battle in Britain was at Culloden Field, Drummossie Moor, near Inverness, Highland, on 16 Apr. 1746. The last Clan battle in Scotland was between Clan Mackintosh and Clan MacDonald at Mulroy, Highland in 1689. The last battle on English soil was the Battle of Sedgemoor, Somerset, on 6 July 1685, when the forces of James II defeated the supporters of Charles II's illegitimate son, James Scott (formerly called Fitzroy or Crofts), the Duke of Monmouth (1649–85). During the Jacobite rising of 1745–46, there was a skirmish at Clifton Moor, Cumbria, on 18 Dec. 1745, when the British forces under Prince William, the Duke of Cumberland (1721–65), brushed with the rebels of Prince Edward Stuart (1720–88) with about 12 killed on the King's side and 5 Highlanders. This was a tactical victory for the Scots under Lord George Murray.

Bloodiest battle *Modern*
The battle with the greatest recorded number of fatalities was the First Battle of the Somme, France from 1 July to 19 Nov. 1916, with more than 1,030,000—614,105 British and French and *c.* 420,000 (*not* 650,000) German. The gunfire was heard on Hampstead Heath, London. The greatest battle of World War II and the greatest ever conflict of armour was the Battle of Kursk and Oryol which raged for 50 days on 5 July–23 Aug. 1943 on the Eastern front, which involved 1,300,000 Red Army troops with 3,600 tanks, 20,000 guns and 3,130 aircraft in repelling a German Army Group which had 2,700 tanks. The final investment of Berlin by the Red Army on 16 Apr.–2 May 1945 involved 3,500,000 men; 52,000 guns and mortars; 7,750 tanks and 11,000 aircraft on both sides.

Ancient
Modern historians give no credence to the casualty figures attached to ancient battles, such as the 250,000 reputedly killed at Plataea (Greeks *v.* Persians) in 479 B.C. or the 200,000 allegedly killed in a single day.

British
The bloodiest battle fought on British soil was the Battle of Towton, in North Yorkshire, on 29 Mar. 1461, when 36,000 Yorkists defeated 40,000 Lancastrians. The total loss has been estimated at between 28,000 and 38,000 killed. A figure of 80,000 British dead was attributed by Tacitus to the battle of A.D. 61 between Queen Boudicca (Boadicea) of the Iceni and the Roman Governor of Britain Suetonius Paulinus, for the reputed loss of only 400 Romans in an army of 10,000. The site of the battle is unknown but may have been near Borough Hill, Daventry, Northamptonshire, or more probably near Hampstead Heath, Greater London. Prior to this battle the Romans had lost up to 70,000 in Colchester and London.

Greatest naval battle
The greatest number of ships and aircraft ever involved in a sea-air action was 231 ships and 1,996 aircraft in the Battle of Leyte Gulf, in the Philippines. It raged from 22 to 27 Oct. 1944, with 166 Allied and 65 Japanese warships engaged, of which 26 Japanese and 6 U.S. ships were sunk. In addition 1,280 U.S. and 716 Japanese aircraft were engaged. The greatest naval battle of modern times was the Battle of Jutland on 31 May 1916, in which 151 Royal Navy warships were involved against 101 German warships. The Royal Navy lost 14 ships and 6,097 men and the German fleet 11 ships and 2,545 men. The greatest of ancient naval battles was the Battle of Salamis, Greece on 23 Sept. 480 B.C. There were an estimated 800 vessels in the defeated Persian fleet and 310 in the victorious Greek fleet with a possible involvement of 190,000 men. The death roll at the Battle of Lepanto on 7 Oct. 1571 has been estimated at 33,000.

Invasion Greatest *Seaborne*
The greatest invasion in military history was the Allied land, air and sea operation against the Normandy coasts of France on D-day, 6 June 1944. Thirty-eight convoys of 745 ships moved in on the first three days, supported by 4,066 landing craft, carrying 185,000 men and 20,000 vehicles, and 347 minesweepers. The air assault comprised 18,000 paratroopers from 1,087 aircraft. The 42 available divisions possessed an air support from 13,175 aircraft. Within a month 1,100,000 troops, 200,000 vehicles and 750,000 tons of stores were landed. The Allied invasion of Sicily on 10–12 July 1943 involved the landing of 181,000 men in 3 days.

Airborne

The largest airborne invasion was the Anglo-American assault of three divisions (34,000 men), with 2,800 aircraft and 1,600 gliders, near Arnhem, in the Netherlands, on 17 Sept. 1944.

Last on the soil of Great Britain

The last invasion of Great Britain occurred on 12 Feb. 1797, when the Irish-American adventurer General Tate landed at Carreg Gwastad with 1,400 French troops. They surrendered near Fishguard, Dyfed, to Lord Cawdor's force of the Castlemartin Yeomanry and some local inhabitants armed with pitchforks. The U.K. Crown Dependency of the Channel Islands were occupied by German armed forces from 30 June 1940 to 8 May 1945.

Greatest evacuation

The greatest evacuation in military history was that carried out by 1,200 Allied naval and civil craft from the beach-head at Dunkerque (Dunkirk), France, between 27 May and 4 June 1940. A total of 338,226 British and French troops were taken off.

Worst sieges

The worst siege in history was the 880-day siege of Leningrad, U.S.S.R. by the German Army from 30 Aug. 1941 until 27 Jan. 1944. The best estimate is that between 1.3 and 1.5 million defenders and citizens died. The longest recorded siege was that of Azotus (now Ashdod), Israel which according to Herodotus was invested by Psamtik I of Egypt for 29 years in the period 664–610 B.C.

DEFENCE

The estimated level of spending on armaments throughout the world in 1978 was $400,000 million £200,000 million. This represents £48 per person per annum, or more than 6 per cent of the world's total production of goods and services. It was estimated in 1978 that there were 22½ million full-time armed force regulars or conscripts.

The budgetted expenditure on defence by the U.S. government for the year ending 30 June 1979 was $126,000 million (£66,300 million) or 6.9 per cent of the country's Gross National Product.

The official Chinese estimate for 1977 was that the defence burden on the U.S.S.R's G.N.P. was in excess of 15% of Gross National Product *i.e.* more than double that of the U.S.A.

ARMED FORCES

Largest

Numerically the largest regular armed force in the world is that of the People's Republic of China with 4,325,000. Her para-military forces of armed and unarmed militias have been estimated also by the Institute of Strategic Studies at some 115,000,000. Their mid-1978 estimates for the world's two principal military powers are U.S.S.R. (3,638,000) and U.S.A. (2,068,800).

Navies *Largest*

The largest navy in the world in terms of man power is the United States Navy, with a manpower of 532,000 and 191,500 Marines in mid-1978. The active strength in 1978 included 13 aircraft carriers, 41 Strategic Missile Submarines, 68 attack nuclear submarines and 10 diesel attack submarines, 71 Guided Missile Warships (26 cruisers, 38 destroyers and 6 frigates) and 62 amphibious warfare ships. The U.S.S.R. navy has a larger submarine fleet of 360 boats of which 85 are nuclear powered, and 90 carry strategic atomic missiles. It has 243 major surface combat ships.

The strength of the Royal Navy in mid-1978 included 4 nuclear submarines with strategic atomic missiles, 6 other nuclear and 17 diesel attack submarines and 2 anti-submarine commando carriers, 2 helicopter cruisers, 11 guided weapon destroyers, 55 frigates and 2 assault ships in a fleet of 72 major surface combat vessels. The uniformed strength was 67,770 including Fleet Air Arm and Royal Marines in mid-1978. In 1914 the Royal Navy had 542 warships including 72 capital ships with 16 building.

Armies *Oldest*

The oldest army in the world is the 83-strong Swiss Guard in the Vatican City, with a regular foundation dating back to 21 Jan. 1506. Its origins, however, extend back before 1400.

Largest

Numerically, the world's largest army is that of the People's Republic of China, with a total strength of some 3,625,000 in mid-1978. The total size of the U.S.S.R.'s army in mid-1978 was estimated by The International Institute of Strategic Studies at 1,825,000 men, believed to be organised into about 170 divisions with a maximum strength of 12,700 each. The strength of the British Army was 160,837 in mid-1978. The NATO agreement requires not less than 55,000 in West Germany. The basic strength maintained in Northern Ireland is 14,500 but this fluctuates.

Oldest soldiers

The oldest old soldier of all time was probably John B. Salling of the army of the Confederate States of America and the last accepted survivor of the U.S. Civil War (1861–65). He died in Kingsport, Tennessee, U.S.A., on 16 Mar. 1959, aged 113 years 1 day. The oldest Chelsea pensioner, based *only* on the evidence of his tombstone, was the 111-year-old William Hiseland (b. 6 Aug. 1620, d. 7 Feb. 1732). The longest serving British soldier has been Field Marshal Sir William Maynard Gomm G.C.B. (1784–1875), who was an ensign in 1794 and the Constable of the Tower to his death aged 91.

Youngest Soldiers

Dr. Kenneth Vernon Bailey M.C. (b. 14 Dec. 1897) served as a 2nd Lieutenant in the 2/8th Battn. Manchester Regt. for some 6 weeks before his 17th birthday.

Probably the youngest enlistment in the 20th century was of William Frederick Price, (b. 1 June 1891), who was enlisted into the Army at Aldershot on 23 May 1903, aged 11 years 356 days.

Youngest Conscripts

President Francisco Macias Nguema of Equatorial Guinea decreed in March 1976 compulsory military service for all boys between 7 and 14. Any parent refusing to hand over his or her son "will be imprisoned or shot".

Tallest soldiers

The tallest soldier of all time was Väinö Myllyrinne (1909–63) who was inducted into the Finnish Army when he was 7 ft 3 in 2,21 m and later grew to 8 ft 1¼ in 2,47 m. The British Army's tallest soldier was Benjamin Crow who was signed on at Lichfield in November 1947 when he was 7 ft 1 in 2,15 m tall. Edward Evans (1924–58), who later grew to 7 ft 8½ in 2,34 m was in the Army when he was 6 ft 10 in 2,08 m.

British regimental records

The oldest regular regiment in the British Army is the Royal Scots, raised in French service in 1633, though the Buffs (Royal East Kent Regiment) can trace back their origin to independent companies in Dutch pay as early as 1572. The Coldstream Guards, raised in 1650, were, however, placed on the establishment of the British Army before the Royal Scots and the Buffs. The oldest armed body in the United Kingdom is the Queen's Bodyguard of the Yeoman of the Guard formed in 1495. The Honourable Artillery Company, formed from the Finsbury Archers, received its charter from Henry VIII in 1537 but this lapsed until reformed in 1610. The infantry regiment with most battle honours is The Queen's Lancashire Regiment with 188.

The most senior regiment of the Reserve Army is The Royal Monmouthshire Royal Engineers (Militia) formed on 21 Mar. 1577 and never disbanded, with battle honours at Dunkirk, 1940 and Normandy, 1944.

Greatest Mutiny

In the 1914–18 War 56 French divisions comprising some 650,000 men and their officers refused orders on the Nivelle sector.

185

Longest march

The longest march in military history was the famous Long March by the Chinese Communists in 1934–35. In 368 days, of which 268 days were of movement, from October to October, their force of 90,000 covered 6,000 miles *9 650 km* from Kiangsi to Yenan in Shensi *via* Yünnan. They crossed 18 mountain ranges and six major rivers and lost all but 22,000 of their force in continual rear-guard actions against Nationalist Kuo-min-tang (K.M.T.) forces.

On the night of 12–13 Sept. 1944 a team of nine from B Company 4th Infantry Battalion of the Irish Army made a night march of 42 miles *67,59 km* in full battle order carrying 40 lb. *18,1 kg* in 11 hr. 49 mins.

Air Forces *Oldest*

The earliest autonomous air force is the Royal Air Force whose origin began with the Royal Flying Corps (created 13 May 1912); the Air Battalion of the Royal Engineers (1 Apr. 1911) and the Corps of Royal Engineers Balloon Section (1878) which was first operational in Bechuanaland (now Botswana) in 1884. The Prussian Army used a balloon near Strasbourg, France as early as 24 Sept. 1870.

Largest

The greatest Air Force of all time was the United States Army Air Force (now called the U.S. Air Force), which had 79,908 aircraft in July 1944 and 2,411,294 personnel in March 1944. The U.S. Air Force including strategic air forces had 571,000 personnel and 3,400 combat aircraft in mid-1978. The U.S.S.R. Air Force, including Air Defence Forces, with about 1,005,000 men in mid-1978, had 7,370 combat aircraft. In addition, the U.S.S.R.'s Offensive Strategic Rocket Forces had about 375,000 operational personnel in mid-1977. The strength of the Royal Air Force was 84,646 with some 510 combat aircraft in mid-1978.

BOMBS
Heaviest

The heaviest conventional bomb ever used operationally was the Royal Air Force's "Grand Slam", weighing 22,000 lb. *9 975 kg* and measuring 25 ft 5 in *7,74 m* long, dropped on Bielefeld railway viaduct, Germany, on 14 Mar. 1945. In 1949 the United States Air Force tested a bomb weighing 42,000 lb. *19 050 kg* at Muroc Dry Lake, California, U.S.A.

Atomic

The two atom bombs dropped on Japan by the United States in 1945 each had an explosive power equivalent to that of 20,000 short tons *20 kilotons* of trinitrotoluene ($C_7H_5O_6N_3$), called T.N.T. The one dropped on Hiroshima, known as "Little Boy", was 10 ft *3,04 m* long and weighed 9,000 lb. *4 080 kg*. The most powerful thermo-nuclear device so far tested is one with a power equivalent to 57,000,000 short tons of T.N.T., or 57 megatons, detonated by the U.S.S.R. in the Novaya Zemlya area at 8.33 a.m. G.M.T. on 30 Oct. 1961. The shock wave was detected to have circled the world three times, taking 36 hours 27 min for the first circuit. Some estimates put the power of this device at between 62 and 90 megatons. On 9 Aug. 1961, Nikita Khrushchyov, then the Chairman of the Council of Ministers of the U.S.S.R., declared that the Soviet Union was capable of constructing a 100-megaton bomb, and announced the possession of one in East Berlin, Germany, on 16 Jan. 1963. It has been estimated that such a bomb would make a crater 19 miles *30 km* in diameter and would cause serious fires at a range of from 36 to 40 miles *58–64 km*. Atom bomb theory began with Einstein's publication of the $E = mc^2$ formula in *Annalen der Physik* in Leipzig on 14 May 1907. It became a practicality with the mesothorium experiments of Otto Hahn, Fritz Strassman and Lise Meitner on 17 Dec. 1938. Work started in the U.S.S.R. on atomic bombs in June 1942 although their first chain reaction was not achieved until December

The U.S. XM1 tank, the fastest tank in the world. This prototype attained 45 m.p.h. *72 km/h*. Its 105 mm gun will be replaced by a 120 mm gun in 1984.

1945 by Dr. Igor Vasilyevich Kurchatov. The patent for the fusion or H bomb was filed in the United States on 26 May 1946 by Dr. Janos (John) von Neumann (1903–57), a Hungarian-born mathematician, and Dr. Klaus Julius Emil Fuchs (born in Germany 29 Dec. 1911), the physicist, who defected.

Largest nuclear weapons

The most powerful ICBM are the U.S.S.R.'s SS-18's, each with up to 10 one-megaton M.I.R.V's (multiple independently targetable re-entry vehicles), thus each of power 50 times as great as the Hiroshima bomb. The U.S. Minuteman III has 3 M.I.R.V's each of 335 kiloton force.

No official estimate has been published of the potential power of the device known as Doomsday, but this far surpasses any tested weapon. If it were practicable to construct, it is mooted that a 50,000 megaton cobalt-salted device could wipe out the entire human race except people deep underground and who did not emerge for more than five years.

Largest "conventional" explosion

The largest use of conventional explosive was for the demolition of the fortifications at Heligoland on 18 Apr. 1947. A charge of 3,997 tons *4 061 tonnes* was detonated by Commissioned Gunner E. C. Jellis of the naval demolition team headed by Lt. F. T. Woosnam R.N. aboard H.M.S. *Lasso* lying 9 miles *14,5 km* out to sea.

TANKS

Note—Guinness Superlatives Ltd. has published a specialist volume entitled *The Guinness Book of Tank Facts and Feats* (2nd edition) by Kenneth Macksey (£4.95). This work deals with all the aspects of the development and history of the tank and other armoured fighting vehicles in greater detail.

Earliest

The first fighting tank was "Mother" *alias* "Big Willie" built by William Foster & Co. Ltd. of Lincoln, and completed on 8 Sept. 1915. Tanks were first taken into action by the Machine Gun Corps (Heavy Section), which later became the Royal Tank Corps, at the battle of Flers, in France, on 15 Sept. 1916. The Mark I Male tank, which was armed with a pair of 6-pounders guns and two machine-guns, weighed 28 tons *28,4 tonnes* and was driven by a motor developing 105 horse-power which gave it a maximum road speed of 3 to 4 m.p.h. *4,8–6,4 km/h.*

Heaviest

The heaviest tank ever constructed was the German Panzer Kampfwagen Maus II, which weighed 189 tons *192 tonnes*. By 1945 it had reached only the experimental stage and was not proceeded with.

The heaviest operational tank used by any army was the 81.5 ton *82,8 tonnes* 13-man French Char de Rupture 2C bis of 1923. It carried a 155 mm. howitzer and had two 250 h.p. world's fastest tank is the $1.8 million (£900,000) XM-1 due for U.S. Army service. The prototype reached 45 m.p.h. *72,4 km/h*. The DM3,6 million (£950,000) German Leopard 2 has the greatest fire-power with a 120 mm *4.72 in* gun.

The heaviest British tank ever built was the 78-ton *79 tonnes* prototype "Tortoise". With a crew of seven and a designed speed of 12 m.p.h. *19 km/h*, this tank had a width two inches *5 cm* less than that of the one-time operational 65-ton *66 tonnes* "Conqueror". The most heavily armed is the 52-ton *52,8 tonnes* "Chieftain", put into service in November 1966, with a 120 mm gun.

GUNS
Earliest

Although it cannot be accepted as proved, the best opinion is that the earliest guns were constructed in North Africa, possibly by Arabs, in *c.* 1250. The earliest representation of an English gun is contained in an illustrated manuscript dated 1326 at Oxford. The earliest anti-aircraft gun was an artillery piece on a high angle mounting used in the Franco-Prussian War of 1870 by the Prussians against French balloons.

Largest

The remains of the most massive gun ever constructed were found near Frankfurt am Main, Germany, in 1945. It was the 'Schwerer Gustav" or "Dora", which had a barrel 94.7 ft *28,87 m* long, with a calibre of 800 mm (31.5 in), and a breech weighing 108 tons *109 tonnes*. The maximum charge was 4,409 lb. *2 000 kg* of cordite to fire a shell weighing 4.7 tons *4 800 kg* a distance of 34 miles *55 km*. The maximum projectile was one of 7 tons/*tonnes* with a range of 22 miles *35 km*. Each gun with its carriage weighed 1,323 tons *1 344 tonnes* and required a crew of 1,500 men.

During the 1914–18 war the British army used a gun of 18 in *457 mm* calibre. The barrel alone weighed 125 tons *127 tonnes*. In World War II the "Bochebuster", a train-mounted howitzer with a calibre of 18 in *457 mm* firing a 2,500 lb. *1 133 kg* shell to a maximum range of 22,800 yds *20 850 m*, was used from 1940 onwards as part of the Kent coast defences.

Greatest range

The greatest range ever attained by a gun was achieved by the H.A.R.P. (High Altitude Research Project) gun consisting of two 16.5 in *419 mm* calibre barrels in tandem 36.4 m *119.4 ft* long weighing 150 tonnes at Yuma, Arizona, U.S.A. On 19 Nov. 1966 an 84 kg *185 lb.* projectile was fired to an altitude of 180 km *111.8 miles* or *590,550 ft*. The static V.3 underground firing tubes built in 50 degree shafts near Mimoyecques, near Calais, France to bombard London were never operative due to R.A.F. bombing.

The famous long range gun, which shelled Paris in World War I, was the *Kaiser Wilhelm geschütz* with a calibre of 220 mm (*8.66 in*), a designed range of 79.5 miles *127,9 km* and an achieved range of 76 miles *122 km* from the Forest of Cérpy in March 1918. The Big Berthas were mortars of 420 mm *16.53 in* calibre and with a range of less than 9 miles *14 500 m*.

Mortars

The largest mortars ever constructed were Mallets mortar (Woolwich Arsenal, London, 1857), and the "Little David" of World War II, made in the U.S.A. Each had a calibre of 36¼ in *920 mm*, but neither was ever used in action. The heaviest mortar used was the tracked German 600 mm *23.6 in* siege piece known as "Karl" before Stalingrad, U.S.S.R.

Largest cannon

The highest calibre cannon ever constructed is the *Tsar Puchka* (King of Cannons), now housed in the Kremlin, Moscow, U.S.S.R. It was built in the 16th century with a bore of 920 mm *36.2 in* and a barrel 10 ft 5 in *3,18 m* long. It weighs 2400 *pouds* or 40 tonnes. The Turks fired up to seven shots per day from a bombard 26 ft *7,92 m* long, with an internal calibre of 42 in *1 066 mm* against the walls of Constantinople (now Istanbul) from 12 Apr. to 29 May 1453. It was dragged by 60 oxen and 200 men and fired a stone cannon ball weighing 1,200 lb. *544 kg*.

Military engines

The largest military catapults, or onagers, were capable of throwing a missile weighing 60 lb. *27 kg* a distance of 500 yds *457 m*.

5. JUDICIAL

LEGISLATION AND LITIGATION
Statutes *Oldest*

The earliest known judicial code was that of King Ur-Hammu during the third dynasty of Ur, Iraq, in *c.* 2145 B.C. The oldest English statute in the Statute Book is a section of the Statute of Marlborough of 1267, retitled in 1948 "The Distress Act, 1267". Some statutes enacted by Henry II (d. 1189) and earlier kings are even more durable as they have been assimilated in to the Common Law. An extreme example is Ine's Law concerning the administration of shires *c.* 8 A.D.

Longest in the United Kingdom

Measured in bulk the longest statute of the United Kingdom, is the Income Tax and Corporation Tax Act, 1970, which ran to 540 sections, 15 schedules and 670 pages. It is 1½ in *37 mm* thick and costs £2.80. However, its 540 sections are surpassed in number by the 748 of the Merchant Shipping Act, 1894. Of old statutes, 31 George III xiv, the Land Tax Act of 1791, written on parchment, consists of 780 skins forming a roll 1,170 ft *360 m* long.

Shortest

The shortest statute is the Parliament (Qualification of Women) Act, 1918, which runs to 27 operative words—"A woman shall not be disqualified by sex or marriage from being elected to or sitting or voting as a Member of the Commons House of Parliament". Section 2 contains a further 14 words giving the short title.

Most inexplicable

Certain passages in several Acts have always defied interpretation and the most inexplicable must be a matter of opinion. A Judge of the Court of Session of Scotland has sent the Editor his candidate which reads, "In the Nuts (unground), (other than ground nuts) Order, the expression nuts shall have reference to such nuts, other than ground nuts, as would but for this amending Order not qualify as nuts (unground) (other than ground nuts) by reason of their being nuts (unground)."

Earliest English patent

The earliest of all known English patents was that granted by Henry VI in 1449 to Flemish-born John of Utyman for making the coloured glass required for the windows of Eton College. The peak number of applications for patents filed in the United Kingdom in any one year was 63,614 in 1969. The shortest, concerning a harrow attachment, of 48 words was filed on 14 May 1956 while the longest, comprising 2,318 pages of text and 495 pages of drawings, was filed on 31 Mar. 1965 by I.B.M. to cover a computer.

Most protracted litigation

The longest contested law suit ever recorded ended in Poona, India on 28 Apr. 1966, when Balasaheb Patloji Thorat received a favourable judgment on a suit filed by his ancestor Maloji Thorat 761 years earlier in 1205. The points at issue were rights of presiding over public functions and precedences at religious festivals.

The dispute over the claim of the Prior and Convent (now the Dean and Chapter) of Durham Cathedral to administer the spiritualities of the diocese during a vacancy in the See grew fierce in 1283. It flared up again in 1672 and 1890; an attempt in November 1975 to settle the issue, then 692 years old, was unsuccessful. Neither side admit the legitimacy of writs of appointment issued by the other even though identical persons are named.

Longest British trial

The longest trial in the annals of British justice was the Tichborne personation case. The civil trial began on 11 May 1871, lasted 103 days and collapsed on 6 Mar. 1872. The criminal trial went on for 188 days, resulting in a sentence on 28 Feb. 1874 for two counts of perjury (two 7 year consecutive terms of imprisonment with hard labour) on the London-born Arthur Orton, *alias* Thomas Castro (1834–98), who claimed to be Roger Charles Tichborne (1829–54), the elder brother of Sir Alfred Joseph Doughty-Tichborne, 11th Bt. (1839–66). The whole case, thus spanned 1025 days. The jury were out for only 30 minutes.

The impeachment of Warren Hastings (1732–1818), which began in 1788, dragged on for seven years until 23 Apr. 1795, but the trial lasted only 149 days. He was appointed a member of the Privy Council in 1814.

The £21 million claim against the U.K. government by the Ocean Islanders, Pacific before Mr. Justice Megarry finished after 226 days on 3 Dec. 1976 with 7,000,000 words on evidence.

Murder

The longest murder trial in Britain was that at the Old Bailey, London of Reginald Dudley, 51 and Robert Maynard, 46 in the Torso Murder of Billy Moseley and Micky Cornwall which ran before Mr. Justice Swanwick from 11 Nov. 1976 to 17 June 1977 with 136 trial days. Both men were sentenced to life (minimum 15 years) imprisonment. The costs were estimated to exceed £500,000 and the evidence 3,500,000 words.

Divorce

The longest trial of a divorce case in Britain was *Gibbons v. Gibbons and Roman and Halperin.* On 19 Mar. 1962, after 28 days, Mr. Alfred George Boyd Gibbons was granted a decree *nisi* against his wife Dorothy for adultery with Mr. John Halperin of New York City, N.Y., U.S.A.

Shortest Trials

The shortest recorded British murder hearings were *R. v. Murray* on 28 Feb. 1957 and *R. v. Cawley* at Winchester Assizes on 14 Dec. 1959. The proceedings occupied only 30 sec on each occasion.

An ill-founded prosecution under the Air Navigation Order, 1974 against a pilot at Edinburgh airport was timed at No. 1 Sheriff Court, Edinburgh on 1 Mar. 1977 to have lasted 7 seconds. Sheriff Skae uttered two words—"Not Guilty".

Longest address

The longest address in a British court was in *Globe and Phoenix Gold Mining Co. Ltd. v. Amalgamated Properties of Rhodesia.* Mr. William Henry Upjohn, K.C. (1853–1941) concluded his speech on 22 Sept. 1916, having addressed the court for 45 days.

Highest bail *World*

The highest amount ever demanded as bail was $46,500,000 (*then £16,608,333*) against Antonio De Angelis in a civil damages suit by the Harbor Tank Storage Co. filed in the Superior Court, Jersey City, New Jersey, U.S.A. on 16 Jan. 1964 in the Salad Oil Swindle. He was released on 4 June 1973. Abul Hassen Ebtehaj, later Chairman of the Iranian Bank in Teheran was in 1967 granted bail in excess of $50 million.

Great Britain

The highest bail figure in a British court is £250,000 granted to the former Hong Kong policeman, chief superintendent Peter Godber, 52 at Bow Street Court, Greater London on 16 May 1974 when charged with bribery. This consisted of a maximum of four sureties aggregating £200,000 and £50,000 in his own recognisance.

Longest arbitration

The longest arbitration (under the 1950 Act) on record has been the Royce Arbitration. It lasted 239 days and concerned the Milchell Construction Co. and the East Anglian Regional Hospital Board over the building of Peterborough Hospital.

The longest case before an Industrial Tribunal has been 44 days during more than 13 months (2 May 1977–29 June 1978) when the columnist C. Gordon Tether contested the fairness of his dismissal by *The Financial Times* in person.

Best attended trial

The greatest attendance at any trial was that of Major Jesús Sosa Blanco, aged 51, for an alleged 108 murders. At one point in the 12½ hr trial (5.30 p.m. to 6 a.m., 22–23 Jan. 1959), 17,000 people were present in the Havana Sports Palace, Cuba.

Greatest Damages *Personal injury World*

The greatest personal injury damages ever awarded were to Janelle Lynn Stearns, 12, against Park Avenue Hospital Inc. and an anaesthetist Dr. Howard K. Gifford in settlement for alleged medical malpractice resulting in severe brain damage following a tonsillectomy at Pomona, California in May 1973. If she lives to the average expectation of 63.9 additional years the payments will total $26,541,832. The largest single cash payment settlement for single person has been

$6,800,000 (*then* £3.4 million) to the lawyer John Coates, 42, of Austin, Texas U.S.A. against Remington Arms Co. Inc. *et al.* on 23 Oct. 1978. The case concerned severe injury from a defectively made hunting rifle.

The highest damages ever actually paid have been $14,387,674, following upon the crash of a private aircraft at South Lake, Tahoe, California, U.S.A. on 21 Feb. 1967, to the sole survivor Ray Rosendin, 45, by the Santa Clara Superior Court on 8 Mar. 1972. Rosendin received *inter alia* $1,069,374 for the loss of both legs and disabling arm injuries; $1,213,129 for the loss of his wife and $10,500,000 punitive damages against Avco-Lyconing Corporation which allegedly violated Federal regulations when it rebuilt the aircraft engine owned by Rosendin Corporation.

Great Britain
The highest damages for personal injury ever paid from a United Kingdom court were for £201,786 in the Queen's Bench Division by Mr. Justice Mustill on 6 Apr. 1979 to David Seton, 36 of Leeds against Glenton Elliott, the driver of a car involved in a collision in 1977. Mr. Seton crashed into a bus sign resulting in injuries which effectually ended his career as a chartered surveyor.

An appeal may be pending on the £310,000 damages awarded on 23 May 1979 at Teeside Crown Court by Mr. Justice Smith in favour of David Taylor aged 9 of Whitley Bay, Tyne and Wear. The Medical Union Fund were ordered to pay £150,000 immediately in respect of the admitted liability of a family doctor's failure to diagnose meningitis when David was aged one.

Breach of contract
The greatest damages ever awarded for a breach of contract were £610,392, awarded on 16 July 1930 to the Bank of Portugal against the printers Waterlow & Sons Ltd., of London, arising from their unauthorised printing of 580,000 five-hundred escudo notes in 1925. This award was upheld in the House of Lords on 28 Apr. 1932. One of the perpetrators, Arthur Virgilio Alves Reis, served 16 years (1930–46) in gaol.

Breach of promise
The largest sum involved in a breach of promise suit in the United Kingdom was £50,000, accepted in 1913 by Miss Daisy Markham, *alias* Mrs. Annie Moss (d. 20 Aug. 1962, aged 76), in settlement against the 6th Marquess of Northampton (b. 6 Aug. 1885).

Defamation *World*
A sum of $16,800,000 (£6,720,000) was awarded to Dr. John J. Wild, 58, at the Hennepin District Court, Minnesota, U.S.A., on 30 Nov. 1972 against The Minnesota Foundation and others for defamation, bad-faith termination of a contract, interference with professional business relationship and $10.8 million in punitive damages. These amounts are unappealed.

The largest libel settlement made has been one for $600,000 (*then* £343,000) by the San Francisco Examiner's publishers, the Hearst Corporation in response to a $32 million (£18 million) suit by the Synanon Foundation Inc. and its founder Charles E. Dederich on 1 July 1976 for adverse news articles.

The greatest damages for defamation ever awarded in the United Kingdom have been £302,000 in the Courts in Edinburgh in favour of Capital Life Assurance Co. against the *Scottish Daily Record* and the *Sunday Mail* for articles published in the latter in 1975.

Greatest compensation
William De Palma (b. 1938) of Whittier, California, agreed to a $750,000 settlement for 16 months wrongful imprisonment in McNeil Island Federal Prison, on 12 Aug. 1975 after a 15 year sentence for armed robbery in Buena Park on forged finger print evidence in 1968. The greatest Crown compensation in Britain for wrongful imprisonment has been £17,500 paid to Laszio Virag, 35, who had been sentenced to 10 years imprisonment at Gloucester assizes in 1969 for theft and shooting and wounding a police officer. His acceptance of this sum was announced on 23 Dec. 1974 after his having been released in April 1974 on grounds of mistaken identification.

Greatest Alimony
The highest alimony awarded by a court has been $2,261,000 (*then* £983,000) against George Storer Sr., 74, in favour of his third wife Dorothy, 73, in Miami, Florida on 29 Oct. 1974. Mr Storer, a broadcasting executive, was also ordered to pay his ex-wife's attorney $200,000 (*then* £86,950) in fees.

Greatest Divorce Settlement
The greatest amount ever reported in a divorce settlement is half of the estimated $100 million wealth of the publisher James Kent Cooke (b. 1913) of Las Vegas, Nevada agreed by a Los Angeles court in March 1979 in favour of his wife Mrs. Jeannie Cooke (b. 1917) after 42 years of marriage.

Patent case
The greatest settlement ever made in a patent infringement suit is $9,250,000 (*then* £3,303,000), paid in April 1952 by the Ford Motor Company to the Ferguson Tractor Co. for a claim filed in January 1948.

Largest Suit
The highest amount of damages ever sought is $675,000,000,000,000 (then equivalent to 10 times the U.S. national wealth) in a suit by Mr. I. Walton Bader brought in the U.S. District Court, New York City on 14 Apr. 1971 against General Motors and others for polluting all 50 states.

Highest Costs
The highest costs in English legal history arose from the alleged infringement of a patent owned by General Tire and Rubber Co. of America by the Firestone Tyre and Rubber Co. The case was heard by 17 judges over 5½ years ending on 16 Apr. 1975 in a reduction of damages from £1,388,000 to £311,000 but costs were an estimated £500,000.

Longest Lease
Part of the Cattle Market, Dublin, Ireland was leased by John Jameson to the city's corporation on a lease for 100,000 years expiring on 21st January A.D. 101,863.

Greatest lien
The greatest lien ever imposed by a court is 40,000 million lire (£27 million) on 9 Apr. 1974 upon Vittorio and Ida Riva in Milan for back taxes allegedly due on a chain of cotton mills around Turin, Italy, inherited by their brother Felice (who left for Beirut) in 1960.

Wills *Shortest*
The shortest valid will in the world is "Vše zene", the Czech for "All to wife", written and dated 19 Jan. 1967 by Herr Karl Tausch of Langen, Hesse, Germany. The shortest will contested but subsequently admitted to probate in English law was the case of *Thorn v. Dickens* in 1906. It consisted of the three words "All for Mother".

Longest
The longest will on record was that of Mrs. Frederica Cook (U.S.A.), in the early part of the century. It consisted of four bound volumes containing 95,940 words.

Judges *Most Durable*
The oldest recorded active judge was Judge Albert R. Alexander (1859–1966) of Plattsburg, Missouri, U.S.A. He was the magistrate and probate judge of Clinton County until his retirement aged 105 years 8 months on 9 July 1965. James Russell McElroy (b. 1 Oct. 1901) served 49 years 125 days (1927–1977) on the Circuit Court of Alabama, U.S.A. Judge Vernon D. Hitchings of Norfolk, Virginia disposed of his millionth traffic case from Jan. 1954 to 19 Jan 1977. Of these some 965,000 of his verdicts were unappealed or upheld on appeal.

Great Britain
The greatest recorded age at which any British judge has sat on a bench was 93 years 9 months in the case of Sir William Francis Kyffin Taylor, G.B.E., K.C. (*later* Lord Maenan), who was born on 9 July 1854 and retired as presiding judge of the Liverpool Court of Passage in April 1948, having held that position since 1903. Sir Salathiel Lovell was, however,

A portrait of the Rt Hon Lord Denning, Britain's longest serving judge. He was first appointed to the High Court in 1944. He has been Master of the Rolls since 1962.

still sitting in 1713 in his 94th or 95th year. The greatest age at which a House of Lords judgment has been given is 92 in the case of the 1st Earl of Halsbury (b. 3 Sept. 1823) in 1916.

The longest serving judge in Britain is the Rt. Hon. Lord Denning (b. 23 Jan. 1899), who was appointed a High Court Judge in 1944, a Lord Justice of Appeal in 1948, a Law Lord in 1957 and Master of the Rolls in 1962.

Judge Youngest

No collated records on the ages of judicial appointments exist. However Thomas J. Boynton (b. Amherst, Ohio on 31 Aug. 1838) is known to have been appointed Federal Judge at Key West, Florida on 20 Jan. 1864 aged 25 years 142 days. Judge Susan I. Broyles (b. Alamosa, Colorado, U.S.A., 25 June 1949) was appointed County Judge of Conefos County, Colorado on 9 Jan. 1973 aged 23 years 198 days.

The youngest certain age at which any English judge has been appointed is 31, in the case of Sir Francis Buller (b. 17 Mar. 1746), who was appointed Second Judge of the County Palatine of Chester on 27 Nov. 1777, and Puisne Judge of the King's Bench on 6 May 1778, aged 32 years 1 month. The lowest age of appointment this century has been 42 years 2 months of Lord Hodson in 1937.

Youngest English Q.C.

The earliest age at which a barrister has taken silk this century is 33 years 8 months in the case of Mr. (later the Rt. Hon. Sir) Francis Raymond Evershed (1899–1966) in April 1933. He was later Lord Evershed, Master of the Rolls. Buller (see above) was nepotiscally given silk aged 31 being a nephew of the then Lord Chancellor, Lord Bathurst.

Most successful advocate

Sir Lionel Luckhoo K.C.M.G., C.B.E. senior partner of Luckhoo and Luckhoo of Georgetown, Guyana succeeded in getting his 225th successive murder charge acquittal by May 1979.

Deadliest Prosecutor

Joe Freeman Britt, District Attorney, Sixteenth Judicial District, North Carolina, U.S.A. obtained 23 death verdicts in 28 months to mid-1976 when he had 13 defendants simultaneously on death row.

CRIME

Mass Killings *China*

The greatest massacre ever imputed by the government of one sovereign nation against the government of another is that of 26,300,000 Chinese during the regime of Mao Tse-tung between 1949 and May 1965. This accusation was made by an agency of the U.S.S.R. Government in a radio broadcast on 7 Apr. 1969. The broadcast broke down the figure into four periods:—2.8 million (1949–52); 3.5 million (1953–57); 6.7 million (1958–60); and 13.3 million (1961–May 1965). The highest reported death figures in single monthly announcements on Peking radio were 1,176,000 in the provinces of Anhwei, Chekiang, Kiangsu, and Shantung, and 1,150,000 in the Central South Provinces. Po I-po, Minister of Finance, is alleged to have stated in the organ *For a lasting peace, for a people's democracy* "in the past three years (1950–52) we have liquidated more than 2 million bandits". General Jacques Guillermaz, a French diplomat estimated the total executions between February 1951 and May 1952 at between 1 million and 3 million. In April 1971 the Executive cabinet or *Yuan* of the implacably hostile government of The Republic of China in Taipei, Taiwan announced its official estimate of the mainland death roll in the period 1949–69 as "at least 39,940,000". This figure, however, excluded "tens of thousands" killed in the Great Proletarian Cultural Revolution, which began in late 1966. The Walker Report published by the U.S. Senate Committee of the Judiciary in July 1971 placed the parameters of the total death roll within China since 1949 between 32.25 and 61.7 million. An estimate of 63,784,000 was published by Jean-Pierre Dujardin in *Figaro Magazine* of 19–25 Nov. 1978.

U.S.S.R.

The total death roll in the Great Purge, or *Yezhovshchina*, in the U.S.S.R., in 1936–38 has, not surprisingly, never been published. Evidence of its magnitude may be found in population statistics which show a deficiency of males from *before* the outbreak of the 1941–45 war. The reign of terror was administered by the *Narodny Kommissariat Vnutrennykh Del* (N.K.V.D.), or People's Commissariat of Internal Affairs, the Soviet security service headed by Nikolay Ivanovich Yezhov (1895–1939), described by Nikita Khrushchyov in 1956 as a "degenerate". S. V. Utechin, an expert on Soviet affairs, regarded estimates of 8,000,000 or 10,000,000 victims as "probably not exaggerations".

Nazi Germany

Obersturmbannführer (Lt.-Col.) Karl Adolf Eichmann (b. Solingen, West Germany 19 Mar. 1906) of the S.S. was hanged in a small room inside Ramleh Prison, near Tel Aviv, Israel, at just before midnight (local time) on 31 May 1962, for his complicity in the deaths of an indeterminably massive number of Jews during World War II, under the instruction given in April 1941 by Adolf Hitler (1889–1945) for "the Final Solution" (*Endlösung*). On 17 Aug 1942 Stalin indicated to Churchill in Moscow that 10 million *kulaks* had been liquidated.

At the S.S. (*Schutzstaffel*) extermination camp (*Vernichtungslager*) known as Auschwitz-Birkenau (Oswiecim-Brzezinka), near Oswiecim (Auschwitz), in southern Poland, where a minimum of 920,000 people (Soviet estimate is 4,000,000) were exterminated from 14 June 1940 to 18 Jan. 1945, the greatest number killed in a day was 6,000. The man who operated the release of the "Zyklon B" cyanide pellets into the gas chambers there during this time was Sgt. Major Moll (variously Mold). The Nazi (*Nationalsozialistische Deutsche Arbeiter Partei*) Commandant during the period 1940–43 was Rudolph Franz Ferdinand Höss who was tried in Warsaw from 11 Mar. to 2 Apr. 1947 and hanged, aged 47, at Oswiecim on 15 Apr. 1947.

Forced Labour
No official figures have been published of the death roll in Corrective Labour Camps in the U.S.S.R., first established in 1918. The total number of such camps was known to be more than 200 in 1946 but in 1956 many were converted to less severe Corrective Labour Colonies. An estimate published in the Netherlands puts the death roll between 1921 and 1960 at 19,000,000. The camps were administered by the *Cheka* until 1922, the O.G.P.U. (1922–34), the N.K.V.D. (1934–46), the M.V.D. (1946–53) and the K.G.B. since 1953. Solzhenitsyn's aggregate best estimate is that the number of inmates has been 66 million. The study by S. Grossu published 1975 stated there were then 2 million political prisoners in 96 camps. In China there are no published official statistics on the numbers undergoing *Lao Jiao* (Education through Labour) nor *Lao Dong Gai Zao* (Reform through manual labour). An estimate published by Bao Ruo-wang, who was released in 1964 due to his father having been a Corsican, was 16,000,000 which then approached 3 per cent of the population.

Largest criminal organization
The largest syndicate of organized crime is the Mafia or La Cosa Nostra, which has infiltrated the executive, judiciary and legislature of the United States. It consists of some 3,000 to 5,000 individuals in 24 "families" federated under "The Commission", with an annual turnover in vice, gambling, protection rackets, cigarettes, bootlegging, hijacking, narcotics, loan-sharking and prostitution estimated in the *Time* magazine survey of May 1977 at $48,000 million per annum of which $25.3 billion were profit—$9\frac{1}{2}$ times more than Exxon. The origin in the U.S. dates from the lynching of 11 Mafiosi in New Orleans in 1890 for which a naïve U.S. government paid $30,000 compensation to widows which was seized as the initial funding to prime the whole operation. The biggest Mafia (meaning *swank* from a Sicilian word for beauty or pride) killing was on 11–13 Sept. 1931 when the topmost man Salvatore Maranzano, *Il Capo di Tutti Capi*, and 40 allies were liquidated.

Murder rate *Highest*
The country with the highest recorded murder rate is Mexico, with 46.3 registered homicides per each 100,000 of the population in 1970. It has been estimated that the total number of murders in Colombia during *La Violencia* (1945–62) was about 300,000, giving a rate over a 17-year period of more than 48 a day. A total of 592 deaths was attributed to one bandit leader, Teófilo ("Sparks") Rojas, aged 27, between 1948 and his death in an ambush near Armenia on 22 Jan. 1963. Some sources attribute 3,500 slayings to him.

The highest homicide rates recorded in New York City have been 58 in a week in July 1972 and 13 in a day in August 1972. In 1973 the total for Detroit, Michigan (pop. then 1.5 million) was 751.

Lowest
The country with the lowest officially recorded rate in the world is Spain, with 39 murders (a rate of 1.23 per each million of the population) in 1967, or one murder every 9 days. In the Indian state of Sikkim, in the Himalayas, murder is, however, practically unknown, while in the Hunza area of Kashmir, in the Karakoram, only one definite case by a Hunzarwal has been recorded since 1900.

Great Britain
In Great Britain the total number of homicides and deaths from injuries purposely inflicted by other persons in the year 1977 was 549. This figure compares with a murder total of 124 in 1937 and 125 in 1958.

Most Prolific Murderers *World*
It was established at the trial of Buhram, the Indian thug, that he had strangled at least 931 victims with his yellow and white cloth strip or *ruhmal* in the Oudh district between 1790 and 1840. It has been estimated that at least 2,000,000 Indians were strangled by Thugs (*burtotes*) during the reign of the Thugee cult (pronounced tugee) from 1550 until its final suppression by the British *raj* in 1853. The greatest number of victims ascribed to a murderess has been 610 in the case of Countess Erszebet Bathory (1560–1614) of Hungary. At her trial which began on 2 Jan. 1611 a witness testified to seeing a list of her victims in her own handwriting totalling this number. All were alleged to be young girls from the neighbourhood of her castle at Csejthe where she died on 21 Aug. 1614. She had been walled up in her room for the $3\frac{1}{2}$ years after being found guilty.

20th century
The 20th century's most prolific one-at-a-time murderer has been Bruno Lüdke (Germany) (b. 1909), who confessed to 85 murders of women between 1928 and 29 Jan. 1943. He was executed by injection without trial in a hospital in Vienna on 8 Apr. 1944.

Frans Hooijmaijers, 40, a male nurse at the Luckerheide Geriatric Clinic, Kerkrade, Netherlands admitted to 14 murders of patients in August 1976. In his section since November 1969 there were 245 other deaths of a suspicious nature and an inordinately high consumption of insulin and Valium. He was sentenced to 18 years in April 1977.

John Wayne Gacy was charged with murdering 7 youths and according to the police admitted to assaulting and strangling 25 others. The first of 29 bodies was found on 21 Dec. 1978 under his house at Park Ridge, Chicago, U.S.A.

Great Britain
The publication of *The Legend of Sawney Bean* by Ronald Holmes in 1975 makes it fully evident that the story of a notorious cannibalistic murderer so named from Galloway, Scotland lacks historic reality.

Six men were each charged with 21 murders at Lancaster Crown Court on 9 June 1975 concerning the bombing of the two Birmingham public houses Mulberry Bush and Tavern in the Town on 21 Nov. 1974. They were John Walker, Patrick Hill, Robert Hunter, Noel McIlkenny, William Power and Hugh Callaghan.

Judith Minna Ward, 25 of Stockport, Cheshire was convicted on 11 separate murder charges on 4 Nov. 1974 making 12 in all arising from the explosion in an army coach on the M.62 near Drighlington, West Yorkshire on 4 Feb. 1974. Mary Ann Cotton (*née* Robson) (b. 1832, East Rainton, County Durham), hanged in Durham Jail on 24 Mar. 1873 is believed to have poisoned 14, possibly 20, people.

Gang murders
During the period of open gang warfare in Chicago, Illinois, U.S.A., the peak year was 1926, when there were 76 unsolved killings. The 1,000th gang murder in Chicago since 1919 occurred on 1 Feb. 1967. Only 13 cases have ended in convictions.

"Smelling out"
The greatest "smelling out" recorded in African history occurred before Shaka (1787–1828) and 30,000 Nguni subjects near the River Umhlatuzana, Zululand (now Natal, South Africa) in March 1824. After 9 hrs, over 300 were "smelt out" as guilty of smearing the Royal *Kraal* with blood, by 150 witch-finders led by the hideous female *isangoma* Nobela. The victims were declared innocent when Shaka admitted to having done the smearing himself to expose the falsity of the power of his diviners. Nobela poisoned herself with atropine ($C_{17}H_{23}NO_3$), but the other 149 witch-finders were thereupon skewered or clubbed to death.

Suicide
The estimated daily rate of suicides throughout the world surpassed 1,000 in 1965. The country with the highest suicide rate is Hungary, with 42.6 per each 100,000 of the population in 1977. The country with the lowest recorded rate is Jordan with a single case in 1970 and hence a rate of 0.04 per 100,000.

In England and Wales there were 3,976 suicides in 1977, or an average of 10.89 per day. In the northern hemisphere April and May tend to be peak months.

Robbery

The greatest robbery on record was that of the Reichsbank reserves by a civilian—U.S. military consortium in April–May 1945. The Westphalia bearer bonds repayable in gold were for $400 million. Gold coin and bullion then valued at $3,434,626 and jewels, foreign exchange and securities valued at 23 million gold marks, were stolen from the Berlin Reichsbank.

Art

The greatest recorded art robbery by market valuation was the removal of 19 paintings, valued at £8,000,000 taken from Russborough House, Blessington, County Wicklow, Ireland, the home of Sir Alfred and Lady Beit by 4 men and a woman on 26 Apr. 1974. They included the £3 million Vermeer "Lady Writing a Letter with her maid". The paintings were recovered on 4 May near Glandore, County Cork. Dr. Rose Bridgit Dugdale (b 1941) was convicted. It is arguable that the value of the *Mona Lisa* at the time of its theft from The Louvre, Paris on 21 Aug. 1911 was greater than this figure. It was recovered in Italy in 1913 when Vincenzo Perruggia was charged with its theft. On 1 Sept. 1964 antiquities reputedly worth £10,000,000 were recovered from 3 warehouses near the Pyramids, Egypt.

Bank

During the extreme civil disorder prior to 22 Jan. 1976 in Beirut, Lebanon, a guerilla force blasted the vaults of the British Bank of the Middle East in Bab Idriss and cleared out safe deposit boxes with contents valued by former Finance Minister, Lucien Dahadah, at $50 million and by another source as an 'absolute minimum' of $20 million.

Britain's greatest ever robbery was of an estimated £8,000,000 from the Bank of America, Mayfair, London on 24 Apr. 1975. On 16 Nov. 1976 five men were jailed for between 12 and 23 years. Leonard "The Twirler" Wilde, 51 was the locksmith.

Train

The greatest recorded train robbery occurred between about 3.03 a.m. and 3.27 a.m. on 8 Aug. 1963, when a General Post Office mail train from Glasgow, Scotland, was ambushed at Sears Crossing and robbed at Bridego Bridge near Mentmore, Buckinghamshire. The gang escaped with about 120 mailbags containing £2,631,784 worth of bank notes being taken to London for destruction. Only £343,448 was recovered.

Jewels

The greatest recorded theft of jewels was from safe deposits in Palm Towers, Palm Beach, Florida on 14 Apr. 1976 estimated by the police at about $6,000,000 *(then £3.4 million)* and $1 million for other items. The haul from Carrington & Co. Ltd. of Regent Street, London, on 21 Nov. 1965 was estimated to be £500,000. Jewels are believed to have constituted a major part of the Hotel Pierre "heist" on Fifth Avenue, New York City, U.S.A. on 31 Dec. 1971. An unofficial estimate ran as high as $5,000,000 *(then £2,000,000)*.

Greatest kidnapping ransom

Historically the greatest ransom paid was that for Atahualpa by the Incas to Francisco Pizarro in 1532–33 at Cajamarca, Peru which constituted a hall full of gold and silver worth in modern money some $170 million *(£95 million)*.

The greatest ransom ever reported is 1,500 m pesos *(£25,300,000)* for the release of the brothers Jorge Born, 40 and Juan Born, 39, of Bunge and Born, paid to the left wing urban guerilla group Montoneros in Buenos Aires, Argentina on 20 June 1975.

The youngest person kidnapped has been Carolyn Wharton born at 12.46 p.m. on 19 Mar. 1955 in the Baptist Hospital, Texas, U.S.A. and kidnapped, by a woman disguised as a nurse, at 1.15 p.m. aged 29 minutes.

Greatest hijack ransom

The highest amount ever paid to hijackers has been £2,000,000 in small denomination notes by the West German government to Popular Front for the Liberation of Palestine representatives 30 miles outside Beirut, Lebanon on 23 Feb. 1972. In return a Lufthansa Boeing 747, hijacked an hour out of New Delhi and bound for Athens which had been forced down at Aden, and its 14 crew members were released. The longest air piracy has been one of 8,800 miles *14 160 km* by three Filipino Moslem separatists from Southern Philippines in a BAC 111 changing to a DC8 at Bangkok and arriving at Benghazi, Libya a week later on 14 Apr. 1976.

Largest narcotics haul

The heaviest recorded haul of narcotics was made in The Bahamas on 16 Aug. 1975 when 1049 sacks of high grade Colombian marijuana was discovered with a weight of 86,280 lb 43.14 short tons *38,85 tonnes* worth an estimated $24 million. The most valuable ever haul was of 937 lb *425 kg* of pure heroin worth $106¼ million *(then £44 million)* retail seized aboard the 60 ton shrimp boat *Caprice des Temps* at Marseille, France on 28 Feb. 1972. The captain, Louis Boucan, 57, who tried to commit suicide was sentenced to 15 years on 5 Jan. 1973. Thailand's Prime Minister Gen. Kriangsak Chammanand personally ignited a 13 × 33 ft *4 × 10 m* pit containing heroin (3,585 lb. *1 625 kg*); marijuana (4,409 lb. *2 000 kg*); amphetamines (2,679 lb. *1 215 kg*) and 7,253 lb. *3 290 kg* of other drugs in Bangkok on 31 Jan. 1979. The street worth of the seizures made in 1975–78 was put at "billions of dollars".

It was revealed on 29 Apr. 1978 that 512.5 tons *529,7 tonnes* of marijuana was seized in raids on the Guajira peninsula, Colombia on 27–29 Apr. 1978. The wholesale value was estimated at $200 million *(£105 million)*.

The Home Office disclosed on 23 Dec. 1977 that 13 million LSD tablets with a street value approaching £100 million had been destroyed on the conclusion of "Operation Julie".

Largest bribe

An alleged bribe of £30,000,000 offered to Shaikh Zaid ibn Sultan of Abu Dhabi, United Arab Emirates, by a Saudi Arabian official in August 1955, is the highest on record. The affair concerned oil concessions in the disputed territory of Buraimi on the Persian Gulf.

Greatest banknote forgery

The greatest forgery was the German Third Reich government's forging operation, code name "Bernhard", engineered by SS Sturmbannfuhrer Alfred Naujocks of the Technical Dept. of the German Secret Service Amt VI F in Berlin in 1940–41. It involved £150,000,000 worth of £5 notes.

Biggest Bank fraud

The largest amount of money named in a defalcation case has been a gross £33,000,000 at the Lugano branch of Lloyd's Bank International Ltd. in Switzerland on 2 Sept. 1974. Mr. Mark Colombo was arrested pending charges including falsification of foreign currency accounts and suppression of evidence.

Computer Fraud

Between 1964 and 1973, 64,000 fake insurance policies were created on the computer of the Equity Funding Corporation involving $2,000 million.

Welfare swindle

The greatest welfare swindle yet worked was that of the gypsy Anthony Moreno on the French Social Security in Marseilles. By forging birth certificates and school registration forms, he invented 197 fictitious families and 3,000 children on which he claimed benefits from 1960 to mid-1968. Moreno, nicknamed "El Chorro" (the fountain), was last reported free of extradition worries and living in luxury in his native Spain having absquatulated with an estimated £2,300,000.

CAPITAL PUNISHMENT

Capital punishment was first abolished *de facto* in 1798 in Liechtenstein. The death penalty for murder was formally abolished in Britain on 18 Dec. 1969. Between the 5-4 Supreme Court decision against capital punishment in June 1972 and April 1975, 32 of the 50 States of the U.S.A. voted to restore it.

Capital punishment in the British Isles dates from A.D. 450, but was abolished by William I and re-imposed by Henry I, reaching a peak in the reign of Edward VI (1547–1553), when an average of 560 persons were executed annually at Tyburn alone. Even into the 19th century, there were 223 capital crimes, though people were, in practice, hanged for only 25 of these. Between 1830 and 1955 the most murderers hanged in a year was 27 (24 men, 3 women) in 1903. The least was 5 in 1854, 1921 and 1930. In 1956 there were no hangings in England, Wales or Scotland, since when the highest number in any year to 1964 was 5.

Largest hanging
The most people hanged from one gallows was 38 Sioux Indians by William J. Duly outside Mankato, Minnesota, U.S.A. for the murder of unarmed citizens on 26 Dec. 1862.

Last hangings
The last public execution in England took place outside Newgate Prison, London at 8 a.m. on 26 May 1868, when Michael Barrett was hanged for his part in the Fenian bomb outrage on 13 Dec. 1867, when 12 were killed outside the Clerkenwell House of Detention, London. The earliest non-public execution was of the murderer Thomas Wells on 13 Aug. 1868. The last public hanging in Scotland was that of the murderer Joe Bell in Perth in 1866. The last in the United States occurred at Owensboro, Kentucky in 1936. The last hangings in the United Kingdom were those of Peter Anthony Allen (b. 4 Apr. 1943) at Walton Prison, Liverpool, and John Robson Walby (b. 1 Apr. 1940), *alias* Gwynne Owen Evans, at Strangeways Gaol, Manchester both on 13 Aug. 1964. They had been found guilty of the capital murder of John Alan West, on 7 Apr. 1964. The 14th and last woman executed this century was Mrs. Ruth Ellis (*née* Neilson), 28, for the murder of David Blakely, 25, shot outside the Magdala, Hampstead, on 10 Apr. 1955. She was executed on 13 July at Holloway.

Last from yard-arm
The last naval execution at the yard-arm was the hanging of Private John Dalliger, Royal Marines, aboard H.M.S. *Leven* in the River Yangtze, China, on 13 July 1860. Dalliger had been found guilty of two attempted murders.

Youngest
Although the hanging of persons under 18 was expressly excluded only in the Children's and Young Person's Act, 1933 (Sec. 33), no person under that age was, in fact executed more recently than 1887. The lowest satisfactorily recorded age was of a boy aged 8 "who had malice, cunning and revenge" in firing two barns and who was hanged at Abingdon, Oxfordshire in the 17th century. The youngest persons hanged since 1900 have been 18 years old, the most recent of whom was Francis Robert George ("Flossie") Forsyth on 10 Nov. 1960.

Oldest
The oldest person hanged in the United Kingdom since 1900 was a man of 71 named Charles Frembd (*sic*) at Chelmsford Gaol on 4 Nov. 1914, for the murder of his wife at Leytonstone, Waltham Forest, Greater London. In 1822 John Smith, said to be 80, of Greenwich, Greater London, was hanged for the murder of a woman.

Last public guillotining
The last person to be publicly guillotined in France was the murderer Eugen Weidmann before a large crowd at Versailles, near Paris, at 4.50 a.m. on 17 June 1939. In January 1978 Marcel Chevalier was nominated to succeed his uncle Andre Obrecht as executioner who had in turn succeeded his uncle Henri Desfourneaux. Dr. Joseph Ignace Guillotin (1738–1812) died a natural death. He had advocated the use of the machine designed by Dr. Antoine Louis in 1789 in the French constituent assembly.

Death Row Longest Stay
The longest stay on "death row" in the United States has been one of more than 14 years by Edgar Labat, aged 44, and Clifton A. Paret, aged 38, in Angola Penitentiary, Louisiana, U.S.A. In March 1953 they were sentenced to death, after being found guilty of rape in 1950. They were released on 5 May 1967, only to be immediately re-arrested on a local jury indictment arising from the original charge. Caryl Whittier Chessman, aged 38 and convicted of 17 felonies, was executed on 2 May 1960 in the gas chamber at the California State Prison, San Quentin, California, U.S.A. In 11 years 10 months and one week on "death row", Chessman had won eight stays. John Spenkelink, 30, was the first to be electrocuted since 1967 at Railford Jail, Florida on 25 May 1979.

Executioner
The longest period of office of a Public Executioner was that of William Calcraft (1800–1879), who was in action from 1828 to 25 May 1874 and officiated at nearly every hanging outside and later inside Newgate Prison, London. On 2 Apr. 1868 he hanged the murdress Mrs. Frances Kidder, 25 outside Maidstone Jail, Kent—the last public execution of a woman.

Albert Pierrepoint officiated at the execution of 433 men and 17 women during his career.

Lynching
The worst year in the 20th century for lynchings in the United States has been 1901, with 130 lynchings (105 Negroes, 25 Whites), while the first year with no reported cases was 1952. The last lynching recorded in Britain was that of Panglam Godolan, a suspected murderer, in London on 27 Oct. 1958. The last case previous to this was of a kidnapping suspect in Glasgow in 1922.

Corporal Punishment
The last use of corporal punishment in one of H.M. Prisons was on 26 June 1962 and it was abolished in the United Kingdom by the Criminal Justice Act, 1967. The treadmill which 14 prisons operated in 1878 was finally suspended on 1 Apr. 1902. Men on the 36 man wheel at Northallerton, Yorkshire raised themselves 9,639 ft *2 937 m* in an 8 hour day.

PRISON SENTENCES
Longest sentences *World*
The longest recorded prison sentence is one of 7,109 years awarded to a pair of confidence tricksters by an Iranian court on 15 June 1969. The duration of sentences are proportional to the amount of the defalcations involved. A sentence of 384,912 years was demanded at the prosecution of Gabriel March Grandos, 22, at Palma de Mallorca, Spain on 11 Mar. 1972 for failing to deliver 42,768 letters.

Juan Corona, a Mexican-American was sentenced to 25 consecutive life terms, for murdering 25 farm workers in 1970–71 around Feather River, Yuba City, California, at Fairfield on 5 Feb. 1973. His U.S. 20th century record for victims was surpassed with the discovery on 13 Aug. 1973 of the body of the 27th victim of the pervert Dean Corll, 33, of Houston, Texas.

United Kingdom
Robert Bates, 30, received 16 life sentences for his part in the Shankill butcher's murders of 1975–77 in Belfast from Mr. Justice O'Driscoll on 20 Feb. 1979. It was recommended that he be held for the "rest of his life".

The longest single period served by a reprieved murderer in Great Britain this century was 40 years 11 months by John Watson Laurie, the Goat Fell or Arran murderer, who was reprieved on the grounds of insanity in November 1889 and who died in Perth Penitentiary on 4 Oct. 1930.

The longest specific minimum period recommended by a judge under the Murder (Abolition of Death Penalty) Act 1965 has been 35 years in the case of Patrick Armstrong and Michael Hill on 22 Oct. 1975 for pub bombings (7 killed, 99 injured) at Guildford and Woolwich in 1974.

The longest prison sentence ever passed under British law was one of three consecutive and two concurrent terms of 14 years, thus totalling 42 years, imposed on 3 May 1961 on George Blake *né* Behar (b. Rotterdam, 11 Nov. 1922), for treachery. Blake, formerly U.K. vice–consul in Seoul, South Korea, had been converted to Communism during 34 months' internment there from 2 July 1950 to April 1953. It had been alleged that his betrayals may have cost the lives of up to 42 British agents. He was "sprung" from Wormwood Scrubs Prison, Greater London, on 22 Oct. 1966.

The longest single sentence passed on a woman under English law was 20 years for Mrs. Lona Teresa Cohen née Petra (b. 1913) at the Old Bailey, City of London on 2 Mar. 1961 for conspiring to commit a breach of the Official Secrets Act, 1911. The sentence of this K.G.B. agent was remitted by the Foreign Secretary on no known lawful authority on 24 July 1969. Ward (see Most Prolific Murderers) was sentenced to 20 years for a single offence and an aggregate 30 years on 4 Nov. 1974.

Longest Time Served

Paul Geidel, a prisoner in New York State, overtook the 66 year 11 month total of time served by Johnson VanDyke Grigsby (1908–74 plus 7 months in 1976), in August 1977. Geidel was still serving in April 1979.

Longest in Broadmoor

The longest period for which any person has been detained in the Broadmoor hospital for the criminally insane, near Crowthorne, Berkshire, is 76 years in the case of William Giles. He was admitted as an insane arsonist at the age of 11 and died there on 10 Mar. 1962, at the age of 87.

The longest escape from Broadmoor was one of 39 years by the Liverpool wife murderer James Kelly, who got away on 28 Jan. 1888, using a pass key made from a corset spring. After an adventurous life in Paris, in New York and at sea he returned in April 1927, to ask for re-admission. After some difficulties this was arranged. He died in 1930.

Most Appearances

There are no collected records on the greatest number of convictions on an individual but the highest recently reported is 1,433 for the gentlemanly but alcoholic Edward Eugene Ebzery, who died in Brisbane Jail, Queensland, Australia on 23 Sept. 1967.

Greatest mass arrest

The greatest mass arrest in the United Kingdom occurred on 17 Sept. 1961, when 1,314 demonstrators supporting the unilateral nuclear disarmament of the United Kingdom were arrested for wilfully disregarding the directions of the police and thereby obstructing highways leading to Parliament Square, London, by sitting down. As a consequence of the 1926 General Strike there were 3,149 prosecutions: incitement (1,760) and violence (1,389).

FINES

Heaviest *World*

It was reported in January 1979 that Carlo Ponti, husband of Sophia Loren, was to be fined the equivalent of $26.4 million by the Italian courts in connection with claims for tax alleged to be unpaid.

U.K.

The heaviest fine ever imposed in the United Kingdom was one of £277,500, plus £3,717 costs, on I. Hennig & Co. Ltd., the London diamond merchants, at Clerkenwell Magistrates' Court, London, on 14 Dec. 1949. The amount was later reduced on appeal.

Rarest prosecution

There are a number of crimes in English law for which there have never been prosecutions. Among unique prosecutions are *Rex v. Crook* in 1662 for the praemunire of disputing the King's title and *Rex v. Gregory* for selling honours under the Honours (Prevention of Abuses) Act, 1924, on 18 Feb. 1933. John Maundy Gregory (d. 3 Oct. 1941 in France as "Sir" "Arthur" Gregory) was an honours broker during 6 administrations from 1919 to 1932 and was sentenced to two months in Wormwood Scrubs, London.

PRISONS

Largest *World*

The largest prison in the world is Kharkov Prison, in the U.S.S.R., which has at times accommodated 40,000 prisoners.

Great Britain

The largest prison in Great Britain is Wormwood Scrubs, West London, with 1,208 cells. The highest prison walls in Great Britain are those of Lancaster Prison measuring 36 to 52 ft *11–15,85 m.*

The largest prison in Scotland in Barlinnie, Glasgow, with 753 single cells. Ireland's largest prison is Mountjoy Prison, Dublin, with 808 cells.

Penal camps

The largest penal camp systems in the world were those near Karaganda and Kolyma, in the U.S.S.R., each with a population estimated in 1958 at between 1,200,000 and 1,500,000. The largest labour camp is now said to be the Dubrovlag Complex of 15 camps centred on Pot'ma, Mordovian S.S.R. The official N.A.T.O. estimate for all Soviet camps was "more than one million" in March 1960 compared with a peak of probably 12 million during the Stalinist era.

Devil's Island

The largest French penal settlement was that of St. Laurent du Maroni, which comprised the notorious Îles du Diable, Royale and St. Joseph (for incorrigibles) off the coast of French Guiana, in South America. It remained in operation for 99 years from 1854 until the last group of repatriated prisoners, including Théodore Rouselle, who had served 50 years, was returned to Bordeaux on 22 Aug. 1953. It has been estimated that barely 2,000 *bagnard* (ex-convicts) of the 70,000 deportees ever returned. These, however, include the executioner Ladurelle (imprisoned 1921—37), who was murdered in Paris in 1938.

Highest population

The peak prison population, including Borstals and detention centres, for England and Wales was the figure for Oct. 1976 with 42,419. In Scotland the prison population record was 5,400 in 1972 and in Northern Ireland 2,934 on 16 Nov. 1975.

Most secure prison

After it became a maximum security Federal prison in 1934, no convict was known to have lived to tell of a successful escape from the prison of Alcatraz Island in San Francisco Bay, California, U.S.A. A total of 23 men attempted it but 12 were recaptured, 5 shot dead, one drowned and 5 presumed drowned. On 16 Dec. 1962, just before the prison was closed on 21 Mar. 1963 one man reached the mainland alive, only to be recaptured on the spot. John Chase held the record with 26 years there.

Most Expensive Prison

Spandau Prison, Berlin built 100 years ago for 600 prisoners is now used solely for the Nazi war criminal Rudolf Hess (b. 26 Apr. 1894). The cost of maintenance of the staff of 105 has been estimated at $415,000 (£245,000) per annum.

Longest Escape

The longest recorded escape by a recaptured prisoner was that of Leonard T. Fristoe, 77, who escaped from Nevada State Prison, U.S.A., on 15 Dec. 1923 and was turned in by his son on 15 Nov. 1969 at Compton, California. He had had 46 years of freedom under the name Claude R. Willis. He had killed two sheriff's deputies in 1920. The longest period of freedom achieved by a British gaol breaker is more than 22 years by Irish-born John Patrick Hannan, who escaped from Verne Open Prison at Portland, Dorset, on 22 Dec. 1955 and was still at large in June 1979. He had served only 1 month of a 21-month term for car-stealing and assaulting two policemen.

Greatest gaol break

In February 1979 a retired U.S. Army Colonel Arthur 'Bull' Simons led a band of 14 to break into Gasre prison, Tehran, Iran to rescue two fellow Americans. Some 11,000 other prisoners took advantage of this and the Islamic revolution in history's largest gaol break.

In July 1971, Raoul Sendic and 105 other Tupamaro guerrillas escaped from a Uruguayan prison through a tunnel 91 m *298 ft* long.

The greatest gaol break in Britain was that from Brixton Prison, Lambeth, Greater London on 30 May 1973 when 20 men got out using a rubbish tipping lorry as a battering ram. Eighteen were captured immediately and one other 5 weeks later, nine staff were injured.

6. ECONOMIC

MONETARY AND FINANCE

Largest budget *World*
The greatest annual expenditure budgeted by any country has been $500,200 million (*£250,100 million*) by the United States government for the fiscal year ending 30 Sept. 1979. The highest budgeted revenue in the United States has been $439,600 million (*£219,800 million*) for 1978–79.

In the United States, the greatest surplus was $8,419,469,844 in 1947–48, and the greatest budgeted deficit was $61,800,000 (*£30,900 million*) in 1978–79.

Largest budget *Great Britain*
The greatest budgeted current expenditure of Great Britain has been £69,375 million for the fiscal year 1979–80. The highest budgeted current receipts has been £66,818 million after the budget changes of 12 June 1979.

Foreign aid
The total net foreign aid given by the United States government between 1 July 1945 and 1 Jan. 1978 was $177,681 million. The country which received most U.S. aid in 1977 was Israel with $1,476 million U.S. foreign aid began with $50,000 to Venezuela for earthquake relief in 1812.

Least taxed
The lowest income taxed nations in the world include Bahrain, Kuwait and Qatar where the rate regardless of income is nil.

There is no income tax paid by residents on Lundy Island off North Devon, England. This 1,062.4 acre *429,9 ha* island issued its own unofficial currency of Puffins and Half Puffins between the Wars for which offence the owner was prosecuted.

Highest Taxation Rates
The country with the most confiscatory taxation is Norway where in January 1974 the Labour Party and Socialist Alliance abolished the 80 per cent limit so that some 2,000 citizens were listed in the *Lignings Boka* as paying more than 100 per cent of their taxable income. The shipping magnate Hilmer Reksten was assessed at 491 per cent. In the United Kingdom the former top earned and unearned rates of 83 per cent and 98 per cent were reduced to 60 per cent and 75 per cent in the budget of 12 June 1979. The all-time record ruled in 1967–68, when a "special charge" of up to 9s. (45p) in the £ additional to surtax brought the top rate to 27s 3d. (or 136%) in the £ on investment income.

Highest and lowest rates in Great Britain
Income tax was first introduced in Great Britain in 1799 for incomes above £60 per annum. It was discontinued in 1815, only to be re-introduced in 1842 at the rate of 7d. (3p) in the £. It was at its lowest at 2d. (0.83p) in the £ in 1875, gradually climbing to 1s. 3d. (6p) by 1913. From April 1941 until 1946 the record peak of 10s. (50p) in the £ was maintained to assist in financing of World War II.

National Debt
The largest national debt of any country in the world is that of the United States, where the gross federal public debt of the Federal Government surpassed the "half trillion" dollar mark in 1975 and reached $721,800 million (*£379,800 million*) by 1 Jan. 1978. This amount in dollar bills would make a pile 39,166 miles *63 031 km* high, weighing 548,699 tons *557 661 tonnes*.

The National Debt in Great Britain was less than £1 million during the reign of James II in 1687. It was £86,974 million or £1,557 per person at 31 Mar. 1979. This amount placed in a pile of brand new £1 notes would be 5,300.0 miles *8 529 km* in height.

Gross National Product
The country with the largest Gross National Product is the United States running at $1,965,100 million at 1 Jan. 1978. The G.N.P. of the United Kingdom at factor cost was £141,292 million for 1978.

National Wealth
The richest nation, measured by average per capita is Abu Dhabi with $70,000 (US) (*£41,175*) in 1976. The U.S.A. which took the lead in 1910 is now (1977) third behind Sweden ($9,030 per head) and Switzerland. The United Kingdom stands 20th with $3,455 (*£2,032*) per head. It has been estimated that the value of all physical assets in the U.S.A. in 1976 was $6·2 trillion ($10^{12}$) or $28,800 (*£16,950*) per head. The figure for private wealth in the United Kingdom was £325,000 million (1976) or £5,811 per head.

Biggest Savers
The worlds' top savers are the Swiss with deposits averaging $11,225 per head.

Poorest Country
The lowest published annual income per caput of any country in the world is Rwanda, with $70 (*£41*).

Gold Reserves *World*
The country with the greatest monetary gold reserve is West Germany, whose Treasury had $38,000 million (*then £19,000 million*) on hand in February 1979. The United States Bullion Depository at Fort Knox, 30 miles *48 km* south-west of Louisville, Kentucky, U.S.A. is the principal Federal depository of U.S. gold. Gold is stored in standard mint bars of 400 troy ounces *12,441 kg* measuring 7 by 3⅝ by 1⅝ in, *17,7 × 9,2 × 4,1 cm* and each worth $16,888.

The greatest accumulation of the world's central banks' $50,000 million of gold bullion is now in the Federal Reserve Bank at 33 Liberty Street, New York City, N.Y., U.S.A. Some $17,000 million or 14,000 tons is stored 85 ft *25,90 m* below street level, in a vault 50 ft *15,24 m* by 100 ft *30,48 m* behind a steel door weighing 89 tons/*tonnes*.

Gold and Foreign Currency Reserves *Great Britain*
The lowest published figure for the sterling area's gold and convertible currency reserves was $298,000,000 (*then £74 million*) on 31 Dec. 1940. The valuation on 1 Apr. 1979 was a peak $21,467 million of which $1,027 million was in gold.

Minimum Lending Rate
The highest ever figure for the British bank rate (since 13 Oct. 1972, the Minimum Lending Rate) has been 15% from 7 Oct. to 19 Nov. 1976. The longest period without a change was the 12 years 13 days from 26 Oct. 1939 to 7 Nov. 1951, during which time the rate stayed at 2 per cent. This record low rate was first attained on 22 Apr. 1852.

Balance of Payments
The most unfavourable current balance of payments figure for the United Kingdom has been a deficit of £3,591 million in 1974. The 4th quarter of 1978–79 was the worst with £1,360 million. The greatest surplus for a quarter has been £522 million for the 3rd quarter of 1977. Monthly figures are regarded as too erratic to be significant.

Worst Inflation *World*
The world's worst inflation occurred in Hungary in June 1946, when the 1931 gold pengö was valued at 130 trillion ($1.3 × 10^{20}$) paper pengös. Notes were issued for szazmillio billion (100 trillion or 10^{20}) pengös on 3 June and withdrawn on 11 July 1946. Notes for 1,000 trillion or 10^{21} pengös were printed but not circulated. On 6 Nov. 1923 the circulation of Reichsbank marks reached 400,338,326,350,700,000,000 and inflation 755,700 million fold 1913 levels.

The 1977 Bahamian $2,500 gold coin which contains 1 lb. troy or *435,4 g* of 22 carat gold. (*Royal Canadian Mint*)

Worst Inflation *Great Britain*
The United Kingdom's worst rate in a year has been for Aug. 1974 to Aug. 1975 when inflation ran at a rate of 26.9% compared with 10.1% from May 1978 to May 1979. At a sustained 20% inflation rate the £ would be worth 1p (1977 value) sometime during the year 2002—only 27 years hence.

PAPER MONEY
Earliest
Paper money is an invention of the Chinese first tried in A.D. 910 and prevalent by A.D. 970. The world's earliest bank notes (*banco-sedlar*) were issued in Stockholm, Sweden, in July 1661. The oldest surviving banknote is one for 5 dalers dated 6 Dec. 1662. The oldest surviving printed Bank of England note is one for £555 to bearer, dated 19 Dec. 1699 (4½ × 7½ in, *11,4 × 19,6 cm*).

Largest and smallest
The largest paper money ever issued was the one kwan note of the Chinese Ming dynasty issue of 1368–99, which measured 9 by 13 in *22,8 × 33,0 cm*. The smallest bank note ever issued was the 10 bani note of the Ministry of Finance of Romania, issued in 1917. It measured (printed area) 27,5 × 38 mm *1.09 × 1.49 in.*

Highest denominations *World*
The highest denomination notes in circulation are U.S. Federal Reserve Bank notes for $10,000 (£5,260). They bear the head of Salmon Portland Chase (1808–73). None has been printed since July 1944 and the U.S. Treasury announced in 1969 that no further notes higher than $100 would be issued. Only some 400 $10,000 bills remain in circulation.

Great Britain
Two Bank of England notes for £1,000,000 still exist, dated before 1812, but these were used only for internal accounting. In November 1977 the existence of a Treasury £1 million note dated 30 Aug. 1948 came to light and was sold by private treaty for $A18,500 (*then £11,300*) in Australia.

The highest issued denominations were £1,000 notes, first printed in 1725, discontinued on 22 Apr. 1943 and withdrawn on 30 April 1945. A total of 62 of these notes were still unretired up to May 1973 (last data to be published). Of these only 4 are known to be in the hands of collectors.

Lowest denomination *World*
The lowest denomination banknote issued is the 1 cent Hong Kong note which is worth 1/12th of one new penny.

Great Britain
The lowest denomination Bank of England notes ever printed were half-crown (now 12½p) black on pale blue notes in 1941, signed by K. O. Peppiatt. Very few examples have survived and they are now valued at from £750.

Highest circulation
The highest ever Bank of England note circulation in the United Kingdom was £9,306 million in Dec. 1978—equivalent to a pile of £1 notes 462.54 miles *744,39 km* high.

CHEQUES
Largest *World*
The greatest amount paid by a single cheque in the history of banking has been one for Rs. 16,640,000,000 equivalent to £852,791,660 handed over by Hon. Daniel P. Moynihan, Ambassador of the U.S.A. to India in New Delhi on 18 Feb. 1974. An internal U.S. Treasury check for $4,176,969,623.57 was drawn on 30 June 1954.

Largest *Great Britain*
The largest cheque drawn in Britain was one for £119,595,645, drawn on 24 Jan. 1961 by Lazard Brothers & Co. Ltd., and payable to the National Provincial Bank, in connection with the takeover of the British Ford Motor Company.

COINS
Oldest *World*
The earliest certainly dated coins are the electrum (alloy of gold and silver) staters of Lydia, in Asia Minor (now Turkey), which were coined in the reign of King Gyges (*c.* 685–652 B.C.). Primitive uninscribed "spade" money of the Chou dynasty of China is now *believed* to date from *c.* 770 B.C. A discovery at Tappeh Nush-i-jan, Iran of silver ingot currency in 1972 has been dated to as early as 760 B.C. The earliest dated coin is the Danish coin of the Bishop of Roskilde dated MCCXXXIIII (1234) of which 6 are known. Laos is the only country today without coins.

Oldest *Great Britain*
The earliest coins to circulate in Britain were Gallo-Belgic gold imitations of the Macedonian staters of Philip II (359–336 B.C.). The Bellovaci type has been tentatively dated *c.* 130 B.C. The earliest date attributed to coins minted *in* Britain is *c.* 95 B.C. for the Westerham type gold stater of which 51 examples are known.

Heaviest
A Swedish 10 daler copper plate of 1644 attained a weight of 43 lb 7¼ oz. *19,710 kg.* Of primitive exchange tokens, the most massive are the holed stone discs, or *Fé*, from the Yap Islands, in the western Pacific Ocean, with diameters of up to 12 ft *3,65 m* and weighing up to 185 lb. *84 kg.* A medium-sized one was worth one Yapese wife or an 18 ft *5,18 m* canoe.

Smallest
The smallest coins in the world have been the Nepalese ¼ dam or Jawa struck *c.* 1740 in silver in the reign of Jeya Prakash Malla. The Jawa of between 0.008 and 0.014 g measuring about 2 × 2 mm were sometimes cut into ½ and even ¼ Jawa of 0.002 g or 14,000 to the oz.

Highest denomination *World*
The 1654 Indian gold 200 Mohur (£500) coin of the Mughal Emperor Khurram Shihāb-ud-dīn Muhammad, Shāh Jahān (reigned 1628–57), had the greatest intrinsic worth ever struck. It weighed 2 177 g *70 troy oz.* and hence has an intrinsic worth of £2,800. It had a diameter of 5⅜ in *136 mm*. The only known example disappeared in Patna, Bihar, India, in *c.* 1820, but a plastercast of this coin exists in the British Museum, London. Currently the highest denomination is the Bahamian $2500 1977 gold coin 72 mm *2.8 in* in diameter struck by the Royal Canadian Mint, Ottawa. Each of the 250 examples struck contain 1 lb troy *435,4 g* of 22 carat gold.

Highest denomination *Great Britain*
Gold five-guinea pieces were minted from the reign of Charles II (1660–1685) until 1753 in the reign of George II. A pattern 5 guinea piece of George III dated 1777 also exists.

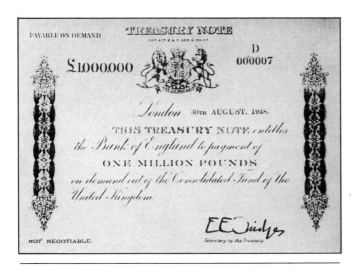

A £1,000,000 Treasury note used in connection with intra-governmental Marshall Aid payments in 1948 (see p. 196).

Lowest denomination *Great Britain*

Quarter farthings (sixteen to the penny) were struck in copper at the Royal Mint, London, in the Imperial coinage for use in Sri Lanka (then Ceylon), in 1839 and 1851–53.

Rarest *World*

There are numerous coins of which but a single example is known. An example of a unique coin of threefold rarity (in alloy, denomination and reign) is one of the rare admixture of bronze with inlaid gold of Kaleb I of Axum (*c.* A.D. 500). Only 700 Axumite coins of any sort are known.

Rarest *Modern British*

Single examples of a Victoria farthing of 1889, a George VI half-crown of 1952 and an Elizabeth II penny of 1954 are known. The penny was sold privately in March 1978 for £23,000.

Most expensive *World*

The highest price paid at auction for a single coin is $272,000 (*then £113,000*) or $314,000 inclusive of commission for an Athenian silver decadrachm in Zurich, Switzerland on 28 May 1974 by Constantinople Fine Arts Inc. The unique U.S. 1907 $20 gold Double Eagle "Indian Head" pattern from the Dr. Wilkison collection was sold by private treaty by the dealer Steven C. Markoff of Beverly Hills, California for $500,000 (*£250,000*) in May 1979.

Most expensive *Great Britain*

The highest auction price paid for a British coin is $67,500 (*then £33,000*) for a James VI of Scotland £20 gold piece of 1576 at the auction of the Dundee Collection by Spink/Bowers & Ruddy in Los Angeles on 19 Feb. 1976.

An unissued silver Crown (5 shillings) piece of Edward VIII owned by Richard Lobel & Co. in London, was sold privately in February 1979 for £50,000. One example of the Edward VIII £5 gold piece is known to be in private hands in Ohio, U.S.A.

Legal tender coins *Oldest*

The oldest legal tender Imperial coins in circulation are the now rare silver shillings (now 5p) and sixpences (now 2½p) of the reign of George III, dated 1816. All gold coinage of or above the least current weight dated onward from 1838 is still legal tender. Scotland's separate coinage dated between 1135 and 1709.

Legal tender coins *Heaviest and highest denomination*

The gold five-pound (£5) piece or quintuple sovereign is both the highest current denomination coin in the United Kingdom and also, at 616.37 grains *1.4066 oz.* the heaviest. The most recent specimens made available to the public were dated 1937, of which only 5,501 were minted. (See Colour photographs 20th edition.)

Legal tender coins *Lightest and smallest*

The silver Maundy (new) penny piece is the smallest of the British legal tender coins and, at 7.27 grains (just under 1/60th of an ounce), the lightest. These coins were so used since 1670 and exist for each date since 1822 and are 0.453 in *11,5 mm* in diameter.

Greatest collection

The highest price paid for a coin collection has been $7,300,000 (*then £3,550,000*) for a hoard of 407,000 U.S. silver dollars from the La Vere Redfield estate in a courtroom auction in Reno, Nevada on 27 Jan. 1976 by Steven C. Markoff of A-Mark Coin Co. Inc. of Beverly Hills, California.

Largest Hoards

The largest hoard ever found was one of about 80,000 aurei in Brescello near Modena, Italy in 1814 believed to have been deposited *c.* 37 B.C. The numerically largest hoard ever found was the Brussels hoard of 1908 containing *c.* 150,000 coins. A hoard of 56,500 Roman coins was found at Cunetio near Marlborough, Wiltshire on 15 Oct. 1978.

It's believed that the greatest under sea recovery of treasure will be made from the wreck of the 140 ft *42,6 m* long Spanish ship "Nuestra Senora de Concepcion" which capsized off the north coast of the Dominican Republic in 1641. The first part of possibly $40 million of treasure was found by Seaquest International on 30 Nov. 1978.

Largest mint

The largest mint in the world is the U.S. Treasury's mint built in 1965–69 on Independence Mall, Philadelphia, covering 11½ acres *4,65 ha* with an annual capacity on a 3 shift seven day week production of 8,000 million coins. A single stamping machine can produce coins at a rate of 10,000 per hour.

Charity Walks

The greatest recorded amount raised by a single charity walk is HK $1.6 million (*then £188,235*) in the Hong Kong Island Walk of December 1976. The most participants on one course were 57,000 in the Kowloon Walk over 14 miles *22,5 km* on 6 Mar. 1977 in which John L. Boyer, general manager of the Hong Kong and Shanghai Bank raised HK $519,680 or £4,367 per mile.

Largest charity collection

The most valuable column of coins amassed for charity was a column of 27,530 ten pence pieces worth £2,753 "knocked over" by Richard Briers for the Handicapped Children's Aid Fund at The Gallon Pot, Great Yarmouth, Norfolk on 30 Jan. 1979. It had been collected by the landlord Gerry Firth. The *longest* line of coins laid was one of 2.36 miles *3,8 km* (200,000 coins) set down by 36 students from Villanova College, Coorparoo, Queensland, Australia on 24 Sept. 1976, to spell the word "Hunger". The highest value line was one of 10 pfg pieces valued at £2,679 laid by the Royal Army Dental Corps in Hameln, West Germany on 3 Sept. 1977.

LABOUR

Trade Union Oldest *Great Britain*

The oldest of the 150 trade unions affiliated to the Trades Union Congress (founded 1868) is the National Society of Brushmakers and General Workers (current membership 1,547) founded in 1747.

Trade Union Largest *World*

The world's largest union is the Industrie-Gewerkschaft Metall (Metal Workers' Union) of West Germany, with a membership of 2,695,312 on 1 Jan. 1979. The union with the longest name is probably the International Association of Marble, Slate and Stone Polishers, Rubbers and Sawyers, Tile and Marble Setters' Helpers and Marble Mosaic and Terrazzo Worker's Helpers of Washington D.C., U.S.A.

Trade Union Largest *Great Britain*

The largest union in the United Kingdom is the Transport and General Workers' Union, with 2,083,959 members at 1 Apr. 1979.

CONSUMPTION

Of all the countries in the world, based on the latest available data, Belgium–Luxembourg has the largest available total of calories per person. The net supply averaged 3645 per day in 1974. The United Kingdom average was 3349 per day in 1974. The lowest *reported* supply figures are 1728 calories per day in Upper Volta in 1974. It has been estimated that Britons eat 7¼ times their own weight in food per annum or 70,000 tons/*tonnes* per day. The highest calorific value of any foodstuff is that of pure animal fat with 930 calories per 100 g *3.5 oz.* Pure alcohol provides 710 calories per 100 g.

Below: The World's greatest consumers, per head, per day.   **Figures in square brackets refer to UK consumption.**

Protein
Australia and New Zealand
106 g *3.79 oz.* (1969)
[*88 g* 3.1 oz. *(1968–9)*]

Tea[2]
Eire 0.36 oz. *10,2 g* (1977)
[*0.314 oz.* 8,9 g *(1977)*]

Cereals[1]
Egypt—600 g *21.95 oz.*
(1966–7) [*7.14 oz.* 202 g
(1977)]

Coffee[3]
Sweden—21,78 g *0.76 oz.*
(1978) [*3,28 g* 0.11 oz.
(1978)]

Sugars
Bulgaria—177 g *6.26 oz.*
(1977) [*4.1 oz.* 116 g
(1977)]

Fresh Water
United States—1,544 gal
7021 l (1974)

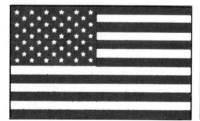

Meat
U.S.—308 g *10.89 oz.*
(1977) [*193 g* 6.8 oz
(1977)]

Beer
W. Germany—41,3 cl
0.716 pints (1977)
[*0.575 pints* 32,5 cl *(1977)*]

Sweets
Britain—1.11 oz. *31,58 g*
(1971)

Wine
France 27,6 cl *0.486 pints*
(1977) [*1,4 cl* 0.026 pints
(1977)]

Spirits
Poland 1,5 cl *0.027 pints*
(1977) [*0.006 pt* 0,34 cl
(1977)]

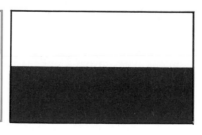

[1] Figures for 1977 from China suggest a possible consumption (including rice) of 890 g 31.3 oz.

[2] The most expensive tea marketed in the U.K. is "Oolong Leaf Bud", specially imported for Fortnum & Mason of Piccadilly, City of Westminster, Greater London. In June 1979 it retailed for £15.20 per lb. or *£3.35/100 g.* It is blended from very young Formosan leaves.

[3] The most expensive coffee in the U.S. is Jamaican High Mountain Supreme which retails for $4.98 per lb *$11 per kg.*

Trade Union Smallest

The smallest T.U.C. affiliated union is the Wool Shear Workers' Trade Union of Sheffield with a membership of 32. The unaffiliated London Handforged Spoon and Fork Makers' Society instituted in July 1874, has a last reported membership of 6.

Labour Dispute *Earliest*

A labour dispute concerning monotony of diet and working conditions was recorded in 1153 B.C. in Thebes, Egypt. The earliest recorded strike was one by an orchestra leader from Greece named Aristos in Rome *c*. 309 B.C. The cause was meal breaks.

Labour Dispute *Largest*

The most serious single labour dispute in the United Kingdom was the General Strike of 4–12 May 1926, called by the Trades Union Congress in support of the Miners' Federation. During the nine days of the strike 1,580,000 people were involved and 14,500,000 working days were lost.

During the year 1926 a total of 2,750,000 people were involved in 323 different labour disputes and the working days lost during the year amounted to 162,300,000, the highest figure ever recorded. The figure for 1978 was 9,306,000 working days involving 939,000 workers.

Labour Dispute *Longest*

The world's longest recorded strike ended on 4 Jan. 1961, after 33 years. It concerned the employment of barbers' assistants in Copenhagen, Denmark. The longest recorded major strike was that at the plumbing fixtures factory of the Kohler Co. in Sheboygan, Wisconsin, U.S.A., between April 1954 and October 1962. The strike is alleged to have cost the United Automobile Workers' Union about $12,000,000 (£4.8 million) to sustain.

Longest Dispatch to Coventry

The longest recorded instance of a worker being "sent to Coventry" by his fellow workers is 4 years 11 months endured by Mr. Tommy Seddon of Droylsden, Greater Manchester from 9 Dec. 1970 until 7 Nov. 1975 at the Wellman Gas Engineering Co.

Unemployment *Highest*

The highest recorded unemployment in Great Britain was on 23 Jan. 1933, when the total of unemployed persons on the Employment Exchange registers was 2,903,065, representing 22.8 per cent of the insured working population. The highest figure for Wales was 244,579 (39.1 per cent) on 22 Aug. 1932.

Unemployment *Lowest*

In Switzerland in December 1973 (pop. 6.6 million), the total number of unemployed was reported to be 81. The lowest recorded peace-time level of unemployment in Britain was 0.9 per cent on 11 July 1955, when 184,929 persons were registered. The peak figure for the total working population in the United Kingdom has been 26,543,000 in September 1977.

Association *Largest*

The largest single association in the world is the Blue Cross system, the U.S.-based hospital insurance organization with a membership of 83,256,601 on 1 Jan. 1979. Benefits paid out in 1978 totalled $15,720,022,000 (£7,860 million). The largest association in the United Kingdom is the Automobile Association (formed 1905) with a membership which reached 5,289,758 on 1 Jan. 1979.

Oldest Club

Britain's oldest club is White's, St. James', London opened *c*. 1697 by Francis White (d. 1711) and moved to its present site in 1755.

CONSUMPTION
Prohibition

The longest lasting imposition of prohibition has been 26 years in Iceland (1908–34). Other prohibitions have been Russia, later U.S.S.R. (1914–24) and U.S.A. (1920–33). The Faroe Islands have had a public (as opposed to private licensed) prohibition since 1918. By way of contrast the Northern Territory of Australia's annual intake has been estimated to be as high as 416 pints *236 litres* per person. A society for the prevention of alcoholism in Darwin had to disband in June 1966 for lack of support.

Biggest round

The largest round of drinks ever recorded was one for 1,222 people stood by the *Sunday Sun* and shouted by Jack Amos in Newcastle upon Tyne, England in October 1974 at the conclusion of the Jack o' Clubs road show.

Largest dish

The largest menu item in the world is roasted camel, prepared occasionally for Bedouin wedding feasts. Cooked eggs are stuffed in fish, the fish stuffed in cooked chickens, the chickens stuffed into a roasted sheep carcass and the sheep stuffed into a whole camel.

Most expensive food

The most expensive non-seasonal food is white truffle of Alba which fetch, according to seasonal rarity, up to $200 per lb. *$440 or £250 per kg* on the U.S. market. Truffles from oak roots in the Périgord district of France require drought between mid-July and mid-August. Only 7 of Europe's 70 species of this hypogeous mycorrhizal fungus are considered edible.

Longest banana split

The longest Banana split ever made was one of 1 700 m *1 mile 99 yds* in length embracing 11,333 bananas; 34,000 scoops of ice cream; 260 gal *1 181 litres* of topping, 160 lb. *72,59 kg* of chopped nuts and 100 gal *453 litres* of whipped cream at the annual fete of the Cleveland State High School, Queensland, Australia on 20 Nov. 1976.

Largest Barbecue

The most monumental spit roast has been one for over 4,000 people at Brisbane, California on 16 Sept. 1973 with a rotisserie with 12 ft *3,65 m* spit length impaling 7 buffalo with a dressed weight of 3,755 lb. *1 703 kg*. John De Marco supervised the 26 hour roast. The 1977 annual Lancaster Sertoma in Pennsylvania, U.S.A. served 18,500 barbecued chickens.

Largest beefburger

The largest beefburger on record is one of 2,859 lb. *1 293 kg* 27½ ft *8,38 m* in circumference exhibited by Tip Top Butchers and Noonan's Bakery Pty. Ltd. at the Perth Royal Show, Western Australia on 24 Sept. 1975.

Largest cake

The largest cake ever assembled was the Baltimore City Bicentennial Cake on 4 July 1976 with ingredients weighing 69,860 lb. or 31.18 tons *31,69 tonnes*. An estimated 10,000 dozen eggs, 21,600 lb. *9 797 kg* of sugar and a 415 lb. *188 kg* pinch of salt were used. The tallest recorded free-standing wedding cake was one of 39 tiers 23 ft 7 in *7,18 m* tall baked and constructed by Mrs. Rhoda Murray and Roy Butterworth on 20 Oct. 1978 in the Halifax Shopping Centre, Halifax, Nova Scotia, Canada.

Largest Easter egg

The largest Easter egg ever made was one weighing 4,484 lb. *2,035 tonnes*, measuring 10 ft 2½ in *3,11 m* high and 24 ft 9 in *7,54 m* in circumference made in Melbourne, Australia on 2–16 Mar. 1978 by Red Tulip Chocolates Pty. Ltd. of Prahran Victoria.

Largest haggis

The largest haggis (encased in 4 ox stomach linings) on record was one weighing 328 lb. *148,77 kg* for Wm. Low & Co. Ltd. (Supermarkets) of Dundee, Scotland by David A. Hall Ltd. of Broxburn. The cooking time was 11 hours.

Longest loaf

The longest one-piece loaf ever baked was one of 684 ft 6 in *208,6 m* baked at Buttercup Bakeries, Unanderra, N.S.W., Australia on 22 July 1978 and sold to the public by the Apex Club of Corrimal.

Largest apple pie

The largest apple pie ever baked was that in a 16 ft 8 in *5,08 m* diameter dish at the Orleans Country Fair, New York State, U.S.A. on 2–3 Aug. 1977. Baking time of the 300 bushels of apples, 5,950 lb. *2,698 tonnes* of sugar was 4 hrs 40 mins. The total weight was 21,210 lb. *9,62 tonnes.*

Largest cherry pie

The largest cherry pie ever made was one weighing a total of 6¼ tons *6 350 kg* and containing 4,950 lb. *2 245 kg* of cherries. It measured 14 ft 4 in *4,36 m* in diameter, 24 in *60,96 cm* in depth, and was baked in the grounds of the Medusa Cement Corporation, Charlevoix, Michigan on 15 May 1976, as part of the town's contribution to America's Bicentennial celebrations.

Largest meat pie

The largest meat pie ever baked weighed 5¾ tons, measuring 18 × 6 ft and 18 in deep *5,48 × 1,83 × 0,45 m*, the eighth in the series of Denby Dale, West Yorkshire pies, to mark four royal births, baked on 5 Sept. 1964. The first was in 1788 to celebrate King George III's return to sanity but the fourth (Queen Victoria's Jubilee, 1887) went a bit "off" and had to be buried in quick-lime.

Largest mince pie

The largest mince pie recorded was one of 2,260 lb. *1 025 kg* 20 × 5 ft *6,09 × 1,52 m*, baked at Ashby-de-la-Zouch, Leicestershire on 15 Oct. 1932.

Largest omelette

The largest verified omelette in the world was one made of 11,145 eggs on a 10 ft *3,048 m* diameter frying pan over a 12 ft *3,65 m* diameter gas ring with 15 litres *3.29 galls* of oil by the Bradford Junior Chamber of Commerce involving 21 chefs cooking for 75 mins on 23 June 1979 at the Civic Precinct, Bradford.

Largest pancake

This category is now discontinued
The largest pancake ever flipped intact on any griddle was one of 12 ft *3,65 m* diameter by the Liberal Jayees at Liberal, Kansas, U.S.A. on 9 Feb. 1975.

Largest pizza pie

The largest pizza ever baked was one measuring 80 ft 1 in *24,4 m* in diameter, hence 5027 ft² *467 m²* in area and 18 664 lb. *8 465 kg* in weight at the Oma Pizza Restaurant, Glen Falls, New York, U.S.A. owned by Lorenzo Amato on 8 Oct. 1978. It was cut into 60,318 slices.

Largest Iced Lollipop

The world's largest iced lollipop was one of 5,750 lb. *2 608 kg* constructed for the Westside Assembly of God Church, Davenport, Iowa, U.S.A. on 7 Sept. 1975.

Blackpool rock

The mightiest piece of Blackpool lettered rock ever produced was a piece weighing more than 3 cwt *152 kg* delivered on 16 Apr. 1975 to the Royal Variety Club of Great Britain in London by Ashton Candy Co. Ltd. of Blackpool.

Largest salami

The largest salami on record was one of 18 ft 10 in *5,74 m* long with a circumference of 28 in *71 cm* weighing 457 lb. *207,2 kg* made by La Ron Meat Co., Cosby, Missouri, U.S.A. on 29 Jan. 1978.

Longest sausage

The longest continuous sausage ever recorded was one of 2 miles *3,21 km*, made by Dewhurst's at Thamesmead on 28 May 1979 and cooked by scouts at the Great Children's Party in Hyde Park, London, on 30–31 May 1979. It was made with pork and seasonings and weighed 2740 lb *1 242 kg, 1.22 tons.*

Largest sundae

The most monstrous ice cream sundae ever concocted is one of 7,250 lb. *3 288,5 kg* constructed by Sealtest foods on 30 Aug. 1976 for the Tavern-on-the-Green restaurant in New York City's Central Park, N.Y., U.S.A.

Largest Yorkshire Pudding

The largest Yorkshire Pudding on record is one measuring 16½ × 3¾ ft *5,02 × 1,14 m* baked for 7 hrs at "The Jester", Alwoodley, Leeds, Yorkshire by Ian Ghiloni and Mark Harries on 4 June 1977.

Top Selling Sweet

The world's top selling sweets (candies) are Life Savers with 25,000 million rolls between 1913 and 14 Nov. 1973. The aggregate depth of the "hole in the middle" exceeds 1,000,000 miles *1,6 million km*. Paul Shirley, 21, of Sydney made one last for 4 hrs 40 min on 15 Feb. 1979.

Spice *Most expensive*

The most expensive of common spices is Mediterranean saffron (*Crocus sativus*). It takes 96,000 stigmas and therefore 32,000 flowers to make a pound *453 g*. Packets of 1,3 g *0.045 oz* are retailed in the United Kingdom for £3.00 —equivalent to £66.66 per oz. *£2.30 per gramme*. Prices for unprocessed ginseng (root of *Panax quinquefolius*), thought to have aphrodisiac qualities were reported in September 1977 to be as high as $2,000 (£1,050) per oz.

Spice "*Hottest*"

The hottest of all spices is claimed to be Siling labuyo from the Philippines.

Most Expensive Fruit

On 5 Apr. 1977 John Synnott of Ashford, Co. Wicklow, Ireland sold 1 lb. *453 g* of strawberries (a punnet of 30 berries) to the restauranteur Mr. Leslie Cooke at auction by Walter L. Cole Ltd. in the Dublin Fruit Market for £530 or £17.70 a berry.

Rarest condiment

The world's most prized condiment is Cà Cuong, a secretion recovered in minute amounts from beetles in northern Vietnam. Owing to war conditions, the price rose to $100 (*now £57*) per ounce *28 g* before supplies virtually ceased in 1975.

ENERGY CONSUMPTION

To express the various forms of available energy (coal, liquid fuels and water power, etc., but omitting vegetable fuels and peat), it is the practice to convert them all into terms of coal.

The highest consumption in the world is in the United States, with an average of 11 500 kg *226.0 cwt* per person. With only 5.3% of the world's population the U.S. consumes 28.6% of the world's gasoline and 32.9% of the world's electric power. The United Kingdom average was 6 046 kg *119.0 cwt* per person in 1977. The lowest recorded average for 1974 was 13 kg *28,6 lb*. per person in Rwanda.

MASS COMMUNICATIONS
Airline

The country with the busiest airlines system is the United States of America where 193,218,837,000 revenue passenger miles were flown on scheduled domestic and local services in 1977. This was equivalent to an annual trip of 891.1 miles *1 434,1 km* for every one of the inhabitants of the U.S.A. The United Kingdom airlines flew 363,107,000 miles *584,348,000 km* and carried 32,567,755 passengers in 1978.

Merchant Shipping

The world total of merchant shipping excluding vessels of less than 100 tons gross, sailing vessels and barges was 69,020 vessels of 406,001,979 tons gross on 1 July 1978. The largest merchant fleet in the world as at mid-1978 was that under the flag of Liberia with 2,523 ships of 80,191,329 tons gross. The U.K. figure for mid-1978 was 3,359 ships of 30,896,606 tons gross.

Largest and busiest ports

Physically, the largest port in the world is New York Harbor, N.Y., U.S.A. The port has a navigable waterfront of 755 miles *121,5 km* (295 miles *474 km* in New Jersey) stretching over 92 miles² *238 km²*. A total of 261 general cargo berths and 130 other piers give a total berthing capacity of 391 ships at one time. The total warehousing floor space is 422.4 acres

170,9 ha. The world's busiest port and largest artificial harbour is the Rotterdam-Europoort in the Netherlands which covers 38 miles² *100 km²*. It handled 31,042 sea-going vessels carrying a total of 280 million tonnes of sea-going cargo, and about 200,000 barges in 1978. It is able to handle 310 sea-going vessels simultaneously of up to 318,000 tonnes and 68 ft *20,72 m* draught.

Railways
The country with the greatest length of railway is the United States, with 200,000 miles *321 860 km* of track at 1 Jan. 1979. The farthest anyone can get from a railway on the mainland island of Great Britain is 110 miles *177 km* by road in the case of Southend, Mull of Kintyre.

The number of journeys made on British Rail in 1977 was 728,270,000 compared with the peak year of 1957, when 1,101 million journeys (average 20.51 miles *33 km*) were made.

Road *Oldest*
The oldest trackway yet discovered in the world is the Sweet track, Shapwick, Somerset which has been dated to 4,000 B.C. The first sod on Britain's first motorway, the M6 Preston By-Pass, was cut by bulldozer driver Fred Hackett on 12 June 1956.

The country with the greatest length of road is the United States (all 50 States), with 3,814,970 miles *6 139 600 km* of graded roads at 1 Jan. 1977. Regular driving licences are issuable at 15, without a driver education course only in Hawaii and Mississippi. Thirteen U.S. States issue restricted juvenile licences at 14.

The United Kingdom has 229,018 miles *368 568 km* of road including 1,490 miles *2 397 km* of motorway at 1 April 1977 and 18,070,057 vehicles in 1978.

The $3,500 million Interstate 75, opened on 21 Dec. 1977, now runs 1,564 miles *2 517 km* from Sault St. Marie, Michigan to Tampa, Florida without a traffic light. The longest uninterrupted dual carriageway is from Plymouth to Exeter (the A.38) and thence by the M5 and M6 for 515 miles *829 km* to Greenloaning, north of Stirling, Scotland.

Traffic Volume *Highest*
The highest traffic volume of any point in the world is at the East Los Angeles interchange (Santa Ana, Pomona, Golden State and Santa Monica Freeways), California, U.S.A. with a 24-hour average on weekdays of 443,000 vehicles in 1976. The most heavily travelled stretch of road is between 43rd and 47th Street on the Dan Ryan Expressway, Chicago with an average daily volume of 254,700 vehicles.

The territory with the highest traffic density in the world is Hong Kong. By 1 Jan. 1977 there were 191,146 motor vehicles on 678 miles *1 091 km* of serviceable roads giving a density of 6.24 yds *5,70 m* per vehicle. The comparative figure for Great Britain in 1977 was 20.22 yds *18,49 m*.

The greatest traffic density at any one point in Great Britain is at Hyde Park Corner, London. The average daytime 8 a.m.–8 p.m. flow in 1970 (last census) was 164,338 vehicles every 12 hours. The busiest Thames bridge in 1976 was Putney Bridge, with a 24-hour average of 63,000 vehicles. The greatest reported aggregation of London buses was 52, bumper to bumper, along Oxford Street on 13 February 1976. The longest traffic jam reported in Britain was one of 35 miles *56 km* out of 42.5 miles *75,6 km* road length between Torquay and Yarcombe, Devon, on 25 July 1964 and 35 miles *56 km* on the A30 between Egham, Surrey and Micheldever, Hampshire on 23 May 1970.

Road *Widest*
The widest street in the world is the Monumental Axis running for 1½ miles *2,4 km* from the Municipal Plaza to the Plaza of the Three Powers in Brasilia, the capital of Brazil. The six-lane Boulevard was opened in April 1960 and is 250 m *273.4 yds* wide. The B Bridge Toll Plaza has 23 lanes (17 west bound) serving the Bay Bridge, San Francisco, California.

The only instance of 17 carriageway lanes side by side in Britain occurs on the M61 at Linnyshaw Moss, Worsley, Greater Manchester.

Road *Narrowest*
The world's narrowest street is in Port Isaac, Cornwall at the junction of Temple Bar and Dolphin Street. It is popularly known as "Squeeze-belly alley" and is 19 5/16 in *49 cm* wide at its narrowest point.

Road *Longest*
The longest motorable road in the world is the Pan-American Highway, which will stretch 17,018 miles *27 387 km* from North West Alaska, to southernmost Chile. There remains a gap known as the Tapon del Darién, in Panama and the Atrato Swamp, Colombia. The first complete traverse was made by the 1972 British Trans-Americas Expedition led by Lt. Col. John Blashford-Snell M.B.E., R.E. which emerged from the Atrato Swamp after 99 days. The Range Rover VXC 868K which left Alaska on 3 Dec. 1971 arrived in Tierra del Fuego on 9 June 1972.

Most complex interchange
The most complex interchange on the British road system is that at Gravelly Hill, north of Birmingham on the Midland Link Motorway section of the M6 opened on 24 May 1972. There are 18 routes on 6 levels together with a diverted canal and river, which consumed 26,000 tons/*tonnes* of steel, 250,000 tons/*tonnes* of concrete, 300,000 tons/*tonnes* of earth and cost £8,200,000.

Street *Longest World*
The longest designated street in the world is Yonge Street running north and west from Toronto, Canada. The first stretch completed on 16 Feb. 1796 ran 34 miles 53 chains *55,783 km*. Its official length now extended to Rainy River at the Manitoba-Minnesota border is 1,178.3 miles *1 896,2 km*.

Longest Great Britain
The longest designated road in Great Britain is the A1 from London to Edinburgh of 404 miles *650 km*. The longest Roman roads were Watling Street, from Dubrae (Dover) 215 miles *346 km* through Londinium (London) to Viroconium (Wroxeter), and Fosse Way, which ran 218 miles *350 km* from Lindum (Lincoln) through Aquae Sulis (Bath) to Isca Dumnoniorum (Exeter). However, a 10 mile *16 km* section of Fosse Way between Ilchester and Seaton remains indistinct. The commonest street name in Greater London is High Street (153) followed by Station Road (114).

Shortest
The shortest reported measurement of a street in Britain is 58 ft *17,67 m* of Tolbooth Street, Falkirk, Central, Scotland. The shortest length of restricted road is probably Kelbrook Road, Salterforth, Lancashire with 336½ ft *102,5 m* between 30 m.p.h. signs, seemingly too short to sustain a speeding conviction.

Steepest
The steepest streets in the world are Filbert Street, Russian Hill and 22nd Street, Dolores Heights, San Francisco with gradients of 31.5% or 1 in 3.17. Lombard Street between Leavenworth and Hyde with 5 consecutive hairpins is described as the "Crookedest street in the world". Britain's steepest is 26.3% or 1 in 3.8 at a point in Vale Street, Bristol.

Longest hill
The longest steep hill on any road in the United Kingdom is on the road westwards from Lochcarron towards Applecross in Highland, Scotland. In 6 miles *9,6 km* this road rises from sea-level to 2,054 ft *626 m* with an average gradient of 1 in 15.4, the steepest part being 1 in 4.

Of the five unclassified roads with 1 in 3 gradients the most severe is Hard Knott Pass between Boot and Ambleside, Cumbria.

Road *Highest World*
The highest trail in the world is an 8 mile *13 km* stretch of the Kang-ti-suu between Khaleb and Hsin-chi-fu, Tibet

which in two places exceeds 20,000 ft *6 080 m*. The highest carriageable road in the world is one 1,180 km *733.2 miles* long between Tibet and south western Sinkiang, completed in October 1957, which takes in passes of an altitude up to 18,480 ft *5 632 m* above sea-level. Europe's highest pass (excluding the Caucasian passes) is the Col de Restefond (9,193 ft *2 802 m*) completed in 1962 with 21 hairpins between Jausiers and Saint Etienne-de-Tinée, France. It is usually closed between early October and early June. The highest motor road in Europe is the Pico de Veleta in the Sierra Nevada, southern Spain. The shadeless climb of 36 km *22.4 miles* brings the motorist to 11,384 ft *3 469 m* above sea-level and became, on completion of a road on its southern side in Summer 1974, arguably Europe's highest "pass".

Road *Highest Great Britain*
The highest road in the United Kingdom is the A6293 tarmac extension at Great Dun Fell, Cumbria, (2,780 ft *847 m*) leading to a Ministry of Defence radar installation. A permit is required to use it. The highest classified road in England is the B6293 at Killhope Cross (2,056 ft *626 m*) on the Cumbria-Durham border near Nenthead. The highest classified road in Scotland is the A93 road over the Grampians through Cairnwell, a pass between Blairgowrie, Tayside, and Braemar, Grampian, which reaches a height of 2,199 ft *670 m*. The highest classified road in Wales is the Rhondda-Afan Inter-Valley road (A4107), which reaches 1,750 ft *533 m* 2½ miles *4 km* east of Abergwynfi, Mid Glamorgan. An estate track exists to the summit of Ben a'Bhuird (3,860 ft *1 176 m*) in Grampian, Scotland. The highest motorway in Great Britain is the trans-Pennine M62, which, at the Windy Hill interchange, reaches an altitude of 1,220 ft *371 m*. Its Dean Head cutting is the deepest roadway cutting in Europe at 183 ft *55,7 m*.

Road *Lowest*
The lowest road in the world is that along the Israeli shores of the Dead Sea, 1,290 ft *393 m* below sea-level. The lowest surface roads in Great Britain are just below sea-level in the Holme Fen area of Cambridgeshire. The world's lowest "pass" is Rock Reef Pass, Everglades National Park, Florida which is 3 ft *91 cm* above sea-level.

Longest viaduct
The longest elevated road viaduct on the British road system is the 2.97 mile *4 779 m* Gravelly Hill to Castle Bromwich section of the M6. It was completed in May 1972.

Biggest square
The Tian an men (Gate of Heavenly Peace) Square in Peking, described as the navel of China, extends over 98 acres *39,6 ha*. The Maiden e Shah in Isfahan, Iran extends over 20.1 acres *8,1 ha*. The oldest London Square is Bloomsbury Square planned in 1754.

Traffic lights
Semaphore-type traffic *signals* had been set up in Parliament Square, London in 1868 with red and green gas lamps for night use. It was not an offence to disobey traffic signals until assent was given to the 1930 Road Traffic Bill. Traffic *lights* were introduced in Great Britain with a one day trial in Wolverhampton on 11 Feb. 1928. They were first permanently operated in Leeds, West Yorkshire on 16 Mar. and in Edinburgh, Scotland on 19 Mar. 1928. The first vehicle-actuated lights were installed at the Cornhill-Gracechurch Junction, City of London in 1932.

Parking meters
The earliest parking meters ever installed were those put in the business district of Oklahoma City, Oklahoma, U.S.A., on 19 July 1935. They were the invention of Carl C. Magee (U.S.A.) and reached London in 1958.

Worst driver
It was reported that a 75-year-old *male* driver received 10 traffic tickets, drove on the wrong side of the road four times, committed four hit-and-run offences and caused six accidents, all within 20 minutes, in McKinney, Texas, U.S.A., on 15 Oct. 1966. The most heavily banned driver in Britain was John Hogg, 28, who, in the High Court, Edinburgh on 27 Nov. 1975, received 5¾ years in gaol and his 3rd, 4th and 5th life bans for drunken driving in a stolen car while disqualified. For his previous 40 offences he had received bans of 71½ years plus two life bans.

Milestone
Britain's oldest milestone *in situ* is a Roman stone dating from A.D. 150 on the Stanegate, at Chesterholme, near Bardon Mill, Northumberland.

Longest Ford
The longest ford in any classified road in England is that at Bilbrook, Old Cleeve parish, Somerset which measures 90 yds *82 m* in width.

Inland Waterways
The country with the greatest length of inland waterways is Finland. The total length of navigable lakes and rivers is about 50,000 km *31,000 miles*. In the United Kingdom the total length of navigable rivers and canals is 3,940 miles *6 340 km*.

Longest navigable river
The longest navigable natural waterway in the world is the River Amazon, which sea-going vessels can ascend as far as Iquitos, in Peru, 2,236 miles *3 598 km* from the Atlantic seaboard. On a National Geographic Society expedition ending on 10 Mar. 1969, Helen and Frank Schreider navigated downstream from San Francisco, Peru, a distance of 3,845 miles *6 187 km* to Bélem.

TELECOMMUNICATIONS
Telephones
There were 398,182,000 telephones in the world at 1 Jan. 1977 as estimated by The American Telephone & Telegraph Co. The country with the greatest number was the United States, with 155,173,000 instruments, equivalent to 718 for every 1,000 people, compared with the United Kingdom figure of 22,012, 304 (third largest in the world to the U.S.A. and Japan), or 394 per 1,000 people, at 31 Mar. 1977. The territory with fewest reported telephones is Pitcairn Island with 29.

The country with the most telephones per head of population is Monaco, with 965 per 1,000 of the population at 1 Jan. 1977. The country with the least was Rwanda with less than 1 telephone per 1,000.

The greatest total of calls made in any country is in the United States, with 210,715 million (979 calls per person) in 1976. The United Kingdom telephone service connected 16,220,000,000 calls in the year 1976–77, an average of 290 per person.

The city with most telephones is New York City, N.Y., U.S.A., with 5,945,045 (802 per 1,000 people) at 1 Jan. 1977. In 1977 Washington D.C. reached the level of 1,458 telephones per 1,000 people though in some small areas there are still higher densities such as Beverley Hills, Los Angeles County with a return of about 1,600 per 1,000.

Telephones *Busiest Phone*
The pay phone with the heaviest usage in the world is one in the Greyhound bus terminal, Chicago, which averages 270 calls a day thus used each 5 min 20 secs round the clock all year.

Telephones *Longest telephone cable*
The world's longest submarine telephone cable is the Commonwealth Pacific Cable (COMPAC), which runs for more than 9,000 miles *14 480 km* from Australia, *via* Auckland, New Zealand and the Hawaiian Islands to Port Alberni, Canada. It cost about £35,000,000 and was inaugurated on 2 Dec. 1963.

Telephones *Bill Most Incorrect*
On 18 Aug. 1975 the landlord of the Blue Bell Inn, Lichfield Staffordshire received a bill for £1,494,000,000. The Post Office admitted it contained "an arithmetical error".

Postal Services

The country with the largest mail in the world is the United States, whose population posted over 92 billion letters and packages in 1977 when the U.S. Postal Service employed 655,097 people. The United Kingdom total was 9,484.5 million letters and 159.9 million parcels in the year ending 31 Mar. 1978.

The United States also takes first place in the average number of letters which each person posts during one year. The figure was 427 in 1977. The United Kingdom figure was 169 per head in 1977–78.

Postal Address *Highest numbering*

The practice of numbering houses began in 1463 on the Pont Notre Dame, Paris, France. The highest numbered house in Britain is No. 2,679 Stratford Road, Hockley Heath, West Midlands, owned since 1964 by Mr. & Mrs. Howard Hughes. The highest numbered house in Scotland is No. 2,629 London Road, Mount Vernon, Glasgow, which is part of the local police station.

Pillar-boxes *Oldest*

The oldest site on which one is still in service is one dating from 8 Feb. 1853 in Union Street, St. Peter Port Guernsey though the present box is not the original. The oldest original box in Great Britain is another Victorian example at Barnes Cross, Bishop's Caundle, Dorset, also dating from probably later in 1853. It is now no longer in use.

Post Offices

The Post Office's northernmost post office is at Haroldswick, Unst, Shetland Islands. The most southerly in the British Isles is at Samarès, Jersey. The oldest is at Sanquhar, Dumfries and Galloway which was first referred to in 1763. In England the Post Office at Shipton-Under-Wychwood, Oxfordshire dates back to April 1845.

The longest counter in Britain is one of 185 ft *56,38 m* with 33 positions opened in 1962 at Trafalgar Square, London. It is open 24 hrs a day, 7 days a week. The biggest sorting office is that of 17½ acres *6,75 ha* in Birmingham with a capacity of 3,500,000 items per day.

Telegrams

The country where most telegrams are sent is the U.S.S.R., whose population sent 478;535,000 telegrams in 1977. The United Kingdom total was 8,487,000 including 5,286,000 sent overseas, in the year ending 31 Mar. 1978.

Britain's oldest original pillar box with a contemporary postman at Barnes Cross, Bishop's Caundle, Dorset. (*Post Office*)

POSTAGE STAMPS

EARLIEST	Issued 1 May 1840	1d Black of Great Britain, Queen Victoria, 68,158,080 printed. Put on sale 6 May 1840 two days before the 2d Blue.
HIGHEST PRICE (AUCTION) (WORLD)	£272,000 (1 million D Mks)	Swedish 3 skilling banco yellow colour error of 1855 by anonymous buyer in Hamburg, West Germany on 17 Oct. 1978.
HIGHEST PRICE (AUCTION) (U.K.)	£50,000 £50,000	1d "Perot" of Bermuda, 1854, at Stanley Gibbons, London on 4 Oct. 1973. 1d orange-red of Mauritius, 1847, by M. René Berlingen at Stanley Gibbons, London on 25 Nov. 1976.
HIGHEST PRICE (PHILATELIC ITEM) (U.K.)	£75,000	Pair of 2 cent "Cotton Reels" of British Guiana (now Guyana) on envelope dated 26 Nov. 1851 sold by F. T. Small, by Robson Lowe at Christie's, London on 21 Mar. 1970.
LARGEST (SPECIAL PURPOSE) **(STANDARD POSTAGE)**	9¾ × 2¾ in *247,5 × 69,8 mm* 4⅜ × 3½ in *111 × 90 mm*	Express Delivery of China, 1913. 250 mils of Cyprus, 2 July 1974.
SMALLEST	0.31 × 0.37 in *8 × 9,5 mm*	10 cent and 1 peso Colombian State of Bolivar, 1863–66.
HIGHEST DENOMINATION (WORLD) (U.K.)	£100 £5	Red and black, George V, of Kenya, 1925–27. Orange, Victoria, issued 21 Mar. 1882. Pink and Blue Elizabeth II definitive 2 Feb 1977.
LOWEST DENOMINATION	3,000 pengö of Hungary	Issued 1946 when 150 million million pengö = 1p.
RAREST (WORLD)	Unique examples include	British Guiana (now Guyana) 1 cent black on magenta of 1856 and Swedish 3 skilling banco yellow colour error of 1855. (see above) The former was priced by Stanley Gibbons in their 1979 Catalogue at £350,000.
RAREST (U.K.)	11 or 12	6d dull purple Inland Revenue Edward VII, issued and withdrawn on 14 May 1904. Only unused specimen in private hands from W. H. Harrison-Cripps sold by Stanley Gibbons for £10,000 on 27 Oct. 1972.

The world's first adhesive postage stamp, the classic Great Britain Victoria One Penny Black put on sale on 6 May 1840. Although more than 68 million were printed a perfect mint specimen is today worth £2,000 (see p. 203).

The rarest of all Great Britain stamps—the 6d dull purple Edward VII stamp of 1904, overprinted "Official Inland Revenue". It was withdrawn on its day of issue and only 11 or 12 examples have survived (see p. 203).

7. EDUCATION

Illiteracy
Literacy is variously defined as "ability to read simple subjects" and "ability to read and write a simple letter". The looseness of definition and the scarcity of data for many countries preclude anything more than approximations, but the extent of illiteracy among adults (15 years old and over) is estimated to have been 34.7 per cent in 1969. The continent with the greatest proportion of illiterates is Africa, where 81.5 per cent of adults are illiterate. The last published figure for Mali in 1960 showed 97.8 per cent of people over 15 were unable to read.

University Oldest *World*
Probably the oldest educational institution in the world is the University of Karueein, founded in A.D. 859 in Fez, Morocco.

University Oldest *Great Britain*
The oldest university in the United Kingdom is the University of Oxford, which came into being in *c.* 1167. The oldest of the existing colleges is probably University College (1249), though its foundation is less well documented than that of Merton College in 1264. The earliest college at Cambridge University is Peterhouse, founded in 1284. The largest college at either university is Trinity College, Cambridge. It was founded in 1546. The oldest university in Scotland is the University of St. Andrews, Fife. It was established in 1411.

University *Greatest enrolment*
The university with the greatest enrolment in the world is the State University of New York, U.S.A., with 344,000 students enrolled in 1978. Its oldest college at Albany, New York was founded in 1844. Britain's largest university is the University of London with 39,337 internal students and 25,191 external students (in 1978–79) so totalling 64,528.

Largest University
Tenders for the $3.4 billion (*£1,790 million*) University of Riyadh, Saudi Arabia closed in June 1978. The University will house 15,000 families and have its own mass transport system.

The largest existing university building in the world is the M. V. Lomonosov State University on the Lenin Hills, south of Moscow, U.S.S.R. It stands 240 m *787.4 ft* tall, has 32 storeys and contains 40,000 rooms, it was constructed in 1949–53.

Largest Court or Quadrangle
The largest College quadrangle at any Oxford or Cambridge college is the Great Court, Trinity College, Cambridge completed in 1605. Its dimensions average 325 ft × 273 ft *99,06 m × 83,2 m.*

Professor *Youngest*
The youngest at which anybody has been elected to a chair in a university is 19 years in the case of Colin MacLaurin (1698–1746), who was admitted to Marischal College, Aberdeen as Professor of Mathematics on 30 Sept. 1717. In 1725 he was made Professor of Mathematics at Edinburgh University on the recommendation of Sir Isaac Newton. In July 1967 Dr. Harvey Friedman, Ph.D., was appointed Assistant Professor of Mathematics at Stanford University, California, U.S.A. aged just 19 years.

Professors *Most durable*
The longest period for which any professorship has been held is 63 years in the case of Thomäs Martyn (1735–1825), Professor of Botany at Cambridge University from 1762 until his death. His father, John Martyn (1699–1768), had occupied the chair from 1733 to 1762. Dr. Joel Hildebrand (b. 16 Nov. 1881), Professor Emeritus of Physical Chemistry at the University of California, Berkeley, became first an Assistant Professor in 1913 and was still researching in 1978.

Senior Wranglers
Since 1910 the Wranglers (first class honours students in the Cambridge University mathematical Tripos, part 2) have been placed in alphabetical order only. In 1890 Miss P. G. Fawcett of Newnham was placed "above the Senior Wrangler".

Youngest undergraduate and graduate
The most extreme recorded case of undergraduate juvenility was that of William Thomson (1824–1907), later Lord Kelvin, O.M., G.C.V.O., who entered Glasgow University aged 10 years 4 months in October 1834 and matriculated on 14 Nov. 1834. Dr. Merrill Kenneth Wolf (b. 28 Aug. 1931) of Cleveland, Ohio took his B.A. in music from Yale University in Sept. 1945 in the month of his 14th birthday.

School *Oldest in Britain*
The title of the oldest existing school in Britain is contested. It is claimed that King's School in Canterbury, Kent, was a foundation of Saint Augustine, some time between his arrival in Kent in A.D. 597 and his death in *c.* 604. Cor Tewdws (College of Theodosius) at Llantwit Major, South Glamorgan, reputedly burnt down in A.D. 446, was refounded after an elapse of 62 years, by St. Illtyd in 508 and flourished into the 13th century.

School Largest *World*
At the time of its highest enrolments the largest school in the world was the De Witt Clinton High School in the Bronx, New York City, N.Y., U.S.A., with a peak of 12,000 in 1934. It was founded in 1897 and now has an enrolment of 4,500.

Great Britain
The school with the most pupils in Great Britain was Exmouth Comprehensive, Devon with 2,552 (Mar. 1979). The highest enrolment in Scotland has been at Our Lady's Roman Catholic High School, Motherwell, Strathclyde with a peak of 2,325 in August 1977. The total in Holy Child School, Belfast, Northern Ireland reached 2,752 in 1973 before being split up.

School Most Expensive *World*
L'Institut 'Le Rosey' at Rolle Switzerland charges annual fees of at least 25,000 Sw Fr or £7,700.

Great Britain
The most expensive school in Great Britain is Millfield

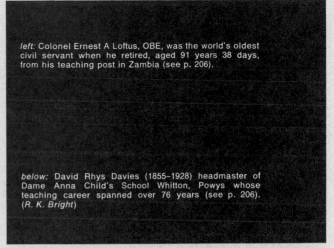

left: Colonel Ernest A Loftus, OBE, was the world's oldest civil servant when he retired, aged 91 years 38 days, from his teaching post in Zambia (see p. 206).

below: David Rhys Davies (1855–1928) headmaster of Dame Anna Child's School Whitton, Powys whose teaching career spanned over 76 years (see p. 206). (R. K. Bright)

in Street, Somerset (headmaster C. R. M. Atkinson). The terminal fee for boarding entries for the winter term 1979 is £1,250 presaging an annual rate of some £3,750. The most expensive girls' school in 1979–80 was Cranbourne Chase School, Tisbury, Wilts, (founded 1946) with annual fees of £2,250.

Oldest old school tie

The practice of wearing distinctive neckties bearing the colours of registered designs of schools, universities, sports clubs, regiments, etc., appears to date from c. 1880. The practice originated in Oxford University, where boater bands were converted into use as "ribbon ties". The earliest definitive evidence stems from an order from Exeter College for college ties, dated 25 June, 1880.

PTA Oldest

The Parent-Teacher Association with the earliest foundation date in Britain is St. Christopher School, Letchworth, Parents' Circle formed in 1919.

Most Schools

The greatest documented number of schools attended by a pupil is 265 by Wilma Williams, now Mrs. R. J. Horton, from 1933–43 when her parents were in show business in the U.S.A.

Most "O" and "A" levels

Francis L. Thomason of Tottenham, London had by January 1977 accumulated 37 "O", 8 "A" and 1 "S" levels making a total of 46. A. F. Prime, a prisoner in H.M. Prison Portsmouth, has a total of 10 A's and 33 O's to July 1977. Environmental difficulties make study far harder in prison than elsewhere.

Robert Pidgeon (b. 7 Feb. 1959) of St. Peter's School, Bournemouth, secured 13 "O" level passes at Grade A at one sitting in the summer of 1975. Subsequently he passed

THE HUMAN WORLD

3 "A" levels at Grade A and 2 "S" levels with firsts. Stephen Murell of Crown Woods School, Eltham passed 11 "A" levels at one sitting in June 1978 achieving 6 at grade A.

Youngest headmaster

The youngest headmaster of a major public school was Henry Montagu Butler (b. 2 July 1833), appointed Head-master of Harrow School on 16 Nov. 1859, when aged 26 years 137 days. His first term in office began in January 1860.

Most Durable Teachers

David Rhys Davies (1835–1928) taught as a pupil teacher and latterly as teacher and headmaster of Dame Anna Child's School, Whitton, Powys (1879–1928) for a total of 76 years 2 months. Col. Ernest Achay Loftus C.B.E., T.D., D.L. (b. 11 Jan. 1884) served as a teacher over a span of 73 years from September 1901 in York, England until 18 Feb. 1975 in Zambia retiring as the world's oldest civil servant aged 91 years 38 days. His father John was born in Hull in the reign of William IV in 1832.

Most Durable Don

Dr. Martin Joseph Routh (b. Sept. 1755) was President of Magdalen College, Oxford, from April 1971 for 63 years 8 months, until his death in his 100th year on 22 Dec. 1854.

---

8. RELIGIONS

Oldest

The oldest major formal religion is Hinduism. Its Vedic precursor was brought to India by Aryans c. 1500 B.C. The Rig Veda Hindu hymnal was codified c. 900 B.C. or earlier.

Largest

Religious statistics are necessarily only approximate. The test of adherence to a religion varies widely in rigour, while many individuals, particularly in the East, belong to two or more religions.

Christianity is the world's prevailing religion, with some 1,070,000,000 adherents in 1978. The Vatican statistics office reported that in 1978 there were 724,434,000 Roman Catholics. The largest non-Christian religion is Islam (Muslim) with some 550,000,000 followers.

In the United Kingdom the Anglicans comprise members of the Established Church of England, the Dis-established Church in Wales, the Episcopal Church in Scotland and the Church of Ireland. In mid 1973 there were 27,484,000 (58.9% of the home population) baptized in the Church of England, which has two provinces (Canterbury and York), 43 dioceses, 11,549 full-time diocesan clergymen (1978) and 13,950 parish churches (1978).

In Scotland the most numerous group is the Church of Scotland (46 Presbyteries), which had 1,002,945 members as at 1 Jan. 1978.

Largest clergies

The world's largest religious organization is the Roman Catholic Church, with 1,494,090 clergy, (1978 est.) 401,168 professional priests and 956,734 nuns. The total number of cardinals, archbishops and bishops is 2,947. There are about 420,000 churches.

Jews

The total of world Jewry was estimated to be 14.3 million in 1978. The highest concentration is in the United States, with 5.8 million, of whom 2.0 million are in the New York area. The total in Israel is 3,060,000. The total of British Jewry is 410,000 of whom 280,000 are in Greater London, and 13,000 in Glasgow. The total in Tokyo, Japan, is less than 1,000.

PLACES OF WORSHIP

Earliest *World*

The earliest known shrine dates from the proto-neolithic Natufian culture in Jericho, where a site on virgin soil has been dated to the ninth millennium B.C. A simple rectilinear red-plastered room with a niche housing a stone pillar be-

The tallest cathedral spire in the world at Ulm, West Germany. This 528 ft *160,9 m* Gothic was under construction at the time of the birth there of Albert Einstein in 1879 (see p. 208).

The memorial stone inscribed in Latin in the crypt of St. Peter's in the Vatican unveiled to commemorate England's only Pope—Nicholas Breakspear who was elected Pope Adrian IV in 1154 (see p. 209).

Great Britain's largest cathedral, the Anglican Cathedral of Christ the King, Liverpool, completed in 1978, after 74 years in building. (*Sydney W. Newbury*)

lieved to be the shrine of a Pre-Pottery fertility cult dating from *c.* 6500 B.C. was also uncovered in Jericho (now Arihã) in Jordan. The oldest surviving Christian church in the world is Qal'at es Salihiye in eastern Syria, dating from A.D. 232.

Oldest *Great Britain*
The oldest ecclesiastical building in the United Kingdom is a 6th century cell built by St. Brendan in A.D. 542 on Eileachan Naoimh (pronounced Noo), Garvelloch Islands, Strathclyde. The Church in the United Kingdom with the oldest origins is St. Martin's Church in Canterbury, Kent. It was built in A.D. 560 on the foundations of a 1st century Roman church. The oldest church in Ireland is the Gallerus Oratory, built in *c.* 750 at Ballyferriter, near Kilmalkedar, County Kerry, Britain's oldest nunnery is St. Peter and Paul Minster, on the Isle of Thanet, Kent. It was founded in *c.* 748 by the Abbess Eadburga of Bugga. The oldest wooden church in Great Britain is St. Andrew's, Greensted, near Ongar, Essex dating to A.D. 845 though some of the timbers date to the original building of *c.* A.D. 650.

Temple Largest
The largest religious structure ever built is Angkor Wat (City Temple), enclosing 402 acres *162,6 ha* in Cambodia, south-east Asia. It was built to the God Vishnu by the Khmer King Suryavarman II in the period 1113–50. Its curtain wall measures 1,400 by 1,400 yds *1 280 × 1 280 m* and its population before it was abandoned in 1432, was 80,000. The largest Buddhist temple in the world is Borobudur, near Jogjakarta, Indonesia built in the 8th century.

The largest Mormon temple is in Kensington, Maryland U.S.A. dedicated in November 1974 with a floor area of 159,000 ft² *14 770 m²*.

Cathedral Largest *World*
The world's largest cathedral is the cathedral church of the Diocese of New York, St. John the Divine, with a floor area of 121,000 ft² *11 240 m²* and a volume of 16,822,000 ft³ *476 350 m³*. The corner stone was laid on 27 Dec. 1892, and the Gothic building was still uncompleted in 1977. In New York it is referred to as "Saint John the Unfinished". The nave is the longest in the world, 601 ft *183,18 m* in length, with a vaulting 124 ft *37,79 m* in height.

The cathedral covering the largest area is that of Santa Mariá de la Sede in Sevilla (Seville), Spain. It was built in Spanish Gothic style between 1402 and 1519 and is 414 ft *126,18 m* long, 271 ft *82,60 m* wide and 100 ft *30,48 m* high to the vault of the nave.

Cathedral Largest *Great Britain*
The largest cathedral in the British Isles is the Anglican Cathedral of Christ the King, Liverpool. Built in modernized Gothic style, work was begun on 18 July 1904, and was completed in October 1978 after 74 years (*cf.* Exeter 95 years) using ½ million stone blocks and 12 million bricks at a cost of £65 million (1978 prices). The building encloses 100,000 ft² *9 300 m²* and has an overall length of 671 ft *204,52 m*. The Vestey Tower is 331 ft *100,88 m* high.

Cathedral Smallest
The smallest cathedral in the world is the Cathedral Chapel of St. Francis of the American Catholic Church built in 1933 at Laguna Beach, California with an area of 1,008 ft² *93,6 m²* and seating for 42 people. The smallest cathedral in use in the United Kingdom (of old foundation) is St. Asaph in Clwyd, Wales, It is 182 ft *55,47 m* long, 68 ft *20,72 m* wide and has a tower 100 ft *30,48 m* high. Oxford Cathedral in Christ Church (College) is 155 ft *47,24 m* long. The nave of the Cathedral of the Isles on the Isle of Cumbrae. Strathclyde measures only 40 × 20 ft *12,19 × 6,09 m*. The total floor area is 2,124 ft² *197,3 m²*.

Church Largest *World*
The largest church in the world is the basilica of St. Peter, built between 1492 and 1612 in the Vatican City, Rome. The length of the church, measured from the apse, is 611 ft 4 in

186,33 m. The area is 162,990 ft² *15 142 m².* The inner diameter of the famous dome is 137 ft 9 in *41,98 m* and its centre is 119 m *390 ft 5 in* high The external height is 457 ft 9 in *139,52 m.*

The elliptical Basilique of St. Pie X at Lourdes, France, completed in 1957 at a cost of £2,000,000 has a capacity of 20,000 under its giant span arches and a length of 200 m *656 ft.*

The crypt of the underground Civil War Memorial Church in the Guadarrama Mountains, 45 km *28 miles* from Madrid, Spain, is 260 m *853 ft* in length. It took 21 years (1937–58) to build, at a reported cost of £140,000,000 and is surmounted by a cross 150 m *492 ft* tall.

Church Largest *Great Britain*
The largest Church in the United Kingdom is the Collegiate Church of Saint Peter at Westminister built AD 1050–1745. Its maximum dimensions are overall: length 530 ft *161,5 m;* breadth across transept 203 ft *61,87 m* and internal height 101 ft 8 in *30,98 m.* The largest parish church is the Parish Church of the Most Holy and Undivided Trinity at Kingston-upon-Hull covering 27,235 ft² *2 530 m²* and with an external length and width of 288 ft × 124 ft *87,7 × 37,7 m.* It is also believed to be the country's oldest brick building serving its original purpose dating from *c.* 1285. Both the former Cathedral of Saint Mungo, Glasgow and Beverley Minster, Humberside are now used as Parish Churches. The largest school chapel is that of the 150 ft *45,7 m* high Lancing College, West Sussex.

Church Smallest *World*
The world's smallest church is the Union Church at Wiscasset, Maine, U.S.A., with a floor area of 31½ ft² *2,92 m²* (7 × 4½ ft *2,13 × 1,37 m*). Les Vauxbelets Church in Guernsey has an area of 16 × 12 ft *4,87 × 3,65 m,* room for one priest and a congregation of two.

Church Smallest *Great Britain*
The smallest church in use in England is Bremilham Church, Cowage Farm, Foxley near Malmesbury, Wiltshire which measures 12 × 12 ft *3,65 × 3,65 m* and is used for service once a year. The smallest completed medieval English church in regular use is that at Culbone, Somerset, which measures 35 × 12 ft *10,66 × 3,65 m.* The smallest Welsh chapel is St. Trillo's Chapel, Rhôs-on-Sea (Llandrillo-yn-Rhos), Clwyd, measuring only 12 × 6 ft *3,65 × 1,83 m.* The smallest chapel in Scotland is St. Margaret's, Edinburgh, measuring 16½ × 10½ ft *5,02 × 3,20 m,* giving a floor area of 173¼ ft² *16,09 m².*

Synagogue Largest *World*
The largest synagogue in the world is the Temple Emanu-El on Fifth Avenue at 65th Street, New York City, N.Y., U.S.A. The temple, completed in September 1929, has a frontage of 150 ft *45,72 m* on Fifth Avenue and 253 ft *77,11 m* on 65th Street. The Sanctuary proper can accommodate 2,500 people, and the adjoining Beth-El Chapel seats 350. When all the facilities are in use, more than 6,000 people can be accommodated.

Synagogue Largest *Great Britain*
The largest synagogue in Great Britain is the Edgware Synagogue, Barnet, Greater London, completed in 1959, with a capacity of 1,630 seats. That with highest registered membership is Ilford Synagogue with 2,631 at 21 May 1979.

Mosque Largest
The largest mosque ever built was the now ruinous al-Malawiya mosque of al-Mutawakil in Samarra, Iraq built in A.D. 842–852 and measuring 9.21 acres *3,72 ha* with dimensions of 784 × 512 ft *238,9 × 156,0 m.* The world's largest mosque in use is the Umayyad Mosque in Damascus, Syria built on a 2,000 year old religious site measuring 157 × 97 m *515 × 318 ft* thus covering an area of 3.76 acres *1,52 ha.* The largest mosque will be the Merdeka Mosque in Djakarta, Indonesia, which was begun in 1962. The cupola will be 45 m *147.6 ft* in diameter and the capacity in excess of 50,000 people.

Minaret *Tallest*
The world's tallest minaret is the Qutb Minar, south of New Delhi, India, built in 1194 to a height of 238 ft *72,54 m.*

Pagoda *Tallest and Oldest*
The world's tallest pagoda is the Shwe Dagon Pagoda in Rangoon, Burma which was increased to its present height of 326 ft *99,36 m* and perimeter of 1,420 ft *432,8 m* by Hsinbyushin, King of Ava (1763–1776). The oldest pagoda in China is Sung-Yo Ssu in Honan built with 15 12-sided storeys in A.D. 523.

Nave *Longest*
The longest nave in the United Kingdom is that of St. Albans Cathedral, Hertfordshire, which is 285 ft *86,86 m* long. The central tower of Liverpool's Anglican Cathederal (internal overall length 619 ft *188,6 m*) interrupts the nave with an undertower space.

Spire Tallest *World*
The tallest cathedral spire in the world is that of the Protestant Cathedral of Ulm in Germany. The building is early Gothic and was begun in 1377. The tower, in the centre of the west façade, was not finally completed until 1890 and is 160,90 m *528 ft* high. The world's tallest church spire is that of the Chicago Temple of the First Methodist Church on Clark Street, Chicago, Illinois, U.S.A. The building consists of a 22-storey skyscraper (erected in 1924) surmounted by a parsonage at 330 ft *100,5 m,* a "Sky Chapel" at 400 ft *121,92 m* and a steeple cross at 568 ft *173,12 m* above street level.

Great Britain
The highest spire in Great Britain is that of the church of St. Mary, called Salisbury Cathedral, Wiltshire. The Lady Chapel was built in the years 1220–25 and the main fabric of the cathedral was finished and consecrated in 1258. The spire was added later, *ante* 1305, and reaches a height of 404 ft *123,13 m.* The Central Spire of Lincoln Cathedral completed in *c.* 1307 and which fell in 1548 was 525 ft *160,02 m* tall.

Stained glass *Oldest*
The oldest stained glass in the world represents the Prophets in a window of the cathedral of Augsburg, Bavaria, Germany, dating from *c.* 1050. The oldest datable stained glass in the United Kingdom is represented by 12th century fragments in the Tree of Jesse in the north aisle of the nave of York Minster, dated *c.* 1150, and medallions in Rivenhall Church, Essex which appear to date from the first half of that century. Dates late in the previous century have been attributed to glass in a window of the church at Compton, Surrey, and a complete window in St. Mary the Virgin, Brabourne, Kent.

Stained glass *Largest*
The largest stained glass window is the complete mural of The Resurrection Mausoleum in Justice, Illinois, measuring 22,381 ft² *2 079 m²* in 2,448 panels completed in 1971. The largest single stained glass window in Great Britain is the East window in Gloucester Cathedral measuring 72 × 38 ft *21,94 × 11,58 m,* set up to commemorate the Battle of Crécy (1346), while the largest area of stained glass is 125 windows, totalling 25,000 ft² *2 322 m²* in York Minster.

Brasses
The world's oldest monumental brass is that commemorating Bishop Ysowilpe in St. Andrew's Church, Verden, near Hanover, West Germany, dating from 1231. The oldest in Great Britain is of Sir John D'Abernon at Stoke D'Abernon, near Leatherhead, Surrey, dating from 1277.

CHURCH PERSONNEL
Saints
There are 1,848 "registered" saints (including 60 St. Johns) of whom 628 are Italians, 576 French and 271 from the British Isles. The total includes 15 Popes. Britain's first Christian martyr was St. Alban executed *c.* AD 209. The first U.S. born saint is Mother Elizabeth Ann Bayley Seton (1774–1821) canonized 14 Sept. 1975.

Most and least rapidly Canonized
The shortest interval that has elapsed between the death of a Saint and his canonization was in the case of St. Anthony of Padua, Italy, who died on 13 June 1231 and was canonized 352 days later on 30 May 1232. The other extreme is repre-

sented by St. Bernard of Tiron for 20 years Prior of St. Sabinus, who died in 1117 and was made a Saint in 1861—744 years later.

Pope *Reign Longest and Shortest*

The longest reign of any of the 264 Popes has been that of Pius IX (Giovanni Maria Mastai-Ferretti), who reigned for 31 years 236 days from 16 June 1846 until his death aged 85, on 7 Feb. 1878. Pope Stephen II was elected on 24 Mar. 752 and died two days later.

Pope *Oldest*

It is recorded that Pope St. Agatho (reigned 678–681) was elected at the age of 103 and lived to 106, but recent scholars have expressed doubts. The oldest of recent Pontiffs has been Pope Leo XIII (Gioacchino Pecci), who was born on 2 Mar. 1810, elected Pope at the third ballot on 20 Feb. 1878 and died on 20 July 1903, aged 93 years 140 days.

Pope *Youngest*

The youngest of all Popes was Pope Benedict IX (d. 1056) (Theophylact), who had three terms as Pope; 1032–44; April to May 1045; and 8 Nov. 1047 to 17 July 1048. It would appear that he was aged only 11 or 12 in 1032, though the Catalogue of the Popes admits only to his "extreme youth".

Last non-Italian, ex-Cardinalate and English Popes

The current Pope John-Paul II, elected on 16 Oct. 1978, (born Karol Wojtyla 18 May 1920 at Wadowice, nr. Cracow, Poland) is the first non-Italian pope since Cardinal Adrian Florenz Boeyens (Pope Adrian VI) of the Netherlands crowned on 31 Aug. 1522. The last Pope elected from outside the College of Cardinals was Bartolomeo Prignano (1318–89), Archbishop of Bari, who was elected Pope Urban VI on 8 April 1378. The only Englishman to be elected Pope was Nicholas Breakspear (born at Abbots Langley, near Watford, Hertfordshire, in *c*. 1100), who, as Cardinal Bishop of Albano, was elected Pope Adrian IV on 4 Dec. 1154, and died on 1 Sept. 1159.

Last married Pope

The first 37 Popes had no specific obligation to celibacy. Pope Hormisdas (514–523) was the father of Pope Silverius (536–537). The last married Pope was Adrian II (867–872). Rodrigo Borgia (1431–1503) was the father of at least six children before being elected Pope Alexander VI in 1492.

Slowest papal election

After 31 months without declaring *Habemus Papam* ("We have a Pope"), the cardinals were subjected to a bread and water diet and the removal of the roof of their conclave by the Mayor of Viterbo before electing Tabaldo Visconti (*c*. 1210–1276), the Archbishop of Liège, as Pope Gregory X on 1 Sept. 1271. The papacy was, however, vacant for at least 3 years 214 days in A.D. 304–308. The shortest conclave was that of 21 Oct. 1503 for the election of Pope Julius II on a first ballot.

Cardinal *Oldest*

By 2 Feb. 1973 the Sacred College of Cardinals contained a record 145 declared members compared with 135 on 25 May 1979. The oldest was James Francis L. McIntyre, former Archbishop of Los Angeles (b. 25 June 1886). The record length of service of any cardinal has been 60 years 10 days by the Cardinal York, a grandson of James VII of Scotland and II of England, from 3 July 1747 to 13 July 1807.

The oldest Cardinal of all time was probably Giorgio da Costa (b. Portugal, 1406), who died in Rome on 18 Sept. 1508 aged 102.

Cardinal *Youngest*

The youngest Cardinal of all time was Luis Antonio de Bourbon (b. 25 July 1727) created on 19 Dec. 1735 aged 8 years 147 days. His son Luis was also made a Cardinal but aged 23. The youngest Cardinal is Jaime L Sin, Archbishop of Manila (b. 31 Aug. 1928).

Bishopric *Longest tenure*

The longest tenures of any Church of England bishopric is 57 years in the case of the Rt. Rev. Thomas Wilson, who was consecrated Bishop of Sodor and Man on 16 Jan. 1698 and died in office on 7 Mar. 1755. Of English bishoprics the longest tenure, if one excludes the unsubstantiated case of Aethelwulf, reputedly Bishop of Hereford from 937 to 1012, are those of 47 years by Jocelin de Bohun (Salisbury) 1142–1189 and Nathaniel Crew or Crewe (Durham) 1674–1721.

Bishop *Oldest*

The oldest serving bishop (excluding Suffragans and Assistants) in the Church of England at 22 May 1979 was the Most Reverend and Right Honourable Frederick Donald Coggan, Archbishop of Canterbury who was born on 9 Oct. 1909.

The oldest Roman Catholic bishop in recent years has been Bishop Angelo Teutonico, formerly Bishop of Aversa (b. 28 Aug. 1874), who died aged 103 years 275 days on 30 May 1978. He had celebrated Mass about 24,800 times. Bishop Herbert Welch of the United Methodist Church who was elected a bishop for Japan and Korea in 1916 died on 4 Apr. 1969 aged 106.

Bishop *Youngest*

The youngest bishop of all time was H.R.H. The Duke of York and Albany K.G., G.C.B., G.C.H., the second son of George III, who was elected Bishop of Osnabrück, through his father's influence as Elector of Hanover, at the age of 196 days on 27 Feb. 1764. He resigned after 39 years' enjoyment.

The youngest serving bishop (excluding Suffragans and Assistants) in the Church of England at 22 May 1979 was the Rt. Rev. David Young (b. 2 Sept. 1931), Bishop of Ripon.

Longest incumbency

The longest incumbency on record is one of 76 years by the Rev. Bartholomew Edwards, Rector of St. Nicholas, Ashill, Norfolk from 1813 to 1889. There appears to be some doubt as to whether the Rev. Richard Sherinton was installed at Folkestone from 1524 or 1529 to 1601. If the former is correct it would surpass the Norfolk record. The parish of Farrington, Hampshire had only two incumbents in the 122 year period from 28 Mar. 1797 to 5 Apr. 1919.

Longest serving chorister

Alfred Ernest Pick (d. 23 Dec. 1973, aged 95) served in the choir of St. Helen's Church, Sandal, Wakefield, West Yorkshire from August 1886 to April 1973—a stretch of 86¾ years. Having become a choirster in 1876 at the age of 9, Thomas Rogers was appointed vicar's warden in 1966 at Montacute, Somerset.

Oldest parish register

The oldest part of any parish register surviving in England is a sheet from that of Alfriston, East Sussex recording a marriage on 10 July 1504. Scotland's oldest surviving register is that for Anstruther-Wester, Fife, with burial entries from 1549.

Crowds *Largest*

The greatest recorded number of human beings assembled with a common purpose was an estimated 12,700,000 at the Hindu festival of Kumbh-Mela, which was held at the confluence of the Yamuna (formerly called the Jumna), the Ganges and the invisible "Sarasvati" at Allahabad, Uttar Pradesh, India, on 19 Jan. 1977. The holiest time during this holiest day since 1833 was during the planetary alignment between 9.28 and 9.40 a.m. during which only 200,000 achieved immersion to wash away the sins of a lifetime.

Largest funeral

The greatest attendance at any funeral is the estimated 4 million who thronged Cairo, Egypt, for the funeral of President Gamal Abdel Nasser (1918–1970) on 1 Oct. 1970.

Biggest demonstrations

A figure of 2.7 million was published from China for the demonstration against the U.S.S.R. in Shanghai on 3–4 Apr. 1969 following the border clashes, and one of 10 million for the May Day celebrations of 1963 in Peking.

ACCIDENTS & DISASTERS Death Tolls

WORST IN THE WORLD

Category	Death toll	Description	Date
Pandemic	75,000,000	The Black Death (bubonic, pneumonic and septicaemic plague)	1347–1351
		Influenza	April–Nov. 1918
Famine	21,640,000	Northern China	Feb. 1877–Sept. 1878
Flood	9,500,000[1]	Hwang-ho River, China	Aug. 1931
Circular Storm[2]	3,700,000	Ganges Delta Islands, Bangladesh	12–13 Nov. 1970
Earthquake	1,000,000	Shensi Province, China (duration 2 hours)	23 Jan. 1556
Landslide	830,000	Kansu Province, China	16 Dec. 1920
Atomic Bomb	180,000 141,000	Hiroshima, Japan	6 Aug. 1945
Conventional Bombing[3]	c 25,000	Dresden, Germany	13–15 Feb. 1945
Alluvion Flood	c. 25,000[4]	Yungay, Huascarán, Peru	31 May 1970
Marine (single ship)	c. 7,700	Wilhelm Gustloff (25,484 tons) German liner torpedoed off Danzig by U.S.S.R. submarine S-13	30 Jan. 1945
Panic	c. 4,000[5]	Chungking (Zhong qing) China air raid shelter	c. 8 June 1941
Dam Burst	2,209	South Fork Dam, Johnstown, Pennsylvania	31 May 1889
Explosion	1,963[6]	Halifax, Nova Scotia, Canada	6 Dec. 1917
Fire[7] (single building)	1,670	The Theatre, Canton, China	May 1845
Mining[8]	1,572	Honkeiko Colliery, China (coal dust explosion)	26 April 1942
Riot	c. 1,200	New York City anti-conscription riots	13–16 July 1863
Crocodiles	c. 900	Japanese soldiers, Ramree I., Burma (disputed)	19–20 Feb. 1945
Fireworks	>800	Dauphine's Wedding, Seine, Paris	16 May 1770
Tornado	689	South Central States, U.S.A. (3 hours)	18 Mar. 1925
Aircraft (Civil)	582	KLM-Pan Am Boeing 747 ground crash, Tenerife	27 Mar. 1977
Railway	543[9]	Modane, France	12 Dec. 1917
Man-eating Animal[10]	436	Champawat district, India, tigress shot by Col. Jim Corbett	
Hail	246	Moradabad, Uttar Pradesh, India	20 April 1888
Submarine	129	Le Surcouf rammed in Caribbean	18 Feb. 1942
	129	U.S.S. Thresher off Cape Cod, Massachusetts, U.S.A.	10 April 1963
Road (single vehicle)[11]	127	Bus crashed into irrigation canal, Egypt	9 Aug. 1973
Helicopter	54	Israeli military "Sea Stallion", West Bank	10 May 1977
Mountaineering	40[12]	U.S.S.R. Expedition on Mount Everest	Dec. 1952
Ski Lift (Cable car)	42	Cavalese resort, Northern Italy	9 Mar. 1976
Lightning (single bolt)	21	Hut in Chinamasa Kraal nr. Umtali, Rhodesia	23 Dec. 1975
Space Exploration	3	Apollo oxygen fire, Cape Kennedy, Fla., U.S.A.	27 Jan. 1967
	3	Soyuz II re-entry over U.S.S.R.	29 June 1971

WORST IN THE UNITED KINGDOM

Category	Description	Death toll	Date
Pandemic	The Black Death (bubonic, pneumonic and septicaemic plague)	800,000	1347–1350
	Influenza	225,000	Sept.–Nov. 1918
Famine	Ireland (famine and typhus)	1,500,000[13]	1846–1851
Flood	Severn Estuary	c. 2,000[14]	20 Jan. 1606
Circular Storm	"The Channel Storm"	c. 8,000	26 Nov. 1703
Earthquake	East Anglian Earthquake	4	22 April 1884
Landslide	Pantglas coal tip No. 7, Aberfan, Mid Glamorgan	144	21 Oct. 1966
Conventional Bombing	London	1,436	10–11 May 1941
Alluvion Flood	Lewes, East Sussex (snowdrifts)		27 Dec. 1836
Marine (single ship)	H.M.S. Royal George, off Spithead	c. 800[15]	29 Aug. 1782
Panic	Victoria Hall, Sunderland, Tyne and Wear	183	16 June 1883
Dam Burst	Bradfield Reservoir, Dale Dyke, near Sheffield, South Yorkshire, (embankment burst)	250	12 Mar. 1864
Explosion	Chilwell, Notts. (explosives factory)	134[16]	1 July 1918
Fire (single building)	Theatre Royal, Exeter	188[17]	5 Sept. 1887
Mining	Universal Colliery, Senghenydd, Mid Glamorgan	439	14 Oct. 1913
Riot	London anti-Catholic Gordon riots	565 (min)	2–13 June 1780
Tornado	Widecombe, Devon (casualty figure)	60	21 Oct. 1638
Aircraft (Civil)	B.E.A. Trident 1C, Staines, Surrey	118[18]	18 June 1972
Railway	Triple collision, Quintins Hill, Dumfries & Galloway	227[19]	22 May 1915
Submarine	H.M.S. Thetis, during trials, Liverpool Bay	99	1 June 1939
Road (single vehicle)	Coach crash, River Dibb, nr. Grassington, North Yorks	33	27 May 1975
Mountaineering	On Cairngorm, Scotland (4,084 ft)	6	21 Nov. 1971
Lightning (single bolt)	Worst year on record (annual av. 12)	31	1914

[1] In 1770 the great Indian famine carried away a proportion of the population estimated as high as one third, hence a figure of tens of millions. The figure for Bengal alone was also probably about 10 million. It has been estimated that more than 5,000,000 died in the post-World War I famine of 1920–21 in the U.S.S.R. The U.S.S.R. government in July 1923 informed Mr. (later President) Herbert Hoover that the A.R.A. (American Relief Administration) had since August 1921 saved 20,000,000 lives from famine and famine diseases.

[2] This figure published in 1972 for the East Pakistan disaster was from Dr. Afzal, Principal Scientific Officer of the Atomic Energy Authority Centre, Dacca. One report asserted that less than half of the population of the 4 islands of Bhola, Charjabbar, Hatia and Ramagati (1961 Census 1.4 million) survived. The most damaging hurricane recorded was the billion dollar Betsy (name now retired) in 1965 with an estimated insurance pay-out of $750 million.

[3] The number of civilians killed by the bombing of Germany has been put variously as 593,000 and "over 635,000". A figure of c. 140,000 deaths in the U.S.A.F. fire raid on Tokyo of 10 Mar. 1945 has been attributed. Total Japanese fatalities were 600,000 (conventional) and 220,000 (nuclear).

[4] A total of 10,000 Austrian and Italian troops is reported to have been lost in the Dolomite valley of Northern Italy on 13 Dec. 1916 in more than 100 snow avalanches. The total is probably exaggerated though bodies were still being found in 1952.

[5] It was estimated that some 5,000 people were trampled to death in the stampede for free beer at the coronation celebration of Czar Nicholas II in Moscow in May 1896.

[6] Some sources maintain that the final death roll was over 3,000 on 6–7 Dec.

[7] Worst ever hotel fire 162 killed. Hotel Taeyonkak, Seoul, South Korea 25 Dec. 1971.

[8] The worst gold mining disaster in South Africa was 152 killed due to flooding in the Witwatersrand Gold Mining Co. Gold Mine in 1909.

[9] Between 500 and 800 died in the Torro Tunnel, Leon, Spain on 3 Jan. 1944.

[10] In the period 1941–42 c. 1,500 Kenyans were killed by a pride of 22 man-eating lions. Eighteen of these were shot by a hunter named Rushby.

[11] The worst ever years for road deaths in the U.S.A. and the U.K. have been respectively 1969 (56,400) and 1941 (9,169). The global aggregate death roll was put at 25 million in Sept. 1975. The world's highest death rate is said to be in Queensland, Australia. The greatest pile-up on British roads was on the M6 near Lymm Interchange, near Thelwell, involving 200 vehicles on 13 Sept. 1971 with 11 dead and 60 injured.

[12] According to Polish sources, not confirmed by the U.S.S.R. Also 23 died on Mount Fuji, Japan, in blizzard and avalanche on 20 Mar. 1972.

[13] Based on the net rate of natural increase between 1841 and 1851, a supportable case for a loss of population of 3 million can be made out if rates of under-enumeration of 25 per cent (1841) and 10 per cent (1851) are accepted. Potato rot (Phytophthora infestans) was first reported on 13 Sept. 1845.

[14] Death rolls of 100,000 were reputed in England and Holland in the floods of 1099, 1421 and 1446.

[15] c. 2,800 were lost on H.M. Troopship Lancastria 16,243 tons off St. Nazaire on 17 June 1940. The Princess Alice collision in the Thames with the Bywell Castle off Woolwich on 6 Sept. 1878 killed 786.

[16] H.M. Armed Cruiser Natal blew up off Invergordon killing 428 on 30 Dec. 1915.

[17] In July 1212, 3,000 were killed in the crush, burned or drowned when London Bridge caught fire at both ends. The death roll in the Great Fire of London of 1666 was only 8. History's first "fire storm" occurred in the Quebec Yard, Surrey Docks, Southwark, London during the 300-pump fire in the Blitz on 7–8 Sept. 1940. Dockland casualties were 306 killed.

[18] The worst crash by a U.K. operated aircraft was that of the B.O.A.C. Boeing 707 which broke up in mid-air near Mount Fuji, Japan, on 5 March 1966. The crew of 11 and all 113 passengers (total 124) were killed. The cause was violent CAT (Clear Air Turbulence).

[19] The 213 yd long troop train was telescoped to 67 yds. Signalmen Meakin and Tinsley were sentenced for manslaughter. Britain's worst underground train disaster was the Moorgate Tube disaster of 28 Feb. 1975 when 43 were killed.

HUMAN ACHIEVEMENTS

1. ENDURANCE AND ENDEAVOUR

Lunar conquest

Neil Alden Armstrong (b. Wapakoneta, Ohio, U.S.A. of Scoto-Irish and German ancestry, on 5 Aug. 1930), command pilot of the Apollo XI mission, became the first man to set foot on the Moon on the Sea of Tranquillity at 02.56 and 15 sec G.M.T. on 21 July 1969. He was followed out of the Lunar Module *Eagle* by Col. Edwin Eugene Aldrin, Jr. U.S.A.F. (b. Glen Ridge, New Jersey, U.S.A. of Swedish, Dutch and British ancestry, on 20 Jan. 1930), while the Command Module *Columbia* piloted by Lt.-Col. Michael Collins, U.S.A.F. (b. Rome, Italy, of Irish and pre-Revolutionary American ancestry, on 31 Oct. 1930) orbited above.

Eagle landed at 20.17 hours 42 sec G.M.T. on 20 July and lifted off at 17.54 G.M.T. on 21 July, after a stay of 21 hours 36 min. The Apollo XI had blasted off from Cape Canaveral, Florida at 13.32 G.M.T. on 16 July and was a culmination of the U.S. space programme, which, at its peak, employed 376,600 people and attained in the year 1966–67 a peak budget of $5,900,000,000 (*then £2,460 million*).

Altitude *Man*

The greatest altitude attained by man was when the crew of the ill-fated Apollo XIII were at apocynthion (*i.e.* their furthest point) 158 miles *254 km* above the lunar surface and 248,655 miles *400 187 km* above the Earth's surface at 1.21 a.m. B.S.T. on 15 Apr. 1970. The crew were Capt. James Arthur Lovell, Jr. U.S.N. (b. Cleveland, Ohio 25 Mar. 1928), Fred Wallace Haise Jr. (b. Cleveland, Ohio, 25 Mar. 1928) and John L. Swigert Jr. (b. Biloxi, Miss. 14 Nov. 1933).

Altitude *Woman*

The greatest altitude attained by a woman is 231 km *143.5 miles* by Jnr. Lt. (now Lt. Col.) Valentina Vladimirovna Tereshkova-Nikolayev (b. 6 Mar. 1937) of the U.S.S.R., during her 48-orbit flight in *Vostok 6* on 16 June 1963. The record for an aircraft is 24 336 m *79,842 ft* by Natalia Prokhanova (U.S.S.R.) (b. 1940) in an E-33 jet, on 22 May 1965.

Speed *Man*

The fastest speed at which any human has travelled is 24,791 m.p.h. *39 897 km/h* when the Command Module of Apollo X carrying Col. (*now* Brig-Gen.) Thomas Patten Stafford,

U.S.A.F. (b. Weatherford, Okla. 17 Sept. 1930), and Cdr. Eugene Andrew Cernan (b. Chicago, 14 Mar. 1934) and Cdr. (*now* Capt.) John Watts Young, U.S.N. (b. San Francisco, 24 Sept. 1930), reached this maximum value at the 400,000 ft *121,9 km* altitude interface on its trans-Earth return flight on 26 May 1969.

Speed *Woman*

The highest speed ever attained by a woman is 28 115 km/h *17,470 m.p.h.* by Jnr. Lt. (now Lt. Col.) Valentina Vladimirovna Tereshkova-Nikolayev (b. 6 Mar. 1937) of the U.S.S.R. in *Vostok 6* on 16 June 1963. The highest speed ever achieved by a woman aircraft pilot is 2 687,42 km/h *1,669.89 m.p.h.* by Svetlana Savitskaya (U.S.S.R.) reported on 2 June 1975.

Land Speed *Man*

The highest speed ever achieved on land is 650 m.p.h. *1 046 km/h* momentarily during the faster of the two runs of *The Blue Flame* driven by Gary Gabelich (b. San Pedro, California, 29 Aug. 1940) on Bonneville Salt Flats, Utah, U.S.A., on 23 Oct. 1970 (when setting the world land speed record of 622.287 m.p.h. *1001,473 km/h*). The car was built by Reaction Dynamics Inc. of Milwaukee, Wisconsin. (See also p. 135)

Land Speed *Woman*

The highest land speed recorded by a woman is 524.016 m.p.h. *843,323 km/h* by Mrs. Kitty Hambleton *née* O'Neil (U.S.) in the 48,000 h.p. rocket-powered 3 wheeled S.M.1 *Motivator* over the Alvard Desert, Oregon, U.S.A. on 6 Dec. 1976. Her official two-way record was 512.710 m.p.h. *825,126 km/h* and she probably touched 600 m.p.h. *965 km/h* momentarily.

Water Speed *Man*

The highest speed ever achieved on water is an estimated 300 knots *555,9 km/h* by Kenneth Peter Warby, M.B.E., (b. 9 May 1939) on the Blowering Dam Lake, N.S.W. Australia on 20 Nov. 1977 in his unlimited hydroplane *Spirit of Australia*. The official world water speed record is 514.39 km *319.627 mph* set on 8 Oct. 1978 by Kenneth Warby on Blowering Dam Lake.

Woman

Sue Williams, 28 drove the unlimited hydroplane U-96 KYYX through a measured mile on Lake Washington, Seattle, U.S.A. at 163.043 m.p.h. *262,392 km/h* on 26 July 1977 for a world record.

Water speed *Propeller driven*
The world record for propeller-driven craft is 202.42 m.p.h. *325,76 km/h* set by Larry Hill in his supercharged hydroplane *Mr. Ed* off Long Beach, California. On a one-way run *Climax* recorded 205.19 m.p.h. *330,22 km/h.*

Most travelled *Man*
The man who had visited more countries than anyone was Jesse Hart Rosdail (1914–77) of Elmhurst, Illinois, U.S.A., a teacher of children in the 5th grade. Since 1934, of the *then* 161 sovereign countries and 60 non-sovereign territories, listed by the *U.N. Population Report*, making a total of 221, he had visited all but two, namely North Korea, and French Antarctic Territories. He estimated his mileage was 1,626,605 statute miles *2 617 766 km.*

Though he has not visited so many *currently* existing countries, Mehmet S. Ersöz (b. 1904 in Turkey) has travelled much more widely within some 210 countries. Mrs. Ersöz's total was 163 by mid 1978.

Horseback
The most travelled man in the horseback era was probably the Methodist preacher Francis Asbury (b. Birmingham, England), who travelled 264,000 miles *424 850 km* in North America from 1771–1815 preaching 16,000 sermons.

Disabled Person
The most countries visited by a disabled person is 115 sovereign and 59 non-sovereign countries by Professor Daniel J. Crowley of Davis, California, U.S.A. who has been confined to a wheelchair since March 1946.

Most Isolated *Man*
The farthest any human has been removed from his nearest living fellow man is 2,233.2 miles *3596,4 km* in the case of the Command Service Module pilot Alfred M. Worden on the U.S. Apollo 15 lunar mission of 30 July–1 Aug. 1971.

Passport Records
The world's most expensive passports are those from the U.S.S.R. which in 1974 at the official rate of exchange were priced at £225 payable in advance. If applications involved a whole family or travel to the West however the necessary accompanying visa was refused, 996 times in each 1,000 applications.

Round the World
The fastest time for a round the world trip on scheduled flights for a circumnavigation is 53 hr 34 min by Alec E. Prior and Terry Sloane eastabout from Sydney via Los Angeles, London, Bombay, Perth and Melbourne on 10–12 Mar. 1978 over 38 884 km *24,161 miles.*

The F.A.I. allows any flight taking off and landing at the same point, which is as long as the Tropic of Cancer (viz 22,858.754 miles 36 787,599 km) as a circumnavigational flight.

North Pole conquest
The claims of neither of the two U.S. Arctic explorers, Dr. Frederick Albert Cook (1865–1940) nor Cdr. (later Rear Ad.) Robert Edwin Peary (1856–1920), of the U.S. Naval Civil Engineering branch in reaching the North Pole are subject to positive proof. Cook, accompanied by the Eskimos, Ah-pellah and Etukishook, two sledges and 26 dogs, struck north from a point 60 miles *96,5 km* north of Svartevoeg, on Axel Heiberg I., Canada, 460 miles *740 km* from the Pole on 21 Mar. 1908, allegedly reaching Lat. 89° 31′ N on 19 April and the Pole on 21 April. Peary, accompanied by his negro assistant, Matthew Alexander Henson (1866–1955) and the four Eskimos, Ooqueah, Eginwah, Seegloo, and Ootah (1875–1955), struck north from his Camp Bartlett (Lat. 87° 44′ N.) at 5 a.m. on 2 Apr. 1909. After travelling another 134 miles *215 km*, he allegedly established his final camp, Camp Jessup, in the proximity of the Pole at 10 a.m. on 6 April and marched a further 42 miles *67,5 km* quartering the sea-ice before turning south at 4 p.m. on 7 April. On excellent pack ice Wally Herbert's 1968–69 Expedition (see below) attained a best day's route mileage of 23 miles *37 km* in 15 hours. Cook

claimed 26 miles *41,8 km* twice while Peary claimed a surely unsustainable average of 38 miles *61 km* for 8 consecutive days.

The earliest indisputable attainment of the North Pole over the sea-ice was at 3 p.m. (Central Standard Time) on 19 Apr. 1968 by Ralph Plaisted (U.S.) and three companions after a 42-day trek in four Skidoos (snow-mobiles). Their arrival was independently verified 18 hours later by a U.S. Air Force weather aircraft. The sea bed is 13,410 ft *4 087 m* below the North Pole.

Naomi Uemura (b. 1941) the Japanese explorer and mountaineer became the first person to reach the North Pole in a solo trek across the Arctic Ice Cap at 0445 G.M.T. on 1 May 1978. He had travelled 450 miles *7 25 km* setting out on 7 March from Cape Edward, Ellesmere Island in northern Canada. He averaged over 8 miles *13 km* per day with his sled "Aurora" drawn by 17 huskies. He had hoped to average 17 km *10.5 miles* per day.

The first woman to set foot on the North Pole was Mrs. Fran Phipps, wife of the Canadian bush pilot Weldy Phipps on 5 Apr. 1971. Galina Aleksandrovna Lastovskaya (b. 1941) and Lilia Vladislavovna Minina (b. 1959) were crew members of the U.S.S.R. atomic icebreaker Arktika which reached the Pole on 17 Aug. 1977.

South Pole conquest
The first ships to cross the Antarctic circle (Lat. 66° 30′ S.) were the 193 crew of the *Resolution* (462 tons) (Capt. James Cook R.N. (1728–79)) and *Adventure* (336 tons) (Lt. T. Furneaux) on 17 Jan. 1773 in 39° E. The first person to sight the Antarctic *mainland*—on the best available evidence and against claims made for British and Russian explorers—was Nathaniel Brown Palmer (U.S.) (1799–1877). On 17 Nov. 1820 he sighted the Orleans Channel coast of the Palmer Peninsula from his 45 ton/tonnes sloop *Hero.*

The South Pole (alt. 9,186 ft *2 779 m* on ice and 336 ft *102 m* bed rock) was first reached at 11 a.m. on 16 Dec. 1911 by a Norwegian party led by Capt. Roald Amundsen (1872–1928), after a 53-day march with dog sledges from the Bay of Whales, to which he had penetrated in the *Fram.* Subsequent calculations showed that Olav Olavson Bjaaland, (the last survivor, dying in June 1961, aged 88) and Helmer Hanssen probably passed within 400–600 metres of the exact pole. The other two members were Sverre H. Hassell and Oskar Wisting.

Women
The first woman to set foot on Antarctica was Mrs. Klarius Mikkelsen on 20 Feb. 1935. No woman stood on the South Pole until 11 Nov. 1969. On that day Lois Jones, Kay Linsay, Eileen McSavenay, Jean Pearson, Tarry Lee Tickhill and Pam Young, all of U.S.A. arrived by air.

Arctic crossing
The first crossing of the Arctic sea-ice was achieved by the British Trans-Arctic Expedition which left Point Barrow, Alaska on 21 Feb. 1968 and arrived at the Seven Island Archipelago north-east of Spitzbergen 464 days later on 29 May 1969 after a haul of 2,920 statute miles *4 699 km* and a drift of 700 miles *1 126 km* compared with the straight line distance of 1,662 miles *2 674 km.* The team was Wally Herbert (leader), 34, Major Ken Hedges, 34, R.A.M.C., Allan Gill, 38, and Dr. Roy Koerner, 36 (glaciologist), and 40 huskies. This was the longest sustained journey ever made on polar pack ice and the first indisputable attainment of the North Pole by sledge. Temperatures sank to −47° F *−43,8° C* during the trek.

Antarctic crossing
The first crossing of the Antarctic continent was completed at 1.47 p.m. on 2 Mar. 1958, after a trek of 2,158 miles *3 473 km* lasting 99 days from 24 Nov. 1957, from Shackleton Base to Scott Base *via* the Pole. The crossing party of twelve was led by Dr. (now Sir) Vivian Ernest Fuchs (born 11 Feb. 1908).

MILESTONES IN ABSOLUTE
HUMAN ALTITUDE & SPEED RECORDS

Altitude Ft	m	Pilot	Vehicle	Place	Date
80*	24	Jean Francois Pilâtre de Rozier (France)	Hot Air Balloon (tethered)	Fauxbourg, Paris	15 & 17 Oct. 1783
c. 330	c. 100	de Rozier and the Marquis d'Arlandes (1742–1809) (France)	Hot Air Balloon (free flight)	LaMuette, Paris	21 Nov. 1783
c. 3,000	c. 900	Dr. Jacques-Alexander-Cesar Charles (1746–1823) and Ainé Robert (France)	Charliere Hydrogen Balloon	Tuileries, Paris	1 Dec. 1783
c. 9,000	c. 2 750	J.-A.-C. Charles (France)	Hydrogen Balloon	Nesles, France	1 Dec. 1783
c. 13,000	c. 4 000	James Sadler (G.B.)	Hydrogen Balloon	Manchester	May 1785
25,400[1]	7 740	James Glaisher (1809–1903) (U.K.)	Hydrogen Balloon	Wolverhampton	17 July 1862
31,500	9 615	Prof. A. Berson (Germany)	Hydrogen Balloon Phoenix	Strasbourg, France	4 Dec. 1894
36,565	11 145	Sadi Lecointe (France)	Nieuport Aircraft	Issy-les-Moulineaux, France	30 Oct. 1923
51,961	15 837	Prof. Auguste Piccard and Paul Kipfer (Switzerland)	F.N.R.S. 1 Balloon	Augusburg, Germany	27 May 1931
72,395	22 066	Capts. Orvill A. Anderson and Albert W. Stevens (U.S. Army Air Corps)	U.S. Explorer II Helium Balloon	Rapid City, South Dakota, U.S.A.	Nov. 11 1935
79,600	24 262	William Barton Bridgeman (U.S.A.)	U.S. Douglas D558—11 Skyrocket	California, U.S.A.	15 Aug. 1951
126,200	38 465	Capt. Iven C. Kincheloe, Jr. (U.S.A.F.)	U.S. Bell X-2 Rocket 'plane	California, U.S.A.	7 Sept. 1956
169,600	51 694	Joseph A. Walker (U.S.A.)	U.S. X-15 Rocket 'plane	California, U.S.A.	30 Mar. 1961

Statute miles	Km				
203.2	327	Flt.-Major Yuriy A. Gagarin (U.S.S.R.)	U.S.S.R. Vostok I Capsule	Orbital flight	12 Apr. 1961
234,672	377 268,9	Col. Frank Borman, U.S.A.F., Capt. James Arthur Lovell, Jr., U.S.N. and Major William A. Anders, U.S.A.F.	U.S. Apollo VIII Command Module	Circum-lunar flight	25 Dec. 1968
248,655	400 187	Capt. James Arthur Lovell Jr., U.S.N. Frederick Wallace Haise Jr. and John L. Swigert Jr.	U.S. Apollo XIII	Abortive lunar landing mission	15 Apr. 1970

* There is some evidence that Father Bartolomeu de Gusmao flew in his hot-air balloon in his 4th experiment post Aug. 1709 in Portugal.
[1] Glaisher, with Henry Tracey Coxwell (1819–1900). claimed 37,000 ft 11 275 m from Wolverhampton on 5 Sept. 1862. Some writers accept 30,000 ft 9 145 m.

Speed m.p.h.	Km/h	Person and Vehicle	Place	Date
25	40	Sledging	Southern-Finland	c. 6500 B.C.
35	55	Horse-riding	Anatolia, Turkey	c. 1400 B.C.
45	70	Mountain Sledging	Island of Hawaii (now U.S.A.)	ante A.D. 1500
50	80	Ice Yachts (earliest patent)	Netherlands	A.D. 1600
56¾	95	Grand Junction Railway 2-2-2 :Lucifer	Madeley Banks, Staffs., England	13 Nov. 1830
87.8	141,3	Tommy Todd, downhill skier	La Porte, California, U.S.A.	Mar. 1873
90.0	144,8	Midland Railway 4–2–2 7 ft 9 in single	Ampthill, Bedford, England	Mar. 1897
130.61	210,2	Siemens and Halske electric engine	Marienfeld-Zossen, near Berlin	27 Oct. 1903
c. 150	c. 257,5	Frederick H. Marriott (fl. 1957) Stanley Steamer Wogglebug	Ormond Beach, Florida, U.S.A.	26 Jan. 1907
210.64	339	Sadi Lecointe (France) Nieuport-Delage 29	Villesauvage, France	25 Sept. 1921
415.2	668,2	Flt. Lt. (later Wing Cdr.) George Hedley Stainforth A.F.C. Supermarine S.6B	Lee-on-Solent, England	29 Sept. 1931
623.85	1 004	Flugkapitan Heinz Dittmar Me. 163V-1	Peenemunde, Germany	2 Oct. 1941
967	1 556	Capt. Charles Elwood Yeager, U.S.A.F. Bell XS-1	Muroc Dry Lake, California	26 Mar. 1948
2,905	4 675,1	Major Robert M White, North American X-15	Muroc Dry Lake, California	7 Mar. 1961
c. 17,560	c. 28 260	Flt. Maj. Yurly Alekseyevich Gagarin, Vostok 1	Earth orbit	12 Apr. 1961
24,226	38 988	Col. Frank Borman, U.S.A.F., Capt. James Arthur Lovell, Jr., U.S.N. Major William A. Anders, U.S.A.F. Apollo VIII	Trans-lunar injection	21 Dec. 1968
24,790.8	39 897,0	Cds. Eugene Andrew Cernan and John Watts Young, U.S.N. and Col. Thomas P. Stafford, U.S.A.F. Apollo X	Re-entry after lunar orbit	26 May 1969

Longest sledge journeys

The longest totally self-supporting Polar sledge journey ever made, was one of 1,080 miles 1 738 km from West to East across Greenland on 18 June to 5 Sept. 1934 by Capt. M. Lindsay (now Sir Martin Lindsay, Bt., C.B.E., D.S.O.); Lt. Arthur S. T. Godfrey, R.E., (later Lt. Col., k. 1942), Andrew N. C. Croft (later Col., D.S.O.) and 49 dogs. The same crossing was first made but with man hauled sledges by the inter Services 1974 Trans Greenland Expedition, led by Flt. Lt. D. R. Gleed in 36 days.

Greatest Ocean Descent

The record ocean descent was achieved in the Challenger Deep of the Marianas Trench, 250 miles 400 km south-west of Guam, in the Pacific Ocean, when the Swiss-built U.S. Navy bathyscaphe Trieste, manned by Dr. Jacques Piccard (b. 1914) (Switzerland) and Lt. Donald Walsh, U.S.N., reached the ocean bed 35,820 ft (6.78 miles 10 917 m) down, at 1.10 p.m. on 23 Jan. 1960 (see page 63). The pressure of the water was 16,883 lbf/in² 1 183 kg f/cm² and the temperature 37.4° F 3° C. The descent required 4 hours 48 min and the ascent 3 hours 17 min.

Deep diving records

The record depth for the extremely dangerous activity of breath-held diving is 282 ft 85,9 m by Jacques Mayol (France) off Elba, Italy, on 9 Nov. 1973 for men and 147½ ft 45 m by Giuliana Treleani (Italy) off Cuba in September 1967 for women. The pressure on Mayol's thorax was 136.5 lb f/in² 9,6 kg/cm² and his pulse fell to 36. Enzo Maiorca (Italy) surfaced unconscious from a dive of 87 m 285 ft off Sorrento, Italy on 27 Sept. 1974. The record dive with Scuba (self-contained under-water breathing apparatus) is 437 ft 133 m by John J. Gruener and R. Neal Watson (U.S.A.) off Freeport, Grand Bahama on 14 Oct. 1968. The record dive utilizing gas mixtures is a simulated dive of 2,001 ft 609 m in a dry chamber by Patrice Chemin and Robert Gauret (France) at the Comex Chamber, Marseille, France reported in June 1972. Some divers have survived free swimming for short intervals at depths of 1,400 ft 426 m.

Deepest Underwater Escape

The deepest underwater rescue achieved was of the Pisces III in which Roger R. Chapman, 28 and Roger Mallinson, 35 were trapped for 76 hours when it sank to 1,575 ft 480 m 150

MARINE CIRCUMNAVIGATION RECORDS (Compiled by Sq. Ldr. D. H. Clarke, D.F.C., A.F.C.)

A true circumnavigation entails passing through two antipodal points (which are at least 12,429 statute miles *20 000 km* apart).

CATEGORY	VESSEL	NAME	START PLACE AND DATE	FINISH DATE AND DURATION
Earliest*	*Vittoria* Expedition of Fernão de Magalhães, *c.* 1480–k. 1521	Juan Sebastion de Elcano or Del Cano (d. 1526) and 17 crew	Seville, Spain 20 Sept. 1519	San Lucar, 6 Sept. 1522 30,700 miles *49 400 km*
Earliest British	*Golden Hind* (ex *Pelican*) 100 tons/tonnes	Francis Drake (*c.* 1540–1596)· (Knighted 4 April 1581)	Plymouth, 13 Dec. 1577	26 Sept. 1580
Earliest Woman	*Etoile*	Crypto-female valet of M. de Commerson, named Baré	St. Malo, 1766	1769
Earliest fore-and-aft rigged vessel	*Union* 98 tons (Sloop)	John Boit Junior, 19–21, (U.S.)	Newport, R.I. 1794 (via Cape Horn westabout)	Newport, R.I. 1796
Earliest Yacht	*Sunbeam* 170 ft *51,8 m* 3 Mast Topsail schooner	Lord and Lady Brassey (G.B.) passengers and crew	Cowes, Isle of Wight 1876	Cowes, Isle of Wight 1877
Earliest Solo	*Spray* 36 ¾ ft *11,20 m* gaff yawl	Capt. Joshua Slocum, 51, (U.S.) (a non-swimmer)	Newport, R.I., via Magellan Straits, 24 Apr. 1895	3 July 1898 46,000 miles *74 000 km*
Earliest Motor Boat	*Speejacks* 98 ft *29,87 m*	Albert Y. Gowen (U.S.) wife and crew	New York City 1921	New York City 1922
Earliest Woman Solo	*Mazurek* 31 ft 2 in *9,5 m* Bermudan Sloop	Krystyna Chojnowska-Liskiewicz. (Poland)	Las Palmas 28 Mar. 1976 Westabout *via* Panama	Tied knot 21 Mar. 1978
Earliest woman Solo (via Cape Horn)	*Express Crusader* 53 ft *16,15 m* Bermuda Sloop	Naomi James (N.Z./G.B.)	Dartmouth 9 Sept. 1977 (Cape Horn 19 Mar. 1978)	Dartmouth 8 June 1978 (266 days 19 hrs)
Smallest Boat	*Ahodori II* 20 ft 8 in *6,3 m* Bermudan Yawl	Hiroshi Aoki (Japan)	Osaka, Japan, 13 June, Cape Horn 12 Jan. 1973	Osaka, Japan 29 July 1974
Earliest Submerged	*U.S. Submarine Triton*	Capt. Edward L. Beach U.S.N. plus 182 crew	New London, Connecticut 16 Feb. 1960	10 May 1960 30,708 miles *49 422 km*
Earliest non-stop Solo (Port to Port)	*Suhaili* 32.4 ft *9,87 m* Bermuda Ketch	Robin Knox Johnston C.B.E. (b. 1939)	Falmouth, 14 June 1968	22 Apr. 1969 (312 days) Longest alone at sea
Fastest Solo (multihull)	*Manureva* (ex *Pen Duick IV*) 70 ft *21,33 m* Trimaran	Alain Colas (France)	Saint Malo *via* Sydney	29 Mar. 1974 (167 days)
Fastest Solo (monohull)	*Egregious* 37.5 ft *11,4 m* Bermuda Sloop	Webb Chiles (U.S.)	San Diego 18 Oct. 1974 (Cape Horn 12 Dec. 1975)	San Diego 1 Oct. 1976 (202 days)
Fastest	*Great Britain II* 77 ft 2 in *23,52 m* Ketch	1st Mike Gill (13 crew) 2nd R. Mullender (15 crew)	Thames 31 Aug. 1975 *via* Sydney (Change crews)	67 days 5 hrs 19 min 66 days 22 hrs 31 min 26,380 miles 209.9 m.p.d.
Fastest Solo Westabout (*via* Cape Horn)	*Mermaid III* 28 ft *8,80 m* sloop	Kenichi Horie (Japan) (b. 1939)	Osaka, Japan 1 Aug. 1973	5 May 1974 (275 days 13 hrs)
Fastest-ever (Cape Horn)	*Awahnee II* 53 ft *16,15 m*	Bob Griffith (U.S.) (5 crew)	Bluff, N.Z., 1970 (eastabout)	Bluff, N.Z., 1971 (84 days)

* Eduard Roditi author of *Magellan of the Pacific* advances the view that Magellan's slave Enrique was the first circumnavigator. He had been purchased in Malacca but knew the Filipino dialect Vizayan, when he reached the Philippines from the east in 1521.

---

miles *240 km* south-east of Cork, Ireland on 29 Aug. 1973. She was hauled to the surface by the cable ship *John Cabot* after work by Pisces V, Pisces II and the remote control recovery vessel U.S. C.U.R.V. on 1 Sept. The greatest depth of an actual escape without any equipment has been from 225 ft *68,58 m* by Richard A. Slater from the rammed submersible *Nekton Beta* off Catalina Island, California, U.S.A. on 28 Sept. 1970.

Deepest salvage
The greatest depth at which salvage has been achieved is 16,500 ft *5 029 m* by the bathyscaphe *Trieste II* (Lt.-Cdr. Mel Bartels U.S.N.) to attach cables to an "electronic package" on the sea bed 400 miles *645 km* north of Hawaii on 20 May 1972. Project Jennifer by U.S.S. *Glomar Explorer* in June/July 1974 to recover a Golfclass U.S.S.R. submarine, 750 miles *1 200 km* N.W. of Hawaii, cost $550 million but was not successful.

Flexible dress divers
The deepest salvaging operation ever carried out was on the wreck of the S.S. *Niagara*, sunk by a mine in 1940, 438 ft *133,5 m* down off Bream Head, Whangarei North Island, New Zealand. All but 6 per cent of the £2,250,000 of gold in her holds was recovered in 7 weeks. The record recovery was that from the White Star Liner *Laurentic*, which was mined in 132 ft *40,2 m* of water off Malin Head, Donegal, Ireland, in 1917, with £5,000,000 of gold ingots in her Second Class baggage room. By 1924, 3,186 of the 3,211 gold bricks had been recovered with immense difficulty.

Greatest penetration into the Earth
Man's deepest penetration made into the ground is in the Western Deep Levels Mine at Carltonville, Transvaal, South Africa. By May 1975 a record depth of 12,600 ft *3 840 m* had been attained. The rock temperature at this depth is 131° F *55° C*.

Shaft sinking record
The one month (31 days) world record is 1,251 ft *381,3 m* for a standard shaft 26 ft *7,92 m* in diameter at Buffelsfontein Mine, Transvaal, South Africa, in March 1962. The British record of 410 ft *124,9 m* of 18 ft 1 in *5,51 m* diameter shaft was set in the Boulby Mine, Whitby, North Yorkshire on 18 Jan.–17 Feb. 1971 (30 days). The rock shaft at this potash mine at 3,765 ft *1 147,5 m* is the deepest in Great Britain.

Longest on a raft
The longest recorded survival alone on a raft is 133 days (4½ months) by Second Steward Poon Lim (born Hong Kong) of the U.K. Merchant Navy, whose ship, the S.S. *Ben Lomond*, was torpedoed in the Atlantic 565 miles *910 km* west of St. Paul's Rocks in Lat. 00° 30′ N Long. 38° 45′ W at 11.45 a.m. on 23 Nov. 1942. He was picked up by a Brazilian fishing boat off Salinópolis, Brazil, on 5 April 1943 and was able to walk ashore. In July 1943, he was awarded the B.E.M. and now lives in New York City.

Maurice and Maralyn Bailey survived 118¼ days in an inflatable dinghy 4½ ft *1,37 m* in diameter in the north-east Pacific from 4 Mar. to 30 June 1973.

Most Marriages *World*
The greatest number of marriages accumulated in the monogamous world is 20 by the former minister of religion Glynn de Moss Wolfe (U.S.) (b. 1908) who married for the 20th time since 1931 his 18th wife Maria Valez aged 18 in October 1977. His total number of children is, he says, 34. He has long kept two wedding dresses (different sizes) in his closet for ready use. He has additionally suffered 16 mothers-in-law. The most often marrying millionaire was Thomas F. Manville (1894–1967) who contracted his 13th marriage to his 11th wife Chrstine Erdlen Popa (1940–71) aged 20, in New York City, U.S.A., on 11 Jan. 1960 when aged 65. His shortest marriage (to his seventh wife) effectively lasted only 7½ hours.

TRANS-ATLANTIC MARINE RECORDS (Compiled by Sq. Ldr. D. H. Clarke, D.F.C., A.F.C.)

Earliest Canoe	"Finn-Man" (Eskimo)	Kayak 11 ft 10 in *3,6 m*	Greenland	Humber, England	Time not known	1613
Earliest rowing (partial)	Six British deserters from garrison	Ship's boat *c.* 20 ft *6,1 m*	St. Helena (10 June)	Belmonte, Brazil	28 days (83 m.p.d.)	1799
Earliest crossing (2 men)	C. R. Webb + 1 crew (U.S.)	*Charter Oak* 43 ft *13,1 m*	New York	Liverpool	35 days	1857
Earliest Trimaran	John Mikes + 2 crew (U.S.)	*Non Pareil*, 25 ft *7,62 m*	(New York 4 June)	Southampton	51 days	1868
Earliest Solo Sailing	Alfred Johnson (U.S.)	*Centennial* 20 ft *6,09 m*	Glos., Mass	Wales	46 days	1876
Earliest Woman (with U.S. husband)	Mrs. Joanna Crapo (b. Scotland)	*New Bedford* 20 ft *6,09 m*	Chatham, Mass.	Newlyn, Cornwall	51 days	1877
Earliest Single-handed race	J. W. Lawlor (U.S.) (winner)	*Sea Serpent* 15 ft *4,57 m*	Boston (21 June)	Coverack, Cornwall	45 days	1891
Earliest Rowing by 2 men (Northern)	George Harbo and Frank Samuelson (U.S.)	*Richard K. Fox* 18¼ ft *5,58 m*	New York City (6 June)	Isles of Scilly (1 Aug.)	55 days (56 m.p.d.)	1897
Fastest Solo Sailing West–East	J. V. T. McDonald (G.B.)	*Inverarity* 38 ft *11,58 m*	Nova Scotia	Ireland	16 days	1922
Earliest Canoe (with sail)	F. Romer (Germany)	*Deutscher Sport*	Las Palmas	St. Thomas,	58 days (47 m.p.d.)	1928
Earliest Woman Solo (East-West)	Mrs. Ann Davison (G.B.)	*Felicity Ann* 23 ft *7,01 m*	Las Palmas (20 Nov 1952)	Portsmouth, Dominica	65 days	1952/ 1953
Earliest Woman Solo (West-East)	Gladys Gradley (U.S.)	Lugger 18 ft *5,5 m*	Nova Scotia	Hope Cove, Devon	60 days	1903
Fastest Woman Solo	Clare Francis now Mrs. Redon M.B.E. (G.B.)	*Robertson's Golly* 37½ ft *11,43 m*	Plymouth	Newport, R.I.	29 days 1 hr 52 mins	1976
Longest Non-Stop Woman Solo	Anna Woolf (S.Af.)	*Zama Zulu* 43 ft *13,10 m*	Cape Town Ascension Is.	Ascension Is. Bowling, Scot.	1,800 miles 29 days 7,120 miles 80 days	1976
Smallest (Across 2 oceans)	John Riding (G.B.)	*Sjo Ag* 12 ft *3,65 m*	Plymouth *via* Panama	New Zealand, 1973	Lost in Tasman Sea	1964/ 1974
Smallest West-East	William Verity (U.S.)	*Nonoalca* 12 ft *3,65 m*	Ft. Lauderdale, Florida	Tralee, Kerry (12 July)	68 days	1966
Smallest (East-West) (Southern)	Hugo S. Vihien (U.S.)	*The April Fool* 5 ft 11⅞ in *1,83 m*	Casablanca (29 Mar.)	Ft. Lauderdale, Florida (21 June)	85 days	1968
Fastest Crossing Sailing (multihull)	Eric Tabarly (France) + 2 crew Wilson Marshall (U.S.) & crew	*Pen Duick IV* 67 ft *20,42 m*	Tenerife	Martinique	251.4 miles *404,5 km/* day (10 days 12 hours)	1968
Fastest Crossing Sailing (monohull) (East-West)	Wilhelm Hirte & crew (Ger.)	*Kriter II* 80 ft *24,38 m*	Canary Is.	Barbados	13 days 8 hrs	1977
Fastest Crossing Sailing (Monohull) (West-East)	Wilson Marshall (U.S.) & crew	*Atlantic* 185 ft *56,38 m*	Sandy Hook, N.J.	Lizard, Cornwall (3,054 miles)	12 days 4 hr (fastest noon to noon 341 miles)	1905
Fastest Solo East–West (Northern) (monohull)	Jean-Yves Terlain (France)	*Vendredi 13*, 128 ft *39 m*	Plymouth 13 June	Newport, R.I. 8 July	21 days 5¼ hr	1972
Fastest Solo East–West (Southern) (monohull)	Sir Francis Chichester K.B.E. (G.B.)	*Gipsy Moth V* 57 ft *17,37 m*	Portuguese Guinea	Nicaragua	179.1 miles *288,2 km/* day (22.4 days)	1970
Fastest Solo East-West (Northern) (multihull)	Alain Colas (France)	*Pen Duick IV* 70 ft *21,33 m* trimaran	Plymouth (17 June)	Newport, Rhode I. (7 July)	20 days 13¼ hrs	1972
Fastest Solo Rowing East–West	Sidney Genders, 51 (G.B.)	*Khaggavisana* 19¾ ft *6,02 m*	Penzance, Cornwall	Miami, Florida *via* Antigua	37.3 miles *60 km*/day 162 days 18 hr	1970
Earliest Solo Rowing East–West	John Fairfax (G.B.)	*Britannia* 22 ft *6,70 m*	Las Palmas (20 Jan.)	Ft. Lauderdale, Florida (19 July)	180 days	1969
Earliest Solo Rowing West–East	Tom McClean (Ireland)	*Super Silver* 20 ft *6,90 m*	St. John's, Newfoundland (17 May)	Black Sod Bay, Ireland (27 July)	70.7 days	1969
Youngest Solo Sailing	David Sandeman (17½ years)	*Sea Raider* 35 ft *10,67 m*	Jersey, C.I.	Newport, R.I.	43 days	1976
Oldest Solo Sailing	Jean Gau (72 years)	*Atom* 30 ft *9,14 m*	New York	France (wrecked N. Africa)	50 days	1975

TRANS-PACIFIC MARINE RECORDS

Fastest	Bill Lee (U.S.)	*Merlin* 67 ft *20,42 m* sloop	Los Angeles, Cal.	Honolulu, Hawaii	8 days 11 hr 1 min	1977
Fastest Solo	Andrew Urbanczyk	*Nord III* 27 ft Sloop	Yohosuba, Japan 23 Apr.	San Francisco, California 11 June	49 days	1979
Earliest Solo (Woman)	Sharon Sites Adams (U.S.)	*Sea Sharp II* 31 ft *9,45 m*	Yokohama, Japan	San Diego, Cal.	75 days (5,911 miles)	1969
Earliest Rowing	John Fairfax (G.B.) Sylvia Cook (G.B.)	*Britannia II* 35 ft *10,66 m*	San Francisco, Cal. 26 Apr. 1971	Hayman I., Australia 22 Apr. 1972	362 days	1971/ 1972
Earliest Rowing Solo	Anders Svedlund (Sweden)	*Roslagena* 20 ft *6,10 m* 21½ ft *6,55 m*	Chile (2 June)	Samoa, West Indies	118 days	1974

N.B.—The earliest single-handed Pacific crossings were achieved East–West by Bernard Gilboy (U.S.) in 1882 in the 18 ft *5,48 m* double-ender *Pacific* and West–East by Fred Rebel (Latvia) in the 18 ft *5,48 m Elaine*, and Edward Miles (U.S.) in the 36¾ ft *11,2 m Sturdy II* both in 1932.

His fortune of $20 million came from asbestos, neither of which he could take with him.

Mrs. Beverly Nina Avery, then aged 48 a bar-maid from Los Angeles, California, U.S.A., set a monogamous world record in October 1957 by obtaining her sixteenth divorce from her fourteenth husband, Gabriel Avery. She alleged outside the court that five of the 14 had broken her nose.

Great Britain

The only monogomous citizen married eight times is Olive Joy Wilson of Marston Green, Birmingham. She has consecutively been Mrs. John Bickley; Mrs. Don Trethowan; Mrs. George Hundley; Mrs. Raymond Ward; Mrs. Harry Latrobe; Mrs. Leslie Harris; Mrs. Ray Richards and now Mrs. John Graffick. All were divorced except Mr. Hundley, who died.

Oldest Bride and Bridegroom

The British record was set by Edward Reuben Simpson, (1873–1973), who married Mrs. Eva. J. Midwinter, 83, at Swindon, Wiltshire, on 8 Dec. 1971 when aged 98 years 10 months.

Dyura Avramovich reportedly aged 101, married Yula Zhivich, admitting to 95, in Belgrade, Yugoslavia in November 1963.

Longest Engagements

The longest engagement on record is one of 67 years between Octavio Guillen, 82 and Adriana Martinez, 82. They finally took the plunge in June 1969 in Mexico City, Mexico.

Longest Marriage *World*

The longest recorded marriage is one of 86 years between Sir Temulji Bhicaji Nariman and Lady Nariman from 1853 to 1940 resulting from a cousin marriage when both were five. Sir Temulji (b. 3 Sept. 1848) died, aged 91 years 11 months, in August 1940 at Bombay. The only reliable instance of an 83rd anniversary celebrated by a couple marrying at normal ages is that between the late Edd (105) and Margaret (99) Hollen, who celebrated their 83rd anniversary on 7 May 1972. They were married in Kentucky on 7 May 1889.

Great Britain
James Frederick Burgess (born 3 March 1861, died 27 Nov. 1966) and his wife Sarah Ann, *née* Gregory (born 11 July 1865, died 22 June 1965) were married on 21 June 1883 at St. James's, Bermondsey, London, and celebrated their 82nd anniversary in 1965.

The most recent example of a marriage with both partners being centenarians was that of John and Harriet Orton aged 102 and 100 of Great Gidding, Cambridgeshire, who celebrated their 78th anniversary on 9 July 1978.

Most married
Jack V. and Edna Moran of Seattle, Washington, U.S.A. have married each other 40 times since the original and only really necessary occasion on 27 July 1937 in Seaside, Oregon. Subsequent ceremonies have included those at Banff, Canada (1952), Cairo, Egypt (1966) and Westminster Abbey, London (1975).

Mass ceremony
The largest mass wedding ceremony was one of 1,800 couples officiated over by Sun Myung Moon of the Holy Spirit Association for the Unification of World Christianity in Seoul, South Korea on 14 Feb. 1975. The response to the question "Will you swear to love your spouse for ever?" is "Ye".

Eating out
The world champion for eating out is Fred E. Magel of Chicago, Illinois, U.S.A. who since 1928 has dined in 41,355 restaurants in 60 nations as a restaurant grader (to August, 1978). He asserts the one serving the largest helpings is Zehnder's Hotel, Frankenmuth, Michigan, U.S.A. Mr. Magel's favourite dishes are South African rock lobster and mousse of fresh English strawberries.

Party giving
The most expensive private party ever thrown was that of Mr. and Mrs. Bradley Martin of Troy, N.Y., U.S.A. staged at the Waldorf Hotel, Manhattan in February 1897. The cost to the host and hostess was estimated to be $369,200 in the days when dollars were made of gold.

Estimates as high as $600 million (*then £325 million*) were made for the 49 nation Organization of African Unity summit conference staged in Libreville, Gabon in July 1977.

The "International Year of the Child" children's party in Hyde Park, London was attended by Royal Family and 160,000 children on 30–31 May 1979.

Toastmasters
The Guild of Professional Toastmasters (founded 1962) has only 12 members. Its founder and President, Ivor Spencer, listened to a speech in excess of 2 hours by the maudlin guest of honour of a retirement luncheon. The Guild also elects the most boring speaker of the year, but for professional reasons, will not publicize the winners' names until a decent interval has elapsed. Red coats were introduced by the pioneer professional, William Knight-Smith (d. 1932) *c.* 1900.

Lecture Agency
The world's largest lecture agency is the American Program Bureau of Boston, Mass., U.S.A., with 400 Personalities on 40 Topics and a turnover of some $5 million. The top rate is $4,000 (£1,600) per hour commanded by Ralph Nader (b. Winsted, Connecticut, 27 Feb. 1934). This is $66.66 (£26.66) per min.

Working week
Dr. Adrian Caro of Norfolk and Norwich Hospital, gave evidence in November 1971, that some housemen and registrars in hospitals have an active working week in extreme cases of 139 hours, allowing only 4 hours 8½ mins

sleep per night. Some contracts for University lecturers call for a 3 hour week or a 72 hours year spread over 24 weeks.

Working career
Edward King Gaylord (b. 5 Mar. 1873, Muscotah, Kansas) worked for 90 years from being a strawberry picker aged 11 until the age of 101, as the millionaire President of The Oklahoma Publishing Co. He died on 30 May 1974.

The longest recorded working career one in job in Britain was that of Miss Polly Gadsby who started work with Archibald Turner & Co. of Leicester aged 9. In 1932, after 86 years service, she was still at her bench wrapping elastic, at the age of 95. Mr. Theodore C. Taylor (1850–1952) served 86 years with J. T. & T. Taylor of Batley, West Yorkshire including 56 years as chairman.

Milkman, Longest serving
Britain's longest serving milkman was Mr. John Baggs (b. August 1884) of Horndean, near Portsmouth, Hampshire, who had been on his round for over 80 years ("I don't like sitting about"). He was assisted by his boy John Baggs Junior, aged 64.

Most Durable Coal Miner
David Davies (*né* David) (b. 19 Feb. 1842 Pontrhyfen, Afan Valley, South Wales) worked underground as a collier for 73 years from 1849 to 1922 from the age of 7 to his retirement aged 80.

Longest pension
Miss Millicent Barclay, daughter of Col. William Barclay was born posthumously on 10 July 1872 and became eligible for a Madras Military Fund pension to continue until her marriage. She died unmarried on 26 Oct. 1969 having drawn the pension for every day of her life of 97 years 3 months.

Doctors *Oldest*
Dr. Frederick Walter Whitney Dawson Q.S.M. (1876–1977) was the first doctor to be registered this century in London on 1 Jan. 1901. He was still practising in Whangarei, New Zealand in his 101st year.

Doctors *Most in a family*
Eight sons of John Robertson of Benview, Dumbarton, Scotland graduated as medical doctors between 1892 and 1914. The family of David L. Bernie of Dayton, Ohio contains 27 members who are qualified M.D.'s with 5 more in medical school.

MISCELLANEOUS ENDEAVOURS
Accordion Playing
Stas Szezesnak played an accordion for 64 hrs 13 mins at Westchester, Pennsylvania on 20–22 Apr. 1979.

Apple peeling
The longest single unbroken apple peel on record is one of 172 ft 4 in *52,51 m* peeled by Kathy Wafler, 17 of Wolcott, New York, U.S.A. in 11 hours 30 min at Long Ridge Mall, Rochester, N.Y. on 16 Oct. 1976. The apple weighed 20 oz *567 g*.

Apple picking
The greatest recorded performance is 341 U.S. bushels (330.4 Imperial bushels *120,14 hectolitres*) picked in 8 hours by Geoffrey Cash at N. & E. Hides, Batlow, N.S.W., Australia on 3 Apr. 1977.

Bag carrying
The greatest non-stop bag-carrying feat carrying 1 cwt. *50,8 kg* of household coal in an open bag is 22.2 miles *35,72 km* by Brian Newton, 29 from Leicester to Rearsby and back in 6 hr 7 mins on 12 Nov. 1976.

The record for the 1012,5 m *1,107.2 yd* course annual Gawthorpe, West Yorkshire race is 4 min 19 sec by Terry Lyons, 36 on 16 Apr. 1979.

Bag-pipes
The longest duration pipe has been one of 100 hours by

Neville Workman, Clive Higgins, Patrick Forth and Paul Harris of Churchill School Pipe Band, Salisbury, Rhodesia on 9–13 July 1976.

Balancing on one foot
The longest recorded duration for continuous balancing on one foot is 27 hours 3 mins by K. Ranganathan at Puttalam, Sri Lanka on 20–21 Apr. 1979. The disengaged foot may not be rested on the standing foot nor may any sticks be used for support or balance.

Ball punching
Ron Renaulf (Australia) equalled his own world duration ball punching record of 125 hours 20 min at 10.20 p.m. on 31 Dec. 1955, at the Esplanade, Southport, Australia.

Balloon flights
The longest reported toy balloon flight is one of 9,000 miles *14 500 km* from Atherton, California (released by Jane Dorst on 21 May 1972) and found on 10 June at Pietermaritzburg, South Africa. The longest recorded hydrogen-filled balloon flight from the geographical British Isles is one of 5,880 miles *9 460 km* from Jersey which was returned from Camps Bay, Cape Province, South Africa on 28 Apr. 1974, 43 days after release by Gerard Wankling.

Balloon racing
The largest balloon release on record has been one of 130,000 helium balloons at Baltimore Memorial Stadium, Baltimore, Maryland, U.S.A. on 10 Oct. 1976.

Band marathons
The longest recorded "blow-in" is 100 hrs 2 min by the Du Val Senior High School, Lanham, Maryland, U.S.A. on 13–17 May 1977.

Band One-Man
Don Davis of Hollywood, California was the first one-man band able to play 4 melody and 2 percussion instruments simultaneously without electronics in 1974. For his rendition of the 4th movement of Beethoven's Fifth, he utilizes his unique 8-prong pendular perpendicular piano pounder and semicircular chromatic radially-operated centrifugally sliding left-handed glockenspiel. The greatest number of instruments played in a single tune is 75 in 2 mins 11.2 secs by Rory Blackwell at the E.M.I. Bingo and Social Club, Derry's Cross, Plymouth, Devon on 6 Sept. 1977. The Professor of Music at the University of Connecticut, U.S.A. certified on 11 Aug. 1978 that James Blain played 8 intsruments (4 melodic and 4 percussion) simultaneously. Rob Stewart of Kissimmee, Florida, U.S.A., played his one man band (which must include at least 3 instruments played simultaneously) for 38 hrs 1 min on 5–6 May 1979.

Barrel jumping
The greatest reported distance achieved by a barrel-jumper on ice skates is 32 ft *9,75 m* (over 13 barrels) by T. Karl Milne (b. 1900) at Albany, N.Y., U.S.A. on 31 Jan. 1930.

Barrel rolling
The record for rolling a full 36 gallon metal beer barrel over a measured mile is 9 min 52 secs by a team of six from Haunchwood Collieries Institute and Social Club, Nuneaton, Warwickshire on 30 Oct. 1977.

Barrow pushing
The heaviest loaded barrow pushed for a minimum 20 ft (actually 22 ft 9½ in *6,94 m*) is one loaded with 232 bricks weighing a gross 18½ cwt. (2,076 lb.) *941,65 kg* by Steven Draper at Dapto, N.S.W. Australia on 11 Mar. 1978.

Bath Tub Racing
The record for the annual international 36 miles *57,9 km* Nanaimo to Vancouver, British Columbia bath tub race is 1 hr 29 min 40 sec by Gary Deathbridge (Astralian) on 30 July 1978. Tubs are limited to 75 in *1,90 m* and 6 h.p. motors. The greatest distance for paddling a hand propelled bath tub in 24 hours is 36 miles 1,072 yds *58,91 km* by 25 scouts at Priory Park, Malvern, Hereford and Worcester on 10–11 May 1975.

James Blain, in action when claiming to be playing 8 instruments simultaneously in August 1978.

Baton Twirling
Shelia Cline, Donnetta Cline and Rebeckah Peery of Tazewell High School, Tazewell, Virginia, U.S.A. twirled for 50 hrs 30 min on 2–4 Dec. 1978.

Beard of Bees
The heaviest recorded beard of bees was one of 17,500 which swarmed around a queen bee on the chin of Don Cooke of Ohio in Los Angeles on 6 Apr. 1979.

Bed making
The record time set under the rigorous rules of the Australian Bedmaking Championships is 28.2 secs by Wendy Wall, 34, of Hebersham, Sydney, N.S.W. on 30 Nov. 1978.

The British record with 1 blanket, 2 sheets, an undercsheet, an uncased pillow, 1 counterpane and "hospital" corners is 24.0 secs by Judith Strange and Catheryn Marsden of High Peak College, Buxton, Derbyshire on 11 Mar. 1978.

Bed of nails
The duration record for non-stop lying on a bed of nails (sharp 6-inch *15,2 cm*; 2 in *5* cm apart) is 65 hours 43 min 21 sec by Tim Robinson (Strombo, The Maniac) at Oval House Theatre Club, London, on 16–19 June 1977. The female record is 30 hours (non-stop) set by Geraldine Williams (Miranda, Queen of the fakirs) of Welwyn Garden City, Hertfordshire, on 18–19 Mar. 1977. Much longer durations are claimed by uninvigilated *fakirs*—the most extreme case being *Silki* who claimed 111 days in São Paulo, Brazil ending on 24 Aug. 1969.

Note: Now that weights in Bed of Nails contests have attained

¾ ton 762 kg *this category has been retired. No further claims for publication will be entertained or published.*

The ultimate weight in an Iron Maiden, being sandwiched between two beds of nails, was 1,642½ lb. *745,02 kg* endured by Komar (Vernon E. Craig) at Old Chicago Towne, Chicago, Illinois on 6 Mar. 1977.

Bed pushing
The longest recorded push of a normally sessile object is of 3,000 miles *4 828 km* in the case of a wheeled hospital bed by a team of 12 from the Swansea Hospitals Radio Service, Swansea, S. Wales on 1–25 Aug. 1978.

Bed race
The record time for the annual Knaresborough Bed Race (established 1966) in North Yorkshire is 14 min 7.0 sec for the 1.96 mile *3,15 km* course crossing the River Nidd by the I.C.I. Fibres Flying Fiasco team on 10 June 1978.

Beer Label Collecting
The greatest collection of different British Beer labels is 22,000 by Keith Osborne, Hon. Sec. of The Labologists Society (founded by Guinness Exports Ltd in 1958). His oldest is a Bass label of 1869.

Beer Mat Flipping
Lack of standardisation of the size and weight of beer mats has bedevilled the chronicling of records in this international pursuit.

A figure of 72 was reported from Roy Clarke, 36 of Fleetwood on 9 Feb. 1979 at Leek, Staffordshire but rules have not been codified.

Best man
The world's champion "best man" is Mr. Wally Gant, a bachelor fishmonger from Wakefield, West Yorkshire, who officiated for the 50th time since 1931 in December 1964.

Bicycle *Most mounting simultaneously*
In August 1977 Chinese circus acrobats demonstrated the ability of a troupe of 12 (sometimes 13) to mount and ride a single bicycle in Peking.

Big Wheel riding
The endurance record for riding a Big Wheel is 37 days by Rena Clark and Jeff Block at Frontier Village Amusement Park, San Jose, California, U.S.A. on 1 July–7 Aug. 1978.

Billiard table jumping
Joe Darby (1861–1937) cleared a full-sized 12 ft *3,65 m* billiard table lengthwise, taking off from a 4 in *10 cm* high solid wooden block, at Wolverhampton, West Midlands on 5 Feb. 1892.

Bomb defusing
The highest reported number of unexploded bombs defused by any individual is 8,000 by Werner Stephan in West Berlin, Germany, in the 12 years from 1945 to 1957. He was killed by a small grenade on the Grunewald blasting site on 17 Aug. 1957.

Bond signing
The greatest historical feat of bond signing was that performed by L. E. Chittenden (d. 1902), the Registrar of the United States Treasury. In 48 hours (20–22 March 1863) he signed 12,500 bonds worth $10,000,000 (*now £4 million*), which had to catch a steam packet to England. He suffered years of pain and the bonds were never used.

Boomerang throwing
The earliest mention of a word similar to *boomerang* is *wo-mur-rang* in Collins *Acct. N.S. Wales Vocab.* published in 1798. The earliest certain Australian account of a returning boomerang (term established, 1827) was in 1831 by Major (later Sir Thomas) Mitchell. Curved throwing sticks for wild fowl hunting were found in the tomb of Tutankhamun dating from the mid 14th century B.C.

World championships and codified rules were not established until 1970. Jeff Lewry has won in 1970–71–72–73 and also the Australian title in 1974. The Boomerang Association of Australia's official record for distance reached from the thrower before the boomerang returns is 88,2 m *289 ft 4 in* diameter (orbital path 270 m *885 ft*) by Leo Meier (Switzerland) at Darlington Point, N.S.W. on 6 Nov. 1976. Herb A. Smith won a contest at Crawley Sussex on 6 Aug. 1978 with a throw of 105,5 m *346.1 ft.*

Brick carrying
The greatest distance achieved for carrying a brick 8 lb. 15 oz. *4,053 kg* in a nominated ungloved hand in an uncradled downward pincher grip is 45 miles *72,4 km* by David and Kym Barger of Lamar, Missouri, U.S.A. on 21 May 1977.

The feminine record for an 9 lb. 12 oz. *4,422 kg* brick is 19.2 miles *30,89 km* by Cynthia Ann Smolko of Denville, New Jersey, U.S.A. on 14 May 1977. The British record for a 6 lb. *2,72 kg* smooth-sided brick is 2.24 miles *3,60 km* by Mrs. Jane Reynolds of Salisbury, Wiltshire at the B.B.C. T.V. Centre London on 10 Nov. 1974.

Bricklaying
Andy Lundie of Aldershot, Hants won the first National Bricklaying Championship held on 25 Oct. 1978. He laid 619 bricks in one hour according to the rules of the Guild of Bricklayers.

Brick Racing
The record times recorded at the Annual N.F.B.T.E. Young Builders Dry-brick championship in Leicester are 100 metres: 1 min 25.0 sec + 22 penalty points giving a gross 1 min 47.0 sec by Steve Mee, and 1 mile (team): 23 min 52 sec + 89 penalties giving an overall time of 25 min 21 sec by William Davis & Company (Leicester) Ltd. Both were established on 21 May 1978.

Brick throwing
The greatest reported distance for throwing a standard 5 lb. *2,268 kg* building brick is 146 ft 1 in *44,54 m* by Geoffrey Capes at Braybrook School, Orton Goldhay, Cambridgeshire on 19 July 1978.

Bubble Gum Blowing
The greatest reported diameter for a bubble gum bubble is 17 in *43 cm* by Rhodessa Ruffin and Cindy McNeil of California, Andy Berrick of Pennsylvania and Brett Nichols of Georgia, U.S.A. The British record also using "Bubble Yum" is 15¾ in *40 cm* by John Burnside, 15, in Portsmouth on 6 Aug. 1978.

Burial alive
Voluntary burial alive (for which claims up to 217 days have been published) are inadmissible unless the depth of the coffin is a minimum 2 m *6 ft 6¾ in* below ground; the coffin has a maximum cubic capacity of 1,5 million cc or 54 cubic feet and the aperture for communication and feeding has a maximum dimension of 10 cm or *4 inches.*

"Country" Bill White, 44, used an inadmissible 8 inch square *20,3 × 20,3 cm* aperture in his 134 day 2 hr 5 min burial at New Bedford, Massachusetts on 29 Jan.–12 June 1978 but the Sheriff of Bristol County certified that he remained underground throughout.

Camping Out
Graeme Hurry (38th Coventry Central Scout Group) completed four years sleeping out on 19 June 1978. He had earlier shared first place in the *Scouting* magazine national contest on 19 June 1975 but just carried on.

Can Top Collecting
The longest recorded one-man chain of can tops is one of 11.2 miles *18,02 km* collected since 4 July 1969 by Arthur J. Jordan Sr. of Yorkstown, Virginia, U.S.A. to the estimated number of 710,000 as of 14 May 1979.

Card Throwing
Tommy Jackson threw a standard playing card 166 ft

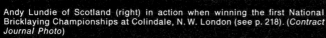

Andy Lundie of Scotland (right) in action when winning the first National Bricklaying Championships at Colindale, N.W. London (see p. 218). (*Contract Journal Photo*)

Don Cooke (USA) sporting a beard of 17,500 swarming bees (see p. 217).

50,59 m at Glenwood School, Phoenix City, Alabama, U.S.A. on 8 Sept. 1977.

Car Wrecking
The greatest number of cars wrecked in a stunting career is 1,470 to 1 June 1979 by Dick Sheppard of Gloucester, England.

Catapulting
The greatest recorded distance for a catapult shot is 1,362 ft *415 m* by James F. Pfotenhauer using a patented 16½ ft *5,02 m* "Monarch IV Supershot" and a 53 calibre lead shot on Ski Hill, Escanaba, Michigan, U.S.A. on 10 Sept. 1977.

Champagne Fountain
The tallest successfully filled column of champagne glasses is one 19 high filled from the top by Martin Moore, Annabel Lee, Christine Price and Susan Brooklyn of Butlin's, Brighton, Sussex on 17 Apr. 1979.

Clapping
The duration record for continuous clapping (sustaining an average of 140 claps per min audible at 100 yd *91 m*) is 39 hrs 15 min by James Dutton, Steven Passmore, Melody Goodrich and Tammy Robertson of Richmond, Virginia, U.S.A. on 19–20 Aug. 1977.

Club swinging
Bill Franks set a world record of 17,280 revolutions (4.8 per sec) in 60 min at Webb's Gymnasium, Newcastle, N.S.W., Australia on 2 Aug. 1934. M. Dobrilla swung continuously for 144 hours at Cobar, N.S.W. finishing on 15 Sept. 1913.

Coal cutting
The first coal mine in Britain to achieve more than 5 tons output per man-shift for a whole year has been Bagworth Colliery, Leicestershire announced on 5 Apr. 1975. The individual record for filling is 218 tons in a week of 5 shifts by Jim Marley (b. 1914) at East Walbottle Colliery, Tyne and Wear, England in 1949. This included 47½ tons in 6 hours.

Coal shovelling
The record for filling a half-ton *508 kg* hopper with coal is 42 sec by Robert Taylor of Dobson, New Zealand on 3 Feb. 1979.

Coin balancing
The greatest recorded feat of coin-balancing is the stacking of 130 coins on top of a silver U.S. dollar on edge by Alex Chervinsky, of Lock Haven, Pennsylvania in 1974 after 26 years practice.

Coin snatching
The greatest number of 10p pieces clean caught from being flipped from the back of a forearm into the same palm is 62 by Andrew Gleed at the *Evening Star* offices, Ipswich on 22 Sept. 1978. The North American record using 25 cent pieces or "quarters" is 120 by Gene Basta of Liverpool, N.Y., U.S.A., set on 12 May 1978.

Competition winnings
The largest individual competition prize win on record is $307,500 (*then £109,821*) by Herbert J. Idle, 55, of Chicago in an encyclopaedia contest run by Unicorn Press Inc. on 20 Aug. 1953. The highest value first prize offered in Britain has been a fully furnished house worth £27,000 featured in *Women's Own* in the autumn of 1974. The winner came from more than 150,000 entrants.

Complainer Most successful
Ralph Charell (b. 3 Dec. 1929), author of *How I Turn Ordinary Complaints into Thousands of Dollars*, between January

1963 and June 1977 amassed a total of $80,710.46 (£42,480) ranging between $6.95 and $25,000 in refunds and compensations. A recent complaint was against this publication for failing to list his 51 consecutive profitable transactions in "option trading".

Cow Chip tossing

The record distance for throwing a dried cow chip depends on whether or not the projectile may or may not be "moulded into a spherical shape". Purists do not permit "sphericalization". The greatest distance achieved under the "non-alteration" rule (established in 1970) is 199 ft 1 in 60,68 m by Mr Robert D. Fleming, 25, of Taylorville, Illinois on 27 Aug. 1977. These increasing distances are anxiously studied by party political campaign managers who are also in support of a rule which precludes the common practice of mixing cement kiln dust into the cow feed prior to contests.

Crawling

The longest continuous voluntary crawl (progression with one or other knee in unbroken contact with the ground) on record is 12.6 miles 20,27 km by Peter Holroyd of Bath University, Avon on 1 Nov. 1978. The Baptist lay preacher Hans Mullikin, 39 arrived at the White House, Washington D.C. on 23 Nov. 1978 having crawled all but 8 of the 1,600 miles 2 575 km from Marshall, Texas.

Crochet

The longest recorded crocheted chain is one of 4 ply yarn measuring 25.70 miles 41,3 km completed by Mrs. Theresa Bloxsome of Mortlake in April 1978. Mrs. Sybille Anthony bettered all knitting marathons in a 120 hour crochet marathon at Toombul Shopping-town, Australia on 3–7 Oct. 1977.

Cucumber slicing

Norman Johnson of Blackpool College of Art and Technology set a record of 24.2 sec for slicing a 12 in cucumber 1½ in diameter at 20 slices to the inch (total 240 slices) on B.B.C. T.V. Record Breakers on 28 Sept. 1973.

Custard Pie throwing

The most times champion in the annual World Custard Pie Championships at Coxheath, Kent (instituted 1967) have been the "The Birds" and the Coxheath Man each with 3 wins. The target (face) must be 8 ft 3⅞ in 2,53 m from the thrower who must throw a pie no more than 10¾ in 27,3 cm in diameter. Six points are scored for a square hit full in the face.

DANCING

In future editions Go-Go *and* Twist *categories will be deleted and* Disco-Dancing *will encompass these styles of dance.*

Largest Dance

The largest dance ever staged was that put on by the Houston Livestock Show at the Astro Hall, Houston, Texas, U.S.A. on 8 Feb. 1969. The attendance was more than 16,500 with 4,000 turned away.

Marathon dancing must be distinguished from dancing mania, which is a pathological condition. The worst outbreak of dancing mania was at Aachen, Germany, in July 1374, when hordes of men and women broke into a frenzied and compulsive choreomania in the streets which lasted for hours till injury or complete exhaustion ensued.

The most severe marathon dance staged as a public spectacle in the U.S.A. was one lasting 4,152½ hours (24 weeks 5 days) completed by Tony Alteriri and Vera Mikus (now Mrs. Oglesby of Springdale, Pennsylvania) at Motor Square Garden, Pittsburgh from 6 June to 30 Nov. 1932. The rest allowance of 15 min per hour was progressively cut to 10, 7, 6, 5, and in the final weeks to 3 min. per hour until this Marathon Dance "Classic" was finally stopped by the authorities. The prize of $1,000 was equivalent to 24 cents per hour.

Ballet

In the *entrechat* (a vertical spring from the fifth position with the legs extended criss-crossing at the lower calf), the starting and finishing position each count as one such that in an *entrechat douze* there are *five* crossings and uncrossings. This was performed by Wayne Sleep for the B.B.C. *Record Breakers* programme on 7 Jan. 1973. He was in the air for 0.71 of a second.

Ballet *Most turns*

The greatest number of spins called for in classical ballet choreography is the 32 *fouettés rond de jambe en tournant* in "Swan Lake" by Pyotr Ilyich Chaykovskiy (Tschaikovsky) (1840–1893). Miss Rowena Jackson (later Chatfield), M.B.E. (b. Invercargill, N.Z., 1925) achieved 121 such turns at her class in Melbourne, Victoria, Australia, in 1940.

Ballet *Most curtain calls*

The greatest recorded number of curtain calls ever received by ballet dancers is 89 by Dame Margaret Evelyn Arias, D.B.E. *née* Hookham (born Reigate, Surrey, 19 May 1919), *alias* Margot Fonteyn, and Rudolf Hametovich Nureyev (born on a train near Irkutsk, U.S.S.R., 17 Mar. 1938) after a performance of "Swan Lake" at the Vienna Staatsoper, Austria, in October 1964.

Ballet *Largest Cast*

The largest number of ballet dancers used in a production in Britain has been 2,000 in the London Coster Ballet of 1962, directed by Lillian Rowley, at the Royal Albert Hall, London.

Ballroom *Marathon*

The individual continuous world record for ballroom dancing is 106 hours 5 min 10 sec by Carlos Sandrini in Buenos Aires, Argentina, in September 1955. Three girls worked shifts as his partner.

Ballroom *Champions*

The world's most successful professional ballroom dancing champions have been Bill Irvine, M.B.E. and Bobbie Irvine, M.B.E., who won 13 world titles between 1960 and 1972.

The most consecutive national titles won is 10 in the New Zealand Old Time Championship by Mr. Maurice Fox and his wife Royce (*née* Miles) of Palmerston North in 1959–68.

The oldest competitive ballroom dancer is Albert J. Sylvester C.B.E., J.P. (b. 24 Nov. 1889) of Corsham, Wiltshire. In 1977 he won the topmost amateur Alex Moore award for a 10 dance test with his partner Paula Smith in Bath on 26 Apr. 1977.

Belly Dancing

The longest recorded belly dance was one of 100 hours by Sabra Starr at Teplitzki's Hotel, Atlantic City, New Jersey, U.S.A. on 4–8 July 1977.

Charleston

The Charleston duration record is 110 hours 58 mins by Sabra Starr of Lansdowne, Pennsylvania, U.S.A. on 15–20 Jan. 1979.

Conga

The longest recorded conga was one comprising a "snake" of 8,128 people in Sidmouth, Devon on 25 Aug. 1978.

Disco

The longest recorded disco dancing marathon is one of 329 hrs 30 min by Keith Leriche of Port Aux Basques, Newfoundland, Canada on 16–30 Apr. 1979.

Flamenco

The fastest flamenco dancer ever measured is Solero de Jerez aged 17 who in Brisbane, Australia in September 1967 in an electrifying routine attained 16 heel taps per second or a rate of 1,000 a minute.

Go-go

The duration record for go-go dancing (Boogoloo or Reggae) is 200 hrs 7 min by Nitro (Sabra Starr) and Rhiannon (Beverly Rainey) at Kelly's Bar, Wrightstown, New Jersey, U.S.A. on 1–8 July 1978.

Veronica Evans, who set the still unrivalled world record for high kicks with 8,005 in 4 hrs 40 min in 1939.

High Kicking
The world record for high kicks is 8,005 in 4 hrs 40 min by Veronica Evans (*née* Steen), (b. Liverpool, 20 Feb. 1910) at the Pathétone Studios, Wardour Street, London in summer 1939.

Jiving
The duration record for non-stop jiving is 96 hrs 49 min by Richard Rimmer of Caterham, Surrey on 20–24 Nov. 1978.

Limbo
The lowest height for a bar under which a limbo dancer has passed under a flaming bar is 6⅛ in *15,5 cm* off the floor by Marlene Raymond, 15 at the Port of Spain Pavilion, Toronto, Canada on 24 June 1973. Strictly no part of the body other than the sole or side of the foot should touch the ground though the brushing of a shoulder blade does not in practice usually result in disqualification.

Tap
The fastest *rate* ever measured for any tap dancer has been 1,440 taps per min (24 per sec) by Roy Castle on the B.B.C. T.V. *Record Breakers* programme on 14 Jan. 1973.

The greatest ever assemblage of tap dancers in a single routine is 528 from Brenda Kalatze's Tap Studio, Los Angeles for the Guinness Spectacular T.V. transmission on 7 Apr. 1979. Ages ranged from 4 to 84.

Twist
The duration for the twist is 145 hours 30 mins by Anetta Roussou of Simonstown, Cape Province, South Africa on 12–18 Dec. 1977.

Dance band
The most protracted session for a dance band is one of 321 hours (13 days 9 hours) by the Black Brothers of West Germany at Bonn ending on 2 Feb. 1968. Never less than a quartet were in action during the marathon.

Demolition work
Fifteen members of the International Budo Association (Japanese martial arts) led by Phil Milner (3rd Dan Karate) demolished, a 6-roomed early Victorian house at Idle, Bradford, West Yorkshire by head, foot and empty hand in 6 hours on 4 June 1972. On completion they bowed to the rubble.

Disc-Jockey
The longest continuous period of acting as a disc-jockey is 1,500 hours by Mickie Gee in Reykjavik, Iceland from 22 Jan.–25 Mar. 1979. L.P.'s are limited to 50% of total playing time.

Domino Toppling
The greatest number of dominoes toppled is 169,713 by Michael Cairney, 23, at the Mid-Hudson Civic Center, Plaza, Poughkeepsie, New York on 9 June 1979 for the National Hemophilia Foundation. The dominoes stretching 4.3 miles *6,9 km* fell at 2¼ m.p.h. *3,6 km/h* having taken 13 days to set up.

Drumming
The world's duration drumming record is 720 hours by Clifford Marshall Van Buren of Ridgefield, Conn., U.S.A. on 26 Dec. 1977–25 Jan. 1978.

Ducks and Drakes
The best accepted ducks and drakes (stone-skipping) record is 24 skips (10 plinkers and 14 pitty-pats) by Warren Klope, 20 of Troy, Michigan with a 4 in *10 cm* thin flat limestone at the annual Mackinac Island, Michigan, U.S.A. stone skipping tournament on 5 July 1975. This was equalled by John S. Kolar of Birmingham, Michigan and Glenn Loy Jr. of Flint, Michigan on 4 July 1977.

Egg dropping
The greatest height from which fresh eggs have been dropped and remained intact is 600 ft *182 m* by David S. Donoghue and John Cartwright from a helicopter on 8 Feb. 1974.

Egg and spoon racing
Gerry O'Kane, 21, from Carfin, Motherwell, Strathclyde completed a 27-mile *43,45 km* fresh egg and dessert spoon marathon in 5 hours 27 min on 7 Apr. 1977.

Egg shelling
Two kitchen hands, Harold Witcomb and Gerald Harding shelled 1,050 dozen eggs in a 7¼ hour shift at Dwyers, Trowbridge, Wiltshire on 23 Apr. 1971. Both are blind.

Egg throwing
The longest recorded distance for throwing a fresh hen's egg without breaking is 350 ft *106,68 m* on their 58th exchange between William Cole and Jonathan Heller in Central Park, New York, U.S.A. on 17 Mar. 1979.

Escapology
The most renowned of all escape artists has been Erich Weiss *alias* Harry Houdini (1874–1926), who pioneered underwater escapes from locked, roped and weighted containers while handcuffed and shackled with irons.

One of the major manufacturers of strait-jackets acknowledges that an escapologist "skilled in the art of bone and muscle manipulation" could escape from a standard jacket in seconds. The extreme acknowledged claim is 1.68 secs by Bill Shirk on 19 June 1979 at the Marion County Sheriff's Dept. Training Center, Indianapolis, Indiana, U.S.A. Shirk also set the record for the highest escape suspended in a strait jacket below a helicopter at 1,610 ft *490 m* altitude over Indianapolis on 7 Aug. 1977 (in 22.5 sec).

Bill Shirk was imprisoned in a cell in Hamilton County Jail, Indiana on 31 Oct. 1977. He was locked with 3 handcuffs behind his back, tied by 5 millimetre chain, fastened in foot-cuffs and a further 44 lb *20 kg* of 5 mm and 10 mm chain (tensile strength 5.94 tons). He broke out in 3 hrs 49 min 42 sec.

Family Tree
The largest family tree on record is the Borton tree of 6,820 names compiled by Nellaray "Borton" Holt of Union Gap, Washington, U.S.A. over 16 years. It measures 18 × 15 ft *5,48 × 4,57 m* and extends back to 1562. She also constructed a 340 ft *103,6 m* long pedigree chart covering 16 generations commissioned by Maxine Bremermans.

Fashion Show *longest*
The longest fashion show ever recorded was one which lasted 48 hrs on the Roseland catwalk, Sydney, Australia on 16–18 June 1977, compèred by Patrick Bollen. Lyn Snowdon, Kay Hammond and Virginia Connor all completed 41.4 miles *66,6 km* on the catwalk.

Faux Pas
If measuring by financial consequence, the greatest *faux pas* on record was that of the young multi-millionaire, James Gordon Bennett, committed on 1 Jan. 1877 at the family mansion of his demure fiancée one Caroline May, in Fifth Avenue, New York City. Bennett arrived in a two-horse cutter late and obviously in wine. By dint of intricate foot-work, he gained the portals to enter the withdrawing room where he was the cynosure of all eyes. He mistook the fire-place for a plumbing fixture more usually reserved for another purpose. The May family broke the engagement and Bennett (1841–1918) was obliged to spend the rest of his foot-loose and fancy-free life based in Paris with the resultant non-collection of millions of tax dollars by the U.S. Treasury.

Feminine Beauty
Female pulchritude being qualitative rather than quantitative does not lend itself to records. It has been suggested that, if the face of Helen of Troy (*c.* 1200 B.C.) was capable of launching 1,000 ships, a unit of beauty sufficient to launch one ship should be a millihelen. The pioneer beauty contest was staged

---

above: Arild Støre (encircled) diving from a height of 38 m *124½ ft* from a bridge at Vrengenbroen near Oslo. This gives a dramatic idea of the height of the 36 m *118 ft* cliffs at La Quebrada, Acapulco, Mexico from which divers regularly perform (see p. 223). (*Ottar Rogne: Express Forlag*) *below:* Steve McPeak, the world's highest high-wire artist, in action in a race up a 39 degree gradient with Farrell Hettig in Los Angeles (see p. 224).

at Atlantic City, New Jersey, U.S.A. in 1921 and was won by a thin blue-eyed blonde with a 30 in *76,2 cm* chest, Margaret Gorman. The Miss World contest began in London in July 1951. The maximum dimensions of any winner were those of Miss Egypt, Antigone Costanda, in 1954 whose junoesque characteristics were at 40-26-38 in *101-66-96 cm* in advance of the classic Western idea of allure. The United Kingdom is the only country to have produced four winners. They were Rosemarie Frankland (1961); Ann Sidney (1964); Lesley Langley (1965) and Helen Morgan (1974), who resigned. The maximum number of contestants was 68 in November 1975.

The tallest girl to win the Miss United Kingdom title has been Madelene Stringer (now Mrs Chandler), the 6 ft *1,82 m* tall 1977 winner from Tyne and Wear.

The world's largest beauty pageant is the annual Miss Universe contest inaugurated in Long Beach California in 1952. The most successful country has been the U.S.A. with winners in 1954–56–60–67. The number of countries represented has reached 75 with Miss South Africa reigning in 1978.

Fire Pumping
The greatest gallonage stirrup-pumped by a team of 8 in an 80 hour charity pump is 7,494 galls *340,6 hectolitres* by the Witney Brigade, Oxfordshire on 26–30 Aug. 1977.

Fire Pump pulling
The longest unaided tow of a fire appliance in excess of 10 cwt *508 kg* in 24 hrs is 168.3 miles *270,8 km* by a team of 32 men from the Dublin Fire Brigade who reached Cork City in 23 hrs 55 min on 29–30 March 1978.

Flute marathon
The longest recorded marathon by a flautist is 48 hours by Joe Silmon in H.M.S. *Grampus* in Gosport, Hampshire on 19–20 Feb. 1977.

Frisbee throwing
A Frisbee is a concave plastic throwing plate. Competitive Frisbee throwing began in 1957. The International Frisbee Association indoor records are Men: 296.3 ft *90,3 m* by Joseph Youngman, 22 Aug. 1978, Los Angeles; and Women: 222.5 ft *67,8 m* Monika Lou in Los Angeles on 24 Aug. 1977. The outdoor records are: Men: 444 ft *135,3 m* by John Kirkland, 30 Apr. 1978, Dallas; and Women: 283.5 ft *86,4 m* by Susane Lempert, 24 July 1976 at Boston. The throw, run and catch record is 254.9 ft *77,7 m* by Bob Reeve on 24 Mar. 1979 at Santa Barbara. The group marathon record is 1001 hours by The Alhambra Frisbee disc club on 7 May–18 June 1978 at Alhambra, California.

Gladiatorial Combat
Emperor Trajan of Rome (A.D. 98–117) staged a display involving 4,941 pairs of gladiators over 117 days. Publius Ostorius, a freedman, survived 51 combats in Pompeii.

Gold panning
The fastest time recorded for "panning" 8 planted gold nuggets in a 10 in *25,4 cm* diameter pan is 14.45 secs by Lance Murray and 15.27 secs by Mrs. Carolyn Box both of Ahwahnee, California in the 1978 18th World Gold Panning Championships held at Tropico Gold Mine, Rosamond, California on 5–4 Mar. 1978.

Golf Ball Balancing
Lang Martin, 16, balanced 6 golf balls vertically without adhesive at Charlotte, North Carolina, U.S.A. on 10 July 1977.

Grape catching
The longest recorded distance for catching a thrown grape in the mouth is 259 ft *78,9 m* by Arden Chapman at Northeast Louisiana University, Louisiana, U.S.A. on 7 Nov. 1977. The grape-thrower was Benny David Jones.

Grave digging
It is recorded that Johann Heinrich Karl Thieme, sexton of Aldenburg, Germany, dug 23,311 graves during a 50-year career. In 1826 *his* understudy dug his grave.

Guitar playing
The longest recorded solo guitar playing marathon is one of 200 hrs 2 min by Dave Hathaway in Marion, Indiana, U.S.A., on 20–28 July 1978.

Gum Boot throwing
The longest recorded distance (a Size 8 Challenger Dunlop Boot) for "Wellie wanging" is 173 ft *52,73 m* by Tony Rodgers of Warminster, Wilts on 9 Sept. 1978. Rosemary Payne established the feminine record at Cannon Hill Park, Birmingham on 21 June 1975 with 129 ft 11 in *39,60 m.*

Gun running
The record for the Royal Tournament Naval Field Gun competition (instituted 1907, with present rules since 1913) is 2 min 44.6 secs by the Devonport Crew at Earl's Court, Kensington & Chelsea, Greater London on 24 July 1978. The barrel alone weighs 8 cwt. *406 kg*. The wall is 5 ft *1,52 m* high and the chasm 28 ft *8,53 m* across. The Portsmouth crew returned 2 min 40.7 sec in a training practice run at Whale Island, Portsmouth, Hampshire in 1972.

Haggis Hurling
The longest recorded distance for throwing a haggis (min. weight 1 lb. 8 ozs. *680 g* is 158 ft 2 in *48,2 m* by Robin Durant in Edzell, Tayside, Scotland on 12 August 1978.

Hair-dressing
Gerry Stupple of Dover, Kent cut, set and styled hair continuously for 341 hours 58 min on 5–19 March 1979.

Hair splitting
The greatest reported achievement in hair splitting has been that of the former champion cyclist and craftsman Alfred West (b. London, 14 Apr. 1901) who has succeeded in splitting a human hair 15 times into 16 parts in 1977.

Handbell ringing
The longest recorded handbell ringing recital has been one of 43 hrs 2 min by the Bluebells of Paradise United Church of Christ, Louisville, Ohio, U.S.A. on 8–10 June 1978.

Handshaking
A world record for handshaking was set up by Theodore Roosevelt (1858–1919), President of the U.S.A., when he shook hands with 8,513 people at a New Year's Day, White House Presentation in Washington, D.C., U.S.A. on 1 Jan. 1907. Mayor Joseph Lazarow shook hands with 11,030 people on the Boardwalk, Atlantic City, New Jersey, U.S.A. in 11 hrs 5 mins on 3 July 1977. Outside public life the record has become meaningless because aspirants merely tend to arrange circular queues or wittingly or unwittingly shake the same hands repetitively.

Hand writing
The longest recorded hand written letter writing marathon is one of 505 hours and 3,998 letters with their envelopes by Raymond L. Cantwell of Littlemore, Oxford, England in raising money for the Radcliffe Infirmary on 25 Aug.–16 Sept. 1978.

High Diving
The highest regularly performed dive is that of professional divers from La Quebrada ("the break in the rocks") at Acapulco, Mexico, a height of 118 ft *36 m*. The leader of the 27 divers in the exclusive Club de Clavadistas is Raul Garcia (b. 1928) with more than 35,000 dives. The base rocks, 21 ft *6,40 m* out from the take-off, necessitate a leap of 27 ft *8,22 m* out. The water is 12 ft *3,65 m* deep. The *Wide World of Sports* record is 130 ft 6 in *39,77 m* jointly set by Donnie Vick, Pat Sucher and John Tobler in March 1974.

On 8 May 1885, Sarah Ann Henley, aged 24, jumped from the Clifton Suspension Bridge, which crosses the Avon, England. Her 250 ft *76 m* fall was slightly cushioned by her voluminous dress and petticoat acting as a parachute. She landed, bruised and bedraggled, in the mud on the north bank and was carried to hospital by four policemen. On 11 Feb. 1968 Jeffrey Kramer, 24, leapt off the George Washington Bridge 250 ft *76 m* above the Hudson River, New York

City, N.Y. and survived. Of the 511 (to 25 Apr. 1974) people who have made 240 ft *73 m* suicide dives from the Golden Gate Bridge, San Francisco, California, U.S.A. since 1937 seven survived. On 10 July 1921 a stuntman named William H. Bailey leapt from a seaplane into the Ohio River at Louisville, Kentucky. The alleged altitude was 310 ft *94,5 m*.

Samuel Scott (U.S.A.) is reputed to have made a dive of 497 ft *151,48 m* at Pattison Fall (now Manitou Falls) in Wisconsin, U.S.A., in 1840, but this would have entailed an entry speed of 86 m.p.h. *138 km/h*. The actual height was probably 165 ft *50,30 m*. Col. Harry A. Froboess (Switzerland) jumped 110 m *360 ft* into the Bodensee from the airship *Graf Hindenburg* on 22 June 1936.

The greatest height reported for a dive into a flaming tank is one of 100 ft *20,4 m* into 7½ ft *2,28 m* by Bill McGuire, 48 at the Holiday Inn, Chicago City Center, Michigan, U.S.A. on 14 Aug. 1975. Kitty O'Neil dived 127 ft *38,70 m* from the 12th floor of the Valley Hilton Hotel, Sherman Oaks, California onto an airbag in March 1979.

Highest Shallow Dive
Henri La Mothe (b. 1904) set a record by diving 28 ft *8,53 m* into 12¾ in *31,43 cm* of water in a child's paddling pool in Northridge, California, on 7 Apr. 1979. He struck the water chest first at a speed of more than 25 mph *40 km/h*.

High-wire act *Highest and Steepest*
Steve McPeak, (b. Sept. 1945) made a 300 ft *91,4 m* crossing on a high wire 1,800 ft *550 m* above the Yosemite Valley Falls, California, U.S.A. on 5 July 1976. Farrell Hettig of Sarasota, Florida and McPeak raced up a wire ascending to 57 ft *17,37 m* at an angle of 39° in Los Angeles on the Guinness Spectacular T.V. Show in April 1979.

The greatest height above street level of any high wire performance has been from a 140 ft *42,6 m* wire between the 1,350 ft *411 m* twin towers of the World Trade Center, New York City by Philippe Petit, 24 of Nemours, France on 7 Aug. 1974. He was charged with criminal trespass after a 75 minute display of at least 7 crossings. The police psychiatrist opined "Anyone who does this 110 storeys up can't be entirely right".

Hitch-hiking
The title of world champion hitch-hiker is claimed by Devon Smith who from 1947 to 1971 thumbed lifts totalling 291,000 miles *468 300 km*. In 1957 he covered all the then 48 U.S. States in 33 days. It was not till his 6,013th "hitch" that he got a ride in a Rolls-Royce. The hitch-hiking record for the 873 miles *1 405 km* from Land's End, Cornwall, to John o' Groats, Highland, Scotland, is 21 hrs 55 min by John Repton and Rosemary Grounds of Eaton Hall College, Retford, Nottinghamshire (in reverse direction) on 13–14 Apr. 1978. The time before the first "hitch" on the first day is excluded. The fastest time recorded for the round trip is 45 hours 34 min by Guy Hobbs of Bradford-on-Avon, Wiltshire on 14–16 June 1978.

Hod Carrying
John Pitson of Oxford carried fifty-six 4.4 lb. *2 kg* Fletton bricks totalling 246 lb. *111,7 kg* up a 12 ft *3,65 m* ladder on 31 May 1978.

Hoop rolling
In 1968 it was reported that Zolilio Diaz (Spain) had rolled a hoop 600 miles *965 km* from Mieres to Madrid and back in 18 days.

Hop Scotch
The longest recorded hop scotch marathon is one of 54 hr 15 min by Sharon Wright and Sandra Burchett of Streamwood High School, Streamwood, Illinois, U.S.A. on 23–26 July 1978.

Hot Water Bottle Bursting
The highest lung power measurement in bursting hot water bottles is 28½ lb./in² *139 kg/m²* by Mel Robson of Newcastle upon Tyne in February 1977. He and Stuart Hughes have both extended a Suba Seal Safety Bottle to 5 ft 6 in *1,67 m* before rupture. Franco Columbu burst this type of bottle in

55 secs in Los Angeles on 6 Apr. 1979 for the Guinness Spectacular T.V. Show.

House of cards
The greatest number of storeys achieved in building free standing houses of playing cards is 61 in the case of a tower using 3,650 cards to a height of 11 ft 7 in *3,53 m* built by James Warnock at Cantley, Quebec, Canada, on 8 Sept. 1978.

Hula hooping
The highest claim for sustaining gyrating hoops is 62 set by Jo Ann Barnes 15, of Inglewood, California co-champion of the 1976 U.S. National contest at Six Flags Over Georgia U.S.A. on 3 Oct. 1976. The longest recorded marathon is 54 hrs by Kym Coberly of Denton, Texas, U.S.A. on 7–9 Oct. 1978.

Human cannonball
The record distance for firing a human from a cannon is 175 ft *53,3 m* in the case of Emanuel Zacchini in the Ringling Bros. and Barnum & Bailey Circus, Madison Square Gardens New York City, U.S.A., in 1940. His muzzle velocity has been estimated at 54 m.p.h. *86,9 km/h*. On his retirement the management were fortunate in finding that his daughter Florinda was of the same calibre. An experiment on Yorkshire T.V. on 17 Aug. 1978 showed that when Miss Sue Evans, 17 was fired she was ⅜ in *9,5 mm* shorter on landing.

In the Halifax explosion of 6 Dec. 1917 (see page 210) A. B. William Becker, A.M. (d. 1969) was blown some 1,600 yd *1,46 km* but was found breathing in a tree.

Human Fly
The greatest climb achieved on the vertical face of a building occurred on 26 May 1977 when George Willig, 27, scaled the outside of the 1,350 ft *411,48 m* high World Trade Centre, New York City in 3½ hours at a rate of 6.4 ft/min *1,95m/min*. On descending by elevator he was led to a waiting police car and charged with criminal trespass and reckless endangerment. The name of the masked "human fly", who has ridden at *240 m.p.h.* 380 km/h atop a DC-8 jetliner in April 1977 has not been disclosed. It is however believed unlikely that he is a member of the jet set.

Joke cracking
G. David Howard cracked jokes unremittingly for 13 hrs 18 min on 24–25 June 1978 at the Hilton Inn, Clearwater Beach, Florida, U.S.A. The duration record for a duo is 52 hours by Wayne Malton and Mike Hamilton at the Howard Johnson Motor Hotel, Toronto airport, Ontario, Canada on 13–16 Nov. 1975.

Juggling
The only juggler in history able to juggle—as opposed to "shower"—10 balls or eight plates was the Italian Enrico Rastelli, who was born in Samara, Russia, on 19 Dec. 1896 and died in Bergamo, Italy, on 13 Dec. 1931.

Jumble Sale
Britain's largest Jumble Sale was "Jumbly' 79" sponsored by *Woman's Own* at Alexandra Palace, London on 5–7 May 1979 in aid of Save The Children Fund. The attendance was 60,000 and the gross takings in excess of £60,000. The Winnetka Congregational Church, Illinois, U.S.A. raised $70,037.98 (then £36,860) in a one-day rummage sale on 11 May 1978.

Kraate Chop
Claims for breaking bricks and wooden slats etc. are unsatisfactory because of the lack of any agreed standards of friability and the spacing of fulcrums upon which comparisons can be made. Karatekas have been measured to exert a force of 3,000 newtons *675 lb f* and can develop a speed of 14,4 m/sec *32.2 m.p.h.*

Kiss of Life
Five members of the St. John Ambulance, York maintained a "kiss of life" for 132 hours with 140,742 inflations on 26–31 Dec. 1978. The "patient" was a dummy. 108 members of the Hawthorne Ambulance Service, Farmington, Maine, U.S.A. completed a 168 hr "Kiss of Life" marathon on 17–24 Sept. 1978.

Kissing

The most prolonged osculatory marathon in cinematic history is one of 185 sec by Regis Toomey and Jane Wyman in *You're In the Army Now* released in 1940. In a "Smoochathon" in Pittsburgh, Pennsylvania Bobbi Sherlock and Ray Blazina kissed for 130 hrs 2 mins (in aid, they say, of Cystic Fibrosis) on 1–6 May 1978. James Whale, 27, of Metro Radio, Newcastle-upon-Tyne kissed 4,049 girls in 8 hours in Tyneside on 22 Sept. 1978—a rate of one per 7.11 secs.

Kite Flying *Largest*

The largest kite on record was built in Naruto City, Japan in 1936 of 3,100 panes of paper weighing 8½ tons/*tonnes*. The largest hand-launched kite was one 91 ft *27,7 m* long and of 2,640 ft² *245,2 m²* by Mr. & Mrs. Don Shearing at San Pedro, California on 17 Oct. 1975.

Kite Flying *Greatest number*

The most kites flown on a single line is 4128 by Kazuhiko Asaba, 55 at Kamakura, Japan on 21 Sept. 1978.

Kite Flying *Altitude*

The single kite record is 22,500 ft (min)–28,000 ft (max) *6 860 to 8 535 m* by Prof. Phillip R. Kunz and Jay P. Kunz at Laramie, Wyoming, U.S.A. on 21 Nov. 1967. A claim for a chain of 8 kites reaching 31,955 ft *9 470 m* was made from Lindenburg, East Germany on 1 Aug. 1919.

Kite Flying *Duration*

The longest recorded flight is one of 169 hours by the Sunrise Inn team, Fort Lauderdale, Florida managed by Will Yolen on 30 Apr.–7 May 1977.

Knitting

The world's most prolific hand-knitter of all time has been Mrs. Gwen Matthewman of Featherstone, West Yorkshire, who in 1975 knitted 885 garments involving 10,530 oz. *298,52 kg* of wool (equivalent to the fleece of 85 sheep). She had been timed to average 108 stitches per min in a 30-min test. Her technique has been filmed by the world's only Professor of Knitting—a Japanese.

Knot-tying

The fastest recorded time for tying the six Boy Scout Handbook Knots (square knot, sheet bend, sheep shank, clove hitch, round turn and two half hitches and bowline) on individual ropes is 8.1 sec by Clinton R. Bailey Sr., 52, of Pacific City, Oregon, on 13 Apr. 1977.

Leap frogging

Fourteen members of Hanover High School, Hanover, New Hampshire, U.S.A. covered 555.25 miles *888,9 km* in 148 hours on 4–10 June 1978.

Life Saving

In November 1974 the City of Galveston, Texas and the Noon Optimist Club unveiled a plaque to the deaf-mute lifeguard Leroy Colombo (1905–1974) who saved 907 people from drowning in the waters around Galveston Island from 1917 to his death.

Lightning most times struck

The only living man in the world to be struck by lightning 7 times is ex-Park Ranger Roy C. Sullivan (U.S.), the human lightning conductor of Virginia. His attraction for lightning began in 1942 (lost big toe nail), and was resumed in July 1969 (lost eyebrows), in July 1970 (left shoulder seared), on 16 Apr. 1972 (hair set on fire), on 7 Aug. 1973 (new hair refired and legs seared), on 5 June 1976 ankle injured, and sent to Waynesboro Hospital with chest and stomach burns on 25 June 1977 after being struck while fishing.

Waiting for the "Off" for the largest ever game of musical chairs with 3,728 holiday makers at Butlin's, Filey, North Yorkshire (see p 226).

Lion-taming

The greatest number of lions mastered and fed in a cage by an unaided lion-tamer was 40, by "Captain" Alfred Schneider in 1925. Clyde Raymond Beatty handled more than 40 "cats" (mixed lions and tigers) simultaneously. Beatty (b. Bainbridge, Ohio, 10 June 1903, d. Ventura, California, 19 July 1965) was the featured attraction at every show he appeared with for more than 40 years. He insisted upon being called a lion-trainer. More than 20 lion-tamers have died of injuries since 1900.

Log rolling

The record number of International Championships is 10 by Jubiel Wickheim (of Shawnigan Lake, British Columbia, Canada) between 1956 and 1969. At Albany, Oregon on 4 July 1956 Wickheim rolled on a 14 inch *35,5 cm* log against Chuck Harris of Kelso, Washington U.S.A. for 2 hrs 40 mins before losing.

Merry Go Round

The longest merry go round marathon on record is one of 312 hours 43 min by Gary Mandau, Chris Lyons and Dana Dover in Portland, Oregon, U.S.A. on 20 Aug.–2 Sept. 1976.

Message in a bottle

The longest recorded interval between drop and pick up is 64 years between 7 Aug. 1910 ("please write to Miss Gladys Potter") in Grand Lake and August 1974 from Lake Huron. Miss Potter was traced as Mrs. Oliver Scheid, 76 of Columbus, Ohio. A bottle apparently bearing a message written on 19 Nov. 1899 by Capt. Charles Weieerishen of the S.S. "Crown Princess Cecilia" off Varberg, Sweden was reportedly picked up on the coast of Victoria, B.C. Canada on 9 Dec. 1936.

Milk Bottle Balancing

The greatest distance walked by a person continuously balancing a full pint milk bottle on the head is 18 miles 880 yds *29,7 km* by Willie Hollingsworth of Freeport, New York, U.S.A. on 24 March 1979.

Model *Highest Paid*

The largest contract in the history of modelling was for $1,000,000 *£588,200* between Fabergè and Miss Margaux Hemingway (b. 1955) of Ketchum, Idaho, U.S.A. for 5 years on 20 May 1975. She is described as "corn-fed pretty" and describes her height as "five foot twelve". Lauren Hutton is reported to be on a higher *rate* at $500,000 for 2 years from Revlon. The modelling rate of Cheryl Tiegs (Mrs Stan Dragoti), proponent of the California look, was last reported to be $2,000 per day in early 1978.

Morse

The highest recorded speed at which anyone has received morse code is 75.2 words per minute—over 17 symbols per second. This was achieved by Ted R. McElroy of the United States in a tournament at Asheville, North Carolina, U.S.A. on 2 July 1939.

Musical Chairs

The largest game on record was one starting with 3,728 participants and ending with Paul Morgan, on the last chair at Butlin's Holiday Centre, Filey, N. Yorkshire on 20 July 1978.

Needle threading

The record number of strands of cotton threaded through a number 13 needle (eye $\frac{1}{2}$ in by $\frac{1}{16}$ of an in *12,7 mm × 1,6 mm*) in 2 hours is 3,795 times by Miss Brenda Robinson of the College of Further Education, Chippenham, Wiltshire on 20 Mar. 1971.

Noodle making

Stephen Yim (b. Shanghai, China, 1949) made 256 noodle strings (over 5 ft *1,52 m*) in 63 sec on the B.B.C. T.V. *Record Breakers* programme on 21 Oct. 1973.

Omelette making

The greatest number of two-egg omelettes made in 30 min is 217 by Howard Helmer of New York City, U.S.A., at Disneyland, Anaheim, California on 14 July 1978.

Onion Peeling

The record for onion peeling is 50 lb. *22,67 kg* in 25 min 7 sec by Alan Benn at the EMI Bingo and Social Club, Newcastle-upon-Tyne on 29 March 1979.

Organ

The longest recorded electric organ marathon is one of 411 hours by Vince Bull at the Comet Hotel, Scunthorpe, South Humberside on 2–19 June 1977. The longest church organ recital ever sustained has been 90 hours by Frank Hughes at Wesley College Chapel, Dublin, Ireland on 31 Oct.–4 Nov. 1975.

PARACHUTING RECORDS

Record	Name	Detail	Place	Date
First from Tower	Louis-Sébastian Lenormand (1757–1839)	quasi-parachute	Montpellier France	1783
First from Balloon	André-Jacques Garnerin (1769–1823)	2,230 ft *680 m*	Monceau Park, Paris	22 Oct. 1797
First from Aircraft (man)	Capt. Albert Berry	U.S. Army	St. Louis, Missouri	1 Mar. 1912
(woman)	Mrs. Georgina 'Tiny' Broadwick (b. 1893)		Griffith Park, Los Angeles	21 June 1913
First Free Fall	Mrs. Georgina 'Tiny' Broadwick	Pilot Glenn L. Martin	North Island, San Diego, California	13 Sept. 1914
Lowest Escape	S/Ldr. Terence Spencer, D.F.C., R.A.F.	30–40 ft *9–12 m*	Wismar Bay, Baltic	19 April 1945
Longest Duration Fall	Lt. Col. Wm. H. Rankin U.S.M.C.	40 min due to thermals	North Carolina	26 July 1956
Highest Escape	Flt. Lt. J. de Salis and Fg. Off. P. Lowe, R.A.F.	56,000 ft *17 068 m*	Monyash, Derby	9 April 1958
Longest Delayed Drop (man)	Capt. Joseph W. Kittinger[1]	84,700 ft 16.04 miles *25 816 m* from balloon at 102,800 ft *31 333 m*	Tularosa, New Mexico	16 Aug. 1960
(woman)	O. Kommissarova (U.S.S.R.)	14 100 m *46,250 ft*	over U.S.S.R.	21 Sept. 1965
(civilian, over U.K.)	John Noakes (G.B.)	22,000 ft from 25,000 ft *7 620 m*	Salisbury Plain, Wiltshire	15 May 1973
(civilian, world)	R. W. K. Beckett (G.B.) Harry Ferguson (G.B.)	30,000 ft *9 144 m* from 32 000 ft *9 753 m*	D. F. Malan Airport, Capetown	23 Nov. 1969
Most Southerly	T/Sgt. Richard J. Patton (d. 1973)	Operation Deep Freeze	South Pole	25 Nov. 1956
Most Northerly	Ray Munro (Canada)	−39° F (−39,4° C)	In 89° 39′ N	31 Mar. 1969
Career Total (man)	Anotolyi Osipov (U.S.S.R.)	8,000	over U.S.S.R.	April 1978
(woman)	Patty Wilson	More than 1,000	Elsinore paracenter, California	Nov. 1973
Highest Landing	Ten U.S.S.R. parachutists[2]	23,405 ft *7 133 m*	Lenina Peak	May 1969
Heaviest Load	U.S.A.F. C-130 Hercules	22.52 tons *22,88 tonnes* steel plates 6 parachutes	El Centro, California	28 Jan. 1970
Highest from Bridge	Donald R. Boyles	1,053 ft *320 m*	Royal Gorge, Colorado	7 Sept. 1970
Highest Tower Jump	Herbert Leo Schmidtz (U.S.A.)	KTUL-TV Mast 1,984 ft *604 m*	Tulsa, Oklahoma	4 Oct. 1970
Biggest Star (5 sec. hold)	32 Enquirer Team	Formation held 5 secs (FAI rules)	Tahlequah, Oklahoma	14 July 1975
Highest column	8 man Enquirer Team	170 ft *52 m*	over California, U.S.A.	Oct. 1978
Most Travelled	Kevin Seaman from a Cessna Skylane (pilot Charles E. Merritt)	12,186 miles *19 611 km*	Jumps in all 50 U.S. States	26 July–15 Oct. 1972
Oldest Man	Bob Broadbere (G.B.) (1892–1977)	85 years (broke glasses)	Honiton, Devon, England	10 July 1977
Woman	Mrs. Ardath Evitt (U.S.)	74 years 6 months	Mooresville, Indiana, U.S.A.	6 Aug. 1978
24 Hour Total[3]	David Parchment (G.B.)	233 (18 hrs 7 mins)	Shobdon Air Centre, nr. Leominster, Here. & Worcs.	19 June 1979

[1] *Maximum speed in rarified air was 625.2 m.p.h. 1006 km/h. at 90,000ft 27,430 m – marginally supersonic.*
[2] *Four were killed.*
[3] *First estimates of the sponsored income due for the charity Age Concern were £1 million.*

Parachuting *Longest fall without*

The greatest altitude from which anyone has bailed out without a parachute and survived is 6 700 m *21,980 ft.* This occurred in January 1942, when Lt. (now Lt.-Col.) I. M. Chisov (U.S.S.R.) fell from an Ilyushin 4 which had been severely damaged. He struck the ground a glancing blow on the edge of a snow-covered ravine and slid to the bottom. He suffered a fractured pelvis and severe spinal damage. It is estimated that the human body reaches 99 per cent of its low level terminal velocity after falling 1,880 ft *573 m* which takes 13 to 14 sec. This is 117–125 m.p.h. *188–201 km/h* at normal atmospheric pressure in a random posture, but up to 185 m.p.h. *298 km/h* in a head down position.

Vesna Vulovic, 23 a Jugoslavenski Aerotransport hostess, survived when her DC-9 blew up at 33,330 ft *10 160 m* over the Czechoslovak village of Ceská Kamenice on 26 Jan. 1972. She fell inside a section of tail unit. She was in hospital for 16 months after emerging from a 27 day coma and having many bones broken.

The British record is 18,000 ft *5 485 m* by Flt.-Sgt. Nicholas Stephen Alkemade, aged 21, who jumped from a blazing R.A.F. *Lancaster* bomber over Germany on 23 Mar. 1944. His headlong fall was broken by a fir tree near Oberkürchen and he landed without a broken bone in a snow bank 18 in *45 cm* deep.

Piano-playing

The longest piano-playing marathon has been one of 1,172 hours 27 min (48 days 20 hours 27 min) playing 22 hours every day (with 5 min intervals each playing hour) from 6 Jan. to 24 Feb. 1978 by Roger Lavern at the Osborne Tavern, London.

The women's world record in the discontinued non-stop category was 133 hours (5 days 13 hours) by Mrs. Marie Ashton aged 40, in a theatre in Blyth, Northumberland, on 18–23 Aug. 1958.

Piano smashing

The record time for demolishing an upright piano and passing the entire wreckage through a circle 9 in *22,8 cm* in diameter is 1 min 37 secs by six members of the Tinwald Rugby Football Club, Ashburton, New Zealand led by David Young on 6 Nov. 1977. Messrs Anthony Fukes, Mike Newman, Terry Cullington and Malcolm Large smashed a piano with bare hands in 7 min in Nottingham on 6 June 1977. Messrs C. Crain, R. Crain, O. Richards and M. Cording took 7 min. 7 sec. in Nottingham on 16 Dec. 1978. (All wreckage was passed through the circle).

Piano tuning

The record time for pitch raising (one semi-tone or 100 cents) and then returning a piano to a musically acceptable quality is 9 min 57 sec by Sebastian Verdolino at the A. & C. Piano Craft Company in New York City, U.S.A. on 9 Feb. 1979.

Pillar box standing

The record number of people to pile on top of a pillar box (oval top of 6 ft² *0,55 m²*) is 29, all students of the City of London College, Moorgate, in Finsbury Circus, City of London on 21 Oct. 1971.

Pin Ball marathon

The most protracted pin ball game was one of 216 hours played by Jon Wood and David Irvine of Luton, Bedfordshire on 1–9 March 1979.

Pipe smoking

The duration record for keeping a pipe (3.3 g *0.1 oz* of tobacco) continuously alight with only an initial match is 253 min 28 sec by Yrjö Pentikäinen of Kuopio, Finland on 15–16 Mar. 1968.

Plate spinning

The greatest number of plates spun simultaneously is 53 by Shukuni Sasaki of Takamatsu, Japan on 3 Jan. 1979.

Pogo stick jumping

The greatest number of jumps achieved is 100,013 by Steve Ennis (b. 1 Nov. 1960) in 16 hr 15 min at St Jude's Church, Chalfont, Pennsylvania, U.S.A. on 1–2 Apr. 1977.

Pole-squatting

Modern records do not, in fact, compare with that of St. Simeon the Younger, (*c.* 521–597 A.D.) called Stylites (Greek, *stylos* = pillar) a monk who spent his last 45 years up a stone pillar on The Hill of Wonders, near Antioch, Syria. This is probably the earliest example of record setting.

There being no international rules, the "standards of living" atop poles vary widely. The record squat is 399 days by Frank Perkins from 1 June 1975–4 July 1976 in 8 × 8 ft *2,43 × 2,43 m* box atop a 50 ft *15,24 m* telegraph pole in San Jose, California, U.S.A.

The British record is 32 days 14 hours by John Stokes, aged 32, of Moseley, West Midlands in a barrel on a 45 ft *13,70 m* pole in Birmingham, ending on 27 June 1966. This is claimed as a world record for a barrel.

Pop group

The duration record for a 4-man pop-playing group is 144 hours by "Rocking Ricky and the Velvet Collars" at The Talardy Hotel, St. Asaph, Clwyd, North Wales on 12–18 Nov. 1976.

Potato peeling

The peeling of 170 lb. *77,1 kg* of potatoes to an institutional cookery standard by 5 teenagers (aged 14–16) with standard kitchen knives in 45 minutes was set in Sydney, Australia on 11 June 1977. They were Julie Morris, Chris Hughes, Kerry White, Angus McKinnon and Julian Morgan.

Pram pushing

The greatest distance covered in pushing a pram in 24 hours is 319 miles *513 km* on a track by a 60 strong team from the White Horse Sports and Social Club, Stony Stratford, Buckinghamshire on 19–20 May 1973. A team of 10 with an adult "baby" from "Flore Moderns" covered 226.1 miles *363,8 km* at Flore, Northamptonshire in 24 hours on 28–29 June 1975.

"Psychiatrist" fastest

The world's fastest "psychiatrist" was Dr. Albert L. Weiner of Erlton, New Jersey, U.S.A., who was trained solely in osteopathy but who dealt with up to 50 psychiatric patients a day in four treatment rooms. He relied heavily on narcoanalysis, muscle relaxants and electro-shock treatments. In December 1961 he was found guilty on 12 counts of manslaughter from using unsterilized needles.

Quoit throwing

The world's record for rope quoit throwing is an unbroken sequence of 4,002 pegs by Bill Irby, Snr. of Australia in 1968.

Ramp Jumping

The longest distance ever achieved for motor cycle long jumping is *64,60 m 212 ft* by Alain Jean Prieur (b. 4 July 1939) of France at Montlhéry near Paris over 16 buses on 6 Feb. 1977. The pioneer of this form of exhibition—Evel Knievel (b. Robert Craig Knievel, 17 Oct. 1938 at Butte, Montana, U.S.A.) had suffered 433 bone fractures by his 1975 season. His abortive attempt to cross the Snake River Canyon, Idaho on 8 Sept. 1974 in a rocket reputedly increased his life-time earnings by $6 million (*then £2½ million*) The longest jump achieved in Britain is 190 ft *57,9 m* by Eddie Kidd at Radlett Airfield, Hertfordshire on 4 April 1978.

Riding in armour

The longest recorded ride in full armour is one of 167 miles *268,7 km* from Edinburgh to Dumfries in 3 days (riding time 28 hrs 30 min) by Dick Brown, 48, on 13–15 June 1979.

Riveting

The world's record for riveting is 11,209 in 9 hours by J. Moir at the Workman Clark Ltd. shipyard, Belfast, Northern Ireland, in June 1918. His peak hour was his seventh with 1,409, an average of nearly 23½ per min.

Rocking chair

The longest recorded duration of a "Rockathon" is 432 hours by Mrs. Maureen Weston of Petreburgh Athletics Club, Peterborough, Cambridge on 14 Apr.–2 May 1977.

Rolling pin

The record distance for a woman to throw a 2 lb. *907 g* rolling pin is 157 ft 6 in *48,00 m* by Janet Thompson at West London Stadium, Wormwood Scrubs, Greater London on 6 July 1975.

Rope tricks

The only man to demonstrate the ability to spin 12 ropes simultaneously (without extensions) has been Roy Vincent (b. 1910) of Gloversville, N.Y. in the period 1933–53. He used all limbs, both hands, his back and his teeth.

Scooter riding

The greatest distance covered by a team of 25 in 24 hours is 331 miles 95 yds *532,7 km* by Carnforth High School, Carnforth, Lancashire on 14–15 April 1979.

Search *Longest*

In October 1972 Frank Jones of Lowestoft, Suffolk ended a 68 year long search by locating his missing brother Arthur Jones.

See-saw

George Partridge and Tamara Marquez of Auburn High School, Washington, U.S.A. on a suspension see-saw completed 1,101 hrs 40 min (indoor) on 28 Mar.–13 May 1977. Georgia Chaffin and Tammy Adams of Goodhope Jr. High School, Cullman Alabama, U.S.A. completed 730 hrs 30 min (outdoor) on 25 June–25 July 1975.

Sermon

The longest sermon on record was delivered by the Rev. Donald Thomas of Brooklyn, New York, U.S.A. on 18–22 Sept. 1978 for 93 hrs. From 31 May to 10 June 1969 the 14th Dalai Lama (b. 6 July 1934 as Tenzin Gyalto) the exiled ruler of Tibet, completed a sermon on Tantric Buddhism for five to seven hours per day to total 60 hours in India.

Shaving

The fastest demon barber on record is Gerry Harley, who shaved 130 men in 60 min with a *cut-throat* razor at The Plough, Gillingham, Kent on 1 Apr. 1971. In an attempt to set a marathon he ran out of volunteer subjects.

Sheaf tossing

The world's best performance for tossing an 3,63 kg *8 lb.* sheaf for height is 19,77 m *64.86 ft* by Trond Ulleberg of Skolleborg, Norway on 11 Nov. 1978. Such pitchfork contests date from 1914.

Shoeshine Boys

In this category (limited to a team of 4 teenagers; duration of 8 hours; shoes 'on the hoof') the record is 6,334 pairs by the Bedford North (Newnham) Scout Group on 16 July 1977.

Shorthand fastest

The highest recorded speeds ever attained under championship conditions are: 300 words per min (99.64 per cent accuracy) for five minutes and 350 w.p.m. (99.72 per cent accuracy, that is, two insignificant errors) for two minutes by Nathan Behrin (U.S.A.) in tests in New York in December 1922. Behrin (b. 1887) used the Pitman system invented in 1837. Morris I. Kligman, official court reporter of the U.S. Court House, New York has taken 50,000 words in five hours (a sustained rate of 166.6 w.p.m.). Rates are much dependent upon the nature, complexity and syllabic density of the material. Mr. G. W. Bunbury of Dublin, Ireland held

the unique distinction of writing at 250 w.p.m. for 10 min on 23 Jan. 1894.

In Great Britain only four shorthand writers have passed the official Pitman test at 250 w.p.m. for five min:

Miss Edith Ulrica Pearson of London, on 30 June 1927.
Miss Emily Doris Smith of London, on 22 Mar. 1934.
Miss Beatrice W. Solomon of London, in March 1942.
Mrs. Audrey Boyes (*née* Bell) of Finchley, Barnet, Greater London, in 1956.

Emily Smith has a unique 250 w.p.m. certificate from an independent examining body, the National Union of Teachers. She has given demonstrations from unseen current newspaper material in excess of 300 w.p.m.

Shouting

The greatest number of wins in the national town criers' contest is 11 by Ben Johnson of Fowey, Cornwall, who won in 1939, 1949–55, 1966, 1969 and 1973. (See also Longest-ranged voice, Chapter I page 21.)

Showering

The most prolonged continuous shower bath on record is one of 336 hours by Arron Marshall of Rockingham Park, Western Australia on 29 July–12 Aug. 1978. The feminine record is 120 hours 1 min by Penny Cresswell of Waikiki, Western Australia on 7–12 Sept. 1977. Desquamation can be a positive danger.

Singing

The longest recorded solo singing marathon is one of 132 hrs 45 min by Eamonn McGirr in Belfast, Northern Ireland on 1–6 Jan. 1979. The marathon record for a choir has been 61 hours by the Clinton High School Choir, Saline, Michigan, U.S.A., on 20–22 Jan. 1979. Acharya Prem Bhikuji started chanting the Akhand Ram Dhum in 1964 and devotees took this up in rotation completing their devotions 13 years later on 31 July 1977 at Jamnagar, India.

Skate Boarding

"World" championships have been staged intermittently since 1966. Mike Kinney won a marathon contest at Reseda, California on 26 May 1979 with 217.3 miles *349,7 km* in 30 hrs 35 mins.

The highest speed recorded on a skate board is 71.79 m.p.h. under U.S.S.A. rules on a course at Mt. Baldy, California in a prone position by Richard K. Brown, 33, on 17 June 1979. The stand-up record is 53.45 m.p.h. *86,01 km/h* by John Hutson, 23 at Signal Hill, Long Beach, California on 11 June 1978. The high jump record is 5 ft. 0 in *1,52 m* by Bryan Beardsly (U.S.) at Signal Hill on 24–25 Sept. 1977. At this same 4th U.S. Skateboard Association championship Tony Alva, 19, jumped 17 barrels (17 ft *5,18 m*).

Skipping

The longest recorded non-stop skipping marathon was one of 6 hrs 12 mins (58,869 turns) by Katsumi Suzuki of Saitama, Japan on 1 Jan. 1979.

Other records made without a break:

Most turns in one jump	5 by Katsumi Suzuki, Saitama, Japan, 29 May 1975
Most turns in 1 min	290 by Brian D. Christensen, East Ridge, Tennessee, 30 May 1978
Most turns in 10 secs	108 by A. Rayner, Wakefield, W. Yorks, 28 June 1978
Most doubles (with cross)	96 by K. A. Brooks, Gosford, N.S.W., 5 Dec. 1978
Double turns	6,851 by Katsumi Suzuki, Tokyo, 4 July 1976
Treble turns	381 by Katsumi Suzuki, Saitama, Japan, 29 May 1975
Quadruple turns	51 by Katsumi Suzuki, Saitama, Japan, 29 May 1975
Duration	1,264 miles *2 034 km* by Tom Morris, Brisbane–Cairns, Queensland, 1963
Most children, single rope (11 turns)	62, from Air Academy High School Colorado Springs, Colorado, U.S.A., 31 Jan. 1979.

Slinging

The greatest distance recorded for a sling-shot is 1,147 ft 4 in *349,70 m* using a 34 in *86 cm* long sling and a 7½ oz. *212 g* stone by Melvyn Gaylor on Newport Golf Course, Shide, Isle of Wight on 25 Sept. 1970.

right: Brian Christensen, in action breaking the record for most turns in one minute with 290 or nearly 5 per second (see p 228).

below: Atsuhiro Nakamura producing an unrivalled 441 formed smoke rings from a single pull of a cigarette in December 1978.

Smoke ring blowing

The highest recorded number of smoke rings formed from a single pull of a cigarette is 441 rings by Atsuhiro Nakamura of Nara, Japan on 21 Dec. 1978.

Snakes and Ladders

The longest recorded game of Snakes and Ladders has been one of 204 hours by a team of six (four always in play) from Baulkham Hills High School, Baulkham Hills, N.S.W., Australia on 15–23 June 1976.

Snow Shoeing

The fastest officially recorded time for covering a mile *1 609,34 m* is 6 min 23.8 sec by Richard Lemay (Frontenac Club, Quebec, Canada) at Manchester, New Hampshire, U.S.A. in 1973.

Spinning

The duration record for spinning a clock balance wheel by hand is 5 min 26.8 sec by Philip Ashley, aged 16, of Leigh, Greater Manchester on 20 May 1968.

Spitting

The greatest distance achieved at the annual tobacco spitting classic (instituted 1955) at Raleigh, Mississippi is 31 ft 1 in *9,47 m* by Don Snyder, 28 on 26 July 1975. In the 3rd International Spittin', Belchin' and Cussin' Triathlon Harold Fielden reached 34 ft 0¼ in *10,36 m* at Central City, Colorado U.S.A. on 13 July 1973. Distance is dependent on the quality of salivation, absence of cross wind, two finger pucker and the coordination of the back arch and neck snap. Sprays or wads smaller than a dime are not measured. The record for projecting a melon seed is under WCWSSCA rules is 59 ft 1½ in *18,02 m* by Brian Dunne at Savemore Centre, Yeppoon, Queensland, Australia on 11 Dec. 1976. The highest reported distance for a cherry stone is 49 ft 2 in *14,98 m* by William A. Mobley at Eau Claire, Michigan, U.S.A. on 8 July 1978. Spitters who care about their image wear 12 in *30,4 cm* block-ended boots so practice spits can be measured without a tape.

Stair Climbing

The 100 storey record for stair climbing was set by Dennis W. Martz in the Detroit Plaza Hotel, Detroit, Michigan, U.S.A., on 26 June 1978 at 11 min 23.8 sec. Richard Black, 44, President of the Maremont Corporation ran a vertical mile on the stairs of Lake Point Tower, Chicago on 13 July 1978 in continuous action with 1 hr 25 min 6 sec ascent time and 44 min 39 sec descent time. *These records can only be attempted in buildings with a minimum of 70 storeys.*

Jerry Rafferty, 26, raced up the 1,575 steps of the Empire State Building, New York City on 15 Feb. 1979 in 12 min 19.8 sec.

In the line of duty Bill Stevenson has mounted 334 of the 364 steps of the tower in the Houses of Parliament, 2,829 times in 10 years (1968–78)—equivalent to 17.63 ascents of Everest.

Standing

The longest period on record that anyone has continuously stood is for more than 17 years in the case of Swami Maujgiri Maharij when performing the *Tapasya* or penance from 1955 to November 1973 in Shahjahanpur, Uttar Pradesh, India. When sleeping he would lean against a plank.

Stilt-walking

Hop stringers use stilts up to 15 ft *4.57 m*. In 1892 M. Garisoain of Bayonne stilt-walked 8 km *4,97 miles* into Biarritz in 42 min to average 11,42 km/h *7.10 m.p.h.* In 1891 Sylvain Dornon stilt-walked from Paris to Moscow *via* Vilno in 50 stages for the 1,830 miles *2 945 km.* Another source gives his time as 58 days. Even with a safety wire very high stilts are extremely dangerous—25 steps are deemed to constitute "mastery". Joe Long (b. Kenneth Caesar), who has suffered 5 fractures, mastered 56 lb. *25,4 kg* stilts 24 ft *7,31 m* from ground to ankle at the B.B.C. T.V. Centre, London on 8 Dec. 1978.

Emma Sian Disley (b. 17 May 1965) walked up Snowdon (3,560 ft *1085 m*) covering 2,500 vertical feet *762 m* in 4 hrs 5 min 45 sec on stilts in aid of the International Fund for Animal Welfare on 19 Aug. 1977.

Stowaway

The most rugged stowaway was Socarras Ramirez who escaped from Cuba on 4 June 1969 by stowing away in an

unpressurized wheel well in the starboard wing of a Boeing 707 from Havana to Madrid in a 5,600 mile *9 010 km* Iberian Airlines flight. He survived 8 hours at 30,000 ft *9 145 m* where temperatures were −8° F −*22,2° C.*

Stretcher bearing

The longest recorded carry of a stretcher case with a 10 st. *63,5 kg* "body" is 100.4 miles *161,5 km* in 25 hrs 20 min by two 4 man teams from 6th Battalion The Royal Australian Regiment, Australian Army, in Enoggera, Queensland, Australia on 29–30 Sept. 1978.

The record limited to Youth Organizations (under 20 yrs of age) and 8 hours carrying is 35.4 miles *56,97 km* by 8 members of the Vulcan Venture Scout Unit, Marlow, Bucks on 26 March 1977.

String Ball Largest

The largest balls of string on record are ones both of 11 ft *3,35 m* in diameter, weighing 5 tons/*tonnes* amassed by Francis A. Johnson of Darwin, Minnesota, U.S.A., since 1950 and Frank Stoeber of Cawker City, Kansas since at least 1962.

Submergence

The most protracted underwater endurance record (excluding the use of diving bells) is 141 hrs 24 min established by L/Cpl Steven Cook, R.E., 22 of Romsley near Birmingham in a 22 500 litre *4,950 gall* tank in Confederation Square, Ottawa, Canada in 83–84°F *28,5°C* water on 12–18 Aug. 1978.

Suggestion boxes

The most prolific example on record of the use of any suggestion box scheme is that of John Drayton (b. 18 Sept. 1907) of Newport, Gwent who has plied British Rail and the companies from which it was formed with a total of 28,186 suggestions from 1924 to May 1979 of which one in seven were accepted.

above: John Massis stopping the take-off of a helicopter by holding it down with a teeth-bit. The dynometer read a pull of 375 lb *170 kg* (see p 231).

below: Thomas Hunt covering 50 yd *45,7 m* in an inverted sprint in 18.7 seconds (see p 232).

The U.S. Postal Service champion John Kingston has had an acceptance rate of one in 5.3 (284 out of 1,500) to January 1976.

Swinging
The record duration for continuous swinging is 185 hours by Mollie Jackson of Tarrytown, New York, U.S.A. on 25 March–1 April 1979.

Switchback riding
The endurance record for rides on a roller coaster is 168 hours by Jim King at Panama City, Florida, U.S.A., on 28 Aug–4 Sept. 1978. He covered a distance of 1,946.5 miles *3 132,5 km.*

Tailoring
The highest speed in which the making of a 2 piece suit has been made from sheep to finished article is 1 hour 52 min 18.5 sec to the order of Bud Macken of Mascot, N.S.W., Australia on 23 Dec. 1931. The shearing took 35 sec, the carding and teasing 19 min and weaving 20 min.

Talking
The world record for non-stop talking is 150 hours by Raymond Cantwell at Trust House Forte's Travel Lodge, Oxford on 4–10 Dec. 1977. A feminine non-stop talking record was set by Mrs. Mary E. Davis, who on 2–7 Sept. 1958 started at a radio station in Buffalo, New York and did not draw breath until 110 hours 30 min 5 secs later in Tulsa, Oklahoma U.S.A. The longest continuous political speech on record was one of 33 hrs 5 min by Marvin Eakman of Minneapolis, Minnesota, U.S.A. on 6–7 Nov. 1978. The longest recorded lecture was one of 56½ hours on "The Old Testament: Mirror of Theocracy" by Wayne P. Morrow at Grants Pass High School, Oregon, on 3–5 June 1978.

Historically the longest recorded after-dinner speech with unsuspecting victims was one of 3 hours by the Rev. Henry Whitehead (d. March 1896) at the Rainbow Tavern, Fleet Street, London on 16 Jan. 1874. Both Nicholas Parsons and Gyles Brandreth spoke for 11 hours from 8 p.m. to 7 a.m. on 13–14 Feb. 1978 at the Hyde Park Hotel, London in aid of Action Research, to tie a longest after-dinner speech contest.

T-bone dive
The so-called T-bone dives or Dive Bomber crash by cars off ramps over and on to parked cars are often measured by the number of cars, but owing to their variable size and that their purpose is purely to cushion the shock, distance is more significant. The longest recorded distance is 176 ft *53,6 m* by Dusty Russell in a 1963 Ford Falcon at Athens, Georgia in April 1973.

Teeth-pulling
The man with "the strongest teeth in the world" is "Hercules" John Massis (b. Wilfried Oscar Morbée, 4 June 1940) of Oostakker, Belgium, who on 8 Nov. 1978 demonstrated the ability to pull 3 railway carriages weighing 126,3 tonnes *124.7 tons* on a level track outside Stockholm, Sweden. At Evry, France on 19 Mar. 1977 Massis raised a weight of 233 kg *513⅗ lb.* 15 cm *6 in* from the ground with a teeth bit. Massis prevented a helicopter from taking off using only a teeth-bit harness in Los Angeles on 7 Apr. 1979 for a Guinness Spectacular T.V. Show.

Tightrope walking
The greatest 19th century tightrope walker was Jean François Gravelet, *alias* Charles Blondin (1824–1897), of France, who made the earliest crossing of the Niagara Falls on a 3 in *76 mm* rope, 1,100 ft *335 m* long, 160 ft *48,75 m* above the Falls on 30 June 1859. He also made a crossing with Harry Colcord, pick-a-back on 15 Sept. 1860. Though other artists still find it difficult to believe, Colcord was his agent.

Tightrope walking *Endurance*
The world tightrope endurance record is 185 days by Henri Rochetain (b. 1926) of France on a wire 394 ft *120 m* long, 82 ft *25 m* above a supermarket in Saint Etienne, France, on 28 Mar.–29 Sept. 1973. His ability to sleep on the wire has left doctors puzzled. He walked some 500 km *310 miles* on the wire to keep fit.

Tightrope walking *Longest*
The longest walk by any funambulist was achieved by Henri Rochetain (b. 1926) of France on a wire 3,790 yds *3 465 m* long slung across a gorge at Clermont Ferrand, France on 13 July 1969. He required 3 hours 20 min to negotiate the crossing. On 19 Mar. 1977 Steve McPeak ascended a 44 mm *1.7 in* cable 2,400 ft *731 m* long up to the Sugar Loaf, Rio de Janeiro, Brazil in 65 min. The climb was 675 ft *205 m.*

The first crossing of the River Thames was achieved by Charles Elleano (b. 1911) of Strasbourg, France on a 1,050 ft *320 m* wire 60 ft *18,2 m* above the river in 25 min on 22 Sept. 1951.

Tree-climbing
The fastest speed climb up a 100 ft *30,4 m* fir spar pole and return to the ground is one of 31.1 sec by Marvin Trudeau of Honeymoon Bay, B.C. at Haywood, Wisconsin, U.S.A. in July 1977.

The fastest time up a 40 foot *12,2 m* coconut tree barefoot is 8.4 sec by Kini Marawai in Suva, Fiji on 2 Sept. 1977.

Tree-Sitting
The duration record for sitting in a tree is 182 days 2 min by Glen T. Woodrich 23 at Golf N'Stuff Amusement Park, Norwalk, Calif., U.S.A. from 1 Jan.–2 July 1978.

Typewriting *Fastest*
The highest recorded speeds attained with a ten-word penalty per error on a manual machine are:

One Min: 170 words, Margaret Owen (U.S.A.) (Underwood Standard), New York, 21 Oct. 1918.
One Hour: 147 words (net rate per min) Albert Tangora (U.S.A.) (Underwood Standard), 22 Oct. 1923.

The official hour record on an electric machine is 9,316 words (40 errors) on an I.B.M. machine, giving a net rate of 149 words per min, by Margaret Hamma, now Mrs. Dilmore (U.S.A.), in Brooklyn, New York City, N.Y., U.S.A. on 20 June 1941. Mrs. Barbara Blackburn of Everett, Washington can maintain 150 w.p.m. for 50 min (37,500 key strokes) and attain speeds of 170 w.p.m. using the Dvorak Simplified Keyboard (D.S.K.) system.

In an official test in 1946 Stella Pajunas now Mrs. Garnard attained a rate of 216 words in a minute on an I.B.M. machine.

Typewriting *Longest*
The world duration record for typewriting on an electric machine is 162 hrs 1 min by Robin Heil of Sherman E. Burroughs High School, Ridgecrest, Calif. U.S.A. on 6–13 April 1976. Mrs. Marva Drew, 51, of Waterloo, Iowa, U.S.A. between 1968 and 30 Nov. 1974 typed number 1 to 1,000,000 in words on a manual typewriter on 2,473 pages. Asked why she replied "But I love to type".

The longest duration typing marathon on a manual machine is 120 hours 15 min by Mike Howell, a 23 year-old blind office worker from Greenfield, Oldham, Greater Manchester on 25–30 Nov. 1969 on an Olympia manual typewriter in Liverpool. In aggregating 561,006 strokes he performed a weight movement of 2,482 tons *2 521 tonnes* plus a further 155 tons *157 tonnes* on moving the carriage for line spacing.

Tyre Lifting
The greatest number of motor tyres lifted is 60 by Gary Windebank at Braishfield Country Fair, Romsey, Hants on 3 June 1979. The total weight was 840 lb *381 kg.* The tyres used were Michelin 155-13 XZX

Unsupported Circle
The highest recorded number of people who have demonstrated the physical paradox of all being seated without a chair

is an unsupported circle of 3,394 for 60 sec at Balment Park, Cranbrook, British Columbia, Canada on 14 May 1978.

Walking on hands
The duration record for walking on hands is 1 400 km *871 miles* by Johann Hurlinger, of Austria, who in 55 daily 10-hour stints, averaged 1.58 m.p.h. *2,54 km/h* from Vienna to Paris in 1900. Cadet Thomas P. Hunt of U.S.A.F. Academy, Colorado Springs completed a 50 yd *45,7 m* inverted sprint in 18.7 sec on 20 May 1978.

Wall of death
The greatest endurance feat on a wall of death was 3 hours 4 min by the motorcyclist Louis W. "Speedy" Babbs (1908–1976) on a silo, 32 ft *9,75 m* in diameter refuelling in motion, at the Venice Amusement Pier, California on 11 Oct. 1929. In 1934 Babbs performed in a globe 18 ft *5,48 m* at Ocean Park Pier, California, U.S.A. Britain's most durable performer is Doug. Murphy of Colne, Lancashire who completed his 33rd season in 1978 billed in West Germany as *Der Welte bester steilwand faher.*

Whip cracking
The longest stock whip ever "cracked" (*i.e.* the end made to travel above the speed of sound—760 m.p.h. *1 223 km/h*) is one of 97 ft *29,66 m* wielded by Noel Harris on the steps of Parliament House, Melbourne, Australia on 7 Aug. 1978. The dry weight of the red hide plaited whip was 12 kg *26.4 lb.*

Window Cleaning
The fastest time in the annual Top Shiner contest has been 46.5 sec plus three ½ sec smear penalties to equal 48 sec by Richard Baterip for 3 standard 1040 × 1153 mm *40.94 × 45.39 in* office windows with a 300 mm *11.8 in* long squeegee and 9 litres *15.83 pts* of water.

Wood-cutting

The earliest competitions date from Tasmania in 1874. The records set at the Lumberjack World Championships at Hayward, Wisconsin (founded 1960) are

Power Saw	11.55 sec	Ron Johnson (U.S.)	1976
One-Man Bucking	23.06 sec	Ron Hartill (N.Z.)	1976
Standing Block Chop	26.9 sec	Ron Wilson (Aust.)	1973
Underhand Block Chop	20.3 sec	Jim Alexander (Aust.)	1973
Two-Man Bucking	10.40 sec	Dave Green and Rudy Dettmer (U.S.)	1976

White pine logs 14 in *35,5 cm* diameter are used for chopping and 20 in *50,8 cm* for sawing.

Writing Minuscule
In 1926 an account was published of Alfred McEwen's pantograph record in which the 56 word version of the Lord's Prayer was written by diamond point on glass in the space of 0.0016 × 0.0008 in *0,04 × 0,02 mm.* Frank C. Watts of Felmingham, Norfolk demonstrated for photographers on 24 Jan. 1968, his ability, without mechanical or optical aid, to write the Lord's Prayer 34 times (9,452 letters) within the size of a definitive U.K. postage stamp (viz.) 0.84 × 0.71 of an inch *21,33 × 18,03 mm.*

Writing under handicap
The ultimate feat in "funny writing" would appear to be the ability to write extemporaneously and decipherably backwards, upside down, laterally inverted (mirror-style) while blindfolded with both hands simultaneously. One claim to this ability with both hands and feet simultaneously is under investigation.

Yodelling
The most protracted yodel on record was that of Donn Reynolds for 7 hrs 29 min in Brampton, Ontario, Canada on 27 Nov. 1976.

Yo-yo
The yo-yo originates from a Filipino jungle fighting weapon recorded in the 16th century weighing 4 lb. with a 20 ft *6 m* thong. The word means "come-come". Though illustrated in a book in 1891 as a bandalore the craze did not begin until it was started by Donald F. Duncan of Chicago, U.S.A. in 1926. The most difficult modern yo-yo trick is the "Whirlwind" incorporating both inside and outside horizontal loop-the-loops. The individual continuous endurance record is 120 hours by John Winslow of Gloucester, Virginia, U.S.A. on 23–28 Nov. 1977. Dr. Allen Bussey in Waco, Texas on 23 Apr. 1977 completed 20,302 loops in 3 hours (including 6,886 in a single 60 min period). He used a Duncan Imperial with a 34½ in *87,6 cm* nylon string.

CIRCUS RECORDS
Largest circus
The world's largest permanent circus is Circus Circus, Las Vegas, Nevada, U.S.A. opened on 18 Oct. 1968 at a cost of $15,000,000 (*then £6,250,000*). It covers an area of 129,000 ft² *11 984 m²* capped by a tent-shaped flexiglass roof 90 ft *27,43 m* high. The largest travelling circus is the Circus Vargas in the U.S.A. which can accommodate 5,000 people under its Big Top. (see also page 233).

WEALTH AND POVERTY
The comparison and estimations of extreme personal wealth are beset with intractable difficulties. Quite apart from reticence and the element of approximation in the valuation of assets, as Jean Paul Getty (1892–1976) once said "if you can count your millions you are not a billionaire". The term millionaire was invented *c.* 1740 and billionaire in 1861. The earliest dollar billionaires were John Davison Rockfeller (1839–1937); Henry Ford (1863–1947) and Andrew William Mellon (1855–1937). In 1937, the last year in which all 3 were alive, a billion U.S. dollars were worth £205 million but that amount of sterling would today have a purchasing power of in excess £2,000 million.

Richest Men *World*
There is currently only one surviving dollar billionaire (a billion dollars is now £500,000,000) of the seven U.S. citizens so described in the 20th century, namely Daniel K. Ludwig (b. South Haven, Mich., June 1897), whose fortune was estimated at $3,000 million in 1977. Mr Ludwig reportedly began in business aged 9 by buying a sunken boat for $25 and now has the world's third largest tanker fleet and much real estate. (Henry) Ross Perot of Texas (b. Texarkana, Texas, 1930) was, in December 1969, worth in excess of a billion dollars on paper.

Europeans with family assets in excess of the equivalent of a billion dollars, include the Wallenberg family in Sweden.

Richest Man *Great Britain*
The richest man in Great Britain is reputed to be John Moores, C.B.E. the co-founder of Littlewoods football pools in 1923. In 1973 he was estimated to be worth about £400 million (hence £850 million in 1979). His first job after leaving school at 14 was as a telephone operator. He was born in Eccles, Lancashire in 1896.

Highest Incomes
The greatest incomes derive from the collection of royalties per barrel by rulers of oil-rich sheikhdoms, who have not abrogated personal entitlement. Before his death in 1965, H. H. Sheikh Sir Abdullah as-Salim as-Sabah G.C.M.G., C.I.E. (b. 1895), the 11th Amir of Kuwait was accumulating royalties payable at a rate of £2.6 million per week or £135 million a year.

The highest gross income ever achieved in a single year by a private citizen is an estimated $105,000,000 (*then £21½ million*) in 1927 by the Neapolitan born Chicago gangster Alphonse ("Scarface Al") Capone (1899–1947). This was derived from illegal liquor trading and alky-cookers (illicit stills); gambling establishments, dog tracks, dance halls, "protection" rackets and vice. On his business card Capone described himself as a "Second Hand Furniture Dealer".

Proved Wills and Death Duties
Sir John Reeves Ellerman, 2nd Bt., (1909–1973) left £53,238,370 on which all-time record death duties were

left: Circus aerobat Roberto Tabak, 11, uniquely performing his double full-twisting somersault onto a 2 in *5,08 cm* diameter flexible pole. *right:* The highest trapeze act in the world with Ryan Kelly performing his helicopter, no hands, calf-hang.

The following circus acrobatic feats represent the greatest performed, either for the first time or, if marked with an asterisk, uniquely. A "mechanic" is a safety harness.

FLYING TRAPEZE	Earliest Act	Jules Léotard (France)	Circus Napoléon, Paris	12 Nov. 1859
	Double back somersault	Eddie Silbon	Paris Hippodrome	1879
	Triple back somersault (female)	Lena Jordan (Latvia) to Lew Jordan (U.S.A.)	Sydney, Australia	April 1897
	Triple back somersault (male)	Ernest Clarke to Charles Clarke	Publiones Circus, Cuba	1909
	Triple and half back somersault	Tony Steel to Lee Strath Marilees	Durango, Mexico	30 Sept. 1962
	Quadruple back somersault (in practice)	*Ernest Clarke to Charles Clarke	Orrin Bros. Circus, Mexico City, Mexico	1915
	Double Pass with back somersault	Buster and Anne Melzora with Paul Garee (catcher)	Labrobe, Pennsylvania	1935
	Triple back somersault (with 1½ twists)	Terry Cavarette Lemus (b. 6 Mar. 1953, Buffalo, N.Y.)	Circus Circus, Las Vegas	16 Mar. 1969
	Head to head stand on swinging bar (no holding)	*Ed and Ira Millette (né Wolf)	Europe and U.S.A.	1910–20
	Downward circles or "Muscle grinding"	306 by Denise La Grassa (U.S.)	Circus World Museum, Baraboo, Wisconsin	9 May 1976
	Highest trapeze act	Ryan Kelly (U.S.)	Calf-hang from helicopter	1978
HORSE BACK	Running leaps on and off	*26 by "Poodles" Hanneford	New York	1915
	Three-high column without "mechanic" with a pad	*Willy, Beby and Rene Fredianis	Nouveau Cirque, Paris	1908
	Double back somersault mounted	(John or Charles) Frederic Clarke	Various	c. 1905
	Double back somersault from a 2-high to a trailing horse with "mechanic"	Aleksandr Sergey	Moscow Circus	1956
FIXED BARS	Pass from 1st to 3rd bar with a double back somersault	Phil Shevette, Andres Atayde	Woods Gymnasium, New York, European tours	1925–27
	Triple fly-away to ground (male)	Phil Shevette	Folies Bergere, Paris	May 1896
	Triple fly-away to ground (female)	Loretto Twins, Ora and Pauline	Los Angeles	1914
GIANT SPRING BOARD	Running forward triple back somersault	John Cornish Worland (1855–1933) of the U.S.A.	St. Louis, Missouri	1874
RISLEY (HUMAN JUGGLING)	Back somersault feet to feet	Richard Risley Carlisle (1814–74) and son (U.S.A.)	Theatre Royal, Edinburgh	Feb. 1844
	Seat to seat triple back somersault	The 5 Draytons		1896
TEETER BOARD	Quadruple back somersault to a chair	Sylvester Mezzetti (voltiger) to Butch Mezzetti (catcher)	New York Hippodrome	1915–17
	Five high column	The Yacopi-Goucho troupe with 3 understanders, 3 second layer understanders, 1 middleman, 1 upper middleman and somersaulting top mounter (Bernard Armstrong)	Ringling Bros., Barnum & Bailey circuit	1941
	Six man high perch pyramid	Emilia Ivanova (Bulgaria) of Kehaiovi Troupe	Inglewood, California	21 July 1976
AERIALIST	One arm swings or planges 305 (no net) 40 ft *12,2 m* up	Janet May Klemke (U.S.A.)	Medina Shrine Circus, Chicago	21 Jan 1938
WIRE-JUGGLING	16 hoops (hands and feet)	Ala Naito (Japan) (female)	Madison Square Garden, N.Y.	1937
LOW WIRE (*7 ft 2 m*)	Feet to feet forward somersault	Con Colleano	Empire Theatre, Johannesburg	1923
		Ala Naito (Japan) (female)	Madison Square Garden, N.Y.	1937
HIGH WIRE (30–40 ft *9–12 m*)	Four high column (with mechanic)	*The Solokhin Brothers (U.S.S.R.)	Moscow Circus	1962
	Three layer, 7 man pyramid	Great Wallendas (Germany)	U.S.A.	1961
GROUND ACROBATICS	Stationary double back somersault	Francois Gouleau (France)		1905
	Four high column	The Picchianis (Italy)		1905
HAND TO HAND BALANCE	Longest horizontal dive 22 ft *6,7 m*	Harry Berry (top mounter) to Nelson Soule (understander)	Bell-Thazer troupe, State Fair in the U.S.	1908–17
TRAMPOLINE	Septuple twisting back somersault	Marco Canestrelli (U.S.)	St. Petersburg, Florida, U.S.A.	5 Jan. 1979
	5 twisting back to shoulders	Marco to Belmonte Canestrelli	Madison Square, N.Y., U.S.A.	28 Mar. 1979
FLEXIBLE POLE	Double full-twisting somersault on to a 2 in *5,08 cm* diameter pole	The Robertos Roberto Tabak (aged 11)	Jarasota, Florida, U.S.A.	1977

payable. This is the largest will ever proved in the United Kingdom. The greatest will proved in Ireland was that of the 1st Earl of Iveagh (1847–1927), who left £13,486,146.

Millionairesses
The world's wealthiest woman was probably Princess Wilhelmina Helena Pauline Maria of Orange-Nassau (1880–1962), formerly Queen of the Netherlands from 1890 to her abdication, 4 Sept. 1948, with a fortune which was estimated at over £200 million. The largest amount proved in the will of a woman in the United Kingdom has been the £4,075,550 (duty paid £3,233,454) of Miss Gladys Meryl Yule, daughter of Sir David Yule, Bt. (1858–1928), in August 1957. Mrs. Anna Dodge (later Mrs. Hugh Dillman) who was born in Dundee, Scotland, died on 3 June 1970 in the United States, aged 103, and left an estate of £40,000,000.

The cosmetician Madame Charles Joseph Walker *née* Sarah Breedlove (b. Louisiana Delta, U.S.A. 23 Dec. 1867) is reputed to have become the first self-made millionairess. She was an uneducated negro orphan scrub-woman whose fortune was founded on a hair straightener.

It was estimated in 1978 that 50.4% of the U.S.A's 250,000 millionaires are in fact millionairesses.

Millionaire and Millionairess *Youngest*
The youngest person ever to accumulate a million dollars was the child film actor Jackie Coogan (b. Los Angeles, 26 Oct. 1914) co-star with Sir Charles Chaplin (1889–1977) in "The Kid" made in 1920. Shirley Temple (b. Santa Monica, California 23 Apr. 1928), formerly Mrs. John Agar, Jr., now Mrs. Charles Black accumulated wealth exceeding $1,000,000 (*then £209,000*) before she was 10. Her child actress career spanned the years 1934–39.

Richest families *World*
It has been tentatively estimated that the combined value of the assets nominally controlled by the Du Pont family of some 1,600 members may be of the order of $150,000 million. The family arrived penniless in the U.S.A. from France on 1 Jan. 1800.

Largest dowry
The largest recorded dowry was that of Elena Patiño daughter of Don Simón Iturbi Patiño (1861–1947), the Bolivian tin millionaire, who in 1929 bestowed £8,000,000 from a fortune at one time estimated to be worth £125,000,000.

Greatest miser
If meaness is measurable as a ratio between expendable assets and expenditure then Henrietta (Hetty) Howland Green (*née* Robinson) (1835–1916), who kept a balance of over $31,400,000 (*then £6.2 million*) in one bank alone, was the all-time world champion. Her son had to have his leg amputated because of her delays in finding a *free* medical clinic. She herself lived off cold porridge because she was too thrifty to heat it and died of apoplexy in an argument over the virtues of skimmed milk. Her estate proved to be of $95 million (*then £19 million [and now worth £240 million*]).

Return of cash
The largest amount of *cash* ever found and returned to its owners was $500,000 (U.S.) found by Lowell Elliott, 61 on his farm at Peru, Indiana, U.S.A. It had been dropped in June 1972 by a parachuting hi-jacker.

Greatest bequests
The greatest bequests in a life-time of a millionaire were those of the late John Davison Rockefeller (1839–1937), who gave away sums totalling $750,000,000 (*now £312.5 million*). The greatest benefactions of a British millionaire were those of William Richard Morris, later the Viscount Nuffield, G.B.E., C.H. (1877–1963), which totalled more than £30,000,000 between 1926 and his death on 22 Aug. 1963. The Scottish-born U.S. citizen Andrew Carnegie (1835–1919) is estimated to have made benefactions totalling £70 million during the last 18 years of his life. These included 7,689 church organs and 2,811 libraries. He had started life in a bobbin factory at $1.20 per week.

The largest bequest made in the history of philanthropy was the $500,000,000 (*£178,570,000*) gift, announced on 12 Dec. 1955, to 4,157 educational and other institutions by the Ford Foundation (established 1936) of New York City, N.Y., U.S.A.

Salary Highest *World*
The highest paid executive in the United States in 1978 was David Mahoney, chairman of Norton Simon with $917,000 (*£458,500*) in salary, $2,037,000 (*£1,018,500*) in total, including stock options. In 1977 Archie R. McCardell as president of both Xerox (Jan.–Aug.) and International Harvester (Sept.–Dec.) earned $1,496,000 (*then £787,000*) in salary.

Salary Highest *Great Britain*
Britain's highest paid business executive has been Mr. G. Richard F. Tompkins (b. 1918) Chairman of Green Shield Trading Stamp Company which he founded in 1958. His service agreement entitled him to 15 per cent of profits which for the year ending 31 Oct. 1971 would have earned him £395,000. He waived £135,000. Norman Castle, chairman of the produce brokers S & W Berisford was believed to have Britain's highest salary in 1978/79 with £272,672 gross.

The Chairman of Shell Trading and Transport in 1978–79 drew £109,634 gross—barely half that of the top paid director, who is a a U.S. citizen, who was paid £216,779.

Golden Handshake
The highest carat handshake in Britain has been one of £139,000 for Basil Glass 64, Honorary President of Vantora textile company resident in Monaco, in October 1974.

Lowest Incomes
The poorest people in the world are the Tasaday tribe of cave-dwellers of central Mindanao, Philippines who were "discovered" in 1971 without any domesticated animals, agriculture, pottery, wheels or clothes.

GLUTTONY RECORDS
Records for eating and drinking by trenchermen do not match those suffering from the rare disease of bulimia (morbid desire to eat) and polydipsia (pathological thirst). Some bulimia patients have to spend 15 hours a day eating, with an extreme consumption of 384 lb. 2 oz. *174,236 kg* of food in six days by Matthew Daking, aged 12, in 1743 (known as Mortimer's case). Fannie Meyer of Johannesberg, after a skull fracture, was stated in 1974 to be unsatisfied by less than 160 pints of water a day. By October 1978 he was down to 52 pints. Miss Helge Andersson (b. 1908) of Lindesberg, Sweden was reported in January 1971 to have been drinking 40 pints *22,73 litres* of water a day since 1922—a total of 87,600 gal *3 982 hectolitres*.

The world's greatest trencherman has been Edward Abraham ("Bozo") Miller (b. 1909) of Oakland, California, U.S.A. He consumed up to 25,000 calories per day or more than 11 times that recommended. He stands 5 ft 7½ in *1,71 m* tall but weighs from 20 to 21½ st. *127–139 kg* with a 57 in *144 cm* waist. He had been undefeated in eating contests since 1931 (see below). The bargees on the Rhine are reputed to be the world's heaviest eaters with 5,200 calories a day. However the New Zealand Sports Federation of Medicine reported in December 1972 that a long-distance road runner consumed 14,321 calories in 24 hours.

While no healthy person has been reported to have succumbed in any contest for eating or drinking non-alcoholic or non-toxic drinks, such attempts, from a medical point of view, must be regarded as *extremely* inadvisable, particularly among young people. Gluttony record attempts should aim at improving the rate of consumption rather than the *volume*. Guinness Superlatives will not list any records involving the consumption of more than 2 litres *3.52 Imperial pints*

above: Alan Peterson the "mega-hamburgerologist" in action consuming 20¾ in 30 minutes. (*Brian Drake*)

left: Bobby Acland, holder of the epicurean record of 3 bottles of Champagne per day every day.

of beer nor any at all involving spirits. Nor will records for such potentially dangerous categories as live ants, chewing gum, marsh mallow or raw eggs with shells be published. The ultimate in stupidity—the eating of a bicycle—has however been recorded since it is unlikely to attract competition.

Specific records have been claimed as follows:

Baked Beans
2,353 cold baked beans one by one with a cocktail stick in 30 min by John Lawrence in Petersfield, Hants on 4 Mar. 1978.
Bananas
17 (edible weight minimum 4½ oz *128 g* each) in 2 mins by Dr. Ronald L. Alkana at the University of California, Irvine on 7 Dec. 1973.
Beer
Steven Petrosino drank one litre of beer in 1.3 sec on 22 June 1977 at "The Gingerbreadman", Carlisle, Pennsylvania.
Peter G. Dowdeswell (b. London 29 July 1940) of Earls Barton, Northamptonshire holds the following records:
2 pints—2.3 sec Zetters Social Club, Wolverton, Bucks   11 June 1975
2 litres—6.0 sec Carriage Horse Hotel, Higham Ferrers, Northants   7 Feb. 1975
Yards of Ale
2½ pints—5.0 sec R.A.F. Upper Heyford, Oxfordshire   4 May 1975
3 pints—5.4 sec Corby Town S.C., Northamptonshire   23 Jan. 1976
Upsidedown
2 pints—6.4 sec Top Rank Club, Northants   25 May 1975
Bicycle
15 days by Monsieur "Mangetout" (M. Lotito) (tyres and metal filings) at Every, France on 17 Mar–2 Apr. 1977.
Champagne
1,000 bottles per annum by Bobby Acland of the "Black Raven", Bishopsgate, City of London.
Cheese
16 oz. *453 g* of Cheddar in 1 min 13 sec by Peter Dowdeswell (see above) in Earls Barton, Northants on 14 July 1978.
Chicken
27 (2 lb. *907 g* pullets) by "Bozo" Miller (see above) at a sitting at Trader Vic's, San Francisco, California, U.S.A. in 1963.
Clams
424 (Littlenecks) in 8 min by Dave Barnes at Port Townsend Bay, Washington, U.S.A. on 3 May 1975.
Doughnuts
29 in 7 min 16 sec by Hany Rizk of Chedstone, Melbourne, Australia on 10 Apr. 1976. (total weight 2 lb. 12½ oz.).
Eels
1 lb. *453 g* of elvers in 13.7 secs by Peter Dowdeswell at Reeves Club, Bristol on 20 Oct. 1978.
Eggs
(Hard Boiled) 14 in 58 sec by Peter Dowdeswell (see above) at the Stardust Social Club, Corby, Northants on 18 Feb. 1977.
(Soft Boiled) 32 in 78 secs by Peter Dowdeswell in Northampton, on 8 Apr. 1978.
(Raw) 13 in 2.2 secs by Peter Dowdeswell at B.B.C., Norwich on 26 Jan. 1978.

Frankfurters
23 (2 oz. *56,6 g*) in 3 min 10 sec by Lynda Kuerth, 21, at the Veterans Stadium, Philadelphia, on 12 July 1977.
Gherkins
1 lb. *453 g* in 43.6 sec by Rex Barker of Elkhorn, Nebraska, U.S.A. on 30 Oct. 1975.
Grapes
3 lb. 1 oz. of grapes in 34.6 sec by Jim Ellis of Montrose, Michigan, U.S.A. on 30 May 1976.
Haggis
26 oz. *737 g* in 50 sec by Peter Dowdeswell at Reeves Club, Bristol on 21 Dec. 1978.
Hamburgers
20¾ hamburgers (each weighing 3½ oz. *100 g* totalling *2,07 kg* of meat) and buns in 30 mins by Alan Peterson at Longview, Washington, U.S.A. on 8 Feb. 1979.
Ice Cream
3 lb. 6 oz *1,530 kg* in 90 sec by Bennett D'Angelo at Dean Dairy, Waltham, Massachusetts, U.S.A. on 7 Aug. 1977.
Kippers
25 (self-filleted) in 60 min by Bob Ibbotson at Scarborough, North Yorkshire on 10 Aug. 1973.
Lemons
12 quarters (3 lemons) whole (including skin and pips) in 22.9 sec by Peter Dowdeswell at Reeves Club, Bristol on 20 Oct. 1978.
Meat
One whole roast ox in 42 days by Johann Ketzler of Munich, Germany in 1880.
Meat Pies
22 (each weighing 5½ oz. *156 g*) in 18 min 13 sec by Peter Dowdeswell in Northampton on 5 Oct. 1978.
Milk
2 pt (1 Imperial quart or *113.5 centilitres*) in 3.2 sec by Peter Dowdeswell (see above) at Dudley Top Rank Club, West Midlands on 31 May 1975.
Oysters
218 in 5 min by Mickey Rigdon at Fat City, Metairie, Louisiana, U.S.A. on 6 July 1977. The record for opening oysters is 100 in 3 min 1 sec by Douglas Brown, 31 at Christchurch, New Zealand on 29 Apr. 1975.
Pancakes
(6 in *15,2 cm* diameter buttered and with syrup) 62 in 6 min 58.5 sec by Peter Dowdeswell (see above) at The Drapery, Northampton on 9 Feb. 1977.
Peanuts
100 (whole unshelled) singly in 47.32 sec by Dan Blackwell in South Lake Tahoe, California, U.S.A. on 10 Feb. 1979
Pickled Onions
91 pickled onions (total weight 30 oz. *850 g*) in 1 min 8 sec by Pat Donahue in Victoria, British Columbia on 9 Mar. 1978.
Potatoes
3 lb. *1,36 kg* in 1 min 22 sec by Peter Dowdeswell in Earls Barton, Northants on 25 Aug. 1978.
Potato Crisps
30 2 oz. *56,6 g* bags in 24 min 33.6 sec, without a drink, by Paul G. Tully of Brisbane University in May 1969. Charles Chip Inc. of Mountville, Pennsylvania produced crisps 4 × 7 in *10 × 17,5 cm* from outsize potatoes in Feb. 1977.
Prunes
144 in 65 sec by Douglas Mein at Dundee University, Tayside, Scotland on 19 Oct. 1978.
Ravioli
324 (first 250 in 70 min) by "Bozo" Miller (see above) at Rendezvous Room, Oakland, California, U.S.A. in 1963.

Sandwiches
40 in 17 min 53.9 sec (jam "butties" 6 × 3¾ × ½ in *15,2 × 9,5 × 1,2 cm*) by Peter Dowdeswell on 17 Oct. 1977 at The Donut Shop, Reedley, California, U.S.A.

Sausage Meat
96 1 oz. *28,3 g* sausages in 6 min by Steve Meltzer of Brooklyn, New York, U.S.A. on 14 Oct. 1974. No "Hot Dog" contests results have been remotely comparable.

Shrimps
3 lb. *1,36 kg* in 4 min 8 sec by Peter Dowdeswell of Earls Barton, Northants on 25 May 1978.

Snails
124 in 15 mins (Moroccan snails) by Mrs. Nicky Bove at 6th Great Escargot Eating Contest, Houston, Texas, U.S.A. 1 Apr. 1974. The style prize was won by Rex Miller.

Spaghetti
100 yds *91,44 m* in 28.73 sec by Steve Weldon of Austin, Texas, U.S.A., on 1 May 1977.

Tortilla
74 (total weight 4 lb. 1½ oz. *1,85 kg*) in 30 min by Tom Nall in the 2nd World Championship at Mariano's Mexican Restaurant, Dallas, Texas, U.S.A. on 16 Oct. 1973.

Whelks
81 (unshelled) in 15 min by William Corfield, 35 at the Helyar Arms, East Coker, Somerset on 6 Sept. 1969.

2. HONOURS, DECORATIONS AND AWARDS

Oldest Order
The earliest of the orders of chivalry is the Venetian order of St. Marc, reputedly founded in A.D. 831. The Castilian order of Calatrava has an established date of foundation in 1158. The prototype of the princely Orders of Chivalry is the Most Noble Order of the Garter founded by King Edward III in *c.* 1348. A date of A.D. 809 has been attributed to the Most Ancient Order of the Thistle but is of doubtful provenance.

Eponymous record
The largest object to which a human name is attached is the universe itself—in the case of the "standard" cosmological model devised in 1922 by the Russian mathematician Aleksandr Aleksandrovitch Friedman (1888–1925) and known as Friedman's Universe. The claim that Lord Rutherford named the proton (of which there are some 10^{85} in the observable universe) with the scientist William Prout in mind is not now supported.

Most titles
The most titled person in the world is the 18th Duchess of Alba (Alba de Tormes), Doña Maria del Rosario Cayetana Fitz-James Stuart y Silva. She is 8 times a duchess, 15 times a marchioness, 21 times a countess and is 19 times a Spanish grandee.

Versatility
The only person to win a Victoria Cross and an Olympic Gold Medal has been Lt. Gen. Sir Philip Neame V.C., K.B.E., C.B., D.S.O. (1888–1978). He won the V.C. in 1914 and was an Olympic gold medalist for Britain for rifle shooting in 1924 though under the illusion at the time that he was shooting for the British Empire.

Victoria Cross *Double awards*
The only three men ever to have been awarded a bar to the Victoria Cross (instituted 1856) are:

Surg.-Capt. (later Lt.-Col.) Arthur Martin-Leake, V.C.*, V.D., R.A.M.C. (1874–1953) (1902 and bar 1915).
Capt. Noel Godfrey Chavasse, V.C.*, M.C., R.A.M.C. (1884–1917) (1916 and bar posthumously 14 Sept. 1917).
Second Lieut. (later Capt.) Charles Hazlitt Upham, V.C.*, N.Z.M.F. (born 1911) (1941 and bar 1942).

Victoria Cross *Youngest*
The lowest established age for a V.C. is 15 years 100 days for Hospital Apprentice Andrew (wrongly gazetted as Arthur) Fitzgibbon (born at Peteragurh, northern India, 13 May 1845) of the Indian Medical Services for bravery at the Taku Forts in northern China on 21 Aug. 1860. The youngest living V.C. is Lance-Corporal Rambahadur Limbu (b. Nepal, 1939) of the 10th Princess Mary's Own Gurkha Rifles. The award was for his courage while fighting in the Bau district of Sarawak, East Malaysia, on 21 Nov. 1965.

Victoria Cross *Longest lived*
The longest lived of all the 1,349 winners of the Victoria Cross was Captain (later General Sir) Lewis Stratford Tollemache Halliday, V.C. K.C.B., of the Royal Marine Light

BRITISH GALLANTRY AWARDS

The record number of bars (repeat awards) ever awarded to British gallantry awards are

DSO	3rd bar	16	QPM	2nd bar	1
RRC	2nd bar	1	DSM	3rd bar	1
DSC	3rd bar	1	MM	3rd bar	1
MC	3rd bar	4	DFM	2nd bar	1
DFC	2nd bar	54	AFM	1st bar	7
AFC	2nd bar	12	SGM	1st bar	1
DCM	2nd bar	11	QGM	1st bar	2
CGM (naval)	1st bar	1	BEM	1st bar	4
GM	1st bar	25			

No bars have ever been awarded to the GC or the CGM (Flying)

For fuller details see British Gallantry Awards by Abbott and John Taplin (Guinness Superlatives, £6.00).

Infantry. He was born on 14 May 1870, won his V.C. in China in 1900, and died on 9 Mar. 1966, aged 95 years 299 days.

Most Highly Decorated
The only four living persons to have been twice decorated with any of the United Kingdom's topmost decorations are Capt. C. H. Upham V.C. and bar; the Viscount De L'Isle V.C., K.G.; H.R.H. the Duke of Edinburgh K.G., K.T. and H.R.H. Prince Charles K.G., K.T.

George Cross
The highest award ever given to a woman is the George Cross. The oldest female recipient was Miss Emma Josie Townsend (formerly E.G.M.) aged 53 in 1932 and the youngest is Mrs. Doreen Ashburnham-Ruffner (formerly A.M.) aged 11 in 1916.

Order of Merit
The Order of Merit (instituted on 23 June 1902) is limited to 24 members. Up to 30 June 1978 there have been 128 awards including only 3 women, plus 9 honorary awards to non-British citizens. The longest lived holder has been the Rt. Hon. Bertrand Arthur William Russell, 3rd Earl Russell, who died on 2 Feb. 1970 aged 97 years 260 days. The oldest recipient was Admiral of the Fleet the Hon. Sir Henry Keppel, G.C.B., O.M. (1809–1904), who received the Order aged 93 years 56 days on 9 Aug. 1902. The youngest recipient has been H.R.H. the Duke of Edinburgh, K.G., K.T., O.M., G.B.E. who was appointed on his 47th birthday on 10 June 1968.

Most mentions in despatches
The record number of "mentions" is 24 by Field Marshal the Rt. Hon. Sir Frederick Sleigh Roberts Bt., the Earl Roberts, V.C., K.G., K.P., G.C.B., O.M., G.C.S.I., G.C.I.E., V.D. (1832–1914).

Most post-nominal letters
Lord Roberts was the only subject with 8 sets of *official* post-nominal letters. Currently the record number is seven by Admiral of the Fleet the Earl Mountbatten of Burma (born 25 June 1900) K.G., G.C.B., O.M., G.C.S.I., G.C.I.E., G.C.V.O., D.S.O.

U.S.S.R.
The U.S.S.R.'s highest award for valour is the Gold Star of a Hero of the Soviet Union. Over 10,000 were awarded in World War II. Among the 109 awards of a second star were those to Marshall Iosif Vissarionovich Dzhugashvili, *alias* Stalin (1879–1953) and Lt.-General Nikita Sergeyevich Khrushchyov (1894–1971). The only war-time triple awards were to Marshal Georgiy Konstantinovich Zhukov, Hon. G.C.B. (1896–1974) (subsequently awarded a fourth Gold Star unique until Mr. Khrushchyov's fourth award) and the leading air aces Guards' Colonel (now Marshal Aviation Aleksandr Ivanovich Pokryshkin and Aviation Maj.-Gen. Ivan Nikitovich Kozhedub. Zhukov also had the Order of Victory, twice, the Order of Lenin 4 times and the Order of

the Red Banner, thrice. Leonid Brezhnev received a third Gold Star on 19 Dec. 1978.

Germany
The only man to be awarded the Knight's Cross of the Iron Cross with swords, diamonds and golden oak-leaves was Col. Hans-Ulrich Rudel for services on the Eastern Front.

U.S.A.
The highest U.S. decoration is the Congressional Medal of Honor. Five marines received both the Army and Navy Medals of Honor for the same acts in 1918 and 14 officers and men from 1863 to 1915 have received the medal on two occasions.

Top Scoring Air Aces (World Wars I and II)
World
80 Rittmeister Manfred, Freiherr (Baron) von Richthofen (Germany).
352[1] Major Erich Hartman (Germany).

United Kingdom
73 Capt. (acting Major) Edward Mannock, V.C., D.S.O.**, M.C.*.
38[2] Wg.-Cdr. (now Air Vice Marshal) James Edgar Johnson, C.B., C.B.E., D.S.O.**, D.F.C.
A compilation of the top air aces of 13 combatant nations in World War I and of 22 nations in World War II was included in the 13th edition of *The Guinness Book of Records*.

[1] *All except one of the aircraft in this unrivalled total were Soviet combat aircraft on the Eastern Front in 1942–45. The German air ace with most victories against the R.A.F. was Oberleutnant Hans-Joachim Marseille (killed 30 Sept. 1942), who in 388 actions shot down 158 Allied aircraft, 151 of them over North Africa.*

[2] *The greatest number of successes against flying bombs (V.I's) was by Sqn. Ldr. Joseph Berry, D.F.C.** (b. Nottingham, 1920, killed 2 Oct. 1944), who brought down 60 in 4 months. The most successful R.A.F. fighter pilot was Sqn. Ldr Marmaduke Thomas St. John Pattle, D.F.C.*, of South Africa, with a known total of at least 40.*

Top jet ace
The greatest number of kills in jet to jet battles is 16 by Capt. Joseph Christopher McConnell, Jr., U.S.A.F. (b. Dover, New Hampshire, 30 Jan. 1922) in the Korean war (1950–53). He was killed on 25 Aug. 1954. It is possible that an Israeli ace may have surpassed this total in the period 1967–70 but the identity of pilots is subject to strict security.

Top woman ace
The record score for any woman fighter pilot is 12 by Jnr. Lt. Lydia Litvak (U.S.S.R.) (b. 1921) on the Eastern Front between 1941 and 1943. She was killed in action on 1 Aug. 1943.

Anti Tank successes
Major Hans-Ulrich Rudel, the German *Stuka* pilot, in 2,530 combat missions destroyed 519 Soviet armoured vehicles and was uniquely awarded the golden oak-leaves to the Knight's Cross of the Iron Cross on 1 Jan. 1945. (see above).

Anti-submarine successes
The highest number of U-boat kills attributed to one ship in the 1939–45 war was 13 to H.M.S. *Starling* (Capt. Frederick J. Walker, C.B., D.S.O.***, R.N.). Captain Walker was in overall command at the sinking of a total of 25 U-boats between 1941 and the time of his death on 9 July 1944. The U.S. Destroyer Escort *England* sank six Japanese submarines in the Pacific between 18 and 30 May 1944.

Most successful U-boat captain
The most successful of all World War II submarine commanders was Leutnant Otto Kretschmer, captain of the U.23 and U.99 who up to March 1940 sank one destroyer and 44 Allied merchantmen totalling 266,629 gross registered tons.

In World War I Kapitän-Leutnant Lothar von Arnauld de la Periere, in the U.35 and U.139, sank 194 allied ships totalling 453,716 gross tons. The most successful boats were U.48, which in World War I sank 54 ships of 90,350 g.r.t. in a single voyage and 535,900 g.r.t. all told, and U.53 which sank 53 ships of 318,111 g.r.t. in World War II.

NOBEL PRIZE
The Nobel Foundation of £3,200,000 was set up under the will of Alfred Bernhard Nobel (1833–96), the unmarried Swedish chemist and chemical engineer, who invented dynamite, in 1866. The Nobel Prizes are presented annually on 10 December, the anniversary of Nobel's death and the festival day of the Foundation. Since the first Prizes were awarded in 1901, the highest cash value of the award, in each of the six fields of Physics, Chemistry, Medicine and Physiology, Literature, Peace and Economics (inst. 1969) was $160,000 (*then £94,100*) in 1976 compared with $161,000 (*£80,500*) in 1978.

Most awards by countries (shared awards count as one)
United States citizens have won outright or shared in the greatest number of awards (including those made in 1978) with a total of 144 made up of 39 for Physics, 21 for Chemistry, 52 for Medicine-Physiology, 9 for Literature, 17 for Peace and 6 for Economics.

The United Kingdom has shared in 69 awards, comprising 20 for Physics, 20 for Chemistry, 13 for Medicine-Physiology, 9 for Peace, 5 for Literature and 2 for Economics.

By classes, the United States holds the record for Medicine-Physiology with 52, for Physics with 39, for Peace with 17 and Economics with 6; Germany and the U.S.A. for Chemistry with 21 each and France for Literature with 12.

Individuals
Individually the only person to have won two Prizes outright is Dr. Linus Carl Pauling (b. 28 Feb. 1901), Professor of Chemistry at the California Institute of Technology, Pasadena, California, U.S.A. since 1931. He was awarded the Chemistry Prize for 1954 and the Peace Prize for 1962. The only other persons to have won two prizes are Madame Marie Curie (1867–1934), who was born in Poland as Marja Sklodowska. She shared the 1903 Physics Prize with her husband Pierre Curie (1859–1906) and Antoine Henri Becquerel (1852–1908), and won the 1911 Chemistry Prize outright. Professor John Bardeen (b. 23 May 1908) shared the Physics Prize in 1956 and 1972. The Peace Prize has been awarded three times to the International Committee of the Red Cross (founded 29 Oct. 1863), of Geneva, Switzerland, namely in 1917, 1944 and in 1963, when it was shared with the International League of Red Cross Societies.

Oldest
The oldest prizeman has been Professor Francis Peyton Rous (1879–1970) of the United States. He shared the Medicine Prize in 1966, at the age of 87.

Youngest
The youngest laureate has been Professor Sir William Lawrence Bragg, C.H., O.B.E., M.C. (1890–1971), of the U.K., who at the age of 25, shared the 1915 Physics Prize with his father, Sir William Henry Bragg, O.M., K.B.E. (1862–1942), for work on X-rays and crystal structures. Bragg and also Theodore William Richards (1868–1928) of the U.S.A., who won the 1914 Chemistry Prize, carried out their prize work when aged 23. The youngest Literature prizeman has been Joseph Rudyard Kipling (1865–1936) at the age of 41 in 1907. The youngest Peace prize-winner has been the Rev. Dr. Martin Luther King, Jr. (1929–68) of the U.S.A., in 1964 at the age of 35.

Most statues
The world record for raising statues to oneself was set by Generalissimo Dr. Rafael Leónidas Trujillo y Molina (1891–1961), former President of the Dominican Republic. In March 1960 a count showed that there were "over 2,000". The country's highest mountain was named Pico Trujillo (now Pico Duarte). One province was called Trujillo and another Trujillo Valdez. The capital was named Ciudad Trujillo (Trujillo City) in 1936, but reverted to its old name of Santo Domingo de Guzmán on 23 Nov. 1961. Trujillo was assassinated in a car ambush on 30 May 1961, and 30 May is now celebrated annually as a public holiday. The man to whom most statues have been raised is undoubtedly Vladimir Ilyich Ulyanov, *alias* Lenin (1870–1924), busts of whom have been mass-produced as also in the case of Mao Tse-tung (1893–1976) and Ho Chi Minh (1890–1969).

PEERAGE
Most ancient
The oldest extant peerage is that of the premier Earl of Scot-

land, the Rt. Hon. Margaret of Mar, the Countess of Mar and 31st holder of this Earldom, (b. 19 Sept. 1940), who is the heir-at-law of Roderick or Rothri, 1st Earl (or Mormaer) of Mar, who witnessed a charter in 1114 or 1115 as "Rothri *comes*".

Oldest creation

The greatest age at which any person has been raised to the peerage is 93 years 337 days in the case of Sir William Francis Kyffin Taylor, G.B.E., K.C. (b. 9 July 1854), who was created Baron Maenan of Ellesmere, County Salop (Shropshire), on 10 June 1948, and died, aged 97, on 22 Sept. 1951. The oldest elevation to a Life Peerage has been that of Emmanuel Shinwell C.H. (b. 18 Oct. 1884) on 2 June 1970 when aged 85 years 227 days.

Longest lived peer

The longest lived peer ever recorded was the Rt. Hon. Frank Douglas-Pennant, the 5th Baron Penrhyn (b. 21 Nov. 1865), who died on 3 Feb. 1967, aged 101 years 74 days. The oldest peeress recorded was the Countess Desmond, who was alleged to be 140 when she died in 1604. This claim is patently exaggerated but it is accepted that she may have been 104. Currently the oldest holder of a peerage, and the oldest Parliamentarian, is the Rt. Hon. Walter Egerton George Lucian Keppel M.C., the 9th Earl of Albemarle who was 97 on 28 Feb. 1979.

Youngest peers

Twelve Dukes of Cornwall became (in accordance with the grant by the Crown in Parliament) peers at birth as the eldest son of a Sovereign; and the 9th Earl of Chichester posthumously inherited his father's (killed 54 days previously) earldom at his birth on 14 Apr. 1944. The youngest age at which a person has had a peerage conferred on them is 7 days old in the case of the Earldom of Chester on H.R.H. the Prince George (later George IV) on 19 Aug. 1762.

Longest and shortest peerages

The peer who has sat longest in the House of Lords was Lt.-Col. Charles Henry FitzRoy, O.B.E., the 4th Baron Southampton (b. 11 May 1867), who succeeded to his father's title on 16 July 1872, took his seat on 23 Jan. 1891, 18 months before Mr. W. E. Gladstone's fourth administration began, and died, aged 91, on 7 Dec. 1958, having held the title for 86 years 144 days.

The shortest enjoyment of a peerage was the "split second" by which the law assumes that the Hon. Wilfrid Carlyle Stamp (b. 28 Oct. 1904), the 2nd Baron Stamp, survived his father, Sir Josiah Charles Stamp, G.C.B., G.B.E., the 1st Baron Stamp, when both were killed as a result of German bombing of London on 16 Apr. 1941. Apart from this legal fiction, the shortest recorded peerage was one of 30 minutes in the case of Sir Charles Brandon, K.B., the 3rd Duke of Suffolk, who died, aged 13 or 14, just after succeeding his brother, Sir Henry, the 2nd Duke, when both were suffering a fatal illness, at Buckden, Cambridgeshire, on 14 July 1551.

Highest numbering

The highest succession number borne by any peer is that of the present 35th Baron Kingsale (John de Courcy, b. 27 Jan. 1941), who succeeded to the then 746-year-old Barony on 7 Nov. 1969.

Most creations

The largest number of new hereditary peerages created in any year was the 54 in 1296. The record for all peerages (including 40 life peerages) is 55 in 1964. The greatest number of extinctions in a year was 16 in 1923 and the greatest number of deaths was 44 in 1935.

Most prolific

The most prolific peers of all time are believed to be the 1st Earl Ferrers (1650–1717) and the 3rd Earl of Winchelsea (*c.* 1620–1689) each with 27 legitimate children. In addition, the former reputedly fathered 30 illegitimate children. Currently the peer with the largest family is the Rt. Hon. Bryan Walter Guinness, 2nd Baron Moyne (b. 27 Oct. 1905) with 6 sons and 5 daughters.

The most prolific peeress is believed to be Elizabeth (*née*

Barnard), who bore her husband, Lord Chandos of Sudeley (1642–1714), 22 children.

Baronets

The greatest age to which a baronet has lived is 101 years 188 days, in the case of Sir Fitzroy Donald Maclean, 10th Bt., K.C.B., (1835–1936). He was the last survivor of the Charge of the Light Brigade at Balaclava in the Crimea. The only baronetess in her own right is Dame Maureen Dunbar of Hampriggs, who succeeded as 8th in line of a 1706 baronetcy in 1965.

Knights

The greatest number of knights dubbed in a single day was 432 by James I in the Royal Garden, Whitehall on 23 July 1603. On his coronation day two days later, he appointed 62 Knights of the Garter.

Youngest and oldest

The youngest age for the conferment of a knighthood is 29 days for H.R.H. the Prince Albert Edward (b. 9 Nov. 1841) (later Edward VII) by virtue of his *ex officio* membership of the Order of the Garter (K.G.) consequent upon his creation as Prince of Wales on 8 Dec. 1841. The greatest age for the conferment of a knighthood is on a 100th birthday in the case of Sir Robert Meyer made a K.C.V.O. by the Queen at the Royal Festival Hall, London on 5 June 1979.

Most freedoms

Probably the greatest number of freedoms ever conferred on any man was 57 in the case of Andrew Carnegie (1835–1919), who was born in Dumfermline, Fife but emigrated to the United States in 1848. The most freedoms conferred upon any citizen of the United Kingdom is 42, in the case of Sir Winston Churchill, (1874–1965).

Most honorary degrees

The greatest number of honorary degrees awarded to any individual is 89, given to Herbert Clark Hoover (1874–1964), former President of the United States (1929–33).

Greatest vote

The largest monetary vote made by Parliament to a subject was the £400,000 given to the 1st Duke of Wellington (1769–1852) on 12 Apr. 1814. He received in all £864,000. The total received by the 1st, 2nd and 3rd Dukes to January 1900 was £1,052,000.

Who's Who

The longest entry in *Who's Who* (founded 1848) was that of the Rt. Hon. Sir Winston Leonard Spencer Churchill, K.G., O.M., C.H., T.D. (1874–1965), who appeared in 67 editions from 1899 (18 lines) and had 211 lines by the 1965 edition. Currently the longest entry is that of Barbara Cartland, the romantic novelist, with 114 lines. Apart from those who qualify for inclusion by hereditary title, the youngest entry has been Yehudi Menuhin, Hon. K.B.E. (b. New York City, U.S.A. 22 Apr. 1916), the concert violinist, who first appeared in the 1932 edition aged 15. The longest entry of the 66,000 entries in *Who's Who in America* is that of Dr. Glen T. Seaborg (b. 12 Apr. 1912) whose all-time record of 97 lines compares with the 16 line sketch on President Carter.

Most brothers

The most brothers having entries in *Who's Who* is five in the case of the Barrington-Wards: Frederick Temple (1880–1938), Sir Lancelot (1884–1953), Sir Michael (1887–1972), Robert McGowan (1891–1948) and John Grosvenor (1894–1946). Their father Canon Mark James (died 1924) of Duloe, Cornwall was himself in *Who's Who*.

Oxford and Cambridge Unions

Four brothers were Presidents of the Union in the case of the sons of the Rt. Hon. Isaac Foot. Sir Dingle Foot (Balliol, 1927–28); John (Lord Foot) (Balliol, 1930–31) and Rt. Hon. Michael (Wadham, 1933–34) at Oxford and Hugh (Lord Caradon) (St. John's, 1929) at Cambridge. The last named's son Paul was President at Oxford (University College, 1960–61).

WATER SKIING: Longest jump
YACHTING: Olympic title

SPORTS, GAMES AND PASTIMES

ALL SPORTS

Earliest

The origins of sport stem from the time when self-preservation ceased to be the all-consuming human preoccupation. Archery was a hunting skill in mesolithic times (by *c.* 8000 B.C.), but did not become an organized sport until *c.* A.D. 300, among the Genoese. The earliest dated evidence for sport is *c.* 2450 B.C. for fowling with throwing sticks, similar to return boomerangs, and hunting. Ball games by girls depicted on Middle Kingdom murals at Beni Hasan, Egypt have been dated to *c.* 2050 B.C.

Fastest

The highest speed reached in a non-mechanical sport is in sky-diving, in which a speed of 185 m.p.h. *298 km/h* is that a single bout once lasted for 11 hrs 40 min. In the lower atmosphere. In delayed drops speeds of 614 m.p.h. *988 km/h* have been recorded at high rarefied altitudes. The highest projectile speed in any moving ball game is *c.* 180 m.p.h. *289 km/h* in pelota. This compares with 170 m.p.h. *273 km/h* (electronically-timed) for a golf ball driven off a tee.

Slowest

In wrestling, before the rules were modified towards "brighter wrestling", contestants could be locked in holds for so long that a single bout once lasted for 11 hrs 40 min. In the extreme case of the 2 hrs 41 min pull in the regimental tug o' war in Jubbulpore, India, on 12 Aug. 1889, the winning team moved a net distance of 12 ft *3,6 m* at an average speed of 0.00084 m.p.h. *0,00135 km/h*.

Longest

The most protracted sporting test was an automobile duration test of 222,618 miles *358 268 km* by Appaurchaux and others in a Ford Taunus. This was contested over 142 days in 1963. The distance was equivalent to 8.93 times around the equator.

The most protracted non-mechanical sporting event is the *Tour de France* cycling race. In 1926 this was over 3,569 miles *5 743 km* lasting 29 days. The total damage to the French national economy due to the interest in this annual event, now reduced to 23 days, is immense, and is currently estimated to be in excess of £1,000,000,000.

Largest stadium

For details of the world's largest stadium see p. 116.

Largest pitch

The largest pitch of any ball game is that of polo, with 12.4 acres *5,0 ha,* or a maximum length of 300 yd *274 m* and a width, without side boards, of 200 yd *182 m*. Twice a year in the Parish of St. Columb Major, Cornwall, England, a game called Hurling (not to be confused with the Irish game) is played on a "pitch" which consists of the entire Parish, approximately 25 square miles *64,7 km²*.

Largest trophy

The world's largest trophy for a particular sport is the Bangalore Limited Handicap Polo Tournament Trophy. This massive cup is 6 ft *1,83 m* tall and was presented in 1936 by the Raja of Kolanka.

Heaviest sportsmen

The heaviest sportsman of all-time was the professional wrestler William J. Cobb of Macon, Georgia, U.S.A., who in 1962 was billed as the 802 lb. (57 st 4 lb. *363 kg*) "Happy Humphrey". The heaviest player of a ball-game was the 487 lb *221 kg* Bob Pointer, the U.S. Football tackle formerly on the 1967 Santa Barbara High School Team, California, U.S.A. The current heaviest in British sport is professional wrestler "Giant Haystacks" (Luke McMasters) at 492 lb *223 kg*.

Youngest and oldest world record breakers

The youngest age at which any person has broken a world record is 12 years 298 days in the case of Gertrude Caroline Ederle (U.S.A.) (b. 23 Oct. 1906) who broke the women's 880 yd freestyle world record with 13 min 19.0 sec at Indianapolis, U.S.A., on 17 Aug. 1919. Irish-born John J. Flanagan (1868–1938), triple Olympic hammer throw champion for the U.S., 1900–1908, set his last world record of 184 ft 4 in *56,18 m* at New Haven, Conn., U.S.A., on 24 July 1909 41 years 196 days.

Most prolific record breaker

Between 24 Jan. 1970 and 1 Nov. 1977 Vasili Alexeyev (U.S.S.R.) (b. 7 Jan. 1942) broke a total of 80 official world records in weightlifting.

Youngest and oldest internationals

The youngest age at which any person has won international honours is eight years in the case of Joy Foster, the Jamaican singles and mixed doubles table tennis champion in 1958.

The largest television sporting audience saw Argentina beat the Netherlands 3–1 in the 1978 World Cup Final in Buenos Aires. (*All Sport Photographic*)

The youngest British international has been diver Beverley Williams (b. 5 Jan. 1957), who was 10 yr 268 days old when she competed against the U.S.A. at Crystal Palace, London, on 30 Sept. 1967. It would appear that the greatest age at which anyone has actively competed for his country was 72 yr 280 days in the case of Oscar G. Swahn (Sweden) (1847–1927) who won a silver medal for shooting in the Olympic Games at Antwerp on 26 July 1920. He qualified for the 1924 Games but was unable to participate due to illness. Britain's oldest international was Hilda Lorna Johnstone (b. 4 Sept. 1902) who was 69 yr 358 days when she competed in the Dressage competition at the 1972 Games.

Most versatile

All-round ability is measured by level of attainment in highly varied pursuits. By these parameters Charlotte (Lottie) Dod (1871–1960) stands supreme. She won the Wimbledon Singles title five times between 1887 and 1893, the British Ladies Golf Championship in 1904, an Olympic silver medal for archery in 1908, and represented England at hockey in 1899. She also excelled at skating and tobogganing. Among current sportsmen, Chief Petty Officer Alan Robert Cronin (b. 20 Sept. 1946) has represented Great Britain in track and field (hurdles), karate, and bobsleigh.

Youngest and oldest champions

The youngest successful competitor in a world title event was a French boy, whose name is not recorded, who coxed the Netherlands' Olympic pair at Paris on 26 Aug. 1900. He was not more than ten and may have been as young as seven. The youngest individual Olympic winner was Marjorie Gestring (U.S.A.), who took the springboard diving title at the age of 13 years 9 months at the Olympic Games in Berlin in 1936. Oscar Swahn (see above) was aged 65 yr 258 days when he won a gold medal in the 1912 Olympic Running Deer team shooting competition.

Longest reign

The longest reign as a world champion is 33 years (1829–62) by Jacques Edmond Barre (France) (1802–73) at real tennis. The longest reign as a British champion is 41 years by the archer Alice Blanche Legh (1855–1948) who first won the Championship in 1881 and for the 23rd and final time in 1922 aged 67.

Greatest earnings

The greatest fortune amassed by an individual in sport is an estimated $60 million by the boxer Muhammad Ali Haj (U.S.A.) to August 1979. The highest paid woman athlete in the world is ice skater Janet Lynn (U.S.A.) (b. 6 Apr. 1953), who, in 1974, signed a $1.5 million £652,000 three year contract. In 1974 she earned more than $750,000 £325,000. The greatest purse won for a single sports contest is $6½ million by Muhammad Ali Haj (U.S.A.) when he defeated Ken Norton (U.S.A.) in New York on 28 Sept. 1976.

Most expensive

The most expensive of all sports is the racing of large yachts —"J" type boats, last built in 1937, and International 12-metre boats. The owning and racing of these is beyond the means of individual millionaires and is confined to multi-millionaires or syndicates.

Largest crowd

The greatest number of live spectators for any sporting spectacle is the estimated 2,000,000 who lined the route of the New York Marathon in Oct. 1978. The race was won by Bill Rodgers (U.S.A.) for the third consecutive time. However, spread over 23 days, it is estimated that more than 10,000,000 see the annual *Tour de France* along the route (see also above).

The largest crowd travelling to any sporting venue is "more than 400,000" for the annual *Grand Prix d'Endurance* motor race on the Sarthe circuit near Le Mans, France. The record stadium crowd was one of 199,854 for the Brazil *v.* Uruguay match in the Maracaña Municipal Stadium, Rio de Janeiro, Brazil, on 16 July 1950.

Most participants

The *Stramilano* 22 km run around Milan, Italy attracted over 50,000 runners on 16 Apr. 1978. In May 1971, the "Ramblin' Raft Race" on the Chattahoochee River, at Atlanta, Georgia, U.S.A., attracted 37,683 competitors on 8,304 rafts.

Largest following

The sport with most regular participants in Britain is angling with 2¾ million. Over 30 million spectators watched Association Football matches in Britain in 1978–79. The largest television audience for a single sporting event, excluding Olympic events, was an estimated 400 million who saw the final of the 1978 Soccer World Cup (see also p. 110).

Most sportsmen

According to a report in 1978, 55 million people are active in sports in the U.S.S.R. The country has 3,282 stadiums, 1,435 swimming pools and over 66,000 indoor gymnasia. It is estimated that some 29% of the population of East Germany participate in sport regularly.

Worst disasters

The worst sports disaster in recent history was when an estimated 604 were killed after some stands at the Hong Kong Jockey Club racecourse collapsed and caught fire on 26 Feb. 1918. During the reign of Antoninus Pius (A.D. 138–161) the upper wooden tiers in the Circus Maximus, Rome, collapsed during a gladiatorial combat killing some 1,112 spectators. Britain's worst sports disaster was when 66 were killed and 145 injured at the Rangers *v.* Celtic football match at Exit 13 of Ibrox Park stadium, Glasgow on 2 Jan. 1971.

AEROBATICS

Earliest

The first aerobatic "manoeuvre" is generally considered the sustained inverted flight in a Bleriot of Célestin-Adolphe Pégoud, at Buc, France on 21 Sept. 1913, but Lieut. Peter Nikolayevich Nesterov, of the Imperial Russian Air Service, performed a loop in a Nieuport Type IV monoplane at Kiev, USSR on 27 Aug. 1913.

World Championships

Held biennially since 1960 (excepting 1974), scoring is based on the system devised by Col José Aresti of Spain. The competitions consist of two compulsory and two free programmes.

Most titles

The world championships Team competition has been won on four occasions by the USSR. No individual has won more than one title, the most successful competitor being Igor Egorov (USSR) who won in 1970, was second in 1976, fifth in 1972 and eleventh in 1968. The most successful in the women's competition has been Lidia Leonova (USSR) with first place in 1976, second in 1978, third in 1972 and fifth in 1970. The only medal achieved by Britain has been a bronze in the team event at Kiev, USSR in 1976. The highest individual placing by a Briton is fourth by Neil Williams (1935–77) in 1976.

Inverted Flight

The duration record for inverted flight is 2 hr 15 min 4 sec by John Leggatt in a Champion Decathlon on 28 May 1974 over the Arizona Desert, U.S.A.

Loops

On 16 Dec. 1973, John "Hal" McClain performed 1,501½ inside loops in a Pitts S-2A over Long Beach, Cal., U.S.A. He also achieved 180 outside loops in a Bellanca Super Decathlon on 2 Sept. 1978 over Houston, Texas, U.S.A.

ANGLING

Catch *Largest Single*

The largest officially ratified fish ever caught on a rod is a

Richard Walker with his record carp—the biggest coarse fish on the British record list. (*Angling News Service*)

man-eating great white shark (*Carcharodon carcharias*) weighing 2,664 lb. *1 208 kg* and measuring 16 ft 10 in *5,13 m* long, caught on a 130 lb. *58 kg* test line by Alf Dean at Denial Bay, near Ceduna, South Australia, on 21 Apr. 1959. A white pointer shark weighing 3,388 lb. *1 537 kg* was caught by Clive Green off Albany, Western Australia, on 26 Apr. 1976 but will remain unratified as whale meat was used as bait. The biggest ever rod-caught fish by a British angler is a 1,260 lb. *571,5 kg* black marlin caught by Edward A. Crutch off Cairns, Queensland, Australia on 19 Oct. 1973.

Capt. Frank Mundus (U.S.A.) harpooned a 17 ft *5,18 m* long 4,500 lb. *2,040 kg* great white shark off Montauk Point, New York, U.S.A. on 6 June 1964 and, assisted by Peter Brandenberg, Gerald Mallow, Frank Bloom and Harvey Ferston, landed it after a five hour battle.

The largest marine animal ever killed by *hand* harpoon was a blue whale 97 ft *29,56 m* in length, killed by Archer Davidson in Twofold Bay, New South Wales, Australia, in 1910. Its tail flukes measured 20 ft *6,09 m* across and its jaw bone 23 ft 4 in *7,11 m*.

Catch *Smallest*

The smallest fish to win a competition is a smelt, weighing $\frac{1}{16}$ of an ounce *1 dram*, caught by Peter Christian at Buckenham Ferry, Norfolk, England on 9 Jan. 1977, in defeating 107 other competitors. For the smallest full-grown fish see p. 42.

Spear fishing

The largest fish ever taken underwater was an 804 lb. *364 kg* giant black grouper or jewfish by Don Pinder of the Miami Triton Club, Florida, U.S.A., in 1955. The British spear-fishing record is 89 lb. *40,36 kg* for an angler fish by J. Brown (Weymouth Association Divers) in 1969.

Championship records *World*

The *Confederation Internationale de la Pêche Sportive* championships were inaugurated as European championships in 1953. They were recognised as World Championships in 1957. France won ten times between 1956 and 1978 and

Robert Tesse (France) took the individual title uniquely three times, in 1959–60, 1965. The record weight (team) is 57 lb 13 oz. 4 dr. in three hours by Italy on the Danube, near Belgrade, Yugoslavia on 29 Sept. 1957. The individual record is 29 lb. 13 oz. 9 dr. by Fausto Pasinetti (Italy) at Varna, Bulgaria on 3 Oct. 1976. The most fish caught is 652 by Jacques Isenbaert (Belgium) at Dunajvaros, Yugoslavia on 27 Aug. 1967.

Championship records *British*
The National Angling Championship (instituted 1906) has been won seven times by Leeds (1909–10, 1914, 1928, 1948–49, 1952). Only James H. R. Bazley (Leeds) has ever won the individual title twice (1909, 1927). The record catch is 76 lb. 9 oz. *34 kg 720* by David Burr (Rugby) in the Huntspill, Somerset in 1965. The largest single fish caught in the Championships is a carp of 14 lb. 2 oz. *6 kg 406* by J. C. Essex in Sept. 1975. The team record is 136 lb. 15¼ oz. *62 kg 120* by Sheffield Amalgamated also in the Huntspill in 1955.

Match Fishing
In the Fermanagh Angling Festival on the River Erne, Ulster, Northern Ireland, on 27 May 1979, Dennis Willis weighed in 207 lb. 7½ oz. of fish in a 5 hr match.

Casting records
The longest freshwater cast ratified under I.C.F. (International Casting Federation) rules is 175,01 m *574 ft 2 in* by Walter Kummerow (West Germany), for the Bait Distance Double-Handed 30 g event held at Lenzerheide, Switzerland in the 1968 Championships. The British National record is 148,78 m *488 ft 1 in* by A. Dickison on the same occasion. The longest Fly Distance Double-Handed cast is 78,38 m *257 ft 2 in* by S. Scheen (Norway), also at Lenzerheide in 1968. Peter Anderson set a British National professional record of 70,90 m *232 ft 7 in* on water at Scarborough in 1977, and Mike Weddell cast 73,15 m *240 ft* on land at Oslo, Norway in 1977.

Longest fight
The longest recorded individual fight with a fish is 32 hrs 5 min by Donal Heatley (b. 1938) (New Zealand) with a black marlin (estimated length 20 ft *6,09 m* and weight 1,500 lb. *680 kg*) off Mayor Island off Tauranga, North Island on 21–22 Jan. 1968. It towed the 12 ton/*tonnes* launch 50 miles *80 km* before breaking the line.

Marathon
John Reader fished for 504 hr at Hutton Pond, Weston-super-Mare, Avon from 20 Aug.–10 Sept. 1978.

WORLD RECORDS

(Selected Sea and Freshwater fish [All Tackle] from the complete list ratified by the International Game Fish Association to Jan. 1979)

Species	Weight lb. oz.	kg/g	Name of Angler	Location	Date
Amberjack	149 0	67,585	Peter Simons	Bermuda	21 June 1964
Barracuda[1]	83 0	37,648	K. J. W. Hackett[2]	Lagos, Nigeria	13 Jan. 1952
Bass (Giant Sea)	563 8	255,599	James D. McAdam Jr.	Anacapa Is., California, U.S.A.	20 Aug. 1968
Black Runner (Cobia)	110 5	50,035	Eric W. Tinworth	off Mombasa, Kenya	8 Sept. 1964
Carp[3]	55 5	25,089	Frank J. Ledwein	Clearwater Lake, Minnesota, U.S.A.	10 July 1952
Cod	98 12	44,792	Alphonse J. Bielevich	Isle of Shoals, New Hampshire, U.S.A.	8 June 1969
Marlin (Black)	1,560 0	707,604	Alfred C. Glassell, Jr.	Cabo Blanco, Peru	4 Aug. 1953
Marlin (Atlantic Blue)	1,282 0	581,505	Larry Martin	off St Thomas, Virgin Is.	6 Aug. 1977
Marlin (Pacific Blue)	1,153 0	522,992	Greg D. Perez	Ritidian Point, Guam	21 Aug. 1969
Marlin (Striped)	417 8	189,374	Phillip Bryers	off Cavalli I., New Zealand	14 Jan. 1977
Marlin (White)	174 3	79,000	Otavia Cunha Reboucas	Vitoria, Brazil	1 Nov. 1976
Pike (Northern)	46 2	20,921	Peter Dubuc	Sacandaga Reservoir, N.Y., U.S.A.	15 Sept. 1940
Sailfish (Atlantic)	128 1	58,088	Harm Steyn	Luanda, Angola	27 Mar. 1974
Sailfish (Pacific)	221 0	100,243	C. W. Stewart	Santa Cruz I., Galapagos Is.	12 Feb. 1947
Salmon (Chinook)[4]	93 0	42,184	Howard C. Rider	Kelp Bay, Alaska, U.S.A.	24 June 1977
Shark (Blue)	437 0	198,220	Peter Hyde	Catherine Bay, N.S.W., Australia	2 Oct. 1976
Shark (Shortfin Mako)[5]	1,061 0	481,261	James B. Penwarden	Mayor Island, New Zealand	17 Feb. 1970
Shark (White or Man-eating)	2,664 0	1 208,370	Alfred Dean	Denial Bay, Ceduna, South Australia	21 Apr. 1959
Shark (Porbeagle)	465 0	210,920	Jorge Potier	Padstow, Cornwall, England	23 July 1976
Shark (Thresher)[6]	739 0	335,204	Brian Galvin	Tutukaka, New Zealand	17 Feb. 1975
Shark (Tiger)	1,780 0	807,394	Walter Maxwell	Cherry Grove, South Carolina, U.S.A.	14 June 1964
Sturgeon (White)[7]	360 0	163,293	Willard Cravens	Snake River, Idaho, U.S.A.	24 Apr. 1956
Swordfish	1,182 0	536,146	Lou E. Marron	Iquique, Chile	7 May 1953
Tarpon	283 0	128,366	M. Salazar	Lago de Maracaibo, Venezuela	19 Mar. 1965
Trout (Lake)[8]	65 0	29,483	Larry Daunis	Great Bear Lake, N.W.T., Canada	8 Aug. 1970
Tuna (Allison or Yellowfin)	388 12	176,333	Curt Wiesenhutter	San Benedicto Is., Mexico	1 Apr. 1977
Tuna (Atlantic bigeye)	375 8	170,323	Cecil Browne	Ocean City, Md., U.S.A.	26 Aug. 1977
Tuna (Pacific bigeye)	435 0	197,312	Dr. Russel V. A. Lee	Cabo Blanco, Peru	17 Apr. 1957
Tuna (Bluefin) Tunny	1,235 0	560,186	Michael MacDonald	North Lake, P.E.I., Canada	17 Oct. 1978
Wahoo	149 0	67,585	John Pirovano	Cat Cay, Bahamas	15 June 1962

[1] A barracuda weighing 103 lb. 4 oz. 46 kg 826 was caught on an untested line by Chester Benet at West End, Bahamas, on 11 Aug. 1932. Another of 48 lb. 6 oz. 21 kg 942, was caught barehanded by Thomas B. Pace at Panama City Beach, Florida, U.S.A. on 19 April 1974.
[2] Aged 11 yrs 137 days at the time.
[3] A carp weighing 83 lb. 8 oz. 37 kg 874 was taken (not by rod) near Pretoria, South Africa.
[4] A salmon weighing 126 lb. 8 oz. 57 kg 379 was taken (not by rod) near Petersburg, Alaska, U.S.A.
[5] A 1,295 lb. 587 kg specimen was taken by two anglers off Natal, South Africa on 17 Mar. 1939 and a 1,500 lb. 680 kg specimen harpooned inside Durban Harbour, South Africa in 1933.
[6] W. W. Dowding caught one of 922 lb. 418 kg in 1937 on an untested line.
[7] Glenn Howard caught one of 394 lb 178 kg on the Snake River, Idaho in 1954.
[8] A 102 lb. 46 kg 266 trout was taken from Lake Athabasca, northern Saskatchewan, Canada, on 8 Aug. 1961.

BRITISH RECORDS

(Selected from the complete list ratified by the British Record [rod-caught] Fish Committee of the National Anglers' Council to Jan. 1979)

Species SEA FISH	Weight lb. oz. dr.	kg/g	Name of Angler	Location	Year
Angler Fish	82 12	37,534	K. Ponsford	off Mevagissey, Cornwall	1977
Bass	18 6	8,334	R. G. Slater	off Eddystone Reef	1975
Bream (Black)	6 14 4	3,125	J. A. Garlick	off Devon coast	1977
Bream (Red)	9 8 12	4,330	B. H. Reynolds	Mevagissey, Cornwall	1974
Brill	16 0	7,257	A. H. Fisher	Derby Haven, Isle of Man	1950
Bull Huss	21 3	9,610	J. Holmes	Hat Rock, Looe, Cornwall	1955
Cod	53 0	24,039	G. Martin	off Start Point, Devon	1972
Conger	109 6	49,609	Robin. W. Potter	S. E. of Eddystone	1976
Dab	2 12 4	1,254	Robert Islip	Gairloch, Wester Ross	1975
Flounder	5 11 8	2,593	A. G. L. Cobbledick	Fowey, Cornwall	1956

Species	Weight lb. oz.	kg/g	Name of Angler	Location	Year
Garfish	2 13 14	*1,300*	S. Claeskens	off Newton Ferrers, Devon	1971
Gurnard (Red)	5 0	*2,268*	B. D. Critchley	off Rhyl, Clwyd	1973
Gurnard (Yellow)	12 3	*5,528*	G. J. Reynolds	Langland Bay, Wales	1976
Haddock	13 11 4	*6,209*	G. Bones	Falmouth Bay, Cornwall	1978
Hake	25 5 8	*11,494*	H. W. Steele	Belfast Lough, N. Ireland	1962
Halibut	212 4	*96,270*	J. A. Hewitt	off Dunnet Head, Highland	1975
John Dory	11 14	*5,386*	J. Johnson	off Newhaven, East Sussex	1977
Ling	57 2 8	*25,924*	H. Solomons	off Mevagissey, Cornwall	1975
Mackerel	5 6 8	*2,452*	S. Beasley	N. of Eddystone Lighthouse	1969
Monkfish	66 0	*29,936*	G. C. Chalk	Shoreham, West Sussex	1965
Mullet (Red)	3 10	*1,644*	J. E. Martel	St. Martin's, Guernsey	1967
Mullet (Thick Lipped)	10 1	*4,564*	P/O. P. C. Libby	Portland, Dorset	1952
Plaice	10 3 8	*4,635*	Master H. Gardiner	Longa Sound, Scotland	1974
Pollack	25 0	*11,339*	R. J. Hosking	off Eddystone Lighthouse	1972
Ray (Spotted)	7 12	*3,515*	P. R. Dower	Stoke Beach, Plymouth, Devon	1977
Ray (Sting)	59 0	*26,761*	J. M. Buckley	Clacton-on-Sea, Essex	1952
Ray (Thornback)	38 0	*17,236*	J. Patterson	Rustington, East Sussex	1935
Rockling (Three bearded)	3 2	*1,417*	N. Docksey	off Portand Breakwater, Dorset	1976
Shad (Allis)	4 12 7	*2,166*	P. B. Gerrard	off Chesil Beach, Dorset	1977
Shad (Thwaite)	3 2	*1,417*	T. Hayward	Deal, Kent	1949
	3 2	*1,417*	S. Jenkins	Tor Bay, Devon	1954
Shark (Blue)	218 0	*98,878*	N. Sutcliffe	Looe, Cornwall	1959
Shark (Mako)	500 0	*226,786*	Mrs. J. Yallop	off Eddystone Lighthouse	1971
Shark (Porbeagle)	see world record list				
Shark (Thresher)	295 0	*133,809*	H. Jim Aris	off Dunose Head, Isle of Wight	1978
Skate (Common)	226 8	*102,733*	R. S. Macpherson	Dury Voe, Shetland	1970
Sole	4 8	*2,041*	H. C. L. Pike	Platte Saline Beach, Alderney, C.I.	1978
Spurdog	21 3 7	*9,622*	P. R. Barrett	off Porthleven, Cornwall	1977
Tope	74 11	*33,876*	A. B. Harries	Caldy Island, Dyfed	1964
Tunny (Tuna bluefin)	851 0	*385,989*	L. Mitchell-Henry	Whitby, North Yorkshire	1933
Turbot	32 3	*14,599*	Derrick Dyer	off Plymouth, Devon	1976
Whiting	6 4	*2,834*	S. Dearman	West Bay, Bridport, Dorset	1977
Wrasse (Ballan)	8 6 6	*3,808*	R. W. Le Page	Bordeaux Beach, Guernsey, C.I.	1976

FRESHWATER FISH

Species	Weight lb. oz.	kg/g	Name of Angler	Location	Year
Barbel	13 12	*6,237*	J. Day	Royalty Fishery, Christchurch, Dorset	1962
Bleak	0 3 15	*0,111*	D. Pollard	Staythorpe, Nottinghamshire	1971
Bream (Common)	13 8	*6,123*	A. R. Heslop	Private water, Staffs.	1977
Carp	44 0	*19,957*	Richard Walker	Redmire Pool, Hereford and Worcester	1952
Carp (Crucian)	5 10 8	*2,565*	G. Halls	near King's Lynn, Norfolk	1976
Chub	7 6	*3,345*	W. L. Warren	River Avon, Hampshire	1957
Dace	1 4 4	*0,574*	J. L. Gasson	Little Ouse, Thetford, Norfolk	1960
Eel	11 2	*5,046*	S. Terry	Kingfisher Lake, Hants.	1978
Gudgeon	0 4 4	*0,120*	M. J. Bowen	Fish pond, Ebbw Vale, Gwent	1977
Gwyniad (Whitefish)	1 4	*0,567*	J. R. Williams	Llyn Tegid, Gwynedd	1965
Loch Lomond Powan	1 7	*0,652*	J. M. Ryder	Loch Lomond, Strathclyde/Central	1972
Perch	4 12	*2,154*	S. F. Baker	Oulton Broad, Suffolk	1962
Pike[1]	40 0	*18,143*	Peter D. Hancock	Horsey Mere, Norfolk	1967
Roach	4 1	*1,842*	Richard G. Jones	Gravel pits, Colwich, Notts.	1975
Rudd	4 8	*2,041*	Rev. E. C. Alston	Mere, near Thetford, Norfolk	1933
Ruffe	0 5	*0,141*	P. Barrowcliffe	River Bure, Norfolk	1977
Salmon[2]	64 0	*29,029*	Miss G. W. Ballantyne	River Tay, Tayside	1922
Tench	10 1 2	*4,567*	L. W. Brown	Brick pit, Peterborough	1975
Trout (Brown)[3]	19 9 4	*8,880*	J. A. F. Jackson	Loch Quoich, Inverness-shire	1978
Trout (Rainbow)	19 8	*8,844*	A. Pearson	Avington Trout Fisheries, Itchen Abbas, Hampshire	1977

[1] *A pike of allegedly 52 lb.* 23 kg *was recovered when Whittlesea Mere, Cambridgeshire was drained in 1851. A pike of reputedly 72 lb.* 32 kg 650 *was landed from Loch Ken, Dumfries and Galloway, by John Murray in 1777.*

[2] *The 8th Earl of Home is recorded as having caught a 69¾ lb.* 31 kg 638 *specimen in the River Tweed in 1730. J. Wallace claimed a 67-pounder* 30 kg *at Barjarg, Dumfries and Galloway in 1812.*

[3] *In 1866 W. C. Muir caught a 39½ lb.* 17 kg 916 *specimen in Loch Awe, Strathclyde and in 1816 a 36 lb* 16 kg *specimen was reported from the R. Colne, near Watford, Hertfordshire.*

IRISH RECORDS

(Selected from the complete list as ratified by the Irish Specimen Fish Committee to 30 June 1978)

Species	Weight lb. oz.	kg/g	Name of Angler	Location	Date
SEA FISH					
Angler Fish	71 8	*32,431*	Michael Fitzgerald	Cork (Cóbh) Harbour	5 July 1964
Bass	17 1¼	*7,746*	Malcolm Tucker	Whiting Bay, Ardmore	27 Apr. 1977
Sea Bream (Red)	9 6	*4,252*	P. Maguire	Valentia, Kerry	24 Aug. 1963
Coalfish	24 7	*11,084*	J. E. Hornibrook	Kinsale, Cork	26 Aug. 1967
Cod	42 0	*19,050*	I. L. Stewart	Ballycotton, Cork	1921
Conger	72 0	*32,658*	J. Greene	Valentia, Kerry	June 1914
Dab	1 12½	*0,807*	Ian V. Kerr	Kinsale, Cork	10 Sept. 1963
Dogfish (Greater Spotted)	21 4	*9,638*	Drew Alexander	Malin Head, Co. Donegal	3 Sept. 1975
Dogfish (Spur)	18 12	*8,504*	John Murnane	Bantry	10 Sept. 1977
Flounder	4 3	*1,899*	J. L. McMonagle	Killala Bay, Co. Mayo	5 Aug. 1963
Garfish	3 10¼	*1,651*	Evan G. Bazzard	Kinsale, Cork	16 Sept. 1967
Gurnard (Grey)	3 1	*1,389*	Brendan Walsh	Rosslare Bay	21 Sept. 1967
Gurnard (Red)	3 9½	*1,630*	James Prescott	Belmullet, Co. Mayo	17 July 1968
Gurnard (Tub)	12 3½	*5,542*	Robert J. Seaman	Achill, Co. Mayo	8 Aug. 1973
Haddock	10 13½	*4,918*	F. A. E. Bull	Kinsale, Cork	15 July 1964
Hake	25 5½	*11,495*	Herbert W. Steele	Belfast Lough	28 Apr. 1962
Halibut	156 0	*70,760*	Frank Brogan	Belmullet, Co. Mayo	23 July 1972
John Dory	7 1	*3,203*	Stanley Morrow	Tory Island, Co. Donegal	6 Sept. 1970
Ling	46 8	*21,092*	Andrew J. C. Bull	Kinsale, Cork	26 July 1965
Mackerel	3 8	*1,587*	Roger Ryan	Clogherhead Pier, Co. Louth	1 July 1972
Monkfish	69 0	*31,297*	Mgr. Michael Fuchs	Westport, Co. Mayo	1 July 1958
Mullet (Grey)	7 12	*3,515*	Colm Quinn	Brittas Bay, Co. Wicklow	7 Sept. 1975
Plaice	7 2½	*3,246*	Cecil Pratt	Youghal	27 May 1973
Pollack	19 3	*8,703*	J. N. Hearne	Ballycotton, Cork	1904
Pouting	4 10	*2,097*	W. G. Pales	Ballycotton, Cork	1937
Ray (Blonde)	36 8	*16,556*	D. Minchin	Cork (Cóbh) Harbour	9 Sept. 1964
Ray (Sting)	51 0	*23,133*	John K. White	Kilfenora Strand, Fenit	8 Aug. 1970
Ray (Thornback)	37 0	*16,782*	M. J. Fitzgerald	Kinsale, Cork	28 May 1961

	lb	oz	g	Angler	Location	Date
Shark (Blue)	206	0	93,440	J. L. McMonagle	Achill, Co. Mayo	7 Oct. 1959
Shark (Porbeagle)	365	0	165,561	Dr. M. O'Donel Browne	Keem Bay, Achill, Co. Mayo	28 Sept. 1932
Skate (Common)	221	0	100,243	T. Tucker	Ballycotton, Cork	1913
Skate (White)	165	0	74,842	Jack Stack	Clew Bay, Westport, Co. Mayo	7 Aug. 1966
Tope	60	12	27,555	Crawford McIvor	Strangford Lough, Co. Down	12 Sept. 1968
Turbot	26	8	12,020	J. F. Eldridge	Valentia, Kerry	1915
Whiting	4	8½	2,055	Eddie Boyle	Kinsale, Cork	4 Aug. 1969
Wrasse (Ballan)	7	8½	3,869	Anthony J. King	Killybegs, Donegal	26 July 1964
FRESHWATER FISH						
Bream	11	12	5,329	A. Pike	River Blackwater, Co. Monaghan	July 1882
Carp	18	12	8,504	John Roberts	Abbey Lake	6 June 1958
Dace	1	2	0,510	John T. Henry	River Blackwater, Cappoquin	8 Aug. 1966
Eel (River)	5	15	2,693	Edmund Hawksworth	River Shannon, Clondra	25 Sept. 1968
Perch	5	8	2,494	S. Drum	Lough Erne	1946
Pike (River)[1]	42	0	19,050	M. Watkins	River Barrow	22 Mar. 1964
Roach	2	13½	1,289	Lawrie Robinson	River Blackwater, Cappoquin	11 Aug. 1970
	2	13½	1,289	Ronald Frost	River Blackwater, Cappoquin	29 Aug. 1972
Rudd	3	1	1,389	A. E. Biddlecombe	Kilglass Lake	27 June 1959
Rudd-Bream hybrid	5	13½	2,650	P. J. Dighton	River Shannon, Lanesboro, Co. Longford	12 Apr. 1975
Salmon[2]	57	0	25,854	M. Maher	River Suir	1874
Tench	7	13½	3,550	R. Webb	River Shannon, Lanesboro, Co. Longford	25 May 1971
Brown Trout (Lake)[3]	26	2	11,850	William Meares	Lough Ennell	15 July 1894
Brown Trout (River)	20	0	9,071	Major Hugh Ll. Place	River Shannon, Corbally	22 Feb. 1957
Sea Trout	14	3	6,435	Dr. Eoin Bresnihan	Dooagh Beach, Achill, Co. Mayo	8 June 1973

[1] A pike in excess of 92 lb. 41 kg is reputed to have been landed from the Shannon at Portumna, County Galway, in c. 1796.

[2] A 58 lb. 26 kg salmon was reported from the River Shannon in 1872 while one of 62 lb. 28 kg was taken in a net on the lower Shannon on 27 Mar. 1925.

[3] A 35½ lb. 16 kg 102 brown trout is reputed to have been caught at Turlaghvan near Tuam, in August 1738. "Pepper's Ghost", the 30 lb. 8 oz. 13 kg 834 fish caught by J. W. Pepper in Lough Derg in 1860 has now been shown to have been a salmon.

ARCHERY

Earliest references
The discovery of stone arrow heads at Border Cave, Northern Natal, South Africa in deposits exceeding the Carbon 14 dating limit indicates the invention of the bow as *ante* 46,000 B.C. Archery developed as an organized sport at least as early as the 3rd century A.D. The oldest archery body in the British Isles is the Royal Company of Archers, the Sovereign's bodyguard for Scotland, dating from 1676, though the Ancient Scorton Arrow meeting in North Yorkshire was first staged in 1673. The world governing body is the *Fédération Internationale de Tir à l'Arc* (FITA), founded in 1931.

World records
The world records for a single FITA Round are: men 1,318 points (possible 1,440) by Giancarlo Ferrari (Italy) at Viareggio, Italy, on 15–16 Oct. 1977, and women 1304 points (possible 1,440) by Zebiniso Rustamova (U.S.S.R.) at Milan, Italy on 3 Oct. 1977.

Highest Championship scores
There are no world records for Double FITA Rounds but the highest scores achieved in either a world or Olympic championship were: men, 2,571 points (possible 2,880) by Darrell Pace (U.S.A.) at the 1976 Olympic Games in Montreal, Canada, on 29–30 July 1976; and women, 2,515 points by Luann Ryon (U.S.A.) at Canberra, Australia, 11–12 Feb. 1977.

British records
York Round,—possible 1,296 pts: Single Round, 1,142 Peter Waterton at Oxford on 29 June 1977. Double Round, 2,238 Peter Waterton at Oxford on 29 June 1977.

Hereford (Women)—possible 1,296 pts: Single Round, 1,148 Sue Wilcox at Winchester, Hants, on 11 May 1978. Double Round, 2,227 Patricia Conway at Dunster 18–19 June 1977.

FITA Round (Men): Single Round, 1,258 Mark Blenkarne at Strasbourg, France, 24 June 1979. Double Round, 2,406 David Pink at Stoneleigh, Warwick, 22–23 May 1976.

FITA Round (Women's): Single Round, 1,271, Rachel Fenwick at Southampton, Hants., 3 June 1979. Double Round, 2,520 Rachel Fenwick at Brussels, Belgium 12–13 Aug. 1978.

Most titles *World*
The greatest number of world titles (instituted 1931) ever won by a man is four by Hans Deutgen (Sweden) in 1947–50.

The greatest number won by a woman is seven by Janina Spychajowa-Kurkowska (Poland) in 1931–34, 1936, 1939 and 1947. Oscar Kessels (Belgium) has participated in 21 world championships since 1931.

Most titles, *Olympic*
Hubert van Innis (1866–1961) (Belgium) won six gold and three silver medals in archery events at the 1900 and 1920 Olympic Games.

Most titles *British*
The greatest number of British Championships is 12 by Horace Alfred Ford (1822–1880) in 1849–59 and 1867, and 23 by Alice Blanche Legh (1855–1948) in 1881, 1886–1892 1895, 1898–1900, 1902–09, 1913 and 1921–22. Miss Legh was inhibited from winning from 1882 to 1885—because her mother Piers Legh was Champion—and also for four further years 1915 to 1918 because there were no Championships held owing to the first World War.

Flight shooting
Sultan Selim III (1761–1808) shot 1,400 Turkish *Pikes* or *gez* near Istanbul, Turkey in 1798. The equivalent is arguably between 953–972 yd *871–888 m*. The longest recorded distance ever shot is 1 mile 268 yd *1 854,40 m* in the unlimited footbow class by the professional Harry Drake (b. 7 May 1915) of Lakeside, California, U.S.A. at Ivanpah Dry Lake, California on 24 Oct. 1971. Don Brown (b. 13 Nov. 1945) (U.S.A.) set the flight record for the handbow with 1,164 yd 2 ft 9 in *1 065,19 m* at Wendover, Utah, U.S.A. on 18 Sept. 1977. April Moon (U.S.A.) set a women's record of 810 yd 1 ft 9 in *741,19 m* at the same venue on 17 Sept. 1977. Drake holds the crossbow flight record with 1,359 yds 2 ft 5 in *1 243,4 m* at Ivanpah Dry Lake on 14–15 Oct. 1967.

The British record (Men) is 774 yd 17½ in *708,2 m* by Alan Webster at Burton Constable, nr Hull, Humberside on 15 May 1977 and (Women) 446 yd *407,82 m* by Monica Thorley at Burton Constable, in 1976.

Greatest draw
Gary Sentman, of Roseburg, Oregon, U.S.A. drew a longbow weighing a record 176 lb. *79,83 kg* to the maximum draw on the arrow of 28¼ in *72 cm* at Forksville, Penn., on 20 Sept. 1975.

24 Hours
The highest recorded score over 24 hours by a pair of archers is 51,633 during 48 Portsmouth Rounds by Jimmy Watt and Gordon Danby at the Epsom Showgrounds, Auckland N.Z., on 18th–19th Nov. 1977

BADMINTON

Origins
A similar game was played in China in the 2nd Millenium B.C. The modern game was devised c. 1863 at Badminton Hall in Avon, the seat of the Dukes of Beaufort. The oldest club is the Newcastle Badminton Club formed as the Armstrong College Club on 24 Jan. 1900.

Thomas Cup
The International Championship or Thomas Cup (instituted 1948) has been won seven times by Indonesia in 1957–58, 1960–61, 1963–64, 1969–70, 1972–73, 1975–76 and 1978–79.

Uber Cup
The Ladies International Championship or Uber Cup (instituted 1956) has been won four times by Japan (1966, 1969, 1972 and 1978).

Inter County Championship
The most successful county has been Surrey with 19 wins between 1955 and 1975. The championships were instituted on 30 Oct. 1930.

Most titles
The men's singles in the All-England Championships (instituted 1899) have been won a record eight times by Rudy Hartono (Indonesia) (b. 1949) in 1968–74 and 1976. The greatest number of championships won (incl. doubles) is 21 by G. A. Thomas (later Sir George Alan Thomas, Bt.) (1881–1972) between 1903 and 1928. The women's title has been won ten times by Judy Hashman (née Devlin) (U.S.A.) (b. 1935) in 1954, 1957–58, 1960–64, 1966–67. She also equalled the greatest number of championships won of 17 by Mary Lucas (later Mrs. King Adams) from 1899 to 1910.

MOST INTERNATIONAL APPEARANCES

	Times	Men
England	100	Anthony Derek Jordan, M.B.E., 1951 to 1970
Ireland	45	Ken Carlisle, 1954 to 1970
Scotland	67	Robert S. McCoig, M.B.E., 1956 to 1976
Wales	50	David Colmer, 1964 to 1979

	Times	Women
England	67	Gillian M. Gilks M.B.E. (née Perrin), 1966 to 1979
Ireland	57	Yvonne Kelly, 1955 to 1976
Scotland	50	Christine Stewart (née Evans), 1970 to 1979
Wales	46	Angela Dickson, 1964 to 1979

Shortest game
In the 1969 Uber Cup in Jakarta, Indonesia, Noriko Takagi (later Mrs. Nakayama) (Japan) beat P. Tumengkol in 9 min.

Darrell Pace (U.S.A.)—World and Olympic champion as well as world record holder. (*Don Morley, All-Sport Photographic*)

Longest hit
Frank Rugani drove a shuttlecock 79 ft 8½ in *24,29 m* in indoor tests at San Jose, California, U.S.A., on 29 Feb. 1964.

Marathon
The longest singles match is 72 hrs 30 min by Will Nayar and Gary Miles at Sorrento/Duncraig Community Centre, W.A., Aust. on 1–4 June 1979.

An English international on a record 67 occasions, Gillian Gilks has twice been All-England champion. (*Sporting Pictures (UK) Ltd.*)

BASEBALL

Earliest game

The Rev. Thomas Wilson, of Maidstone, Kent, England, wrote disapprovingly, in 1700, of baseball being played on Sundays. It is also referred to in *Northanger Abbey* by Jane Austen, *c.* 1798. The earliest baseball game under the Cartwright (Alexander Joy Cartwright Jr. 1820–1892) rules was at Hoboken, New Jersey, U.S.A., on 19 June 1846, with the New York Nine beating the Knickerbockers 23–1 in four innings.

Highest batting average

The highest average in a career is .367 by Tyrus Raymond Cobb (1886–1961), the "Georgia Peach" from Augusta who played with Detroit (1905–26) and Philadelphia (1927–28). During his career Ty Cobb made a record 2,244 runs from a record 4,191 hits made in 3,033 major league games. Lin Wen-Nsiung (Taiwan) was reported to have an average of .727.

Home runs *Most*

Henry Louis "Hank" Aaron (Atlanta Braves) (b. 5 Feb. 1934) holds the major league career home run record of 755 from 1954 to 1976. On 30 Aug. 1978 Sadaharu Oh (b. 20 May 1940) hit his 800th for Yomiuri Giants *v.* Taiyo Whales in Tokyo, Japan. George Herman "Babe" Ruth's (1895–1948) record for home runs in one year is 60 in 154 games between 15 Apr. and 30 Sept. 1927. Roger Eugene Maris (b. 10 Sept. 1934) (New York Yankees) hit 61 homers in a 162-game schedule in 1961. Joshua Gibson (1911–1947) of Homestead Grays and Pittsburgh Crawfords, Negro League clubs, achieved a career total of 800 homers and 84 in one season, and in 1972 was elected to the Hall of Fame.

Longest home run

The longest home run ever measured was one of 618 ft *188,4 m* by Roy Edward "Dizzy" Carlyle (1900–56) in a minor league game at Emeryville Ball Park, California, U.S.A., on 4 July 1929. In 1919 Babe Ruth hit a 587 ft *178,9 m* homer in a Boston Red Sox *v.* New York Giants match at Tampa, Florida, U.S.A.

At 6 ft 2 in and 195 lb, Dizzy Carlyle had the physical makeup for his record breaking home run.

Longest throw

The longest throw (ball weighs 5–5¼ oz *141–148 g*) is 445 ft 10 in *135,88 m* by Glen Edward Gorbous (b. Canada 8 July 1930) on 1 Aug. 1957. The longest throw by a woman is 296 ft *90,2 m* by Mildred "Babe" Didrikson (later Mrs. George Zaharias) (U.S.) (1914–56) at Jersey City, New Jersey, U.S.A. on 25 July 1931.

Fastest base runner

The fastest time for circling bases is 13.3 sec by Ernest Evar Swanson (1902–73) at Columbus, Ohio, in 1932, at an average speed of 18.45 m.p.h. *29,70 km/h.*

Pitching

The only "perfect game" (no hits, no runs, no walks) pitched in a World Series was by Don Larsen (New York Yankees) (b. 7 Aug. 1929) with 97 pitches (71 in the strike zone) against Brooklyn Dodgers on 8 Oct. 1956.

Fastest pitcher

The fastest pitcher in the world is Lynn Nolan Ryan (California Angels) (b. 31 Jan. 1947) who, on 20 Aug. 1974 at Anaheim Stadium, California, U.S.A., was measured to pitch at 100.9 m.p.h. *162,3 km/h.*

Youngest player

The youngest major league player of all time was the Cincinnati pitcher, Joseph Henry Nuxhall (b. 30 July 1928) who started his career in June, 1944, aged 15 years 10 months 11 days.

Record attendances and receipts

The World Series record attendance is 420,784 (six games with total receipts of $2,626,973.44) when the Los Angeles (ex-Brooklyn) Dodgers beat the Chicago White Sox 4–2 on 1–8 Oct. 1959. The single game record is 92,706 for the fifth game (receipts $552,774.77) at the Memorial Coliseum, Los Angeles, California, on 6 Oct. 1959. The highest seating capacity in a baseball stadium is 76,977 in the Cleveland Municipal Stadium, Ohio, U.S.A. The all-time season record for attendances for both leagues has been 29,193,417 in 1971.

An estimated 114,000 spectators watched a game between Australia and an American Services team in a "demonstration" event during the Olympic Games at Melbourne, 1 Dec. 1956.

BATTING RECORDS (see also above)			
Batting av., season	.438	Hugh Duffy (NL)	1894
,, ,,	.422	Napoleon Lajoie (AL)	1901
RBIs, career	2,297	Henry "Hank" Aaron	1954–76
,, season	190	Lewis Rober "Hack" Wilson	1930
,, game	12	James LeRoy Bottomley	16 Sept 1924
,, innings	7	Edward Cartwright	23 Sept. 1890
Base hits, season	257	George Harold Sisler	1920
Hits, consecutive	12	Michael Franklin "Pinky" Higgins	19–21 June 1938
,, ,,	12	Walter "Moose" Dropo	14–15 July 1952
Consecutive games batted safely	56	Joseph Paul DiMaggio	15 May–16 July 1941
Stolen bases, career	899	Louis Clark Brock	1961–77
,, ,, season	118	Louis Clark Brock	1974
Consecutive games played	2,130	Henry Louis "Lou" Gehrig	1 June 1925–30 Apr. 1939
PITCHING RECORDS			
Games won, career	511	Denton True "Cy" Young	1890–1911
,, ,, season	60	Charles Gardner Radbourn	1884
Consecutive games won	24	Carl Owen Hubbell	1936–37
Shutouts, career	113	Walter Perry Johnson	1907–27
,, season	16	George W. Bradley	1876
	16	Grover Cleveland Alexander	1916
Strikeouts, career	3,508	Walter Perry Johnson	1907–27
,, season	383	Lynn Nolan Ryan	1973
No-hit games, career	4	Sanford "Sandy" Koufax	1955–66
	4	Lynn Nolan Ryan	1966–77
Earned run av, season	0.90	Ferdinand Schupp (140 inn)	1916
,, ,,	1.01	Hubert "Dutch" Leonard (222 inn)	1914
,, ,,	1.12	Robert Gibson (305 inn)	1968
Complete games, career	751	Denton True "Cy" Young	1890–1911

BASKETBALL

Origins

The game of "Pok-ta-Pok" was played in the 10th century B.C., by the Olmecs in Mexico, and closely resembled basketball in its concept. "Ollamalitzli" was a variation of this game played by the Aztecs in Mexico as late as the 16th century. If the solid rubber ball was put through a fixed stone ring the player was entitled to the clothing of all the spectators. Modern basketball (which may have been based on the German game of *Korbball*) was devised by the Canadian-born Dr. James A. Naismith (1861–1939) at the Training School of the International Y.M.C.A. College at Springfield, Massachusetts, U.S.A., in mid-December 1891. The first game played under modified rules was on 20 Jan. 1892. The International Amateur Basketball Federation (F.I.B.A.) was founded in 1932, and the English Basket Ball Association was founded in 1936.

Most titles *Olympic*

The U.S.A. won all seven Olympic titles from the time the sport was introduced to the Games in 1936 until 1968, without losing a single match. In 1972 in Munich their run of 64 consecutive victories in matches in the Olympic Games was broken when they lost 50–51 to the U.S.S.R. in the disputed Final match. They won their eighth title in 1976.

Most titles *World*

Brazil, U.S.S.R. and Yugoslavia have won the World Men's Championship (instituted 1950) twice. Brazil won in 1959 and 1963, the U.S.S.R. in 1967 and 1974 and Yugoslavia in 1970 and 1978. In 1975 the U.S.S.R. won the Women's Championship (instituted 1953) for the fifth consecutive time since 1959.

Most titles *European*

The most European Champions Cup (instituted 1957) wins is six by Real Madrid, Spain. The women's title has been won 16 times by Daugawa, Riga, U.S.S.R. The most wins in the European Nations Championships for men is 11 by the U.S.S.R., and in the Women's event 14 also by the U.S.S.R.

Most titles *British*

England has won six British Championship titles, out of the 13 competitions since the championship was introduced in 1960.

Most titles *American Professional*

The most National Basketball Association titles (instituted 1947), played for between the leading professional teams in the United States, have been won by the Boston Celtics with 13 victories between 1957 and 1976.

Most titles *English*

The most English National championship wins (instituted 1936) have been by London Central Y.M.C.A., with eight wins in 1957–58, 1960, 1962–64, 1967 and 1969. On 6 Apr. 1974 Sutton and Crystal Palace beat Embassy All Stars in a record score for the final of 120–100. The English National League title has been won four times by Crystal Palace 1974, 1976–78.

Most titles *English Women's Cup*

Most English Women's cups (instituted 1965) have been won by Tigers D.S.C. (Hertfordshire) with six wins.

Highest score *International*

The highest score recorded in an international match is 164 by Romania against Wales (50) on 15 May 1975, in the European Men's Championship at Hagen, West Germany. The highest by a women's team is 153 by U.S.S.R. against Switzerland (25) on 4 June 1956 in the European Championships. The highest in a British Championship is 125 by England when beating Wales (54) on 1 Sept. 1978. England beat Gibraltar 130–45 on 31 Aug. 1978.

Highest score *match*

The highest aggregate score in an N.B.A. match is 316 in a match between the Philadelphia Warriors (169 points) and the New York Knickerbockers (147 points) at Hershey,

Britain's tallest basketball player, Chris Greener, is nearly seven inches shorter than the world's tallest player. (*The Times*)

Pennsylvania on 2 Mar. 1962, and in a match between the Cincinnati Royals (165 points) and the San Diego Rockets (151 points) on 12 Mar. 1970. In an A.B.A. match between the San Diego Conquistadors (176 points) and the New York Nets (166 points) on 14 Feb. 1975, the score totalled 342 points after four periods of overtime.

Highest score *United Kingdom*

The highest score recorded in a match is 250 by the Nottingham Y.M.C.A. Falcons *v.* Mansfield Pirates at Nottingham, England on 18 June 1974. It was a handicap competition and Mansfield received 120 points towards their total of 145. The highest score in a National League or Cup match is 165 by Crystal Palace *v* Bedford (40) on 3 Dec. 1977.

Highest score *Individual*

Mats Wermelin, 13, (Sweden) scored all 272 points in a 272–0 win in a regional boys' tournament in Stockholm, Sweden on 5 Feb. 1974. The highest single game score in an N.B.A. game is 100 points by Wilton Norman Chamberlain (b. 21 Aug. 1936) for Philadelphia *v.* New York on 2 Mar. 1962. The most in a college game is 113 points by Clarence (Bevo) Francis, for Rio Grande College, Ohio *v* Hillsdale on 2 Feb. 1954.

The highest individual score in an English National League (Div. One) or Cup match is 68 points by Bobby Cooper of London Central YMCA *v* Exeter on 2 Mar. 1979.

Most points

Wilt Chamberlain, scored a career total of 31,419 points in N.B.A. matches between 1960–73. The record for the most points scored in a college career is 4,045 by Travis Grant for Kentucky State in 1969–1972. In the English National League, Peter Sprogis (b. 31 Oct. 1949) has scored 2,096 points in 84 games, 1973–78.

Tallest players

The tallest player of all time is reputed to be Suleiman Ali Nashnush (b. 1943) who played for the Libyan team in 1962 when measuring 2,45 m *8 ft*. The tallest woman player is

Iuliana Semenova (U.S.S.R.) (b. 1951) at a reported 7 ft 2 in *2,18 m* and weighing 281 lb. *127,4 kg.*. The tallest British player has been the 7 ft 5¼ in *226,6 cm* tall Christopher Greener (see p. 10) of London Latvians whose International debut for England was *v.* France on 17 Dec. 1969.

Most accurate
The greatest goal shooting demonstration has been by Ted St. Martin of Jacksonville, Florida, who, on 25 June 1977, scored 2,036 consecutive free throws. In a 24 hour period, 31 May to 1 June 1975 Fred L. Newman of San José, California, U.S.A. scored 12,874 baskets out of 13,116 throws (98.15% accuracy). Newman also holds the record for consecutive blindfold free throws with 88 straight at the San José Y.M.C.A. on 5 Feb. 1978.

Longest recorded goal
The longest recorded field goal in a match is a measured 89 ft *27,12 m* by Rudy Williams (b. 16 Dec. 1957) at Providence College, Rhode Island, U.S.A., on 17 Feb. 1979

Most travelled team
The Harlem Globetrotters (U.S.A.) have travelled over 6,000,000 miles *9 600 000 km*, visited 94 countries on six continents, and have been watched by an estimated 80,000,000 since their foundation on 7 Jan. 1927 at Hinckley, Illinois. They have won over 12,000 games (losing less than 350), but many were not truly competitive.

Largest ever gate
The Harlem Globetrotters (U.S.A.) played an exhibition in front of 75,000 in the Olympic Stadium, West Berlin, Germany, in 1951. The largest indoor basketball attendance was at the Astrodome, Houston, Texas, U.S.A., where 52,693 watched the match between University of Houston and University of California at Los Angeles (U.C.L.A.), on 20 Jan. 1968.

Marathon
The longest game is 89 hr by two teams of five at Kwinana High School, W. Aust. on 18–21 May 1979.

BILLIARDS
Earliest mention
The earliest recorded mention of billiards was in France in 1429, while Louis XI, King of France 1461–83, is reported to have had a billiard table. The first recorded public billiards room in England was the Piazza, Covent Garden, London, in the early part of the 19th century. Rubber cushions were introduced in 1835 and slate beds in 1836.

Most titles *Professional*
The greatest number of world championship titles (instituted 1870) won by one player is eight by John Roberts, Jnr.

Equally at home in either game, Joe Davis made 87 breaks of a thousand at billiards, and 687 centuries at snooker. (*Keystone Press*)

(1847–1919) (England) in 1870 (twice), 1871, 1875 (twice), 1877 and 1885 (twice). The greatest number of United Kingdom titles (instituted 1934) won by any player is seven (1934–39 and 1947) by Joe Davis, O.B.E. (1901–78) (England), who also won four world titles (1928–30 and 1932) before the series was discontinued in 1934. William F. Hoppe (U.S.A.) (1887–1959) won 51 "world" titles in the United States variant of the game between 1906 and 1952.

Most titles *Amateur*
The record for world amateur titles is four by Robert Marshall (Australia) (b. 10 Apr. 1910) in 1936, 1938, 1951 and 1962. The greatest number of English Amateur Championships (instituted 1888) ever won by Norman Dagley (b. 1930) in 1965–66, 1970–75, 1978–79. The record number of women's titles is eight by Vera Selby 1970–78.

Highest breaks
Tom Reece (1873–1953) made an unfinished break of 499,135, including 249,152 cradle cannons (two points each), in 85 hrs 49 min against Joe Chapman at Burroughes' Hall, Soho Square, London, between 3 June and 6 July 1907. This was not recognized because press and public were not continuously present. The highest certified break made by the anchor cannon is 42,746 by W. Cook (England) from 29 May to 7 June 1907. The official world record under the then baulk-line rule is 1,784 by Joe Davis, O.B.E. in the United Kingdom Championship on 29 May 1936. Walter Lindrum O.B.E. (Australia) (1898–1960) made an official break of 4,137 in 2 hrs 55 min against Joe Davis at Thurston's on 19–20 Jan. 1932, before the baulk-line rule was in force. Davis has an unofficial personal best of 2,502 (mostly pendulum cannons) in a match against Tom Newman (1894–1943) (England) in Manchester in 1930. The amateur record is 1,149 by Michael Ferreira (India) at Calcutta, India on 15 Dec. 1978.

Fastest century
Walter Lindrum, O.B.E. of Australia made an unofficial 100 break in 27.5 sec in Australia on 10 Oct. 1952. His official record is 100 in 46.0 sec set in Sydney in 1941.

BAR BILLIARDS
Highest scoring rate
Thomas Morrison Clayton of Earlsfield, Greater London scored 11,700 in 10 min on a timed table at the Greyhound, Battersea High Street on 18 June 1974. The record scoring rate in a league match has been 24,340 in 17 min by John Stevens at the Ampthill Hotel, Freemantle, Southampton, Hampshire on 25 Jan. 1979.

24 hours
The highest bar billiards score in 24 hr by a team of five is 1,359,370 by the G. D. Searle 'A' team at High Wycombe, Bucks., on 16–17 Mar. 1979.

POOL
Pool or championship pocket billiards with numbered balls began to become standardized *c.* 1890. The greatest exponents were Ralph Greenleaf (U.S.A.) (1899–1950) who won the "world" professional title 19 times (1919–1937) and William Mosconi (U.S.A.) (b. 27 June 1913) who dominated the game from 1941–1957.

The longest consecutive run in an American straight pool match is 625 balls by Michael Eufemia at Logan's Billiard Academy, Brooklyn, N.Y., on 2 Feb. 1960. The greatest number of balls pocketed in 24 hours is 10,752 (a rate of one per 8.03 secs) by Patrick D. Young (b. 17 March 1932) at the Camden Arms, Newham, Greater London, on 2–3 May 1978.

Marathon
The longest game is 151 hr by Roy Sadd and Richard Smith at The Sandringham, Brislington, Bristol, Avon on 12–19 Apr. 1979.

3 CUSHION
This pocketless variation dates back to 1878. The world governing body, the *Union Mondiale de Billiard* (U.M.B.) was formed in 1928. The most successful exponent spanning the pre and post international era from 1906–1952 was Willie

Hoppe who won 51 billiards championships in all forms. Most U.M.B. titles have been won by Raymond Ceulemans (Belgium) (b. 1937) with 14 (1963–66, 1968–73, 1975–78, with a peak average of 1.479 in 1973.

BOBSLEIGH AND TOBOGGANING

BOBSLEDDING
Origins
The oldest known sledge is dated c. 6500 B.C. and came from Heinola, Finland. The first known bobsleigh race took place at Davos, Switzerland in 1889. The International Federation of Bobsleigh and Tobogganing was formed in 1923, followed by the International Bobsleigh Federation in 1957.

Most titles *Olympic*
The Olympic four-man bob title (inst. 1924) has been won four times by Switzerland (1924, 1936, 1956 and 1972). The U.S.A. (1932, 1936), Italy (1956, 1968) and West Germany (1952 and 1972) have won the Olympic boblet (inst. 1932) event twice. The most medals won by an individual is six (two gold, two silver, two bronze) by Eugenio Monti (Italy) (b. 23 Jan. 1928) from 1956 to 1968. The only British victory has been the two-man bob in 1964 by Hon. Robin Thomas Valerian Dixon (b. 21 Apr. 1935) and Anthony James Dillon Nash (b. 18 Mar. 1936).

Most titles *World*
The world four-man bob title has been won 12 times by Switzerland (1924, 1936, 1939, 1947, 1954–57, 1971–73 and 1975). Italy won the two-man title 14 times (1954, 1956–63, 1966, 1968–69, 1971 and 1975). Eugenio Monti has been a member of eleven world championship crews, eight two-man and three four-man.

TOBOGGANING
Cresta Run
The word toboggan comes from the Micmac American Indian word *tobaakan*. The St. Moritz Tobogganing Club,

The winner of many Cresta Run titles, Nino Bibbia had possibly his proudest moment when his son, Gianni, won the 1975 Brabazon Trophy. (*Gerry Cranham*)

Switzerland, founded in 1887 is the oldest toboggan club in the world. It is unique in being the home of the Cresta Run, which dates from 1884 and for the introduction of the one-man racing toboggan skeleton. The course is 3,977 ft *1212,25 m* long with a drop of 514 ft *157 m* and the record is 53.24 sec (av. 50.92 m.p.h. *81,96 km/h*) by Poldi Berchtold of Switzerland on 9 Feb. 1975. The record from the Junction (2,913 ft *888 m*) is 42.96 sec, by Berchtold on 22 Feb. 1975. Speeds of 90 m.p.h. *145 km/h* are occasionally attained.

The greatest number of wins in the Grand National (inst. 1885) is eight by the 1948 Olympic champion Nino Bibbia (Italy) (b. 9 Sept. 1924) in 1960–64, 1966, 1968 and 1973. The greatest number of wins in the Curzon Cup (inst. 1910) is eight by Bibbia in 1950, 1957–58, 1960, 1962–64, and 1969, who hence won the double in 1960 1962 and 1963–64. The most descents made in a season is 7,832 during 65 days in 1976.

Lugeing
In lugeing the rider adopts a sitting, as opposed to a prone position. Official international competition began at Klosters, Switzerland, in 1881. The first European championships were at Reichenberg, East Germany, in 1914 and the first world championships at Oslo, Norway, in 1953. The International Luge Federation was formed in 1957. Lugeing became an Olympic sport in 1964. Speeds of more than 80 m.p.h. *128 km/h* have been recorded at Krynica, Poland.

Most titles *World and Olympic*
The most successful rider in the world championships is Thomas Köhler (East Germany) (b. 25 June 1940), the only double Olympic gold medallist, who won the single-seater title in 1962, 1964 (Olympic), 1966 and 1967 and shared the two seater title in 1967 and 1968 (Olympic). In the women's championship Margit Schumann (East Germany) (b. 14 Sept. 1952) has won five times, in 1973–75, 1976 (Olympic) and 1977.

BOWLING (TENPIN)
Origins
The ancient German game of nine-pins (*Heidenwerfen*—knock down pagans) was exported to the United States in the early 17th century. In about 1845 the Connecticut and New Haven State Legislatures prohibited the game so a tenth pin was added to evade the ban; but there is some evidence of ten pins being used in Suffolk about 300 years ago.

In the United States there were 8,640 bowling establishments with 147,237 bowling lanes and 65,000,000 bowlers in 1977. The world's largest bowling centre (now closed) was the Tokyo World Lanes Centre, Japan with 252 lanes. Currently the largest centre is the Willow Grove Park Lanes, Philadelphia, U.S.A. which has 116 lanes. The largest in Europe is the Nottingham Bowl at Nottingham, England, where the game was introduced in 1960, with 48 lanes on two floors (24 on each floor).

World championships
The world (Fédération Internationale des Quilleurs) championships were instituted in 1954. The highest pinfall in the individual men's event is 5,963 (in 28 games) by Ed Luther (U.S.) at Milwaukee, Wisconsin, on 28 Aug. 1971. In the women's championships (instituted 1963) the record is 4,615 pins (in 24 games) by Annedore Haefker (West Germany) at Tolworth, Surrey on 11 Oct. 1975.

Highest scores *World*
The highest individual score for three sanctioned games (possible 900) is 886 by Albert "Allie" Brandt of Lockport, New York, U.S.A., on 25 Oct. 1939. The record by a woman is 818 by Bev Ortner in Galva, Iowa, U.S.A. in 1968. The record for consecutive strikes in sanctioned match play is 33 by John Pezzin (b. 1930) at Toledo, Ohio, U.S.A. on 4 Mar. 1976. The highest number of sanctioned 300 games is 26 (till 1975) by Elvin Mesger of Sullivan, Missouri, U.S.A. The maximum 900 for a three-game series has been recorded

three times in unsanctioned games—by Leo Bentley at Lorain, Ohio, U.S.A., on 26 Mar. 1931; by Joe Sargent at Rochester, New York State, U.S.A., in 1934, and by Jim Margie in Philadelphia, Pennsylvania, U.S.A., on 4 Feb. 1937. Such series must have consisted of 36 consecutive strikes (*i.e.* all pins down with one ball).

The highest average for a season attained in sanctioned competition is 239 by Jim Lewis, of Schenectady, N.Y., U.S.A., for 88 games in 1975–76.

Highest scores *Great Britain*
The United Kingdom record for a three-game series is 775 by Geoffrey Liddiard at Harrow, Greater London on 3 Oct. 1971. The record score for a single game is 300, first achieved by Albert Kirkham (b. 1931) of Burslem, Staffordshire, on 5 Dec. 1965, which has since been equalled on several occasions. The best by a woman is 299 by Carole Cuthbert at the Airport Bowl, West London on 16 Mar. 1972. The three-game series record for a woman player is 724 by Joyce Presland at the Humber Bowl, Ilkeston, Derby on 8 Oct. 1974.

12 hours
The Cossacks Bowling Team (five men), of Somerset, England, totalled 19,694 pins at Weston-super-Mare, Somerset on 20 Jan. 1979.

Longest career
William H. Bailey (b. 4 Jan. 1891) has been bowling for 70 consecutive years in the Hamilton City Ten Pin League, Ontario, Canada.

Marathon
Tom Destowet bowled for 150 hr 15 min on 2–8 Apr. 1978 in Dublin, Calif., U.S.A. He bowled 709 games with a 16 lb. ball.

SKITTLES
24 Hours
Eight players from South Molton Round Table knocked down 49,543 West Country skittles on 6–7 May 1979. The highest hood skittle score in 24 hr is 107,487 pins by 12 players from the Plume of Feathers, Daventry, Northamptonshire, on 19–20 Mar. 1976. The highest table skittle score claimed in 24 hr is 148,048 skittles by 12 players from the Alleyn Old Boys Athletic Club, Herne Hill, Greater London, on 20–21 Nov. 1976.

Marathon
The duration record for knocking down skittles (9-pins) is 120 hr by seven skittlers from the Rotaract Club of Bristol North-West, Avon, England ending on 4 May 1977.

BOWLS
OUTDOOR
Origins
Bowls can be traced back to at least the 13th century in England. The Southampton Town Bowling was formed in 1299. A green dating back to 1294 is claimed by the Chesterfield Bowling Club. After falling into disrepute, the game was rescued by the bowlers of Scotland who, headed by W. W. Mitchell, framed the modern rules in 1848–49.

Most titles *World*
In the inaugural World Championship held in Sydney, Australia in October 1966 the singles title was won by David John Bryant M.B.E. (b. 1931) (England) and the team title (Leonard Cup) by Australia. In the second Championships at Worthing in 1972 the singles was won by Malwyn Evans (Wales) and Scotland won the Leonard Cup. At Johannesburg, South Africa, in February 1976, the South African team achieved an unprecedented clean sweep of all four titles and the Leonard Cup.

Most titles *International Championship*
In the annual International Championships (instituted 1903) Scotland have won 32 times to England's 19. The most consecutive wins are 11 by Scotland from 1965 to 1975.

Most titles *English*
The record number of English Bowls Association (founded 8 June 1903) championships is 15 won or shared by David Bryant, M.B.E., including six singles, three pairs (1965, 1969, 1974), and two triples (1966, 1977), who uniquely was involved in all four titles with four rinks or fours championships (1957, 1968, 1969 and 1971). He has also won six British Isles titles (four singles, one pairs, one fours) in the period 1957–74.

International appearances
The greatest number of international appearances by any bowler is 78 reached by Syd Thompson for Ireland in 1973. The youngest bowler to represent England was David J. Cutler (b. 1 Aug. 1954) in 1975, who was the youngest ever E.B.A. champion.

Most eights
Freda Ehlers and Linda Bertram uniquely scored three consecutive eights in the Southern Transvaal pairs event at Johannesburg, South Africa on 30 Jan. 1978.

Marathon
The longest game is 70 hr 20 min by Berowra Bowling Club, N.S.W., Aust. from 13–16 Apr. 1979.

INDOOR
The English Indoor Bowling Association became an autonomous body in 1971. Prior to that it was part of the English Bowling Association.

Most titles
The four-corner international championship was first held in 1936. England have won most titles with 16 wins. The National Singles title (inst. 1960) has been won most often by David Bryant M.B.E. with eight wins (1960, 1966, 1971–73, 1975, 1978–79).

Highest score
The highest score in a British International match is 52 by Scotland *v.* Wales (3) at Teeside in 1972.

Marathon
Two fours teams from the Western Indoor Bowling Ass., New Lynn, Auckland, N.Z., played for 72 hr on 21–24 Oct. 1977.

BOXING
Earliest references
Boxing with gloves was depicted on a fresco from the Isle of Thera, Greece which has been dated 1520 B.C. The earliest prize-ring code of rules was formulated in England on 16 Aug. 1743 by the champion pugilist Jack Broughton (1704–1789), who reigned from 1734 to 1750. Boxing, which had, in 1867, come under the Queensberry Rules formulated for John Sholto Douglas, 9th Marquess of Queensberry (1844–1900) was not established as a legal sport in Britain until after the ruling, R. *v.* Roberts and Others, of Mr. Justice Grantham, following the death of Billy Smith (Murray Livingstone) as the result of a fight on 24 Apr. 1901.

Longest fights
The longest recorded fight with gloves was between Andy Bowen of New Orleans (k. 1894) and Jack Burke in New Orleans, Louisiana, U.S.A., on 6–7 Apr. 1893. The fight lasted 110 rounds and 7 hr and 19 min from 9.15 p.m. to 4.34 a.m., and was declared no contest (later changed to a draw) when both men were unable to continue. The longest bare knuckle fight was 6 hr 15 min between James Kelly and Jack Smith at Fiery Creek, Dalesford, Victoria, Australia on 3 Dec. 1855. The longest bare knuckle fight in Britain was 6 hr 3 min (185 rounds) between Bill Hayes and Mike Madden at Edenbridge, Kent, on 17 July 1849. The greatest number of rounds was 276 in 4 hr 30 min when Jack Jones beat Patsy Tunney in Cheshire in 1825.

Shortest fights
There is a distinction between the quickest knock-out and the shortest fight. A knock-out in 10½ sec (including a 10 sec

count) occurred on 26 Sept. 1946, when Al Couture struck Ralph Walton while the latter was adjusting a gum shield in his corner at Lewiston, Maine, U.S.A. If the time was accurately taken it is clear that Couture must have been more than half-way across the ring from his own corner at the opening bell. The shortest fight on record appears to be one in a Golden Gloves tournament at Minneapolis, Minnesota, U.S.A., on 4 Nov. 1947 when Mike Collins floored Pat Brownson with the first punch and the contest was stopped, without a count, four secs after the bell.

The fastest officially timed knock-out in British boxing is 11 sec (including a doubtless fast 10 sec count) when Jack Cain beat Harry Deamer, both of Notting Hill, Greater London at the National Sporting Club on 20 Feb. 1922.

The shortest world heavyweight title fight occurred when Tommy Burns (b. Noah Brusso) (1881–1955) of Canada knocked out Jem Roche in 1 min 28 sec in Dublin, Ireland, on 17 Mar. 1908. The duration of the fight between Cassius Clay (b. Louisville, Kentucky, U.S.A., 17 Jan. 1942 who later took the name Muhammad Ali Haj) and Charles "Sonny" Liston (1932–1970) at Lewiston, Maine, U.S.A., on 25 May 1965 was 1 min 52 sec (including the count) as timed from the video tape recordings, despite a ringside announcement giving a time of 1 min. The shortest world title fight was when Al McCoy knocked out George Chip in 45 sec for the middleweight crown in New York on 7 Apr. 1914. The shortest ever British title fight was one of 40 sec (including the count), when Dave Charnley knocked out David "Darkie" Hughes in a lightweight championship defence in Nottingham on 20 Nov. 1961.

Most British titles
The most defences of a British heavyweight title is 14 by "Bombardier" Billy Wells (b. 31 Aug. 1889–1967) from 1911 to 1919. The only British boxer to win three Lonsdale Belts outright has been Henry William Cooper, O.B.E. (b. Camberwell, London, 3 May 1934), heavyweight champion (1959–69, 1970–71). He retired after losing to Joe Bugner (b. Hungary, 13 Mar. 1950), having held the British heavyweight title from 12 Jan. 1959 to 28 May 1969 and from 24 Mar. 1970 to 16 Mar. 1971.

Tallest
The tallest boxer to fight professionally was Gogea Mitu (b. 1914) of Romania in 1935. He was 7 ft 4 in *223 cm* and weighed 23 st. 5 lb. *148 kg* (327 lb.). John Rankin, who won a fight in New Orleans, Louisiana, U.S.A., in November 1967, was reputedly also 7 ft 4 in *223 cm*.

Longest career
The heavyweight Jem Mace (G.B.), known as "the gypsy" (1831–1910), had a career lasting 35 years from 1855 to 1890, but there were several years in which he had only one fight. Bobby Dobbs (U.S.A.) (1858–1930) is reported to have had a 39 yr career from 1875 to 1914. Walter Edgerton, the "Kentucky Rosebud", knocked out John Henry Johnson aged 45 in four rounds at the Broadway A.C., New York City, N.Y., U.S.A., on 4 Feb. 1916, when aged 63.

Most fights
The greatest recorded number of fights in a career is 1,024 by Bobby Dobbs (U.S.A.) (see above). Abraham Hollandersky, *alias* Abe the Newsboy (U.S.A.) is reputed to have had up to 1,309 fights from 1905 to 1918, but many of them were exhibition bouts.

Most fights without loss
Hal Bagwell, a lightweight, of Gloucester, England, was reputedly undefeated in 180 consecutive fights, of which only five were draws, between 15 Aug. 1938 and 29 Nov. 1948. His record of fights in the war-time period (1939–46), is however very sketchy. He never contested a British title. Of boxers with complete records Packey McFarland (U.S.A.) (1888–1936) had 97 fights in 1905–1915 without a defeat.

Most knock-outs
The greatest number of finishes classed by the rules prevailing as "knock-outs" in a career (1936 to 1963) is 141 by

The "Father of Boxing" Jack Broughton, drew up the first rules and invented the first boxing gloves or "mufflers". (*Radio Times Hulton Picture Library*)

Archie Moore (b. Archibald Lee Wright, Collinsville, Illinois, U.S.A., 13 Dec. 1913 or 1916). The record for consecutive K.O.'s is 44, set by Lamar Clark of Utah at Las Vegas, Nevada, U.S.A., on 11 Jan. 1960. He knocked out six in one night (five in the first round) at Bingham, Utah, on 1 Dec. 1958.

Largest purse
The greatest purse won is a reported $6,500,000 by Muhammad Ali Haj for his heavyweight title fight against Ken Norton (U.S.A.) in the Yankee Stadium, New York on 28 Sept. 1976.

Highest bare knuckle stake
The largest stake ever fought for in this era was $22,500 *then* £4,633 in the 27-round fight between Jack Cooper and Wolf Bendoff at Port Elizabeth, South Africa on 29 July 1889.

Highest earnings in career
The largest fortune ever made in a fighting career is an estimated $60 million (including exhibitions) amassed by Muhammad Ali from Oct. 1960–Aug. 1979 in 59 fights comprising 529 rounds.

Two Olympic light-heavyweight champions, Muhammad Ali (1960) and Leon Spinks (1976), were watched by boxing's largest ever indoor audience in Ali's last title fight. (*All-Sport Photographic*)

Attendances *Highest*

The greatest paid attendance at any boxing fight has been 120,757 (with a ringside price of $27.50) for the Tunney *v.* Dempsey world heavyweight title fight at the Sesqui-centennial Stadium, Philadelphia, Pennsylvania, U.S.A., on 23 Sept. 1926. The indoor record is 63,350 at the Ali *v.* Leon Spinks fight in the Superdome, New Orleans, Louisiana, on 15 Sept. 1978. The British attendance record is 82,000 at the Len Harvey *v.* Jock McAvoy fight at White City, London, on 10 July 1939.

The highest non-paying attendance is 135,132 at the Tony Zale *v.* Billy Pryor fight at Juneau Park, Milwaukee, Wisconsin, U.S.A., on 18 Aug. 1941.

Attendances *Lowest*

The smallest attendance at a world heavyweight title fight was 2,434 at the Clay *v.* Liston fight at Lewiston, Maine, U.S.A., on 25 May 1965.

WORLD HEAVYWEIGHT CHAMPIONS
Earliest title fight

The first world heavyweight title fight, with gloves and three min rounds, was that between John Lawrence Sullivan (1858–1918) and "Gentleman" James J. Corbett (1866–1933) in New Orleans, Louisiana, U.S.A., on 7 Sept. 1892. Corbett won in 21 rounds.

Longest and shortest reigns

The longest reign of any world heavyweight champion is 11 years 8 months and 7 days by Joe Louis (b. Joseph Louis Barrow, Lafayette, Alabama, 13 May 1914), from 22 June 1937, when he knocked out James J. Braddock in the eighth round at Chicago, Illinois, U.S.A., until announcing his retirement on 1 Mar. 1949. During his reign Louis made a record 25 defences of his title. The shortest reign was by Leon Spinks (U.S.A.) (b. 11 July 1953) for 212 days from 15 Feb.–15 Sept. 1978.

Oldest and youngest

The oldest man to win the heavyweight crown was Jersey Joe Walcott (b. Arnold Raymond Cream, 31 Jan. 1914 at Merchantville, New Jersey, U.S.A.) who knocked out Ezzard Mack Charles (1921–1975) on 18 July 1951 in Pittsburgh, Pennsylvania, when aged 37 years 168 days. Walcott was the oldest holder at 38 years 7 months 23 days losing his title to Rocky Marciano (1923–69) on 23 Sept. 1952. The youngest age at which the world title has been won is 21 years 331 days by Floyd Patterson (b. Waco, North Carolina, 4 Jan. 1935). After the retirement of Marciano, Patterson won the vacant title by beating Archie Moore in five rounds in Chicago, Illinois, U.S.A., on 30 Nov. 1956.

Most recaptures

Muhammad Ali Haj is the only man to regain the heavy-weight championship twice. Ali first won the title on 25 Feb. 1964 defeating Sonny Liston. He defeated George Foreman on 30 Oct. 1974 having been stripped of the title by the world boxing authorities on 28 Apr. 1967. He then won the W.B.A. title from Leon Spinks on 15 Sept. 1978 having previously lost to him on 15 Feb. 1978.

Undefeated

Rocky Marciano (b. Rocco Francis Marchegiano) (1923–1969) is the only world heavyweight champion to have been undefeated during his entire career (1947–56).

Heaviest and lightest

The heaviest world champion was Primo Carnera of Italy, the "Ambling Alp", who won the title from Jack Sharkey in six rounds in New York City, N.Y., U.S.A., on 29 June 1933. He scaled 267 lb. *121 kg* for this fight but his peak weight was 270 lb. *122 kg*. He had an expanded chest measurement of 53 in *134 cm*, the longest reach at 85½ in *217 cm* (finger tip to finger tip) and also the largest fists with a 14¾ in *37 cm* circumference. The lightest champion was Robert James (Bob) Fitzsimmons (1863–1917), from Helston,

Cornwall, England, who at a weight of 167 lb. *75 kg*, won the title by knocking out James Corbett in 14 rounds at Carson City, Nevada, U.S.A., on 17 Mar. 1897.

The greatest differential in a world title fight was 86 lb. *39 kg* between Carnera (270 lb. *122 kg*) and Tommy Loughran (184 lb. *83 kg*) of the U.S.A., when the former won on points at Miami, Florida, U.S.A., on 1 Mar. 1934.

Tallest and shortest
The tallest world champion according to measurements by the Physical Education Director of the Hemingway Gymnasium, Harvard University, was Carnera at 6 ft 5.4 in *196,59 cm* although he was widely reported and believed to be up to 6 ft 8½ in *204 cm*. Jess Willard (1881–1968) who won the title in 1915, often stated to be 6 ft 6¼ in *199 cm* was in fact 6 ft 5¼ in *196,21 cm*. (Willard was the longest lived of heavyweight champions at 86 yr 351 days). The shortest was Tommy Burns, world champion from 23 Feb. 1906 to 26 Dec. 1908, who stood 5 ft 7 in *170 cm* and weighed 179 lb. *81 kg*.

WORLD CHAMPIONS (any weight)
Longest and shortest reign
Joe Louis's heavyweight duration record of 11 years 252 days stands for all divisions. The shortest reign has been 54 days by the French featherweight Eugène Criqui (1893–1977) from 2 June to 26 July 1923. The disputed flyweight champion Emile Pladner (France) (b. 2 Sept. 1906) reigned only 47 days from 2 Mar. to 18 Apr. 1929, as did also the disputed featherweight champion Dave Sullivan, from 26 Sept. to 11 Nov. 1898.

Youngest and oldest
The youngest age at which any world championship has been won is 17 years 180 days by Wilfredo Benitez (b. 8 Sept. 1958) of Puerto Rico, who won the W.B.A. light welterweight title in San Juan, P.R., on 6 Mar. 1976. The oldest world champion was Archie Moore who was recognized as a light heavyweight champion up to 10 Feb. 1962 when his title was removed. He was then believed to be between 45 and 48. Bob Fitzsimmons had the longest career of any official world titleholder with over 32 years from 1882 to 1914. He won his last world title aged 40 years 183 days in San Francisco, California on 25 Nov. 1903. He was an amateur from 1880 to 1882.

Longest fight
The longest world title fight (under Queensberry Rules) was that between the lightweights Joe Gans (1874–1910), of the U.S.A., and Oscar Matthew "Battling" Nelson (1882–1954), the "Durable Dane", at Goldfield, Nevada, U.S.A., on 3 Sept. 1906. It was terminated in the 42nd round when Gans was declared the winner on a foul.

Most recaptures
The only boxer to win a world title five times at one weight is "Sugar" Ray Robinson (b. Walker Smith, Jr., in Detroit, 3 May 1920) of the U.S.A., who beat Carmen Basilio (U.S.A.) in the Chicago Stadium on 25 Mar. 1958, to regain the world middleweight title for the fourth time. The other title wins were over Jake LaMotta (U.S.A.) in Chicago on 14 Feb. 1951, Randolph Turpin (United Kingdom) in New York on 12 Sept. 1951, Carl "Bobo" Olson (U.S.A.) in Chicago on 9 Dec. 1955, and Gene Fullmer (U.S.A.) in Chicago on 1 May 1957. The record number of title bouts in a career is 33 or 34, at bantam and featherweight, by George Dixon (1870–1909), *alias* "Little Chocolate", of Canada, between 1890 and 1901.

Greatest weight span
The only man to hold world titles at three weights *simultaneously* was Henry "Homicide Hank" Armstrong (b. 12 Dec. 1912), now the Rev. Henry Jackson, of the U.S.A., at featherweight, lightweight and welterweight from August to December 1938.

Greatest "tonnage"
The greatest "tonnage" recorded in any fight is 700 lb. *317 kg* when Claude "Humphrey" McBride (Oklahoma) 340 lb. *154 kg* knocked out Jimmy Black (Houston), who weighed 360 lb. *163 kg* in the third round at Oklahoma City on 1 June 1971. The greatest "tonnage" in a world title fight was 488¾ lb. *221½ kg*, when Carnera, then 259¼ lb. *117½ kg* fought Paolino Uzcudun 229½ lb. *104 kg* of Spain in Rome on 22 Oct. 1933.

Smallest champion
The smallest man to win any world title has been Pascual Perez (1926–77) who won the flyweight title in Tōkyō on 26 Nov. 1954 at 107 lb. *48½ kg* and 4 ft 11½ in *1,51 m*. Jimmy Wilde (1892–1969) who held the flyweight title from 1916–23 was reputed never to have fought above 108 lb. *49 kg*.

Most knock-downs in Title fights
Vic Toweel (South Africa) knocked down Danny O'Sullivan of London 14 times in ten rounds in their world bantamweight fight at Johannesburg on 2 Dec. 1950, before the latter retired.

AMATEUR
Most Olympic titles
The only amateur boxer to win three Olympic gold medals is the southpaw László Papp (b. 25 Mar. 1926) (Hungary), who took the middleweight (1948) and the light-middleweight titles (1952 and 1956). The only man to win two titles in one celebration was Oliver L. Kirk (U.S.A.), who took both the bantam and featherweight titles in St. Louis, Missouri, U.S.A., in 1904, when the U.S. won all the titles. In 1908 Great Britain won all the titles. Harry W. Mallin (1892–1969) (G.B.) was in 1924 the first boxer ever to defend successfully an Olympic title in retaining the middleweight title.

Oldest gold medallist
Richard K. Gunn (b. 1870) (G.B.) won the Olympic featherweight gold medal on 27 Oct. 1908 in London aged 38.

MOST A.B.A. TITLES WON IN EACH CLASS				
Class	**Instituted**	**Wins**	**Name**	**Years**
Light-Flyweight (7st. 8lb. *48 kg* or under)	1971	3	M. Abrams	1971–73
Flyweight (8 st. *51 kg* or under)	1920	5	T. Pardoe	1929–33
Bantamweight (8 st. 7 lb. *54 kg* or under)	1884	4	W. W. Allen	1911–12, 1914, 1919
Featherweight (9 st. *57 kg* or under)	1884	5	G. R. Baker	1912–14, 1919, 1921
Lightweight (9 st. 7 lb. *60 kg* or under)	1881	4	M. Wells	1904–7
		4	F. Grace	1909, 1913, 1919–20
Light-Welterweight (10 st. *63,5 kg* or under)	1951	2	D. Stone	1956–57
		2	R. Kane	1958–59
		2	L/Cpl. B. Brazie	1961–62
		2	R. McTaggart	1963, 1965
Welterweight (10 st. 8 lb. *67 kg* or under)	1920	3	N. Gargano	1954–56
		3	T. Waller	1970, 1973–74
Light-Middleweight (11 st. 2 lb. *71 kg* or under)	1951	2	B. Wells	1953–54
		2	B. Foster	1952, 1955
		2	S. Pearson	1958–59
		2	T. Imrie	1966, 1969
		2	R. Maxwell	1973–74
Middleweight (11 st. 11 lb. *75 kg* or under)	1881	5	R. C. Warnes	1899, 1901, 1903, 1907, 1910
		5	H. W. Mallin	1919–23
		5	F. Mallin	1928–32
Light-Heavyweight (12 st. 10 lb. *81 kg* or under)	1920	4	H. J. Mitchell	1922–25
Heavyweight (over 12 st. 10 lb. *81 kg*)	1881	5	F. Parks	1899, 1901–02, 1905–06

Most titles

The greatest number of A.B.A. titles won by any boxer is six by Joseph Steers at middleweight and heavyweight between 1890 and 1893. A. Watson of Leith, Scotland won the Scottish heavyweight title in 1938, 1942–3, and the light-heavyweight championship 1937–39, 1943–45 and 1947, making ten in all. He also won the A.B.A. light-heavyweight title in 1945 and 1947.

Longest span

The greatest span of A.B.A. title-winning performances is that of the heavyweight Hugh "Pat" Floyd (b. 23 Aug. 1910), who won in 1929 and gained his fourth title 17 years later in 1946.

BULLFIGHTING

Earliest

In the latter half of the Second Millenium B.C. bull leaping was practised in Crete. Bullfighting in Spain was first reported by the Romans in Baetica (Andalusia) in the third century B.C.

The first renowned professional *espada* was Francisco Romero of Ronda, in Andalusia, Spain, who introduced the *estoque* and the red muleta c. 1700. Spain now has some 190 active matadors. Since 1700, 42 major matadors have died in the ring.

Most successful matadors

The most successful matador measured by bulls killed was Lagartijo (1841–1900), born Rafael Molina, whose lifetime total was 4,867. The longest career as a full matador was by Bienvenida (1922–1975), born Antonio Mejías, from 1942 to 1974. Recent Spanish law requires compulsory retirement at 55 years of age.

Most kills in a day

In 1884 Romano set a record by killing 18 bulls in a day in Seville and in 1949 El Litri (Miguel Báes) set a Spanish record with 114 *novilladas* in a season.

Highest paid

The highest paid bullfighter in history was El Cordobés (b. Manuel Benítez Pérez, probably on 4 May 1936, Palma del Rio, Spain), who became a sterling millionaire in 1965, when he fought 111 *corridas* up to 4 October of that year. In 1970 he received an estimated £750,000 for 121 fights. Paco Camino (b. 19 Dec. 1941) has received up to 2,000,000 pesetas £16,000 for a *corrida*. He retired in 1977.

Largest stadiums

The world's largest bullfighting ring, the Plaza, Mexico City, with a capacity of 48,000, was closed in Mar. 1976. The largest of Spain's 312 bullrings is Las Ventas, Madrid with a capacity of 24,000.

CANOEING

Origins

The acknowledged pioneer of canoeing as a modern sport was John Macgregor, a British barrister, in 1865. The Canoe Club was formed on 26 July 1866.

Most titles *Olympic*

Gert Fredriksson (b. 21 Nov. 1919) of Sweden has won mos Olympic gold medals with six in 1948, 1952, 1956 and 1960 The most by a woman is three by Ludmila Pinayeva (ne Khvedosyuk) (b. 14 Jan. 1936) (U.S.S.R.), in 1964, 1968 and 1972. The Olympic 1,000 m best performance of 3 mi 06.46 sec by the 1976 Spanish K.4 represents an averag speed of 11.99 m.p.h. *19,30 km/h* and a striking rate of abou 125 strokes per min.

Most titles *World*

In addition to his six Olympic championships Gert Fredriks son has three other world titles in non-Olympic years for record total of nine. This has been equalled by Yuri Lobano (U.S.S.R.) (b. 29 Sept. 1952) from 1972 to 1977, an Ludmila Pinayeva, who added six other world titles to he three Olympic golds, from 1966 to 1973.

The only British canoeists to win world titles have bee the late Paul Farrant of Chalfont Park Canoe Club, the cano slalom at Geneva, Switzerland, in August 1959, Alan Emus the canoe sailing at Hayling Island, Hampshire, in Augus 1961 and on the Boden See (Lake of Constance) in Augus 1965, and Albert Kerr, the Whitewater kayak slalom a Spittal, Austria on 24 July 1977.

Most titles *British*

The most British Open titles (instituted 1936) ever won is 32 by John Laurence Oliver (Lincoln Canoe Club) (b. 12 Jan 1943) from 1966 to 1976 including 12 individual events. Davi Mitchell (Chester S. & C.C.) won eight British slalom titles i 1963–68, 1970–71.

Longest journey

The longest journey ever made by canoe is one of 7,516 mile 12 096 km around the eastern U.S.A. by paddle and portage from Lake Itasca, Minn. via New Orleans, Miami, New Yor and Lake Ontario, by Randy Bauer (b. 15 Aug. 1949) and Jerry Mimbach (b. 22 May 1952) of Coon Rapids, Minn. from 8 Sept. 1974 to 30 Aug. 1976.

The longest journey without portages or aid of any kind is on of 6,102 miles 9 820 km by Richard H. Grant and Ernest "Moose" Lassy circumnavigating the eastern United State via Chicago, New Orleans, Miami, New York and the Grea Lakes from 22 Sept. 1930 to 15 Aug. 1931.

Cross-Channel

The singles record across the English Channel is 3 hr 33 min 47 sec by Andrew William Dougall Samuel (b. 12 July 1937) of Glasgow, from Shakespeare Bay, Dover, to Wissant, France, on 5 Sept. 1976. The doubles record is 3 hr 20 min 30 sec by Capt. William Stanley Crook and the late Ronald Ernest Rhodes in their glass-fibre K.2 *Accord*, from St. Margaret's Bay, Dover, to Cap Blanc Nez, France on 20 Sept. 1961.

The record for a double crossing is 12 hr 47 min in K.1 canoes by nine members of the Canoe Camping Club, G.B., on 7 May 1976.

Longest open sea voyage

Beatrice and John Dowd, Ken Beard and Steve Benson

DOWNSTREAM CANOEING

River	Miles	Km	Name and Country	Route	Date	Duration
Rhine	714	1 149	Sgt. Charles Kavanagh (G.B.)	Chur, Switzerland to Willemstad, Neth.	13 Feb.–2 Apr. 1961	17½ days
	714	1 149	Four Royal Marine Reservists (G.B.)	Chur to Willemstad	9–14 Mar. 1974	10 days 11 hr.
Murray-Darling	1,980	3 186	Six students of St. Albert's College, UNE. (Australia)	Gunnedah, N.S.W. to Lake Alexandrina, S.A.	Dec. 1975	—
Mississippi	2,500	4 023	Royal Air Force team of three two-man canoes (G.B.)	Lake Itasca, Minnesota to Gulf of Mexico	23 Aug–4 Oct. 1978	42 days 5 hr
Zaire (Congo)	2,600	4 185	John and Julie Batchelor (G.B.)	Moasampanga to Banana	8 May–12 Sept. 1974	128 days
Amazon	3,400	5 470	Stephen Zsolnay Bezuk (U.S.) (Kayak)	Atalaya to Ponta do Céu	21 June–4 Nov. 1970	136 days
Mississippi–Missouri	3,810	6 132	Nicholas Francis (G.B.)	Three Forks, Montana to New Orleans, La.	13 July–25 Nov. 1977	135 days
Nile	4,000	6 500	John Goddard (U.S.), Jean Laporte and André Davy (France)	Kagera to the Delta	Nov. 1953–July 1954	9 months

(Richard Gillett replaced him mid-journey) paddled 2,170 miles *3 491 km* (of a total 2,192 miles *3 527 km*) from Venezuela to Miami, Florida, U.S.A., via the West Indies 11 Aug. 1977–29 Apr. 1978 in two Klepper Aerius 20 kayaks.

Devizes-Westminster
The Senior Class record for the annual Challenge Cup race (instituted officially 1949) over 125 miles *201 km* with 77 locks is 15 hr 34 min 12 sec by B. R. Greenham and T. J. Cornish (Reading/Leighton Park/Richmond) to win the 1975 race. The Junior Class record is 15 hr 34 min 43 sec by A. R. Ayres and J. Q. West (Royal C.C.) to win the 1979 race from 60 crews.

Loch Ness
The fastest time for a K.1 from Fort Augustus to Lochend (22.7 miles *36,5 km*) is 3 hrs 33 min 4 sec by Andrew Samuel (Trossachs Canoe and Boat Club) on 19 Oct. 1975.

Highest altitude
In Sept. 1976 Dr. Michael Jones (1951–78) and Michael Hopkinson of the British Everest Canoe Expedition canoed down the River Dudh Kosi, Nepal from an altitude of 17,500 ft *5 334 m*.

Longest race
The longest regularly held canoe race in the U.S.A. is the Texas Water Safari (inst. 1963), 419 miles *674 km* from San Marcos to Seadrift on the San Marcos and Guadalupe rivers. Butch Hodges and Robert Chatham set a record of 37 hr 18 min on 5–6 June 1976.

Eskimo rolls
The record for Eskimo rolls is 1,000 in 65 min 39.3 sec by Bruce Parry (b. 25 Sept. 1960) on Lake Lismore, N.S.W., Australia on 17 Dec. 1977. A "hand-rolling" record of 100 rolls in 3 min 44.0 sec was set in the Strathclyde University Pool, Scotland on 18 June 1979 by Peter Turcan (21).

CAVING (see also p. 67)

Duration (trogging)
The endurance record for staying in a cave is 463 days by Milutin Veljkovic (b. 1935) (Yugoslavia) in the Samar Cavern, Svrljig Mountains, northern Yugoslavia from 24 June 1969 to 30 Sept. 1970. The British record is 130 days by David Lafferty, (b. 1939) of Hampstead, who stayed in Boulder Chamber, Goughs' Cave, Cheddar Gorge, Somerset, from 27 Mar. to 4 Aug. 1966. He was alone until 1 Aug. when he thought it was 7 July.

COURSING

Origins
The sport of dogs chasing hares was probably of Egyptian origin in *c.* 3000 B.C. and brought to England by the Normans in 1067. The first club was the Swaffham Coursing Club formed in 1776. The classic event is the annual Waterloo Cup,

The late Dr Mike Jones took his canoe to a record height of over three miles above sea level. (*Leo Dickinson*)

instituted at Altcar, Merseyside in 1836. A government bill to declare the sport illegal was "lost" owing to the dissolution of Parliament on 29 May 1970. The number of clubs in Britain had dwindled from 169 in 1873 to 25 in 1973.

Most successful dog
The most successful Waterloo Cup dog recorded was Colonel North's *Fullerton*, sired by *Greentich*, who tied for first in 1889 and then won outright in 1890–92. He died on 4 June 1899.

Longest course
The longest authenticated course is one of 4 min 10 sec, when Major C. Blundell's *Blackmore* beat *Boldon* in a Barbican Cup decider on 2 Mar. 1934.

BEAGLING
The oldest beagle hunt is the Royal Rock Beagle Hunt, Wirral, Merseyside, whose first outing was on 28 Mar. 1845. The

PROGRESSIVE WORLD DEPTH RECORDS

Compiled by Dr. A. C. Waltham, Trent Polytechnic, Nottingham.

ft	m	Cave	Country	Cavers	Date	
453	138	Macocha	Czechoslovakia	J. Nagel et al.		1748
741	226	Grotta di Padriciano	Italy	A. Lindner et al.		1839
1,076	328	Grotta di Trebiciano	Italy	A. Lindner et al.		1841
1,509	460	Geldloch	Austria	—		1923
1,574	480	Antro di Corchia	Italy	E. Fiorentino Club		1934
1,978	603	Trou du Glaz	France	P. Chevalier et al.		1947
2,418	737	Reseau de la Pierre St. Martin	France	G. Lepineux et al.	July	1953
2,962	903	Gouffre Berger	France	F. Petzl et al.	Sept.	1954
3,123	952	Gouffre Berger	France	L. Potié et al.	Aug.	1955
3,681	1 122	Gouffre Berger	France	F. Petzl et al.	July	1956
3,715	1 133	Gouffre Berger	France	K. Pearce	Aug.	1963
3,842	1 171	Reseau de la Pierre St. Martin	France	A.R.S.I.P.	Aug.	1966
4,370	1 332	Reseau de la Pierre St. Martin	France	A.R.S.I.P.	Aug.	1975

N.B. The Reseau de la Pierre St. Martin was explored via a number of entrances and was never entirely descended at any one time until 1978; consequently after Aug. 1963 the "sporting" records for the greatest descent into a cave should read:

3,743	1 141	Gouffre Berger	France	Spéléo Club de Seine	July	1968
4,370	1 332	Reseau de la Pierre St. Martin	France	P. Courbon *et al.*	Sept.	1978

Newcastle and District Beagles claim their origin from the municipally-supported Newcastle Harriers existing in 1787. The Royal Agricultural College beagle pack killed 79½ brace of hares in the 1968–69 season.

CRICKET

Origins

The earliest evidence of the game of cricket is from a drawing depicting two men playing with a bat and ball dated *c.* 1250. The game was played in Guildford, Surrey, at least as early as 1550. The earliest major match of which the score survives was one in which a team representing England (40 and 70) was beaten by Kent (53 and 58 for 9) by one wicket at the Artillery Ground in Finsbury, London, on 18 June 1744. Cricket was played in Australia as early as 1803.

BATTING RECORDS—TEAMS

Highest innings *World*

The highest recorded innings by any team was one of 1,107 runs by Victoria against New South Wales in an Australian inter-State match at Melbourne, Victoria, on 27–28 Dec. 1926.

Highest innings *England*

The highest innings made in England is 903 runs for 7 wickets declared, by England in the Fifth Test against Australia at the Oval, London, on 20, 22 and 23 Aug. 1938. The highest innings in a county championship match is 887 by Yorkshire *versus* Warwickshire at Edgbaston on 7–8 May 1896.

Lowest innings

The lowest recorded innings is 12 made by Oxford University *v.* the Marylebone Cricket Club (M.C.C.) at Oxford on 24 May 1877, and 12 by Northamptonshire *v.* Gloucestershire at Gloucester on 11 June 1907. On the occasion of the Oxford match, however, the University batted a man short. The lowest score in a Test innings is 26 by New Zealand *v.* England in the second innings of the Second Test at Auckland on 28 Mar. 1955.

The lowest aggregate for two innings is 34 (16 in first and 18 in second) by Border *v.* Natal in the South African Currie Cup at East London on 19 and 21 Dec. 1959.

Greatest victory

The greatest recorded margin of victory is an innings and 851 runs, when Pakistan Railways (910 for 6 wickets declared) beat Dera Ismail Khan (32 and 27) at Lahore on 2–4 Dec. 1964. The largest margin in England is one of an innings and 579 runs by England over Australia in the Fifth Test at the Oval on 20–24 Aug. 1938 when Australia scored 201 and 123 with two men short in both innings. The most one-sided county match was when Surrey (698) defeated Sussex (114 and 99) by an innings and 485 runs at the Oval on 9–11 Aug. 1888.

Most runs in a day *World*

The greatest number of runs scored in a day is 721 all out (ten wickets) in 5 hrs 48 min by the Australians *v.* Essex at Southchurch Park, Southend-on-Sea on 15 May 1948.

Most runs in a day *Test match*

The Test record for runs in a day is 588 at Old Trafford on 27 July 1936 when England put on 398 and India were 190 for 0 in their second innings by the close.

Fastest 200 or more

The fastest recorded exhibition of hitting occurred in a Kent *v.* Gloucestershire match at Dover on 20 Aug. 1937, when Kent scored 219 runs for two wickets in 71 min, at the rate of 156 runs for each 100 balls bowled.

BATTING RECORDS—INDIVIDUALS

Highest innings

The highest individual innings recorded is 499 in 10 hrs 40 min by Hanif Mohammad (b. Junagadh, India, now Pakistan, 21 Dec. 1934) for Karachi *v.* Bahawalpur at Karachi, Pakistan, on 8, 9 and 11 Jan. 1959. The highest score in England

is 424 in 7 hrs 50 min by Archibald Campbell MacLaren (1871–1944) for Lancashire *v.* Somerset at Taunton on 15–16 July 1895. The record for a Test match is 365 not out in 10 hrs 8 min by Sir Garfield St. Aubrun Sobers (b. Bridgetown, Barbados, 28 July 1936) playing for the West Indies in the Third Test against Pakistan at Sabina Park, Kingston, Jamaica, on 27 Feb.–1 Mar. 1958. The England Test record is 364 by Sir Leonard Hutton (b. Fulneck, Pudsey, West Yorkshire, 23 June 1916) *v.* Australia in the Fifth Test at the Oval on 20, 22 and 23 Aug. 1938.

1,000 in May

The most recent example of scoring 1,000 runs *in May* was by Charles Hallows (Lancashire) (1895–1972), who made precisely 1,000 between 5–31 May 1928. Dr. William Gilbert Grace (1848–1915) 9–30 May 1895, and Walter Reginald Hammond (1903–1965) 7–31 May 1927, surpassed this feat with 1,016 and 1,042 runs. The greatest number of runs made *before the end of May* was by Thomas Walter Hayward (1871–1939) with 1,074 from 16 Apr. to 31 May in 1900.

Longest innings

The longest innings on record is one of 16 hrs 10 min for 337 runs by Hanif Mohammad (Pakistan) *v.* the West Indies in the First Test at Bridgetown, Barbados, on 20–23 Jan. 1958. The English record is 13 hrs 17 min by Len Hutton.

Most runs *Season*

The greatest number of runs ever scored in a season is 3,816 in 50 innings (8 not out) by Denis Charles Scott Compton C.B.E. (b. Hendon, Greater London, 23 May 1918) of Middlesex and England in 1947. His batting average was 90.85.

Most runs *Career*

The greatest aggregate of runs in a career is 61,237 in 1,315 innings (106 not out) between 1905 and 1934 by Sir John (Jack) Berry Hobbs (1882–1963) of Surrey and England. His career average was 50.65.

Most runs *Test matches*

The greatest number of runs scored in Test matches is 8,032 in 160 innings (21 not out) by Sir Garfield Sobers of Barbados and Nottinghamshire playing for the West Indies between 1953 and 1974. His average is 57.78.

Most runs *Off an over*

The only batsman to score the possible of 36 runs off a six-ball over was Sir Garfield Sobers (Nottinghamshire) off Malcolm Andrew Nash (Glamorgan) at Swansea on 31 Aug. 1968. The ball (recovered from the last hit from the road by a small boy) resides in Nottingham's Museum.

Most runs *Off a ball*

The most runs scored off a single hit is ten by Samuel Hill Wood (later Sir Samuel Hill Hill-Wood) (1872–1949) off Cuthbert James Burnup (1875–1960) in the Derbyshire *v.* M.C.C. match at Lord's, City of Westminster, Greater London, on 26 May 1900.

Most sixes *In an innings*

The highest number of sixes hit in an innings is 15 by John Richard Reid, O.B.E. (b. 3 June 1928), in an innings of 296, lasting 3 hrs 47 min, for Wellington *v.* Northern Districts in the Plunket Shield Tournament at Wellington, New Zealand, on 14–15 Jan. 1963. The Test record is ten by Walter Hammond in an innings of 336 not out for England *v.* New Zealand at Auckland on 31 Mar. and 1 Apr. 1933.

Most sixes *In a match*

The highest number of sixes in a match is 17 (ten in the first and seven in the second innings) by William James Stewart (b. 31 Aug. 1934) for Warwickshire *v.* Lancashire at Blackpool on 29–31 July 1959. His two innings were of 155 and 125.

Most boundaries in an innings

The highest number of boundaries in an innings was 68 (all in fours) by Percival Albert Perrin (1876–1945) in an innings of 343 not out for Essex *v.* Derbyshire at Chesterfield on 18–19 July 1904.

In addition to his one day batting performances, South Africa's Barry Richards scored 79 hundreds in his first class career. (*Syndication International*)

Though achieving notoriety at the receiving end of a record 36 run over, Malcolm Nash is no mean bowler, as evidenced by his John Player League hat-trick. (*Sporting Pictures*)

Highest score by a No. 11

The highest score by a No. 11 batsman is 163 by Thomas Peter Bromly Smith (1908–67) for Essex *v.* Derbyshire at Chesterfield in August 1947.

Most centuries *Season*

The record for the greatest number of centuries in a season is held by Denis Compton with 18 in 1947.

Most centuries *Career*

The most centuries in a career is 197 by Sir Jack Hobbs between 1905 and 1934.

Most centuries *Test matches*

The greatest number of centuries scored in Test matches is 29 by Sir Donald George Bradman (Australia) (b. Cootamundra, N.S.W., 27 Aug. 1908) between 1928 and 1948. The English record is 22 by Walter Hammond of Gloucestershire, between 1927 and 1947, and 22 by Michael Colin Cowdrey, C.B.E. (b. Bangalore, India 24 Dec. 1932) (Kent) between 1954 and 1975.

Double centuries

The only batsman to score double centuries in both innings is Arthur Edward Fagg (1915–77), who made 244 and 202 not out for Kent *v.* Essex at Colchester on 13–15 July 1938. Sir Donald Bradman scored a career record 37 double centuries 1927–49.

Highest averages

The highest recorded seasonal batting average in England is 115.66 for 26 innings (2,429 runs) by Sir Donald Bradman (Australia) in England in 1938. The English record is 100.12 by Geoffrey Boycott (b. 21 Oct. 1940) of Yorkshire and England for 30 innings (2,503 runs) including 13 centuries and five times not out in 1971. The world record for a complete career is 95.14 for 338 innings (28,067 runs) by Bradman between 1927 and 1949. The record for Test matches is 99.94 in 80 innings (6,996 runs) by Bradman in 1928–48. The English career record is 56.37 for 500 innings (62 not out) by Kumar Shri Ranjitsinhji (1872–1933) later H. H. the Jam Saheb of Nawanagar, with 24,692 runs between 1893 and 1920.

Fastest scoring

The fastest 50 ever hit was completed in 8 min (1.22 to 1.30 p.m.) and in 11 scoring strokes by Clive C. Inman (b. Colombo, Ceylon, 29 Jan. 1936) in an innings of 57 not out for Leicestershire *v.* Nottinghamshire at Trent Bridge, Nottingham on 20 Aug. 1965.

The fastest century ever hit was completed in 35 min by Percy George Herbert Fender (b. 22 Aug. 1892), when scoring 113 not out for Surrey *v.* Northamptonshire at Northampton on 26 Aug. 1920. The most prolific scorer of centuries in an hour or less was Gilbert Laird Jessop (1874–1955), with 11 between 1897 and 1913. The fastest Test century was one of 70 min by Jack Morrison Gregory (1895–1973) of New South Wales, for Australia *v.* South Africa in the Second Test at Johannesburg on 12 Nov. 1921. Edwin Boaler Alletson (1884–1963) scored 189 runs in 90 min for Nottinghamshire *v.* Sussex at Hove on 20 May 1911.

A double century in 120 min was achieved by Gilbert Jessop (286) for Gloucestershire *v.* Sussex at Hove on 1 June 1903 and equalled by Clive Hubert Lloyd (West Indies) (b. Georgetown, now Guyana, 31 Aug. 1944) *v.* Glamorgan at Swansea, West Glamorgan, on 9 Aug. 1976.

The fastest treble century was completed in 181 min by Denis Compton, C.B.E. (Middlesex) who scored 300 for the M.C.C. *v.* North-Eastern Transvaal at Benoni on 3–4 Dec. 1948.

Slowest scoring

The longest time a batsman has ever taken to open his scoring is 1 hr 37 min by Thomas Godfrey Evans (b. Finchley, Greater London, 18 Aug. 1920) of Kent, who scored ten not out for England v. Australia in the Fourth Test at Adelaide on 5–6 Feb. 1947. Richard Gorton Barlow (1850–1919) utilized 2½ hrs to score five not out for Lancashire v. Nottinghamshire at Nottingham on 8 July 1882. During his innings his score remained unchanged for 80 min.

The slowest century on record is by Mudassar Nazar (b. 6 Apr. 1956) of Pakistan in the First Test v. England at Lahore on 15–16 Dec. 1977. He required 9 hrs 51 min for 114 reaching the 100 in 9 hrs 17 min. The slowest double century recorded is one of 10 hrs 8 min by Robert Baddeley Simpson (b. 3 Feb. 1936) of New South Wales, during an innings of 311, lasting 12 hrs 42 min, for Australia v. England in the Fourth Test at Old Trafford on 23–24 July 1964.

Greatest partnership

The record stand for any partnership is the fourth wicket stand of 577 by Gul Muhammad (b. 15 Oct. 1921), who scored 319, and Vijay Samuel Hazare (b. 11 Mar. 1915) 288 in the Baroda v. Holkar match at Baroda, India, on 8–10 Mar. 1947.

The highest stand in English cricket is the first-wicket partnership of 555 by Percy Holmes (1886–1971) (224 not out) and Herbert Sutcliffe (1894–1978) (313) for Yorkshire v. Essex at Leyton on 15–16 June 1932.

Longest hit

The longest measured drive is one of 175 yds *160 m* by Walter (later the Rev.) Fellows (1834–1901) of Christ Church, Oxford University, in a practice on their ground off Charles Rogers in 1856. J. E. C. Moore made a measured hit of 170 yds 1 ft 5 in *155,59 m* at Griffith, New South Wales, Australia, in February 1930.

BOWLING

Most wickets *Season*

The largest number of wickets ever taken in a season is 304 by Alfred Percy "Tich" Freeman (1888–1965) of Kent, in 1928. Freeman bowled 1,976.1 overs, of which 423 were maidens, with an average of 18.05 runs per wicket.

Most wickets *Career*

The greatest wicket-taker in history was Wilfred Rhodes (1877–1973) who took 4,187 wickets for 69,993 runs (average 16.71 runs per wicket) between 1898 and 1930. He also holds the record for first-class appearances with 1,107. The highest percentage of wickets gained unassisted is 73.50% (1,479 from 2,012) by Schofield Haigh (1871–1921), who played for Yorkshire from 1895 to 1913.

Most wickets *Tests*

The greatest number of wickets taken in Test matches is 309 for 8,989 runs (average 29.09) by Lancelot Richard Gibbs (b. Georgetown, now Guyana, 29 Sept. 1934) in 79 Tests between 1958 and 1976. The lowest bowling average in a Test career (minimum 15 wickets) is 112 wickets for 1,205 runs (10.75 runs per wicket) by George Alfred Lohmann (1865–1901) in 18 Tests for England between 1886 and 1896.

Most wickets *In an innings*

The taking of all ten wickets by a single bowler has been recorded many times but only one bowler has achieved this feat on three occasions—Alfred Freeman of Kent, against Lancashire at Maidstone on 24 July 1929, against Essex at Southend on 13–14 Aug. 1930 and against Lancashire at Old Trafford, Greater Manchester on 27 May 1931. The fewest runs scored off a bowler taking all ten wickets is ten, when Hedley Verity (1905–43) of Yorkshire dismissed (eight caught, one l.b.w., one stumped) every Nottinghamshire batsman in 118 balls at Leeds on 12 July 1932. The only bowler to have "clean bowled" a whole side out was John Wisden (1826–84) of Sussex, playing for the North v. the South at Lord's in 1850.

Most wickets *Match*

James Charles Laker (b. Frizinghall, West Yorkshire, 9 Feb. 1922) of Surrey took 19 wickets for 90 runs (9–37 and 10–53) for England v. Australia in the Fourth Test at Old Trafford, on 26–31 July 1956. No other bowler has taken more than 17 wickets in a first class match.

Most wickets *In a day*

The greatest number of wickets taken in a day's play is 17 by Colin Blythe (1879–1917) for 48 runs, for Kent against Northamptonshire at Northampton on 1 June 1907; by Hedley Verity for 91 runs, for Yorkshire v. Essex at Leyton on 14 July 1933; and by Thomas William John Goddard (1900–66) for 106 runs, for Gloucestershire v. Kent at Bristol, Avon on 3 July 1939.

Most consecutive wickets

No bowler in first class cricket has yet achieved five wickets with five consecutive balls. The nearest approach was that of Charles Warrington Leonard Parker (1884–1959) (Gloucestershire) in his own benefit match against Yorkshire at Bristol on 10 Aug. 1922, when he struck the stumps with five successive balls but the second was called as a no-ball. The only man to have taken four wickets with consecutive balls more than once is Robert James Crisp (b. 28 May 1911) for Western Province v. Griqualand West at Johannesburg on 23–24 Dec. 1931 and against Natal at Durban on 3 Mar. 1934.

Most "hat tricks"

The greatest number of "hat tricks" is seven by Douglas Vivian Parson Wright (b. 21 Sept. 1914) of Kent, on 3 and 29 July 1937, 18 May 1938, 13 Jan. and 1 July 1939, 11 Aug. 1947 and 1 Aug. 1949. In his own benefit match at Lord's on 22 May 1907, Albert Edwin Trott (Middlesex) took four Somerset wickets with four consecutive balls and then later in the same innings achieved a "hat trick".

GILLETTE CUP, JOHN PLAYER LEAGUE AND BENSON & HEDGES CUP RECORDS

	Gillette Cup (Instituted 1963)	John Player League (Instituted 1969)	Benson and Hedges Cup (Instituted 1972)
Highest Individual Innings	177—C. G. Greenidge, Hants v. Glams. Southampton, 1975	163*—C. G. Greenidge, Hampshire v. Warwickshire, Edgbaston, 1979	173*—C. G. Greenidge, Hants v. Minor Counties (South), Amersham, 1973
Best Individual Bowling	7-15—A. L. Dixon, Kent v. Surrey, Oval, 1967	8-26—K. D. Boyce, Essex v. Lancs. Old Trafford, 1971. *N.B.* A. Ward, Derby v. Sussex, Derby 1970, 4 wickets in 4 balls	7-12—W. W. Daniel, Middx. v. Minor Counties (East), Ipswich, 1978.
Highest Innings Total	371 for 4 (off 60 overs), Hants v. Glams. Southampton, 1975	307 for 4 (off 38 overs) Worcs. v. Derbys. Worcester, 1975	350 for 3 (off 55 overs), Essex v. Combined Universities, Chelmsford, 1979
Lowest Innings Total	41 (off 20 overs), Cambs. v. Bucks., Cambridge, 1972 41 (off 19.4 overs), Middlesex v. Essex, Westcliff, 1972 41 (off 36.1 overs), Shropshire v. Essex, Wellington, 1974	23 (off 19.4 overs), Middlesex v. Yorks., Headingley, 1974	61 (off 26 overs), Sussex v. Middlesex Hove, 1978
Highest Partnership	234* for 4th wicket—D. Lloyd and C. H. Lloyd, Lancs. v. Glos., Old Trafford, 1978	218 for 1st wicket—A. R. Butcher and G. P. Howarth, Surrey v. Gloucestershire, Oval, 1976	285* for 2nd wicket—C. G. Greenidge and D. R. Turner, Hants v. Minor Counties (South), Amersham, 1973

* Not Out

Most expensive bowling

The greatest number of runs hit off one bowler in one innings is 362, scored off Arthur Alfred Mailey (1886–1967) in the New South Wales v. Victoria inter-State match at Melbourne on 24–28 Dec. 1926. The greatest number of runs ever conceded by a bowler in one match is 428 by C. S. Nayudu (b. 18 Apr. 1914) in the Holkar v. Bombay match at Bombay on 4–9 Mar. 1945, when he also made the record number of 917 deliveries.

Most maidens

Hugh Tayfield bowled 16 consecutive eight-ball maiden overs (137 balls without conceding a run) for South Africa v. England at Durban on 25–27 Jan. 1957. The greatest number of consecutive six-ball maiden overs bowled is 21 (130 balls) by Ragunath G. "Bapu" Nadkarni (b. 4 Apr. 1932) for India v. England at Madras on 12 Jan. 1964. The English record is 17 overs (105 balls) by Horace L. Hazell (b. 30 Sept. 1909) for Somerset v. Gloucestershire at Taunton on 4 June 1949, and 17 (104 balls) by Graham Anthony (Tony) Richard Lock (b. 5 July 1929) of Surrey, playing for the M.C.C. v. the Governor-General's XI at Karachi, Pakistan, on 31 Dec. 1955. Alfred Shaw (1842–1907) of Nottinghamshire bowled 23 consecutive four-ball maiden overs (92 balls) for North v. the South at Nottingham in 1876.

Most balls

The greatest number of balls sent down by any bowler in one season is 12,234 (651 maidens: 298 wickets) by Alfred Freeman in 1933. The most balls bowled in an innings is 588 (98 overs) by Sonny Ramadhin (b. 1 May 1930) of Trinidad, playing for the West Indies in the First Test v. England at Edgbaston, West Midlands on 30 May and 1, 3 and 4 June 1957. He took two for 179.

Best average

The lowest recorded bowling average for a season is one of 8.61 runs per wicket (177 wickets for 1,525 runs) by Alfred Shaw of Nottinghamshire in 1880.

Fastest

The highest electronically measured speed for a ball bowled by any bowler is 99.7 m.p.h. *160,45 km/h* by Jeffrey Robert Thomson (b. 16 Aug. 1950) (Australia) during the Second Test v. the West Indies in Dec. 1975. Albert Cotter (1883–1917) of New South Wales, Australia, is reputed to have broken a stump more than 20 times.

ALL-ROUNDERS
The "double"

The "double" of 1,000 runs and 100 wickets in the same season was performed a record number of 16 times by Wilfred Rhodes (1877–1973), of Yorkshire and England, between 1903 and 1926. The greatest number of consecutive seasons in which a player has performed the "double" is 11 (1903–1913) by George Herbert Hirst (1871–1954), of Yorkshire and England. Hirst is also the only player to score 2,000 runs (2,385) and take 200 wickets (208) in the same season (1906).

Test Cricket

The only players to achieve 2,000 runs and 200 wickets in their Test careers are Richard (Richie) Benaud, O.B.E. (b. 6 Oct. 1930), of Australia, with 2,201 runs and 248 wickets between 1952 and 1964, and Sir Garfield Sobers, of West Indies, with 8,032 runs and 235 wickets between 1954 and 1974. The only player to score a century and take eight wickets in a single innings in the same Test is Ian Terrence Botham (b. 24 Nov. 1955) with 108 and eight for 34 for England v Pakistan at Lord's in June 1978.

FIELDING
Most catches *Innings and Match*

The greatest number of catches in an innings is seven, by Michael James Stewart (b. 16 Sept. 1932) for Surrey v. Northamptonshire at Northampton on 7 June 1957, and by Anthony Stephen Brown (b. 24 June 1936) for Gloucestershire v. Nottinghamshire at Trent Bridge, Nottingham on 26 July 1966.

Ian Botham's bowling and batting (here bowled at 108) in the Test against Pakistan at Lords in 1978 was the greatest all-round performance ever in Test cricket. (*Keystone Press*)

Walter Hammond held a record total of ten catches (four in the first innings, six in the second) for Gloucestershire v. Surrey at Cheltenham, Gloucestershire on 16–17 Aug. 1928. The record for a wicket-keeper is 11 (see wicket-keeping).

Most catches *Season and career*

The greatest number of catches in a season is 78 by Walter Hammond in 1928, and 77 by Michael James Stewart in 1957. The most catches in a career is 1,015 by Frank Edward Woolley (1887–1978) of Kent in 1906–1938. The Test record is 120 by Colin Cowdrey between 1954 and 1975.

Longest throw

The longest recorded throw of a cricket ball (5½ oz. *155 g*) is 140 yds 2 ft *128,6 m* by Robert Percival, a left-hander, on Durham Sands Racecourse on Easter Monday, 18 Apr. 1881.

WICKET KEEPING
Most dismissals *Season*

The record number of dismissals for any wicket-keeper in a season is 127 (79 caught, 48 stumped) by Leslie Ethelbert George Ames, C.B.E. (b. 3 Dec. 1905) of Kent in 1929. The record for the number stumped is 64 by Ames in 1932. The record for catches is 96 by James Graham Binks (b. 5 Oct. 1935) of Yorkshire in 1960.

Most dismissals *Career*

The highest total of dismissals in a wicket-keeping career is 1,527 (a record 1,270 catches plus 257 stumpings) by John Thomas Murray M.B.E. (b. 1 Apr. 1935) of Middlesex between 1952 and 1975. The most stumpings in a career is 415 by Leslie Ames between 1926 and 1951. The Test record is 252 dismissals (233 catches, 19 stumpings) in 89 Tests by Alan Philip Eric Knott (b. 9 Apr. 1946) for England between 1967 and 30 Aug. 1977.

Most dismissals *Innings*

The most dismissals by a wicket-keeper in an innings is eight (all caught) by Arthur Theodore Wallace Grout (1927–68) for Queensland against Western Australia at Brisbane on 15 Feb. 1960. The most stumpings in an innings is six by Henry "Hugo" Yarnold (1917–1974) for Worcestershire v. Scotland at Broughty Ferry, Tayside, on 2 July 1951. The Test record is seven (all caught) by Wasim Bari (Pakistan) (b. 23 Mar. 1948) for Pakistan v New Zealand at Auckland on 23 Feb. 1978.

Most dismissals *Match*

The greatest number of dismissals by a wicket-keeper in a match is 12 by Edward Pooley (1838–1907), eight caught, four stumped, for Surrey v. Sussex at the Oval on 6–7 July 1868; nine caught, three stumped by Don Tallon (b. 17 Feb. 1916) of Australia for Queensland v. New South Wales at Sydney on 2–4 Jan. 1939; and also nine caught, three stumped by Hedley Brian Taber (b. 29 Apr. 1940) for New South Wales v South Australia at Adelaide 17–19 Dec. 1968. The record for catches is 11, seven in the first innings and four in the second, by Arnold Long (b. 18 Dec. 1940), for Surrey v. Sussex at Hove, East Sussex on 18 and 21 July 1964, and also by Rodney William Marsh (b. 11 Nov. 1947) for Western Australia v. Victoria at Perth on 15–17 Nov. 1975. The most stumpings in a match is nine by Frederick Henry Huish (1872–1957) for Kent v. Surrey at the Oval on 21–23 Aug. 1911. The Test record for dismissals is nine, eight caught, one stumped, by Gilbert Roche Andrews Langley (b. 19 Sept. 1919), playing for Australia v. England in the Second Test at Lord's on 22–26 June 1956.

TEST RECORDS
Most Test appearances

The record number of Test appearances is 114 by Colin Cowdrey C.B.E. for England between December 1954 and February 1975. The highest number of Test captaincies is 41 including 35 consecutive games by Peter Barker Howard May (b. 31 Dec. 1929) of Cambridge University and Surrey, who captained England from 1955 to 1961 and played in a total of 66 Tests. The most innings batted in Test matches is 188 in 114 Tests by Colin Cowdrey. Sir Garfield Sobers (West Indies) holds the record for consecutive Tests, with 85 from April 1955 to April 1972.

Longest match

The lengthiest recorded cricket match was the "timeless" Test between England and South Africa at Durban on 3–14 Mar. 1939. It was abandoned after ten days (eighth day rained off) because the boat taking the England team home was due to leave. The lengthiest in England have been the six-day Fifth England v. Australia Test on 6–12 Aug. 1930, when rain prevented play on the fifth day, and six-day Fifth England v. Australia Test on 10–16 Aug. 1972, when play took place on all six days.

Largest crowds

The greatest recorded attendance at a cricket match is 350,534 (receipts £30,124) for the Third Test between Australia and England at Melbourne on 1–7 Jan. 1937. For the whole series the figure was a record 933,513 (receipts £87,963). The greatest recorded attendance at a cricket match on one day was 90,800 on the second day of the Fifth Test between Australia and the West Indies at Melbourne on 11 Feb. 1961, when the receipts were £A13,132 £10,484 *sterling*. The English record is 159,000 for the Fourth Test between England and Australia at Headingley, Leeds, West Yorkshire, on 22–27 July 1948, and the record for one day probably a capacity of 46,000 for a match between Lancashire and Yorkshire at Old Trafford on 2 Aug. 1926. The English record for a Test series is 549,650 (receipts £200,428) for the series against Australia in 1953.

Greatest receipts

The world record for receipts from a match is £220,384 at the First Test between England and Australia on 16–18, 20–21 June 1977. The Test series record is £735,995 for the five England v. Australia Tests of June–August 1977.

WORLD CUP

The Prudential World Cup held in 1975 and 1979, was won both times by the West Indies. The highest team score was 334 for 4 by England v India at Lords on 7 June 1975, and the lowest 45 by Canada v England at Old Trafford on 14 June 1979. The highest individual score was 171 not out by Glenn Turner for New Zealand v Sri Lanka at Edgbaston on 7 June 1975. The best bowling, 6 wickets for 14 runs by Gary Gilmour for Australia v England at Leeds on 18 June 1975.

ENGLISH COUNTY CHAMPIONSHIP

The greatest number of victories has been secured by Yorkshire with 31 outright wins, and two shared, with Nottinghamshire 1869 and Middlesex 1949. The most "wooden spoons" have been won by Northamptonshire, with ten since 1923. They did not win a single match between May 1935 and May 1939. The record number of consecutive title wins is seven by Surrey from 1952 to 1958. The greatest number of consecutive appearances for one county in county championship matches is 423 by Kenneth George Suttle (b. 25 Aug. 1928) of Sussex in 1954–69. James Graham Binks (b. 5 Oct. 1935) of Yorkshire played in every county championship match for his side between his debut in 1955 and his retirement in 1969—412 matches. The seven sons of the Rev. Henry Foster, of Malvern, uniquely all played county cricket for Worcestershire between 1899 and 1934.

Oldest and youngest county cricketers

The youngest player to represent his county was William Wade Fitzherbert Pullen (1866–1937), for Gloucestershire against Middlesex at Lord's on 5 June 1882, when aged 15 years 346 days. The oldest regular county players have been William "W. G." Quaife (1872–1951) of Sussex and Warwickshire, who played his full season last match for Warwickshire against Hampshire at Portsmouth on 27–30 Aug. 1927, when aged 55, and John Herbert King (1871–1946) of Leicestershire, who played his last match for his county against Yorkshire at Leicester on 5–7 Aug. 1925, when aged 54.

WOMEN'S CRICKET
Earliest

The first recorded women's match took place at Gosden Common, Surrey, England on 26 July 1745. *Circa* 1807 Christina Willes is said to have introduced the roundarm bowling style. The first Test match was Australia v. England at Brisbane on 28 Dec. 1934. The International Women's Cricket Council was formed in 1958.

Batting *Individual*

The highest individual innings recorded is 224 not out by Mabel Bryant for Visitors v. Residents at Eastbourne, East Sussex, England in Aug. 1901. The highest innings in a Test match is 189 by Elizabeth Alexandra (Betty) Snowball for England v. New Zealand at Christchurch, N.Z. on 16 Feb. 1935. The highest Test innings in England is 179 by Rachael Flint M.B.E. (*née* Heyhoe) for England v. Australia at The Oval, Greater London on 27–28 July 1976. Rachael Flint also has scored the most runs in Test cricket with 1,789 in 22 matches from Dec. 1960 to July 1979.

Batting *Team*

The highest innings score by any team is 567 by Tarana v. Rockley, at Rockley, N.S.W., Australia in 1896. The highest Test innings is 503 for five wickets declared by England v. New Zealand at Christchurch, N.Z. on 16 Feb. 1935. The most in a Test in England is 379 by Australia v. England at The Oval, Greater London on 26–27 July 1976. The highest innings total by any team in England is 406 by South v. Australia at Hove, East Sussex in July 1937.

The lowest innings in a Test is 35 by England v. Australia at

Melbourne, Australia in Feb. 1958. The lowest in a Test in England is 63 by New Zealand at Worcester in July 1954.

Bowling
The greatest number of wickets taken in Test matches is 77 by Mary Duggan (England) in 16 Tests from 1949–63. On 26 June 1931 Rubina Winifred Humphries (b. 19 Aug 1915), for Dalton Ladies v. Woodfield S.C., took all ten wickets for no runs. This was equalled by Rosemary White for Wallington L.C.C. v. Beaconsfield L.C.C. in July 1962.

MINOR CRICKET RECORDS
(where excelling those in First Class Cricket)
Highest individual innings
In a Junior House match between Clarke's House (now Poole's) and North Town, at Clifton College, Bristol, 22–23, 26–28 June 1899, A. E. J. Collins (b. India, 1886—k. Flanders, Nov. 1914) scored an unprecedented 628 not out in 6 hrs 50 min, over five afternoons' batting, carrying his bat through the innings of 836. The scorer, E. W. Pegler, gave the score as "628—plus or minus 20, shall we say".

Fastest individual scoring
Stanley Keppel "Shunter" Coen (South Africa) (1902–67) scored 50 runs (11 fours and one six) in 7 min for Gezira v. the R.A.F. in 1942. The fastest century by a prominent player in a minor match was by Vivian Frank Shergold Crawford (1879–1922) in 19 min at Cane Hill, Surrey on 16 Sept. 1899. Cedric Ivan James Smith hit nine successive sixes for a Middlesex XI v. Harrow and District at Rayner's Lane, Harrow, Greater London in 1935. This feat was repeated by Arthur Dudley Nourse in a South African XI v. Military Police match at Cairo in 1942–43. Nourse's feat included six sixes in one over. Greg Beacroft (b. 20 Jan. 1958) scored 268 (including 29 sixes and 11 fours) in 92 min for Yass Wallaroos v. Williamsdale at Canberra, A.C.T., Australia on 21 Jan. 1979.

Fastest and Slowest scoring rates
In the match Royal Naval College, Dartmouth v. Seale Hayne Agricultural College in 1923, K. A. Sellar (now Cdr. "Monkey" Sellar, D.S.O., D.S.C., R.N.) and Leslie Kenneth Allen Block (now Judge Block, D.S.C.) (b. 9 Aug. 1906) were set to score 174 runs in 105 min but achieved this total in 33 min, so averaging 5.27 runs per min. Playing for Gentlemen of Leicestershire C.C. v. Free Foresters, at Oakham, Rutland, on 19 Aug. 1963, Ian H. S. Balfour batted for 100 min without adding to his score of five runs. He went on to make 39.

Consecutive not out centuries
Gerald Vivian William Lukehurst (b. 5 Oct. 1917) of Kent, hit six consecutive not out centuries for Gore Court and F. Day's XI between 3 July and 20 July 1955.

Most runs off a ball
A scoring stroke of 11 (all run, with no overthrows) was achieved by Lt. (later Lt.-Col.) Philip Mitford (1879–1946), Q.O. Cameron Highlanders, in a Governor's Cup match in Malta on 28 May 1903.

Greatest stand
T. Patten and N. Rippon made a third wicket stand of 641 for Buffalo v. Whorouly at Gapsted, Victoria, Australia, on 19 Mar. 1914.

Bowling
Stephen Fleming bowling for Marlborough College "A" XI, New Zealand v. Bohally Intermediate at Blenheim, New Zealand in December 1967 took nine wickets in nine consecutive balls. In February 1931 in a schools match in South Africa Paul Hugo also took nine wickets with nine consecutive balls for Smithfield School v. Aliwal North. In the Inter-Divisional Ships Shield at Purfleet, Essex, on 17 May 1924, Joseph William Brockley (b. 9 Apr. 1907) took all ten wickets, clean bowled, for two runs in 11 balls—including a triple hat trick.

In 1881 Frederick Robert Spofforth (1853–1926) in Australia

clean bowled all ten wickets in *both* innings. J. Bryant for Erskine v. Deaf Mutes in Melbourne on 15 and 22 Oct. 1887, and Albert Rimmer for Linwood School v. Cathedral G.S. at Canterbury, New Zealand in Dec. 1925 repeated the feat. In 1910, H. Hopkinson, of Mildmay C. C. London, took 99 wickets for 147 runs.

Wicket-keeping
In Ceylon, playing for Mahinda v. Galle, W. J. Bennette caught four and stumped six batsmen in one innings in 1954.

Fielding
In a Wellington, New Zealand secondary schools 11-a-side match on 16 Mar. 1974, Stephen Lane, 13, held 14 catches in the field (seven in each innings) for St. Patrick's College, Silverstream v. St. Bernard's College, Lower Hutt.

Marathon
A match under M.C.C. rules was played by 22 members of Clare House, King Charles I School, Kidderminster, Worcs, England for 72 hr on 16–19 July 1979.

CROQUET
Earliest references
Croquet was probably derived from the French game *Jeu de Mail* first mentioned in the 12th century. In its present-day form, it originated as a country-house lawn game in Ireland in the 1830's when it was called "crokey" and was introduced to Hampshire 20 years later. The first club was formed in the Steyne Gardens, Worthing, West Sussex.

Most championships
The greatest number of victories in the Open Croquet Championships (instituted at Evesham, Hereford and Worcester, 1867) is ten by John William Solomon (b. 1932) (1953, 1956, 1959, 1961, 1963–68). He has also won the Men's Championship on ten occasions (1951, 1953, 1958–60, 1962, 1964–1965, 1971 and 1972), the Open Doubles (with Edmond

A game of croquet in the 1860s. (*Radio Times Hulton Picture Library*)

Patrick Charles Cotter) on ten occasions (1954–55, 1958–59, 1961–65 and 1969) and the Mixed Doubles once (with Mrs. N. Oddie) in 1954, making a total of 31 titles. Solomon has also won the President's Silver Cup (inst. 1934) on nine occasions (1955, 1957–59, 1962–64, 1968 and 1971). He has also been Champion of Champions on all four occasions that this competition has been run (1967–70).

Dorothy Dyne Steel (1884–1965), fifteen times winner of the Women's Championship (1919–39), won the Open Croquet Championship four times (1925, 1933, 1935–36). She had also five Doubles and seven Mixed Doubles titles making a total of 31 titles.

International trophy

The MacRobertson International Shield (instituted 1925) has been played for ten times. It has been won most often by Great Britain with six wins (in 1925, 1937, 1956, 1963, 1969 and 1974). The players to make five international appearances are J. C. Windsor (Australia) in 1925, 1928, 1930, 1935 and 1937 and John Solomon (G.B.) in 1951, 1956, 1963, 1969 and 1974.

Lowest handicap

Historically the lowest playing handicap has been that of Humphrey Osmond Hicks (Devon) (b. 1904) with minus $5\frac{1}{2}$. In 1974 the limit was however fixed at minus 5. The player holding the lowest handicap is G. Nigel Aspinall with minus 5.

Marathon

The longest croquet match on record is one of 100 hours by Peter Olsen, Julio Aznarez, Hazell Kelly and Donald Noack at Manly Croquet Club, N.S.W. Australia on 14–18 May 1978.

CROSS-COUNTRY RUNNING

International championships

The earliest recorded international cross-country race took place over 14,5 km *9 miles 18 yds* from Ville d'Avray, outside Paris, on 20 Mar. 1898, between England and France (England won by 21 points to 69). The inaugural International Cross-Country Championships took place at the Hamilton Park Racecourse, Glasgow, on 28 Mar. 1903. The greatest margin of victory is 56 sec or 390 yds *356 m* by Jack T. Holden (England) at Ayr Racecourse, Scotland, on 24 Mar. 1934. The narrowest win was that of Jean-Claude Fayolle (France) at Ostend, Belgium, on 20 Mar. 1965, when the timekeepers were unable to separate his time from that of Melvyn Richard Batty (England), who was placed second. Since 1973 the race has been run under the auspices of the International Amateur Athletic Federation.

The greatest team wins have been those of England, with a minimum of 21 points (the first six runners to finish) on two occasions, at Gosforth Park, Newcastle, Tyne and Wear, on 22 Mar. 1924, and at the Hippodrome de Stockel, Brussels, Belgium, on 20 Mar. 1932.

Most international appearances

The runners of participating countries with the largest number of international championship appearances are:

Belgium	20	Marcel Van de Wattyne, 1946–65
Wales	14	Danny Phillips, 1922, 1924, 1926–37
England	12	Jack T. Holden, 1929–39, 1946
Spain	14	Mariano Haro, 1962–65, 1967–69, 1971–76, 1977
Scotland	14	Jim N. C. Alder, 1962, 1964–1976
France	14	Noel Tijou, 1963–1975, 1977

Margaret Coomber (*née* MacSherry) for Scotland, and Jean Lochhead for Wales, have competed in all 13 women's races, 1967–79.

Most wins

The greatest number of victories in the International Cross-Country Race is four by Jack Holden (England) in 1933–35 and 1939, by Alain Mimoun-o-Kacha (France) in 1949, 1952,

1954 and 1956 and Gaston Roelants (Belgium) in 1962, 1967, 1969 and 1972. England have won 43 times to 1977. Doris Brown-Heritage (U.S.A.) (b. 17 Sept. 1942) has won the women's race five times, 1967–71.

English championship

The English Cross-Country Championship was inaugurated at Roehampton, Wandsworth, Greater London, in 1877. The most individual titles won is four by Percy H. Stenning (1854–92) (Thames Hare and Hounds) in 1877–80 and Alfred E. Shrubb (1878–1964) (South London Harriers) in 1901–04. The most successful club in the team race has been Birchfield Harriers from Birmingham with 27 wins and one tie between 1880 and 1953. The largest field was the 1,672 starters in 1979 at Luton, Bedfordshire, of whom all but 117 finished.

Largest field

The largest recorded field was one of 7,036 starters (6,299 finished) in the 30 km *18.6 miles* Lidingöloppet, near Stockholm, Sweden, on 10 Oct. 1978.

CURLING

Origins

Although a 15th century bronze figure in the Florence Museum appears to be holding a curling stone, the earliest illustration of the sport was in one of the Flemish painter Pieter Bruegel's winter scenes *c.* 1560. The club with the earliest records, dating back to 1716, is that of Kilsyth, Strathclyde which was resuscitated in 1954. The game was introduced into Canada in 1759. Organized administration began in 1838 with the formation in Edinburgh of the Grand (later Royal) Caledonian Curling Club, the international legislative body until the foundation of the International Curling Federation in 1966. The first indoor ice rink to introduce curling was at Southport, Merseyside in 1879.

The U.S.A. won the first Gordon International Medal series of matches, between Canada and the U.S.A., at Montreal in 1884. The first Strathcona Cup match between Canada and Scotland was won by Canada in 1903. Although demonstrated at the Winter Olympics of 1924, 1932 and 1964, curling has never been included in the official Olympic programme.

Most titles

The record for World championships (inst. 1959) for the Air Canada Silver Broom is 12 wins by Canada, in 1959–64, 1966, 1968–72. The most Strathcona Cup wins is seven by Canada (1903, 1909, 1912, 1923, 1938, 1957, 1965) against Scotland.

Perfect games

A unique achievement is claimed by Bernice Fekete, of Edmonton, Alberta, Canada, who skipped her rink to two consecutive eight-enders on the same sheet of ice at the Derrick Club, Edmonton, on 10 Jan. and 6 Feb. 1973.

Largest bonspiel

The largest bonspiel in the world is the Manitoba Bonspiel held in Winnipeg, Canada. There were 728 teams, or rinks, of four players in the Feb. 1977 tournament.

Largest rink

The world's largest curling rink is the Big Four Curling Rink, Calgary, Alberta, Canada opened in 1959 at a cost of $Can. 2,250,000 £867,050. Each of the two floors has 24 sheets of ice, the total accommodating 96 teams and 384 players.

Marathons

The longest recorded curling match is one of 64 hours 28 mins by eight members of the Pine Point Curling Club, N.W.T., Canada on 13–15 Jan. 1979.

The duration record for two curlers is 24 hr 5 min by Eric Olesen and Warren Knuth at Racine Curling Club, Wisconsin, U.S.A. on 30–31 March 1978. The weight handled was 27.72 tons each.

CYCLING

Earliest race
The earliest recorded bicycle race was a velocipede race over 2 km *1.24 miles* at the Parc de St. Cloud, Paris, on 31 May 1868, won by James Moore (G.B.).

Highest speed
The highest speed ever achieved on a bicycle is 140.5 m.p.h. *226,1 km/h* by Dr. Allan V. Abbott, 29, of San Bernadino, California, U.S.A., behind a wind-shield mounted on a 1955 Chevrolet over ¾ mile *1,2 km* at Bonneville Salt Flats, Utah, U.S.A. on 25 Aug. 1973. His speed over a mile *1,6 km* was 138,674 m.p.h. *223,174 km/h.* It should be noted that considerable help is provided by the slipstreaming effect of the lead vehicle. The first Mile a Minute was achieved by Charles Minthorne Murphy (b. 1872) behind a pacing locomotive on the Long Island Railroad on 30 June 1899 in 57⅘ sec for an average of 62.28 m.p.h. *100,23 km/h.* Allan Abbott recorded an official unpaced 9.22 sec for 200 m (48.52 m.p.h. *78,08 km/h*) on a streamlined bicycle at Ontario, California, U.S.A., on 30 Apr. 1977.

The greatest distance ever covered in one hour is 122,862 km *76 miles 604 yd* by Leon Vanderstuyft (Belgium) (1890–1964) on the Montlhery Motor Circuit, France, on 30 Sept. 1928, achieved from a standing start paced by a motorcycle. The 24 hr record behind pace is 860 miles 367 yd *1 384,367 km* by Hubert Opperman (later Hon. Sir) (b. 29 May 1904) in Australia in 1932.

Most titles *Olympic*
Cycling has been on the Olympic programme since the revival of the Games in 1896. The most gold medals won is three by Paul Masson (France) in 1896, Francisco Verri (Italy) (1885–1945) in 1906 and Robert Charpentier (France) (1916–1966) in 1936. In the "unofficial" 1904 cycling programme, Marcus Hurley (U.S.A.) won four events.

Most titles *British*
Beryl Burton, O.B.E. (b. 12 May 1937), 20 times British all-round time trial champion (1959–78), has won 12 B.C.F. road race titles, 14 track pursuit titles and 58 R.T.T.C. titles. Mrs. Burton's career overshadows all male achievements. Albert White (1889–1965) gained 12 individual National track championships from the ¼ mile to 25 miles in 1920–25 and also shared in three tandem titles.

Tour de France
The greatest number of wins in the Tour de France (inaugurated 1903) is five by Jacques Anquetil (b. 8 Jan. 1934) of France, 1957, 1961–64 and by Eddy Merckx (b. Belgium, 17 June 1945), 1969–72 and 1974. The closest race ever was that of 1968 when after 4 665 km *2,898.7 miles* over the 25 days (27 June–21 July) Jan Janssen (Netherlands) (b. 19 May 1940) beat Herman van Springel (Belgium) in Paris by 38 sec. The fastest average speed was 37,3 km/h *23.2 m.p.h.* by Anquetil in 1962. The longest race was 5 745 km *3,569 miles* in 1926, and most participants were in 1928 when 162 started—only 41 finished.

Four times world champion Hugh Porter is married to Olympic swimming champion Anita Lonsbrough. (*Provincial Sports Photography*)

Tour of Britain (Milk Race)
Three riders have won the Tour of Britain twice each—Bill Bradley (1959–60), Les West (1965, 1967) and Fedor den Hertog (Netherlands) (1969, 1971). The closest race ever was in 1976 when after 1,035 miles *1 665,67 km* over 14 days (30 May–12 June) Bill Nickson (G.B.) (b. 30 Jan. 1953) beat Joe Waugh (G.B.) by 5 sec. Den Hertog recorded the fastest average speed of 25.20 m.p.h. *40,55 km/h* in the 1971 race (1,096 miles *1 763,84 km*). The longest Milk Race was in 1969 (1,515 miles *2 438,16 km*) although the longest ever Tour of Britain was in 1953 (1,631 miles *2 624,84 km* starting and finishing in London) under *Daily Express* sponsorship.

Longest one-day race
The longest single-day "massed start" road race is the 265 miles *426,47 km* London–Holyhead event. The record is 10 hr 49 min 4 sec by Tom Simpson (G.B.) (1937–67) in 1965.

Land's End to John o' Groats
The "end to end" record for the 861 miles *1 414 km* is 1 day 23 hr 23 min 2 sec (average speed 18.17 m.p.h. *29,24 km/h*) by Paul Carbutt (b. 4 July 1950) on 11–13 July 1979. The feminine record is 2 days 11 hr 7 min by Eileen Sheridan (b. 1925) on 9–11 June 1954. She completed 1,000 miles *1 609 km* in 3 days 1 hr.

Most World titles
The greatest number of world titles for a particular event won since the institution of the amateur championships in 1893 and the professional championships in 1895 are:

Amateur Sprint	7	Daniel Morelon (France)	1966–67, 1969–71, 1973, 1975
Amateur 100 km Paced	7	Leon Meredith (U.K.)	1904–05, 1907–09, 1911, 1913
Amateur Road Race	2	Giuseppe Martano (Italy)	1930, 1932
	2	Gustave Schur (East Germany)	1958–59
Professional Sprint	7	Jeff Scherens (Belgium)	1932–37, 1947
	7	Antonio Maspes (Italy)	1955–56, 1959–62, 1964
Amateur Pursuit	3	Guido Messina (Italy)	1947–48, 1953
	3	Tiemen Groen (Netherlands)	1964–66
Professional Pursuit	4	Hugh Porter, M.B.E (U.K.)	1968, 1970, 1972–3
Professional 100 km Paced	6	Guillermo Timoner (Spain)	1955, 1959–60, 1962, 1964–65
Professional Road Race	3	Alfredo Binda (Italy)	1927, 1930, 1932
	3	Henri (Rik) Van Steenbergen (Belgium)	1949, 1956–57
	3	Eddy Merckx (Belgium)	1967, 1971, 1974
Women's titles	7	Beryl Burton, O.B.E. (U.K.)	1959–60, 1962–63, 1966 (pursuits) 1960, 1967 (Road)
	7	Yvonne Reynders (Belgium)	1961, 1964–65 (pursuits) 1959, 1961, 1963, 1966 (Road)

Endurance

Tommy Edward Godwin (1912–1975) (G.B.) in the 365 days of 1939 covered 75,065 miles *120 805 km* or an average of 205.65 miles *330,96 km* per day. He then completed 100,000 miles *160 934 km* in 500 days to 14 May 1940.

The greatest mileage amassed in a cycle tour was more than 402,000 miles *643 700 km* by the itinerant lecturer Walter Stolle (b. Sudetenland, 1926) from 24 Jan. 1959 to 12 Dec. 1976. He visited 159 countries starting from Romford, Essex, England. Among his many misadventures were over 1,000 punctures. From 1922 to 25 Dec. 1973 Tommy Chambers (b. 1903) of Glasgow, had ridden a verified total of 799,405 miles *1 286 517 km*. On Xmas Day he was badly injured and has not ridden since.

Ray Reece (b. 13 July 1930), of **Alverstoke, Hants**, circum-navigated the world (13,325 road miles *21 444 km*) between 14 June and 5 Nov. (143 days) in 1971. Visiting every continent, John W. Hathaway (b. England, 13 Jan. 1925) of Vancouver, Canada covered 50,600 miles *81 300 km* from 10 Nov. 1974–6 Oct. 1976. John Joseph Marino (b. 26 Nov. 1948) rode from Santa Monica to New York City, 2,956 miles *4 757 km* in a record 13 days 1 hr 20 min on 13–26 Aug. 1978. Stan N. Kuhl (b. 31 Dec. 1955) and Steve Jeschien (b. 6 Aug. 1956) of Sunnyvale, Calif. travelled 8,026.7 miles *12 918 km* on a tandem around the United States from 29 June–3 Oct. 1976 to celebrate the Bicentennial.

Vivekananda Selva Kumar Anandan (Sri Lanka) cycled for 187 hr 28 min non-stop around Vihara Maha Devi Park, Colombo, on 2–10 May 1979.

WORLD RECORDS (*In events contested by professional and amateur riders only the better mark is given*)

OPEN AIR TRACKS

MEN

Distance	min sec	Name and Country	Place	Date
Professional unpaced standing start:				
5 km	5:51.6	Ole Ritter (Denmark)	Mexico City	4 Oct. 1968
10 km	11:53.2	Eddy Merckx (Belgium)	Mexico City	25 Oct. 1972
20 km	24:06.8	Eddy Merckx (Belgium)	Mexico City	25 Oct. 1972
100 km	2hr 14:02.5	Ole Ritter (Denmark)	Mexico City	15 Nov. 1971
1 hour	30 miles 1,258 yd *49 431 m*	Eddy Merckx (Belgium)	Mexico City	25 Oct. 1972
Professional motor-paced:				
100 km	1hr 03:40.0	Walter Lohmann (W. Germany)	Wuppertal, W. Germany	24 Oct. 1955
1 hour	58 miles 737 yd *94 015 m*	Walter Lohmann (W. Germany)	Wuppertal, W. Germany	24 Oct. 1955
Amateur unpaced standing start:				
1 km	1:02.4	Pierre Trentin (France)	Zürich, Switzerland	15 Nov. 1970
Amateur unpaced flying start:				
200 metres	10.61	Omari Phakadze (U.S.S.R.)	Mexico City	22 Oct. 1967
500 metres	27.85	Pierre Trentin (France)	Mexico City	21 Oct. 1967
1,000 metres	1:01.14	Luigi Borghetti (Italy)	Mexico City	21 Oct. 1967

WOMEN

Distance	min sec	Name and Country	Place	Date
Unpaced standing start:				
1 km	1:15.1	Irena Kirichenko (U.S.S.R.)	Yerevan, U.S.S.R.	8 Oct. 1966
5 km	6:44.75	Keetie Van Oostenhage (Netherlands)	Munich, W. Germany	16 Sept. 1978
10 km	13:34.39	Keetie Van Oostenhage (Netherlands)	Munich, W. Germany	16 Sept. 1978
20 km	27:26.66	Keetie Van Oostenhage (Netherlands)	Munich, W. Germany	16 Sept. 1978
100 km	2hr 41:32.6	Maria Cressari (Italy)	Milan, Italy	17 Oct. 1974
1 hour	26 miles 1,355 yd *43 082 m*	Keetie Van Oostenhage (Netherlands)	Munich, W. Germany	16 Sept. 1978
Unpaced flying start:				
200 metres	12.3	Lyubov Razuvayeva (U.S.S.R.)	Irkutsk, U.S.S.R.	17 July 1955
500 metres	31.7	Galina Tzareva (U.S.S.R.)	Tbilisi, U.S.S.R.	6 Oct. 1978
1,000 metres	1:12.9	Lyubov Razuvayeva (U.S.S.R.)	Irkutsk, U.S.S.R.	17 July 1955

INDOOR TRACKS

MEN

Distance	min sec	Name and Country	Place	Date
Professional unpaced standing start:				
5 km	6:05.6	Ferdinand Bracke (Belgium)	Grenoble, France	5 Dec. 1964
1 hour	29 miles 192 yd *46 847 m*	Siegfried Adler (W. Germany)	Zürich, Switzerland	2 Aug. 1968
Professional unpaced flying start:				
500 metres	28.6	Oscar Plattner (Switzerland)	Zürich, Switzerland	17 Aug. 1956
1,000 metres	1:01.23	Patrick Sercu (Belgium)	Antwerp, Belgium	3 Feb. 1967
Professional motor-paced:				
100 km	1hr 23:59.8	Guillermo Timoner (Spain)	San Sebastian, Spain	12 Sept. 1965
1 hour	76 miles 669 yd *7 4641 m*	Guy Solente (France)	Paris, France	13 Feb. 1955
Amateur unpaced standing start:				
1 km	1:06.76	Patrick Sercu (Belgium)	Brussels, Belgium	12 Dec. 1964
10 km	12:06.29	Hans-Henrik Oersted (Denmark)	Copenhagen, Denmark	28 Nov. 1978
20 km	25:14.6	Ole Ritter (Denmark)	Zürich, Switzerland	30 Oct. 1966
Amateur unpaced flying start:				
200 metres	10.72	Daniel Morelon (France)	Zürich, Switzerland	4 Nov. 1967
500 metres	28.89	Pierre Trentin (France)	Zürich, Switzerland	4 Nov. 1967

WOMEN

Distance	min sec	Name and Country	Place	Date
Unpaced standing start:				
1,000 metres	1:15.5	Elizabeth Eicholz (E. Germany)	E. Berlin, E. Germany	4 Mar. 1964
Unpaced flying start:				
200 metres	13.17	Luigina Bissoli (Italy)	Milan, Italy	6 Dec. 1978
500 metres	34.32	Luigina Bissoli (Italy)	Milan, Italy	6 Dec. 1978

Cycling

Cyclo-cross

The greatest number of world championships (inst. 1950) have been won by Eric de Vlaeminck (Belgium) (b. 23 Aug. 1945) with the amateur and Open in 1966 and six professional titles in 1968–73. British titles (inst. 1955) have been won most often by John Atkins (b. 7 Apr. 1942) with five amateur (1961–62, 1966–68), seven professional (1969–75) and one Open title in 1977.

Pennine Way

John North (b. 18 Aug. 1943) of Rawtenstall, Lancashire, cycled or carried his machine along the 270 mile *434,5 km*

Pennine Way from Edale, Derbyshire to Kirk Yetholm, Borders in 2 days 8 hr 45 min on 9–11 June 1978.

Slow cycling

David Steed, of Tucson, Arizona, U.S.A., stayed stationary without support for 9 hr 15 min on 25 Nov. 1977.

Roller cycling

The four-man 12 hr record is 717.9 miles *1 155,5 km* by a Northampton team at the Guildhall, Northampton, England on 28 Jan. 1978. The 24 hr record by an individual is 792.7 miles *1 275,7 km* by Bruce W. Hall at San Diego University, Calif., U.S.A. on 22–23 Jan. 1977.

BRITISH RECORDS (*Where a rider set up one or more intermediate records during the same attempt, only the figure for the final distance has been given*)

OPEN AIR TRACKS

MEN

Distance	min sec	Name	Place	Date
Professional unpaced flying start:				
500 metres	31.8	Trevor Bull	Leicester, Leicestershire	12 Aug. 1976
Professional unpaced standing start:				
10 km	13:18.8	Phil Bayton	Leicester, Leicestershire	12 Aug. 1976
20 km	27:24.4	Phil Bayton	Wolverhampton, W. Midlands	10 June 1975
Amateur unpaced standing start:				
1 km	1:08.86	Trevor Gadd	Leicester, Leicestershire	24 July 1978
1 hour	27 miles 979 yd *44 348 m*	Phil Griffiths	Newcastle-under-Lyme, Staffordshire	24 Aug. 1978
Amateur motor-paced standing start:				
50 km	42:58.0	Rik Notley	Leicester, Leicestershire	31 July 1976
1 hour	43 miles 1,426 yd *70 506 m*	Rik Notley	Leicester, Leicestershire	31 July 1976

WOMEN

Distance	min sec	Name	Place	Date
Unpaced standing start:				
3 km	4:14.9	Beryl Burton, O.B.E.	Newcastle-under-Lyme, Staffordshire	18 July 1964
5 km	7:19.0	Carol Barton	Leicester, Leicestershire	13 Aug. 1976
20 km	30:11.8	Carol Barton	Leicester, Leicestershire	10 Oct. 1973
1 hour	24 miles 979 yd *39 520 m*	Carol Barton	Leicester, Leicestershire	10 Oct. 1973

ROAD CYCLING RECORDS
(British) as recognized by the Road Time Trials Council (out and-home records)

MEN

Distance	min sec	Name	Course area	Date
10 miles	20:26	Steve Denton	Blyth, Nottinghamshire	26 Aug. 1978
25 miles	49:24	Alf Engers	Kelvedon, Essex	5 Aug. 1978
30 miles	1hr 02:07	Roger Queen	Kelvedon, Essex	12 Aug. 1978
50 miles	1hr 43:46	John Watson	Boroughbridge, North Yorkshire	23 Aug. 1970
100 miles	3hr 45:28	Phil Griffiths	Boroughbridge, North Yorkshire	20 Aug. 1978
12 hours	281.87 miles *453,62 km*	John Watson	Blyth, Nottinghamshire	7 Sept. 1969
24 hours'	507.00 miles *815,93 km*	Roy Cromack	Cheshire	26–27 July 1969

On 10 Sept. 1974 Teuvo Louhivuori (Finland) cycled from Tampere to Kolari, 830,1 km 515.8 miles in 24 hours—an unofficial world's best performance.

WOMEN

Distance	min sec	Name	Course area	Date
10 miles	21:25	Beryl Burton, O.B.E.	Blyth, Nottinghamshire	29 Apr. 1973
25 miles	53:21	Beryl Burton, O.B.E.	Catterick, North Yorkshire	17 June 1976
30 miles	1hr 12:20	Beryl Burton, O.B.E.	St. Neots, Cambridgeshire	3 May 1969
50 miles	1hr 51:30	Beryl Burton, O.B.E.	Boroughbridge, North Yorkshire	25 July 1976
100 miles	3hr 55:05	Beryl Burton, O.B.E.	Essex	4 Aug. 1968
12 hours	277.25 miles *446,19 km*	Beryl Burton, O.B.E.	Wetherby, West Yorkshire	17 Sept. 1967
24 hours	427.86 miles *688,57 km*	Christine Minto (née Moody)	Cheshire	26–27 July 1969

ROAD RECORDS ASSOCIATION'S STRAIGHT-OUT DISTANCE RECORDS

Distance	hr	min	sec	Name	Date
25 miles		46	23	Alan Richards	1 Sept. 1977
50 miles	1	35	45	David Lloyd	26 Oct. 1974
100 miles	3	28	40	Ray Booty	28 Sept. 1956
1,000 miles	2 days 10	40	0	Reg Randell	19–21 Aug. 1960

PLACE TO PLACE RECORDS
(British) as recognized by the Road Records Association

Distance	hr	min	sec	Name	Date
London to Edinburgh (380 miles *610 km*)	18	49	42	Cliff Smith	2 Nov. 1965
London to Bath and back (212 miles *341 km*)	9	07	05	Les West	28 July 1973
London to York (197 miles *317 km*)	7	41	13	Bob Addy	6 Aug. 1972
London to Brighton and back (107 miles *172 km*)	4	15	8	Phil Griffiths	20 July 1977
Land's End to London (287 miles *461 km*)	12	34	0	Robert Maitland	17 Sept. 1954

EQUESTRIAN SPORTS

See also The Guinness Guide to Equestrianism *by Dorian Williams, published by Guinness Superlatives Ltd. (price £8.95).*

Origins
Evidence of horse-riding dates from a Persian engraving dated *c.* 3,000 B.C. Pignatelli's academy of horsemanship at Naples dates from the 16th century. The earliest jumping competition was at the Agricultural Hall, London, in 1869. Equestrian events have been included in the Olympic Games since 1912.

Most Olympic medals
The greatest number of Olympic gold medals is five by Hans-Günter Winkler (b. 24 July 1926) (West Germany) who won four team gold medals as captain in 1956, 1960, 1964 and 1972 and won the individual Grand Prix in 1956. The most team wins in the Prix des Nations is five by Germany in 1936, 1956, 1960, 1964 and 1972. The lowest score obtained by a winner is no faults by Frantisek Ventura (b. 27 Oct. 1895) (Czechoslovakia) on *Eliot*, 1928 and Alwin Schockemöhle (b. 29 May 1937) (West Germany) on *Warwick Rex*, 1976. Pierre Jonqueres d'Oriola (b. 1 Feb. 1920) (France) is the only two time winner of the individual gold medal in 1952 and 1964. Richard John Hannay Meade, O.B.E. (b. 4 Dec. 1938) (Great Britain) is the only British rider to win three gold medals—as an individual in 1972 and team titles in 1968 and 1972, all in the 3-day event.

Most titles *World*
The men's world championships (inst. 1953) have been won twice by Hans-Günter Winkler (W. Germany) (1954–55) and Raimondo d'Inzeo (Italy) (1956 and 1960). The women's title (inst. 1965) has been won twice by Jane "Janou" Tissot (*née* Lefebvre) (France) (b. Saigon, 14 May 1945) on *Rocket* (1970 and 1974).

Most titles *B.S.J.A.*
The most B.S.J.A. championships won is five by Alan Oliver (1951, 1954, 1959, 1969–70). The only horses to have won twice are *Maguire* (Lt.-Col. Nathaniel Kindersley) in 1945 and 1947, *Sheila* (Seamus Hayes) in 1949–50, *Red Admiral* (Oliver) in 1951 and 1954 and *Stroller* (Marion Mould) in 1968 and 1971. The record for the Ladies' Championship is eight by Patricia Smythe (b. 22 Nov. 1928), now Mrs. Samuel Koechlin, O.B.E. (1952–53, 1955, 1957–59, 1961–62). She won on *Flanagan*, owned by Robert Hanson, C.B.E., in 1955, 1958 and 1962—the only three time winner.

Lucinda Prior-Palmer riding *Killaire* on the way to her fourth Badminton Three-Day Event title. (*John Starr, All-Sport Photographic*)

Pierre Jonqueres d'Oriola won the 1966 World championship to add to his two Olympic gold medals. (*Popperfoto*)

George V Gold Cup and Queen Elizabeth II Cup
David Broome (b. 1 Mar. 1940) has won this premier award (first held in 1911) a record four times, in 1960 on *Sunsalve*, 1966 on *Mister Softee*, 1972 on *Sportsman* and 1977 on *Philco*. The Queen Elizabeth II Cup, (first held in 1949) the premier award for women, has been won outright three times by Marion Mould (*née* Coakes) (G.B.) (1965, 1971) on *Stroller* and 1976 on *Elizabeth Ann*. The only horse to win both these trophies is *Sunsalve* in 1957 (with Elisabeth Anderson) and 1960.

President's Trophy
Instituted in 1965, the Trophy has been won most times by Great Britain with eight in 1965, 1967, 1970, 1972–74, 1977–78.

Three-day event
The Badminton Three-Day Event (inst. 1949) has been won four times by Lucinda Prior-Palmer M.B.E. (b. 7 Nov. 1953) in 1973 (on *Be Fair*), 1976 (*Wide Awake*), 1977 (*George*), and 1979 (*Killaire*).

Jumping records
The official *Fédération Equestre Internationale* high jump record is 8 ft 1¼ in *2,47 m* by *Huasó*, ridden by Capt. Alberto Larraguibel Morales (Chile) at Vina del Mar, Santiago, Chile, on 5 Feb. 1949, and 27 ft 2¾ in *8,30 m* for long jump over water by *Amado Mio* ridden by Lt.-Col. Lopez del Hierro (Spain), at Barcelona, Spain on 12 Nov. 1951. *Heatherbloom*, ridden by Dick Donnelly was reputed to have covered 37 ft *11,28 m* in clearing an 8 ft 3 in *2,51 m* puissance jump at Richmond, Virginia, U.S.A. in 1903. H. Plant on *Solid Gold* cleared 36 ft 3 in *11,05 m* over water at the Wagga Show, New South Wales, Australia on 28 Aug. 1936. The official Australian record is 32 ft 10 in *10,00 m* by *Monarch* in Brisbane in 1951. *Jerry M.* allegedly cleared 40 ft *12,19 m* over the water at Aintree in 1912.

At Cairns, Queensland, *Golden Meade* ridden by Jack Martin cleared an unofficially measured 8 ft 6 in *2,59 m* on 25 July 1946. *Ben Bolt* was credited with clearing 9 ft 6 in *2,89 m* at the 1938 Royal Horse Show, Sydney, Australia. The Australian record is 8 ft 4 in *2,54 m* by *Flyaway* (Colin Russell) in 1939 and *Golden Meade* (A. L. Payne) in 1946. The world's unofficial best for a woman is 7 ft 8 in *2,34 m* by Katrina Towns (now Musgrove) (Australia) on *Big John* at Cairns, Queensland, Australia in 1978. The greatest recorded height reached bareback is 6 ft 7 in *2,00 m* by *Silver Wood* at Heidelberg, Victoria, Australia, on 10 Dec. 1938.

The highest British performance is 7 ft 7⁵⁄₁₆ in *2,32 m* by the 16.2 hands *167 cm* grey gelding *Lastic* ridden by Nick Skelton (b. 30 Dec. 1957) at Olympia, Greater London, on 16 Dec. 1978. On 25 June 1937, at Olympia, the Lady Wright (*née* Margery Avis Bullows) set the best recorded height for a British equestrienne on her liver chestnut *Jimmy Brown* at 7 ft 4 in *2,23 m*.

Driving

The biennial World Driving Championships have been held four times since 1972. Great Britain won the team gold medal in 1972 and 1974, and the team bronze in 1978. The best individual performance by a Briton has been a silver medal won by Col. Sir John Miller in 1972.

Longest ride

Aimé Felix Tschiffely rode 10,000 miles *16 093 km* from Buenos Aires, Argentina to Washington D.C., U.S.A. in 504 days starting on 23 Apr. 1925, with two horses, *Mancha* and *Gato*.

Horsemanship marathon

Michael Grealy of Australia rode at all paces (including jumping) for 55 hr 26 min at Blackwater, Queensland on 5–7 May 1978.

FENCING

Origins

"Fencing" (fighting with single sticks) was practised as a sport in Egypt as early as *c.* 1360 B.C. The first governing body for fencing in Britain was the Corporation of Masters of Defence founded by Henry VIII before 1540 and fencing has been practised as sport, notably in prize fights, since that time. The foil was the practice weapon for the short court sword from the 17th century. The épée was established in the mid-19th century and the light sabre was introduced by the Italians in the late 19th century.

Most titles *World*

The greatest number of individual world titles won is four by d'Oriola (see details in table), but note that he also won two individual Olympic titles. Of the three women foilists with three world titles, Heléne Mayer (Germany) (1929, 1931, 1937), Ellen Muller-Preis (Austria) (1947, 1949, 1950) and Ilona Schacherer-Elek (Hungary), (1934–35 1951), only Elek won two individual Olympic titles (1936 and 1948).

Most titles *Olympic*

The most individual Olympic gold medals won is three by Ramón Fonst (Cuba) (1883–1959) in 1900 and 1904 (two) and by Nedo Nadi (Italy) (1894–1952) in 1912 and 1920 (two). Nadi also won three team gold medals in 1920 making a then unprecedented total of five gold medals at one celebration. Edoardo Mangiarotti (Italy) (b. 7 Apr. 1919) with six gold, five silver and two bronze holds the record of 13 Olympic medals. He won them for foil and épée from 1936 to 1960. The most gold medals by a woman is four (three individual, one team) by Elena Novikova–Belova (U.S.S.R.) (b. 28 July 1947) from 1968 to 1976, and the record for all medals is seven (two gold, three silver, two bronze) by Ildikó Sagine-Retjöo (formerly Ujlaki-Retjö) (Hungary) (b. 11 May 1937) from 1960 to 1976.

Italy's Edoardo Mangiarotti (*left*) and France's Christian d'Oriola, who between them have won 19 Olympic fencing medals. (*Popperfoto*)

British Olympic records

The only British fencer to win a gold medal is Gillian Mary Sheen (b. 21 Aug. 1928) in the 1956 foil. A record three Olympic medals has been won by Edgar Seligman with silver medals in the épée team event in 1906, 1908 and 1912. Henry William Furse Hoskyns M.B.E. (b. 19 Mar. 1931) has competed most often for Great Britain with six Olympic appearances, 1956–1976.

FIVES

ETON FIVES

A handball game against the buttress of Eton College Chapel was first recorded in 1825. New courts were built at Eton in 1840, the rules were codified in 1877, rewritten laws were introduced in 1931 and the laws were last drawn up in 1950. There are courts in several countries besides England, with more than a dozen in northern Nigeria.

Most titles

Only one pair has won the Amateur Championship (Kinnaird Cup) eight times—Anthony Hughes and Arthur James Gordon Campbell (1958, 1965–68, 1971, 1973 and 1975). Hughes was also in the winning pair in 1963 making nine

---

MOST OLYMPIC AND WORLD FENCING TITLES

Event	Olympic Gold Medals		World Championships (not held in Olympic years)	
Men's Foil, Individual	2	Christian d'Oriola (France) (b. 3 Oct. 1928) 1952, 56	4	Christian d'Oriola (France) (b. 3 Oct. 1928) 1947, 49, 53–54
	2	Nedo Nadi (Italy) (1894–1952) 1912, 20		
Men's Foil, Team	5	France 1924, 32, 48, 52, 68	12	Italy 1929–31, 33–35, 37–38, 49–50, 54–55
Men's Epée, Individual	2	Ramón Fonst (Cuba) (1883–1959) 1900, 04	3	Georges Buchard (France) (b. 21 Dec. 1893) 1927, 31, 33
			3	Aleksey Nikanchikov (U.S.S.R.) (1940–72) 1966–67, 70
Men's Epée, Team	6	Italy 1920, 28, 36, 52, 56, 60	10	Italy 1931, 33, 37, 49–50, 53–55, 57–58
Men's Sabre, Individual	2	Dr. Jenö Fuchs (Hungary) (b. 29 Oct. 1882) 1908, 12	3	Aladár Gerevich (Hungary) (b. 16 Mar. 1910) 1935, 51, 55
	2	Rudolf Kárpáti (Hungary) (b. 17 July 1920) 1956, 60	3	Jerzy Pawlowski (Poland) (b. 25 Oct. 1932) 1957, 65–66
	2	Jean Georgiadis (Greece) (b. 1874) 1896, 1906	3	Yakov Rylsky (U.S.S.R.) (b. 25 Oct. 1928) 1958, 61, 63
Men's Sabre, Team	9	Hungary 1908, 12, 28, 32, 36, 48, 52, 56, 60	15	Hungary 1930–31, 33–35, 37, 51, 53–55, 57–58, 66, 73, 78
Women's Foil, individual	2	Ilona Schacherer-Elek (Hungary) (b. 1907) 1936, 48	3	Helène Mayer (Germany) (1910–53) 1929, 31, 37
			3	Ilona Schacherer-Elek (Hungary) (b. 17 May 1907) 1934–35, 51
			3	Ellen Muller-Preis (Austria) (b. 6 May 1912) 1947, 49, 50 (shared)
Women's Foil, Team	4	U.S.S.R. 1960, 68, 72, 76	12	U.S.S.R. 1956, 58, 61, 65–66, 70–71, 74–75, 77–78
			12	Hungary 1933–35, 37, 52–55, 59, 62, 67, 73

MOST AMATEUR FENCING ASSOCIATION TITLES

Foil	(Instituted 1898)	7	John Emrys Lloyd (b. 1906)	1928, 1930–33, 1937–38
Epée	(Instituted 1904)	6	Edward O. (Teddy) Bourne (b. 30 Sept. 1948)	1966, 1972, 1974, 1976–78
Sabre	(Instituted 1898)	6	Dr. Roger F. Tredgold (1912–1975)	1937, 1939, 1947–49, 1955
Foil (Ladies)	(Instituted 1907)	10	Gillian M. Sheen (now Mrs. R. G. Donaldson)	1949, 1951–58, 1960

titles in all. The Clubs championship (the Barber Cup) has been won six times by Old Cholmeleians out of ten final appearances.

RUGBY FIVES

As now known, this game dates from c. 1850 with the first inter-public school matches recorded in the early 1870s. The Oxford v. Cambridge contest was inaugurated in 1925 and the Rugby Fives Association was founded in the home of Dr. Cyriax, in Welbeck Street, City of Westminster, Greater London, on 29 Oct. 1927. The dimensions of the Standard Rugby Fives court were approved by the Association in 1931.

Most titles

The greatest number of Amateur Singles Championships (instituted 1932) ever won is six by Wayne Enstone in 1973–78. The record for the Amateur Doubles Championship (instituted 1925) is seven shared by John Frederick Pretlove (1952, 1954, 1956–59, 1961) and David E. Gardner (1960, 1965–66, 1970–72, 1974).

FOOTBALL (ASSOCIATION)

A specialist volume The Guinness Book of Soccer Facts and Feats *(2nd ed.) by Jack Rollin has been published by Guinness Superlatives Ltd. (price £5.95).*

Origins

A game with some similarities termed *Tsu-chu* was played in China in the 3rd and 4th centuries B.C. A football game, Calcio, existed in Italy in 1410. One of the earliest references to the game in England refers to the accidental death of a goal-keeper on 23 Feb. 1582 in Essex. The earliest clear representation of the game is an Edinburgh print dated 1672–73. The game was standardized with the formation of the Football Association in England on 26 Oct. 1863. The oldest club is Sheffield F.C., formed on 24 Oct. 1857. Eleven per side became standard in 1870.

PROFESSIONAL

Longest match

The duration record for first class fixtures was set in the Copa Libertadores in Santos, Brazil, on 2–3 Aug. 1962, when Santos drew 3–3 with Penarol F.C. of Montevideo, Uruguay. The game lasted 3½ hours (with interruptions), from 9.30 p.m. to 1 a.m.

The longest British match on record was one of 3 hours 25 min between Stockport County and Doncaster Rovers in the second leg of the Third Division (North) Cup at Edgeley Park, Stockport, Greater Manchester on 26 Mar. 1946.

HIGHEST SCORES

Teams

The highest score recorded in a British first-class match is 36. This occurred in the Scottish Cup match between Arbroath and Bon Accord on 5 Sept. 1885, when Arbroath won 36–0 on their home ground. But for the lack of nets and the consequent waste of retrieval time the score must have been even higher.

Internationals

The highest margin recorded in an international match is 17. This occurred in the England v. Australia match at Sydney on 30 June 1951, when England won 17–0. This match is not listed by England as a *full* international. The highest in the British Isles was when England beat Ireland 13–0 at Belfast on 18 Feb. 1882.

F.A. Cup

The highest score in an F.A. Cup match is 26, when Preston North End beat Hyde 26–0 at Deepdale, Lancashire on 15 Oct. 1887. This is also the highest score between English clubs. The biggest victory in a final tie is six when Bury beat Derby County 6–0 at Crystal Palace on 18 Apr. 1903, in which year Bury did not concede a single goal in the five Cup matches.

League match

The highest score by one side in a Football League (Division I) match is 12 goals when West Bromwich Albion beat Dar-

wen 12–0 at West Bromwich, West Midlands on 4 Apr. 1892; when Nottingham Forest beat Leicester Fosse by the same score at Nottingham on 21 Apr. 1909; and when Aston Villa beat Accrington 12–2 at Perry Barr, West Midlands on 12 Mar. 1892.

League match aggregate

The highest aggregate in League Football was 17 goals when Tranmere Rovers beat Oldham Athletic 13–4 in a Third Division (North) match at Prenton Park, Merseyside, on Boxing Day, 1935. The record margin in a League match has been 13 in the Newcastle United 13, Newport County 0 (Division II) match on 5 Oct. 1946 and in the Stockport County 13, Halifax 0 (Division III (North)) match on 6 Jan. 1934.

League season

The highest number of goals by any British team in a professional league in a season is 142 in 34 matches by Raith Rovers (Scottish Division II) in the 1937–38 season. The English League record is 134 in 46 matches by Peterborough United (Division IV) in 1960–61.

Individual

The most scored by one player in a first-class match is 16 by Stephan Stanis (*né* Stanikowski, b. Poland, 15 July 1913) for Racing Club de Lens v. Aubry-Asturies, in Lens, France, in a wartime French Cup game on 13 Dec. 1942. The record for any British first-class match is 13 by John Petrie in the Arbroath v. Bon Accord Scottish Cup match in 1885 (see above). The record in League Football is ten by Joe Payne (1914–77) for Luton Town v. Bristol Rovers in a Third Division (South) match at Luton on 13 Apr. 1936. The English First Division record is seven goals by Ted Drake (b. 16 Aug. 1912) for Arsenal v. Aston Villa at Birmingham on 14 Dec. 1935, and James David Ross ("The Little Demon") for Preston North End v. Stoke at Preston on 6 Oct. 1888. The Scottish First Division record is eight goals by James Edward McGrory (b. 26 Apr. 1904) for Celtic v. Dunfermline Athletic at Celtic Park, Glasgow, on 14 Jan. 1928.

The record number of goals scored by one player in an international match is ten by Gottfried Fuchs for Germany who beat Russia 16–0 in the 1912 Olympic tournament (consolation event) in Sweden.

The record for individual goal-scoring in a British home international is six by Joe Bambrick (b. 3 Nov. 1905) for Ireland v. Wales at Belfast on 1 Feb. 1930.

Career

Artur Friedenreich (1892–1969) (Brazil) scored an undocumented 1,329 goals in a 43 yr first class football career. The most goals scored in a specified period is 1,216 by Edson Arantes do Nascimento (b. Baurú, Brazil, 23 Oct. 1940), known as Pelé, the Brazilian inside left, from 7 Sept. 1956 to 2 Oct. 1974 in 1,254 games. His best year was 1958 with 139 and the *milesimo* (1,000th) came in a penalty for his club Santos in the Maracaña Stadium, Rio de Janeiro on 19 Nov. 1969 when playing his 909th first-class match. He later played for New York Cosmos and on his retirement on 1 Oct. 1977 his total had reached 1,281, in 1,363 games. Franz "Bimbo" Binder (b. 1911) scored 1,006 goals in 756 games in Austria and Germany between 1930 and 1950.

The best season League records are 60 goals in 39 League games by William Ralph "Dixie" Dean (b. Birkenhead, 22 Jan. 1907) for Everton (Division I) in 1927–28 and 66 goals in 38 games by Jim Smith for Ayr United (Scottish Division II) in the same season. With three more in Cup ties and 19 in representative matches Dean's total was 82.

The international career record for England is 49 goals by Robert (Bobby) Charlton, O.B.E. (b. Ashington, Northumberland, 11 Oct. 1937). His first was v. Scotland on 19 Apr. 1958 and his last on 20 May 1970 v. Colombia.

The greatest number of goals scored in British first-class football is 550 (410 in Scottish League matches) by James McGrory of Glasgow Celtic (1922–38). The most scored in

The French soccer team Lens, with Stephan Stanis (front row, extreme right) who scored 16 goals in one match for them. (*Presse Sports*)

League matches is 434, for West Bromwich Albion, Fulham, Leicester City and Shrewsbury Town, by George Arthur Rowley (b. Wolverhampton, 21 Apr. 1926) between 1946 and April 1965. Rowley also scored 32 goals in the F.A. Cup and one for England "B".

Fastest goals

The fastest goal on record was one scored in 6 sec. by Albert Mundy for Aldershot in a Fourth Division match *v.* Hartlepools United at Victoria Ground, Hartlepool, Cleveland on 25 Oct. 1958. The same time was recorded by Barrie Jones in a Third Division match *v.* Torquay United on 31 Mar. 1962, and by Keith Smith of Crystal Palace in a Second Division match *v.* Derby County at the Baseball Ground, Derby on 12 Dec. 1964. A hat-trick in 1 min 50 sec is claimed for Maglioni of Independiente *v.* Gimnasia y Escrima de la Plata in Argentina on 18 Mar. 1973. John McIntyre (Blackburn Rovers) scored four goals in 5 min *v.* Everton at Ewood Park, Blackburn, Lancashire on 16 Sept. 1922. W. 'G.' (Ginger) Richardson (West Bromich Albion) scored four goals in 5 min against West Ham United at Upton Park on 7 Nov. 1931. Frank Keetley scored six goals in 21 min in the 2nd half of the Lincoln City *v.* Halifax Town league match on 16 Jan. 1932. The international record is three goals in 3½ min by Willie Hall (Tottenham Hotspur) for England against Ireland on 16 Nov. 1938 at Old Trafford, Greater Manchester.

The fastest goal in World Cup competition was one in 30 sec. by Olle Nyberg for Sweden *v.* Hungary in Paris, 16 June 1938.

Fastest own goal

Torquay United's Pat Kruse equalled the fastest goal on record when he headed the ball into his own net only 6 sec after kick-off *v.* Cambridge United on 3 Jan. 1977.

Longest unbeaten streak

Leeds United were undefeated in 34 consecutive First Division matches from 19 Oct. 1968 to 30 Aug. 1969. In Scottish Football Glasgow Celtic were undefeated in 63 matches, 13 Nov. 1915–21 Apr. 1917.

F.A. CHALLENGE CUP
Most wins

The greatest number of F.A. Cup wins is seven by Aston Villa in 1887, 1895, 1897, 1905, 1913, 1920 and 1957 (nine final appearances). Of the six-time winners Newcastle United have been in the final 11 times. The highest aggregate scores have been 6–1 in 1890, 6–0 in 1903 and 4–3 in 1953.

The greatest number of Scottish F.A. Cup wins is 25 by Celtic in 1892, 1899, 1900, 1904, 1907–08, 1911–12, 1914, 1923, 1925, 1927, 1931, 1933, 1937, 1951, 1954, 1965, 1967, 1969, 1971, 1972, 1974, 1975 and 1977.

Youngest player

The youngest player in a F.A. Cup Final was Howard Kendall (b. 22 May 1946) of Preston North End, who played against West Ham United on 2 May 1964, 20 days before his 18th birthday. Note however, that Derek Johnstone (Rangers) (b. 4 Nov. 1953) was 16 years 11 months old when he played in the Scottish League Cup Final against Celtic on 24 Oct. 1970. The youngest goal scorer in the F.A. Cup Final was John Sissons (b. 30 Sept. 1945) who scored for West Ham United *v.* Preston North End on 2 May 1964. The youngest player ever in the F.A. Cup competition was Scott Endersby (b. 20 Feb. 1962) who was only 15 yrs 288 days old when he played in goal for Kettering *v.* Tilbury on 26 Nov. 1977.

Most medals

Three players have won five F.A. Cup Winner's Medals: James Forrest (Blackburn Rovers) (1884–86, 1890–91); the Hon. Sir Arthur Fitzgerald Kinnaird, K.T. (Wanderers) (1873, 1877–78) and Old Etonians (1879, 1882) and Charles H. R. Wollaston (Wanderers) (1872–73, 1876–78).

Longest tie

The most protracted F.A. Cup tie in the competition proper was that between Stoke City and Bury in the third round with Stoke winning 3–2 in the fifth meeting after 9 hours 22 min of play in January 1955. The matches were at Bury (1–1) on 8 January; Stoke on Trent on 12 January (abandoned after 22 min of extra time with the score 1–1); Goodison Park (3–3) on 17 January; Anfield (2–2) on 19 January; and finally at Old Trafford on 24 January. In the 1972 final qualifying round Alvechurch beat Oxford City after five previous drawn games.

FOOTBALL LEAGUE CUP
Most Wins

The most Football League Cup wins is three by Aston Villa in 1961, 1975 and 1977.

MOST LEAGUE CHAMPIONSHIPS
World

The world record number of successive national League championship wins is nine by Celtic (Scotland) 1966–74, C.S.K.A., Sofia (Bulgaria) 1954–62 and M.T.K. Budapest (Hungary) 1917–25. The Sofia club hold a European post-war record of 19 league titles.

English

The greatest number of League Championships (Division I) is 11 by Liverpool in 1901, 1906, 1922, 1923, 1947, 1964, 1966, 1973, 1976, 1977 and 1979. The record number of points in Division I is 68 by Liverpool in 1978–9. The lowest in the League has been eight by Doncaster Rovers (Division II) in 1904–5. Doncaster Rovers scored 72 points from 42 games in Division III (North) in 1946–7. Lincoln City achieved 74 points from 46 games in Division IV in 1975–6.

"Double"

The only F.A. Cup and League Championship "doubles" are those of Preston North End in 1889, Aston Villa in 1897, Tottenham Hotspur in 1961 and Arsenal in 1971. Preston won the League without losing a match and the Cup without having a goal scored against them throughout the whole competition. Glasgow Rangers have won the Scottish League Championship 35 times between 1899 and 1976 and were joint champions on another occasion. Their 76 points in the Scottish First Division in 1920–1 represents a record in any division.

Closest win

In 1923–24 Huddersfield won the Division I championship over Cardiff by 0.02 of a goal with a goal average of 1.81.

TOURNAMENT RECORDS
World Cup

The *Fédération Internationale de Football* (F.I.F.A.) was founded in Paris on 21 May 1904 and instituted the World Cup Competition on 13 July 1930, in Montevideo, Uruguay.

The only country to win three times has been Brazil in 1958, 1962 and 1970. Brazil was also second in 1950 and third in 1938 and 1978, and is the only one of the 45 participating countries to have played in all eleven competitions. Antonio Carbajal (b. 1923) played for Mexico in goal in the five competitions from 1950 to 1966. The record goal scorer has been Just Fontaine (b. Marrakesh, Morocco, 18 Aug. 1933) (France) with 13 goals in six games in the final stages of the 1958 competition in Sweden. The most goals scored in a final is three by Geoffrey Charles Hurst M.B.E. (b. Ashton-under-Lyne, Greater Manchester, 1941) (West Ham United) for England v. West Germany on 30 July 1966. Gerd Müller (West Germany) (b. 3 Nov. 1945) holds the aggregate record for goals scored in the World Cup Finals with 14 in 1970 and 1974.

World Club Championship

This club tournament was started in 1960 between the winners of the European Cup and the Copa Libertadores, the South American equivalent. Three clubs have won it twice: Penarol, Uruguay in 1961, 1966; Santos, Brazil in 1962, 1963; and Inter-Milan in 1964, 1965.

European Championship (*formerly Nations Cup*)

The European equivalent of the World Cup started in 1958 and is staged every four years. Each tournament takes two years to run with the semi-finals and final in the same country. The U.S.S.R. won the first when they beat Yugoslavia 2–1 in Paris on 10 July 1960 followed by Spain (1964), Italy (1968), West Germany (1972) and Czechoslovakia in 1976.

European Champion Clubs Cup

The European Cup for the League champions of the respective nations was approved by F.I.F.A. on 8 May 1955 and

was run by the European governing body U.E.F.A. (Union of European Football Associations) which came into being in the previous year. Real Madrid won the first final, and have won a record six times, including five times consecutively, 1956–60, 1966.

Glasgow Celtic became the first British club to win the Cup beating Inter-Milan 2–1 in Lisbon, Portugal, on 25 May 1967. They also became the only British club to win the European Cup and the two senior domestic tournaments (League and Cup) in the same season. On 10 May 1978 Liverpool won the Cup for the second successive year, beating F.C. Bruges 1–0 at Wembley.

European Cup Winners Cup

A tournament for the national Cup winners started in 1960–61 with ten entries. Fiorentina beat Glasgow Rangers 4–1 on aggregate in a two-leg final in May 1961. Tottenham Hotspur were the first British club to win the trophy, beating Atletico Madrid 5–1 in Rotterdam in 1963.

U.E.F.A. Cup

Originally known as the International Inter-City Industrial Fairs Cup, this club tournament began in 1955. The first competition lasted three years, the second two years. In 1960–61 it became an annual tournament and since 1971–72 has been replaced by the U.E.F.A. Cup. The first British club to win the trophy were Leeds United in 1968. The most wins is three by Barcelona in 1958, 1960 and 1966.

PLAYERS
Most international appearances

Robert Frederick (Bobby) Moore, O.B.E. (b. Barking, Greater London, 12 Apr. 1941) of West Ham United and Fulham set up a new record of full international appearances by a British footballer by playing in his 108th game for England v. Italy on 14 Nov. 1973 at Wembley. His first appearance was v. Peru on 20 May 1962 and he retired from professional football on 14 May 1977 on his 1,000th appearance in all matches.

Most appearances *England*

The greatest number of appearances for England secured in the International Championship is 38 by William (Billy) Ambrose Wright, C.B.E. (b. Ironbridge, Salop, 6 Feb. 1924) in 1946–1959.

Most appearances *Wales*

The record number of appearances for Wales in the International Championship is 48 by William Henry (Billy) Meredith (1874–1958) (Manchester City and United) in the longest international span of 26 years (1895–1920). This is a record for any of the four home countries. Ivor Allchurch, M.B.E. (b. 29 Dec. 1929) of Swansea, Newcastle, Cardiff City and Worcester City played 68 times for Wales, including 37 times against the home countries, between 15 Nov. 1950 and Feb. 1968.

Most appearances *Scotland*

The Scottish record for International Championship matches is 30 by Alan Morton (1895–1971) (Queen's Park and Glasgow Rangers) from 1920 to 1932. Morton also had a single foreign international making a total of 31 caps. Kenny Dalglish (b. Glasgow, 4 Mar. 1951), of Celtic and Liverpool, has a record total of 65 appearances for Scotland between Nov. 1971 and June 1979.

Most appearances *N. Ireland*

The greatest number of appearances for Ireland is 80 by Patrick Jennings (b. Newry, 12 June 1945) (Watford, Tottenham Hotspur, Arsenal) Apr. 1964 to June 1979.

Oldest cap

The oldest cap has been Billy Meredith who played outside right for Wales v. England at Highbury, Islington, Greater London, on 15 Mar. 1920 when aged 45 years 229 days.

Youngest caps

The youngest cap in the four home countries internationals has been Norman Kernoghan (Belfast Celtic) who played for

top left: As well as scoring a record 14 goals in World Cup finals, Gerd Müller (West Germany) twice won the title of Europe's leading goalscorer. (*Syndication International*)

top right: Ivor Allchurch's 68 international caps included helping Wales reach the quarter finals of the 1958 World Cup. (*Syndication International*)

bottom left: Britain's first million pound player—Trevor Francis—scored the goal which won his new club, Nottingham Forest, the European Champions Cup. (*Provincial Sports Photography*)

bottom right: Jimmy Dickinson has been a stalwart of the Portsmouth Club for over thirty years, as player (a record 764 matches), scout, secretary and manager. (*Syndication International*)

Sixteen times an international himself, Germany's Helmut Schoen went on to become the world's most successful national soccer coach. (*Sporting Pictures*)

Ireland *v*. Wales in 1936 aged 17 years 80 days. It is possible, however, that W. K. Gibson (Cliftonville) who played for Ireland *v*. Wales on 24 Feb. 1894 at 17 was slightly younger. England's youngest home international was Duncan Edwards (b. Dudley, West Midlands, 1 Oct. 1936, d. 21 Feb. 1958, 15 days after the Munich air crash) the Manchester United left half, against Scotland at Wembley on 2 Apr. 1955, aged 18 years 183 days. The youngest Welsh cap was John Charles (b. Swansea, 27 Dec. 1931) the Leeds United centre half, against Ireland at Wrexham on 8 Mar. 1950, aged 18 years 71 days. Scotland's youngest international has been Denis Law of Huddersfield Town, who played against Wales on 18 Oct. 1958, aged 18 years 236 days. David Black of Hurlford, Strathclyde, may have been 17 when he played for Scotland *v*. Ireland in 1889.

Most durable player

The most durable player in League history has been Terence Lionel Paine M.B.E. (b. 23 Mar. 1939) who made 824 league appearances from 1957 to 1977 playing for Southampton F.C. and Hereford Utd. F.C. James William (Jimmy) Dickinson M.B.E. (b. 24 Apr. 1925) made 764 League appearances for one club, Portsmouth, between 1946 and 1965.

Transfer fees *World*

The world's first transfer fee approaching £1 million was the £922,300 paid by F.C. Barcelona, Spain to Ajax Amsterdam, Netherlands, for Johan Cruyff, (b. 25 Apr. 1947) announced on 20 Aug. 1973. On transfer (Sept.) he received a record signing fee of *c*. £400,000.

Transfer fees *British*

The record fee received by a British club was £1 million by Birmingham City from Nottingham Forest for Trevor John Francis (b. Plymouth, 19 Apr. 1954), on 4 Feb. 1979.

Most successful national coach

The most successful national coach has been Helmut Schoen (b. Dresden 1915) of West Germany. His teams won the 1972 European championship and the 1974 World Cup, as well as finishing second in the 1966 World Cup and 1976 European championships, and third in the 1970 World Cup.

Heaviest goalkeeper

The biggest goalkeeper in representative football was the England international Willie J. "Fatty" Foulke (1874–1916), who stood 6 ft 3 in *1,90 m* and weighed 22 st. 3 lb. *141 kg*. His last games were for Bradford, by which time he was 26 st. *165 kg*. He once stopped a game by snapping the cross bar.

Greatest crowds

The greatest recorded crowd at any football match was 205,000 (199,854 paid) for the Brazil *v*. Uruguay World Cup match in the Maracaña Municipal Stadium, Rio de Janeiro, Brazil on 16 July 1950. The record attendance for a European Cup match is 136,505 at the semi-final between Glasgow Celtic and Leeds United at Hampden Park, Glasgow on 15 Apr. 1970.

The British record paid attendance is 149,547 at the Scotland *v*. England international at Hampden Park, Glasgow, on 17 Apr. 1937. It is, however, probable that this total was exceeded (estimated 160,000) on the occasion of the F.A. Cup Final between Bolton Wanderers and West Ham United at Wembley Stadium on 28 Apr. 1923, when the crowd broke in on the pitch and the start was delayed 40 min until the pitch was cleared. The counted admissions were 126,047.

The Scottish Cup record attendance is 146,433 when Celtic played Aberdeen at Hampden Park on 24 Apr. 1937. The record attendance for a League match in Britain is 118,567 for Rangers *v*. Celtic at Ibrox Park, Glasgow on 2 Jan. 1939.

For details of the largest football stadiums, see p. 113.

Smallest crowd

The smallest crowd at a full home international was 4,946 for the Northern Ireland *v*. Wales match of 19 May 1973 at Goodison Park, Everton, Merseyside. The smallest crowd at a Football League fixture was for the Stockport County *v*. Leicester City match at Old Trafford, Greater Manchester, on 7 May 1921. Stockport's own ground was under suspension and the "crowd" numbered 13.

Greatest receipts

The record gross F.A. Cup receipts at Wembley, Brent, Greater London, is £500,000 (excluding radio and television fees) for the finals on 6 May 1978 and 12 May 1979. The "gate" at the first F.A. Cup Final at Kennington Oval on 16 Mar. 1872 was £100.

The greatest receipts at any World Cup final were £204,805, from an attendance of 96,924 for England *v*. West Germany at Wembley, on 30 July 1966.

The record for a British international match is £440,000 for the England *v*. Italy World Cup qualifying match at Wembley on 16 Nov. 1977 (attendance 92,000). The receipts for the Manchester United *v*. Benfica match at Wembley on 29 May 1968 were £118,000 (attendance 100,000).

Most peripatetic fans

In a period of 264 days (10 Aug. 1968–30 Apr. 1969) Michael Jones and Bob Wilson of Shrewsbury, viewed league matches at all 93 English Football League grounds (incl. Berwick Rangers F.C.).

AMATEUR AND MINOR LEAGUES

Most Olympic wins

The only country to have won the Olympic football title three times is Hungary in 1952, 1964 and 1968. The United Kingdom won the unofficial tournament in 1900 and the official tournaments of 1908 and 1912. The highest Olympic score is Denmark 17 *v*. France "A" 1 in 1908.

Most F.A. Amateur Cup wins

The greatest number of F.A. Amateur Cup (1893–1974) wins is ten by Bishop Auckland who won in 1896, 1900, 1914, 1921–22, 1935, 1939, 1955–57.

Most caps

The record number of England amateur caps is held by Rod Haider (b. 23 Jan. 1943), the Hendon captain and half-back, who made his 65th amateur international appearance for England *v*. Scotland on 5 Apr. 1974.

Largest crowd

The highest attendance at an amateur match has been 120,000 in Senayan Stadium, Jakarta, Indonesia, on 26 Feb. 1976 for the Pre-Olympic Group II final, North Korea *v*. Indonesia.

Highest scores *Teams*

The highest aggregate score in a home Amateur International is 11 goals in the England *v*. Scotland match (8–3) at Dulwich on 11 Mar. 1939. The foreign record was when England beat France 15–0 in Paris on 1 Nov. 1906.

The highest score in an F.A. Amateur Cup Final was eight when Northern Nomads beat Stockton 7–1 at Sunderland, Tyne and Wear in 1926, and when Dulwich Hamlet beat Marine (Liverpool) by the same score at Upton Park in 1932.

In 1975, in a Scottish ladies league match, Edinburgh Dynamos F.C. beat Lochend Thistle 42–0.

In an under-14 league match between Midas F.C. and Courage Colts, in Kent, England on 11 Apr. 1976, the full time score after 70 min play was 59–1. Top scorer for Midas was Kevin Graham with 17 goals. Courage had scored the first goal.

Highest scores *Individual*
The highest individual score in amateur internationals is six: by William Charles Jordan (1885–1949) for England *v.* France (12–0) at Park Royal, Brent, Greater London on 23 Mar. 1908; by Vivian John Woodward (1879–1954) for England *v.* Holland (9–1) at Stamford Bridge, Hammersmith, Greater London, on 11 Dec. 1909; and by Harold A. Walden (1889–1949) for Great Britain *v.* Hungary, in Stockholm, Sweden, on 1 July 1912. Kim Barker, 11, of South Hobart, Tasmania, Australia scored 21 goals in his team's 25–0 win over Hutchins in the under-12 competition on 11 May 1974.

Highest scores *International Schoolboys*
The most prolific schoolboy international scorer has been Richard Smith Bell (England) who in the 1935–36 season scored 12 goals in three internationals: three *v.* Scotland, three *v.* Wales and six *v.* Ireland.

Highest scores *Season*
The greatest number of goals in a season reported for an individual player in junior league football is 96 by Tom Duffy, who played centre forward professionally for Ardeer Thistle F.C., Strathclyde in the 1960–61 season. The highest season figure reported in any class of competitive football for an individual is 294 goals in 67 matches by centre forward Michael Jones for Afan Lido F.C., St. Joseph's School and Port Talbot Boys XI in 1972–73. His total (65 headers, 120 right foot and 109 left foot) included an 11, a ten and six triple hat-tricks.

Fastest goals
Wind-aided goals in three sec after kick-off have been scored by a number of players. Tony Bacon, of Schalmont H.S. scored three goals *v.* Icabod Crane H.S. in 63 sec at Schenectady, New York, U.S.A. on 8 Oct. 1975.

Fastest own goal
The fastest own goal on record was one in 5 sec "scored" by Peter Johnson of Chesham United in a match against Wycombe Wanderers on 21 Feb. 1976.

Longest match
A match between Simon Fraser Univ. Clansmen and Quincy College Hawks lasted 4 hr 25 min (221 min 43 sec playing time) at Pasadena, Cal., U.S.A. in Nov. 1976.

Longest ties
The aggregate duration of ties in amateur soccer have not been collated but it is recorded that in the London F.A.

Intermediate Cup first qualifying round Highfield F.C. Reserves had to meet Mansfield House F.C. on 19 and 26 September and 3, 10 and 14 Oct. 1970 to get a decision after 9 hours 50 min play with scores of 0–0, 1–1, 1–1, 3–3, and 0–2.

In the Hertfordshire Intermediate Cup, London Colney beat Leavesden Hospital after 12 hours 41 min play and seven ties from 6 Nov. to 17 Dec. 1971.

Most and Least successful teams
The Home Farm F.C., Dublin, Ireland, between 12 Oct. 1968 and 10 Oct. 1970 won 79 consecutive matches. Fairholme A.F.C., Tyne and Wear, completed a run of 94 league games without defeat between 19 Sept. 1974 and 19 Apr. 1978. In six successive years the Larkswood County Junior School team of 1959–60 was unbeaten, winning 118 games and drawing three. Stockport United F.C., of the Stockport Football League, lost 39 consecutive League and Cup matches from Sept. 1976 to 18 Feb. 1978.

Most disciplined
Coleridge F.C. of the Cambridgeshire F.A. completed 25 years without a single member having been cautioned, sent off or otherwise disciplined since its formation in 1954.

Most indisciplined
In the local Cup match between Tongham Youth Club, Surrey and Hawley, Hampshire, England on 3 Nov. 1969 the referee booked all 22 players including one who went to hospital, and one of the linesmen. The match, won by Tongham 2–0, was described by a player as "A good, hard game".

In a Gancia Cup match at Waltham Abbey, Essex on 23 Dec. 1973, the referee, M. J. Woodhams, sent off the entire Juventus-Cross team and some club officials. Glencraig United, Faifley, nr. Clydebank, had all 11 team members and two substitutes for their match against Goldenhill Boy's Club on 2 Feb. 1975 booked in the dressing room before a ball was kicked. The referee, Mr. Tarbet of Bearsden, took exception to the chant which greeted his arrival. It was not his first meeting with Glencraig. The teams drew 2–2.

Ball control
Adrian Walsh (aged 34) juggled a regulation soccer ball for 4 hr 3 min 43 sec non-stop at The Town Park, Mallow, Co Cork, Ireland on 24 June 1979. He did 23,547 repetitions with feet, legs and head without the ball ever touching the ground.

Istvan Halaszi (b. Hungary, 24 July 1957) headed a regulation football non-stop for 79 min 24 sec (12,374 repetitions) at the Jewish Community Centre, Milwaukee, Wis., U.S.A. on 29 Apr. 1979.

Marathon *11-a-side*
The longest recorded 11-a-side football match is 49 hr by two teams from Blackett United F.C. at Haber Park, N.S.W., Aust. on 20–22 Oct. 1978.

Marathon *5-a-side*
The longest recorded authenticated 5-a-side games have been: outdoors; 62 hr 51 min by two teams (no substitutes) from St. Albans United F.C. at Belmont Hill, St. Albans, Herts. on 22–24 June 1979 and indoors: 91 hr 45 min by two teams (no substitutes) from Liverpool Polytechnic, Merseyside, England on 16–20 Feb. 1978.

Tired but happy, the St. Albans United five-a-side soccer marathon record breakers.

FOOTBALL (GAELIC)

Earliest references

The game developed from inter-parish "free for all" with no time-limit, no defined playing area nor specific rules. Standardisation came with the formation of the Gaelic Athletic Association in Thurles, Ireland, on 1 Nov. 1884.

Most titles

The greatest number of All Ireland Championships ever won by one team is 24 by Ciarraidhe (Kerry) between 1903 and 1978. The greatest number of successive wins is four by Wexford (1915–18) and four by Kerry (1929–32). Leinster has won most Inter-provincial championships (Railway Cup) with 18 between 1928 and 1974. Sean O'Neill (Down) holds the record of eight medals with Ulster (1960–71).

Highest scores

The highest team score in an All-Ireland final was when Dublin, 27 (5 goals, 12 points) beat Armagh, 15 (3 goals, 6 points) on 25 Sept. 1977. The highest combined score was 45 pts when Cork (26) beat Galway (19) in 1973. A goal equals three points. The highest individual score in an All-Ireland final has been 2 goals, 6 points by Jimmy Keaveney (Dublin) in the match against Armagh in 1977.

Lowest scores

In four All-Ireland finals the combined totals have been 7 points; 1893 Wexford (1 goal, till 1894 worth 5 points, 1 point) v. Cork (1 point); 1895 Tipperary (4 points) v. Meath (3 points); 1904 Kerry (5 points) v. Dublin (2 points); 1924 Kerry (4 points) v. Dublin (3 points).

Most appearances

The most appearances in All-Ireland finals is ten by Dan O'Keeffe (Kerry) of which seven (a record) were on the winning side.

Largest crowd

The record crowd is 90,556 for the Down v. Offaly final at Croke Park, Dublin, in 1961.

FOOTBALL (RUGBY LEAGUE)

Origins

The Rugby League was formed originally on 29 Aug. 1895 as "The Northern Rugby Football Union" by the secession of 22 clubs in Lancashire and Yorkshire from the parent Rugby Union. Though payment for loss of working time was a major cause of the breakaway the "Northern Union" did not itself embrace full professionalism until 1898. A reduction in the number of players per team from 15 to 13 took place in 1906 and the present title of "Rugby League" was adopted in 1922.

Most titles

There have been eight World Cup Competitions. Australia were winners in 1957, 1968, 1970, 1975 and 1977. Great Britain/England won in 1954, 1960 and 1972.

Under the one-league Championship system (1907–62 and 1965–71) the club with the most wins was Wigan with nine (1909, 1922, 1926, 1934, 1946, 1947, 1950, 1952 and 1960).

In the Rugby League Challenge Cup (inaugurated 1896–97) the club with the most wins is Leeds with ten in 1910, 1923, 1932, 1936, 1941–42 (wartime), 1957, 1968, 1977–78. Oldham is the only club to appear in four consecutive Cup Finals (1924–27).

Only three clubs have won all four major Rugby League trophies (Challenge Cup, League Championship, County Cup and County League) in one season: Hunslet in 1907–08, Huddersfield in 1914–15 and Swinton in 1927–28.

In addition to the three "All Four Cup clubs", on only five other occasions has a club taken the Cup and League honours in one season: Broughton Rangers (1902); Halifax (1903); Huddersfield (1913); Warrington (1954); and St. Helens (1966). Warrington (1974) and St. Helens (1976) have won the Cup and the newly constituted Club championship.

HIGHEST TEAM SCORES

World Cup

The record aggregate score in a World Cup match is 72 points when Great Britain beat New Zealand at Hameau Stadium, Pau, France by 53 points to 19 on 4 Nov. 1972.

Senior match

The highest aggregate score in Cup or League football in a game where a senior club has been concerned, was 121 points, when Huddersfield beat Swinton Park Rangers by 119 points (19 goals, 27 tries) to 2 points (one goal) in the first round of the Northern Union Cup on 28 Feb. 1914.

Cup Final

The record aggregate in a Cup Final is 47 points when Featherstone Rovers beat Bradford Northern 33–14 at Wembley, Brent, Greater London, on 12 May 1973.

The greatest winning margin was 34 points when Huddersfield beat St. Helens 37–3 at Oldham on 1 May 1915.

Touring teams

The record score for a British team touring the Commonwealth is 101 points by England v. South Australia (nil) at Adelaide in May 1914.

The record for a Commonwealth touring team in Britain is 92 points (10 goals, 24 tries) by Australia against Bramley's 7 points (2 goals, 1 try) at the Barley Mow Ground, Bramley, near Leeds, on 9 Nov. 1921.

HIGHEST INDIVIDUAL SCORES

Most points *Cup*

George Henry "Tich" West (1882–1927) of Hull Kingston Rovers scored 53 points (10 goals and 11 tries) in a First Round Challenge Cup-tie v. Brookland Rovers on 4 Mar. 1905.

Most points *League*

Jimmy Lomas (Salford) scored a record 39 points (5 tries, 12 goals) against Liverpool City (78–0) on 2 Feb. 1907.

Most points *Season*

The record number of points in a season was scored by B. Lewis Jones (Leeds) with 496 in season 1956–57 (he also scored 9 points in a friendly game). David Watkins (Salford) (b. 5 Mar. 1942) scored 493 points in season 1972–73 (he also scored 14 points in two friendly games).

Gilbert Austin of Hull Kingston Rovers helped his club win most of Rugby League's club honours during his record run of games for them.

HIGHEST SCORES

The highest aggregate scores in international Rugby League football are:

Match	Points	Score
Great Britain v. Australia (Test Matches)	62	Australia won 50–12 (Swinton, 9 Nov. 1963)
Great Britain v. New Zealand (Test Matches)	72	Great Britain won 52–20 (Wellington, 30 July 1910)
Great Britain v. France (Test Matches)	65	Great Britain won 50–15 (Leeds, 14 Mar. 1959)
England v. Wales	73	England won 60–13 (St. Helens, 28 May 1978)
England v. France	55	France won 42–13 (Marseilles, 25 Nov. 1951)
England v. Other Nationalities	61	England won 34–27 (Workington, 30 Mar. 1933)
Wales v. France	50	France won 29–21 (Bordeaux, 23 Nov. 1947)
Wales v. Other Nationalities	48	Other Nationalities won 27–21 (Swansea, 31 Mar. 1951)
Australia v. Great Britain	76	Australia won 63–13 (Paris, 31 Dec. 1933)
Australia v. Wales	70	Australia won 51–19 (Wembley, 30 Dec. 1933)
Australia v. France (Test Matches)	62	Australia won 56–6 (Brisbane, 2 July 1960)
Australia v. New Zealand (Test Matches)	74	New Zealand won 49–25 (Brisbane, 28 June 1952)
New Zealand v. France (Test Matches)	53	France won 31–22 (Lyon, 15 Jan. 1956)

Most points *Career*

Neil Fox (Bradford Northern) scored 6,388 points (2,643 goals, 365 tries, 7 drop goals) in a senior Rugby League career from 10 Apr. 1956 to the end of the 1978–79 season.

Most tries *Season*

Albert Aaron Rosenfeld (1885–1970) (Huddersfield), an Australian-born wing-threequarter, scored 80 tries in the 1913–14 season.

Most tries *Career*

Brian Bevan (b. Australia, 1924) a wing-threequarter, scored 834 tries in League, Cup, representative or charity games in the 18 seasons (16 with Warrington, two with Blackpool Borough) from 1946 to 1964.

Most goals *Season*

The record number of goals in a season is 228 by David Watkins (Salford) in the 1972–73 season. His total was made up of 221 in League, Cup, other competitions, and a Salford v. New Zealand match, plus seven in two pre-season friendly fixtures.

Fast scoring

David Watkins scored 13 points (3 tries, 2 conversions) in 5 min for Salford v. Barrow on 1 Dec. 1972.

Longest kick

In April 1940 Martin Hodgson (Swinton) kicked a goal on the Rochdale ground, later measured to be 77¾ yd *71 m* to the goal posts. It thus probably carried another 20 yd or so.

Most international appearances

Test Matches between Great Britain (formerly England) and Australia are regarded as the highest distinction for a R.L. player in either hemisphere and Jim Sullivan (1903–77) (Wigan) holds the Test record for a British player with 15 appearances between 1924 and 1933, though Mick Sullivan (no kin) (b. 1934) of Huddersfield, Wigan, St. Helens and York, played in 16 G.B. v. Australia games in 1954–64, of which 13 were Tests and three World Cup matches.

In all Tests, including those against New Zealand and France, Mick Sullivan made the record number of 47 appearances and scored 43 tries.

Most Cup Finals

Two players have appeared in seven Cup Finals: Alan Edwards (Salford, Dewsbury, and Bradford Northern) between 1938 and 1949, and Eric Batten (Leeds, Bradford Northern and Featherstone Rovers) between 1941 and 1952.

Eric Ashton, M.B.E. (b. 24 Jan. 1935), Wigan and Great Britain centre has the distinction of captaining Wigan at Wembley in six R.L. Cup Finals in nine years 1958–66, taking the trophy three times (1958, 1959 and 1965).

Youngest player

The youngest player in a Cup Final was Reg Lloyd (Keighley) who was 17 years 8 months when he played at Wembley on 8 May 1937.

Most durable player

David Watkins (Salford) played and scored in every club game during seasons 1972–73 and 1973–74—a total of 92 games contributing 41 tries and 403 goals—a total of 929 points. Together with seasons 1970–71 and 1971–72 he played 140 consecutive games.

Gilbert Austin (Hull Kingston Rovers) played in 190 consecutive games (plus five friendlies) for his club between 1918 and 1924.

Most and least successful teams

Hull F.C. won all 26 League Division II matches in the 1978–79 season. Doncaster hold the unenviable record of losing 40 consecutive League games from 16 Nov. 1975 to 21 Apr. 1977.

Record transfer fees

The highest R.L. transfer fee is £20,000 paid to Dewsbury for Michael Stephenson by Penrith, Australia on 17 July 1973. David Watkins (Welsh R.U.) received an £11,000 signing fee and a guaranteed £1,000 p.a. for five years from Salford in October 1967.

Greatest crowds

The greatest attendance at any Rugby League match is 102,569 for the Warrington v. Halifax Cup Final replay at Odsal Stadium, Bradford, on 5 May 1954.

Greatest receipts

The highest receipts for a match in the world have been £332,000 for the Leeds v. St. Helens Cup Final at Wembley on 13 May 1978.

FOOTBALL (RUGBY UNION)

Records are determined in terms of present day scoring values, i.e. a try at 4 points; a dropped goal, penalty or goal from a mark at 3 points; and a conversion at 2 points. The actual score, in accordance with which ever of the eight earlier systems was in force at the time, is also given, in brackets.

Origins

Though there are records of a game with many similarities to Rugby dating back to the Roman occupation, the game is traditionally said to have originated from a breach of the rules of the football played in November 1823 at Rugby School by William Webb Ellis (later the Rev.) (c. 1807–72). This handling code of football evolved gradually and was known to have been played at Cambridge University by 1839. The Rugby Football Union was founded on 26 Jan. 1871.

Most Olympic Gold Medals

Rugby Football was included four times in the Olympic Games: 1900, 1908, 1920 and 1924. Four United States players, in the 1920 winning team won second gold medals in 1924: Charles W. Doe, John T. O'Neil, John C. Patrick and Rudolph J. Scholz. Daniel B. Carroll, who was in the winning Australian team in 1908, won a second gold medal in the 1920 U.S. team.

HIGHEST TEAM SCORES

Internationals

The highest score in any full International was when Wales

Former French captain Benoit Dauga, here (*in white shirt*) grappling Llewelyn of Wales, has another thirteen caps in addition to his record fifty against International Board countries. Coming up behind him is Andy Hill, who holds the British Club try scoring record. (*E. D. Lacey*)

beat Japan by 82 points (10 goals, 4 tries, 2 penalties) to 6 points (2 penalties) in Tokyo, on 24 Sept. 1975.

The International Championship record is 75 points when Wales beat France at Swansea in 1910 by 59 points (8 goals, 1 penalty goal, 2 tries) to 16 (1 goal, 2 penalty goals and 1 try) (49–14).

The highest aggregate score for any International match between the Four Home Unions is 69 when England beat Wales by 69 points (7 goals, 1 drop goal and 6 tries) to 0 at Blackheath, Greenwich, Greater London in 1881. (Note: there was no point scoring in 1881).

The highest score by any Overseas side in an International in the British Isles is 53 points (7 goals, 1 drop goal and 2 tries) to 0 when South Africa beat Scotland at Murrayfield, Edinburgh, on 24 Nov. 1951 (44–0).

Tour match

The record score for any international tour match is 125–0 (17 goals, 5 tries and 1 penalty goal) (103–0) when New Zealand beat Northern New South Wales at Quirindi, Australia, on 30 May 1962.

276

Inter-club

In Denmark, Comet beat Lindo by 194–0 on 17 Nov. 1973. The highest British score is 154–0 by Roundhay Rams *v.* R.A.F. Catterick in 1973.

Schools

Scores of over 200 points have been recorded in school matches, for example Radford School beat Hills Court 214 points (31 goals and 7 tries) to 0 (100–0) on 20 Nov. 1886.

Season

The highest number of points accumulated in a season by a rugby club is 1,454 points by Pontypridd R.F.C., Mid Glamorgan, in 1975–76. In 1970–71 Solihull R.U.F.C's 1st XV scored a record 247 tries.

HIGHEST INDIVIDUAL SCORES
Internationals

The highest individual points score in any match between members of the International Board is 24 by William Fergus "Fergie" McCormick (b. 1940)—1 drop goal, 3 conversions and 5 penalty goals for New Zealand against Wales at Auckland on 14 June 1969.

ALL TIME SCORING RECORDS—AGGREGATE and MARGIN of VICTORY in the ten annual matches in the "International Championship"

Note: Headnote on page 275 on Scoring systems

		Aggregate Record Present Day pts. value		Record Margin Present Day pts. Value
England v. Scotland	Scotland (28) beat England (19) in 1931	57	England (19) beat Scotland (0) in 1924	21
			England (24) beat Scotland (5) in 1947	21
England v. Ireland	England (36) beat Ireland (14) in 1938	61	Ireland (22) beat England (0) in 1947	27
England v. Wales	England beat Wales by 7 goals, 1 drop goal and 6 tries to nil in 1881	69*	England beat Wales by 7 goals, 1 drop goal and 6 tries to nil in 1881	69
England v. France	England (49) beat France (15) in 1907	64	England (37) beat France (0) in 1911	44
Scotland v. Ireland	Scotland (29) beat Ireland (14) in 1913	51	Scotland beat Ireland by 6 goals and 2 tries to nil in 1877	44
Scotland v. Wales	Scotland (20) beat Wales (0) in 1887	56	Scotland (20) beat Wales (0) in 1887	56
Scotland v. France	Scotland (31) beat France (3) in 1912	41	Scotland (31) beat France (3) in 1912	33
Ireland v. Wales	Wales (24) beat Ireland (21) in 1979	45	Wales (29) beat Ireland (0) in 1907	34
Ireland v. France	France (27) beat Ireland (6) in 1964	40	Ireland (24) beat France (0) in 1913	30
Wales v. France	Wales (49) beat France (14) in 1910	75	Wales (47) beat France (5) in 1909	52

* Point scoring was not introduced until 1886.

Ian Scott Smith (Scotland) (1903–1972) scored a record six consecutive international tries in 1925; last three v. France and first three v. Wales two weeks later.

Season
The first class rugby scoring record for a season is 581 points by Samuel Arthur Doble (1944–77) of Moseley, in 52 matches in 1971–72. He also scored 47 points for England in South Africa out of season.

Career
Sam Doble scored a total of 3,703 points (3,651 then) in his first class career, comprising 85 tries, 651 conversions, 661 penalty goals, 26 dropped goals.

Inter Club
Michael Curran scored 64 points (7 tries, 18 conversions) for Broughton Park III v. Nuneaton on 26 Nov. 1977.

Schools
In a junior house match in February 1967 at William Ellis School, Edgware, Greater London, between Cumberland and Nunn, Thanos Morphitis, 12, contributed 90 points (13 tries and 19 conversions) (77) to Cumberland's winning score.

Most international appearances
The totals below are limited to matches between the seven member countries of the "International Rugby Football Board" and France. Including 12 appearances for the British Lions, Mike Gibson has played in 81 international matches. Willie John McBride M.B.E. (b. Co. Antrim, 6 June, 1940) made a record 17 appearances for the British Lions.

Ireland	69	Cameron Michael Henderson Gibson	1964–79
New Zealand	55	Colin Earl Meads	1957–71
France	50	Benoit Dauga	1964–72
Wales	53	Gareth Owen Edwards	1967–78
Scotland	50	Alexander 'Sandy' B. Carmichael M.B.E.	1967–78
England	41	John Vivian Pullin	1966–76
Australia	39	Peter G. Johnson	1958–72
	39	Gregory Victor Davis	1963–72
South Africa	38	Frederick Christoffel Hendrick Du Preez	1960–71

Youngest International
C. Reid (Scotland) was 17 yr 22 days old when he played against England in 1881.

County Championships
The County Championships (instituted in 1889) have been won most often by Gloucestershire with 13 titles (1910, 1913, 1920–22, 1930–32, 1937, 1972, 1974, 1975 and 1976). The most individual appearances is 104 by Richard Trickey for Lancashire between 1964 and 1978.

Seven-a-sides *Origins*
Seven-a-side rugby dates from 28 Apr. 1883 when Melrose R.F.C. Borders in order to alleviate the poverty of a club in such a small town staged a Seven-a-side tournament. The idea was that of Ned Haig, the town's butcher. The popularity of this variation of the game culminated in a world record 16 countries competing in an international Seven-a-side tournament in Hong Kong on 15–16 Apr. 1978.

Middlesex Seven-a-sides
The Middlesex Seven-a-sides were inaugurated in 1926. The most successful side has been Harlequins with eight wins (1926–29, 1933, 1935, 1967, 1978).

The only players to be in five winning "sevens" have been Norman Macleod Hall (1925–73) (St. Mary's Hospital 1944, 1946 and Richmond 1951, 1953, 1955), and James Alexander Pirie Shackleton and Iain Hugh Page Laughland both of London Scottish (1960–63, 1965).

Greatest crowd
The record paying attendance is 104,000 for Scotland v. Wales at Murrayfield, Edinburgh, on 1 Mar. 1975. Scotland won 12 points to 10.

Highest posts
The world's highest Rugby Union goal posts are reputed to be over 98½ ft *30 m* high at the Railway Rugby Club, Nelspruit, South Africa. The posts at Kilmarnock R.F.C., Strathclyde, are 53 ft *16,15 m* high and made of three 20 ft *6,09 m* tubular steel lengths each.

Longest kicks
The longest recorded successful drop-goal is 90 yd *82 m* by Gerry Brand for South Africa v. England at Twickenham, Greater London, on 2 Jan. 1932. This was taken 7 yd *6 m* inside the England "half" 55 yd *50 m* from the posts and dropped over the dead ball line.

The place kick record is reputed to be 100 yd *91 m* at Richmond Athletic Ground, Richmond upon Thames, Greater London, by D. F. T. Morkell in an unsuccessful penalty for South Africa v. Surrey on 19 Dec. 1906. This was not measured until 1932.

In the match Bridlington School 1st XV v. an Army XV at Bridlington, Humberside in 1944, Ernie Cooper, captaining the school, landed a penalty from a measured 81 yd *74 m* from the post with a kick which carried over the dead ball line.

Most tries
On 26 Mar. 1977 Andy Hill scored his 250th try for Llanelli, a British Club Rugby record, since his debut on 3 Nov. 1967.

Longest try
The longest "try" ever executed is by 15 members of Sedgley Park R.U.F.C. Manchester, who scored on 5 May 1979 from a "move" which carried the ball 736 miles 637 yd *1 185,06 km*. There were no forward passes or knock-ons, and the ball was touched down between the posts in the prescribed manner (Law 12).

FOXHUNTING

Earliest references

Hunting the fox in Britain became popular from the second half of the 18th century though it is mentioned very much earlier. Prior to that time hunting was confined principally to the deer and the hare. It is estimated that foxhunters account for some 10,000 of the 50,000 foxes killed each year.

Pack *Oldest*

The Old Charlton Hunt in West Sussex, now extinct. The Duke of Monmouth and Lord Grey of Werke at Charlton, Sussex, and the Duke of Buckingham in north Yorkshire, owned packs which were entered to fox only during the reign (1660–85) of Charles II.

Pack *Largest*

The pack with the greatest number of hounds has been the Duke of Beaufort's hounds maintained at Badminton, Avon, since 1786. At times hunting six days a week, this pack once had 120 couples at hounds.

Longest hunt

The longest recorded hunt was one led by Squire Sandys which ran from Holmbank, northern Lancashire, to Ulpha, Cumbria, a total of nearly 80 miles *128 km* in reputedly only six hours, in January or February 1743. The longest hunt in Ireland was probably a run of 24 miles *38 km* made by the Scarteen Hunt, County Limerick, from Pallas to Knockoura in 1914. The longest duration hunt was one of 10 hours 5 min by the Charlton Hunt of West Sussex, which ran from East Dean Wood at 7.45 a.m. to a kill over 57¼ miles *92 km* away at 5.50 p.m. on 26 Jan. 1738.

Largest fox

The largest fox ever killed by a hunt in England was a 23¾ lb. *10 kg 770* dog on Cross Fell, Cumbria, by an Ullswater Hunt in 1936.

GAMBLING

World's biggest win

The world's biggest gambling win is £1,065,891 for a bet of two cruzeiros (25p) in the Brazilian football pools Loteria Esportiva by Miron Vieira de Sousa, 30, of Ivolandia, Brazil on the results of 13 games in October 1975. The first thing he bought was a set of false teeth. By winning a state lottery in January 1976, Eric C. Leek, of North Arlington, New Jersey, U.S.A., won $1,776 a week for life. Aged 26, he will receive a total of $4.6 million should he live a further 50 years.

World's biggest loss

An unnamed Italian industrialist was reported to have lost £800,000 in five hours at roulette in Monte Carlo, Monaco on 6 Mar. 1974. A Saudi Arabian prince was reported to have lost more than $1 million in a single session at the Metro Club, Las Vegas, U.S.A. in December 1974.

Largest casino

The largest casino in the world is the Casino, Mar del Plata, Argentina with average daily attendances of 14,500 rising to 25,000 during carnivals. The Casino has more than 150 roulette tables running simultaneously.

BINGO

Origins

Bingo is a lottery game which, as keno, was developed in the 1880s from lotto, whose origin is thought to be the 17th century Italian game *tumbule*. It has long been known in the British Army (called Housey-Housey) and the Royal Navy (called Tombola). The winner was the first to complete a random selection of numbers from 1–90. The U.S.A. version called Bingo differs in that the selection is from 1–75. There are six million players in the United Kingdom.

Largest house

The largest "house" in Bingo sessions was staged at the Empire Pool, Wembley, Brent, Greater London, on 25 Apr. 1965 when 10,000 attended.

"Clickety-click" was about all Philip Carter and Timothy Mann could say after their marathon Bingo calling session.

Earliest and latest Full House

A "Full House" call occurred on the 15th number by Norman A. Wilson at Guide Post Workingmen's Club, Bedlington, Northumberland on 22 June 1978. "House" was not called until the 82nd number at the Telstar Club, Bransholme, Hull, Humberside on 13 Nov. 1976. 28 people won £2 each.

Most cards

The highest recorded number of cards played simultaneously (with a call rate of 31.7 secs per call) has been 346 by Robert A. Berg at Pacific Beach, California on 16 Nov. 1973.

Marathon

A session of 240 hr 30 min was held at the Top Rank Club, Kingston-upon-Thames, Surrey, England on 1–4 May 1979 with Philip Carter and Timothy Mann calling.

CARD PLAYING

Dealing marathon

Earl Arnall, dealt at a blackjack table in the King 8 Casino, Las Vegas, Nevada, U.S.A. for 190 hr on 22–30 June 1977.

FOOTBALL POOLS

The winning dividend paid out by Littlewoods Pools in their first week in February 1923 was £2 12s 0d (£2.60). In 1976/77 British Football Pools firms had a total record turnover of £247,374,000 of which Littlewoods contributed over two-thirds.

Progressive list of individual record winnings (in last 20 years)

Amount	Recipient	Date
£265,352	Arthur Webb, 70, of Scarborough, North Yorkshire	24 Nov. 1959
£301,739.45	Lawrence Freedman, 54, of Willesden, Brent, Greater London	8 Dec. 1964
£338,356.80	Percy Harrison, 52, of East Stockwith, Lincolnshire	30 Aug. 1966
£401,792	Albert Crocker, 54, of Dobwalls, Cornwall	20 Apr. 1971
£512,683	Cyril Grimes, 62, of Liss, Hampshire	7 Mar. 1972
£542,252	James Wood, 56, of Bradford, West Yorkshire	27 Feb. 1973
£547,172	A London woman	6 Mar. 1973
£629,801	Colin Carruthers, 24, of Kirkintilloch, Strathclyde	20 Mar. 1973
£680,697	Nell Fletcher, 32, of Furnace, Strathclyde	19 Feb. 1974
£882,528	Irene Powell, 20, of Port Talbot, West Glamorgan	24 Mar. 1979

In order to earn £882,528 post tax in 1978/79 a single person would have to be paid a salary of £5,144,826.18p.

The odds for selecting 8 draws (if there are 8 draws) from 54 matches for an all-correct line are 1,040,465,790 to 1 against. (In practice, the approximate odds of winning a dividend of any size on Littlewoods Pools are 80 to 1.)

SLOT MACHINES

The world's biggest slot machine (or one armed bandit) is Super Bertha (555 ft³ *15,71 m³*) installed by Si Redd at the Four Queens Casino, Las Vegas, Nevada, U.S.A. in September 1973. Once in every 25,000 million plays it may yield $1 million for a $10 feed. The total gambling "take" in 1978 in Nevada casinos was estimated at $1,800,000,000. The biggest beating handed to a "one-armed bandit" was $285,000 by Brian Flattery (U.S.A.) at the Flamingo Hilton, Las Vegas on 23 June 1979.

HORSE RACING

Highest ever odds

The highest recorded odds ever secured were 1,099,299 to 1 by a backer from Otley, West Yorkshire on a seven horse accumulator on 10 May 1975. On a stake of £1.76 in penny bets, he won a total of £12,578.14. The world record odds on a "double" are 24,741 to 1 secured by Montague Harry Parker at Windsor, England, for a £1 each-way "double" on *Ivernia* and *Golden Sparkle* with William Hill.

Biggest tote win

The best recorded tote win was one of £341 2s 6d to 2s (*£341.12½ to 10p*) representing odds of 3,410¼ to 1, by Catharine Unsworth of Blundellsands, Liverpool at Haydock Park on a race won by *Coole* on 30 Nov. 1929. The highest odds in Irish tote history were £184 7s 6d on a 2s 6d (*£184.37½ on a 12½p*) stake, *viz.* 1,474 to 1 on *Hillhead VI* at Baldoyle on 31 Jan. 1970.

Most complicated bet

The most complicated bet is the Harlequin, a compound wager on four horses with 2,028 possible ways of winning. It was invented by Monty H. Preston of London who has been reputed to be the fastest settler of bets in the world. He once completed 3,000 bets in a 4½-hour test.

Largest bookmaker

The world's largest bookmaker is Ladbrokes of London with a turnover from gambling in 1978 of £390 million. The largest chain of betting shops is that of Ladbrokes with 1,005 shops in the United Kingdom in 1979.

Topmost tipster

The only recorded instance of a racing correspondent forecasting ten out of ten winners on a race card was at Delaware Park, Wilmington, Delaware, U.S.A. on 28 July 1974 by Charles Lamb of the *Baltimore News American*.

Greatest pay-out

The greatest published "pay-out" on a single bet is £69,375 by Ladbroke's to the late Bernard Sunley on the Derby victory of *Santa Claus* in 1964. The greatest on a day's racing is £100,000 to P. Joliffe on 19 Aug. 1978. On 12 Dec. 1976 Mr. Lim Chooi Seng won Malaysian $1,112,400 *£258,700* on *Freedom Fighter* in the sixth race at Penang.

ROULETTE

The longest run on an ungaffed (*i.e.* true) wheel reliably recorded is six successive coups (in No. 10) at El San Juan Hotel, Puerto Rico on 9 July 1959. The odds with a double zero were 1 in 38⁶ or 3,010,936,383 to 1.

Longest marathon

The longest "marathon" on record is one of 31 days from 10 Apr. to 11 May 1970 at The Casino de Macao, to test the validity or invalidity of certain contentions in 20,000 spins.

ELECTIONS

The highest ever individual bet was £50,000 on Labour to win the 1964 Election by Sir Maxwell Joseph. He made £37,272 on the odds offered. A bet of £5,000 at 200–1 was placed by Frank Egerton in April 1975 that his political Centre Party would win the next General Election. It didn't.

GLIDING

Emanuel Swedenborg (1688–1772) of Sweden made sketches of gliders c. 1714.

The earliest man-carrying glider was designed by Sir George Cayley (1773–1857) and carried his coachman (possibly John Appleby) about 500 yd *457 m* across a valley near Brompton Hall, North Yorkshire in the summer of 1853. Gliders now attain speeds of 168 m.p.h. *270 km/h* and the Jastrzab aerobatic sailplane is designed to withstand vertical dives at up to 280 m.p.h. *450 km/h.*

Highest standard

A gold C with three diamonds (for goal flight, distance and height) is the highest standard in gliding. This has been gained by 94 British pilots up to June 1979.

Most titles *World*

World individual championships (inst. 1948) have been won five times by West Germans. There have been four British wins by Philip Aubrey Wills C.B.E. (1907–78) in 1952, H. C. Nicholas Goodhart and Frank Foster (2-seater) in 1956 and Douglas George Lee M.B.E. (b. 7 Nov. 1945) in 1976 and 1978.

Most titles *British*

The British national championship (instituted 1939) has been

SELECTED WORLD RECORDS (Single-seaters)	
Distance 907.7 miles *1 460,8 km*	Hans-Werner Grosse (W. Germany) in an ASW-12 on 25 Apr. 1972 from Lübeck to Biarritz
Declared Goal Flight 799.4 miles *1 254,126 km*	Bruce Drake, David Speight, S. H. "Dick" Georgeson (all N.Z.) all in Nimbus 2s, Te Anau to Te Araroa, 14 Jan 1978
Absolute Altitude 46,266 ft *14 102 m*	Paul F. Bikle, Jr. (U.S.A.) in a Schweizer SGS 1-23E over Mojave, California (released at 3,963 ft *1 207 m*) on 25 Feb. 1961 (also record altitude gain—42,303 ft *12 894 m*)
Goal and Return 1,015.7 miles *1 634,7 km*	Karl H. Striedieck (U.S.A.) in an ASW 17 from Lock Haven, Penn. to Tennessee. on 9 May 1977
Speed over Triangular Course 100 km 102.74 m.p.h. *165,35 km/h*	Ross Briegleb (U.S.A.) in a Kestrel 17 over the U.S.A. on 18 July 1974
300 km 95.95 m.p.h. *153,43 km/h*	Walter Neubert (W. Germany) in a Kestrel 604 over Kenya on 3 Mar. 1972
500 km 88.82 m.p.h. *143,04 km/h*	Edward Pearson (GB) in a Nimbus 2 over Namibia on 27 Nov. 1976
750 km 87.69 m.p.h. *141,13 km/h*	G. Eckle (W. Germany) in a Nimbus 2 over South Africa, 7 Jan. 1978
1000 km 90.28 m.p.h. *145,3 km/h**	Hans-Werner Grosse (W. Germany) in an ASW-17 over Australia on 3 Jan. 1979

* awaiting homologation

BRITISH NATIONAL RECORDS¹ (Single-seaters)	
460.5 miles *741 km*	Peter D. Lane in a Skylark 3F, Geilenkirchen to Hiersac, Germany on 1 June 1962
360 miles *579,36 km*	H. C. N. Goodhart in a Skylark 3, Lasham, Hants, to Portmoak, Scotland on 10 May 1959.
37,729 ft *11 500 m*	H. C. N. Goodhart in a Schweizer 1-23 over California, U.S.A. on 12 May 1955
497.7 miles *801,3 km*	Christopher Garton in a Kestrel 19, Lasham to Durham on 22 July 1976
88.99 m.p.h. *143,3 km/h*	E. P. Hodge in a Standard Cirrus over Rhodesia on 30 Oct. 1976
91.2 m.p.h. *146,8 km/h*	Edward Pearson in a Nimbus 2 over S.W. Africa on 30 Nov. 1976
88.82 m.p.h. *143,04 km/h*	Edward Pearson in a Nimbus 2 over Namibia on 27 Nov. 1976
68.2 m.p.h. *109,8 km/h*	Michael R. Carlton in a Kestrel 19 over South Africa on 5 Jan. 1975.

¹ *British National Records may be set up by British pilots in any part of the world*

won most often by Philip A. Wills in 1948–50 and 1955 and by John Delafield (b. 31 Jan. 1938) in 1968, 1972, 1976 and 1978. The first woman to win this title was Anne Burns (b. 23 Nov. 1915) of Farnham, Surrey on 30 May 1966.

HANG GLIDING

Origins

In the eleventh century the monk, Elmer, is reported to have flown from the 60 ft *18,3 m* tower of Malmesbury Abbey, Wiltshire. The earliest modern pioneer was Otto Lilienthal (1848–96) (Germany) with numerous flights between 1893 and 1896. In the 1950's Professor Francis Rogallo of the National Space Agency, U.S.A., developed a "wing" from his space capsule re-entry researches.

Championships

The First World Team Championships, held at Chattanooga, Tenn., U.S.A. in Oct. 1978 were won by Great Britain.

Greatest distance

The official F.A.I. record is 95 miles *153 km* by George Worthington (U.S.A.) in an ASG-21 (Rogallo) over California on 21 July 1977. The best in Britain is 49.6 miles *80 km* by Robert Bailey over the Yorkshire Dales in May 1979.

Greatest ascent and descent

The official F.A.I. height gain record is by George Worthington (U.S.A.) 11,700 ft *3 566 m* over Bishop, Cal., U.S.A. on 22 July 1978.

The greatest altitude from which a hang-glider has descended is 31,600 ft *9 631 m* by Bob McCaffrey, 18, (U.S.A.) in an experimental design from a balloon over the Mojave Desert, California, U.S.A. on 21 Nov. 1976.

GOLF

Origins

Although a stained glass window in Gloucester Cathedral, dating from 1350 portrays a golfer-like figure, the earliest mention of golf occurs in a prohibiting law passed by the Scottish Parliament in March 1457 under which "goff be utterly cryit doune and not usit". The Romans had a cognate game called *paganica* which may have been carried to Britain before A.D. 400. The Chinese Nationalist Golf Association claim the game is of Chinese origin ("*Ch'ui Wan*— the ball hitting game") in the 3rd or 2nd century B.C. Gutta percha balls succeeded feather balls in 1848 and by 1902 were in turn succeeded by rubber-cored balls, invented in 1899 by Haskell (U.S.A.). Steel shafts were authorized in 1929.

Club *Oldest*

The oldest club of which there is written evidence is the Gentlemen Golfers (now the Honourable Company of Edinburgh Golfers) formed in March 1744—ten years prior to the institution of the Royal and Ancient Club of St. Andrews, Fife. The oldest existing club in North America is the Royal Montreal Club (1873).

Club *Largest*

The club with the highest membership in the British Isles is the Royal and Ancient Golf Club of St. Andrews, Fife, Scotland with 1,800 members. The largest in England is 1,600 at the Moor Park G.C., Rickmansworth, Herts., and the largest in Ireland is Royal Portrush, Co. Antrim with 1,215 members.

Course *Highest*

The highest golf course in the world is the Tuctu Golf Club in Morococha, Peru, which is 4 369 m *14,335 ft* above sea-level at its lowest point. Golf has, however, been played in Tibet at an altitude of over 4 875 m *16,000 ft.*

The highest golf course in Great Britain is one of nine holes at Leadhills, Strathclyde, 1,500 ft *457 m* above sea-level.

Course *Lowest*

The lowest golf course in the world was that of the now defunct Sodom and Gomorrah Golfing Society at Kallia (Qulya) on the northern shores of the Dead Sea, 380 m *1,250 ft* below sea-level.

Longest hole

The longest hole in the world is the 17th hole (par 6) of 745 yd *681 m* at the Black Mountain Golf Club, North Carolina, U.S.A. It was opened in 1964. In August 1927 the sixth hole at Prescott Country Club in Arkansas, U.S.A. measured 838 yd *766 m.* The longest hole on a championship course in Great Britain is the sixth at Troon, Strathclyde, which stretches 580 yds *530 m.*

Largest green

Probably the largest green in the world is the fifth green at International G.C. Bolton, Massachusetts, U.S.A. with an area greater than 28,000 ft² *2 600 m².*

Biggest bunker

The world's biggest bunker (called a trap in the U.S.A.) is Hell's Half Acre on the seventh hole of the Pine Valley course, New Jersey, U.S.A., built in 1912 and generally regarded as the world's most trying course.

Longest course

The world's longest course is at Dub's Dread G.C. Piper, Kansas, U.S.A. and is a 78-par 8,101 yd *7 407 m.* Floyd Satterlee Rood used the United States as a course, when he played from the Pacific surf to the Atlantic surf from 14 Sept. 1963 to 3 Oct. 1964 in 114,737 strokes. He lost 3,511 balls on the 3,397.7 mile *5 468 km* trail.

Longest drives

In long-driving contests 330 yd *300 m* is rarely surpassed at sea level. In officially regulated long driving contests over level ground the greatest distance recorded is 392 yd *358 m* by William Thomas (Tommie) Campbell (Foxrock Golf Club) made at Dun Laoghaire, Co. Dublin, in July 1964. On an

'Slammin Sam' Snead's 134 tournament wins included one in which he posted the first under-60 round in top class American golf. (Don Morley, All-Sport Photographic)

airport runway Valentin Barrios (Spain) drove a Slazenger B51 ball 568½ yd *520 m* at Palma, Majorca on 7 Mar. 1977. The greatest recorded drive on an ordinary course is one of 515 yd *471 m* by Michael Hoke Austin (b. 17 Feb. 1910) of Los Angeles, California, U.S.A., in the U.S. National Seniors Open Championship at Las Vegas, Nevada, on 25 Sept. 1974. Austin, 6 ft 2 in *1,88 m* tall and weighing 210 lb. *92,250 kg* drove the ball to within a yard of the green on the par-4 450 yd *412 m* fifth hole of the Winterwood Course and it rolled 65 yd *59 m* past the flagstick. He was aided by an estimated 35 m.p.h. *56 km/h* tailwind.

A drive of 2,640 yd *2 414 m* (1½ miles) across ice was achieved by an Australian meteorologist named Nils Lied at Mawson Base, Antarctica, in 1962. Arthur Lynskey claimed a drive of 200 yd *182 m* horizontal and two miles *3 200 m* vertical off Pikes Peak, Colorado (14,110 ft *4 300 m*) on 28 June 1968. On the Moon the energy expended on a mundane 300 yd *274 m* drive would achieve, craters permitting, a distance of one mile *1,6 km*.

Longest hitter
The golfer regarded as the longest consistent hitter the game has ever known is the 6 ft 5 in *195 cm* tall, 17 st 2 lb. *108 kg 86* George Bayer (U.S.A.), the 1957 Canadian Open Champion. His longest measured drive was one of 420 yd *384 m* at the fourth in the Las Vegas Invitational, Nevada, in 1953. It was measured as a precaution against litigation since the ball struck a spectator. Bayer also drove a ball pin high on a 426 yd *389 m* hole at Tucson, Arizona in 1955. Radar measurements show that an 87 m.p.h. *140 km/h* impact velocity for a golf ball falls to 46 m.p.h. *74 km/h* in 3 seconds.

Longest putt
The longest recorded holed putt in a major tournament was one of 86 ft *26 m* on the vast 13th green at the Augusta National, Georgia by Cary Middlecoff (b. January 1921) (U.S.A.) in the 1955 Masters' Tournament. Robert Tyre (Bobby) Jones Jr. (1902–71) was reputed to have holed a putt in excess of 100 ft *30 m* at the fifth green in the first round of the 1927 Open at St. Andrews.

SCORES
Lowest 9 holes and 18 holes *Men*
The lowest recorded score on any 18-hole course with a par score of 70 or more is 55 (15 under bogey) first achieved by Alfred Edward Smith (b. 1903) the Woolacombe professional, on his home course on 1 Jan. 1936. The course measured 4,248 yd *3 884 m*. The detail was 4, 2, 3, 4, 2, 4, 3, 4, 3 = 29 out, and 2, 3, 3, 3, 3, 2, 5, 4, 1 = 26 in. At least three players are recorded to have played a long course (over 6,000 yd *5 846 m*) in a score of 58. The lowest recorded score on a long course in Britain is 58 by Harry Weetman (1920–72) the British Ryder Cup golfer, for the 6,171 yd *5 642 m* Croham Hurst Course, Croydon, on 30 Jan. 1956.

Nine holes in 25 (4, 3, 3, 2, 3, 3, 1, 4, 2) was recorded by A. J. "Bill" Burke in a round in 57 (32 + 25) on the 6,389 yd *5 842 m* par 71 Normandie course St. Louis, Missouri, U.S.A. on 20 May 1970. The tournament record is 27 by Jose Maria Canizares (Spain) (b. 18 Feb. 1947) for the first nine of the third round in the 1978 Swiss Open on the 6,811 yd *6 228 m* Crans-Sur-Sierre course.

The United States P.G.A. tournament record for 18 holes is 59 (30 + 29) by Al Geiberger (b. 1 Sept. 1937) in the second round of the Danny Thomas Classic, on the 72-par 7,249 yd *6 628 m* course at Memphis, Tennessee on 10 June 1977. Three golfers have recorded 59 over 18 holes in non-P.G.A. tournaments; Samuel Jackson Snead (b. 27 May 1912) in the third round of the Sam Snead Festival at White Sulphur Springs, West Virginia, U.S.A. on 16 May 1959; Gary Player (South Africa) (b. 1 Nov. 1935) in the second round of the Brazilian Open in Rio de Janeiro on 29 Nov. 1974, and David Jagger (G.B.) (b. 9 June 1949) in a Pro-Am tournament prior to the 1973 Nigerian Open.

Lowest 9 holes and 18 holes *Women*
The lowest recorded score on an 18-hole course (over 6,000 yd *5 486 m*) for a woman is 62 (30 + 32) by Mary "Mickey" Kathryn Wright (b. 14 Feb. 1935) of Dallas, Texas, on the Hogan Park Course (6,282 yd *5 747 m*) at Midland, Texas, U.S.A., in November 1964. Wanda Morgan (b. 22 Mar. 1910) recorded a score of 60 (31 + 29) on the Westgate-on-Sea and Birchington Golf Club course over 18 holes (5,002 yd *4 573 m*) on 11 July 1929.

Lowest 9 holes and 18 holes *Great Britain*
The British Tournament 9-hole record is 28 by John Panton (b. 1917) in the Swallow-Penfold Tournament at Harrogate, North Yorkshire, in 1952; by Bernard John Hunt M.B.E. (b. 2 Feb. 1930) of Hartsbourne in the Spalding Tournament at Worthing, West Sussex, in August 1953; by Peter Mills (b. 7 June 1931) in the Bowmaker Tournament at Sunningdale in 1958; by Lionel Platts (b. 10 Oct. 1934, Yorkshire) of Wanstead in the Ulster Open at Shandon Park, Belfast, on 11 Sept. 1965; and by Richard W. Seamer in the Kent Cob at Knole Park, Sevenoaks, Kent on 3 Sept. 1977. This last is the best by an Amateur player. The lowest score recorded in a first class professional tournament on a course of more than 6,000 yd *5 486 m* in Great Britain was set at 61 (29 + 32), by Thomas Bruce Haliburton (1915–75) of Wentworth G.C. in the Spalding Tournament at Worthing, West Sussex, in June 1952. Peter J. Butler (b. 25 Mar. 1932) equalled this record with 61 (32 + 29) in the Bowmaker Tournament on the Old Course at Sunningdale, Berkshire, on 4 July 1967.

Lowest 36 holes
The record for 36 holes is 122 (59 + 63) by Snead in the 1959 Sam Snead Festival on 16–17 May 1959. Horton Smith (1908–1963), twice U.S. Masters Champion, scored 121 (63 + 58) on a short course on 21 Dec. 1928. The lowest score by a British golfer has been 126 (61 + 65) by Tom Haliburton in the Spalding Tournament at Worthing in 1952.

Lowest 72 holes
The lowest recorded score on a first-class course is 257 (27 under par) by Mike Souchak in the Texas Open at Brackenridge Park, San Antonio in February 1955, made up of 60 (33 + 27), 68, 64, 65 (average 64.25 per round) exhibiting, as one critic said: "up and down" form, for a 27 under par with 27 birdies. The temperature on the fourth day was 27 °F *−2.8 °C*.

Horton Smith scored 245 (63, 58, 61 and 63) for 72 holes on the 4,700 yd *4 297 m* course (par 64) at Catalina Country Club, California, U.S.A., to win the Catalina Open on 21–23 Dec. 1928.

The lowest 72 holes in a national championship is 262 (67, 66, 66, 63) by Percy Alliss (G.B.) (1897–1975) in the 1932 Italian Open at San Remo, and by Liang Huan Lu (Taiwan) (b. 1936) in the 1971 French Open at Biarritz. Kelvin D. G. Nagle (b. 21 Dec. 1920) of Australia shot 261 in the Hong Kong Open in 1961. The lowest for four rounds in a British

The long career of British 72 hole record holder Bernard Hunt was highlighted by his third place in the 1960 Open. (*Sporting Pictures*)

top left: Jack Nicklaus was only nineteen years old when he won the first (the 1959 U.S. Amateur) of his record seventeen major tournaments. (*Steve Powell, All-Sport Photographic*)

bottom left: At 6′ 5″ and over fourteen stone, Peter Oosterhuis, who won a record sum in 1974, is one of the biggest players in golf. (*Sporting Pictures*)

right: In her first full year as a professional, Nancy Lopez won nine tournaments and set a record winnings total. (*Tony Duffy, All-Sport Photographic*)

first class tournament is 262 (66, 63, 66 and 67) by Bernard Hunt in the Piccadilly Stroke Play tournament on Wentworth East Course, Virginia Water, Surrey on 4–5 Oct. 1966.

Eclectic record

The lowest recorded eclectic (from the Greek *eklektikos* = choosing) score, i.e. the sum of a player's all-time personal low scores for each hole, for a course of more than 6,000 yd *5 486 m* is 33 by the club professional Jack McKinnon on the 6,538 yd *5 978 m* Capilano Golf and Country Club course, Vancouver, British Columbia, Canada. This was compiled over the period 1937–1964 and reads 2–2–2–1–2–2–2–2–1 (16 out) and 2–1–2–2–1–2–2–2–3 (17 in) = 33. The British record is 34 by John Harrowar (Jock) Morrison (b. 3 Oct. 1929) at West Kilbride G.C., Strathclyde, (6,348 yd *5 804 m*) from 1951–78. This is made up of fourteen 2s, three aces and one 3.

Highest score

The highest score for a single hole in the British Open is 21 by a player in the inaugural meeting at Prestwick in 1860. Double figures have been recorded on the card of the winner only once, when Willie Fernie (1851–1924) scored a ten at Musselburgh, Lothian, in 1883. Ray Ainsley of Ojai, California, took 19 strokes for the par-4 16th hole during the second round of the U.S. Open at Cherry Hills Country Club, Denver, Colorado, on 10 June 1938. Most of the strokes were used in trying to extricate the ball from a brook. Hans Merell of Mogadore, Ohio, took 19 strokes on the par-3 16th (222 yd *203 m*) during the third round of the Bing Crosby National Tournament at Cypress Point Club, Del Monte, California, U.S.A., on 17 Jan. 1959. It is recorded that Chevalier von Cittern went round 18 holes in 316, averaging 17.55 per hole, at Biarritz, France in 1888. Steven Ward took 222 strokes for the 6,212 yd *5 680 m* Pecos Course, Reeves County, Texas, U.S.A., on 18 June 1976—but he was only aged 3 yr 286 days.

Most shots for one hole

A woman player in the qualifying round of the Shawnee Invitational for Ladies at Shawnee-on-Delaware, Pennsylvania, U.S.A., in *c.* 1912, took 166 strokes for the short 130 yd *118 m* 16th hole. Her tee shot went into the Binniekill River and the ball floated. She put out in a boat with her exemplary, but statistically minded husband at the oars. She eventually beached the ball 1½ miles *2,4 km* downstream but was not yet out of the wood. She had to play through one on the home run. In a competititon at Peacehaven, Sussex, England in 1890, A. J. Lewis had 156 puts on one green without holing out.

Rounds fastest *Individual*
With such variations in lengths of courses, speed records, even for rounds under par, are of little comparative value. Bob Williams at Eugene, Oregon, U.S.A., completed 18 holes (6,010 yd *5 495 m*) in 27 min 48.2 sec in 1971 but this test permitted the striking of the ball whilst still moving. The record for a still ball is 30 min 10 sec by Dick Kimbrough (b. 1931) (U.S.A.) at North Platte C.C., Nebraska, U.S.A. (6,068 yd *5 548 m*) on 8 Aug. 1972, using only a 3-iron.

Rounds fastest *Team*
Forty-three players representing Borger High School, Texas, U.S.A., completed the 18 hole 6,109 yd *5 586 m* Huber Golf Course in 10 min 11.4 sec on 11 June 1976.

Rounds slowest
The slowest stroke play tournament round was one of 6 hours 45 min taken by South Africa in the first round of the 1972 World Cup at the Royal Melbourne G.C., Australia. This was a four-ball medal round, everything holed out.

Most rounds
The greatest number of rounds played on foot in 24 hours is 22 rounds and five holes (401 holes) by Ian Colston, 35, at Bendigo G.C. Victoria (6,061 yd *5 542 m*) on 27–28 Nov. 1971. The most holes played on foot in a week (168 hr) is 1,102 by David Shepardson (U.S.A.) 17, at Maple Grove G.C., Wisconsin in Aug. 1976.

Most peripatetic golfer
George S. Salter, of Carmel, Cal., U.S.A. has played in 116 different "countries" around the world from 1964 to 1977.

Throwing the golf ball
The lowest recorded score for throwing a golf ball round 18 holes (over 6,000 yd or 5 500 m) is 82 by Joe Flynn, 21, at the 6,228 yd *5 694 m* Port Royal Course, Bermuda, on 27 Mar. 1975.

CHAMPIONSHIP RECORDS
The Open
The Open Championship was inaugurated in 1860 at Prestwick, Strathclyde, Scotland. The lowest score for 9 holes is 29 by Tom Haliburton (Wentworth) and Peter W. Thomson, M.B.E. (Australia) (b. 23 Aug. 1929) in the first round of the Open on the Royal Lytham and St. Anne's course at Lytham St. Anne's, Lancashire on 10 July 1963 and by Tony Jacklin, O.B.E. (b. 7 July 1944) in the first round of the Open at St. Andrews, Fife, on 8 July 1970.

The lowest round in The Open itself has been 63 by Mark Hayes (b. 12 July 1949) (U.S.A.) at Turnberry, Strathclyde, in the second round on 7 July 1977. Thomas Henry Cotton, M.B.E. (b. Holmes Chapel, Cheshire, 26 Jan. 1907) at Royal St. George's, Sandwich, Kent completed the first 36-holes in 132 (67 + 65) on 27 June 1934. The lowest 72-hole aggregate is 268 (68, 70, 65, 65) by Tom Watson (b. 4 Sept. 1949) (U.S.A.) at Turnberry, ending on 9 July 1977.

U.S. Open
The United States Open Championship was inaugurated in 1894. The lowest 72-hole aggregate is 275 (71, 67, 72 and 65) by Jack Nicklaus (b. 21 Jan. 1940) on the Lower Course (7,015 yd *6 414 m*) at Baltusrol Country Club, Springfield, New Jersey, on 15–18 June 1967 and 275 (69, 68, 69 and 69) by Lee Trevino (b. near Horizon City, Texas, 1 Dec. 1939) at Oak Hill Country Club, Rochester, N.Y., on 13–16 June 1968. The lowest score for 18 holes is 63 by Johnny Miller (b. 29 Apr. 1947) on the 6,921 yd *6 328 m* par-71 Oakmont Country Club course, Pennsylvania on 17 June 1973.

U.S. Masters'
The lowest score in the U.S. Masters' (instituted on the par-72 6,980 yd *6 382 m* Augusta National Golf Course, Georgia, in

1934) has been 271 by Jack Nicklaus in 1965 and Raymond Floyd (b. 4 Sept. 1942) in 1976. The lowest rounds have been 64 by Lloyd Mangrum (1914–74) (first round, 1940), Jack Nicklaus (third round, 1965), Maurice Bembridge (G.B.) (b. 21 Feb. 1945) (fourth round, 1974), Hale Irwin (b. 3 June 1945) (fourth round, 1975), Gary Player (S. Africa) (fourth round, 1978) and Miller Barber (b. 31 Mar. 1931) (second round, 1979).

Amateur
The lowest score for nine holes in the Amateur Championship (inaugurated in 1885) is 29 by Richard Davol Chapman (b. 23 Mar. 1911) of the U.S.A. at Sandwich in 1948.

Michael Francis Bonallack, O.B.E. (b. 31 Dec. 1934) shot a 61 (32 + 29) on the par-71 6,905 yd *6 313 m* course at Ganton, North Yorkshire, on 27 July 1968 in the first 18 of the 36 holes in the final round of the English Amateur championship.

World Cup (formerly Canada Cup)
The World Cup (instituted as the Canada Cup in 1953) has been won most often by the U.S.A. with 14 victories between 1955 and 1978. The only men to have been on six winning teams have been Arnold Palmer (b. 10 Sept. 1929) (1960, 1962–64, 1966–67) and Jack Nicklaus (1963–64, 1966–67, 1971 and 1973). Only Nicklaus has taken the individual title three times (1963–64, 1971). The lowest aggregate score for 144 holes is 545 by Australia, Bruce Devlin (b. 10 Oct. 1937) and David Graham (b. 23 May 1946), at San Isidro, Buenos Aires, Argentina on 12–15 Nov. 1970. The lowest individual score has been 269 by Roberto de Vicenzo (b. Buenos Aires, Argentina, 14 Apr. 1923) also in 1970.

Ryder Trophy
The biennial Ryder Cup professional match between U.S.A. and the British Isles or Great Britain was instituted in 1927. The U.S.A. have won 18½ to 3½ to date. William Earl (Billy) Casper (b. San Diego, California, U.S.A., 24 June 1931) has the record of winning most matches in the Trophy with 20 in 1961–1975. Christy O'Connor Sr. (b. 21 Dec. 1924) (G.B.) played in ten matches up to 1973.

Walker Cup
The U.S.A. *v.* G.B. series instituted in 1921 (for the Walker Cup since 1922 and now biennially) has been won by the U.S.A. 25½–2½ to date. Joseph Boynton Carr (G.B. & I.) (b. February 1922) played in ten contests (1947–67).

Youngest and oldest champions
The youngest winner of The Open was Tom Morris, Jr. (1851–1875) at Prestwick, Strathclyde in 1868 aged 17 yr 5 months. The youngest winners of The Amateur title were John Charles Beharrel (b. 2 May 1938) at Troon, Strathclyde, on 2 June 1956, and Robert (Bobby) Cole (b. 11 May 1958) (South Africa) at Carnoustie, Tayside, on 11 June 1966, both aged 18 years 1 month. The oldest Open Champion was "Old Tom" Morris (1821–1908), aged 46 yr 99 days when he won at Prestwick in 1867. In recent times the 1967 champion, Roberto de Vicenzo was aged 44 years 93 days. The oldest winner of The Amateur was the Hon. Michael Scott at Hoylake, Merseyside in 1933, when 54. The oldest United States Amateur Champion was Jack Westland (b. 1905) at Seattle, Washington, in 1952 aged 47.

Most club championships
D. H. R. (Doug) Adams (b. 16 Oct. 1916) has won 29 club championships at the Port Pirie G.C., South Australia, from 1939–68, including 26 consecutively. The British record for amateur club championships is 20 consecutive wins (1937–39 and 1946–62) by Ronald Warner Hardy Taylor (1912–74) at the Dyke Golf Club, Brighton, East Sussex, who retired unbeaten in July 1963, and by Edward Christopher Chapman (b. 9 Apr. 1909), who won the Tunbridge Wells G.C. Scratch Championship for 20 consecutive years from 1951 to 1971.

Record tie
The longest delayed result in any National Open Championship occurred in the 1931 U.S. Open at Toledo, Ohio.

George von Elm (b. 1901) and Billy Burke (b. 1902) tied at 292, then tied the first replay at 149. Burke won the second replay by a single stroke after 72 extra holes.

Largest tournament

The annual Ford Amateur Golf Tournament in Great Britain attracted a record 100,030 competitors in 1978.

Richest prizes

The greatest first place prize money was $100,000 (total purse $500,000) in the World Open played at Pinehurst, North Carolina, U.S.A., over 144 holes on 8–17 Nov. 1973 won by Miller Barber (b. 31 Mar. 1931), of Texas, U.S.A. The World Series of Golf also carries a prize of $100,000. The highest British prize was £25,000 in the John Player Golf Classic at Hollinwell, Nottinghamshire, England on 3–6 Sept. 1970 won by Christy O'Connor Sr.

Highest earnings US PGA and LPGA circuits

The all time professional money-winner is Jack Nicklaus who, up to 31 Dec. 1978, has won $3,349,393. The record for a year is $362,429 by Tom Watson in 1978. The record for a woman is $189,814 by Nancy Lopez (now Mrs. T. Melton) (b. 6 Jan. 1957) (U.S.A.) in 1978. The record career earnings for a woman is $822,214 by Kathy Whitworth (U.S.A.) (b. 27 Sept. 1939) up to 31 Dec. 1978. The most won in a year by a British golfer is £32,127 by Peter Oosterhuis (b. 3 May 1948) in 1974.

Most tournament wins

The record for winning tournaments in a single season is 19, including a record 11 consecutively, by Byron Nelson (b. 4 Feb. 1912) (U.S.A.), in 1945. Sam Snead has won 84 official U.S. P.G.A. Tour events to Dec. 1978, and has been credited with a total 134 tournament victories since 1934. Mickey Wright has won 82 professional tournaments to Dec. 1978.

Biggest winning margin

The greatest margin of victory in a major tournament is 17 strokes by Randall Colin Vines (b. 22 June 1945) of Australia, in the Tasmanian Open with 274 in 1968.

HOLES IN ONE
Longest

The longest straight hole ever holed in one shot is the tenth (406 m *444 yd*) at Miracle Hills Golf Club, Omaha, Nebraska, U.S.A., by Robert Mitera (b. 1944) on 7 Oct. 1965. Mitera stands 5 ft 6 in *1,68 m* tall and weighs 165 lb. *74,842 kg* (11 st. 11 lb.). He is a two handicap player who can normally drive 245 yd *224 m*. A 50 m.p.h. *80 km/h* gust carried his shot over a 290 yd *265 m* drop-off. The longest "dog-leg" hole achieved in one is the 480 yd *439 m* fifth at Hope Country Club, Arkansas by L. Bruce on 15 Nov. 1962. The feminine record is 393 yd *359 m* by Marie Robie on the first hole of the Furnace Brook Golf Club, Wollaston, Mass., U.S.A., on 4 Sept. 1949. The longest hole in one performed in the British Isles is the seventh (393 yd *359 m*) at West Lancashire G.C. by Peter Parkinson in 1972.

In 1975 *Golf Digest* magazine recorded 26,267 "aces" which averages over 71 per day.

Most

The greatest number of holes-in-one in a career is 41 by Art Wall, Jr. (b. 23 Nov. 1923) between 1936 and 1973. The British record is 31 by Charles T. Chevalier (1902–1973) of Heaton Moor Golf Club, Stockport, Greater Manchester between 20 June 1918 and 1970. Douglas Porteous, 28, holed-in-one four times over 36 consecutive holes (3rd and 6th on 26 Sept.; 5th on 28 Sept. at Ruchill Golf Club, Glasgow; 6th at the Clydebank and District Golf Course on 30 Sept. 1974). Robert Taylor (Leicestershire) holed the 188 yd *172 m* 16th at Hunstanton, Norfolk on three successive days—31 May, 1 and 2 June 1974—in the Eastern Inter-Counties foursomes. Joe Lucius (U.S.A.), 59, holed the 138 yd *126 m* 15th at the Mohawk Golf Club, Tiffin, Ohio, in one for the eighth time on 16 Nov. 1974.

Consecutive

There are at least 15 cases of "aces" being achieved in two consecutive holes of which the greatest was Norman L. Manley's unique "double albatross" on the par-4 330 yd *301 m* seventh and par-4 290 yd *265 m* eighth holes on the Del Valle Country Club Course, Saugus, California, on 2 Sept. 1964. The only woman to record consecutive "aces" is Sue Prell, on the 13th and 14th holes at Chatswood Golf Club, Sydney, Australia on 29 May 1977.

There is no recorded instance of a golfer performing three consecutive holes in one. The closest to achieving it was by Dr. Joseph Boydstone on the 3rd, 4th and 9th at Bakersfield G.C., Cal., U.S.A., on 10 Oct. 1962, and by the Rev. Harold Snider (b. 4 July 1900) who aced the 8th, 13th and 14th holes of the par-3 Ironwood course, Arizona, U.S.A. on 9 June 1976.

Youngest and oldest

The youngest golfer recorded to have shot a hole-in-one was Coby Orr (5 years) of Littleton, Colorado on the 103 yd *94 m* fifth at the Riverside Golf Course, San Antonio, Texas in 1975. The oldest golfers to have performed the feat are 93 yr olds George Miller, on the 116 yd *106 m* 11th at Anaheim G.C., California on 4 Dec. 1970 and Charles Youngman, at the Tam O'Shanter Club, Toronto in 1971.

Shooting your age

The lowest under his age score recorded in a professional competition is 64 by Sam Snead (U.S.A.) at Onion Creek G.C. (6,585 yd *6 021 m*, par 70), Austin, Texas, in April 1978 when one month short of his 66th birthday.

The oldest player to score under his age is C. Arthur Thompson (1869–1975) of Victoria, British Columbia, Canada, who scored 103 on the Uplands course of 6,215 yd *5 682 m* aged 103 in 1973. The youngest player to score his age is Robert Leroy Klingaman (b. 22 Oct. 1914) who shot a 58 when aged 58 on the 5,654 yd *5 170 m* course at the Caledonia G.C., Fayetteville, Penn., U.S.A., on 31 Aug. 1973. Bob Hamilton shot 59, aged 59, on the 6,233 yd *5 699 m* blue course, Hamilton G.C., Evansville, Indiana, U.S.A., on 3 June 1975.

MOST TITLES

The most titles won in the world's major championships are as follows:

The Open	Harry Vardon (1870–1937)	6	1896, 1898–99, 1903, 11, 14
The Amateur	John Ball (1861–1940)	8	1888, 90, 92, 94, 99, 1907, 10, 12
U.S. Open	Willie Anderson (1880–1910)	4	1901, 1903–05
	Robert Tyre Jones, Jr. (1902–71)	4	1923, 26, 1929–30
	Ben William Hogan (b. 13 Aug. 1912)	4	1948, 1950–51, 1953
U.S. Amateur	Robert Tyre Jones, Jr. (1902–71)	5	1924–25, 1927–28, 1930
P.G.A. Championship (U.S.A.)	Walter Charles Hagen (1892–1969)	5	1921, 1924–27
Masters' Championship (U.S.A.)	Jack William Nicklaus (b. 21 Jan. 1940)	5	1963, 1965–66, 1972, 1975
U.S. Women's Open	Elizabeth (Betsy) Earle-Rawls (b. 4 May 1928)	4	1951, 1953, 1957, 1960
	"Mickey" Wright (b. 14 Feb. 1935)	4	1958–59, 1961, 1964
U.S. Women's Amateur	Glenna C. Vare (*née* Collett) (b. 20 June 1903)	6	1922, 1925, 1928–30, 1935
British Women's	Charlotte Cecilia Pitcairn Leitch (1891–1977)	4	1914, 1920–21, 1926
	Joyce Wethered (b. 17 Nov. 1901) (now **Lady** Heathcoat-Amory)	4	1922, 1924–25, 1929

Note: Nicklaus is the only golfer to have won five different major titles (the Open, U.S. Open, Masters, P.G.A. and U.S. Amateur titles) twice and a record 17 all told (1962–78). His remarkable record in the Open is three firsts, five seconds and two thirds.

GREYHOUND RACING

Earliest meeting

In September 1876 a greyhound meeting was staged at Hendon, North London with a railed hare operated by a windlass. Modern greyhound racing originated with the perfecting of the mechanical hare by Owen Patrick Smith at Emeryville, California, U.S.A., in 1919. The earliest greyhound race behind a mechanical hare in the British Isles was at Belle Vue, Manchester, opened on 24 July 1926.

Derby

The only two greyhounds to have won the English Greyhound Derby twice (instituted 1927, now over 500 m *546 yd*) are *Mick the Miller* (whelped in Ireland, June 1926 and died 1939) on 25 July 1929, when owned by Albert H. Williams, and on 28 June 1930 (owned by Mrs. Arundel H. Kempton), and *Patricia's Hope* on 24 June 1972 (when owned by Gordon and Basil Marks and Brian Stanley) and 23 June 1973 (when owned by G. & B. Marks and J. O'Connor). The highest prize was £17,500 to *Balliniska Band* for the Derby on 25 June 1977. The only greyhounds to win the English, Scottish and Welsh Derby "triple" are *Trev's Perfection*, owned by Fred Trevillion, in 1947, *Mile Bush Pride*, owned by Noel W. Purvis, in 1959, and *Patricia's Hope* in 1972. The only greyhound to win the American Derby, at Taunton, Mass., twice was *Real Huntsman* in 1950–51.

Grand National

The only greyhound to have won the Grand National (inst. 1927 over 525 yd *480 m*, now 500 m, and four flights) three times is *Sherry's Prince*, a 75 lb. *32 kg* dog (whelped in April 1967, died July 1978) owned by Mrs. Joyce Mathews of Sanderstead, Surrey, in 1970, 1971 and 1972 when he won by 6¼ lengths.

Fastest greyhound

The highest speed at which any greyhound has been timed is 41.72 m.p.h. *67,14 km/h* (410 yd *374 m* in 20.1 sec) by *The Shoe* on the then straightaway track at Richmond, N.S.W., Australia on 25 Apr. 1968. It is estimated that he covered the last 100 yds *91,44 m* in 4.5 sec or at 45.45 m.p.h. *73,14 km/h*. The highest speed recorded for a greyhound in Great Britain is 39.13 m.p.h. *62,97 km/h* by *Beef Cutlet*, when covering a straight course of 500 yds *457 m* in 26.13 sec at Blackpool, Lancashire, on 13 May 1933.

Fastest 500 m timings

The fastest *photo*-timing is 28.99 sec (38.58 m.p.h. *62,09 km/h*) at Brighton and Hove Stadium, Sussex by *Linacre* on 30 July 1977. The fastest *photo* timing over hurdles is 29.71 sec (37.64 m.p.h. *60,58 km/h*) also at Brighton by *Wotchit Buster* on 22 Aug. 1978.

Winning streak

Westpark Mustard, owned by Mr. & Mrs. Cyril Scotland, set a British record of 20 consecutive wins between 7 Jan. and 28 Oct. 1974. The world record is 28 consecutive victories by an American greyhound *Real Huntsman* in 1950–51.

GYMNASTICS

Earliest references

A primitive form of gymnastics was practised in ancient Greece and Rome during the period of the ancient Olympic Games (776 B.C. to A.D. 393) but Johann Friedrich Simon was the first teacher of modern gymnastics at Basedow's School, Dessau, Germany in 1776.

Most titles *World*

The greatest number of individual titles won by a man in the World Championships is ten by Boris Shakhlin (b. 27 Jan. 1932) (U.S.S.R.) between 1954 and 1964. He also won three team titles. The female record is ten individual wins and five team titles by Larissa Semyonovna Latynina (b. 27 Dec. 1934, retired 1966) of the U.S.S.R., between 1956 and 1964. Japan has won the men's team title a record five times (1962, 1966, 1970, 1974, 1978) and the U.S.S.R. the women's team title on six occasions (1954, 1958, 1962, 1970, 1974, 1978).

Fifty-four year old Lee Chin-yong, the appropriately named chin-ups record holder.

Most titles *Olympic*

Japan (1960, 1964, 1968, 1972 and 1976) have won the men's team title most often. The U.S.S.R. have won the women's title seven times (1952–1976). The only man to win six individual gold medals is Boris Shakhlin (U.S.S.R.), with one in 1956, four (two shared) in 1960 and one in 1964. He was also a member of the winning Combined Exercises team in 1956.

Vera Caslavska-Odlozil (b. 3 May 1942) (Czechoslovakia), has won most individual gold medals with seven, three in 1964 and four (one shared) in 1968. Larissa Latynina won six individual gold medals and was in three winning teams in 1956–64 making nine gold medals. She also won five silver and four bronze medals making 18 in all—an Olympic record for either sex in any sport.

Highest score *Olympics*

Nadia Comaneci (b. Romania, 12 Nov. 1961) achieved seven perfect scores of 10.00 at the Montreal Olympics in July 1976. Nelli Kim (now Mrs. Achasov) (b. U.S.S.R., 29 July 1957) was awarded two such scores on the same occasion.

Youngest International

Anita Jokiel (Poland) was aged only 11 yr 2 days when she competed at Brighton, East Sussex, England on 6 Dec. 1977.

Most titles *British*

The British Gymnastic Championship was won ten times by Arthur J. Whitford in 1928–36 and 1939. He was also in four winning teams. Wray "Nik" Stuart, M.B.E. (b. 20 July 1927) equalled the record of nine successive wins, 1956–64. The women's record is eight by Mary Patricia Hirst (b. 18 Nov. 1918) (1947, 1949–50 and 1952–56).

Most titles *World Cup*

In the first World Cup Competition, in London in 1975,

Ludmilla Tourischeva (now Mrs. Valeriy Borzov) (b. 7 Oct. 1952) (U.S.S.R.) won all five gold medals available.

Rope climbing

The United States Amateur Athletic Union records are tantamount to world records: 20 ft *6,09 m* (hands alone) 2.8 sec, Don Perry (U.S.A.) at Champaign, Illinois, U.S.A., on 3 Apr. 1954; 25 ft *7,62 m* (hands alone) 4.7 sec, Garvin S. Smith at Los Angeles, California, U.S.A., on 19 Apr. 1947.

Chinning the bar

The greatest number of continuous chin-ups (from a dead hang position) is 120 by Lee Chin-yong (b. 15 Aug. 1925) at the Y.M.C.A. Gym Hall, Seoul, Korea on 1 Mar. 1979. William Aaron Vaught (b. 1959) performed 20 one-arm (his right) chin-ups at Finch's Gymnasium, Houston, Texas, U.S.A., on 3 Jan. 1976. Francis Lewis (b. 1896) of Beatrice, Nebraska, U.S.A. in May 1914 achieved seven consecutive chins using only the middle finger of his left hand. His bodyweight was 158 lb. *71 kg 667* (11 st. 4 lb.).

Parallel bar dips

Peter Herbert (aged 33) performed a record 294 consecutive parallel bar dips on 11 July 1979 at the Haverfordwest Sports Centre, Dyfed, Wales. Jack La Lanne is reported to have done 1,000, in Oakland, Calif., U.S.A. in 1945.

Press-ups (Push-ups)

Tommy Gildert (aged 34) did 9,105 consecutive press-ups in 4 hr 17 min 19 sec at the Burnley Boys' Club, Lancashire, England on 1 July 1979. The most in 30 min is 1,834 by Troy Lapic (b. 30 Mar. 1966) of Corsicana, Texas, U.S.A. on 19 Aug. 1978. Tommy Gildert also performed 269 one-arm push-ups in ten minutes at the Burnley Boys' Club on 1 July 1979. Noel Barry Mason, of Burton-on-Trent, Staffs., did 267 finger tip press-ups in 1 min 50 sec on 10 June 1979. Robert Goldman, of Arverne, N.Y., did 80 consecutive hand-stand push-ups in 43 sec on 31 Aug. 1978 at the Brickman Hotel, N.Y., U.S.A.

Sit-ups *Straight-legged*

The greatest recorded number of sit-ups without feet pinned down or knees bent is 26,000 in 11 hr 44 min by Angel Bustamonte (b. 28 Feb. 1959) at Sacramento, Calif., U.S.A. on 17 Dec. 1977. In 2 min, under the same conditions, Darryl Hyek (aged 18) recorded 125 sit-ups at the Golden Triangle Health Spa, Tarentum, Penn., U.S.A. on 31 May 1979.

Jumping Jacks

The greatest recorded number of side-straddle hops is 20,088 performed in 4 hr 30 min by Chris Luther (b. 1947) at Beechwood School, Fort Lewis, Wash., U.S.A., on 12 Nov. 1977.

Vertical jumps

The greatest height in a vertical jump (Sargent Jump) *i.e.* the differential between the height of the finger-tip reach static and in jumping is 42 in *1,06 m* by David "Dr. D" Thompson (U.S.A.) in 1972. Reported higher jumps by athletes Franklin Jacobs (U.S.A.) and Greg Joy (Canada) were probably with an initial run. Olympic Pentathlon champion Mary Peters M.B.E. (G.B.) (b. 6 July 1939) is reported to have done 30 in *76,2 cm* in California in 1972.

Somersaults

James Chelich (b. 12 Mar. 1957, Fairview, Alberta, Canada) performed 8,450 forward rolls over 8.3 miles *13,35 km* on 21 Sept. 1974. Ian Michael Miles (b. 6 July 1960) of Corsham, Wiltshire, made a successful dive and tucked somersault over 33 men at Harrogate, North Yorkshire, on 27 July 1977.

Largest gymnasium

The world's largest gymnasium is Yale University's Payne Whitney Gymnasium at New Haven, Connecticut, U.S.A., completed in 1932 and valued at $18,000,000 £10,285,000. The building, known as the "Cathedral of Muscle" has nine storeys with wings of five storeys each. It is equipped with four basketball courts, three rowing tanks, 28 squash courts, 12 handball courts, a roof jogging track and a 25 yd *22,8 m*

by 14 yd *12,8 m* swimming pool on the first floor and a 55 yd *50,2 m* long pool on the third floor.

Largest crowd

The largest recorded crowd was approximately 18,000 people who packed the Forum, Montreal, Canada, for the final of the women's individual apparatus competitions at the XXI Olympic Games on 22 July 1976. Comparable audiences are reported for the Shanghai Stadium, People's Republic of China.

HANDBALL

Origins

Handball, similar to association football, with hands substituted for feet, was first played *c.* 1895. It was introduced into the Olympic Games at Berlin in 1936 as an 11-a-side outdoor game with Germany winning, but when re-introduced in 1972 it was an indoor game with seven-a-side, the standard size of team since 1952.

By 1977 there were some 70 countries affiliated to the International Handball Federation, (founded 1946), and an estimated ten million participants. The earliest international match was when Sweden beat Denmark on 8 Mar. 1935.

Olympic titles

The most victories in Olympic competition have been those by the U.S.S.R. in winning the men and women's titles at Montreal, Canada in 1976.

World titles

The most victories won in World championship (inst. 1938) competition are by Romania with four men's and three women's titles from 1956 to 1974.

HANDBALL (Court)

Origins

Handball played against walls or in a court is a game of ancient Celtic origin. In the early 19th century only a front wall was used but gradually side and back walls were added. The earliest international contest was in New York City, U.S.A., in 1887 between the champions of the U.S.A. and Ireland. The court is now a standardized 60 ft *18 m* by 30 ft *9 m* in Ireland, Ghana and Australia, and 40 ft *12 m* by 20 ft *6 m* in Canada, Mexico and the U.S.A. The game is played with both a hard and soft ball in Ireland and soft ball only in Australia, Canada, Ghana, Mexico and the U.S.A.

Championships

World championships were inaugurated in New York in October 1964 with competitors from Australia, Canada, Ireland, Mexico and the U.S.A. The most wins have been two by the U.S.A. in 1964 and 1967 (shared with Canada).

Most titles

The U.S. Championship 4-wall singles has been won six times by Jimmy Jacobs in 1955–57, 1960, 1964–65. He also shared in six doubles titles, 1962–63, 1965, 1967–68, 1975.

HARNESS RACING

Origins

Trotting races were held in Valkenburg, Netherlands in 1554. In England the trotting gait (the simultaneous use of the diagonally opposite legs) was known in the 16th century. The sulky first appeared in harness-racing in 1829. Pacers thrust out their fore and hind legs simultaneously on one side.

Most successful driver

The most successful sulky driver in North American harness racing history has been Herve Filion (b. 1 Feb. 1940) of Quebec, Canada who reached a record 6,705 wins by the end of the 1978 season. In 1974 he set year records of 637 wins and earnings of $3,474,315 by horses he drove. He won his tenth North American championship in 1978. William Haughton has won a record $27.1 million in his career to end 1978.

Records against time	Trotting				Pacing		
World (mile 1 609,34 m track)	1:54.8	Nevele Pride (driver Stanley Dancer) (U.S.) Indianapolis, Indiana	31 Aug. 1969		1:52.0	Steady Star (driver Joe O'Brien) (Canada) Lexington, Kentucky	1 Oct 1971
World race record (mile)	1:55.0	Speedy Somolli (driver, Howard Beissinger) (U.S.A.) at Du Quoin, Illinois	2 Sept. 1978		1:53.2	Warm Breeze (driver Dick Farrington) (U.S.) at Sacramento, California	26 June 1977
	1:55.0	Florida Pro (driver, George Sholty) (U.S.A.) at Du Quoin, Illinois	2 Sept. 1978				

Highest price

The highest price paid for a trotter is $3,200,000 for *Green Speed* by the Pine Hollow Stud of New York from Beverley Lloyds, Florida in 1977. The highest price ever paid for a pacer is $3,600,000 for *Nero* in March, 1976 and *Falcon Almahurst* in 1978.

Greatest winnings

The greatest amount won by a trotting horse is $1,960,945 by *Bellino II* (France) up to retirement in 1977. The record for a pacing horse is $1,360,887 by *Rambling Willie* (U.S.A.) to end of 1978 season.

Troika record

The U.S.S.R troika record for the standard 1 600 m (four laps of 400 m) is 1 min 58.0 sec by a bay trio from Nolinsk, trained by Vladimir Kuznetsov in Moscow in February 1974.

HOCKEY

MEN

Origins

A representation of two players with curved snagging sticks apparently in an orthodox "bully" position was found in Tomb No. 17 at Beni Hasan, Egypt and has been dated to *c.* 2050 B.C. There is a British reference to the game in Lincolnshire in 1277. The first country to form a national association was England with the first Hockey Association founded at Cannon Street Hotel, City of London on 16 Apr. 1875.

The oldest club with a continuous history is Teddington H.C. formed in the autumn of 1871. They played Richmond on 24 Oct. 1874 and used the first recorded circle *versus* Surbiton at Bushey Park on 9 Dec. 1876. The first international match was the Wales v. Ireland match at Rhyl on 26 Jan. 1895. Ireland won 3–0.

Most Olympic medals

The Indians were Olympic Champions from the re-inception of Olympic hockey in 1928 until 1960, when Pakistan beat them 1–0 at Rome. They had their seventh win in 1964. Of the six Indians who have won three Olympic team gold medals two have also won a silver medal—Leslie Walter Claudius (b. 25 Mar. 1927) in 1948, 1952, 1956 and 1960 (silver) and Udham Singh (b. 4 Aug. 1928) in 1952, 1956, 1964 and 1960 (silver).

Highest international score

The highest score in international hockey was when India defeated the United States 24–1 at Los Angeles, California, U.S.A., in the 1932 Olympic Games. The greatest number of goals in a home international match was when England defeated France 16–0 at Beckenham on 25 Mar. 1922. The World Cup has been won twice by Pakistan in 1971 and 1978.

Most international appearances

Avtar Singh Sohal (b. 22 Mar. 1938) represented Kenya 167 times between 1957 and 1972. The most by a home countries player is 139 by H. David Judge (b. 19 Jan. 1936) with 124 for Ireland and 15 for Great Britain from 1957 to 1978.

Ireland	124	H. David Judge		1957–78
Wales	90	D. Austin Savage (b. 15 Dec. 1940)		1962–78
England	73	Bernard J. Cotton (b. 30 Jun. 1948)		1970–78
Scotland	66	Kenneth A. H. Dick (b. 17 Nov. 1946)		1969–78
Great Britain	56	John W. Neill (England) (b. 15 May 1934)		1959–68

Greatest scoring feats

M. C. Marckx (Bowdon 2nd XI) scored 19 goals against Brooklands 2nd XI (score 23–0) on 31 Dec. 1910. He was selected for England in March 1912 but declined due to business priorities. Between 1923 and 1958, Fred H. Wagner scored 1,832 goals for Beeston H.C., Nottingham Casuals and the Nottinghamshire county side.

Greatest goalkeeping

Richard James Allen (b. 1902) (India) did not concede a goal during the 1928 Olympic Tournament and only a total of three in the following two Olympics of 1932 and 1936.

Longest game

The longest international game on record was one of 145 min (into the sixth period of extra time), when Netherlands beat Spain 1–0 in the Olympic tournament at Mexico City on 25 Oct. 1968. The longest club match on record was one of 175 min between Perth H.C. and Aberdeen G.S.F.P. at the North Inch, Perth in the Scottish Cup quarter-final on 24 Feb. 1973.

WOMEN

Origins

The earliest women's club was East Molesey in Surrey, England formed in *c.* 1887. The Wimbledon Ladies Hockey

Television's female Superstars champion, Val Robinson, hopes to add an Olympic medal to her hockey appearances record. (*Provincial Sports Photography*)

Club, founded one year later, is still in existence. The first national association was the Irish Ladies' Hockey Union founded in 1894. The All England Women's Hockey Association held its first formal meeting in Westminster Town Hall, London, on 23 Nov. 1895. The first international match was an England v. Ireland game in Dublin in 1896. Ireland won 2–0. The first Championship Tournament of 21 nations was at Edinburgh, Scotland in 1975. England won and hold the Silver Quaich.

Highest scores

The highest score in a women's international match occurred when England defeated France 23–0 at Merton, Greater London, on 3 Feb. 1923. In club hockey, Ross Ladies beat Wyeside, at Ross-on-Wye, Herefordshire, 40–0 on 24 Jan. 1929, when Edna Mary Blakelock (b. 22 Oct. 1904) scored a record 21 goals.

Most international appearances

England	110*	Valerie Robinson	1963–79
Wales	67	Ann Ellis (b. 21 Sept. 1940)	1963–79
Ireland	46	Maeve Esther Enid Kyle (*née* Shankey) (b. 6 Oct. 1928)	1947–66
Scotland	52	Margaret Brown (b. 7 June 1946)	1967–79
* She has also represented Great Britain on eight occasions.			

Highest attendance

The highest attendance at a women's hockey match was 65,165 for the match between England and the U.S.A. at the Empire Stadium, Wembley, Brent, Greater London, on 11 Mar. 1978.

Marathon

Two teams of eleven from Newmarket Hockey Club played for 27 hr 10 min on 19–20 May, 1979, at Coldhams Common, Cambridge.

HORSE RACING

Origins

Horsemanship was an important part of the Hittite culture of Anatolia, Turkey dating from 1400 B.C. The 33rd ancient Olympic Games of 648 B.C. in Greece featured horse racing. The earliest horse race recorded in England was one held in about A.D. 210 at Netherby, North Yorkshire, among Arabians brought to Britain by Lucius Septimius Severus (A.D. 146–211), Emperor of Rome. The oldest race still being run annually is the Lanark Silver Bell, instituted in Scotland by William the Lion (1143–1214).

The Jockey Club was formed in 1750–51; however the original Charleston Jockey Club, Virginia, U.S.A. was the first in the world, organised in 1734. The General Stud Book started in 1791. Racing colours (silks) became compulsory in 1889.

Racecourse *Largest*

The world's largest racecourse is the Newmarket course (founded 1636) on which the Beacon Course, the longest of the 19 courses, is 4 miles 397 yds *6,80 km* long and the Rowley Mile is 167 ft *50 m* wide. The border between Suffolk and Cambridgeshire runs through the Newmarket course. The world's largest grandstand is that opened in 1968 at Belmont Park, Long Island, N.Y., U.S.A. at a cost of $30,700,000 *£12.8 million*. It is 110 ft *33 m* tall, 440 yd *402 m* long, contains 908 mutuel windows and seats 30,000. The highest seating capacity at any racetrack is 40,000 at Atlantic City Audit, New Jersey, U.S.A.

The world's smallest racecourse is the Lebong racecourse, Darjeeling, West Bengal, India (altitude 7,000 ft *2 125 m*), where the complete lap is 481 yd *439 m*. It was laid out c. 1885 and used as a parade ground.

Largest prizes

The richest race ever held is the All-American Futurity, a race for quarter-horses over 440 yds *402 m* (400 yd *366 m* before 1973) at Ruidoso Downs, New Mexico, U.S.A. The prizes in 1978 totalled $1,280,000 *£218,750*. The richest first prize for any horse race was $437,500 won by the *Moon Lark*, the winner of the 1978 All-American Futurity.

above: Lester Piggott winning his record eighth Derby on *The Minstrel* in 1977. (*Tony Duffy, All-Sport Photographic*)

right: The American Triple Crown winner *Affirmed*, here ridden by Steve Cauthen, became the most valuable horse ever when syndicated for $14.4 million. (*All-Sport Photographic*)

The richest prize on the British Turf was £153,980 in the 200th Derby, won by *Troy*, owned by Sir Michael Sobell, on 6 June 1979.

Longest race

The longest recorded horse race was one of 1,200 miles *1 925 km* in Portugal, won by a horse *Emir* bred from Egyptian-bred Blunt Arab stock. The holder of the world's record for long distance racing and speed is *Champion Crabbet*, who covered 300 miles *482 km* in 52 hr 33 min carrying 17½ st. *111,130 kg*, in 1920. In 1831 Squire George Osbaldeston (1787–1866), M.P. of East Retford covered 200 miles *321 km* in 8 hr 42 min at Newmarket, using 50 mounts, so averaging 22.99 m.p.h. *36,99 km/h.*

Most runners

The most horses in a race is 66 in the Grand National of 22 Mar. 1929. The record for the flat is 58 in the Lincolnshire Handicap on 13 Mar. 1948. The most runners at a meeting were 214 (flat) in seven races at Newmarket on 15 June 1915 and 229 (National Hunt) in eight races at Worcester on 13 Jan. 1965.

Dead heats

There is no recorded case in turf history of a quintuple dead heat. The nearest approach was in the Astley Stakes, at Lewes, England, on 6 Aug. 1880 when *Mazurka*, *Wandering Nun* and *Scobell* triple dead-heated for first place a head in front of *Cumberland* and *Thora*, who dead-heated for fourth place. Each of the five jockeys thought he had won. The only three known examples of a quadruple dead heat were between *Honest Harry*, *Miss Decoy*, *a filly by Beningbrough* (later named *Young Daffodil*) and *Peteria* at Bogside, on 7 June 1808, between *Defaulter*, *The Squire of Malton*, *Reindeer* and *Pulcherrima* in the Omnibus Stakes at The Hoo, Herts., England, on 26 Apr. 1851, and between *Overreach*, *Lady Golightly*, *Gamester* and *The Unexpected* at the Houghton Meeting at Newmarket on 22 Oct. 1855. Since the introduction of the photo-finish, the highest number of horses dead-heating has been three, on several occasions.

Horse *Greatest record*

The horse with the best recorded win-loss record was *Kincsem*, a Hungarian mare foaled in 1874, who was unbeaten in 54 races (1876–79), including the Goodwood Cup of 1878. *Camarero* owned by Don José Coll Vidal of Puerto Rico, foaled in 1951, had a winning streak of 56 races from 19 Apr. 1953 to 17 Aug. 1955. He died "from a colic" on 26 Aug. 1956 the day after his 73rd win in 77 starts.

Horse *Tallest*

The tallest horse ever to race is *Fort d'Or*, owned by Lady Elizabeth (Eliza) Nugent (*née* Guinness) of Berkshire, England. He stands 18.2 hands *187 cm* and was foaled in County Wexford, Ireland in April 1963 out of *Golden Sunset*, who stood only 15.1 hands.

Horse *Highest price*

The most expensive horse ever is the 1978 American Triple Crown winner *Affirmed* (foaled 1975). It was announced in Nov. 1978 that he would be syndicated for $14.4 million, in 36 shares of $400,000 each. The highest price for a yearling is $1.6 million for a colt by *Hoist the Flag-Royal Dowry*, bought on 25 July 1979 at Keeneland, Kentucky, U.S.A. by two Japanese buyers.

Horse *Greatest winnings*

The greatest amount ever won by a horse is $2,044,218 by *Affirmed* from 1977 to June 1979. The leading money-winning mare is *Dahlia* (foaled 1970) who, from 1972 to 1976, earned $1,535,443. The most won in a year is $901,541 *£450,770* by *Affirmed* in 1978.

Horse *Shortest price*

The shortest odds ever quoted for any racehorse are 10,000 to 1 on for *Dragon Blond*, ridden by Lester Piggott O.B.E. (G.B.) (b. 5 Nov. 1935) in the Premio Naviglio in Milan, Italy on 1 June 1967. Odds of 100 to 1 on were quoted for the United States horse *Man o' War* (foaled 29 Mar. 1917, died 1 Nov. 1947) on three separate occasions in 1920, and for the two British horses, *Ormonde* (Champion Stakes, 14 Oct. 1886,

three runners), and *Sceptre* (Limekiln Stakes 27 Oct. 1903, two runners).

Jockey *Wins on one card*

The most winners ridden on one card is eight by Hubert S. Jones, 17, from 13 rides at Caliente, Cal., U.S.A. on 11 June 1944, and by Oscar Barattuci, at Rosario City, Argentina, on 15 Dec. 1957. The longest winning streak is 12 by Sir Gordon Richards (b. Oakengates, Salop, 5 May 1904) (last race at Nottingham on 3 Oct., six out of six at Chepstow on 4 Oct. and the first five races next day at Chepstow) in 1933.

Jockey *Youngest and oldest*

The youngest jockey was Frank Wootton (English Champion jockey 1909–1912), who rode his first winner in South Africa aged 9 years 10 months. The oldest jockey was Levi Barlingame (U.S.A.), who rode his last race at Stafford, Kansas, in 1932 aged 80.

The greatest recorded age for a first win has been 67 years in the case of Mr. Victor Morley Lawson on *Ocean King* at Warwick on 16 Oct. 1973.

Jockey *Lightest*

The lightest recorded jockey was Kitchener (d. 1872), who won the Chester Cup on *Red Deer* in 1844 at 3 st. 7 lb. *22,226 kg*. He was said to have weighed only 2 st. 7 lb. *15,875 kg* in 1840.

Jockey *Most successful*

The most successful jockey of all time has been William Lee (Willie) Shoemaker (b. weighing 2½ lb. *1,133 kg* on 19 Aug. 1931) now weighing 98 lb. *44 kg* and standing 4 ft 11½ in *1,51 m*. From March 1949 to end 1978 he rode 7,598 winners from some 32,184 mounts earning $70,020,545.

The greatest amount ever won by any jockey in a year is $6,188,353 by Darrell McHargue (b. 1954) in 1978. The most winners ridden in a year is 546, from a record 2,199 mounts, by Chris McCarron (U.S.A.) (b. 1955) in 1974.

Trainers

The greatest number of wins by a trainer in one year is 494 by Jack Van Berg in 1976. The greatest amount won in a year is $3,314,564 by Lazaro S. Barrera in 1978.

Owners

The most winners in a year by an owner is 494 by Dan R. Lasater (U.S.A.) in 1974 when he also won a record $3,022,960 in prize money.

BRITISH TURF RECORDS
Most successful *Horses*

As the 1,000 Guineas and the Oaks are restricted to fillies, only they can possibly win all five classics. *Sceptre* came closest in 1902 when she won the 2,000 Guineas, 1,000 Guineas, Oaks and St. Leger. In 1868 *Formosa* won the same four but dead-heated in the 2,000 Guineas. The most races won in a season is 23 by three-year-old *Fisherman* in 1856. *Catherina* (foaled 1830) won a career record 79 out of 176 races, 1832–41. The record for this century is by *Le Garcon d'Or* (foaled 1958) with 34 wins out of 181 flat races 1960–73. The only horse to win the same race in seven successive years was *Dr. Syntax* (foaled 1811) in the Preston Gold Cup (1815–21). The most successful sire was *Stockwell* (foaled 1849) whose progeny won 1,153 races (1858–76) and in 1866 set a record of 132 races won. The greatest amount ever won by an English-trained horse is £326,421 by *Grundy* (foaled 1972) in 1974–75 and by a filly, £154,194 by *Highclere* (foaled 1971) in 1973–74.

Most successful *Owners*

The greatest amount of stake money won is £1,025,592 from 784 races by H.H. Aga Khan III (1877–1957) from 1922 until his death. These included 35 classics, of which 17 were English classics. He was leading owner a record thirteen times between 1924 and 1952. The record for a season was set by Robert Sangster, who won £348,023 in first-prize money in 1977. The most wins in a season is 115 by David Robinson in 1973. The most English classics won is 20 by the 4th Duke of Grafton, K.G. (1760–1844), from 1813 to 1831.

Sir Gordon Richards on *Pinza* after he had finally won the Derby in 1953, the year he was champion jockey for the 26th time and received his knighthood. (*Popperfoto*)

Most successful *Trainers*

Sir Charles Francis Noel Murless (b. Malpas, Cheshire, 24 Mar. 1910) earned more than £2,500,000 in winning money and £3,000,000 counting place money for his patrons. The record first-prize money in a season is £439,124 by Vincent O'Brien in 1977. The most classics won by a trainer is 41 by John Scott (1794–1871) including 16 St. Leger winners between 1827 and 1862. Alec Taylor of Manton, Wiltshire headed the trainers' lists for a record 12 seasons between 1907 and 1925. In 1867 John Day won 146 races.

Most successful *Jockeys*

Sir Gordon Richards won 4,870 races from 21,834 mounts from his first mount at Lingfield on 16 Oct. 1920 to 1954. His first win was on 31 Mar. 1921. In 1953, after 27 attempts, he won the Derby, six days after being knighted. In 1947 he won a record 269 races. He was champion jockey a record 26 times between 1925 and 1953. The most classic races won by a jockey is 27 by Francis (Frank) Buckle (1766–1832), between 1792 and 1827.

Triple Crown

The English "Triple Crown" (Two Thousand Guineas, Derby, St. Leger) has been won 15 times, most recently by *Nijinsky* in 1970. The American "Triple Crown" (Kentucky Derby, Preakness Stakes, Belmont Stakes) has been achieved 11 times, most recently by *Affirmed* in 1978.

THE DERBY

For more details see Derby 200 *by Michael Seth-Smith and Roger Mortimer, published by Guinness Superlatives Ltd. (price £5.95).*

The greatest of England's five classics is the Derby Stakes,

inaugurated on 4 May 1780, and named after the 12th Earl of Derby (1752–1834). The distance was increased in 1784 from a mile to 1½ miles *2 414 m*. The race has been run at Epsom Downs, Surrey, except for the two war periods, when it was run at Newmarket, and is for three-year-olds only. Since 1884 the weights have been: colts 9 st. *57 kg*, fillies 8 st. 9 lb. *54 kg 884*. Geldings were eligible until 1904.

GRAND NATIONAL

For more details see The Guinness Guide to Steeplechasing *by Gerry Cranham, Richard Pitman and John Oaksey, published by Guinness Superlatives Ltd. (price £11.95).*

The first official Grand National Steeplechase may be regarded as the Grand Liverpool Steeplechase of 26 Feb. 1839 though the race was not given its present name until 1847. It became a handicap in 1843. Until 1930 five-year-olds were eligible, but since then it has been for six-year-olds and above. Except for the two war periods (1916–18 and 1941–45) the race has been run at Aintree near Liverpool, since 1839, over a course of 4½ miles *7 242 m* and 30 jumps.

Most wins

The only horse to win three times is *Red Rum* (foaled 1965) in 1973–74, and 1977. He also came second in 1975 and 1976 from five runs. *Manifesto* ran eight times (1895–1904) and won twice, came third three times and fourth once.

The only owners with three wins are Captain Henry Machell with *Disturbance* (1873), *Reugny* (1874) and *Regal* (1876); Sir Charles Assheton-Smith (formerly Charles Duff) with *Cloister* (1893), *Jerry M.* (1912) and *Covertcoat* (1913); and Noel Le Mare with *Red Rum* (1973–74, 1977).

The only trainer with four winners is Fred Rimell with *E.S.B.* (1956), *Nicolaus Silver* (1961), *Gay Trip* (1970) and *Rag Trade* (1976). The Hon. Aubrey Hastings won with *Ascetic's Silver* (1906), *Ally Sloper* (1915), and *Master Robert* (1924), and also won a wartime substitute race at Gatwick with *Ballymacad* (1917).

The only jockey to ride five winners was George Stevens on *Free Trader* (1856), *Emblem* (1863), *Emblematic* (1864) and *The Colonel* (1869–70).

Red Rum with his trainer Ginger McCain, the combination which dominated the Grand National for five years. (*Syndication International*)

MAJOR RACE RECORDS

Race	Record Time	Jockey	Trainer	Owner	Largest Field
Derby (1780) 1½ miles	2 min 33.8 sec Mahmoud 1936	8—Lester Piggott O.B.E. 1954, 57, 60, 68, 70, 72, 76, 77	7—John Porter 1868, 82, 83, 86, 90, 91, 99 7—Robert Robson 1793, 1802, 09, 10, 15, 17, 23 7—Fred Darling 1922, 25, 26, 31, 38, 40, 41	5—3rd Earl of Egremont 1782, 1804, 05, 07, 26 5—H. H. Aga Khan III 1930, 35, 36, 48, 52	34 (1862)
1,000 Guineas (1814) 1 mile	1 min 37 sec Camaree 1950	7—George Fordham 1859, 61, 65, 68, 69, 81, 83	8—Robert Robson 1819, 20, 21, 22, 23, 25, 26, 27	8—4th Duke of Grafton 1819, 20, 21, 22, 23, 25, 26, 27	29 (1926)
2,000 Guineas (1809) 1 mile	1 min 35.8 sec My Babu 1948	9—Jem Robinson 1825, 28, 31, 33, 34, 35, 36, 47, 48	5—Fred Darling 1925, 31, 38, 42, 47	5—4th Duke of Grafton 1820, 21, 22, 26, 27 5—Lord Jersey 1831, 34, 35, 36, 37	28 (1930)
Oaks (1779) 1½ miles	2 min 34.6 sec Beam 1927	9—Frank Buckle 1797, 98, 99, 1802, 03, 05, 17, 18, 23	8—Alec Taylor 1910, 17, 18, 19, 21, 22, 25, 26	6—4th Duke of Grafton 1813, 15, 22, 23, 28, 31	26 (1848)
St. Leger (1776) 1 m 6 f 127 yd	3 min 01.6 sec Coronach 1926 Windsor Lad 1934	9—Will Scott 1821, 25, 28, 29, 38, 39, 40, 41, 46	16—John Scott 1827, 28, 29, 32, 34, 38, 39, 40, 41, 45, 51, 53, 56, 57, 59, 62	7—9th Duke of Hamilton 1786, 87, 88, 92, 1808, 09, 14	30 (1825)
Prix de l'Arc de Triomphe (1920) 2400 metres	2 min 28.3 sec Mill Reef 1971 San San 1972	4—Jacqués Doyasbère 1942, 44, 50, 51	4—Charles H. Semblat 1942, 44, 46, 49	6—Marcel Boussac 1936, 37, 42, 44, 46, 49	30 (1967)
Washington, D.C. International (1952) 1½ miles	2 min 23.8 sec Kelso 1964	3—Manuel Ycaza 1959, 60, 67	3—Maurice Zilber 1973, 75, 76	3—Paul Mellon 1967, 70, 71 3—Nelson Bunker Hunt 1973, 75, 76	13 (1955, 1962)
King George VI and Queen Elizabeth Stakes (1951) 1½ miles	2 min 26.98 sec Grundy 1975	6—Lester Piggott 1965, 66, 69, 70, 74, 77	3—Noel Murless 1966, 67, 68 3—Vincent O'Brien 1958, 70, 77	2—Nelson Bunker Hunt 1973, 74	19 (1951)
Kentucky Derby (1875) 1¼ miles	1 min 59.4 sec Secretariat 1973	5—Eddie Arcaro 1938, 41, 45, 48, 52 5—Bill Hartack 1957, 60, 62, 64, 69	6—Ben A. Jones 1938, 41, 44, 48, 49, 52	8—Calumet Farm 1941, 44, 48, 49, 52, 57, 58, 68	23 (1974)

SPEED RECORDS

Distance	Time min. sec.	m.p.h.	km/h	Name	Age	Weight carried lb.	Course	Date
¼ mile	20.8	43.26	69,62	*Big Racket (Mexico)*	4	114	Mexico City, Mexico	5 Feb. 1945
½ mile	44.4	40.54	65,24	*Sonido (Venezuela)*	2	111	‡Caracas, Venezuela	28 June 1970
⅝ mile	53.6†	41.98	67,56	*Indigenous (G.B.)*	4	131	‡*Epsom Surrey	2 June 1960
	53.89††	41.75	67,19	*Raffingora (G.B.)*	5	140	‡*Epsom, Surrey	5 June 1970
	55.4	40.61	65,36	*Zip Pocket (U.S.A.)*	3	122	Turf Paradise, Phoenix, Arizona, U.S.A.	22 Apr. 1967
¾ mile	1:06.2	40.78	65,62	*Gelding by Blink—Broken Tendril (G.B.)*	2	123	*Brighton, East Sussex	6 Aug. 1929
	1:07.2	40.18	64,66	*Grey Papa (U.S.A.)*	6	112	Longacres, Seattle, Washington, U.S.A.	4 Sept. 1972
1 mile	1:31.8	39.21	63,10	*Soueida (G.B.)*	4	126	*Brighton, East Sussex	19 Sept. 1900
	1:31.8	39.21	63,10	*Loose Cover (G.B.)*	3	110	*Brighton, East Sussex	9 June 1966
	1:32.2	39.04	62,82	*Dr. Fager (U.S.A.)*	4	134	Arlington, Illinois, U.S.A.	24 Aug. 1968
1¼ miles	1:57.4	38.33	61,68	*Double Discount (U.S.A.)*	4	116	Santa Anita, Arcadia, California, U.S.A.	9 Oct. 1977
1½ miles	2:23.0	37.76	60,76	*Fiddle Isle (U.S.A.)*	5	124	Santa Anita, Arcadia, California, U.S.A.	21 Mar. 1970
2 miles**	3:15.0	36.93	59,43	*Polazel (G.B.)*	3	142	Salisbury, Wiltshire	8 July 1924
2½ miles	4:14.6	35.35	56,90	*Miss Grillo (U.S.A.)*	6	118	Pimlico, Baltimore, Maryland, U.S.A.	12 Nov. 1948
3 miles	5:15.0	34.29	55,18	*Farragut (Mexico)*	5	113	Aguascalientes, Mexico	9 Mar. 1941

* Epsom and Brighton courses include a sharp descent of ¼ mile.
** A more reliable modern record is 3 min 16.75 sec by Il Tempo (N.Z.) (7 yr, 130 lb.) at Trentham, Wellington, New Zealand on 17 Jan. 1970.
† Hand timed.
†† Electrically timed.
‡ Straight courses.

Highest prize

The highest prize and the richest ever under National Hunt rules was £41,140 for *Red Rum* on 2 Apr. 1977.

Fastest time

The record time is 9 min 1.9 sec set by *Red Rum* carrying 10 st. 5 lb. *65,770 kg* ridden by Brian Fletcher (b. 1947) owned by Noel Le Mare (b. 1887) and trained by Donald McCain (b. 1930) of Southport on 31 Mar. 1973. This represents an average speed of 29.80 m.p.h. *47,96 km/h.*

NATIONAL HUNT

Jockeys *Most successful*

The first National Hunt jockey to reach 1,000 wins is Stan Mellor, M.B.E. (b. Manchester, 10 Apr. 1937). This he achieved on *Ouzo* at Nottingham on 18 Dec. 1971 and retired on 18 June 1972 after 1,049 wins (incl. 14 abroad) in 20 years. He also won three flat races.

The record number of wins in a season is 149 by John "Jonjo" O'Neill (b. 1952) in 1977–78. The record number of successive wins is ten by John Alnam Gilbert (b. 26 July 1920), 8–20 Sept. 1959. The record number of National Hunt Championships is seven by Gerald Wilson (1903–68) from 1933–38 and 1941. Capt. Kenyon Goode owned, trained and rode three successive winners under National Hunt rules at Torquay, Devon on 7 Apr. 1931.

Horse *Greatest winnings*

The greatest amount won by a British-trained jumper is £114,370 by *Red Rum* between 1969 and 1978.

HURLING

Earliest reference

A game of very ancient origin, hurling only became standardized with the formation of the Gaelic Athletic Association in Thurles, Ireland, on 1 Nov. 1884. The Irish Hurling Union was formed on 24 Jan. 1879.

Most titles *All-Ireland*

The greatest number of All-Ireland Championships won by one team is 24 by Cork between 1890 and 1978. The greatest number of successive wins is the four by Cork (1941–44).

Most titles *Inter-provincials*

Munster holds the greatest number of inter-provincial (Railway Cup) championships with 34 (1928–1977).

Most appearances

The most appearances in All-Ireland finals is ten shared by Christy Ring (Cork and Munster) and John Doyle (Tipperary). They also share the record of All-Ireland medals won with eight each. Ring's appearances on the winning side were in 1941–44, 1946 and 1952–54, while Doyle's were in 1949–51, 1958, 1961–62 and 1964–65. Ring also played in a record 22 inter-provincial finals (1942–63) and was on the winning side 18 times.

Highest scores

The highest score in an All-Ireland final (60 min) was in 1896 when Tipperary (8 goals, 14 points) beat Dublin (no goals, 4 points). The record aggregate score was when Cork (6 goals, 21 points) defeated Wexford (5 goals, 10 points) in the 80 min final of 1970. A goal equals three points.

The highest recorded individual score was by Nick Rackard (Wexford), who scored 7 goals and 7 points against Antrim in the 1954 All Ireland semi-final.

Lowest score

The lowest score in an All-Ireland final was when Tipperary (1 goal, 1 point) beat Galway (nil) in the first championship at Birr in 1887.

Longest stroke

The greatest distance for a "lift and stroke" is one of 129 yd *117 m* credited to Tom Murphy of Three Castles, Kilkenny, in a "long puck" contest in 1906. The record for the annual *An Poc Fada* (Long Puck) contest (instituted 1961) in the ravines of the Cooley Hills, north of Dundalk, County Louth, is 65 pucks (drives) plus 87 yd *79 m* over the course of 3 miles 320 yd *5,120 km* by Fionnbar O'Neill (Cork) in 1966. This represents an average of 84.8 yd *77,5 m* per drive.

Largest crowd

The largest crowd was 84,856 for the final between Cork and Wexford at Croke Park, Dublin, in 1954.

ICE HOCKEY

Origins

There is pictorial evidence that a hockey-like game was played on ice in the early 16th century in The Netherlands. The game was probably first played with a puck in North America in 1855 at Kingston, Ontario, Canada, but Halifax also lays claim to priority. The International Ice Hockey Federation was founded in 1908. The National Hockey League of North America was inaugurated 1917. The World Hockey Association was formed in 1971.

Olympic Games and World Championships

Canada has won the Olympic Championship six times (1920–1924–28–32–48–52) and the world title 19 times, the last being at Geneva in 1961. The longest Olympic career is that of Richard Torriani (b. 1 Oct. 1911) (Switzerland) from 1928 to 1948. The most gold medals won by any player is three achieved by Vitaliy Davidov, Anatoliy Firssov, Viktor Kuzkin and Aleksandr Ragulin of the U.S.S.R. teams that won the Olympic titles in 1964, 1968 and 1972. World amateur championships began at Antwerp, Belgium in 1920, and were first opened to professionals in 1976.

Yet another goal to record breaking Anders Hedberg, one of the fine Swedish players who have made their mark on North American ice hockey. (*World Hockey Association*)

Stanley Cup

The Stanley Cup, presented by the Governor-General, Lord Stanley (original cost $48.67), became emblematic of National Hockey League supremacy 33 years after the first contest at Montreal in 1893. It has been won most often by the Montreal Canadiens with 22 wins in 1916, 1924, 1930–31, 1944, 1946, 1953, 1956–60, 1965–66, 1968–69, 1971, 1973, 1976–79.

British Leagues

The defunct British League championship (inst. 1934) was won most often by the Wembley Lions with four victories in 1936–37, 1952 and 1957. Murrayfield Racers have won the Northern League (inst. 1966) four times, 1970–72 and 1976. Streatham Redskins have won the Southern League (inst. 1970) four times, 1975–78.

Most goals *Team*

The greatest number of goals recorded in a world championship match has been 47–0 when Canada beat Denmark in Stockholm, Sweden on 12 Feb. 1949. The National Hockey League record is 21 goals when Montreal Canadiens beat Toronto St. Patrick's, at Montreal, 14–7 on 10 Jan. 1920.

Most goals *Individual*

The most goals by a professional player in a season (W.H.A.) is 83 by Anders Hedberg (b. Sweden, 25 Feb. 1951) (Winnipeg Jets) in 1976–77. Most in the N.H.L. is 80 by Reggie Leach (b. Canada, 23 Apr. 1950) (Philadelphia Flyers) in 1975–76. The most points in a season, including playoffs, is 169 (71 goals and 98 assists) by Marc Tardif (b. 12 June 1949) (Quebec Nordiques) in 1977–78. The North American career record for goals is 1,033 (786 in the N.H.L.) by Gordie Howe (b. 31 Mar. 1928) (Detroit Red Wings, Houston Aeros and New England Whalers) in 30 seasons ending in 1977–78. He took 2,204 games to achieve the 1,000th goal, but Bobby Hull, O.C. (b. 3 Jan. 1939) (Chicago Black Hawks and Winnipeg Jets) scored his 1,000th in 1,600 games on 12 Mar. 1978.

Most goals *British*

The highest score and aggregate in a League match has been 34–0 when Streatham beat Deeside Dragons on 1 Nov. 1975. The most individual goals scored in a senior League game is 13 by John Hudson for Durham Wasps v. Paisley Mohawks on 20 Feb. 1977.

The sacred mountain of Japan, Mount Fuji (12,388 ft *3 776 m*) looming over the largest ice rink complex in the world. (*Fujikyu Highland Amusement Park*)

Fastest scoring *World*

The fastest major league goal was after 4 sec in the second period by Claude Provost (Montreal Canadians) *v.* Boston Bruins at Montreal, 9 Nov. 1957. Kim D. Miles scored in 3 sec for Univ. of Guelph *v.* Univ. of W. Ontario on 11 Feb. 1975. Toronto scored eight goals against the New York Americans in 4 min 52 sec on 19 Mar. 1938. Canadian Bill Mosienko (Chicago Black Hawks) (b. 2 Nov. 1921) scored three goals in 21 sec against New York Rangers on 23 Mar. 1952. In minor hockey three goals in 14 sec was achieved by Kent Guest (b. 1 Jan. 1964) for Bay Ridges *v.* Ajax, at Toronto, Canada, on 19 Mar. 1975.

Fastest scoring *Great Britain*

Kenny Westman (Nottingham Panthers) scored a hat trick in 30 sec *v.* Brighton Tigers on 3 Mar. 1955.

Most points one game

The North American major league record for most points scored in one game is ten (3 goals, 7 assists) by Jim Harrison (b. 9 July 1947) (for Alberta, later Edmonton Oilers) in a W.H.A. match at Toronto on 30 Jan. 1973, and by Darryl Sittler (b. 18 Sept. 1950) (6 goals, 4 assists) for Toronto Maple Leafs in a N.H.L. match at Toronto on 7 Feb. 1976. In Britain, Richard Bacon scored 15 (10 goals, 5 assists) for Streatham *v.* Deeside on 1 Nov. 1975.

Most successful goaltending

The most matches played by a goaltender without conceding a goal is 103 by Terrance (Terry) Gordon Sawchuck (b. 28 Dec. 1929) of Detroit Red Wings, Boston Bruins, Toronto Maple Leafs, Los Angeles Kings and New York Rangers, between 1950 and 1967. Gerry Cheevers (b. 2 Dec. 1940) Boston Bruins, went a record 33 games without defeat in 1971–72.

Fastest player

The highest speed measured for any player is 29.7 m.p.h. *47,7 km/h* for Bobby Hull. The highest puck speed is also attributed to Hull, whose left-handed slap shot has been timed at 118.3 m.p.h. *190,3 km/h*.

Longest match

The longest match was 2 hrs 56 min 30 sec (playing time) when Detroit Red Wings beat Montreal Maroons 1–0 in the sixth period of overtime at the Forum, Montreal, at 2.25 a.m. on 25 Mar. 1936.

ICE SKATING

Origins

The earliest reference to ice skating is in early Scandinavian literature referring to the 2nd century though its origins are believed, on archeological evidence, to be ten centuries earlier still. The earliest English account of 1180 refers to skates made of bone. The earliest known illustration is a Dutch woodcut of 1498. The earliest skating club was the Edinburgh Skating Club formed in 1742. The earliest artificial ice rink in the world was opened at the Baker Street Bazaar, Portman Square, Greater London, on 7 Dec. 1842. The National Skating Association of Great Britain was founded in 1879. The International Skating Union was founded in 1892.

FIGURE SKATING

Most titles *Olympic*

The most Olympic gold medals won by a figure skater is three by Gillis Gråfstrom (1893–1938) of Sweden in 1920, 1924, and 1928 (also silver medal in 1932); and by Sonja Henie (1912–1969) of Norway in 1928, 1932 and 1936.

Most titles *World*

The greatest number of individual world figure skating titles (instituted 1896) is ten by Ulrich Salchow (1877–1949) of Sweden, in 1901–05 and 1907–11. The women's record (instituted 1906) is also ten individual titles by Sonja Henie between 1927 and 1936. Irina Rodnina (b. U.S.S.R., 12 Sept. 1949) has won ten pairs titles (inst. 1908) four with Aleksiy Ulanov (b. 4 Nov. 1947) 1969–72, and six with her husband Aleksandr Zaitsev (b. 16 June 1952) 1973–78. Most ice dance titles (inst. 1950) won is six by Aleksandr Gorshkov (b. 8. Dec. 1946) and Ludmila Pakhomova (b. 31 Dec. 1946) (U.S.S.R.) 1970–74 and 1976.

Most titles *British*

The most individual British titles is 11 by Jack Page (b. 1900) (Manchester S.C.) in 1922–31 and 1933, and six by Cecilia Colledge (b. 28 Nov. 1920) (Park Lane F.S.C., London) in 1935–37 (two), 1938 and 1946. Page also won nine pairs titles, 1923–31.

Triple Crown

The only British skater to win the "Grand Slam" of World, Olympic and European titles in the same year is John Anthony Curry O.B.E. (b. 9 Sept. 1949) in 1976.

World 500 metres record holder and Olympic champion Evgeni Kulikov of the U.S.S.R. (*Tony Duffy, All-Sport Photographic*)

WORLD SPEED SKATING RECORDS (Ratified by the I.S.U. as at 25 July 1979)

	Distance	min. sec.	Name and Country	Place	Date
MEN	500 metres	37.00*	Evgeni Kulikov (U.S.S.R.)	Medeo, U.S.S.R.	29 Mar. 1975
	1,000 metres	1:14.99	Eric Heiden (U.S.A.)	Inzell, West Germany	17 Feb. 1979
	1,500 metres	1:55.18	Jan Egil Storholt (Norway)	Medeo, U.S.S.R.	20 Mar. 1977
	3,000 metres	4:04.06	Dmitri Ogloblin (U.S.S.R.)	Medeo, U.S.S.R.	28 Mar. 1979
	5,000 metres	6:56.90	Kay Arne Stenshjemmet (Norway)	Medeo, U.S.S.R.	19 Mar. 1977
	10,000 metres	14:34.33	Viktor Leskine (U.S.S.R.)	Medeo, U.S.S.R.	3 Apr. 1977
WOMEN	500 metres	40.68	Sheila Young (U.S.A.)	Inzell, West Germany	13 Mar. 1976
	1,000 metres	1:23.46	Tatiana Averina (U.S.S.R.)	Medeo, U.S.S.R.	29 Mar. 1975
	1,500 metres	2:07.18	Khalida Vorobyeva (U.S.S.R.)	Medeo, U.S.S.R.	10 Apr. 1978
	3,000 metres	4:31.00	Galina Stepanskaya (U.S.S.R.)	Medeo, U.S.S.R.	23 Mar. 1976

* *This represents an average speed of 30.22 m.p.h. 48,64 km/h.*

BRITISH OUTDOOR RECORDS

	Distance	min. sec.	Name	Place	Date
MEN	500 metres	39.76	Simon Grenshaw	Inzell, West Germany	10 Feb. 1979
	1,000 metres	1:21.27	Simon Grenshaw	Innsbruck, Austria	13 Jan. 1978
	1,500 metres	2:05.99	Steve Pearce	Madonna di Campiglio, Italy	16 Jan. 1977
	3,000 metres	4:27.53	Geoff Sandys	Madonna di Campiglio, Italy	10 Jan. 1978
	5,000 metres	7:35.42	Geoff Sandys	Inzell, West Germany	6 Jan. 1977
	10,000 metres	16:10.49	Geoff Sandys	Inzell, West Germany	1 Feb. 1976
WOMEN	500 metres	46.64	Kim Ferran	Inzell, West Germany	17 Feb. 1979
	1,000 metres	1:31.85	Kim Ferran	Madonna di Campiglio, Italy	10 Jan. 1979
	1,500 metres	2:23.26	Kim Ferran	Madonna di Campiglio, Italy	9 Jan. 1979
	3,000 metres	4:54.74	Kim Ferran	Inzell, West Germany	6 Jan. 1979

Karl Schäfer (Austria) (1909–1976) and Sonja Henie achieved double "Grand Slams", both in the years 1932 and 1936.

Highest marks

The highest number of maximum six marks awarded for one performance in an international championship was 11 to Aleksandr Zaitsev and Irina Rodnina (U.S.S.R.) in the European pairs in Zagreb, Yugoslavia, in 1974. The most by a soloist was seven to Donald Jackson (b. 2 Apr. 1940) (Canada) in the world men's championship at Prague, Czechoslovakia, in 1962.

Most difficult jump

The first ever triple Axel jump in competition was by Vern Taylor (b. 1958) (Canada) in the World Championships at Ottawa on 10 Mar. 1978. The quadruple twist lift has been performed by only one pair, Sergei Shakrai (b. 1957) and Marina Tcherkasova (b. 1962), of U.S.S.R., in an international championship, at Helsinki, on 26 Jan. 1977. They also were the first skaters to accomplish simultaneous triple jumps at that level, at Strasbourg, France on 1 Feb. 1978.

Largest rink

The world's largest indoor ice rink is in the Moscow Olympic indoor arena which has an ice area of 8 064 m² *86,800 ft²*. The largest artificial outdoor rink is the quintuple complex of the Fujikyu Highland Promenade Rink, Japan (opened 1967) with an area of 26 500 m² *285,244 ft²*.

Marathon

The longest recorded skating marathon is one of 109 hr 5 min by Austin McKinley, of Christchurch, New Zealand on 21–25 June 1977.

SPEED SKATING

Most titles *Olympic*

The most Olympic gold medals won in speed skating is six by Lidia Skoblikova (b. 8 Mar. 1939) of Chelyabinsk, U.S.S.R., in 1960 (two) and 1964 (four). The male record is by Clas Thunberg (b. 5 Apr. 1893) (Finland) with five gold, (including one tied) and also, one silver and one tied bronze in 1924 and 1928.

Most titles *World*

The greatest number of world overall titles (instituted 1893) won by any skater is five by Oscar Mathisen (Norway) in 1908–09 and 1912–14, and Clas Thunberg in 1923, 1925, 1928–29 and 1931. The most titles won by a woman is four by Inga Voronina (*née* Artomonova) (1936–66) of Moscow, U.S.S.R., in 1957, 1958, 1962 and 1964 and Atje Keulen-Deelstra (b. 31 Dec. 1938) (Netherlands) 1970, 1972–74.

Longest race

The longest race regularly held is the "Elfstedentocht" ("Tour of the Eleven Towns") in the Netherlands. It covers 200 km *124 miles 483 yds* and the fastest time is 7 hrs 35 min by Jeen van den Berg (b. 8 Jan. 1928) on 3 Feb. 1954.

ICE AND SAND YACHTING

Origins

The sport originated in the Low Countries from the year 1600 (earliest patent granted) and along the Baltic coast. The earliest authentic record is Dutch, dating from 1768. Land or sand yachts of Dutch construction were first reported on beaches (now in Belgium) in 1595. The earliest International championship was staged in 1914.

Highest speeds *Ice*

The largest known ice yacht was *Icicle*, built for Commodore John E. Roosevelt for racing on the Hudson River, New York, in c. 1870. It was 68 ft 11 in *21 m* long and carried 1,070 ft² *99 m²* of canvas. The highest speed officially recorded is 143 m.p.h. *230 km/h* by John D. Buckstaff in a Class A stern-steerer on Lake Winnebago, Wisconsin, U.S.A., in 1938. Such a speed is possible in a wind of 72 m.p.h. *115 km/h.*

Highest speeds *Sand*

The fastest recorded speed for a sand yacht is 57.69 m.p.h. *92,84 km/h* (measured mile in 62.4 sec) by *Coronation Year Mk. II* owned by R. Millett Denning and crewed by J. Halliday, Bob Harding, J. Glassbrook and Cliff Martindale at Lytham St. Anne's, Lancashire, England in 1956. A speed of 77.47 m.p.h. *125,11 km/h* was attained by Jan Paul Lowe (b. 15 Apr. 1936) of U.S.A. in *Sunkist* at Ivanpaugh Dry Lake, California, U.S.A. on 25 Mar. 1975.

INDOOR PASTIMES

CHESS
Origins

The name chess is derived from the Persian word *shah* (a king or ruler). It is a descendant of the game *Chaturanga*. The earliest reference is from the Middle Persian Karnamak (c. A.D. 590–628), though in December 1972, two ivory chessmen were found in the Uzbek Soviet Republic dateable to A.D. 200. It reached Britain in c. 1255. The *Fédération Internationale des Echecs* was established in 1924. There were an estimated 7,000,000 competitive players in the U.S.S.R. in 1973.

Most World titles

World champions have been generally recognized since 1886. The longest undisputed tenure was 27 years by Dr. Emanuel Lasker (1868–1941) of Germany, from 1894 to 1921. The women's world championship was held by Vera Menchik-Stevenson (1906–44) (G.B.) from 1927 till her death, and was successfully defended a record seven times. Nona Gaprindashvili (U.S.S.R.) has held the title since 1962 and defended four times. Robert J. (Bobby) Fischer (b. Chicago, Illinois, U.S.A., 9 Mar. 1943) is reckoned on the officially adopted Elo System to be the greatest Grand Master of all-time.

Most British titles

Most British titles have been won by Dr. Jonathan Penrose, O.B.E. (b. 1934) of East Finchley, London with ten titles in 1958–63, 1966–69. Rowena M. Bruce (*née* Dew) (b. 1919) of Plymouth won 11 titles between 1937 and 1969. The first British player to attain official International Grand Master status was Anthony Miles, (b. 1956), on 24 Feb. 1976.

Current world champion Anatoli Karpov (right) here playing Viktor Korchnoi in 1971, seven years before their acrimonious series for the supreme title. (*Popperfoto*)

Winning streak

Bobby Fischer won 20 games in succession in Grand Master chess from 2 Dec. 1970 to 30 Sept. 1971. Since 1966 (to Dec. 1977) Anatoli Karpov (U.S.S.R.) (b. 5 May 1951) has only lost 4.3% of his 597 games.

Most opponents

The record for most opponents tackled (with replacements as they are defeated) is held by Branimir Brebrich (Canada) who played 575 games (533 wins, 27 draws, 15 losses) in Edmonton, Alberta, on 27–28 Jan. 1978 during 28 hr of play. Vlastimil Hort (b. 12 Jan. 1944) (Czechoslovakia) in Seltjarnarnes, Iceland on 23–24 Apr. 1977, simultaneously tackled 201 opponents and did not lose a game. Georges Koltanowski (Belgium, now of U.S.A.) (b. 1903) tackled 56 opponents "blindfold", won 50, and drew six in 9¾ hrs at the Fairmont Hotel, San Francisco, California, U.S.A., on 13 Dec. 1960.

Slowest and longest games

The slowest recorded move (before modern rules) was one of 11 hours between Paul Charles Morphy, (1837–84) the U.S. Champion of 1852–62, and the German chess master Louis Paulsen (1833–91).

The master game with most moves on record was one drawn on the 191st move between H. Pilnik (Argentina) and Moshe Czerniak (Israel) at Mar del Plata, Argentina, in April 1950. The total playing time was 20 hrs. A game of 21½ hrs, but drawn on the 171st move (average over 7½ min per move), was played between N. Makagonov and Chekhover at Baku, U.S.S.R., in 1945.

Marathon

The longest recorded session is one of 158 hrs 24 min by Lori Daulton *v.* Marion Selby and Charlotte Rugar *v.* Gayle Fields from Dinwiddie Junior High School, Virginia, U.S.A. on 17–23 Dec. 1977.

CONTRACT BRIDGE
Origins

Bridge (a corruption of Biritch) is thought to be of Levantine origin, similar games having been played there in the early 1870s. The British Museum contains a pamphlet of 1886 entitled "Biritch or Russian Whist".

Auction Bridge (highest bidder names trump) was invented c. 1902. The contract principle, present in several games (notably the French game *Plafond*, c. 1917) was introduced to Bridge by Harold S. Vanderbilt (U.S.A.) on 1 Nov. 1925 during a Caribbean voyage aboard the *s.s. Finland*. It became a world-wide craze after the U.S.A. *v.* Great Britain challenge match between Romanian-born Ely Culbertson (1891–1955) and Lt.-Col. Walter Thomas More Buller (1887–1938) at Almack's Club, London, in Sept. 1930. The U.S.A. won the 200 hand match by 4,845 points.

Most World titles

The World Championship (Bermuda Bowl) has been won most often by Italy's Blue Team (*Squadra Azzurra*), 1957–59, 1961–63, 1965–7, 1969, 1973–75, whose team also won the Olympiad in 1964, 1968 and 1972. Giorgio Belladonna (b. 1923) was in all these winning teams.

Most master points

In 1971 a new world ranking list based on Master Points was instituted. The leading male player in the world was Giorgio Belladonna a member of Italy's Blue team with 1,712 points as at March 1978, followed by five more Italians. The leading Briton is Boris Schapiro (b. 1911) in 17th place with 353 points. The world's leading woman player is Mrs. Rixi R. Markus M.B.E. (G.B.) with 269 points to March 1978. Britain had four more women players in the Top Twenty.

Most brilliant play

Dana de Falco (Italy) was awarded the annual Bols Brilliancy Prize by the International Bridge Press Association for the best play of 1979—for a 'discovery' play in the match against Israel in the European Championships.

Perfect deals

The mathematical odds against dealing 13 cards of one suit are 158,753,389,899 to 1, while the odds against receiving a "perfect hand" consisting of all 13 spades are 635,013,559,596 to 1. The odds against each of the four players receiving a complete suit (a "perfect deal") are 2,235,197,406,895,366,368,301,559,999 to 1.

Marathon

The longest recorded session is one of 180 hr by four students at Edinburgh University on 21–28 Apr. 1972.

HIGHEST POSSIBLE SCORES: BRIDGE

Opponents bid 7 of any suit or 7 No Trumps doubled and redoubled and vulnerable

	Opponents make no trick	
Above Line	1st undertrick	400
	12 subsequent undertricks at 600 each	7,200
	All Honours	150
		7,750

Bid 1 No Trump, doubled and redoubled, vulnerable

Below Line	1st trick (40 × 4)	160
Above Line	6 over tricks (400 × 6)	2,400
	2nd game of 2-Game Rubber	*350
	All Honours	150
	Bonus for making redoubled contract	50
	(Highest Possible Positive Score)	3,110

* In practice, the full bonus of 700 points is awarded after the completion of the second winning game rather than 350 after each game.

CRIBBAGE
Origins

The invention of the game (once called Cribbidge) is credited to the English dramatist Sir John Suckling (1609–42). It is estimated that some ten million people play in the United States alone.

Rare hands

F. Art Skinner, of Alberta, Canada is reported to have had five maximum 29 point hands. Paul Nault of Athol, Mass., U.S.A. had two such hands within eight games in a tournament on 19 Mar. 1977. At Blackpool, Lancs., England, Derek Hearne dealt two hands of six clubs with the turn-up the remaining club on 8 Feb. 1976. Bill Rogers of Burnaby, B.C., Canada scored 29 in the crib in 1975.

Marathon

Four members of the Barley Mow Forever Legless Society, Clifton Hempden, Oxon played for 60 hr on 6–8 Feb. 1979.

DARTS
Origins

The origins of darts date from the use by archers of heavily weighted ten-inch throwing arrows for self-defence in close quarters fighting. The "dartes" were used in Ireland in the 16th century and darts was played on the *Mayflower* by the Plymouth pilgrims in 1620. Today there are an estimated 6,000,000 dart players in the British Isles. The National Darts Association of Great Britain (inst. 1953) is seeking to standardize the throwing distances and treble boards.

Most titles

Re-instituted in 1947, the annual *News of the World* England and Wales individual Championships consist of the best of three legs 501 up, "straight" start and finish on a double with an 8 ft *2,4 m* throwing distance. The only men to win twice are Tommy Gibbons (Ivanhoe Working Men's Club) of Conisbrough, South Yorkshire, in 1952 and 1958; Tom Reddington of New Inn, Stonebroom, Derbyshire in 1955 and of George Hotel, Alfreton, Derbyshire 1960; and Tom M. Barrett (Odco Sports Club, London) in 1964 and 1965.

The National Darts Association of Great Britain Individual title was won by Tom O'Regan of the Northern Star, New Southgate, Greater London in 1970–72.

Longest unbeaten run

Mike Bowell (b. 31 May 1947) of Paulton Darts League, Avon, won 152 successive competition games from 9 Feb. 1971 to 29 Nov. 1974.

Fastest match

The fastest time taken for a match of three games of 301 is 1 min 58 sec by Ricky Fusco (G.B.) at the Perivale Residents Association Club, Middx., England on 30 Dec. 1976.

Fastest "round the board"

The record time for going round the board clockwise in "doubles" at arm's length is 9.2 sec by Dennis Gower at the Millers Arms, Hastings, East Sussex on 12 Oct. 1975 and 14.5 sec in numerical order by Jim Pike (b. 1903) at the Craven Club, Newmarket in March, 1944. The record for this feat at the nine-feet *2,7 m* throwing distance, retrieving own darts, is 2 min 13 sec by Bill Duddy at The Plough, Hornsey Road, Harringey, Greater London on 29 Oct. 1972.

Lowest possible scores

Scores of 201 in four darts, 301 in six darts, 401 in seven darts and 501 in nine darts, have been achieved on various occasions. The lowest number of darts thrown for a score of 1,001 is 19 by Cliff Inglis (160, 180, 140, 180, 121, 180, 40) at the Bromfield Men's Club, Devon on 11 Nov. 1975. A score of 2,001 in 52 darts was achieved by Alan Evans at Ferndale, Glamorgan on 3 Sept. 1976. 3,001 in 81 darts was thrown by Leighton Rees at The Spotted Cow, Bedminster, Avon, on 3 Apr. 1976.

Ten hour scores

The record number of trebles scored in 10 hr is 2,150 (in 9,400 darts) for a percentage of 22.87 by E. Jacky Hughes at Heswell British Legion, Merseyside on 27 Sept. 1974. On 19 Mar. 1978 Nick Korn scored a record 2,814 doubles (out of 9,285 darts) in 10 hr for a 30.31 percentage at Newquay, Cornwall. The greatest score amassed in 10 hr is 487,588 by Bruce Campbell and Peter Dawson at the Waikiki Hotel, W. A., Aust. on 14 Oct. 1978.

Million and one up

Eight players from The Golden Fleece, Edmonton, North London scored 1,000,001 with 41,214 darts in one session from 26–28 May 1979.

Marathon

Stephen Ablett and Chris Dare played for 101 hr at Nienburg Weser, W. Ger. on 29 Mar.–2 Apr. 1975.

DOMINOES
Origins

The National Museum in Baghdad, Iraq contains artifacts from Ur called "dominoes" dated *c.* 2450 B.C. Though unknown in Europe in *c.* 1750, the game reached England *via* France *c.* 1795. The Eskimo game requires 148 pieces while that in Europe utilizes only 28.

Marathon

The longest by two players is 123 hr 4 min by Alan Mannering and David Harrison of Stoke on Trent, Staffs., on 8–13 Feb. 1978.

DRAUGHTS

Origins

Draughts, known as checkers in North America, has origins earlier than chess. It was played in Egypt in the second millennium B.C. The earliest book on the game was by Antonio Torquemada of Valencia, Spain in 1547. There have been three U.S. *v.* Great Britain international matches (crossboard) 1905, 1927 and 1973, two won by the United States and one by Great Britain.

The British Championship (biennial) was inaugurated in 1926. The only man to win five titles has been Jim Marshall (Fife) in 1948, 1950, 1952, 1954 and 1966. The longest tenure of invincibility was that of Melvin Pomeroy (U.S.), who was internationally undefeated from 1914 until his death in 1933.

Most opponents

Newell W. Banks (b. Detroit, U.S.A., 10 Oct. 1887) played 140 games simultaneously, winning 133 and drawing seven, in Chicago, Illinois in 1933. His playing time was 145 min, so averaging about one move per sec.

Longest and shortest games

In competition the prescribed rate of play is not less than 30 moves per hour with the average game lasting about 90 min. In 1958 a match between Dr. Marion Tinsley (U.S.) and Derek Oldbury (G.B.) lasted 7½ hours. The shortest possible game is one of 20 moves composed by Alan M. Beckerson (b. 21 Feb. 1938) (G.B.) on 2 Nov. 1977.

MONOPOLY ®

Origins

The patentee of Monopoly ® the world's most popular proprietary board game of which Parker Bros. have sold 80,000,000 copies, was Charles Darrow (1889–1967). He invented the patented version of the game in 1933, while an unemployed heating engineer, using the street names of Atlantic City, New Jersey where he spent his vacations.

Marathon

The longest game by four players ratified by Parker Bros. is 288 hr by Valerie Schmoltze, Karen and Bob Schmidt and Paul Boyer of Ashland, Penn., U.S.A. on 17–29 Aug. 1978.

SCRABBLE ® Crossword Game

Origins

The crossword game was invented by Alfred M. Butts in 1931 and was developed, refined and trademarked as Scrabble ® Crossword Game by James Brunot in 1948. He sold the North American rights to Selchow & Richter Company, New York, the European rights to J. W. Spears & Sons, London, and the Australian rights to Murfett Pty. Ltd., Melbourne.

Highest scores

The highest competitive game score known is 730 by Ron K. Hendra (G.B.) on 12 July 1978. His opponent scored 360. Ralph Beaman (U.S.A.) made an idealized game score of 4,153 in 1974. The highest competitive single turn score recorded is 380. Ronald E. Jerome, of Bracknell, Berkshire, England made an idealized single turn score of 1,961 in May 1974.

Most titles

British National Championships were instituted in 1971. Olive Behan of Widnes has won twice in 1972 and 1975.

Marathon

The longest Scrabble ® Crossword Game is 120 hours by Norman Hazeldean, Alan Giles, Tom Barton and Keith Ollett at Uckfield, East Sussex, on 4–9 Aug. 1975, and Mark Morris,

Jean-Pierre Burdinat, Robert Emmanuel and Gary Dolton in Sydney, Australia on 27 Aug.–1 Sept. 1975.

TIDDLYWINKS

Origins

This game was only espoused by adults in 1955 when Cambridge University issued a challenge to Oxford.

National Championships

Alan Dean (Southampton) has won the singles title a record five times, 1971–3, 1976, 1978. He has also won the pairs title three times, as have Jon Mapley and Keith Seaman.

Guinness Trophy

England has remained unbeaten against Scotland, Ireland and Wales since the Trophy's inception on 7 May 1960. The closest result has been their 59½–52½ win over Wales at Warwick on 7 Apr. 1968.

Silver Wink Trophy

The *Silver Wink*, presented by H.R.H. The Duke of Edinburgh, for the British University championship has been won a record six times by Cambridge University to 1979.

Speed records

The record for potting 24 winks from 18 in *45 cm* is 21.8 sec by Stephen Williams (Altrincham Grammar School) in May 1966. Allen R. Astles (University of Wales) potted 10,000 winks in 3 hours 51 min 46 sec at Aberystwyth, Cardiganshire in February 1966.

Four Pot Relay

The greatest number of winks potted in 3 min by a relay of four is 29 by Paul Light, Paul Hoffman, Andrew James and Geoff Thorpe at "The Castle", Cambridge on 6 Dec. 1974.

Marathon

The most protracted game on record is one of 240 hr by six players from St. Anselm's College, Birkenhead, Merseyside on 2–12 Aug. 1977.

WHIST

Origins

Whist, first referred to in 1529 (*as trump*), was the world's premier card game until 1930. The rules were standardized in 1742.

Highest score

The highest score claimed for 24 hands is 209 by Mrs. E. Heslop in the Shaldon Over 60 Club, Teignmouth, Devon on 5 Jan. 1973 and by Mrs. A. Lulham at Hurstmonceux, East Sussex, on 21 Jan. 1978.

JUDO

Origins

Judo is a modern combat sport which developed out of an amalgam of several old (pre-Christian era) Japanese fighting arts, the most popular of which was ju-jitsu (jiu-jitsu), which is thought to be of pre-Christian Chinese origin, Judo was greatly developed since 1882, when it was first devised by Dr. Jigoro Kano (1860–1938).

Most titles *World and Olympic*

World championships were inaugurated in Tōkyō on 5 May 1956. The only man to have won four world titles is Wilhelm Ruska (b. 29 Aug. 1940) (Netherlands), who won the 1967 Heavyweight, the 1971 Heavyweight and the 1972 Olympic Heavyweight and Open titles. In the European championships (instituted in 1951) only Great Britain (1957–59) and the U.S.S.R. (1972–74) have won three consecutive team titles.

Most titles *British*

The greatest number of titles (inst. 1966) won is nine by David Colin Starbrook, M.B.E. (b. 9 Aug. 1945) (5th dan) who won the middleweight title 1969–70, the light-heavyweight 1971–75 and the open division 1970–71. The women's championships were instituted in 1971. Christine Child (b. 1946) (5th dan) has won a record six times: the heavyweight in 1971–75 and the open division in 1973.

Trevor Legett (standing) shares with two others the distinction of holding the highest grade—7th dan—among British Judoka. (*Sport & General Press*)

Highest grades

The efficiency grades in Judo are divided into pupil (*kyu*) and master (*dan*) grades. The highest awarded is the extremely rare red belt *Judan* (*10th dan*), given only to seven men so far. The Judo protocol provides for an *11th dan* (*Juichidan*) who also would wear a red belt, a *12th dan* (*Junidan*) who would wear a white belt twice as wide as an ordinary belt and the highest of all, *Shihan*, but these have never been bestowed. The highest British native Judo grades are *7th dan* by Trevor Pryce Leggett (b. 22 Aug. 1914), Charles Stuart Palmer O.B.E. (b. 1930) and Geoff Gleeson.

Marathon

The longest recorded continuous Judo marathon, by two of six Judoka in 5 min stints, is 200 hr by the Dufftown and District Judo Club, Banffshire on 9–17 July 1977.

KARATE

Origins

Based on techniques devised from the sixth century Chinese art of Shaolin boxing (Kempo). Karate was developed by an unarmed populace in Okinawa as a weapon against armed Japanese oppressors *c.* 1500. Transmitted to Japan in the 1920s by Funakoshi Gichin, this method of combat was refined into Karate and organized into a sport with competitive rules. The five major styles of Karate in Japan are: *Shotokan*, *Wado-ryu*, *Goju-ryu*, *Shito-ryu* and *Kyokushinkai*, each of which place different emphasis on speed and power etc. Other styles include *Sankukai*, *Shotokai* and *Shukokai*. The military form of *Tae kwan-do* with nine dans is a Korean equivalent of Karate. *Wu shu* is a comprehensive term embracing all Chinese martial arts. *Kung fu* is one aspect of these arts popularised by the cinema. (See also p. 224).

The Governing Body for the sport in Britain is the Martial Arts Commission upon which all the martial arts are represented.

Great Britain became the first country ever to defeat the Japanese in competition when they beat them in the 1972 World championships in Paris. They repeated the feat in the final of the 1975 World championships at Long Beach, California, U.S.A. and during the 1977 World championships in Tokyo.

Most titles

The only winner of three All-Japanese titles has been Takeshi

Oishi who won in 1969–71. David "Ticky" Donovan (5th dan) has won the British title on three consecutive occasions 1973–75.

Top exponents

The leading exponents among karatekas are a number of 10th dans in Japan. The leading exponents in the United Kingdom are Tatsuo Suzuki (8th dan, *Wado-ryu*) (b. 27 Apr. 1928) chief instructor to the European Karatedo Wadokai; Keinosuke Enoeda (8th dan, *Shotokan*), resident instructor to the Karate Union of Great Britain and Steve Arneil (7th dan, *Kyokushinkai*) British national born in South Africa.

LACROSSE

Origins

The game is of American Indian origin, derived from the inter-tribal game *baggataway*, and was played before 1492 by Iroquois Indians in lower Ontario, Canada and upper New York State, U.S.A. The French named it after their game of *Chouler à la crosse*, known in 1381. It was introduced into Great Britain in 1867. The English Lacrosse Union was formed in 1892. It was included in the Olympic Games of 1908 and featured as an exhibition sport in the 1928 and 1948 Games.

Most titles *World*

The United States won the first two World Championships in 1967 and 1974. Canada won the third in 1978 beating the U.S.A. 17–16 after extra time—this was the first drawn international match.

Most titles *English*

The English Club Championship (Iroquois Cup), instituted in 1890, has been won most often by Stockport with 15 wins between 1897 and 1934. The record score in a final was in 1979 when Cheadle beat Buckhurst Hill, 28–6.

Highest scores

The highest score in any international match was the United States' 28–4 win over Canada at Stockport, England on 3 July 1978. England's highest score was their 19–11 win over Canada at Melbourne in 1974. The highest score in the annual North of England v. South of England match has been 26–2 in 1927.

Most international appearances *Men*

The record number of international representations is 26 for England by Michael Roberts (Urmston), to 1978. He is the only person to play in all three World Championships.

Most international appearances *Women*

The record for women is 52 for Scotland by Caro MacIntosh (1952–1969).

Fastest scoring

Rod Burns scored only 4 sec into the game for South Manchester and Wythenshawe v. Sheffield Univ. on 6 Dec. 1975.

Playing at centre for most of her 52 appearances for the Scottish lacrosse team, Caro MacIntosh was also captain for ten years.

The Silver Wink Trophy, presented by H.R.H. Prince Philip for the British University Tiddlywinks championship. (*English Tiddlywinks Association*)

LAWN TENNIS

Origins

The modern game is generally agreed to have evolved as an outdoor form of the indoor game of Tennis (see separate entry). "Field Tennis" is mentioned in an English magazine—*Sporting Magazine*—of 29 Sept. 1793. The earliest club for such a game, variously called Pelota or Lawn Rackets, was the Leamington Club founded in 1872 by Major Harry Gem. The earliest attempt to commercialise the game was by Major Walter Clopton Wingfield, M.V.O. (1833–1912) who patented a form called 'sphairistike" on 23 Feb. 1874. It soon became called Lawn Tennis. Amateur players were permitted to play with and against professionals in "Open" tournaments in 1968.

Greatest domination

The grand slam is to hold at the same time all four of the world's major championship singles: Wimbledon, the United States, Australian and French championships. The first man to have won all four was Frederick John Perry (G.B.) (b. 18 May 1909) with the French title in 1935. The first man to hold all four championships simultaneously was John Donald Budge (U.S.A.) (b. 13 June 1915) with the French title in 1938. The first man to achieve the grand slam twice was Rodney George Laver M.B.E. (Australia) (b. 9 Aug. 1938) having won in 1962 as an amateur and again in 1969 when the titles were "open" to professionals.

Only two women have achieved the grand slam: Maureen Catherine Connolly (U.S.A.) (1934–69), later Mrs. Norman E. Brinker, in 1953; and Margaret Jean Court, M.B.E., (*née* Smith) (Australia) (b. 16 July 1942) in 1970.

Most Olympic medals

Lawn Tennis was part of the Olympic programme at the first eight celebrations of the Games (including the 1906 Games). The winner of most medals was Max Decugis (1882–1978) (France) with six (a record four gold, one silver and one bronze) in the 1900, 1906 and 1920 tournaments. The most won by a woman is five by Kitty McKane (later Mrs. L. A. Godfree) (b. 7 May 1897) (G.B.), with one gold, two silver and two bronze in 1920 and 1924.

Davis Cup *Most victories*

The greatest number of wins in the Davis Cup (instituted 1900) has been (inclusive of 1978) by the U.S.A. with 25. The British Isles/Great Britain have won nine times, in 1903–06, 1912, 1933–36.

Davis Cup *Individual Performance*

Nicola Pietrangeli (b. 11 Sept. 1933) (Italy) played 164 rubbers, 1954 to 1972, winning 120. He played 110 singles (winning 78) and 54 doubles (winning 42). He took part in 66 ties.

Fastest service

The fastest service ever *measured* was one of 163.6 m.p.h. *263 km/h* by William Tatem Tilden (1893–1953) (U.S.A.) in 1931. Some players consider the service of Robert Falkenburg (U.S.A.) (b. 29 Jan. 1926), the 1948 Wimbledon champion, as the fastest ever produced.

Longest game

The longest known singles game was one of 37 deuces (80 points) between Anthony Fawcett (Rhodesia) and Keith Glass (G.B.) in the first round of the Surrey championships at Surbiton, Surrey, England on 26 May 1975. It lasted 31 min.

Greatest crowd

The greatest crowd at a tennis match was 30,472 at the Astrodome, Houston, Texas, on 20 Sept. 1973, when Billie-Jean King (*née* Moffitt) (b. 22 Nov. 1943) (U.S.A.) beat Robert Larimore Riggs (b. 25 Feb. 1918) (U.S.A.). The record for an orthodox match is 25,578 at Sydney, N.S.W., Australia on 27 Dec. 1954 in the Davis Cup Challenge Round (first day) Australia v. U.S.A.

Highest earnings

Guillermo Vilas (b. 17 Aug. 1952) (Argentina) won a record $800,642 in 1977. The record for a woman player is $454,486 in 1978 by Christine Marie Evert (now Lloyd) (b. 21 Dec. 1954) (U.S.A.). Earnings from special restricted events and team tennis salaries are not included.

The one match record is $500,000 *£217,400* won by Jimmy Connors when he beat John Newcombe (Australia) (b. 23 May 1944) in a challenge match at Caesars Palace, Las Vegas, U.S.A. on 26 Apr. 1975.

Left-hander Guillermo Vilas won most of his record 1977 winnings on clay courts. (*Sporting Pictures*)

Longest span

The championship career of C. Alphonso Smith (b. 18 Mar. 1909) of Charlottesville, Virginia, U.S.A., extended from winning the United States National Boy's title at Chicago, on 14 Aug. 1924, to winning the National 65-and-over Hard Court Doubles title at Aptos, California, exactly 50 years to the day later on 14 Aug. 1974.

Marathons

The longest recorded non-stop lawn tennis singles match is one of 105 hr by Ricky Tolston and Jeff Sutton at Bill Faye Park, Kinston, N.C., U.S.A., on 7–11 May 1979. The duration record for doubles is 80 hr by Paul Blackburn, Terry Mabbitt, Nigel Johnson and Rod Wild at Ilkley Tennis Club, Yorkshire, England on 13–16 June 1979.

WIMBLEDON RECORDS

For more details see *100 Years of Wimbledon* by Lance Tingay, published by Guinness Superlatives Ltd. (price £8.50)

Most wins *Women*

Six time singles champion Billie-Jean King has also won ten women's doubles and four mixed doubles during the period 1961 to 1979, to total a record 20 titles.

Most wins *Men*

The greatest number of wins by a man at Wimbledon has been 13 by Hugh Laurence Doherty (G.B.) (1875–1919) who won five singles titles (1902–06) and a record eight men's doubles (1897–1901, 1903–05) partnered by his brother Reginald Frank (1872–1910).

Most wins *Singles*

The greatest number of singles wins was eight by Helen N. Moody (*née* Wills) (U.S.A.) (b. 6 Oct. 1905), who won in 1927–30, 1932–33, 1935 and 1938. The most men's singles wins since the Challenge Round was abolished in 1922 is four by Rod Laver, in 1961–62, 1968–69, and consecutively, by Bjorn Borg (Sweden) (b. 6 June 1956) in 1976–79. William Charles Renshaw (G.B.) (1861–1904) won seven singles in 1881–86 and 1889.

Most wins *Mixed doubles*

The male record is four wins shared by Elias Victor Seixas (U.S.A.) (b. 30 Aug. 1923) in 1953–56, Kenneth N. Fletcher (Australia) (b. 15 June 1940) in 1963, 1965–66, 1968 and

Owen Keir Davidson (Australia) (b. 4 Oct. 1943) in 1967, 1971, 1973–74.

Most appearances

Arthur William Charles "Wentworth" Gore (1868–1928) (G.B.) made a record 36 appearances at Wimbledon between 1888 and 1927, and was in 1909 at 41 yr 6 months the oldest ever singles winner. In 1964, Jean Borotra (b. 13 Aug. 1898) of France, made his 35th appearance since 1922. In 1977 he appeared in the Veterans' Doubles aged 78.

Youngest champions

The youngest champion was Charlotte (Lottie) Dod (1871–1960), who was 15 years 9 months when she won in 1887 (see also p. 240). Richard Dennis Ralston (b. 27 July 1942) of Bakersfield, California, U.S.A., was 25 days short of his 18th birthday when he won the men's doubles with Rafael H. Osuna (1938–1969) of Mexico in 1960. The youngest male singles champion was Wilfred Baddeley (1872–1929) who won the Wimbledon title in 1891 aged 19 years 175 days. The youngest ever player at Wimbledon is reputedly Mita Klima (Austria) who was 13 yr old in the 1907 singles competition. The youngest of modern times is Tracy Austin (b. 12 Dec. 1962) (U.S.A.), who was only 14 yr 7 months in the 1977 tournament.

Greatest crowd

The record crowd for one day at Wimbledon is 38,295 on 27 June 1979. The record for the whole championship is 338,591 in 1975.

MARBLES

Origins

Marbles may have been a children's game in Ancient Egypt, and was introduced into Britain by the Romans in the 1st Century A.D. It became a competitive sport under the British Marbles Board of Control at the Greyhound Hotel, Tinsley Green, Crawley, West Sussex in 1926. The governing body now is the British Isles Marbles Association.

The game is also played on the Continent (especially Belgium) and in Australia, Brazil (as *Gude*), Canada, China, India, Iran, New Zealand, Syria, the United States and the West Indies.

Most championships

The British Championship (established 1926) has been won most often by the Toucan Terribles with 20 consecutive titles (1956–75). Three founder members, Len Smith, Jack and Charlie Dempsey, have played in every title win. They were finally beaten in 1976 by the Pernod Rams, captained by Len Smith's son, Paul. Len Smith (b. 13 Oct. 1917) has won the individual title 15 times (1957–64, 1966, 1968–73) but lost in 1974 to his son Alan.

Speed record

The record for clearing the ring (between 5¾ and 6¼ ft *1,75–1,90 m* in diameter) of 49 marbles is 2 min 57 sec by the Toucan Terribles at Worthing, West Sussex in 1971.

MODERN PENTATHLON

Points scores in riding, fencing, cross country and hence overall scores have no comparative value between one competition and another. In shooting and swimming (300 m) the scores are of record significance and the best achievements are shown.

The Modern Pentathlon (Riding, Fencing, Shooting, Swimming and Running) was inaugurated into the Olympic Games at Stockholm in 1912. The Modern Pentathlon Association of Great Britain was formed in 1922.

Most titles *World*

The record number of world titles won is six by András Balczó (b. 16 Aug. 1938) (Hungary) in 1963, 1965–67 and 1969. In Olympic years this title also rates as the world title, thus giving Balczó his sixth in 1972. The best British placing is

Four time Wimbledon mixed doubles champion Owen Davidson was Britain's Davis Cup team coach from 1967–70. (*Syndication International*)

the bronze medal by Sgt. (now Capt.) Jeremy Robert "Jim" Fox, M.B.E. (b. 19 Sept. 1941) at Mexico in 1975.

Most titles *Olympic*
The greatest number of Olympic gold medals won is three by András Balczó a member of the winning team in 1960 and 1968 and the 1972 individual champion. Lars Hall (b. 30 Apr. 1927) (Sweden) has uniquely won two individual Championships (1952 and 1956). Balczó has won a record number of five medals (three gold and two silver). The best British performance is the team gold medal at Montreal, Canada 18–22 July 1976 by Jim Fox, Adrian Philip Parker and Daniel Nightingale. The best individual placing is fourth by Jim Fox at Munich in 1972.

Most titles *British*
The pentathlete with most British titles is Jim Fox, with ten (1963, 1965–68, 1970–74).

HIGHEST SCORES

	World			
Shooting	1,132	Danieli Massala (Italy) Jönkoping, Sweden	21 Aug.	1978
Swimming	1,324	Robert L. Nieman (U.S.A.) Montreal, Canada	21 July	1976
	British			
Shooting	1,088	Tim Kenealy, Helsinki, Finland	4 June	1979
Swimming	1,240	Adrian Philip Parker, Montreal, Canada	21 July	1976

MOTORCYCLE RACING

See also The Guinness Book of Motorcycling Facts and Feats by L. J. K. Setright, published by Guinness Superlatives Ltd. (price £6.95).

Earliest race
The first motorcycle race was held over a mile *1,6 km* on an oval track at Sheen House, Richmond, Surrey, on 29 Nov. 1897, won by Charles Jarrott (1877–1944) on a Fournier. The oldest motorcycle races in the world are the Auto-Cycle Union Tourist Trophy (T.T.) series, first held on the 15.81 mile *25,44 km* "Peel" ("St. John's") course in the Isle of Man on 28 May 1907, and still run in the island on the 37.73 mile *60,72 km* long "Mountain" circuit.

Fastest circuits *World*
The highest average lap speed attained on any closed circuit is 160.288 m.p.h. *257,958 km/h* by Yvon du Hamel (Canada) on a modified 903 c.c. four-cylinder Kawasaki Z1 at the 31 degree banked 2.5 mile *4,02 km* Daytona International Speedway, Florida, U.S.A., in Mar. 1973. His lap time was 56.149 sec.

The fastest road circuit is the Francorchamps circuit near Spa, Belgium. It is 8.74 miles *14,120 km* in length and was lapped in 3 min 50.3 sec (average speed 137.150 m.p.h. *220,721 km/h*) by Barry Stephen Frank Sheene M.B.E. (b. Holborn, London, 11 Sept. 1950) on a 495 c.c. four-cylinder Suzuki during the Belgian Grand Prix on 3 July 1977.

Fastest circuits *United Kingdom*
The fastest circuit in the United Kingdom is the Portstewart-Coleraine-Portrush circuit in Londonderry, Northern Ireland. The lap record (10.1 mile *16,26 km* lap) is 4 min 53.2 sec (average speed 124.060 m.p.h. *199,655 km/h*) by John Glyn Williams (1946–78) on a 747 c.c. four-cylinder Yamaha on lap five of the 750 c.c. event of the North West 200, on 21 May 1977.

The lap record for the outer circuit (2.767 miles *4,453 km*) at the Brooklands Motor Course, near Weybridge, Surrey (open between 1907 and 1939) was 80.0 sec (average speed 124.51 m.p.h. *200,37 km/h*) by Noel Baddow "Bill" Pope (later Major) (1909–71) of the United Kingdom on a Brough Superior powered by a supercharged 996 c.c. V-twin "8-80" J.A.P. engine developing 110 b.h.p., on 4 July 1939.

The late John Williams was one of Britain's leading motorcyclists, and lap record holder on the fast Londonderry circuit. (*Syndication International*)

Fastest races *World*
The fastest race in the world was held at Grenzlandring, near Wegberg, W. Germany in 1939. It was won by Georg Meier (b. Germany, 1910) at an average speed of 134 m.p.h. *215 km/h* on a supercharged 495 c.c. flat-twin B.M.W.

The fastest road race is the 500 c.c. Belgian Grand Prix held on the Francorchamps circuit (see above). The record time for this ten lap (87.74 mile *141,20 km*) race is 38 min 58.5 sec (average speed 135.068 m.p.h. *217,370 km/h*) by Barry Sheene, on a 495 c.c. four-cylinder Suzuki, on 3 July 1977.

Fastest races *United Kingdom*
The fastest race in the United Kingdom is the 750 c.c. event of the North-West 200 held on the Londonderry circuit (see above). The record time for this five lap (50.52 mile *81,30 km*) race is 24 min 53.8 sec (average speed 121.751 m.p.h. *195,939 km/h*) by John Williams on a 747 c.c. four-cylinder Yamaha, on 21 May 1977.

Most successful riders *Tourist Trophy*
The record number of victories in the Isle of Man T.T. races is 14 by Stanley Michael Bailey Hailwood, M.B.E., G.M. (b. Oxford, 2 Apr. 1940) between 1961 and 1979. The first man to win three consecutive T.T. titles in two events was James A. Redman, M.B.E. (Rhodesia) (b. Hampstead, Greater London, 8 Nov. 1931). He won the 250 c.c. and 350 c.c. events in 1963–65. Mike Hailwood is the only man to win three events in one year, in 1961 and 1967.

Most successful riders *World championships*
The most world championship titles (instituted by the *Fédération Internationale Motorcycliste* in 1949) won are 15 by Giacomo Agostini (b. Lovere, Italy, 16 June 1942), the 350 c.c. in 1968–1974, and 500 c.c. in 1966–1972, 1975. He is

left: Henk Vink, the Flying Dutchman, here leading John Hobbs, holds two world standing start records. (*Mark Moylan, All-Sport Photographic*)

right: Tom Sneva in his Penske Cosworth set a new record in practice for the 1978 Indianapolis 500 but finished second in the race itself. (*All-Sport Photographic*)

below: Co-record holder for the Le Mans circuit, Jean-Pierre Jaussaud, after the race. (*Sporting Pictures*)

the only man to win two world championships in five consecutive years (350 and 500 c.c. titles in 1968–1972).

Agostini won 122 races in the world championship series between 24 Apr. 1965 and 29 Aug. 1976, including a record 19 in 1970, also achieved by Mike Hailwood in 1966. Klaus Enders (Germany) (b. 1937) won six world side-car titles, 1967, 1969–70, 1972–74.

Most successful riders *Trials*

Samuel Hamilton Miller (b. Belfast, Northern Ireland, 11 Nov. 1935) won eleven A.-C.U. Solo Trials Drivers' Stars in 1959–69.

Most successful riders *Scrambles*

Jeffrey Vincent Smith, M.B.E. (b. Colne, Lancashire, 14 Oct. 1934) won nine A.-C.U. 500 c.c. Scrambles' Stars in 1955–56, 1960–65 and 1967.

Joël Robert (b. Chatelet, Belgium, 11 Nov. 1943) has won six 250 c.c. moto-cross world championships (1964, 1968–72). Between 25 Apr. 1964 and 18 June 1972 he won a record fifty 250 c.c. Grands Prix. He became the youngest moto-cross world champion on 12 July 1964 when he won the 250 c.c. championship aged 20 years 8 months.

Most successful machines

Italian M.V.-Agusta machines won 37 world championships

between 1952 and 1973 and 276 world championship races between 1952 and 1976. Japanese Honda machines won 29 world championship races and five world championships in 1966. In the seven years they contested the championship (1961–67) their annual average was 20 race wins.

Youngest and oldest world champions

Alberto "Johnny" Cecotto (b. Caracas, Venezuela, 25 Jan. 1956) is the youngest to win a world championship. He was 19 years 211 days when he won the 350 c.c. title on 24 Aug. 1975. The oldest was Hermann-Peter Müller (1909–76) of West Germany, who won the 250 c.c. title in 1955 aged 46.

Highest speeds

Official world speed records must be set with two runs over a measured distance made in opposite directions within a time limit. This limit is one hour for F.I.M. records and two hours for A.M.A. records.

Donald A. Vesco (b. Loma Linda, Calif., U.S.A., 8 Apr. 1939) riding his 21 ft long 1500 c.c. *Silver Bird* streamliner, powered by two Yamaha TZ750 four-cylinder engines developing 180 b.h.p., on Bonneville Salt Flats, Utah, U.S.A. on 28 Sept. 1975 set A.M.A. and F.I.M. absolute records. His average time was 11.8495 sec (303.810 m.p.h. *488,935 km/h*) for the A.M.A. record and 11.884 sec (302.928 m.p.h. *487,516 km/h*) for the F.I.M. record. (For details of the individual runs see the 23rd Edition.) On the same day he covered a flying quarter mile in 2.925 sec (307.692 m.p.h. *495,183 km/h*), the highest speed ever achieved on a motorcycle.

The highest speed achieved over two runs in the U.K. is 189.873 m.p.h. *305,571 km/h* by Frederick James Cooper (b. London, 9 Mar. 1925) on his 1,267 c.c. supercharged twin-engined Triumph *Cyclotron* at R.A.F. Fairford, Glos., on 23 Sept. 1972. Average time for the flying 440 yd *402 m* runs was 4.74 sec.

The world record for 1 km *1,093.6 yd* from a standing start is 16.68 sec by Henk Vink (b. 24 July 1939) (Netherlands) on his supercharged 984 c.c. four-cylinder Kawasaki, at Elvington Airfield, North Yorkshire on 24 July 1977. The faster run was made in 16.09 secs.

The world record for 440 yd *402 m* from a standing start is 8.805 sec. by Henk Vink on his supercharged 1,132 c.c. four-cylinder Kawasaki at Elvington Airfield, North Yorkshire on 23 July 1977. The faster run was made in 8.55 sec.

The fastest time for a single run over 440 yd *402 m* from a standing start is 7.62 sec by Russ Collins of Gardena, California, U.S.A. riding a nitro-burning 2000 c.c. 8-cylinder Honda, *Sorcerer*, in the National Hot Rod Association's World Finals at Ontario Motor Speedway, Ontario, California, on 7 Oct. 1978. The highest terminal velocity recorded at the end of a 440 yd *402 m* run from a standing start is 199.55 m.p.h. *321,14 km/h* by Russ Collins at the above meeting on 7 Oct. 1978.

Longest race

The longest race is the Liège 24 hours. The greatest distance ever covered is 2,761.9 miles *4 444,8 km* (average speed 115.08 m.p.h. *185,20 km/h*) by Jean-Claude Chemarin and Christian Leon, both of France, on a 941 c.c. four-cylinder Honda on the Francorchamps circuit on 14–15 Aug. 1976.

Longest circuit

The 37.73 mile *60,72 km* "Mountain" circuit, over which the principal T.T. races have been run since 1911 (with minor amendments in 1920), has 264 curves and corners and is the longest used for any motorcycle race.

MOTOR RACING

Earliest races

There are various conflicting claims, but the first automobile race was the 201 mile *323 km* Green Bay to Madison, Wis-

consin, U.S.A. run in 1878 won by an Oshkosh steamer. In 1887 Count Jules Felix Philippe Albert de Dion de Malfiance (1856–1946) won the *La Velocipede* 19.3 miles *31 km* race in Paris in a De Dion steam quadricycle in which he is reputed to have exceeded 37 m.p.h. *59 km/h*. The first "real" race was from Paris to Bordeaux and back (732 miles *1 178 km*) on 11–13 June 1895. The first to finish was Emile Levassor (1844–1897) of France, in a Panhard-Levassor two-seater, with a 1.2 litre Daimler engine developing 3½ h.p. His time was 48 hr 47 min (average speed 15.01 m.p.h. *24,15 km/h*). The first closed circuit race was held over five laps of a mile *1,6 km* dirt track at Narragansett Park, Cranston, R.I., U.S.A., on 7 Sept. 1896, won by A. H. Whiting, driving a Riker electric.

The oldest race in the world, still regularly run, is the R.A.C. Tourist Trophy, first staged on 14 Sept. 1905, in the Isle of Man. The oldest continental race is the French Grand Prix first held on 26–27 June 1906. The Coppa Florio, in Sicily, has been irregularly held since 1900.

Fastest circuits *World*

The highest average lap speed attained on any closed circuit is 250.958 m.p.h. *403,878 km/h* in a trial by Dr. Hans Liebold (b. 12 Oct. 1929) (Germany) who lapped the 7.85 mile *12,64 km* high-speed track at Nardo, Italy in 1 min 52.67 sec in a Mercedes-Benz C111-IV experimental coupe on 5 May 1979. It was powered by a V8 engine with two KKK turbochargers with an output of 500 hp at 6,200 r.p.m.

The highest average race lap speed for a closed circuit is 214.158 m.p.h. *344,654 km/h* by Mario Gabriele Andretti (U.S.A.) (b. Trieste, Italy, 28 Feb. 1940) driving a 2.6 litre turbocharged Viceroy Parnelli-Offenhauser on the 2 mile *3,2 km*, 22 degree banked oval at Texas World Speedway, College Station, Tex., U.S.A. on 6 Oct. 1973.

The fastest road circuit was the Francorchamps circuit near Spa, Belgium, then 8.761 miles *14,100 km* in length which was lapped in 3 min 13.4 sec (average speed 163.086 m.p.h. *262,461 km/h*) on lap seven of the Francorchamps 1000 km sports car race on 6 May 1973, by Henri Pescarolo (b. Paris, France, 25 Sept. 1942) driving a 2 993 c.c. V12 Matra-Simca MS670 Group 5 sports car. The race lap average speed record at Berlin's AVUS track was 171.75 m.p.h. *276,38 km/h* by Bernd Rosemeyer (Germany) (1909–38) in a 6-litre V16 Auto Union in 1937.

The fastest World championship GP circuit in current use is the 2.932 miles *4,719 km* at Silverstone, Northamptonshire, England opened in 1948. The race lap record is 1 min 14.40 sec (average speed 141.87 m.p.h. *228,31 km/h*) by Gianclaudio (Clay) Regazzoni (Switzerland) (b. 5 Sept. 1939) driving a Saudia-Williams FW07 on 14 July 1979. The practice lap record is 1 min 11.88 sec (146.84 m.p.h. *263,31 km/h*) by Alan Jones (Australia) (b. 2 Nov. 1946) in a Saudia-Williams on 12 July 1979.

The Motor Industry Research Association (MIRA) High Speed Circuit (2.82 mile *4,53 km* lap with 33-degree banking on the bends) at Lindley, Warwickshire, was lapped in 1 min 2.8 sec (average speed 161.655 m.p.h. *260,158 km/h*) by David Wishart Hobbs (b. Leamington, Warwickshire, 9 June 1939) driving a 4 994 c.c. V12 Jaguar XJ13 Group 6 prototype sports car in April 1967.

Fastest races *World*

The fastest race was the NASCAR Grand National 125 mile *201 km* (a qualifying event for the Daytona 500) on the 2.50 mile *4,02 km*, 31-degree banked tri-oval at Daytona International Speedway, Florida, U.S.A. The record time for this race is 40 min 55 sec (average speed 183.295 m.p.h. *294,985 km/h*) by William Caleb "Cale" Yarborough (b. 27 Mar. 1939) of Timmonsville, S. Carolina, U.S.A., driving a 1969 Mercury V8, on 19 Feb. 1970.

The fastest road race was the Francorchamps 1000 km sports car race held on the Francorchamps circuit. The record time for this 71-lap (622.055 mile *1 001,100 km*) race was 4 hr 1

303

min 9.7 sec (average speed 154.765 m.p.h. *249,070 km/h*) by Pedro Rodriguez (1940–71) of Mexico, and Keith Jack "Jackie" Oliver (b. Chadwell Heath, Greater London, 14 Aug. 1942) driving a 4 998 c.c. flat-12 Porsche 917K Group 5 sports car, on 9 May 1971.

Fastest races *United Kingdom*

The fastest currently held race in the United Kingdom is the British Grand Prix race. The record time for this 68 lap (199.37 mile *320,85 km*) race is 1 hr 26 min 11.17 sec (average speed 138.80 m.p.h. *223,37 km/h*) by Clay Regazzoni (Switzerland) driving a Saudia-Williams FW07 at Silverstone on 14 July 1979.

Fastest pit stop

Robert William (Bobby) Unser (b. Colorado Springs, Colorado, U.S.A., 20 Feb. 1934) took 4 sec to take on fuel on lap 10 of the Indianapolis 500 on 30 May 1976.

Toughest circuit *World*

The Targa Florio (first run 9 May 1906) was widely acknowledged to be the most arduous race. Held on the Piccolo Madonie Circuit in Sicily, it covered eleven laps (492.126 miles *792,000 km*) and involved the negotiation of 9,350 corners, over severe mountain gradients, and narrow rough roads. The record time was 6 hr 27 min 48.0 sec (average speed 76.141 m.p.h. *122,537 km/h*) by Arturo Francesco Merzario (b. Civenna, Italy, 11 Mar. 1943) and Sandro Munari (b. Venice, Italy, 1940) driving a 2 998.5 c.c. flat-12 Ferrari 312P Group 5 sports car in the 56th race on 21 May 1972. The lap record was 33 min 36.0 sec (average speed 79.890 m.p.h. *128,570 km/h*) by Leo Juhani Kinnunen (b. Tampere, Finland, 5 Aug. 1943) on lap 11 of the 54th race on 3 May 1970 driving a 2 997 c.c. flat-8 Porsche 908/3 Spyder Group 6 prototype sports car.

Toughest circuit *Grand Prix*

The most gruelling and slowest Grand Prix circuit is that for the Monaco Grand Prix (first run on 14 Apr. 1929), round the streets and the harbour of Monte Carlo. It is 2.058 miles *3,312 km* in length and has eleven pronounced corners and several sharp changes of gradient. The race is run over 76 laps (156.4 miles *251,7 km*) and involves on average about 1,600 gear changes. The record time for the race is 1 hr 55 min 22.48 sec (average speed 81.338 m.p.h. *130,901 km/h*) by Jody Scheckter (b. S. Africa, 29 Jan. 1950) driving a Ferrari 312T4 on 27 May 1979. The race lap record is 1 min 28.65 sec (average speed 83.67 m.p.h. *134,649 km/h*) by Andreas-Nikolaus "Niki" Lauda (b. Austria, 22 Feb. 1949) driving a Brabham-Alfa Romeo BT46 on 7 May 1978. The practice lap record is 1 min 26.45 sec (average speed 85.69 m.p.h. *137,92 km/h*) by Jody Scheckter in a Ferrari 312T4 on 26 May 1979.

Le Mans

The greatest distance ever covered in the 24 hour *Grand Prix d'Endurance* (first held on 26–27 May 1923) on the old Sarthe circuit at Le Mans, France is 3,315.208 miles *5 335,313 km* by Dr. Helmut Marko (b. Graz, Austria, 27 Apr. 1943) and Jonkheer Gijs van Lennep (b. Bloemendaal, Netherlands, 16 Mar. 1942) driving a 4 907 c.c. flat-12 Porsche 917K Group 5 sports car, on 12–13 June 1971. The record for the current circuit is 3,134.52 miles *5 044,52 km* by Didier Pironi (b. 26 Mar. 1952) and Jean-Pierre Jaussaud (b. 3 June 1937) (France) (av. speed 130.60 m.p.h. *210.18 km/h*) in an Alpine Renault on 10–11 June 1978. The race lap record (8.475 mile *13,64 km* lap) is 3 min 34.2 sec (average speed 142.44 m.p.h. *229,244 km/h*) by Jean Pierre Jabouille (b. France, 1 Oct. 1942) driving an Alpine Renault on 11 June 1978. The practice lap record is 3 min 27.6 sec (av. speed 146.97 m.p.h. *236,53 km/h*) by Jacques-Bernard "Jacky" Ickx (b. Belgium, 1 Jan. 1945) in a turbocharged 2.1 litre Porsche 936/78 on 7 June 1978.

Le Mans *Most wins*

The race has been won by Ferrari cars nine times, in 1949, 1954, 1958 and 1960–65. The most wins by one man is four by Olivier Gendebien (b. 1925) (Belgium), 1958, 1960–62, and Jackie Ickx, 1969 and 1975–77.

Le Mans *British wins*

The race has been won 12 times by British cars, thus: Bentley in 1924 and 1927–30, once by Lagonda in 1935, five times by Jaguar in 1951, 1953 and 1955–57 and once by Aston Martin in 1959.

Indianapolis 500

The Indianapolis 500 mile *804 km* race (200 laps) was inaugurated in the U.S.A. on 30 May 1911. The most successful driver has been Anthony Joseph "A.J." Foyt, Jr. (b. Houston, Texas, U.S.A., 16 Jan. 1935) who won in 1961, 1964, 1967 and 1977. The record time is 3 hr 4 min 5.54 sec (average speed 162.962 m.p.h. *262,261 km/h*) by Mark Donohue, Jr. driving a 2 595 c.c. 900 b.h.p. turbocharged Sunoco McLaren M16B-Offenhauser on 27 May 1972. The race lap record is 46.71 sec (average speed 192.678 m.p.h. *310,085 km/h*) by Danny Ongais, driving a 2.6 litre turbocharged Parnelli-Cosworth DFX on lap 42 of the race held on 29 May 1977. The 4–lap qualifying record is 2 min 58.08 sec (average speed 202.156 m.p.h. *325,338 km/h*) by Tom Sneva (b. U.S.A., 1 June 1948) driving a Penske-Cosworth DFX turbocharged PC6 on 20 May 1978.

The record prize fund was $1,271,954 for the 63rd race on 27 May 1979. The individual prize record is $290,363 by Al Unser (b. Albuquerque, New Mexico, U.S.A., 29 May 1939) on 28 May 1978.

Drivers *Most successful*

Based on the World Drivers' Championship, inaugurated in 1950, the most successful driver is Juan-Manuel Fangio y Cia (b. Balcarce, Argentina, 24 June 1911) who won five times in 1951, 1954–57. He retired in 1958, after having won 24 Grand Prix races (two shared). The most successful driver in terms of race wins is Richard Lee Petty (b. Randleman, N. Carolina, U.S.A., 2 July 1937) with 186 NASCAR Grand National wins between 1960 and Apr. 1979. His best season was 1967 with 27 wins.

Three time winner of the Indianapolis 500, Al Unser won the highest ever prize money in the race in 1970. (*Sporting Pictures*)

The most Grand Prix victories is 27 by John Young "Jackie" Stewart, O.B.E. (b. Milton, Dunbartonshire, 11 June 1939) between 12 Sept. 1965 and 5 Aug. 1973. James "Jim" Clark, O.B.E. (1936–68) of Scotland holds the record for Grand Prix victories in one year with seven in 1963. He won a record 61 Formula One and Formula Libre races between 1959 and 1968. The most Grand Prix starts is 176 (out of a possible 184) between 18 May 1958 and 26 Jan. 1975 by the British driver Norman Graham Hill, O.B.E. (1929–1975). Between 20 Nov. 1960 and 5 Oct. 1969 he took part in 90 consecutive Grands Prix.

Oldest and youngest *World champions*
The youngest world champion was Emerson Fittipaldi (b. São Paulo, Brazil, 12 Dec. 1946) who won his first world championship on 10 Sept. 1972 aged 25 years 273 days. The oldest world champion was Juan-Manuel Fangio who won his last world championship on 18 Aug. 1957 aged 46 years 55 days.

Oldest and youngest *G.P. winners and drivers*
The youngest Grand Prix winner was Bruce Leslie McLaren (1937–70) of New Zealand, who won the United States Grand Prix at Sebring, Florida, U.S.A., on 12 Dec. 1959 aged 22 years 104 days. The oldest Grand Prix winner was Tazio Giorgio Nuvolari (1892–1953) of Italy, who won the Albi Grand Prix at Albi, France on 14 July 1946 aged 53 years 240 days. The oldest Grand Prix driver was Louis Alexandre Chiron, O. St-C., L.d'H., C.d'I, (Monaco) (1899–1979), who finished 6th in the Monaco Grand Prix on 22 May 1955 aged 55 years 292 days. The youngest Grand Prix driver was Christopher Arthur Amon (b. Bulls, New Zealand, 20 July 1943) who took part in the Belgian Grand Prix at Spa on 9 June 1963 aged 19 years 324 days.

Hill climbing *Pikes Peak race*
The Pikes Peak Auto Hill Climb, Colorado, U.S.A. (instituted 1916) has been won 13 times by Bobby Unser between 1956 and 1974 (ten championship, two stock and one sports car title). On 30 June 1968, in the 46th race, he set a record time of 11 min 54.9 sec in his 5 506 c.c. Chevrolet championship car for the 12.42 mile *19,98 km* course rising from 9,402 ft to 14,110 ft *2 865–4 300 m* through 157 curves.

Hill climbing *Most successful drivers*
The British National Hill Climb Championship (inaugurated in 1947) has been won six times by Anthony Ernest Marsh (b. Stourbridge, West Midlands, 20 July 1931) 1955–57, 1965–67. Raymond Mays C.B.E. (b. Bourne, Lincolnshire, 1 Aug. 1899) won the Shelsley Walsh hill climb, near Worcester, 19 times between 1923 and 1950.

Rallies *Earliest*
The earliest long rally was promoted by the Parisian daily *Le Matin* in 1907 from Peking, China to Paris over a route of about 7,500 miles *12 000 km*. Five cars left Peking on 10 June. The winner, Prince Scipione Borghese, of Italy, arrived in Paris on 10 Aug. 1907 in his 40 h.p. Itala accompanied by his chauffeur, Ettore, and Luigi Barzini.

Rallies *Longest*
The world's longest ever rally was the *Singapore Airlines* London–Sydney Rally run over 19,329 miles *31 107 km* starting from Covent Garden, Greater London on 14 Aug. 1977 to Sydney Opera House passing through 17 countries. It was won on 28 Sept. 1977 by Andrew Cowan, Colin Malkin and Michael Broad in a Mercedes 280E. The longest held annually is the East African Safari (first run 1953 through Kenya, Tanzania and Uganda) which is up to 3,874 miles *6 234 km* long, as in the 17th Safari held between 8–12 Apr. 1971. It has been won a record three times by Joginder Singh (Kenya) in 1965, 1974 and 1976.

Rallies *Monte Carlo*
The Monte Carlo Rally (first run 1911) has been won a record four times by Sandro Munari (Italy) in 1972, 1975, 1976 and 1977. The smallest car to win was an 851 c.c. Saab driven by Erik Carlsson (b. Sweden 5 Mar. 1929) and Gunnar Häggbom of Sweden on 25 Jan. 1962, and by Carlsson and Gunnar Palm on 24 Jan. 1963.

Dragging *Piston engined*
The lowest elapsed time recorded by a piston-engined dragster is 5.637 sec (terminal velocity 250.69 m.p.h. *403,45 km/h*) by Donald Glenn "Big Daddy" Garlits (b. 1932) of Seffner, Florida, U.S.A. driving his rear-engined AA/F dragster, powered by a 7 948 c.c. supercharged Dodge V8 engine, during the National Hot Rod Association's Super-nationals at Ontario Motor Speedway, Ontario, California, U.S.A., on 11 Oct. 1975. The highest terminal velocity recorded is 255.58 m.p.h. *411,31 km/h* by Shirley Muldowney (U.S.A.) at Pomona, Cal., in Jan. 1979.

The world record for two runs in opposite directions over 440 yd *402 m* from a standing start is 6.70 sec by Dennis Victor Priddle (b. 1945) of Yeovil, Somerset, driving his 6 424 c.c. supercharged Chrysler dragster developing 1,700 b.h.p. using nitromethane and methanol, at Elvington Airfield, North Yorkshire on 7 Oct. 1972. The faster run was made in 6.65 sec.

Dragging *Rocket or jet-engined*
The highest terminal velocity recorded by any dragster is 377.754 m.p.h. *607,936 km/h* (elapsed time 4.65 sec) by Norman Craig Breedlove (b. 23 Mar. 1938) of Los Angeles, Calif., U.S.A., in the rocket powered *English Leather Special* on Bonneville Salt Flats, Utah, U.S.A. in September 1973. The lowest elapsed time recorded by any dragster is 3.94 sec by Samuel A. Miller (b. 15 Apr. 1945) of Wayne, N.J., at Miami, Florida, U.S.A., in Feb. 1979.

Terminal velocity is the speed attained at the end of a 440 yd 402 m run made from a standing start and elapsed time is the time taken for the run.

Highest speeds
For details of the land speed record see pp. 135 and 211.

The world speed record for compression ignition engined cars is 190.344 m.p.h. *306,328 km/h* (average of two runs in opposite directions over a measured mile *1,6 km*) by Robert Havemann of Eureka, California, U.S.A. driving his *Corsair* streamliner, powered by a turbocharged 6 981 c.c. 6-cylinder GMC 6-71 diesel engine developing 746 b.h.p., at Bonneville Salt Flats, Utah, U.S.A., in August 1971. The faster run was made at 210 m.p.h. *337 km/h*.

The most successful land speed record breaker was Major Sir Malcolm Campbell (1885–1948) of the United Kingdom. He broke the official record nine times between 25 Sept. 1924, with 146.157 m.p.h. *235,216 km/h* in a Sunbeam, and 3 Sept. 1935, when he achieved 301.129 m.p.h. *480,620 km/h* in the Rolls-Royce engined *Bluebird*.

Duration records
The greatest distance ever covered in one year is 400 000 km *248,548.5 miles* by François Lecot (1879–1949), an innkeeper from Rochetaillée, near Lyon, France, in a 1 900 c.c. 66 b.h.p. Citroën 11 sedan, mainly between Paris and Monte Carlo, from 22 July 1935 to 26 July 1936. He drove on 363 of the 370 days allowed.

The world's duration record is 185,353 miles 1,741 yd *298 298 km* in 133 days 17 hr 37 min 38.64 sec (average speed 58.07 m.p.h. *93,45 km/h*) by Marchand, Presalé and six others in a Citroën on the Montlhéry track near Paris, France, during March-July 1933.

MOUNTAINEERING

Origins
Although bronze-age artifacts have been found on the summit of the Riffelhorn, Switzerland (9,605 ft *2 927 m*) mountaineering, as a sport, has a continuous history dating back only to 1854. Isolated instances of climbing for its own sake exist back to the 13th century. The Atacamenans built sacrificial platforms near the summit of Llullaillaco (22,058 ft *6 723 m*) in late pre-Columbian times c. 1490. The earliest recorded rock climb in the British Isles was of Stac na Biorrach, St. Kilda by Sir Robert Moray in 1698.

305

Dave Cannon, who won the British marathon running
championship the year after setting the Ben Nevis race record.
(*West Highland News Agency*)

Mount Everest

Mount Everest (29,028 ft *8 848 m*) was first climbed at
11.30 a.m. on 29 May 1953, when the summit was reached
by Edmund Percival Hillary (b. 20 July 1919), created
K.B.E., of New Zealand, and the Sherpa, Tenzing Norgay
(b., as Namgyal Wangdi, in Nepal in 1914, formerly called
Tenzing Khumjung Bhutia), who was awarded the G.M. The
successful expedition was led by Col. (later Hon. Brigadier)
Henry Cecil John Hunt, C.B.E, D.S.O. (b. 22 June 1910),
who was created a Knight Bachelor in 1953, a life Baron on
11 June 1966 and K.G. on 23 Apr. 1979.

Since the first ascent, another 85 climbers have succeeded to
end—June 1979. Franz Oppurg (Austria) made the first
solo climb on 14 May 1978. The first Britons to reach the
summit were Douglas Scott (b. 29 May 1941) and Dougal
Haston (1940–77) on 24 Sept. 1975. Three women have
reached the summit, the first being Junko Tabei (b. 1939)
(Japan) on 16 May 1975.

Greatest walls

The highest final stage in any wall climb is that on the south
face of Annapurna I (26,545 ft *8 091 m*). It was climbed by
the British expedition led by Christian Bonington, C.B.E.
(b. 1934) when from 2 Apr to 27 May 1970, using 18,000 ft
5 500 m of rope, Donald Whillans (b. 1934) and Dougal
Haston scaled to the summit. The longest wall climb is on
the Rupal-Flank from the base camp at 3 560 m *11,680 ft* to
the South Point 8 042 m *26,384 ft* of Nanga Parbat—a
vertical ascent of 4 482 m *14,704 ft*. This was scaled by the
Austro-Germano-Italian Expedition led by Dr. Karl Maria
Herrligkoffer in April 1970.

Europe's greatest wall is the 6,600 ft *2 000 m* north face of
the Eigerwand (Ogre wall) first climbed by Heinrich Harrer
and Fritz Kasparek of Austria and Anderl Heckmair and
Wiggerl Vörg of Germany on 21–24 July 1938. The north-

east face of the Eiger had been climbed on 20 Aug. 1932 by
Hans Lauper, Alfred Zurcher, Alexander Graven and Josef
Knubel. The greatest alpine solo climb was that of Walter
Bonatti (b. Bergamo, Italy, 22 June 1930) of the South West
Pillar of the Dru, Montenvers now called the Bonatti Pillar,
with five bivouacs in 126 hr 7 min on 17–22 Aug. 1955.

There are climbs in the Yosemite Valley, California with a
severity rating of 5.12, regarded as the most demanding free
climbs in the world.

Highest bivouac

Douglas Scott and Dougal Haston bivouaced in a snow hole
at 28,700 ft *8 747 m* on the South Summit of Everest on the
night of 24 Sept. 1975.

MOUNTAIN RACING

Mount Cameroun

Ndumbe Evambe Amos descended from the summit
13,353 ft *4 070 m* to Buea at 3,000 ft *914 m* in 78 min 4 sec
on 26 Feb. 1978 achieving a vertical rate of 132 ft *40,4 m* per
min. In winning for the third successive year, Father Walter
Stifter ran to the summit and back in a record 4 hr 18 min
16 sec in 1978.

Ben Nevis

The record time for the race from Fort William to the summit of Ben Nevis (4,406 ft *1 343 m*) and return is 1 hr 26 min
55 sec by David Cannon (b. 7 Aug. 1950) (Gateshead H.)
on 4 Sept. 1976. The feminine record is 1 hr 53 min 23 sec
by Ros Coats on 2 Sept. 1978. The full course by the bridle
path is about 14 miles *22 km* but distance is saved by crossing
the open hillside. The mountain was first climbed *c.* 1720
and the earliest race was in 1895.

Skiddaw Fell

In the Skiddaw Fell Race (3,053 ft to 250 ft *930 to 107 m*) a

PROGRESSIVE MOUNTAINEERING ALTITUDE RECORDS (See also pp. 67–68)

ft	m	Mountain	Climbers	Date	
17,887	5 452	Popocatépetl, Mexico	Francisco Montano		1521
18,400	5 608	Mana Pass, Zaskar Range	A. de Andrade, M. Morques	July	1624
18,893	5 758	On Chimborazo, Ecuador	Dr. Alexander Von Humboldt, Goujand (France) and C. Montufar	23 June	1802
19,411	5 916	On Leo Pargyal Range, Himalaya	Gerrard and Lloyd		1818
22,260	6 784	On E. Ibi Gamih, Garhwal Himalaya	A. & R. Schlagintweit	Aug.	1855
22,834	6 959	Aconcagua, Andes	Matthias Zurbriggen	14 Jan.	1897
22,606	6 890	Pioneer Peak on Baltoro Kangri	William M. Conway, Matthias Zurbriggen	23 Aug.	1892
23,394	7 130	On Pyramis Peak, Karakoram	William H. Workman, J. Petigax Snr. & Jnr., C. Savoie	12 Aug.	1903
23,787	7 250	On Guria Mandhata, Tibet	Thomas G. Longstaff, Alexis & Henri Brocherel	23 July	1905
c.23,900	c.7 285	On Kabru, Sikkim-Nepal	Carl W. Rubenson and Monrad Aas	20 Oct.	1907
24,607	7 500	On Chogolisa, Karakoram	Duke of the Abruzzi, J. Petigax, H. & E. Brocherel	18 July	1909
c.24,900	c.7 590	Camp V, Everest, Tibet-Nepal	G. L. Mallory, E. F. Norton, T. H. Somervell, H. T. Morshead	20 May	1922
26,986	8 225	On Everest (North Face), Tibet	George L. Mallory, Edward F. Norton, T. Howard Somervell	21 May	1922
c.27,300	c.8 320	On Everest (North Face), Tibet	George I. Finch, J. Granville Bruce	27 May	1922
28,126	8 570	On Everest (North Face), Tibet	Edward Felix Norton	4 June	1924
28,126	8 570	On Everest (North Face), Tibet	P. Wynn Harris, Lawrence R. Wager	30 May	1933
28,126	8 570	On Everest (North Face), Tibet	Francis Sydney Smythe	1 June	1933
28,215	8 599	South Shoulder on Everest, Nepal	Raymond Lambert, Tenzing Norgay	28 May	1952
28,721	8 754	South Shoulder on Everest, Nepal	Thomas D. Bourdillon, Robert C. Evans	26 May	1953
29,028*	8 848*	Everest, Nepal-Tibet	Edmund P. Hillary, Tenzing Norgay	29 May	1953

* First attained without oxygen, by Reinhold Messner (Italy) and Peter Habeler (Austria), 8 May 1978.

PROGRESSIVE LIST OF HIGHEST SUMMITS CLIMBED

The progressive list of highest summits climbed after Aconcagua in 1897 is as follows:

ft	m		Climbers	Date	
23,360	7 120	Trisul, Garhwal Himalaya	Thomas G. Longstaff, Alexis & Henri Brocherel, Karbir	12 June	1907
23,385*	7 127	Pauhunri, Sikkim Himalaya	A. M. Kellas, Sonam and another porter	16 June	1911
23,383	7 127	Pik Lenin, Trans-Alai Pamir	E. Allwein, K. Wien, E. Schneider	25 Sept.	1928
23,442	7 145	Nepal Peak, Sikkim-Nepal	E. Schneider	24 May	1930
24,344	7 417	Jongsong Peak, Nepal-Sikkim-Tibet	E. Schneider, H. Hoerlin	3 June	1930
25,447	7 756	Kamet, Garhwal Himalaya	Francis S. Smythe, R. L. Holdsworth, Eric E. Shipton, Lewa	21 June	1931
25,645	7 816	Nanda Devi, Garhwal Himalaya	N. E. Odell, Harold W. Tilman	29 Aug.	1936
26,492	8 047	Annapurna I, Nepal	Maurice Herzog, L. Lachenal	3 June	1950
29,028	8 848	Mount Everest, Nepal-Tibet	Edmund P. Hillary, Tenzing Norgay	29 May	1953

* Survey of India height now listed as 23,180 ft 7 065 m.

vertical descent rate of 128 ft *39 m* per min was achieved by George Jeffrey Norman (b. 6 Feb. 1945) (Altrincham A.C.) in the 1972 race.

Peak racing
The Lakeland 24-hour record is 72 peaks achieved by Joss Naylor, M.B.E. (b. 10 Feb. 1936) of Wasdale on 22–23 June 1975. He covered 105 miles *168 km* with 40,000 ft *12 190 m* of ascents and descents in 23 hr 11 min. Naylor won the Ennerdale mountain race over 23 miles *37 km* nine times from 1968 to 1977 setting a record time of 3 hr 30 min 40 sec in 1972. The Yorkshire three peak record is 2 hr 29 min 53 sec by Jeff Norman on 28 Apr. 1974.

The "Three Thousander" record over the 14 Welsh peaks of over 3,000 ft *914 m* is 4 hr 46 min 22 sec with pacemakers, by Joss Naylor on 17 June 1973 despite misty conditions.

Three peaks record
The Three Peaks route from sea level at Fort William, Inverness-shire, to sea level at Caernarvon, *via* the summits of Ben Nevis, Scafell Pike and Snowdon, was covered by Metropolitan Police Constable Arthur Eddleston (b. 6 Dec. 1939) (Cambridge H.) who walked it in 7 days 11 hr 40 min on 22–29 Apr. 1978. Five members of the Vauxhall Motors Recreation Club, Luton, Beds., ran the distance in relay in 54 hr 57 min 47 sec, on 21–23 May 1977.

The fastest individual total time for climbing the three mountains is 4 hr 16 min by Joss Naylor on 8–9 July 1971.

Ten peaks record
The Ten Peaks race is from Barnthwaite Farm, Wasdale Head, Cumbria to the top of Skiddaw *via* England's nine other highest mountains and tops: Great Gable, Sca Fell, Scafell Pike, Ill Crags, Broad Crag, Great End, Bow Fell, Helvellyn and Lower Man. The record time is 6 hr 8 min by Michael Fieldhouse (b. 20 July 1960) of Grange-over-Sands, Cumbria, on 31 July 1977.

Pennine Way
The record for traversing the 271 mile *436 km* long Pennine Way is 3 days 1 hr 48 min by Peter Dawes (b. 1939) of Kendal A.C. on 18–21 July 1975.

Guides Race
Bill Teasdale, M.B.E., won the Guides' Race at the Grasmere Sports, Cumbria, for the eleventh time in 1966. It involves running to a turning point on Butter Crag (966 ft *294 m* above sea level) and back, a distance of about 1½ miles *2,4 km*. The record time for this race is 12 min 21.6 sec by Frederick Leslie Reeves (b. 25 Feb. 1945) on 24 Aug. 1978.

NETBALL

Origins
The game was invented in the U.S.A. in 1891 and introduced into England in 1895 by Dr. Toles. The All England Women's Netball Association was formed in 1926. The oldest club in continuous existence is the Polytechnic Netball Club of London founded in 1907.

Most titles *World*
World championships were inaugurated in August 1963. Australia has won on three occasions, 1963, 1971 and 1975.

Most titles *National*
The National Championships (inst. 1966) have been won most often by Sudbury Netball Club with five titles (1968–70, 1971 (shared) and 1973).

Most titles *County*
Surrey have won the County Championships a record 17 times 1949–64, 1966, 1969 (shared).

Most international appearances
The record number of internationals is 65 by Anne Miles (b. 9 Apr. 1942) of England 1965–1975.

Highest scores
England has never been beaten in a senior Home international. The World Tournament record score was in Auckland, New Zealand in 1975 when England beat Papua New Guinea 114

goals to 16. The record number of goals in the World Tournament is 402 by Judith Heath (England) (b. 1942) in 1971. The highest international score recorded was when New Zealand beat Singapore 117–9 in Oct. 1974.

OLYMPIC GAMES

Note: These records now include the un-numbered Games held at Athens in 1906, which some authorities ignore. Although inserted between the regular III Games in 1904 and the IV Games in 1908, the 1906 Games though unnumbered, were officially run by the International Olympic Committee and were of a higher standard than all three of those that preceded them.

Origins

The earliest celebration of the ancient Olympic Games of which there is a certain record is that of July 776 B.C., when Coroibos, a cook from Elis, won a foot race, though their origin dates from c. 1370 B.C. The ancient Games were terminated by an order issued in Milan in A.D. 393 by Theodosius I, "the Great" (c. 346–395), Emperor of Rome. At the instigation of Pierre de Fredi, Baron de Coubertin (1863–1937), the Olympic Games of the modern era were inaugurated in Athens on 6 Apr. 1896.

Modern celebrations

Modern celebrations have been voted for by the International Olympic Committee as follows. Dates indicate the span of Olympic competitions (excluding elimination contests). The first date is not necessarily that of the opening ceremony.

| I | 1896 | Athens, Greece | 6–15 April |
| II | 1900 | Paris, France | 20 May–28 Oct. |

The unique winner of four consecutive individual Olympic gold medals, Al Oerter, who intends to try for a fifth at the Moscow Games, twelve years after retiring. (*All-Sport Photographic*)

III	1904	St. Louis, U.S.A.	1 July–23 Nov.
*	1906	Athens, Greece	22 April–2 May
IV	1908	London, England	27 April–31 Oct.
V	1912	Stockholm, Sweden	5 May–22 July
VI	1916	Berlin, Germany	not celebrated owing to war
VII	1920	Antwerp, Belgium	20 April–12 Sept.
VIII	1924	Paris, France	4 May–27 July
IX	1928	Amsterdam, Holland	17 May–12 Aug.
X	1932	Los Angeles, U.S.A.	30 July–14 Aug.
XI	1936	Berlin, Germany	1–16 Aug.
XII	1940	Tokyo, then Helsinki, Finland	not celebrated owing to war
XIII	1944	London, England	not celebrated owing to war
XIV	1948	London, England	29 July–14 Aug.
XV	1952	Helsinki, Finland	19 July–3 Aug.
XVI	1956	Melbourne, Australia[1]	22 Nov.–8 Dec.
XVII	1960	Rome, Italy	25 Aug.–11 Sept.
XVIII	1964	Tokyo, Japan	10–24 Oct.
XIX	1968	Mexico City, Mexico	12–27 Oct.
XX	1972	Munich, W. Germany	26 Aug.–10 Sept.
XXI	1976	Montreal, Canada	17 July–1 Aug.
XXII	1980	Moscow, U.S.S.R.	19 July–3 Aug.
XXIII	1984	Los Angeles, U.S.A.	To be scheduled

* This celebration (to mark the tenth anniversary of the modern Games) was officially intercalated but is not numbered.

[1] The equestrian events were held in Stockholm, Sweden, 10–17 June 1956.

Separate Winter Olympics (there had been ice skating events in 1908 and 1920 and ice hockey in 1920) were inaugurated in 1924 and have been voted for as follows:

I	1924	Chamonix, France	25 Jan.–4 Feb.
II	1928	St. Moritz, Switzerland	11–19 Feb.
III	1932	Lake Placid, New York, U.S.A.	4–15 Feb.
IV	1936	Garmisch-Partenkirchen, Germany	6–16 Feb.
V	1948	St. Moritz, Switzerland	30 Jan.–8 Feb.
VI	1952	Oslo, Norway	14–25 Feb.
VII	1956	Cortina d'Ampezzo, Italy	26 Jan.–5 Feb.
VIII	1960	Squaw Valley, California, U.S.A.	18–28 Feb.
IX	1964	Innsbruck, Austria	29 Jan.–9 Feb.
X	1968	Grenoble, France	6–18 Feb.
XI	1972	Sapporo, Japan	3–13 Feb.
XII	1976	Innsbruck, Austria	4–15 Feb.
XIII	1980	Lake Placid, New York, U.S.A.	13–24 Feb.
XIV	1984	Sarajevo, Yugoslavia	1–12 Feb.

The first Winter Games in 1924 attracted 294 competitors from 16 nations.

Most medals *Individual gold*

In the ancient Olympic Games victors were given a chaplet of wild olive leaves. Leonidas of Rhodos won 12 running titles 164–152 B.C. The most individual gold medals won by a male competitor in the modern Games is ten by Raymond Clarence Ewry (U.S.A.) (1874–1937) (see Track and Field Athletics). The female record is seven by Vera Caslavska-Odlozil (Czechoslovakia) (see Gymnastics). The most won by a British competitor is four by Paul Radmilovic (1886–1968) in water polo, 1908, 1912 and 1920 and the 4 × 200 m freestyle relay in 1908, and swimmer Henry Taylor (1885–1951) in 1906 and 1908. The Australian swimmer Ian Murray Rose, who won four gold medals, was born in Birmingham, England on 6 Jan. 1939. The only Olympian to win four consecutive individual titles in the same event has been Alfred A. Oerter (b. 19 Sept. 1936, Astoria, N.Y.) of the U.S.A., who won the discus title in 1956–68.

Most medals *National*

The total figures for most medals and most gold medals for all Olympic events (including those now discontinued) for the summer (1896–1976) and Winter Games (1924–76):

	Gold	Silver	Bronze	Total
1. U.S.A.	658*	511½	438½	1,608
2. U.S.S.R. (formerly Russia)	311	255	244	810
3. G.B. (including Ireland to 1920)	165½	202½	178	546

* The A.A.U. (U.S.) reinstated James F. Thorpe (1888–1953) the disqualified highest scorer in the 1912 decathlon and pentathlon events on 12 Oct. 1973 but no issue of medals has yet been authorised by the I.O.C.

(A unique table of all medals won by nations is contained in *The Guinness Book of Answers*, 1978 edition).

Youngest and oldest gold medallists

The youngest ever winner was a French boy (whose name is not recorded) who coxed the Netherlands pair in 1900. He was not more than ten and may have been as young as seven. He substituted for Dr. Hermanus Brockmann, who coxed in the heats but proved too heavy. The youngest-ever female gold medal winner is Marjorie Gestring (U.S.A.) (b. 18 Nov. 1922, now Mrs. Bowman), aged 13 yr 9 months, in the 1936 women's springboard event. Oscar Swahn (see p. 240) was a member of the winning Running Deer shooting team in 1912 aged 65 yr 258 days.

Youngest and oldest *Great Britain*
The youngest competitor to represent Britain in the Olympic Games was Magdalena Cecilia Colledge (b. 28 Nov. 1920) aged 11 yr 24 days when she skated in the 1932 Games. The oldest was Hilda Lorna Johnstone (b. 4 Sept. 1902) aged 64 yr 358 days in the Equestrian Dressage in the 1972 Games.

Longest span
The longest span of an Olympic competitor is 40 years by Dr. Ivan Osiier (Denmark) (1888–1965) who competed as a fencer in 1908–32 and 1948, and Magnus Konow (Norway) (1887–1972) in yachting, 1908–20, and 1936–48. The longest feminine span is 24 years (1932–56) by the Austrian fencer Ellen Müller-Preis (b. 6 May 1912). Raimondo d'Inzeo (b. 8 Feb. 1925) competed for Italy in equestrian events at a record eight celebrations from 1948 to 1976, gaining one gold, two silver and three bronze medals. Janice Lee York Romary (b. 6 Aug. 1928) the U.S. fencer, competed in all six Games from 1948 to 1968, and Lia Manoliu (Romania) (b. 25 Apr. 1932) competed from 1952 to 1972 winning the discus title in 1968.

The longest span of any British competitor is 28 years by Enoch Jenkins who appeared in the 1924 and the 1952 Games in the clay pigeon shooting event, and the longest feminine span by Dorothy J. B. Tyler (*née* Odam) (b. 14 Mar. 1920) who high-jumped in 1936, 1948, 1952 and 1956. The record number of appearances for Great Britain is six by fencer Bill Hoskyns from 1956 to 1976. Durward Randolph Knowles (b. 2 Nov. 1917) competed in yachting for Britain in 1948 and in the following six Games for the Bahamas.

Most countries and participants
The greatest number of competitors in any summer Olympic Games has been 7,147 at Munich in 1972. A record 122 countries competed at Munich in 1972. The fewest was 311 competitors from 13 countries in 1896. In 1904 only 12 countries participated. France entered the largest ever team of 880 men and four women in the 1900 Games at Paris.

Ever present
Five countries have never failed to be represented at the 19 celebrations of the Games: Australia, Greece, Great Britain, Switzerland and the United States of America.

Largest crowd
The largest crowd at any Olympic site was 150,000 at the 1952 ski-jumping at the Holmenkollen, outside Oslo, Norway. Estimates of the number of spectators of the marathon race through Tōkyō, Japan on 21 Oct. 1964 have ranged from 500,000 to 1,500,000.

ORIENTEERING
Origins
Orienteering as now known was invented by Major Ernst Killander in Sweden in 1918. It was based on military exercises of the 1890s. The term was first used for an event at Oslo, Norway on 7 Oct. 1900. World championships (inst. 1966) are held biennially. Annual British championships were instituted in 1967 following the formation of the British Orienteering Federation.

Most titles *World*
Sweden has won the men's relay five times 1966–76 and the women's relay four times, 1966, 1970, 1974–76. Ulla Lindkvist (Sweden) gained the women's individual titles in 1966 and 1968. The men's title has been won twice by Åge Hadler (Norway) in 1966 and 1972 and Egil Johansen (Norway) 1976 and 1978.

Most titles *British*
The men's relay has been won twice by Oxford University,

1955, 1979, and the women's relay twice by Manchester and District, 1976, 1977, and Derwent Valley Orienteers, 1975, 1979. Geoffrey Peck (b. Blackpool, 27 Sept. 1949) (Interlopers) has won the men's individual title a record five times, 1971, 1973, 1976–77 and 1979. Carol McNeill of the same club has won the women's title six times, 1967, 1969, 1972–76.

PARACHUTING
Origins
Parachuting became a regulated sport with the institution of world championships in 1951. A team title was introduced in 1954 and women's events were included in 1956.

Most titles *World*
The U.S.S.R. won the men's team titles in 1954, 1958, 1960, 1966, 1972 and 1976 and the women's team title in 1956, 1958, 1966, 1968, 1972 and 1976. No individual has ever won a second world overall title.

Most titles *British*
John Meacock (Peterborough) has won the British title three times in 1969, 1971–72.

Greatest accuracy
Jacqueline Smith (G.B.) (b. 29 Mar. 1951) scored ten consecutive dead centre strikes (10 cm *4 in* disc) in the World Championships at Zagreb, Yugoslavia, 1 Sept. 1978. At Yuma, Arizona, U.S.A., in March 1978, Dwight Reynolds scored a record 105 daytime dead centres, and Bill Wenger and Phil Munden tied with 43 nighttime DCs, competing as members of the U.S. Army team, the Golden Knights.

Most jumps
The greatest number of consecutive jumps completed is 233 in 24 hours by David Parchment at Shobdon Airfield, Hereford, England on 19 June 1979.

World champion parachutist, Jacqueline Smith, did ten perfect jumps from 2,500 ft on to a 4 inch disc.

PELOTA VASCA
(Jaï Alaï)

Origins

The game, which originated in Italy as *longue paume* and was introduced into France in the 13th century, is said to be the fastest of all ball games. The glove or *gant* was introduced *c.* 1840 and the *chistera* was invented by Jean "Gantchiki" Dithurbide of Ste. Pée, France. The *grand chistera* was invented by Melchior Curuchague of Buenos Aires, Argentina in 1888.

The world's largest *frontón* (enclosed stadium) is the World Jaï-Alaï at Miami, Florida, U.S.A., which had a record attendance of 15,052 on 27 Dec. 1975.

Various games are played in a *frontón* the most popular being *main nue, remonte, rebot, pala, grand chistera* and *cesta punta*. Internationally the sport is governed by the Federación Internacional de Pelota Vasca in Madrid, Spain.

Highest speed

An electronically measured ball velocity of 180 m.p.h. *289 km/h* was recorded by José Ramon Areitio at the Palm Beach Jai Alai, Florida, U.S.A. on 2 Feb. 1978.

Longest domination

The longest domination as the world's No. 1 player was enjoyed by Chiquito de Cambo (*né* Joseph Apesteguy) (France), (1881–1955) from the beginning of the century until succeeded in 1938 by Jean Urruty (France) (b. 19 Oct. 1913).

A record 15,000 spectators packed the Miami Jaï-Alaï *frontón* in December 1975.

PIGEON RACING

Earliest references

Pigeon Racing developed from the use of homing pigeons for carrying messages—a quality utilised in the ancient Olympic Games (776 B.C.–A.D. 393). The sport originated in Belgium and the earliest long-distance race was from London to Antwerp in 1819, involving 32 pigeons. The earliest recorded occasion on which 500 miles *804 km* was flown in a day was by *Motor* (owned by G. P. Pointer of Alexander Palace Racing Pigeon Club) which was released from Thurso, Scotland on 30 June 1896 and covered 501 miles *806 km* at an average speed of 1,454 yd *1 329 m* per min (49½ m.p.h. *79,6 km/h*).

Longest flights

The greatest recorded homing flight by a pigeon was made by one owned by the 1st Duke of Wellington (1769–1852). Released from a sailing ship off the Ichabo Islands, West Africa, on 8 April, it dropped dead a mile from its loft at Nine Elms, Wandsworth, Greater London on 1 June 1845, 55 days later, having flown an airline route of 5,400 miles *8 700 km*, but an actual distance of possibly 7,000 miles *11 250 km* to avoid the Sahara Desert. The official British duration record (into Great Britain) is 1,141 miles *1 836 km* in 27 days by A. Bruce's bird in the 1960 Barcelona Race. In the 1975 Palamos Race, *The Conqueror*, owned by Alan Raeside, homed to Irvine, Strathclyde, 1,010 miles *1 625 km*, in 43 hr 56 min.

Highest speeds

In level flight in windless conditions it is very doubtful if any pigeon can exceed 60 m.p.h. *96 km/h*. The highest race speed recorded is one of 3,229 yds *2 952 m* per min (110.07 m.p.h. *177,14 km/h*) in the East Anglian Federation race from East Croydon on 8 May 1965 when the 1,428 birds were backed by a powerful south south-west wind. The winner was owned by A. Vidgeon & Son, Wickford, Essex.

The highest race speed recorded over a distance of more than 1 000 km *621.37 miles* is 2,432.70 yds *2 224,5 m* per min (82.93 m.p.h. *133,46 km/h*) by a hen pigeon in the Central Cumberland Combine race over 683 miles 147 yds *1 099,316 km* from Murray Bridge, South Australia to North Ryde, Sydney on 2 Oct. 1971.

24 hour records

The world's longest reputed distance in 24 hours is 803 miles *1 292 km* (velocity 1,525 yd *1 394 m* per min) by E. S. Petersen's winner of the 1941 San Antonio R.C. event in Texas, U.S.A.

The best 24-hour performance into the United Kingdom is 724 miles 219 yd *1 165,3 km* by E. Cardno's *Mormond Lad*, on 2 July 1977, from Nantes, France to Fraserburgh,

An old print of Persian *Pulu*, the forerunner of the modern game of polo. (*British Library*)

Grampian. Average speed 1,648 yd *1 507 m* per min (56.18 m.p.h. *90,41 km/h*).

Lowest speed
A pigeon *Blue Clip*, belonging to Harold Hart released in Rennes, France arrived home in its loft in Leigh, Greater Manchester, on 29 Sept. 1974, seven years and two months later. It had covered the distance of 370 miles *595 km* at an average speed of 0.00589 m.p.h. *0,00948 km/h* which is slower than the world's fastest snail (see page 48).

Most first prizes
Owned by R. Green, of Walsall Wood, West Midlands, *Champion Breakaway* had won a record 56 first prizes from 1972 to May 1979.

Highest priced bird
The highest recorded price paid for a pigeon is approximately £25,000 by a Japanese Fancier for *De Wittslager* to Georges Desender (Belgium) in Oct. 1978.

POLO

Earliest games
Polo is usually regarded as being of Persian origin having been played as *Pulu c.* 525 B.C. Other claims have come from Tibet and the Tang Dynasty of China A.D. 250. The earliest polo club of modern times was the Kachar Club (founded in 1859) in Assam, India. The game was introduced into England from India in 1869 by the 10th Hussars at Aldershot, Hampshire and the earliest match was one between the 9th Lancers and the 10th Hussars on Hounslow Heath, Greater London, in July 1871. The earliest international match between England and the U.S.A. was in 1886.

The game is played on the largest pitch of any ball game in the world. A ground measures 300 yd *274 m* long by 160 yd *146 m* wide with side boards, or 200 yd *182 m* wide without boards.

Most Olympic medals
Polo has been part of the Olympic programme on five occasions: 1900, 1908, 1920, 1924, and 1936. Of the 21 gold medallists, a 1920 winner, the Rt. Hon. Sir John Wodehouse, Br., C.B.E., M.C., the 3rd Earl of Kimberley (b. 1883 k. 1941) uniquely also won a silver medal (1908).

Most international appearances
The most times any player has represented England is four in the case of Frederick Maitland Freake in 1900, 1902, 1909 and 1913. Thomas Hitchcock, Jr. (1900–44) played five times for the U.S.A. *v.* England (1921, 1924, 1927, 1930, 1939) and twice *v.* Argentina (1928 and 1936).

Highest handicap
The highest handicap based on eight 7½-min "chukkas" is ten goals introduced in the U.S.A. in 1891 and in the United Kingdom and in Argentina in 1910. The latest of the 39 players ever to receive ten-goal handicaps are Alberto Heguy and Alfredo Harriott of Argentina, and in England, Eduardo Moore (Argentina). The last (of six) ten-goal handicap players from Great Britain was Gerald Balding in 1939. A match of two 40-goal teams was staged for the first time ever, at Palermo, Buenos Aires, Argentina, in 1975.

The highest handicap of the United Kingdom's 500 players is eight, held by brothers, Julian and Howard Hipwood. Claire Tomlinson of Gloucestershire has a handicap of three, thought to be the highest ever attained by a woman.

Highest score
The highest aggregate number of goals scored in an international match is 30, when Argentina beat the U.S.A. 21–9 at Meadow Brook, Long Island, New York, U.S.A., in September 1936.

Oldest pony
The oldest known polo pony, still playing regularly, is *Rustum*, a Barb gelding aged 36 yr at Stourhead, Wiltshire, England.

Largest trophy
For details see p. 239.

Largest crowd
World record crowds of more than 50,000 have watched floodlit matches at the Sydney Agricultural Show, Australia. A crowd of 40,000 watched a game played at Jaipur, India, in 1976 using elephants instead of ponies. The length of the polo sticks used has not been ascertained.

POWERBOAT RACING

See also The Guinness Book of Motorboating Facts and Feats *by Kevin Desmond, published by Guinness Superlatives Ltd. (price £7.95).*

Origins
The earliest application of the petrol engine to a boat was by Jean Joseph Etienne Lenoir (1822–1900) on the River Seine, Paris, France, in 1865. The sport was given impetus by the presentation of an international championship cup by Sir Alfred Harmsworth in 1903, which was also the year of the first off-shore race from Calais to Dover.

Harmsworth Cup
Of the 25 contests from 1903 to 1961, the United States has won the most with 16. The greatest number of wins is eight, by Commodore Garfield A. Wood (1881–1971) 1920–21, 1926, 1928–30, 1932–33. The only boat to win three times is *Miss Supertest III*, owned by James G. Thompson (Canada), driven by Jack Regas (Canada), in 1959–61. This boat also achieved the record speed of 119.27 m.p.h. *191,94 km/h* at Picton, Ontario, Canada in 1961. The trophy is now awarded to the British Commonwealth driver with the highest points score in the World Off-shore Championships.

Gold Cup
The Gold Cup (instituted 1903) has been won seven times by Bill Muncey (b. 1929) (U.S.A.) (1956–57, 1961–62, 1972, 1977–78). The record speed is 128.338 m.p.h. *206,539 km/h* for a 2½ mile *4 km* lap by the unlimited hydroplane *Atlas Van Lines*, driven by Bill Muncey in a qualifying round on the Columbia River, Washington, U.S.A., in July 1977, and again in July 1978.

Cowes-Torquay race
The record average for the *Embassy/Daily Express* International Off-shore Race (instituted 1961) is 77.42 m.p.h. *124,59 km/h* by *Kaama* driven by Betty Cook (U.S.A.) (b. 1924) over the 199.1 mile *320,4 km* course from Cowes, Isle of Wight to Torquay, Devon and back in 2 hr 58 min 55 sec on 27 Aug. 1978. The only three time winner has been Thomas Edward Brodie (Tommy) Sopwith (b. 1933) (G.B.) in 1961, 1968, and 1970.

Highest speeds
The fastest off-shore record, as recognised by the Union Internationale Motonautique, is 92.99 m.p.h. *149,65 km/h* by a Class IIID Frode, driven by Mikael Frode (Sweden) on 5 Nov. 1977. The R6 inboard engine record of 128.375 m.p.h. *206,599 km/h* was set by the hydroplane *Vladivar I*, driven by Tony Fahey (G.B.) on Lake Windermere, Cumbria, on 23 May 1977. The Class ON record is 136.38 m.p.h. *219,48 km/h* by J. F. Merten (U.S.A.) 1973.

Longest races
The longest race has been the Port Richborough London to Monte Carlo Marathon Off-Shore International event. The race extended over 2,947 miles *4 742 km* in 14 stages on 10–25 June 1972. It was won by *H.T.S.* (G.B.) driven by Mike Bellamy, Eddie Chater and Jim Brooks in 71 hrs 35 min 56 sec (average 41.15 m.p.h. *66,24 km/h*). The *Daily Telegraph and B.P.* Round Britain race, 26 July–7 Aug. 1969, 1,403 miles *2,257 km* (from Portsmouth in ten stages west and *via* the Caledonian Canal) was won by *Avenger Too* (Timo Makinen, Alan Pascoe Watson and Brian Hendicott) in 39 hr 9 min 37.7 sec. Of 42 starters, 24 finished.

Longest journey
The Dane, Hans Tholstrup (b. 1946), circumnavigated Australia (11,500 miles *18 500 km*) in a 17 ft Caribbean

Larry Mahan, six times world all-round rodeo champion, won his first contest, calf-riding, at the age of six.

Couger fibreglass runabout with a single 80 h.p. Mercury outboard motor from 11 May to 25 July 1971.

Longest jump

The longest jump achieved by a powerboat has been 110 ft *32,5 m* by Jerry Comeaux (b. 1943) in a Glastron GT-150 with a 135 h.p. Evinrude Starflite on an isolated waterway in Louisiana, U.S.A. in mid-October 1972. The take-off speed was 56 m.p.h. *90 km/h*. The jump was required for a sequence in the eighth James Bond film *Live and Let Die*.

Dragsters

The first drag boat to attain 200 m.p.h. *321 km/h* was Sam Kurtovich's *Crisis* which attained 200.44 m.p.h. *322,57 km/h* in California in October 1969 at the end of a one-way run. *Climax* has since been reported to have attained 205.19 m.p.h. *330,22 km/h*.

RACKETS

Origins

There is record of the sale of a racket court at Southernhay, Exeter, Devon dated 12 Jan. 1798. The game which is of 17th century origin was played by debtors in the Fleet Prison, London in the middle of the 18th century, and an inmate, Robert Mackay, claimed the first "world" title in 1820. The first closed court champion was Francis Erwood at Woolwich in 1860. A new court has been constructed at the Sea Court Club, Hayling Island, Hants., England.

Longest reign

Of the 20 world champions since 1820 the longest reign is by British-born U.S. resident Geoffrey W. T. Atkins (b. 1926) who held the title after beating the professional James Dear in 1954 and retired after a fourth successful defence of it in April 1970.

Most Amateur titles

Since the Amateur singles championship was instituted in 1888 the most titles won by an individual is nine by Edgar M. Baerlein (1879–1971) between 1903 and 1923. Since the institution of the Amateur doubles championship in 1890 the most shares in titles has been eleven by David Sumner Milford (b. 7 June 1905), between 1938 and 1959 and John R. Thompson (b. 1918) between 1948 and 1966. Milford has also seven Amateur singles titles (1930–52), an Open title (1936) and held the World title from 1937 to 1946. Thompson has additionally won an Open singles title and five Amateur singles titles.

RODEO

Origins

Rodeo which developed from 18th century *fiestas* came into being in the early days of the North American cattle industry. The earliest reference to the sport is at Santa Fe, New Mexico, U.S.A., on 10 June 1847. Steer wrestling came in with Bill Pickett (1870–1932) of Texas, in 1900.

The largest rodeo in the world is the Calgary Exhibition and Stampede at Calgary, Alberta, Canada. The record attendance has been 1,069,830 on 8–17 July 1977. The record for one day is 141,670 on 13 July 1974. The oldest continuously-held rodeo is that at Payson, Arizona, first held in Aug. 1887.

Most world titles

The record number of all-round titles in the Association of Professional Rodeo Cowboys world championships is six by Larry Mahan (U.S.A.) (b. 21 Nov. 1943) in 1966–70 and 1973. Jim Shoulders (b. 1928) of Henryetta, Okla., has won a record 16 world championships between 1949 and 1959. The record figure for prize money in a single season is $131,233 by Tom Ferguson (b. 20 Dec. 1950) from Miami, Oklahoma, U.S.A. in 1978.

Youngest champion

The youngest winner of a world title is Metha Brorsen, of Oklahoma, who was only 11 yr when she won the International Rodeo Association Cowgirls barrel racing event in 1975.

Time records
Records for timed events, such as calf-roping and steer-wrestling, are meaningless, because of the widely varying conditions due to the size of arenas and amount of start given the stock. The fastest time recorded for roping a calf is 5.7 sec by Bill Reeder at Assiniboia, Saskatchewan, Canada in 1978, and the fastest time for overcoming a steer is 2.4 sec by James Bynum of Waxahachie, Texas, at Marietta, Oklahoma, U.S.A., in 1955.

The standard required time to stay on in bareback, saddle bronc and bull riding events is 8 sec. In the now discontinued ride-to-a-finish events, rodeo riders have been recorded to have survived 90+ min, until the mount had not a buck left in it.

Champion bull
The top bucking bull was probably *Honky Tonk*, an 11 yr old Brahma, who unseated 187 riders in an undefeated eight-year career to his retirement in Sept. 1978.

Champion bronc
Traditionally a bronc called *Midnight* owned by Jim McNab of Alberta, Canada was never ridden in 12 appearances at the Calgary Stampede.

ROLLER SKATING

Origins
The first roller skate was devised by Joseph Merlin of Huy, Belgium, in 1760 and first worn by him in public in London. James L. Plimpton of New York produced the present four-wheeled type and patented it in Jan. 1863. The first indoor rinks were opened in London, in the Strand and at Floral Hall, Covent Garden, in 1857. The great boom periods were 1870–75, 1908–12 and 1948–54, each originating in the United States.

Most titles
Most world speed titles have been won by Alberta Vianello (Italy) with 16 between 1953 and 1965. Most world pair titles have been taken by Dieter Fingerle (W. Germany) with four in 1959, 1967–67. The records for figure titles are five by Karl Heinz Losch in 1958–59, 1961–62 and 1966, and four by Astrid Bader, also of West Germany, in 1965–68. Leslie E. Woodley of Birmingham won 12 British national individual titles over the three regulation distances (880 yds *804 m*, 1 mile *1,6 km* and 5 miles *8 km*) between 1957 and 1964. Jimmy Reed won 11 amateur and one professional title from 1929 to 1937. Chloe Ronaldson (b. 30 Nov. 1939) has won 40 ladies' titles from 1958 to 1979.

Speed skating
The fastest speed put up in an official world record is 25.78 m.p.h. *41,48 km/h* when Giuseppe Cantarella (Italy) recorded 34.9 sec for 440 yds *402 m* on a road at Catania, Sicily on 28 Sept. 1963. The world mile record on a rink is 2 min 25.1 sec by Gianni Ferretti (Italy) at Inzell, W. Germany on 28 Sept. 1968. The greatest distance skated in one hour on a rink by a woman is 35,399 km *21.995 miles* by Marisa Danesi (Italy) at Inzell, W. Germany on 28 Sept. 1968. The men's record on a track is 37,230 km *23.133 miles* by Alberto Civolani (Italy) at Inzell, W. Germany on 28 Sept. 1968, who went on to skate 50 miles *80,46 km* in 2 hr 20 min 33.1 sec.

Roller hockey
Roller hockey (previously known as Rink Hockey in Europe) was first introduced in this country as Rink Polo, at the old Lava rink, Denmark Hill, Greater London in the late 1870s. The Amateur Rink Hockey Association was formed in 1908, and in 1913 became the National Rink Hockey (now Roller Hockey) Association. Britain won the inaugural World Championship in 1936 since when Portugal has won most titles with 11 between 1947 and 1973. The European Championship (inst. 1926) was won by Britain a record 12 consecutive times prior to 1939.

Largest rink
The greatest indoor rink ever to operate was located in the Grand Hall, Olympia, Hammersmith, Greater London. Opened 1890 and closed in 1912 it had an actual skating area of 68,000 ft² *6 300 m²*. The current largest is the Fireside Roll-Arena, Illinois, U.S.A. which has a total skating surface of 29,859 ft² *2 774 m²*.

Endurance
Clinton Shaw (b. Canada, 1942) skated from Victoria, British Columbia to St. John's Newfoundland (4,900 miles *7 900 km* on the Trans-Canadian Highway *via* Montreal) from 1 Apr. to 11 Nov. 1967. On 23 April 1979 at Savannah, Georgia, U.S.A. Jackie Jacobs (21) completed a coast to coast 2,389 miles *3 844 km* skate having started at San Diego, Calif. on 18 Mar. Her longest stint in a day was 110 miles *177 km* on 17 Apr.

Marathon
The longest recorded continuous roller skating marathon was one of 322 hr 20 min performed by Randy Reed of Springfield, Oregon, U.S.A., on 12–26 June 1977.

ROWING

Oldest race
The Sphinx stela of Amenhotep II (1450–1425 B.C.) records that he *stroked* a boat for some three miles. The earliest established sculling race is the Doggett's Coat and Badge, which was first rowed on 1 Aug. 1716 from London Bridge to Chelsea and is still contested annually. Although rowing regattas were held in Venice in 1300 the first English regatta probably took place on the Thames by the Ranelagh Gardens, near Putney in 1775. Boating began at Eton in 1793, 72 years before the "song". The Leander Club was formed *c*. 1818.

Most Olympic medals
Since 1900 there have been 119 Olympic finals of which the U.S.A. have won 26, Germany (now West Germany) 15 and Great Britain 14.

Four oarsmen have won three gold medals: John B. Kelly (U.S.A.) (1889–1960), father of H.S.H. Princess Grace of Monaco, in the sculls (1920) and double sculls (1920 and 1924); his cousin Paul V. Costello (U.S.A.) (b. 27 Dec. 1899) in the double sculls (1920, 1924 and 1928); Jack Beresford, Jr., C.B.E. (G.B.) (1899–1977) in the sculls (1924), coxless fours (1932) and double sculls (1936) and Vyacheslav Ivanov (U.S.S.R.) (b. 30 July 1938) in the sculls (1956, 1960 and 1964). Beresford competed in five games and additionally won two silver medals.

Boat race *Earliest*
The earliest University Boat Race, which Oxford won, was from Hambledon Lock to Henley Bridge on 10 June 1829. Outrigged eights were first used in 1846. In the 125 races to 1979, Cambridge won 68 times, Oxford 56 times and there was a dead heat on 24 Mar. 1877.

Boat race *Record times*
The race record time for the course of 4 miles 374 yd *6,779 km* (Putney to Mortlake) is 16 min 58 sec by Oxford on 20 Mar. 1976. This represents an average speed of 14.89 m.p.h. *23,97 km/h*. The smallest winning margin was Oxford's win by a canvas in 1952. The greatest margin (apart from sinking) was Cambridge's win by 20 lengths in 1900.

The record to the Mile Post is 3 min 31 sec (Oxford 1978) an average speed of 17.06 m.p.h. *27,45 km/h*; Hammersmith Bridge 6 min 24 sec (Oxford 1978); Chiswick Steps 10 min 18 sec (Oxford 1976); and Barnes Bridge 14 min 09 sec (Oxford 1976).

Boat race *Heaviest and lightest oarsmen*
The heaviest man ever to row in a University boat has been Stephen G. H. Plunkett (Queen's) the No. 5 in the 1976 Oxford boat at 16 st. 5 lb. *104 kg*. The 1976 Oxford crew averaged a record 14 st. 0⅜ lb. *89 kg*. The lightest oarsman was the 1882 Oxford Stroke, Alfred Herbert Higgins, at

MEN—Fastest times over 2 000 m course (still water)				
	min sec	Country	Place	Date
Single Sculls	6:49.68	Nikolai Dovgan, U.S.S.R.	Amsterdam, Netherlands	26 Aug. 1978
Double Sculls	6:12.48	Norway	Montreal, Canada	23 July 1976
Coxed Pairs	6:56.94	East Germany	Copenhagen, Denmark	— Aug. 1971
Coxless Pairs	6:33.02	East Germany	Montreal, Canada	23 July 1976
Coxed Fours	6:09.17	East Germany	Amsterdam, Netherlands	30 June 1979
Coxless Fours	5:53.65	East Germany	Montreal, Canada	23 July 1976
Quadruple Sculls	5:47.83	U.S.S.R.	Montreal, Canada	18 July 1976
Eights	5:32.17	East Germany	Montreal, Canada	18 July 1976
WOMEN—Fastest times over 1 000 m course (still water)				
Single Sculls	3:34.31	Christine Scheiblich, East Germany	Amsterdam, Netherlands	21 Aug. 1977
Double Sculls	3:16.83	East Germany	Amsterdam, Netherlands	21 Aug. 1977
Coxless Pairs	3:26.32	East Germany	Amsterdam, Netherlands	21 Aug. 1977
Coxed Fours	3:14.05	U.S.S.R.	Mannheim, West Germany	20 May 1979
Quadruple Sculls	3:08.49	East Germany	Montreal, Canada	19 July 1976
Eights	2:59.00	U.S.S.R.	Mannheim, West Germany	19 May 1979

9 st. 6½ lb. *60 kg*. The lightest cox was Francis Henry Archer (Cambridge) (1843–89) in 1862 at 5 st. 2 lb. *32,6 kg*.

Henley Royal Regatta
The annual regatta at Henley-on-Thames, Oxfordshire, was inaugurated on 26 Mar. 1839. Since then the course, except in 1923, has been about 1 mile 550 yd *2 212 m* varying slightly according to the length of boat. In 1967 the shorter craft were "drawn up" so all bows start level. Prior to 1922 there were two slight angles.

The most wins in the Diamond Challenge Sculls (inst. 1844) is six consecutively by Stuart A. Mackenzie (b. 5 Apr. 1937) (Australia and G.B.) 1957–62. The record time is 7 min 40 sec by Sean Drea (Neptune R.C., Ireland) on 5 July 1975. The Grand Challenge Cup (inst. 1839) for eights, has been won 27 times by Leander R.C. crews between 1840 and 1953. The record time for the event is 6 min 13 sec by Harvard Univ., U.S.A., and a combined Leander/Thames Tradesmen crew, both on 5 July 1975.

Sculling
The record number of wins in the Wingfield Sculls (instituted on the Thames 1830) is seven by Jack Beresford, Jr. from 1920 to 1926. The fastest time (Putney to Mortlake) has been 21 min 11 sec by Leslie Southwood (b. 1906) in 1933. The most world professional sculling titles (instituted 1831) won is seven by William Beach (Australia) between 1884 and 1887.

Highest speed
The highest recorded speed on non-tidal water for 2,000 m *2,187 yd* is by an East German eight in 5 min 32.17 sec (13.46 m.p.h. *21.67 km/h*) at Montreal, Canada on 18 July 1976. A team from Penn A.C., U.S.A., was timed in 5 min 18.8 sec (14.03 m.p.h. *22,58 km/h*) in the F.I.S.A. Championships on the River Meuse, Liege, Belgium, on 17 Aug. 1930.

Cross Channel
The Rev. Sidney Swann (1862–1942) sculled across the Channel in a record 3 hr 50 min on 13 Sept. 1911.
For trans-Atlantic rowing records see p. 214.

Loch Ness
Loch Ness, the longest stretch of inland water in Great Britain (22.7 miles *36,5 km*), was rowed by George G. Parsonage, 31, of Whitehill Secondary School, Glasgow in 2 hr 43 min 34.1 sec on 17 May 1975. A coxed junior eight (average age 15 yr 7 months) from Sir Thomas Rich's School, Gloucester, rowed the distance in 2 hr 35 min 38.2 sec on 25 Aug. 1975.

Longest race
The longest annual rowing race is the Ringvaart Regatta 100 km *62 miles* for eights, at Delft, Netherlands. The record time is 7 hr 3 min 29 sec by the Njord team on 31 May 1979.

Oxford–London
The fastest time registered between Folly Bridge, Oxford through 33 locks and 112 miles *180 km* to Westminster Bridge, London is 14 hr 35 min 46 sec by an eight (no substitutes) of Guy's Hospital on 28 Apr. 1974.

Punting
The earliest reference to punting as a sport was in 1793. Amateur and professional championships were instituted in the 1870s. Victorians argued about the two styles of pole planting and running *versus* pricking. Abel Beasley, the foremost exponent of the latter, won the Professional Championship 14 times (1877–90). In winning the 1896 Amateur title B. Rixon achieved a record average speed of 7.6 m.p.h. *12,2 km/h*. The longest recorded punt is one of 300 miles *482 km* from Kingston upon Thames to Cambridge via Reading, Oxford, Northampton and Ely by Peter Stickland and Chris Hampson from 10 Sept. to 3 Oct. 1973.

SHINTY
Origins
Shinty (from the Gaelic *sinteag*, a leap) was recorded in the West and Central Highlands in 1769 when it was known as *lomain* (driving forward). Games were contested between whole clans or parishes without limit as to numbers or time until darkness stopped play among the walking wounded. The field of play was undelineated except by the occasional pail of *uisge-beatha* "breath of life" (i.e. whisky). In an inter-clan match a combatant who had failed to disable at least one opponent within a reasonable time had his curved stick (*caman*) confiscated as a punishment by the Chieftain so that he could only kick the ball (*cnaige*) or his opponents.

This ungovernable game was first given rules in 1879 and the Camanachd Association was set up by C. I. Macpherson of Balavil near Kingussie, Highland on 10 Oct. 1893.

Most titles
Newtonmore, Highland has won the Camanachd Association Challenge Cup (instituted 1896) a record 21 times (1896–1975). In 1923 the Furnace Club, Argyll won the Cup without conceding a goal throughout the competition.

Highest scores
The highest Cup Final score was in 1909 when Newtonmore beat Furnace 11–3 at Glasgow, Dr. Johnnie Cattanach scoring eight hails or goals. In 1938 John Macmillan Mactaggart scored ten hails for Mid-Argyll in a Camanachd Cup match.

SHOOTING
Earliest club
The Lucerne Shooting Guild (Switzerland) was formed *c.* 1466 and the first recorded shooting match was at Zurich in 1472.

Most Olympic medals
The record number of medals won is 11 by Carl Townsend Osburn (U.S.A.) (b. 5 Nov. 1884) in 1912, 1920 and 1924, consisting of five gold, four silver and two bronze. Six other marksmen have won five gold medals. The only marksman to win three individual gold medals has been Gulbrandsen Skatteboe (Norway) (b. 18 July 1875) in 1906, 1908 and 1912.

Bisley
The National Rifle Association was instituted in 1859. The Queen's (King's) Prize has been shot since 1860 and has only once been won by a woman—Miss Marjorie Elaine Foster,

INDIVIDUAL WORLD RECORDS
(for Olympic Games programme events)
(as ratified by the International Shooting Union (U.I.T.)). * awaiting ratification.

			Possible—Score				
Free Rifle	300 m	3 × 40 shots	1,200—1,160	Lones W. Wigger (U.S.A.)	Seoul, S. Korea	Oct.	1978
Small-bore Rifle	50 m	3 × 40 shots	1,200—1,170*	Sven Johansson (Sweden)	Suhl, East Germany	27 May	1979
Small-bore Rifle	50 m	60 shots prone	600— 599	Eight men			
Free Pistol	50 m	60 shots	600— 577	Moritze Minder (Switzerland)	Seoul, S. Korea	28 Sept.	1978
Rapid Fire Pistol	25 m	60 shots	600— 600	Weissenberger (W. Ger.)	Suhl, East Germany	27 May	1979
				Ian Corneliu (Romania)	Bucharest, Romania		1977
Running (Boar) Target	50 m	60 shots "normal runs"	600— 581	Thomas Pfeffer (E. Ger.)	Seoul, S. Korea	Sept.	1978
Trap	200 birds		200— 199	Angelo Scalzone (Italy)	Munich, W. Germany	29 Aug.	1972
			200— 199	Michel Carrega (France)	Thun, Switzerland	23 Sept.	1974
Skeet	200 birds		200— 200	Yevgeniy Petrov (U.S.S.R.)	Phoenix, Arizona, U.S.A.		1970
			200— 200	Yuri Tzuranov (U.S.S.R.)	Bologna, Italy		1971
			200— 200	Tariel Zhgenti (U.S.S.R.)	Turin, Italy		1973
			200— 200	Kjeld Rasmussen (Denmark)	Vienna, Austria		1975
			200— 200	Wieslaw Gawlikowski (Poland)	Vienna, Austria		1975
Centre-fire Pistol	25 m	60 shots	600— 597	Thomas D. Smith (U.S.A.)	Sao Paulo, Brazil		1963

LARGEST BRITISH BAGS

Hare	1,215	11 guns	Holkham, Norfolk	19 Dec.	1877
Rabbit	6,943	5 guns	Blenheim, Oxfordshire	17 Oct.	1898
Geese (Brent)	704[1]	32 punt-guns	Colonel Russell i/c, River Blackwater, Essex	c.	1860
Grouse	1,070	1 gun	Lord Walsingham in Yorkshire	30 Aug.	1888
Grouse	2,929	8 guns	Littledale and Abbeystead, Lancashire	12 Aug.	1915
Partridge (Wild)	2,015[2]	6 guns	Rothwell, Lincolnshire	3 Oct.	1952
Pheasant	3,937	7 guns[3]	Hall Barn, Beaconsfield, Buckinghamshire	18 Dec.	1913
Pigeon	561	1 gun	K. Ransford, Salop-Powys	22 July	1970
Snipe	1,108	2 guns	Tiree Inner Hebrides	25 Oct.–3 Nov.	1906
Woodcock	228	6 guns	Ashford, County Galway, Ireland	28 Jan.	1910
Woodpigeon	550	1 gun	Major A. J. Coates, near Winchester, Hampshire	10 Jan.	1962

[1] *Plus about 250 later picked up.*
[2] *Plus 104 later picked up.*
[3] *Including H.M. King George V.*

M.B.E. (1894–1974) (score 280) on 19 July 1930. Arthur G. Fulton, M.B.E. (1887–1972) won a record three times (1912, 1926, 1931). Both his father and his son also won the Prize.

The highest score (possible 300) is 293 by Richard P. Rosling (City R.C.) and Alain Marion (Canada) on 28–29 July 1972 and by Keith Martin Pilcher on 20–21 July 1973. The record for the Silver Medal is 150 (possible 150) by Martin John Brister (City Rifle Club) and the Lord Swansea on 24 July 1971. Brister won the tie shoot.

Small Bore

The National Small-Bore Rifle Association, of Britain, was formed in 1901. The British team record (1966 target) is 1988 × 2000 by Lancashire in the Inter-County Association League, 1968–69. The British individual record is by John Palin (b. 16 July 1934) who shot 600 × 600 prone with a .22 rifle in Switzerland in 1972, and by Barry Dagger (b. 19 May 1937) at Bisley, in June 1976. The record score for a round in the British Schools' Small Bore Rifle Association (B.S.S.R.A.) contest is a team possible of 500 × 500 by Gresham's School, Holt, Norfolk in Lent Term, 1972. S. J. Carter scored 500 × 500 in the five rounds in this .22 contest. Richard Hansen shot 5,000 bullseyes in 24 hr at Fresno, Cal., U.S.A. on 13 June 1929.

Air weapons

The individual world record for air rifle (40 shots at 10 m) is 393 by Olegario Vasquez (Mexico) at Mexico City, 1975 and for Air Pistol (40 shots at 10 m) is 394 by Uwe Potteck (b. 1 May 1955) (East Germany) at Graz, Austria in Mar. 1979.

Clay pigeon

Most world titles have been won by S. De Lamniczer (Hungary) in 1929, 1933 and 1939. The only woman to win two world titles has been Gräfin von Soden (West Germany) in 1966–67. The record number of clay birds shot in an hour is 1,904 by Tom Kreckman, 36, at Cresco, Penn., U.S.A., on a Skeet range, 28 Sept. 1975. Jerry Teynor shot 1,735 birds on a Trapshooting range at Bucyrus, Ohio, U.S.A., on 30 July 1977.

Bench rest shooting

The smallest group on record at 1,000 yds *914 m* is 6.125 in

155 mm by Kenneth A. Keefer, Jr., with a 7 mm 300 Remington Action in Williamstown, Pennsylvania, U.S.A., on 22 Sept. 1974.

Highest score in 24 hours

The Central Lancashire Rifle Club team of John Jepson, Graham Sharples, Derek Byron and Joseph Graham, scored 85,752 points (averaging 94.03 per card) on 26–27 Nov. 1976.

Rapid firing

Using a Soper single-loading rifle, Private John Warrick, 1st Berkshire Volunteers, loaded and fired 60 rounds in one minute at Basingstoke, Hants., in April 1870.

Trick shooting

The greatest revolver firing feat was that of Ed McGivern (U.S.A.), who twice fired from 15 ft *4,5 m* five shots which could be covered by a silver half-dollar piece (diameter 1.205 in *3,060 cm*) in 0.45 sec at the Lead Club Range, South Dakota, U.S.A., on 20 Aug. 1932. On 13 Sept. 1932 at Lewiston, Montana, McGivern fired ten shots in 1.2 sec from two guns at the same time double action (no draw) all ten shots hitting two 2¼ × 3½ in *5,7 × 8,9 cm* playing cards at 15 ft *4,57 m*.

In between winning Olympic gold (1968) and silver (1972) medals, Evgeni Petrov set an unbeatable record in skeet shooting. (*Novosti Press Agency*)

The most renowned trick shot of all-time was Phoebe Anne Oakley Mozee (Annie Oakley) (1860–1926). She demonstrated the ability to shoot 100 × 100 in trap shooting for 35 years aged between 27 and 62. At 30 paces she could split a playing card end-on, hit a dime in mid-air or shoot a cigarette from the lips of her husband—one Frank Butler.

Record heads
The world's finest head is the 23-pointer stag in the Maritzburg collection, East Germany. The outside span is 75½ in *191 cm* the length 47½ in *120 cm* and the weight 41½ lb *18 kg 824*. The greatest number of points is probably 33 (plus 29) on the stag shot in 1696 by Frederick III (1657–1713), the Elector of Brandenburg, later King Frederick I of Prussia.

The record head for a British Red Deer is a 47-pointer (length 33½ in *85 cm*) from the Great Warnham Deer Park, West Sussex in 1892. The record for a semi-feral stag is a 20-pointer with an antler length of 45⅜ in *115 cm* from Endsleigh Wood, Devon, found in December 1950 and owned by G. Kenneth Whitehead.

Biggest bag
The largest animal ever shot by any big game hunter was a bull African elephant (*Loxodonta africana africana*) shot by E. M. Nielsen, of Columbus, Nebraska, U.S.A., 25 miles *40 km* north-north-east of Mucusso, Angola, on 7 Nov. 1974. The animal, brought down by a Westley Richards 0.425 stood 13 ft 8 in *4,16 m* at the shoulders (see also p. 25). In November 1965 Simon Fletcher, 28, a Kenyan farmer, claimed to have killed two elephants with one 0.458 bullet.

The greatest recorded lifetime bag is 556,000 birds, including 241,000 pheasants, by the 2nd Marquess of Ripon (1852–1923). He himself dropped dead on a grouse moor after shooting his 52nd bird on the morning of 22 Sept. 1923.

Largest shoulder guns
The largest bore shoulder guns made were 2-bore. Less than a dozen of these were made by two English wildfowl gunmakers c. 1885. Normally the largest guns made are double-barrelled 4-bore weighing up to 26 lb *11 kg* which can be handled only by men of exceptional physique. Larger smooth-bore guns have been made, but these are for use as punt-guns.

SKIING

Origins
The most ancient ski in existence was found well preserved in a peat bog at Höting, Sweden, dating from *c.* 2,500 B.C. A rock carving of a skier at Bessovysledki, U.S.S.R., dates from 6000 B.C. The earliest recorded military use of skiing was in Norway in 1199. Skiing did not develop into a sport until 1843 at Tromsø, Norway. The Trysil Shooting and Skiing Club, founded in Norway in 1861, claims it is the world's oldest. Skiing was not introduced into the Alps until 1883, though there is some evidence of earlier use in the Carniola district. The earliest formal downhill race was staged at Montana, Switzerland in 1911. The first Slalom event was run at Murren, Switzerland, on 21 Jan. 1922. The International Ski Federation (F.I.S.) was founded on 2 Feb. 1924. The Winter Olympics were inaugurated on 25 Jan. 1924. The Ski Club of Great Britain was founded on 6 May 1903. The National Ski Federation of Great Britain was formed in 1964.

Most titles *World Championships*
The world Alpine championships were inaugurated at Mürren, Switzerland, in 1931. The greatest number of titles won is 12 by Christel Cranz (b. 1 July 1914) of Germany, with four Slalom (1934, 1937–39), three Downhill (1935, 1937, 1939) and five Combined (1934–35, 1937–39). She also won the gold medal for the Combined in the 1936 Olympics. The most won by a man is seven by Anton (Toni) Sailer (b. 17 Nov. 1935) (Austria) who won all four in 1956 (Giant Slalom, Slalom, Downhill and the non-Olympic Alpine Combination) and the Downhill, Giant Slalom and Combined in 1958.

In the Nordic events Sixten Jernberg (b. 6 Feb. 1929)

(Sweden) won eight titles, including relays, in 1956–64. Johan Grøttumsbraaten (1899–1942) of Norway won six individual titles in 1926–32. The most by a woman is nine by Galina Koulakova (b. 29 Apr. 1942) (U.S.S.R.) in 1968–78. The record for a jumper is five by Birger Ruud (b. 23 Aug. 1911) of Norway, in 1931–32 and 1935–37.

Most titles *World Cup*
The Alpine World Cup, (inst. 1967), has been won four times by Gustavo Thoeni (Italy) (b. 28 Feb. 1951) in 1971–73 and 1975. The women's cup has been won six times by the 1,67 m *5 ft 6 in* 68 kg *150 lb*. Annemarie Moser *née* Proell (b. 27 Mar. 1953) of Austria in 1971–75 and 1979. In 1973 she completed a record sequence of 11 consecutive downhill wins and in ten seasons, 1970–79, has won a total of 62 individual events. The most individual events won by a man is 42 by Ingemar Stenmark (Sweden) in 1974–79, including a record 14 in one season in 1979. The Nordic World Cup (inst. 1979) was first won by Oddvar Braa (Norway) with the women's title won by Galina Koulakova (U.S.S.R.).

Most titles *British*
The most British skiing overall titles won is four by Stuart Fitzsimmons (b. 28 Dec. 1956) in 1973, 1975–76 and 1979.

The most ladies' titles won is four by Isobel M. Roe (1938–39, 1948–49) and Gina Hathorn (b. 6 July 1949) (1966, 1968–70).

Ski-jumping
The longest ski-jump ever recorded is one of 181 m *593 ft 10 in* by Bogdan Norcic (Yugoslavia) who fell on landing at Planica, Yugoslavia in Feb. 1977. The official record is 176 m *577 ft 5 in* by Toni Innauer (b. 1 Apr. 1958) (Austria) at Oberstdorf, West Germany, on 6 Mar. 1976. The female record is 98 m *321 ft 6 in* jumped by Anita Wold (b. 21 Sept. 1956) (Norway) at Okura, Sapporo, Japan on 14 Jan. 1975. The longest jump achieved in the Olympics is 111 m *364 ft* by Wojciech Fortuna (Poland) at Sapporo on 11 Feb. 1972.

The British record is 61 m *200 ft 1 in* by Guy John Nixon (b. 9 Jan. 1909) at Davos on 24 Feb. 1931. The record at Hampstead, Camden, Greater London, on artificial snow is 28 m *91 ft 10 in* by Reidar Anderson (b. 20 Apr. 1911) of Norway on 24 Mar. 1950.

The most wins in the British Ski-jumping championship (discontinued 1936) was three, by Colin Wyatt (1931, 1934 and 1936).

Highest speed
The highest speed claimed for any skier is 124.412 m.p.h. *200,222 km/h* by Steve McKinney (b. 1953) (U.S.A.) at Portillo, Chile on 1 Oct. 1978. The fastest by a woman is 103.084 m.p.h. *165,898 km/h* by Catherine Breyton (France) at Portillo on 1 Oct. 1978. The average speed in the 1976 Olympic downhill race on the Iglis-Patscherkofel course, Innsbruck, Austria by Franz Klammer (b. 3 Dec. 1953) of Austria was 102,828 km/h *63.894 m.p.h.* on 5 Feb. 1976.

Highest altitude
Yuichiro Miura (Japan) (b. 1933) skied 2,5 km *1.6 miles* down Mt. Everest on 6 May 1970 starting from 26,200 ft *7 985 m*.

Greatest descent
Sylvain Saudan (b. Lausanne, Switzerland, 23 Sept. 1936) skied down the 23,400 ft *7 132 m* Nun peak in the Ladakh Himalayas on 26 June 1977.

The greatest reported aggregate elevation descended in 12 hr is 416,000 ft *126 796 m* by Sarah Ludwig, Scott Ludwig and Timothy B. Gaffney at Mount Brighton, Brighton, Michigan, U.S.A. on 16 Feb. 1974.

Steepest descent
The steepest descents in alpine skiing history have been by Sylvain Saudan. At the start of his descent from Mont Blanc on the north-east side down the Couloir Gervasutti from 4 248 m *13,937 ft* on 17 Oct. 1967 he skied to gradients in excess of 60°.

Since his 1976 Olympic bronze medal Ingemar Stenmark has dominated World Cup slalom skiing. (*All-Sport Photographic*)

Longest run

The longest all-downhill ski run in the world is the Weiss-fluhjoch-Küblis Parsenn course, near Davos, Switzerland, which measures 12,23 km *7.6 miles.* The run from the Aiguille du Midi top of the Chamonix lift (vertical lift 2 492 m *8,176 ft* across the Vallée Blanche is 20,9 km *13 miles.*

Largest race

The world's greatest Nordic ski race is the "Vasa Lopp", which commemorates an event of 1521 when Gustav Vasa (1496–1560), later King Gustavus Eriksson, skied 85,8 km *53.3 miles* from Mora to Sälen, Sweden. The re-enactment of this journey in reverse direction is now an annual event, with a record 11,596 starters on 5 March 1978. The fastest time is 4 hr 5 min 58 sec by Ola Hassis (Sweden) on 4 Mar. 1979.

Longest lift

The longest chair lift in the world is the Alpine Way to Kosciusko Châlet lift above Thredbo, near the Snowy Mountains, New South Wales, Australia. It takes from 45 to 75 min to ascend the 3.5 miles *5,6 km,* according to the weather. The highest is at Chacaltaya, Bolivia, rising to 5 029 m *16,500 ft.* The longest gondola ski lift, at Killington, Vermont, U.S.A., is 3.4 miles *5,48 km* long.

Backflip

The greatest number of skiers to perform a back layout flip while holding hands is 21 at Mont St. Saveur, Quebec, Can. on 12 Mar. 1977.

Marathons

The longest non-stop nordic skiing marathon was one lasting 48 hr by Onni Savi, aged 35, of Padasjoki on 19–21 Apr. 1966. In 24 hr Ahti Nevada (Finland) covered 280,90 km *174.5 miles* at Rovaniemi, Finland on 30 March 1977.

Pat Purcell and John McGlynn (U.S.A.) completed 81 hr 12 min of alpine skiing at Holiday Mountain, Monticello, N.Y., U.S.A. on 1–4 Feb. 1979.

MOST OLYMPIC TITLES

Men Alpine	3	Anton (Toni) Sailer (Austria) (b. 17 Nov. 1935)	Downhill, slalom, giant slalom, 1956
	3	Jean-Claude Killy (France) (b. 30 Aug. 1943)	Downhill, slalom, giant slalom, 1968
Men Nordic	4[1]	Sixten Jernberg (Sweden) (b. 6 Feb. 1929)	50 km, 1956, 30 km, 1960, 50 km and 4 × 10 km, 1964
Women Alpine	2	Andrea Mead-Lawrence (U.S.A.) (b. 19 Apr. 1932)	Slalom, giant slalom, 1952
	2	Marielle Goitschel (France) (b. 28 Sept. 1945)	Giant slalom, 1964; slalom, 1968
	2	Marie-Therese Nadig (Switz.) (b. 8 Mar. 1954)	Downhill, giant slalom, 1972
	2[2]	Rosi Mittermaier (W. Germany) (b. 5 Aug. 1950)	Downhill, slalom, 1976
Women Nordic	4[3]	Galina Koulakova (U.S.S.R.) (b. 29 Apr. 1942)	5 km, 10 km and 3 × 5 km relay, 1972; 4 × 5 km relay, 1976

[1] *Jernberg also won three silver and two bronze medals for a record nine Olympic medals.*
[2] *Also won silver medal in Giant Slalom in 1976.*
[3] *Koulakova also won one silver and two bronze medals in 1968 and 1976.*

Ski-Parachuting

The greatest recorded vertical descent in parachute ski-jumping is 3,300 ft *1006 m* by Rick Sylvester (b. 1943) (U.S.) who on 28 July 1976 skied off the 6,600 ft *2 011 m* summit of Mt. Asgard in Auyuittuq National Park, Baffin Island, Canada, landing on the Turner Glacier, the jump for a sequence in the James Bond film "The Spy Who Loved Me".

Ski-Bob *Origins*

The ski-bob was invented by Mr. Stevens of Hartford, Connecticut, U.S.A., and patented (No. 47334) on 19 Apr. 1892 as a "bicycle with ski-runners". The Fédération Internationale de Skibob was founded on 14 Jan. 1961 in Innsbruck, Austria and the first world championships were held at Bad Hofgastein, Austria in 1967. The Ski-Bob Association of Great Britain was registered on 23 Aug. 1967. The highest speed attained is 166 km/h *103.4 m.p.h.* by Erich Brenter (b. 1940) (Austria) at Cervinia, Italy, in 1964.

Ski-Bob *World Championships*

The only ski-bobbers to retain a world championship are Alois Fischbauer (Austria) who won the men's title in 1973 and 1975, Gerhilde Schiffkorn (Austria) who won the women's title in 1967 and 1969, and Gertrude Geberth (Austria) who won in 1971 and 1973.

Snowmobile

A world record speed of 135.93 m.p.h. *218,75 km/h* was set up by Donald J. Pitzen (U.S.A.) at Union Lake, Michigan, U.S.A., on 27 Feb. 1977.

SNOOKER

Origins

Research shows that snooker was originated by Colonel Sir Neville Francis Fitzgerald Chamberlain, K.C.B., K.C.V.O. (1856–1944) as a hybrid of "black pool", "pyramids" and billiards, in the Ootacamund Club, Nilgiris, Madras, India in the summer of 1875. It did not reach England until 1885, where the modern scoring system was adopted in 1891. Championships were not instituted until 1916. The World Professional Championship was instituted in 1927.

Highest breaks

It is possible in a combination of highly unlikely circumstances to score 155. Alex Higgins (b. 18 Mar. 1949) (N. Ireland) became the first player ever to make a "16 red" clearance with a break of 146 at Leicester Y.M.C.A., Leicester, England in 1976. The official world record break (commonly referred to as a maximum) is 147 set by Joe Davis, O.B.E. (1901–78) against Willie Smith at Leicester Square Hall, City of Westminster, Greater London on 22 Jan. 1955, and by Rex Williams (b. 1934) (G.B.) against Manuel Francisco at Cape Town, South Africa, on 22 Dec. 1965. Over 80 other "perfect" frames have been achieved under less rigorous conditions. The only maximum compiled in a major tournament was by John Spencer at Slough, Berks., on 13 Jan. 1978. The first man to compile a 147 break was E. J. "Murt" O'Donoghue (b. New Zealand, 1901) in Griffiths, N.S.W., Australia on 26 Sept. 1934.

The official world amateur record break is 140 set by Joe Johnson (England) in the T.U.C. Club, Middlesbrough, Cleveland in 1978. David Taylor (b. 9 July 1943) made three consecutive frame clearances of 130, 140 and 139 (total 409) at Minehead, Somerset, on 1 June 1978.

Marathon

The snooker endurance record is 134 hr 59 min by Paul G. Revell B.Sc. and Michael A. C. Craigen at Guys Hospital, London on 16–22 Feb. 1979 during Guy's Hospital charities week.

above: Although over eighty maximums have been recorded, only three-time World champion John Spencer has achieved one in a major snooker tournament. (*Sporting Pictures*)

below: In an eighteen year career in top class squash Heather McKay has never lost a match and only lost a total of six games. (*Syndication International*)

SOFTBALL

Origins

Softball, the indoor derivative of baseball, was invented by George Hancock at the Farragut Boat Club of Chicago, Illinois in 1887. Rules were first codified in Minneapolis, Minnesota in 1895 as Kitten Ball. International rules were set in 1933 when the name Softball was officially adopted and the ISF was formed in 1952 as governing body for both fast pitch and slow pitch.

Most titles

The U.S.A. has won the men's world championship (inst. 1966) three times, 1966, 1968 and 1976 (shared). Japan has twice won the women's title (inst. 1965) in 1970 and 1974.

WORLD CHAMPIONSHIPS RECORDS

Mens

Most runs	12	Lopez (Venezuela)	1966
Most home runs	4	Burrows (Canada)	1976
Most hits	17	McLean (New Zealand)	1976
RBIs	14	Teuscher (U.S.A.)	1966
"	14	Burrows (Canada)	1976
Highest average	.522	Stewart (U.S.A.)	1968
Most wins	6	Walford (New Zealand)	1976
Most innings pitched	59	Stofflet (U.S.A.)	1976
Most strikeouts	98	Stofflet (U.S.A.)	1976
Most perfect games	1	Lynch (U.S.A.); Richard (U.S.A.);	1976
		Ruthowsky (Canada)	1968

WOMEN

Most runs	13	Elliott (U.S.A.)	1974
Most hits	17	Naruse (Japan)	1974
RBIs	11	Naruse (Japan); Usui (Japan);	
		Elliott (U.S.A.)	1974
Highest average	.515	Naruse (Japan)	1974
Most wins	6	Wooley (Australia)	1965
" "	6	Welborn (U.S.A.)	1970
Most innings pitched	50	Welborn (U.S.A.)	1970
Most strikeouts	76	Joyce (U.S.A.)	1974
Most perfect games	2	Joyce (U.S.A.)	1974

Marathon

The longest fast pitch marathon is 55 hr 50 min by the Y.C.W. Softball Assn., Melbourne, Aust. on 16–18 Dec. 1978. The longest for slow pitch is 72 hr 3 sec by two teams of ten players from the U.S. Navy in Singapore on 28–31 Dec. 1977.

SPEEDWAY

Origins

Motorcycle racing on large dirt track surfaces has been traced back to 1902 in the United States. The first organized "short track" races were at the West Maitland (New South Wales, Australia) Agricultural Show in November 1923. The sport evolved in Great Britain with small diameter track racing at Droylsden, Greater Manchester on 25 June 1927 and a cinder track event at High Beech, Essex, on 19 Feb. 1928. The National League was instituted in 1932. The best record is that of the Wembley Lions who won in 1932, 1946–47, 1949–53, making a record total of eight victories. Since the National Trophy knock-out competition was instituted in 1931, Belle Vue (Manchester) have been most successful with nine victories in 1933–37, 1946–47, 1949 and 1958. In 1965 the National League was replaced by the British League which Belle Vue have won three times in succession (1970–72).

Most world titles

The world speedway championship was inaugurated at Wembley, Brent, Greater London in September 1936. The most wins have been five by Ove Fundin (Sweden) (b. 23 May 1933) in 1956, 1960–61, 1963, 1967, and Ivan Gerald Mauger, M.B.E. (b. Christchurch, N.Z., 4 Oct. 1939) in 1968–70, 1972, 1977. Barry Briggs, M.B.E. (b. Christchurch, N.Z., 30 Dec. 1934) made a record 17 consecutive appearances in the finals (1954–70) and won the world title in 1957–58, 1964 and 1966. He also scored a record 201 points in world championship competition. New Zealanders have won the title on 11 occasions.

Highest speed

The fastest recorded speed on a British speedway track is 54.62 m.p.h. *87,90 km/h* on the 470 yd *429 m* 2nd Division track at Crewe by Barry Meeks in 1970. The current fastest track record on a British circuit is an average of 52.57 m.p.h. *84,60 km/h* on the Exeter track by Scott Autrey (U.S.A.) (b. 1953) of the Exeter Falcons on 19 June 1978.

SQUASH RACKETS

Earliest champion

Although rackets (U.S. spelling racquets) with a soft ball was played in 1817 at Harrow School, Harrow, Greater London, there was no recognized champion of any country until John A. Miskey of Philadelphia won the American Amateur Singles Championship in 1906.

Most World Amateur titles

Australians have won the individual title (inst. 1967) five times and the team title four times. Geoffrey B. Hunt (b. Feb. 1947) (Australia) won the individual title three times (1967, 1969 and 1971).

World Open title

The world Open championship (inst. 1976) has been won twice by Geoffrey Hunt (Australia) in 1976 and 1977.

Most titles *Open Championship*

The most wins in the Open Championship (amateurs or professionals), held annually in Britain, is seven by Hashim Khan (Pakistan) (b. 1915) in 1950–55 and 1957. He also twice won the Vintage title in 1977–78.

Most titles *Amateur Championship*

The most wins in the Amateur Championship is six by Abdel Fattah Amr Bey (b. Egypt, 1910) later appointed Ambassador in London, who won in 1931–33 and 1935–37. Norman F. Borrett (b. 1919) of England won in 1946–50.

Most titles *Women*

The most wins in the Women's Squash Rackets Championship is 16 by Heather Pamela McKay, M.B.E. (*née* Blundell) (b. Australia, 31 July 1941) from 1961 to 1976. She also won the first World Open title in 1978. Since 1961 she has not lost a match.

Most titles *Professional Championship*

The most wins in the Professional Championship of Britain is ten by J. H. (Jack) Giles M.B.E. from 1954 to 1963. He relinquished the title in 1964 undefeated.

Longest and shortest championship matches

The longest recorded championship match was one of 2 hr 35 min in the British Amateur Championships at Wembley on 12 Dec. 1976 when Murray Lilley (N.Z.) beat Barry O'Connor (Kent) 9–3, 10–8, 2–9, 7–9, 10–8. The second game lasted 58 min and there were 98 lets in the match. Sue Cogswell beat Teresa Lawes (Kent) in only 16 min in a British Women's title match at Dallington, Northants., on 12 Dec. 1977.

Most international appearances

The record for international selection is 61 by Robert Anthony Dolman (b. 15 Oct. 1945) for Wales from 1960–1978. The record for England is 51 by Philip N. Ayton from 1968 to 1976; A. Kim Bruce-Lockhart (Scotland) gained 59 between 1968 and 1978, and Robert J. S. Weir totalled 53 for Ireland between 1969 and 1977. The most appearances by a woman representing one of the Home Countries is 51 by Brenda Carmichael of Scotland from 1958 to 1978.

Longest span of internationals

Sheila Macintosh (*née* Speight), the 1960 British Champion, played for England v. Wales in April 1949 and in December 1971—a span of 22 years. Among men Paul Harding-Edgar first played for Scotland in 1938 and last played 21 years later in 1959.

Marathons

The longest squash marathon has been 120 hr 51 min by Peter Fairlie at the Bridge of Allan Sports Club, Stirling, Scotland on 30 June–5 July 1979. George Deponselle and William de Bruin played for 106 hr 43 min at Sutterheim Country Club, Cape Province, South Africa on 1–5 Oct. 1978. (*This category will now be confined to two players only.*)

SURFING

Origins

The traditional Polynesian sport of surfing in a canoe (*ehorooe*) was first recorded by Captain James Cook, R.N., F.R.S. (1728–79) on his first voyage at Tahiti in December 1771. Surfing on a board (*Amo Amo iluna ka lau oka nalu*) was first described "most perilous and extraordinary . . . altogether astonishing and is scarcely to be credited" by Lt. (later Capt.) James King, R.N., F.R.S. in March 1779 at Kealakekua Bay, Hawaii Island. A surfer was first depicted by this voyage's official artist John Webber. The sport was revived at Waikiki by 1900. Hollow boards were introduced in 1929 and the light plastic foam type in 1956.

Most titles

World Championships were inaugurated in May 1964 at Sydney, Australia. The only surfer to win two titles has been Joyce Hoffman (U.S.) in 1965 and 1966.

Highest waves ridden

Makaha Beach, Hawaii provides the reputedly highest consistently high waves often reaching the rideable limit of

30–35 ft *9–10 m.* The highest wave ever ridden was the *tsunami* of "perhaps 50 ft *15,24 m*", which struck Minole, Hawaii on 3 Apr. 1868, and was ridden to save his life by a Hawaiian named Holua.

Longest ride *Sea wave*
About four to six times each year rideable surfing waves break in Matanchen Bay near San Blas, Nayarit, Mexico which makes rides of *c.* 5,700 ft *1 700 m* possible.

Longest ride *River bore*
The longest recorded rides on a river bore have been set on the Severn bore, England. In 1968 local residents reported a ride of four to six miles *6–9 km* by Rodney Sumpter of Sussex. In September 1971 Mick Evans of Towyn Surfing Club, Gwynedd succeeded in making a run from Rea to Maisemore Weir a distance of four miles *6,4 km.*

SWIMMING

Earliest references
In Japan, swimming in schools was ordered by Imperial edict of Emperor Go-Yoozei in 1603 but competition was known from 36 B.C. Sea water bathing was fashionable at Scarborough, North Yorkshire as early as 1660. In Great Britain competitive swimming originated in London *c.* 1837, at which time there were five or more pools, the earliest of which had been opened at St. George's Pier Head, Liverpool in 1828.

Largest pools
The largest swimming pool in the world is the sea-water Orthlieb Pool in Casablanca, Morocco. It is 480 m *1,547 ft* long and 75 m *246 ft* wide, and has an area of 3.6 ha *8.9 acres.* The largest land-locked swimming pool with heated water was the Fleishhacker Pool on Sloat Boulevard, near Great Highway, San Francisco, California, U.S.A. It measured 1,000 × 150 ft *304,8 × 45,7 m* and up to 14 ft *4,26 m* deep and contained 7,500,000 U.S. gallons *28 390 hectolitres* of heated water. It was opened on 2 May 1925 but has now been abandoned to a few ducks. The world's largest competition pool is that at Osaka, Japan, which accommodates 13,614 spectators. The largest in use in the United Kingdom is the Royal Commonwealth Pool, Edinburgh, completed in 1970 with 2,000 permanent seats but the unused pool at Earls Court, London (opened 1937) is 200 ft *60,96 m* by 100 ft *30,48 m* and has seating for over 12,000 spectators.

Fastest swimmer
Excluding relay stages with their anticipatory starts, the highest speed reached by a swimmer is 5.19 m.p.h. *8,35 km/h* by Joe Bottom (b. 18 Apr. 1955) (U.S.A.), who recorded 19.70 sec for 50 yd *45,72 m* in a 25 yd *22,86 m* pool at Cleveland, Ohio, on 24 Mar. 1977. The fastest by a woman is 4.42 m.p.h. *7,11 km/h* by Sue Hinderaker (U.S.A.) who clocked 23.14 for 50 yd at Pittsburgh, Pa., on 16 Mar. 1979.

Most world records
Men 32, Arne Borg (Sweden) (b. 18 Aug. 1901), 1921–29. Women, 42, Ragnhild Hveger (Denmark) (b. 10 Dec. 1920), 1936–1942.

Most world titles
In the world championships (inst. 1973) the most medals won is ten by Kornelia Ender (now Matthes) (E. Germany) eight gold and two silver in 1973 and 1975. The most by a man is seven by James Montgomery (U.S.A.) (b. 24 Jan. 1955), six gold and a bronze in 1973 and 1975. The most medals in a single championships is six by Tracy Caulkins (U.S.A.) (b. 11 Jan. 1963) in 1975 with five golds and a silver.

OLYMPIC RECORDS
Most gold medals *Men*
The greatest number of Olympic gold medals won is nine by Mark Andrew Spitz (U.S.A.) (b. 10 Feb. 1950):—

100 m and 200 m freestyle	1972
100 m and 200 m butterfly	1972
4 × 100 m freestyle	1968 and 1972
4 × 200 m freestyle	1968 and 1972
4 × 100 m medley	1972

All but one of these performances (the 4 × 200 m freestyle of 1968) were also new world records.

Most gold medals *Women*
The record number of gold medals won by a woman is four shared by Patricia McCormick (*née* Keller) (U.S.A.) (b. 12 May 1930) with the high and springboard diving double in 1952 and 1956 (also the female record for individual golds), Dawn Fraser, O.B.E. (later Mrs. Gary Ware) (b. Sydney, Australia, 4 Sept. 1937) with the 100 m freestyle (1956, 1960 and 1964) and the 4 × 100 m freestyle (1956) and Kornelia Ender (b. Plauen, E. Germany, 25 Oct. 1958) with the 100 and 200 m freestyle, 100 m butterfly and 4 × 100 m medley in 1976. Dawn Fraser is the only swimmer to win the same event on three successive occasions.

Most gold medals *British*
The record number of gold medals won by a British swimmer (excluding Water Polo *q.v.*) is four by Henry Taylor (1885–1951) in the mile freestyle (1906), 400 m freestyle (1908), 1,500 m freestyle (1908) and 4 × 200 m freestyle (1908). None of the seven British women who have won a gold medal won a second title.

Most medals *Men*
The most medals won is 11 by Mark Spitz who in addition to his nine golds (see above), won a silver (100 m butterfly) and a bronze (100 m freestyle) both in 1968.

Most medals *Women*
The most medals won by a woman is eight by Dawn Fraser, who in addition to her four golds (see above) won four silvers (400 m freestyle 1956, 4 × 100 m freestyle 1960 and 1964, 4 × 100 m medley 1960), Kornelia Ender (see above) who in addition to her four golds won four silvers (200 m individual medley 1972, 4 × 100 m medley 1972, 4 × 100 m freestyle 1972 and 1976) and Shirley Babashoff (U.S.A.) (b. 3 Jan. 1957), who won two golds (4 × 100 m freestyle 1972 and 1976) and six silvers (100 m freestyle 1972, 200 m freestyle 1972 and 1976, 400 m and 800 m freestyle 1976, 4 × 100 m medley 1976).

Most medals *British*
The British record is eight by Henry Taylor who in addition to his four golds (see above) won a silver (400 m freestyle 1906) and three bronzes (4 × 200 m freestyle 1906, 1912, 1920). The most medals by a British woman is four by M. Joyce Cooper (later Mrs. John Badcock) (b. 18 Apr. 1909) with one silver (4 × 100 m freestyle 1928) and three bronze (100 m freestyle 1928, 100 m backstroke 1928, 4 × 100 m freestyle 1932).

Most individual gold medals
The record number of individual gold medals won is four by Charles M. Daniels (U.S.A.) (1884–1973) (100 m freestyle 1906 and 1908, 220 yd freestyle 1904, 440 yd freestyle 1904); Roland Matthes (E. Germany) (b. 17 Nov. 1950) with 100 m and 200 m backstroke 1968 and 1972; Mark Spitz and Pat McCormick (see above). The most individual golds by a British swimmer is three by Henry Taylor (see above).

Closest verdict
The closest recorded win in the Olympic Games was in the Munich 400 m individual medley final of 30 Aug. 1972 when Gunnar Larsson (Sweden) (b. 12 May 1951) got the verdict over Tim McKee (U.S.A.) (b. 14 Mar. 1953) by 2/1,000th of a second in 4 min 31.981 sec to 4 min 31.983 sec—a margin of 3 mm or the length grown by a finger nail in three weeks.

DIVING
Most Olympic medals *World*
The most medals won by a diver are five (three gold, two silver) by Klaus Dibiasi (b. Austria, 6 Oct. 1947) (Italy) in four Games from 1964 to 1976. He is also the only diver to win the same event (highboard) at three successive Games

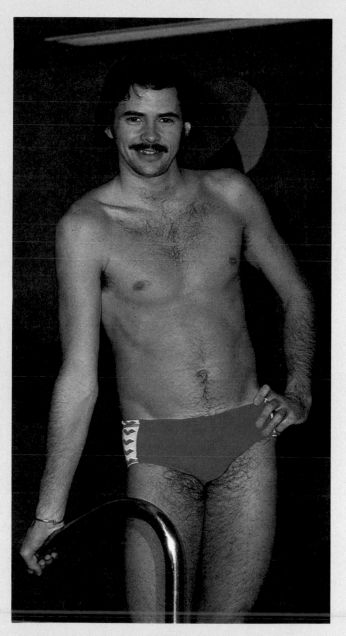

Above: World champion and record holder in the 200 metres breaststroke, Lina Kachushite of the U.S.S.R. (*Tony Duffy, All-Sport Photographic*)

Right: David Wilkie achieved all his goals in breaststroke swimming with an Olympic gold medal, three world championships and a world record. (*Syndication International*)

Below left: World 100 metres butterfly stroke record holder, Joe Bottom, is also the fastest freestyle swimmer. (*All-Sport Photographic*)

Below right: America's Tracy Caulkins achieved her world records in winning three gold medals at the 1978 World Swimming Championships. (*All-Sport Photographic*)

(1968, 1972 and 1976). Pat McCormick (see p. 320) won four gold medals.

Most Olympic medals *British*
The highest placing by a Briton has been the silver medal by Eileen Armstrong (b. 1896) in the 1920 highboard event. The best placings by male divers are the bronze medals by Harold Clarke (b. 1888) (plain high diving, 1924) and Brian Phelps (b. 21 Apr. 1944) (highboard, 1960).

Most world titles
Phil Boggs (U.S.A.) (b. 29 Dec. 1949) has won three gold medals, in 1973, 1975 and 1978 but Klaus Dibiasi (Italy) won four medals (two gold, two silver) in 1973 and 1975.

321

Irina Kalinina (U.S.S.R.) (b. 8 Feb. 1959) has won five medals (three gold, one silver, one bronze) in 1973, 1975 and 1978.

Perfect dive

In the 1972 U.S. Olympic Trials, in Chicago, Illinois, Michael Finneran (b. 21 Sept. 1948) was awarded a score of 10 by all seven judges for a backward 1½ somersault, 2½ twist, free, dive from the 10 m board, an achievement without precedent. (See also p. 223).

CHANNEL SWIMMING

Earliest *Men*

The first man to swim across the English Channel (without a life jacket) was the Merchant Navy captain Matthew Webb (1848–83) who swam breaststroke from Dover, England to Calais Sands, France, in 21 hr 45 min from 12.56 p.m. to 10.41 a.m., 24–25 Aug. 1875. He swam an estimated 38 miles *61 km* to make the 21-mile *33 km* crossing. Paul Boyton (U.S.A.) had swum from Cap Gris-Nez to the South Foreland in his patent life-saving suit in 23 hr 30 min on 28–29 May 1875. There is good evidence that Jean-Marie Saletti, a French soldier, escaped from a British prison hulk off Dover by swimming to Boulogne in July or August 1815. The first crossing from France to England was made by Enrico Tiraboschi, a wealthy Italian living in Argentina, who crossed in 16 hr 33 min on 12 Aug. 1923, to win the *Daily Sketch* prize of £1,000.

Earliest *Women*

The first woman to succeed was Gertrude Caroline Ederle (b. 23 Oct. 1906) (U.S.A.) who swam from Cap Gris-Nez, France to Deal, England on 6 Aug. 1926, in the then overall record time of 14 hr 39 min. The first woman to swim from England to France was Florence Chadwick (b. 1918) of California, U.S.A., in 16 hr 19 min on 11 Sept. 1951. The first Englishwoman to succeed was Ivy Gill on 14 Oct. 1927.

Fastest

The official Channel Swimming Association (founded 1927) record is 7 hr 40 min by Penny Dean (b. 21 Mar. 1955) of California, U.S.A., from Shakespeare Beach, Dover to Cap Gris-Nez, France, on 29 July 1978.

Slowest

The slowest crossing was the third ever made, when Henry Sullivan (U.S.A.) swam from England to France in 26 hr 50 min on 5–6 Aug. 1923. It is estimated that he swam some 56 miles *90 km*.

Earliest and latest

The earliest date in the year on which the Channel has been swum is 6 June by Dorothy Perkins (England) (b. 1942) in 1961, and the latest is 14 October by Ivy Gill. Both swims were from France to England.

Youngest and Oldest

The youngest conqueror is Markus Hooper (b. 14 June 1967) of Elton, Kent who swam from Dover to Sangatte, France in 14 hr 37 min on 5/6 Aug. 1979, when he was aged 12 yr 53 days. The oldest has been William E. (Ned) Barnie, aged 55, when he swam from France to England in 15 hr 1 min on 16 Aug. 1951. The youngest woman was Abla Adel Khairi (b. Egypt, 26 Sept. 1960), aged 13 yr 326 days when she swam from England to France in 12 hr 30 min on 17 Aug. 1974, and the oldest was Stella Ada Rosina Taylor (b. Bristol, Avon, 20 Dec. 1929) aged 45 yr 350 days when she did the swim in 18 hr 15 min on 26 Aug. 1975.

Double crossing *First*

Antonio Abertondo (b. Buenos Aires, Argentina, 1919), swam from England to France in 18 hr 50 min (8.35 a.m. on 20 Sept. to 3.25 a.m. on 21 Sept. 1961) and after about 4 min rest returned to England in 24 hr 16 min, landing at St. Margaret's Bay at 3.45 a.m. on 22 Sept. 1961, to complete the first "double crossing" in 43 hr 10 min. Kevin Murphy (b. Bushey Heath, Herts, 1949) completed the first double crossing by a Briton in 35 hr 10 min on 6 Aug. 1970. The first swimmer to achieve a crossing both ways was Edward Harry Temme (1904–78) on 5 Aug. 1927 and 19 Aug. 1934.

Double crossing *Fastest*

The fastest double crossing was one of 19 hr 12 min by Cynthia Nicholas (b. 20 Aug. 1957) of Scarborough, Ont., Canada, on 4–5 Aug. 1979. The fastest by a relay team is 16 hr 5½ min (including a 2 min rest) by six Saudi Arabian men on 11 Aug. 1977.

Most conquests

The greatest number of Channel conquests is 14 by Desmond Renford, M.B.E. (b. 1927) (Australia) from 9 Aug. 1970 to 4 Aug. 1979. Cindy Nicholas made her first crossing on 29 July 1975 and her eighth on 5 Aug. 1979.

Underwater

The first underwater cross-Channel swim was achieved by Fred Baldasare (b. 1924) (U.S.A.), who completed a 42 mile *67,5 km* distance from France to England with Scuba equipment in 18 hr 1 min on 10–11 July 1962.

LONG DISTANCE SWIMMING

Longest ocean swim

The longest recorded ocean swim is one of 128.8 miles *207,3*

WORLD RECORDS
recognised by the *Fédération Internationale de Natation Amateur* (as at 24 Aug. 1979)

MEN

Event	Time Min. sec.	Name and Country	Place	Date
FREESTYLE				
100 metres	49.44	Jonty Skinner (S.A.)	Philadelphia, U.S.A.	14 Aug. 1976
200 metres	1:49.83†	Serge Kopliakov (U.S.S.R.)	Potsdam, East Germany	7 Apr. 1979
400 metres	3:51.41	Vladimir Salnikov (U.S.S.R.)	Potsdam, East Germany	6 Apr. 1979
800 metres	7:56.49	Vladimir Salnikov (U.S.S.R.)	Minsk, U.S.S.R.	23 Mar. 1979
1,500 metres	15:02.40	Brian Stuart Goodell (U.S.A.)	Montreal, Canada	20 July 1976
4 × 100 metres	3:19.74	United States (Jack Babashoff, Ambrose Gaines, James Montgomery, David McCagg)	Berlin, West Germany	22 Aug. 1978
4 × 200 metres	7:20.82	United States (Bruce Furniss, William Forrester, Bobby Hackett, Ambrose Gaines)	Berlin, West Germany	24 Aug 1978
† First leg of relay				
BREASTSTROKE				
100 metres	1:02.86	Gerald Moerken (West Germany)	Jonkoping, Sweden	17 Aug. 1977
200 metres	2:15.11	David Andrew Wilkie M.B.E. (G.B.)	Montreal, Canada	24 July 1976
BUTTERFLY				
100 metres	54.18	Joseph Bottom (U.S.A.)	East Berlin, East Germany	27 Aug. 1977
200 metres	1:59.23	Michael Bruner (U.S.A.)	Montreal, Canada	18 July 1976
BACKSTROKE				
100 metres	55.49	John Naber (U.S.A.)	Montreal, Canada	19 July 1976
200 metres	1:59.19	John Naber (U.S.A.)	Montreal, Canada	24 July 1976

km by Walter Poenisch Snr. (U.S.A.) (b. 1914) from Havana, Cuba, to Little Duck Key, Florida, U.S.A. (in a shark cage and wearing flippers) in 34 hr 15 min on 11–13 July 1978.

In 1966 Mihir Sen of Calcutta, India uniquely swam the Palk Strait from Sri Lanka to India (in 25 hr 36 min on 5–6 April); the Straits of Gibraltar (in 8 hr 1 min on 24 August); the length of the Dardanelles (in 13 hr 55 min on 12 September) and the length of the Panama Canal (in 34 hr 15 min on 29–31 October). He swam the English Channel in 14 hr 45 min on 27 Sept. 1958.

Irish Channel
The swimming of the 23 mile *37 km* wide North Channel from Donaghadee, Northern Ireland to Portpatrick, Scotland was first accomplished by Tom Blower of Nottingham in 15 hr 26 min in 1947. A record time of 11 hr 21 min was set by Kevin Murphy on 11 Sept. 1970. The first Irish-born swimmer to achieve the crossing was Ted Keenan on 11 Aug. 1973 in 52–56 °F *11–13 °C* water in 18 hr 27 min.

Bristol Channel
The first person to achieve a crossing of the Bristol Channel was Kathleen Thomas (now Mrs. F. Day) (b. Apr. 1906) who swam from Penarth, South Glamorgan to Weston-super-Mare, Avon in 7 hr 20 min on 5 Sept. 1927. The record for the longer swim from Glenthorne Cove, Devon to Porthcawl, Mid-Glamorgan is 10 hr 46 min by Jane Luscombe (b. 13 Jan. 1961) of Jersey, C.I., on 19 Aug. 1976.

Solent
The fastest time for swimming the Solent (Ryde, Isle of Wight to Southsea) has been 1 hr 6 min 27 sec by Ron Evans (b. 3 June 1958) (Wimbledon) in 1977. The greatest number of official crossings has been 36, including two double crossings, by Brian M. Rann (b. 23 May 1934) from 1954 to 1978.

Lake swims
The fastest time for swimming the length of Great Britain's longest lake, the 22.7 mile *36,5 km* long Loch Ness, is 10 hr 30 min by Kevin Murphy on 14 July 1976. The first successful swim was by Brenda Sherratt (b. 1948) of West Bollington, Cheshire on 26–27 July 1966. The fastest time for the Lake Windemere International Championship, 16.5 miles *26,5 km*, is 6 hr 10 min 33 sec. by Mary Beth Colpo (U.S.A.) (b. 1961) on 5 Aug. 1978.

Island circumnatation
The fastest swim round the Isle of Wight (55 miles *88 km*) is 24 hr 36 min 25 sec by Michael P. Read (Norwich) in Aug.

1976. David Angus Minty (b. 1963) swam round the Island of Jersey, Channel Islands (40 miles *64 km*) in 10 hr 54½ min on 17 Aug. 1977.

Palk Strait
The first person to achieve a double crossing of the Palk Strait, 40 miles *64 km*, between India and Sri Lanka, was V. S. C. Anandan (Sri Lanka) on 18–20 Apr. 1975.

Longest swims
The greatest recorded distance ever swum is 1,826 miles *2 938 km* down the Mississippi, U.S.A. between Ford Dam near Minneapolis and Carrollton Ave, New Orleans, Louisiana, by Fred P. Newton, (b. 1903) of Clinton, Oklahoma from 6 July to 29 Dec. 1930. He was 742 hours in the water.

The greatest distance covered in a continuous swim is 292 miles *469,9 km* by Joe Maciag (b. 26 Mar. 1956) from Billings to Glendive, Montana in the Yellowstone River in 64 hr 50 min on 1–4 July 1976.

Longest duration
The longest duration swim ever achieved was one of 168 continuous hours, ending on 24 Feb. 1941, by the legless Charles Zibbelman, *alias* Zimmy (b. 1894) of the U.S.A., in a pool in Honolulu, Hawaii, U.S.A. The longest duration swim by a woman was 87 hours 27 min in a salt water pool by Myrtle Huddleston (U.S.A.) at Raven Hall, Coney Island, N.Y., U.S.A., in 1931. Margaret "Peggy" Byrne (U.S.A.) (b. 17 Dec. 1949), a Minnesota State Representative, swam for 60 hr 15 min in a freshwater pool at Saint Paul, Minn., on 18–20 Dec. 1978.

Relays
The longest recorded mileage in a 24 hr swim relay is 85 miles 837.5 yds *137,56 km* by a team of five from Hamline University at St. Paul, Minn, U.S.A. on 21–22 Jan. 1978. The fastest time recorded for 100 miles *160 km* by a team of 20 swimmers is 22 hr 38 min at the Atlantis Swim Centre, Plympton Park, S.A. Aust. on 14–15 Oct. 1978.

Sponsored swimming
The greatest amount of money collected in a charity swim was £26,641.28 by the Lions Club of Jersey, C.I. on 23–25 Feb. 1979, using 1,746 swimmers.

Treading water marathon
The duration record for treading water (vertical posture without touching the lane markers in an 8 ft *2,43 m* square) is 64 hr by Norman Albert at Pennsylvania State University, U.S.A. on 1–4 Nov. 1978.

Event	Time Min. sec.	Name and Country	Place	Date
MEDLEY				
200 metres	2:03.29	Jesse Vassallo (U.S.A.)	San Juan, Puerto Rico	6 July 1979
400 metres	4:20.05	Jesse Vassallo (U.S.A.)	Berlin, West Germany	22 Aug. 1978
4 × 100 metres	3:42.22	United States (John Naber, John Hencken, Matthew Vogel, James Montgomery)	Montreal, Canada	22 July 1976
WOMEN				
FREESTYLE				
100 metres	55.41	Barbara Krause (East Germany)	East Berlin, East Germany	5 July 1978
200 metres	1:58.43	Cynthia Woodhead (U.S.A.)	San Juan, Puerto Rico	4 July 1979
400 metres	4:06.28	Tracey Wickham, M.B.E. (Australia)	Berlin, West Germany	24 Aug. 1978
800 metres	8:24.62	Tracey Wickham, M.B.E. (Australia)	Edmonton, Canada	6 Aug. 1978
1,500 metres	16:06.63	Tracey Wickham, M.B.E. (Australia)	Perth, Australia	25 Feb. 1979
4 × 100 metres	3:43.43	United States (Tracy Caulkins, Stephanie Elkins, Jill Sterkel, Cynthia Woodhead)	Berlin, West Germany	26 Aug. 1979
BREASTSTROKE				
100 metres	1:10.31	Julia Bogdanova (U.S.S.R.)	Berlin, West Germany	22 Aug. 1978
200 metres	2:28.36	Lina Kachushite (U.S.S.R.)	Potsdam, East Germany	6 Apr. 1979
BUTTERFLY				
100 metres	59.46	Andrea Pollack (East Germany)	East Berlin, East Germany	3 July 1978
200 metres	2:07.01	Mary Meagher (U.S.A.)	Fort Lauderdale, U.S.A.	17 Aug. 1979
BACKSTROKE				
100 metres	1:01.51	Ulrike Richter (East Germany)	East Berlin, East Germany	5 June 1976
200 metres	2:11.93	Linda Jezek (U.S.A.)	Berlin, West Germany	24 Aug. 1978

Event	Time Min sec	Name and Country	Place	Date
MEDLEY				
200 metres	2:14.07	Tracy Caulkins (U.S.A.)	Berlin, West Germany	20 Aug. 1978
400 metres	4:40.83	Tracy Caulkins (U.S.A.)	Berlin, West Germany	23 Aug. 1978
4 × 100 metres	4:07.95	East Germany (Ulrike Richter, Hannelore Anke, Andrea Pollack, Kornelia Ender)	Montreal, Canada	18 July 1976

World records can only be set in 50 m pools. FINA has not recognised records for Imperial distances since 30 Apr. 1969.

BRITISH NATIONAL (long course) RECORDS
as ratified by the Amateur Swimming Federation of Great Britain as at 24 Aug. 1979

MEN

Event	Time Min sec	Name	Place	Date
FREESTYLE				
100 metres	52.26†	Martin Smith	Berlin, West Germany	22 Aug. 1978
200 metres	1:52.47	Gordon Downie	Montreal, Canada	19 July 1976
400 metres	3:56.47	Andrew Astbury	Fort Lauderdale, U.S.A.	17 Aug. 1979
800 metres	8:16.50	Simon Gray	Berlin, West Germany	24 Aug. 1978
1,500 metres	15:31.42	Simon Gray	Berlin, West Germany	24 Aug. 1978
4 × 100 metres	3:28.76	National team (Martin Smith, Mark Taylor, Ricky Burrell, David Dunne)	Berlin, West Germany	22 Aug. 1978
4 × 200 metres	7:32.11	National team: (Alan McClatchley, David Dunne, Gordon Downie, Brian Brinkley)	Montreal, Canada	21 July 1976

† First leg of relay

Event	Time Min sec	Name	Place	Date
BREASTSTROKE				
100 metres	1:03.43	David Andrew Wilkie, M.B.E.	Montreal, Canada	20 July 1976
200 metres	2:15.11	David Andrew Wilkie, M.B.E.	Montreal, Canada	24 July 1976
BUTTERFLY				
100 metres	55.52	Philip Hubble	Coventry, W. Midlands	21 Apr. 1979
200 metres	2:01.28	Philip Hubble	Coventry, W. Midlands	22 Apr. 1979
BACKSTROKE				
100 metres	58.34	Gary Abraham	Crystal Palace, London	11 Aug. 1979
200 metres	2:06.87	James Carter	Long Beach, U.S.A.	1 Apr. 1976
INDIVIDUAL MEDLEY				
200 metres	2:06.25	David Andrew Wilkie, M.B.E.	Long Beach, U.S.A.	4 Apr. 1976
400 metres	4:27.70	Simon Gray	Edmonton, Canada	5 Aug. 1978
4 × 100 metres	3:49.06	National team: (Gary Abraham, Duncan Goodhew, John Mills, Martin Smith)	Berlin, West Germany	28 Aug. 1978

WOMEN

Event	Time Min sec	Name	Place	Date
FREESTYLE				
100 metres	57.5	Cheryl Brazendale	Blackpool, Lancashire	23 Aug. 1977
200 metres	2:04.11	Sharron Davies	Edmonton, Canada	7 Aug. 1978
400 metres	4:18.59	Sharron Davies	Coventry, W. Midlands	25 July 1979
800 metres	8:51.40	Jackie Willmott	Utrecht, Netherlands	12 Aug. 1979
1,500 metres	17:14.26	Maxine Charles	Edinburgh, Scotland	22 June 1979
4 × 100 metres	3:53.27	England team: (Kaye Lovatt, Heidi Turk, Cheryl Brazendale, Sharron Davies)	Edmonton, Canada	5 Aug. 1978
BREASTSTROKE				
100 metres	1:11.73	Margaret Mary Kelly, M.B.E.	Berlin, West Germany	22 Aug. 1978
200 metres	2:35.64	Debbie Rudd	Berlin, West Germany	24 Aug. 1978
BUTTERFLY				
100 metres	1:02.74	Ann Osgerby	Berlin, West Germany	23 Aug. 1978
200 metres	2:15.45	Susan Jenner	Jonkoping, Sweden	18 Aug. 1977
BACKSTROKE				
100 metres	1:05.70	Helen Jameson	Crystal Palace, London	15 Apr. 1979
200 metres	2:19.29	Jane Admans	Crystal Palace, London	16 Apr. 1979
INDIVIDUAL MEDLEY				
200 metres	2:17.55	Sharron Davies	Amersfoort, Netherlands	2 Feb. 1979
400 metres	4:47.67	Sharron Davies	Amersfoort, Netherlands	3 Feb. 1979
4 × 100 metres	4:19.83	National team: (Helen Jameson, Margaret Kelly, Ann Osgerby, Sharron Davies)	Coventry, W. Midlands	22 Apr. 1979

TABLE TENNIS

Origins
The earliest evidence relating to a game resembling table tennis has been found in the catalogues of London sports goods manufacturers in the 1880s. The old Ping Pong Association was formed in 1902 but the game proved only a temporary craze until resuscitated in 1921. The English Table Tennis Association was formed on 24 Apr. 1927.

Most English titles
The highest total of English men's titles (instituted 1921) is 20 by G. Viktor Barna (1911–72) (b. Hungary, Gyözö Braun). The women's record is 17 by Diane Rowe (b. 14 Apr. 1933), now Mrs. Eberhard Scholer. Her twin Rosalind (now Mrs. Cornett) has won nine (two in singles).

TABLE TENNIS
MOST WINS IN WORLD CHAMPIONSHIPS (Instituted 1926–27)

Event	Name and Nationality	Times	Years
Men's Singles (St. Bride's Vase)	G. Viktor Barna (Hungary) (1911–72)	5	1930, 1932–35
Women's Singles (G. Geist Prize)	Angelica Rozeanu (Romania) (b. 15 Oct. 1921)	6	1950–55
Men's Doubles	G. Viktor Barna (Hungary)	8	1929–35, 1939
Women's Doubles	Maria Mednyanszky (Hungary) (1901–79)	7	1928, 1930–35
Mixed Doubles (Men)	Ferenc Sido (Hungary) (b. 1923)	4	1949–50, 1952–53
(Women)	Maria Mednyanszky (Hungary)	6	1927–28, 1930–31, 1933–34

G. Viktor Barna gained a personal total of 15 world titles, while 18 have been won by Maria Mednyanszky.
Note: With the staging of championships biennially the breaking of the above records would now be virtually impossible.

MOST TEAM TITLES

Event	Team	Times	Years
Men's Team (Swaythling Cup)	Hungary	12	1927–31, 1933–35, 1938, 1949, 1952, 1979
Women's Team (Marcel Corbillon Cup)	Japan	8	1952, 1954, 1957, 1959, 1961, 1963, 1967, 1971

MOST WINS IN ENGLISH OPEN CHAMPIONSHIPS (Instituted 1921)

Event	Name and Nationality	Times	Years
Men's Singles	Richard Bergmann (Austria, then G.B.) (1920–70)	6	1939–40, 1948, 1950, 1952, 1954
Women's Singles	Maria Alexandru (Romania) (b. 1941)	6	1963–64, 1970–72, 1974
Men's Doubles	G. Viktor Barna (Hungary, then G.B.)	7	1931, 1933–35, 1938–39, 1949
Women's Doubles	Diane Rowe (G.B.) (now Scholer) (b. 14 Apr. 1933)	12	1950–56, 1960, 1962–65
Mixed Doubles (Men)	G. Viktor Barna (Hungary, then G.B.)	8	1933–36, 1938, 1940, 1951, 1953
(Women)	Diane Rowe (G.B.) (now Scholer)	4	1952, 1954, 1956, 1960, 1969

Youngest international
The youngest ever international was Joy Foster, aged 8, the 1958 Jamaican singles and mixed doubles champion.

Longest match
In the Swaythling Cup final match between Austria and Romania in Prague, Czechoslovakia, in 1936, the play lasted for 25 or 26 hours, spread over three nights.

Longest rally
In a 1936 Swaythling Cup match in Prague between Alex Ehrlich (Poland) and Paneth Farcas (Romania) the opening rally lasted 2 hr 12 min. On 30 July 1978 Robert Siegel and Donald Peters staged an 8 hr 33 min rally at Stamford, Conn. U.S.A.

Counter hitting
The record number of hits in 60 sec is 162 by English Internationals Nicky Jarvis (b. 7 Mar. 1954) and Desmond Douglas (b. 20 July 1955) at the Eccentric Club, London on 1 Dec. 1976. This was equalled by Douglas and Paul Day (b. 20 Oct. 1958) at Butlins, Blackpool, Lancs., England on 21 Mar. 1977. The most by women is 148 by Linda Howard and Melodi Ludi at Blackpool, Lancs., on 11 Oct. 1977. With a bat in each hand, Gary D. Fisher of Olympia, Wash., U.S.A., completed 5,000 consecutive volleys over the net in 44 min 28 sec on 25 June 1979.

Highest speed
No conclusive measurements have been published but in a lecture M. Sklorz (West Germany) stated that a smashed ball had been measured at speeds up to 170 km/h *105,6 m.p.h.*

Marathons
The longest marathon singles match is 132 hr 31 min by Danny Price and Randy Nunes at Cherry Hill, N.J., U.S.A. on 20–26 Aug. 1978.

The longest doubles marathon is 101 hr 1 min 11 secs by Lance, Phil and Mark Warren and Bill Weir at Sacramento, Calif., U.S.A. on 9–13 April 1979.

TENNIS (Real or Royal)
Origins
The game originated as *jeu de paume* in French monasteries *c.* 1050. A tennis court is mentioned in the sale of the Hôtel de Nesle, Paris in 1308. The oldest court in the world is one built in Paris in 1496.

The oldest of the 17 surviving active Tennis Courts in the British Isles is the Royal Tennis Court at Hampton Court Palace, which was built in 1529–30 and rebuilt in 1660. There are estimated to be 3,000 players and 32 active courts throughout the world. The latest court was opened at Bordeaux, France in 1979.

Most titles *World*
The first recorded World Tennis Champion was Clerge (France) *c.* 1740. Jacques Edmond Barre (France) (1802–73) held the title for a record 33 yr from 1829 to 1862. Pierre Etchebaster (b. 1893) a Basque, holds the record for the greatest number of successful defences of the title with eight between 1928 and 1952.

Most titles *British*
The Amateur Championship of the British Isles (instituted 1888) has been won 14 times by Howard R. Angus (b. 1945) consecutively 1966–79. Angus, a left-hander, is also the first British amateur to win a World title, in 1975, which he retained in 1977 and 1979.

TRACK AND FIELD ATHLETICS
See also The Official Centenary History of the A.A.A. *by Peter Lovesey, published by Guinness Superlatives Ltd., (price £7.95).*

Origins
Track and field athletics date from the ancient Olympic Games. The earliest accurately known Olympiad dates from July 776 B.C., at which celebration Coroibos won the foot race. The oldest surviving measurements are a long jump of 7,05 m *23 ft 1¼ in* by Chionis of Sparta in *c.* 656 B.C. and a discus throw of 100 cubits (about 46.30 m *152 ft*) by Protesilaus.

Earliest landmarks
The first time 10 sec ("even time") was bettered for 100 yds under championship conditions was when John Owen recorded 9⅘ sec in the United States A.A.U. Championship at Analostan Island, Washington, D.C., U.S.A., on 11 Oct. 1890. The first recorded instance of 6 ft *1,83 m* being cleared in the high jump was when Marshall Jones Brooks (1855–1944) jumped 6 ft 0⅛ in *1,832 m* at Marston, near Oxford, England, on 17 Mar. 1876. The breaking of the "four-minute barrier" in the one mile *1 609,34 m* was first achieved by Dr. (now Sir) Roger Gilbert Bannister, C.B.E. (b. Harrow, Greater London, England, 23 Mar. 1929), when he recorded 3 min 59.4 sec on the Iffley Road track, Oxford, at 6.10 p.m. on 6 May 1954.

Fastest runner
Robert Lee Hayes (b. 20 Dec. 1942) of Jacksonville, Florida, U.S.A., may have reached a speed of over 27 m.p.h. *43,5*

km/h during his then world record run of 9.1 sec in a 100 yard event at St. Louis, Missouri, on 21 June 1963. Marlies Göhr (*née* Oelsner) (b. East Germany, 21 Mar. 1958) reached a speed of over 24 m.p.h. *38,6 km/h* in her world record 100 m in 10.88 sec at Dresden, East Germany on 1 July 1977.

Highest jumper

There are several reported instances of high jumpers exceeding the official world record height of 7 ft 8 in *2,34 m*. The earliest of these came from unsubstantiated reports of Tutsi tribesmen in Central Africa (see page 12) clearing up to 8 ft 2½ in *2,50 m*, definitely however, from inclined take-offs. The greatest height cleared above an athlete's own head is 23¼ in *59 cm* by Franklin Jacobs (U.S.) (b. 31 Dec. 1957), who cleared 7 ft 7¼ in *2,32 m* at New York, U.S.A., on 28 Jan. 1978. He is only 5 ft 8 in *1,73 m* tall. The greatest height cleared by a woman above her own head is 26 cm *10¼ in* by Tamami Yagi (Japan) (b. 15 Nov. 1958) who stands 1,64 m *5 ft 4½ in* and jumped 1,90 m *6 ft 2¾ in* at Matsumoto, Japan on 19 Oct. 1978.

WORLD RECORDS—MEN

A list of World's Records for the 32 scheduled men's events (excluding the walking records—see under WALKING) passed by the International Amateur Athletic Federation as at 24 Aug. 1979. Fully automatic electric timing is mandatory for the six events up to the 400 metre distance.
* Denotes awaiting ratification.

RUNNING

RUNNING	Min	sec	Name and Country	Place	Date
100 metres		9.95	James Ray Hines (U.S.A.)	Mexico City, Mexico	14 Oct. 1968
200 metres		19.83	Tommie C. Smith (U.S.A.)	Mexico City, Mexico	16 Oct. 1968
400 metres		43.86	Lee Edward Evans (U.S.A.)	Mexico City, Mexico	18 Oct. 1968
800 metres		1:42.4*	Sebastian Newbold Coe (G.B.)	Oslo, Norway	5 July 1979
1,000 metres		2:13.9	Richard Charles Wohlhuter (U.S.A.)	Oslo, Norway	30 July 1974
1,500 metres		3:32.1*	Sebastian Newbold Coe (G.B.)	Zurich, Switzerland	15 Aug. 1979
1 mile		3:49.0*	Sebastian Newbold Coe (G.B.)	Oslo, Norway	17 July 1979
2,000 metres		4:51.4	John George Walker O.B.E. (N.Z.)	Oslo, Norway	30 June 1976
3,000 metres		7:32.1	Henry Rono (Kenya)	Oslo, Norway	27 June 1978
5,000 metres		13:08.4	Henry Rono (Kenya)	Berkeley, Cal., U.S.A.	8 Apr. 1978
10,000 metres		27:22.5	Henry Rono (Kenya)	Vienna, Austria	11 June 1978
20,000 metres		57:24.2	Jos Hermens (Netherlands)	Papendal, Netherlands	1 May 1976
25,000 metres		1 hr 14:11.8	William Rodgers (U.S.A.)	Saratoga, Cal., U.S.A.	21 Feb. 1979
30,000 metres		1 hr 31:30.4	James Noel Carroll Alder (G.B. & N.I.)	Crystal Palace, London	5 Sept. 1970
1 hour	20 944 m *13 miles 24 yd 2 ft*		Josephus Hermens (Netherlands)	Papendal, Netherlands	1 May 1976

HURDLING

HURDLING	sec	Name and Country	Place	Date
110 metres (3′ 6″ *106 cm*)	13.00	Renaldo Nehemiah (U.S.A.)	Westwood, Cal., U.S.A.	6 May 1979
400 metres (3′ 0″ *91,4 cm*)	47.45	Edwin Corley Moses (U.S.A.)	Westwood, Cal., U.S.A.	11 June 1977
3,000 metres steeplechase	8:05.4	Henry Rono (Kenya)	Seattle, Wash., U.S.A.	13 May 1978

MARATHON

There is no offical marathon record because of the varying severity of courses. The best time recorded over 26 miles 385 yards *42,195 km* (standardised in 1924) is 2 hr 08 min 33.6 sec (av. 12.24 m.p.h. *19,69 km*) by Derek Clayton (b. 17 Nov. 1942, Barrow-in-Furness, England) of Australia, at Antwerp, Belgium, on 30 May 1969. The best time by a British international is 2 hr 09 min 12.2 sec by Ian Thompson (b. 16 Oct. 1949) at Christchurch, New Zealand, 31 Jan. 1974. The fastest time by a female is 2 hr 32 min 30 sec (av. 10.31 m.p.h. *16,60 km/h*) by Grete Waitz (Norway) (b. 1 Oct. 1953) at New York, U.S.A., 22 Oct. 1978. The fastest by a British woman is 2 hr 41 min 37 sec by Joyce Esther Smith (*née* Byatt) (b. 26 Oct. 1937) at Sandbach, Cheshire, on 17 June 1979.

RELAYS

RELAYS	sec	Name and Country	Place	Date
4 × 100 metres (two turns)	38.03	United States National Team (William Collins, Steven Earl Riddick, Clifford Wiley, Steven Williams)	Dusseldorf, West Germany	3 Sept. 1977
4 × 200 metres	1:20.3†	University of Southern California, U.S.A. (Joel Andrews, James Sanford, William Mullins, Clancy Edwards)	Tempe, Ariz., U.S.A.	27 May 1978
4 × 400 metres	2:56.1	United States National Team (Vincent Edward Matthews, Ronald J. Freeman, George Lawrence James, Lee Edward Evans)	Mexico City, Mexico	20 Oct. 1968
4 × 800 metres	7:08.1	U.S.S.R. Team (Vladimir Podoliakov, Nikolai Kirov, Vladimir Malosemlin, Anatoli Reschetniak)	Podolsk, U.S.S.R.	13 Aug. 1978
4 × 1,500 metres	14:38.8	West German Team (Thomas Wessinghage, Harald Hudak, Michael Lederer, Karl Fleschen)	Cologne, West Germany	17 Aug. 1977

† *The time of 1:20.2 achieved by the Tobias Striders (Guy Abrahams, Mike Simmons, Donald O'Riley Quarrie, James Gilkes) at Tempe, Ariz., U.S.A. on 27 May 1978 was not ratified as the team was composed of varied nationalities.*

FIELD EVENTS

FIELD EVENTS	ft	in	m	Name and Country	Place	Date
High Jump	7	8	*2,34†*	Vladimir Ilych Yashchenko (U.S.S.R.)	Tbilis, U.S.S.R.	16 June 1978
Pole Vault	18	8¼	*5,70*	David Luther Roberts (U.S.A.)	Eugene, Oregon, U.S.A.	26 June 1976
Long Jump	29	2½	*8,90*	Robert Beamon (U.S.A.)	Mexico City, Mexico	18 Oct. 1968
Triple Jump	58	8½	*17,89*	João Carlos de Oliveira (Brazil)	Mexico City, Mexico	15 Oct. 1975
Shot Putt	72	8	*22,15††*	Udo Beyer (East Germany)	Gothenburg, Sweden	6 July 1978
Discus Throw	233	5	*71,16*	Wolfgang Schmidt (East Germany)	East Berlin, East Germany	9 Aug. 1978
Hammer Throw	263	6	*80,32*	Karl Hans Riehm (West Germany)	Heidenheim, West Germany	6 Aug. 1978
Javelin Throw	310	4	*94,58*	Miklós Németh (Hungary)	Montreal, Canada	26 July 1976

† *Yaschenko cleared 7 ft 8½ in 2,35 m indoors at Milan, Italy on 12 Mar. 1978.*

†† *Note: One professional performance is superior to the I.A.A.F. mark, but the same highly rigorous rules as to measuring and weighing were not necessarily applied.*

	ft	in	m	Name and Country	Place	Date
	75	0	*22,86*	Brian Ray Oldfield (U.S.A.)	El Paso, Texas, U.S.A.	10 May 1975

Everybody's favourite for the Olympic title, 20-year-old Renaldo 'Skeets' Nehemiah (U.S.A.), world record holder in the high hurdles. (*Steve Sutton, All-Sport Photographic*)

Franklin Jacobs (U.S.A.), whose 23¼ inch differential between his height and the height he can jump, would put the world record way over eight feet if equalled by most high jumpers. (*Fairleigh Dickinson University*)

DECATHLON
8,618 points

William Bruce Jenner (U.S.A.)
(1st day: 100 m 10.94 sec, Long Jump 7,22 m *23′ 8¼″*,
Shot Putt 15,35 m *50′4½″*, High Jump 2,03 m *6′ 8′*,
400 m 47.51 sec)

Montreal, Canada   29–30 July 1976
(2nd day: 110 m hurdles 14.84 sec,
Discus 50,04 m *164′ 2″*, Pole Vault 4,80 m *15′ 9″*,
Javelin 68,52 m *224′ 10″*, 1,500 m 4:12.61 sec)

WORLD RECORDS—WOMEN

A list of World's Records for the 19 scheduled women's events passed by the International Amateur Athletic Federation as at 24 Aug. 1979. The same stipulation about electrically timed events applies in the six events up to 400 metres as in the men's list. * Denotes awaiting ratification.

RUNNING	Min sec	Name and Country	Place	Date
100 metres	10.88	Marlies Oelsner (now Göhr) (East Germany)	Dresden, East Germany	1 July 1977
200 metres	21.71*	Marita Koch (East Germany)	Karl Marx Stadt, East Germany	10 June 1979
400 metres	48.60	Marita Koch (East Germany)	Turin, Italy	4 Aug. 1979
800 metres	1:54.9	Tatyana Kazankina (U.S.S.R.)	Montreal, Canada	26 July 1976
1,500 metres	3:56.0	Tatyana Kazankina (U.S.S.R.)	Podolsk, U.S.S.R.	28 June 1976
1 mile	4:22.1	Natalia Marasescu (*née* Andrei) (Romania)	Auckland, New Zealand	27 Jan. 1979
3,000 metres	8:27.2	Ludmila Bragina (U.S.S.R.)	College Park, Md., U.S.A.	7 Aug. 1976

HURDLING				
100 metres (2′ 9″ *84 cm*)	12.48	Grazyna Rabsztyn (Poland)	Fuerth, West Germany	10 June 1978
400 metres (2′ 6″ *76 cm*)	54.78*	Marina Makeyeva (U.S.S.R.)	Moscow, U.S.S.R.	27 July 1979

RELAYS				
4 × 100 metres	42.09*	East German Team (Romy Schneider, Ingrid Auerswald Marlies Göhr (*née* Oelsner), Marita Koch)	Karl Marx Stadt, East Germany	10 June 1979
4 × 200 metres	1:30.8*	Ukraine, U.S.S.R. (Raisa Maklova, Nina Zuskova, Tatyana Provrochenko, Maria Kulchunova)	Moscow, U.S.S.R.	29 July 1979
4 × 400 metres	3:19.2	East German National Team (Doris Maletzki, Brigitte Röhde, Ellen Streidt (*née* Stropahl), Christina Brehmer)	Montreal, Canada	31 July 1976
4 × 800 metres	7:52.3	U.S.S.R. National Team (Tatyana Providokhina, Valentina Gerasimova, Svetlana Styrkina, Tatyana Kazankina)	Podolsk, U.S.S.R.	16 Aug. 1976

FIELD EVENTS

Event	ft	in	m	Name and Country	Place	Date
High Jump	6	7	2,01	Sara Simeoni (Italy)	Brescia, Italy	4 Aug. 1978
Long Jump	23	3¼	7,09	Vilma Bardauskiene (U.S.S.R.)	Prague, Czechoslovakia	29 Aug. 1978
Shot Putt	73	2¾†	22,32	Helena Fibingerova (Czechoslovakia)	Nitra, Czechoslovakia	20 Aug. 1977
Discus Throw	232	0	70,72	Evelin Jahl (*née* Schlaak) (East Germany)	Dresden, East Germany	12 Aug. 1978
Javelin Throw	228	1	69,52*	Ruth Fuchs (*née* Gamm) (East Germany)	Dresden, East Germany	13 June 1979

† Helena Fibingerova set an indoor record of 22,50 m 73 ft 10 in at Jablonec, Cz. on 19 Feb. 1977.

PENTATHLON (with 800 m)

4,839 points (1971 Scoring Tables)	Nadezda Tkachenko (U.S.S.R.) (100 m hurdles 13.49 sec; Shot 15,93 m *52 ft 3¼ in;* High Jump 1,80 m *5 ft 10¾ in;* Long Jump 6,49 m *21 ft 3½ in;* 800 m 2 min 10.62 sec)	Lille, France	18 Sept. 1977

Most Olympic titles *Men*

The most Olympic gold medals won is ten (an absolute Olympic record) by Ray C. Ewry (U.S.A.) (1874–1937) in the Standing High, Long and Triple Jumps in 1900, 1904, 1906 and 1908.

Most Olympic titles *Women*

The most gold medals won by a woman is four shared by Francina E. Blankers-Koen (Netherlands) (b. 26 Apr. 1918) with 100 m, 200 m, 80 m hurdles and 4 × 100 m relay, 1948, and Betty Cuthbert (Australia) (b. 20 Apr. 1938) with 100 m, 200 m, 4 × 100 m relay, 1956 and 400 m, 1964.

Most wins at one Games

The most gold medals at one celebration is five by Paavo Johannes Nurmi (Finland) (1897–1973) in 1924, and the most individual is four by Alvin C. Kraenzlein (U.S.A.) (1876–1928) in 1900, with 60 m, 110 m hurdles, 200 m hurdles and long jump.

Most Olympic titles *British*

The most gold medals won by a British athlete (excluding Tug of War and Walking q.v.) is two by: Charles Bennett (1871–1949) (1,500 m and 5,000 m team, 1900); Alfred Tysoe (1874–1901) (800 m and 5,000 m team, 1900); John Rimmer (1879–1962) (4,000 m steeplechase; and 5,000 m team, 1900); Albert G. Hill (1889–1969) (800 m and 1,500 m, 1920) and Douglas Gordon Arthur Lowe (b. 7 Aug. 1902) (800 m 1924 and 1928).

Most Olympic medals *Men*

The most medals won is 12 (nine gold and three silver) by Paavo Nurmi (Finland) in the Games of 1920, 1924 and 1928.

Most Olympic medals *Women*

The most medals won by a woman athlete is seven by Shirley de la Hunty (*née* Strickland) M.B.E. (Australia) (b. 18 July 1925) with three gold, one silver and three bronze in the 1948, 1952 and 1956 Games. A recently discovered photo-finish indicates that she finished third, not fourth, in the 1948 200 metres event, thus unofficially increasing her medal haul to eight. Irena Szewinska (née Kirszenstein) (Poland) (b. 24 May 1946) won three gold, two silver and two bronze in 1964, 1968, 1972 and 1976, and is the only woman athlete to win a medal in four successive games.

Most Olympic medals *British*

The most medals won by a British athlete is four by Guy M. Butler (b. 25 Aug. 1899) with a gold medal for the 4 × 400 m relay and a silver in the 400 m in 1920 and a bronze medal for each of these events in 1924. Two British women athletes have won three medals: Dorothy Hyman, M.B.E. (b. 9 May 1941) with a silver (100 m, 1960) and a bronze (200 m, 1960 and 4 × 100 m relay, 1964) and Mrs. Mary Denise Rand, M.B.E. (now Toomey, *née* Bignal), (b. 10 Feb. 1940) with a gold (long jump), a silver (pentathlon) and a bronze (4 × 100 m relay) all in 1964.

Olympic champions *Oldest and youngest*

The oldest athlete to win an Olympic title was Irish-born Patrick J. "Babe" McDonald (U.S.A.) (1878–1954) who was aged 42 yr 26 days when he won the 56 lb. *25,4 kg* weight throw at Antwerp, Belgium on 21 Aug. 1920. The oldest female champion was Lia Manoliu (Romania) (b. 25 Apr. 1932) aged 36 yr 176 days when she won the discus at Mexico City on 18 Oct. 1968. The youngest gold medallist was Barbara Jones (U.S.A.) (b. 26 Mar. 1937) who was a member of the winning 4 × 100 m relay team, aged 15 yr 123 days, at Helsinki, Finland on 27 July 1952. The youngest male champion was Robert Bruce Mathias (U.S.A.) (b. 17 Nov. 1930) aged 17 yr 263 days when he won the decathlon at London on 5–6 Aug. 1948.

World record breakers *Oldest and youngest*

For the greatest age at which anyone has broken a world record in a standard Olympic event see p. 239. The female record is 35 yr 255 days in the case of Dana Zátopkova, *née* Ingrova (b. 19 Sept. 1922) of Czechoslovakia, who broke the women's javelin record with 182 ft 10 in in *55,73 m* at Prague, Czechoslovakia, on 1 June 1958. The youngest individual record breaker is Ulrike Meyfarth (b. 4 May 1956) of West Germany who equalled the women's high jump mark with 1.92 m *6 ft 3½ in* in winning the gold medal on 4 Sept. 1972 at the Munich Olympics aged 16 yr 123 days. Barbara Jones (see Olympic champions above), aged 15 yr 123 days, was in a team event.

Most records in a day

Jesse Owens (b. 12 Sept. 1913) (U.S.A.) set six world records in 45 min at Ann Arbor, Michigan on 25 May 1935 with a 9.4 sec 100 yd at 3.15 p.m., a 26 ft 8¼ in *8,13 m* long jump at 3.25 p.m., a 20.3 sec 220 yd (and 200 m) at 3.45 p.m. and a 22.6 sec 220 yd low hurdles (and 200 m) at 4.00 p.m.

Most national titles

The greatest number of national A.A.A. titles (excluding those in tug of war events) won by one athlete is 14 individual and two relay titles by Emmanuel McDonald Bailey (b. Williamsville, Trinidad 8 Dec. 1920), between 1946 and 1953.

The greatest number of consecutive title wins is seven by Denis Horgan (1871–1922) (Ireland) (shot putt, 1893–99), Albert Arthur Cooper (1910–74) (2 miles walk, 1932–38), Donald Osborne Finlay, D.F.C., A.F.C. (1909–70) (120 yd hurdles, 1932–38), Harry Whittle (b. 2 May 1922) (440 yd hurdles, 1947–53) and Maurice Herriott (b. 8 Oct. 1939) (3,000 m steeplechase, 1961–67). The record for consecutive W.A.A.A. titles is nine by Judy Undine Farr (Trowbridge & District A.C.) (b. 24 Jan. 1942), who won the 1½ mile *2 414 m/2 500 m 1 mile 974 yd* walk from 1962–70.

Most international appearances

The greatest number of full Great Britain outdoor internationals won by a British male athlete is 61 by **Andrew Howard Payne** (b. South Africa, 17 Apr. 1931). Michael Anthony Bull (b. 11 Sept. 1946) has gained 66 full international appearances, including indoor matches, between Aug. 1965 and Feb. 1977. The feminine record is 68 full internationals, including indoor matches, by Brenda Rose Bedford (*née* Sawyer) (b. 4 Sept. 1937, London) from Sept. 1961 to June 1978.

UNITED KINGDOM (NATIONAL) RECORDS—MEN (as at 24 Aug. 1979)

* Denotes awaiting ratification.

RUNNING	Min sec	Name	Place	Date
100 metres	10.15	Allan Wipper Wells	Edinburgh, Scotland	15 July 1978
200 metres (turn)	20.42*	Allan Wipper Wells	Zurich, Switzerland	15 Aug. 1979
400 metres	44.93	David Andrew Jenkins	Eugene, Oregon, U.S.A.	21 June 1975
800 metres	1:42.4*	Sebastian Newbold Coe	Oslo, Norway	5 July 1979
1,000 metres	2:18.2	John Peter Boulter	London (Crystal Palace)	6 Sept. 1969
1,500 metres	3:32.1*	Sebastian Newbold Coe	Zurich, Switzerland	15 Aug. 1979
1 mile	3:49.0*	Sebastian Newbold Coe	Oslo, Norway	17 July 1979
2,000 metres	4:57.8	Steven Michael James Ovett	London (Crystal Palace)	3 June 1978
3,000 metres	7:35.2	Brendan Foster, M.B.E.	Gateshead, Tyne and Wear	3 Aug. 1974
5,000 metres	13:14.6	Brendan Foster, M.B.E.	Christchurch, New Zealand	29 Jan. 1974
10,000 metres	27:30.5†	Brendan Foster, M.B.E.	London (Crystal Palace)	23 June 1978
20,000 metres	58:39.0	Ronald Hill	Leicester	9 Nov. 1968
25,000 metres	1hr 15:22.6	Ronald Hill	Bolton, Lancashire	21 July 1965
30,000 metres	1hr 31:30.4	James Noel Carroll Alder	London (Crystal Palace)	5 Sept. 1970
1 hour	12 miles 1,268 yds *20 472 m*	Ronald Hill	Leicester	9 Nov. 1968

† *Film evidence indicates that time should be 27:30.3*

HURDLING				
110 metres	13.69	Berwyn Price	Moscow, U.S.S.R.	18 Aug. 1973
400 metres	48.12	David Peter Hemery, M.B.E.	Mexico City, Mexico	15 Oct. 1968
3,000 metres Steeplechase	8:19.0	Dennis Malcolm Coates	Montreal, Canada	25 July 1976

RELAYS				
4 × 100 metres	38.95	United Kingdom Team (Allan Wipper Wells, Trevor Hayter, Stephen Green, Andrew Emlyn McMaster)	Turin, Italy	4 Aug. 1979
4 × 200 metres	1:24.1	Great Britain (Brian William Green, Roger Walters, Ralph Banthorpe, Martin Edward Reynolds)	Paris, France	2 Oct. 1971
4 × 400 metres	3:00.5	United Kingdom National Team (Martin Edward Reynolds, Alan Peter Pascoe, M.B.E., David Peter Hemery, M.B.E., David Andrew Jenkins)	Munich, West Germany	10 Sept. 1972
4 × 800 metres	7:17.4†	United Kingdom National Team (Martin Bilham, David Cropper, Michael John Maclean, Peter Miles Browne)	London (Crystal Palace)	5 Sept. 1970
4 × 1,500 metres	14:56.8*	United Kingdom Team (Alan David Mottershead, Geoffrey Michael Cooper, Stephen John Emson, Roy Wood)	Bourges, France	24 June 1979

† *A time of 7:14.6 by a U.K. team* (*Graeme Grant, G. Michael Varah, Christopher Carter, John Peter Boulter*) *at Crystal Palace, London on 22 June 1966 was not ratified on a technicality.*

FIELD EVENTS	ft	in	m	Name	Place	Date
High Jump	7	2½	*2,20*†	Brian Burgess	London (Crystal Palace)	11 June 1978
Pole Vault	17	9¼	*5,42*	Brian Roger Leslie Hooper	Gateshead, Tyne and Wear	17 Sept. 1978
Long Jump	27	0	*8,23*	Lynn Davies, M.B.E.	Bern, Switzerland	30 June 1968
Triple Jump	55	0	*16,76*	Keith Leroy Connor	Edmonton, Canada	12 Aug. 1978
Shot Putt	70	8½	*21,55*	Geoffrey Lewis Capes	Gateshead, Tyne and Wear	28 May 1976
Discus Throw	213	1	*64,94*	William Raymond Tancred	Loughborough, Leicester	21 July 1974
Hammer Throw	246	0	*74,98*	Christopher Francis Black	Edinburgh, Scotland	21 Aug. 1976
Javelin Throw	278	7	*84,92*	Charles Philip Clover	Christchurch, New Zealand	2 Feb. 1974

† *Mark Naylor jumped 7 ft 3¼ in 2,22 m indoors at West Berlin, West Germany on 3 Feb. 1979*

DECATHLON (1962 Scoring Table)

8,289 (points) — Francis Morgan (Daley) Thompson — Prague, Czechoslovakia — 30–31 Aug. 1978

(1st day: 100 m 10.69 sec, Long Jump 26′ 0¼″ *7,93 m*, Shot Putt 48′ 2½″ *14,69 m*, High Jump 6′ 8¼″ *2,04 m*, 400 m 47.77 sec)

(2nd day: 110 m Hurdles 15.28 sec, Discus 142′ 9″ *43,52 m*, Pole Vault 13′ 9¼″ *4,20 m*, Javelin 196′ 0½″ *59,80 m*, 1,500 m 4:22.8 sec)

UNITED KINGDOM (NATIONAL) RECORDS—WOMEN (as at 24 Aug. 1979)

* Denotes awaiting ratification.

RUNNING	Min sec	Name	Place	Date
100 metres	11.16	Andrea Joan Caron Lynch M.B.E.	London (Crystal Palace)	11 June 1975
200 metres	22.75	Donna-Marie Louise Hartley (*née* Murray)	Birmingham, W. Midlands	17 June 1978
400 metres	51.28	Donna-Marie Louise Murray (now Hartley)	Sofia, Bulgaria	12 July 1975
800 metres	1:59.1	Christina Boxer	Turin, Italy	3 Sept. 1972
1,500 metres	4:01.6*	Christine Benning (*née* Tranter)	Zurich, Switzerland	15 Aug. 1979
1 mile	4:30.2*	Christina Boxer	Gateshead, Tyne and Wear	8 July 1979
3,000 metres	8:48.7†	Paula Fudge (*née* Yeoman)	Prague, Czechoslovakia	29 Aug. 1978

RELAYS	Min sec	Name	Place	Date
4 × 100 metres	42.72	United Kingdom Team (Beverley Lanita Goddard, Kathryn Jane Smallwood, Sharon Colyear, Sonia May Lannaman)	Prague, Czechoslovakia	3 Sept. 1978
4 × 200 metres	1:31.6	United Kingdom National Team (Donna-Marie Louise Hartley [née Murray], Verona Marolin Elder [née Bernard], Sharon Colyear, Sonia May Lannaman)	London (Crystal Palace)	20 Aug. 1977
4 × 400 metres	3:26.6	United Kingdom National Team (Jannette Veronica Roscoe [née Champion], Gladys Taylor [now McCormack], Verona Marolin Elder [née Bernard], Donna-Marie Louise Murray [now Hartley])	Nice, France	17 Aug. 1975
4 × 800 metres	8:23.8	Great Britain (Joan Florence Allison, Sheila Janet Carey [née Taylor], Patricia Barbara Lowe [now Cropper], Rosemary Olivia Stirling [now Wright])	Paris, France	2 Oct. 1971

HURDLING				
100 metres	13.08	Lorna Marie Boothe	London (Crystal Palace)	11 June 1978
400 metres	56.06	Christine Anne Warden (née Howell)	London (Crystal Palace)	28 July 1979

FIELD EVENTS	ft	in	m	Name	Place	Date
High Jump	6	1½	1,87	Barbara Jean Inkpen (now Lawton)	London (Crystal Palace)	22 Sept. 1973
Long Jump	22	2¼	6,76	Mary Denise Rand M.B.E. (now Toomey, née Bignal)	Tokyo, Japan	14 Oct. 1964
Shot Putt	54	10¼	16,72*††	Judith Miriam Oakes	London (Crystal Palace)	3 June 1979
Discus Throw	199	6	60,80	Margaret Elizabeth Ritchie	Edinburgh, Scotland	15 Apr. 1978
Javelin Throw	220	6	67,20	Theresa Ione Sanderson	Dublin, Rep. of Ireland	17 July 1977

† Current rules relating to the rounding up of performances electrically timed to hundredths would have made this time 8:48.8.

†† Judith Oakes achieved 54 ft 11¼ in 16,74 m indoors at Cosford, England on 11 Feb. 1978.

PENTATHLON (with 800 m)				
4,385 points (1971 Tables)		Susan Jane Longden (née Wright)	Sittard, Netherlands	31 July 1977

Oldest and youngest internationals

Of full Great Britain (outdoor) internationals the oldest have been Hector Harold Whitlock (b. 16 Dec. 1903) at the 1952 Olympic Games, aged 48 yr 218 days, and Rosemary Payne (née Charters) (b. 19 May 1933) in the Great Britain v. Sweden match, 22 Sept. 1973, aged 40 yr 126 days. The youngest have been Ross Hepburn (b. 14 Oct. 1961) v. the U.S.S.R. in 1977, aged 15 yr 316 days, and Janis Walsh (b. 28 Mar. 1960) v. Belgium (indoor) at 60 m and 4 × 200 m relay on 15 Feb. 1975, 41 days short of her 15th birthday.

Longest career

Duncan McLean (b. Gourock, Strathclyde, 3 Dec. 1884) set a world age—92—record of 100 m in 21.7 sec in August 1977, over 73 years after his best ever sprint of 100 yd in 9.9 sec in South Africa in February 1904. At Athens, Greece, on 10 Oct. 1976, Dimitrion Yordanidis, aged 98, completed a marathon race in 7 hr 33 min.

Ambidextrous shot putt

The best recorded distance is 121 ft 6¾ in by Allan Feuerbach (b. 14 Jan. 1948) (U.S.A.) (left 51 ft 5 in 15,67 m, right 70 ft 1¾ in 21.38 m) at Malmo, Sweden on 24 Aug. 1974.

Highland Games

The weight and height of cabers (Gaelic cabar) vary considerably. Extreme values are 25 ft 7,62 m and 280 lb 127 kg. The Braemar caber (19 ft 3 in 5,86 m and 120 lb 54,4 kg) in Grampian, Scotland, was untossed from 1891 until 1951 when it was tossed by George Clark. The best authentic mark recorded for throwing the 56 lb. weight for height is 16 ft 5½ in 5,02 m over a bar by Hreinn Halldorsson (b. Iceland, 3 Mar. 1949) at Edinburgh, Scotland on 20 Aug. 1977. The best throw recorded for the Scots hammer is 151 ft. 2 in 46,08 m by William Anderson, M.B.E., (b. 6 Oct. 1938) at Lochearnhead, 26 July 1969.

Standing jumps

The best amateur standing high jump is 5 ft 10¾ in 1,80 m by Rune Almen (b. 20 Oct. 1952) (Sweden) at Orebro, Sweden on 8 Dec. 1974. Joe Darby (1861–1937), the famous Victorian professional jumper reportedly cleared 6 ft 1,83 m with ankles tied at Church Cricket Ground, Dudley, West Midlands on 11 June 1892. Joe Darby long jumped a measured 12 ft 1½ in 3,69 m without weights at Dudley Castle, on 28 May 1890. Johan Christian Evandt (Norway) achieved 3,65 m 11 ft 11¾ in as an amateur in Reykjavik, Iceland on 11 Mar. 1962.

Highest one-legged jump

One legged Arnie Boldt, (b. 1958) of Saskatchewan, Canada cleared 2.00 m 6 ft 6¾ in indoors at Saskatoon, Canada in 1977.

Fastest three-legged race

The fastest recorded time for a 100 yd three-legged race is 11.0 sec by Harry L. Hillman (1881–1945) and Lawson Robertson (1883–1951) at Brooklyn, New York City, N.Y., U.S.A., on 24 Apr. 1909.

Fastest run backwards

The fastest time recorded for running the 100 yd backwards is 13.3 sec by Paul Wilson (N.Z.) at Hastings, New Zealand on 10 Apr. 1977.

Fastest blind sprinting

Graham Henry Salmon (b. 5 Sept. 1952) of Loughton, Essex, England ran 100 m 109 yd in 11.4 sec at Grangemouth, Scotland on 2 Sept. 1978.

Pancake race record

The annual Housewives' Pancake Race at Olney, Buckinghamshire, was first mentioned in 1445. The record for the winding 415 yd 380 m course (three tosses mandatory) is 61.0 sec, set by Sally Ann Faulkner, (b. 1958) on 26 Feb. 1974. The record for the counterpart race (inst. 1949) at Liberal, Kansas, U.S.A. is 58.5 sec by Sheila Turner (b. 9 July 1953) on 11 Feb. 1975.

Longest runs

Mensen Ernst (1799–1846) of Norway is reputed to have run from Istanbul, Turkey, to Calcutta, in West Bengal,

India, and back in 59 days in 1836, so averaging an improbable 92.4 miles *151,6 km* per day. Max Telford (N.Z.) ran 5,110 miles *8 224 km* from Anchorage, Alaska to Halifax, Nova Scotia, in 106 days 18 hr 45 min from 25 July–9 Nov. 1977. The fastest time for the cross-America run is 53 days 7 min for 3,046 miles *4 902 km* by Tom McGrath (N. Ireland) from 29 Aug–21 Oct. 1977.

Longest non-stop run

The greatest non-stop run recorded is 186 miles *300 km* in 31 hr 33 min 38 sec by Max Telford (b. Hawick, Scotland, 2 Feb. 1935) of New Zealand at Wailuku, Hawaii, U.S.A. on 19–20 Mar. 1977. No rest breaks were taken.

Six-day races

The greatest distance covered by a man in six days (*i.e.* the 144 permissible hours between Sundays in Victorian times) was 623¾ miles *1 003,828 km* by George Littlewood (England), who required only 141 hr 57 min 30 sec for this feat on 3–8 Dec. 1888 at the old Madison Square Gardens, New York City, U.S.A.

Greatest mileage

The greatest racing mileage is the 5,926 miles *9 537 km* in 192 races of marathon distance or more by Ted Corbitt (U.S.A.) (b. 31 Jan. 1920) from Apr. 1951 to end 1978.

The greatest life-time mileage recorded by any runner is 195,855 miles *315 198 km* by Earle Linwood Dilks (b. 20 Sept. 1894) of New Castle, Pennsylvania, U.S.A., up to end–1977.

Longest running race

The longest race ever staged was the 1929 Trans-continental Race (3,665 miles *5 898 km*) from New York City, N.Y., to Los Angeles, California, U.S.A. The Finnish-born Johnny Salo (1893–1931) was the winner in 79 days, from 31 March to 18 June. His elapsed time of 525 hr 57 min 20 sec (averaging 6.97 m.p.h. *11,21 km/h*) left him only 2 min 47 sec ahead of Englishman Pietro (Peter) Gavuzzi (b. Kent, 28 Sept. 1905).

Oldest race

The oldest continuously held foot race is the "Red Hose Race" held at Carnwath, Lanarkshire, Scotland since 1507. The prize is a pair of hand-knitted knee length red hose.

24 hour record

The greatest distance run on a standard track in 24 hr is 161 miles 545 yd *259,60 km* by Ron Bentley (b. 10 Nov. 1930) at Walton-on-Thames, Surrey, on 3–4 Nov. 1973. The best distance by a 19th century "wobbler" was 150 miles 395 yd *241 762 km* by Charles Rowell (G.B.) (1853–1909) in 22 hr 28 min 25 sec in New York City on 27 Feb. 1882.

Fastest 100 miles

On 15 Oct. 1977 Donald A. Ritchie (b. 6 July 1944) (Birchfield H.) ran 100 miles *160,9 km* in a record 11 hr 30 min 51 sec at Crystal Palace, Greater London, England. The best by a woman is 16 hr 50 min 47 sec by Ruth Anderson (b. 1929) at Woodside, Cal., U.S.A. on 15–16 June 1978.

Mass relay records

The record for 100 miles *160,9 km* by 100 runners belonging to one club is 7 hr 56 min 55.6 sec by Shore A.C., New Jersey, U.S.A., on 5 June 1977. The feminine record is held by a team from San Francisco Dolphins Southend Running Club, U.S.A. with 10 hr 47 min 9.3 sec on 3 Apr. 1977. The best club time for a 100 × 400 metres relay is 1 hr 29 min 11.8 sec (average 53.5 sec) by the Physical Training Institute, Leuven, Belgium on 19 Apr. 1978.

A 13-man relay team from the Los Angeles Police Revolver and Athletic Club, California, U.S.A., started from the Capitol steps, Washington, D.C., on 10 May 1974, and ran 3,871.6 miles *6230,7 km* to the Los Angeles City Hall in 20 days 5 hr 20 min.

The longest relay ever run, and that with the most participants, was by 1,607 students and teachers who covered 6,014.65 miles *9 679,645 km* at Trondheim, Norway, 21 Oct.–23 Nov. 1977.

TRAMPOLINING

Origins

Trampolines were used in show business at least as early as "The Walloons" of the period 1910–12. The sport of trampolining (from the Spanish word *trampolin*, a springboard) dates from 1936, when the prototype "T" model trampoline was developed by George Nissen (U.S.A.).

Most titles

Four men have won a world title (instituted 1964) twice; Dave Jacobs (U.S.A.) in 1967–68, Wayne Miller (b. 1946) (U.S.A.), in 1966 and 1970, Richard Tison (France) in 1974 and 1976 (shared), and E. Janes (U.S.S.R.), 1976 (shared) and 1978. Judy Wills (b. 1948) (U.S.A.) won the first five women's titles (1964–68). Two European titles (1969 and 1971) have been won by Paul Luxon (b. 1952) (G.B.), the 1972 world champion. A record seven United Kingdom titles have been won by Wendy Wright (1969–70, 1972–75, 1977). The most by a man have been four, by David Curtis (1966–67, 1969, 1975) and Stewart Matthews (1976–79).

Marathons

The longest trampoline bouncing marathon is one of 1,248 hours (52 days) set by a team of six in Phoenix, Arizona, U.S.A. on 24 June to 15 Aug. 1974. The solo record is 179 hours by Geoffrey Morton, of Broken Hill, N.S.W., Australia, on 7–14 Mar. 1977.

One world and two European titles are among the many championships won by British trampolinist, Paul Luxon

TUG OF WAR

Origins
Though ancient China and Egypt have been suggested as the originators of the sport, it is known that neolithic flint miners in Norfolk, England practiced "rope-pulling". The first rules were those framed by the New York A.C. in 1879. In 1958 the Tug-of-War Association was formed to administer Britain's 600 clubs.

Most Olympic medals
An Olympic event from 1908 to 1920, three men won two gold medals (1908 and 1920) (all also won a silver medal in 1912)—John James Shepherd (1884–1954) Frederick H. Humphreys (1878–1954) and Edwin A. Mills (1878–1946) (all G.B.).

Most titles
The Wood Treatment team (formerly the Bosley Farmers) of Cheshire, have represented England since 1964, winning two World and ten European Championships at 720 kg *1,587 lb*. They have also won 20 consecutive A.A.A. Catchweight Championships 1959–78. Hilary Brown has been in every team. Trevor Brian Thomas (b. 1943), of British Aircraft Corporation Club is the only holder of three winners medals in the European Open club championships.

Longest pulls
The longest recorded pull (prior to the introduction of A.A.A. rules) is one of 2 hrs 41 min between "H" Company and "E" Company of the 2nd Battalion of the Sherwood Foresters (Derbyshire Regiment) at Jubbulpore, India, on 12 Aug. 1889. "H" Company won. The longest recorded pull under A.A.A. Rules (in which lying on the ground or entrenching the feet is not permitted) is one of 11 min 23 sec for the first pull between the Isle of Oxney and St. Claret's at Chertsey, Surrey on 26 May 1979. The record time for "The Pull" (inst. 1898), across the Black River, between freshman and sophomore teams at Hope College, Holland, Mich., U.S.A., is 3 hr. 51 min on 23 Sept. 1977, but the method of bracing the feet precludes the replacing of the preceding records.

VOLLEYBALL

Origins
The game was invented as *Minnonette* in 1895 by William G. Morgan at the Y.M.C.A. gymnasium at Holyoke, Massachusetts, U.S.A. The International Volleyball Association was formed in Paris in April 1947. The Amateur (now English) Volleyball Association of Great Britain was formed in May 1955.

Most world titles
World Championships were instituted in 1949. The U.S.S.R. has won five men's titles (1949, 1952, 1960, 1962 and 1978). The U.S.S.R. won the women's championship in 1952, 1956, 1960 and 1970.

Most Olympic medals
The sport was introduced to the Olympic Games for both men and women in 1964. The only player to win four medals is Inna Ryskal (U.S.S.R.) (b. 15 June 1944), who won silver medals in 1964 and 1976 and golds in 1968 and 1972. The record for men is held by Yuriy Poyarkov (U.S.S.R.) (b. 10 Feb. 1937) who won gold medals in 1964 and 1968 and a bronze in 1972.

Highest attendance
The record crowd is 60,000 for the 1952 world title matches in Moscow, U.S.S.R.

Marathon
The record by two teams of six is 70 hr 33 min by the 2nd Military Hospital at Ingleburn, N.S.W., Aust. on 4–7 May 1979.

WALKING

Most Olympic medals
Walking races have been included in the Olympic events since 1906 but walking matches have been known since 1589. The only walker to win three gold medals has been Ugo Frigerio (Italy) (1901–68) with the 3,000 m and 10,000 m in 1920 and 1924. He also holds the record of most medals with four (having additionally won the bronze medal in the 50,000 m in 1932) which total is shared with Vladimir Golubnichiy (U.S.S.R.) (b. 2 June 1936), who won gold medals for the 20,000 m in 1960 and 1968, the silver in 1972 and the bronze in 1964.

The best British performance has been two gold medals by George Edward Larner (1875–1949) for the 3,500 m and the 10 miles in 1908, but Ernest J. Webb (1872–1937) won three medals being twice "walker up" to Larner and finishing second in the 10,000 m in 1912.

Most titles
Four time Olympian, Ronald Owen Laird (b. 31 May 1938) of the New York A.C., U.S.A., won a total of 65 National titles from 1958 to 1976, plus four Canadian championships. The greatest number of U.K. National titles won by a British walker is 27 by Vincent Paul Nihill M.B.E. (b. 5 Sept. 1939) from 1963 to 1975.

Road walking
The world's best performances for road walking are: 20,000 m 1 hr 22 min 16 sec by Daniel Bautista (b. 4 Aug. 1952) (Mexico) at Valencia, Spain on 19 May 1979; and 50,000 m 3 hrs 41 min 19.2 sec by Raul Gonzalez (b. 29 Feb. 1952) (Mexico) at Podebrady, Czechoslovakia on 11 June 1978.

Walking backwards
The greatest ever exponent of reverse pedestrianism has been Plennie L. Wingo (b. 24 Jan. 1895) then of Abilene, Texas,

---

OFFICIAL WORLD RECORDS (Track Walking)
(As recognised by the International Amateur Athletic Federation)

Distance	Time hr min sec	Name and Country	Place	Date
20,000 metres	1 20 58.6	Domingo Colin (Mexico)	Fana, Norway	26 May 1979
30,000 metres	2 08 00.0	Jose Marin (Spain)	Barcelona, Spain	8 Apr. 1979
50,000 metres	3 41 39.0	Raul Gonzalez (Mexico)	Fana, Norway	8 Apr. 1979
2 hours	28 165 m *17 miles 881 yd*	Jose Marin (Spain)	Barcelona, Spain	25 May 1979

UNITED KINGDOM RECORDS (Track Walking)

Distance	Time hr min sec	Name and Country	Place	Date
20,000 metres	1 28 46	Kenneth Matthews, MBE	Walton	6 June 1964
30,000 metres	2 24 19	Roy Thorpe	Hamburg, West Germany	25 May 1974
50,000 metres	4 11 22	Robert Dobson	Paris, France	10 Aug. 1974
2 hours	26 037 m *16 miles 314 yd*	Ronald Wallwork,	Stretford	31 July 1971

Top left: Britain's Daley Thompson, has his eyes on the Olympic title and the world record. (*Tony Duffy, All-Sport Photographic*)

Top right: In thirty days, Britain's Sebastian Coe set three records. (*Tony Duffy, All-Sport Photographic*)

Centre: Two of the greatest female sprinters the world has known, Irena Szewinska (Poland) (*left*) and her successor, Marita Koch (East Germany). (*Tony Duffy, All-Sport Photographic*)

Bottom left: Vladimir Yashchenko set the world high jump record using the "old fashioned" straddle style. (*Tony Duffy, All-Sport Photographic*)

Bottom right: Grete Waitz (No. 5) of Norway, with Christine Benning (G.B. No. 2). (*Tony Duffy, All-Sport Photographic*)

William Baker's record London to Brighton and back walk represents over 100 miles at an average of 5.8 miles per hour.

1904, but the first verified achievement was by David Kunst, of Waseca, Minnesota from 10 June 1970 to 5 Oct. 1974. Tomas Carlos Pereira (b. Argentine, 16 Nov. 1942) spent ten years, 6 Apr. 1968–8 Apr. 1978, walking 29,825 miles *48,000 km* around all five continents. Georgyi Bushuyev (b. 1924) walked 6,800 miles *10 940 km* from Riga, Latvia to Vladivostok, U.S.S.R., in 238 days in 1973–74. The Trans-Canada (Halifax to Vancouver) record walk of 3,764 miles *6 057 km* is 96 days by Clyde McRae, 23, from 1 May to 4 Aug. 1973. John Lees, (b. 23 Feb. 1945) of Brighton, East Sussex, England between 11 Apr. and 3 June 1972, walked 2,876 miles *4 628 km* across the U.S.A. from City Hall, Los Angeles to City Hall, New York City in 53 days 12 hr 15 min (average 53.746 miles *86,495 km* a day). The longest continuous walk in Britain is one of 6,824 miles *10 982 km*, around the British coast by John N. Merrill, from 3 Jan. to 8 Nov. 1978.

"End to end"

The reported time to walk from John o'Groats to Land's End (route varies between 876 and 891 miles *1 409 and 1 433 km*) is 10 days 23 hrs 53 min by Malcolm Taylor of Milnsbridge, Huddersfield, Yorkshire on 28 July–7 Aug. 1973. The feminine record is 17 days 7 hours by Miss Wendy Lewis ending on 15 Mar. 1960. End to end and back has twice been achieved. Frederick E. Westcott, aged 31, finished on 18 Dec. 1966 and David Tremayne (Australia), aged 27, finishing on 28 May 1971. The Irish "End to End" record over the 376 miles *605 km* from Mizen Head, Cork to Malin Head, Donegal is 7 days 16 hr 34 min, set by Roy Dickson on 2–9 June 1979.

London to Brighton

The record time for the 53 miles *85 km* walk is 7 hr 35 min 12 sec by Donald James Thompson, M.B.E. (b. 20 Jan. 1933) on 14 Sept. 1957. The record time to Brighton and back is 18 hr 5 min 51 sec by William Frederick Baker (b. 5 Apr. 1889) on 18–19 June 1926. Richard Esmond Green (b. 22 Apr. 1924) has completed the course a record 43 times from 1950 to 1978.

Longest non-stop walk

Fred Jago (b. 1935) (G.B.) walked 317.155 miles *510,411 km* at Vivary Park, Taunton, Somerset, England in 148 hr 31 min on 13–16 July 1979. He did not permit himself any stops for resting and was moving 98.3% of the time.

24 hours

The best performance for distance walked in 24 hours is 142 miles 448 yd *228,93 km* by Jesse Castañeda (U.S.A.) at the New Mexico State Fair, Albuquerque, N.M., U.S.A., on 18–19 Sept. 1976. The best by a woman is 187,7 km *116.6 miles* by Ann Sayer (G.B.) at Rouen, France on 28–29 Apr. 1979.

who completed his 8,000 mile *12,875 km* trans-continental walk from Santa Monica, California to Istanbul, Turkey, from 15 Apr. 1931 to 24 Oct. 1932. The longest distance recorded for walking backwards in 24 hours is 80.5 miles *129,55 km* by Veikko Matias (b. 23 Apr. 1941) of Kangasala, Finland, at Kankaapää Airfield, Niinisalo, Finland on 7–8 Oct. 1978.

Longest annual race

The Strasbourg–Paris event (inst. 1926 in the reverse direction) over 504–554 km *313–344 miles* is the world's longest annual race walk. The fastest performance is by Robert Rinchard (Belgium) (b. 29 May 1931) who walked 523 km *325 miles* in the 1974 race in 63 hrs 29 min (deducting 4 hrs compulsory stops). This represents an average speed of 8.24 km/h *5.12 m.p.h.* Gilbert Roger (France) (b. 1914) won six times (1949, 1953–54, 1956–1958). The only Briton to have completed the course is Colin Young (b. 20 Jan. 1935) (Essex Beagles) in 1971 averaging 7.46 km/h *4.63 m.p.h.*, covering 520 km *323.1 miles* in 73 hr 38 min.

Greatest mileage

Dimitru Dan (b. 13 July 1890 *fl* 1976) of Romania was the only man of 200 entrants to succeed in a contest in walking 100,000 km *62,137 miles* organised by the Touring Club de France on 1 Apr. 1910. He covered 96,000 km *59,651 miles* up to 24 Mar. 1916 so averaging 43,85 km *27.24 miles* a day.

Longest walks

The first person reported to have "walked round the world" is George Matthew Schilling (U.S.A.) from 3 Aug 1897–

WATER POLO

Origins

Water Polo was developed in England as "Water Soccer" in 1869 and first included in the Olympic Games in Paris in 1900.

Most Olympic titles

Hungary has won the Olympic tournament most often with six wins in 1932, 1936, 1952, 1956, 1964 and 1976. Great Britain won in 1900, 1908, 1912 and 1920.

Five players share the record of three gold medals: Britons, George Wilkinson (1879–1946) in 1900, 1908, 1912; Paulo (Paul) Radmilovic (1886–1968), and Charles Sidney Smith (1879–1951) in 1908, 1912, 1920; and Hungarians Deszo Gyarmati (b. 23 Oct. 1927) and György Kárpáti (b. 23 June 1935) in 1952, 1956, 1964. Gyarmati's wife and daughter won gold and silver medals respectively in swimming. Paul Radmilovic also won a gold medal for the 4 × 200 m freestyle relay in 1908.

A.S.A. championships

The greatest number of Amateur Swimming Association titles is eleven, by Plaistow United S.C. from 1928 to 1954 and London Polytechnic from 1956 to 1978. The National League (formed 1963) has been won a record nine times by London Polytechnic.

Most goals
The greatest number of goals scored by an individual in a home international is eleven by Terry Charles Miller (b. 2 Mar. 1932) (Plaistow United), when England defeated Wales 13–3 at Newport, Gwent, in 1951.

Most international appearances
The greatest number of internationals is 244 by Ozren Bonacic (b. 5 Jan. 1942) (Yugoslavia) from 1964 to Sept. 1975. The British record is 126 by Martyn Thomas, of Cheltenham, 1964–1978.

Marathon
The longest match on record is one of 67 hr 36 min between two teams of 15 from the Townsville Amateur Water Polo Assn, Qld., Aust. on 1–4 Dec. 1978.

WATER SKIING

A specialist volume entitled The Guinness Guide to Water Skiing *by David Nations, O.B.E. and Kevin Desmond has been published by Guinness Superlatives Ltd. (price £8.50).*

Origins
The origins of water skiing lie in walking on planks and aquaplaning. A 19th century treatise on sorcerers refers to Eliseo of Tarentum who, in the 14th century, "walks and dances" on the water. The first report of aquaplaning was on America's Pacific coast in the early 1900's. At Scarborough, Yorks, England, on 15 July 1914, a single plank-gliding contest was won by H. Storry.

The present day sport of water skiing was pioneered by Ralph W. Samuelson (1904–77) on Lake Pepin, Minnesota, U.S.A., on two curved pine boards in the summer of 1922, though claims have been made for the birth of the sport on Lake Annecy (Haute Savoie), France at about the same time. The first world organisation, the Union Internationale de Ski Nautique, was formed in Geneva on 27 July 1946. The British Water Ski Federation was founded in London in 1954.

Most titles
World Overall championships (instituted 1949) have been won twice by Alfredo Mendoza (U.S.A.) in 1953 and 1955, Mike Suyderhoud (U.S.A.) in 1967 and 1969 and George Athans (Canada) in 1971 and 1973, and three times by Willa McGuire (*née* Worthington) of the U.S.A. in 1949–50 and 1955 and Elizabeth (Liz) Allan-Shetter (U.S.A.) in 1965, 1969 and 1975. Liz Allan-Shetter has won a record eight individual championship events. The most British Overall titles (instituted 1953) ever won by a man is five by Michael Hazelwood M.B.E. (b. Lincolnshire 14 Apr. 1958) in 1974, 1976–79; the most by a woman is seven by Karen Jane Morse (b. 1956) in 1971–76 and 1978.

Jumping
The first recorded jump on water skis was made by Ralph Samuelson off a greased ramp, on Lake Pepin in 1925. The longest jump ever recorded is one of 55,18 m *181 ft* by Sammy Duvall, (U.S.A.) at Callaway Gardens, Georgia, U.S.A. on 15 July 1979. The women's record is 39.02 m *128 ft* by Linda Giddens (U.S.A.) in Miami, Florida, U.S.A. on 22 Aug. 1976.

The British record is 54,70 m *179 ft 5 in* by Mike Hazelwood M.B.E. at Nancy, France in September 1976. The women's record is 37,75 m *123 ft 10 in* by Karen Morse at Thorpe Water Park, Surrey on 28 July 1979.

Slalom and Tricks
The world record for slalom is 4 buoys on a 11,25 m *37 ft* line by Kris LaPoint (U.S.A.) at Horton Lake, U.S.A., on 15 July 1975, and Bob LaPoint (U.S.A.), his brother, at Miami in Aug. 1976. The record for women is 3 buoys on a 12 m *39 ft* line by Cindy Hutcherson Todd (U.S.A.) at Groveland, Fla., 16 July 1977. The tricks record is 7,840

points by Cory Pickos (U.S.A.) at Lakeland, Florida, U.S.A. on 6 May 1979. The women's record is 5,880 points by Maria Victoria Carrasco (Venezuela), also at Lakeland on 6 May 1979. The British record for tricks is 6,870 points by Mike Hazelwood at Moomba, Australia on 12 Mar. 1978.

Highest speed
The water skiing speed record is 202,27 km/h *125.69 m.p.h.* by Danny Churchill at the Oakland Marine Stadium, California, U.S.A. in 1971. A claim of 216,18 km/h *134.33 m.p.h.* by Grant Torrens (Australia) in February 1978 is awaiting ratification. Donna Patterson Brice (b. 1953), set a feminine record of 178,81 km/h *111.11 m.p.h.* at Long Beach, California on 21 Aug. 1977. The fastest recorded speed by a British skier over a measured kilometre is 131,217 km/h *81.535 m.p.h.* (average) on Lake Windermere, Cumbria on 18 Oct. 1973 by Billy Rixon. The fastest by a British woman is 111,80 km/h *69.47 m.p.h.* by Elizabeth Hobbs on Windermere, 19 Oct. 1979.

Longest run
The greatest distance travelled non-stop is 1 809 km *1,124 miles* by Will Coughey, of New Zealand, on Lake Karapiro, N.Z., in 30 hr 34 min on 26–27 Feb. 1977.

Barefoot
The first person to water ski barefoot is reported to be Dick Pope Jr. at Lake Eloise, Florida, on 6 Mar. 1947. The barefoot duration record is 2 hr 42 min 39 sec by Billy Nichols (U.S.A.) (b. 1964) on Lake Weir, Florida, on 19 Nov. 1978. The backward barefoot record is 39 min by Paul McManus (Aust.). The British duration record is 67 min 5 sec by John Doherty on 1 October 1974. The official barefoot speed record (two runs) is 177,06 km/h *110.02 m.p.h.* by Lee Kirk (U.S.A.) at Firebird Lake, Phoenix, Ariz. on 11 June 1977. His fastest run was 182,93 km/h *113.67 m.p.h.* The fastest by a woman is 98.79 km/h *61,39 m.p.h.* by Haidee Jones (now Lance) (Australia). Richard Mainwaring (G.B.) reached 114,86 km/h *71.37 m.p.h.* at Holme Pierrepoint, Nottinghamshire on 2 Dec. 1978.

The best officially recorded barefoot jump is 15,85 m *52 ft* by Keith Donnelly at Baronscourt, N. Ireland on 9 July 1978. This is also the current British record.

WEIGHTLIFTING

Origins
Amateur weightlifting is of comparatively modern origin and the first "world" championship was staged at the Cafe Monico, Piccadilly, City of Westminster, Greater London, on 28 Mar. 1891. Prior to that time, weightlifting consisted of

Russia's Yurik Vardanyan won the 1977 world middleweight lifting title, then moved up to light-heavyweight, winning that world title and setting world records. (*Novosti Press Agency*)

professional exhibitions in which some of the advertised poundages were open to doubt. The first to raise 400 lb. *181 kg* was Karl Swoboda (1882–1933) (Austria), in Vienna, with 401¼ lb. *182 kg* in 1910, using the Continental clean and jerk style.

Most Olympic Medals

The winner of most Olympic medals is Norbert Schemansky (U.S.A.) (b. 30 May 1924) with four: Gold, middle-heavyweight 1952; Silver, heavyweight 1948; Bronze, heavyweight 1960 and 1964. Schemansky achieved a world record—the heavyweight snatch at 361½ lb. *163,75 kg* on 28 Apr. 1962 at Detroit—at the record age of 37 years and 10 months.

Most successful British lifter

The only British lifter to win an Olympic title has been Launceston Elliot (1874–1930), the open one-handed lift champion in 1896 at Athens.

Louis George Martin, M.B.E. (b. Jamaica, 11 Nov. 1936) won four World and European mid-heavyweight titles in 1959, 1962–63, 1965. He won an Olympic silver medal in 1964 and a bronze in 1960 and also three Commonwealth gold medals in 1962, 1966, 1970. His total of British titles was 12.

Greatest lift

The greatest weight ever raised by a human being is 6,270 lb. *2 844 kg* (2.80 tons *2,84 tonnes*) in a back lift (weight raised off trestles) by the 26 st. *165 kg* Paul Anderson (U.S.A.) (b. 17 Oct. 1932), the 1956 Olympic heavyweight champion, at Toccoa, Georgia, U.S.A., on 12 June 1957. The greatest lift by a woman is 3,564 lb. *1 616 kg* with a hip and harness lift by Josephine Blatt (*née* Schauer) (1869–1923) at the Bijou Theatre, Hoboken, New Jersey, U.S.A., on 15 Apr. 1895.

Greatest overhead lifts

The greatest overhead lifts made from the ground are the clean and jerks achieved by super-heavyweights which now exceed 5 cwt (560 lb.) *254 kg*. The greatest overhead lift ever made by a woman is 286 lb. *129 kg* in a continental jerk by Katie Sandwina (*née* Brummbach, later Mrs. Max Heymann) (1884–1952) of Germany, in *c.* 1911. She stood 5 ft 11 in *1,80 m* tall, weighed 210 lb. *95 kg* (15 st.) and is

WORLD WEIGHTLIFTING RECORDS (as at 24 Aug. 1979)

Bodyweight Class	Lift	Lifted kg	Lifted lb	Name and Country	Place	Date
Flyweight	Snatch	111	*244½*	Han Sen-bi (N. Korea)	Leningrad, U.S.S.R.	25 July 1979
(*52 kg* 114½ lb.)	Jerk	142	*313*	Alexander Voronin (U.S.S.R.)	Varna, Bulgaria	19 May 1979
	Total	247,5	*545½*	Alexander Voronin (U.S.S.R.)	Stuttgart, West Germany	17 Sept. 1977
Bantamweight	Snatch	121,5	*267¾*	Anton Kodiabashev (Bulgaria)	Sofia, Bulgaria	8 July 1979
(*56 kg* 123¼ lb.)	Jerk	152	*335*	Anton Kodiabashev (Bulgaria)	Sofia, Bulgaria	8 July 1979
	Total	265	*584¼*	Anton Kodiabashev (Bulgaria)	Sofia. Bulgaria	8 July 1979
Featherweight	Snatch	130	*286½*	Gyorgyi Todorov (Bulgaria)	Sofia, Bulgaria	25 May 1976
(*60 kg* 132¼ lb)	Jerk	166	*365¾*	Nikolai Kolesnikov (U.S.S.R.)	Varna, Bulgaria	21 May 1979
	Total	292,5	*644¾*	Nikolai Kolesnikov (U.S.S.R.)	Varna, Bulgaria	21 May 1979
Lightweight	Snatch	147	*324*	Yanko Rusev (Bulgaria)	Sofia, Bulgaria	10 July 1979
(*67,5 kg* 148¾ lb.)	Jerk	186	*410*	Gyorgyi Todorov (Bulgaria)	Leningrad, U.S.S.R.	29 July 1979
	Total	325	*716½*	Yanko Rusev (Bulgaria)	Sofia, Bulgaria	10 July 1979
Middleweight	Snatch	157,5	*347*	Yurik Vardanyan (U.S.S.R.)	Rostov, U.S.S.R.	7 May 1977
(*75 kg* 165¼ lb.)	Jerk	196,5	*433*	Alexander Logoutov (U.S.S.R.)	Simferopol, U.S.S.R.	16 Nov. 1978
	Total	347,5	*766*	Yurik Vardanyan (U.S.S.R.)	Rostov U.S.S.R.	7 May 1977
Light-heavyweight	Snatch	175,5	*386¾*	Yurik Vardanyan (U.S.S.R.)	Leningrad, U.S.S.R.	30 July 1979
(*82,5 kg* 181¾ lb.)	Jerk	212	*473¾*	Yurik Vardanyan (U.S.S.R.)	Leningrad, U.S.S.R.	30 July 1979
	Total	390	*859¾*	Yurik Vardanyan (U.S.S.R.)	Leningrad, U.S.S.R.	30 July 1979
Middle-heavyweight	Snatch	180,5	*398*	David Rigert (U.S.S.R.)	Havirov, Czechoslovakia	16 June 1978
(*90 kg* 198¼)	Jerk	222,5	*490½*	Rolf Milser (West Germany)	Varna, Bulgaria	25 May 1979
	Total	400	*881¾*	David Rigert (U.S.S.R.)	Karaganda, U.S.S.R.	14 May 1976
(100 *kg 220½ lb.*)	Snatch	180	*396¾*	David Rigert (U.S.S.R.)	Varna, Bulgaria	26 May 1979
	Jerk	230	*507*	Viktor Kanonov (U.S.S.R.)	Lipetzk, U.S.S.R.	9 June 1979
	Total	402,5	*887¼*	David Rigert (U.S.S.R.)	Varna, Bulgaria	26 May 1979
Heavyweight	Snatch	185	*407¾*	Valentin Khristov (Bulgaria)	E. Berlin, East Germany	10 Apr. 1976
(*110 kg* 242½ lb.)	Jerk	237,5	*523½*	Valentin Khristov (Bulgaria)	Moscow, U.S.S.R.	22 Sept. 1975
	Total	417,5	*920¼*	Valentin Khristov (Bulgaria)	Moscow, U.S.S.R.	22 Sept. 1975
Super-heavyweight	Snatch	200,5	*442*	Sultan Rakhmanov (U.S.S.R.)	Kiev, U.S.S.R.	25 Apr. 1978
(Over 110 kg *242½ lb.*)	Jerk	256†	*564¼*	Vasili Alexeev (U.S.S.R.)	Moscow, U.S.S.R.	1 Nov. 1977
	Total	445	*981*	Vasili Alexeev (U.S.S.R.)	Moscow, U.S.S.R.	1 Sept. 1977

† *This was Alexeev's 80th world record* (*See p. 239*)

SELECTED POWER LIFTING RECORDS (as recognised by the International Power Lifting Federation), as at 1 July 1979

52 kg	Squat	217,5	*479½*	Chuck Dunbar (U.S.A.)	Honolulu, Hawaii	4 May 1979
	Bench Press	135	*297½*	Chuck Dunbar (U.S.A.)	Honolulu, Hawaii	4 May 1979
	Dead Lift	224,5	*494¾*	Hideaki Inaba (Japan)	Honolulu, Hawaii	10 Apr. 1979
	Total	552,5	*1,218*	Hideaki Inaba (Japan)	Turku, Finland	2 Feb. 1979
60 kg	Squat	242,5	*534½*	Eddie Pengelley (G.B.)	Birmingham, England	17 June 1979
	Bench Press	162,5	*358¼*	Yoshinobu Tominaga (Japan)	Tokyo, Japan	28 May 1978
	Dead Lift	282,5	*622¾*	Lamar Gant (U.S.A.)	Turku, Finland	3 Nov. 1978
	Total	645	*1,421¾*	Eddie Pengelley (G.B.)	Birmingham, England	17 June 1979
82,5 kg	Squat	332,5	*733*	Ron Collins (G.B.)	Birmingham, England	17 June 1979
	Bench Press	230,5	*508*	Mike McDonald (U.S.A.)	Oklahoma City, U.S.A.	30 Sept. 1978
	Dead Lift	340	*749½*	Vince Anello (U.S.A.)	Bedford, Ohio, U.S.A.	16 Dec. 1973
	Total	842,5	*1,857¼*	Ron Collins (G.B.)	Birmingham, England	12 June 1977
Over 110 kg	Squat	422,5	*931¼*	Don Reinhoudt (U.S.A.)	Findlay, Ohio, U.S.A.	15 Apr. 1976
	Bench Press	277,5	*611¼*	Doug Young (U.S.A.)	Arlington, Texas, U.S.A.	4 Mar. 1978
	Dead Lift	400	*881¾*	Don Reinhoudt (U.S.A.)	Chattanooga, Tenn., U.S.A.	3 May 1975
	Total	1097,5	*2,419½*	Don Reinhoudt (U.S.A.)	Chattanooga, Tenn., U.S.A.	3 May 1975

Jim Mills, the Derbyshire traffic warden, setting the world cue levering record using the traditional grip.

reputed to have unofficially lifted 312½ lb. *141,747 kg* and to have shouldered a cannon, which allegedly weighed 1,200 lb. *544 kg*.

Greatest power lifts

Paul Anderson, as a professional, has bench-pressed 627 lb. *284 kg* and has achieved 1,200 lb. *544 kg* in a squat so aggregating, with an 820 lb. *371 kg* dead lift, a career total of 2,647 lb. *1 200 kg*. Ronald Collins (G.B.) with 1,655 lb. *750,5 kg* at Liverpool on 15 Dec. 1973, weighing 165 lb. *74,8 kg*, became the first man to lift a total ten times his own bodyweight. Nine other lifters have since achieved this but only Collins has repeated in more than one weight division. The newly instituted two-man deadlift record was raised to 1,439 lb. *652½ kg* by Clay and Doug Patterson in El Dorado, Arkansas, U.S.A., on 3 Mar. 1979.

Hermann Görner (1891–1956) (Germany) performed a one-handed dead lift of 734½ lb. *333,1 kg* in Dresden on 20 July 1920. Peter B. Cortese (U.S.A.) achieved a one-armed dead lift of 370 lb. *167 kg i.e.* 22 lb. *9,9 kg* over triple his bodyweight at York, Pennsylvania on 4 Sept. 1954. Görner also raised 24 men weighing 4,123 lb. *1 870 kg* on a plank on the soles of his feet in London on 12 Oct. 1927 and carried on his back a 1,444 lb. *654 kg* piano for 52½ ft *16 m* at Leipzig on 3 June 1921.

The highest competitive two-handed dead lift by a woman is 463 lb. *210 kg* by Jan Suffolk Todd (b. 22 May 1952) (U.S.A.) at Honolulu, Hawaii on 4 May 1979. She also holds the three-lift record total of 1,125 lb. *510,29 kg* set at Stephenville Crossing, Newfoundland, Canada, on 24 June 1978.

A deadlifting record of 2,100,000 lb. *952 543 kg* in 24 hr was set by a 10-man team from the Darwen Weightlifting Club, Lancs. on 19 Aug. 1978.

Cue Levering

Traffic warden Jim Mills (b. 24 May 1923) levered eight 16 oz *453 g* billiard cues simultaneously by their tips through 90 degrees to the horizontal, at Alfreton Police Station, Derbyshire, England on 9 June 1979. On 3 Aug. 1979 he went on to lever a 22 oz *623 gr* cue 564 times consecutively at Alfreton Police Station, by the same method.

Strandpulling

The International Steel Strandpullers' Association was founded by Gavin Pearson (Scotland) in 1940. The greatest ratified poundage to date is a super-heavyweight right arm push of 815 lb. *369,5 kg* by Malcolm Bartlett, of Oldham, Lancashire. The record for the Back Press Anyhow is 645 lb. *292,5 kg* by Barry Anderson, of Leeds, in 1975.

Oldest and Youngest

Harry Sawyer (Ashford Common) set a world 12 stone dislocation record of 353 lb *160 kg* in 1972 aged 52 and David

Hoar (Ossett, West Yorkshire) set a world 11 stone right arm push record of 601 lb *272,5 kg* aged 17.

WRESTLING

Origins

The earliest depictions of wrestling holds and falls on the walls of the tomb of Ptahhotep (5th Dynasty) indicate that organised wrestling dates from before *c.* 2350 B.C. It was the most popular sport in the ancient Olympic Games and victors were recorded from 708 B.C. The Greco-Roman style is of French origin and arose about 1860. The International Amateur Wrestling Federation (F.I.L.A.) was founded in 1912.

Most titles *Olympic*

Three wrestlers have won three Olympic titles: Carl Westergren (1895–1958) (Sweden) in 1920, 1924, 1932; Ivar Johansson (b. 31 Jan. 1903) (Sweden) in 1932 (two), 1936; and Aleksandr Medved (b. 16 Sept. 1937) (U.S.S.R.) in 1964, 1968, 1972.

The only wrestler with more medals is Imre Polyák (Hungary) (b. 16 Apr. 1932) who won the silver medal for the Greco-Roman featherweight class in 1952, 1956, 1960 and the gold in 1964.

Most titles *World*

The greatest number of world championships won by a wrestler is ten by the freestyler Aleksandr Medved (U.S.S.R.) (b. 16 Sept. 1937) with the light-heavyweight titles in 1964 (Olympic) and 1966, the heavyweight 1967 and 1968 (Olympic), and the super-heavyweight in 1969–72 (Olympic). The only wrestler to win the same title in six successive years has been Abdollah Movahed (Iran) (b. 10 Mar. 1940) in the lightweight division in 1965–70. The record for successive Greco-Roman titles is five by Roman Rurua (U.S.S.R.) (b. 25 Nov. 1942) with the featherweight 1966–68 (Olympic), 1969 and 1970.

Most titles *British*

The most British titles won is ten by heavyweight Kenneth Alan Richmond (b. 10 July 1926) between 1949 and 1960.

Longest span

The longest span for B.A.W.A. titles is 24 years by George Mackenzie (1890–1957) who won his first in 1909 and his last in 1933. Mackenzie represented Great Britain in five successive Olympiads from 1908 to 1928.

Most wins

In international competition, Osamu Watanabe (b. 21 Oct. 1940), of Japan, the 1964 Olympic freestyle featherweight champion, was unbeaten and unscored-upon in 187 consecutive matches. Wade Schalles (U.S.A.) has won 615 bouts from 1964 to end–1977.

Longest bout

The longest recorded bout was one of 11 hr 40 min between Martin Klein (1885–1947) (Estonia representing Russia) and Alfred Asikáinen (1888–1942) (Finland) for the Greco-Roman middleweight "A" event silver medal in the 1912 Olympic Games in Stockholm, Sweden. It was won by Klein.

Heaviest heavyweight

The heaviest wrestler in Olympic history is Chris Taylor (1950–79), bronze medallist in the super-heavyweight class in 1972, who stood 6 ft 5 in *1,96 m* and weighed over 420 lb. *190 kg*. The record for a British heavyweight champion is held by Archibald (Archie) Dudgeon (1914–73) (Scotland), who won the 1936 and 1937 B.A.W.A. heavyweight titles at 6 ft 2 in *1,88 m* and 308 lb. *139 kg*.

Cumberland and Westmoreland wrestling

The British amateur championships were established in 1904. The only six time champions have been J. Baddeley (middleweight in 1905–06, 1908–10, 1912) and E. A. Bacon (lightweight in 1919, 1921–23, 1928–29).

Professional wrestling

Professional wrestling dates from 1874 in the U.S.A. Georges Karl Julius Hackenschmidt (U.S.S.R.) (1877–1968), Estonian-born, was undefeated at Greco-Roman contests from 1900 to his retirement in 1911. (See also p. 105).

Sumo wrestling

The sport's origins in Japan certainly date from c. 23 B.C. The heaviest ever *sumotori* were probably Dewagatake, a wrestler of the 1920s who was 6 ft 7¾ in *2,03 m* tall and weighed up to 430 lb. *195 kg* and Odachi, of the 1950s, 6 ft 7½ in *2,02 m* who weighed about 441 lb. *200 kg*. Weight is amassed by over alimentation with a high protein stew called *chankonabe*. The tallest was probably Ozora, an early 19th century performer, who stood 7 ft 3 in *2,20 m* tall. The most successful wrestlers have been Totaro Koe *alias* Umegatani I who had the highest winning percentage among grand champions of .951 in the 1880s, Sadaji Akiyoshi (b. 1912) *alias* Futabayama, winner of 69 consecutive bouts in the 1930s, Koki Naya (b. 1940) *alias* Taiho ("Great Bird"), who won the Emperor's Cup 32 times up to his retirement in 1971 and the *ozeki* Torokichi *alias* Raiden who in 21 years (1789–1810) won 254 bouts and lost only ten. The youngest of the 56 men to attain the rank of *Yokozuna* (Grand Champion) was Toshimitsu Ogata (b. 16 May 1953) *alias* Kitanoumi, in July 1974 aged 21 years and two months. Jesse Kuhaulua (b. Hawaii, 16 June 1944) *alias* Takamiyama was the first non-Japanese to win an official tournament in July 1972.

YACHTING

The Guinness Book of Yachting Facts and Feats by Peter Johnson, published by Guinness Superlatives Ltd (price £4.95) provides more data on the sport.

Origins

Yachting in England dates from the £100 stake race between Charles II and his brother James, Duke of York, on the Thames on 1 Sept. 1661 over 23 miles from Greenwich to Gravesend. The earliest club is the Royal Cork Yacht Club (formerly the Cork Harbour Water Club), established in Ireland in 1720. The oldest yacht club in Britain which still is active is the Starcross Yacht Club at Powderham Point, Devon. Its first regatta was held in 1772. The word yacht is from the Dutch to hunt or chase.

Olympic titles *World*

The first sportsman ever to win individual gold medals in four successive Olympic Games was Paul B. Elvström (b. 24 Feb. 1928) (Denmark) in the Firefly class in 1948 and the Finn class in 1952, 1956 and 1960. He has also won eight other world titles in a total of six classes. The lowest number of penalty points by the winner of any class in an Olympic regatta is three points (five wins, one disqualified and one second in seven starts) by *Superdocius* of the Flying Dutchman class (Lt. Rodney Stuart Pattisson, M.B.E., R.N. (b. 5 Aug. 1943) and Iain Somerled Macdonald-Smith, M.B.E. (b. 3 July 1945)) at Acapulco Bay, Mexico in October 1968.

Olympic titles *British*

The only British yacht to win two titles was *Scotia* in the Open class and Half-One Ton class at the 1900 Regatta with Lorne C. Currie, helmsman and crewed by John H. Gretton (1867–1947) and Linton Hope (1863–1920). The only British yachtsman to win in two Olympic regattas is Rodney Pattisson in 1968 (see above) and again with *Superdoso* crewed by Christopher Davies (b. 29 June 1946) at Kiel, West Germany in 1972. He gained a silver medal in 1976 with Julian Brooke Houghton (b. 16 Dec. 1946).

Admiral's Cup

The ocean racing series to have attracted the largest number of participating nations (three boats allowed to each nation) is Admiral's Cup held by the Royal Ocean Racing Club in the English Channel in alternate years. A record 19 nations competed in 1975, 1977 and 1979. To 1979, Britain had won seven times, U.S.A. and Australia twice and West Germany once.

America's Cup

The America's Cup was originally won as an outright prize by the schooner *America* on 22 Aug. 1851 at Cowes and was later offered by the New York Yacht Club as a challenge trophy. On 8 Aug. 1870 J. Ashbury's *Cambria* (G.B.) failed to capture the trophy from the *Magic*, owned by F. Osgood (U.S.A.). Since then the Cup has been challenged by Great Britain in 15 contests, in 2 contests by Canada, and by Australia four times, but the United States have never been defeated. The closest race ever was the fourth race of the 1962 series, when the 12 metre sloop *Weatherly* beat her Australian challenger *Gretel* by about three and a half lengths, a margin of only 26 sec, on 22 Sept. 1962. The fastest time ever recorded by a 12 metre boat for the triangular course of 24 sea miles is 2 hr 46 min 58 sec by *Gretel* in 1962.

London to Sydney

The *Great Britain II*, a 77 ft 2 in *23,5 m* ketch manned by a British joint services crew, sailed from the Thames estuary to Sydney, Australia in 67 days 5 hr 19 min 49 sec from 31 Aug.–7 Nov. 1975, beating the previous record of the clipper *Patriarch* in 1870 by nearly two days. The return journey to Dover took only 66 days 22 hr 31 min 35 sec. The total round-the-world passage of up to 30,000 miles *42,280 km* was accomplished in a record time of 134 days 3 hr 51 min 24 sec. For other record passages see pp. 214–215.

24 Hour Dinghy Race

The greatest distance covered in the West Lancashire Y.C. 24 hr race is 140 nautical miles by an Enterprise from the Grimsby and Cleethorpes Yacht Club on 3–4 Sept. 1978. The Betio Boating Community sailed an Osprey, *Tamaroa*, 149 nautical miles at Tarawa, Gilbert Islands, on 24–25 Sept. 1977.

Highest speeds

The official world sailing speed record is 33.4 knots (38.46 m.p.h. *61,89 km/h*) by the 73½ ft *22,40 m* proa *Crossbow II* over a 500 m *547 yd* course in Portland Harbour, Dorset, on 4 Oct. 1977. The vessel (sail area 1,400 ft² *130,06 m²*) was designed by Rod McAlpine-Downie and owned and steered by Timothy Colman. In an unsuccessful attempt on the record in Oct. 1978, *Crossbow II* is reported to have momentarily attained a speed of 45 knots (51 m.p.h. *83 km/h*).

The fastest 24 hr single-handed run by a sailing yacht was recorded by Nick Keig (b. 13 June 1936), of the Isle of Man, who covered 340 nautical miles in a 37½ ft *11,43 m* trimaran *Three Legs of Mann I* during the Falmouth to Punta, Azores race on 9–10 June 1975, averaging 14.16 knots (16.30 m.p.h. *26,23 km/h*). The fastest bursts of speed reached were about 25 knots (28.78 m.p.h. *46,32 km/h*).

Most successful yacht

The most successful racing yacht in history was the Royal Yacht *Britannia* (1893–1935), owned by King Edward VII, when Prince of Wales and subsequently by King George V, which won 231 races in 625 starts.

Largest sail

The largest sail ever made was a parachute spinnaker with an area of 18,000 ft² *1 672 m²* (more than two-fifths of an acre *0,1 ha*) for Vanderbilt's *Ranger* in 1937.

Marinas, *Largest*

The largest marina in the world is that of Marina Del Rey, Los Angeles, California, U.S.A., which has 7,500 berths. The largest in Britain is the Brighton Marina, Sussex, with 2,313 berths.

Most competitors

The most competitors ever to start in a single race was 1,261 sailing boats in the Round Zealand (Denmark) race in June 1976, over a course of 375 km *233 miles*. The greatest number to start in a race in Britain was 742 keeled yachts and multi-hulls on 16 June 1979 from Cowes in the Annual Round-the-Island race.

Highest

The greatest altitude at which sailing has taken place is 16,109 ft *4 910 m* on Laguna Huallatani, Bolivia, in Mirror Dinghy 55448, variously by Peter Williams, Gordon Siddeley, Keith Robinson and Brian Barrett, on 19 Nov. 1977.

The world's fastest sailing craft, *Crossbow II*, which has attained a speed of over ten knots in excess of her official record. *(Alastair Black)*

STOP PRESS

CHAPTER 1

Tallest Giantess Living (page 10). In Dec. 1978 an unconfirmed height of 7 ft 6½ in *229,8 cm* was reported for a 17 year old girl named Hu Chun-Rhang living in Shashih, Hupeh province, central China. She is reportedly still growing.

Tallest Giants (page 10). In 1979 the circus giant Gabriel Monjane was credited with a new measurement of 2,65 m *8 ft 8⅓ in* by his promoters, but his true height is believed to be nearer 2,45 m *8 ft 0¾ in.*

Tallest giants England (page 10). Chris Greener was re-measured on 5 Aug. 1979 and found to be 7 ft 6¼ in *2,29 m.*

Heaviest Man World (page 12). Jon Brower Minnoch (b. 1941) of Bainbridge Island, Washington, was carried, immobile, into the University Hospital, Seattle on plywood planking in March 1978. Dr Robert Schwartz, the endocrinological consultant, estimated (from extrapolating his intake and elimination rates) that he weighed 1,400 lb *635 kg (100 stone)* and "probably more". By July 1979 he was down to 475 lb *215,4 kg* after nearly 16 months on a 1,200 calories per day diet.

Oldest Dwarf (page 12). Susanna Bokoyni celebrated her 100th birthday on 6 Apr. 1979 weighing 37 lb *16,78 kg* and standing 3 ft 4 in *1,01 m* at Merriam House Retirement Home in Newton, New Jersey.

Heaviest Twins (page 13). Billy McCrary died at Niagara Falls, Ontario, Canada on 13 July, 1979 aged 32 years after falling from his mini motorcycle.

Most living ascendants (page 17). Kurt Diekrager (b. 17 May 1978) of Winona, Minnesota, USA, had a full set of grandparents and great-grandparents and one great-great-grandmother, making fifteen direct ascendants.

Most Proximate Births and Shortest Pregnancies (page 17). Mrs Gloria Kuehn of Lemay, Missouri, USA gave birth to a daughter, Amy Elizabeth, on 9 June 1978 and a son, Gregory Charles, on 19 Jan. 1979, 224 days later.

The first ever photograph taken of a human on his proven 114th birthday. Mr. Izumi (see pages 15–16) now greets mere mortal mortals with word *Banzai* (long life).

The greatest number of places of π (page 20). Creighton Carvello of Cleveland, England memorised and recited pi to 15,186 places on 12 July 1979.

Longest Fasting (page 24). Andreas Mihavecz, 18, was put into a holding cell on 1 Apr. 1979 in a local government building in Hochst, Austria but was totally forgotten by the police. On 18 Apr. 1979 he was discovered close to death having had neither food nor water. He had been a passenger in a crashed car.

Most voracious fire eaters (page 24). On 15 Apr. 1979 at The Dolphin, Kingston-upon-Thames, Surrey, Darryl Hayden extinguished 2,509 torches of flame successively in his mouth in 1 hr 52 mins.

Longest Operation (page 25). James Boydston, 24, underwent arterial surgery for 47 hr on 15–17 June 1979 at the Veterans Administration Hospital, Des Moines, Iowa, USA.

CHAPTER 2

Largest Pet Litters (page 36). Gerbil-10-Rosemary Burdon, Selsdon, Surrey.

Birds—Highest Flying (page 38). On 9 Dec. 1967, 30 Whooper swans (*Cygnus c. cygnus*) flying in from Iceland were spotted by an airline pilot over the Outer Hebrides at an altitude of 27,000 ft *8 230 m.* The height was also confirmed by air traffic control in Northern Ireland after they had picked up the skein on radar.

Chicken Flying (page 38). The record distance flown by a chicken is 302 ft 8 in *92,25 m* by Lola B at the 8th Annual International Chicken Flying Contest in June 1979.

Picture Corrections (page 43) Heaviest Starfish. *Thromidia catalai* is a member of the genus *Thromidia* (anagram of *Mithrodia*). The Rhinoceros starfish are the smaller 5-armed specimens shown in the photograph. (*Elizabeth C. Pope*) Credit for the stonefish (*J. Kenfield*).

Largest Extinct Amphibian (page 50). For 11 m *36 ft* read 9 m *29.5 ft.*

Tallest Broadleaf Tree (page 52). For Euculyptus read Eucalyptus.

Main Table—Pear Footnote (page 53). A specimen weighing 1,405 kg *3.09 lb* was harvested on 10 May 1979 at Messrs K. & R. Yeomans, Arding, Armidale, NSW, Australia.

Main Table—Petunia (page 53). Ultimate height 8 ft 4 in *2,53 m.*

Largest Wreath (page 56). The largest wreath constructed was the wreath built by the Interflora Australian Unit Ltd, District 4 at Mt. Lawley, W. Australia in May 1979. It measured 13,37 m *43.8 ft* in diameter.

Earliest life form (page 58). Traces of yeast-like cells, *Isuasphaera,* from cherty layers of quartzite from S.W. Greenland dated to 3,800 million years ago were announced on 9 Aug. 1979.

CHAPTER 3

Highest Waterspout (page 62). The Spithead waterspout off Ryde, Isle of Wight of 21 Aug. 1878 was measured by sextant to be "about a mile" or *1600 m* in height.

Northernmost land (page 67). On 26 July 1978 Uffe Petersen of the Danish Geodetic Institute observed an as yet unnamed islet 30 m *100 ft* across, 1,36 km *1,487 yds* north of Kaffeklubben Ø off Pearyland, Greenland in Long 83° 40′ 32.5″ N. Lat 30° 40′ 10.1″ W.

CHAPTER 4

Progressive Rocket Altitude Records (page 74). Caption—9th line. For 9,500 m read 9 500 m.

Highest Pay Load (page 77). Skylab I fell to Earth on its 34,981 st orbit over the Western Australian coast on 11 July 1979 thus leaving Salyut 6 as the heaviest object in space.

Longest manned spaceflight (page 78). The longest time spent in space is 175 days, from 25 Feb. to 19 Aug. 1979 by Valeriy Ryumin, 40, and Vladimir Lyakhov, 38, on board the Salyut-Soyuz orbital research station.

Astronaut Oldest and Youngest (page 78). There have been 92 people in space from 12 Apr. 1961 to 1 Aug. 1979.

CHAPTER 5

Elements Most and Least Stable (page 80). 5th line: For three read four.

Most Expensive Perfume (page 80). The most expensive perfume in England is *Mille* by Jean Patou, retailing at £115.00 per oz.

Most Expensive Wine (page 81). A bottle of 1806 Château Lafite-Rothschild was bought by Charles F. Maras for $28,000 (*£14,000*) at the 11th annual Heublein Premiere National Auction of Rare Wines on 24 May 1979. There is allegedly only one other bottle surviving.

Most Expensive Spirits (page 81). 2nd line: For *Grande Fine Champagne Cognac 1811* read *Grand Armée Fine Champagne Cognac 1811.*

Miniature Bottles (page 81). Mrs Ivy Grant of Stonegate, Wadhurst, Sussex, has an unduplicated collection of 2,307 as at 1 Aug. 1979.

Precious Stone Records (page 83). Sapphire: A 63 000 carat (12,6 kg *27 lb 12¼ oz*) star sapphire was found near Mogok, Upper Burma in 1966.

Highest Prime Number (page 84). $2^{44497}-1$ was announced as a prime number on 30 May 1979 after a two month long run on a Cray One computer at the University of California's Lawrence Livermore Laboratory by Harry Nelson, 47 and David Slowinski, 25.

Time Measure Shortest (page 85). Penultimate line: Before "Light" insert, "In that time" . . .

CHAPTER 6

World's largest poster (page 87). A poster 800ft *243,8 m* long and 10ft *3,048 m* high was painted by 480 artists for the British Safety Council at South Bank, London, on 26–29 July 1979.

Painting Smallest (page 87). José M. Salas executed an "oil painting" with a diameter of 0.11 mm (1/231) *of an inch* in Apr.1979 in Orillia, Ontario, Canada. *No further claims for this category will be considered.*

Painting—Auction Price by a Woman Artist (page 88). For Pensylvania read Pennsylvania.

Commonest Family Name World (page 94). Last line. For 159 read 164.

Largest Publication (page 94). For £21,000 read £25,000.

Birthday Card—Most Parsimonious (page 96). For New Jersey read New York.

Best Sellers Fiction (page 98). Nicholas Monsarrat died on 8 Aug. 1979.

Libraries Largest World (page 98). The New York Public Library has 9,210,630 volumes, 10,993,975 manuscripts and 331,804 maps.

Crossword Largest (page 99). The world's largest published crossword is one compiled by Marvin Ryder of Aylmer, Ontario and published in the *Courier Press* of Wallaceberg, Ontario, Canada on 28 Mar. 1979. It contained 5,585 clues across and 5,358 down and covered 18.28 ft² *1,7 m²*.

Crossword Longest (page 99). A crossword based on the *Guinness Book of Records* published in 1979 by Onsworld Ltd. with over 1200 clues, measures 7 ft 2 in *2,18 m* in length.

Greatest Attendance Classical Concert (page 101). Arthur Fiedler died on 10 July 1979.

Most Gold Discs (pages 106–107). Paul McCartney's total of RIAA Gold record awards reached 60 with his "Back to the Egg" in August 1979.

Most Expensive Film Rights (page 108). For Andrea McCordle read Andrea McCardle.

Longest Radio Broadcasts (page 109). Add: David Carter of BBC Radio London broadcast for 48 hrs. 30 min. on 6–8 May 1979. Glynn Perkins of Radio Thamesmead, London, completed a 52-hr broadcast on 2–4 July 1979. Tony Richards broadcast for 101 hrs on Hospital Radio Crawley, Sussex, on 15–19 June 1979.

Largest TV Prizes (page 110). For El Dorado read Forrest City.

Highest TV Advertising Rates (page 110). For 1977 read 1979.

Smallest TV Set (page 110). Sinclair Radionics now manufacture in Great Britain a TV set weighing 20oz *567 g* with dimensions of 3½ × 2 × 7 in *8,9 × 5,08 × 17,7 mm*, a screen measuring 2 in *5,08 mm* and costing £99.95 + VAT.

Highest Paid TV Commercial (page 110). Brooke Shields (b. 31 May 1965) was reportedly paid $250,000 (*£125,000*) for one minute of film by a Japanese TV commercial film maker in 1979. Faye Dunaway was reported in May 1979 to have been paid $900,000 (*£450,000*) for uttering 6 words for a Japanese department store TV commercial.

CHAPTER 7

Largest Building demolished by Explosives (page 125). The largest building demolished by explosives has been the 21 storey Traymore Hotel, Atlantic City New Jersey, USA on 26 May 1972 by Controlled Demolition Inc of Towson, Maryland. This 600 room hotel had a cubic capacity of 6,405,500 ft³ *181 339,7 m³*. The tallest chimney ever demolished by explosives was the American Smelting and Refining Co Chimney at Crockett, California on 14 June 1973. It stood 605 ft 5 in *184,5 m* and was brought down by the same company.

Deepest drilling (page 128). A drilling 31,911 ft (6.04 miles) *9 726 m* deep on the Kola peninsula, USSR, was announced in July 1979. The intention is to persist to 10 500 m *34,450 ft*.

Oil Spill Greatest (page 128). The collision of the supertankers *Atlantic Empress* and *Aegean Captain* off Tobago on 19 July 1979 resulted in an oil spill of an estimated 236,000 tons. The slick from the Mexican marine blow-up in Campeche Bay, Gulf of Mexico, on 3 June 1979 reached 400 miles *640 km* by 5 Aug. 1979.

Copper Mine (page 130). The San Manuel Mine, Arizona, USA, owned by Magma Copper Co., has underground workings 355.8 miles *572,7 km* long and in 1972–77 averaged an extraction of 17,589,285 long tons.

CHAPTER 8

Car Registrations (page 135). On 9 Dec. 1978 Sir Run Run Shaw CBE bid HK$330,000 (then £34,800) for a 'Good Fortune' number plate at a Hong Kong Government charity auction.

Largest Engines (page 136). 3rd paragraph, for Jameson-Concorde read Jameson-Merlin.

Oldest Driver (page 137). Mr Roy Marek Rawlins, died on 9 July 1975, one day short of his 105th birthday.

Most Expensive Car (page 137). The Rolls Royce *Camargue* retailed in the USA in July 1979 for $130,000 (*£65,000*).

Cars least expensive (page 137). The only car listed under £2,000 in Aug. 1979 was the Skoda Super Estelle 1055 at £1,970.

Most on one Machine (page 140). On 18 May 1979 at the Brisbane Show Grounds, Sgt John Patrick Toohey drove a Kawasaki 1,000 cc motorcycle, with 18 other policemen mounted on it, a distance of 805 m *880 yds*. The total weight was 2 104,8 kg *2.07 tons*.

Greatest Mileage (page 143). The greatest mileage covered with a 7 day all-line roving ticket on British Rail is 10,371 miles *16 690,5 km* on 30 June–6 July 1979 by Dick Godwin of Hockley, Essex.

Most take-offs and Landings (page 151). Al Yates and Bob Phoenix of Texas, USA made 193 take-offs and daylight landings in 14 hr 57 min in a Piper Seminole, on 15 June 1979.

Human Powered Flight (page 151). The world distance record for human powered flight was set on 12 June 1979 by Dr Paul MacReady's man powered aircraft *Gossamer Albatross*, piloted and pedalled by Bryan Allen. The *Albatross* took off from Folkestone at 05.51 hrs and landed 23 miles *37 km* distant at Cap Gris Nez, France at 08.40 hrs. The duration was 2 hr 49 min, and they won the £100,000 prize offered by Henry Kremer.

Watch Thinnest (page 156). Eterna of Grenchen, Switzerland manufacture a watch which measures 1,98 mm *1/16 in* thick.

CHAPTER 9

Biggest Take Over Bids (page 158). A bid of U.S.$1,125 million (*£562.5 million*) made by Brascan Ltd of Canada for F. W. Woolworth Co. interest was still being resisted in May 1979. Exxon Corporation bid $1,165 million (*£582.5 million*) for Reliance Electric Co. in May 1979.

Greatest Bankruptcy (page 158). William G. Stern (b. Hungary, 1936), a US citizen since 1957, who set up Wilstar Group Holding Co. in the London property market in 1971 for £104,390,248 in Feb. 1979 was declared bankrupt for £104,390,248 in Feb. 1979.

Aircraft Manufacturer (page 159). Cessna Aircraft Company of Wichita, Kansas, USA produced a record 9,197 civil aircraft in 1978 with total sales of $759 million (*£379.5 million*). The company has produced more than 150,000 aircraft since Clyde Cessna's first was built in 1911.

Chair Largest (page 165). For 9 ft 6¼ in read 29 ft 6¼ in.

Cigars Largest (page 165). For Scmidt read Schmidt.

Furniture (page 166). The highest price ever paid for a single piece of furniture is 7,600,000 francs (*£844,440*) by the J. Paul Getty Museum in Malibu, California, for a 10 ft *3,048 m* high marquetry and ormulu Louis XV corner cabinet made by Dubois, at Sotheby, Parke Bernet, Monte Carlo on 25 June 1979.

Paperweight (page 168). The highest price ever paid for a glass paperweight is £48,000 at Christie's, London on 10 July 1979 for a St Louis 19th century paperweight.

Snuff box (page 168). For Meissonnier read Meissonier.

Sofa Largest (page 168). The longest sofa manufactured for market is the King Talmage Sofa, 12 ft 2 in *3,7 m* in length made by the Talmageville Furniture Manufacturers, California, USA.

Chicken Ranch (page 170). For Jules read Julius. For 3.1 million chickens read 3,160,000 hens.

Sheep Shearing (page 170). Peter Casserly of Christchurch, New Zealand, achieved a solo blade (i.e. hand-shearing) record of 353 lambs in 9 hours on 13 Feb. 1976.

CHAPTER 10

Most Populous Country (page 174). The mid–1979 census for the People's Republic of China was 958,050,000.

Most populous city (pages 176–7). The estimated population of the Greater Tokyo Metropolitan area in 1977 was 27,717,000.

Best Attendance Record (page 180). Lucille McCollough has maintained her perfect attendance record up to June 1979.

Communist Parties (page 181). The British Communist Party membership announced on 15 July 1979 was 20,599.

STOP PRESS

Largest Agenda Item (page 183). All the weight of evidence indicates that the heaviest agenda item in the history of local government was a 950 page, 6 in *15,2 cm* thick, 6½ lb *2,95 kg* report produced for Lambeth Borough Council's Community Liaison Sub-Committee in May 1979 at a reproduction cost of £728.

Mass Suicide (page 191). The final total of the mass cyanide poisoning of the People's Temple cult near Port Kaituma, Guyana on 18 Nov. 1978 was 910. The leader was the paranoid "Rev." Jim Jones of San Francisco, California who had deposited "millions of dollars" overseas.

Largest budget (page 196). US budget deficit 1978/9. For $61,800,000 read $61,800 million.

Largest Barbecue (page 199). The 1979 annual Lancaster Sertoma in Pennsylvania, USA, served 20,500 barbecued chickens.

Largest Omelette (page 200). The largest omelette in the world was one made of 12,440 eggs on a pan measuring 30 × 10 ft *9,1 × 3,04 m* cooked by students of Conestoga College, Kitchener, Ontario, Canada on 29 June 1979.

Largest ice cream sundae (page 200). The largest ice cream sundae ever concocted is one of 8,100 lb *3674 kg* plus 90 lb *40,8 kg* of walnuts, 160 lb *72,5 kg* of chocolate syrup and 12 gallons *54,55 l.* of whipped topping, constructed by the Class of '82 at Smiths College, Northampton, Mass., USA on 29 April 1979.

Telephones (page 202). As of 1 Jan. 1978 there were 423,082,000 telephones in the world, the US with 162,076,000 equivalent to 744 per 1000 people, compared with the UK figure of 23,182,239 (3rd in the world) or 415 per 1000 people. Pitcairn has fewest telephones with 32 (total). The country with most telephones per head of population is Midway Islands with 129.6 per 100. Those with the least were Chad, Rwanda, Upper Volta and Nepal with less than 1 per 100. The greatest total of calls made is in the US with 221,482 million (975 calls per person) compared with UK, 17,453,537,000 (312 per person). The city with most telephones is New York with 5,936,829 (808 per 1000 people). Washington DC reached a density of 1495 per 1000 people).

Most Expensive Stamp (page 203). Controversy has arisen on whether the price revised to £270,219.14 was a true purchase price or a knock-down price on which no commission was in fact paid.

Most 'A' levels (page 206). For Stephen Murell read Murrell.

Fire Pump Pulling (page 223). A team of 32 men from the Hamburg Fire Brigade pulled a fire appliance weighing 510 kg *10 cwt*, 217.5 miles *350 km* in 23 hrs 55 min on 22–23 June 1979.

Feminine Beauty (page 223). The number of countries represented in the July 1979 Miss Universe contest held in Perth, Australia reached 78. Miss Venezuela was declared the winner.

Hitchhiking (page 224). The hitchhiking record for the 873 miles *1405 km* from John O'Groats to Land's End, Cornwall, is 21 hrs 50 min by Cpl J. C. Fuller of R.A.F. Coningsby, Lincoln, Lincs on 15–16 July 1979.

Joke Cracking (page 224). G. David Howard cracked jokes unremittingly for 16 hours on 14–15 July 1979 at Clearwater Beach, Florida, USA.

Jumble Sale (page 224). The Winnetka Congregational Church in Illinois, USA broke its own record on 10 May 1979 when it raised $73,200.79 (£36,600) in a one-day rummage sale.

Karate Chop (page 224). For Kraate read Karate.

Parachuting (page 226). Footnote 3 to table: The £1 million target has been changed to £100,000. By 1 Aug. 1979 £20,000 had been raised.

Pram Pushing (page 227). The greatest distance covered in pushing a pram in 24 hours is 345.25 miles *555,62 km* by Runner's Factory of Los Gatos, California, USA with an All-Star team of 57 California runners on 23–24 June 1979.

Singing (page 228). The longest solo singing marathon is one of 134 hrs 54 mins by L/Cpl S.A. Perera of the Sri Lankan Army on 8–13 May 1979.

Skipping (page 228). Most doubles (with cross)—386 by K. A. Brooks at Gold Coast City, Queensland, Australia on 23 Dec. 1978.

Stilt Walking (page 229). Eddy Wolf (Steady Eddy) of Loyal, Wisconsin, U.S.A. mastered 30 ft 3 in *9,22 m* long aluminium stilts without touching two horizontal safety wires.

Snake Pit Duration (page 229). Arguably the least competitive record in the history of record-breaking was set by Peter Snyman, 24, who stayed 50 days 7 hours (except for 30 minute rest breaks per 24 hours) in a 10 ft × 8 ft cage with 24 venomous snakes (6 black mambas, 6 cobras, 6 puff adders and 6 boomslangs (tree snakes)) at Hartbeesport, South Africa, from 7 Apr. to 27 May 1979.

Oldest Peer (page 238). With the death of the Earl of Albemarle in July 1979, the 7th Baron Henniker (b. 18 Jan. 1883) who sits as Lord Hartismere, became the oldest peer.

CHAPTER 11

Altitude Man (page 211). Hayes was born 14 Nov. 1933 at Biloxi, Miss., and Swigert was born on 30 Aug. 1931 at Denver, Col.

Water speed record (page 211). For 514 km *read* 514 km/h.

Desert walk longest. The longest desert walk ever recorded is one of 316 miles *508 km* by Bill Collins (b. 22 Oct. 1923) of Las Vegas, through Death Valley, California in 10 days 10 hours on 28 July–6 Aug. 1972.

Most Marriages (page 214). Glynn Wolfe, 71, filed his 23rd marriage licence application on 22 June 1979. Co-signatory was Guadalupe Reyes Chavez, 20. His total of children was, he claimed, 39.

Transatlantic Marine Records (page 215). Smallest West–East, Gerry Spiess, 39(US)—*Yankee Girl* 10 ft *3,048 m*—Norfolk, Virginia 1 June – Falmouth 24 July—54 days (3,800 miles *6115 km*)—1979.

Balancing On One Foot (page 217). Anton Christy of Jaffna, Sri Lanka balanced for 31 hrs 45 min on 27–28 May 1979.

Barrow Pushing (page 217). Bill Richardson of Pontefract, Yorkshire pushed a barrow containing 289 bricks weighing 2,347 lb *1064,5 kg* the minimum distance of 20 ft *6,09 m* on 30 June 1979.

Barrow Racing (page 217). The fastest time reached for a one mile *1,609 km* wheelbarrow race is 5 min 1.59 sec by Bryan Zellweger ("charger") and Jack Zellweger ("rider") at the Ladner Centennial Sports Festival, Delta, BC, Canada on 1 July 1979.

Bed Pushing (page 218). The longest recorded push of a normally sessile object is of 3,233 miles, 1,150 yds *5 204 km* in the case of a wheeled hospital bed by a team of 9, all employees of Bruntsfield Bedding Centre, Edinburgh on 21 June to 26 July 1979.

Brick Throwing (page 218). Robin Tait of Auckland, New Zealand threw a standard 5 lb *2,268 kg* brick a distance of 43,94 m *144 ft* on 30 June 1979.

Card Throwing (page 218). Kevin St Onge threw a standard playing card 185 ft 1 in *56,4 m* at the Henry Ford Community College Campus, Dearborn, Michigan, USA on 12 June 1979.

Crawling (page 220). Wayne Forsyth equalled the crawling record of 12.6 miles *20,27 km* in Christchurch, New Zealand on 12 May 1979.

Disc Jockey (page 221). Dave Belmondo of Brocton, New York, USA acted as a disc jockey for 2016 hours from 15 Sept.–7 Dec. 1978. *No further disc jockey marathons results will be listed in the future editions of the Guinness Book of Records.*

CHAPTER 12

Angling Marathon (page 242). John Reader fished for 552 hr at Hunstrete Lake, Weston-super-Mare, Avon on 7–30 July 1979.

British Angling Records (page 243). Mullet (Thick Lipped) 10 lb 1 oz 4 dr caught by R. Gifford on 30 Aug. 1978 at Lagoon Leys, Glamorgan, Wales.

Archery British Records (page 244). FITA Round (Men): Double round 2,410 by Mark Blenkarne at Berlin, West Germany on 19–20 July, 1979. Hereford Round (Women): Single Round 1,177 by Sue Willcox at Oxford on 28 June 1979.

Basketball Most points (page 247). Pearl Moore of Francis Marion College, Florence, South Carolina, USA, scored 4,061 points in her college career, 1975–79.

Pool (page 248). The greatest number of balls pocketed in 24 hr is 11,700 (one per 7.5 sec) by Gary Mounsey (b. 1947) at Hamilton, New Zealand on 30 June–1 July 1979.

Badminton Marathon (page 249). 50 hr by Richard and Margarette Jones, Sarah Moss and Neelam Sarpal at Ilkley Grammar School, West Yorkshire on 1–3 Aug. 1979.

Indoor Bowls Marathon (page 250). 73 hr 30 min by the Tauranga District Indoor Bowling Association, N.Z. on 13–16 Apr. 1979.

Football (page 273). Needing to improve their goal average to gain promotion in 1979, Ilinden FC of Yugoslavia, with the collusion of the opposition, Mladost, and the referee, won their final game of the season by 134–1. Their rivals in the promotion race won their match, under similar circumstances, by 88–0.

Hockey (page 287). The longest recorded club match occurred in the Hong Kong Hockey Association Holland Cup semi-final between HKFC 'C' and Prisons Sports Dept HC on 11 Mar. 1979 which ended at 2–2 at full time. After 20 min of extra time, it took 115 min of 'sudden death' play before the Football Club scored.

Mountaineering (page 307). Brian Harney (b. 11 May 1945) of Dark Peak Fell Runners and Rotherham Harriers ran the Pennine Way in 3 days 42 min on 9–12 Aug. 1979.

Pelota (page 310). Jose Areitio recorded a speed of 188 mph *302 km/h* at the Newport Jai Alai, Rhode Island, U.S.A. on 3 Aug. 1979.

Swimming (page 323). Women's 1500 m freestyle 16:4.49, Kim Linehan, Fort Lauderdale, 20 Aug. 1979.

An asterisk indicates a further reference in the Stop Press.

INDEX

INDEX

An asterisk indicates a further reference in the Stop Press.

An asterisk indicates a further reference in the Stop Press.

INDEX

An asterisk indicates a further reference in the Stop Press.

Indexing by

Anna Pavord